SOCIAL PSYCHOLOGY

SIXTH EDITION

SOCIAL PSYCHOLOGY:

Theories, Research, and Applications

Daniel A. Miller
Purdue University Fort Wayne

Kenneth S. Bordens
Purdue University Fort Wayne—Emeritus

Irwin A. Horowitz
Oregon State University—Emeritus

Social Psychology: Theories, Research, and Applications, 6th Edition, Daniel A. Miller, Kenneth S. Bordens, and Irwin A. Horowitz

Cover photo: topform/Shutterstock

Paperback (b/w)	ISBN–13:	978-1-955543-26-2
	ISBN–10:	1-955543-26-7
Paperback (4c)	ISBN–13:	978-1-955543-30-9
	ISBN–10:	1-955543-30-5
Loose-leaf version (b/w)	ISBN–13:	978-1-955543-31-6
	ISBN–10:	1-955543-31-3
Online eBook	ISBN–13:	978-1-955543-10-1
	ISBN–10:	1-955543-10-0

Copyright © 2023 by Academic Media Solutions

All Rights Reserved. No part of this publication may be reproduced, stored in a retrieval system, or transmitted, in any form or by any means, electronic, mechanical, recording, photocopying, or otherwise, without the prior written permission of the publisher.

Printed in the United States of America by Academic Media Solutions.

Dedication

This book is dedicated to the memory of Dr. Irwin A. Horowitz (1939–2019), mentor, colleague, and friend.

Kenneth S. Bordens

Brief Contents

Preface   xix

About the Authors   xxv

1. Understanding Social Behavior   1
2. The Social Self   31
3. Social Perception: Understanding Other People   71
4. Prejudice and Discrimination   105
5. Attitudes   167
6. Persuasion and Attitude Change   201
7. Conformity, Compliance, and Obedience   251
8. Group Processes   305
9. Interpersonal Attraction and Close Relationships   343
10. Interpersonal Aggression   391
11. Prosocial Behavior and Altruism   441
12. Applying Social Psychology: Law, Business, and Health   493

Answers to Discussion Questions, Social Psychology in Action Boxes   A-1

Answers to Chapter Quiz Questions   A-5

Glossary   G-1

References   R-1

Name Index   I-1

Subject Index   I-13

Contents

Preface xix
About the Authors xxv

1 Understanding Social Behavior 1

Social Psychology and the Understanding of Social Behavior 2
A Model for Understanding Social Behavior 4
Expanding Lewin's Model 6

Social Psychology and Related Fields 8

Research in Social Psychology 10
Experimental Research 13
Correlational Research 17
Settings for Social Psychological Research 19
The Role of Theory in Social Psychological Research 21
What Do We Learn from Research in Social Psychology? 22
Can Findings in Social Psychology Be Replicated? 23
Ethics and Social Psychological Research 24

Trinidad Beach Revisited 25

2 The Social Self 31

Self-Concept 33
Self-Knowledge: How Do You Know Thyself? 33
The Self and Memory 36
The Self: The Influence of Groups and Culture 39

Self-Esteem: Evaluating the Self 48
Internal Influences on Self-Esteem 48
Self-Esteem and Stigma 51
Self-Esteem and Cultural Influences 53
What's So Good about High Self-Esteem? 53
Implicit and Explicit Self-Esteem 54

Self-Control: How People Regulate Their Behavior   54
    Self-Control and Self-Regulation   54
    The Cost and Ironic Effects of Self-Control   57

Thinking about Ourselves   58
    Self-Serving Cognitions   58
    Maintaining Self-Consistency   59

Self-Awareness   60
    Self-Knowledge and Self-Awareness   61

Managing Self-Presentations   61
    Self-Esteem and Impression Management   62
    Self-Monitoring and Impression Management   62
    Self-Handicapping   63

The Impression We Make on Others   65

The Life of Serena Williams Revisited   67

3   Social Perception: Understanding Other People   71

Automatic and Controlled Processing   73
    Automatic Processing   73
    Controlled Processing   74

Impression Formation   74
    How Accurate Are Our Impressions?   75
    Confidence and Impression Formation   76
    The Importance of First Impressions   77
    Social Media and Impression Formation   80
    Person Perception: Reading Faces and Catching Liars   80

The Attribution Process: Deciding Why People Act As They Do   84
    Heider's Early Work on Attribution   84
    Correspondent Inference Theory   85
    Covariation Theory   85
    Dual-Process Models   88
    Perceptions of Responsibility and Attributions   89

Attribution Biases   91
    Misattributions   91
    The Fundamental Attribution Error   92
    The Actor-Observer Bias   94
    The False Consensus Bias   95

Schemas   96
- Assimilating New Information into a Schema   97
- Origins of Schemas   97
- The Relationship Between Schemas and Behavior   97
- Shortcuts to Reality: Heuristics   99

The *Vincennes* Revisited   101

4 Prejudice and Discrimination   105

The Dynamics of Prejudice, Stereotypes, and Discrimination   107
- Prejudice   107
- Stereotypes   110
- Discrimination   118

The Persistence and Recurrence of Prejudice and Stereotypes   118

Individual Differences and Prejudice: Personality and Gender   120
- The Authoritarian Personality   120
- Social Dominance Orientation   123
- Openness to New Experience and Agreeableness   124
- Other Personality Correlates of Prejudice   124
- Gender and Prejudice   125

The Social Roots of Prejudice   126
- Explicit and Implicit Prejudice   128
- Changing Social Norms   132

The Cognitive Roots of Prejudice: From Categories to Stereotypes   133
- Identification with the In-Group   135
- The Role of Language in Maintaining Bias   137
- System Justification and Prejudice   139
- Illusory Correlations   140
- The Confirmation Bias   142
- The Out-Group Homogeneity Bias   143
- The Difference Between Prejudiced and Nonprejudiced Individuals   143

The Consequences of Being a Target of Prejudice   145
- Ways Prejudice Can Be Expressed   145
- Prejudice-Based Jokes   145
- Stereotype Threat   147
- Collective Threat   150
- Expecting to Be a Target of Prejudice   151

Coping with Prejudice   151
    Raising the Value of a Stigmatized Group   151
    Making In-Group Comparisons   152
    Anticipating and Confronting Prejudice   152
    Compensating for Prejudice   153

Reducing Prejudice   154
    Contact Between Groups   154
    Personalizing Out-Group Members   156
    Reducing the Expression of Prejudice Through Social Norms   157
    Reducing Prejudice Through Training   158

The Mormon Experience Revisited   160

5   Attitudes   167

What Are Attitudes?   169
    Allport's Definition of Attitudes   169
    Attitude Structures   170
    Attitudes as an Expression of Values   171
    Explicit and Implicit Attitudes   172

How Are Attitudes Measured?   173
    The Attitude Survey   173
    Behavioral Measures   174
    Implicit Measures   174

How Are Attitudes Formed?   175
    Mere Exposure   175
    Direct Personal Experience   176
    Operant and Evaluative Conditioning   176
    Observational Learning   178
    The Effect of the Mass Media   178
    The Heritability Factor   181
    Social Networks   184

Attitudes and Behavior   185
    An Early Study of Attitudes and Behavior   185
    Theory of Planned Behavior   186
    The Importance of Attitude Strength   188
    The Nonrational Actor   190

Ideology and How We Feel About Those Who Think Differently from Us   192
  Ideology   193
  Ideology and Political Polarization   193
  Ideology as Motivated Social Cognition   195
  Does Ideology Predict Behavior?   195

Ida Tarbell Revisited   197

6 Persuasion and Attitude Change   201

The Persuasion Process   203

The Yale Communication Model   203
  The Communicator   204
  The Message and the Audience   209

The Cognitive Approach to Persuasion   216
  The Elaboration Likelihood Model   216
  The Effect of Mood on Processing   218
  The Effect of Personal Relevance on Processing   221
  The Impact of Attitude Accessibility on Elaboration   223
  Do Vivid Messages Persuade Better Than Nonvivid Messages?   224
  The Need for Cognition and Affect   225
  The Heuristic Model of Persuasion   227

Cognitive Dissonance Theory: A Model of Self-Persuasion   227
  Cognitive Dissonance Theory   228
  Does Inconsistency Lead to Cognitive Dissonance?   228
  Alternatives to Cognitive Dissonance Theory   237

Persuading the Masses Through Propaganda   241
  Propaganda: A Definition   241
  Characteristics of Propaganda   242
  The Aims of Propaganda   243
  Propaganda Techniques   243
  Hitler's Rise to Power   244

COVID-19 Vaccine Hesitancy Revisited   247

7 Conformity, Compliance, and Obedience   251

Conformity: Going Along with the Crowd   253
- Informational and Normative Social Influence   254
- Social Norms: The Key to Conformity   255
- Classic Studies in Conformity   256
- How Does Social Influence Bring About Conformity?   258
- Different Forms of Conformity   260
- Factors That Affect Conformity   261

Minority Influence   266
- Can a Minority Influence the Majority?   266
- Majority and Minority Influence: Two Processes or One?   268

Compliance: Responding to a Direct Request   269
- Foot-in-the-Door Technique   270
- Door-in-the-Face Technique   274
- Compliance Techniques: Summing Up   276

Obedience   278
- Defining Obedience   278
- Destructive Obedience and the Social Psychology of Evil   279
- Milgram's Experiments on Obedience   283
- The Role of Gender in Obedience   289
- Obedience or Aggression?   289
- Obedience Across Culture, Situation, and Time   289
- Reevaluating Milgram's Findings   292
- Critiques of Milgram's Research   292

Disobedience   294
- Breaking with Authority   294
- Reassessing the Legitimacy of the Authority   295
- Strength in Numbers   297

To Mask or Not to Mask Revisited   299

8 Group Processes   305

What Is a Group?   307
- Characteristics of Groups   307
- What Holds a Group Together?   308

How and Why Do Groups Form?   309
- Meeting Basic Needs   309
- Roles in Groups   310

How Do Groups Influence the Behavior of Individuals? 311
The Effects of an Audience on Performance 311
Group Performance: Conditions That Decrease or Increase Motivation of Group Members 314

Groups, Self-Identity, and Intergroup Relationships 317
The Power of Groups to Punish: Social Ostracism 318
Deindividuation and Anonymity: The Power of Groups to Do Violence 321

Group Performance 323
Individual Decisions and Group Decisions 323
The Harder the Problem, the Better the Group 325
The Effect of Leadership Style on Group Decision Making 327

Factors That Affect the Decision-Making Ability of a Group 330
Group Composition 330
Group Size 332
Group Cohesiveness 332

The Dynamics of Group Decision Making: Decision Rules, Group Polarization, and Groupthink 333
Group Decisions: How Groups Blend Individual Choices 333
Group Polarization 334
Groupthink 335

The *Challenger* Explosion Revisited 338

9 Interpersonal Attraction and Close Relationships 343

The Roots of Interpersonal Attraction and Close Relationships 344
Affiliation and Intimacy 345

Loneliness and Social Anxiety 346
Loneliness 346
Social Anxiety 348

Love and Close Relationships 349
Love's Triangle 349
Types of Love 351
The Formation of Intimate Relationships 353

Determinants of Interpersonal Attraction 356
Physical Proximity: Being in the Right Place 356
Similarity 359
Physical Attractiveness 361

Dynamics of Close Relationships   369
    Relationship Development   370
    Dating Scripts and Relationship Formation   371
    Evaluating Relationships   373
    Love over Time   376
    Sculpting a Relationship   377
    Responses to Conflict   378
    Love in the Lab   381

Friendships   382
    Gender Differences in Friendships   383
    Friendships over the Life Cycle   384

Gertrude and Alice Revisited   385

10   Interpersonal Aggression   391

What Is Aggression?   393
    Levels and Types of Aggression   393
    Gender Differences in Aggression   394

Biological Explanations for Aggression   397
    Ethology   397
    Sociobiology   398
    Genetics and Aggression   399
    The Physiology of Aggression   400
    Alcohol and Aggression   403
    Physiology and Aggression: Summing Up   406

The Frustration-Aggression Link   406
    Components of the Frustration-Aggression Sequence   407
    Factors Mediating the Frustration-Aggression Link   408

The Social Learning Explanation for Aggression   411
    The Socialization of Aggression   412
    Aggressive Scripts: Why and How They Develop   414
    The Role of the Family in Developing Aggressive Behaviors   414
    Child Abuse and Neglect   417
    Family Disruption   418
    The Role of Culture in Violent Behavior   419

Exposure to Media Violence and Aggression   423
    The Role of Television in Teaching Aggression   424
    Violent Video Games and Aggression   427
    Viewing Sexual Violence: The Impact on Aggression   430

Reducing Aggression 433
Reducing Aggression in the Family 433
Reducing Aggression with Cognitive Intervention and Therapy 434

The Valley Transportation Authority Case Revisited 436

11 Prosocial Behavior and Altruism 441

Why Do People Help? 443
Empathy: Helping in Order to Relieve Another's Suffering 444
Empathy and Egoism: Two Paths to Helping 444
Biological Explanations: Helping in Order to Preserve Our Own Genes 449

Helping in Emergencies: A Five-Stage Decision Model 451
Stage 1: Noticing the Situation 452
Stage 2: Labeling the Situation as an Emergency 453
Stage 3: Assuming Responsibility to Help: The Bystander Effect 454
Stage 4: Deciding How to Help 459
Stage 5: Implementing the Decision to Help 460
Increasing the Chances of Receiving Help 469

Courageous Resistance and Heroism 469
Explaining Courageous Resistance and Heroism:
The Role of Personality 472
Righteous Rescuers in Nazi-Occupied Europe 473
A Synthesis: Situational and Personality Factors in Altruism 479

Altruistic Behavior from the Perspective of the Recipient 483
Seeking Help from Others 483
Reacting to Help When It Is Given 485

Irene Opdyke Revisited 488

12 Applying Social Psychology: Law, Business, and Health 493

Social Psychology and the Law 494
Eyewitness Testimony 494
Juries: Group Processes in Action 502
Intergroup Bias in Court 504
Confessions: Are They Always What They Seem? 505
Summary of This Section 508

The Social Psychology of Work: Industrial Organizational Psychology   508
    Personnel Selection   508
    Performance Appraisals   510
    Motivation at Work   512
    Organizational Citizenship Behaviors   514

Social Psychology and Health   515
    Perceived Stress and Health   516
    Coping with Stress   519
    Optimism and Health   521

Answers to Discussion Questions, Social Psychology in Action Boxes   A-1

Answers to Chapter Quiz Questions   A-5

Glossary   G-1

References   R-1

Name Index   I-1

Subject Index   I-13

Preface

When we set out to write the first edition of *Social Psychology: Theories, Research, and Applications,* our goal was to provide teachers and students with a book that covered the important research and theoretical areas in social psychology in a concise fashion. Through the next five editions, and in this most current edition, our goal has not changed. In this new edition of the book, we continue to present the field of social psychology in a clear, concise way with an emphasis on the science of the field. We have also continued our tradition of showing how research and theory in social psychology can help students understand events that affect their lives. We have drawn parallels between what social psychology has to offer and events that have occurred in the past and current events. We hope that students will come away from their reading of this book and their course in social psychology with a better understanding of their immediate social world and the wider world around them.

Social psychology is a diverse field, and any attempt to present a totally comprehensive overview of all of its content area would be difficult to execute in a single volume or course. Instead, we take the approach of presenting students with information concerning three questions:

1. What is social psychology?
2. What do we know about social psychological phenomena?
3. How do we know what we know about social psychological phenomena?

This sixth edition of *Social Psychology: Theories, Research, and Applications* maintains the basic structure of the fifth. Chapters 1–11 cover the core topics in social psychology. Each of these chapters has been updated to include citations to new research, and many new topics are explored. Chapter 12 focuses on how social psychology applies to the law, to business, and to health. This edition also marks some changes from the previous edition. Each chapter now has a Social Psychology in Action box (see "Changes to the Sixth Edition") that organizes information relevant to each chapter on applications of social psychological research and theory to applied issues. Another change is that, sadly, Dr. Irwin A. Horowitz passed away in 2019. His expertise and wit will be missed. Although Dr. Horowitz did not participate in this edition, his past contributions can still be seen throughout this text. Dr. Daniel A. Miller of Purdue University Fort Wayne (Indiana) has joined as the first author of this edition. Dr. Miller brings his expertise in various aspects of social psychology (e.g., stereotyping and prejudice, the psychology of work, and effects of social media) and made significant contributions to each chapter in this book.

Social psychology is important, interesting, relevant to the current world, and exciting. We hope to communicate to this generation of social psychology students the excitement that we felt as budding social psychologists when we first learned about Milgram's obedience research or Darley and Latané's bystander intervention research. Intrigued by the results of such studies, we began to wonder how they could be applied to real-life situations that confront each of us daily. In this edition, we communicate the excitement of the field so that new students will be as intrigued with social psychological research and theory as we are.

Most social psychology texts approach the field from the perspective of research and theory, using examples from everyday life as illustrations of social psychological phenomena. This approach often leaves students without a full appreciation of the applications of social psychology. By applications, we mean not only the usual applied social psychology topics that are interesting in their own right, but also the theory and research of social psychology that can be used to understand the complexities of cultural, historical, and current events. Social psychology can help us understand how we, as individuals, fit in with the wider social environment. Students will come away from this text with a sense that they are truly social creatures, subject to the influence of the social and physical environment.

Changes to the Sixth Edition

Key pedagogical elements from previous editions, such as the chapter-opening vignettes, opening questions, running glossary, focused chapter summaries, lists of key terms keyed to the text pages, and study breaks, have been retained. The study breaks include a list of key questions to answer on the material just read, offering a chance for students to review the content and providing a break in the text's narrative. One major change is the addition of a Social Psychology in Action box to each chapter. In some cases, the boxes contain expanded and updated material that appeared in the fifth edition. In others, the boxes contain entirely new material. Each box includes a set of questions for students to answer about the content covered. These boxes are as follows:

- Chapter 1: Distinguishing Science from Pseudoscience
- Chapter 2: The Internet Self
- Chapter 3: Body Art and Impressions
- Chapter 4: The Disarming of Racism in the U.S. Army
- Chapter 5: Toe the Party Line
- Chapter 6: Cognitive Dissonance and Cult Membership
- Chapter 7: Using the Foot-in-the-Door Technique to Increase Desired Behavior
- Chapter 8: Why Group Members Obey Leaders: The Psychology of Legitimacy
- Chapter 9: Internet Relationships
- Chapter 10: Social Media and Aggression
- Chapter 11: When a Good Thing Is Taken Too Far
- Chapter 12: What Makes Us Happy?

Additionally, each chapter now concludes with a 10-question quiz for students to test their knowledge of the material in the chapter. Answers are organized in an appendix at the back of the book.

Some major changes to the chapters include the following:

Chapter 1

A new opening vignette focusing on a rescue at Trinidad State Beach in California replaces the Sandy Hook shooting vignette. The section on the scientific method has been updated to include new views from the Next Generation Science Standards, which are summarized in the new Table 1.1. Figure 1.2, depicting the steps of the scientific method, has been deleted. An updated example of experimental research replaces the old one at the beginning of the section on manipulating independent variables. The new section "Can Findings in Social Psychology Be Replicated?" has been added to the section on what we learn from social psychology research. Table 1.2 summarizing the American Psychological Association (APA) code of ethics has been deleted, and a link to the APA Web site on ethics has been added instead.

Chapter 2

We added material on the imposter phenomenon to the section on self-concept, material on optimal distinctiveness theory to the section on distinctiveness theory, and material on autobiographical memory and mood to the section on autobiographical memory. We added information on the autobiographical memory incongruence effect and added a new figure showing results from an experiment on incongruence (Figure 2.1). The short section on religion and the self has been deleted. We updated the section on the Internet self and organized the material into a Social Psychology in Action box. Material under the heading "Who Am I?" in the fifth edition has been deleted. The section "Culture and the Expression of the Self" has been reorganized, along with the addition of material on the self and the COVID-19 pandemic, as well as material on gays, lesbians, and bisexuals in the military. Information on internalized weight bias has been added to the section on self-esteem and stigma. Material is now included on the relationship between implicit self-esteem and anxiety and depression, as well as research on the relationship between self-esteem, weight, and Internet addiction. Research citations on ego-depletion, dishonesty, and individual differences in trait self-control have also been added.

Chapter 3

We updated the discussion of automatic and controlled processing at the beginning of the chapter. We removed the discussion of priming studies because of the controversies about replication in that literature. We added new information on the effects of a target's well-being on impression formation. We updated the section on tattoos and impression formation and organized the material into a Social Psychology in Action box. We also added a new section on social media and impression formation. The section on detecting deception has new additional material on using pupil dilation to detect deception. The section on intentionality and attribution has been updated to include an example of individuals' perceptions of a passenger with COVID-19 and attributions of responsibility, citing a 2021 study on this topic. Also, a new paragraph on ideology and attributions of responsibility has been added to this section. The section has been renamed "Responsibility and Attribution." We updated several aspects of the section on the fundamental attribution error. We added a study showing that Protestants are more likely to attribute behavior internally than are Catholics. We also added a citation to a study showing that the fundamental attribution error can be reduced by making information on situational factors more easily accessible, especially for people prone to the error. We updated the section on the false-consensus bias, adding a citation to a study showing that prejudiced individuals are more prone to the false-consensus bias than are nonprejudiced individuals. We also added a new section on social media and the false-consensus bias. Finally, we removed the section on positive psychology and incorporated some of the content from this section into Chapter 12.

Chapter 4

We reordered and updated the opening section on prejudice. We also updated and expanded the discussion of skin tone bias and updated the information on the stereotype content model. We updated the discussion of the shooter bias and added a new figure (Figure 4.4). The section on implicit versus explicit prejudice now includes a discussion about the current issues of validity surrounding implicit measures of prejudice. We updated the section on Right-Wing authoritarianism (RWA) to include a discussion of how labels for same-sex relationships (*homosexual* vs. *gay and lesbian*) affect those high in RWA. We also updated the section and accompanying figure (Figure 4.7) discussing the racial divide between Black and Whites concerning the perception of how fairly Blacks are treated. We moved the discussion of the U.S. Army's attempt to eliminate racial prejudice within its ranks to a Social Psychology in Action box. Finally, we updated the section on stereotype threat.

Chapter 5

We updated the discussion of implicit attitudes and their measurement. We removed detailed discussion of different types of questionnaire items and added information about direct experience and attitudes toward the COVID-19 vaccine. The section on the influence of the mass media has been updated to reflect current shifts from traditional television to streaming and other technology sources. We added a Social Psychology in Action box about how political parties influence attitudes, including updated information on this topic. We also updated the section on social media and attitudes. The section on attitude conviction has been modified to use the term *attitude strength*, which is a much more common term. We also updated the ideology and political polarization section and added a new figure (Figure 5.4) that displays the widening partisan gap in presidential approval. New information has been added on the relationship between social media and political polarization.

Chapter 6

A new vignette replaces the one from the fifth edition. The new vignette focuses on vaccine hesitancy; it discusses historical and current attempts to persuade hesitant populations to receive vaccinations. We added a new section discussing the hedonic contingency model and its predictions about the impact of mood on the processing of persuasive messages, as well as a new section discussing how goals (epistemic or hedonic) can moderate the relationship between personal relevance and elaboration.

We also updated the section on fear appeals in persuasion and included a new figure (Figure 6.3). A new section was added explaining a study (Nyhan et al., 2004) that demonstrates the possible ironic effects of dissonance on attitude change. In this study, when vaccine-hesitant parents were exposed to information that debunked false claims about the measles, mumps, and rubella (MMR) vaccine, the dissonance produced by this information led to more negative attitudes toward the MMR vaccine (rather than less negative). The information about cognitive dissonance and cult membership was incorporated into a Social Psychology in Action box. Finally, we added a new section on reactance and vaccine hesitancy.

Chapter 7

A new vignette replaces the one from the fifth edition. The new, more contemporary vignette focuses on complying with COVID-19 mandates. In the section on explaining conformity, research has been added showing that remaining independent in a conformity situation is more physiologically arousing than conforming. We added research on the nature of the first request in a foot-in-the-door (FITD) situation to the section on factors affecting the FITD effect. The material on using the FITD to increase blood and organ donations has been organized into a Social Psychology in Action box. Finally, new material on the belief in pure evil has been added to the section "Banality of Evil."

Chapter 8

We updated the opening of the chapter vignette, incorporating Dr. Miller's memories of the event as a child. We also added new information about how increased social isolation as a result of the COVID-19 pandemic has had a negative impact on people's mental health. The section on ostracism has been updated to include a discussion of the effects of ostracism on the ostracizers. We added a section discussing the social identity model of deindividuation and its relationship with the deindividuation theory. We also added a section on the contextual antecedents of transactive memory systems. The section on the hidden profile paradigm was updated. The section titled "Why Group Members Obey Leaders: The Psychology of Legitimacy" was incorporated into a Social Psychology in Action box. The section on group polarization was updated to include a discussion of group polarization with respect to the elaboration likelihood model.

Chapter 9

We added material on the negative aspects of the implicit and explicit need for affiliation in the section on the need for affiliation. Material has been added on the relational mobility of one's heritage culture and loneliness experiences among migrant students. The section on Internet friendships has been organized and updated into a Social Psychology in Action box for this chapter. Material was added to the section on the limits of the similarity effect on the role of diversity in the formation of diverse friendships. Material was also added to the section on accommodation for relationship conflict and the relationship between hope and accommodation. We also added information on gender differences in friendship transgression and forgiveness in the section on friendship.

Chapter 10

A new vignette focusing on a contemporary act of aggression replaces the old vignette. The new vignette centers on a mass shooting that occurred in 2021 at the Valley Transportation Authority in California. We added new research on gender differences in brain functioning relating to gender differences in aggression. The sections on genetics and aggression and alcohol and aggression were updated with new research. A more recent study is cited (Zapolski et al., 2018) to support the role of perceived injustice and aggression in the frustration-aggression section. New material and research were added to the section on the relationship between physical punishment and aggression. We added material on the relationship between watching pornography and coercive sexual aggression in women, as well as a Social Psychology in Action box containing new material on social media and aggression.

Chapter 11

The previous edition's section on pathological altruism has been expanded and set off in a Social Psychology in Action box. Figure 11.2 has been updated to better reflect the processes involved in the five-stage model of helping. Material has been added to the section on modeling and helping behavior and the effects of prosocial modeling on young children. A reference was added concerning a meta-analysis of the prosocial modeling literature showing a moderate effect of modeling on helping. In the section on gratitude, material was added on the effects on helping of making gratitude mindful. We added research to the section on heroism that raises questions about what should be relevant when designating behavior as heroic when it is performed by people in roles where risk is expected (e.g., doctors and nurses during the pandemic). The section on the decision model for seeking help has been deleted.

Chapter 12

The section on weapon focus was updated to include research on novelty versus threat of weapon presence. Also, a study was added showing that for Black suspects, the weapon focus effect is weaker than for White suspects. The material on the explanations for the own-race effect has been updated to include information on perceptual expertise and processing in visual working memory. Research has been added to the section on confessions and how people perceive the appropriateness of coercive and psychologically manipulative tactics. A new introduction was added to the section on industrial/organizational psychology. New information about the Internet and employee recruitment and screening practices was added, as well as a new section on bona fide occupational qualifications and their relationship to adverse impact. U.S. health statistics were updated, and a new figure was added. New material on the relationship between sleep, stress, and health was added. Material about optimism and health, as well as positive emotions as a preventative measure, was deleted from Chapter 3, updated, and added to this chapter. A new section on what contributes to happiness was added as a Social Psychology in Action box.

A Note on APA Style

As we have gone through multiple editions of *Social Psychology: Theories, Research, and Applications*, there have been numerous changes in APA style, which we use as our major guide for this book. Many of these changes have been to the format of citations and references. We have followed the seventh edition of the APA manual for in-text citations. This means all multiple-authorship citations now use the "et al." convention. In the reference section, we have used a hybrid of the new APA format and older formats. Issue numbers and DOI numbers are not included in our reference section. To modify old references to include these features would have been a daunting task. The exclusion of these features does not significantly hinder the ability of a reader to find the original sources cited in the book.

Online and in Print

Student Options: Print and Online Versions

This sixth edition of *Social Psychology: Theories, Research, and Applications* is available in multiple versions: online, in PDF, and in print as either a paperback or looseleaf text. The content of each version is identical.

The most affordable version is the online book, with upgrade options including the online version bundled with a print version. What's nice about the print version is that it offers you the freedom of being unplugged—away from your computer. The people at Academic Media Solutions recognize that it's difficult to read from a screen at length and that most of us read much faster from a piece of paper. The print options are particularly useful when you have extended print passages to read.

The online edition allows you to take full advantage of embedded digital features, including search and notes. Use the search feature to locate and jump to discussions anywhere in the book. Use the notes feature to add personal comments or annotations. You can move out of the book to follow Web links. You can navigate within and between chapters using a clickable table of contents. These features allow you to work at your own pace and in your own style as you read and surf your way through the material. (See "Harnessing the Online Version" for more tips on working with the online version.)

Harnessing the Online Version

The online version of *Social Psychology: Theories, Research, and Application,* 6e, offers the following features to facilitate learning and to make using the book an easy, enjoyable experience:

- *Easy-to-navigate/clickable table of contents*—You can surf through the book quickly by clicking on chapter headings, or first- or second-level section headings. And the Table of Contents can be accessed from anywhere in the book.

- *Key terms search*—Type in a term, and a search engine will return every instance of that term in the book; then jump directly to the selection of your choice with one click.

- *Notes and highlighting*—The online version includes study apps such as notes and highlighting. Each of these apps can be found in the tools icon embedded in the Academic Media Solutions/Textbook Media's online eBook reading platform: (http://www.academicmediasolutions.com).

Instructor Supplements

In addition to its student-friendly features and pedagogy, the variety of student formats available, and the uniquely affordable pricing options that are designed to provide students with a flexibility that fits any budget and/or learning style, *Social Psychology: Theories, Research, and Applications,* 6e, comes with the following teaching and learning aids:

- *Test Item File*—An extensive set of multiple-choice, short answer, and essay questions for every chapter for creating original quizzes and exams.

- *Instructor's Manual*—An enhanced version of the book offering assistance in preparing lectures, identifying learning objectives, developing essay exams and assignments, and constructing course syllabi.

- *PowerPoint Presentations*—Key points in each chapter are illustrated in a set of PowerPoint files designed to assist with instruction.

- *Online Video Labs with Student Worksheets*—A collection of high-quality video segments, organized by chapter and accessed via the web, which illustrate key topics and issues. Instructors are provided with suggested answers for each worksheet (for questions not based on student opinion).

Student Supplements and Upgrades (Additional Purchase Required)

- *Lecture Guide*—This printable lecture guide is designed for student use and is available as an in-class resource or study tool. Note: Instructors can request the PowerPoint version of these slides to use as developed or to customize.

- *Study Guide*—A printable version of the online study guide is available via downloadable PDF chapters for easy self-printing and review.

- *Quizlet Study Set*—Quizlet is an easy-to-use online learning tool built from all the key terms from the textbook. Students can turbo charge their studying via digital flashcards and other types of study apps, including tests and games. Students are able to listen to audio, as well as create their own flashcards. Quizlet is a cross-platform application and can be used on a desktop, tablet, or smartphone.

Acknowledgments

A project of this scope requires much hard work and the support of many people. First and foremost, we would like to thank our wives, Lori Miller, Ricky Karen Bordens, and Kay F. Schaffer, who now and in the past provided much-needed love and support while we toiled on this book. We would also like to thank Dan Luciano of Academic Media Solutions and Victoria Putman of Putman Productions, LLC. We would also like to give a special thanks to Amber Garcia, assistant professor of psychology at the College of Wooster, for writing Chapter 12. Her contribution significantly adds to the depth and breadth of the this book.

About the Authors

Dr. Daniel A. Miller is an associate professor of psychology at Purdue University Fort Wayne, where he has taught for 16 years. He received his bachelor of science degree in psychology from The Ohio State University in 1998. He earned a master of science (2002) and a doctor of philosophy degree (2005) in social psychology from Purdue University. During his time at Purdue University Fort Wayne, he has taught courses on stereotyping and prejudice, social psychology, industrial/organizational psychology, statistics, introductory psychology, and the history of psychology. Dr. Miller's research interests include prejudice, social media and online behavior, and protest behaviors. Dr. Miller has authored or coauthored 14 scholarly publications, has given several invited addresses, and has presented over 40 papers at professional conferences.

Dr. Kenneth S. Bordens is a professor emeritus of psychology at Purdue University Fort Wayne, where he taught for 37 years. Dr. Bordens taught courses in social psychology, research methods, the history of psychology, developmental psychology, human learning and memory, psychology and law, and introductory psychology. He taught online sections of social psychology, introductory psychology, and the history of psychology. He received his bachelor of arts degree in psychology from Fairleigh Dickinson University (Teaneck, NJ, campus) in 1975. He earned a master of arts (1978) and doctor of philosophy degree in social psychology from the University of Toledo in 1979. Dr. Bordens's research interests were in the areas of psychology and law, prejudice, the history of psychology, and psychology and the arts. He has coauthored five textbooks: *Research Design and Methods: A Process Approach* (11th edition), *Social Psychology* (5th edition), *General Psychology* (5th edition), *Basic Psychology* (4th Edition), and *Psychology of Law: Integrations and Applications* (2nd edition). He has also authored or coauthored 17 scholarly publications and has presented numerous papers at professional conferences. Dr. Bordens retired from Purdue University in Fort Wayne in 2016.

Dr. Irwin A. Horowitz (1939–2019) was a professor emeritus at Oregon State University. He received his bachelor of science and master's degrees from the Brooklyn College of the City University of New York and a doctorate degree from Michigan State in 1966. Dr. Horowitz held positions as a professor of psychology at the University of Toledo and Oregon State University, as well as a courtesy professor of law appointment at the University of Oregon College of Law. He was a fellow of both the American Psychological Association and the American Psychological Society and was recognized by the American Judicature Society as one of the foremost jury scholars in the United States. He coauthored textbooks in social psychology and in psychology and law.

He published nearly 70 research articles in a variety of journals, including *Law and Human Behavior, Personality and Social Psychology, Journal of Personality and Social Psychology, Journal of Applied Psychology, Psychology,* and *Public Policy and Law*. His areas of research interest included the ability of jurors to process complex evidence in civil trials, the effectiveness of various jury-aid innovations that may increase the competence of the civil jury, and the circumstances that provoke juries in criminal (and civil) trials to disobey the law (jury nullification). Dr. Horowitz passed away on December 23, 2019.

Understanding Social Behavior

Few people are capable of expressing with equanimity opinions which differ from the prejudices of their social environment. Most people are even incapable of forming such opinions.

—Albert Einstein

CHAPTER 1

Source: Fran Middendorf/Shutterstock.

Key Questions

As you read this chapter, find the answers to the following questions:

1. What is social psychology?
2. How do social psychologists explain social behavior?
3. How does social psychology relate to other disciplines that study social behavior?
4. How do social psychologists use science to describe and explain social behavior?
5. What is pseudoscience, and why is it important to learn about it?
6. What is experimental research, and how is it used?
7. What is correlational research?
8. What is the correlation coefficient, and what does it tell you?
9. Where is social psychological research conducted?
10. What is the role of theory in social psychology?
11. What can we learn from social psychological research?
12. What is the replication crisis, and how have social psychologists responded to it?
13. What ethical standards must social psychologists follow when conducting research?

On a misty, foggy morning in November 2019, four teenage friends, Narayan Weibel, Spenser Stratton, Adrian York, and Taj Ortiz-Beck, were out surfing at Trinidad State Beach outside the small coastal city of Trinidad in northern California. Things were going pretty well, and after surfing for a while, the four friends decided to take a break. They stayed out in the water and floated on their surfboards, resting, before resuming their surfing.

Nearby, two brothers who were on an outing with four other family members had waded into the California waters. Unfortunately, they ventured too far out into the surf (*The Press Democrat*, 2019). They were about 50 feet from shore when they were caught in one of California's notorious rip currents. A rip current is a powerful channeled current moving from shore out to sea, much like a flowing river. Rip currents are not only strong but swift as well, moving up to 8 feet per second (National Oceanic and Atmospheric Administration, 2021). The brothers were dressed in shorts and T-shirts, hardly adequate in the 50-degree November waters (Simmons, 2020). Suddenly, the two brothers (ages 15 and 20) were caught in the rip current and were being quickly pulled out into deeper water. They screamed desperately for help. However, because it was so foggy, their relatives and others on the beach could not see far enough to locate the struggling brothers (*The Press Democrat*, 2019).

1

Source: TheLazyPineapple/Shutterstock.

Recognizing the seriousness of their situation, the two brothers continued to scream for help. Fortunately for the brothers, the four surfers were not far off. The surfers peered through the fog, looking toward the source of the screams. Then, they saw two heads bobbing in and out of the water. They knew that time was of the essence because of the cold temperature of the water. It would not be long before the two brothers would be overcome by hypothermia, lose consciousness, and drown. Without hesitation, Ortiz-Beck, Weibel, and Stratton paddled toward the struggling swimmers. Meanwhile, York swam to shore and had a bystander call 911. He then swam back out to assist his friends. Ortiz-Beck observed that "it was pretty stressful, but there wasn't any time to think about it, and that helped me keep my cool" (Simmons, 2019, para. 5). Ortiz-Beck reached the younger brother and grabbed him under his arms, pulling him up onto his surfboard. It was a difficult task because the victim was in a panic and weighed over 250 pounds. But Ortiz-Beck managed to rescue him. Weibel noted, "We told them to calm down, we got you . . . they thought they were going to die" (Simmons, 2020, para. 7). York arrived on the scene in time to rescue the older brother, getting him onto a surfboard.

After securing the panicked brothers onto the surfboards, the friends headed for shore, where medical help awaited. The brothers were scared and cold, but they were fine thanks to the quick action of the four friends. Had the surfers not been there, it is highly likely that the two brothers would have died. It was also fortunate that two of the surfers, Stratton and York, had lifeguard training. York was a certified lifeguard, whereas Stratton went through a junior lifeguard training program (Sukheja, 2019). Lifeguard Dillon Cleavinger, who responded to the 911 call, said that hypothermia normally begins in seconds, and without the quick action of the four surfers, the brothers would have drowned. Cleavinger also noted that in such cases, by the time they get a 911 call and arrive at the scene, it is already too late. He was proud that the four friends acted quickly and were willing to risk their own lives to save two total strangers in distress (Simmons, 2019).

Social Psychology and the Understanding of Social Behavior

The events that occurred at Trinidad Beach raise many questions in our minds about the behaviors of those involved and why things happened the way they did. In the days and weeks after the event, the four teen surfers were hailed as heroes. We might ask ourselves a number of questions about why Weibel, Stratton, York, and Ortiz-Beck acted the way they did. Did they, for example, possess special personality characteristics that made them bolder and more likely to take risks than others? Did Stratton's and York's special training contribute? Or was it something unique about the situation in which they found themselves? We can also ask questions about the actions of the two brothers. Did they have any idea how dangerous it was to wade into the surf on a foggy day? Were they accomplished swimmers? Finally, we might speculate on whether we would have acted as the four surfers did on that day. Would you be willing to risk your life to save a perfect stranger?

As human beings, we are inherently curious. When something like the Trinidad Beach rescue takes place, we inevitably ask questions about why such things happen. We want an explanation for such events to satisfy our curiosity and to restore order to our world. Most of the time the first explanation we come up with is a "commonsense" explanation based on our experiences and our views of life and the world around us. So, we are likely to label the four teens as "brave," "resourceful," or "heroic." However, as is often the case, such simple commonsense explanations often fall short and do not give us final answers about why people behave the way they do. This is why we turn to science to help us better understand and explain events such as the Trinidad Beach rescue.

One science that can help us make sense out of the things that happen to us and around us is *psychology*, which is the study of behavior and the motives and cognitions that underlie that behavior. By studying "cognitive psychology," "personality psychology," and other areas of psychology, we can begin to piece together rational explanations for events such as Trinidad Beach. One branch of psychology can give us a unique perspective on behavior and perhaps help us best understand events that occur to us and around us: social psychology. **Social psychology** is the scientific study of how individuals think and feel about, interact with, and influence one another, individually and in groups. It is the branch of psychology that studies social behavior—the thinking and behavior of individuals as they relate to other human beings.

social psychology
The scientific study of how individuals think about, interact with, and influence each other.

Social psychology provides tools to help you understand things that happen in your personal life. It can help you make sense of your day-to-day interactions—your friendships, love relationships, interactions at work, and performance at school. It can give you insight, for example, into why your most recent romantic relationship did not succeed, and why you find yourself attracted to one person in your afternoon math class but not to another. It can also help you understand why you may behave aggressively when someone cuts ahead of you in a line, or why you get annoyed when someone sits right next to you in a theater when there are plenty of other empty seats. Social psychology can also help you understand why *other* people act the way they do. For example, social psychology can help you understand the behavior of the four teens at the Trinidad Beach rescue. You could ask if the four teens would have acted the same had they not known each other.

Your life also is touched by events beyond your immediate, day-to-day affairs—events that occur in the community, the nation, and the world. Although these events are more distant, you may still feel strongly about them and find a link between them and your personal life. If your friend's father were very sick, for example, you might want to share with him knowledge about a man whose determination kept him alive for 6 years. Perhaps the story would encourage him to keep on with his life. If a terrorist attack happened in your hometown, you would experience directly the consequences of people driven to acts of murder by a radical ideology. You probably would hear many people decrying terrorism and talking about ways to deal with such acts.

In one form or another, all the events such as mass shootings, riots, and even heroic rescues represent recurring themes in human history. Violence and aggression date back thousands of years. As soon as humans began to claim ownership of territory, they began to fight with each other. Humans have always been both aggressive and altruistic toward one another. Human beings have always had to find ways to live with each other. We have always functioned together in groups; had love relationships; tried to persuade others of our point of view; followed or rebelled against authority; and sought ways to resolve conflicts, whether through negotiation or through coercion. We help each other, and we hurt each other. We display prejudice and discrimination; we even have tried to kill entire populations. History is a tapestry of the best and the worst that human beings can do. Studying social psychology will give you the knowledge and tools to help you better understand this human tapestry.

It's important to note, however, that social psychologists do not simply wonder and speculate about social behavior. Instead, they use scientific methods involving carefully designed and executed research studies to help explain complex, uncertain social issues. Social psychology is first and foremost a science. Through theory, research, and thoughtful application of concepts and principles to real-life situations, social psychologists provide insights into everyday events, both past and present, as well as those monumental events that are the stuff of history.

More than any other branch of psychology, social psychology offers a broad perspective on human behavior. Rather than focusing on the personal histories of individuals (as would a personality psychologist), or on how individuals respond to their environment (as would a strict behaviorist), it looks at how people interact with and relate to each other *in social contexts*. It is within these social contexts that a wide range of behaviors and events fall.

Chapter 1 Understanding Social Behavior

A Model for Understanding Social Behavior

Social psychologists are interested in the forces that operate on individuals and cause them to engage in specific social behaviors. But social behavior is typically complex and has many contributing causes. Consequently, explaining social behavior is a difficult task. To simplify this task, we can assign the multiple causes of social behavior to one of two broad categories: the situation and the individual. According to a formula first proposed by Kurt Lewin (1936), one of the founders of social psychology, social behavior is a function of the interaction of the situation and the individual's characteristics, or

$$\text{Behavior} = f(\text{social situation} \times \text{individual characteristics})$$

Lewin's model of social behavior was inspired by his observation that the individual's perception of a situation is influenced by the tasks he or she has to accomplish. Lewin was a soldier in the German army during World War I. He noticed that as he came nearer to the battlefield, his view of the world changed. Where he once might have seen beautiful flowers and beckoning forests, he now saw boulders to hide behind and gullies from which he could ambush the enemy. Lewin came to believe that a person's perception of the world is influenced by what he or she has to do in that situation. He termed the combination of individual needs and situational factors the *psychological field* in which the individual lives (Pratkanis & Aronson, 1992).

According to this view, individuals with different needs and tasks would come to see the same event in dissimilar ways (Pratkanis & Aronson, 1992). Although Lewin looked at the individual's needs and tasks, he emphasized the importance of social context in producing the forces that control the individual's actions. Lewin was aware that we often fail to take situational factors into account when we try to explain why people behave as they do (Ross & Nisbett, 1991). For example, there were undoubtedly other young men with similar backgrounds and characteristics as the Trinidad Beach rescuers. However, those individuals may never risk their lives to save the lives of total strangers. They may react in different ways. So, each person reacts to the same situation differently.

Research supports the idea that one's personal characteristics interact with the nature of the social context to influence behavior. In one study, for example, individuals with high scores on a measure of extraversion used more gestures to communicate information to others than those with lower scores on this personality dimension did. However, individuals low in extraversion use more gestures to communicate when audience members can see them than if audience members cannot see them. This difference was smaller for individuals high in extraversion (Hostetter & Potthoff, 2012). Thus, personality (extraversion) interacted with the social situation (audience visibility) to affect behavior.

Thus far we have seen that the situation and individual characteristics are central to the understanding of social behavior in a general way. How do social psychologists define *situation* and *individual characteristics*? Let's take a closer look.

The Social Situation

The *social situation* comprises all influences on behavior that are external to the individual. A situational factor might be any aspect of the physical and/or social environment (the presence of other people, real or imagined) that influences behavior. Different individuals will react differently to the social situation. For example, Weibel, Straton, and Ortiz-Beck went directly to the two drowning brothers. York, on the other hand, swam to shore to get help, ensuring that medical assistance would be on the way.

Sometimes the situation works on us in subtle ways. We may modify our behavior even if there is no pressure on us to do so. We may imagine or believe that we are expected to act a certain way in a certain situation, and those beliefs can be as powerful as the situation itself. For example, let's say that you are in a restaurant with a group of friends. You are trying to decide what to order. You are leaning toward the sautéed buffalo, but the stewed rabbit sounds good too. When the server comes to the table, you order last, intending to try the buffalo. However, each of your friends orders the rabbit. When your turn comes, you also order the rabbit. You modified your behavior based on your friends' actions, because you didn't want to appear different. You felt and responded to social pressure of your own making!

Situational or social determinants of behavior exist on several levels simultaneously. Sometimes the social environment leads to temporary changes in behavior, as was the case in the restaurant. Ordering the rabbit may be specific to that one situation; you may never order rabbit again. In other cases, the social environment is a more pervasive influence and may lead to relatively permanent, enduring patterns of behaviors. One's culture exerts a long-lasting influence over a wide range of behaviors. Culture influences the foods we like, how we relate to members of the other sex, the amount of personal space we require (the area immediately surrounding us that we claim and defend), what we plan and expect to accomplish in life, and a host of other behaviors. It may also influence one's decision concerning shooting innocent children in a school or kill innocent co-workers at their place of employment.

Individual Characteristics

Individual characteristics include sex, age, race or ethnicity, personality characteristics, attitudes, self-concept, ways of thinking, and so on. In short, individual characteristics consist of anything internal to the person that might influence behavior. Physical traits are individual characteristics that are relatively enduring and for the most part known to others. Personality characteristics also tend to be enduring, but they are not necessarily obvious to others. Other internal characteristics, such as attitudes, opinions, self-concept, and so on, can change over time. People often have some choice about how much of these areas of themselves they reveal to others.

Let's consider our four rescuers again. Did they possess some special personality characteristic that impelled them to risk their lives to save the two brothers? Were they higher in what social psychologists call *dispositional empathy* (which we will discuss in Chapter 11) than other people? Would everyone with their level of dispositional empathy act the same way? Others at Trinidad Beach reacted differently than the four teenagers. How did their personal characteristics differ from the rescuers'? These are all questions relating to individual characteristics that affect behavior within a situation.

Another important individual characteristic that is somewhat different from personality characteristics is the particular way each individual perceives and thinks about his or her social world. **Social cognition** refers to a general process we use to make sense out of social events, which may or may not include other people. For example, if you read about the Trinidad Beach rescue on the Internet, you would probably begin to interpret the events, attempting to explain the rescuers' behavior. Eventually, you would probably begin to make inferences about the motives of the individuals involved and to form impressions of them. Social psychologists call this process **social perception**. For example, thinking about the four rescuers who risked their lives to save others may lead you to the inference that they were highly empathic, caring individuals acting in a way that many others would not. Once you infer these characteristics and form an impression that they were caring, compassionate individuals, you then settle on these internal characteristics as the primary motivation for their behavior.

Social cognition and social perception are central to our interpretation of situations. How we interpret social situations depends, in part, on our individual characteristics. For example, how would you respond if you discovered that your significant other was cheating on you? Most would say that they would be angry and feel betrayed. This is undoubtedly the case. However, how individuals respond to such a situation depends on who is involved. A common finding is that men are more upset by sexual infidelity, while women are more upset by emotional infidelity (Miller & Maner, 2009). So, how a person perceives infidelity is related to his or her gender. However, it gets more complicated when we consider another individual difference factor. Miller and Maner also found that the gender difference is more pronounced for individuals who are prone to chronic jealousy. So, the degree to which a man or woman is upset by sexual or emotional infidelity, respectively, depends on another individual characteristic. The bottom line is that every individual has a slightly different view of the world because everyone has unique personal traits and a unique history of life experiences. Each of us actively constructs our own view of our social world, based on interpretations of social information (which we discuss in detail in Chapter 3).

social cognition The general process we use to make sense out of social events, which may or may not include other people.

social perception The social processes by which we come to comprehend the behavior, words, and actions of other people.

Before we look at how Lewin's model has been expanded, we must make an important point about how individuals perceive the relative effects of the social situation and individual characteristics on behavior. Although one of the major lessons of social psychology (which we explore throughout this text) is that the social situation exerts a powerful effect on social behavior, individuals may minimize or deny this effect. We tend to see ourselves as individualists or free thinkers who will not go along with the crowd. For example, Spanos et al. (2015) investigated the degree to which participants were willing to admit that the social situation affected food intake. They found that participants who were more attuned to the social environment were more likely to acknowledge that the social situation affected food intake, compared to those who were less attuned. Interestingly, denial that the social situation affects food intake is not related to the degree to which the situation actually affects food intake (Spanos et al., 2015). The late social psychologist Stanley Milgram issued a challenge to those who deny that their behavior is affected by the social environment. He challenged students who fancied themselves to be free thinkers to go somewhere crowded (e.g., a food court at a mall on a busy Saturday), stand on a chair, and sing their favorite song at the top of their lungs. If you are, in fact, free from the effects of others, you should be more than willing to do this. In reality, very few students are willing to sing at the mall!

The social situation exerts a powerful effect on behavior. The late social psychologist Stanley Milgram once issued the challenge that if you believe that you are not affected by others, go to a crowded place (like a mall food court), stand up on a chair, and loudly sing your favorite song. Would you?
Source: conrado/Shutterstock.

Expanding Lewin's Model

Lewin's model tells us that both the social situation (physical setting, the presence of other people, real or imagined) and individual characteristics (physical traits, personality traits, attitudes and habitual ways of thinking, perceptual and cognitive processes, needs and tasks) influence social behavior. Lewin's model, however, does not specify how situational factors and individual characteristics fit together into a broad, general model of social behavior. We need to expand on Lewin's original model to gain a better understanding of the forces that shape social behavior. An expansion of Lewin's original model is shown in Figure 1.1.

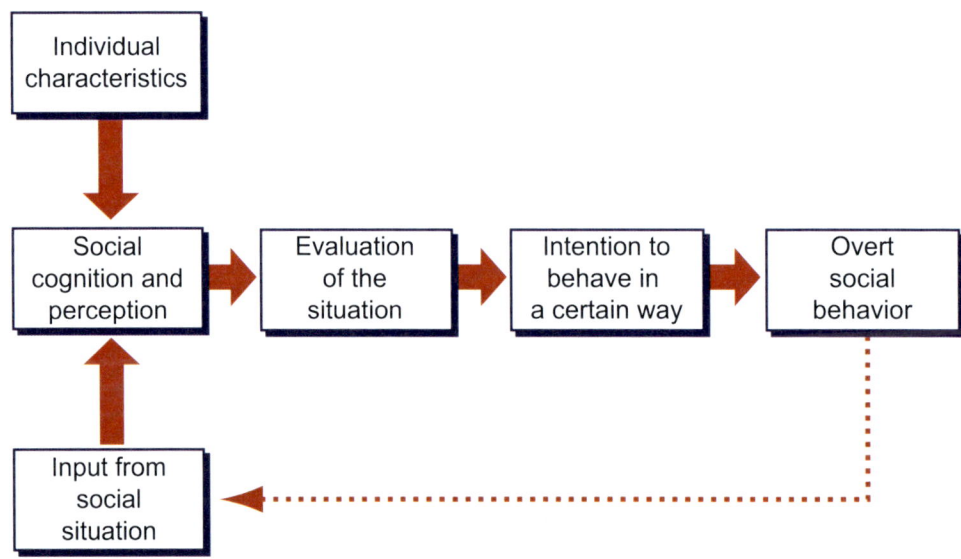

FIGURE 1.1

An expanded model of social behavior. How we act in a given situation depends on input from the situation and individual characteristics that are mediated by the processes of social cognition and perception and the formation of an intention to behave in a certain way.

As shown in this model, input from the social situation and individual characteristics do not influence social behavior directly. Instead, they both contribute to how we process information via mechanisms of social cognition and social perception. How that information is processed yields a particular evaluation of the situation. For example, in the wake of a mass shooting, controversy swirls around how to best prevent mass shootings. Some want to ban certain firearms and high-capacity magazines. Others want to increase security at schools and place more emphasis on mental health services. Even those who favor more gun control laws cannot agree on what shape those laws should take. Some people may favor banning so-called "assault rifles" and high-capacity magazines. Others may be more in favor of tightening up background check laws to make it more difficult for a mentally ill person to obtain a gun. According to Figure 1.1, our evaluation of the social situation does not translate immediately into overt social behavior. Instead, based on our evaluation of the situation, we form a behavioral intention. For example, after 17 students were killed in a mass shooting at Marjory Stoneman Douglas High School in Parkland, Florida, David Hogg (a student) became a strong advocate for gun control to address such shootings. He spoke out often on the need for gun-control measures. On the other hand, Andrew Pollack, whose daughter Meadow was killed at the school, became an advocate for school safety and tightening security in schools. In these cases, the same event led two different individuals to form different behavioral intentions, leading to different behaviors.

It is important to realize that just because we form a behavioral intention does not mean we will act on that intention. For example, a person can form the intention of advocating for gun bans but never follow through, thinking that perhaps attempting to pass gun ban laws will be futile in the current political atmosphere.

This view of social behavior implies that it is a dynamic process. Our monitoring of the social situation does not end with an evaluation of the situation, or the formation of an intention, or social behavior. Instead, we are constantly monitoring the social situation (our own behavior and that of others) and may modify our assessment of it on a moment-to-moment basis. Thus, we fine-tune our behavioral intentions up to the point that we engage in social behavior. So, even though the various processes underlying social behavior are presented in Figure 1.1 in a sequence of discrete boxes, they are really quite fluid and involve constant updating of our evaluation of the situation.

One final aspect of this model needs to be addressed. Notice that in Figure 1.1 there is a dotted arrow going from social behavior to the social situation. In any social situation in which we are directly involved, our own behavior influences the social environment and probably will cause changes in the behavior of others. For example, imagine that you are talking to someone you have just met. Based on the first thing she says, you determine that she is not very friendly. Consequently, you become defensive (you fold your arms, lean away from her) and respond to her in a cold way. She picks up on your behavior and becomes colder herself. This cycle continues until one of you breaks off the conversation. How might this situation have played out if you had interpreted her initial behaviors as nervousness and responded to her in a positive way? You may have made a new friend. Thus, your own interpretations and behaviors had a profound effect on the situation.

Study Break

This section defined *social psychology* and introduced you to the basic model for understanding social behavior. Before you begin the next section, answer the following questions:

1. What is the definition of social psychology, and what does each element of the definition mean?
2. What is Kurt Lewin's model for explaining social behavior? Define each of the crucial components of the model.
3. How have social psychologists expanded upon Lewin's model?
4. How can your social behavior affect the social situation, requiring a re-evaluation of the situation? Give an example.

Social Psychology and Related Fields

We have seen that social psychology is a field of study that seeks to understand and explain social behavior—how individuals think and act in relation to other people. Yet many other disciplines are also concerned with the thoughts and actions of human beings, both individually and in groups. In what ways does social psychology differ from its two parent disciplines, sociology and psychology? And how is it similar to and different from other fields of study, such as biology, anthropology, and history?

To see how these fields differ in their approaches, let's consider a single question: Why do groups of people, including nations, display hostility toward one another? Although social psychologists are interested in this social problem, they have no unique claim to it (nor to others). Biologists, psychologists, anthropologists, sociologists, historians, and others all have explanations for the never-ending cycle of human violence. Let's consider first those fields that look for the causes of violent behavior within the individual and then move on to fields that focus increasingly on factors in the environment.

Many biologists say the answer to the puzzle of human violence resides not in our social situations, organizations, or personalities but rather in our genetic structure. For example, scientists have identified a tiny genetic defect that appears to predispose some men toward violence. Scientists studied a large Dutch family with a history of violent and erratic behavior among many, although not all, of the males. They found that those males who were prone to violence had an enzyme deficiency due to a mutation of a gene carried by the X chromosome (Brunner et al., 1993). Because men have only one X chromosome, they were the only ones who manifested the defect. Women may be carriers of the deficiency, but they are protected from expressing it by their second X chromosome with its backup copy of the gene. Geneticists do not argue that genetic defects are the sole cause of violence, but they do say that these factors play a definite role in determining who is violent. To complicate the genetic picture, we now know that one's epigenetic code, which determines how a particular genetic predisposition is expressed, also has an influence. *Epigenetics* refers to a complex biochemical system that exists above the basic level of one's DNA code (genetics) that can affect the overt expression of genetically influenced traits. Epigenetics influence the expression of genetic codes by switching genes on or off and can affect the expression of genetic predispositions (Pennisi, 2001; Tremblay, 2010). Scientists have discovered that your epigenetic code is influenced by environmental factors (Dolinoy et al., 2006). So, for example, exposure to a violent environment may lead to the expression of a genetic predisposition toward violence. Another person with the same genetic predisposition who is not exposed to a violent environment may not express the predisposition.

Although social psychology is not the only science to study group behavior, social psychologists focus on small groups, such as a jury.
Source: bikeriderlondon/Shutterstock.

Another biologically oriented view of this question comes from developmental psychologists (who study the development of human beings across the lifespan). They suggest that human beings may have an innate fear of strangers. They point out that at about 4 or 5 months, infants begin to react with fear to novel or unusual stimuli, such as the faces of strangers (Hebb & Thompson, 1968). Between 6 and 18 months, infants may experience intense *stranger anxiety*. These psychologists, as well as some biologists, argue that fear of strangers may be part of our genetic heritage. Early humans who possessed this trait may have been more likely to survive than those who didn't, and they passed the trait down to us. On a group or societal level, this innate mistrust of strangers might be elaborated into hostility, aggression, or even warfare. Other psychologists, however, are not convinced that fear of the novel is inborn (Hebb & Thompson, 1968).

Along similar lines, anthropologists (who study the physical and cultural development of the human species) have documented that some tribal societies view strangers with suspicion and may even attempt to kill them. Some anthropologists argue that hostility to strangers may have benefited early human groups by helping them unite against threats from the outside.

Other scientists emphasize the psychological makeup of individuals as a way of explaining behavior. Personality psychologists suggest that aggressiveness (or any other behavioral trait) is a characteristic of the individual. The person carries the trait from situation to situation, expressing it in any number of different circumstances (Derlega et al., 1991). Personality psychologists would argue that some internal characteristic drove the four rescuers to behave altruistically at Trinidad Beach, just as some other personality traits affected the behavior of the two drowning brothers.

One researcher studied the aggressive behavior of adolescent boys in Sweden over 3 years (Olweus, 1984). He found that boys who were aggressive (started fights, were bullies) in the sixth grade were also physically aggressive in the ninth grade. Personality researchers take this as evidence that individual factors are an important determinant of aggression. Over the course of the 3 years, the boys had different teachers, were in different buildings, and had a variety of classmates. Yet their behavior remained consistently aggressive, despite the change in their social situation (Derlega et al., 1991).

Social psychologists study the individual in the social situation. They are concerned with determining what characteristics of a situation increase or decrease the potential for violence. In looking at the question of hostility between groups, social psychologists focus on the forces both in individuals and in situations that lead to this outcome.

Whereas psychology (including social psychology) focuses on the role of the individual, other fields look for causes of behavior in more impersonal and general causes outside the individual. For example, sociologists are concerned primarily, although not exclusively, with larger groups and systems in society. A sociologist interested in violence might study the development of gangs. Interviews with gang members, observation of gang activity, or even participation in a gang as a participant, if possible, would be potential methods of study.

Although sociology and social psychology are related, there are important differences between them. The sociologist asks what it is about the structure of society that promotes violence; the social psychologist, in contrast, looks at the individual's particular social situation as the potential cause of violence. The social psychologist is interested primarily in the behavior of individuals or of small groups, such as a jury. Sociology may be empirical in the sense that it attempts to gather quantitative information. A sociologist might compare rates of violent behavior in two societies and then try to determine how those societies differ. Social psychology is much more an experimental, laboratory-based science.

Historians take an even broader view of intergroup hostility than sociologists. They are primarily concerned with the interplay of large forces such as economic, political, and technological trends. Historians have shown, for example, that one nation can express power against other nations only if it has sufficient economic resources to sustain armed forces and if it has developed an adequate technological base to support them (Kennedy, 1987; O'Connell, 1989). One historian documented the importance of a single technological advance—the invention of stirrups—in accelerating violence between groups in the early Middle Ages (McNeill, 1982). Before stirrups were invented, knights on horseback were not very effective fighters. But once they were able to steady themselves in the saddle, they became capable of delivering a powerful blow with a lance at full gallop. The use of stirrups quickly spread throughout Europe and led to the rise of cavalry as an instrument of military power.

History and sociology focus on how social forces and social organization influence human behavior. These fields tend to take a *top-down perspective*; the major unit of analysis is the group or the institution, whether a nation, a corporation, or a neighborhood organization. Psychology, with its emphasis on individual behavior and the individual's point of view, offers a *bottom-up perspective*. Social psychology offers a distinct perspective on social behavior. Social psychologists look at how social forces affect the individual's thinking and behavior. Although the field takes a bottom-up perspective, focusing on the individual as the unit of analysis, behavior is always examined in social situations. Social psychology, therefore, tries to take into account individual factors, such as personality, as well as social and historical forces that have shaped human behavior.

As indicated earlier, social psychology is a science. The use of scientific methods is the primary contribution of social psychology to the understanding of complex, uncertain social behaviors such as intergroup hostility.

Research in Social Psychology

On January 27, 2013, hundreds of patrons were enjoying themselves in the Kiss nightclub in Santa Maria, Brazil. The popular country band Gurizada Fandangueira was just about to perform their sixth song of the night. The band's guitarist Rodrigo Martins noticed embers falling from the club's foam ceiling. The ceiling was on fire, and the fire was spreading quickly. Once patrons noticed the rapidly spreading fire, they began to rush for the exit. In the ensuing panic, patrons surged toward the only exit. Several patrons burst through a restroom door, believing it was an exit. At least 30 patrons died in the restroom, their bodies piled on top of another. The scene within the club rapidly degenerated into a mass panic that one survivor described as a scene out of hell. In the rush to the only exit, a person fell, then another and then another. Soon, the exit was blocked and hundreds of patrons continued to surge toward the exit. When the dust cleared, 233 patrons lay dead, most crushed to death in the panic.

Even if you only read about this on the Internet, you probably would wonder how it could happen and try to come up with an explanation. Could it be possible that the nightclub was filled with selfish, aggressive people who would do anything to survive? Could it be that Brazilians are more prone to panic than others? That does not seem likely since similar panics have happened in other countries as well.

When we devise explanations for events like the one in Brazil, based on our prior knowledge and experiences, our attitudes and biases, and the limited information the Internet provides, we don't know if they are accurate or not. Such *commonsense explanations*—simplistic explanations for social behavior that are based on what we believe to be true of the world (Bordens & Abbott, 2021)—serve us well in our day-to-day lives, providing easy ways to explain complex events. People would be hopelessly bogged down in trying to understand events if they didn't devise these explanations and move on to the next concern in their lives. Unfortunately, commonsense explanations are usually inadequate; that is, there is no evidence or proof that they pinpoint the real causes of events.

The aim of social psychology is to provide valid, reliable explanations for events such as the one in Santa Maria, Brazil. Rather than relying on conjecture, rumor, and simplistic reasoning, social psychologists approach the problem of explaining complex social behavior in a systematic, scientific way. Like other scientists, social psychologists seek to develop scientific explanations for social behavior. These explanations are based on careful scientific observations and/or experimentation rather than on casual observations that underlie commonsense explanations. To accomplish this, social psychologists use **science**, which is a set of activities designed to generate a systematic, reliable body of knowledge and explanations for social behavior (Bordens & Abbott, 2021).

Traditionally, the scientific method has been an organizing principle guiding how research is carried out. The *scientific method* involves four steps. The first step in the scientific method is to identify a phenomenon to study. This can come from observation of everyday behavior, research literature, or your own previous research. Next, a testable research **hypothesis** must be formed. A hypothesis is a tentative statement about the relationship between variables. The third step is to design a research study to test your hypothesis. Finally, the study is actually carried out, and the data are analyzed.

Although it is still beneficial to use the scientific method to guide research, a new approach has been developed that moves away from the conception of science as a series of steps. This approach is the **Next Generation Science Standards**, which set out eight practices for science and engineering to guide scientific research. These eight practices are summarized in Table 1.1. It is important to understand that there is no particular order in which scientists apply the eight principles. Also, scientists in one field may rely on some practices more than scientists in other fields. Even within a particular science, some scientists may use some practices more than others. The eight practices allow for a great deal of flexibility in how science is conceptualized and practiced.

Throughout this book, we refer to and describe research that social psychologists have conducted to test their ideas, to gain information about events, and to discover the causes of social behavior. We turn now to some of the basic principles of research, including the major research methods, the role of theory in research, the settings for social psychological research, and the importance of ethical conduct in research involving human participants.

science A set of activities designed to generate a systematic, reliable body of knowledge and explanations for social behavior.

hypothesis A tentative and testable statement about the relationship between variables.

Next Generation Science Standards An approach to science setting out eight practices for science and engineering to guide scientific research.

TABLE 1.1 Eight Principles of Science

Practice	Definition
Asking questions and defining problems	Scientists ask and refine questions, leading to descriptions of and explanations for events that can be tested empirically.
Developing and using models	Scientists use and build models to represent ideas and explanations (e.g., diagrams, mathematical representations, simulations).
Planning and carrying out investigations	Scientists plan and carry out systematic studies in the laboratory or field, either individually or in collaboration with other scientists.
Analyzing and interpreting data	Scientists analyze data resulting from their studies to derive meaning using a range of tools (e.g., statistical analysis, tabulation, graphing).
Using mathematical and computational thinking	Scientists use mathematics and computation as tools for representing variables and relationships among them, including performing statistical analysis, constructing simulations, and characterizing quantitative relationships.
Constructing explanations and designing solutions	The products of the practice of science are explanations and solutions to problems.
Engaging in argument from evidence	Scientists use arguments from evidence obtained from research to develop explanations and solutions.
Obtaining, evaluating, and communicating information	Scientists must communicate clearly and persuasively any ideas and methods they develop and critique ideas through professional activity.

Based on National Science Teaching Association (2014).

The principal aim of the science of social psychology is to uncover scientific explanations for social behavior. A scientific explanation is an interpretation of the causes of social behavior that is based on objective observation and logic and is subject to empirical testing (Bordens & Abbott, 2021). To this end, social psychologists use a wide variety of techniques to study social behavior. Generally, they favor two research strategies in their quest for scientific knowledge: *experimental research* and *correlational research*. Let's consider the characteristics of each of these methods, along with their advantages and disadvantages.

SOCIAL PSYCHOLOGY IN ACTION

Distinguishing Science from Pseudoscience

We have taken great pains to point out that social psychology is a science because it adheres to the rules and methods employed in science to acquire knowledge. Does this mean that everything you encounter relating to social psychology and its phenomena is based on careful scientific scrutiny? Unfortunately, the answer to this question is no. There is a great deal of dross out there (dross means "worthless, commonplace, or trivial" matters), especially in the popular media, that is not based on careful scientific research. For example, is it really possible that you will experience greater physical and psychological well-being if you tape a patch to the bottom of your foot at night to draw out toxins from the body? Will you actually get more and higher quality sleep if you take a pill with a special blend of herbs and enzymes before you go to bed? Does a polygraph actually detect when someone is lying? The polygraph is used in employment screening and by law enforcement to detect deception. Some scientists claim that the polygraph amounts to nothing more than pseudoscience, pointing out that best estimates of accuracy show a relatively low rate (65%; Barber, 2013). Many of the claims made in commercials and by seemingly legitimate psychologists are simply false because they are based on pseudoscientific claims and not on carefully conducted scientific studies.

What exactly is pseudoscience? Well, the term literally translates to "false science." You can think of it as nonscience masquerading as a true science (Hansson, 2017). However, we really need a more formal definition to better understand exactly what pseudoscience means. One definition that we particularly like states that "pseudoscience is [a] set of ideas based on theories put forth as scientific when they are not scientific" (Carrol, 2006). The term pseudoscience dates backw to 1796 when alchemy was called a "fantastic pseudoscience." The term pseudoscience has been used widely since the 1880s and has a negative connotation (Hansson, 2017). Hansson maintains that in order for an endeavor to be considered pseudoscience, it must meet two criteria. First, the endeavor is not scientific. Second, the major proponents of the endeavor attempt

In the 19th century the pseudoscience of phrenology became very popular. It fell from favor when brain scientists found evidence against its main assumptions.
Source: Everett Collection/Shutterstock.

to give the impression that the endeavor is actually scientific.

Scott Lilienfeld (2005) enumerates several additional characteristics that comprise pseudoscience. For example, in pseudoscience, disconfirmed ideas are not adjusted based on new information. The burden of proof to falsify a claim is shifted from the person making the claim to the critic. Claims are largely based on anecdotal evidence (e.g., "My aunt sleeps better while wearing a magnetic bracelet"), and published findings are not reviewed by experts before publication. Additionally, impressive-sounding jargon is often used to give credibility to dubious claims. It is important to understand that not every instance of pseudoscience will have all of Lilienfeld's characteristics. However, the more of them present, the more likely a claim or finding is the product of pseudoscience.

Why is it important for you to understand the difference between true science and pseudoscience? There are two reasons: theoretical and practical (Hansson, 2017). According to Hansson, on a theoretical level, an understanding of pseudoscience contributes to our understanding of the philosophy of science. On a practical level, understanding the distinction can help guide decisions in your everyday life and decisions made by

(continued)

TABLE 1.2 Real Science versus Pseudoscience

Real Science	Pseudoscience
Findings published in scientific, peer-reviewed journals.	Findings published in publications for the general public that do not involve peer review.
Methods used in experiments must be specified clearly, and results must be reproducible.	Vague descriptions of methods are provided, and results cannot be easily reproduced.
Failures in prediction are scrutinized carefully.	Failures are downplayed, rationalized away, hidden, ignored, or avoided.
With time, more and more is learned about a phenomenon being studied.	Little, if any progress, is made over time with respect to a phenomenon or claim.
Persuasion is based on scientific evidence, and old ideas are discarded when they are shown to be incorrect.	Persuasion is often through belief or faith. Conversion is sought rather than convincing others with evidence. Ideas are adhered to, regardless of conflicting evidence.
No advocacy of unproven products or claims.	Person making claim or advocating product likely to make money based on unproven claims or products.

Based on Coker (2001).

policymakers (e.g., on health care issues). In your personal life, understanding this distinction can help you better critically analyze what appear to be scientific claims made in sales pitches, on your newsfeed, or in an article you might read online. By critically thinking about the claims made in these and other sources, you will be in a better position to separate the gold from the dross and make more informed decisions about your world. Also, it can possibly save you money! You might not shell out your hard-earned cash on those pads for the bottoms of your feet or that magnetic bracelet. How can you distinguish real science from pseudoscience? It takes work. However, a place to start is with the information in Table 1.2, which presents some clues you can use to distinguish science from pseudoscience.

Discussion Questions

1. What is pseudoscience and what are its characteristics?
2. Why is it important to learn about pseudoscience?

Study Break

This section showed how social psychology relates to other fields that also study social behavior and how social psychologists apply the scientific method to study social behavior. Before you begin the next section, answer the following questions:

1. How does social psychology differ from other disciplines that study social behavior? Give examples.
2. What are *commonsense explanations,* and how do they form?
3. How does a scientific explanation differ from a commonsense explanation, and why do social psychologists prefer scientific explanations?
4. How do social psychologists use science to describe and explain social behavior?
5. What is pseudoscience, and why is it important to learn about it?

Experimental Research

One goal of research in social psychology is to understand the causes of social behavior. The researcher usually has an idea he or she wants to test about how a particular factor affects an event or a behavior—that is, whether a particular factor *causes* a particular behavior. To establish a causal relationship between factors, researchers have to use the

experimental research
Research involving manipulating a variable suspected of influencing behavior to see how that change affects behavior; results show causal relationships among variables.

research method known as the experiment. Because **experimental research** is the only kind of study that can establish causality, it is the method most social psychologists prefer. An experiment has three essential features: manipulating a variable, ensuring that groups comprising the experiment are equivalent at the beginning of the experiment, and exercising control over extraneous variables.

Manipulating Variables

In an experiment, a researcher manipulates, or changes the value or nature of, a variable. For example, Nicolas Guéguen (2015) investigated whether a woman's hairstyle would affect a person's willingness to help another. Guéguen had a female confederate (someone working for the researcher) walk in front of a participant and drop a glove. The confederate's hairstyle was manipulated between being up in a bun, tied in a ponytail, or down on her shoulders. Guéguen measured whether the participant picked up the glove to return to the confederate. Guéguen found that hairstyle affected male participants' willingness to help (but not female participants' willingness). The male participants were more likely to help when the confederate's hair fell naturally on her shoulders.

In this experiment, Guéguen (2015) manipulated the hairstyle of the confederate between three different styles. This variable that the researcher manipulates is called the **independent variable**. The researcher wants to determine whether changes in the value of the independent variable cause changes in the participant's behavior. To this end, the researcher obtains some measure of behavior. For example, Guéguen measured the participants' willingness to help the confederate. This second variable is called the **dependent variable**: It is the measure the researcher assesses to determine the influence of the independent variable on the participant's behavior. The essence of experimental research is to manipulate an independent variable (or two or even more independent variables) and look for related changes in the value of the dependent variable.

independent variable
The variable that the researcher manipulates in an experiment.

dependent variable
The measure the researcher assesses to determine the influence of the independent variable on the participants' behavior.

The Equivalence of Groups

The second essential characteristic of an experiment is that there are at least two groups involved who are comparable at the outset of the experiment. In the simplest type of experiment, one group of participants receives a treatment (for example, the hairstyle to which they are exposed). The participants who receive the experimental treatment comprise the **experimental group**. To know for sure that an experimental treatment (the independent variable) is causing a particular effect, you have to compare the behavior of participants in the experimental group with the behavior of participants who do not receive the treatment. The participants who do *not* receive the experimental treatment comprise the **control group**. A simple example of this strategy is an experiment testing the effects of a drug on aggressive behavior. Participants in the experimental group would receive a dose of an active drug (e.g., norepinephrine), whereas participants in the control group would not receive the drug. The researcher then compares the behavior of the participants in the experimental and control groups. In essence, the control group provides a baseline of behavior in the absence of the treatment against which the behavior of the treated participants is compared.

experimental group
A group comprised of participants who receive the experimental treatment in an experiment.

control group A group in an experiment comprised of participants who do not receive the experimental treatment.

In the real world of research, the distinction between the experimental and control groups may not be this obvious. For example, in the Guéguen (2015) experiment, there is no true control group in the true sense of the concept. Instead, participants in all three groups received a "treatment" (i.e., bun, ponytail, or hair falling on the shoulders). Most experiments you will encounter will follow this model. In order to establish a clear cause-and-effect relationship between the independent and dependent variables in an experiment, the participants in the groups must have the same characteristics at the outset of the experiment. For example, in an experiment on norepinephrine and aggression, you would not want to assign individuals with bad tempers to the 15-mg experimental group. If you did this and found that norepinephrine produces the highest levels of aggression, one could argue that the heightened aggression was due to the fact that all of the participants in that group were hotheads.

random assignment
A method of assigning participants to groups in an experiment that involves each participant's having an equal chance of being in the experimental or control group.

The best way to ensure that two or more groups will be comparable at the outset of an experiment is **random assignment** of individuals to groups, which means that each participant has an equal chance of being assigned to the experimental or control group.

Researchers can then be fairly certain that participants with similar characteristics or backgrounds are distributed among the groups. If the two or more groups in an experiment are comparable at the outset, the experiment is said to have *internal validity*, and it can legitimately demonstrate a causal relationship.

Researchers are also concerned about another kind of validity, known as *external validity*, or generality. When researchers study how experimental treatments affect groups of participants, they want to be able to generalize their results to larger populations. To do so, they have to be reasonably sure that the participants in their experiments are representative (typical) of the population to which they wish to generalize their results. For example, if the participants of a study were all male science majors at a small religious college, the researchers could not legitimately generalize the results to females or mixed populations, to younger or older people, or to music majors. If the researchers have gotten a representative sample of their population of interest, then they can legitimately generalize the results to that population, and the study is said to have external validity.

Controlling Extraneous Variables

The goal of any experiment is to show a clear, unambiguous causal relationship between the independent and dependent variables. In order to show such a relationship, the researcher must ensure that no other variables influence the value of the dependent variable. The researcher must tightly control any **extraneous variable** that might influence the value of the dependent variable. An extraneous variable is any variable not controlled by the researcher that could affect the results. For example, Guéguen (2015) controlled an extraneous variable by using the same confederate with the same hair color for all participants. Had he used three different confederates (blonde, brunette, redhead) with different hair colors, the results might have been affected by hair color.

extraneous variable
Any variable not controlled by the researcher that could affect the results of a study.

As just described, extraneous variables affect the outcome of an experiment by adding a random influence on behavior. In short, extraneous variables make it more difficult to establish a causal connection between your independent and dependent variables. In some cases, an extraneous variable can exert a systematic effect on the outcome of an experiment. This happens when the extraneous variable varies systematically with the independent variable. The result is that a **confounding variable** exists in the experiment. For example, if Guéguen (2015) had a blonde confederate wear the bun hairstyle, a brunette wear the ponytail, and a redhead wear the on-the-shoulders style, there would be no way to know if it were the hairstyle or hair color that affected helping behavior. There is no way to separate the effect of hairstyle from the effect of hair color. There is no way to tell if more participants helped because of hairstyle (shoulder) or hair color (red). An obvious way to avoid this problem is to do what Guéguen did: use the same confederate with the same hair color for all participants.

confounding variable
An extraneous variable in an experiment that varies systematically with the independent variable, making it difficult or impossible to establish a causal connection between the independent and dependent variables.

In the real world of research, confounding is seldom as obvious and blatant as in our example. More often, confounding results because a researcher is careless when designing an experiment. Confounding variables often creep into experiments because independent variables are not clearly defined or executed. The presence of confounding variables in an experiment renders the results useless. The confounding variable provides an alternative explanation for any results that emerge. Because of this, a clear causal connection between the independent and dependent variables cannot be established. Consequently, it is essential that a researcher identify potential sources of confounding and take steps to avoid them. The time to do this is during the design phase of an experiment. Careful attention to detail when designing an experiment can go a long way toward achieving an experiment that is free from confounding variables.

Factorial Experiments

An important aspect of real-world research is that experiments are usually more complex than the simple experimental group/control group design we discussed previously. In fact, a vast majority of research in social psychology has two or more independent variables. A design with two or more independent variables is a **factorial experiment**.

As an example of a simple factorial experiment, consider one conducted by Patricia Oswald (2002) that investigated the effects of two independent variables on willingness

factorial experiment
An experimental design in which two or more independent variables are manipulated.

to help. Oswald had participants watch a videotape of a person presented as an older adult (Michelle), who was discussing some of her thoughts and emotions about returning to college. The first independent variable was whether participants were instructed to focus on Michelle's thoughts (cognitions) or emotions (affect) while watching her on the videotape. The second independent variable was the type of affect (positive or negative) and cognitions (positive or negative) Michelle displayed on the videotape. Participants filled out several measures after watching the videotape, including how much time they would be willing to devote to helping the student shown on the tape. Before we get to Oswald's results, let's analyze the benefits of doing a factorial experiment.

The principal benefit of doing a factorial experiment as compared to separate one-factor (i.e., one independent variable each) experiments is that you obtain more information from the factorial experiment. For example, we can determine the independent effect of each independent variable on the dependent variable. In Oswald's experiment we can determine the effect of participant focus (the focus on either Michelle's affect or cognition) on willingness to help. This is called a *main effect* of one independent variable on the dependent variable. We could also determine, independently, the main effect of the second independent variable (positive or negative cognition or affect) on the dependent variable.

The main advantage of the factorial experiment lies in the third piece of information that would not be available if you ran two separate experiments: the interaction between independent variables. An **interaction** exists if the effect of one independent variable (e.g., focus of attention) changes over levels of a second (e.g., type of affect or cognition displayed). The presence of an interaction indicates a complex relationship between independent variables. In other words, an interaction shows that there is no simple effect of either independent variable on the dependent variable. For this reason, most social psychological experiments are designed to discover interactions between independent variables.

Let's go back to Oswald's experiment to see what she found. First, Oswald found a statistically significant main effect of focus of attention on willingness to help. Participants who focused on Michelle's affect volunteered more time than those who focused on Michelle's cognitions. If this were all that Oswald found, we would be content with the conclusion that focus of attention determines helping. However, Oswald also found a statistically significant interaction between focus of attention and the type of affect (positive or negative) Michelle displayed. This interaction is shown in Figure 1.2.

interaction When the effect of one independent variable in a factorial experiment changes over levels of a second, indicating a complex relationship between independent variables.

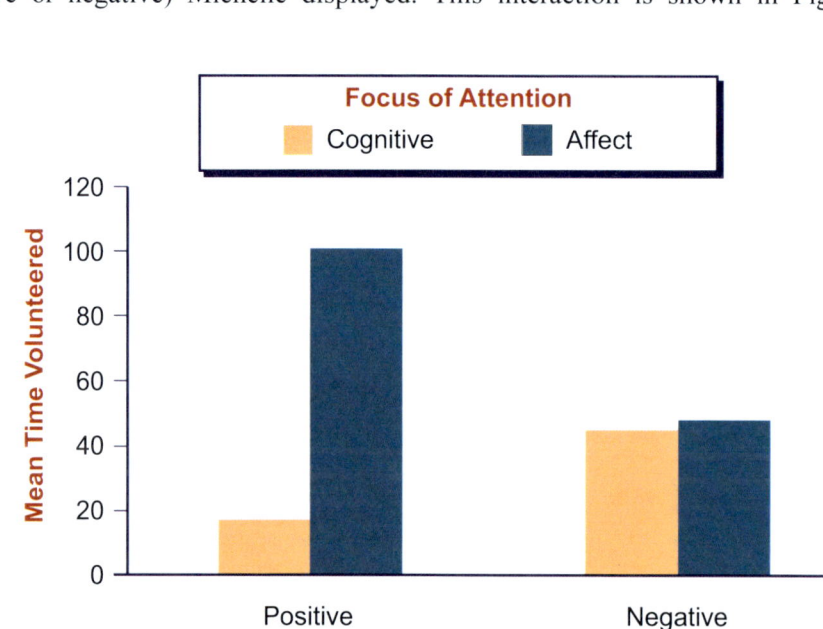

FIGURE 1.2

The interaction between type of affect and focus of attention.
Based on data from Oswald (2002).

As you can see, focus of attention had a significant effect when Michelle displayed positive affect or cognition, but not when she displayed negative affect or cognition. In the light of this interaction, would you still be confident in the broad conclusion that focus of attention affects helping? Probably not, because whether focus of attention affects helping depends on the type of affect or cognition displayed.

Evaluating Experiments

Most of the research studies described in this book are experimental studies. When evaluating these experiments, ask yourself these questions:

- What was the independent variable, and how was it manipulated?
- What were the experimental and control groups?
- What was the dependent variable?
- What methods were employed to test the hypothesis, and were the methods sound?
- Were there any confounding variables that could provide an alternative explanation for the results?
- What was found? That is, what changes in the dependent variable were observed as a function of manipulation of the independent variable?
- What was the nature of the sample used? Was the sample representative of the general population, or was it limited with respect to demographics, such as age, gender, culture, or some other set of characteristics?

Study Break

This section introduced you to experimental research. Because experimental research helps social psychologists to discover the causes of social behavior, it is the most widely used research method in social psychology. Before you begin the next section, answer the following questions:

1. What makes up the most basic experiment, and why is a control group needed?
2. How do social psychologists ensure that groups in an experiment are equivalent before an experiment begins? Why is this important?
3. What are extraneous and confounding variables, and why are steps taken to control them?
4. What is a factorial experiment? Give an example. What is an interaction, and why do social psychologists focus on interactions?

Correlational Research

Although most research in social psychology is experimental, some research is correlational. In **correlational research**, researchers do not manipulate an independent variable. Instead, they measure two or more dependent variables and look for a relationship between them. If changes in one variable are associated with changes in another, the two variables are said to be correlated. When the values of two variables change in the same direction, increasing or decreasing in value, there is a **positive correlation** between them. For example, if you find that crime increases along with increases in temperature, a positive correlation exists. When the values change in opposite directions, one increasing and the other decreasing, there is a **negative correlation** between the variables. For example, if you find that less help is given as the number of bystanders to an emergency increases, a negative correlation exists. When one variable does not change systematically with the other, they are uncorrelated.

Even if correlations are found, however, a causal relationship cannot be inferred. For example, height and weight are correlated with each other—the greater one is, the greater the other tends to be—but increases in one do not cause increases in the other. Changes in both

correlational research
Research that measures two or more dependent variables and looks for a relationship between them; causal relationships among variables cannot be established.

positive correlation
The direction of a correlation in which the values of two variables increase or decrease in the same direction.

negative correlation
The direction of a correlation in which the value of one variable increases whereas the value of a second decreases.

are caused by other factors, such as growth hormone and diet. Correlational research indicates whether changes in one variable are related to changes in another, but it does not indicate *why* the changes are related. Cause and effect can be demonstrated only by experiments.

In correlational studies, researchers are interested in both the direction of the relationship between the variables (whether it is positive or negative) and the degree, or strength, of the relationship. They measure these two factors with a special statistical test known as the **correlation coefficient** (symbolized as r). The size of the correlation coefficient, which can range from -1 through 0 to $+1$, shows the degree of the relationship. A value of r that approaches -1 to $+1$ indicates a stronger relationship than a value closer to 0.

In Figure 1.3, the five graphs illustrate correlations of varying strengths and directions. Figure 1.3A shows a 0 correlation: Points are scattered at random within the graph. Figures 1.3B and 1.3C show positive correlations of different strengths. As the correlation gets stronger, the points start to line up with each other (Figure 1.3B). In a perfect positive correlation ($r = +1$), all the points line up along a straight line (Figure 1.3C). Notice that in a positive correlation, the points line up along a line that slopes in an upward direction, beginning at the lower left of the graph and ending at the upper right.

In a negative correlation (shown in Figures 1.3D and 1.3E), the same rules concerning strength apply that held for the positive correlation. Figure 1.3E shows a perfect negative correlation (-1).

An excellent example of a correlational study is one conducted by Del Barrio et al. (2004). Del Barrio et al. investigated the relationship between personality characteristics and an individual's capacity to feel empathy for someone in need. Del Barrio et al. administered a measure of empathy and a personality inventory measuring the "Big Five" personality dimensions (energy, friendliness, conscientiousness, emotional stability, and openness) to Spanish adolescents. Del Barrio et al. found that "friendliness" correlated most strongly with empathy for both boys and girls. High scores on the "friendliness" dimension related

correlation coefficient
A statistical technique used to determine the direction and strength of a relationship between two variables.

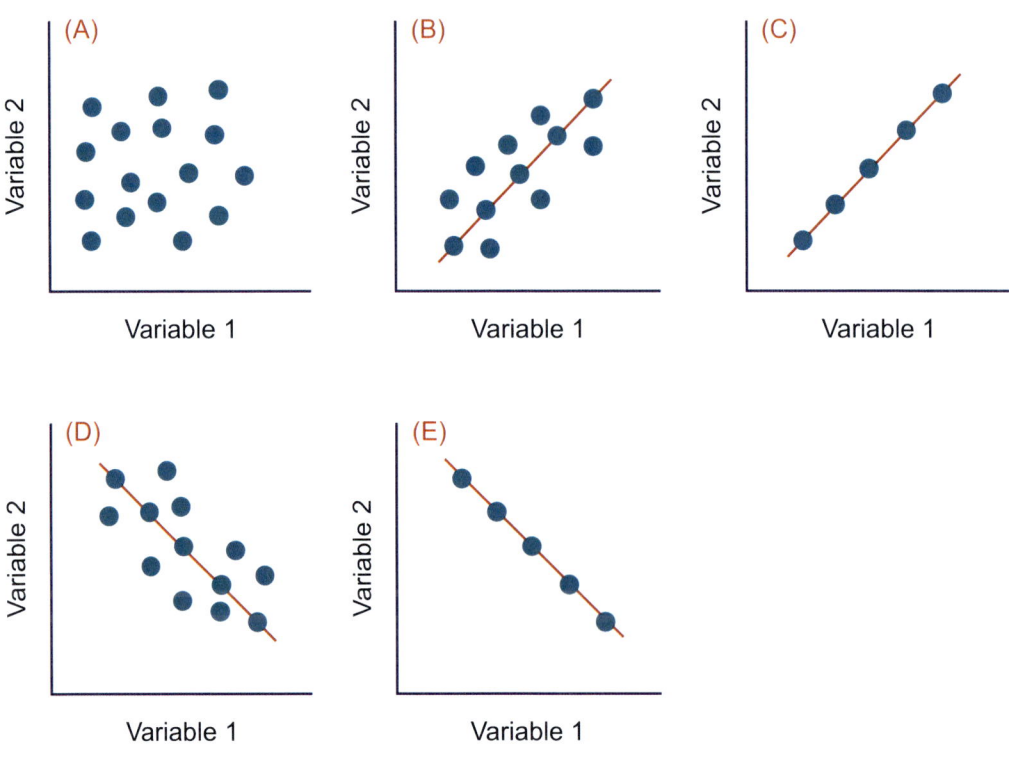

FIGURE 1.3

Scatterplots showing correlations of different directions and strength: (a) correlation of 0 indicated by dots randomly arrayed; (b) strong positive correlation; (c) perfect positive correlation (+1) indicated by the dots lined up perfectly, sloping from bottom left to upper right; (d) strong negative correlation; (e) perfect negative correlation indicated by the dots lined up perfectly, sloping from upper left to lower right.

to higher empathy scores. They also found that "energy," "conscientiousness," and "openness" all positively correlated with empathy for girls and boys, although not as strongly as "friendliness." "Emotional stability" did not significantly correlate with empathy.

Based on this brief summary, you can see that six variables were measured: five personality dimensions and empathy. However, notice that Del Barrio and her colleagues did not manipulate any of the variables. Therefore, there were no independent variables.

Although correlational research does not demonstrate causal relationships, it does play an important role in science. Correlational research is used in situations where it is not possible to manipulate variables. Any study of individual characteristics (age, sex, race, and so on) is correlational. After all, you cannot manipulate someone's age or sex. Correlational research is also used when it would be unethical to manipulate variables. For example, if you were interested in how alcohol consumption affects the human fetus, it would not be ethical to expose pregnant women to various dosages of alcohol and see what happens. Instead, you could measure alcohol consumption and the rate of birth defects and look for a correlation between those two variables. Finally, correlational research is useful when you want to study variables as they occur naturally in the real world.

Settings for Social Psychological Research

Social psychological research is done in one of two settings: the laboratory or the field. *Laboratory research* is conducted in a controlled environment created by the researcher; participants come into this artificial environment to participate in the research. *Field research* is conducted in the participant's natural environment; the researcher goes to the participant, in effect taking the study on the road. Observations are made in the participant's natural environment; sometimes, independent variables are even manipulated in this environment.

Laboratory Research

Most research in social psychology is conducted in the laboratory. This allows the researcher to exercise tight control over extraneous (unwanted) variables that might affect results. For example, the researcher can maintain constant lighting, temperature, humidity, and noise level within a laboratory environment. This tight control over the environment and over extraneous variables allows the researcher to be reasonably confident that the experiment has *internal validity*—that is, that any variation observed in the dependent variable was caused by manipulation of the independent variable. However, that tight control also has a cost: The researcher loses some ability to apply the results beyond the tightly controlled laboratory setting (*external validity*). Research conducted in highly controlled laboratories may not generalize very well to real-life social behavior, or even to other laboratory studies.

Field Research

Field research comes in three varieties: the field study, the field survey, and the field experiment. In a **field study**, the researcher makes unobtrusive observations of the participants without making direct contact or interfering in any way. The researcher simply watches from afar. In its pure form, the participants should be unaware that they are being observed, because the very act of being observed tends to change the participants' behavior. The researcher avoids contaminating the research situation by introducing any changes in the participants' natural environment.

Jane Goodall's original research on chimpanzee behavior was a field study. Goodall investigated social behavior among chimpanzees by observing groups of chimps from a distance, initially not interacting with them. However, as Goodall became more accepted by the chimps, she began to interact with them, even to the point of feeding them. Can we be sure that Goodall's later observations are characteristic of chimp behavior in the wild? Probably not, because she altered the chimps' environment by interacting with them.

In the **field survey**, the researcher directly approaches participants and asks them questions. For example, he or she might stop people in a shopping mall and collect information on which make of car they plan to buy next. The ubiquitous political polls we see all the time, especially during election years, are examples of field surveys.

field study A descriptive research strategy in which the researcher makes unobtrusive observations of the participants without making direct contact or interfering in any way.

field survey A descriptive research strategy in which the researcher directly approaches participants and asks them questions.

field experiment
A research setting in which the researcher manipulates one or more independent variables and measures behavior in the participant's natural environment.

Field studies and surveys allow us to describe and catalogue behavior. Political polls, for example, may help us discover which candidate is in the lead, whether a proposition is likely to pass, or how voters feel about important campaign issues. However, they cannot tell us what causes the differences observed among voters, because we would need to conduct an experiment to study causes. Fortunately, we can conduct experiments in the field.

The field experiment is probably the most noteworthy and useful field technique for social psychologists. In a **field experiment**, the researcher manipulates independent variables and collects measures of the dependent variables (the participant's behavior). In this sense, a field experiment is like a laboratory experiment. The main difference is that in the field experiment, the researcher manipulates independent variables under naturally occurring conditions. The principal advantage of the field experiment is that it has greater external validity—that is, the results can be generalized beyond the study more legitimately than can the results of a laboratory experiment.

Hendren and Blank (2009) conducted a field experiment to investigate the effect of sexual orientation on helping. In this experiment, a confederate of the experimenter (a confederate is someone working for the experimenter) approached a participant in a parking garage and asked for money for a parking meter. The confederate was wearing either a T-shirt with the words "Gay Pride" printed on it or a blank T-shirt. Hendren and Blank also manipulated the gender of the person making the request: Sometimes, the confederate was male; at other times, the confederate was female. Hendren and Blank found that more participants were willing to help the confederate perceived to be heterosexual (wearing the blank T-shirt) than the confederate perceived to be same-sex orientation (wearing the "Gay Pride" T-shirt).

Field experiments have advantages and disadvantages. One advantage is that because the experiment is conducted in the participant's natural environment, it is realistic and has a high degree of external validity. Often, participants do not know that they are in an experiment until it is over. For example, Hendren and Blank (2009) did not tell participants that they were taking part in an experiment when the confederate approached them. Consequently, the results have more generality than would the same experiment conducted in a laboratory where participants know that that they are in an experiment.

A disadvantage of the field experiment is that you cannot control extraneous variables as effectively as in the laboratory. Thus, internal validity may be compromised. For example, Hendren and Blank had no control over such factors as the amount of traffic in the parking lot or the presence of other people. Consequently, the internal validity of the experiment—the legitimacy of the causal relationship discovered—may suffer. The field experiment also poses some ethical problems, one of which is obtaining informed consent. Hendren and Blank did not tell potential participants that they were being recruited for an experiment. Obtaining informed consent prior to participation is a requirement for ethical research practice (although exceptions can be made). Should experimenters doing research like Hendren and Blank be obligated to inform people that they are participants in an experiment before participation? We discuss the ethics of research in more detail in a later section of this chapter.

Although most research in social psychology is conducted in a laboratory setting, field research is conducted in an individual's natural environment, such as on a city street.
Source: blvdone/Shutterstock.

> **Study Break**
>
> In contrast to experimental research (in which an independent variable is manipulated), correlational research involves measuring two (or more) dependent variables and exploring an association between them. Correlational research cannot be used to establish causal relationships among variables. This section also introduced you to different settings for social psychological research. Before you begin the next section, answer the following questions:
>
> 1. What is the difference between a positive correlation and a negative correlation? Give an example of each.
> 2. What is the correlation coefficient, and what information do you obtain from it?
> 3. Why are participant characteristics (such as age, gender, and personality) considered correlational variables, and how does that limit what you can say about them?
> 4. How does field research differ from laboratory research? What are the different types of field research? Describe each.

The Role of Theory in Social Psychological Research

On many occasions throughout this book, we refer to social psychological theories. A **theory** is a set of interrelated statements or propositions about the causes of a particular phenomenon. Theories help social psychologists organize research results, make predictions about how certain variables influence social behavior, and give direction to future research. In these ways, social psychological theories play an important role in helping us understand complex social behaviors.

There are a few important points to keep in mind as you read about these theories. First, a theory is not the final word on the causes of a social behavior. Theories are developed, revised, and sometimes abandoned according to how well they fit with research results. Rather than tell us how things are in an absolute sense, theories help us understand social behavior by providing a particular perspective. Consider attribution theories—theories about how people decide what caused others (and themselves) to act in certain ways in certain situations. Attribution theories do not tell us exactly how people assign or attribute causality. Instead, they suggest rules and make predictions about how people make such inferences in a variety of circumstances. These predictions are then tested with research.

The second important point about social psychological theories is that often, more than one theory can apply to a particular social behavior. For example, social psychologists have devised several attribution theories to help us understand how we make decisions about the causes for behaviors. Each theory helps provide a piece of the puzzle of social behavior. However, no single theory may be able to account for all aspects of a social behavior. One theory helps us understand how we infer the internal motivations of another individual; a second theory examines how we make sense of the social situation in which that individual's behavior took place.

theory A set of interrelated propositions concerning the causes for a social behavior that helps organize research results, make predictions about the influence of certain variables, and give direction to future social research.

Theory and the Research Process

Theories in social psychology are usually tested by research, and much research is guided by theory. Research designed to test a particular theory or model is referred to as **basic research**. In contrast, research designed to address a real-world problem is called **applied research**. The distinction between these two categories is not rigid, however. The results of basic research can often be applied to real-world problems, and the results of applied research may affect the validity of a theory.

For example, research on how stress affects memory may be primarily basic research, but the findings of this research apply to a real-world problem: the ability of an eyewitness to recall a violent crime accurately. Similarly, research on how jurors process evidence in complex trials (e.g., Horowitz & Bordens, 1990) has implications for predictions made by various theories of how people think and make decisions in a variety of situations. Both types of research have their place in social psychology.

basic research Research that has the principal aim of empirically testing a theory or a model.

applied research Research that has a principal aim to address a real-world problem.

Theory and Application

Application of basic theoretical ideas may take many forms. Consider, for example, the idea that it is healthy for individuals to confront and deal directly with psychological traumas from the past. Although various clinical theories have made this assumption, evidence in support of it was sparse.

In one study, social psychologist Jamie Pennebaker (1989) measured the effects of disclosure on mind and body. The research showed that when the participants confronted past traumas, either by writing or talking about them, their immunological functioning improved and their skin conductance rates were lowered. This latter measure reflects a reduction in autonomic nervous system activity, indicating a lessening of psychological tension. In other words, people were "letting go" as they fully revealed their feelings about these past traumas. Those who had trouble revealing important thoughts about the event—who could not let go of the trauma—showed heightened skin conductance rates. Pennebaker's work shows that the act of confiding in someone protects the body from the internal stress caused by repressing these unvoiced traumas. Thus, this is an example of basic research that had clear applications for real-life situations.

What Do We Learn from Research in Social Psychology?

Two criticisms are commonly made of social psychological research. One is that social psychologists study what we already know, the "intuitively obvious." The other is that because exceptions to research results can nearly always be found, many results must be wrong. Let's consider the merits of each of these points.

Do Social Psychologists Study the Obvious?

William McGuire (1973), a prominent social psychologist, once suggested that social psychologists may appear to study "bubba psychology"—things we learned on our grandmother's knee. That is, social psychologists study what is already obvious and predictable based on common sense. Although it may seem this way, it is not the case. The results of research seem obvious only when you already know what they are. This is called **hindsight bias**, or the "I-knew-it-all-along" phenomenon (Slovic & Fischoff, 1977; Wood, 1978). With the benefit of hindsight, everything looks obvious. For example, after the terrorist attacks on September 11, 2001, some commentators asked why President Bush or the CIA did not "connect the dots" and see the attacks coming. Unfortunately, those dots were not so clear in the months and years leading up to the attacks. In hindsight, the signs seemed to point to an attack, but before the incident, things were not so clear. In fact, the 9/11 Commission pointed out that hindsight can bias our perceptions of events:

hindsight bias Also known as the "I-knew-it-all-along" phenomenon; shows that with the benefit of hindsight, everything looks obvious.

The hindsight bias is when we see events that have already occurred as being obvious and predictable. For example, some believed that President George Bush should have "connected the dots" and predicted the terrorist attacks on September 11, 2001.
Source: Frontpage/Shutterstock.

> Commenting on Pearl Harbor, Roberta Wohlstetter found it "much easier after the event to sort the relevant from the irrelevant signals. After the event, of course, a signal is always crystal clear; we can now see what disaster it was signaling since the disaster has occurred. But before the event it is obscure and pregnant with conflicting meanings." As time passes, more documents become available, and the bare facts of what happened become still clearer. Yet the picture of how those things happened becomes harder to reimagine, as that past world, with its preoccupations and uncertainty, recedes and the remaining memories of it become colored by what happened and what was written about it later. (The 9/11 Commission Report, 2004, p. 339)

Although the results of some research may seem obvious, studies show that when individuals are given descriptions of research without results, they can predict the outcome of the research no better than chance (Slovic & Fischoff, 1977). In other words, the results were not so obvious when they were not already known!

Do Exceptions Mean Research Results Are Wrong?

When the findings of social psychological research are described, someone often points to a case that is an exception to the finding. Suppose a particular study shows that a person is less likely to get help when there are several bystanders present than when there is only one. You probably can think of a situation in which you were helped with many bystanders around. Does this mean that the research is wrong or that it doesn't apply to you?

To answer this question, you must remember that in a social psychological experiment, groups of participants are exposed to various levels of the independent variable. In an experiment on the relationship between the number of bystanders and the likelihood of receiving help, for example, one group of participants is given an opportunity to help a person in need with no other bystanders present. A second group of participants gets the same opportunity but with three bystanders present. Let's say that our results in this hypothetical experiment show that seven out of 10 participants in the no-bystander condition helped (70%), whereas only 2 out of 10 helped in the three-bystander condition (20%). Thus, we would conclude that you are more likely to get help when there are no other bystanders present than if there are three bystanders.

Notice, however, that we do not say that you will never receive help when three bystanders are present. In fact, two participants helped in that condition. Nor do we say that you always receive help when there are no bystanders present. In fact, in three instances no help was rendered.

The moral to the story is that the results of experiments in social psychology represent differences between groups of participants, not differences between specific individuals. Based on the results of social psychological research, we can say that *on the average*, groups differ. Within those groups, there are nearly always participants who do not behave as most of the participants behaved. We can acknowledge that exceptions to research findings usually exist, but this does not mean that the results reported are wrong.

Can Findings in Social Psychology Be Replicated?

Throughout this book, we cite research to support the points we make. A hallmark of science is that its research findings can be repeated or *replicated*. That is, we should be able to reproduce a finding of a study if the second study is conducted using the same or highly similar methods and measures. For example, if a researcher finds that research participants are less likely to help someone in need when there are bystanders present than if the participants are alone, another researcher should be able to find the same thing under the same or highly similar conditions. In the early days of psychology, the reliability of research findings was established through replication. With the development of inferential statistics toward the end of the 19th century and into the early 20th century, statistical analysis of data largely replaced replication to determine the reliability of findings. Journals quickly established the unwritten rule that only statistically significant findings (defined as those significant at the level of at least $p < .05$) would be published. Any research in which statistical reliability fell below $p < .05$ was relegated to the file drawer, rarely to be seen again.

Although scientists pay lip service to replication, actual replication research is relatively rare for a variety of reasons. For example, scientists who replicate the work of others are often seen as journeymen and as not contributing to the advancement of scientific knowledge (Earp & Trafimow, 2015). Scientists started paying more serious attention to replication when some researchers started questioning whether the statistically significant findings reported in journals were valid and whether they could be replicated. For example, John Ioannidis (2005) estimated that nearly 50% of the findings reported in published research could be false positives. That is, the statistically significant findings reported might not be significant at all. By extension, we would expect such findings not to replicate. This idea was echoed by Simmons et al. (2011) in an article titled "False-Positive Psychology: Undisclosed Flexibility in Data Collection and Analysis Allows Presenting Anything as Significant." Critics traced the problem to "suspect practices" used by researchers to massage data to obtain statistical significance. For example, a researcher might run a few participants in an experiment, run a statistical test, and stop the experiment if significance is found. If not, the experiment is continued until significance is obtained.

To assess the reliability of research in psychology, a group of researchers set out to determine if the findings reported in major psychology journals could be replicated (Open Science Collaboration, 2015). Open Science Collaboration researchers attempted replications of studies published in *Psychological Science* ($N = 40$), the *Journal of Personality and Social Psychology* ($N = 32$), and the J*ournal of Experimental Psychology: Learning, Memory, and Cognition* ($N = 28$). The results were not pretty: Only 39% of the replications produced statistically significant results. Additionally, the effect sizes for the replications were half (.197) of those of the original studies (.403). So, when results were replicated, they were weaker than those reported in the original studies.

Another finding was that the replication success rate varied according to the area of psychology. Studies in cognitive psychology replicated at a 50% rate, but studies in social psychology replicated at only 25%, sometimes even lower for some of the more prominent findings in the area (e.g., behavioral priming). The replication rate for studies using within-subjects designs was higher than for those using between-subjects designs. Critics started to point to a *replication crisis* in psychology based on these shocking findings. However, Ulrich Schimmack (2020) pointed out that it is not fair to say that psychology, in general, faces this crisis. Instead, he maintained that social psychology and other disciplines using less powerful research designs might suffer from such a crisis. Also, replication failures have been found in other sciences, such as medicine and biochemistry.

It is evident that social psychology has a problem with its research findings. How have researchers responded to this problem? Some have tried to downplay the failure to replicate or rationalize it away (Schimmack, 2020). Others have made efforts to change research practices to reduce the problem. Researchers are now taking steps to increase the power of their studies. For example, larger participant samples are being used, as are more within-subjects designs, which are more sensitive to effects than between-subjects designs (Schimmack, 2020). The crisis is also being addressed by journal publication policies. Some journals now use *preregistration* so that even studies that do not find statistical significance are published, cutting down on the false-positive problem discussed previously. With preregistration, you submit your research design to a journal before running your study. If approved, the journal editor agrees to publish your results, regardless of statistical significance. Another strategy is moving away from traditional null hypothesis significance testing (NHST), which relies on inferential statistics to evaluate the validity of a null hypothesis stating that no difference exists between groups in an experiment. Instead, *new statistics* are employed that emphasize estimation, confidence intervals, and meta-analysis instead of NHST (Bordens & Abbott, 2021).

Ethics and Social Psychological Research

Unlike research in chemistry and physics, which does not involve living organisms, research in social psychology uses living organisms, both animal and human. Because social psychology studies living organisms, researchers must consider research ethics. They have to concern themselves with the treatment of their research participants and with the potential long-range effects of the research on the participants' well-being. In every study conducted in social psychology, researchers must place the welfare of the research participants among their top priorities.

Questions about ethics have been raised about some of the most famous research ever done in social psychology. For example, you may be familiar with the experiments on obedience conducted by Stanley Milgram (1963; described in detail in Chapter 7). In these experiments, participants were asked to administer painful electric shocks to an individual who was doing poorly on a learning task. Although no shocks were actually delivered, participants believed they were inflicting intense pain on an increasingly unwilling victim. Following the experiment, participants reported experiencing guilt and lowered self-esteem as well as anger toward the researchers. The question raised by this and other experiments with human participants is how far researchers can and should go to gain knowledge.

Research conducted by social psychologists is governed by an ethical code of conduct developed by the American Psychological Association (APA). The code mandates that participation in psychological research is voluntary. This means that participants cannot be compelled to participate in research. Researchers must also obtain **informed consent** from the participants, which means that they must inform them of the nature of the study, the requirements for participation, and any risks or benefits associated with participating in the study. Subjects must also be told they have the right to decline or withdraw from participation with no penalty.

Additionally, the APA code restricts the use of deception in research. *Deception* occurs when researchers tell their participants they are studying one thing but actually are studying another. Deception can be used only if no other viable alternative exists. When researchers use deception, they must tell participants about the deception (and the reasons for it) as soon as possible after participation.

Following ethical codes of conduct protects subjects from harm. In this sense, ethical codes help the research process. However, sometimes ethical research practice conflicts with the requirements of science. For example, in a field experiment on helping, it may not be possible (or desirable) to obtain consent from participants before they participate in the study. When such conflicts occur, the researcher must weigh the potential risks to the participants against the benefits to be gained. You can find the APA ethical code for researchers at https://www.apa.org/ethics/code.

informed consent An ethical research requirement that participants must be informed of the nature of the study, the requirements for participation, any risks or benefits associated with participating in the study, and the right to decline or withdraw from participation with no penalty.

Study Break

This section introduced you to various topics related to social psychological research, including the role of theory in research, making sense of social psychological research, and ethics in research. Before you read the Chapter Review, answer the following questions:

1. What is a scientific theory, and how does it relate to research done in social psychology?
2. What is the hindsight bias, and how can it influence how a person interprets social psychological research?
3. What do exceptions to social psychological research findings say about the implications of research results?
4. What is the "replication crisis," and how has it been addressed?
5. What are the basic ethical principles that apply to social psychological research, and why is it important to follow them?

Trinidad Beach Revisited

How can we explain the behavior of the main actors at Trinidad Beach? Social psychologists would begin by pointing to the two factors that contribute to social behavior: individual characteristics and the social situation. Was there something about the four rescuers' personalities, attitudes, or other characteristics that predisposed them to act altruistically? Or was it the social environment that was more important? Social psychologists focus on the latter. After the rescue was publicized, the four teens were hailed as heroes. From their behavior people inferred that they possessed the personality characteristics necessary to risk their lives for strangers. However, many people might possess those very same characteristics. Yet, they might not risk their lives by directly aiding the two brothers. They may choose to act in other ways (e.g., call for help). Social psychology is not the only discipline that would be interested in explaining the rescuers' behavior. Biologists studying ethology would look at their behavior in the light of what altruism does to help a species survive. Each discipline has its own way of collecting information about issues of interest. Social psychology would face the daunting task of explaining the rescuers' behavior by conducting carefully designed research. Through the use of scientific research, one could isolate the variables that contribute to altruistic acts such as those that occurred at Trinidad Beach on that foggy November day.

Chapter Review

1. **What is social psychology?**

   Social psychology is the scientific study of how we think and feel about, interact with, and influence each other. It is the branch of psychology that focuses on social behavior—specifically, how we relate to other people in our social world. Social psychology can help us understand everyday things that happen to us, as well as past and present cultural and historical events.

2. **How do social psychologists explain social behavior?**

   An early model of social behavior proposed by Kurt Lewin suggested that social behavior is caused by two factors: individual characteristics and the social situation. This simple model has since been expanded to better explain the forces that shape social behavior. According to modern views of social behavior, input from the social situation works in conjunction with individual characteristics to influence social behavior through the operation of social cognition (the general process of thinking about social events) and social perception (how we perceive other people). Based on our processing of social information, we evaluate the social situation and form an intention to behave in a certain way. This behavioral intention may or may not be translated into social behavior. We engage in social behavior based on our constant changing evaluation of the situation. Once we behave in a certain way, it may have an effect on the social situation, which in turn will affect future social behavior.

3. **How does social psychology relate to other disciplines that study social behavior?**

   There are many scientific disciplines that study social behavior. Biologists, developmental psychologists, anthropologists, personality psychologists, historians, and sociologists all have an interest in social behavior. Although social psychology has common interests with these disciplines, unlike biology and personality psychology, social psychology focuses on the social situation as the principal cause of social behavior. Whereas sociology and history focus on the broader situation, social psychology takes a narrower view, looking at the individual in the social situation rather than the larger group or society. In other words, history and sociology take a top-down approach to explaining social behavior, making a group or institution the focus of analysis. Social psychology takes a bottom-up approach, focusing on how individual behavior is influenced by the situation.

4. **How do social psychologists use science to describe and explain social behavior?**

   Unlike the layperson who forms commonsense explanations for social behavior based on limited information, social psychologists rely on the scientific method to formulate scientific explanations—tentative explanations based on observation and logic that are open to empirical testing. The scientific method involves identifying a phenomenon to study, developing a testable research hypothesis, designing a research study, and carrying out the research study. Only after applying this method to a problem and conducting careful research will a social psychologist be satisfied with an explanation.

5. **What is pseudoscience, and why is it important to learn about it?**

   Pseudoscience is a set of ideas based on theories put forth as scientific when they are not scientific. It is important to learn about pseudoscience because it helps us better understand the philosophy of science (theoretical reason) and it may help guide decisions by policymakers and you in your everyday life (practical reason).

6. **What is experimental research, and how is it used?**

   Experimental research is used to uncover causal relationships between variables. Its main features are (1) the manipulation of an independent variable and the observation of the effects of this manipulation on a dependent variable, (2) the use of two or more initially comparable groups, and (3) exercising control over extraneous and confounding variables. Every experiment includes at least one independent variable with at least two levels. In the simplest experiment, one group of participants (the experimental group) is exposed to an experimental treatment, and a second group (the control group) is not. Researchers then compare the behavior of participants in the experimental group with the behavior of participants in the control group. Independent variables can be manipulated by varying their quantity or quality. Researchers use random assignment to ensure that the groups in an experiment are comparable before applying any treatment to them.

The basic experiment can be expanded by adding additional levels of an independent variable or by adding a second or third independent variable. Experiments that include more than one independent variable are known as factorial experiments.

7. **What is correlational research?**

In correlational research, researchers measure two or more dependent variables and look for a relationship between them. When two variables both change in the same direction, increasing or decreasing in value, they are positively correlated. When they change in opposite directions, one increasing and the other decreasing, they are negatively correlated. When one variable does not change systematically with the other, they are uncorrelated. Even if a correlation is found, a causal relationship cannot be inferred.

8. **What is the correlation coefficient, and what does it tell you?**

Researchers evaluate correlational relationships between variables with a statistic called the correlation coefficient (symbolized as r). The sign of r (positive or negative) indicates the direction of the relationship between variables; the size of r (ranging from -1 through 0 to $+1$) indicates the strength of the relationship between variables.

9. **Where is social psychological research conducted?**

Social psychologists conduct research either in the laboratory or in the field. In laboratory research, researchers create an artificial environment in which they can control extraneous variables. This tight control allows the researchers to be reasonably confident that any variation observed in the dependent variable was caused by manipulation of the independent variable. However, results obtained this way may not generalize well beyond the laboratory setting.

There are several kinds of field research. In the field study, the researcher observes participants but does not interact with them. In the field survey, the researcher has direct contact with participants and interacts with them. Both of these techniques allow the researcher to describe behavior, but causes cannot be uncovered. In the field experiment, the researcher manipulates an independent variable in the participant's natural environment. The field experiment increases the generality of the research findings. However, extraneous variables may cloud the causal relationship between the independent and dependent variables.

10. **What is the role of theory in social psychology?**

A theory is a set of interrelated statements or propositions about the causes of a phenomenon that helps organize research results, makes predictions about how certain variables influence social behavior, and gives direction to future research. A theory is not the final word on the causes of a social behavior. Theories are developed, revised, and sometimes abandoned according to how well they fit with research results. Theories do not tell us how things are in an absolute sense. Instead, they help us understand social behavior by providing a particular perspective. Often, more than one theory can apply to a particular social behavior.

Sometimes, one theory provides a better explanation of one aspect of a particular social behavior, and another theory provides a better explanation of another aspect of that same behavior. Some research, called basic research, is designed to test predictions made by theories. Applied research is conducted to study a real-world phenomenon (e.g., jury decisions). Basic and applied research are not necessarily mutually exclusive. Some basic research has applied implications, and some applied research has theoretical implications.

11. **What can we learn from social psychological research?**

Two common criticisms of social psychological research are that social psychologists study things that are intuitively obvious and that because exceptions to research results can nearly always be found, many results must be wrong. However, these two criticisms are not valid. The findings of social psychological research may *appear* to be intuitively obvious in hindsight (the hindsight bias), but individuals cannot predict how an experiment will come out if they don't already know the results. Furthermore, exceptions to a research finding do not invalidate that finding. Social psychologists study groups of individuals. Within a group, variation in behavior will occur. Social psychologists look at average differences between groups.

12. **What is the replication crisis, and how have social psychologists responded to it?**

The replication crisis began when some scientists questioned whether research in psychology in general, and social psychology in particular, could be replicated. Some critics pointed out that because of suspect research practices, much of the published research in psychology represented false positives that could not be replicated. This was confirmed when researchers tried to replicate research published in three major psychology journals. They found that only 39% of the replication attempts yielded statistically significant results and that the results that were replicated were weaker than the original results. The replication crisis is most pronounced in social psychology, where only 25% of the replications produced statistically significant results. Social psychologists have responded to the crisis by modifying research practices to strengthen their findings. For example, larger samples are used, and more researchers are using more powerful within-subjects designs.

13. What ethical standards must social psychologists follow when conducting research?

Social psychologists are concerned with the ethics of research—how participants are treated within a study and how they are affected in the long term by participating. Social psychologists adhere to the code of research ethics established by the American Psychological Association. Ethical treatment of participants involves several key aspects, including informing participants about the nature of a study and requirements for participation prior to participation (informed consent), protecting participants from short-term and long-term harm, and ensuring anonymity.

Key Terms

Applied research (p. 21)
Basic research (p. 21)
Confounding variable (p. 15)
Control group (p. 14)
Correlation coefficient (p. 18)
Correlational research (p. 17)
Dependent variable (p. 14)
Experimental group (p. 14)
Experimental research (p. 14)
Extraneous variable (p. 15)
Factorial experiment (p. 15)
Field experiment (p. 20)
Field study (p. 19)
Field survey (p. 19)
Hindsight bias (p. 22)
Hypothesis (p. 11)
Independent variable (p. 14)
Informed consent (p. 25)
Interaction (p. 16)
Negative correlation (p. 17)
Next Generation Science Standards (p. 11)
Positive correlation (p. 17)
Random assignment (p. 14)
Science (p. 11)
Social cognition (p. 5)
Social perception (p. 5)
Social psychology (p. 3)
Theory (p. 21)

Chapter Quiz

1. The scientific study of how individuals think and feel about, interact with, and influence each other is the definition of _____ offered in your text.
   A. social psychology
   B. sociology
   C. history
   D. anthropology

2. According to your text, the two categories of influence used to understand social behavior are
   A. biology and environment.
   B. biology and culture.
   C. the situation and individual characteristics.
   D. the situation and culture.

3. _____ is the process by which we make sense out of behavior; it involves inferring motives and attributing causes.
   A. Social categorization
   B. Social cognition
   C. Impression formation
   D. Social perception

4. According to your text, social psychologists attempt to determine
   A. what characteristics of the situation increase or decrease the potential for social behaviors.
   B. what characteristics of the person increase or decrease the potential for social behaviors.
   C. how the situation affects a person's personality.
   D. how large groups, such as an entire society, increase or decrease the potential for social behaviors.

5. An explanation that is based on objective observation and logic and is subject to empirical testing is a
   A. commonsense explanation.
   B. hypothetical explanation.
   C. theoretical explanation.
   D. scientific explanation.

6. _____ research involves changing the value of one variable and evaluating how that change affects the value of another variable.
   A. Correlational
   B. Experimental
   C. Nonexperimental
   D. None of the above

7. Eight practices for science and engineering to guide research are set out in the
   A. New Generation Scientific Method Protocol.
   B. scientific method.
   C. Next Generation Science Standards.
   D. hypo-deductive method.

8. A set of ideas based on theories put forth as scientific when they are not scientific is known as
   A. protoscience.
   B. false science.
   C. pseudoscience.
   D. correlational research.

9. According to your text, studies in social psychology replicated at _____, sometimes even lower for some of the more prominent findings in the area.
   A. 15%
   B. 25%
   C. 35%
   D. 50%

10. Research primarily conducted to test a theory is called _____ research.
    A. theoretical
    B. applied
    C. systematic
    D. basic
    E. fundamental

Answers can be found in the end-of-book Answers section.

The Social Self

Though I am not naturally honest, I am so sometimes by chance.
—William Shakespeare

CHAPTER 2

Source: Igor Shmanko/Shutterstock.

Serena Williams is probably the greatest female tennis player ever to set foot on a tennis court. By age 39, Williams had won 39 major professional tennis titles, including 23 in singles, 14 in women's doubles, and 2 in mixed doubles. She is one of only three professional tennis players (male or female) to have won all four major tournaments in a row *twice* in her career. She holds the record in the "open era" of 23 major singles titles. To top it off, Williams also has won three Olympic medals, including one gold. In addition to being a dominant tennis professional, Williams is an actress, businesswoman, and philanthropist.

The road to her success has not always been easy. Williams was born in Saginaw, Michigan, on September 26, 1981, the youngest of five sisters. At a young age, she and her family moved to Compton, California, a city located outside of Los Angeles. Life in Compton was difficult for the Williams family. Their neighborhood could be characterized as "rough," and Serena and her sisters often heard gunshots and saw violence all around them. Serena shared a bedroom with her four sisters. Despite the rough surroundings, Serena's parents provided a warm, loving home. They homeschooled Serena and her sisters and encouraged them to excel. Her father, Richard, always dreamed of his daughters becoming tennis stars, even before they

Key Questions

As you read this chapter, find the answers to the following questions:

1. What is the self?
2. How do we know the self?
3. What is distinctiveness theory?
4. What is autobiographical memory?
5. How do groups and culture relate to the self?
6. How do social media relate to one's self-concept, and what factors affect how the self is expressed on the Internet?
7. How is the self organized through schemas?
8. What is self-esteem?
9. How do we evaluate the self?
10. What is self-evaluation maintenance (SEM) theory?
11. How does self-esteem relate to coping with disaster and stigma?
12. What is so good about high self-esteem?
13. What are implicit and explicit self-esteem?
14. What is self-regulation, and how does it relate to behavior?
15. What are the self-serving bias and self-verification?
16. What is meant by self-awareness?

17. How do we present the self to others?
18. What is self-monitoring?
19. What is self-handicapping?
20. How accurate are we in assessing the impression we convey?
21. What are the spotlight effect and the illusion of transparency?

Tennis has had a significant impact on the development of Serena Williams's sense of self.
Source: Ritu Manoj Jethani/Shutterstock.

were born. He purchased books, videotapes, and instructional materials on tennis for them. Eventually, he (along with Serena's mother, Oracene) became Serena's tennis coach.

It was in Compton that Williams first picked up a tennis racquet at the age of three. Serena took to the game quickly and showed her talent early. She competed in her first tournament at age four-and-a-half. She, along with her older sister Venus, became quite the sensation on the junior tennis circuit in southern California. Over the course of the next 5 years, Serena won 46 of the 49 tournaments in which she competed. Serena and Venus rose to the number-one positions in their respective age groups. As the sisters' skills developed, word got around, and they started to receive endorsement offers and invitations to the best tennis camps in the country. Eventually, Richard Williams pulled his daughters off the junior tennis circuit and accepted an invitation from Rick Macci (a teaching tennis professional) to attend his tennis academy in Florida. The family packed up and moved to Florida.

In 1995, at age 14 and still in high school, Serena became a professional tennis player. Unfortunately, the Women's Tennis Association (WTA) would not recognize someone of Serena's young age. So Serena played her first professional tournament in Quebec, Canada. Serena lost to Lindsay Davenport in the semifinals. However, she did beat Monica Seles, who was ranked fourth that year, in an earlier match. By 1999, Serena was the fourth-ranked women's player in the world and won two grand-slam events with her sister Venus (doubles titles). The following year, she suffered from injuries that set her career back somewhat. She fought through these injuries, and many others in the years to come, to capture numerous titles, including 39 major titles and the number-one ranking in women's tennis.

On the court, Serena is a fierce, often merciless competitor. She has been known to drop multiple "f-bombs" during a match. She has gotten into arguments with officials. At a U.S. Open, she threatened a judge over a foot-fault call, resulting in an $82,500 fine. Her drive to win exceeds that of most. She has played injured and sick and still won. For example, after her third match during the 2015 French Open, Serena came down with the flu and had a 101-degree fever. She could not take medication because she was afraid that she would fail a drug screening. She could hardly move and almost withdrew. She did play and won the match, defeating her opponent 6–0 in the final set. Off the court, Serena is much different. Her friends and family variously report that she is warm, funny, loyal, and curious. She showed great empathy and concern for a friend when her husband was killed in an accident.

The darkest day in Serena's tennis career came in 2001 at the Indian Wells Tournament in California. Both she and Venus were playing in the singles matches, and as fate had it, they ended up scheduled to face each other in the semifinal match. Tennis fans greatly anticipated the showdown between the two sisters, and emotions were running high. Unfortunately, Venus had injured her knee in an earlier match and had to withdraw from the match. Rumors began to circulate that the "fix was in" and that Venus withdrew to help Serena. When Venus and her father came into the arena, the crowd booed. Nobody told Serena about the booing, and when she entered the arena, the crowd booed even louder. Serena had no idea why they were booing. All through the match, they cheered each time that Serena made a mistake and booed when she scored points. Richard, Venus, and Serena all reported hearing racial slurs as well (although this was not independently verified). This treatment devastated Serena, and she vowed never to return to Indian Wells, a promise she kept for the next 14 years, despite threats of fines and loss of ranking points.

Over the next several years, Serena had a number of experiences that eventually led to her return to Indian Wells. In 2006, she visited Africa and saw much suffering and injustice. She saw a film about the life of Nelson Mandela, which also inspired her. In 2014, the high-profile cases involving African Americans being shot by White police officers had a profound effect on Serena. These and other experiences forced Serena to face the notion of injustice and how to confront it. She felt that she had to return to Indian Wells and make a statement about injustice and racism. So, against her family's advice, she returned to Indian Wells and played in the tournament. Before the match, Serena was nervous and concerned about being booed again. However, her reception was much different this time. She entered the arena to cheers and great applause. She went on to win the tournament, much to the delight of the crowd.

In Serena Williams's life, we can see the interplay of the various parts of the self: The personal self—her personal strength, determination, and personality—and that part of the self influenced by her relationships with family, friends, and competitors. We also see the impact of a variety of events on Serena. Her early experience at age 19 at Indian Wells and her subsequent experiences with racism and injustice all helped shape her sense of self.

Self-Concept

How do we develop a coherent sense of who we are? The chapter-opening vignette describing Serena Williams suggests that our personal experiences, interactions with others, and cultural forces all play some role in our definition of self. Who am I? The answer to this question is the driving force in our lives. If you were asked to define yourself, you most likely would use sentences containing the words *I, me, mine,* and *myself* (Cooley, 1902; Schweder et al., 1997).

The *self* may be thought of as a structure that contains the organized and stable contents of one's personal experiences (Schlenker, 1987). In this sense, the self is an object, something inside us that we may evaluate and contemplate. The self is "me," the sum of what I am. A significant part of what we call the *self* is knowledge. All the ideas, thoughts, and information that we have about ourselves—about who we are, what characteristics we have, what our personal histories have made us, and what we may yet become—make up our **self-concept**.

self-concept All the ideas, thoughts, and information we have about ourselves.

Self-Knowledge: How Do You Know Thyself?

We use several sources of social information to forge our self-concept. One comes from our view of how other people react to us. These **reflected self-appraisals** shape our self-concept (Cooley, 1902; Jones & Gerard, 1967). Reflected self-appraisals have implications for self-concept as well as actual performance. For example, Bouchey and Harter (2005) report that reflected self-appraisals of adults (e.g., parents and teachers) regarding

reflected self-appraisal A source of social information involving our view of how other people react to us.

a student's performance in math and science related significantly to that student's beliefs about his or her competence and performance in these subjects. The more positive the adult reflected self-appraisal, the better was the student's performance. Interestingly, positive reflected self-appraisals from peers were not as strongly related to a student's perceived competence and performance as adult reflected self-appraisals.

A second source of social information regarding our self-concept is how we compare ourselves to other people (Festinger, 1954). Self-knowledge comes from the **social comparison process** by which we compare our reactions, abilities, and attributes to others (Festinger, 1954). We do this because we need accurate information so that we may succeed. We need to know if we are good athletes or students or race car drivers so that we can make rational choices. Social comparison is a control device because it makes our world more predictable.

Social comparison can lead to either positive or negative views of the self, depending on who serves as the comparison group. For example, within a school environment, a student who is placed in a high-achieving class may develop a negative academic self-concept, especially if that student questions his or her academic competence (Trautwein et al., 2009). In this case, a social comparison is made with peers that the student perceives to be of higher competence than the self, leading to a negative self-appraisal.

A third source of information comes from the self-knowledge gained by observing our behavior. Daryl Bem (1967) suggested that people really do not know why they do things, so they simply observe their behavior and assume that their motives are consistent with their behavior. Someone who rebels against authority may simply observe his or her behavior and conclude, "Well, I must be a rebel." Therefore, we obtain knowledge of our self simply by observing ourselves behave and then inferring that our private beliefs must coincide with our public actions.

Another method of knowing the self is through **introspection**, the act of examining our thoughts and feelings. Introspection is a method we all use to understand ourselves, but evidence suggests that we may get a somewhat biased picture of our internal state. Thinking about our attitudes and the reasons we hold them can sometimes be disruptive and confusing (Wilson et al., 1989). More generally, the process of introspection—of looking into our mind, rather than just behaving—can have this effect. For example, if you are forced to think about why you like your romantic partner, you might find it disconcerting if you are not able to think of any good reasons why you are in this relationship. This doesn't mean that you don't have reasons, but they may not be accessible or easy to retrieve. Much depends on the strength of the relationship. If the relationship is not strong, thinking about the relationship could be disruptive because you might not think up many positive reasons in support of the relationship. If it is pretty strong, then reasoning might further strengthen it. The stronger our attitude or belief, the more likely that thinking about it will increase the consistency between the belief and our behavior (Fazio, 1986).

We use all of the previously described tools to form a relatively coherent sense of who we are. However, sometimes we find ourselves in a situation that causes us to doubt our self-concept. Imagine, for example, a person starting medical school, which is a very difficult and demanding endeavor. During the first few days, she may begin to doubt whether she has the knowledge, skills, and abilities to succeed. In short, she may begin to feel that she is an imposter who doesn't belong in medical school. Instead of attributing her success in gaining entry into medical school to her abilities, our medical student may come to believe that there must have been an error in the admission process or that she somehow fooled others into believing in her abilities (Clance & Imes, 1978). The feeling that one lacks the skills and abilities to succeed is known as the **imposter phenomenon** (Clance & Imes, 1978). The imposter phenomenon is stronger in individuals who strive for perfection and have a family history stressing high achievement (Sakulku & Alexander, 2011). Do you ever feel like an imposter? How strongly do you have those feelings? You can test the degree to which you experience the imposter phenomenon at https://paulineroseclance.com/pdf/IPTestandscoring.pdf.

Feeling like an imposter can lead a person to not perform well in endeavors related to the feelings of being an imposter (Badaway et al., 2018), as well as feelings of depression

---

social comparison process A source of social knowledge involving how we compare our reactions, abilities, and attributes to others.

introspection The act of examining our thoughts and feelings to understand ourselves, which may yield a somewhat biased picture of our internal state.

imposter phenomenon The feeling that one lacks the skills and abilities to succeed.

(Bernard et al., 2017). Whether one feels like an imposter can be affected by the situation one is in. For example, Black students attending a predominantly White university showed a stronger relationship between the imposter phenomenon and decreased well-being than those attending a historically Black college or university (Bernard et al., 2020). Although both men and women can experience the imposter phenomenon, some research shows that women experience greater feelings of being an imposter than men (McGregor et al., 2008; Cokley et al., 2015). Interestingly, the imposter phenomenon does not appear to relate directly to race. However, if a minority individual experiences racial discrimination, feeling like an imposter relates to stronger feelings of depression (Bernard et al., 2017).

Personal Attributes and Self-Concept

Now that we know some of the methods for forming and gaining access to our self-concept, let's see what is inside. What kind of information and feelings are contained in the self? First of all, the self-concept contains ideas and beliefs about **personal attributes**. A person may think of herself as female, American, young, smart, compassionate, the daughter of a single mother, a good basketball player, reasonably attractive, hot-tempered, artistic, patient, and a movie fan. All of these attributes and many more go into her self-concept.

Researchers investigated the self-concepts of American schoolchildren by asking them the following kinds of questions (McGuire & McGuire, 1988, p. 99):

- Tell us about yourself.
- Tell us what you are not.
- Tell us about school.
- Tell us about your family.

These open-ended probes revealed that children and adolescents often defined themselves by characteristics that were unique or distinctive. Participants who possessed a distinctive characteristic were much more likely to mention that attribute than were those who were less distinctive on that dimension (McGuire & McGuire, 1988).

According to **distinctiveness theory**, people think of themselves in terms of those attributes or dimensions that make them different, that are distinctive, rather than in terms of attributes they have in common with others. People, for example, who are taller or shorter than others, or wear glasses, or are left-handed are likely to incorporate that characteristic into their self-concept.

People usually are aware of the attributes they have in common with other individuals. A male going to an all-male high school is aware that he is male. But being male may not be a defining part of his self-concept because everybody around him has that same characteristic. He will define himself by attributes that make him different from other males, such as being a debater or a football player. Being male may certainly be important in another social context, however, such as when taking part in a debate about changing gender roles. People who belong to nondominant or minority groups are more likely to include their gender, ethnicity, or other identity in their self-concept than are those in dominant, majority groups (e.g., White males).

Although we may define ourselves according to distinctive personal attributes, we still have a strong need to fit in with others. In fact, an important part of our self-concept is our *social identity,* which is made up of the social groups (e.g., occupational groups, culture, etc.) with which we identify. The need to fit in may conflict with the competing need to perceive ourselves as distinct from others and thus create a sense of tension within ourselves (Guion Peoples, 2017). According to *optimal distinctiveness theory,* we try to reconcile this tension by creating optimal distinctiveness to strike a balance between the needs for inclusion and distinctiveness (Leonardelli et al., 2010). It is important to understand that the process of creating optimal distinctiveness is a dynamic one that changes over time and with changing situations and may vary across individuals and cultures (Guion Peoples, 2017). For example, a new musician might

personal attributes
An aspect of the self-concept involving the attributes we believe we have.

distinctiveness theory
The theory suggesting that individuals think of themselves in terms of those attributes or dimensions that make them different—rather than in terms of attributes they have in common with others.

satisfy the need for inclusion early in his career by performing shows at small venues for little money while retaining his unique style. Later in his career, after achieving some success, he may only perform at larger venues for more pay while retaining his unique style (Guion Peoples, 2017).

Of course, not all knowledge about the self is conscious simultaneously. At any given time, we tend to be aware of only parts of our overall self-concept. This *working self-concept* varies, depending on the nature of the social situation and how we feel at that moment (Markus & Kunda, 1986). So when we are depressed, our working self-concept would likely include all those thoughts about ourselves that have to do with failure or negative traits. In addition, we tend to unconsciously synchronize our self-concepts with the nature of the social situation. For example, if you are hanging around a group of "jocks," you may automatically begin to think about yourself in ways that are consistent with athleticism (e.g., disciplined, competitive; Kawakami et al., 2012).

Although the self-concept is relatively stable, the notion of a working self-concept suggests that the self can vary from one situation to another. As the late Ziva Kunda (1999) pointed out, if you are shy but are asked to give examples of when you were very outgoing, at least momentarily you might feel less shy than usual. Working self-concept is also affected by affiliation with groups. When a group with which we closely identify is made salient, we are likely to identify characteristics associated with the group as being characteristics of the individual self (Sim, et al., 2014). However, Sim et al., report that these group-based characteristics do not replace characteristics that individuals normally say describe them. Instead, they appear to exist alongside those more stable individual characteristics. However, the ease with which the self may change may depend on how self-knowledge is organized and how important the behavior is.

Study Break

This section defined self-concept. It also discussed how information related to self-concept is acquired. Before you begin the next section, answer the following questions:

1. What is the definition of self-concept?
2. How do reflected appraisals, social comparison, and introspection help define self-concept?
3. What are personal attributes, and how do they relate to self-concept?
4. What is distinctiveness theory, and why is it important in understanding self-concept?

The Self and Memory

autobiographical memory Memory for information relating to the self that plays a powerful role in recall of events.

In addition to personal attributes, the self-concept contains memories, the basis for knowledge about oneself. The study of **autobiographical memory**—memory for information relating to self—shows that the self plays a powerful role in the recall of events (Woike et al., 1999). The self is an especially powerful memory system because events and attributes stored in the self contain many associations (Greenwald & Banaji, 1989). Events in autobiographical memory are stored in an organized manner and on at least two levels: general events and broad lifetime periods (Grysman & Hudson, 2011). The level of general events includes events that have occurred in your life (e.g., going to college, meeting your future spouse), whereas lifetime periods refer to important times in your life (e.g., childhood, early adulthood). Events in autobiographical memory are embedded within lifetime periods. So, for example, if you and your future spouse attended a lot of movies when you dated in college, these events would be embedded within the lifetime period of your college years. Generally, autobiographical memories at higher levels of organization have fewer details than those at lower levels (Grysman & Hudson, 2011). So, for example, your memories for events (e.g., going to the movies) will have more detail than those associated with more general lifetime periods. Grysman and Hudson also report that when we start thinking about autobiographical events, we tend to make more connections to the meaning of those events than we do to the specifics of who, where, and when. Finally, autobiographical memory helps us maintain a well-organized sense of self (self-concept clarity) and connections between the past and present (self-concept continuity). When we experience low levels of self-concept clarity and continuity, we rely on autobiographical memories to enhance them (Jiang et al., 2019).

The self is concerned with maintaining positive self-feelings, thoughts, and evaluations. One way it does this is by influencing memory. Anthony Greenwald (1980) suggested that the self functions as a kind of unconscious monitor that enables people to avoid disquieting or distressing information. The self demands that we preserve what we have, especially that which makes us feel good about ourselves. Is it true, as Greenwald predicted, that the self is a kind of filter that makes us feel good by gathering self-serving information and discarding information that makes us feel uncomfortable?

Most people take only about 2 seconds to answer questions about their traits (Klein et al., 1992). This is because we have a kind of summary knowledge of our self-traits, especially the most obvious ones. Such a handy summary makes it harder to access memories that conflict with our positive self-concept, however. As noted earlier, memories that match a person's self-concept are recalled more easily than those that clash with that concept (Neimeyer & Rareshide, 1991). If you perceive yourself as an honest person, you will have trouble digging up memories in which you have behaved dishonestly.

A research study of social memory of everyday life among college students had similar findings (Skowronski et al., 1991). Participants were asked to keep two diaries: In one, they recorded events that occurred in their lives, and in the other, they recorded events that occurred in the life of a close relative or friend, someone they saw on a daily basis. The students had to ask the consent of the other person, and they recorded the events discreetly. Participants made entries in the diaries for self and other for roughly 10 weeks, the length of the academic quarter. At the end of the quarter, the participants took a memory test on the events recorded in the two diaries. They were presented with the recorded events from the diaries in a random order and were asked to indicate how well they remembered the event, the date it occurred, and whether it was a unique episode.

The researchers found that participants recalled recent events more quickly than earlier ones, with faster retrieval of the oldest episodes than of those in the middle. They also found that pleasant events were recalled better than unpleasant ones and that extreme events—both pleasant and unpleasant—were recalled better than neutral episodes. Pleasant events that especially fit the person's self-concept were most easily recalled. The self, then, monitors our experiences, processing information in ways that make us look good to ourselves. We interpret, organize, and remember interactions and events in self-serving ways, recalling primarily pleasant, self-relevant events that fit our self-concept. Obviously, this built-in bias influences the manner in which we understand our social world

Important events in your life, such as graduating from college, are organized in the "general events" section of your autobiographical memory.
Source: Syda Productions/Shutterstock.

and how we interact with other people. Without realizing it, we are continually constructing a view of the world that is skewed in our favor.

Emotions and Autobiographical Memories

Some of you may be thinking as you read this, "These findings don't square with what happens to me when I think about my past." It is true that you don't always retrieve memories that are positive or pleasant, or that bolster good feelings. Indeed, sometimes the precise opposite is true. McFarland and Buehler (1998) examined how negative moods affect autobiographical memory. Generally, the memories you may recall seem to fit the mood that you are in. The explanation for this mood-congruence recall is that our mood makes it more likely that we will find memories of events that fit that mood: positive mood, positive recall; negative mood, negative recall. People who experience lots of negative moods can enter into a self-defeating cycle wherein their negative moods prime or key negative memories that in turn make them even more sad or depressed.

The idea that we recall autobiographical memories that are congruent with our present mood does not always hold true. Sometimes when we are experiencing something negative, we conjure up a positive autobiographical memory to make ourselves feel better. For example, if you just received a negative performance evaluation at work, you might think back to other instances when you received positive evaluations. This *incongruence effect* was shown in an experiment by Sezin Öner and Sami Gülgöz (2018). They had participants recall an event from the past 5 years that made them sad, an event that made them angry, or some everyday event (unspecified condition). Those memories were rated for how positive or negative they were. Later, participants were told to recall another specific event. These memories were also rated for how positive or negative they were. What they found, shown in Figure 2.1, is consistent with autobiographical incongruence recall. As you can see in Figure 2.1, participants recalling sad or angering events initially recalled more positive events later on. The opposite was true for the unspecified initial recall condition. Öner and Gülgöz suggest that individuals in the sadness and anger conditions used the subsequent positive memories to compensate for the negative mood they created.

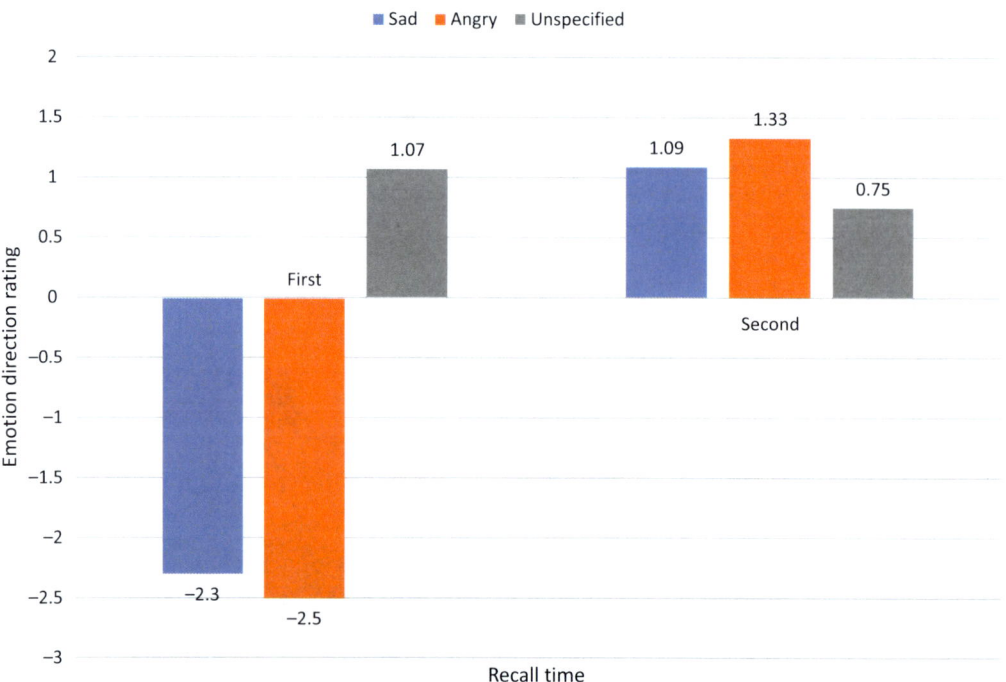

FIGURE 2.1

Results from Sezin Öner and Sami Gülgöz's (2018) experiment.
Based on data from Öner and Gülgöz (2018).

So, it appears that autobiographical memories have a powerful functional component. That is, they *do something* for us. Autobiographical memories may be called up at certain times to perform specific functions (Wolf & Demiray, 2019). Tabea Wolf and Burcu Demiray point out that autobiographical memories serve several functions: regulating mood, enhancing self-continuity, directing behavior, and enhancing self-esteem, as well as a social function (sharing memories with others). Wolf and Demiray found that mood-enhancing memories tend to be more positive than those serving a directive or social function. Interestingly, they also found that mood-enhancing memories often serve self-focused and directive functions but not a social function. That is, we may use memories to enhance mood, bolster self-continuity, and direct behavior while not necessarily sharing those memories with others.

Why do some people in negative moods perpetuate that mood and others make themselves feel better? It appears that the approach to how we retrieve these memories is the key (Lyubomirsky et al., 1998). If you adopt a focused *reflective* attitude, which means that you may admit that you failed at this task, you explore the nature of why you feel bad and work to regulate that mood. This is in contrast to people who *ruminate* over their moods. That is, they focus neurotically and passively on negative events and feelings (McFarland & Buehler, 1998).

Of course, over our lifetimes our experiences may very well alter, sometimes dramatically, our sense of ourselves. If this change is significant, we may look back and wonder if we are in fact the same person we once were. William James (1890), the renowned 19th-century psychologist and philosopher, observed that the self was both a "knower" ("I") and an object ("me"). For college students, the transition from high school to university may produce a conflict between the person's current sense of self and that other person who existed before the transition: "I am not the same person that I was 2 years ago."

Psychologists Lisa Libby and Richard Eibach (2002) investigated what happened when people thought about behaviors that conflicted with their current self-concept. When this happens, individuals refer to their "old self" in the third person, as if it were an object that is no longer part of the psyche. Autobiographical memory, then, is not static, but may be altered by our current self-concept. For example, someone who recalls that he was a chronic overeater in the past may transform that bit of autobiographical memory into motivation not to overindulge at this Thanksgiving's meal (Libby & Eibach, 2002). Major life changes often require that people disengage from their past. For example, a "born again" religious experience, or surviving a deadly cancer, or dealing with a divorce and the resultant radical change in lifestyle are all events that can make people "disidentify" with their autobiographical memories of their past selves (Libby & Eibach, 2002). It is not as if we create a brand-new self, but rather, we place the old one in a kind of cold storage.

Study Break

This section explored the relationship between memory and self-concept. It also introduced the concept of autobiographical memory and how it relates to self-concept. Before you begin the next section, answer the following questions:

1. What is the relationship between memory and self-concept?
2. What is autobiographical memory, and what two subsystems make it up?
3. How does emotion relate to autobiographical memory?

The Self: The Influence of Groups and Culture

Thus far, we have focused on the **individual self**, that part of the self that refers to our self-knowledge, including our private thoughts and evaluations of who and what we are. But as we have seen, the groups to which we belong and the culture in which we live play crucial roles in sculpting our self-concept.

individual self The part of the self that refers to our self-knowledge, including our private thoughts and evaluations of who and what we are.

collective self The part of the self-concept that comes from membership in groups.

The **collective self** is that part of our self-concept that comes from our membership in groups. This collective self is reflected in thoughts such as, "In my family I am considered the responsible, studious one." It reflects the evaluation of the self by important and specific groups to which the person belongs (Greenwald & Pratkanis, 1984). Basic research on groups shows that the groups we belong to have a strong influence on self-concept (Gaertner et al., 1999). Our behavior is often changed by what other group members demand of us.

These two representations, the individual and the collective selves, do not occupy equal space in or have equal influence on the self-concept. The relative importance of each component for an individual is determined in large part by the culture in which the person lives. In some cultures, the individual self is dominant. Cultures that emphasize individual striving and achievement—societies that are concerned with people "finding themselves"—produce individuals in which the individual self is highly complex, containing many traits and beliefs. Other cultures may emphasize specific groups, such as family or religious community, and therefore, the collective self is primary. Collectivist societies show a pattern of close links among individuals who define themselves as interdependent members of groups such as family, coworkers, and social groups (Vandello & Cohen, 1999).

However, even within societies, the degree of collectivism may vary. Vandello and Cohen (1999) argued that collectivist tendencies in the United States would be highest in the Deep South because that region still maintains a strong regional identity. Vandello and Cohen also thought that the greatest individualistic tendencies would be found in the West and mountain states. The map in Figure 2.2 identifies regional differences in collectivism and confirms Vandello and Cohen's predictions. Note that the states with the highest collectivism scores contain either many different cultures (e.g., Hawaii) or a strong and dominant religion (e.g., Utah). In another study contrasting Australian and Japanese individuals, results showed that Australians scored higher on two measures of the individual self (agency and assertiveness) than Japanese (Kashima et al., 2004). This study also found differences in emphasis on the collective self when large metropolitan areas were compared to smaller "regional" cities in Japan and Australia. Residents of smaller regional cities placed more emphasis on the collective self than residents of larger metropolitan areas. Individuals in cultures that emphasize the collective self are also less likely to view themselves as the focus of attention in social interactions (Markus & Kitayama, 1991; Ross & Nisbett, 1991). For example,

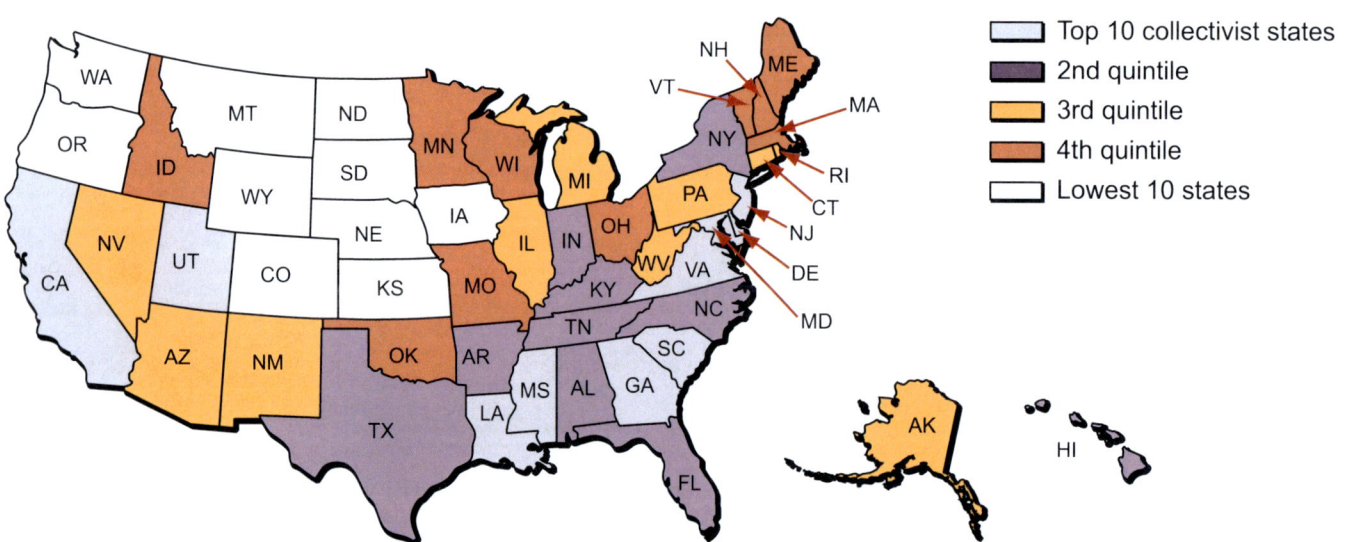

FIGURE 2.2

Map of the United States showing regional patterns of collectivism.
Based on Vandello and Cohen (1999).

Japanese individuals appear to view their peers, rather than themselves, as the focus of attention. Consequently, social interactions in Japan are quite different from those in a society such as the United States.

One way to determine whether the individual or collective self is the dominant representation of who we are is to observe what occurs when one or another of these images of the self is threatened. Is a threat to the individual self more or less menacing than a threat to our collective self? If the status of the important groups to which we belong is threatened, is this more upsetting to us than if our individual, personal self is under attack?

Social media have provided a modern-day outlet for the expression of the self.
Source: Rawpixel.com/Shutterstock.

In a series of experiments, Gaertner et al. (1999) tried to answer these questions by comparing individuals' responses to threats to the collective or individual self. For example, in one study, women at a university were given a psychological test and were told either that they personally had not done very well on the test or that an important group to which they belonged (women at the university) had not done well. Similar procedures were used in other experiments. Gaertner and his colleagues found that, compared to a threat to the collective self, a threat to the individual self resulted in the perception that the threat was more severe, a more negative mood, more anger, and the participants' denial of the accuracy or validity of the test or source of the threat.

The results suggest that the individual self is primary and that the collective self is less so. Of course, this does not mean that the collective self is not crucial. It and our group memberships provide protection and financial and social rewards. But all things being equal, it appears that, in the United States, our individual self is more important to us than our collective self.

SOCIAL PSYCHOLOGY IN ACTION

Social Psychology in Action: The Internet Self

Traditionally, social psychologists have talked about the self within the context of one's physical existence. However, technology and social media (e.g., Facebook and Twitter) have opened up a whole new dimension of the self. Not only do we have a self that we project to others in face-to-face social interactions, but we may also have an alternative self that exists in cyberspace, such as on Facebook or in a virtual world. On Facebook, for example, people post personal information about themselves; photos of themselves, friends, and family; information about attitudes; and other material important to them. In other words, people engage in self-disclosure of important information about themselves. Social media content is just as much an expression of the self as any other manner of self-expression. We might refer to this self as the *Internet self*.

Do people express the self on Facebook in the same way as they do in face-to-face situations? One study suggests that they do not (Chen & Marcus, 2012). In this study, college students completed an online survey concerning their use of social media. Chen and Marcus found that the most important reasons for using social media were to stay in touch with friends and classmates. Participants also indicated that they disclosed more information on social media sites than they did in person. However, more extraverted (outgoing) people were more likely to disclose information about themselves on social media than were less extraverted people. This difference was most pronounced for extraverted people who also had a stronger "collectivist" self-definition. More introverted (shy and reserved) people with a collectivist orientation disclosed less honest information.

In the face-to-face world of interpersonal relationships, individuals are more likely to self-disclose to others if they perceive that those others will be responsive to that self-disclosure (Reis & Shaver, 1988). According to Reis and Shaver's interpersonal

(continued)

model of intimacy, responsiveness to self-disclosure helps promote intimacy in a relationship. Does this idea extend to self-disclosure on social media? That is, will individuals engage in more self-disclosure on social media if they perceive that others will respond to those disclosures? A study by Rebecca Walsh and colleagues (2020) addressed this question. Walsh et al. had Facebook users provide their 10 most recent updates to their pages. They also had them complete measures of how responsive and supportive they perceived their Facebook network of friends to be. They found that, just like in face-to-face situations, Facebook users who perceived their network of friends to be more responsive and supportive were more likely to self-disclose than those who did not. In another study, individuals who received social support for a self-disclosure on an instant messenger platform continued to receive social support even 6 months after the disclosure. Interestingly, those who received such social support were more willing than those who did not to engage in future self-disclosure (Trepte et al., 2018).

There are gender differences in how men and women present themselves on social media. Women are more likely to use carefully chosen pictures to present themselves, whereas men are more likely to use verbal descriptions (Mehdizadeh, 2010). Men are more likely than women to present self-promotional information in the "About" section on Facebook. However, women are more likely to use a self-promotional photograph as their main photograph than are men (Mehdizadeh, 2010).

There is also a gender difference in the importance of various controls used on Facebook. For males, privacy (e.g., posting with a privacy setting) and image (e.g., being able to update profile pictures) controls were strongly related to using Facebook for the presentation of information about the self. For females, expressive information control (e.g., updating personal status) was most strongly related to using Facebook to present information about the self (Kuo et al., 2013).

Self-disclosure on social media presents an especially challenging problem for individuals who must manage sensitive identities presented to a virtual audience made up of a number of subgroups. One example is how LGBTQ individuals manage what they disclose on social media. Often, these individuals must be very careful regarding what and how much they disclose to others about their identities on social media (McConnell et al., 2018). Generally, nonheterosexual individuals often disclose their sexual identity on social media platforms, most notably Facebook (Twist et al., 2017). Some studies have examined

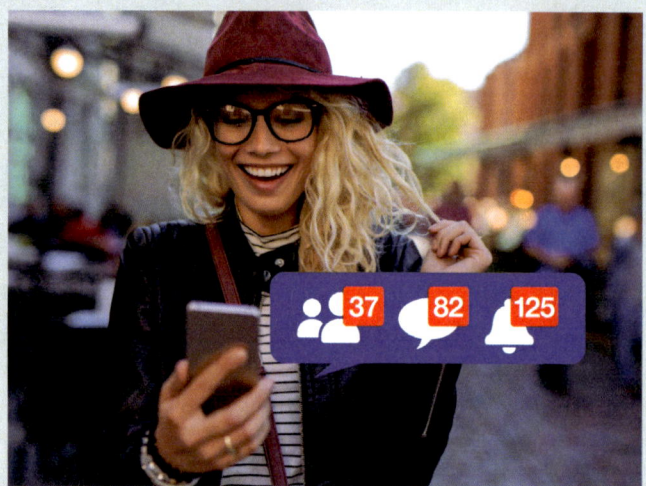

For many people, a version of the self exists in cyberspace as the Internet self. People express their Internet self differently from face-to-face situations.
Source: Kaspara Grinvalds/Shutterstock.

how gay men have used social media to "come out" to others. In one study, gay men reported a number of benefits of using Facebook to come out, including efficiency (reaching others easily), increased authenticity, and decreased ambiguity about their sexuality (Chester et al., 2016). However, disclosing information about one's sexual orientation can be complex. In one study, LGBTQ youth and young adults reported using multiple Facebook accounts for different audiences, most notably for family and work associates. Others reported carefully censoring and monitoring what information they disclose due to fears over how others might react (McConnell et al., 2018). McConnell et al. also found that LGBTQ individuals reported receiving both positive (likes) and negative (homophobic comments) feedback for their posts, causing a degree of stress and anxiety.

There are also cultural differences in the information disclosed on Facebook pages. For example, one study found that British and Italian social media users differed in the content they posted on social media. British individuals were more likely to post information about alcohol and drug use, whereas Italian individuals were more likely to post offensive content and personal information (White et al., 2018). In another study, Black students posted more psychological characteristics and more self-descriptive statements about themselves than either White or Asian students (who did not differ; DeAndrea et al., 2010). Black students also used more words relating to their families than White or Asian students. Finally, White students were three times more likely to post a photograph of themselves than either Black or Asian students (who did not differ).

(continued)

> Generally, a number of global cultural factors relate to the willingness to self-disclose on social media (Reed et al., 2016). For example, cultures stressing greater gender egalitarianism are associated with fewer concerns over privacy issues and may have increased self-disclosure. Cultures with high levels of assertiveness show more privacy concerns, which may reduce self-disclosure (Reed et al., 2016). Individuals who live in a culture stressing honor (i.e., maintaining respect and esteem of others) are less willing to post potentially improper pictures (e.g., showing one's boyfriend or girlfriend) on social media than those who do not live in such a culture (Günsoy et al., 2015). There was no difference between an honor and non-honor culture in terms of willingness to post pictures showing an achievement (e.g., a graduation picture; Günsoy et al., 2015). In an honor culture, posting an inappropriate picture may lead to a loss of respect and esteem from others, which may account for the difference observed.
>
> **Discussion Questions**
>
> 1. What is the Internet self?
> 2. Do people express aspects of the Internet self in the same way as they do in face-to-face situations?
> 3. Do all people express the Internet self in the same way?

Study Break

This section examined how group affiliation, access to social media, and culture relate to self-concept. Before you begin the next section, answer the following questions:

1. What are the characteristics of the individual and collective selves, and how do they relate to one another?
2. How does group affiliation affect self-concept?
3. How do social media relate to one's self-concept, and what factors affect how the self is expressed on the Internet?

Culture and the Expression of the Self

Individual-self societies emphasize self-fulfillment at the expense of communal relationships; collective-self societies are more concerned with meeting shared obligations and helping others. In Haiti, for example, where the culture emphasizes the collective self, people are willing to share houses and food with relatives and friends for long periods of time.

Members of individual and collective cultures may react differently to a negative situation that arises. For example, the COVID-19 pandemic of 2020–2021 highlighted differences between Asian cultures (collectivist) and Western cultures (individualistic). Members of Asian cultures, for example, had little trouble adapting to and accepting wearing masks to help prevent the spread of the virus. Members of Western cultures showed much more resistance (Scalabrini et al., 2021). According to Scalabrini et al., Asian individuals see wearing a mask as benefiting other members of society by reducing their risk of illness or death. On the other hand, those in Western cultures are more likely to react negatively to the highly valued "individual freedom" infringed upon by mask mandates. Situational factors can sometimes determine whether the collective or individual self is dominant. Gardner et al. (1999) showed that the individual self may be temporarily more dominant in a collectivist culture when people are focused on personal issues—say, one's intelligence or one's goals in life. Similarly, people who live in an individualistic culture may temporarily focus on collectivist factors when confronted by issues involving group belongingness (e.g., "I am an American"). This was evident in the aftermath of the September 11, 2001, terrorist attacks in the United States. For many, the threat posed by the attacks enhanced their feelings of nationalism. However, whatever the effects of temporary situational factors, the thoughts and traits that make up the core of the self of a person from a collectivist culture are likely to differ from those making up someone from an individualistic culture.

Members of individual and collective cultures reacted differently to wearing masks during the COVID-19 pandemic of 2020–2021. Members of Asian cultures, for example, had little trouble adapting to and accepting wearing masks to help prevent the spread of the virus.

Source: CGN089/Shutterstock.

Another example of how culture relates to defining the self is how gay and lesbian individuals define themselves relative to culture. Historically, gays and lesbians have been marginalized by the wider culture in the United States. However, this has changed. Gays and lesbians have become more accepted within the wider American culture, as evidenced by the greater acceptance of gay rights issues such as same-sex marriage. Have these changes brought about a change in how gays and lesbians define themselves? A study conducted by Weststrate and McLean (2010) shows that this has occurred. Gays and lesbians from five age cohorts (1960s, 1970s, 1980s, 1990s, and 2000s) reported on a significant cultural event (e.g., a gay rights march) and a personal event related to their sexuality (e.g., when they "came out" with respect to their sexuality). Weststrate and McLean found that individuals in the older cohorts were more likely to report a "cultural event" as being important to their sexual identities than were those in the younger cohorts. Conversely, individuals in the younger cohorts were more likely to report a "personal event." When Weststrate and McLean looked at the nature of the cultural events reported as being important, older and younger gays and lesbians reported different types of events. Those in the older cohort were more likely to report a specific cultural event, whereas those in the younger cohort were more likely to report a more personal cultural experience (e.g., college or school influence). Finally, the researchers found that gays and lesbians differed on the types of cultural events reported as important. Gays were more likely to report more general cultural events such as homophobia or HIV/AIDS, whereas lesbians were more likely to report exposure to other gays and lesbians.

Despite the wider acceptance of gays and lesbians in American culture, there are still subcultures in which gay and lesbian self-concept conflicts with situational factors. For example, having a same-sex orientation in the U.S. military creates problems for many and may result in individuals denying and suppressing their sexual identity. In one study, gay, lesbian, and bisexual (GLB) U.S. military members and veterans were interviewed about their experiences (Van Gilder, 2019). Van Gilder found that there were several factors about the military that delegitimized GLB identity. These included dehumanization (being viewed as less than human), stereotype proliferation, and discrimination. This resulted in difficulty integrating identities related to being GLB and being a member of the military. Consequently, GLB individuals had to find ways to reconcile their sexual and military identities using various strategies. Interviewees reported the need to suppress their sexual identities in favor of their military identities as a coping mechanism. Another strategy was to segment their military and personal lives. Some developed a group of friends in the military (to whom they did not come out) and another outside the military (to whom they did come out). Another strategy was attempting to reconcile their sexual and military identities after the military allowed openly GLB individuals to serve. Individuals adopting this strategy were willing to come out despite the potential stereotyping and discrimination they would face. This illustrates how difficult it can be if individuals cannot fully integrate a social role with their internal self-concept and identity.

Organizing Knowledge: Self-Schemas

Whatever the culture one lives in, people don't think of themselves as just chaotic masses of attributes and memories. Instead, they arrange knowledge and information about themselves and their attributes into **self-schemas** (Markus, 1977; Markus & Zajonc, 1985). A *schema* is an organized set of related cognitions—bits of knowledge and information—about a particular person, event, or experience. A self-schema is an arrangement of information, thoughts, and feelings about ourselves, including information about our gender, age, race or ethnicity, occupation, social roles, physical attractiveness, intelligence, talents, and so on. People have many different self-schemas for the different areas of life activities.

Self-schemas serve a very important function: They organize our self-related experiences so that we can respond quickly and effectively in social situations. They help us interpret situations, and they guide our behavior. Schemas also help us understand new events (Scheier & Carver, 1988). You may have a self-schema about how you act in an emergency, for example. From past experience and from your ideals and expectations about yourself, you may believe that you are a person who stays calm, acts responsibly, and takes care of others, or one who panics and has to be taken care of by others. These beliefs about yourself influence your behavior when an emergency arises in the future. Or perhaps you have a self-schema about being a runner. When you hear people talking about keeping fit or eating the right foods, you know what they are talking about and how it relates to you. In these ways, self-schemas contribute to our sense of control over our social world.

Self-schemas lend order to our past experiences as well. They guide what we encode (place) into memory and influence how we organize and store that memory. Memories that match our self-schemas are recalled more easily than are those that do not (Neimeyer & Rareshide, 1991). Self-schemas also influence how we think we will behave in the future. A person who thinks of himself as socially awkward, for example, may behave inappropriately in social situations. And based on his behavior in the past, he expects to behave inappropriately in future social situations.

People tend to have elaborate schemas about areas of life that are important to their self-concepts. Markus (1977) observed that people may be either schematic or aschematic with respect to various attributes that are in the self-concept. The term *schematic* means that the individual has an organized self-schema in an activity that the individual rates as important. In other areas of life—those that are not important to us or that may not even exist for us—people are said to be *aschematic*. That is, they do not have an organized self-schema in that domain.

Sexuality and Self-Schemas

Sexuality is clearly a fundamental behavior, and therefore, we expect people to have **sexual self-schemas** of varying degrees of organization. A sexual self-schema refers to how we think about the sexual aspects of the self. Sexual schemas are derived from past sexual knowledge and experience and, as all schemas do, they guide our future (sexual) activity. Cyranowski and Andersen (1998) studied the sexual self-schemas of university women and found that four different schemas emerged. Women who were schematic—that is, had well-developed schemas—displayed either positive or negative schemas. These positive and negative schemas reflected their individual past sexual history as well as their current sexual activity. As the sexual schema graph shows, positive-sexual-schema women had more previous sexual relationships (Figure 2.3) and scored higher measures of passionate attachment to their partners (Figure 2.4). These women were more likely to be in a current sexual relationship. Negative-sexual-schema women displayed an avoidance of intimacy and passion and were much more anxious about sexual activity.

Some women had both negative and positive aspects to their self-schemas, and they were labeled *co-schematic*. Whereas co-schematic women see themselves as open, passionate, and romantic (as do the positive-schema women), they differ from the positive-schema women in that they hold negative self-views, and this leads to anxieties about being rejected or abandoned by their partners.

Aschematic women, like negative-schema women, have fewer romantic attachments, experience less passionate emotions about love, and avoid emotional intimacy. Aschematic women tend to avoid sexual situations and display anxiety about sex. A major

---

self-schemas Self-conceptions that guide us in ordering and directing our behavior involving how we represent our thoughts and feelings about our experiences in a particular area of life.

sexual self-schema How we think about the sexual aspects of the self, derived from past sexual knowledge and experience, and which guides future sexual activity.

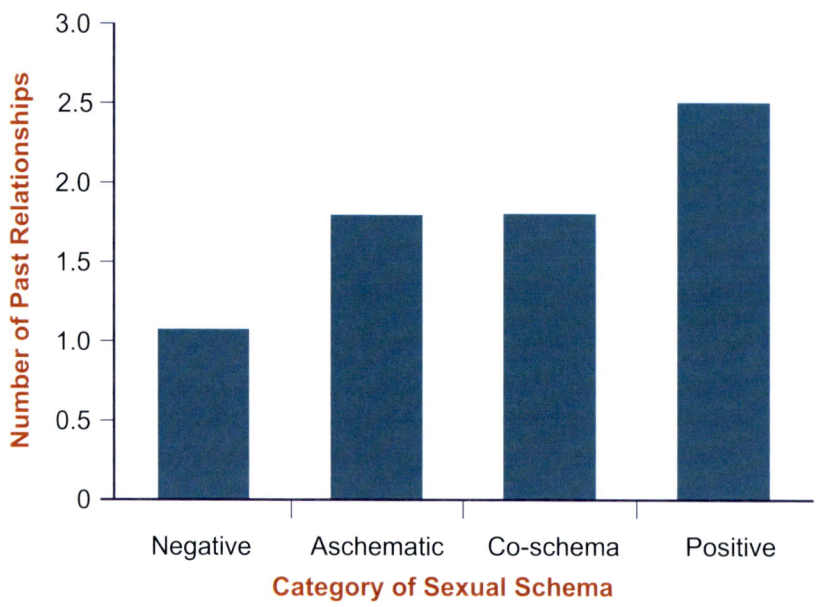

FIGURE 2.3

The relationship between an individual's sexual schema and the number of his or her first relationships.
Based on data from Cyranowski and Anderson (1998).

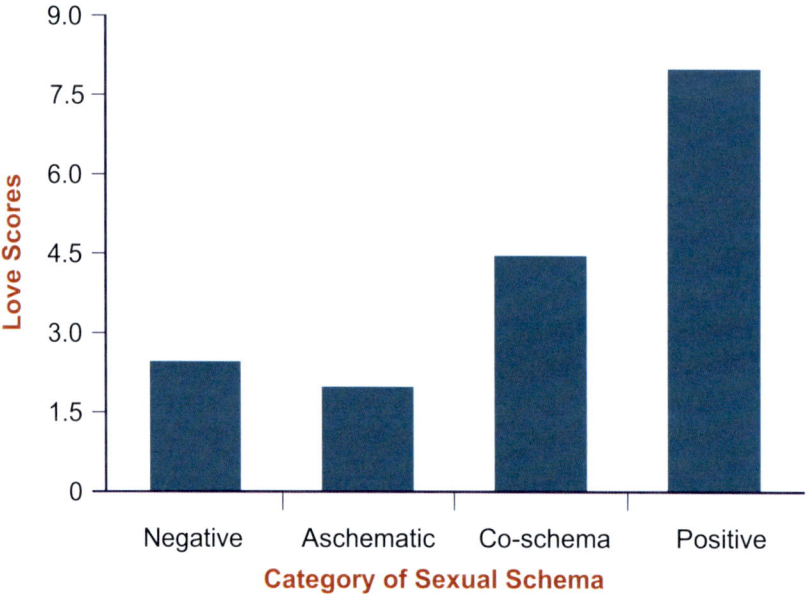

FIGURE 2.4

The relationship between an individual's sexual schema and his or her passionate love score.
Based on data from Cyranowski and Anderson (1998).

difference between aschematic women and negative-schema women is that aschematic women do not have negative self-views. They are just less interested in sexual activity. Table 2.1 summarizes these findings.

Whereas women express sexual self-schemas that fit roughly into categories, men's sexual self-schemas appear to flow along a continuum, ranging from highly schematic to aschematic (Andersen et al., 1999). Men who are schematic have sexual schemas that reflect strong emotions of passion and love, attributes shared with positive-schematic women. However, these men see themselves as strong and aggressive, with liberal sexual attitudes

TABLE 2.1 Sexual Schemas and Sexual Behaviors

	Schematic			
Sexual Behaviors	Positive	Negative	Co-Schematic	Aschematic
Previous sex experiences	Many	Few	Moderate	Few
Passionate	High	Low	High	Low
Intimacy	High	Low	Low	Low
Anxiety	Low	High	High	High
Self-views	Positive	Negative	Negative	Moderate

(Andersen et al., 1999). Schematic men lead varied sexual lives and may engage in quite casual sex, but are also capable of strong attachments. On the other end of the scale are aschematic men, who lead quite narrow sexual lives and have few if any sexual partners.

Do men's and women's sexual self-schemas differ from one another? Although there are some small gender differences, men's and women's sexual self-schemas are for the most part more alike than they are different. For example, Hill (2007) reported a small, but significant gender difference on two dimensions defining the sexual self-schemas of men and women. Women scored higher than men on the dimensions of loving/warm and reserved/conservative. This gender difference was confirmed in a study by Staša Kukulj and Gordana Kereteš (2019). Kukulj and Kereteš also found that men scored higher than women on the dimension of direct/outspoken. Additionally, they found that students with high scores on the direct/outspoken dimension and low scores on the reserved/conservative dimension were more likely to have had a recent sexual partner than those with the opposite profile. However, they did not find a gender difference in the relationship between sexual self-schema dimensions and the likelihood of having a recent sexual partner.

As you might expect, sexual self-schemas can be quite complex and can be affected by a number of factors. For example, sexual self-schemas are related to one's prior sexual history. Amelia Stanton (2015) compared the sexual self-schemas of women with and without a history of childhood sexual abuse. Stanton found that the schemas of women with a history of abuse tended to incorporate that history into their sexual self-schemas, and it appeared that those themes remained an enduring component well into adulthood. Women with no history of sexual abuse tended to incorporate themes related to loss of virginity and sexual relationships into their sexual self-schemas more than did women with a history of sexual abuse. Other research shows that women with a history of childhood sexual abuse see themselves as less passionate and romantic and have higher levels of sexual anxiety than those with no such history. Stanton also found that relationship status affected the theme of women's sexual self-schemas. Women in more-committed relationships focused on virginity less and sexual activity more than women in less-committed relationships. Finally, Stanton found that older women focused less on any childhood abuse and sexual activity and more on attraction than did younger women.

The vast majority of research on sexual self-schemas relates to individuals with a heterosexual orientation. What little research has been done on those with other sexual orientations suggests that the sexual self-schemas of heterosexuals and individuals with same-sex orientations share many characteristics (Peixoto & Nobre, 2015). Elder et al. (2015) interviewed gay men and found that their sexual self-schemas showed conflict between a desire to avoid vulnerability coupled with a desire for an emotional connection with another person (Elder et al., 2015). In addition, the narratives of the gay men in this study suggested that gay men may use casual sex as a way to experience the intimacy of a relationship without having to disclose intimate details about the self. Interestingly, Elder et al. found that the sexual self-schemas of gay men evolved to become more integrated into the gay orientation. For example, early on, there was a period of sexual exploration involving frequent, casual sex. Eventually, the men became involved in a relationship, where they first fully identified themselves as gay. Finally, they reached a point where they had to decide whether to become involved in a committed relationship or an open relationship. Clearly, more research is needed in this area, since the Elder et al. study was based on a small sample of gay men.

The more varied and complex our self is, the more self-schemas we will have. We can see that men and women have sexual self-schemas of varying degrees of organization, and these schemas reflect their sexual past and guide their current (and future) sexual behavior. These cognitive representations or self-schemas reflect both the importance of the behavior represented and the emotional tone of the behavior.

People differ in the number of attributes, memories, and self-schemas that are part of their self-concept. Some people have highly complex selves, others much less complex. Self-complexity is important in influencing how people react to the good and bad events in life. A woman who is, say, an engineer, an opera lover, a mother, and an artist can absorb a blow to one of her selves without much damage to her overall self-concept (Linville, 1985, 1987). If her latest artistic endeavors meet unfavorable reviews, this woman's sense of self is buffered by the fact that there is much more to her than being an artist. She is still a mother, an engineer, an opera lover, and much more. People who are low in self-complexity may be devastated by negative events because there is little else to act as a buffer.

Study Break

This section explored how culture and our concepts of sexuality relate to self-concept. Before you begin the next section, answer the following questions:

1. How does culture, in general, contribute to self-concept?
2. How does an individual's sexual orientation relate to self-concept?
3. What is a self-schema, and how does it relate to self-concept?
4. What is a sexual self-schema, and how do individuals of different genders and sexual orientations express it?

Self-Esteem: Evaluating the Self

The self is more than a knowledge structure. It also has a larger sense of our overall worth, a component that consists of both positive and negative self-evaluations. This is known as **self-esteem**. We evaluate, judge, and have feelings about ourselves. Some people possess high self-esteem: They regard themselves highly and are generally pleased with who they are. Others have low self-esteem, feel less worthy and good, and may even feel that they are failures and incompetent.

self-esteem An individual's evaluation of the self, which can be positive or negative.

Self-esteem is affected both by our ideas about how we are measuring up to our standards and by our ability to control our sense of self in interactions with others. Both of these processes—one primarily internal, the other primarily external—have important repercussions on our feelings about ourselves.

Internal Influences on Self-Esteem

Our feelings about ourselves come from many sources. We carry some, perhaps most, forward from childhood, when our basic self-concepts formed from interactions with our parents and other adults. Research in child development indicates that people develop basic feelings of trust, security, and self-worth, or mistrust, insecurity, and worthlessness from these early relationships and experiences.

Self-Esteem and Emotional Intelligence

Our emotions are important sources of information. They serve as a kind of early warning system to tell us that important things are happening in our environment.

One characteristic that relates to self-esteem is **emotional intelligence**, a person's ability to perceive, use, understand, and manage emotions (Salovey & Grewal, 2005). Individuals who are emotionally intelligent appear to be more successful in personal and work relationships. According Salovey and Grewal (2005), emotionally intelligent people are able to monitor their emotions and those of the people with whom they interact. They then use that information to guide the way they think and behave. So, the emotionally intelligent person knows when to express anger and when not to do so. Such individuals are also good at manipulating their moods. Certain tasks and interactions, for example, may be better accomplished when in a sad mood than a good mood, and emotionally intelligent people seem to know how to manipulate their moods to reach their goals. They are also proficient at reading the emotions of other people. In other words, emotionally intelligent people trust their emotions and use those emotions as information. Others "do not take counsel" of their emotions because they think that emotions are untrustworthy.

Lopes et al. (2005) investigated the relationship between individuals' emotional intelligence and their abilities to regulate their emotions, to choose good interaction strategies, and to accurately read others' emotions, with the quality of their friendships and social interactions. Those people who were high on emotion regulation abilities (high emotional intelligence) were more favorably rated by their friends and acquaintances, and were more likely to be nominated by their peers as people who were sensitive and helpful to others.

What does this have to do with self-esteem? The connection may be that individuals with high self-esteem take greater account of their emotions than do people with lower self-esteem. Emotions seem to be very useful in a variety of areas, including understanding other people, creative thinking, and even good health (Harber, 2005). It appears that emotional intelligence is strongly related to self-esteem (Harber, 2005). The research showing that self-esteem is positively related to effective processing of emotional information suggests that for those high in self-esteem, emotions provide important information. It is certainly true that a lot of the time we do not have the facts of the situation, and all we have to go on are our "gut" feelings.

Okay, so high-self-esteem people use their emotions. Is that good? Well, it depends. The evidence suggests that high-self-esteem individuals are much more likely to act on their anger (Harber, 2005). In other words, sometimes they may pay too much attention to internal emotional cues and not enough to what is going on in the environment. As Kent Harber neatly puts it, "How we feel about our emotions may be shaped by how we feel about ourselves" (p. 287).

Maintaining Self-Esteem in Interactions with Others

When interacting with others, human beings have two primary self-related motives: to enhance self-esteem and to maintain self-consistency (Berkowitz, 1988). Obviously, people have a powerful need to feel good about themselves. They prefer positive responses from the social world. They become anxious when their self-esteem is threatened. What steps do they take to maintain and enhance self-esteem?

Enhancing the Self According to Abraham Tesser's **self-evaluation maintenance (SEM) theory** (1988), the behavior of other people, both friends and strangers, affects how we feel about ourselves, especially when the behavior is in an area that is important to our self-concept. The self carefully manages emotional responses to events in the social world, depending on how threatening it perceives those events to be. Tesser gave this example to illustrate his theory: Suppose, for example, that Jill thinks of herself as a math whiz. Jill and Joan are close friends; Joan receives a 99 and Jill a 90 on a math test. Because math is relevant to Jill, the comparison is important. Therefore, Joan's better performance is a threat, particularly since Joan is a close other. Jill can do a variety of things about this threat. She can reduce the relevance of Joan's performance. If math were not important to Jill's self-definition, she could bask in the reflection of Joan's performance. Jill could also reduce her closeness to Joan, thus making Joan's performance less consequential. Finally, Jill could try to affect their relative performance by working harder or doing something to handicap Joan (Tesser & Collins, 1988).

---

emotional intelligence A person's ability to perceive, use, understand, and manage emotions.

self-evaluation maintenance (SEM) theory A theory explaining how the behavior of other people affects how you feel about yourself, especially when they perform some behavior that is important to your self-concept.

If you believe that you are really good at math, you would be most threatened if a friend who is not good at math outscored you on an important math test.
Source: CREATISTA/Shutterstock.

This story neatly captures the basic elements of SEM theory. The essential question that Jill asks about Joan's performance is: "What effect does Joan's behavior have on my evaluation of myself?" Notice that Jill compares herself to Joan on a behavior that is important to Jill's self-concept. If Joan excelled at bowling, and Jill cared not a fig about knocking down pins with a large ball, she would not be threatened by Joan's rolling a 300 game or winning a bowling championship. In fact, she would *bask in the reflected glory* (BIRG) of her friend's performance; Jill's self-esteem would be enhanced because her friend did so well.

The comparison process is activated when you are dealing with someone who is close to you. If you found out that 10% of high school students who took the math SAT did better than you, it would have less emotional impact on your self-esteem than if you learned that your best friend scored a perfect 800, putting her at the top of all people who took the exam (provided, that is, that math ability was important to your self-concept).

SEM theory is concerned with the self's response to threat, the kinds of social threats encountered in everyday life. Tesser formulated SEM theory by investigating people's responses to social threats in terms of the two dimensions just described—relevance of the behavior to the participant's self-concept and closeness of the participant to the other person (Tesser & Collins, 1988). Participants were asked to remember and describe social situations in which a close or distant other performed better or worse than they did. Half of the time, the task was important to the participant's self-concept, and half of the time the task was unimportant. The participants also reported the emotions they felt during those episodes.

Results indicated that when the behavior was judged relevant to the self, emotions were heightened. When participants did better than the other, distant or close, they felt happier, and when they did worse, they felt more personal disgust, anger, and frustration. When the behavior was not particularly relevant to the self, emotions varied, depending on the closeness of the relationship. When a close friend performed better than the participant, the participant felt pride in that performance. As you would expect, participants felt less pride in the performance of a distant person, and, of course, they felt less pride in the friend's performance when the behavior was self-relevant.

One conclusion we can draw from this research and from SEM theory is that people are willing to make *some* sacrifices to accuracy if it means a gain in self-esteem. People undoubtedly want and need accurate information about themselves and how they compare to significant others, but they also display an equally powerful need to feel positive about themselves. This need for self-enhancement suggests that in appraising our performances and in presenting ourselves to others, we tend to exaggerate our positive attributes.

In sum, then, one way the self maintains esteem is by adjusting its responses to social threats. If a friend does better than we do at something on which we pride ourselves, we experience a threat to that part of our self-concept. Our friend's achievement suggests that we may not be as good in an important area as we thought we were. To preserve the integrity and consistency of the self-concept and to maintain high self-esteem, we can try to downplay the other's achievement, put more distance between ourselves and the other so that we feel less threatened by the performance, or try to handicap our friend. In each case, the self subtly adjusts our perceptions, emotions, and behaviors in the service of enhancing self-esteem.

Self-Enhancement and Coping with Disaster: The Survivors of September 11, 2001

An estimated 2,800 individuals lost their lives in the World Trade Center (WTC) buildings on that traumatic and horrifying day in 2001. Thousands of other individuals in the near vicinity or in the WTC survived but were exposed to both physical and psychological trauma. Bonanno et al. (2005) investigated how some survivors coped with this massive trauma. These researchers were very interested in those people who, while directly exposed to the attacks, showed few psychological effects of their experience. The study focused on those "resilient" individuals who used a kind of unrealistic self-enhancement strategy to deal with the trauma. These people, in fact, used self-enhancing strategies all of their lives so they did not alter their approach to deal with 9/11. The researchers wanted to know whether these self-enhancing "resilients" were truly in control of their emotions.

Self-enhancement in this context refers to the tendency to have overly positive or unrealistic self-serving biases (Bonanno et al., 2005). Research shows that individuals with a pre-existing tendency toward self-enhancement cope better with traumatic events than those not so inclined (Gupta & Bonanno, 2010). With respect to coping with the 9/11 attacks, self-enhancers who were directly exposed to the attack on the World Trade Center showed fewer posttraumatic and depressive symptoms than other individuals who were at the scene on September 11th. Self-enhancers have a very positive view of themselves and believe that they are in total control of themselves. They tend to project very positive feelings. Are these feelings real, or are they just a front for underlying problems? Bonanno and associates (2005) found that while other people were rather annoyed at the "resilient" self-enhancers and their remarkably upbeat attitudes in the face of the tragedy, the self-enhancers did not seem to be aware of this and, in fact, recovered from the trauma quicker than most, with fewer psychological scars. So if you don't mind that your friend might not appreciate your attitude, self-enhancement seems to be a pretty good approach to life's vicissitudes.

Study Break

This section defined self-esteem. It also introduced the concept of emotional intelligence and how the self can be enhanced. Before you begin the next section, answer the following questions:

1. What is the definition of self-esteem, and what characterizes a person with high or low self-esteem?
2. What is emotional intelligence, and how does it relate to self-esteem?
3. What is self-evaluation maintenance (SEM) theory, and why is it important in self-esteem?
4. How does self-enhancement help a person cope with traumatic events?

Self-Esteem and Stigma

We have seen that people often define themselves in terms of attributes that distinguish themselves from others. Sometimes these attributes are positive ("I was always the best athlete"), and sometimes they are negative ("I was always overweight"). Some individuals have characteristics that are stigmatized—marked by society—and therefore they risk rejection whenever those aspects of themselves are recognized. One would expect that culturally defined stigmas would affect a person's self-esteem.

Frable et al. (1998) wondered what effect stigmas that were either visible or concealable had on self-esteem. These researchers had Harvard University undergraduates rate their momentary self-esteem and feelings during everyday situations in their lives. Some of these students had concealable stigmas; that is, these culturally defined faults were hidden from the observer. The individuals were gay, bulimic, or came from poor families. Others had more visible socially defined stigmas; they were African American, or stutterers, or 30 pounds overweight.

Frable and her coworkers thought that those people with concealable stigmas would be most prone to low self-esteem because they rarely would be in the company of people who had similar stigmas. Other people who belong to the "marked" group can provide social support and more positive perceptions of the membership of the stigmatized group than can nonmembers. For example, cancer patients who belong to support groups and have other strong social support generally have more favorable prognoses than do those patients who remain isolated (Frable et al., 1998). In fact, these researchers found that those who were gay, poor, bulimic, or had other concealable stigmas had lower self-esteem and more negative feelings about themselves than both those with visible stigmas or people without any social stigmas at all. In addition, the degree to which a person identifies with a group with a similar stigma relates to that person's collective and individual self-esteem (Nario-Redmond et al., 2013). The more that individuals identify with a stigmatized group, the better they feel about themselves personally and about being affiliated with the group. These studies suggest that group membership that offers support and positive feelings raises our self-esteem and buffers us against negative social evaluations.

Although the Frable study indicates that visible stigmas have a less negative influence on self-esteem than do the concealable ones, conspicuous stigmas, such as being overweight, have definite negative effects on self-esteem as well. Early in life, we get a sense of our physical self. Western culture pays particular attention to physical attractiveness, or lack of the same, and thus, our sense of our physical appearance affects our self-esteem. As an aspect of appearance, body weight plays a role in self-esteem. Interestingly, the relationship between being overweight and having reduced self-esteem has behavioral consequences. Being overweight, and its accompanying low self-esteem, is related to higher levels of Internet addiction (Gentile et al., 2021).

Miller and Downey (1990) examined the relationship between self-esteem and body weight. They found that individuals who were classified as "heavyweights" (as opposed to individuals who were obese because of glandular problems) reported lower self-esteem. This finding was particularly true for females, but heavyweight males also tended to have lower self-esteem. Interestingly, those individuals who were, in fact, in the heavyweight category but who did not *think* that they were did not have lower self-esteem. This suggests that what is important is whether the individual is marked with disgrace—stigmatized—in his or her own eyes. It may be that heavyweights who do not feel that they have to match some ideal body type do not carry the same psychological burden that other heavyweights do. Feelings about ourselves, then, may come from personal evaluations of ourselves in terms of our internal standards, our self-guides. Heavyweights who had higher self-esteem probably had a better match between their ideal and actual selves than did other overweight individuals. Research confirms the link between feelings about oneself and weight-related self-esteem loss. In one study, for example, overweight individuals who experienced the negative emotions of guilt and shame showed the greatest drop in personal self-esteem (Pila et al., 2015).

What is the source of the negative self-esteem experienced by many overweight individuals? Much of it comes from cultural messages communicating that being thin and glamorous is highly desirable. Just look at advertisements using male or female models. Traditionally, they have been thin, fit, and physically attractive individuals. The implicit message is that unless individuals match this ideal, they are less desirable. This leads to an *internalized weight bias* in which overweight individuals internalize negative beliefs, attitudes, and stereotypes about themselves (Selensky & Carels, 2021). In recent years, advertisers have made an effort to show larger-sized models in a positive light. Can exposure to such media affect one's self-esteem? Selensky and Carels investigated this question. Female participants were randomly assigned to watch one of five videos. One video was the Aerie Real campaign showing larger-sized models in a positive way. The second video (Dove video) was from a documentary designed to show the negative effects of weight bias. The third video was a clip from an HBO documentary on weight stigma showing negative images of overweight people. The fourth video was a clip from a Victoria's Secret "Dream Angels" broadcast showing very thin models. The fifth video was a clip from a neutral nature documentary. Participants completed several measures, including self-esteem, internalized weight bias, body image, and positive or negative affect. Selensky and Carels found that women who watched the Aerie and Dove videos showed significant increases in self-esteem compared with those watching the other videos. They also showed higher levels of positive affect and found the videos to be positive, empowering, and uplifting. Interestingly, they did not find an effect on the measure of internalized weight bias. So, improvement in self-esteem was not related to changes in the internalized self-perception of weight bias.

Self-Esteem and Cultural Influences

Self-esteem, as you might think, is influenced by factors other than our personal experiences. After all, we live and identify with certain groups, small and large. We are students or professors at certain colleges and universities, we root for various sports teams, and we have various religious, social, and national affiliations. All of these things influence our self-esteem.

Schmitt and Allik (2005) studied the relationship between culture and *global self-esteem,* which is one's general sense of how worthy one is as a person. These researchers employed a commonly used measure of self-esteem known as the Rosenberg Self-Esteem Scale (RSES). They had this instrument translated into 28 different languages and had 17,000 people in 53 different countries take the test. Schmitt and Allik found that people in all nations have generally positive self-esteem. It seems that positive self-esteem appears to be culturally universal.

A closer analysis of the data led Schmitt and Allik to conclude that, while individuals in all of these 53 countries had meaningful concepts of what self-esteem meant, there was also evidence that in some countries (African and Asian cultures), people were less likely to engage in self-evaluation, which, of course, is the basis of self-esteem. Nevertheless, feeling positive about oneself seems to be universal, and the assumption that self-esteem is usually higher or more positive in individualistic cultures (e.g., the United States) as opposed to collectivist cultures (e.g., Indonesia) in which the group tends to be more important seems not to be true (Schmitt & Allik, 2005).

What's So Good about High Self-Esteem?

In the latter part of the 20th century, a self-esteem craze swept across the United States, with the underlying message that having high self-esteem was related to all that was good (Singal, 2017). The resulting push to improve self-esteem permeated just about everything, from education to industry. The result of this craze was an increase in self-esteem among American middle school, high school, and college students between 1988 and 2008 (Gentile et al., 2010). No such increase in self-esteem occurred in Australian culture, which places more emphasis on equality between the self and others than does American culture. In contrast, American culture places more value on the pursuit of self-esteem as an end in itself (Hamamura et al., 2017). However, researchers such as Jennifer Crocker have raised doubts about these conclusions and have suggested, based upon a closer review of the research, that the real benefits of high self-esteem are "small and limited" (Crocker & Park, 2004). Baumeister et al. (2003) have argued that high self-esteem may lead to good feelings and may make people more resourceful but that it does not cause high academic achievement, good job performance, or leadership; nor does low self-esteem cause violence, smoking, drinking, taking drugs, or becoming sexually active at an early age.

Crocker, and Park (2004) examined the effects of the pursuit of self-esteem, rather than just evaluating who has low or high self-esteem scores. Most individuals tend to judge their self-worth by what they need to do to be seen as a person of worth and value. In other words, they judge their self-esteem by external reactions. It often means competing with others. This explains to some extent the observation that high-self-esteem individuals are quick to react violently when their self-esteem is questioned.

While we tend to think that high self-esteem is a positive attribute, we have not, as Roy Baumeister (2001) noted, looked closely at the consequences, good and bad, of self-esteem on behavior. Indeed, according to Baumeister, the evidence suggests that high-self-esteem individuals are more likely to be violent when their self-esteem is threatened. This pursuit apparently only produces rather temporary emotional benefits but imposes high costs. Crocker and Park (2004) argued that the pursuit of self-esteem inhibits relationships with others, learning, self-regulation, personal autonomy, and both physical and mental health.

Others have observed that while high self-esteem is related to all kinds of positive behaviors, it seems to be based upon what people believe is the best way to live (their "worldview"). For that reason, high self-esteem can also be a cause of horrible and tragic events, not unlike September 11, 2001. After all, in one worldview, "heroic martyrdom" is a good thing (Pyszczynski et al., 2004, p. 461). So high self-esteem in and of itself may not be good or bad. It depends upon the way one behaves (Pyszczynski et al., 2004).

Implicit and Explicit Self-Esteem

The resolution to the question of what's so good about high self-esteem may be found in the idea that there are really two kinds of self-esteem. **Implicit self-esteem** "refers to a very efficient system of self-evaluation that is below our conscious awareness" (Jordan et al., 2005, p. 693). Implicit self-esteem comes from parents who nurture their children but do not overprotect them, and it is unconscious and not controlled by the individual (DeHart et al., 2006). Implicit self-esteem is automatic and less likely to be affected by day-to-day events.

In comparison, the kind of high self-esteem we've been talking about—more fairly called **explicit self-esteem**—arises primarily from interactions with people in our everyday life. The relationship between implicit and explicit self-esteem is unclear. Some studies (e.g., DeHart et al., 2006) find little relationship between the two forms of self-esteem. However, others suggest that there is a relationship between them, but that the relationship is mediated by a number of factors, such as gender, culture, and individualism (QuanIei et al., 2015). High levels of explicit and implicit self-esteem relate to health outcomes. For example, Lorena Desdentado and her colleagues (2021) found that high levels of explicit self-esteem related to lower levels of anxiety and depression after a brain injury. They also found that high levels of implicit self-esteem related to reductions in anxiety and depression over and above the reduction accounted for by high explicit self-esteem. More generally, although explicit self-esteem is a predictor of anxiety and depressive disorders, low implicit self-esteem at the onset of these disorders is an important predictor of their recurrence after 3 years (van Tuijl et al., 2020). High implicit self-esteem is related to very positive health and social attributes, while explicit self-esteem seems to be more fragile or defensive, which accounts for the emotional reactions that threats to individuals with high explicit self-esteem evoke.

implicit self-esteem An efficient system of self-evaluation that is below our conscious awareness.

explicit self-esteem Self-esteem that arises primarily from interactions with people in our everyday life.

Study Break

This section examined how stigma and culture influence self-esteem. Discussion also focused on the impact of self-esteem and on implicit and explicit self-esteem. Before you begin the next section, answer the following questions:

1. How does having a stigma relate to self-esteem?
2. What is the relationship between culture and self-esteem?
3. What is so good about self-esteem? Explain.
4. What are implicit and explicit self-esteem, and how do they relate to one another?

Self-Control: How People Regulate Their Behavior

Maintaining self-esteem is a very powerful motive. However, an equally powerful motive is to maintain self-control, a very good predictor of success in life.

Self-Control and Self-Regulation

Social psychologist E. Troy Higgins (1989) proposed that people think of themselves from two different standpoints: their own perspective and that of a significant other, such as a parent or a close friend. He also suggested that people have three selves that guide their behavior. The first is the **actual self**, the person's current self-concept. The second

actual self A person's current self-concept.

is the **ideal self**, the mental representation of what the person would like to be or what a significant other would like the person to be. The third is the **ought self**, the mental representation of what the person believes he or she should be.

Higgins (1989) assumed that people are motivated to reach a state in which the actual self matches the ideal and the ought selves. The latter two selves thus serve as guides to behavior. In Higgins's *self-discrepancy theory*, when there is a discrepancy between the actual self and the self-guides, we are motivated to try to close the gap. That is, when our actual self doesn't match our internal expectations and standards, or when someone else evaluates us in ways that fail to match our standards, we try to narrow the gap. We try to adjust our behavior to bring it into line with our self-guides. The process we use to make such adjustments is known as **self-regulation**. Self-regulation is our attempt to match our behavior or our self-guides to the expectations of others, and it is a critical control mechanism.

A form of self-regulation is self-control. **Self-control** operates within self-regulation processes and occurs when we consciously try to override a behavior that is dominant for us (vanDellen et al., 2012). How do self-regulation and self-control relate to one another? Self-regulation is a general process of managing our thoughts, identity, goals, and behavior, and it often occurs automatically. Self-control is a specific form of self-regulation used when we consciously try to override a dominant behavior (vanDellen et al., 2012). For example, if you are an aggressive driver and someone cuts you off on a highway, you exercise self-control when you suppress an urge to retaliate or to yell an obscenity at the offending driver. Self-regulation requires cognitive effort, which reduces our ability to exercise self-control, especially on a task that we perceive to be difficult (vanDellen et al., 2012).

Not only do individuals differ on the need to self-regulate, so do people who live in different cultures. Heine and Lehman (1999) observed that whereas residents of the United States and Canada showed a strong bias toward adapting to others' expectations, Japanese citizens are less likely to try to self-regulate. Heine and Lehman found that Japanese participants were much more self-critical than were North Americans and had greater discrepancies between their actual self and the ideal or ought selves, but that these differences were less distressing to the Japanese and did not motivate them to change.

The closer the match among our various self-concepts, the better we feel about ourselves. Additionally, the more information we have about ourselves and the more certain we are of it, the better we feel about ourselves. This is especially true if the self-attributes we are most certain of are those that are most important to us (Pelham, 1991). Our ability to self-regulate—to match our performance to our expectations and standards—also affects our self-esteem. In sum, then, we tend to have high self-esteem if we have a close

ideal self The mental representation of what a person would like to be or what a significant other would like the person to be.

ought self The mental representation of what a person believes he or she should be.

self-regulation A critical control mechanism individuals use to match behavior to internal standards of the self or to the expectations of others.

self-control A form of self-regulation involving the conscious and effortful suppression of a dominant behavior.

You exercise self-control when you over-ride a dominant behavior such as yelling at another driver on the road.
Source: tommaso79/Shutterstock.

match among our selves, strong and certain knowledge about ourselves (especially if it includes attributes that we value), and the ability to self-regulate.

We know that the inability to regulate our self leads to negative emotions. Higgins (1998) investigated the emotional consequences of good matches versus discrepancies among the selves. When there is a good match between our actual self and our ideal self, we experience feelings of satisfaction and high self-esteem. When there is a good match between our actual self and our ought self, we experience feelings of security. (Recall that the actual self is what you or another person currently thinks you are; the ideal self is the mental representation of the attributes that either you or another would like you to be or wishes you could be; and the ought self is the person that you or others believe you should be.) Good matches may also allow people to focus their attention outside themselves, on other people and activities.

But what happens when we can't close the discrepancy gap? Sometimes, of course, we simply are not capable of behaving in accord with our expectations. We might not have the ability, talent, or fortitude. In this case, we may have to adjust our expectations to match our behavior. And sometimes it seems to be in our best interests not to focus on the self at all; to do so may be too painful, or it may get in the way of what we're doing.

In general, however, these discrepancies, if sizable, lead to negative emotions and low self-esteem. As with good matches, the exact nature of the negative emotional response depends on which self-guide we believe we are not matching (Higgins & Tykocinsky, 1992). Higgins et al. (1997) reported that the larger the differences between the actual and ideal selves, the more dejected and disappointed individuals felt, but only if they were aware of that difference. In a similar vein, the larger the discrepancy between the actual self and the ought self, the more people felt agitated and tense, just as the theory predicts. Again, this was true only for those people who were aware of the discrepancy. These findings mean that when self-guides are uppermost in people's minds, then the emotional consequences of not meeting the expectations of those guides have their strongest effects. People who indicated, for instance, that they were punished or criticized by their parents for not being the person they ought to be reported that they frequently felt anxious or uneasy (Higgins, 1998).

It turns out that discrepancies between what you are and what you would like to be can serve as a very positive motivating force. For example, Ouellete and her colleagues studied the effect of possible selves on exercise. They reasoned that a possible self is a person's idea of what he or she might become. Now, that might be both good and bad. If you flunk out of college, you might have to work in a factory. That's one possible self. These researchers, however, asked individuals to conjure up images of the significant positive bodily and mental changes that would occur from successful completion of an exercise program. The results showed that these health images had a significant impact on the behavior of these individuals. The possible self motivated them to actually attain that image (Ouellette et al., 2005).

Of course, if we are not aware of the discrepancies between what we are and what we'd like to be or what we should be, the negative emotions that self-discrepancy theory predicts will not come to pass (Phillips & Silvia, 2005). Research has shown that when people are not particularly focused on themselves, self-discrepancies go unnoticed. One might imagine that a combat soldier would be untroubled by these psychological differences. However, when self-awareness is high, discrepancies become very noticeable (Philips & Silvia, 2005).

Having positive self-esteem does not mean that people have only positive self-evaluations. They do not. When normal people with positive self-esteem think about themselves, roughly 62% of their thoughts are positive and 38% are negative (Showers, 1992). What is important is how those thoughts are arranged. People with high self-esteem blend the positive and negative aspects of their self-concept. A negative thought tends to trigger a counterbalancing positive thought. A person who learns she is "socially awkward," for example, may think, "But I am a loyal friend." This integration of positive and negative self-thoughts helps to control feelings about the self and maintain positive self-esteem.

But some people group positive and negative thoughts separately. The thought "I am socially awkward" triggers another negative thought, such as "I am insecure." This is what happens in people who are chronically depressed: A negative thought sets off a chain reaction of other negative thoughts. There are no positive thoughts available to act as a buffer.

The Cost and Ironic Effects of Self-Control

We have seen that the self has the capacity to engage in effortful behavior to deal with the external world. The part of the self that carries out this executive function probably does it in an automatic, nonconscious fashion, dealing with the world in neutral gear (Bargh & Chartrand, 1999). But when the self has to actively control and guide behavior, much effort is required. Baumeister et al. (1998) wondered whether the self had a limited amount of energy to do its tasks. If this is so, what would be the implications of self-energy as a limited resource?

To explore the possibility that expending energy on one self-related task would diminish the individual's ability (energy) to do another self-related task, Baumeister and his coworkers did a series of experiments in which people were required to exercise self-control or to make an important personal choice or to suppress an emotion. For example, in one study, some people forced themselves to eat radishes rather than some very tempting chocolates. This, as you might imagine, was an exercise in self-control. Others were allowed to have the chocolates without trying to suppress their desires and without having to eat the radishes. All were then asked to work on unsolvable puzzles. As shown in Figure 2.5, those who suppressed their desire for the chocolate and ate the radishes quit sooner on the puzzle than those who did not have to suppress their desire to eat the chocolate. Baumeister argued that the "radish people" depleted self-energy. He called this **ego-depletion**, using the Freudian term *ego* for the executive of the self.

ego-depletion The loss of self-energy that occurs when a person has to contend with a difficult cognitive or emotional situation.

Doing something that leads to ego-depletion affects our ability to regulate behavior later on. For example, in one study, participants were given a difficult cognitive task to perform and were asked to suppress any thoughts of a white bear, which requires a

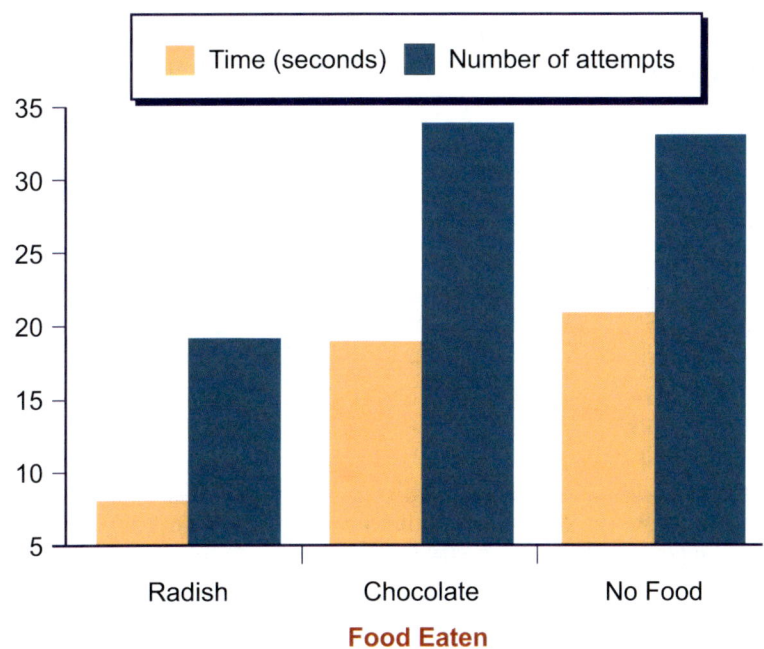

FIGURE 2.5
Persistence on an unsolvable puzzle as a function of the type of food eaten.
Based on data from Baumeister et al. (1998).

great deal of cognitive effort (Wegner, 1993). Try not thinking of a white bear for the next 5 minutes, and you will see what we mean. After doing this task, the individuals were shown a funny movie but were told not to show amusement. People who had expended energy earlier on by suppressing their thoughts were unable to hide their expressions of amusement, whereas those who did not have to suppress their thoughts before seeing the movie were better able to hide their amusement (Muraven et al., 1998). Engaging in an ego-depleting task also increases subsequent dishonesty (Mead et al., 2009). Nicole Mead and her colleagues found that ego-depleted individuals were more likely to cheat for monetary gain to a greater extent than those not ego-depleted. They also found that depleted individuals were more likely to put themselves in a position to cheat than those not depleted. Interestingly, ego-depletion does not appear to reduce our *ability* to regulate dishonest behavior. Rather, it decreases our *willingness* or motivation not to cheat (Wu et al., 2019). All of this suggests that active control of behavior is costly. The irony of efforts to exercise self-control is that the end result may be exactly what we are trying so desperately to avoid.

It is important to understand that ego-depletion may not always occur. Ego-depletion is most likely when we engage in conscious, effortful *self*-control; it is less likely under conditions of more automatic self-regulation (vanDellen et al., 2012). Trying to suppress thoughts of that white bear requires conscious and effortful regulation of behavior. It is under these types of conditions when ego-depletion may be at its maximum. Additionally, not everyone has a strong need for self-control. Some people are higher in *trait self-control* than others. For those high in trait self-control, ego depletion is more likely to affect performance than for those low in trait self-control (Lindner et al., 2017).

Study Break

This section introduced the ideas of self-regulation and self-control. It also explored how these two processes relate to one another and what role they play in behavior. Before you begin the next section, answer the following questions:

1. What are the actual, ideal, and ought selves, and how do they relate to one another?
2. What are self-regulation and self-control, and how do they relate to each other?
3. What factors affect self-regulation and self-esteem?
4. What is ego-depletion, and how does it relate to self-control?

Thinking about Ourselves

Self-Serving Cognitions

In Garrison Keillor's mythical Minnesota town of Lake Woebegon, all the women are strong, all the men are good-looking, and all the children are above average. In thinking so well of themselves, the residents of Lake Woebegon are demonstrating the **self-serving bias**, which leads people to attribute positive outcomes to their own efforts and negative results to situational forces beyond their control. A person typically thinks, I do well on examinations because I'm smart; or I failed because it was an unfair examination. We take credit for success and deny responsibility for failure (Mullen & Riordan, 1988; Weiner, 1986).

There is a longstanding controversy about why the self-serving bias occurs in the attribution process (Tetlock & Levi, 1982). One proposal—the *motivational strategy*—assumes that people need to protect self-esteem and therefore take credit for successes (Fiske & Taylor, 1984). We know that protecting and enhancing self-esteem is a natural function of the self, which filters and shapes information in self-serving ways.

Another way of looking at self-serving biases emphasizes *information-processing strategies*. When people expect to do well, success fits their expectations; when success occurs, it makes sense, and they take credit for it. This bias, however, does not always

self-serving bias
Our tendency to attribute positive outcomes of our behavior to internal, dispositional factors and negative outcomes to external, situational forces.

occur and is not always "self-serving." Sedikides and his colleagues noted that people in close relationships did not demonstrate the self-serving bias. According to these researchers, the bias takes a gracious turn for people who are close and is reflected in the following quote: "If more than one person is responsible for a miscalculation and the persons are close, both will be at fault" (Sedikides et al., 1998, p. 385). What this means is that neither you nor your partner is likely to take more credit for success; nor will you or your partner give more blame to the other for failure. Less close pairs, however, do show the self-serving bias (taking credit for success or giving blame for failure). The closeness of a relationship puts a barrier in place against the individual's need to self-enhance, as revealed by the self-serving bias.

Yet another approach to explaining the self-serving bias is the *self-threat model*, which focuses on the role of positive emotions in the bias (Coleman, 2011). According to this model, when we experience positive emotions, we also experience a boost to our self-esteem. Under these conditions, we have more to lose when we fail at something. As a way of protecting our self-esteem, we attribute the cause for the failure to some external factor (e.g., the difficulty of an exam we failed). Conversely, negative emotions signal that we have less to lose and lead to a lower tendency to engage in the self-serving bias. Coleman found evidence for this. He found that individuals who did well on a test (success) and experienced negative emotions (guilt and revulsion) showed a lower need to use the self-serving bias.

Maintaining Self-Consistency

Another driving motive of the self in social interactions is to maintain high self-consistency—agreement between our self-concept and the views others have of us. We all have a great investment in our self-concepts, and we make a strong effort to support and confirm them. Motivated by a need for **self-verification**—confirmation of our self-concept from others—we tend to behave in ways that lead others to see us as we see ourselves (Swann et al., 1992). The need for self-verification is more than just a simple preference for consistency over inconsistency. Self-verification lends orderliness and predictability to the social world and allows us to feel that we have control (Swann et al., 1992).

self-verification A method of supporting and confirming your self-identity.

People seek to confirm their self-concepts, regardless of whether others' ideas are positive or negative. One study showed that people with unfavorable self-concepts tended to pick roommates who had negative impressions of them (Swann et al., 1989). In other words, people with negative self-concepts prefer to be with people who have impressions of them that are consistent with their own negative views of themselves.

Another study tested the idea that people search for partners who will help them self-verify (Swann et al., 1992). Half the participants in this experiment had positive self-concepts, and half had negative self-concepts. All participants were told that they would soon have the chance to converse with one of two people (an "evaluator") and could choose one of the two. Every participant then saw comments that these two people had made about the participant. One set of comments was positive; the other set was negative (all comments were fictitious).

People with negative self-concepts preferred to interact with an evaluator who had made negative comments, whereas people with positive self-concepts preferred someone who had made positive comments. Why would someone prefer a negative evaluator? Here is one participant's explanation: "I like the (favorable) evaluation, but I am not sure that is, ah, correct, maybe. It *sounds* good, but the (unfavorable evaluator) . . . seems to know more about me. So I'll choose the (unfavorable evaluator)" (Swann et al., 1992, p. 16).

Self-verification is a significant factor predicting relationship satisfaction, especially among married couples (Letzring & Noftle, 2010). Letzring and Noftle compared married, cohabitating, and dating couples and found that self-verification was a stronger predictor of relationship satisfaction among married couples than either cohabitating or dating couples. This difference may be related to the importance of accurate assessments of one's partner in a long-term marital relationship. In less-committed dating relationships, accurate assessments appear to be less important than favorable ones (Letzring & Noftle, 2010).

In another study, spouses with positive self-concepts were found to be more committed to their marriage when their mates thought well of them. No surprise there. But in keeping with self-verification theory, spouses with negative self-concepts were more committed to their partners if their mates thought poorly of them (Swann et al., 1992).

People with low self-esteem do appreciate positive evaluations, but in the end, they prefer to interact with people who see them as they see themselves (Jones, 1990). It is easier and less complicated to be yourself than to live up to someone's impression of you that, although flattering, is inaccurate.

Individuals tend to seek self-verification in fairly narrow areas of the self-concept (Jones, 1990). You don't seek out information to confirm that you are a good or bad person, but you may seek out information to confirm that your voice is not very good or that you really are not a top-notch speaker. If your self-concept is complex, such negative feedback gives you accurate information about yourself but doesn't seriously damage your self-esteem.

People not only choose to interact with others who will verify their self-concepts but also search for situations that will serve that purpose. If, for example, you think of yourself as a storehouse of general knowledge, you may be the first to jump into a game of Trivial Pursuit. You have control over that kind of situation. But if you are the kind of person who can't remember a lot of trivial information or who doesn't care that FDR had a dog name Fala, then being forced to play Trivial Pursuit represents a loss of control.

Finally, keep in mind that most people have a positive self-concept. Therefore, when they self-verify, they are, in essence, enhancing their self-image because they generally get positive feedback. So for most of us, self-verification does not contradict the need for self-enhancement. But as Swann's research shows, people also need to live in predictable and stable worlds. This last requirement is met by our need for self-verification.

Study Break

This section examined how we use various cognitive processes to maintain self-esteem. It also explored why these processes are so important to us and how they work. Before you begin the next section, answer the following questions:

1. What is the self-serving bias, and how does it help maintain self-esteem?
2. What strategies help us understand how the self-serving bias works?
3. What is self-verification, and how does it relate to self-esteem?
4. How does self-verification relate to how we interact with others and our interpersonal relationships?

Self-Awareness

Self-verification suggests that at least some of the time, we are quite aware of how we are behaving and how other people are evaluating us. In fact, in some situations, we are acutely aware of ourselves—monitoring, evaluating, and perhaps adjusting what we say and do. Although sometimes our behavior is mindless and unreflective, we probably spend a surprising amount of time monitoring our own thoughts and actions. Of course, there are some situations that force us to become more self-aware than others. When we are in a minority position in a group, for example, we become focused on how we respond (Mullen, 1986). Other situations that increase **self-focus** include looking in a mirror, being in front of an audience, and seeing a camera (Scheier & Carver, 1988; Wicklund, 1975).

When people become more aware of themselves, they are more likely to try to match their behavior to their beliefs and internal standards. In one study, two groups of participants—one in favor of the death penalty, the other opposed—had to punish another participant, a confederate of the experimenter (Carver, 1975). Some participants held a small mirror up to their faces as they administered an electric shock (no shock was actually transmitted).

When participants self-focused (looked into the mirror), they were truer to their beliefs: Their attitudes and their actions were more in harmony. Highly punitive

self-focus The extent to which one has a heightened awareness of oneself in certain situations (e.g., when a minority within a group).

individuals (those who favored capital punishment) gave much more shock when the confederate made errors than did the less punitive, anti-death-penalty individuals. No such differences existed when participants did not self-focus.

Self-focus means that the individual tends to be more careful in assessing his or her behavior and is more concerned with the self than with others (Gibbons, 1990). Self-focused individuals are concerned with what is proper and appropriate, given their self-guides. Self-focused individuals probably have an increased need for accuracy and try to match their behavior to their self-guides. That is, they try to be more honest or moral. There is also evidence that self-focus can block the effects of automatically activated stereotypes (Dijksterhuis & Knippenberg, 2000). That is, when we self-focus, we are less likely to act upon a stereotype, although the stereotype still exists.

Self-focusing may lead to positive or negative outcomes, depending on how difficult it is to match performance with the self's standards and with the expectations of others. Sometimes, for example, sports teams perform better on the road, especially in important games, than they do at home. There is a definite home-field advantage—that is, teams generally win more games at home than on the road. However, baseball teams win fewer final games of the World Series than expected when they play on their home fields (Baumeister, 1984). Their performance declines due to the pressure of the home fans' expectations ("choking").

Does audience pressure always lead to choking? It depends on whether the performer is more concerned with controlling the audience's perceptions or with living up to internal standards. If concern centers on pleasing the audience, the pressure may have a negative effect on performance. If concern centers on meeting personal standards, then audience pressure will have less impact (Heaton & Sigall, 1991).

Self-Knowledge and Self-Awareness

Accurate information about ourselves as we actually are is essential to effective self-regulation (Pelham & Swann, 1989). Such knowledge may lead us to adjust our self-guides, to lower our expectations or standards, for instance, in order to close the gap between what we are and what we want to be or think we ought to be. Although it is effortful to adjust our standards, it is important to minimize discrepancies between the actual and the other selves. Small discrepancies—that is, good matches between the actual self and self-guides—promote a strong sense of who we really are (Baumgardner, 1990). This knowledge is satisfying because it helps us predict accurately how we will react to other people and situations. It is therefore in our best interest to obtain accurate information about ourselves (Pelham & Swann, 1989).

Research confirms that people want to have accurate information about themselves, even if that information is negative (Baumgardner, 1990). It helps them know which situations to avoid and which to seek out. If you know that you are lazy, for example, you probably will avoid a course that promises to fill your days and nights with library research. There is evidence, however, that people prefer some sugar with medicine of negative evaluation; they want others to evaluate their negative attributes a little more positively than they themselves do (Pelham, 1991).

People who are not certain about their attributes can make serious social blunders. If you are unaware that your singing voice has the same effect on people as someone scratching a fingernail on a chalkboard, then you might one day find yourself trying out for the choir, thereby making a fool of yourself. Greater knowledge of your vocal limitations would have saved you considerable humiliation and loss of face.

Managing Self-Presentations

Eventually, we all try to manage, to some degree, the impressions others have of us. Some of us are very concerned about putting on a good front, others less so. Several factors, both situational and personal, influence how and when people try to manage the impressions they make on others. Situational factors include such variables as the social context, the "stakes" in the situation, and the supportiveness of the audience. Personal factors include such variables as whether the person has high or low self-esteem, and whether the person has a greater or lesser tendency to self-monitor (to be very aware of how he or she appears to other people).

Self-Esteem and Impression Management

One research study looked at how people with high and low self-esteem differed in their approaches to making a good impression (Schlenker et al., 1990). People with low self-esteem were found to be very cautious in trying to create a positive impression. In general, they simply are not confident of their ability to pull it off. When presenting themselves, they focus on minimizing their bad points. On the other hand, people with high self-esteem tend to focus on their good points when presenting themselves.

As might be expected, people with low self-esteem present themselves in a less egotistical manner than those with high self-esteem. When describing a success, they tend to share the credit with others. People with high self-esteem take credit for success even when other people may have helped them (Schlenker et al., 1976). Interestingly, all people seem to have an **egotistical bias**; that is, they present themselves as responsible for success whether they are or are not.

Social context makes a difference in how people present themselves in different ways for people with high and low self-esteem. When participants were told to try to make a good impression in front of an audience, people with high self-esteem presented themselves in a very egotistical and boastful way, pointing out their sterling qualities (Schlenker et al., 1990). People with low self-esteem toned down egotistical tendencies in this high-pressure situation, becoming more timid. When the social stakes increase, people with high self-esteem appear to become more interested in enhancing their self-presentation, whereas their low-self-esteem counterparts are more concerned with protecting themselves from further blows to the self (Schlenker, 1987).

egotistical bias
The tendency to present yourself as responsible for success, whether you are or not, and the tendency to believe these positive presentations.

Self-Monitoring and Impression Management

Another factor that influences impression management is the degree to which a person engages in **self-monitoring**—that is, focuses on how he or she appears to other people in different situations. Some people are constantly gathering data on their own actions. These high self-monitors are very sensitive to the social demands of any situation and tend to fit their behavior to those demands. They are always aware of the impressions they are making on others; low self-monitors are much less concerned with impression management.

High self-monitors are concerned with how things look to others. For example, they tend to choose romantic partners who are physically attractive (Snyder et al., 1985). Low self-monitors are more concerned with meeting people with similar personality traits and interests. Most high self-monitors are aware that they fit their behavior to the expectations of others. If they were to take a self-assessment like the one presented in Table 2.2, they would agree with the "high self-monitor" statements (Snyder, 1987).

High self-monitors are more prone to sex-based discrimination when they are in a position to hire someone in a business situation. High self-monitors offer higher salaries to job candidates applying for a sex-appropriate job (a woman applying to be a receptionist)

self-monitoring
The degree, ranging from low to high, to which a person focuses on his or her behavior when in a given social situation.

TABLE 2.2 Self-Monitoring Scale

1. I would probably make a good actor. (H)
2. My behavior is usually an expression of my true inner feelings. (L)
3. I have never been good at games like charades or improvisations. (L)
4. I'm not always the person I appear to be. (H)
5. I can deceive people by being friendly when I really dislike them. (H)
6. I can argue only for ideas that I already believe in. (L)
7. I find it hard to imitate the behavior of other people. (L)
8. In order to get along and be liked, I tend to be what people expect me to be rather than anything else. (H).

Source: Adapted from Snyder and Gangestad (1986).

than low self-monitors. Similarly, high self-monitors offer lower salaries to applicants for a less sex-appropriate job (a woman applying to be a hardware store clerk) than low self-monitors (Sheets & Bushardt, 1994).

Study Break

This section introduced you to self-awareness and how we manage self-presentations. It also explored the processes of egotistical bias and self-monitoring, and showed how these processes relate to impression management. Before you begin the next section, answer the following questions:

1. What is self-focus, and how does it relate to behavior and lead to positive or negative outcomes?
2. How does the accuracy of self-knowledge relate to behavior?
3. What is egotistical bias, and how does it relate to the way in which we present ourselves to others?
4. What is self-monitoring, and how does it relate to the way in which we present ourselves to others?

Self-Handicapping

When people engage in impression management, their goal is to make a favorable impression on others. We have seen that people work hard to create favorable impressions on others. Yet we all know people who seem determined to make a poor impression and to behave in ways that are ultimately harmful to themselves. Why might these kinds of behavior occur?

Have you ever goofed off before an important exam, knowing that you should study? Or have you ever slacked off at a sport, even though you have a big match coming up? If you have—and most of us have at one time or another—you have engaged in what social psychologists call **self-handicapping** (Berglas & Jones, 1978). People self-handicap when they are unsure of future success; by putting an obstacle in their way, they protect their self-esteem if they should perform badly.

People use self-handicapping to help maintain self-esteem in the face of failure. Convincing yourself that your failure on an important exam was the result of a lack of effort rather than a lack of ability helps you preserve your positive view of yourself. After all, you can correct the problem next time by studying harder. This may be most important if you perceive yourself as possessing some inherent high ability. Failure in this case would be especially damaging to your self-esteem. Kate Snyder and her colleagues (2014) demonstrated this in an interesting experiment. College students at an elite university received one of two messages about the origins of being gifted. In the "entity" condition, participants were told that giftedness was genetically determined: You either have it or don't. Participants in the "incremental" condition were told that although some giftedness is genetically determined, it can also be achieved through hard work. All participants then completed a task on which they either succeeded (worked on solvable problems) or failed (worked on unsolvable problems). They were then given another set of problems to work on with the opportunity to self-handicap. Snyder et al. found that participants who failed at the first task and were given the entity instructions engaged in more self-handicapping on the second task than those receiving the incremental instructions. They concluded that "an entity-focused message about giftedness appears to elicit the use of behavioral self-handicapping among both males and females when failure threatens gifted status, likely due to self-worth concerns" (p. 238).

Although the aim of self-handicapping is to protect the person's self-esteem, it does have some dangers. After all, what are we to make of someone who goes to a movie, rather than studying for a final exam? In one research study, college students negatively evaluated the character of a person who did not study for an important exam (Luginbuhl & Palmer, 1991).

self-handicapping
Self-defeating behavior when one is uncertain about success or failure at a task to protect self-esteem in the face of failure.

Self-handicapping occurs when you do things that interfere with success, like taking a nap instead of getting your work done.
Source: KPG Ivary/Shutterstock.

The self-handicappers succeeded in their self-presentations in the sense that the student evaluators were not sure whether the self-handicappers' bad grades were due to lack of ability or lack of preparation. But the students did not have high opinions of someone who would not study for an exam. Therefore, self-handicapping has mixed results for impression management.

Still, people are willing to make this trade-off. They are probably aware that their self-handicapping will be seen unfavorably, but they would rather have people think they are lazy or irresponsible than dumb or incompetent. A study found that people who self-handicapped and failed at a task had higher self-esteem and were in a better mood than people who did not handicap and failed (Rhodewalt et al., 1991).

Self-handicapping can take two forms (Baumeister & Scher, 1988). The first occurs when the person really wants to succeed but has doubts about the outcome. This person will put some excuse in place. An athlete who says that she has a nagging injury even though she knows she is capable of winning is using this kind of impression-management strategy. People will really be impressed if she wins despite her injury; if she loses, they will chalk it up to that Achilles tendon problem.

The second form of self-handicapping also involves the creation of obstacles to success but is more self-destructive. In this case, the individual fears that some success is a fluke or a mistake and finds ways to subvert it, usually by handicapping himself in a destructive and internal manner. For example, a person who is suddenly propelled to fame as a movie star may start showing up late for rehearsals, or blowing his lines, or getting into fights with the director. It may be because he doesn't really believe he is that good an actor, or he may fear he won't be able to live up to his new status. Perhaps being rich and famous doesn't match his self-concept. Consequently, he handicaps himself in some way.

Alcohol and drug abuse may be an example of self-handicapping (Berglas & Jones, 1978). Abusers may be motivated by a need to have an excuse for possible failure. They prefer that others blame substance abuse for their (anticipated) failure rather than lack of ability. Like the athlete with the injured leg, they want ability to be discounted as the reason for failure but credited as the basis for success. Because the self-handicapper will be embarrassed if the excuse that clouds the link between performance and outcome is absurd, the excuse must be reasonable and believable. Self-handicapping is thus another way people attempt to maintain control over the impression others have of them.

Not everyone engages in self-handicapping to an equal degree. Individual differences related to personal characteristics can increase or decrease the likelihood that someone will engage in self-handicapping. For example, Finez et al. (2012) had athletes report on instances in which they used self-handicapping as a self-protective or self-enhancement strategy against potential failure. The researchers also collected information about personal characteristics, including self-esteem. Finez et al. found that athletes with low self-esteem were more likely to engage in self-handicapping for both reasons, compared to high self-esteem athletes. This self-esteem effect extended to physical capabilities. In a second study, Finez et al. had athletes take part in a test they believed would assess either high or low physical capability (creating either high or low physical self-esteem). Before beginning the test, the athletes were given the opportunity to provide self-handicapping reasons for their potential performance. Once again, low self-esteem athletes engaged in more self-handicapping than high self-esteem athletes.

Self-Handicapping in Academics

Although self-handicapping may have short-term benefits (if you fail at something, it is not really your fault because you already have an excuse), the behavior has some long-term drawbacks. One area in which self-handicapping can interfere with success is in academics. A meta-analysis shows a moderately strong relationship between self-handicapping and academic performance (Schwinger et al., 2014). Schwinger et al. also report that the relationship between self-handicapping and performance was strongest among younger students. Zuckerman et al. (1998) did a long-term study of individuals who used self-handicapping strategies and found that self-handicappers performed less well academically because of bad study habits and had poorer adjustment scores. They also tended to have more negative feelings and withdrew more from other people than did others who did not self-handicap. As you might have predicted, all of this negativity started a vicious cycle that led to even more self-handicapping.

Edward Hirt and his colleagues at the University of Indiana thought that perhaps self-handicapping was really an impression management technique. That is, people put an excuse in place so that if they fail or just do poorly, their failure will not be attributed to their ability. If you don't take the practice test offered by the professor and go to a movie the night before the exam, then maybe your poor performance will be attributed to something other than your lack of academic skills. Indeed, Hirt et al. (2003) set up such a scenario and found that while other students did not attribute failure to a movie-going student's (lack of) ability, their general evaluations of this individual were very negative. So the moviegoer's attempt to manage others' impressions at least partially failed.

As Hirt and his colleagues showed in a series of three studies, there are trade-offs when one uses self-handicapping as a strategy. In one sense, it accomplishes the person's goal of avoiding the dunce cap ("I did not do well because I am a goof-off, but at least I am not stupid"). But there are serious interpersonal costs for self-handicapping. People observing the actions of a student who doesn't study and gets drunk the night before the big test conclude that the student is irresponsible or, just as likely, trying to manipulate others' perceptions of his or her behavior (Hirt et al., 2003).

The Impression We Make on Others

How accurate are we in assessing the impression we convey? In general, most people seem to have a good sense of the impression they make on others. In one study designed to look at this question, participants interacted with partners whom they had not previously met (DePaulo et al., 1987). After each interaction with their partners, participants reported on the impressions they had conveyed to the partner. The researchers found that the participants were generally accurate in reporting the kind of impression their behavior communicated. Participants also were aware of how their behavior changed over time during the interaction and how it changed over time with different partners.

Another study also found that people are fairly accurate in identifying how they come across to others (Kenny & Albright, 1987); they also consistently communicate the same impression over time (Colvin & Funder, 1991). People tend to overestimate how favorably other people view them, however. When they err, it is on the side of believing that they have made a better impression than they actually have.

Sometimes, we assume that other people recognize how we are really feeling, especially when we wish they could not. According to research by Thomas Gilovich and his coworkers, we believe that our internal feelings show more than they actually do (Gilovich et al., 1998). In general, we seem to overestimate the ability of others to "read"

spotlight effect
A phenomenon occurring when we overestimate the ability of others to read our overt behavior—how we act and dress—suggesting that we think others notice and pay attention to whatever we do.

our overt behavior—how we act and dress. Gilovich and his colleagues called this the **spotlight effect**, suggesting that we as actors think others have us under a spotlight and notice and pay attention to what we do. Interestingly, the spotlight effect varies according to a person's race, gender, and social situation. In one experiment, Crosby et al. (2014) had Black, Latino/Latina, and female participants rate the degree to which a confederate of the experimenter looked at them after either hearing a neutral recording or a recording focused on their group. (In reality, the confederate did not look at the participants any differently in either condition.) Crosby et al. found that members of all three groups reported that the confederate looked at them more when the recording focused on their group. This increased self-consciousness seems to be the basis of adult shyness: Shy people are so aware of their actions and infirmities that they believe others are focused (have a spotlight) on them and little else. The reality of social life is quite different, and most of us would be relieved to know that few in the crowd care what we do or think. For example, in one study (Gilovich et al., 2000), college students wore a T-shirt with the ever-popular Barry Manilow on the front, and the wearers highly overestimated the probability that others would notice the T-shirt. The spotlight does not shine as brightly as we think.

illusion of transparency
The belief that observers can read our private thoughts and feelings because they somehow leak out.

Gilovich and colleagues (1998) believe that we have the same preoccupation (that others notice and pay attention to our external actions and appearance) with respect to our hidden, internal feelings. They called this the **illusion of transparency**: the belief that observers can read our private thoughts and feelings because they somehow "leak out." In one of the studies designed to test the illusion of transparency, Gilovich and colleagues hypothesized that participants who were asked to tell lies in the experiment would think that the lies were more obvious than they really were. Indeed, that was the result. In a second experiment, participants had to taste something unpleasant but keep a neutral expression. If, say, your host at a dinner party presented a dish you thoroughly disliked, you might try to eat around the edges for politeness' sake and not express disgust. How successful might you be at disguising your true feelings? The tasters in the Gilovich studies thought that they would not be very successful at all. Instead, observers were not likely to discern that the tasters were disgusted with the food or drink. Again, people overestimated the ability of others to determine their true, internal feelings.

Although most people seem to have a good sense of the impression they make on other people, some do not. In fact, some people never figure out that they are creating a bad impression. In a study designed to look at why some people do not seem to pick up on the cues that they are making a bad impression, individuals were observed interacting with people who had continually made either good or bad impressions (Swann et al. 1992). Swann and his coworkers found that participants said basically the same generally positive things to both types of individuals. However, they acted differently toward the two types of individuals. They directed less approving nonverbal cues (such as turning away while saying nice things) at negative-impression individuals than at those who made positive impressions.

The researchers concluded that there are two reasons why people who continually make bad impressions do not learn to change. First, we live in a "white-lie" society in which people are generally polite, even to someone who acts like a fool. Second, the cues that people use to indicate displeasure may be too subtle for some people to pick up (Swann et al., 1992).

Study Break

This section examined self-handicapping and how we evaluate the impression we make on others. The section also introduced the spotlight effect and the illusion of transparency. Before you read the Chapter Review, answer the following questions:

1. What is self-handicapping, and how does it relate to self-esteem?
2. How does self-handicapping relate to success and failure and to academic performance?
3. What is the spotlight effect, and how does it relate to the impression we make on others?
4. What is the illusion of transparency, and how does it relate to the impression we make on others?

The Life of Serena Williams Revisited

In our brief examination of the life and achievements of champion tennis player Serena Williams at the beginning of this chapter, we had the opportunity to see how her personal life—her family, her teachers and coaches, her race, and the social events that occurred during her formative years and during her career—shaped and influenced both her personal and social selves. Certainly, Serena Williams's personality and response to others and events in her social world contributed to her success on the tennis court.

Chapter Review

1. **What is the self?**

   The self is, in part, a cognitive structure, containing ideas about who and what we are. It also has an evaluative and emotional component because we judge ourselves and find ourselves worthy or unworthy. The self guides our behavior as we attempt to make our actions consistent with our ideas about ourselves. Finally, the self guides us as we attempt to manage the impression we make on others.

2. **How do we know the self?**

   Several sources of social information help us forge our self-concept. The first is our view of how other people react to us. From earliest childhood and throughout life, these reflected appraisals shape our self-concept. We also get knowledge about ourselves from comparisons with other people. We engage in a social comparison process—comparing our reactions, abilities, and personal attributes to those of others—because we need accurate information to succeed. The third source of information about ourselves is observation of our own behavior. Sometimes, we simply observe our behavior and assume that our motives are consistent with our behavior. Finally, we can know our self through introspection, the act of examining our own thoughts and feelings.

3. **What is distinctiveness theory?**

   Distinctiveness theory suggests that people think of themselves in terms of the characteristics or dimensions that make them different from others, rather than in terms of characteristics they have in common with others. An individual is likely to incorporate the perceived distinctive characteristic into his or her self-concept. Thus, distinctive characteristics help define our self-concept.

4. **What is autobiographical memory?**

   The study of autobiographical memory—memory information relating to the self—shows that the self plays a powerful role in the recall of events. Researchers have found that participants recalled recent events more quickly than older ones, pleasant events more quickly than unpleasant ones, and extreme events—both pleasant and unpleasant—more quickly than neutral episodes. Pleasant events that especially fit the person's self-concept were most easily recalled. Events in autobiographical memory are stored on at least two levels: general events and broad lifetime periods. The general events level would include events that have occurred in your life (e.g., going to college, meeting your future spouse), whereas lifetime periods refer to important times in your life (e.g., childhood, early adulthood).

5. **How do groups and culture relate to the self?**

   In contrast to the individual self (which focuses on personal characteristics), the collective self is relevant to how we relate to groups and culture. Some cultures place more emphasis on the collective and the community than others. In these cultures, the collective self is more important than in cultures that stress individual achievement. One relatively recent cultural phenomenon is the increased popularity of social media. This has led to individuals adopting an Internet self, expressed via social media. People portray the self differently on social media than they do in face-to-face situations.

6. **How do social media relate to one's self-concept, and what factors affect how the self is expressed on the Internet?**

   Technology and social media (e.g., Facebook and Twitter) have opened up a whole new dimension of the self. People have a self that exists in cyberspace that differs from the self that is expressed in face-to-face situations. Women are more likely to use carefully chosen pictures to present themselves, whereas men are more likely to use verbal descriptions. Men are more likely than women to present self-promotional information in the "About" section on Facebook. LGBTQ individuals face a dilemma in what to include on social media not faced by heterosexuals. LGBTQ individuals may have a social media self in which they have not "come out" to others. Finally, there are cultural differences with how different content is displayed on social media (e.g., pictures).

7. **How is the self organized through schemas?**

   People arrange knowledge and information about themselves into self-schemas. A self-schema contains information about gender, age, race or ethnicity, occupation, social roles, physical attractiveness, intelligence, talents, and so on. Self-schemas help us interpret situations and guide our behavior. One important self-schema is the sexual self-schema, which refers to how we think about the sexual aspects of the self. Sexual schemas are derived from past sexual knowledge and experience and, like all schemas, they guide our future (sexual) activity.

8. **What is self-esteem?**

   Self-esteem is an evaluation of our overall worth that consists of both positive and negative self-evaluations. We evaluate, judge, and have feelings about ourselves. Some people possess high self-esteem, regard themselves positively, and are generally pleased with who they are. Others have low self-esteem, feel less worthy and good, and may even feel that they are failures and incompetent.

9. **How do we evaluate the self?**

   We evaluate the self by continually adjusting perceptions, interpretations, and memories. The self works tirelessly behind the scenes to maintain positive self-evaluations, or high self-esteem. Self-esteem is affected both by our ideas about how we are measuring up to our standards and by our ability to control our sense of self in interactions with others. Positive evaluations of the self are enhanced when there is a good match between who we are (the actual self) and what we think we'd like to be (the ideal self) or what others believe we ought to be (the ought self). When there are differences between our actual self and either what we would like to be or what we ought to be, we engage in self-regulation, our attempts to match our behavior to what is required by the ideal or the ought self.

10. **What is self-evaluation maintenance (SEM) theory?**

    According to Abraham Tesser's self-evaluation maintenance (SEM) theory, the high achievement of a close other in a self-relevant area is perceived as a threat. In response, we can downplay the other's achievement, put more distance between ourselves and the other, work hard to improve our performance, or try to handicap the other.

11. **How does self-esteem relate to coping with disaster and stigma?**

    Self-esteem and self-enhancement relate to how a person copes with a disaster such as the September 11, 2001, terrorist attacks. Self-enhancement is a tendency to have overly positive or unrealistic self-serving biases. Some people are more prone to self-enhancement than others. Research shows that self-enhancers who were directly exposed to the attack on the World Trade Centers showed fewer post-traumatic and depressive symptoms than other individuals who were at the scene on September 11. Self-enhancers have high self-esteem and believe that they are in total control of themselves.

    Some individuals have characteristics that are stigmatized and may risk rejection whenever others recognize the stigma. Research shows that individuals with concealable stigmas (e.g., sexual orientation) have lower self-esteem and more negative feelings about themselves than individuals with visible stigmas (e.g., being overweight). This suggests that group membership that can offer support and positive feelings raises our self-esteem and buffers us against negative social evaluations.

12. **What is so good about high self-esteem?**

    Researchers have found that while high self-esteem may lead to good feelings and may make people more resourceful, it does not cause high academic achievement, good job performance, or leadership; nor does low self-esteem cause violence, smoking, drinking, taking drugs, or becoming sexually active at an early age.

13. **What are implicit and explicit self-esteem?**

    Implicit self-esteem refers to a very efficient system of self-evaluation that is below our conscious awareness. Implicit self-esteem comes from parents who nurture their children but do not overprotect them. This kind of self-esteem is unconscious and automatic and is less likely to be affected by day-to-day events.

    In comparison, the more well-known conception of self-esteem—explicit self-esteem—arises primarily from interactions with people in our everyday lives. High implicit self-esteem is related to positive health and social attributes, while explicit self-esteem seems to be a more fragile or defensive self-esteem, which accounts for the emotional reactions that threats to these individuals evoke.

14. **What is self-regulation, and how does it relate to behavior?**

    The ideal and ought selves serve as guides to behavior. When there is discrepancy between the actual self and self-guides, we try to reduce the discrepancy. Self-regulation is the process we use to reduce discrepancy between our actual self and self-guides. The general process of self-regulation often occurs automatically for well-ingrained behaviors. Self-control is a form of self-regulation and is used when we consciously try to override a behavior that is dominant for us. Self-control requires a good deal of cognitive energy and often results in ego-depletion, which is loss of self-energy that occurs when a person has to contend with a difficult cognitive or emotional situation. Ego-depletion is most likely to occur when we must engage in conscious, effortful self-control and is less likely under conditions of more automatic self-regulation conditions.

15. **What are the self-serving bias and self-verification?**

    The self-serving bias leads people to attribute positive outcomes to their own efforts and negative results to situational forces beyond their control. According to the maintenance strategy explanation, the self-serving bias helps a person maintain positive self-esteem in the face of failure. In contrast, the information-processing strategy explanation for the bias is that when expected success occurs, it makes sense, and a person takes credit for it.

    An important driving motive of the self in social interactions is to maintain high self-consistency—agreement between our self-concept and the views others have of us. Motivated by a need for self-verification—confirmation of our self-concept—we tend to behave in ways that lead others to see us as we see ourselves. Self-verification suggests that, at least some of the time, we are quite aware of how we are behaving and how other people are evaluating us. In fact, when people become more aware of themselves—when they self-focus—they are more likely to try to match their behavior to their beliefs and internal standards.

16. **What is meant by self-awareness?**

    Self-awareness refers to the degree to which we are aware of ourselves. It involves monitoring ourselves, evaluating what we are doing, and adjusting our behavior to the situation. We spend a good deal of time monitoring our thoughts and actions. Some situations require us to become more self-aware than others. When we are in a situation that requires high levels of self-focus, we are more likely to try to match our behavior to our beliefs and internal standards. Self-focusing may lead to positive or negative outcomes, depending on how difficult it is to match performance with the self's standards and with the expectations of others.

17. **How do we present the self to others?**

    We engage in impression management, the process of presenting ourselves in certain ways to control the impressions that others form of us. People with low self-esteem are cautious in trying to create a positive impression and focus on minimizing their bad points. Those with high self-esteem focus on maximizing their good points. Everyone, however, demonstrates an egotistical bias—the tendency to take credit for successes, whether appropriate or not.

18. **What is self-monitoring?**

    Another factor that influences impression management is the degree to which a person engages in self-monitoring—that is, focuses on his or her own behavior in a given social situation. High self-monitors are very sensitive to the social demands of any situation and tend to fit their behavior to those demands; low self-monitors are much less concerned with impression management.

19. **What is self-handicapping?**

    Self-handicapping involves actions that are harmful but that the person believes may produce some positive outcomes. An excuse is put in place that masks the relationship between performance and ability. It is an attempt to manage the impressions others have of the individual, but in the end, it is self-defeating. Not everyone engages in self-handicapping to the same degree. People with low self-esteem are more likely to engage in self-handicapping than people with high self-esteem.

20. **How accurate are we in assessing the impression we convey?**

    In general, most people seem to have a good sense of the impression they make on others, although they tend to overestimate how favorably others view them. When they err, it is on the side of believing that they have made a better impression than they actually have.

21. **What are the spotlight effect and the illusion of transparency?**

    We sometimes assume that other people can recognize how we are really feeling, especially when we wish they could not. This spotlight effect suggests that we think others have us under a spotlight and notice and pay attention to what we do. This increased self-consciousness seems to be the basis of adult shyness. Some individuals harbor the belief that others can read their hidden, internal feelings. This is the illusion of transparency, or the belief that observers can read our private thoughts and feelings because they somehow leak out. Despite this illusion, people usually overestimate the ability of others to determine their true, internal feelings.

Key Terms

Actual self (p. 54)
Autobiographical memory (p. 36)
Collective self (p. 40)
Distinctiveness theory (p. 35)
Ego-depletion (p. 57)
Egotistical bias (p. 62)
Emotional intelligence (p. 49)
Explicit self-esteem (p. 54)
Ideal self (p. 55)
Illusion of transparency (p. 66)
Implicit self-esteem (p. 54)
Imposter phenomenon (p. 34)

Individual self (p. 39)
Introspection (p. 34)
Ought self (p. 55)
Personal attributes (p. 35)
Reflected self-appraisal (p. 33)
Self-concept (p. 33)
Self-control (p. 55)

Self-esteem (p. 48)
Self-evaluation maintenance (SEM) theory (p. 49)
Self-focus (p. 60)
Self-handicapping (p. 63)
Self-monitoring (p. 62)
Self-regulation (p. 55)

Self-schemas (p. 45)
Self-serving bias (p. 58)
Self-verification (p. 59)
Sexual self-schema (p. 45)
Social comparison process (p. 34)
Spotlight effect (p. 66)

Chapter Quiz

1. The process whereby we judge our attitudes, beliefs, and behaviors against those of others is called
   A. social comparison.
   B. reflected appraisal.
   C. egocentrism.
   D. social matching.

2. Rona sees herself as a smart, strong, self-assured young woman. These characteristics that Rona ascribes to herself are
   A. personal constructs.
   B. personal attributes.
   C. reflected appraisals.
   D. central traits.

3. For most people, it only takes approximately 2 seconds to answer questions about themselves. According to your text, this is because
   A. we know ourselves very well.
   B. autobiographical memories are superficial.
   C. we don't have to worry about whether autobiographical information is accurate.
   D. we have an easily accessed summary of our autobiographical memories.

4. The aspect of your self that is derived through identification with groups is known as the
   A. social self.
   B. collective self.
   C. biographical self.
   D. cultural self.

5. According to your text, advances in new technologies have led to the emergence of the
   A. social self.
   B. Twitter self
   C. Internet self.
   D. virtual self.

6. Sandra thinks of herself as a bright, attractive, and smart woman. These characteristics comprise Sandra's
   A. self-schema.
   B. individual self.
   C. idealized schema.
   D. personal fable.

7. Self-esteem comprises
   A. the characteristics individuals believe they possess.
   B. the characteristics a person would like to have.
   C. the emotional component of the self, including positive and negative self-evaluations.
   D. the emotional component of self that includes only positive self-evaluations.

8. Which is true according to the self-evaluation maintenance (SEM) theory?
   A. Only our own behavior is important in determining how we feel about ourselves.
   B. The behavior of others is important in determining how we feel about ourselves, especially for a behavior important for our self-concept.
   C. The behavior of others is important in determining how we feel about ourselves, but only for unimportant behaviors.
   D. We disregard the opinions of others when evaluating how we feel about ourselves.

9. Our tendency to attribute positive outcomes of our own behavior to internal, dispositional factors and negative outcomes to external, situational forces is known as
   A. ego-depletion.
   B. the self-serving bias.
   C. the egotistical bias.
   D. the self-effacement bias.

10. According to your text, which of the following characteristics is associated with higher levels of self-handicapping?
    A. Narcissism
    B. Shyness
    C. High self-esteem
    D. Low self-esteem

Answers can be found in the end-of-book Answers section.

Social Perception: Understanding Other People

Nobody outside of a baby carriage or a judge's chamber believes in an unprejudiced point of view.

—Lillian Helman

CHAPTER 3

Source: Dean Drobot/Shutterstock.

In July 1988, the U.S. guided missile frigate *Vincennes* was on patrol in the Persian Gulf. A state-of-the-art ship carrying the most sophisticated radar and guidance systems, the *Vincennes* became embroiled in a skirmish with some small Iranian naval patrol boats. During the skirmish, Captain Will Rogers III received word from the radar room that an unidentified aircraft was heading toward the ship. The intruder was on a descending path, the radar operators reported, and appeared to be hostile. It did not respond to the ship's IFF (identify friend or foe) transmissions, nor were further attempts to raise it on the radio successful. Captain Rogers, after requesting permission from his superior, ordered the firing of surface-to-air missiles; the missiles hit and destroyed the plane. The plane was not an Iranian fighter. It was an Iranian Airbus, a commercial plane on a twice-weekly run to Dubai, a city across the Strait of Hormuz. The airbus was completely destroyed, and all 290 passengers were killed.

Following the tragedy, Captain Rogers defended his actions. But Commander David Carlson of the nearby frigate *Sides*, 20 miles away, reported that his crew accurately identified the airbus as a passenger plane. His crew saw on their radar screen that the aircraft was climbing from 12,000 to 14,000 feet (as tapes later verified) and that its flight pattern resembled that of a civilian aircraft (*Time*, August 15, 1988).

Key Questions

As you read this chapter, find the answers to the following questions:

1. What is automatic processing?
2. What is meant by a cognitive miser?
3. What is controlled processing and when do we use it?
4. What is impression formation?
5. Are our impressions of others accurate?
6. What is the importance of first impressions?
7. What is the sample bias?
8. How does body art affect the impressions formed of those who have it?
9. Can we catch liars?
10. What is the attribution process?
11. What are internal and external attributions?
12. What is the correspondent inference theory, and what factors enter into forming a correspondent inference?
13. What are covariation theory and the covariation principle?
14. How do consensus, consistency, and distinctiveness information lead to an internal or external attribution?

15. What is the dual-process model of attribution, and what does it tell us about the attribution process?
16. What is meant by attribution biases?
17. What is the fundamental attribution error?
18. What is the actor-observer bias?
19. What is the false consensus bias?
20. What are schemas, and what role do they play in social cognition?
21. What are the self-fulfilling prophecy and the confirmation bias and how do they relate to behavior?
22. What are the various types of heuristics that often guide social cognition?

Biases in social perception led one ship captain to "see" a passenger jet as a military plane and another ship captain to "see" the same jet as a passenger plane.
Source: ThomasLENNE/Shutterstock.

The crew of the *Sides* did not interpret the plane's actions as threatening, nor did they think an attack was imminent. When Commander Carlson learned that the *Vincennes* had fired on what was certainly a commercial plane, he was so shocked he almost vomited (*Newsweek*, July 13, 1992). Carlson's view was backed up by the fact that the "intruder" was correctly identified as a commercial aircraft by radar operators on the USS *Forrestal*, the aircraft carrier and flagship of the mission (*Newsweek*, July 13, 1992).

What happened during the *Vincennes* incident? How could the crew of the *Vincennes* have "seen" a commercial plane as an attacking enemy plane on their radar screen? How could the captain have so readily ordered the firing of the missiles? And how could others—the crews of the *Sides* and the *Forrestal*, for instance—have seen things so differently?

The answers to these questions reside in the nature of human cognition. The captain and crew of the *Vincennes* constructed their own view of reality based on their previous experiences, their expectations of what was likely to occur, and their interpretations of what was happening at the moment—as well as their fears and anxieties. All these factors were in turn influenced by the context of current international events, which included a bitter enmity between the United States and what was perceived by Americans as an extremist Iranian government.

The captain and crew of the *Vincennes* remembered a deadly attack on an American warship (the *Stark*) the previous year in the same area. They strongly believed that they were likely to be attacked by an enemy aircraft, probably one carrying advanced missiles that would be very fast and very accurate. If this occurred, the captain knew he would need to act quickly and decisively. They had also been recently involved in a skirmish with the Iranian navy, which primed them for hostile action on the part of the Iranians. When the radar crew saw an unidentified plane on their screen, they were primed to see it as hostile. Suddenly they called out that the aircraft was descending, getting in position to attack. The plane didn't respond to their radio transmissions. Weighing the available evidence, Captain Rogers opted to fire on the intruder.

The commander and crew of the *Sides* had a different view of the incident. They saw the incident through the filter of their belief that the *Vincennes* was itching for a fight. The crew of the *Sides* had not had a recent skirmish with the Iranians. From their point of view, a passenger plane was shot down and 290 lives were lost as a result of the hair-trigger reaction of the overly aggressive crew.

These different views and understandings highlight a crucial aspect of human behavior: Each of us constructs a version of social reality that fits with our perception and interpretation of events (Jussim, 1991). We come to understand our world through the processes of social perception, the strategies and methods we use to understand the motives and behavior of other people.

Automatic and Controlled Processing

Just like the captain of the *Vincennes*, when we are confronted with information from the world, we try to interpret it, make sense of it, and decide how to act upon it. Each of us acts like a naïve scientist, doing the best we can to make use of the information the world provides us. Each of us uses the information available to us to construct a version of social reality that will give direction to behavior. The captain of the *Vincennes* made the decision to launch a missile at what he believed to be a hostile aircraft based on the conditions that existed at the time and the information presented to him. In this case, the version of social reality he constructed was incorrect and he ended up shooting down a civilian aircraft.

This chapter looks at the tools and strategies people use to construct social reality. We ask about the cognitive processes involved when individuals are attempting to make sense of the world. What mechanisms come into play when we form impressions of others and make judgments about their behavior and motives? How accurate are these impressions and judgments? And what accounts for errors in perception and judgment that seem to inevitably occur in social interactions? How do we put all of the social information together to get a whole picture of our social world?

Social psychologists interested in cognition are primarily concerned with how the individual tries to make sense out of what is occurring in his or her world under the uncertain conditions that are a part of normal life (Mischel, 1999). As we make sense of our social world and form impressions, we use two forms of processing: automatic and controlled (which we shall define in more detail below).

Automatic Processing

Automatic processing is any type of information processing that primarily occurs without conscious intention or control. Automatic processes have largely two origins. Some automatic processes seem to be innate. We automatically interpret an upturned mouth as a smile, and we automatically infer that the smiling person is pleased or happy (Fiske & Taylor, 1991). Such interpretations and inferences, which may be built into our genetic makeup, are beyond our conscious control. The second type of automatic process is the product of well-practiced activities. For example, try not to read the next few words in this sentence; that request should have been impossible. By this point in your life, you have learned to read so well that you read without effort automatically. That is, you automatically access the semantic meaning of the words on this page without effort.

Running through all our social inference processes—the methods we use to judge other people—is a thread that seems to be part of our human makeup: our tendency to prefer the least effortful means of processing social information (Taylor, 1981). This is not to say we are lazy or sloppy; we simply have a limited capacity to understand information and can deal with only relatively small amounts at any one time (Fiske, 1993). We tend to be cognitive misers in the construction of social reality. Being a **cognitive miser** means that because humans have a limited capacity to understand information, we deal with only small amounts of social information and prefer the least effortful means of processing it. Unless motivated to do otherwise, we use just enough effort to get the job done. In this business of constructing our social world, we are pragmatists (Fiske, 1992). Essentially, we ask ourselves: What is my goal in this situation, and what do I need to know to reach that goal?

automatic processing
Any type of information processing that primarily occurs without conscious intention or control.

cognitive miser
The idea that because humans have a limited capacity to understand information, we deal only with small amounts of social information and prefer the least effortful means of processing it.

Controlled Processing

controlled processing
Processing involving conscious awareness, attention to the thinking process, and effort.

Although automatic processing is the preferred method of the cognitive miser, this does not mean that we are not capable of more deliberative conscious processing of information and behavior. If the conditions are right, we will bring our willful, conscious information processes online. In this case, we would be using controlled processing. **Controlled processing** involves conscious awareness, attention to the thinking process, and effort. It is defined by several factors: First, we know we are thinking about something; second, we are aware of the goals of the thought process; and third, we know what choices we are making. For example, if you meet someone, you may be aware of thinking that you need to really pay attention to what this person is saying. Therefore, you are aware of your thinking process. You will also know that you are doing this because you expect to be dealing with this person in the future. You may want to make a good impression on the person, or you may need to make an accurate assessment. In addition, you may be aware that by focusing on this one person, you are giving up the opportunity to meet other people. People are motivated to use controlled processing—that is, to allocate more cognitive energy to perceiving and interpreting. They may have goals they want to achieve in the interaction, for example, or they may be disturbed by information that doesn't fit their expectancies. Processing becomes more controlled when thoughts and behavior are intended (Wegner & Pennebaker, 1993).

Even though we may speak about automatic and controlled processes as if they are dichotomies, there is no clear line between automatic and controlled processing. Rather, they exist on a continuum, ranging from totally automatic (e.g., reflexes) to totally controlled (e.g., figuring out a difficult math problem), with degrees of more and less automatic thinking in between. Many of our daily activities, such as driving, consist of both automatic and controlled processes. Driving is one of those well-practiced activities that can become automatic, especially if you are driving a route that is familiar. When driving your normal route, you may arrive at home and not remember if you stopped at a particular stop sign or red light. This happened because your concentration and attention were directed elsewhere (e.g., thinking about something else) while the activity of driving was automatized. However, there are other times, such as driving in unfamiliar locations or in heavy traffic, when your full attention and concentration are needed. These are times in which your driving is operating as a more controlled rather than automatic process.

Dual processing (automatic and controlled) of information is an important distinction and a central idea in social psychology. You will see in this chapter and throughout this book that many of the phenomena and effects studied in social psychology can largely be categorized as automatic or controlled processes. As you will see in the next section, when we form impressions of others, sometimes we rely on our "gut" (automatic), whereas at other times, we take a more deliberative approach (controlled) to understanding others.

Study Break

This section defined automatic and controlled processing. Before you begin the next section, answer the following questions:

1. What is automatic processing? Give an example.
2. What does it mean to be a cognitive miser?
3. What is controlled processing? Give an example.
4. What factors define controlled processing, and under what conditions are we likely to use it?

Impression Formation

impression formation
The process by which we make judgments about others.

The process by which we make judgments about others is called **impression formation**. We are primed by our culture to form impressions of people, and Western culture emphasizes the individual, the importance of "what is inside the person," as the cause of behavior (Jones, 1990). We also may be programmed biologically to form impressions of those who might help or hurt us. It is conceivable that early humans who survived were better at making accurate inferences about others and thus had superior survival chances—and those abilities are part of our genetic heritage (Flohr, 1987). It makes sense that those who survived were able to form relatively accurate impressions of others rather effortlessly. Because grossly inaccurate impressions—is this person dangerous or not, trustworthy or not, friend or foe—could be life threatening, humans learned to make those judgments efficiently. Those who could not were less likely to survive. So, efficiency and effortlessness in perception are critical goals of human cognition.

How Accurate Are Our Impressions?

How many times have you heard, "I know just how you feel"? Well, do we really know how someone else feels? When we evaluate how accurate our impressions of others are, we need to consider two forms of accuracy (Human & Biesanz, 2011). *Distinctive accuracy* refers to one's ability to correctly determine another person's traits that make him or her a unique person. *Normative accuracy* on the other hand refers to one's ability to determine the degree to which an individual represents the "average person" (Human & Biesanz, 2011). In their study of impression accuracy, Human and Biesanz obtained measures of personality from participants and people outside of the study who were close to the participants (e.g., family members). Human and Biesanz found that when evaluating others, participants showed both distinctive and normative accuracy. However, participants were generally higher on normative accuracy. They also found a tendency for participants to project some of their own positive personality characteristics onto others. Generally, Human and Biesanz concluded that participants were accurate when it came to forming impressions of others.

As you might expect, forming an accurate impression of others is more complex than meets the eye. Impression accuracy depends on a few factors. For example, Human and Biesanz report that well-adjusted individuals show higher levels of normative accuracy than less well-adjusted individuals. Well-adjusted individuals also saw more similarity between their own personality characteristics and those of others than did less well-adjusted individuals.

Another factor contributing to impression accuracy is one's level of emotionality. King (1998) noted that the ability to recognize the emotions of others is crucial to social interaction and an important marker of interpersonal competence. King found that our ability to accurately read other individuals' emotions depends on our own emotional socialization. That is, some individuals have learned, because of their early experiences and feedback from other people, that it is safe to clearly express their emotions. Others are more conflicted, unsure, and ambivalent about expressing emotions. Perhaps they were punished somehow for emotional expression and learned to adopt a poker face. This personal experience with emotional expressivity, King reasoned, should have an effect on our ability to determine the emotional state of other people.

King (1998) examined the ability of people who were unsure or ambivalent about emotional expressivity to accurately read others' emotions. She found that compared to individuals who had no conflict about expressing emotions, those who were ambivalent about their own emotional expression tended to be confused about other people's expression of emotion. The ambivalent individuals, when trying to read people in an emotional situation or to read their facial expressions, quite often inferred the opposite emotion than the one the individuals actually felt and reported. Ambivalent individuals who spend much energy in being inexpressive or suppressing emotional reactions quite easily inferred that others also were hiding their emotions and what they saw was not what was meant. This simply may mean that people who are comfortable with their own emotional expressiveness are more accurate in reading other people's emotional expressions.

King's work, then, suggests that in our ability to accurately read other people, much depends on our own emotional life. Consider another example of this: Weary and Edwards (1994) suggested that mild or moderately depressed people are much more anxious than others to understand social information. This is because depressives often feel that they have little control over their social world and that their efforts to effect changes meet with little success.

Ambivalent individuals spend a lot of energy being inexpressive or suppressing emotional reactions and are often confused about how others express emotions and misread them.

Source: Leon Rafael/Shutterstock.

Edwards and his coworkers have shown that depressed people are much more tuned to social information and put more effort into trying to determine why people react to them as they do. Depressed individuals are highly vigilant processors of social information (Edwards et al., 1999). One would think that a depressed person's vigilance would make them more accurate in reading people. Depressed people often have problems with social interactions, and this vigilance is aimed at trying to figure out why and perhaps alter these interactions for the better. But here again, we can see the importance of nonconscious behavior. Edwards and colleagues pointed out that depressed people behave in ways that "turn others off." For example, depressed people have trouble with eye contact, voice pitch, and other gestures, which arouses negative reactions in others. In fact, Edwards and colleagues suggested that all this effortful processing detracts depressed individuals from concentrating on enjoyable interactions.

If depressed perceivers have more accurate impressions of targets, does a target's psychological well-being affect how accurately others form impressions of them? Recent research by Kerr et al. (2020) addresses this very issue. Kerr et al. had 378 participants interact in a speed-dating event. Participants participated in 3-minute unstructured interactions with 15 different partners. Prior to the interactions, participants also completed a questionnaire assessing their personal and psychological well-being. Kerr et al. found that the impressions formed of well-adjusted people were generally more accurate. It seems that it may be easier to form accurate impressions of well-adjusted people. Well-adjusted people just seem to be easier "books to read"; perhaps this is because they engage in more effective self-presentation.

The accuracy of our impressions of others also relates to the target person's characteristics. In Chapter 9 we will explore what is known as the "physical attractiveness stereotype." Generally, we can boil this bias down to the following statement: "What is beautiful is good." In other words we tend to assume that physically attractive individuals have a wide range of positive characteristics (e.g., more friendly, warm, and intelligent) than less attractive individuals. Can physical attractiveness affect the accuracy of the impressions we form of these people? Lorenzo et al. (2010) had individuals participate in a group experiment involving groups ranging in size from 5 to 11. Each group member met with each other member for 3 minutes, after which they rated the other members on a number of measures (e.g., receives good grades, is intelligent, is bright). Participants also rated each member's level of physical attractiveness. Lorenzo et al. found that a group member's level of physical attractiveness was positively related to the accuracy of the impression formed by other group members. That is, impressions of attractive members were more accurate than those of less attractive members. Additionally, they also found evidence for an "eye of the beholder" effect. Subjective perceptions of attractiveness were related to impression accuracy. If you think another person is attractive (even if others don't necessarily agree), you will form a more accurate impression of that person. Lorenzo et al. suggest that this attractiveness effect may occur because we may be more motivated to pay attention to the characteristics of attractive versus unattractive others.

Confidence and Impression Formation

We have seen that our impressions of others can be accurate and are mediated by a number of factors. However, how confident are we in the accuracy of our impressions? Confidence in our impressions of other people is important because, as with other beliefs held with great conviction, we are more likely to act on them. If, for example, we are sure that our friend would not lie to us, we then make decisions based on that certainty. The commander of the *Vincennes* certainly was confident in his interpretation of the deadly intent of the aircraft on his radar screen. The confidence we have in our impressions of others appears to depend, not surprisingly, on how much we think we know about the other person.

However, confidence in our judgment may not necessarily mean that it is accurate. Wells (1995) showed that the correlation between accuracy and confidence in eyewitness identification is very modest, and sometimes there is no relationship at all. Similarly, Swann and Gill (1997) reported that confidence and accuracy of perception among dating partners and among roommates were not very good.

Gill and his colleagues found that when individuals were required to form a careful impression of an individual, including important aspects of the target's life—intellectual ability, social skills, physical attractiveness, and so forth—and they had access to information derived from a videotaped interview with the target person, they had high confidence in their judgments of the target. This is not surprising, of course. But what might be surprising is that confidence had no impact on the accuracy of the participants' judgment (experiment 1; Gill et al., 1998). In another series of studies, these researchers demonstrated that having much information about a target makes people even more confident of their judgments, because they can recall and apply information about these people easily and fluently. But, the judgments are no more accurate than when we have much less information about someone. What is most disturbing about these findings is that it is precisely those situations in which we have much information and much confidence that are most important to us. These situations involve close relationships of various kinds with people who are very significant in our lives. But the research says we make errors nevertheless, even though we are confident and possess much information.

Our modest ability to read other people accurately may be due to the fact that our attention focuses primarily on obvious, expressive cues at the expense of more subtle but perhaps more reliable cues. Bernieri et al. showed in a series of experiments that observers pay much attention to overt cues such as when people are extraverted and smile a great deal. Bernieri et al. suggested that expressivity (talking, smiling, gesturing) drives social judgment but that people may not recognize that expressivity determines their judgments (Bernieri et al., 1996).

The Importance of First Impressions

Most of us are familiar with the old adages that "first impressions matter" and that you can "never take back a first impression." It is generally true that first impressions do matter and may affect everything from whom we become friends with to whether or not we get a job we want. Researchers have consistently demonstrated a **primacy effect** in the impression-formation process, which is the tendency of early information to play a powerful role in our eventual impression of an individual.

primacy effect
The observation that information encountered early in the impression formation process plays a powerful role in our eventual impression of an individual.

belief perseverance
The tendency for initial impressions to persist despite later conflicting information, accounting for much of the power of first impressions.

Furthermore, first impressions can, in turn, bias the interpretation of later information. This was shown in a study in which individuals watched a person take an examination (Jones et al., 1968). Some of the observers saw the test-taker do very well at the start and then get worse as the test continued. Other observers saw the test-taker do poorly at the beginning and then improve. Although both test-takers wound up with the same score, the test-taker who did well in the beginning was rated as more intelligent than the test-taker who did well at the end. In other words, the initial impression persisted even when later information began to contradict it.

This **belief perseverance**, the tendency for initial impressions to persist despite later conflicting information, accounts for much of the power of first impressions. A second reason that initial impressions wear well and long is that people often reinterpret incoming information in light of the initial impression. We try to organize information about other people into a coherent picture, and later information that is inconsistent with the first impression is often reinterpreted to fit the initial belief about that person. If your first impression of a person is that he is friendly, you may dismiss a later encounter in which he is curt and abrupt as an aberration—"He's just having a bad day."

The first impressions we make on others, such as on a first date, are important because they can affect how we are perceived later.
Source: fizkes/Shutterstock.

SOCIAL PSYCHOLOGY IN ACTION

Body Art and Impressions

There is a trend in modern American culture toward self-expression through body art (e.g., tattoos and body piercings). Does your choice about adorning yourself with body art affect the first impressions that others form of you? The answer to this question is yes. In one study, for example, Acor (2001) had employers view videotapes of potential job applicants and evaluate them. The potential job applicants were portrayed with or without a pierced eyebrow. Acor found that applicants with an eyebrow piercing were rated less favorably than applicants without the piercing. A similar effect was found for the presence or absence of a tattoo. In two experiments, Resenhoeft et al. (2008) had participants judge a photograph of a female model with or without a tattoo on a number of dimensions. Resenhoeft et al. found that the model with the tattoo was rated more negatively than the same model without the tattoo. In experiment 1, the model without the tattoo was rated as more fashionable, athletic, attractive, caring, and intelligent but less creative than the model with the tattoo. The type of tattoo didn't matter much. In experiment 1, the model had a dragon tattoo, and in experiment 2, she had a dolphin tattoo. In both studies, the model with the tattoo was rated more negatively than the model without the tattoo. The size and placement of a tattoo also matter. Larger tattoos and those on the face are perceived more negatively than smaller ones and ones elsewhere on the body (Howard et al., 2012).

In another study, Timming et al. (2017) investigated both body piercings and tattoos in relation to ratings of hireability for jobs. Timming et al. manipulated frontal face photographs of men and women (of equal attractiveness) by adding either a star tattoo on the left side of the neck or a silver stud piercing on the left side of the lower lip. Participants were instructed to play the role of a recruiter making a hiring decision. They rated the faces for the likelihood of hiring the person with the face shown. Participants were told to consider some of the faces for a customer-facing job (e.g., cashier) and others for a non-customer-facing job (e.g., night janitor). Timming et al. found that faces with a piercing or a tattoo were rated as less hireable than the control faces (no piercing or tattoo). They also found that the pierced faces were rated differently depending on the type of job being evaluated. When participants were judging the faces for customer-facing jobs, the control face was rated as more hireable ($M = 5.16$) than if there

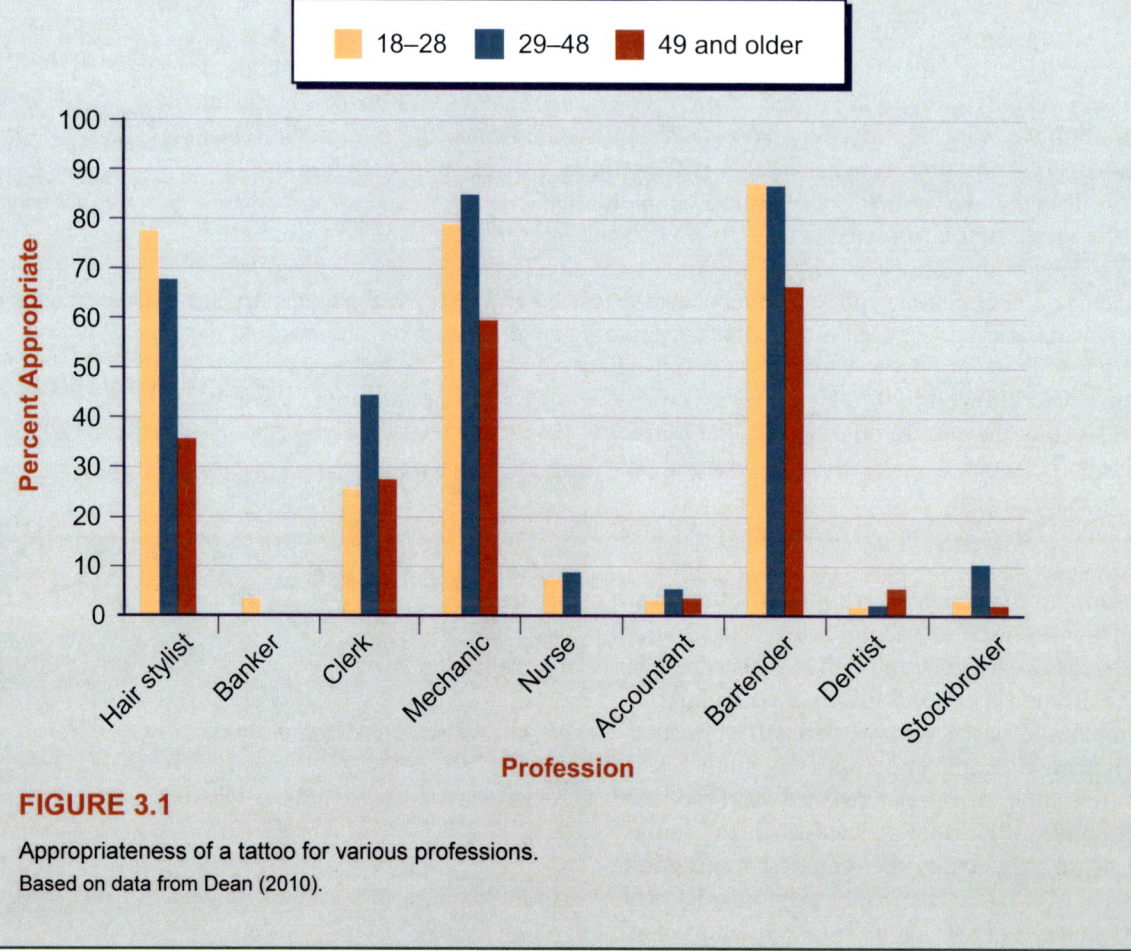

FIGURE 3.1

Appropriateness of a tattoo for various professions.
Based on data from Dean (2010).

(continued)

was a piercing (*M* = 4.67) or a tattoo (*M* = 4.59). No difference was found for non-customer-facing jobs.

Why would body art elicit negative evaluations? Despite the increasing popularity of body art, the presence of body art activates negative perceptions and stereotypes of the person with the art. For example, a person with a tattoo is seen as less attractive, intelligent, and caring than a person without a tattoo. Other negative stereotypes that are activated when a woman has a tattoo are that the woman is less attractive, more sexually promiscuous, and more likely to abuse alcohol than a person without a tattoo (Swami & Furnham, 2007). It appears that once a person believes that you have these types of negative characteristics (whether they are true or not), that person will assume that you have all kinds of other negative characteristics.

Negative perceptions of individuals with tattoos are not universal. The appropriateness of tattoos varies according to the profession of the person with the tattoo (Dean, 2010). Passersby on a street were asked to indicate how appropriate tattoos were for various professions. The results of Dean's study are shown in Figure 3.1. Generally, tattoos were seen as less appropriate for so-called white-collar professions (e.g., bank loan officer, accountant, stockbroker) and health care professionals (dentist and nurse) than for blue-collar workers (e.g., barber/hairstylist, grocery store clerk, bartender). Participants in this study were also more likely to attribute negative characteristics to white-collar workers (e.g., unprofessional and untrustworthy) and health care workers (unsanitary and dirty) with tattoos than to blue-collar workers with tattoos, who were more likely to be described as artistic and rebellious. Dean also found that, especially for blue-collar workers, younger respondents were more positive than older respondents toward people with tattoos.

A tattoo on a professional person does not always lead to a negative first impression. In another study,

There is a trend for people to express themselves through body art, including tattoos. Research suggests body art may affect impressions formed by others.
Source: Alexander Supertramp/Shutterstock.

a college professor with one or two tattoos was rated more positively on three of nine dimensions by college students (student motivation, the instructor being more imaginative, and students being more likely to recommend the instructor; Wiseman, 2010). Additionally, in some industries, having visible body art can be an asset. For example, stores that sell trendy, alternative, and hip kinds of clothing and merchandise (e.g., Hot Topic) often intentionally hire people with visible body art. These employees help the organization project the "brand" they are trying to convey (Timming, 2014).

Discussion Questions

1. Can body art affect another person's first impressions of another person?
2. Is body art always perceived negatively?

One problem with first impressions is that it can lead to a "sampling bias," which happens when the level of interaction between people is determined by first impressions (Denrell, 2005). This sample bias goes something like this: Imagine you are a member of a newly formed group, and you begin to interact with others in the group. You meet Person A, who has low social skills. Your interaction with him is limited, and your tendency, understandably, is to avoid him in the future. Now Person B is different. She has excellent social skills, and conversation with her is easy and fluid. You will obviously sample more of Person B's behavior than Person A's. As a result, potentially false negative impressions of Person A never get changed, while a false positive impression of B could very well be changed if you were to "sample" more of her behavior (Denrell, 2005).

An important point that Denrell (2005) makes, then, about impression formation is that if there are biases in the sampling (the kind and amount of interaction with somebody), then systematic biases in impression formation will occur. This may be especially true of individuals who belong to groups with which we have limited contact. We never get the opportunity to interact with those members in enough situations to form fair impressions based upon a representative sample of their behavior. Therefore, we never have enough evidence to correct a negative or a positive false first impression because we rarely interact again with a person with whom we have had a negative initial interaction (Plant & Devine, 2003). So, for example, an employer who does not hire a person because he or she has a tattoo will never get to know if that person would have made a good employee or not.

If it is true that first impressions can influence how we react to and judge others, it would seem important that those first impressions be reasonably accurate. How accurate are our first impressions of others? For a good part of the history of social psychology, the answer to this question was that they were not all that accurate (Ames et al., 2010). However, this wisdom has been called into question, based on more recent research using *thin-slice methodology*. In this method, participants form impressions of others based on a small slice of a social interaction (e.g., 5 minutes). Research shows that thin-slice impressions can be quite accurate (Ambady, 2010; Ames et al., 2010). In addition, the accuracy of these thin-slice impressions can actually be reduced if a person more carefully processes information (Ambady, 2010).

Social Media and Impression Formation

In 2005, only about 5% of American adults had a profile on social media. Today, almost three-quarters of American adults have a profile on at least one social networking site. YouTube and Facebook are the most popular of these social media sites (Pew Research Center, 2020). If you are like most college students, you probably have a few friends on social media whose stories are full of self-aggrandizing posts (e.g., exotic vacation pictures, recent career or school accomplishments). Obviously, people like to put their best foot forward on social media and present a positive image of themselves. Because our social media profiles are selective snapshots of what we want to present to others, can we form accurate impressions of people from just these profiles? The answer to this question is yes. Researchers have demonstrated that people's assessments of the personality of profile owners are largely consistent with the profile owner's own self-assessment of personality (Back et al., 2010; Gosling et al., 2011; Marcus et al., 2006).

It seems that different elements of a user profile can provide perceivers with clues to different aspects of the profile owner's personality. For example, observers use the number of friends a person has on social media as a clue to accurately estimate that person's level of extraversion (Antheunis & Schouten, 2011; Tong Van Der Heide & Langwell, 2008). Your friends' comments can also be an accurate clue as to how conscientious you are. People whose friends' comments on their posts are generally supportive are viewed as more conscientious (Hall et al., 2013). In addition to what you post online, what you don't post can be a clue to your personality. Hall et al. (2013) found that people who posted excessive political or news stories were accurately seen as less agreeable. One personality trait that seems hard to accurately predict from a social media profile is neuroticism (Gosling et al., 2011). Although there are many clues that people use to predict a person's level of neuroticism (e.g., less friendly pictures, frequent posting), none of these clues seems to be an accurate predictor of neuroticism (Hall et al., 2013).

Person Perception: Reading Faces and Catching Liars

When we say that we can "read" others' emotions, what we really mean is that we can "read" their faces. The face is the prime stimulus for not only recognizing someone but forming an impression of them as well. Recent neuroscience research has yielded a wealth of information about face perception and its neural underpinnings. For example, we know that human face processing occurs in the occipital temporal cortex and that other parts of the brain are involved in determining the identity of the person (Macrae et al., 2005). We also know that we are quite good at determining basic information about people from their faces even under conditions that hinder optimal perception. For example, Macrae and his colleagues, in a series of three experiments, presented a variety of male, female, and facelike photographs, some in an inverted position, and in spite of the "suboptimal" presentation of these stimuli, their subjects could reasonably report the age and sex of the person. In this case, Macrae et al. suggest that acquisition of fundamental facial characteristics (age, sex, race) appears to be automatic.

So we know that getting information from faces is hard-wired in our brains and we know where that wiring is. But there is also evidence for the early start of facial perception. Even newborns have rudimentary abilities that allow them to distinguish several facial expressions, although it is only at the end of the first year that infants seem to be able to assign meaning to emotional expressions (Gosselin, 2005). Can our impression formation and face-reading skills help us to catch a person in a lie? Let's find out.

It Is Hard to Catch a Liar: Detecting Deception

Imagine that you are considering buying a used car and the salesperson tells you that the car you are looking at has just been checked over and is reliable. Would you be able to determine if the salesperson was lying to you? Although we would like to think we could detect deception in situations like this, the truth is that we are not very good at detecting deception (Bond & DePaulo, 2006). At best, people are just slightly above chance levels (i.e., guessing) when detecting deception (Bond & DePaulo, 2006). However we are slightly better at detecting the truth (Bond & DePaulo, 2006). Ironically, Bond and DePaulo report that we are actually worse at detecting deception when we have visual cues available to us.

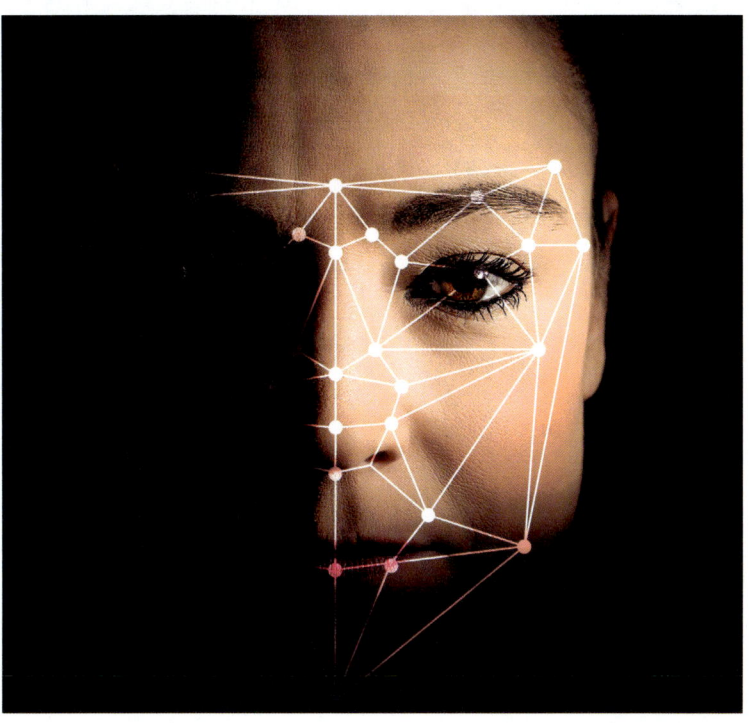

The face is an important source of information for recognizing and forming impressions of others. The ability to read faces is "hard wired" into our brains and is even present in newborns.
Source: steved_np3/Shutterstock.

Some individuals are better at detecting deception than others. Paul Ekman and his coworkers asked 20 males (ages 18 to 28) to indicate how strongly they felt about a number of controversial issues. These males were then asked to speak to an interrogator about the social issue about which they felt most strongly. Some were asked to tell the truth; others were asked to lie about how they felt (Ekman et al., 1999). If the truth tellers were believed, they were rewarded with $10; liars who were believed were given $50. Liars who were caught and truth tellers who were disbelieved received no reward. So, the 20 males were motivated to do a good job. Ekman and his colleagues filmed the faces of the 20 participants and found that there were significant differences in facial movements between liars and truth tellers.

The researchers were interested in whether people in professions in which detection of lies is important were better than the average person in identifying liars and truth tellers. Ekman tested several professional groups, including federal officers (CIA agents and others), federal judges, clinical psychologists, and academic psychologists. In previous research, the findings suggested that only a small number of U.S. Secret Service agents were better at detecting lies than the average person, who is not very effective at recognizing deception. Figure 3.2 shows that federal officers were most accurate at detecting whether a person was telling the truth. Interestingly, these officers were more accurate in detecting lies than truth. Clinical psychologists interested in deception were next in accuracy, and again, they were better at discerning lies than truth telling.

The best detectors focused not on one cue but rather on a battery of cues or symptoms. Ekman notes that no one cue is a reliable giveaway. Perhaps the most difficult obstacle in detecting liars is that any one cue or series of cues may not be applicable across the board. Each liar is different; each detector is different as well. Ekman found a wide range of accuracy within each group, with many detectors being at or below chance levels.

If people are not very good at detecting lies, then they ought not to have much confidence in their ability to do so. But as DePaulo and her colleagues have shown, people's confidence in their judgments as to whether someone else is telling the truth is not

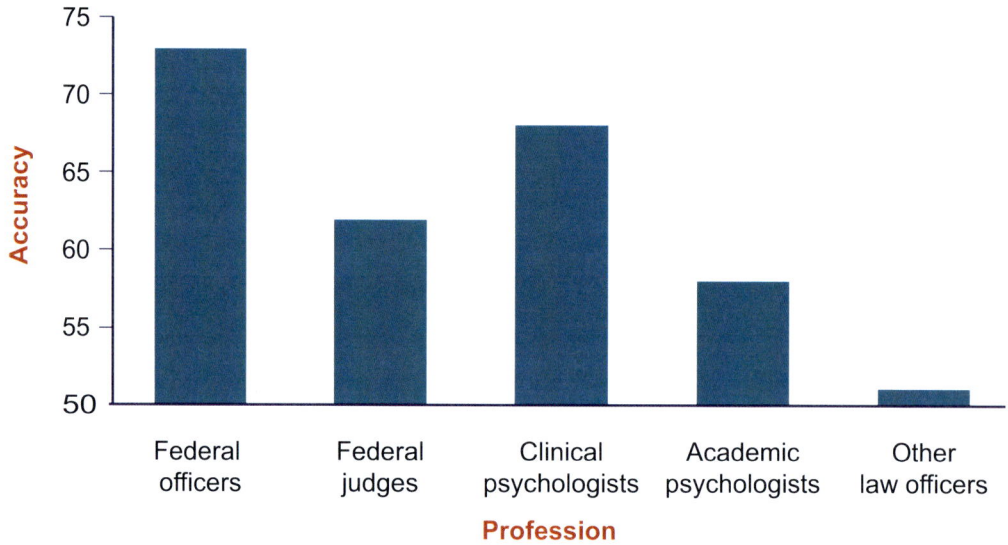

FIGURE 3.2

Accuracy of individuals in various professions in detecting who is deceptive. Based on data from Ekman et al. (1999).

reliably related to the accuracy of their judgments (DePaulo et al., 1997). People are more confident in their judgments when they think that the other person is telling the truth, whether that person is or not, and men are more confident, but not more accurate, than are women. The bottom line is that we cannot depend on our feelings of confidence to tell us someone is lying or not. As suggested by the work of Gill and colleagues (1998) discussed earlier, being in a close relationship and knowing the other person well is no great help in detecting lies (Anderson et al., 1998). However, we can take some comfort in the results of research that shows that people tell fewer lies to the individuals with whom they feel closer and are more uncomfortable if they do lie. When people lied to close others, the lies were other-oriented, aimed at protecting the other person or making things more pleasant or easier (DePaulo & Kashy, 1999).

In a book by neurologist Oliver Sacks, *The Man Who Mistook His Hat for His Wife*, there is a scene in which brain-damaged patients, all of whom had suffered a stroke, accident, or tumor to the left side of the brain (aphasics) and therefore had language disorders, were seen laughing uproariously while watching a TV speech by President Ronald Reagan. Dr. Sacks speculated that the patients were picking up lies that others were not able to catch.

There is now some evidence that Sacks's interpretation may have been right. Etcoff et al. (2000) suggested that language may hide the cues that would enable us to detect lying, and therefore those with damage to the brain's language centers may be better at detecting lies. The indications are that when people lie, their true intent is reflected by upper facial expressions, whereas the part of the face around the mouth conveys the false emotional state the liar is trying to project. It may be that aphasics use different brain circuitry to detect liars. For the rest of us, it's pretty much pure chance.

An examination of over 1,300 studies concerning lying has shown how faint the traces of deception are (DePaulo et al., 2003). This massive review indicates that there are "158" cues to deception, but many of them are faint or counterintuitive—things that you might not expect. So, liars say less than truth tellers and tell stories that are less interesting, less compelling. The stories liars tell us, however, are more complete, more perfect. Clearly, liars think more about what they are going to say than do truth tellers. Cues that would allow us to detect lying are stronger when the liar is deceiving us about something that involves his or her identity (personal items) as opposed to when the liar is deceiving about nonpersonal things.

To illustrate the difficulties, consider the eyes. People often focus on the eyes when trying to detect deception. One cue to deception might be the willingness to make eye contact. According to DePaulo et al. (2003), motivated liars avoid eye contact more than truth tellers and unmotivated liars. So, the motivation of the liar is important. One reliable eye-related cue for detecting deception is pupil dilation (Kim et al., 2019). In their experiment, Kim et al. had participants complete either an innocent mission (use a research assistant's computer to send an email) or a guilty mission (steal a research assistant's wallet from her bag). Guilty and innocent participants were then asked a series of questions and instructed to answer "no" when asked if they stole the wallet. While they answered the questions, their eyes were monitored using an eye-tracking device. The results showed that guilty participants' (but not innocent participants') pupils dilated (got larger) when they lied. To further complicate matters, other potential cues to lying, such as nervousness, may not help much in anxiety-provoking circumstances. Is the liar or the truth teller more nervous when on trial for her life? Perhaps nervousness is a cue in traffic court but maybe not in a criminal court (DePaulo et al., 2003).

We know, then, that the motivation of the liar may be crucial in determining which cues to focus on. Those who are highly motivated may just leave some traces of their deception. DePaulo's question about what cues liars signal if they are at high risk and therefore highly motivated was examined by Davis and her colleagues (2005), who used videotaped statements of criminal suspects who were interviewed by assistant district attorneys (DAs). This was after the suspects had been interviewed by the police, who had determined that a crime had been committed by these individuals. These were high-stakes interviews because the assistant DAs would determine the severity of the charge based on the results of the interviews. All the criminals claimed some mitigating circumstances (Davis et al., 2005).

Detecting deception in others is not as easy as people think. We are better at detecting the truth than a lie. Federal officers are best at detecting deception.
Source: pathdoc/Shutterstock.

In this study, the researchers knew the details of the crimes so they, by and large, knew when the criminal was lying and could match his or her behavior (language and gestures) against truthful and deceitful statements. While the researchers determined that the criminals made many false statements, the deception cues were few, limited, and *lexical* (e.g., saying no and also shaking the head no) (Davis et al., 2005, p. 699). The lady "doth protest too much, methinks," as William Shakespeare wrote in Act 3 of "Hamlet," has the ring of truth, for those criminals who did protest too much by repeating phrases and vigorous head shaking were in fact lying. Curiously, nonlexical sounds (sighing, saying *umm* or *er*) were indicators of truth telling. This latter finding may relate to DePaulo et al.'s observation that liars try to present a more organized story then do truth tellers.

And sometimes, the liar may be a believer. True story: Not long ago an elderly gentleman was unmasked as a liar when his story of having won a Medal of Honor in combat during World War II was shown to be false. By all newspaper accounts, he was a modest man, but every Memorial Day he would wear his medal and lead the town's parade. The medal was part of his identity, and the town respected his right not to talk about his exploits. It is a federal crime to falsely claim to be a Medal of Honor winner. Those who questioned the man about his false claims came to understand that he had played the role for so long it truly became a part of him, and thus after a while, he was not being deceptive. He came to believe who he said he was.

Study Break

This section explored impression formation. It also discussed the accuracy of impressions, the importance of first impressions, and how to detect liars. Before you begin the next section, answer the following questions:

1. What is impression formation, and how accurate are our impressions?
2. What is the relationship between confidence and accuracy in impression formation?
3. Why are first impressions important?
4. How does body art affect the impressions formed of those who have it?
5. How good are we at detecting lies, and what factors relate to the ability to detect lies?

The Attribution Process: Deciding Why People Act As They Do

As human beings we are inherently curious about why things happen the way that they do. Having explanations for events and behavior contributes to a perception that we live in a predictable and controllable world, which we like. Because we rarely have insight into exactly what motivates a person to behave in the way that he or she does, we have to make inferences about underlying motivations based on observable behavior. We make these inferences because we are interested in the cause of that behavior. When a person is late for a meeting, we want to know if the individual simply didn't care or if something external, beyond his or her control, caused the late appearance. Although there is a widespread tendency to overlook external factors as causes of behavior, if you conclude that the person was late because of, say, illness at home, your inferences about that behavior will be more moderate than if you determined he or she didn't care (Vonk, 1999).

attribution The process of assigning causes of behavior, both your own and that of others.

The process by which we assign causes to behavior is called **attribution**. Social psychologists have developed a number of theories to help understand how we make attributions about the causes for behavior (the behavior of others and our own). Each of the theories developed to explain the process provides an important piece of the puzzle in how we assign causes and understand behavior. The aim of these theories is to illuminate how people decide what caused a particular behavior. The theories are not concerned with finding the true causes of someone's behavior. They are concerned with determining how we, in our everyday lives, think and make judgments about the perceived causes of behaviors and events.

In this section, two basic influential attribution theories or models are introduced. These are correspondent inference theory and covariation theory. We shall also introduce extensions to these theories that help us better understand the attribution process. These are dual-process models and assessment of intention in the attribution process. Correspondent inference theory and covariation theory are the oldest and most general attempts to describe the attribution process. The others represent more recent, less formal approaches to analyzing attribution.

Heider's Early Work on Attribution

internal attribution The process of assigning the cause of behavior to some internal characteristic rather than to outside forces.

external attribution The process of assigning the cause of behavior to some situation or event outside a person's control rather than to some internal characteristic.

The first social psychologist to systematically study causal attribution was Fritz Heider. He assumed that individuals trying to make sense out of the social world would follow simple rules of causality. The individual, or perceiver, operates as a kind of "naïve scientist," applying a set of rudimentary scientific rules (Heider, 1958). Attribution theories are an attempt to discover exactly what those rules are.

Heider made a distinction between an **internal attribution**, assigning causality to something about the person, and an **external attribution**, assigning causality to something about the situation. He believed that decisions about whether an observed behavior has an internal (personal) or external (situational) source emerge from our attempt to analyze why others act as they do (causal analysis). Internal sources involve things about the individual—character, personality, motives, dispositions, beliefs, and so on. External sources involve things about the situation—other people, various environmental stimuli, social pressure, coercion, and so on. Heider (1944, 1958) examined questions about the role of internal and external sources as perceived causes of behavior. His work defined the basic questions that future attribution theorists would confront. Heider (1958) observed that perceivers are less sensitive to situational (external) factors than to the behavior of the individual they are observing or with whom they are interacting (the actor). We turn now to the two theories that built directly on Heider's work.

Correspondent Inference Theory

Assigning causes for behavior also means assigning responsibility. Of course, it is possible to believe that someone caused something to happen yet not consider the individual responsible for that action. A 5-year-old who is left in an automobile with the engine running, gets behind the wheel, and steers the car through the frozen food section of Joe's convenience store caused the event but certainly is not responsible for it, psychologically or legally.

Nevertheless, social perceivers have a strong tendency to assign responsibility to the individual who has done the deed—the actor. Let's say your brakes fail, you are unable to stop at a red light, and you plow into the side of another car. Are you responsible for those impersonal brakes failing to stop your car? Well, it depends, doesn't it? Under what circumstances would you be held responsible, and when would you not?

How do observers make such inferences? What sources of information do people use when they decide someone is responsible for an action? In 1965, Edward Jones and Keith Davis proposed what they called **correspondent inference theory** to explain the processes used in making internal attributions about others, particularly when the observed behavior is ambiguous—that is, when the perceiver is not sure how to interpret the actor's behavior. We make a **correspondent inference** when we conclude that a person's overt behavior is caused by or corresponds to the person's internal characteristics or beliefs. We might believe, for example, that a person who is asked by others to write an essay in favor of a tax increase really believes that taxes should be raised (Jones & Harris, 1967). There is a tendency not to take into account the fact that the essay was determined by someone else, not the essayist. What factors influence us to make correspondent inferences? According to correspondent inference theory, two major factors lead us to make a correspondent inference:

correspondent inference theory A theory to explain how internal attributions are made about others.

correspondent inference An inference that occurs when we conclude that a person's overt behavior is caused by or corresponds to the person's internal characteristics or beliefs.

1. We perceive that the person freely chose the behavior.
2. We perceive that the person intended to do what he or she did.

For example, early in the Persian Gulf War of 1991, several U.S.-coalition aircraft were shot down over Iraq. A few days later, some captured pilots appeared in front of cameras and denounced the war against Iraq. From the images, we could see that it was likely the pilots had been beaten. Consequently, it was obvious that they did not freely choose to say what they did. Under these conditions, we do not make a correspondent inference. We assume that the behavior tells us little or nothing about the true feelings of the person. Statements from prisoners or hostages always are regarded with skepticism for this reason. The perception that someone has been coerced to do or say something makes an internal attribution less likely. The second factor contributing to an internal attribution is intent. If we conclude that a person's behavior was intentional rather than accidental, we are likely to make an internal attribution for that behavior. To say that a person intended to do something suggests that the individual wanted the behavior in question to occur. To say that someone did not intend an action, or did not realize what the consequences would be, is to suggest that the actor is less responsible for the outcome.

Covariation Theory

Whereas correspondent inference theory focuses on the process of making internal attributions, **covariation theory**, proposed by Harold Kelley (1967, 1971), looks at both

covariation theory An attribution theory explaining how person and situational attributions are made.

internal and external attributions—how we make sense of a situation, the factors beyond the person that may be causing the behavior in question (Jones, 1990). The attribution possibilities that covariation theory lays out are similar to those that correspondent inference theory proposes. What is referred to as an internal attribution in correspondent inference theory is referred to as a *person attribution* in covariation theory. What is called an external attribution in correspondent inference theory is called a *situational attribution* in covariation theory.

Like Heider, Kelley (1967, 1971) viewed the attribution process as an attempt to apply some rudimentary scientific principles to causal analysis. In correspondent inference theory, in contrast, the perceiver is seen as a moral or legal judge of the actor. Perceivers look at intent and choice, the same factors that judges and jurors look at when assigning responsibility. Kelley's perceiver is more a scientist: just the facts, ma'am.

According to Kelley, the basic rule applied to causal analysis is the **covariation principle**, which states that if a response is present when a situation (person, object, event) is present and absent when that same situation is absent, then that situation is the cause of the response (Kelley, 1971). In other words, people decide that the most likely cause of any behavior is the factor that covaries—occurs at the same time—most often with the appearance of that behavior.

As an example, let's say your friend Keisha saw the hit movie *Avengers: Endgame* and raved about it. You are trying to decide whether you would like it too and whether you should go see it. The questions you have to answer are: What is the cause of Keisha's reaction? Why did she like this movie? Is it something about the movie? Or is it something about Keisha?

In order to make an attribution in this case, you need information, and there are three sources or kinds of relevant information available to us:

1. Consensus information
2. Distinctiveness information
3. Consistency information

Consensus information tells us about how other people reacted to the same event or situation. You might ask: How did my other friends like *Avengers: Endgame*? How are the reviews? How did other people in general react to the movie? If you find high consensus—everybody liked it—well, then, it is probably a good movie. In causal attribution terms, it is the movie that caused Keisha's behavior. High consensus leads to a situational attribution.

Now, what if Keisha liked the movie but nobody else did? Then it must be Keisha and not the movie: Keisha always has strange tastes in movies. Low consensus leads to a person attribution (nobody but Keisha liked it, so it must be Keisha).

The second source of information we use to make attributions is *distinctiveness information*. Whereas consensus information deals with what other people think, distinctiveness information concerns the situation in which the behavior occurred. We ask if there is something unique or distinctive about the situation that could have caused the behavior. If the behavior occurs when there is nothing distinctive or unusual about the situation (low distinctiveness), then we make a person attribution. If Keisha likes all movies, then we have low distinctiveness: There's nothing special about *Avengers: Endgame*—it must be Keisha. If there is something distinctive about the situation, then we make a situational attribution. If this is the only movie Keisha has ever liked, we have high distinctiveness and there must be something special about the movie. Low distinctiveness leads us to a person attribution; high distinctiveness leads us to a situational attribution. If the situation is unique—very high distinctiveness—then the behavior probably was caused by the situation and not by something about the person. The combination of high consensus and high distinctiveness always leads to a situational attribution. The combination of low consensus and low distinctiveness always leads to a person attribution.

covariation principle
The rule that if a response is present when a situation (person, object, or event) is present and absent when that same situation is absent, the situation is presumed to be the cause of the response.

Attribution theories help us understand how we attribute the causes of success or failure to internal or external factors.
Source: VGstockstudio/Shutterstock.

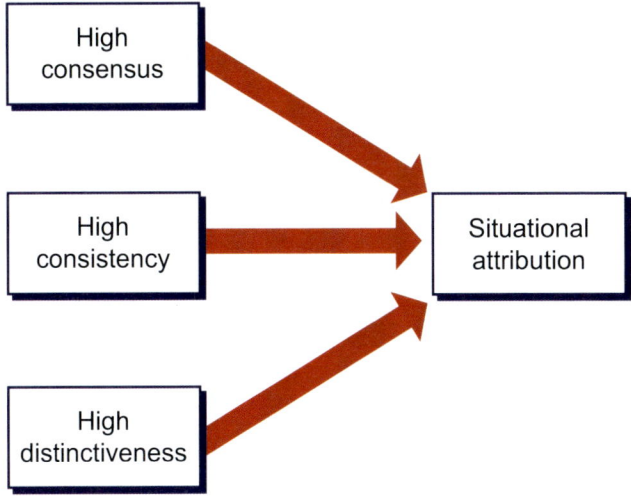

FIGURE 3.3

Information mix leading to a situational attribution.

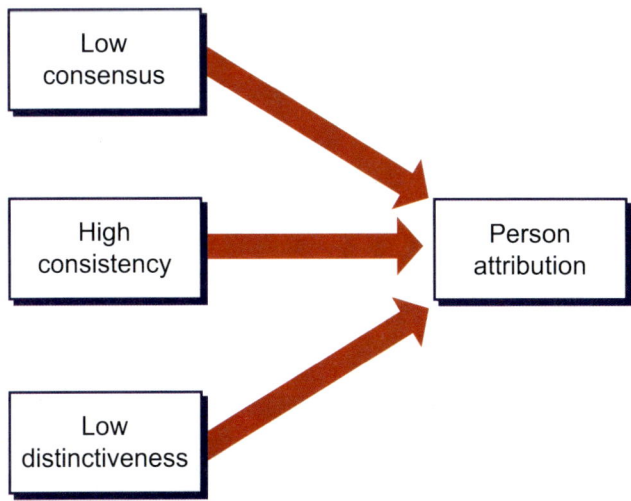

FIGURE 3.4

Information mix leading to a person attribution.

The third source of information is *consistency information*, which confirms whether the action occurs over time and situations (Chen et al., 1988). We ask, Is this a one-time behavior (low consistency), or is it repeated over time (high consistency)? In other words, is this behavior stable or unstable? Consistency is a factor that correspondent inference theory fails to take into account.

What do we learn from knowing how people act over time? If, for example, the next time we see Keisha, she again raves about *Avengers: Endgame* after seeing it for a second time, we would have evidence of consistency over time (Jones, 1990). We would have less confidence in her original evaluation of the movie if she told us she now thought the movie wasn't very good (low consistency). We might think that perhaps Keisha was just in a good mood that night and that her mood affected her evaluation of the movie. Consistency has to do with whether the behavior is a reliable indicator of its cause.

The three sources of information used in making attributions are shown in Figures 3.3 and 3.4. Figure 3.3 shows the combination of information—high consensus, high consistency, and high distinctiveness—that leads us to make a situational attribution. Go see the movie: Everybody likes it (high consensus); Keisha, who likes few, if any, movies, likes it as well (high distinctiveness of this movie); and Keisha has always liked it (high consistency of behavior).

Figure 3.4 shows the combination of information—low consensus, high consistency, and low distinctiveness—that leads us to a person attribution. None of our friends likes the movie (low consensus); Keisha likes the movie, but she likes all movies, even *The Thing That Ate Newark* (low distinctiveness); and Keisha has always liked this movie (high consistency). Maybe we ought to watch TV tonight.

Not surprisingly, research on covariation theory shows that people prefer to make person rather than situational attributions (McArthur, 1972). This conforms with the (correspondence) bias we found in correspondence inference theory and highlights again the tendency toward overemphasizing the person in causal analysis. It also fits with our tendency to be cognitive misers and take the easy route to making causal attributions.

Dual-Process Models

We have emphasized that people are cognitive misers, using the least effortful strategy available. But they are not cognitive fools. We know that although impression formation is mainly automatic, sometimes it is not. People tend to make attributions in an automatic way, but there are times when they need to make careful and reasoned attributions (Chaiken & Trope, 1999).

Trope (1986) proposed a theory of attribution that specifically considers when people make effortful and reasoned analyses of the causes of behavior. Trope assumed, as have other theorists, that the first step in our attributional appraisal is an automatic categorization of the observed behavior, followed by more careful and deliberate inferences about the person (Trope et al., 1991).

The first step, in which the behavior is identified, often happens quickly, automatically, and with little thought. The attribution made at this first step, however, may be adjusted in the second step. During this second step, you may check the situation to see if the target was controlled by something external to him. If "something made him do it," then you might hold him less (internally) responsible for the behavior. In such instances, an inferential adjustment is made (Trope et al., 1991).

What information does the perceiver use to make these attributions? Trope plausibly argued that perceivers look at the behavior, the situation in which the behavior occurs, and prior information about the actor. Our knowledge about situations helps us understand behavior even when we know nothing about the person. When someone cries at a wedding, we make a different inference about the cause of that behavior than we would if the person cried at a wake. Our prior knowledge about the person may lead us to adjust our initial impression of the person's behavior.

A somewhat different model was developed by Gilbert (1989, 1991) and his colleagues. Influenced by Trope's two-step model, they proposed a model with three distinct stages. The first stage is the familiar automatic categorization of the behavior (that action was aggressive); the second is characterization of the behavior (George is an aggressive guy); and the third, correction, consists of adjusting that attribution based on situational factors (George was provoked needlessly). Gilbert essentially divided Trope's first step, the identification process, into two parts: categorization and characterization. The third step is the same as Trope's inferential-adjustment second step.

For example, if you say "Good to see you" to your boss, the statement may be categorized as friendly, and the speaker may be characterized as someone who likes the other person; finally, this last inference may be corrected because the statement is directed at someone with power over the speaker (Gilbert et al., 1992). The correction is based on the inference that you had better be friendly to your boss. Gilbert suggests that categorization is an automatic process; characterization is not quite automatic but is relatively effortless, requiring little attention; but correction is a more cognitively demanding (controlled and effortful) process (Gilbert & Krull, 1988). Of course, we need to have the cognitive resources available to make these corrections. If we become overloaded or distracted, then we are not able to make these effortful corrections, and our default response is to make internal and dispositional attributions and to disregard situational information (Gilbert & Hixon, 1991; Trope & Alfieri, 1997).

Perceptions of Responsibility and Attributions

During the COVID-19 pandemic of 2020–2021, in a number of instances, the virus was spread by a person with the virus behaving in a way that might be considered questionable. For example, in September 2020, a passenger with COVID-19 infected 15 passengers on a flight from London to Hanoi. The female passenger boarded the flight with a sore throat and cough. As the flight progressed, her symptoms worsened, and 4 days later, she tested positive for COVID-19 (Wong, 2021). Knowing these facts, how do you feel about the female passenger? Are you angry with her? Do you feel sorry for her? How you answer these questions depends on whether you see the woman as responsible for spreading the virus. When making such an assessment of responsibility, we consider two relevant questions: First, we may ask whether the woman intended to spread the virus (*intentionality*). Second, we may ask if she had control over spreading the virus (*controllability*). How we answer these questions will affect how we attribute the woman's behavior. Making an internal attribution is likely if we conclude that the person intended to spread the virus and had control over her behavior. Making an internal attribution might lead to judging her harshly and being angry at her. Does this really happen this way? A study by Elvin Yao and Jason Siegel (2021) conducted in China tested this very scenario.

Yao and Siegel (2021) had participants read a scenario much like the one we just presented. They manipulated the intentionality and controllability exhibited by an infected passenger (referred to as Wang) by providing different information about the circumstances surrounding the spread of the COVID-19 virus. In the high-controllability condition (HC), participants read from a police report that the infected passenger said: "I made the choice to take the flight, but it was not something I had to do." In the low-controllability condition (LC), Wang said, "My Visa expired, so I had no choice but to take the flight." In the high-intentionality (HI) condition, Wang was quoted as saying, "I knew I was contagious. My test came back positive. Since someone gave it to me, I thought I would pass coronavirus to others." Finally, in the low-intentionality (LI) condition, Wang said, "I did not know I had it. My test came back negative. I would never want to pass coronavirus to anyone." Yao and Siegel measured participants' anger and sympathy expressed toward Wang and how much they wanted to punish him. Yao and Siegel found that participants in the HI group expressed more anger and less sympathy toward Wang than those in the LI group. As shown in Figure 3.5, there was an interaction between controllability and intentionality with respect to anger ratings. As you can see, intentionality did not affect ratings when controllability was high. Participants were equally, and highly, angry with Wang when he had control over his behavior. The lowest level of anger was expressed in the LI/LC condition. Participants were less angry when Wang had low controllability and intentionality. But they were angrier with low intentionality when controllability was higher. Finally, high levels of controllability and intentionality relate to high perceptions of responsibility. This, in turn, relates to high levels of anger and low levels of sympathy toward Wang and a corresponding higher desire to punish him for his actions.

Malle (2006) has filled some gaps in our understanding of how individuals make attributions by considering the relationship between intentionality (Did the individual intend to do what she actually did?) and judgments about the causes of a behavior. Judging intent has many implications for our sense of what defines blame and morality. The infected passenger who cries, "I didn't know I was infected," however falsely, is making a claim on our understanding of intentionality and blame. If I did not know I was infected, I could not have meant to spread the virus, and hence, I am blameless or should be held blameless legally, if not morally.

Malle asked: What constitutes ordinary folks' notions of what is an "intentional" action? The responses to Malle's question revealed four factors: *desire, belief, intention,* and *awareness. Desire* refers to a hope for a particular outcome; *belief* was defined as thoughts about what would happen before the act actually took place; *intention* meant that the action was meant to occur; and *awareness* was defined as "awareness of the act while the person was performing it" (Malle, 2006, p. 6). Further research, however, showed that there was a fifth component of ordinary notions of intentionality. We judge whether the person actually has the skill or ability to do what was desired. Thus, if I am a lousy tennis player, which I am, and I serve several aces in a row, it is clear that while I desired to do so, observers, knowing my skill level, will be unlikely to conclude that I intended to serve so well. Note here: There is a difference between attributions of intention and attributions of intentionality. An intention to do something is defined by wanting to do something (desire) and beliefs about which actions will provide me with the outcome that I want. But intentionality requires the first two components plus the skill or ability to be able to do what is desired as well as the intention to do it.

Malle offers us the following situation: A nephew plans to kill his uncle by running him over with his car. While driving around, the nephew accidentally hits and kills a man who turns out, unbeknownst to the nephew, to be his uncle. So what we have here is the comparison between actions performed as intended (he planned to kill the uncle) and actions that were unintended (he accidentally ran someone over who happened to be his uncle). Malle asked people to judge whether the killing was intentional murder or unintentional manslaughter.

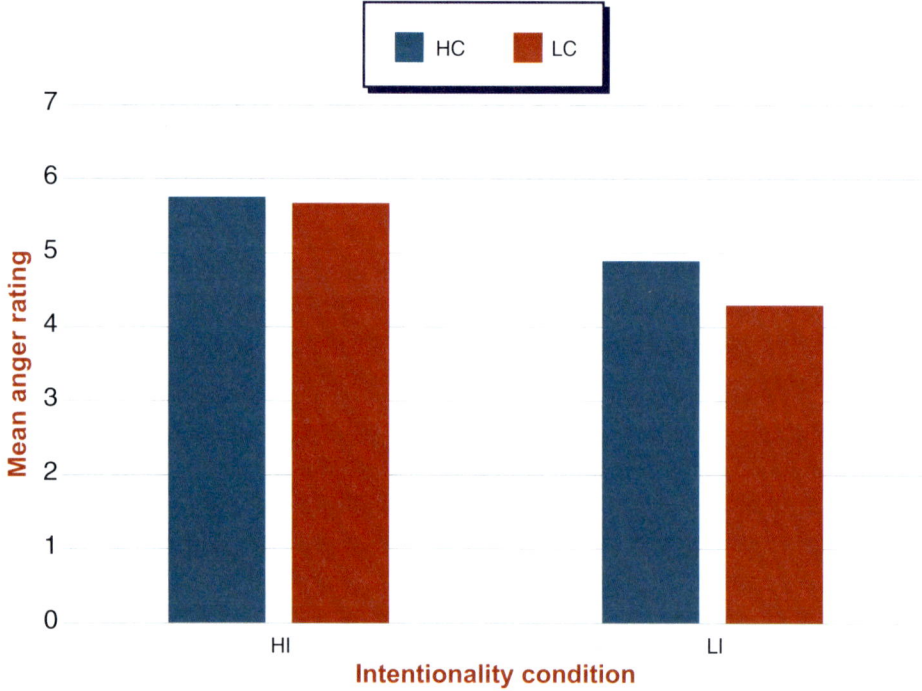

FIGURE 3.5

Results from Yao and Siegel's (2021) experiment.
Based on data from Yao and Siegel (2021).

There is no right answer here, but when people returned a murder verdict, it was because they concluded that the intent to murder had been there and the actual event, the accident, was less crucial than the attribution of the original murderous intent. Others who voted for "unintentional" manslaughter concluded that the action (running uncle over) was separate from the intent to murder (Malle, 2006). Although the circumstances of the case Malle has used are rather unusual, the results show that observers may make attributions based on different interpretations of intent.

Finally, not everyone perceives responsibility the same way. Wesley Wehde and Matthew Nowlin (2021) used survey data to investigate how people attribute responsibility for hurricane preparedness along the Gulf and South Atlantic coasts of the United States. To what extent do respondents assign responsibility to the federal, state, and local governments and to individual homeowners? Wehde and Nowlin found that respondents tended to assign low levels of responsibility to government agencies and more responsibility to individual residents. They also found that conservative respondents assigned more responsibility to individual residents than did liberal respondents. A similar ideological divide exists for responsibility attributions for poverty (Zucker & Weiner, 1993). Zucker and Weiner found that conservatives are more likely than liberals to attribute the causes for poverty to the individual (internal attribution) and less likely to attribute them to society (external attribution) than liberals. Conversely, liberals are more likely to assign responsibility to society and less to the individual. Attributing poverty internally elicits feelings of anger in conservative individuals (Weiner & Osborne, 2011).

Study Break

This section examined attribution theories and how we make attributions for behavior (our own and the behavior of others). Before you begin the next section, answer the following questions:

1. What are internal and external attributions?
2. How does correspondent inference theory account for making internal attributions?
3. What is covariation theory, and how does it account for internal and external attributions?
4. What are the dual-process models, and how do they help understand the attribution process?
5. How does intentionality relate to the attribution process?

Attribution Biases

We know that individuals are not always accurate in determining what other people are really like. Although these attribution models assume people generally can make full use of social information, much of the time we take shortcuts, and we make a number of predictable errors. These errors or biases are examples of the cognitive miser as social perceiver. We deviate from the rules that a "pure scientist" would apply as outlined in the correspondent inference and especially the covariation models. Note, however, that some theorists argue that these biases are a consequence of the fact that people use a somewhat different attribution model than earlier theorists had assumed. In other words, there are no biases in the sense that people do something wrong in the way they make attributions; people just use the models in a different way than the earlier theorists thought they did.

Misattributions

A famous example of how our attributions may be misdirected is illustrated by a classic experiment by Schachter and Singer (1962). Schachter and Singer demonstrated that two conditions are required for the production of an emotional response: physiological arousal and cognitions that label the arousal and therefore identify the emotion for the person experiencing it. Schachter and Singer injected participants with epinephrine, a hormone that produces all the symptoms of physiological arousal—rapid breathing, increased heart rate, palpitations, and so on. Half these people were accurately informed that the injection would create a state of arousal, and others were told the injection was only a vitamin and would not have any effect. In addition, subjects in a control group were not given any drug.

Participants were then placed in a room to await another part of the experiment. Some subjects were in a room with a confederate of the experimenters, who acted in a happy, excited, even euphoric manner, laughing, rolling up paper into balls, and shooting the balls into the wastebasket. Others encountered a confederate who was angry and threw things around the room. All subjects thought that the confederate was just another subject.

Schachter and Singer (1962) argued that the physiological arousal caused by the injection was open to different interpretations. The subjects who had been misinformed about the true effects of the injection had no reasonable explanation for the increase in their arousal. The most obvious stimulus was the behavior of the confederate. Results showed that aroused subjects who were in a room with an angry person behaved in an angry way; those in a room with a happy confederate behaved in a euphoric way. What about the subjects in the group who got the injection and were told what it was? These informed subjects had a full explanation for their arousal, so they simply thought that the confederate was strange and waited quietly.

The research shows that our emotional state can be manipulated. When we do not have readily available explanations for a state of arousal, we search the environment to find a probable cause. If the cues we find point us toward anger or aggression, then perhaps that is how we will behave. If the cues suggest joy or happiness, then our behavior may conform to those signals. It is true, of course, that this experiment involved a temporary and not very involving situation for the subjects. It is probable that people are less likely to make misattributions about their emotions when they are more motivated to understand the causes of their feelings and when they have a more familiar context for them.

The Fundamental Attribution Error

One pervasive bias found in the attribution process is the tendency to attribute behavior to internal forces rather than to external forces. This bias is referred to as the **fundamental attribution error**.

fundamental attribution error The tendency to automatically attribute the causes for another person's behavior to internal rather than external forces.

If you have ever watched the television game show *Jeopardy*, you probably have seen the following scenario played out in various guises: A nervous contestant selects "Russian history" for $500. The answer is, "He was known as the 'Mad Monk.'" A contestant rings in and says, "Who was Molotov?" Alex Trebek, the late host, replied, "Ah, noooo, the correct question is 'Who was Rasputin?'" As the show continues, certain things become evident. The contestants, despite knowing a lot of trivial and not so trivial information, do not appear to be as intelligent or well informed as Trebek.

Sometimes we make attributions about people without paying enough attention to the roles they are playing. Of course, Trebek looked smart—and in fact, he may have been smart, but he also had all the answers in front of him. Unfortunately, this last fact is sometimes lost on us. This so-called *quiz show phenomenon* was vividly shown in an experiment in which researchers simulated a TV game show for college students (Ross et al., 1977). A few subjects were picked to be the questioners, not because they had any special skill or information but by pure chance, and had to devise a few fairly difficult but common-knowledge questions. A control group of questioners asked questions formulated by others. Members of both groups played out a simulation quiz game. After the quiz session, all subjects rated their own knowledge levels, as well as the knowledge levels of their partners.

Now, all of us can think of some questions that might be hard for others to answer. Who was the Dodgers' third baseman in the 1947 World Series? Where is Boca Grande? When did Emma Bovary live? Clearly, the questioners had a distinct advantage: They could rummage around in their storehouse of knowledge, trivial and profound, and find some nuggets that others would not know.

When asked to rate the knowledge levels of the questioners as opposed to the contestants, both the questioners and the contestants rated the questioners as more knowledgeable, especially in the experimental group in which the questioners devised their own questions. Only a single contestant rated herself superior in knowledge to the questioner.

The fundamental attribution error can be seen clearly in this experiment: People attribute behavior to internal factors, even when they have information indicating situational factors are at work. Because the questioners appeared to know more than the contestants, subjects thought the questioners were smarter. The great majority of participants failed to account for the situation.

The quiz show phenomenon occurs in many social situations. The relationship between doctor and patient or teacher and student can be understood via this effect. When we deal with people in positions of high status or authority who appear to have all the answers, we attribute their behavior to positive internal characteristics such as knowledge and intelligence. Such an attribution enhances their power over us.

Why We Make the Fundamental Attribution Error

Why do we err in favor of internal attributions? Several explanations have been offered for the fundamental attribution error, but two seem to be most useful: a focus on personal responsibility and the salience of behavior. Western culture emphasizes the importance of individual personal responsibility (Gilbert & Malone, 1995); we expect individuals to take responsibility for their behavior. We expect to be in control of our fates—our behavior—and we expect others to have control as well. We tend to look down on those who make excuses for their behavior. It is not surprising, therefore, that we perceive internal rather than external causes to be primary in explaining behavior (Forgas et al., 1990).

As we discussed in Chapter 2, some cultures take an individualistic view (e.g., personal responsibility for one's actions), whereas others take a more collectivist view (more focus on the group than the individual). Generally, there is a greater tendency for members of individualistic cultures (e.g., North Americans) to make the fundamental attribution error than members of collectivist cultures (e.g., Chinese). For example, Lee et al. (1996) found that people in the United States (individualistic culture) favored internal attributional explanations for behavior more than people from Hong Kong (collectivist culture). In another study, similar cultural differences were found when members of a Caribbean culture were compared to people from the United States (Joseph, 2003). Interestingly, Caribbeans who immigrated to the United States and self-identified as Americans actually showed a stronger tendency to make the fundamental attribution error than immigrants who maintained a stronger Caribbean identity (Joseph, 2003). Finally, Krull et al. (1999) found that Taiwanese and Chinese people showed a stronger tendency toward situational attributions than American people when attributions alone were assessed. However, when they looked at attributions that were tied to specific behaviors, little difference was found across cultures in the tendency to make the fundamental attribution error.

There is even a difference in the degree to which Protestants and Catholics make the fundamental attribution error (Li et al., 2012). In this study, Protestants and Catholics read scenarios of people in situations that could be attributed internally or externally. Li et al. (2012) found that Protestants were more likely to attribute the behavior of a target person in the scenario internally than were Catholics. There was no difference between the groups when making external attributions. This difference was not due to the "Protestant work ethic," which emphasizes hard work and individual responsibility. The difference in making internal attributions was found when the researchers controlled for the work ethic. In a series of follow-up studies, Li et al. (2012) found that this difference related to Protestants having a stronger belief in the existence of a soul than Catholics. Because of this difference, it appears that Protestants are more likely than Catholics to make the fundamental attribution error.

The second reason for the prevalence of the fundamental attribution error is the salience of behavior. In social situations as in all perception situations, our senses and attention are directed outward. The "actor" becomes the focus of our attention. His or her behavior is more prominent than the less commanding background or environment. The actor becomes the "figure" (focus in the foreground) and the situation, the "ground" (the total background) in a complex figure-ground relationship. A well-established maxim of perceptual psychology is that the figure stands out against the ground and thus commands our attention.

The perceiver tends to be "engulfed by the behavior," not the surrounding circumstances (Heider, 1958). If a person is behaving maliciously, we conclude that he or she is a nasty person. Factors that might have brought on this nastiness are not easily available or accessible to us, so it is easy, even natural, to disregard or slight them. Thus, we readily fall into the fundamental attribution error.

Correcting the Fundamental Attribution Error

So, are we helpless to resist this common misattribution of causality? Not necessarily. As you probably already know from your own experience, the fundamental attribution error does not always occur. There are circumstances that increase or decrease the chances of making this mistake. For example, you are less likely to make the error if you become more aware of information external to another person that is relevant to explaining the causes for his or her behavior. However, even under these circumstances, the error does not disappear; it simply becomes weaker. Although the error is strong and occurs in many situations, it can be lessened when you have full information about a person's reason for doing something and are motivated to make a careful analysis. We are also less likely to make the fundamental attribution error if we will be held accountable for our attributions (Tetlock, 1985). So, as long as our attributions are private, we will have a greater tendency to make the error. Even the mood you are in can affect your tendency to make the fundamental attribution error. If you are in a "happy mood," you are more likely to make the error, whereas if you are in a "sad mood," you are less likely to make the error (Forgas, 1998). So, if you want to reduce the likelihood of making the error, think of something sad! Finally, the bias toward making internal attributions can be reduced by making information concerning situational influences on behavior more readily accessible, especially for individuals who are strongly prone to this bias (Scopelliti et al., 2018).

The Actor-Observer Bias

Actors prefer external attributions for their own behavior, especially if the outcomes are bad, whereas observers tend to make internal attributions for the same behavior. The **actor-observer bias** is especially strong when we are trying to explain negative behaviors, whether our own or that of others. This bias alerts us to the importance of perspective when considering attributional errors, because differing perspectives affect the varied constructions of reality that people produce.

A simple experiment you can do yourself demonstrates the prevalence of the actor-observer bias (Fiske & Taylor, 1984). Using a list of adjectives such as those shown in Table 3.1, rate a friend on the adjectives listed and then rate yourself. If you are like most people, you will have given your friend higher ratings than you gave yourself.

Why these results? It is likely that you see your friend's behavior as relatively consistent across situations, whereas you see your own behavior as more variable. You probably were more likely to choose the 0 category for yourself, showing that sometimes you see yourself as aggressive, thoughtful, or warm and other times not. It depends on the situation. We see other people's behavior as more stable and less dependent on situational factors.

The crucial role of perspective in social perception situations can be seen in a creative experiment in which the perspectives of both observer and actor were altered (Storms, 1973). Using videotape equipment, the researcher had the actor view his own behavior from the perspective of an observer. That is, he showed the actor a videotape of himself as seen by somebody else. He also had the observer take the actor's perspective by showing the observer a videotape of how the world looked from the point of view of the actor. That is, the observer saw a videotape of herself as seen by the actor, the person she was watching.

When both observers and actors took these new perspectives, their attributional analyses changed. Observers who took the visual perspective of the actors made fewer person attributions and more situational ones. They began to see the world as the actors saw it. When the actors took the perspective of the observers, they began to make fewer situational attributions and more personal ones. Both observers and actors got to see themselves as others saw them—always an instructive, if precarious, exercise. In this case, it provided insight into the process of causal analysis.

actor-observer bias
An attribution bias showing that we prefer external attributions for our own behavior, especially if outcomes are negative, whereas observers tend to make internal attributions for the same behavior performed by others.

The actor-observer bias tells us that we will attribute a negative event, like a car accident, internally for someone else, but externally for ourselves.
Source: Robert Crum/Shutterstock.

TABLE 3.1 Self-Test Demonstrating the Actor-Observer Bias

Rating Scale
−2 Absolutely does not describe
−1 Typically does not describe
0 Sometimes describes, sometimes does not
+1 Often describes
+2 Absolutely describes

	Friend	Self
Domineering	_____	_____
Controlling	_____	_____
Authoritative	_____	_____
Argumentative	_____	_____
Considerate	_____	_____
Aspiring	_____	_____
Extroverted	_____	_____
Amicable	_____	_____

The False Consensus Bias

When we analyze the behavior of others, we often find ourselves asking, What would I have done? This is our search for consensus information (What do other people do?) when we lack such information. In doing this, we often overestimate the frequency and popularity of our own views of the world (Ross et al., 1977). The **false consensus bias** is simply the tendency to believe that everyone else shares our own feelings and behavior (Harvey & Weary, 1981). We tend to believe that others hold similar political opinions, find the same movies amusing, and think that baseball is the distinctive American game.

The false consensus bias may be an attempt to protect our self-esteem by assuming that our opinions are correct and are shared by most others (Zuckerman et al., 1982). That is, the attribution that other people share our opinions serves as an affirmation and a confirmation of the correctness of our views. However, this overestimation of the trustworthiness of our own ideas can be a significant hindrance to rational thinking, and if people operate under the false assumption that their beliefs are widely held, the false consensus bias can serve as a justification for imposing one's beliefs on others (Fiske & Taylor, 1991).

Not everyone is equally likely to believe in a false consensus bias. Prejudiced individuals are more likely to overestimate support for their prejudiced views than actually exists compared with nonprejudiced individuals (Watt et al., 2010). Watt et al. found that prejudiced individuals believed more people agreed with their prejudiced attitude toward native Aboriginal Australians (70.9%) than nonprejudiced individuals believed supported their nonprejudiced attitude (38.7%). Watt et al. pointed out that this finding concerning prejudiced individuals is troubling because it may make them more likely to express their negative attitudes and act on those attitudes.

The false consensus bias can also contribute to unethical behavior. Ethical practices—for example, in businesses—are derived from what is agreed upon as ethical behavior

false consensus bias The tendency to believe that our own feelings and behavior are shared by everyone else.

(Flynn & Wiltermuth, 2010). One would hope that decisions would be based on established ethical standards. However, Flynn and Wiltermuth found that ethical decisions are often guided by a false consensus bias where a person believes that there is greater agreement with his or her moral choices than actually exists. False consensus reasoning was strongest when an individual was in the position of a "broker" and had control over the flow of information over others in a network. If decision makers in business assume that there is more ethical agreement than actually exists, those individuals may be more prone to making seriously unethical decisions. In short, if one believes that everyone thinks that a decision is ethically sound, then the decision must be ethically sound.

The false consensus bias also manifests itself in social media. If you have a social media profile, you probably know that these networks have a reputation as "echo chambers." Social networks allow users to select the people and the types of information they receive in their newsfeeds. This results in social network users communicating with others who hold similar attitudes and excluding or blocking users who hold differing opinions (Quattrociocchi et al., 2016). This echo chamber effect is also magnified by the algorithms that social media companies use to supply users with additional information and news stories tailored to their existing attitudes.

Robert Luzsa and Susanne Mayr (2021) tested whether the echo chamber of social media produces a false consensus effect. In two separate studies, participants were exposed to artificially created newsfeeds about marijuana legalization. Prior to exposure to the newsfeeds, the participants' own attitudes toward marijuana legalization were measured. These newsfeeds were either congruent (similar) or incongruent (dissimilar) with the participants' existing attitudes. After exposure to the newsfeed, participants were asked to estimate the percentage of the population in favor of legalizing marijuana. Participants who received the congruent newsfeed were more likely to estimate that a higher percentage of the population shared their views about marijuana legalization—demonstrating a false consensus effect.

Study Break

This section discussed various biases in the attribution process. Before you begin the next section, answer the following questions:

1. What are misattributions?
2. What is the fundamental attribution error, and why do we make it?
3. How can we correct the fundamental attribution error?
4. What are the actor observer and false consensus biases?

Schemas

The aim of social perception is to gain enough information to make relatively accurate judgments about people and social situations. To accomplish this we need ways of organizing the information we already have. Perceivers have strategies that help them know what to expect from others and how to respond. For example, when a father hears his infant daughter crying, he does not have to make elaborate inferences about what is wrong. He has in place an organized set of cognitions—related bits of information—about why babies cry and what to do about it. Psychologists call a set of organized cognitions a **schema**. A schema concerning crying babies might include cognitions about dirty diapers, empty stomachs, pain, or anger. Schemas also direct our search for additional information from the world (Neisser, 1976). For example, if we want to find out more about a political candidate, our schema for that person or his or her political party will direct us to seek out certain types of information. A supporter of the candidate will search for positive information based on the existing schema, whereas a nonsupporter will seek out negative information.

schema A set of organized cognitions that help us interpret, evaluate, and remember a wide range of social stimuli, including events, persons, and ourselves.

Assimilating New Information into a Schema

Schemas have some disadvantages because people tend to accept information that fits their schemas and reject information that doesn't fit. For example, politically conservative people will read conservative publications and watch Fox News for information (we discuss this further in Chapter 5). Politically liberal people will read liberal publications and listen to National Public Radio (NPR). This reduces uncertainty and ambiguity, but it also increases errors. Early in the formation of a schema of persons, groups, or events, we are more likely to pay attention to information that is inconsistent with our initial conceptions because we do not have much information (Bargh & Thein, 1985). Anything that doesn't fit the schema surprises us and makes us take notice. However, once the schema is well formed, we tend to remember information that is consistent with that schema. Remembering schema-consistent evidence is another example of the cognitive miser at work. Humans prefer the least effortful method of processing and assimilating information; it helps make a complex world simpler (Fiske, 1993).

If new information continually and strongly suggests that a schema is wrong, the perceiver will change it. Much of the time we are uncomfortable with schema-inconsistent information. Often we reinterpret the information to fit with our schema, but sometimes we change the schema because we see that it is wrong.

Origins of Schemas

Where do schemas come from? They develop from information about or experience with some social category or event. You can gain knowledge about sororities, for example, by hearing other people talk about them or by joining one. The more experience you have with sororities, the richer and more involved your schema will be. When we are initially organizing a schema, we place the most obvious features of an event or a category in memory first. If it is a schema about a person or a group of people, we begin with physical characteristics that we can see: gender, age, physical attractiveness, race or ethnicity, and so on.

We have different types of schemas for various social situations (Gilovich, 1991). We have self-schemas, which help us organize our knowledge about our own traits and personal qualities. Person schemas help us organize people's characteristics and store them in our memory. People often have a theory—known as an **implicit personality theory**—about what kinds of personality traits go together. Intellectual characteristics, for example, are often linked to coldness, and strong and adventurous traits are often thought to go together (Higgins & Stangor, 1988). An implicit personality theory may help us make a quick impression of someone, but, of course, there is no guarantee that our initial impression will be correct. For example, recall our discussion of how tattoos influence first impression. Once a person (e.g., a potential employer) forms a negative first impression based on a person having a tattoo, implicit personality theory predicts that additional negative characteristics will be inferred to exist as well.

implicit personality theory
A common person-schema belief that certain personality traits are linked together and may help us make a quick impression of someone, but there is no guarantee that initial impression will be correct.

The Relationship Between Schemas and Behavior

Schemas sometimes lead us to act in ways that serve to confirm them. In one study, for example, researchers convinced subjects that they were going to interact with someone who was hostile (Snyder & Swann, 1978). When the subjects did interact with that "hostile" person (who really had no hostile intentions), they behaved so aggressively that the other person was provoked to respond in a hostile way. Thus, the expectations of the subjects were confirmed, an outcome referred to as a **self-fulfilling prophecy** (Jussim, 1986; Rosenthal & Jacobson, 1968). The notion of self-fulfilling prophecies suggests that we often create our own realities through our expectations. If we are interacting with members of a group we believe to be hostile and dangerous, for example, our actions may provoke the very behavior we are trying to avoid.

self-fulfilling prophecy
A tendency to expect ourselves to behave in ways that lead to confirmation of our original expectation.

This does not mean that we inhabit a make-believe world in which there is no reality to what we think and believe. It does mean, however, that our expectations can alter the nature of social reality. Consider the effect of a teacher's expectations on students. How important are these expectations in affecting how students perform? In one study,

A self-fulfilling prophecy occurs when expectations about others are confirmed by that person. Our expectations can alter the nature of social reality. A teacher may believe that a girl has lower math ability than a boy and believe that a girl works harder than a boy in math, resulting in a higher math grade for the girl.
Source: Monkey Business Images/Shutterstock.

behavioral confirmation
A tendency for perceivers to behave as if their expectations are correct and the targets then respond in ways that confirm the perceivers' beliefs.

involving nearly 100 sixth-grade math teachers and 1,800 students, researchers found that about 20% of the results on the math tests were due to the teachers' expectations (Jussim & Eccles, 1992). Twenty percent is not inconsiderable: It can certainly make the difference between an A and a B or a passing and a failing grade. The researchers also found that teachers showed definite gender biases. They rated boys as having better math skills and girls as trying harder. Neither of these findings appeared to have been correct in this study, but it showed why girls got better grades in math. The teachers incorrectly thought that girls tried harder, and therefore rewarded them with higher grades because of the girls' presumed greater effort.

The other side of the self-fulfilling prophecy is **behavioral confirmation** (Snyder, 1992). This phenomenon occurs when perceivers behave as if their expectations are correct, and the targets then respond in ways that confirm the perceivers' beliefs. Although behavioral confirmation is similar to the self-fulfilling prophecy, there is a subtle distinction. When we talk about a self-fulfilling prophecy, we are focusing on the behavior of the perceiver in eliciting expected behavior from the target. When we talk about behavioral confirmation, we are looking at the role of the target's behavior in confirming the perceiver's beliefs. In behavioral confirmation, the social perceiver uses the target's behavior (which is partly shaped by the perceiver's expectations) as evidence that the expectations are correct. The notion of behavioral confirmation emphasizes that both perceivers and targets have goals in social interactions. Whether a target confirms a perceiver's expectations depends on what they both want from the interaction.

As an example, imagine that you start talking to a stranger at a party. Unbeknownst to you, she has already sized you up and decided you are likely to be uninteresting. She keeps looking around the room as she talks to you, asks you few questions about yourself, and doesn't seem to hear some of the things you say. Soon you start to withdraw from the interaction, growing more and more aloof. As the conversation dies, she slips away, thinking, "What a bore!"

You turn and find another stranger smiling at you. She has decided you look very interesting. You strike up a conversation and find you have a lot in common. She is interested in what you say, looks at you when you're speaking, and laughs at your humorous comments. Soon you are talking in a relaxed, poised way, feeling and acting both confident and interesting. In each case, your behavior tends to confirm the perceiver's expectancies. Because someone shows interest in you, you become interesting. When someone thinks you are unattractive or uninteresting, you respond in kind, confirming the perceiver's expectations (Snyder et al., 1977).

As can be seen, whether the perceiver gets to confirm her preconceptions depends on what the target makes of the situation. To predict the likelihood of behavioral confirmation, we have to look at social interaction from the target's point of view. If the goal of the interaction from the target's viewpoint is simply to socialize with the other person, behavioral confirmation is likely. If the goal is more important, then behavioral disconfirmation is likely (Snyder, 1992). Note that the decision to confirm or disconfirm someone's expectations is by no means always a conscious one.

When we try to determine the cause or causes of an event, we usually have some hypothesis in mind. Say your college football team has not lived up to expectations, or you are asked to explain why American students lag behind others in standardized tests. When faced with these problems, we may begin by putting forth a tentative explanation. We may hypothesize that our football team has done poorly because the coach is incompetent. Or we may hypothesize that the cause of American students' poor performance is that they watch too much TV. How do we go about testing these hypotheses in everyday life?

When we make attributions about the causes of events, we routinely overestimate the strength of our hypothesis (Sanbonmatsu et al., 1993). We do this by the way we search for information concerning our hypothesis, typically tending to engage in a search strategy that confirms rather than disconfirms our hypothesis. This is known as the **confirmation bias**.

One researcher asked subjects to try to discover the rule used to present a series of three numbers, such as 2, 4, 6. The question was: What rule is the experimenter using? What is your hypothesis? Let's say the hypothesis is consecutive even numbers. Subjects could test their hypothesis about the rule by presenting a set of three numbers to see if it fit the rule. The experimenter would tell them if their set fit the rule, and then they would tell the experimenter what they hypothesized the rule was.

How would you test your hypothesis? Most individuals would present a set such as 8, 10, 12. Notice the set is aimed at confirming the hypothesis, not disconfirming it. The experimenter would say, Yes, 8, 10, 12 fits the rule. What is the rule? You would say: Any three ascending even numbers. The experimenter would say: That is not the rule. What happened? You were certain you were right.

The rule could have been any three ascending numbers. If you had tried to disconfirm your hypothesis, you would have gained much more diagnostic information than simply trying to confirm it. If you had said 1, 3, 4 and were told it fit the rule, you could throw out your hypothesis about even numbers. We tend to generate narrow hypotheses that do not take into account a variety of alternative explanations.

In everyday life we tend to make attributions for causes that have importance to us. If you hate the football coach, you are more likely to find evidence for his incompetence than to note that injuries to various players affected the team's performance. Similarly, we may attribute the cause of American students' poor performance to be their TV-watching habits, rather than search for evidence that parents do not motivate their children or that academic performance is not valued among students' peers. Of course, we should note that there may be times that confirmation of your hypothesis is the perfectly rational thing to do. But, to do nothing but test confirmatory hypotheses leaves out evidence that you might very well need to determine the correct answer.

Shortcuts to Reality: Heuristics

As cognitive misers, we have a grab bag of tools that help us organize our perceptions effortlessly and automatically. These shortcuts—handy rules of thumb that are part of our cognitive arsenal—are called **heuristics**. Like illusions, heuristics help us make sense of the social world, but also like illusions, they can lead us astray.

If you are asked how many of your friends know people who are serving in the armed forces, you quickly will think of those who do. The **availability heuristic** is defined as a shortcut used to estimate the frequency or likelihood of an event based on how quickly examples of it come to mind (Tversky & Kahneman, 1973). If service in the military is uncommon in your community, you will underestimate the overall number of soldiers; if you live in a community where many serve in the military, you will overestimate the incidence of military service.

The availability heuristic tends to bias our interpretations because the ease with which we can imagine an event affects our estimate of how frequently that event occurs. Television and newspapers, for example, tend to cover only the most visible, violent events. People therefore tend to overestimate incidents of violence and crime as well as the number of deaths from accidents and murder because these events are most memorable (Kahneman et al., 1982). As with all cognitive shortcuts, a biased judgment occurs, because the sample of people and events that we remember is unlikely to be fair and full. The crew and captain of the *Vincennes* undoubtedly had the example of the *Stark* (the American ship bombed previously) in mind when they had to make a quick decision about the Iranian airbus.

Sometimes we make judgments about the probability of an event or a person falling into a category based on how representative it or the person is of the category (Kahneman & Tversky, 1982). When we make such judgments, we are using the **representativeness heuristic**.

confirmation bias A tendency to engage in a search strategy that confirms rather than disconfirms our hypothesis.

heuristics Handy rules of thumb that serve as shortcuts to organizing and perceiving social reality automatically.

availability heuristic A shortcut used to estimate the frequency or likelihood of an event based on how quickly examples of it come to mind.

representativeness heuristic A rule used to judge the probability of an event or a person falling into a category based on how representative it or the person is of the category.

This heuristic gives us something very much like a prototype (an image of the most typical member of a category).

To understand how this heuristic works, consider Steve, a person described to you as ambitious, argumentative, and very smart. Now, if you are told that Steve is either a lawyer or a dairy farmer, what would you guess his occupation to be? Chances are, you would guess that he is a lawyer. Steve seems more representative of the lawyer category than of the dairy farmer category. Are there no ambitious and argumentative dairy farmers? Indeed there are, but a heuristic is a shortcut to a decision—a best guess.

Let's look at Steve again. Imagine now that Steve, still ambitious and argumentative, is 1 of 100 men; 70 of these men are dairy farmers, and 30 are lawyers. What would you guess his occupation to be under these conditions? The study that set up these problems and posed these questions found that most people still guess that Steve is a lawyer (Kahneman & Tversky, 1982). Despite the odds, they are misled by the powerful representativeness heuristic.

The participants who made this mistake failed to use base-rate data, information about the population as opposed to information about just the individual. They knew that 70 of the 100 men in the group were farmers; therefore, there was a 7 out of 10 chance that Steve was a farmer, no matter what his personal characteristics. This tendency to underuse base-rate data and to rely on the special characteristics of the person or situation is known as the *base-rate fallacy*.

Another heuristic involves the tendency to run scenarios in our head—to create positive alternatives to what actually happened. This is most likely to occur when we easily can imagine a different and more positive outcome. For example, let's say you leave your house a bit later than you had planned on your way to the airport and miss your plane. Does it make a difference whether you miss it by 5 minutes or by 30 minutes? Yes, the 5-minute miss causes you more distress because you can easily imagine how you could have made up those 5 minutes and could now be on your way to Acapulco. Any event that has a negative outcome but allows for a different and easily imagined outcome is vulnerable to **counterfactual thinking**, an imagined scenario that runs opposite to what really happened.

counterfactual thinking
The tendency to create positive alternatives to a negative outcome that actually occurred, especially when we can easily imagine a more positive outcome.

As another example, imagine that you took a new route home from school one day because you were tired of the same old drive. As you drive this unfamiliar route, you are involved in an accident. It is likely that you will think, "If only I had stuck to my usual route, none of this would have happened!" You play out a positive alternative scenario (no accident) that contrasts with what occurred. The inclination of people to do these counterfactual mental simulations is widespread, particularly when dramatic events occur (Wells & Gavanski, 1989).

Generally, we are most likely to use counterfactual thinking if we perceive events to be changeable (Miller et al., 1989; Roese & Olson, 1997). As a rule, we perceive dramatic or exceptional events (taking a new route home) as more mutable than unexceptional ones (taking your normal route). Various studies have found that it is the mutability of the event—the event that didn't have to be—that affects the perception of causality (Gavanski & Wells, 1989; Kahneman & Tversky, 1982). People's reactions to their own misfortunes and those of others may be determined, in great part, by the counterfactual alternatives evoked by those misfortunes (Roese & Olson, 1997).

Study Break

This section covered schemas and how they relate to social cognition and behavior. Before you begin the next section, answer the following questions:

1. What is a schema, and how is new information incorporated into one?
2. What are the origins of schemas?
3. Describe the mechanisms linked to the relationship between schemas and behavior?
4. What are the different heuristics, and how do they relate to social cognition?

The *Vincennes* Revisited

The events that resulted in the firing of a missile that destroyed a civilian aircraft by the USS *Vincennes* are clear in hindsight. The crew members of the *Vincennes* constructed their own view of reality, based on their previous experiences, their expectations of what was likely to occur, and their interpretations of what was happening at the moment, as well as their fears and anxieties. All of these factors were in turn influenced by the context of current international events, which included a bitter enmity between the United States and what was perceived by Americans as an extremist Iranian government. The crew members of the *Vincennes* had reason to expect an attack from some quarter and that is the way they interpreted the flight path of the aircraft. This is true despite that fact that later analysis showed that the aircraft had to be a civilian airliner. The event clearly shows the crucial influence of our expectations and previous experience on our perception of new events.

Much of what we discussed in this chapter suggests that we, as social perceivers, make predictable errors. Also, much of what we do is automatic, not under conscious control. The bottom line is that we are cognitive tacticians who expend energy to be accurate when it is necessary but otherwise accept a rough approximation. Accuracy in perception is the highest value, but it is not the only value; efficiency and conservation of cognitive energy also are important. And so, we are willing to make certain trade-offs when a situation does not demand total accuracy. The more efficient any system is, the more its activities are carried out automatically. But when we are motivated, when an event or interaction is really important, we tend to switch out of this automatic, nonconscious mode and try to make accurate judgments. Given the vast amount of social information we deal with, most of us are pretty good at navigating our way.

Chapter Review

1. **What is automatic processing?**

   Much of our social perception involves automatic processing, or forming impressions without much thought or attention.

2. **What is meant by a cognitive miser?**

   The notion of a cognitive miser suggests that humans process social information by whatever method leads to the least expenditure of cognitive energy. Much of our time is spent in the cognitive miser mode. Unless motivated to do otherwise, we use just enough effort to get the job done.

3. **What is controlled processing and when do we use it?**

   Thinking that is conscious and requires effort is referred to as controlled processing. If, however, we have important goals that need to be obtained, then we will switch to more controlled processing and allocate more energy to understanding social information. Automatic and controlled processing are not separate categories but rather form a continuum, ranging from complete automaticity to full allocation of our psychic energy to understand and control the situation.

4. **What is impression formation?**

   Impression formation is the process by which we form judgments about others. Biological and cultural forces prime us to form impressions, which may have adaptive significance for humans.

5. **Are our impressions of others accurate?**

   There are significant differences among social perceivers in their ability to accurately evaluate other people. Those who are comfortable with their own emotions are best able to express those emotions and to read other people. Individuals who are unsure of their own emotions, who try to hide their feelings from others, are not very good at reading the emotions of other people.

   Despite distinct differences in abilities to read others, most of us are apparently confident in our ability to accurately do so. This is especially true if we have a fair amount of information about that person. However, research shows that no matter the information at our disposal, our accuracy levels are less than we think. In part, this appears to be true because we pay attention to obvious cues but do not attend to more subtle nonverbal ones. We are especially incompetent at determining if someone is lying, even someone very close to us.

6. **What is the importance of first impressions?**

   First impressions can be powerful influences on our perceptions of others. Researchers have consistently demonstrated a primacy effect in the impression-formation process, which is the tendency of early information to play a powerful role in our eventual impression of an individual. Furthermore, first impressions, in turn, can bias the interpretation of later information.

7. What is the sample bias?

The sample bias suggests that our initial interaction with individuals is crucial to whether any further interaction will occur. Imagine you are a member of a newly formed group, and you begin to interact with others in the group. You meet Person A, who has low social skills. Your interaction with him is limited, and your tendency, understandably, is to avoid him in the future. Now Person B is different. She has excellent social skills, and conversation with her is easy and fluid. You will obviously sample more of Person B's behavior than Person A's. As a result, potentially false negative impressions of Person A never get changed, while a false positive impression of B could very well be changed if you "sample" more of her behavior. That is, the initial interaction determines whether you will sample more of that person's behavior or not. This seems especially true for persons belonging to different racial or ethnic groups.

8. How does body art affect the impressions formed of those who have it?

Individuals with body art (a body piercing or a tattoo) are evaluated more negatively than those without body art. Larger tattoos and those on the face are perceived more negatively than smaller ones and ones elsewhere on the body. One reason for the negative impressions is that the presence of body art activates negative perceptions and stereotypes of the person with the art. Body art is viewed more negatively for individuals holding some jobs compared to other. A person with no facial piercings or tattoos is rated as more hireable than a person with a piercing or a tattoo for a customer service job requiring face-to-face interaction with the customer. Individuals with tattoos are seen as less appropriate for white-collar professions (e.g., bank loan officer, accountant, stockbroker) and health care professionals (dentist and nurse) than for blue-collar workers.

9. Can we catch liars?

Not very well. A massive review of all the literature on detecting lies shows that while there are many cues to lying, they are unusual and unexpected cues and very subtle. When people lie about themselves, the cues may be a bit stronger, but it is still a guessing game for most of us.

10. What is the attribution process?

The attribution process involves assigning causes for the behavior we observe, both our own and that of others. Several theories have been devised to uncover how perceivers decide the causes of other people's behaviors. The correspondent inference and the covariation models were the most general attempts to describe the attribution process.

11. What are internal and external attributions?

When we make an internal attribution about an individual, we assign the cause for behavior to an internal source. For example, one might attribute failure on an exam to a person's intelligence or level of motivation. External attribution explains the cause for behavior as an external factor. For example, failure on an exam may be attributed to the fact that a student's parents were killed in an automobile accident a few days before the exam.

12. What is the correspondent inference theory, and what factors enter into forming a correspondent inference?

Correspondent inference theory helps explain the attribution process when perceivers are faced with unclear information. We make a correspondent inference if we determine that an individual entered into a behavior freely (versus being coerced) and conclude that the person intended the behavior. In this case, we make an internal attribution. Research shows that the perceiver acting as a cognitive miser has a strong tendency to make a correspondent inference—to assign the cause of behavior to the actor and downplay the situation—when the evidence suggests otherwise.

13. What are covariation theory and the covariation principle?

The covariation principle states that people decide that the most likely cause for any behavior is the factor that covaries, or occurs at the same time, most often with the appearance of that behavior. Covariation theory suggests that people rely on consensus (What is everyone else doing?), consistency (Does this person behave this way all the time?), and distinctiveness (Does this person display the behavior in all situations or just one?) information.

14. How do consensus, consistency, and distinctiveness information lead to an internal or external attribution?

When consensus (Everyone acts this way), consistency (The target person always acts this way), and distinctiveness (The target person only acts this way in a particular situation) are high, we make an external attribution. However, if consensus is low (Nobody else behaves this way), consistency is high (The target person almost always behaves this way), and distinctiveness is low (The target person behaves this way in many situations), we make an internal attribution.

15. **What is the dual-process model of attribution, and what does it tell us about the attribution process?**

    Trope's two-stage model recognized that the initial stage of assigning causality is an automatic categorization of behavior; a second stage may lead to a readjustment of that initial categorization, especially when the behavior or the situation is ambiguous. Trope's model led theorists to think about how and when people readjust their initial inferences.

16. **What is meant by attribution biases?**

    Both the correspondent inference and covariation models emphasize that people often depart from the (causal) analysis of the attribution models they present and make some predictable errors in their causal analyses.

17. **What is the fundamental attribution error?**

    The fundamental attribution error highlights the fact that people prefer internal to external attributions of behavior. The fundamental attribution error may be part of a general tendency to confirm what we believe is true and to avoid information that disconfirms our hypotheses. This is known as the confirmation bias. We make the fundamental attribution error because Western culture (individualistic) leads us to look at the person as being responsible for his or her behavior. Additionally, we make the error because behavior is salient and we pay attention to people when they behave, leading to an internal attribution.

18. **What is the actor-observer bias?**

    The actor-observer bias occurs when observers emphasize internal attributions, whereas actors favor external attributions. That is, when we observe someone else, we make the familiar internal attribution, but when we ourselves act, we most often believe that our behavior was caused by the situation in which we acted. This seems to occur because of a perspective difference. When we observe other people, what is most obvious is what they do. But when we try to decide why we did something, what is most obvious are extrinsic factors, the situation.

19. **What is the false consensus bias?**

    The false consensus bias occurs when people tend to believe that others think and feel the same way they do.

20. **What are schemas, and what role do they play in social cognition?**

    The aim of social perception is to gain enough information to make relatively accurate judgments about people and social situations. One major way we organize this information is by developing schemas, sets of organized cognitions about individuals or events. One type of schema important for social perception is implicit personality theories, schemas about what kinds of personality traits go together. Intellectual characteristics, for example, are often linked to coldness, and strong and adventurous traits are often thought to go together.

21. **What are the self-fulfilling prophecy and the confirmation bias, and how do they relate to behavior?**

    Schemas also influence behavior, as is illustrated by the notion of self-fulfilling prophecies. This suggests that we often create our own realities through our expectations. If we are interacting with members of a group we believe to be hostile and dangerous, for example, our actions may provoke the very behavior we are trying to avoid, which is the process of behavioral confirmation. This occurs when perceivers behave as if their expectations are correct and the targets of those perceptions respond in ways that confirm the perceivers' beliefs.

    When we make attributions about the causes of events, we routinely overestimate the strength of our hypothesis concerning why events happened the way they did. This bias in favor of our interpretations of the causes of behavior occurs because we tend to engage in a search strategy that confirms our hypothesis rather than disconfirms it. This is known as the confirmation bias.

22. **What are the various types of heuristics that often guide social cognition?**

    A heuristic is a shortcut, or a rule of thumb, that we use when constructing social reality. The availability heuristic is defined as a shortcut used to estimate the likelihood or frequency of an event based on how quickly examples of it come to mind. The representativeness heuristic involves making judgments about the probability of an event or of a person's falling into a category based on how representative it or the person is of the category. The simulation heuristic is a tendency to play out alternative scenarios in our heads. Counterfactual thinking involves taking a negative event or outcome and running scenarios in our head to create positive alternatives to what actually happened.

Key Terms

Actor-observer bias (p. 94)
Attribution (p. 84)
Automatic processing (p. 73)
Availability heuristic (p. 99)
Behavioral confirmation (p. 98)
Belief perseverance (p. 77)
Cognitive miser (p. 73)
Confirmation bias (p. 99)
Controlled processing (p. 74)
Correspondent inference (p. 85)
Correspondent inference theory (p. 85)
Counterfactual thinking (p. 100)
Covariation theory (p. 85)
Covariation principle (p. 86)
External attribution (p. 84)
False consensus bias (p. 95)
Fundamental attribution error (p. 92)
Heuristics (p. 99)
Implicit personality theory (p. 97)
Impression formation (p. 74)
Internal attribution (p. 84)
Primacy effect (p. 77)
Representativeness heuristic (p. 99)
Schema (p. 96)
Self-fulfilling prophecy (p. 97)

Chapter Quiz

1. _____ involves forming impressions without much thought or attention, whereas _____ involves forming impressions through attention to the thinking process and effort.
   A. Automatic processing; controlled processing
   B. Controlled processing; automatic processing
   C. Mindless processing; mindful processing
   D. Thoughtful processing; thoughtless processing

2. The process whereby we make judgments about the motives and behaviors of others is
   A. impression management.
   B. impression formation.
   C. schematic representation.
   D. none of the above.

3. With respect to detecting liars, research leads to the conclusion that we
   A. rely too heavily on nonfacial cues.
   B. are not very good at detecting liars.
   C. more easily catch subtle liars than obvious ones.
   D. can accurately determine when someone is lying to us.

4. According to your text, _____ accounts for much of the power of first impressions.
   A. belief perseverance
   B. priming
   C. controlled processing
   D. a recency effect

5. Jennifer has just gotten a tattoo. The impressions others will form of Jennifer will be most negative if Jennifer is a
   A. mechanic.
   B. hair stylist.
   C. doctor.
   D. cashier at a grocery store.

6. After you find out that a classmate of yours failed a really easy exam, you conclude that he must not be terribly smart. In this case you made a(n)
   A. external attribution.
   B. internal attribution.
   C. noncorrespondent inference.
   D. situational attribution.

7. When trying to attribute the cause for your poor grade on a test, you ask around to see how others in your class did on the test. This source of information for attribution is known as
   A. consensus.
   B. distinctiveness.
   C. validity.
   D. consistency.

8. The tendency to automatically attribute the causes for another person's behavior to internal rather than situational forces is the definition of the
   A. sinister attribution error.
   B. ultimate attribution error.
   C. fundamental attribution error.
   D. correspondence error.

9. Which descriptions accurately characterize a schema?
   A. Helps organize related bits of information
   B. Contains prior knowledge of events
   C. Helps us interpret situations and guide behavior
   D. All of the above

10. _____ are handy rules of thumb that serve as shortcuts to organizing and perceiving social reality.
    A. Prophecies
    B. Schemas
    C. Heuristics
    D. Biases

Answers can be found in the end-of-book Answers section.

Prejudice and Discrimination

If we were to wake up some morning and find that everyone was the same race, creed and color, we would find some other cause for prejudice by noon.

—George Aiken

CHAPTER 4

Source: YAKOBCHUK VIACHESLAV/Shutterstock.

Key Questions

As you read this chapter, find the answers to the following questions:

1. How are prejudice, stereotypes, and discrimination defined?
2. What is the relationship among prejudice, stereotypes, and discrimination?
3. What evidence is there for the prevalence of these three concepts from a historical perspective?
4. What are the personality roots of prejudice?
5. How does gender relate to prejudice?
6. What are the social roots of prejudice?
7. What is modern racism, and what are the criticisms of it?
8. What are the cognitive roots of prejudice?
9. How do cognitive biases contribute to prejudice?
10. Are stereotypes ever accurate, and can they be overcome?
11. How do prejudiced and nonprejudiced individuals differ?
12. What is the impact of prejudice on those who are its target?

The seeds for conflict and prejudice were planted somewhere in the hills of Palmyra, New York, in 1830. There a young man named Joseph Smith, Jr., received a vision from the angel Moroni. Centuries before, Moroni, as a priest of the Nephites, wrote the history of his religion on a set of golden plates and buried them in the hills of Palmyra. When Moroni appeared to Smith, he revealed the location of the plates and gave him the ability to transcribe the ancient writings into English. This translated text became the *Book of Mormon*, the cornerstone of the Mormon religion. The *Book of Mormon* contained many discrepancies from the Bible. For example, it suggested that God and Jesus Christ were made of flesh and bone.

The conflicts between this newly emerging religion and established Christianity inevitably led to hostile feelings and attitudes between the two groups. Almost from the moment of Joseph Smith's revelations, the persecution of the Mormons began. Leaving Palmyra, the Mormons established a settlement in Kirtland, Ohio, in 1831, but it was a disaster. The Mormons didn't fit in well with the existing community. For example, the Mormons supported the Democratic Party, whereas most of the Christian population in Kirtland supported the Whigs. Mormonism also was a threat to the colonial idea of a single religion in a community. At a time when heresy was a serious crime, the Mormons were seen as outcast heretics. As a result, the Mormons were the targets of scathing newspaper

13. How can a person who is the target of prejudice cope with being a target?
14. What can be done about prejudice?
15. How did the U.S. Army reduce prejudice?

Historically, the Mormons have been the target of prejudice. In 1873, Missouri Governor Boggs authorized the state militia to expel Mormons from the state.
Source: Everette Historical/Shutterstock.

MASSACRE OF MORMONS AT HAUN'S MILL.

articles that grossly distorted their religion. Mormons were socially ostracized, were denied jobs, became the targets of economic boycotts, and lived under constant threat of attack.

Because of the hostile environment in Kirtland, the Mormons moved on, splitting into two groups. One group began a settlement in Nauvoo, Illinois, and the other in Independence, Missouri. In neither place did the Mormons find peace. Near Nauvoo, for example, a Mormon settlement was burned to the ground, and its inhabitants were forced to take cover in a rain-soaked woods until they could make it to Nauvoo. At the Independence settlement in 1833, Mormon Bishop Edward Partridge was tarred and feathered after refusing to close a store and print shop he supervised. The tensions in Missouri grew so bad that then Governor Lilburn W. Boggs issued the following order: "The Mormons must be treated as enemies and must be exterminated or driven from the State if necessary, for the public peace" (Arrington & Bitton, 1979).

As a result of the prejudice experienced by the Mormons, they became more clannish, trading among themselves and generally keeping to themselves. As you might imagine, this further enraged the Christian community that hoped to benefit economically from the Mormon presence. It was not uncommon for Mormons to become the targets of vicious physical attacks or even to be driven out of a territory. There was even talk of establishing an independent Mormon state, but eventually, the Mormons settled in Utah.

The fate of the Mormons during the 1800s eerily foreshadowed the treatment of other groups later in history (e.g., Armenians in Turkey, Jews in Europe, ethnic Albanians in Yugoslavia). How could the Mormons have been treated so badly in a country with a Constitution guaranteeing freedom of religion and founded on the premise of religious tolerance?

Attitudes provide us with a way of organizing information about objects and a way to attach an affective response to that object (e.g., like or dislike). Under the right circumstances, attitudes predict one's behavior. In this chapter, we explore a special type of attitude directed at groups of people: prejudice. We look for the underlying causes of incidents such as the Mormon experience and the other acts of prejudice outlined. We ask: How do prejudiced individuals arrive at their views? Is it something about their personalities that leads them to prejudice-based acts? Or do the causes lie more in the social situations? What cognitive processes cause them to have negative attitudes toward those they perceive to be different from themselves? How pervasive and unalterable are those processes in human beings? What are the effects of being a target of prejudice and discrimination? What can we do to reduce prejudice and bring our society closer to its ideals?

The Dynamics of Prejudice, Stereotypes, and Discrimination

When we consider prejudice we really must consider two other interrelated concepts: stereotyping and discrimination. Taken together, these three make up a triad of processes that contribute to negative attitudes, emotions, and behaviors directed at members of certain social groups. First, we define just what social psychologists mean by the term *prejudice* and the related concepts of stereotype and discrimination.

Prejudice

The term **prejudice** refers to a biased, often negative, but sometimes positive attitude toward a group of people. Prejudicial attitudes include belief structures, which contain information about a group of people, expectations concerning their behavior, and emotions directed at them. When negative prejudice is directed toward a group, it leads to prejudgment of the individual members of that group and negative emotions directed at them as well. It is important to note that the nature of the emotion directed at a group of people depends on the group to which they belong (Cottrell & Neuberg, 2005). In fact, Cottrell and Neuberg have constructed "profiles" characterizing the emotions directed at members of various groups. For example, African Americans (relative to European Americans) yield a profile showing anger/resentment, fear, disgust, and pity. In contrast, Native Americans mostly elicited pity with low levels of anger/resentment, disgust, and fear.

prejudice A biased attitude, positive or negative, based on insufficient information and directed at a group, which leads to prejudgment of members of that group.

Prejudice also involves cognitive appraisals that are tied to different emotions directed at members of stigmatized groups (Nelson, 2002). For example, fear might be elicited if you find yourself stranded late at night in a neighborhood with a sizeable minority population. On the other hand, you might feel respect when at a professional meeting that includes members from that very same minority group. In short, we appraise (evaluate) a situation and experience an emotion consistent with that appraisal. This can account for the fact that we rarely exhibit prejudice toward all members of a stigmatized group (Nelson, 2002). We may display prejudice toward some members of a group, but not toward others in that group.

Of course, prejudice can be either positive or negative. Fans of a particular sports team, for example, are typically prejudiced in favor of their team. They often believe calls made against their team are unfair, even when the referees are being impartial. Social psychologists, however, have been more interested in prejudice that involves a negative bias—that is, when one group assumes the worst about another group and may base negative behaviors on these assumptions. It is this latter form of prejudice that is the subject of this chapter.

In addition to being either positive or negative, prejudice can also be explicit or implicit (Greenwald & Banaji, 1995). *Explicit prejudice* is overt and easily detectable. For example, a person in a Ku Klux Klan or Nazi uniform is easily spotted as having prejudices. In these instances, the prejudiced individuals are readily displaying their prejudicial attitudes. On the other hand, *implicit prejudice* is more subtle and not as easily spotted. Implicit prejudice is often activated automatically when a member of a stereotyped group is encountered. The individual directing the prejudice may not even be aware that he or she is being prejudiced. For example, a personnel manager may evaluate a majority group job candidate more positively than an equally qualified minority candidate, all the while denying that he or she would ever discriminate in this situation. We will explore the distinction between explicit and implicit prejudice in greater detail later in this chapter.

What Exactly Does *Race* Mean?

An important note should be added here about the concept of race. Throughout history, racial categories have been used to distinguish groups of human beings from one another. However, biologically speaking, race is an elusive and problematic concept. A person's race is not something inherited as a package from his or her parents; nor are biological characteristics such as skin color, hair texture, eye shape, facial features, and other such features valid indicators of one's racial, ethnic, or cultural background. Consider, for example, an individual whose mother is Japanese and whose father is African American, or a blond, blue-eyed person who is listed by the U.S. Census Bureau as Native American because her maternal grandmother was Cherokee. To attempt to define these individuals by race is inaccurate and inappropriate. Although many scientists maintain that race does not exist as a biological concept, it does exist as a social construct.

People perceive and categorize others as members of racial groups and often act toward them according to cultural prejudices. In this social sense, race and racism are very real and important factors in human relations. When we refer to *race* in this book, such as when we discuss race-related violence, it is this socially constructed concept, with its historical, societal, and cultural significance, that we mean.

Different Forms of Prejudice

Prejudice comes in a variety of forms, the most visible of which are racism and sexism. *Racism* is the negative evaluation of others primarily because of their skin color. It includes the belief that one racial group is inherently superior to another. *Sexism* is the negative evaluation of others because of their gender (Lips, 1993). Of course, other forms of prejudice exist, such as religious and ethnic prejudice, and homophobia (negative attitudes toward gay men and lesbians), and transphobia (prejudice against transgender individuals).

In this book, we use the scientific definitions of prejudice, racism, and discrimination avoiding the more politicized ones we encounter regularly.
Source: Colored Lights/Shutterstock.

We must be very careful to approach the issue of prejudice from a *scientific* perspective and not get caught up in the web of definitions of prejudice floating around in our culture. A search of the internet reveals a range of definitions for prejudice and racism. Some of them are straightforward, whereas others have a political flavor. Partisan political groups and some media have propagated definitions for prejudice that encompass behaviors that a more scientific definition would not. These politicized definitions and applications can serve to diminish the true meaning and problem of prejudice. In this chapter and throughout this book, we use the scientific definitions of prejudice and racism, avoiding the more politicized ones we encounter regularly.

Part of the reason for the politicization of prejudice is because Western culture has primed us to think of prejudice in terms of certain groups being the perpetrators of prejudice and other groups being the targets of prejudice. For example, it is common to think of Whites as being perpetrators of prejudice against Blacks or for Christians to direct prejudice against Muslims. However, none of us is immune to prejudice. As you will learn in this chapter, prejudice has many causes. Prejudice can be learned, it can be the result of our social histories, and it can result from how we think about ourselves and even how we process information. Because prejudice has such diverse causes, some of which are the result of the way our minds process information, we are all influenced by race to some extent. Even though we all can fall prey to prejudicial attitudes, the psychological literature has focused on White prejudice toward Blacks. This has occurred primarily because the prejudice of Whites against Blacks has historically been a larger societal problem than the reverse. That is, in the past, White prejudice was institutionalized into laws that systematically oppressed Blacks for generations (e.g., slavery, Jim Crow). The relative lack of interest in Black prejudice isn't because it does not exist. There is evidence, for example, that Blacks can direct prejudice against Whites (Stephan et al., 2002; Montieth & Spicer, 2000). Stephan et al. found that Black college students had more negative racial attitudes toward Whites and perceived greater status differences between racial groups than White students. Montieth and Spicer reported that even though both Whites and Blacks expressed generally positive interracial attitudes, Blacks (especially students at a historically Black college) expressed more negative feelings toward Whites than Whites did toward Blacks. Johnson and Leci (2003) looked at the dimensions underlying Black on White prejudice and found the following four:

1. Expectation of racism from Whites, which includes beliefs such as Whites wanting to return to pre–civil rights days and Whites supporting the views of racist political groups
2. Negative beliefs about Whites, such as Whites destroying things made by Blacks and the success of Whites being due to their color
3. Negative beliefs about interracial relationships, including the beliefs that Whites are responsible for the problems of Blacks and looking negatively at interracial relationships
4. Negative verbal expressions toward Whites, including having referred to Whites as "crackers" and speaking negatively about Whites

There is also evidence for prejudice among Blacks relating to a skin tone bias. The *skin tone bias* (also called *colorism*) is a bias that Blacks (and Whites) show toward other Blacks based on the tone of their skin. Generally, the bias is that darker-skinned Blacks are perceived more negatively than lighter-skinned Blacks (Maddox, 2004; Maddox & Gray, 2002). For example, Maddox and Gray found that Blacks and Whites ascribed more negative stereotypes and characteristics to darker-skinned than lighter-skinned Blacks. Brown (1998) found that compared to darker-skinned Blacks, lighter-skinned Blacks were more likely to have higher income (on average 65% higher), more likely to be employed (especially in a profession), and that lighter-skinned Black women are seen as more attractive. Also, research has shown that the skin tone bias operates on an implicit level as well as an explicit level (White-Means et al., 2009).

Maddox argues that this skin tone bias is the result of Blacks living in a culture that values White skin tones and Blacks internalizing these values. As you can see, prejudice is a complex issue; even Blacks can hold anti-Black attitudes. Further, the skin tone bias is not limited to the United States and Blacks. Analyzing existing data from the Implicit Association Test (IAT). Jacqueline Chen and Andrew Francis-Tan (2021) found a skin tone bias among Asians. In their study, they looked at implicit skin tone bias directed at Asian targets in a number of regions across the globe and found that implicit skin tone bias

The skin-tone bias means that Blacks and Whites show a preference for Blacks with a lighter skin tone over those with a darker skin tone.
Source: Bricolage/Shutterstock.

was the highest in East Asia and the lowest in the Caribbean and sub-Saharan Africa. They also found that males showed more implicit skin tone bias in all regions except for East Asia (where males and females showed equal bias). Chen and Francis-Tan conducted a series of experimental studies looking at explicit skin tone bias. Participants evaluated job applicant profiles on a number of dimensions (e.g., competence and attractiveness). Each profile included a photograph of the applicant that was computer manipulated to vary skin tone (light, medium, dark). The results showed that female participants rated a dark-skinned applicant as less competent and less attractive than a light-skinned applicant. Male participants did not show this bias. The skin tone bias shows how complex prejudice and issues of race can be. Understanding these complexities, rather than superficially casting aspersions of racism, will be needed to truly address the problems of race and prejudice.

Stereotypes

Prejudicial attitudes do not stem from perceived physical differences among people, such as skin color or gender. Rather, prejudice relates more directly to the characteristics we assume members of a different racial, ethnic, or other group have. In other words, it relates to the way we think about others.

People have a strong tendency to categorize objects based on perceptual features or uses. We categorize chairs, tables, desks, and lamps as *furniture*. We categorize love, hate, fear, and jealousy as *emotions*. And we categorize people on the basis of their race, gender, nationality, and other obvious features. Of course, categorization is adaptive in the sense that it allows us to direct similar behaviors toward an entire class of objects or people. We do not have to choose a new response each time we encounter a categorized object.

Categorization is not necessarily the same as prejudice, although the first process powerfully influences the second. We sometimes take our predisposition to categorize too far, developing rigid and overgeneralized images of groups. This rigid categorization—this rigid set of positive or negative beliefs about the characteristics or attributes of a group—is a **stereotype** (Judd & Park, 1993; Stangor & Lange, 1994). For example, we may believe that all lawyers are smart, a positive stereotype; or we may believe that all lawyers are devious, a negative stereotype. Many years ago, the political journalist Walter Lippmann (1922) aptly called stereotypes "pictures in our heads." When we encounter someone new who has a clear membership in one or another group, we reach back into our memory banks of stereotypes, find the appropriate picture, and fit the person to it. But, as we shall see, stereotypes play more roles than just being pictures in our heads.

In general, stereotyping is simply part of the way we do business cognitively every day. It is part of our cognitive "toolbox" (Gilbert & Hixon, 1991). We all have made judgments about individuals (Boy Scout leader, police officer, college student, feminist) based solely on their group membership. Stereotyping is a time saver; we look in our toolbox, find the appropriate utensil, and characterize a person. For example, if we meet someone new who is a college student, we will use our internalized image of what we believe to be true of a college student and characterize the person as a *college student*. It certainly takes less time and energy than trying to get to know that person (individuation; Macrae et al., 1994). Again, this is an example of the cognitive miser at work. Of course, this means we will make some very unfair, even destructive judgments of individuals. All of us recoil at the idea that we are being judged solely on the basis of some notion that the evaluator has of group membership.

stereotype A set of beliefs, positive or negative, about the characteristics or attributes of a group, resulting in rigid and overgeneralized images of members of that group.

The Content of Stereotypes

What exactly constitutes a stereotype? Are all stereotypes essentially the same? What kinds of emotions do different stereotypes elicit? The answers to these questions can inform us on the very nature of stereotypes. Regardless of the actual beliefs and information that underlie a stereotype, there appear to be two dimensions underlying stereotypes: warmth (liking or disliking) and competence (respect or disrespect) (Fiske, 2012; Fiske et al., 2002). According to this *stereotype content model* (Fiske, 2012), these two dimensions combine to define different types of stereotypes. For example, high warmth and high competence yield a positive stereotype involving admiration and pride. Low warmth and low competence results in a negative stereotype involving resentment and anger. Finally, there can be mixed stereotypes involving high competence and low warmth or low competence and high warmth. According to Fiske, members of our own group and groups similar to our own are typically higher on the dimensions of warmth and competence. Conversely, members of groups that are different from our own are lower on warmth and competence. Consequently, positive feelings are directed at members of our group and negative feelings toward members of other groups. In addition to applying to groups typically thought of as being targets of stereotyping and prejudice (e.g., Jews, Blacks, Asians, etc.), these dimensions can also be used to describe perceptions of individuals with mental illnesses (Sadler et al., 2012). As shown in Figure 4.1, various disorders are characterized by differing mixes of warmth and competence. For example, disorders characterized as low on warmth and high on competence are sociopaths and violent criminals. People with eating disorders, depression, and obsessive-compulsive disorder are characterized as high in both competence and warmth. Finally, social class seems to be an area where there are mixed stereotypes involving high competence and low warmth or low competence and high warmth. Wealthy people are viewed as high in competence but cold, whereas poorer people are viewed as less competent but warmer (Durante et al., 2017).

Does the content of stereotypes affect a person's behavior? Research suggests that it does. David Rast and his colleagues (2018) conducted a study of Asian minority members working for a large international corporation in the United Kingdom. Participants completed a survey of their experiences as minorities working as immigrants in a foreign country. Rast et al. obtained measures of the participants' perception of the warmth and competence of their majority group coworkers, the degree of uncertainty they felt, and their willingness to interact with their majority group coworkers. Rast et al. found that participants' willingness

	Competence Higher	Competence Lower
Warmth Higher	Eating disorders Obsessive-compulsive disorder Depression Bipolar disorder Anxiety disorder	Alzheimer's disease Mental retardation
Warmth Lower	Sociopaths Violent criminals	Schizophrenia Multiple personality Addictions Homelessness

FIGURE 4.1

Competence and warmth of individuals with mental disorders.
Based on data from Sadler et al. (2012).

to interact with their majority coworkers related to the perceived competence and warmth of the coworkers. Participants indicated that they were more willing to interact with majority coworkers when competence was high, especially when warmth was low. Participants were less willing to interact with majority coworkers when they perceived them to be incompetent and cold. In another study, Milena Micevski et al. (2021) found that Hungarian citizens expressed a stronger intention to visit tourist destinations for which they held stereotypes of high competence and high warmth. The impact of competence and warmth on intentions to visit a country was indirect, working through eliciting positive emotions. In other words, high competence and warmth elicit positive affect, which then increases the intention to visit a country. In a world in which people are living in increasingly diverse situations, it is important to understand how stereotypes relating to perceived warmth and competence can affect their interactions with others. For example, understanding how minority members perceive majority coworkers can help facilitate interactions between groups.

Explicit and Implicit Stereotypes

Stereotypes, like prejudicial attitudes, exist on the explicit and implicit level. *Explicit stereotypes* are those of which we are consciously aware, and they are under the influence of controlled processing. *Implicit stereotypes* (also referred to as automatic stereotypes) operate on an unconscious level and are activated automatically when a member of a minority group is encountered in the right situation. The operation of implicit stereotypes was demonstrated in an interesting experiment conducted by Banaji et al. (1993). Participants first performed a "priming task," which involved unscrambling sentences indicating either a male stereotype (aggressiveness), a female stereotype (dependence), or neutral sentences (neutral prime). Later, in a supposedly unrelated experiment, participants read a story depicting either a dependent (male or female) or an aggressive (male or female) target person. Participants then rated the target person in the story for the stereotypic or nonstereotypic trait.

The results of this experiment are shown in Figure 4.2. Notice that for both the male and female stereotypic traits, the trait was rated the same when the prime was neutral, regardless of the gender of the target. However, when the prime activated an implicit gender stereotype, the female stereotypic trait (dependence) was rated higher for female targets than for male targets. The opposite was true for the male stereotypic trait (aggressiveness). Here, aggressiveness

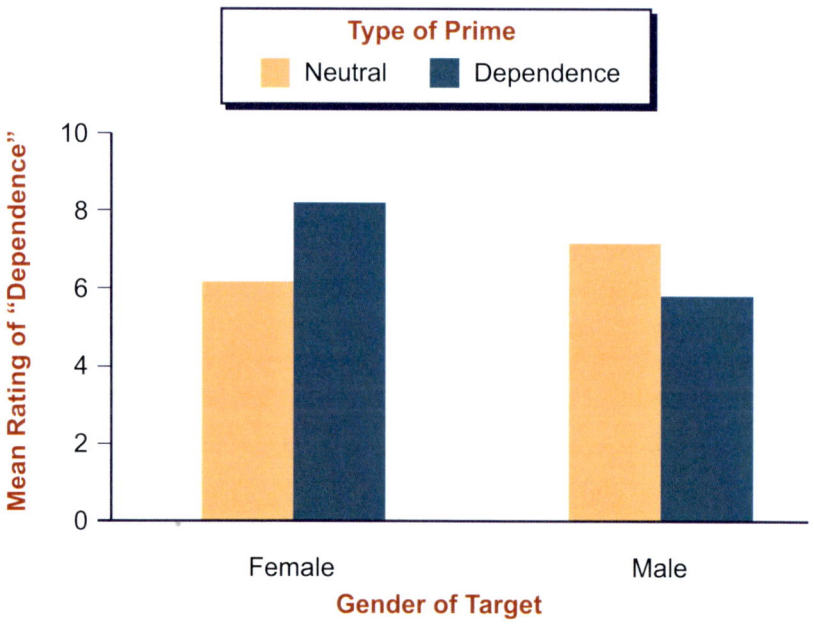

FIGURE 4.2

Results from an experiment on implicit stereotypes. When a prime activates an implicit female gender stereotype, a female stereotypic trait (dependence) was rated higher for female than for male targets. The opposite was true for the implicit male stereotypic trait (aggressiveness).
Based on data from Banaji et al. (1993).

was rated higher for male targets than for female targets. An incidental encounter with a stereotype (in this experiment, the prime) can affect evaluations of an individual who is a member of a given social category (e.g., male or female). Participants judged a stereotypic trait more extremely when the stereotype had been activated with a prime than when it had not. Thus, stereotyped information can influence how we judge members of a social group even if we are not consciously aware that it is happening (Banaji et al., 1993).

The activation of implicit stereotypes may have implications beyond believing that members of certain groups have given characteristics. In a study reported by Moskowitz et al. (2012), doctors associated certain diseases with a Black patient more readily than with a White patient, all on an implicit level. In this study, doctors were subliminally exposed to a face of either a White or Black person. Names of diseases or treatments were then presented "stereotypic"—associated with a particular racial group—or "nonstereotypic"). The speed with which a word could be identified as either a disease or treatment was recorded. Moskowitz et al. found that when subliminally primed by the face of a Black person, doctors identified stereotypically Black diseases faster than when primed by a White face. So, when doctors walk into an examination room to see a Black or White patient, they may be "primed" to automatically look for certain diseases. Furthermore, this effect is not isolated to artificial laboratory studies. In a review of the literature, FitzGerald and Hurst (2017) found evidence of implicit bias in the majority of the studies examining the issue. They noted that implicit bias was evident in the diagnosis, treatment, number of tests ordered, and questions asked of the patient.

Explicit and implicit stereotypes operate on two separate levels (controlled processing or automatic processing) and affect judgments differently, depending on the type of judgment a person is required to make (Dovidio et al., 1997). Dovidio and colleagues found that when a judgmental task required some cognitive effort (in this experiment, to determine whether a Black defendant was guilty or not guilty of a crime), explicit racial attitudes correlated with judgments. However, implicit racial attitudes were not correlated with the outcome on the guilt-judgment task. Conversely, on a task requiring a more spontaneous, automatic response (in this experiment, a word-completion task on which an ambiguous incomplete word could be completed in a couple of ways—e.g., b_d could be completed as *bad* or *bed*), implicit attitudes correlated highly with outcome judgments. Thus, explicit and implicit racial attitudes relate to different tasks. Explicit attitudes related more closely to the guilt-innocence task, which required controlled processing. Implicit attitudes related more closely to the word-completion task, which was mediated by automatic processing.

Can implicit stereotypes translate into overt differences in *behavior* directed at Blacks and Whites? In one experiment, Correll et al. (2002) had college students play a simple video game. The task was for participants to shoot only armed suspects in the game. The race of the target varied between Black and White, some of whom were armed and some unarmed. The results of their first experiment, shown in Figure 4.3, showed that White participants shot at a Black armed target more quickly than a White armed target. They also decided NOT to shoot at an unarmed target more quickly if the target was White as compared to Black. Correll et al. also provided evidence that the observed "shooter bias" was more related to an individual adhering to cultural biases about Blacks as violent and dangerous rather than personally held prejudice or stereotypes. We should note that not all research shows such a bias against Black suspects. For example, a study by Lois James and her colleagues (2013) using a more realistic shooter paradigm task found just the opposite. James et al. used a realistic simulator and had participants use a laser pistol to shoot at suspects. They also included a sample of untrained civilians and trained police and military personnel. The main finding of interest was that White participants took *longer* to shoot Black suspects than White suspects and were more likely *not* to shoot armed Black suspects than armed White suspects. However, they were more likely to shoot unarmed White than Black suspects. Interestingly, the shooter effect also applies to other groups for which negative stereotypes exist. In one experiment, for example, participants were quicker to shoot a non-Black target dressed in Muslim garb (a turban or hijab) than a target not so dressed (Unkelbach et al., 2008). This was especially true when the "Muslim" target was depicted as a male (i.e., wearing a turban) rather than a female (i.e., wearing a hijab).

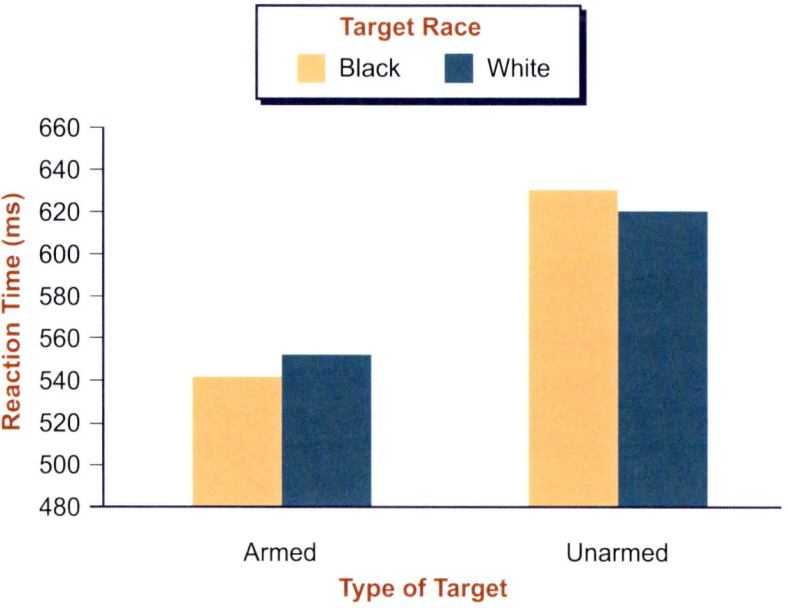

FIGURE 4.3

Reaction times to shoot armed or unarmed Black or White suspects.
Based on data from Correll et al. (2002).

The automatic activation of stereotypes has been characterized as being a normal part of our cognitive toolboxes that improves the efficiency of our cognitive lives (Sherman, 2001). However, as we have seen, this increased efficiency isn't always a good thing. Can this predisposition toward automatic activation of stereotypes be countered? Fortunately, the answer is yes. Automatic stereotypes can be inhibited under a variety of conditions (Sassenberg & Moskowitz, 2005), including thinking of a counter-stereotypic image or if stereotype activation is perceived to threaten one's self-esteem. Sassenberg and Moskowitz suggest that it is possible to train a person to inhibit automatic activation of stereotypes on a general level so that a wide variety of automatic stereotypes can be inhibited, not just specific ones.

Sassenberg and Moskowitz (2005) investigated the impact of inducing participants to "think different" when it comes to members of minority groups. Thinking different means "one has a mindset in which one is avoiding the typical associations with those groups—one's stereotypes" (p. 507). In their first experiment, Sassenberg and Moskowitz had participants adopt one of two mindsets. The first mindset was a "creative mindset" in which participants were told to think of two or three times that they were creative. The second mindset was a "thoughtful mindset" in which participants were told to think of two or three times they behaved in a thoughtful way. After doing this, all participants completed a stereotype activation task. Sassenberg and Moskowitz found that stereotypes were inhibited when the "creative mindset" was activated, but not when the "thoughtful mindset" was activated. By encouraging participants to think creatively, the researchers were able to inhibit the activation of automatic stereotypes about African Americans. Sassenberg and Moskowitz suggest that encouraging people to "think differently" can help them inhibit a wide range of automatically activated stereotypes.

The "shooter bias" just discussed also can be modified with some work (Plant & Peruche, 2005). Plant and Peruche found that police officers showed the shooter bias during early trials with a computer game that presented armed or unarmed Black or White suspects. However, after a number of trials, the bias was reduced. The average number of errors of shooting at an unarmed suspect was different for Blacks and Whites during early trials, but not during late trials. During the early trials the officers were more likely to shoot at an unarmed Black suspect than an unarmed White suspect. During the later trials the rate of error was equivalent for the unarmed Black and White suspects.

Thus, training can attenuate the shooter bias; however, research suggests that the training must contain specific elements, or it can enhance shooter bias (Sim et al., 2013). Training

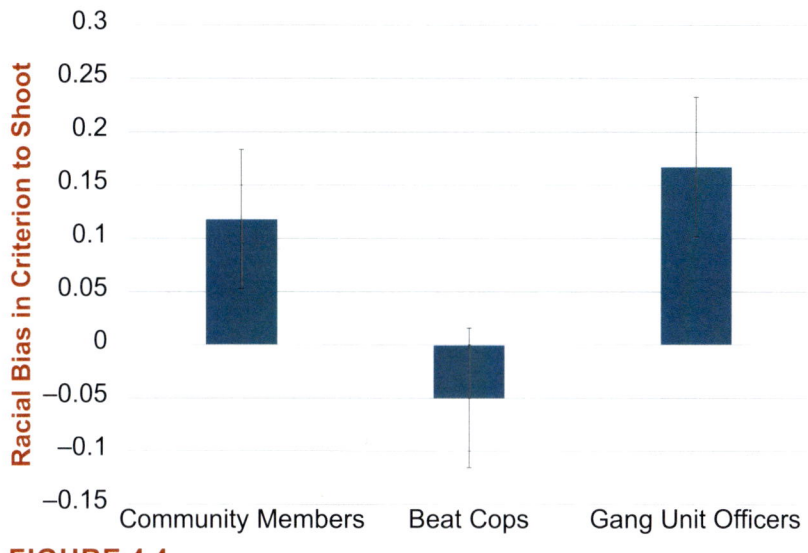

FIGURE 4.4

Racial bias in criterion to shoot as a function of participant sample.
Based on data from Sim et al. (2013).

only reduces shooter bias when the race of the shooter is not a relevant diagnostic piece of information. In the Plant and Peruche (2005) study, when officers "played the game," they saw an equal number of armed Whites and Blacks. Thus, race was not a factor that helped them decide to shoot or not to shoot. Because race was not diagnostic, the officers learned to ignore it, and their bias was reduced. But what if the training was manipulated so that race was related to whether the suspect was armed? Sim and colleagues (2013) found that when the training task reinforced the Black-dangerousness stereotype (i.e., where Black targets were disproportionally likely to be armed and White targets were disproportionately likely to be unarmed), the training did not eliminate the shooter bias but actually slightly increased the bias. In a subsequent study, Sim and colleagues (2013) found a similar pattern in the shooter paradigm with respect to "beat cops" and police officers who work in special gang units (see Figure 4.4). Beat cops work a particular neighborhood and encounter a diverse set of people. The one thing these people have in common is that they are usually not dangerous. Thus, a beat cop's experiences on the job tend to be inconsistent with the Black-dangerousness stereotype. In contrast, the daily experiences of police officers who work in special gang units tend to reinforce the Black-dangerousness stereotype. That is, the gangs they are in contact with are often composed of minorities. Sims and colleagues found that bias on the shooter task was reduced for beat cops as compared to general community members. However, this reduction in bias was not present for police officers who work in special gang units.

Even when the training environment is inconsistent with the Black-dangerousness stereotype, there are still limiting conditions. As you have learned in previous chapters, we tend to process information in one of two ways: automatic and controlled processing. It appears that counter-stereotypical training reduces bias by altering the focus of our attention. We stop attending to race because it is not a diagnostic piece of information. However, this altering of our attention and information processing appears to require effort and cognitive resources. Thus, it is a controlled process. When people are put under a cognitive load (given another distracting task), the gains in bias reduction from training are lost (Singh et al., 2020). The bias reduction that results from training appears to be the result of resource-intensive, effortful processing, and when those cognitive resources are not available, people resort to relying on their stereotypes once again.

Stereotype Accuracy and Malleability

Historically, social psychologists have characterized stereotypes as inaccurate and rigid (not easily changed). Is it, in fact, true that these two characterizations are true? In this section, we will explore this question. As a preview, let's just say that there is mounting evidence that these characterizations are not wholly accurate. It turns out that some aspects of stereotypes (but not all) are accurate. Also, stereotypes are malleable (can be changed) to some degree. We will start by reviewing the issue of stereotype accuracy.

The issue of stereotype accuracy has been addressed by Judd and Park (1993). They suggested several technical standards against which the accuracy of a stereotype can be measured. For example, consider the notion that Germans are efficient. One standard that Judd and Park suggested to measure the accuracy of that stereotype is to find data that answers the questions: Are Germans in reality more or less efficient than the stereotype? Is the group attribute (efficiency) exaggerated? Of course, to apply these standards, we need some objective data about groups. We need to know how groups truly behave with respect to various characteristics. For some attributes, say, kindness or sensitivity, it is probably impossible to obtain such information. For others, there may be readily available data.

Whether stereotypes are accurate or not depends on the definition for stereotypes that one adopts. According to Jussim et al. (2005), social psychologists have focused on the irrational and inaccurate nature of social stereotypes. Jussim et al. note that if one defines stereotypes in terms of inaccuracy, then we can only consider inaccurate beliefs about a group to be stereotypes. Jussim et al. favor a definition of a stereotype that is more "agnostic" and simply defines stereotypes in terms of the beliefs that comprise them. So, for example, we can empirically assess whether beliefs about groups match what is actually true of those groups. Therefore, we can assess the stereotype that women are worse at math than men by comparing women and men on the results of math assessments (e.g., the SAT). We can also test the belief that Jews are rich by comparing the relative wealth of Jews against that of other groups (Jussim et al., 2005).

Using the more "agnostic" and neutral definition of accuracy, research shows that many, but not all, beliefs about groups are accurate. For example, in one experiment Diekman et al. (2001) asked students on a college campus about the political attitudes of men and women (e.g., abortion, health care, defense spending) and then compared those beliefs against the actual political attitudes of men and women. Diekman et al. found a moderate degree of accuracy between the beliefs of the college students and the actual political attitudes of men and women. They also found that the college students were more accurate about the attitudes of women than men. In another study, assessments of women's performance on 12 cognitive tasks matched actual performance on those tasks. Interestingly, participants had a tendency to underestimate performance (Halpern et al., 2011). This effect has also been found for ethnic differences. Ashton and Esses (1994) found that students made fairly accurate estimates of the academic performance (and relative rankings) of the academic performance of ethnic minorities in Canada. Coupled with a number of other areas in which beliefs about a group match actual characteristics reported by Jussim (Jussim, 2015; Jussim et al., 2005), it appears that beliefs relating to stereotypes are fairly accurate.

Is it important to know if a stereotype is accurate? Technically it is, because many of the earlier definitions of stereotypes assume that inaccuracy is part of the definition of the concept (Stangor & Lange, 1994). Most stereotypes are unjustified generalizations; that is, they are not accurate. But, even if they are accurate, stereotypes still have a damaging effect on our perception of others. None of us would wish to be judged as an individual by the worst examples of the group(s) to which we belong.

Now, let's look at the malleability of stereotypes. There is considerable evidence, reviewed below, that overt forms of prejudice have decreased in recent years. Does this extend to stereotypes? Research in this area shows that stereotypes are malleable under certain conditions, and not all stereotypes are equally malleable. In one study, implicit and explicit stereotypes were compared before and after the 2008 presidential election. The results showed that although a change occurred in implicit stereotypes about Blacks after the election of Barack Obama, no significant change occurred in explicit stereotypes (Bernstein et al., 2010). Why was there no appreciable reduction in explicit stereotypes? Remember, explicit stereotypes are under conscious control. As such, individuals go through "mental gymnastics" to preserve consciously mediated beliefs. For example, a person could consider Obama an exception to the general stereotype of Blacks. Another strategy is to subtype the individual who deviates from an established stereotype (Richards & Hewstone, 2001). So, for Barack Obama, a person creates a subcategory of Blacks to include examples who show counter-stereotypical traits. A person can also use subgrouping, which involves organizing groups of individuals according to their similarities and differences. Within a subgroup can be individuals who disconfirm and confirm social stereotypes (Richards & Hewstone, 2001). Interestingly, the strategy adopted (subtyping versus subgrouping) has a different effect on a stereotype. According to Richards and Hewstone, subtyping helps preserve the stereotype, and subgrouping caused differentiation of the stereotype. With subgrouping, the person is likely to end up with a more differentiated view of members of a stereotyped group, with the negative traits making up the stereotype being applied to fewer members of the group.

The idea that automatic stereotypes are malleable is confirmed in other studies. One study found that women exposed to counter-stereotypical models showed a reduction in automatically activated gender stereotypes of women (Dasgupta & Asgari, 2004). Exposure to diversity information also reduces implicit (and explicit) stereotypes (Rudman et al., 2001). However, the effect of exposure to counter-stereotypical information or images has its limits. For example, exposing someone to a successful business woman leads to reductions in implicit stereotypes of women in a business context, but not in a domestic context (Hugenberg et al., 2010). The amount of implicit stereotype reduction also depends on culture and the type of intervention used to reduce the stereotype (Lenton et al., 2009). A meta-analysis by Lenton et al. shows that the impact of an intervention is larger in the United States than it is in Europe. They also found that stereotype reduction achieved using exposure to counter-stereotypic information is more effective than strategies encouraging individuals to suppress stereotypes.

Implicit but not explicit stereotypes of Blacks changed after Barack Obama's successful campaign in 2008.
Source: Steve Adamson/Shutterstock.

Stereotypes as Judgmental Heuristics

Another way that implicit stereotypes manifest themselves is by acting as *judgmental heuristics* (Bodenhauser & Wyer, 1985). For example, if a person commits a crime that is stereotype consistent (compared to one that is not stereotype consistent), observers assign a higher penalty, recall fewer facts about the case, and use stereotype-based information to make a judgment (Bodenhauser & Wyer, 1985). Generally, when a negative behavior is stereotype consistent, observers attribute the negative behavior to internal, stable characteristics. Consequently, the crime or behavior is seen as an enduring character flaw likely to lead to the behavior again.

This effect of using stereotype-consistent information to make judgments is especially likely to occur when we are faced with a difficult cognitive task. Recall from Chapter 3 that many of us are cognitive misers, and we look for the path of least resistance when using information to make a decision. When faced with a situation in which we have both stereotype-consistent and stereotype-inconsistent information about a person, more stereotype-consistent information than inconsistent information is likely to be recalled (Macrae et al., 1993). As Macrae and colleagues suggested, "when the information-processing gets tough, stereotypes (as heuristic structures) get going" (p. 79).

There are also individual differences in the extent to which stereotypes are formed and used. Levy et al. (1998) suggested that individuals use implicit theories to make judgments about others. That is, individuals use their past experience to form a theory about what members of other groups are like. According to Levy and colleagues, there are two types of implicit theories: *entity theories* and *incremental theories*. Entity theorists adhere to the idea that another person's traits are fixed and will not vary according to the situation. Incremental theorists do not see traits as fixed. Rather, they see them as having the ability to change over time and situations (Levy et al., 1998). A central question addressed by Levy and colleagues was whether entity and incremental theorists would differ in their predisposition to form and use stereotypes. Based on the results of five experiments, Levy and colleagues concluded that compared to incremental theorists, entity theorists:

- Were more likely to use stereotypes.
- Were more likely to agree strongly with stereotypes.
- Were more likely to see stereotypes as representing inborn, inherent group differences.
- Tended to make more extreme judgments based on little information about the characteristics of members of a stereotyped group.
- Perceived a stereotyped group as having less intramember diversity.
- Were more likely to form stereotypes.

In addition to the cognitive functions of stereotypes, there is also an emotional component (Jussim et al., 1995). According to Jussim and colleagues, once you stereotype a person, you attach a label to that person that is used to evaluate and judge members of that person's group. Typically, a label attached to a stereotyped group is negative. This negative label generates negative affect and mediates judgments of members of the stereotyped group. Jussim and colleagues pointed out that this emotional component of a stereotype is more important in judging others than is the cognitive function (information storage and categorization) of the stereotype.

Discrimination

discrimination Overt behavior—often negatively directed toward a particular group and often tied to prejudicial attitudes—which involves behaving in different ways toward members of different groups.

Discrimination is the behavioral component accompanying prejudice. Discrimination occurs when members of a particular group are subjected to behaviors that are different from the behaviors directed at other groups. For example, if members of a certain racial group are denied housing in a neighborhood open to other groups, that group is being discriminated against. Discrimination takes many forms. For example, it was not uncommon in the 19th through mid-20th centuries to see job advertisements that said "Irish need not apply" or "Jews need not apply." It was also fairly common practice to restrict access to public places, such as beaches, for Jews and Blacks. And in the U.S. South, there were separate bathroom facilities, drinking fountains, and schools, and minorities were denied service at certain businesses. This separation of people based on racial, ethnic, religious, or gender groups is discrimination.

It is important to point out that discrimination often is a product of prejudice. Negative attitudes and assumptions about people based on their group affiliation have historically been at the root of prejudice. So, it is clear that many instances of discrimination can be traced directly to underlying prejudicial attitudes. However, discrimination can occur even in the absence of underlying prejudice. Consider the following example, based on Simpson's Paradox. Two departments in the same company offer to hire for new positions (Plous, 2016), with both receiving the same number of applicants. Suppose that Department 1 offers jobs to 10% of its applicants and Department 2 offers to 5%. Further, the two departments offer an equal number of jobs to White and Black candidates. At the department level, there is no discrimination in hiring. However, when the job offerings are combined and reported at the company level, discrimination appears to be occurring, even though there is no actual discrimination (see Plous, 2016, for a detailed explanation of this example). Additionally, just like prejudice and stereotyping, discrimination can be positive or negative. Most of the previous examples describe instances of negative discrimination (e.g., denying a person a job because of their race or ethnicity). However, there are times when we may give a person a job or some other benefit just because of their group membership. For example, an employer may give preference to an applicant because the applicant was in the same sorority as the employer in college. These positive forms of discrimination are often the result of positive prejudices that give us an overly optimistic view of a person.

The Persistence and Recurrence of Prejudice and Stereotypes

Throughout history, members of *majority* groups (those in power) have held stereotypical images of members of *minority* groups (those not in power). These images supported prejudicial feelings, discriminatory behavior, and even wide-scale violence directed against minority group members.

History teaches us that stereotypes and prejudicial attitudes are quite enduring. For example, some stereotypes of Jews and Africans are hundreds of years old. Prejudice appears to be an integral part of human existence. However, stereotypes and feelings may change, albeit slowly, as the context of our feelings toward other groups changes. For example, during and just after World War II, Americans had negative feelings toward the Japanese. For roughly the next 70 years, the two countries were at peace and had a harmonious relationship. This was rooted in the fact that the postwar American occupation of Japan (1945–1951) was benign. The Americans helped the Japanese rebuild their war-shattered factories, and the Japanese began to compete in world markets. But in the difficult economic times of the 1980s and early 1990s, many of the beliefs that characterized Japanese-American relations during World War II reemerged, although in somewhat modified form. Compared to how Japanese view Americans, Americans tend to see Japanese as more competitive, hardworking, prejudiced, and crafty (see Figure 4.5). Japanese have a slight tendency to see Americans as undereducated, lazy, and not terribly hard working. Americans see Japanese as unfair, arrogant, and overdisciplined, as grinds who do nothing but work hard because of their conformity to group values (Weisman, 1991). Japanese, for their part, see Americans as arrogant and lacking in racial purity, morality, and dedication (Weisman, 1991). The stereotypes on both sides have been altered and transformed by the passage of time, but like short skirts and wide ties, they tend to recycle. The periodicity of stereotypes suggests that they are based more on external factors such as economics and competition than on any stable characteristics of the group being categorized.

It is interesting to note that stereotypes and the cues used to categorize individuals change over time. Some historians of the ancient Mediterranean suggest that there was a time

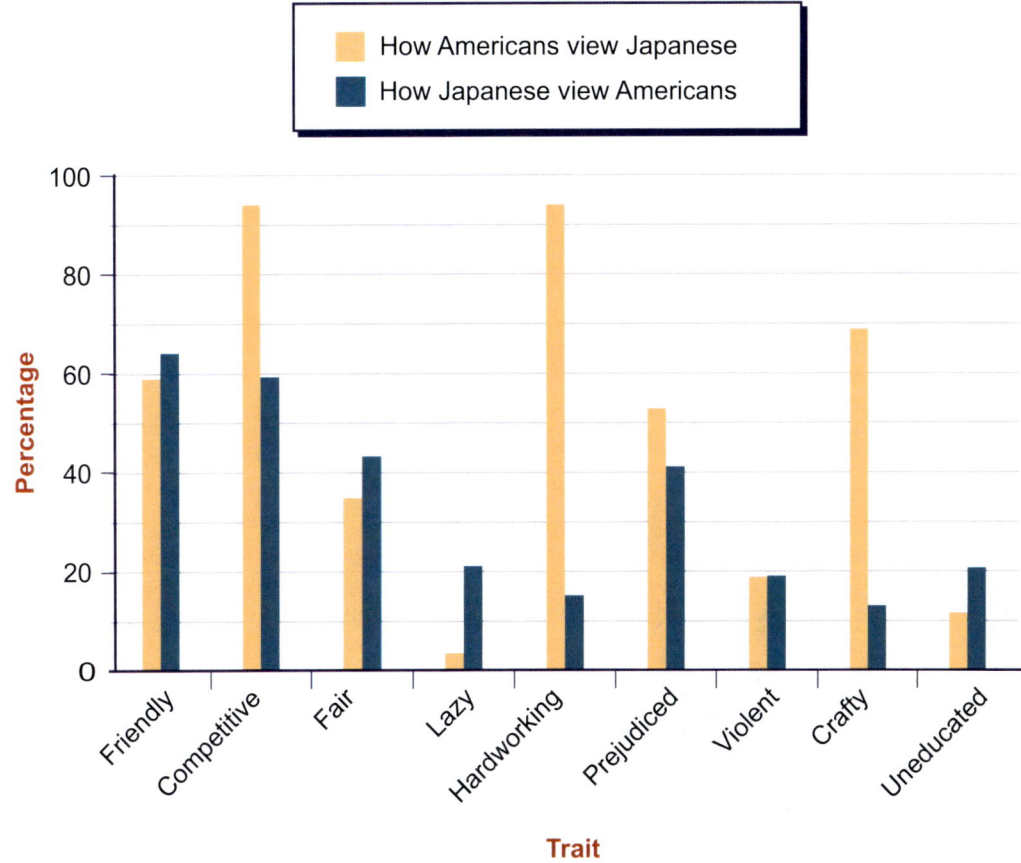

FIGURE 4.5

How the Americans and Japanese view one another. Both Americans and Japanese hold stereotypical views of the other group.

Based on data from a 1992 Times/CNN poll, cited in Holland (1992).

before color prejudice. The initial encounter of Black Africans and White Mediterraneans is the oldest chapter in the chronicle of Black–White relations. Snowden (1983) traced the images of Africans as seen by Mediterraneans from the Egyptians to Roman mercenaries. Mediterraneans knew that these Black soldiers came from a powerful independent African state, Nubia, located in what today would be southern Egypt and northern Sudan. Nubians appear to have played an important role in the formation of Egyptian civilization (Wilford, 1992). Positive images of Africans appear in the artwork and writings of ancient Mediterranean peoples (Snowden, 1983)

The first encounters between Blacks and Whites were encounters between equals. The Africans were respected for their military skill and their political and cultural sophistication. Slavery existed in the ancient world but was not tied to skin color; anyone captured in war might be enslaved, whether White or Black (Snowden, 1983). Prejudice, stereotyping, and discrimination existed too. Athenians may not have cared about skin color, but they cared deeply about national origin. Foreigners were excluded from citizenship. Women were also restricted and excluded. Only males above a certain age could be citizens and participate fully in society.

It is not clear when color prejudice came into existence. It may have been with the advent of the African–New World slave trade in the 16th century. Whenever it began, it is likely that race and prejudice were not linked until some real power or status differences arose between groups. Although slavery in the ancient world was not based exclusively on skin color, slaves were almost always of a different ethnic group, national origin, religion, or political unit than their owners. In the next sections, we explore the causes of prejudice, focusing first on its roots in personality and social life and then on its roots in human cognitive functioning.

Study Break

The previous sections defined three related processes: prejudice, stereotypes, and discrimination. Before you begin the next section, answer the following questions:

1. What is the definition of prejudice, and why is it important to define it from a scientific perspective?
2. What is a stereotype, and what does one contain?
3. What is the difference between implicit and explicit stereotypes?
4. What is discrimination, and how does it relate to prejudice?

authoritarianism
A personality characteristic that relates to a person's unquestioned acceptance of and respect for authority.

With an authoritarian personality, individuals are prejudiced against all groups perceived to be different from themselves. Members of hate groups such as the Ku Klux Klan most likely have authoritarian personalities.
Source: Jon Rehg/Shutterstock.

Individual Differences and Prejudice: Personality and Gender

What are the causes of prejudice? In addressing this question, social psychologists have looked not only at our mental apparatus, our inclination to categorize, but also at characteristics of the individual. Is there such a thing as a prejudiced personality? Are men or women more prone to prejudice? We explore the answers to these questions in this section.

Social psychologists and sociologists have long suspected a relationship between personality characteristics and prejudice. One important personality dimension relating to prejudice, stereotyping, and discrimination is **authoritarianism**. Authoritarianism is a personality characteristic that relates to unquestioned acceptance of and respect for authority. Authoritarian individuals tend to identify closely with those in authority and also tend to be prejudiced.

The Authoritarian Personality

In the late 1940s, Adorno and other psychologists at the University of California at Berkeley studied people who might have been the prototypes of Eric Cartman (a character on the popular TV show *South Park*)—individuals who wanted different ethnic groups to be suppressed and degraded, preferably by an all-powerful government or state. Eric Cartman embodies many of the characteristics of the **authoritarian personality**, which is characterized by submissive feelings toward authority; rigid, unchangeable beliefs; and racism and sexism (Adorno et al., 1950).

> **authoritarian personality**
> A personality dimension characterized by submissive feelings toward authority, rigid and unchangeable beliefs, and a tendency toward prejudicial attitudes.

Motivated by the tragedy of the murder of millions of Jews and other Eastern Europeans by the Nazis, Adorno and his colleagues (1950) conducted a massive study of the relationship between the authoritarian personality and the Nazi policy of *genocide*, the killing of an entire race or group of people. They speculated that the individuals who carried out the policy of mass murder were of a personality type that predisposed them to do whatever an authority figure ordered, no matter how vicious or monstrous.

The massive study produced by the Berkeley researchers, known as *The Authoritarian Personality*, was driven by the notion that there was a relationship, and interconnectedness, between the way a person was reared and various prejudices he or she later came to hold. The study surmised that prejudiced people were highly *ethnocentric*; that is, they believed in the superiority of their own group or race (Dunbar, 1987). The Berkeley researchers argued that individuals who were ethnocentric were likely to be prejudiced against a whole range of ethnic, racial, and religious groups in their culture. They found this to be true, that such people were indeed prejudiced against many or all groups that were different from themselves. A person who was anti-color tended to be anti-Semitic as well. These people seemed to embody a prejudiced personality type, the authoritarian personality.

The Berkeley researchers discovered that authoritarians had a particularly rigid and punishing upbringing. They were raised in homes in which children were not allowed to express any feelings or opinions except those considered correct by their parents and other authority figures. People in authority were not to be questioned and, in fact, were to be idolized. Children handled pent-up feelings of hostility toward these suppressive parents by becoming a kind of island, warding these feelings off by inventing very strict categories and standards. They became impatient with uncertainty and ambiguity and came to prefer clear-cut and simple answers. Authoritarians had very firm categories: This was good; that was bad. Any groups that violated their notions of right and wrong were rejected.

This rigid upbringing engendered frustration and a strong concealed rage, which could be expressed only against those less powerful. These children learned that those in authority had the power to do as they wished. If the authoritarian obtained power over someone, the suppressed rage came out in full fury. Authoritarians were at the feet of those in power and at the throats of those less powerful. The suppressed rage was usually expressed against a *scapegoat*, a relatively powerless person or group, and tended to occur most often during times of frustration, such as during an economic slump.

There is also evidence that parental attitudes relate to a child's implicit and explicit prejudice (Sinclair et al., 2005). Sinclair et al. had parents of fifth and sixth graders complete a racial attitudes measure. The children completed measures of strength of identification with the parent and tests of implicit and explicit prejudice. The results showed that parental prejudice was significantly related to the child's implicit prejudice when the child's identification with the parent was high. So, it is children who have a strong desire to identify (take on the parent's characteristics) with the parent who are most likely to show implicit prejudice. A similar effect was found when the child's explicit prejudice was considered. When the child identified strongly with the parent, the parent's prejudice was positively associated with the child's explicit prejudice. This effect was the opposite for children who did not closely identify with the parents, perhaps indicating a rejection of parental prejudice among this latter group of children.

The authoritarian personality, the individual who is prejudiced against all groups perceived to be different, may gravitate toward hate groups. On July 2, 1999, Benjamin Smith went on a drive-by shooting rampage that killed two and injured several others. Smith took his own life while being chased by police. Smith had a history of prejudicial attitudes and acts. Smith came under the influence of the philosophy of Matt Hale, who became the leader of the World Church in 1996. Hale's philosophy was that the White race was the elite race in the world and that members of any other races or ethnic groups (which he called "inferior mud races") were the enemy. Smith himself believed that Whites should take up arms against those inferior races. The early research on prejudice, then, emphasized the role of irrational emotions and thoughts that were part and parcel of the prejudiced personality. These irrational emotions, simmered in a pot of suppressed rage, were the stuff of prejudice, discrimination, and eventually, intergroup violence. The violence was usually set off by frustration, particularly when resources, such as jobs, were scarce.

Political Orientation, Authoritarianism, and Prejudice

The search for personality correlates of prejudice has extended to investigations of whether one's political ideology relates to prejudice. Altemeyer (1981) developed an updated version of the older authoritarianism scale, which measured *right-wing authoritarianism* (RWA). Although the scale was not intended to focus specifically on right-wing ideology and prejudice, research has found that political conservatives score higher on the RWA measure than liberals or moderates. RWA is characterized by a high degree of submission to legitimate authorities (authoritarian submission), aggressiveness directed against groups believed to be sanctioned by established authority (authoritarian aggression), and adherence to social conventions endorsed by society or authority figures (conventionalism) (Altemeyer, 1994). Generally, people high in RWA tend to be prejudiced against a wide variety of groups, including feminists (Duncan et al., 1997), lesbians and gay men (Whitley & Lee, 2000), Native Americans (Altemeyer, 1998), immigrants (Quinton et al., 1996), and overweight people (Crandall, 1994).

It is interesting to note that RWA appears to relate to the threat posed by groups (e.g., racial, sexual orientation) rather than the individuals making up those groups (Rios, 2013). Kimberly Rios did an interesting experiment in which participants could express prejudice against either "homosexuals" or against "gays and lesbians." She found that high-RWA individuals expressed greater prejudice toward a person labeled as "homosexual" than when labeled as "gay and lesbian." Low-RWA participants expressed lower levels of prejudice, regardless of the label used. Rios suggests that high-RWA individuals perceive homosexuals (but to a lesser extent, gays and lesbians) as a threat to their values as heterosexuals. She also suggests that the label "homosexual" is more likely than "gays and lesbians" to highlight differences between the social categories of homosexual and heterosexual. Both of these processes are involved in the effect she observed.

Attempts to establish a link between a left-wing, liberal political ideology and prejudice have met with mixed success. Initially, researchers attempted to measure left-wing authoritarianism (LWA) (e.g., Altemeyer, 1996). It proved much more difficult to pin down exactly what characterized an LWA person and to establish a link with prejudice. However, research indicates that prejudice exists on the left wing of the political spectrum. For example, Yancy (2010) found that politically liberal participants expressed less warmth for religious fundamentalists than politically conservative participants. In another study, liberal participants made internal attributions for the misconduct of Marines and police accused of committing a crime; whereas conservative participants made external attributions. This is a reversal of the usual pattern of attributions made for wrongdoing where conservatives make internal attributions and liberals external attributions for wrongdoing of minority members. Generally, individuals on both ends of the political spectrum show the most positive feelings toward members of groups that align with their ideology (Brandt et al., 2014). Brandt et al. summarize this effect within their *ideological-conflict hypothesis,* which states that "conservatives and liberals will be similarly intolerant against social groups whose values and beliefs are inconsistent with their own" (p. 28). Brandt et al. report research findings in support of this hypothesis. For example, they report research results showing that compared to a liberal target, liberal students show a greater willingness to discriminate, more political intolerance, and less liking. The converse was true for conservative participants and a liberal target.

Other evidence indicates that prejudice and intolerance exist on the liberal end of the political spectrum as well as on the right end. LaVasseur (1997) developed a measure of LWA and investigated whether LWA related to how participants performed on a simulated jury task. LaVasseur found that LWAs showed a bias in favor of a low-status defendant, recommending a less severe sentence than for a higher-status defendant. Chambers et al. (2012) had liberal and conservative participants evaluate targets that varied in race (Black or White) and political ideology (liberal or conservative). Chambers et al. found that participants of either political ideology rated Black targets equally positively. However, participant ideology was affected by targets' political ideology. Liberal participants rated liberal targets more favorably than conservative targets. The reverse was true for conservative participants. In another study in which participants completed a left-wing belief scale (LWB) and measures of warmth toward members of various groups (Jews, Chinese, Christians), participants with a liberal belief system showed prejudice against all three groups (Miller et al., 2012). Conway et al. (2018), using a methodology very similar to that of the previous study, also found a positive correlation between LWA and prejudice against religious minorities. Finally, Inbar and Lammers (2012) found that social psychologists (a primarily liberal group) expressed willingness to discriminate against conservative colleagues in hiring and paper review decisions. The more liberal the social psychologist, the more likely he or she was to discriminate.

Summing up. The research on political ideology and prejudice shows that prejudice exists on both ends of the political spectrum. Researchers have focused more on the right wing of the political spectrum, mainly because it is easier to identify individuals with RWA than to identify LWAs. However, a body of research shows that, although you have to look harder, there is bias and prejudice on the left wing of the political spectrum.

Social Dominance Orientation

Another personality dimension that has been associated with prejudicial attitudes is **social dominance orientation (SDO)**. A social dominance orientation is defined as "the extent to which one desires that one's in-group dominate or be superior to out-groups" (Pratto, Sidanius et al., 1994, p. 742). In other words, individuals with a high SDO would like to see their group (e.g., racial or ethnic group) be in a dominant position over other groups.

Research shows that one's SDO correlates with prejudicial attitudes. For example, Pratto et al. (1994) found that a high SDO score was related to anti-Black and anti-Arab prejudice. The higher the SDO score, the more prejudice was manifested. In a later study SDO was found to correlate with a wide range of prejudices, including a generalized prejudice, and specific prejudices against individuals with a same-sex orientation and the mentally disabled. SDO was also found to correlate with racism and sexism (Ekehammar, Akrami et al., 2004). Additionally, SDO is negatively correlated with stereotype change (Tausch & Hewstone, 2010). Tausch and Hewstone found that high SDO individuals were less likely to modify a stereotype in the face of moderately counter-stereotypic information than were low SDO individuals.

In another experiment (Kemmelmeier, 2005), White mock jurors were asked to judge a criminal case in which the defendant was Black or White. The results showed no difference in how the White participants judged the Black or White defendant. However, participants who scored high on a measure of social dominance showed more bias against the Black defendant than participants who scored low on the social dominance measure. In fact, low SDO individuals showed a bias in favor of the Black defendant.

Interestingly, SDO is related to the perceived status differences between the groups (Levin, 2004). For example, Levin found that among American and Irish participants, individuals with high SDO scores saw a greater status difference between their group and an out-group (e.g., Irish Catholics versus Irish Protestants). In other words, an Irish Catholic person with a high SDO score saw a greater status difference between Irish Catholics and Irish Protestants than an Irish Catholic with a lower SDO score. A similar, but nonsignificant, trend was found for Israeli participants.

If we consider the SDO dimension along with authoritarianism, we can identify a pattern identifying highly prejudiced individuals. In a study by Altemeyer (2004), participants completed measures of SDO and right-wing authoritarianism (RWA). Altemeyer found modest correlations between the SDO scale and RWA scale and prejudice when the scales were considered separately. However, when the two scales were considered

social dominance orientation (SDO) Desire to have one's in-group in a position of dominance or superiority to out-groups. High social dominance orientation is correlated with higher levels of prejudice.

together (i.e., identifying individuals who were high on both SDO and RWA), stronger correlations were found with prejudice. Altemeyer concluded that individuals with both SDO and RWA are among the most prejudiced people you will find. Fortunately, Altemeyer points out, there are very few such individuals.

There is also evidence that SDO and RWA may relate differently to different forms of prejudice. Whitley (1999), for example, found that an SDO orientation was related to stereotyping, negative emotion, and negative attitudes directed toward African Americans and individuals with a same-sex orientation. However, RWA was related to negative stereotypes and emotion directed at individuals with a same-sex orientation, but not African Americans. In fact, RWA was related to positive emotions concerning African Americans.

Openness to New Experience and Agreeableness

A popular model of personality is the "big five" model of personality (McCrae & Costa, 1987). According to this approach, there are five dimensions underlying personality: extraversion/introversion, agreeableness, conscientiousness, neuroticism, and openness to experience and culture. As we shall see, two of these dimensions (agreeableness and openness to experience) relate to prejudice. Briefly, agreeableness is a "friendliness dimension" including characteristics such as altruism, trust, and willingness to give support to others (Gerow & Bordens, 2015). Openness to experience includes curiosity, imagination, and creativity, along with a willingness to try new things and divergent thinking (Flynn, 2005).

Ekehammar and Akrami (2003) evaluated participants on the big five personality dimensions and measures of classic prejudice (overt, old-fashioned prejudice) and modern prejudice (prejudice expressed in subtle ways). Ekehammar and Akrami found that two of the big five personality dimensions correlated significantly with prejudice: agreeableness and openness to experience. Those participants high on the agreeableness and openness dimensions showed less prejudice. The remaining three dimensions did not correlate significantly with prejudice.

In another study, Flynn (2005) explored more fully the relationship between openness to experience and prejudice. The results of her three experiments confirmed that individuals who had high scores on openness to experience displayed less prejudice. For example, individuals who are open to new experiences rated a Black interviewee as more intelligent, responsible, and honest than individuals who are less open to new experiences.

Other Personality Correlates of Prejudice

Social psychologists have also looked at whether there is a prejudiced personality (Dunbar, 1995; Gough, 1951). Gough developed a prejudiced scale (PR scale) using items from the Minnesota Multiphasic Personality Inventory. Gough (1951) reported that the PR scale correlated with anti-Semitic attitudes among Midwestern high school students.

Dunbar (1995) administered the PR scale and two other measures of racism to White and Asian American students. He also administered a measure of anti-Semitism to see if the PR scale still correlated with prejudiced attitudes. Dunbar found that Asian Americans had higher scores on both the PR scale and the measure of anti-Semitism than did Whites, indicating greater anti-Semitism among Asians than Whites. However, the only significant relationships on the PR scale between anti-Semitic and racist attitudes were among the White participants.

Another personality factor that relates to prejudice is the *dark personality triad*, which comprises narcissism (excessive self-love), Machiavellianism (manipulating and exploiting others), and psychopathy (callus affect, interpersonal manipulation, erratic lifestyles, and antisocial behavior) (Hodson et al., 2009). Hodson et al. found that all three components of the triad were correlated with prejudice. Further, they found that the dark personality triad/prejudice relationship was mediated by two other factors: SDO and perception of intergroup threat (see Figure 4.6). Individuals exhibiting the dark triad also had SDO scores and tended to see out-groups as posing a threat. This, in turn, increased prejudice toward members of out-groups.

FIGURE 4.6

Illustration showing how SDO and intergroup threat mediate the relationship between the dark personality triad and prejudice.
Based on data from Hodson et al. (2009).

Gender and Prejudice

Another characteristic relating to prejudice is gender. Research shows that men tend to be higher than women on SDO (Dambrun et al., 2004; Pratto et al., 1994). This gender difference appears to be rooted in different patterns of social identity orientations among men and women. Although men and women show in-group identification at equivalent levels (i.e., men identifying with the male in-group and women identifying with the female in-group), men more strongly identify with the male in-group than women with the female in-group (Dambrun et al., 2004).

Research on the relationship between gender and prejudice has concentrated on male and female attitudes toward gays and lesbians. Generally, males tend to have more negative attitudes toward gays and lesbians than women (Kite, 1984; Kite & Whitley, 1998). Do men and women view gay men and lesbians differently? There is evidence that males have more negative attitudes toward gay men than toward lesbians (Gentry, 1987; Kite, 1984; Kite & Whitley, 1998). The findings for females are less clear. Kite and Whitley, for example, reported that women tend not to make distinctions between gay men and lesbians. Other research, however, shows that females show more negative attitudes toward lesbians than gay men (Gentry, 1987; Kite, 1984). Interestingly, male (but not female) prejudice against homosexuals is mediated by SDO. Males with higher levels of SDO show more homophobia than males with lower levels (MacInnis & Hodson, 2015).

Baker and Fishbein (1998) investigated the development of gay and lesbian prejudice among a sample of seventh, ninth, and 11th graders. They found that males tended to be more prejudiced against gays and lesbians than females were, and male participants showed greater prejudice against gay males than against lesbians. Prejudice against gays and lesbians increased between seventh and ninth grade for both males and females; however, between the ninth and 11th grades, gay prejudice *decreased* for female participants, whereas it *increased* for male participants. Baker and Fishbein suggested that the increase in male antigay prejudice may be rooted in the male's increased defensive reactions to intimate relationships.

The same gender difference emerges when transphobia is assessed: Men show more transphobia than women (Tebbe & Moradi, 2012). Tebbe and Moradi report that although men and women differ in the level of transphobia, the same factors relate to prejudice for both genders (e.g., prejudice against gays and lesbians, SDO, and traditional gender roles). In another study, transphobia was positively correlated with RWA, religious fundamentalism, and hostile sexism (Nagoshi et al., 2008). Nagoshi et al. found that for men transphobia and homophobia were closely related. When homophobia was controlled for, the relationship between RWA, religious fundamentalism, and transphobia disappeared. For women, controlling for homophobia did not affect the relationship between RWA, religious fundamentalism, and transphobia.

A central question emerging from this research is whether there are gender differences in other forms of prejudice (racism, anti-Semitism, etc.).

Prejudice against gays and lesbians increased between seventh and ninth grade for both males and female.
Source: TheVisualsYouNeed/Shutterstock.

One study, for example, confirmed that males show more ethnic prejudice than females on measures concerning friendship and allowing an ethnic minority to live in one's neighborhood. Males and females did not differ when interethnic intimate relations were considered (Hoxter & Lester, 1994). There is relatively little research in this area, and clearly, more is needed to investigate the relationship between gender and prejudice for a wide range of prejudices.

Study Break

One way to explain prejudice is to point to personality and other individual differences, such as gender. Before you begin the next section, answer the following questions:

1. What is the authoritarian personality, and how does it relate to prejudice?
2. How is social dominance orientation defined, and how does it relate to prejudice?
3. How do the big five personality dimensions and the dark personality triad relate to prejudice?
4. What is the relationship between gender and prejudice?

The Social Roots of Prejudice

The research on personality and gender provides an important piece of the puzzle of prejudice, stereotyping, and discrimination. However, it is only one piece. Prejudice, stereotyping, and discrimination are far too complex and prevalent to be explained by personality-based factors. Prejudice occurs in a social context, and another piece of the puzzle can be found in the evolution of feelings that form the basis of relations between dominant and other groups in a particular society.

To explore the social roots of prejudice, let's consider the situation of African Americans in the United States. During the years before the Civil War, Black slaves were considered the property of White slave owners, and this arrangement was justified by the notion that Blacks were in some way less human than Whites. Their degraded condition was used as proof of their inferiority.

In 1863, in the middle of the Civil War, President Lincoln issued the Emancipation Proclamation, setting slaves free. But abolition did little to end prejudice and negative attitudes toward Blacks. The Massachusetts 54th Regiment, for example, was an all-Black Union Army unit—led by an all-White officer corps. Blacks were said to lack the ability to lead; thus no Black officers were allowed. Because of these stereotypes and prejudices, members of the 54th were also paid less than their White counterparts in other regiments. Initially also, they were not allowed in combat roles; they were used instead for manual labor, such as for building roads.

At one time the overt expression of prejudice was more acceptable than it is today. Social changes have made it unacceptable to express prejudices openly, but they still exist.
Source: Everette Historical/Shutterstock.

Despite prejudice, some Blacks did rise to positions of prominence. Frederick Douglass, who escaped from slavery and became a leader and spokesperson for African Americans, was instrumental in convincing President Lincoln to issue the Emancipation Proclamation and to allow Black troops to fight in the Civil War. Toward the end of the war, over 100,000 Black troops were fighting for the North, and some historians maintain that without these troops, the result of the Civil War may have been different.

Over the course of the next hundred years, African Americans made strides in improving their economic and social status. The U.S. Supreme Court ruled in *Brown v. Board of Education* that segregated (separate but equal) schools violated the Constitution and mandated that schools and other public facilities be integrated. Since then, the feelings of White Americans toward African Americans have become more positive (Goleman, 1991). For example, between 1972 and 2008 fewer Whites reported a belief that Blacks are less intelligent or less hardworking than Whites. There was also a drop in endorsements of various forms of discrimination (Wihbey, 2014). This change in attitude and behavior reflects the importance of social norms in influencing and regulating the expression of feelings and beliefs.

Although definite improvements have been made in racial attitudes over the past decades, an undercurrent of negativity still exists. For example, a sizeable percentage (28%) of Whites in 2008 still endorsed the idea that a person should be able to discriminate based on race when selling his or her house (Wihbey, 2014). Additionally, a similarly sizeable percentage (36%) of White students oppose affirmative action on campus (compared to only 8% of Black and 15% of Hispanic students) (Pew Research Center, 2014). It may be that these still-negative views are related to the idea that Whites may pay lip service to the idea of equality. They perceive African Americans as being *both* disadvantaged by the system *and* deviant. In other words, White Americans are aware that African Americans may have gotten a raw deal, but they also see them as responsible for their own plight (Katz et al., 1986). Remember that the human tendency to attribute behavior to internal rather than external causes makes it more likely that people will ascribe the reasons for achievement or lack of it to the character of an individual or group.

A racial divide also still exists on a range of issues. According to a 2019 Pew Research Organization survey, Blacks and Whites differ in their perceptions of how fairly Blacks are treated. As shown in Figure 4.7, Blacks are more likely than Whites to say that Blacks are treated less fairly by the police, the criminal justice system, in hiring, when applying

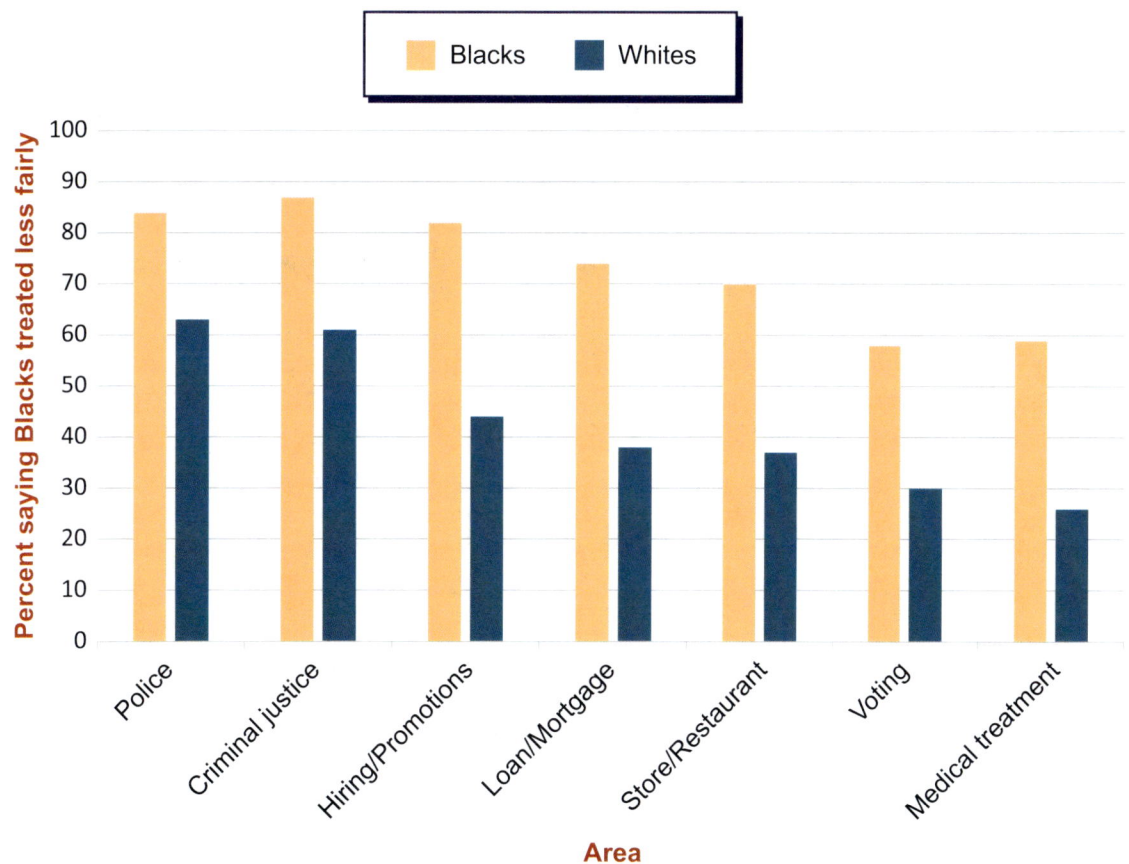

FIGURE 4.7

Percentage of Blacks and Whites saying that Blacks are treated less fairly than Whites.
Based on data from the Pew Research Organization (2019b).

for a loan, in stores or restaurants, when voting, and when seeking medical treatment. The divide was also shown in 2015 over the Confederate flag controversy. In this case, Blacks were more likely than Whites to say that it was right to take down the flag, that retailers should stop selling the flag, that it is fine for the government to ban the flag, and that the flag is a symbol of hate (Newseum Institute, 2015; Pew Research Center, 2015).

Given the importance of racial issues in U.S. history and given the way people process information in a categorical and automatic way, some observers assume that racist feelings are the rule for Americans (Gaertner & Dovidio, 1986).

Explicit and Implicit Prejudice

Although racist beliefs and prejudicial attitudes still exist, they have certainly become less prevalent than they once were. For example, according to data from the General Social Survey (1999), attitudes toward Blacks improved between 1972 and 1996. Figure 4.8 shows some of the data from this survey. As shown in Figure 4.8, responses reflecting more positive racial attitudes can be seen in questions concerning whether Whites have a right to keep Blacks out of their neighborhood ("Blacks out"), whether one would vote for a Black presidential candidate ("Black president"), whether Whites would send their children to a school where more than 50% of the children were Black ("Send children"), whether they would vote to change a rule excluding Blacks from a social club ("Change rule"), and whether they would support a law preventing housing discrimination ("Housing law"). These trends have maintained themselves or improved since 1996 (Moberg et al., 2019). For example, Moberg et al. reported that

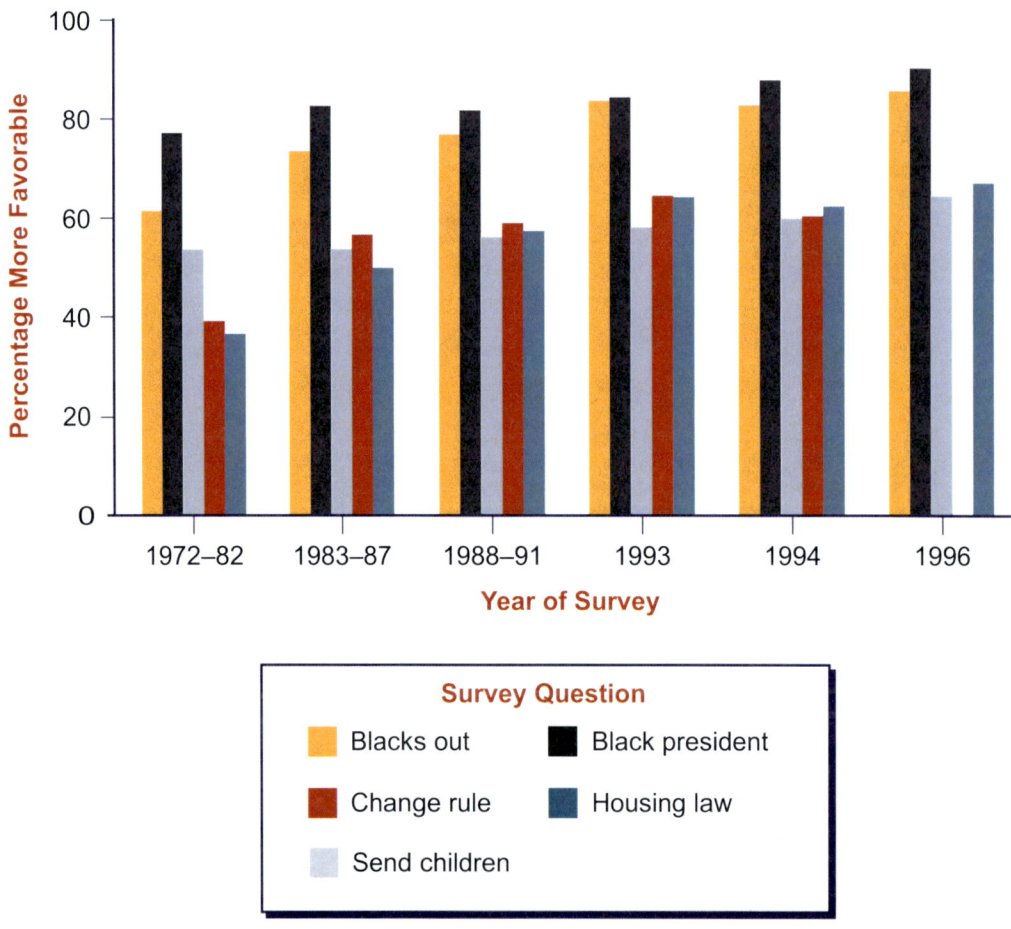

FIGURE 4.8

The changing face of racial prejudice. Between the years 1972 and 1996, Whites have shown more favorable attitudes toward Blacks.

Based on data from General Social Survey (1999).

support for interracial marriage increased from around 45% in 1995 to over 80% by 2015. At the same time, opposition by Whites against laws preventing interracial marriages remained at just under 80% between 1995 and 2015. Despite these actual improvements, there is a general perception that race relations have gotten worse lately. A Gallup poll (2021c) tracking trends in race relations showed that among both Blacks and Whites, the percentage of people saying that race relations are somewhat or very good declined from the early 2000s to 2020. For example, in 2001, 70% of Blacks and 62% of Whites characterized race relations as very or somewhat good. This dropped to 36% of Blacks and 46% of Whites by 2020. These overt forms of racism that have been significantly reduced in the past decades represent *explicit prejudice*. Changes in laws, social norms, and greater sensitivity toward diversity issues have led to a significant reduction in expression of explicit prejudice. However, this does not mean that prejudice has gone away entirely.

Even though we are no longer as likely to express prejudice overtly and blatantly discriminate, prejudice still exists on a more subtle level. As we noted earlier stereotypes exist on both an explicit (overt, conscious) and implicit (unconscious, automatic) level. Prejudice also exists on both levels. *Implicit prejudice*, like implicit stereotypes, is under control of unconscious, automatic processes and is expressed in much more subtle ways than explicit prejudice. Although a person may claim to be nonprejudiced and would never discriminate, subtle signs of prejudice and discrimination may still be detected, when we look carefully for it.

One of the most prominent measures of implicit prejudice is the IAT (Greenwald et al., 1998). Greenwald and colleagues developed the IAT to solve a specific problem. The problem was that self-report explicit measures of prejudice were becoming less useful (as discussed previously). By the late 1990s, researchers had noticed that people seemed unwilling to express their prejudices because of the strong societal norms that had developed against such expressions. They wanted to develop a measure that could tap into people's attitudes that was immune to social desirability. The IAT was developed as such a measure. Hundreds of studies have been published using the IAT, most of which are concentrated on measuring implicit prejudice. The IAT measures how fast and accurately participants can categorize various stimuli. For example, in the standard race, IAT participants are asked to use the "e" and "i" keys on a keyboard to categorize faces and words across a series of trials. In the first series, participants are asked to identify White and Black faces that appear on the screen. In the second series, participants are asked to identify a series of words that flash on the screen that are unambiguously good or bad (i.e., *terrific* vs. *horrific*). Following the initial rounds, the categories are mixed. In these subsequent series, the participants must identify both faces and words using just the "e" and "i" key. Now the "e" key would be pressed when presented with either a Black face or a good word, and the "i" key would be pressed when presented with either a White face or a bad word. In a final series, these categories are reversed. Black faces are now paired with bad words and White faces are paired with good words. A person's level of implicit prejudice is based on how much easier it is for them to do the task (i.e., faster with fewer mistakes) when White faces are paired with good than when Black faces are paired with good.

Although there have been hundreds of published studies using the IAT, and it has even made its way into popular culture, appearing on an episode of *King of the Hill*, the IAT has come under attack. Particularly concerning to researchers are the psychometric properties and validity of the IAT. Schimmack (2021) demonstrated that only about 20% of the variance in the race IAT reflects racial preferences and that most of the differences in race IATs reflect measurement errors. Furthermore, meta-analytic reviews of the literature have revealed that the race IAT is a relatively weak predictor of behaviors and other types of prejudice measures (Greenwald et al., 2009; Kurdi et al., 2019; Oswald et al., 2013). This is particularly disheartening because the main reason the IAT was developed was because of the low predictive validity of traditional self-report measures. Meissner and colleagues (2019) have proposed various solutions that may help to address these issues, from restructuring the order of the trials in the IAT to changing how the scores are computed mathematically. The field of social psychology is in the middle of reexamining many of the implicit processes documented in the last 20 years, and the IAT is one of those. As you know from Chapter 1, this is how the process of science works. It is self-correcting: As we learn more about a phenomenon, we revisit how we thought about it in the past and adjust our understanding.

Beyond the IAT, there have been other attempts to develop more subtle, unobtrusive measures of prejudice. One such measure of prejudice is known as **aversive racism**. Aversive racism involves people who truly believe they are unprejudiced, who want to do the right thing but, in fact, feel very uneasy and uncomfortable in the presence of someone from a different racial group (Gaertner & Dovidio, 1986). When they are with members of other groups, they smile too much, are overly friendly, and are sometimes very fearful. These feelings do not lead the aversive racist to behave in a negative way toward members of other groups; rather, they lead him or her to avoid them. Let's look at an example of how aversive racism can be manifested.

Imagine that you are a personnel manager who has to decide between two equally qualified job candidates, one of whom is Black and one White. Would you discriminate against the Black candidate? Most of us, thankfully, would say "no." What would happen, however, if people were given this choice without knowing that they were overtly choosing between a Black or White candidate? This is what was done by Dovidio and Gaertner (2000) in an imaginative experiment. Participants in this experiment were given a resume from a Black or a White job candidate who varied in the strength of his qualifications (strong, weak, or unclear). In this experiment, a participant judged only one job candidate (e.g., a White candidate with strong credentials) and did not choose between a White or Black candidate. Participants had to decide whether to recommend the job candidate for the job. The results of this experiment (combining results from two decades) are shown in Figure 4.9. As you can see, when the candidates had strong or weak qualifications, there was no significant difference between the Black and White candidates. A qualified candidate was recommended and an unqualified candidate rejected, regardless of race. If anything, the Black candidate was given a slight edge. However, when the qualifications were unclear, the White candidate was recommended significantly more often than the Black candidate. In this case, participants displayed an implicit prejudice against the Black candidate.

Modern racism is another form of subtle prejudice marked by an uncertainty in feeling and action toward people from different racial groups (McConahay, 1986). Modern racists moderate their responses to individuals from different racial groups to avoid showing

aversive racism Racism involving a person who believes he or she is unprejudiced, but feels uneasy and uncomfortable in the presence of someone from a different racial group.

modern racism Subtle racial prejudice, expressed in a less open manner than is traditional overt racial prejudice and characterized by an uncertainty in feeling and action toward minorities.

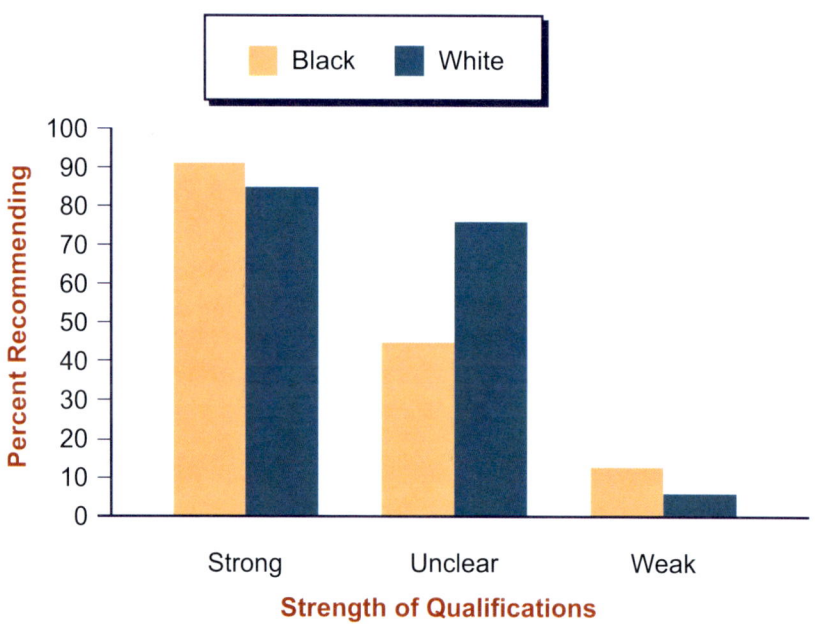

FIGURE 4.9

Percentage of participants recommending a job candidate based on race and strength of the candidate's qualifications.

Based on data from Dovidio and Gaertner (2000).

obvious prejudice; they express racism but in a less open manner than was formerly common. Modern racists would say that yes, racism is a bad thing and a thing of the past; still, it is a fact that African Americans "are pushing too hard, too fast, and into places where they are not wanted" (p. 93).

McConahay devised a scale to measure modern racism. In contrast to older scales, the modern racism scale presents items in a less racially charged manner. For example, an item from the modern racism scale might ask participants whether African Americans have received more economically than they deserve. On an old-fashioned scale, an item might ask how much you would mind if an African American family moved in next door to you. According to McConahay, modern racists would be more likely to be detected with the less racist items on an old-fashioned scale. McConahay found that the modern racism scale is sensitive enough to pick up more subtle differences in an individual's racial feelings and behaviors than the older scales. The modern racism scale tends to reveal a more elusive and indirect form of racism than the older scales.

In one of McConahay's experiments, participants (all of whom were White) were asked to play the role of a personnel director of a major company. All had taken a version of the modern racism scale. The "personnel director" received a resume of a graduating college senior who was a very ordinary job candidate. The race of the candidate was manipulated: for half of the participants, a photograph of an African American was attached, and for the other half, a photograph of a White person was attached.

Another variable was added to the experiment in addition to the race of the applicant. Half of each group of participants were told that there were no other qualified candidates for the job. This was called the *no anchor* condition, because the personnel directors had no basis for judgment, no other candidate against which to evaluate the ordinary candidate. The other half of each group saw the resumes of two other candidates, both White, who were far superior to the ordinary candidate, White or African American. This was called the *anchor* condition, because the personnel directors now had a basis for comparison.

Personnel directors in all four groups were asked to make a decision about the candidate on a scale ranging from "definitely would hire" to "definitely would not hire." McConahay's findings revealed that individuals who have high scores on the modern racism scale (indicating that they are prejudiced) do not treat White candidates any differently than their nonprejudiced counterparts.

Whether they scored 0 or 25 or somewhere in between on the scale, all participants rated the White candidates in both the anchor and the no-anchor condition in a similar way. Participants with low scores (near 0) rated White candidates about the same, whereas high scorers (closer to 25) rated the White no-anchor candidate a little higher than the White anchor candidate.

More interesting are the ratings of African American candidates. For nonprejudiced participants, African Americans, anchored or not, were rated precisely the same. But there was a very large difference between candidates for the prejudiced participants. An unanchored African American candidate was absolutely dismissed, whereas the anchored African American candidate, compared to more qualified Whites, was given the highest rating.

Why these differences? Recall that modern racists are rather uncertain about how to feel or act in situations with members of different racial or ethnic groups. They particularly do not want to discriminate when others will find out about it and can label what they did as racist (Donnerstein & Donnerstein, 1973). To reject a very ordinary African American candidate when there were no other candidates probably would not be seen as prejudiced, because the candidate was not qualified. Note how much more favorably the modern racist judged the White candidate in the same anchor circumstances.

But when there is a chance that his or her behavior might be termed racist, the modern racist overvalues African Americans. This is seen when there were qualified White candidates (anchor condition). The modern racist goes out of his or her way to appear unprejudiced and therefore gives the ordinary African American candidate the highest rating. Participants who scored low on the modern racism scale felt confident about how to feel and act in racial situations. People from different racial groups do not make them uncomfortable; they "call it like they see it" (Hass et al., 1991).

The concept of modern racism is not without its critics. Some suggest that it is illogical to equate opposition to an African American candidate or affirmative action programs with racism (Sykes, 1992). Other critics point out that modern racism researchers have not adequately defined and measured modern racism (Tetlock, 1986). They also point out that high correlations exist (ranging from about r = .6 to .7) between old-fashioned racism and modern racism. That is, if a person is a modern racist, he or she also is likely to be an old-fashioned racist. According to these critics, there simply may not be two forms of racism.

The fact is that race is a complex issue and contains many facets. In the past, according to public opinion surveys, Whites were essentially either favorable or unfavorable to the cause of African Americans. But racial feelings are more subtle now. Someone might be against busing of schoolchildren but not opposed to having an African American neighbor (Sniderman & Piazza, 1994). Additionally, a person's racial attitudes are often affected by his or her politics. Individuals who have favorable attitudes toward African Americans but who perceive affirmative action policies to be unfair may come to dislike African Americans as a consequence (Sniderman & Piazza, 1994).

Changing Social Norms

What accounts for the changes we see in the expression of overt, explicit racist sentiments and for the appearance of modern racism? Our society, primarily through its laws, has made the obvious expression of racism undesirable. Over the past 30 years, social norms have increasingly dictated the acceptance of members of different racial and ethnic groups into mainstream society. Overt racism has become socially unacceptable. But for many individuals, deeply held racist sentiments remain unchanged. Their racism has been driven underground by society's expectations and standards.

Because of changed social norms, charges of prejudice and discrimination are taken seriously by those against whom they are made. In 2002, the Cracker Barrel restaurant chain was sued by the Justice Department on behalf of several patrons who claimed they had been discriminated against because of their race. In the lawsuit, the plaintiffs alleged that Cracker Barrel showed a pattern of discrimination against African Americans by refusing them

Changing social norms no longer allow overt discrimination against Blacks in restaurants. There was a time before the civil rights era when Blacks were not allowed to sit at "Whites Only" lunch counters.
Source: Everette Historical/Shutterstock.

service, allowing White waitstaffers not to serve Blacks, seating Black patrons in a segregated area, and making Black patrons wait longer than White patrons to be seated (NAACP, 2002). In 2004 Cracker Barrel settled the suit with the Justice Department. Cracker Barrel agreed to overhaul its manager and employee training (Litchblau, 2004).

Despite such cases, hate messages still proliferate on the internet. It is nearly impossible to get an accurate count of the number of hate sites on the internet. Various researchers have studied how hate groups such as Neo-Nazis, Skinheads, and the Ku Klux Klan are using the internet to spread their message of hate (Adams & Roscigno, 2005; Chau & Xu, 2007; Douglas et al., 2005; McNamee et al., 2010). The internet has allowed hate speech and the advocacy of violence against minorities to cross national boundaries. For example, on one Web site, one can peruse a variety of racist cartoons and purchase hate-related products. Hate-based "educational materials" are also easily obtained on the internet. One program called *The Jew Rats* portrays Jews as rats who are indoctrinated to hate others and take over the world. Racist video games are also readily available. One game called *Bloodbath in Niggeria* involves shooting caricatures of Africans who pop up in huts. Yet another called *Border Patrol* allows gamers to shoot illegal Mexican immigrants running across the U.S. border. In addition, the internet provides a medium that can help hate groups organize more easily. In addition to organizing on a local level, hate sites can now easily link hate groups across land and ocean, making the spread of hate and prejudice much easier.

There is evidence that attitudes, although not necessarily behavior, toward specific groups have become more positive. As noted previously, a drop has occurred in the past decades in the belief by Whites that Blacks lack intelligence and motivation for hard work. In this case, social norms in favor of greater equality seem to be holding. Finally, it is worth noting that social norms operate on a number of levels simultaneously. It is generally true that societal norms have turned against the overt expression of prejudice, and this has reduced prejudice. However, norms also operate on a more "local" level. We not only are affected by societal norms but are also influenced by the norms of those closest to us (e.g., family and friends). If it is normative within your immediate group of family and friends not to be prejudiced or express prejudices, then odds are you won't. If, however, your immediate family and friends are prejudiced and express prejudices, then you will probably do the same. This effect was shown in an experiment in which pro-gay rights and anti-gay rights participants participated in a group discussion with others who did not agree with them (actually confederates of the researchers). The results showed that anti-gay rights participants showed more hesitancy to express their views than pro-gay rights participants (Walker et al., 2015). In a social context in which the expression of prejudice is not allowed, we are less likely to express it than if in a context where it is accepted (Zitek & Hebl, 2007). Generally, we strive to be "good group" members, which often means following the norms established by that group, whether positive or negative (Crandall et al., 2002).

Study Break

Social psychologists have investigated how social factors relate to prejudice, stereotype, and discrimination. Before you go on to the next section, answer the following questions:

1. How have social norms relating to prejudice and discrimination changed over the past decades, and how have those changes changed the expression of prejudice?
2. What are implicit and explicit prejudice, and how do they relate to behavior?
3. What are modern and aversive racism, and how do they relate to behavior?
4. How do social norms affect the expression of prejudice?

The Cognitive Roots of Prejudice: From Categories to Stereotypes

Cognitive social psychologists believe that one of the best ways to understand how stereotypes form and persist is to look at how humans process information. As we saw in

Chapters 2 and 3, human beings tend to be cognitive misers, preferring the least effortful means of processing social information (Taylor, 1981). We have a limited capacity to deal with social information and therefore can deal with only relatively small amounts at any one time (Fiske & Taylor, 1991).

Given these limitations, people try to simplify problems by using shortcuts, primarily involving category-based processes (Bodenhausen & Wyer, 1985; Brewer, 1988). In other words, it is easier to pay attention to the group to which someone belongs than to the individual traits of the person. It takes less effort and less time for someone to use category-based (group-based) information than to try to deal with people on an individual basis (Macrae et al., 1994). Research studies of the cognitive miser demonstrate that when people's ability or motivation to process information is diminished, they tend to fall back on available stereotypes. For example, in one study, when a juror's task was complex, he or she recalled more negative things about a defendant if the defendant was Hispanic than if the defendant did not belong to an identifiable group. When the juror's task was simple, no differences in judgment were found between a Hispanic and a non-Hispanic defendant (Bodenhausen & Lichtenstein, 1987). When the situation gets more complicated, individuals tend to rely on these stereotypes.

Individuals are more likely to fall back on stereotypes when they are not at the peak of their cognitive abilities (Bodenhausen, 1990; Zhang & Peng, 2020). Bodenhausen tested participants to determine if they were "night people"—individuals who function better in the evening and at night—or "day people"—individuals who function better in the morning. He then had participants make judgments about a student's misconduct. Sometimes the student was described in nonstereotypic terms (his name was "Robert Garner"), and in other situations he was portrayed as Hispanic ("Roberto Garcia"), as African American, or as an athlete.

The experiment showed that when people are not at their peak (morning people at night or night people in the morning), they tend to solve problems by using stereotypes. As shown in Figure 4.10, morning types relied on the stereotype to judge the student

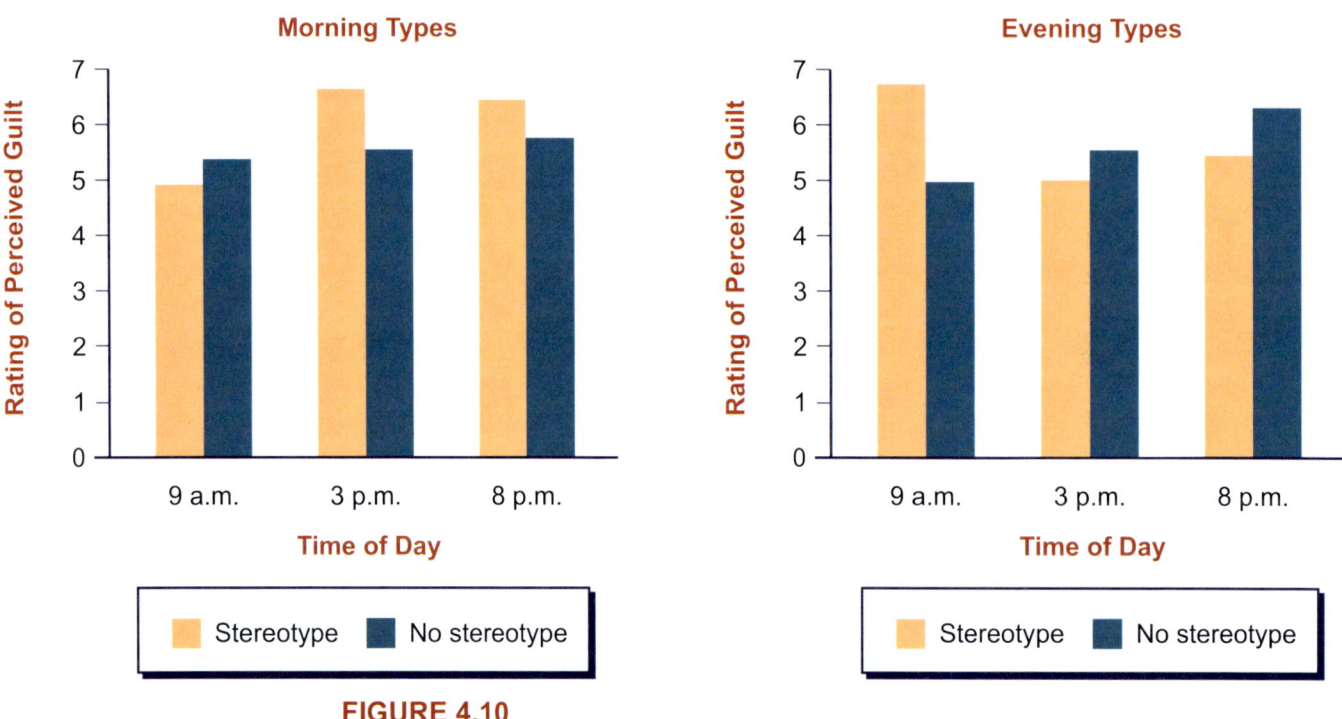

FIGURE 4.10

Ratings of perceived guilt as a function of time of day, personality type, and stereotype activation. When individuals are not at their cognitive peak, they are more likely to rely on stereotypes when making judgments.

Based on data from Bodenhausen (1990).

when presented with the case in the evening; evening types fell back on stereotypes in the morning. These findings suggest that category-based judgments take place when we do not have the capacity, the motivation, or the energy to pay attention to the target, and these lead human beings into a variety of cognitive misconceptions and errors.

Identification with the In-Group

One of the principal cognitive processes common to all human beings seems to be the tendency to categorize people either as belonging to an *in-group* (us) or an *out-group* (them) (Allport, 1954). This tendency has implications beyond simple categorization. We tend to identify with and prefer members of the in-group. We also tend to ascribe more uniquely "human emotions" (e.g., affection, admiration, and pride) to the in-group than the out-group (Leyens et al., 2000). Taken together, these tendencies comprise the **in-group bias**. This tendency to favor the in-group is accompanied by a simultaneous tendency to identify "different" others as belonging to a less favored out-group, which we do not favor.

in-group bias The powerful tendency of humans to favor in-group members over out-group members.

Our tendency to favor the in-group and vilify the out-group is related to the type of emotions we experience about those groups. When we feel good about something that the in-group does or is associated with and feel anger over what the out-group does, then we are most likely to strongly identify with the in-group (Kessler & Hollbach, 2005). So, for example, if our country is associated with something good (e.g., winning an Olympic medal) and another country is associated with something bad (e.g., a judging scandal at the Olympics), we feel the most in-group pride and are likely to strongly identify with the in-group. Conversely, we are less likely to identify with the in-group when it is associated with something bad and the out-group is associated with something good (Kessler & Hollbach, 2005). In other words, we are likely to bask in reflected glory (BIRG) when the in-group does something good and cut off reflected failure (CORF) when the in-group does something bad (Kessler & Hollbach, 2005). This might explain why so many people change attitudes quickly (e.g., about the 2003 Iraq War) when news is bad (CORFing). However, when things are going well (e.g., the early stages of the Iraq War), we experience a sense of national pride and are happy with our BIRGing.

How we perceive and judge members of an out-group depends, at least in part, on how we perceive the in-group. The in-group is normally used as a standard by which the behavior of out-group members is judged (Gawronski et al., 2005). In fact, a contrast effect occurs when in-group and out-group members are compared on the same traits. For example, if members of an in-group perceive that their group possesses a trait, they are likely to perceive that out-group members do not (Gawronski et al., 2005). In short, the way we perceive our own group (the in-group) has a lot to do with how we perceive the out-group.

Henri Tajfel, a social psychologist, studied the phenomenon of in-group favoritism as a way of exploring out-group hostility. He was preoccupied with the issue of genocide, the systematic killing of an entire national or ethnic group. As a survivor of Nazi genocide of European Jews from 1939 to 1945, Tajfel had a personal as well as a professional interest in this issue (Brown, 1986).

Unlike earlier researchers, who emphasized the irrational thoughts and emotions of the prejudiced personality as the source of intergroup violence, Tajfel believed that cognitive processes were involved. He believed that the process of categorizing people into different groups led to loyalty to the in-group, which includes those people one perceives to be similar to oneself in meaningful ways. Inevitably, as in-group solidarity forms, those who are perceived to be different are identified as members of the out-group (Allport, 1954; Billig, 1992).

Tajfel was searching for the minimal social conditions needed for prejudice to emerge. In his experiments with British schoolboys, he found that there was no situation so minimal that some form of in-group solidarity did not take shape. He concluded that the need to favor the in-group was a basic component of human nature. What are the reasons for this powerful bias?

As noted in Chapter 2, we derive important aspects of our self-concepts from our membership in groups (Turner, 1987). These memberships help us establish a sense of positive social identity. Think of what appears to be a fairly inconsequential case of group membership: being a fan of a sports team. When your team wins a big game, you experience a boost, however temporary, to your sense of well-being (by BIRGing). You don't just root for the team; you become part of the team. You say, "We beat the heck out of them." Think for a moment about the celebrations that have taken place in Detroit, New York, Boston, and elsewhere after home teams won professional sports championships. It is almost as if it wasn't the Tigers or the Mets or the Celtics who won, but the fans themselves.

When your team loses the big game, on the other hand, you feel terrible. You're tempted to jump ship. It is hard to read the newspapers or listen to sportscasts the next day. When your team wins, you say, "We won." When your team loses, you say, "They lost" (Cialdini et al., 1975). It appears that both BIRGing and jumping ship serve to protect the individual fan's self-esteem. The team becomes part of the person's identity.

Social Identity Theory

social identity theory (SIT) An assumption that we all need to have a positive self-concept, part of which is conferred on us through identification with certain groups.

Tajfel's (1982) **social identity theory (SIT)** assumes that human beings are motivated to positively evaluate their own groups and value them over other groups, in order to maintain and enhance self-esteem. The group confers on the individual a social identity, that part of a person's self-concept that comes from her membership in social groups and from her emotional connection with those groups (Tajfel, 1981).

Fundamental to social identity theory is the notion of categorizing the other groups, pigeonholing them, by the use of stereotypes—those general beliefs that most people have about members of particular social groups (Turner, 1987). People are motivated to hold negative stereotypes of out-groups; by doing so, they can maintain the superiority of their own group and thereby maintain their positive social (and self) identity.

Generally, any threat to the in-group, whether economic, military, or social, tends to heighten in-group bias. Additionally, anything that makes a person's membership in a group more salient, more noticeable, will increase in-group favoritism. One series of experiments showed that when people were alone, they were likely to judge an out-group member on an individual basis, but when they were made aware of their in-group membership by the presence of other members of their group, they were likely to judge the out-group person solely on the basis of stereotypes of the out-group (Wilder & Shapiro, 1984, 1991). The increase of in-group feelings promoted judgments of other people on the basis of social stereotypes. When group membership gets switched on, as it does, for example, when you are watching the Olympics or voting for a political candidate, then group values and social stereotypes play a larger role in how you react.

Finally, getting people to engage in group-affirmation (focusing on characteristics of one's group) leads to greater attribution of negative traits to an out-group than if you get people to engage in self-affirmation, especially if the in-group is an important one to the person (Ehrlich & Gramzow, 2015).

Self-Categorization Theory

self-categorization theory (SCT) A theory suggesting that people need to reduce uncertainty about whether their perceptions of the world are "correct" and seek affirmation of their beliefs from fellow group members.

Increase in self-esteem as a result of group membership is central to SIT (Grieve & Hogg, 1999). To increase members' self-esteem, the in-group needs to show that it is distinct from other groups in positive ways (Mummenday & Wenzel, 1999). Central to an extension of SIT, **self-categorization theory (SCT)** is the notion that self-categorization is also motivated by the need to reduce uncertainty (Hogg & Mullin, 1999). The basic idea is that people need to feel that their perceptions of the world are correct, and this correctness is defined by people—fellow group members—who are similar to oneself in important ways. In a study by Haslam et al. (1999), when the category Australian was made salient for a group of Australian students, it tended to reduce uncertainty about the characteristics that comprise one's social group. Consequently, it regulated and structured the members' social cognition. This is consistent with SCT. When reminded of their common category or group membership, the Australian students were more likely to agree on what it meant to be Australian.

What are the consequences of uncertainty? Grieve and Hogg (1999) showed that when uncertainty is high (i.e., when group members did not know if their performance was adequate or would be successful in achieving group goals), groups were more likely to downgrade or discriminate against other groups. In other words, uncertainty is a threat. Uncertainty was also accompanied by increased group identification. So threat creates a kind of rally-round-the-flag mentality. Self-categorization theory suggests, then, that only when the world is uncertain does self-categorization lead to discrimination against other groups (Grieve & Hogg, 1999). Self-categorization theory adds a bit of optimism to its parent theory's (SIT) outlook by suggesting that categorization does not always lead to discrimination, and if threat can be managed or alleviated, little discrimination or intergroup antagonism need occur.

A Biological Perspective on the In-Group Bias

Tajfel's research has shown us that the formation of an in-group bias serves basic social and self needs primarily by maintaining personal self-esteem. Some scientists, specifically sociobiologists—scientists who take a biological approach to social behavior—believe that ethnocentrism (the increased valuation of the in-group and the devaluation of out-groups) has a foundation in human biological evolution. They point out that for the longest part of their history, humans lived in small groups ranging from 40 to 100 members (Flohr, 1987). People had to rely on the in-group and gain acceptance by its members; it was the only way to survive. It would make sense, then, that a strong group orientation would be part of our human heritage: Those who lacked this orientation would not have survived to pass their traits on to us.

Sociobiologists also point out that people in all cultures seem to show a naturally occurring *xenophobia,* or fear of strangers. This fear may also be part of our genetic heritage. Because early populations were isolated from one another (Irwin, 1987), people may have used similar physical appearance as a marker of blood relationship (Tonnesmann, 1987). Clearly, there was always the possibility that people who looked different could be a threat to the food supply or other necessities of survival. Sociobiologists argue that it is reasonable to expect that people would be willing to cooperate only with humans of similar appearance and biological heritage and that they would distrust strangers (Barkow, 1980).

In modern times, as Tajfel showed, we still derive much of our identity from group membership; we fear being excluded from groups (Baumeister & Tice, 1990). High respect for our own groups often means a devaluing of other groups. This is not necessarily a big problem until groups have to compete for resources. Because the world does not appear to offer a surplus of resources, competition among groups is inevitable. Of particular interest to sociobiologists is a study by Tajfel (1982) and his coworkers in which it was demonstrated that children show a preference for their own national group long before they have a concept of country or nation. Children ranging in age from 6 to 12 years old were shown photographs of young men and were asked how much they liked those men. Two weeks later, the children were shown the same photographs again. They were also told that some of the men belonged to their nation and others did not. The children had to decide which young men were "theirs" (belonged to their country) and which were not. The researchers found that the children were more likely to assign the photographs they liked to their own nation. Therefore, liking and in-group feelings go together at an age when children cannot really comprehend fully the idea of a nation (Flohr, 1987).

In sum, those who offer a biological perspective on intergroup prejudice say that strong in-group identification can be understood as an evolutionary survival mechanism. We can find examples throughout human history of particular ethnic, racial, and religious groups that have strengthened in-group bonds in response to threats from the dominant group (Eitzen, 1973; Myrdal, 1962). Strengthening of these in-group bonds may help the group survive, but this is only one way of looking at the in-group bias. Acceptance of this notion does not require us to neglect our social psychological theories; it simply gives us some idea of the complexity of the issue (Flohr, 1987).

The Role of Language in Maintaining Bias

Categorization is, generally, an automatic process. It is the first step in the impression formation process. As mentioned earlier, it is not the same as stereotyping and prejudice, but it powerfully affects these other processes. One way in which categorizing can lead to prejudice is through language. The way we sculpt our world via the words and labels we use to describe people connects the category to prejudice. Social psychologist Charles Perdue and his colleagues tested the hypothesis that the use of words describing in-groups and out-groups unconsciously forms our biases and stereotypes (Perdue et al., 1990).

Perdue suggested that the use of collective pronouns—*we, us, ours, they, their, theirs*—is very influential in how we think about people and groups. We use these terms to assign people to in-groups and out-groups. In one study, Perdue and his colleagues showed participants a series of nonsense syllables (*xeh, yof, laj*) paired with pronouns designating in-group or out-group status (*we, they*). Participants were then asked to rate each of the nonsense syllables they had just seen in terms of the pleasantness or unpleasantness of the feelings they evoked. As shown in Figure 4.11, nonsense words paired with in-group pronouns were rated much more favorably than the same nonsense words paired with out-group pronouns or with control stimuli. Out-group pronouns gave negative meaning to previously unencountered and neutral nonsense syllables.

In a second experiment, these investigators demonstrated that in-group and out-group pronouns bias the processing of information about those groups. Participants saw a series of positive- and negative-trait words, such as *helpful, clever, competent, irresponsible, sloppy*, and *irritable*. Now, a positive trait ought to be positive under any circumstances, and the same should hold true for negative traits, wouldn't you agree? *Skillful* is generally positive; *sloppy* is generally negative. But as Figure 4.12 shows, it took participants longer to describe a negative trait as negative when that trait had been associated with an in-group pronoun. Similarly, it took participants longer to describe a positive trait as positive when it had been associated with an out-group pronoun. It took them little time to respond to a positive trait associated with an in-group pronoun and to a negative trait associated with an out-group pronoun.

These findings suggest that we have a nonconscious tendency (after all, the participants were not aware of the associations) to connect in-group labels with positive attributes rather than negative ones and out-group labels with negative attributes rather than positive ones. These associations are so strong that they shape the way we process subsequent information. They also seem to be deep and long lasting, a fact that may help explain why stereotypes remain so tenacious.

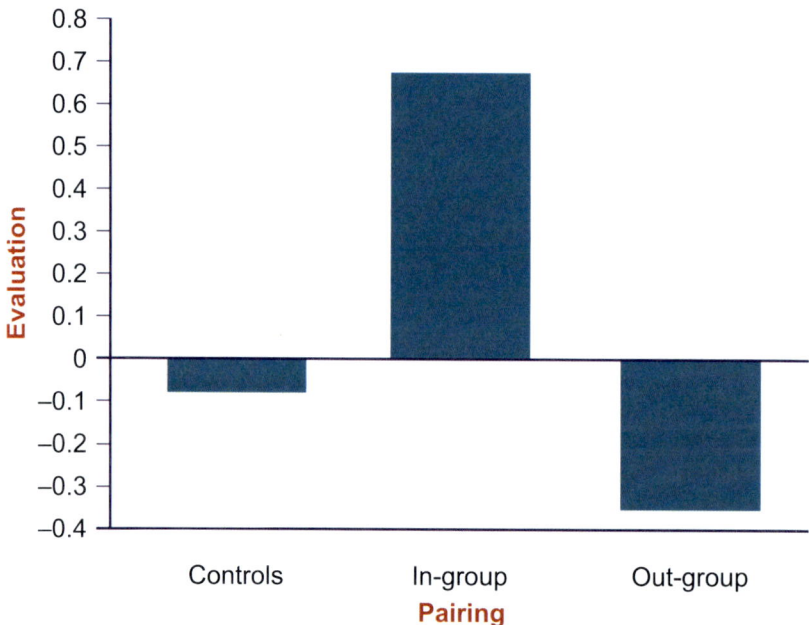

FIGURE 4.11

Standardized ratings of target syllables as a function of pronoun pairing. Syllables paired with in-group pronouns were judged more pleasant than those paired with outgroup pronouns.
Based on Perdue et al. (1990).

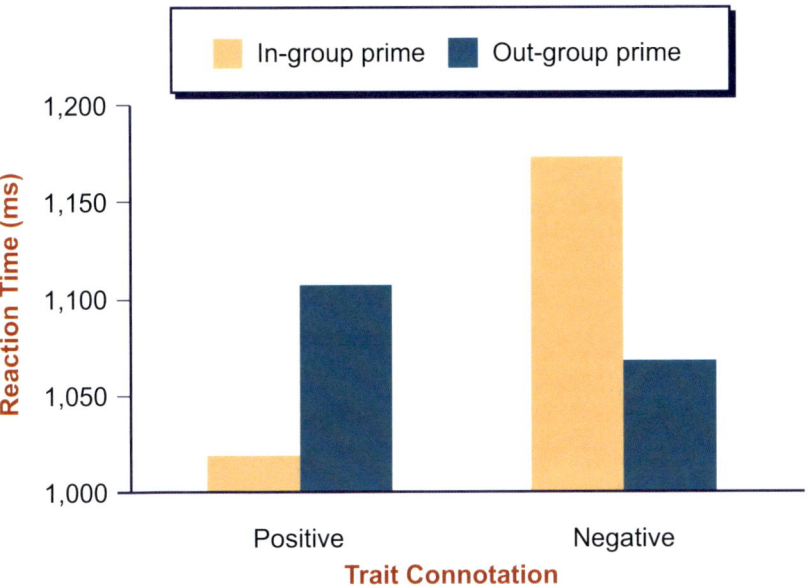

FIGURE 4.12

Reaction times to positive and negative trait descriptors as a function of pronoun type (in-group or out-group). Information processing is affected by in-group and out-group thinking.
Based on Perdue et al. (1990).

System Justification and Prejudice

Social identity theory and self-categorization theory both take the same basic approach to explaining the roots of prejudice. They both assume that a major factor underlying prejudice is the dynamic that develops between in-group solidarity and attitudes toward out-groups. Jost et al. (2004) refer to these approaches as *group justification theories*. Traditionally, social psychologists have emphasized group justification theories when trying to explain stereotyping and prejudice. Jost et al. point out that there is another way to explain stereotyping and prejudice that does not rely on group justification. The alternative approach is known as **system justification theory**. According to system justification theory, prejudice can occur when members of groups justify the existence of social arrangements at the expense of interpersonal and group interests.

From a system justification perspective, stereotyping and prejudice relate to the motivation to maintain existing social order and relationships among groups. Because this motive exists for both members of groups in power (majority groups) and stigmatized groups (minority groups), existing negative stereotypes and prejudices maintain themselves. This tendency to maintain intergroup relations is demonstrated by the fact that oftentimes members of marginalized groups endorse the negative stereotypes about their groups to an even greater extent than do members of the majority group (Sniderman & Piazza, 1993). By endorsing own-group negative stereotypes, the status quo of intergroup perceptions and relations is maintained. Stronger motivations toward system justification are associated with more "stereotypic differentiation" between groups (Jost et al., 2005). Jost et al. (2005) also found that the relationship between system justification beliefs

If a doctor believes that a patient is likely to have a certain disease based on race, the doctor might misdiagnose the patient due to an illusory correlation.
Source: Rocketclips, Inc./Shutterstock.

system justification theory
A theory stating that prejudice can occur when members of groups justify the existence of social arrangements at the expense of interpersonal and group interests.

and stereotyping was found to cut across different cultural groups. Finally, we should note that these system justification processes are stronger on the implicit than explicit level (Essien et al., 2020; Jost et al., 2004).

Illusory Correlations

illusory correlation
An error in judgment about the relationship between two variables in which two unrelated events are believed to covary.

The tendency to associate negative traits with out-groups is explained by one of the fundamental cognitive bases of stereotyping, the illusory correlation. An **illusory correlation** is an error in judgment about the relationship between two variables or, in other words, a belief that two unrelated events covary (are systematically related) (Hamilton & Sherman, 1989). For example, a person may notice that each time he wears his old high school bowling shirt when he goes bowling, he bowls very well. He may come to believe that there is a connection between the two events. Similarly, if you think that members of a minority group are more likely than members of a majority group to have a negative trait, then you perceive a correlation between group membership and behavior relating to that trait (Schaller, 1991).

Sometimes this cognitive bias crops up even among trained professionals. For example, a physician diagnosed a young, married African American woman with chronic pelvic inflammatory disease, an ailment related to a previous history of sexually transmitted disease. This diagnosis was made despite the fact that there was no indication in her medical history that she had ever had such a disease. As it turned out, she actually had endometriosis, a condition unrelated to sexually transmitted diseases *(Time,* June 1, 1992). The physician's beliefs about young Black women, that they are sexually promiscuous, led to a diagnosis consistent with those beliefs. Research supports this anecdote. For example, participants have been found to ascribe different abilities to a girl depending on whether she is portrayed as having a lower or higher socioeconomic-status background (Darley & Gross, 1983).

These examples illustrate the human tendency to overestimate the co-occurrence of pairs of distinctive stimuli (Sherman et al., 1989). In the case of the misdiagnosis, the presence of two distinctive stimuli—a young Black woman and a particular symptom pattern—led the physician to conclude that the woman's disorder was related to her sexual history. The tendency to fall prey to this illusion has been verified in other experiments (Chapman & Chapman, 1967).

The illusory correlation helps explain how stereotypes form. The reasoning goes like this: Minority groups are distinctive because they are encountered relatively infrequently. Negative behavior is also distinctive because it is, in general, encountered less frequently than positive behavior. Because both are distinctive, there is a tendency for people to overestimate the frequency with which they occur together, that is, the frequency with which minority group members do undesirable things (Sherman et al., 1989).

Research shows that if people are presented with information about a majority group and a minority group and these groups are paired with either rare or common traits, people associate the smaller group with the rarer trait (Hamilton & Sherman, 1989). If both a minority and majority group have the same negative trait, say a tendency toward criminal behavior, the negative behavior will be more distinctive when paired with the minority as compared to the majority group. Our cognitive apparatus seems to lead us to make an automatic association between negative behavior and minority group membership.

How many encounters with a minority group member are required for an illusory correlation to form? Common sense would suggest that such correlations would only form after many encounters with minority group members. However, this is not the case. It turns out that an illusory correlation can form after only one encounter with a minority group member (Risen et al., 2007). To demonstrate this, Risen et al. had participants watch a video in which a South Asian or Caucasian student behaved in a "pushy" manner. Next, participants had to form an impression of either a different South Asian or Caucasian person by completing incomplete words. These words could be completed to indicate either pushiness or not (e.g., D _ _ _ nd can be completed as "demand" or "depend). Finally, participants had to select a group of questions to ask either a South Asian or Caucasian in an online interview (some of the questions dealt with pushiness and some did not). Risen et al. found that participants exposed to the pushy South Asian in the video were more like to complete the words in a pushy direction and select more pushy questions than participants exposed to the pushy Caucasian. Participants had formed a "one-shot" illusory correlation after the single exposure to the pushy South Asian student in the video.

Distinctive characteristics are also likely to play a critical role in the formation of category-based responses. In any gathering of people, we pay more attention to those who appear to be different from others, such as a White in an otherwise all-Black group, or a man in an all-woman group. Skin color, gender, and ethnicity are salient characteristics.

One function of automatic evaluation is to point to events that may endanger the perceiver (Pratto & John, 1991). Certainly, sociobiologists would agree with that notion. The human ability to recognize friend from foe, safety from danger, would have fundamental survival value (Ike, 1987). For example, people automatically responded to an angry (salient) face in a happy crowd (Hansen & Hansen, 1988). An angry person among friends is dangerous. Another study demonstrated that individuals automatically turn their attention from a task to words, pictures, or events that might be threatening (Pratte & John, 1991).

Participants attended more rapidly to salient negative traits than to positive ones. This automatic vigilance may lead people to weigh undesirable attributes in those around them differently than positive attributes.

When we encounter other groups, then, it is not surprising that we pay more attention to the bad things about them than the good. Negative social information grabs our attention. This greater attention to negative information may protect us from immediate harm, but it also helps perpetuate stereotypes and may contribute to conflict between groups (Pratto & John, 1991).

From Illusory Correlations to Negative Stereotypes via the Fundamental Attribution Error

The fact that a negative bit of information about a different group has grabbed our attention does not necessarily lead to discrimination against that group. There must be a link between the salience of negative information and prejudiced behavior. The fundamental attribution error—the tendency to overestimate internal attributes and underestimate the effect of the situation—supplies this link and plays a role in the formation of discriminatory stereotypes. This is particularly true when perceivers do not take into account the roles assigned to people. Recall the quiz show study described in Chapter 3 in which participants thought that the quiz show questioners were smarter than the contestants (Ross et al., 1977), even though roles had been randomly assigned.

This confusion between internal dispositions and external roles has led to punishing negative stereotypes of different groups. Let's consider just one example, the experience of the Jews in Europe over the past several hundred years (Ross & Nisbitt, 1991). Historically, Jews had many restrictions imposed on them in the countries where they resided. They were prevented from owning land; they often had to be in certain designated areas; they could not enter politics; and many professions were closed to them.

This exclusion from the greater society left the Jews with two options: either convert to Christianity or maintain their own distinctive culture. Most Jews opted for the latter, living within the walls of the ghetto (in fact, the word *ghetto* is derived from the Venetian word *Gheto*, which referred to a section of the city where iron slag was cooled and Jews were forced to live) assigned to them by the Christian majority and having little to do with non-Jews. Exclusion and persecution strengthened their in-group ties and also led the majority to perceive them as clannish. However, one segment of the Jewish population was highly visible to the mainstream society—the money lenders. Money lending was a profession forbidden to Christians and open to Jews (Ross & Nisbett, 1991). Although it was held in contempt, it was an essential function in national and international business, especially as capitalism began to develop. Jewish money lenders became important behind-the-scenes figures in the affairs of Europe. Thus, the most distinctive members of the group—distinctive for their visibility, their economic success, and their political importance—were invariably money lenders.

The distinctive negative role of money lending, although restricted to only a few Jews, began to be correlated with Jews in general. Jews were also seen as distinctive because of their minority status, their way of life, their unique dress, and their in-group solidarity. All of these characteristics were a function of the situation and roles thrust on the Jews by the majority, but they came to be seen, via the fundamental attribution error, as inherent traits of Jewish people in general. These traits were then used as a justification for discrimination, based on the rationale that Jews were different, clannish, and money grubbing.

Jews have been depicted in negative ways throughout history. For example, in Shakespeare's *The Merchant of Venice,* the Jewish money lender, Shylock, is depicted as a bloodthirsty person who will stop at nothing to extract his pound of flesh for repayment of a defaulted debt. However, do these stereotypes still crop up today in "enlightened" American communities? Movie director Steven Spielberg grew up in New Jersey and Arizona but never experienced anti-Semitism until his family moved to Saratoga, California, during his senior year in high school:

> He encountered kids who would cough the word *Jew* in their hands when they passed him, beat him up, and throw pennies at him in study hall. "It was my six months of personal horror. And to this day I haven't gotten over it nor have I forgiven any of them." (*Newsweek,* December 20, 1993, p. 115)

Jews were not the only group to suffer from majority exclusion and the fundamental attribution error (Ross & Nisbett, 1991). The Armenians in Turkey, the Indians in Uganda, and the Vietnamese boat people were all money middlemen who took on that role because no other positions were open to them. All of these groups suffered terrible fates.

The Confirmation Bias

As you learned in Chapter 3, the *confirmation bias* is the tendency to look for evidence that confirms already existing beliefs. It also involves interpreting new information as confirming preexisting beliefs. People dealing with Jews in the 18th century in Europe or with Armenians in Turkey at the turn of the 20th century found it easy to confirm their expectancies about these groups; perceivers could recall the money lenders, the strange dress, and the different customs. Stereotypes are both self-confirming and resistant to change.

Numerous studies show that stereotypes can influence social interactions in ways that lead to their confirmation. In one study, some participants were told that a person with whom they would soon talk was in psychotherapy; other participants were told nothing about the person (Sibicky & Dovidio, 1986). In actuality, the individuals they talked to were randomly chosen students from basic psychology courses; none were in therapy. After the interviews, participants were asked to evaluate the person with whom they had interacted. Those individuals identified as therapy clients were rated less confident, less attractive, and less likable than the individuals not described as being in therapy.

We can see from this study that once people have a stereotype, they evaluate information within the context of that stereotype. After all, none of the people being interviewed in the experiment was in fact in therapy. The differences between the ratings had to be due to the participants' stereotypical view of what somebody in therapy must be like. Describing a person as being in therapy seems to lead to a negative perception of that person. People who hold negative stereotypes about certain groups may behave so that group members act in a way that confirms the stereotype (Crocker & Major, 1989). The confirmation bias contributes in many instances to self-fulfilling prophecies. If you expect a person to be hostile, your very expectation and the manner in which you behave may bring on that hostility. In the study just described, participants who thought they were interacting with someone in therapy probably held a stereotypical view of all people with psychological problems. It is likely that they behaved in a way that made those individuals uneasy and caused them to act in a less confident manner.

The Out-Group Homogeneity Bias

An initial effect of categorization is that members of the category are thought to be more similar to each other than is the case when people are viewed as individuals. Because we have a fair amount of information about the members of our own group (the in-group), we are able to differentiate among them. But we tend to view members of other groups (out-groups) as being very similar to one another (Wilder, 1986). This phenomenon of perceiving members of the out-group as all alike is called the **out-group homogeneity bias** (Linville et al., 1989).

out-group homogeneity bias The predisposition to see members of an out-group as having similar characteristics or being all alike.

The out-group homogeneity hypothesis was tested in one study involving students from Princeton and Rutgers Universities (Quattrone & Jones, 1980). Participants, who were either Rutgers or Princeton students, saw a videotape of a student supposedly from the other school. The videotaped person had to decide whether he wanted to wait alone or with other people before being a participant in a psychological experiment. The actual participant then had to predict what the average student at the target university (Rutgers for Princeton students and Princeton for Rutgers students) would do in a similar situation.

Would the participants see students at the other university as similar to the student they had viewed? Would they predict that most Princeton students (or Rutgers students) would make the same choice as the Princeton student (or Rutgers student) in the film clip? These questions get at the issue of whether people see out-group members as more similar to one another than to the in-group members. In fact, this is pretty much what the study showed, although there was a greater tendency to stereotype Princeton students than Rutgers students. That seems logical, because it is probably easier to conjure up a stereotype of Princeton student. In general, however, results supported the notion that the out-group homogeneity bias leads us to think that members of out-groups are more similar to one another than to members of in-groups.

A second outcome of out-group homogeneity bias is the assumption that any behavior of an out-group member reflects the characteristics of all group members. If a member of an out-group does something bad, we tend to conclude, "That's the way those people are." In contrast, when an in-group member does something equally negative, we tend to make a dispositional attribution, blaming the person rather than our own in-group for the negative behavior. This has been referred to as the **ultimate attribution error**: We are more likely to give in-group members the benefit of the doubt than out-group members (Pettigrew, 1979).

ultimate attribution error The tendency to give in-group, but not out-group, members the benefit of the doubt for negative behaviors.

Once we construct our categories, we tend to hold on to them tenaciously, which may be both innocent and destructive. It is innocent because the process is likely to be automatic and nonconscious. It is destructive because stereotypes are inaccurate and often damaging; individuals cannot be adequately described by reference to the groups to which they belong.

In previous chapters, we have seen how automatic and controlled processing enter into the social cognition process. Some people use controlled processing to readjust initial impressions of others in instances where new information conflicts with existing categorization (Fiske & Neuberg, 1990; Trope, 1986). Automatic and controlled processing again come into play when we consider how stereotypes are maintained and how prejudiced and nonprejudiced individuals differ.

The Difference Between Prejudiced and Nonprejudiced Individuals

Devine (1989) contends that stereotypes are automatically activated when we encounter a member of a particular social group. According to Devine, some people are able to consciously alter their prejudiced responses, whereas others are not. Devine found that those interested in being nonprejudiced think differently from those who are not. For example, prejudiced individuals are more willing to indulge in negative thoughts and behaviors toward members of different racial and ethnic groups than nonprejudiced individuals. Devine also found that both high- and low-prejudiced Whites hold almost the same stereotypes of African Americans. However, nonprejudiced individuals think those stereotypes are wrong.

Devine also found that the main difference between prejudiced and nonprejudiced Whites was that nonprejudiced Whites are sensitive to and carefully monitor their stereotypes. The nonprejudiced person wants his or her behavior to be consistent with his or her true beliefs rather than his or her stereotypes. When given a chance to use controlled processing, nonprejudiced individuals show behavior that is more consistent with nonprejudiced true beliefs than stereotyped beliefs. In contrast, the behavior of prejudiced individuals is more likely to be guided by stereotypes. In another study, nonprejudiced individuals were more likely than prejudiced individuals to feel bad when they had thoughts about gay men and lesbians that ran counter to their beliefs (Monteith et al., 1993). When nonprejudiced individuals express prejudicial thoughts and feelings, they feel guilty about doing so (Devine et al., 1991).

What happens if automatic processing takes over? According to Devine, activating a stereotype puts a person into automatic mode when confronting a person from the stereotyped group. The automatically activated stereotype will be acted on by both prejudiced and nonprejudiced individuals unless there is an opportunity to use controlled processing (Devine, 1989). Devine found that when participants in an experiment were prevented from switching to controlled processing, both prejudiced and nonprejudiced individuals evaluated the behavior of an African American negatively.

We can draw several conclusions from Devine's research. First, prejudiced individuals are less inhibited about expressing their prejudice than nonprejudiced individuals. Second, no differences exist between prejudiced and nonprejudiced individuals when stereotype activation is beyond conscious control. Third, nonprejudiced people work hard to inhibit the expression of negative stereotypes when they have the opportunity to monitor behavior and bring stereotypes under conscious control. Fourth, nonprejudiced individuals realize that there is a gap between their stereotypes and their general beliefs about equality, and they work continually to change their stereotyped thinking.

How easy is it to identify a prejudiced person? If you see a person in a Ku Klux Klan outfit distributing hate propaganda or burning a cross on someone's lawn, that's pretty easy. However, many people do not express prejudices in such obvious ways. When we encounter someone who makes racist or sexist comments, we can pretty easily identify that person as prejudiced (Mae & Carlston, 2005). Further, we will express dislike for that person, even if he or she is expressing ideas with which we agree (Mae & Carlston, 2005). So, it seems we are pretty adept at identifying individuals who express negative prejudices. However, when it comes to detecting positive prejudices, we are less adept. Speakers who espouse negative prejudices are more likely to be identified as prejudiced than those who espouse positive prejudices (Mae & Carlston, 2005).

Study Break

A third way that social psychologists explain prejudice, stereotypes, and discrimination is through cognitive factors. Specifically, our tendency to define the world in terms of in-groups (us) and out-groups (them) contributes to prejudice. Before you begin the next section, answer the following questions:

1. What are in-groups and out-groups, and how do they relate to prejudice?
2. What are social-identity theory and self-categorization theory, and why are they important in understanding prejudice?

3. How do illusory correlations and the confirmation bias help maintain prejudice?
4. What is the out-group homogeneity bias, and how does it relate to prejudice?
5. How do prejudiced and nonprejudiced individuals differ?

The Consequences of Being a Target of Prejudice

Imagine being awakened several times each night by a telephone caller who inundates you with racial or religious slurs. Imagine being a second-generation Japanese American soldier on December 8, 1941 (the day after the Pearl Harbor attack), and being told you are no longer trusted to carry a gun in defense of your country. Imagine being an acknowledged war hero who is denied the Medal of Honor because of race-related suspicions of your loyalty to the country for which you had just fought. In each of these instances, a person becomes the target of prejudicial attitudes, stereotypes, and discriminatory behavior directed at him or her. What effect does being the target of such prejudice have on an individual? To be sure, being a target of discrimination generates a great deal of negative affect and has serious emotional consequences for the target (Dion & Earn, 1975). Next, we explore some of the effects that prejudice has on those who are its targets.

Ways Prejudice Can Be Expressed

In his monumental work on prejudice called *The Nature of Prejudice,* Gordon Allport (1954) suggested that there are five ways that prejudice can be expressed. These are *antilocution,* talking in terms of prejudice or making jokes about an out-group; *avoidance,* avoiding contact with members of an out-group; *discrimination,* actively doing something to deny members of an out-group something they desire; *physical attack,* beatings, lynchings, and the like; and *extermination,* an attempt to eliminate an entire group. One issue we must address is the reaction shown by members of an out-group when they are targeted with prejudice. It is fairly obvious that those faced with overt discrimination, physical attack, and extermination will respond negatively. But what about reactions to more subtle forms of prejudice? What toll do they take on a member of a minority group?

Swim et al. (1998) characterized some forms of prejudice as *everyday prejudice*: "recurrent and familiar events that can be considered commonplace" (p. 37). These include short-term interactions such as remarks and stares, and incidents that can be directed at an individual or an entire group. According to Swim and colleagues, such incidents can be initiated either by strangers or by those with intimate relationships with the target and have a cumulative effect and contribute to the target's experience with and knowledge of prejudice.

Prejudice-Based Jokes

How do encounters with everyday prejudice affect the target? Let's start by looking at one form of antilocution discussed by Allport that most people see as harmless: prejudice-based jokes. Most of us have heard (and laughed at) jokes that make members of a group the butt of the joke. Many of us may have even told such jokes, assuming that they do no harm. But how do those on the receiving end feel? Women, for example, find sexist jokes less funny and less amusing than nonsexist jokes (LaFrance & Woodzicka, 1998). They also tend to report feeling more disgusted, angry, hostile, and surprised by sexist versus nonsexist jokes. They also tend to roll their eyes (indicating disgust) and touch their faces (indicating embarrassment) more in response to sexist than to nonsexist jokes (LaFrance & Woodzicka, 1998).

Ryan and Kanjorski (1998) directly compared the reactions of men and women to sexist jokes. They found that compared to men, women enjoyed sexist humor less and found it less acceptable and more offensive. Interestingly, men and women did not differ in terms of telling sexist jokes. A more ominous finding was that for men, there were

One form of prejudicial antilocution is prejudice-based jokes. Although they may be funny, they have a negative effect on individuals from the targeted group.
Source: GenerationClash/Shutterstock.

significant positive correlations between enjoyment of sexist humor and rape myth acceptance, adversarial sexual beliefs, acceptance of interpersonal violence, likelihood of engaging in forced sex, and sexual aggression. In another study, the exposure of men with sexist attitudes to sexist jokes was related to tolerance for sexism and fewer negative feelings about behaving in a sexist manner (Ford et al. 2001). These findings may lend some credence to Allport's (1954) idea that antilocution, once accepted, sets the stage for more serious expressions of prejudice.

A study reported by Thomas and Esses (2004) confirms the relationship between sexist attitudes and enjoyment of sexist humor. Male participants completed measures of sexism and authoritarianism. They then evaluated two types of sexist jokes. Half of the jokes were degrading to women and half degrading to men. The results showed that male participants who scored highly on the sexism scale found the jokes degrading females funnier and were more likely to repeat them than male participants who were low on the sexism measure. Sexism did not relate to the evaluation of the jokes that degraded men.

The relationship between sexist attitudes and enjoyment of sexist humor is complicated by the fact that sexism takes a variety of forms. Sexism has two main components: hostile and benevolent (Greenwood & Isbell, 2002). *Hostile sexism* consists of hostile attitudes toward women such as beliefs that women manipulate men to gain power and are too easily offended (Greenwood & Isbell, 2002). *Benevolent sexism* consists of positive attitudes toward women such as women are more pure than men and women should be put on a pedestal (Greenwood & Isbell, 2002). Based on these two components, sexism can be classified as hostile (high on hostile and low on benevolent sexism), ambivalent (high on hostile and benevolent sexism), nonsexist (low on both hostile and benevolent sexism), and benevolent (low on hostile and high on benevolent sexism) (Greenwood & Isbell, 2002). As shown in Figure 4.13, Greenwood and

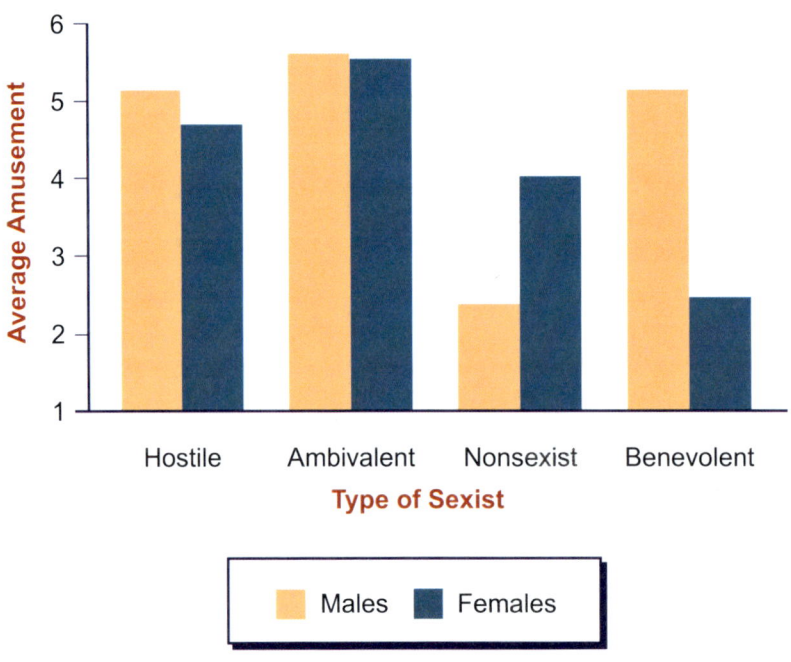

FIGURE 4.13

Average rating of amusement of dumb blonde jokes by different types of male and female sexists. Based on data from Greenwood and Isbell (2001).

Isbell found that men and women who were hostile and ambivalent sexists enjoyed dumb blonde sexist jokes (no significant difference was found between hostile and ambivalent male and female sexists). For nonsexist males and females, females were slightly more likely to enjoy sexist humor than males (the difference here was marginally significant). Finally, there was a clear difference between male and female benevolent sexists: male benevolent sexists enjoyed the dumb blonde jokes more than female benevolent sexists. Greenwood and Isbell found a very similar pattern was found for the degree to which males and females found the jokes offensive.

Stereotype Threat

Many stereotypes exist about a wide range of groups. Women are not supposed to do as well as men in math, Blacks are not supposed to do as well as Whites academically, older people are supposed to be worse drivers than younger people, and Asians are supposed to do better than others academically. What impact can such stereotypes have on a person who is required to do a task that relates to a stereotype about that person's group? Will a person react to that stereotype with poor performance? The answer to this question is yes. For example, if an elderly person does a simulated driving task after being told that a study focuses on why elderly drivers are bad drivers (activating a stereotype), they do more poorly on the simulated driving task than if they are not told what the study is about (Joanisse et al., 2013).

The effect of activating a stereotype about one's group has been extensively studied in the area of racial stereotypes. For example, one intriguing hypothesis about why Blacks might not score well on standard tests of IQ comes from an experiment conducted by Steele and Aronson (1995). According to Steele and Aronson, when a person is asked to perform a task for which there is a negative stereotype attached to their group, that person will perform poorly because the task is threatening. They called this idea a **stereotype threat**. To test this hypothesis, Steele and Aronson conducted the following experiment. Black and White participants took a test comprising items from the verbal section of the Graduate Record Exam. One-third of the participants were told that the test was diagnostic of their intellectual ability (diagnostic condition). One-third were told that the test was a laboratory tool for studying problem solving (nondiagnostic condition). The final third were told that the test was of problem solving and would present a challenge to the participants (nondiagnostic—challenge condition). Steele and Aronson then determined the average number of items answered correctly within each group.

stereotype threat The condition that exists when a person is asked to perform a task for which there is a negative stereotype attached to their group and performs poorly because the task is threatening.

The results of this experiment showed that when the test was said to be diagnostic of one's intellectual abilities, Black and White participants differed significantly, with Black participants performing more poorly than White participants. However, when the *same* test was presented as nondiagnostic, Black and White participants did equally well. There was no significant difference between Blacks and Whites in the nondiagnostic-challenge condition. Overall across the three conditions, Blacks performed most poorly in the diagnostic condition. In a second experiment, Steele and Aronson (1995) produced results that were even more pronounced than in their first. They also found that Black participants in the diagnostic condition finished fewer items and worked more slowly than Black participants in the nondiagnostic condition. Steele and Aronson pointed out that this is a pattern consistent with impairments caused by test anxiety, evaluation apprehension, and competitive pressure.

In a final experiment, Steele and Aronson (1995) had participants perform word-completion tasks (e.g., — — ce; la — —; or — — ack) that could be completed in a racially stereotyped way (e.g., race; lazy; Black) or a nonstereotyped way (e.g., pace; lace; track). This was done to test if stereotypes are activated when participants were told that a test was either diagnostic or nondiagnostic. Steele and Aronson found that there was greater stereotype activation among Blacks in the diagnostic condition compared to the nondiagnostic condition. They also found that in the diagnostic condition, Blacks were more likely than Whites to engage in self-handicapping strategies (i.e., developing behavior patterns that actually interfere with performance, such as losing sleep the night before a test). Blacks and Whites did not differ on self-handicapping behaviors in the nondiagnostic condition.

These findings help us understand why Blacks consistently perform more poorly than Whites on intelligence tests. Intelligence tests by their very nature and purpose are diagnostic of one's intellectual abilities. According to Steele and Aronson's (1995) analysis, when a Black person is faced with the prospect of taking a test that is diagnostic of intellectual ability, it activates the common stereotype threat that Blacks are not supposed to perform well on tests of intellectual ability. According to Steele and Aronson, the stereotype threat impairs performance by generating evaluative pressures. Recall that participants who were under stereotype threat in the diagnostic condition spent more time doing fewer items. As they became more frustrated, performance was impaired. It may also impair future performance, because more self-handicapping strategies are used by Blacks facing diagnostic tests. In short, the stereotype threat creates an impairment in the ability to cognitively process information adequately, which in turn inhibits performance. So, lower scores on IQ tests by Blacks may relate more to the activation of the stereotype threat than to any genetic differences between Blacks and Whites.

Steele and his colleagues extended the notion of the stereotype threat to other groups. For example, Spencer et al. (cited in Aronson et al. 1998) found that men and women equated for math ability performed differently on a math test, depending on whether they were told that there were past results showing no gender differences in performance on the test (alleviating the stereotype threat) or given no information about gender differences (allowing the stereotype threat to be activated). Specifically, when the "no gender differences" information was given, men and women performed equally well on the test. However, when the stereotype threat was allowed to be activated (i.e., that women perform more poorly on math tests than do men), men scored significantly higher than women. Aronson and Alainas reported similar effects for Latino versus White participants and White males versus Asian males (cited in Aronson et al., 1998).

In a more direct test of the relationship between gender, stereotype threat, and math performance, Brown and Josephs (1999) told male and female students that they would be taking a math test. One-half of the participants of each gender were told that the test would identify exceptionally strong math abilities, whereas the other half were told that the test would uncover especially weak math skills. Brown and Josephs reasoned that for males the test for strong math skills would be more threatening, because it plays into the stereotype that males are strong in math. On the other hand, the test for weakness would be more threatening to females, because females stereotypically are viewed as being weak in math. Their results were consistent with Steele and Aronson's stereotype threat notion. Males performed poorly on the test that supposedly measured exceptional math skills. Conversely, females performed poorly on the test that was said to identify weak math skills. In both cases, a stereotype was activated that was relevant to gender, which inhibited performance. According to Brown and Josephs, the stereotype threat for math performance is experienced differently for males and females. Males feel more threatened when faced with having to prove themselves worthy of the label of being strong in math skills, whereas females feel more threatened when they face a situation that may prove a stereotype to be true.

Stereotype threat also operates by reducing positive expectations a person has going into a situation. For example, based on a person's previous experience, he or she may feel confident about doing well on the SATs, having a positive expectation about his or her performance on the exam. Now, let's say that a stereotype of this person's group is activated prior to taking the exam. The resulting stereotype threat may lower that person's expectations about the test, and as a consequence, the person does not do well.

The fact that this scenario can happen was verified in an experiment by Stangor, Carr, and Kiang (1998). Female participants in this experiment all performed an initial task of identifying words. Afterward, some participants were told that their performance on the task provided clear evidence that they had an aptitude for college-level work. Other participants were told that the evidence concerning college performance was unclear.

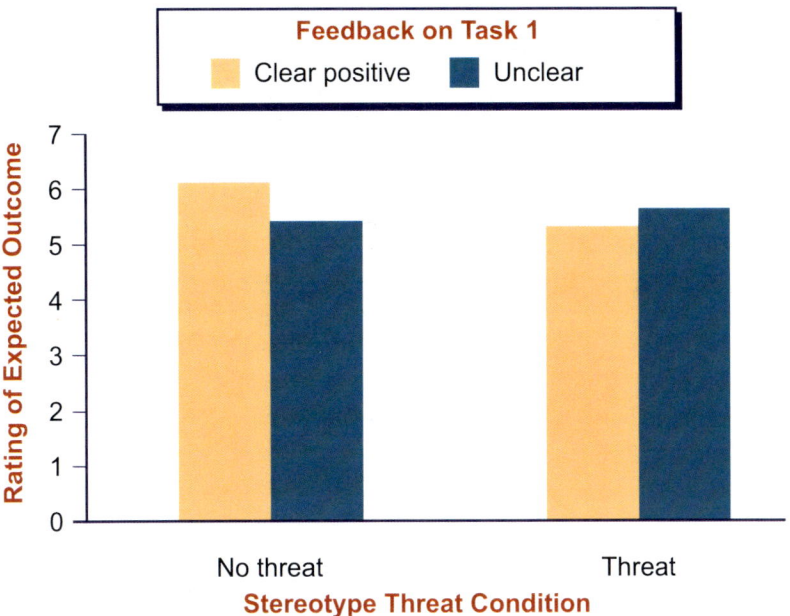

FIGURE 4.14

Task performance as a function of feedback about prior performance and activation of a stereotype threat. When no threat was activated, participants used performance on a prior task to form expectations about further performance. When a threat was activated, performance was affected by what was expected based on the stereotype.

Based on Stangor et al. (1998).

Next, participants were told that there was either strong evidence that men did better than women on the second test (stereotype threat) or that there were no sex differences (no stereotype threat). Before working on the second task, participants were asked to rate their ability to perform the second task successfully. The results of this experiment, shown in Figure 4.14, were clear. When a stereotype threat was not activated, performance was affected by the feedback given after the first task. Those participants who believed that there was clear, positive evidence of college aptitude had higher expectations of success than those given unclear feedback. In the stereotype threat condition, the two groups did not differ in their expectations concerning the second task.

Thus, in addition to arousing anxiety about testing situations, stereotype threats also lower one's expectations about one's performance. Once these negative expectations develop, a self-fulfilling prophecy is most likely developed that "Because I am a female, I am not expected to do well on this task." Poor performance then confirms that prophecy.

Whether the arousal related to a stereotype threat adversely affects performance depends, in part, on the nature of the task individuals must perform. A consistent finding in social psychology is that arousal enhances performance on a simple task but inhibits performance on a more difficult task (we discuss this effect in detail in Chapter 8). Ben Zeev et al. (2005) conducted a study to investigate this effect. Participants performed either a simple task (writing their names in cursive several times) or difficult task (writing their names in cursive backwards) under stereotype threat or no threat. Ben Zeev et al. found that the arousal associated with the stereotype threat enhanced performance on the simple task and inhibited performance on the difficult task.

In a second experiment Ben Zeev et al. found that how participants attributed the cause for their arousal affected performance. Once again, participants were exposed to either a stereotype threat condition or no-threat condition. Participants were told that one purpose of the study was to investigate performance while being exposed to subliminal noise. Participants in the misattribution condition were told that the subliminal noise would produce physical

Chapter 4 Prejudice and Discrimination

symptoms such as arousal and nervousness. Participants in the control group were told that the subliminal noise would have no physical side effects. All participants completed a moderately difficult math test while being exposed to the noise. The results showed that participants in the control group showed the usual stereotype threat effect (poorer performance under threat versus no threat). However, in the misattribution condition there was no significant threat effect on performance. Hence, if you can attribute your arousal to something other than a stereotype, you will perform well. Arousal related to stereotype threat appears to be an important mediator of performance, as is how the source of the arousal is attributed.

Although arousal appears to be an important mediator of stereotype threat, it is not the only mediator. Over the last 20 years, researchers have identified over a dozen mediators of stereotype threat. Stereotype threat has been shown to impair performance by increasing anxiety (Chung et al., 2010), decreasing the capacity of working memory (Schmader & Johns, 2003), and inducing intrusive negative thoughts (Cadinu et al., 2005), and these are just a few examples. There appears to be no single mechanism by which stereotype threat produces its effects on performance. Rather, it appears that stereotype threat may be mediated by different mechanisms depending on who is experiencing the threat and in what context the threat is experienced (Pennington et al., 2016).

Finally, it is not just minorities who experience stereotype threat. For example, White men experienced stereotype threat and had lowered mathematical performance when they believed their performance would be compared with that of Asian men (Aronson et al., 1995). Additionally, White men also have altered performance on motor tasks when the tasks are related to "natural athletic ability" and their performance will be compared to that of Black men (Stone et al., 1999). Thus, stereotype threat is possible anytime a negative stereotype becomes self-relevant, even when the group is generally not stigmatized (e.g., White men).

Collective Threat

The preceding studies show how being the target of a stereotype can affect individual behavior in a very specific context (i.e., testing). Stereotypes can also have a broader, more general effect by making members of stereotyped groups sensitive to the stigmatizing effects of the stereotype. In other words, a person from a stereotyped group may become overly concerned that a transgression by a member of one's group may reflect badly on him or her as an individual (Cohen & Garcia, 2005). Cohen and Garcia refer to this as **collective threat**. Collective threat flows from "the awareness that the poor performance of a single individual in one's group may be viewed through the lens of a stereotype and may be generalized into a negative judgment of one's group" (Cohen & Garcia, 2005, p. 566).

collective threat
The awareness that the poor performance of a member of one's group may be evaluated with a stereotype and may be generalized into a negative judgment of one's entire group.

Cohen and Garcia conducted a series of studies to assess the effects of collective threat. In their first study junior and senior high school students completed a questionnaire that included measures of collective threat (concern that behavior of other members of one's group will reflect badly on the group as a whole), stereotype threat (concern that one's own behavior will reflect badly on one's group), and a more generalized threat of being stereotyped (concern that people will judge the participant based on what they think of the participant's racial group). Cohen and Garcia (2005) compared the responses from students representing three racial/ethnic groups: Blacks, Whites, and Latinos. Garcia and Cohen found that minority students (Blacks and Latinos) were more likely to experience each of the three types of threats than White students. They also found that experiencing collective threat was negatively related to self-esteem. The more a student experienced collective threat, the lower the student's self-esteem, regardless of the race of the student. Collective threat was also related to a drop in student grade point averages. High levels of perceived collective threat were related to significant drops in grade point average.

A series of follow-up experiments confirmed the results from the questionnaire study. Black students who were randomly assigned to a condition that created collective threat (compared to control students) experienced lower self-esteem and also performed more poorly on a standardized test. Additionally, the students tended to distance themselves from a group member who caused the collective threat. Finally, Cohen and Garcia (2005) found that the effects of collective threat were not limited to racial groups. In their last experiment reported, the effects of collective threat were replicated using gender stereotypes (lower math ability than men) rather than racial stereotypes. Women distanced themselves (sat further way) from another woman who confirmed the math inability stereotype.

Expecting to Be a Target of Prejudice

Another way that being the target of prejudice can affect behavior occurs when people enter into a situation in which they expect to find prejudice. Imagine, for example, that you are a minority student who will be meeting his White roommate for the first time. Could your behavior be affected by your belief that your White roommate might harbor prejudices and negative stereotypes about your group? The answer to this question is that it certainly could.

Research reported by Shelton et al. (2005) confirmed this very effect. They found a relationship between the expectation of encountering prejudice and how they perceived interracial interactions. Specifically, Shelton et al. found that the more a minority student expected prejudice from another White student, the more negative they viewed interaction with that person. This relationship was found in a diary study (students kept a diary of their experiences with their White roommates) and in a laboratory experiment in which prejudice was induced. Shelton et al. also assessed the perceptions of the White students in their studies. Interestingly, they found that the more the minority student expected the White student to be prejudiced, the more *positive* the encounter was seen by the White student. This latter finding suggests a major disconnect between the perceptions of the minority and White students. Minority students who expect prejudice (and probably experienced it in the past) may Misinterpret White students' behaviors as indicative of prejudice, making the interaction seem more negative than it actually is. White students who do not have the history of experiencing prejudice may be operating in a state of ignorant bliss, not realizing that innocent behaviors may be misconstrued by their minority counterparts.

Study Break

The previous sections discussed the consequences of being a target of prejudice, which are highly negative. Before you begin the next section, answer the following questions:

1. Define Allport's different ways that prejudice can be expressed.
2. What are the effects of being the target of prejudice-based jokes?
3. What is stereotype threat, and how does it affect behavior?
4. What is collective threat, and how does it relate to being a target of prejudice?
5. What is the impact of expecting to be the target of prejudice?

Coping with Prejudice

It should be obvious from our previous discussion that being a target of prejudice has a variety of negative consequences. Individuals facing instance after instance of everyday prejudice must find ways to deal with its effects. How, for example, can an overweight person who is constantly the target of prejudice effectively manage its consequences? In this section, we explore some strategies that individuals use to cope with being a target of prejudice.

Raising the Value of a Stigmatized Group

One method of coping with prejudice when your group is stigmatized, oppressed, or less valued than other groups is to raise its value. This is done by first convincing group members of their own self-worth and then convincing the rest of society of the group's worth. The function of all consciousness-raising efforts and positive in-group slogans is to persuade the members of scorned or less-valued groups that they are beautiful or smart or worthy or competent. This first step, maintaining and increasing self-esteem, can be approached in at least two ways (Crocker & Major, 1989; Crocker et al., 1991): attributing negative events to prejudice of the majority and comparing oneself to members of one's own group.

First, for example, suppose that an African American woman is denied a job or a promotion. She can better maintain her self-esteem if she attributes this outcome to the prejudice of the person evaluating her. Of course, people are usually uncertain about the true motives of other people in situations like this. Although a rejection by a majority group member can be attributed to the evaluator's prejudice, the effects on the self-esteem of the minority person are complex.

Some of these effects were investigated in a study in which African American participants were evaluated by White evaluators (Crocker & Major, 1989). When participants thought that evaluators were uninfluenced by their race, positive evaluations increased their self-esteem. But when participants knew that evaluators were influenced by their race, positive evaluations decreased their self-esteem. Compared to Whites, African Americans were more likely to attribute both positive and negative evaluations to prejudice. Any judgment, positive or negative, that the recipient thought was based on racism led to a decrease in self-esteem (Crocker et al., 1991).

Uncertainty about such evaluations thus has important consequences for self-esteem. In our society, African Americans are often evaluated primarily by Whites, which suggests that they may always feel uncertain about their evaluators' motives (Crocker et al., 1991). This uncertainty may be exacerbated for African American females who are evaluated by White males (Coleman et al., 1991).

Even when race (or some other characteristic) works in one's favor, uncertainty or *attributional ambiguity* may be aroused. For example, a minority group member who receives a job where an affirmative action program is in effect may never know for certain whether he or she was hired based on qualifications or race. This attributional ambiguity generates negative affect and motivation (Blaine et al., 1995). In one study participants who believed that they received a job due to sympathy over a stigma experienced lower self-esteem, negative emotion, and reduced work motivation than those who believed they received the job based on qualifications (Blaine et al., 1995).

Making In-Group Comparisons

Second, members of less-favored groups can maintain self-esteem by comparing themselves with members of their own group, rather than with members of the more favored or fortunate groups. In-group comparisons may be less painful and more rewarding for members of stigmatized groups. Research supports this hypothesis in a number of areas, including pay, abilities, and physical attractiveness (Crocker & Major, 1989). Once group members have raised their value in their own eyes, the group is better placed to assert itself in society.

As the feelings of cohesiveness and belonging of the in-group increase, there is often an escalation in hostility directed toward the out-group (Allport, 1954). History teaches us that self-identifying with an in-group and identifying others with an out-group underlies many instances of prejudice and intergroup hostility.

Anticipating and Confronting Prejudice

Swim et al. (1998) suggested that another strategy for individuals from a stigmatized group is to try to anticipate situations in which prejudice will be encountered. By doing this, the individual can decide how to best react to or minimize the impact of prejudice. The individual may decide to alter his or her demeanor, manner of dress, or even where he or she goes to school or lives in an effort to minimize the likelihood of encountering prejudice (Swim et al., 1998).

Once a person has made an assessment of a situation for anticipated prejudice, that person must next decide what course of action to take. The individual could choose to confront the prejudice and move toward the original goal or choose to avoid the prejudiced situation and find some alternative (Swim et al., 1998). Confronting prejudice means "a volitional process aimed at expressing one's dissatisfaction with discriminatory treatment to a person or group of people who are responsible for engaging in a discriminatory event" (Kaiser & Miller, 2004, p. 168). For example, a woman who has just been told a nasty, sexist joke can confront the joke teller and point out the inappropriateness of the joke. Although it may be noble to confront prejudice and discrimination, the reality is that many of us don't do it. In one experiment, for example, in which women were subjected to sexist comments, only 45% of the women confronted the offender. However, privately, a vast majority of the women expressed private distaste for the comments and the person who made them (Swim & Hyers, 1999). Why would the women who experienced sexism be reluctant to confront it? Unfortunately, there is not a lot of research on this issue. One study (Kaiser & Miller, 2004), however, did look into this question. Women were asked to recall instances of sexism that they had encountered in their lives (e.g., sexism in the workplace, experiencing demeaning comments, or exposure to stereotyped sex role concepts). The women also completed measures of optimism and cognitive appraisals of confronting sexism. The results showed that women who perceived confronting prejudice as cognitively difficult (e.g., not worth the effort, anxiety producing) were less likely to have reported confronting the sexism they had experienced. Kaiser and Miller also found a relationship between optimism and cognitive appraisals. Women with a more optimistic outlook viewed confrontation as less threatening than women with a pessimistic outlook. In short, women with optimistic outlooks are more likely to confront prejudice than those with a pessimistic outlook. Thus, both personality characteristics and cognitive evaluations are involved in the decision to confront prejudice. Of course, this conclusion is tentative at this time, and we don't know if similar psychological mechanisms apply to coping with other forms of prejudice.

Compensating for Prejudice

Members of a stigmatized group can also engage in *compensation* to cope with prejudice (Miller & Myers, 1998). According to Miller and Myers, there are two modes of compensation in which a person can engage. When **secondary compensation** is used, individuals attempt to change their mode of thinking about situations to psychologically protect themselves against the outcomes of prejudice. For example, a person who wants to obtain a college degree but faces prejudice that may prevent reaching the goal would be using secondary compensation if he or she devalued the goal (a college education is not all that important) or disidentified with the goal (members of my group usually don't go to college). On the other hand, **primary compensation** reduces the actual threats posed by prejudice. Coping strategies are developed that allow the targets of prejudice to achieve their goals. For example, the person in the example could increase his or her effort (study harder in school), use latent skills (become more persistent), or develop new skills to help achieve goals that are blocked by prejudice. When primary compensation is used, it reduces the need for secondary compensation (Miller & Myers, 1998).

Interestingly, coping with prejudice is different if you are talking about individual coping as opposed to group coping. Mummendey et al. (1999) tested coping strategies tied to two theories relating to being a target of prejudice: social identity theory and relative deprivation theory. As you read earlier, social identity theory proposes that individuals derive part of their self-concept from affiliation with a group. If the group with which you affiliate has negative stereotypes attached to it, the social identity will be negative. According to *relative deprivation theory,* members of a stereotyped group recognize that they are undervalued and reap fewer benefits from society than more preferred groups. In theory, negative social identity should lead to individually based coping strategies,

secondary compensation
A method of handling prejudice involving attempts to change one's mode of thinking about situations to psychologically protect oneself against the outcomes of prejudice.

primary compensation
A method by targets of prejudice that reduces threats posed by using coping strategies that allow the targets of prejudice to achieve their goals.

whereas perceived relative deprivation should lead to group-based coping (Mummendey et al., 1999).

To test this hypothesis, residents of former East Germany were administered a questionnaire concerning social identity and relative deprivation. The questionnaire also measured several identity management strategies. Mummendey and colleagues (1999) found that social identity issues were handled with management strategies (e.g., mobility and recategorization of the self to a higher level in the group) that stressed one's individual attachment with an in-group. Management techniques relating to relative deprivation were more group based, focusing on group-based strategies such as collective action to reduce relative deprivation. In addition, social identity issues were tied closely with cognitive aspects of group affiliation, whereas relative deprivation was mediated strongly by emotions such as anger.

Study Break

Individuals who are the target of prejudice often find ways to cope with being such a target. Some of these coping strategies can have negative consequences for a person. Before you begin the next section, answer the following questions:

1. How can raising the value of stigmatized groups help cope with prejudice?
2. How does making in-group comparisons help a person cope with prejudice?
3. In what ways can anticipating and confronting prejudice help cope with prejudice?
4. What are the ways that a person can use to compensate for prejudice, and how do they affect behavior?

Reducing Prejudice

A rather gloomy conclusion that may be drawn from the research on the cognitive processing of social information is that normal cognitive functioning leads inevitably to the development and maintenance of social stereotypes (Mackie et al., 1992). Social psychologists have investigated the strategies that people can use to reduce prejudice and intergroup hostility. In the following sections, we explore some of these actions.

Contact Between Groups

contact hypothesis
A hypothesis that contact between groups will reduce hostility, which is most effective when members of different groups have equal status and a mutual goal.

In his classic book *The Nature of Prejudice* (1954), Gordon Allport proposed the **contact hypothesis**. According to this hypothesis, contact between groups will reduce hostility when the participants have equal status and a mutual goal. There is research supporting the contact hypothesis (Van Laar et al., 2005). Van Laar et al. looked at the effects of living with a roommate from a different racial or ethnic group. They found that students who were randomly assigned to live with an out-group roommate showed increasingly positive feelings as the academic year progressed. The most positive effect of contact was found when the out-group roommate was African American. Even better, the increasing positive attitudes toward African Americans were found to generalize to Latinos. Interestingly, however, both White and Black participants showed increasingly *negative* attitudes toward Asian roommates as the year progressed. Such intergroup contact extends to prejudice against individuals with a same-sex orientation as well. In one study conducted in Jamaica (which has a high level of antigay prejudice), West and Hewstone (2012) found that intergroup contact was effective in reducing this prejudice. In fact, it was more effective among the highly prejudiced Jamaicans than it was among less prejudiced British people.

Another potential benefit of intergroup contact is that it may help slow down the intergenerational transmission of prejudice. Research shows that prejudice is transmitted from parents to children (Rodríguez-García & Wagner, 2009) and that many of the transmitted prejudices are related to authoritarian personality characteristics transmitted from parent to child (Dhont & van Heil, 2012). Dhont and van Heil had Belgian parent-adolescent dyads complete a number of measures of right-wing authoritarianism, prejudice against immigrants, and the amount of positive contact with immigrants. Dhont and van Heil found that positive intergroup contact moderated the amount of prejudice directed at immigrants by the adolescents. They also found that the contact served as a buffer between right-wing authoritarian attitudes and prejudice. Interestingly, Dhont and van Heil found that lower levels of intergroup contact were more effective at buffering against prejudice than higher levels of contact.

In one early study, two groups of boys at a summer camp were made to be competitive and then hostile toward each other (Sherif et al., 1961). At the end of the camp experience, when the researchers tried to reduce the intergroup hostility, they found that contact between the groups and among the boys was not sufficient to reduce hostility. In fact, contact only made the situation worse. It was only when the groups had to work together in pulling a vehicle out of the mud so that they could continue on a long-awaited trip that hostility was reduced. This cooperation on a goal that was important to both groups is called a *superordinate goal,* which is essentially the same as Allport's notion of a mutual goal.

Further evidence that under certain circumstances contact does lead to a positive change in the image of an out-group member comes from other research. In one study, for example, college students were asked to interact with another student described as a former patient at a mental hospital (Desforges et al., 1991). Students were led to expect that the former patient would behave in a manner similar to a typical mental patient. Some of the participants were initially prejudiced toward mental patients, and others were not. After working with the former mental patient in a 1-hour-long cooperative task, the initially prejudiced participants showed a positive change in their feelings about the former patient.

As shown in Figure 4.15, participants experienced a three-stage alteration. At first, they formed a category-based impression: "This is a former mental patient, and this is the

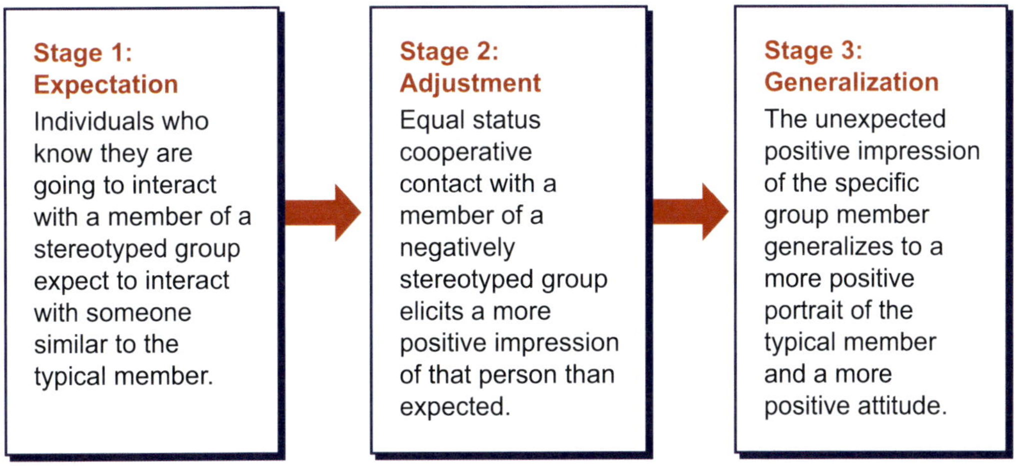

The contact hypothesis says that prejudice can be reduced by encouraging contact between different groups, such as in an integrated classroom. The strategy can work if it is done under the right conditions.
Source: Rawpixel.com/Shutterstock.

Stage 1: Expectation	Stage 2: Adjustment	Stage 3: Generalization
Individuals who know they are going to interact with a member of a stereotyped group expect to interact with someone similar to the typical member.	Equal status cooperative contact with a member of a negatively stereotyped group elicits a more positive impression of that person than expected.	The unexpected positive impression of the specific group member generalizes to a more positive portrait of the typical member and a more positive attitude.

FIGURE 4.15

Three stages in the alteration of characteristics attributed to the typical group member and general attitudes toward the group through structured contact with a group member.
Based on Desforges (1991).

way mental patients behave." But equal status and the necessity for cooperation (Allport's two conditions) compelled the participants to make an adjustment in their initial automatically formed impression (Fiske & Neuberg, 1990). This is the second stage. Finally, once the adjustment was made, participants generalized the change in feelings to other mental patients (although they might have concluded, as tends to be more common, that this patient was different from other former mental patients). Note that the readjustment of the participants' feelings toward the former mental patient was driven by paying attention to the personal characteristics of that individual.

In another setting (a schoolroom), Eliot Aronson found that the use of tasks that require each person to solve some part of the whole problem reduces prejudice among schoolchildren (Aronson et al., 1978). This approach, called the *jigsaw classroom,* requires that each group member be assigned responsibility for a part of the problem. Group members then share their knowledge with everyone else. The concept works because the problem cannot be solved without the efforts of all members; thus each person is valued. This technique also tends to increase the self-esteem of members of different ethnic groups because their efforts are valued.

Interestingly, contact does not even have to be real in order for it to work! Crisp and Turner (2009) investigated the effectiveness of *imagined intergroup contact* in reducing intergroup hostility. In a series of experiments reported in their 2009 article, Crisp and Turner found that imagined intergroup contact reduced negative perceptions of out-groups such as the elderly and individuals with a same-sex orientation. In a later study, West et al. (2012) found that imagined contact can also reduce prejudice directed at patients with schizophrenia. Crisp and Turner suggest that imagined contact is not a substitute for actual contact. They maintain that imagined contact can be used as a way to encourage people to make subsequent actual contact with members of out-groups and can be especially beneficial when opportunities for actual intergroup contact are not possible for some reason.

Although there is considerable support for the contact hypothesis, there is some evidence against the hypothesis (Miller & Brewer, 1984). Even if there is friendly contact, people still manage to defend their stereotypes. Friendly interaction between individual members of different racial groups may have little effect on their prejudices, because the person they are interacting with may be seen as exceptional and not representative of the out-group (Horwitz & Rabbie, 1989).

Ultimately, does the contact hypothesis work? Yes, but with very definite limits. It seems that both parties have to have a goal they both want and cannot achieve without the other. This superordinate goal also has to compel both to attend to each other's individual characteristics. It also seems to be important that they be successful in obtaining that goal. A recent meta-analysis confirms that contact strategies that conform to the optimal conditions have a greater effect on prejudice than those that do not (Tropp & Pettigrew, 2005a). Additionally Tropp and Pettigrew (2005a) found that the prejudice-reducing effects of contact were stronger for majority-status groups than minority-status groups.

Even when all these conditions are met, individuals may revert to their prior beliefs when they leave the interaction. Palestinians and Israelis meeting in Egypt to resolve differences and negotiate peace may find their stereotypes of the other side lessening as they engage in face-to-face, equal, and (perhaps) mutually rewarding contact. But when they go home, pressure from other members of their groups may compel them to take up their prior beliefs again.

Finally, research has investigated how contact reduces prejudice. Recent evidence suggests that intergroup contact mediates prejudice through emotional channels rather than directly reducing stereotypes and other cognitive aspects of prejudice (Miller et al., 2004; Tropp & Pettigrew, 2005b).

Personalizing Out-Group Members

According to Henri Tajfel (1982), the Nazis attempted to deny Jews and others their individuality, their identity, by defining them as outside the category of human beings, as *Untermenschen,* subhumans. This dehumanization made it easy for even humane individuals to brutalize and kill because they did not see the individual men, women, and children who were their victims (Horwitz & Rabbie, 1989).

If dehumanizing people makes it easier to be prejudiced, even to carry out the worst atrocities, then perhaps humanizing people, personalizing them, can reduce stereotyping and prejudice. Research clearly shows that this is so; personalizing out-group members reduces prejudice (Ensari et al., 2012). People are less likely to use gender stereotypes, for example, when they have the time to process information that tells them about the distinctive traits of individual males and females (Pratto & Bargh, 1991). Humanizing members of a group does not necessarily mean that we must know or understand each individual in that group (Bodenhausen, 1993). It means we understand that we and they have a shared humanity and that we all feel the same joys and pains. Also, personalization works best when it targets emotions (e.g., empathy) rather than the more cognitive elements of prejudice (e.g., categorization) (Ensari et al., 2012). Overall, although personalization is not always successful, especially if the individual is disliked, it does make it more difficult for people to act in a prejudiced manner (Fiske & Neuberg, 1990).

Reducing the Expression of Prejudice Through Social Norms

In the spring of 1989, four African American students at Smith College received anonymous notes containing racial slurs. The incident led to campus-wide protests. It also inspired an experiment designed to determine the most effective way to deter such expressions of hatred (Blanchard et al., 1991). The answer? Attack the behaviors—the acts of hatred themselves—not people's feelings about racial issues.

In one experiment, students were asked how they felt the college should respond to these anonymous notes. Some participants then "overheard" a confederate of the experimenters express the opinion that the letter writer, if discovered, should be expelled. Other participants "overheard" the confederate justify the letters by saying the African American students probably did something to deserve it. The study showed that clear antiracist statements (the person should be expelled) set a tone for other students that discouraged the expression of racial sentiment. Because, as we have seen, racial stereotypes are automatically activated and resistant to change, the best way to discourage racial behavior is through the strong expression of social norms—disapproval from students, campus leaders, and the whole college community (Cook, 1984).

Media exposure can also contribute to changing social norms. This was demonstrated in an ambitious field experiment conducted in Rwanda by Paluck (2009). Paluck randomly assigned communities in Rwanda to listen to one of two radio programs. One group listened to a reconciliation program called *New Dawn* in which messages were woven into stories about two communities representing the sides in the Rwandan genocide. The messages were intended to reduce negative attitudes and perceptions that each group had of each other. The second group listened to a radio broadcast of the same show, but with health-related messages substituted for the reconciliation messages. Paluck assessed personal beliefs, perceived social norms, and behaviors before and after the radio broadcasts. Paluck found shifts in the perceptions of social norms related to the radio broadcasts. Those who listened to the reconciliation broadcast were more likely to endorse intermarriage, that it is OK to trust other groups, and showed greater empathy than those who listened to the health message. Despite this positive outcome for social norms, differential exposure to the radio broadcasts did not have a significant effect on participants' personal beliefs.

Another kind of prejudice, *homophobia,* has been deflected in recent years by appeal to social norms as well as by the threat of social sanctions. The Gay and Lesbian Alliance Against Defamation (GLAAD), increasingly supported by public opinion, has targeted pop musicians who sing antigay lyrics and make antigay statements. In 2004, GLAAD issued a statement denouncing singer Beenie Man for his antigay lyrics. One of Man's songs included lyrics such as "I'm dreaming of a new Jamaica; we've come to execute all the gays" (Testone, 2004). As a result of pressure from gay rights groups, MTV cancelled an appearance by Man on its music awards show in 2005.

At what point does canceling a performance or firing someone for statements made become a problem? The idea of using social pressure and canceling individuals has become more prominent recently. So-called *cancel culture* seems to happen to someone almost every day. For example, in 2021 Mike Richards was tapped to replace the late Alex Trebek as host of the game show Jeopardy. That is until a number of disparaging statements were uncovered about women, Jews, and Hattian people on his podcast *The Ringer* eight years earlier. He was subsequently fired as Executive Producer of Jeopardy and a number of other shows. His firing came on the heels of several other celebrities being criticized for long-past statements or behavior. How do people feel about this tactic? Well, as you might expect, it breaks down along ideological lines. Generally, liberals are more accepting of cancel culture than conservatives, with independents between the two (Schaeffer, 2021). For example, conservatives (26%) are more likely than liberals (6%) to view cancel culture as censorship of speech or history. Conversely, liberals (59%) are more likely than conservatives (36%) to view cancel culture as actions taken to hold others accountable. The Pew poll also showed that these ideological differences have widened between 2017 and 2020. It seems that whether one sees cancel culture positively or negatively is in the eye of the beholder.

Perhaps there is no better example of shifting social norms and prejudice reduction than the issue of same-sex marriage. Over a period of time, acceptance of gay marriage increased markedly in the United States. For example, a poll done in 2003 showed that 58% of Americans opposed same-sex marriage. Another poll taken in 2013 showed that percentage dropped to 44%. In the decade between 2003 and 2013 a number of states had legalized same-sex marriage and there was increasing acceptance among the U.S. population for same-sex marriage. This increasing acceptance culminated in a 2015 Supreme Court decision legalizing same-sex marriage.

Reducing Prejudice Through Training

Another strategy employed to reduce prejudice is training individuals to associate positive characteristics with out-group members or to dissociate negative traits from those members. This strategy has been adopted in many contexts. Industries, colleges and universities, and even elementary and high school programs emphasize diversity and attempt to improve intergroup relations and reduce prejudice and stereotyping. In this section we will see if such strategies are effective.

Evidence for the effectiveness of training against stereotypes was found in an experiment by Kawakami et al. (2000). Kawakami et al. had participants respond to photographs of Black and White individuals associated with stereotypic and nonstereotypic traits. Half of the participants received training to help them suppress automatic activation of stereotypes. These participants were trained to respond "No" to a White photograph associated with stereotypical White characteristics and "No" to a Black photograph associated with stereotypical Black characteristics. They were also trained to respond "Yes" when a photograph (Black or White) was associated with a nonstereotypic trait. The other half of the participants were provided with training that was just the opposite. The results showed that after extensive training participants who were given stereotype suppression training were able to suppress stereotypes that were usually activated automatically.

In a similar experiment, Kawakami et al. (2005) investigated whether such training effects extended to gender stereotypes. During the training phase of the experiment, some participants were told that they would see a photograph of a face along with two traits at the bottom of the photograph. Participants were instructed to indicate which of the two traits was *not* culturally associated with the person depicted. So, for example, a face of a female was shown with the traits "sensitive" (a trait stereotypically associated with females) and "strong" (a trait not stereotypically associated with females). The correct answer for this trial would be to select "strong." Participants in the "no training" condition did not go through this procedure. All participants then evaluated four potential job candidates (all equally qualified). Two of the applicants were male and two were female. Participants were told to pick the best candidate for a job that involved leadership and supervising doctors. Half of the participants in the training condition did the applicant rating task immediately after the training, whereas the other half completed a filler task before completing the applicant rating task (this introduced a delay between the training and rating task).

Kawakami et al. (2005) found that participants in the no training and the training with no delay before the rating task were more likely to pick a male candidate than female candidate for the leadership position. These participants displayed sexist preferences. However, when the training and application-rating task were separated by a filler task, sexist preferences were significantly reduced. Kawakami et al. (2005) suggest that when there was no filler task, participants may have felt unduly influenced to pick a female applicant. Because of psychological reactance (i.e., not liking it when we are told to do something), these participants selected the male applicants. Reactance was less likely to be aroused when the training and task were separated.

How about more realistic training exercises? In one study, Stewart et al. (2003) exposed participants to a classic racial sensitivity exercise. This exercise involves using eye color as a basis for discrimination. For example, blue-eyed individuals are set up as the preferred group and brown-eyed individuals in the subordinate group. During the exercise the blue-eyed individuals are treated better, given more privileges, and given preferential treatment. Participants in a control group did not go through this exercise. The results showed that participants in the exercise group showed more positive attitudes toward Asians and Latinos than participants in the control group (the exercise produced only marginally better attitudes toward African Americans). Participants in the exercise group also expressed more displeasure with themselves when they caught themselves thinking prejudicial thoughts.

Hogan and Mallot (2005) assessed whether students enrolled in a course on race and gender experienced a reduction in prejudice (measured by the Modern Racism Scale). Participants in the study were students who were either currently enrolled in the course, had taken the course in the past, or had not taken the course. Hogan and Mallot found that participants who were currently enrolled in the class showed less racial prejudice than participants in the other two groups. The fact that the participants who had completed the course showed more prejudice than those currently enrolled suggested to Hogan and Mallot that the effects of the race/gender course were temporary.

There is emerging evidence that training exercises intended to improve intergroup relations and reduce prejudice may have unintended consequences. One training exercise used in some institutions has participants attempt to build an ideal community (Archie Bunker's Neighborhood). In this exercise some participants are assigned to a condition where they are faced with discrimination while trying to build the ideal community. Other participants are assigned to a condition where they are members of an advantaged group facing no discrimination. After participating in the exercise, participants are supposed to be more sensitive to the problems facing disadvantaged groups. Miller et al. (2013) subjected this exercise to empirical test in a laboratory experiment. Participants were randomly assigned to either the advantaged or disadvantaged groups described above. Participants also completed measures of opposition to equality (OEQ) and group-based dominance (GBD). The results of this experiment showed that participants in the disadvantaged group showed more opposition to equality than those in the advantaged group. Interestingly, this difference was evident when participants were reassessed for OEQ a week later. So, in this instance an exercise that was supposed to increase intergroup equality had the opposite effect.

What is clear from these studies is that there is no simple, consistent effect of training on racial prejudice. Of course, this conclusion is based on only a few studies. More research is needed to determine the extent to which diversity or racial sensitivity training will reduce prejudice.

SOCIAL PSYCHOLOGY IN ACTION

The Disarming of Racism in the U.S. Army

During the Vietnam War, race relations in the U.S. Army were abysmal (Moskos, 1991). Fights between White and African American soldiers were commonplace in army life in the 1970s. By the early 1980s, the army was making an organized and determined effort to eliminate racial prejudice and animosities. It appears to have succeeded admirably. Many of the strategies the army used are based on principles discussed in this chapter. Let's consider what they were.

One important strategy used by the army was the *level playing field* (Moskos, 1990, 1991). This means that from basic training onward, everyone is treated the same—the same haircuts, the same uniforms, the same rules and regulations. This helps to reduce advantages and handicaps and makes everyone equal. The army also has a basic remedial education program that is beneficial for those with leadership qualities but deficits in schooling.

A second factor is a rigid non-discrimination policy. Any expression of racist sentiments results in an unfavorable rating and an end to a military career. This is not to say that officers are free of racist sentiments; it merely means that officers jeopardize their careers if they express or act on such sentiments. A racial insult can lead to a charge of incitement to riot and is punishable by time in the brig. The army uses social scientists to monitor the state of racial relations. It also runs training programs for equal-opportunity instructors, whose function is to see that the playing field remains level.

The army's ability to enforce a nonracist environment is supported enormously by the *hierarchy* that exists both within the officer corps and among the noncommissioned officers. The social barriers that exist in the army reflect rank rather than race. A sergeant must have a stronger identification with his or her peer sergeants than with members of the same race in lower ranks.

Finally, the army's nondiscriminatory environment is visible in its leadership. Many African Americans have leadership roles in the army, including General Colin Powell, the former chairman of the Joint Chiefs of Staff.

What lessons can we learn from the U.S. Army's experience? First, a fair implementation of the contact

The U. S. Army successfully addressed the problem of racism by leveling the playing field, adopting a rigid no-discrimination policy, and enforcing a nonracist environment within the hierarchy of ranks.
Source: lev radin/Shutterstock.

hypothesis is a good starting point for reducing prejudice. Equal-status interactions and clear mutual goals, even superordinate goals, are essential ingredients of effective contact. Clear and forceful support of the program by leadership is another ingredient. Anyone who violates the policy suffers. At the same time, positive action is taken to level prior inequalities. The army's special programs ensure that everyone has an equal chance. Some of these lessons cannot be transferred from the army setting. Civilian society does not have the army's strict hierarchy, its control over its members, or its system of rewards and punishments. But the fundamental lesson may be that race relations can best be served by strengthening positive social norms. When social norms are very clear, and when there is a clear commitment to nondiscrimination by leadership—employers, politicians, and national leaders—individual members of society have the opportunity to transcend their prejudices and act on their shared humanity.

Discussion Questions

1. What did the U.S. Army do to address racism within its ranks?
2. What can we learn from the U.S. Army's experience?

The Mormon Experience Revisited

We opened this chapter with a discussion of the experience of the Mormons in the 1800s. The Mormons were the victims of stereotyping (branded as heretics), prejudice (negative attitudes directed at them by the population and the press), and discrimination (economic boycotts). They were viewed as the out-group by Christians (the in-group) to the extent that they began living in their own homogeneous enclaves and even became the target of an extermination order. Once the "us" versus "them" mentality set in, it was easy enough for the Christian majority to pigeonhole Mormons and act toward individual Mormons based on what was believed about them as a group. This is what we would expect based on social identity theory and self-categorization theory. By perceiving the Mormons as evil and themselves as the protectors of all that is sacred, the Christian majority undoubtedly was able to enhance the self-esteem of its members.

The reaction of the Mormons to the prejudice also fits nicely with what we know about how prejudice affects people. Under conditions of threat, we tend to band more closely together as a protection mechanism. The Mormons became more clannish and isolated from mainstream society. This is an example of using primary compensation to cope with the prejudice. The Mormons decided to keep to themselves and tried not to antagonize the Christian majority. Unfortunately, this increased isolation was viewed by the majority as further evidence for the stereotypes about the Mormons. Ultimately, the cycle of prejudice continued until the Mormons were driven to settle in Utah.

Study Break

Social psychologists have investigated methods that can be used to reduce prejudice. Before you read the chapter review, answer the following questions:

1. What is the contact hypothesis, and under what conditions can contact between groups reduce prejudice?
2. How can personalizing out-group members help reduce prejudice?
3. How can changing social norms reduce prejudice?
4. What are the effects of training programs on prejudice, and what are some of the downsides to this strategy?,
5. How did the U.S. Army reduce prejudice?

Chapter Review

1. **How are prejudice, stereotypes, and discrimination defined?**

   Prejudice is defined as a biased, often negative, attitude about a group of people. Prejudicial attitudes include belief structures housing information about a group and expectations concerning the behavior of members of that group. Prejudice can be positive or negative, with negative prejudice—dislike for a group—being the focus of research and theory. A stereotype is a rigid set of positive or negative beliefs about the characteristics of a group. A stereotype represents pictures we keep in our heads. When a prejudiced person encounters a member of a group, he or she will activate the stereotype and fit it to the individual. Stereotypes are not abnormal ways of thinking. Rather, they relate to the natural tendency for humans to categorize. Categorization becomes problematic when categories become rigid and overgeneralized. Stereotypes may also form the basis for judgmental heuristics about the behavior of members of a group. Discrimination is the behavioral component of a prejudicial attitude. Discrimination occurs when prejudicial feelings are turned into behavior. Like stereotyping, discrimination is an extension of a natural tendency to discriminate among stimuli. Discrimination becomes a problem when it is directed toward people simply because they are members of a group. It is important to note that discrimination can occur in the absence of prejudice, and prejudice can exist without discrimination.

2. **What is the relationship among prejudice, stereotypes, and discrimination?**

   Prejudice, stereotypes, and discrimination are related phenomena that help us understand why we treat members of certain groups with hostility. Prejudice comes in a variety of forms, with sexism (negative feelings based on gender category) and racism (negative feelings based on apparent racial category) being most common. Stereotyped beliefs about members of a group often give rise to prejudicial feelings, which may give rise to discriminatory behavior.

   Stereotypes also may serve as judgmental heuristics and affect the way we interpret the behavior of members of a group. Behavior that is seen as stereotype-consistent is likely to be attributed internally and judged more harshly than behavior that is not stereotype-consistent.

3. **What evidence is there for the prevalence of these concepts from a historical perspective?**

History tells us that stereotyping, prejudice, and discrimination have been with human beings for a long time. Once formed, stereotypes and prejudices endure over time. Stereotyped views of Japanese by Americans (and vice versa) endured from the World War II era through the present. Prejudicial feelings also led to religious persecution in the United States against groups such as the Mormons.

4. **What are the personality roots of prejudice?**

One personality dimension identified with prejudice is authoritarianism. People with authoritarian personalities tend to feel submissive toward authority figures and hostile toward different ethnic groups. They have rigid beliefs and tend to be racist and sexist. Social psychologists have also explored how members of different groups, such as Whites and Blacks, perceive each other. An updated version of the authoritarian personality is right-wing authoritarianism (RWA), which also relates to prejudice. Research also shows that there is also prejudice on the left wing of the political spectrum. Social dominance orientation (SDO) is another personality dimension that has been studied. People high on social dominance want their group to be superior to others. SDO is also related to prejudice. When SDO and RWA are considered together, they are associated with the highest levels of prejudice. Finally, two dimensions of the "big five" approach to personality (agreeableness and openness) are negatively related to prejudice. There is also evidence that SDO and RWA may relate differently to different forms of prejudice. SDO is related to stereotyping, negative emotion, and negative attitudes directed toward African Americans and individuals with a same-sex orientation, and RWA is related to negative stereotypes and emotion directed at individuals with a same-sex orientation, but not African Americans. Two of the big five personality characteristics also relate to prejudice. Individuals low in agreeableness and openness to new experience tend to be prejudiced. Finally, the three components of the dark personality triad correlate with prejudice, operating through SDO and perceptions of intergroup threat.

5. **How does gender relate to prejudice?**

Research shows that males are higher on SDO than females and tend to be more prejudiced than females. Research on male and female attitudes about gays and lesbians generally shows that males demonstrate a more prejudiced attitude toward gays and lesbians than do females. Males tend to have more negative feelings toward gay men than toward lesbians. Whether females show more prejudice against lesbians than against gay men is not clear. Some research shows that women don't make a distinction between gays and lesbians, whereas other research suggests greater prejudice against lesbians than against gay men. Other research shows that males tend to show more ethnic prejudices than females.

6. **What are the social roots of prejudice?**

Prejudice must be considered within the social context within which it exists. Historically, dominant groups have directed prejudice at less dominant groups. Although most Americans adhere to the notion of equity and justice toward minorities such as African Americans, they tend to oppose steps to reach those goals and only pay lip service to the notion of equity. It is no longer acceptable to express explicit prejudice. However, prejudice still exists on a more subtle, often implicit, level. Some examples are aversive racism and modern racism. Even people who claim to be nonprejudiced show prejudice under the right circumstances.

7. **What is modern racism, and what are the criticisms of it?**

In modern culture, it is no longer acceptable to express prejudices overtly, as it was in the past. However, prejudice is still expressed in a more subtle form: modern racism. Adherents of the notion of modern racism suggest that opposing civil rights legislation or voting for a candidate who opposes affirmative action are manifestations of modern racism.

Critics of modern racism point out that equating opposition to political ideas with racism is illogical and that the concept of modern racism has not been clearly defined or measured. Additionally, the correlation between modern racism and old-fashioned racism is high. Thus, modern and old-fashioned racism may be indistinguishable.

8. **What are the cognitive roots of prejudice?**

Cognitive social psychologists have focused on stereotypes and intergroup perceptions when attempting to understand prejudice. As humans, we have a strong predisposition to categorize people into groups. We do this even when we have only the most minimal basis on which to make categorizations. We classify ourselves and those we perceive to be like us in the in-group, and others whom we perceive to be different from us we classify in the out-group. As a result of this categorization, we tend to display an in-group bias: favoring members of the in-group over members of the out-group.

Tajfel proposed his social identity theory to help explain in-group bias. According to this theory, individuals are motivated to maintain a positive self-concept, part of which comes from membership in groups. Identification with the in-group confers us with a social identity. Categorizing dissimilar others as members of the out-group is another aspect of the social identity process. When we feel threatened, in-group bias increases, thereby enhancing our self-concept. Self-categorization theory suggests that self-esteem is most likely to be enhanced when members of the in-group distinguish themselves from other groups in positive ways.

The in-group bias may also have biological roots. We have a strong wariness of the unfamiliar, called xenophobia, which sociobiologists think is a natural part of our genetic heritage. It may have helped us survive as a species. It is biologically adaptive, for example, for a child to be wary of potentially dangerous strangers. The in-group bias may serve a similar purpose. Throughout history there are examples of various groups increasing solidarity in response to hostility from the dominant group to ensure group survival. Prejudice, then, may be seen as an unfortunate by-product of natural, biologically based behavior patterns.

Because it is less taxing to deal with a person by relying on group-based stereotypes than to find out about that individual, categorizing people using stereotypes helps us economize our cognitive processing effort. Quick categorization of individuals via stereotypes contributes to prejudicial feelings and discrimination. Automatic language associations, by which we link positive words with the in-group and negative words with the out-group, contribute to these negative feelings.

Social identity theory and self-categorization theory both take the same basic approach to explaining the roots of prejudice. There is another way to explain stereotyping and prejudice that do not rely on group justification. The alternative approach is system justification theory which states that prejudice can occur when members of groups justify the existence of social arrangements at the expense of interpersonal and group interests.

9. How do cognitive biases contribute to prejudice?

Cognitive biases and errors that lead to prejudice include the illusory correlation, the fundamental attribution error, the confirmation bias, the out-group homogeneity bias, and the ultimate attribution error. An illusory correlation is the tendency to believe that two unrelated events are connected if they are systematically related. If you have a tendency to believe that members of a minority group have a negative characteristic, then you will perceive a relationship between group membership and a behavior related to that trait. Additionally, illusory correlations help form and maintain stereotypes. A prejudiced person will overestimate the degree of relationship between a negative trait and a negative behavior. The fundamental attribution error (the tendency to overestimate the role of internal characteristics in the behavior of others) also helps maintain stereotypes and prejudice. Because of this error, individuals tend to attribute negative behaviors of a minority group to internal predispositions rather than to situational factors. The confirmation bias maintains prejudice because individuals who hold negative stereotypes about a group look for evidence to confirm those stereotypes. If one expects a minority group member to behave in a negative way, evidence will be sought to confirm that expectation. The out-group homogeneity bias is the tendency to see less diversity among members of an out-group than among members of an in-group. As a consequence, a negative behavior of one member of an out-group is likely to be seen as representative of the group as a whole. The ultimate attribution error occurs when we attribute a negative behavior of a minority group to the general characteristics of individuals who make up that group, whereas we attribute the same behavior of an in-group member to situational factors.

10. Are stereotypes ever accurate, and can they be overcome?

There are studies that show that some stereotypes sometimes are accurate. However, accurate or not, stereotypes are still harmful, because they give us a damaging perception of others. There is a tendency to judge individuals according to the worst example of a group represented by a stereotype. Stereotypes can be overcome if one uses controlled processing rather than automatic processing when thinking about others.

11. How do prejudiced and nonprejudiced individuals differ?

One important way in which more- and less-prejudiced individuals differ is that the latter are aware of their prejudices and carefully monitor them. Less-prejudiced persons tend not to believe the stereotypes they hold and act accordingly. Prejudiced individuals are more likely to use automatic processing and energize stereotypes than are less-prejudiced individuals who use controlled processing. However, even nonprejudiced persons will fall prey to stereotyping if stereotypes are activated beyond their conscious control.

12. What is the impact of prejudice on those who are its target?

There are many ways that prejudice can be expressed, some more serious than others. However, it is safe to say that even the lowest level of expression (antilocution) can have detectable emotional and cognitive consequences for targets of prejudice. Everyday prejudice has a cumulative effect on a person and contributes to the target's knowledge and experience with prejudice. Targets of prejudice-based jokes report feelings of disgust, anger, and hostility in response to those jokes.

Another way that targets of prejudice are affected is through the mechanism of the stereotype threat. Once a stereotype is activated about one's group, a member of that group may perform poorly on a task related to that threat, a fact confirmed by research. Another form of threat is collective threat, which occurs when a person from a stereotyped group becomes overly concerned that a transgression by a member of one's group may reflect badly on him or her as an individual. Collective threat comes from a concern that poor performance by one member of one's group may be viewed as a stereotype and generalized to all members of that group.

13. **How can a person who is the target of prejudice cope with being a target?**

Usually, individuals faced with everyday prejudice must find ways of effectively managing it. If one's group is devalued, stigmatized, or oppressed relative to other groups, prejudice can be countered by raising the value of the devalued group. This is done by first convincing group members of their own self-worth and then by convincing the rest of society of the worth of the group. Another strategy used by individuals from a stigmatized group is to try to anticipate situations in which prejudice will be encountered. Individuals can then decide how to best react to or minimize the impact of prejudice, for example, by modifying their behavior, the way they dress, or the neighborhood in which they live. A third way to cope with stress is through the use of compensation. There are two modes of compensation in which a person can engage. When secondary compensation is used, an individual attempts to change his or her mode of thinking about situations to psychologically protect him- or herself against the outcomes of prejudice. For example, a person who wants to obtain a college degree but faces prejudice that may prevent him or her from reaching the goal would be using secondary compensation if he or she devalued the goal (a college education is not all that important) or disidentified with the goal (members of my group usually don't go to college). On the other hand, primary compensation reduces the actual threats posed by prejudice. Coping strategies are developed that allow the target of prejudice to achieve his or her goals.

14. **What can be done about prejudice?**

Although prejudice has plagued humans throughout their history, there may be ways to reduce it. The contact hypothesis suggests that increased contact between groups should increase positive feelings. However, mere contact may not be enough. Positive feelings are enhanced when there is a superordinate goal toward which groups work cooperatively. Contact need not be physical in nature. Imagined contact can also reduce prejudice. Contact can also help reduce the transmission of intergenerational prejudice. Another strategy is to personalize out-group members; this prevents falling back on stereotypes. It is also beneficial to increase the frequency of antiracist statements that people hear, a form of strengthening social norms. A strong expression of social norms, disapproval of prejudice in all of its variations, is probably the best way to discourage and reduce prejudiced acts. Prejudice may also be reduced through training programs that seek to dissociate negative traits from minority group members. Although these programs have met with some success, there is no simple, consistent effect of training on racial prejudice.

15. **How did the U.S. Army reduce prejudice?**

The army reduced prejudice using three strategies. First, the army leveled the playing field by treating everyone the same. The army reduced advantages and disadvantages through extensive training. Second, the army set a rigid no-discrimination policy. Expressions of prejudice and discriminatory actions were not tolerated and could be dealt with severely—including ending an officer's career. Finally, the U.S. Army's rigid hierarchy allowed the first two strategies to be effective.

Key Terms

Authoritarian personality (p. 121)
Authoritarianism (p. 120)
Aversive racism (p. 130)
Collective threat (p. 150)
Contact hypothesis (p. 154)
Discrimination (p. 118)
Illusory correlation (p. 140)
In-group bias (p. 135)

Modern racism (p. 130)
Out-group homogeneity bias (p. 143)
Prejudice (p. 107)
Primary compensation (p. 153)
Secondary compensation (p. 153)
Self-categorization theory (SCT) (p. 136)

Social dominance orientation (SDO) (p. 123)
Social identity theory (SIT) (p. 136)
Stereotype (p. 110)
Stereotype threat (p. 147)
System justification theory (p. 139)
Ultimate attribution error (p. 143)

Chapter Quiz

1. A biased, often negative, attitude about a group of people is the definition of
   A. discrimination.
   B. a stereotype.
   C. an attitude.
   D. prejudice.

2. Prejudice that is overt and easily spotted is known as
   A. explicit.
   B. unconscious.
   C. implicit.
   D. indirect.

3. According to your text, a positive stereotype associated with admiration would result from which of the following combinations?
   A. Low warmth and high competence
   B. High warmth and high competence
   C. Low warmth and low competence
   D. High warmth and low competence

4. Explicit stereotypes are most likely to relate to behavior for a task requiring
   A. little cognitive effort.
   B. automatic processing.
   C. a single judgment.
   D. considerable cognitive effort.

5. Overt behavior directed toward people simply because they are presumed to be members of a particular group is known as
   A. discrimination.
   B. generalization.
   C. behavioral bias.
   D. stereotyping.

6. According to your text, which conclusion can we draw about the relationship between political ideology and prejudice?
   A. Prejudice exists on both ends of the political spectrum.
   B. Liberals actually show a stronger racial bias than conservatives.
   C. Only conservatives show prejudice.
   D. None of the above.

7. According to your text, even though it is no longer socially acceptable to express prejudice overtly, _____ still exists.
   A. private prejudice
   B. clandestine prejudice
   C. implicit prejudice
   D. explicit prejudice

8. Bob gives members of his own religious sect special discounts at his store, but he does not give similar discounts to members of other religions. This illustrates the
   A. own-group bias.
   B. in-group bias.
   C. out-group homogeneity bias.
   D. out-group bias.

9. According to self-categorization theory, in which case is prejudice less likely?
   A. If uncertainty can be managed
   B. If people can be prevented from categorizing each other
   C. If uncertainty can be rationalized
   D. None of the above

10. Major Johnson uses racial slurs when he chews out a Black soldier. He is reprimanded, and a permanent notation of the incident is placed in his service record. This is an example of the U.S. Army using _____ to reduce prejudice.
    A. a level playing field
    B. jigsaw training
    C. hierarchy
    D. a rigid non-discrimination policy

Answers can be found in the end-of-book Answers section.

Attitudes

The ultimate determinant in the struggle now going on for the world will not be bombs and rockets but a test of wills and ideas—a trial of spiritual resolve: the values we hold, the beliefs we cherish and the ideals to which we are dedicated.

—Ronald Reagan

CHAPTER 5

Source: VanHart/Shutterstock.

Key Questions

As you read this chapter, find the answers to the following questions:

1. What is an attitude?
2. What is the relationship of attitudes to values?
3. What are implicit and explicit attitudes?
4. How are attitude surveys conducted?
5. What are the potential sources of bias in a survey?
6. What are behavioral measures of attitudes?
7. What is the Implicit Attitude Test (IAT)?
8. What does the IAT tell us about our prejudices?
9. How are attitudes formed?
10. Can attitudes be inherited?
11. What is agenda setting?
12. How do groups influence one's attitudes?
13. How do social networks influence a person's attitudes?
14. What is the relationship between attitudes and behavior?
15. What is the notion of the nonrational actor?
16. How has the controversy over the rational and nonrational actor been resolved?
17. What is ideology, and how does it relate to behavior?
18. What is naïve realism, and how does it influence our political attitudes?

Ida Tarbell is not a name most of us recognize. A history of American women doesn't give her even a single line (Hymowitz & Weissman, 1984). Yet, she was at the center of American life for the first three decades of the 20th century. Teddy Roosevelt hurled the mocking epithet "muckraker" at her. It was a label she eventually wore proudly, for she, perhaps more than anyone else, told the American people about the corruption, conspiracies, strong-arm tactics, and enormous greed that went into "business as usual" at the turn of the 20th century (Fleming, 1986).

Tarbell grew up in Titusville, Pennsylvania. In the last decades of the 19th century, it was the center of the booming oil industry. It was also the town that would make Standard Oil Company and its founder, John D. Rockefeller, richer than anyone could imagine.

Tarbell grew up among derricks and oil drums, in oil-cloaked fields, under oil-flecked skies. In 1872 her father's business was threatened by a scheme devised by Rockefeller and his partners that would allow them to ship their oil via the railroads at a much cheaper fare than any other producer, thus driving their competition out of the business. Frank Tarbell and the others fought this scheme and forced the railroads to treat everyone fairly, at least temporarily. Ida was well informed about the conspiracy and, possessing her father's strong sense of justice, was outraged. She vowed that if she were given the

167

Source: spatuletail/Shutterstock.

chance, she would make people aware of the greed and dishonesty she had witnessed. At this time she was 15 years old (Weinberg & Weinberg, 1961).

In college, Tarbell was a free spirit. She became friends with whomever she wanted, ignored all the unwritten social rules, learned to be critical and disciplined in her work, and graduated with a degree in natural science. After working as a schoolteacher, she went off to Paris to become a writer. For years, she wrote articles and biographies, but in 1900, she started to write about oil. She began to form an idea about a series of articles on the Standard Oil Company, which supplied almost all the oil that was used to light American homes in the days before electricity. Although Standard Oil had been investigated on charges of bribery and other illegal tactics by authorities for almost the entire 30 years of its existence, very little evidence existed in the public domain. Tarbell got around that by getting to know one of the company's vice presidents, Henry Rogers, who let her have access to private records. Rogers was unapologetic about his role. He cheerfully admitted that Rockefeller lied, cheated, double-dealt, and used violence or the threat of it to build an enormously successful, powerful, and efficient company (Fleming, 1986).

Tarbell's book, *The History of the Standard Oil Company*, published in 1904, appeared in monthly installments in *McClure's* magazine. It was a sensation. It read like a suspense story, and readers couldn't wait until the next month's issue. The book had a ready-made villain: John D. Rockefeller. He was portrayed as a money-hungry rogue without a shred of humanity, and that is the image of him that has come down to us 100 years later. After the book came out, he tried to restore his image by giving over $35 million to charity. At the time, he was estimated to be worth over $900 million, a sum equivalent to many billions in today's currency.

Tarbell's work had a tremendous impact on the nation. It led not only to a number of lawsuits against the oil industry for its monopolistic practices, but also to federal antitrust laws that dismantled the original Standard Oil Company. Today, we have a number of independent Standard Oil companies (Ohio, New Jersey, etc.) as a result of Tarbell's work.

Even more remarkable than what Tarbell did was the way she did it. She was entirely skeptical of all the common beliefs of her time. She did not believe in the theory of the inferiority of women, prevalent in the early years of her life, nor did she believe in the early 20th-century theory that women were morally superior and evolutionarily more advanced. She joined no organizations or social reform movements. Yet she took on the most powerful men in the country and became a formidable adversary (Fleming, 1986).

Tarbell was determined, controlled, and unafraid, but her attitudes and behavior were also shaped and informed by her experience. She grew up in a family that supported her in her independent ways and encouraged her to do what she thought was right. She was powerfully influenced by her father, within whom she saw a strong sense of justice. Events that occurred during her formative years motivated and inspired her and forever altered the way she viewed the world.

The attitudes that Tarbell held played a fundamental role in the way she perceived the world around her. Like other mechanisms of social cognition, they organized her experiences, directed her behavior, and helped define who she was. We begin by exploring what attitudes are and what role they play in our lives. What are the elements that go into attitudes? How do they flow from and express our deepest values? What are the processes by which we acquire or develop attitudes? And what is the relationship between attitudes and behavior in our day-to-day lives? How do attitudes express the relationships among what we think, what we feel, what we intend to do, and what we actually do? These are some of the questions addressed in this chapter.

What Are Attitudes?

The study of attitudes has been of fundamental concern to social psychologists throughout the history of the field. In fact, Gordon Allport (1954b) once characterized attitudes as "the most distinctive and indispensable concept in contemporary social psychology" (p. 43). Today, we have no reason to disagree with him. Other issues may come and go, dictated by fashion in theory and research and influenced by current events, but interest in attitudes remains. This preoccupation with attitudes is easy to understand. The concept of attitudes is central to explaining our thoughts, feelings, and actions with regard to other people, situations, and ideas.

In this section, we explore the basic concept of attitudes. First we look at and elaborate on a classic definition of the term. Then we consider how attitudes relate to values, what functions attitudes serve, and how attitudes can be measured.

Allport's Definition of Attitudes

The word *attitude* crops up often in our everyday conversation. We speak of having an attitude about someone or something. In this usage, attitude usually implies feelings that are either positive or negative. We also speak of someone who has a "bad attitude." You may, for example, think that a coworker has an "attitude problem." In this usage, attitude implies some personality characteristic or behavior pattern that offends us.

Social psychologists use the term *attitude* differently than this. In order to study and measure attitudes, they need a clear and careful definition of the term. Gordon Allport, an early attitude theorist, formulated the following definition: "An **attitude** is a mental and neural state of readiness, organized through experience, exerting a directive or dynamic influence upon the individual's response to all objects and situations with which it is related" (1935, p. 798). This is a rich and comprehensive definition, and although there have been many redefinitions over the years, Allport's definition still captures much that is essential about attitudes (see Figure 5.1).

attitude A mental and neural state of readiness, organized through experience, exerting a directive or dynamic influence on the individual's response to all objects and situations with which it is related.

Attitude

| A mental state of readiness, | organized through experience, | exerting a directive influence on one's responses to related objects and situations. |

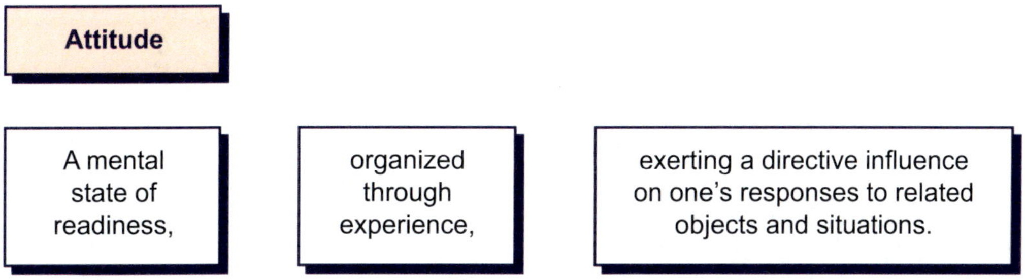

FIGURE 5.1
A schematic diagram of Allport's definition of an attitude showing the important components of an attitude.

Consequently, we adopt it here as our central definition. The definition can be broken into three parts, each with some important implications (Rajecki, 1990).

First, because attitudes are mental or neural states of readiness, they are necessarily private. Scientists who study attitudes cannot measure them directly in the way, for example, that medical doctors can measure blood pressure. Only the person who holds an attitude is capable of having direct access to it. The social psychological measures of an attitude must be indirect.

Second, if attitudes are organized through experience, they are presumably formed through learning from a variety of experiences and influences. Our attitudes about, say, appropriate roles for men and women are shaped by the attitudes passed on by our culture, especially by parents, friends, and other agents of socialization, such as schools and television. Recall that even though the wider society was not supportive of women in nontraditional roles in Ida Tarbell's time, her parents were very supportive. The notion that our attitudes arise only from experience is too limiting, however. There is also increasing evidence that some attitudes also have a genetic element (Tesser, 1993). Finally, because attitudes exert a directive or dynamic influence on a person's response to objects, people, and situations, attitudes are directly related to our actions or behavior.

A person's attitude toward an issue such as gun control is made up of affect, behavior, cognitions, and intentions.
Source: Jacob Lund/Shutterstock.

Attitude Structures

An attitude is made up of four interconnected components: cognitions, affective responses, behavioral intentions, and behaviors. To understand this interconnectedness, let's consider the attitude of someone opposed to gun-control legislation. Her attitude can be stated as, "I am opposed to laws in any way controlling the ownership of guns."

This attitude would be supported by cognitions, or thoughts, about laws and gun ownership. For example, she might think that unrestricted gun ownership is a basic right guaranteed by the Second Amendment of the Constitution. The attitude would also be supported by affective responses, or feelings. She might feel strongly about her right to do what she wants to do without government interference, or she might feel strongly about protecting her family from intruders.

The attitude, and the cognitions and feelings that support it, can result in behavioral intentions and behaviors. Our hypothetical person might intend to send money to the National Rifle Association or to call her representative to argue against a gun-control bill. Finally, she might turn that intention into some real action and send the money or call her legislator.

An attitude is really a summary of an **attitude structure**, which consists of these interconnected components (Zimbardo & Leippe, 1992). Thus, the attitude "I oppose laws that restrict handgun ownership" comprises a series of interrelated thoughts, feelings, and intentions.

attitude structure
The fact that attitudes comprise a cognitive, affective, and behavioral component in their basic structure.

A change in one component of an attitude structure might very well lead to changes in the others (Zimbardo & Leippe, 1992), because an attitude structure is dynamic, with each component influencing the others. For example, if a person's close relative lost his job because of a new gun-control law, that person who favors strong gun-control laws may change her mind. The attitude structure would now be in turmoil. New feelings about guns might lead to new thoughts; intentions might change and, with them, behaviors.

Generally, the affective component dominates the attitude (Breckler & Wiggins, 1989). When we think of a particular object or person, our initial response is usually some expression of affect, as in, "I feel women will make good political candidates." We do not simply have attitudes about war, or the president, or baseball: We like these things, or we do not. When an attitude is evoked, it is always with positive or negative feeling, although, to be sure, the feeling varies in intensity. It is likely that our most intensely held attitudes in particular are primarily affective in nature (Ajzen, 1989). Thus, you might think of an attitude as primarily a response emphasizing how you feel about someone or something, as primarily an evaluation of the person or object. But keep in mind also that this evaluation is based on all the thoughts, intentions, and behaviors that go into the structure of the attitude (Zanna & Rempel, 1988).

Attitudes as an Expression of Values

Our attitudes flow from and express our values (Ball-Rokeach et al., 1984). A **value** is a conception of what is desirable; it is a guideline for a person's actions, a standard for behavior. Thus, for example, the attitude that more women and members of different ethnic groups should be elected to office might flow from the value of equality. The attitude that public officials who lie or cheat should be punished severely might flow from the value of honesty. Ida Tarbell placed a high value on fairness and justice and was outraged by the actions of Standard Oil Company.

value A concept closely related to an attitude that is a standard of what is desirable for one's actions.

Notice that attitudes are directed toward objects, people, and situations; values are broad, abstract notions. Because values are more general than attitudes, there are few values but many attitudes. Just as an attitude can be seen as a system of cognitive, affective, and behavioral components, so a value can be seen as containing many interrelated attitudes. The value of equality could give rise not only to the attitude, say, that more women and members of different ethnic groups should hold office but also to countless other attitudes relating to the innumerable people, objects, issues, and ideas toward which one might direct thoughts, feelings, and behaviors.

Milton Rokeach (1973, 1979), a social psychologist who spent most of his professional life studying how people organize their value systems, argued that there are two distinct categories of values. He called one category *terminal values*. Terminal values, according to Rokeach (1973), refer to desired "end states." For example, equality, freedom, a comfortable life, and salvation would all be end states. The other category he called *instrumental values*. Instrumental values, which flow from our preferred end states, could be values such as being forgiving, broadminded, and responsible. According to Rokeach, two fundamental terminal values, equality and freedom, are especially predictive of a whole range of attitudes. Attitudes about the role of government, for example, often can be predicted by knowing how someone ranks these two values. A person who values equality more highly probably would want the government to take an active role in education, health, and other social welfare issues. A person who values freedom more highly probably would prefer that government stay out of the way and let everyone fend for themselves. Consider a person who rates equality higher than freedom. How might this affect her attitudes on specific issues? A high value placed on equality implies that the individual is more concerned with the common good than with individual freedoms (although freedom might still be ranked relatively highly by that person). This individual might be in favor of "sin taxes" (such as high tobacco and alcohol taxes) to raise money for national health care and also might be in favor of stronger gun-control laws. A person who considers freedom to be more desirable than equality probably would be against sin taxes ("It's none of the government's business if people want to kill themselves") and also against government regulation of gun ownership.

When asked, do people account for their attitudes by referring to specific values? And do people on opposing sides of an issue hold opposing values? In one study, researchers measured participants' attitudes toward two issues, abortion and nuclear weapons (Kristiansen & Zanna, 1988). Next, participants were asked to rank the (personal) importance of 18 values, such as freedom, equality, an exciting life, family security, and so on, and then relate each value to their attitudes on these two issues.

People with different attitudes consider different values important. People who oppose the right to abortion, for example, give a higher ranking to certain values (e.g., mature love, wisdom, true friendship, salvation, and a world of beauty) than do people who support the right to abortion. Those who support the right to abortion give a higher ranking to other values (e.g., happiness, family security, a comfortable life, pleasure, an exciting life, and a sense of accomplishment) than do those who oppose the right to abortion.

At the same time, both groups shared many values. Both ranked freedom, inner harmony, and equality as the values most important to their attitude. Differences in the rankings of other values were slight. The results also suggest that people on either side of volatile issues might be much closer in their values than they realize.

Explicit and Implicit Attitudes

In many cases we freely express and are aware of our attitudes and how they influence our behavior. An attitude falling into this category is known as an **explicit attitude**. Explicit attitudes operate on a conscious level, so we are aware of them—aware of the cognitive underpinnings of them—and are conscious of how they relate to behavior. They operate via controlled processing and take some cognitive effort to activate. For example, you may know how you feel toward a given political candidate and match your behavior (e.g., voting for him or her) to that attitude. It is these explicit attitudes that we often find having a directive effect on behavior.

explicit attitude An attitude that operates on a conscious level via controlled processing.

Although many of our attitudes operate on this conscious level, there are others that operate unconsciously. This form of an attitude is known as an **implicit attitude**. Specifically, an implicit attitude is defined as "actions or judgments that are under control of automatically activated evaluation without the performer's awareness of that causation" (Greenwald et al., 1998, p. 1464). In other words, implicit attitudes affect behaviors automatically, without conscious thought, and below the level of awareness. For example, an individual may have a quick negative reaction toward a member of a minority group, even though the individual professes positive and tolerant attitudes toward that group. The "gut-level" reaction occurs without thought and is often distasteful to the individual (Wilson et al., 2000).

implicit attitude An attitude that affects behavior automatically, without conscious thought and below the level of awareness via automatic processing.

As you may recall from Chapter 4, the relationship between explicit and implicit attitudes is complex and still not fully understood. However, there are some elements of implicit and explicit attitudes for which there is strong agreement. First, implicit and explicit attitudes are distinct from one another. That is, implicit and explicit attitudes are separate but related constructs (Nosek & Smyth, 2007). The distinction between implicit and explicit attitudes coincides well with a large literature in social psychology differentiating automatic versus controlled processes, which are concepts appearing throughout this book. Although there is agreement that implicit and explicit attitudes are related, ideas about the strength of this relationship vary.

There seem to be numerous factors that can affect the relationship between explicit and implicit attitudes. Self-presentation—or altering a response for personal or social purposes—appears to moderate the relationship between implicit and explicit attitudes (Nosek, 2007). For example, a person may be reluctant to express a negative attitude about Blacks; thus, we might expect a weak correlation between implicit and explicit attitudes about Blacks. However, that person may have no reservations about expressing a dislike of mint ice cream; in this case, we might expect a strong correlation between implicit and explicit attitudes. Additionally, for bipolar attitudes (i.e., those that vary strongly from positive to negative), implicit and explicit attitudes are more strongly related than for more complex, multidimensional attitudes. For example, if one has a strong positive attitude toward abortion rights (pro-choice), this would imply a strong dislike of strong pro-life attitudes. We would expect these bipolar attitudes to have higher correlations between implicit and explicit attitudes than attitudes that are less bipolar (e.g., racial attitudes). As our understanding of implicit attitudes expands, we will undoubtedly gain a better understanding of all the factors that influence the relationships between implicit and explicit attitudes.

Study Break

The previous sections introduced you to the concept of an attitude and explored how attitudes are structured. Before you begin the next section, answer the following questions:

1. What is the definition of an attitude?
2. What is an attitude structure, and what are its components (define each)?

3. What are values, and how do they relate to attitudes?
4. What are implicit and explicit attitudes, and how do they relate to each other?

How Are Attitudes Measured?

What happens when investigators want to learn about people's attitudes on a particular issue, such as affirmative action, immigration, or capital punishment? As pointed out earlier in this chapter, attitudes are private; we can't know what a person's attitudes are just by looking at her or him. For this reason, social psychologists use a variety of techniques to discover and measure people's attitudes. Some of these techniques rely on direct responses, whereas others are more indirect.

The Attitude Survey

The most commonly used techniques for measuring attitudes are attitude surveys. In an **attitude survey**, the researcher mails or emails a questionnaire to a potential respondent, conducts a face-to-face interview, or asks a series of questions on the telephone or on the Internet. Because respondents report on their own attitudes, an attitude survey is a self-report measure. A respondent indicates his or her attitude by answering a series of questions.

In evaluating election preferences or other attitudes, social psychologists usually are interested in the attitudes of a large group. Because it is not possible to survey every member of the group, researchers conducting an attitude survey select a *sample* or small subgroup of individuals from the larger group, or *population*. Don't think that you need a huge sample to have a valid survey. In fact, most nationwide surveys use a sample of only about 1,500 individuals.

Although a sample need not be large, it must be representative of the population. As you recall from Chapter 1, a representative sample is one that resembles the population in all important respects. Thus, for any category that is relevant to the attitude being measured (e.g., race and ethnicity, socioeconomic class, gender, age), the sample would contain the same proportion of people from each group within the category (e.g., from each race and ethnic group) as does the population whose attitudes are being measured. A representative sample contrasts with a biased sample, which is skewed toward one or more characteristics and does not adequately represent the larger population.

attitude survey A self-report method of measuring attitudes that involves a researcher's mailing a questionnaire to a potential respondent, conducting a face-to-face interview, or asking a series of questions on the telephone or on the Internet.

Potential Biases in Attitude Surveys

Although attitude surveys, containing various types of questions, are very popular, they do have several problems that may make any responses made by research participants invalid. Schwarz (1999) suggested that the way a person responds to a survey question depends on a variety of factors, including question wording, the format of the question, and the context within which the question is placed.

For example, presidential candidate Ross Perot commissioned a survey in March 1993 that included the following question: Should laws be passed to eliminate all possibilities of special interests giving huge sums of money to candidates? Ninety-nine percent of the people who responded to the survey said yes. A second survey done by an independent polling firm asked the same question in a different way: Do groups have the right to contribute to the candidate they support? In response to this question, only 40% favored limits on spending. This is a textbook example of how the wording of the question can influence polling data (Goleman, 1993).

Phrasing is important, but so are the specific words used in a question. For example, in one survey commissioned some years ago by the American Stock Exchange, respondents were asked how much stock they owned. Much to everyone's surprise, the highest stock ownership was found in the Southwest. It seems that the respondents were thinking of stock of the four-legged kind, not the Wall Street type. The moral is that you must consider the meaning of the words from the point of view of the people answering the questions.

Finally, respondents may lie, or to put it somewhat differently, they may not remember what they actually did or thought. Williams (1994) and his students asked voters whether they had voted in an election; almost all said they had. Williams was able to check the actual rolls of those who had voted (not how they voted) and found that only about 65% of his respondents had voted. Now, some may have forgotten, but many simply did not want to admit they had failed to do a socially desirable thing: to vote in an election (Paulhus & Reid, 1991).

Behavioral Measures

Because of the problems associated with self-report techniques, social psychologists have developed behavioral techniques of measuring attitudes. These techniques, in one way or another, avoid relying on responses to questions.

unobtrusive measure
A method of assessing attitudes such that the individuals whose attitudes you are measuring are not aware of your interest in them.

Unobtrusive measures assess attitudes by indirect means; the individual whose attitudes are being measured simply is never aware of it. For example, in one early study, investigators measured voting preferences by tallying the number of bumper stickers for a particular candidate on cars in a parking lot (Wrightsman, 1969). Other researchers measured attitudes toward competing brands of cola by searching through garbage cans. Still others attempted to determine the most popular exhibit at a museum by measuring the amount of wear and tear on various parts of the carpet (Webb et al., 1981).

Behavioral measures of attitudes often use unobtrusive methods to assess attitudes, such as counting bumper stickers on cars. For example, one could measure support for political candidates by counting the number of bumper stickers on cars supporting each candidate.
Source: Lawrence Glass/Shutterstock.

Another example of unobtrusive measurement of attitudes is the lost-letter technique (Milgram et al., 1965). If a researcher wants to measure a community's attitudes toward, say, its foreign residents, she might not get honest answers on a questionnaire. But, if she has some stamps and envelopes, she can try the lost-letter technique. This is what the researcher does: She addresses an envelope to someone with a foreign-sounding name at a local address. She puts a stamp on the envelope and then drops it on a crowded street near the post office so that it can easily be found and mailed. As her baseline control, she drops a stamped envelope addressed to someone whose name doesn't sound foreign. She repeats the procedure as many times as necessary to get a large enough sample. Then all she has to do is count the envelopes that turn up in the mail and compare the number with the names that sound foreign to the number with names that doesn't. This is her measure of that community's attitude toward foreigners.

Implicit Measures

Implicit Association Test (IAT) The most widely known measure of implicit attitudes.

Over the last 20 years, several implicit attitude measures have been created. These measures include priming tasks, the Go/No-Go association task (GNAT; Nosek & Banaji, 2001), the Affect Misattribution Procure (AMP; Payne et al., 2005), and the **Implicit Association Test (IAT)** (Greenwald et al., 1998). Although the procedures for these tasks vary somewhat, all of them rely primarily on measuring a participant's reaction time to the presentation of a stimulus or pairs of stimuli. The most well-known implicit measures test is the IAT (https://implicit.harvard.edu/implicit/). As you will recall from Chapter 4, the IAT aims to determine the strength of connection between two concepts. For example, the IAT asks test-takers to assign a stimulus, which can be words or pictures, as quickly as they possibly can, to a pair of targets.

As stated in Chapter 4, the field of social psychology is in the process of reevaluating many of the implicit processes documented in the last 20 years. In reexamining these measures, researchers are beginning to ask whether these various implicit measures are actually measuring the same construct. For example, a study by Bar-Anan and Nosek (2012) found that most correlations between the IAT, AMP, and GNAT were below .5, and only a few correlations for political attitudes were above .7. These moderate correlations indicate that these measures are not tapping into the same constructs. There is no doubt that implicit attitudes are a valuable construct in social psychology, and in the next few years, our understanding of the construct and its measurement will continue to improve.

Study Break

Social psychologists have devised a number of methods for measuring attitudes. Before you begin the next section, answer the following questions:

1. What is an attitude survey, and what kinds of questions might you find on one?
2. What are the sources of potential bias in an attitude survey, and how can they affect the results of a survey?
3. How are behavioral measures used to assess attitudes?
4. What are implicit measures of attitudes, and how are they used to measure implicit attitudes?

How Are Attitudes Formed?

We can see now that attitudes affect how we think, feel, and behave toward a wide range of people, objects, and ideas that we encounter. Where do our attitudes come from? Are they developed, as Allport suggested, through experience? If so, just how do our attitudes develop through experience? And are there other ways in which we acquire our attitudes?

Attitude formation refers to the movement we make from having no attitude toward an object to having some positive or negative attitude toward that object (Oskamp, 1991). How you acquire an attitude plays a very important role in how you use it. In this section, we explore a range of mechanisms for attitude formation. Most of these mechanisms—mere exposure, direct personal experience, operant and evaluative conditioning, and observational learning—are based on experience and learning. However, the last mechanism we will look at is based on genetics.

Mere Exposure

Some attitudes may be formed and shaped by what Zajonc (1968) called **mere exposure**, which means that simply being exposed to an object increases our feelings, usually positive, toward that object. The mere-exposure effect has been demonstrated with a wide range of stimuli, including foods, photographs, words, and advertising slogans (Bornstein, 1989).

In one early study, researchers placed ads containing nonsense words such as NAN-SOMA in college newspapers (Zajonc & Rajecki, 1969). Later, they gave students lists of words that included NANSOMA to rate. Mere exposure to a nonsense word, such as NANSOMA, was enough to give it a positive rating. In another study, participants were exposed to nonsense syllables and to Chinese characters (Zajonc, 1968). Repeated exposure increased the positive evaluations of both the nonsense syllables and the Chinese characters.

Generally, this means that familiarity, in fact, may not breed contempt. Familiar faces, ideas, and slogans become comfortable old friends. Think of the silly commercial jingle you sometimes find yourself humming almost against your will.

In fact, repeated exposures often work very well in advertising. The Marlboro man, invented to convince male smokers that taking a drag on a filtered cigarette would enhance their manhood, lasted through a generation of smokers. (The ad lasted, the original model didn't—he died of lung cancer.) When we walk down the aisle to buy a product, be it cigarettes or soap suds, the familiar name brand stands out and says, "Buy me." And we do.

The mere-exposure effect also works on a subliminal level. That is, when novel stimuli are presented below the level of a person's awareness, increased exposure increases liking (Monahan et al., 2000). Interestingly, Monahan et al. also found that subliminally generated positive affect to one stimulus can generalize to a new one. Other research shows that subliminal mere exposure produces changes in both explicit and implicit positive affect (Hicks & King, 2011).

mere exposure
The phenomenon that being exposed to a stimulus increases one's feelings, usually positive, toward that object; repeated exposure can lead to positive attitudes.

Now, there are limits to the effect, at least in the experimental studies. A review of the mere-exposure research concluded that the effect is most powerful when it occurs randomly over time and that too many exposures actually will decrease the effect (Bornstein, 1989; Montoya et al., 2017). A constant bombardment does not work very well.

Repeated exposures increase liking when the stimuli are neutral or positive to begin with. What happens when the stimuli are negative? It seems that continual exposure to some object that was disliked initially increases that negative emotion (Bornstein, 1989; Perlman & Oskamp, 1971). Say, for example, a person grew up disliking a different ethnic group because of comments she heard her parents make. Then, on repeated encounters with members of that group, she might react with distaste and increasing negativity. Over time, these negative emotions are likely to produce hostile beliefs about the group (Krosnick et al., 1992). Thus, negative feelings of which a person might hardly be aware can lead, with repeated exposure to the object of those feelings, to increased negative emotions and, ultimately, to a system of beliefs that support those emotions. Stimuli, ideas, and values to which we are exposed shape us in ways that are not always obvious to us.

The mere exposure effect occurs when repeated exposure to something increases liking. For example, you might initially be lukewarm about a new song, but after listening to it a few times you might come to like it more and more.

Source: Dean Drobot/Shutterstock.

Direct Personal Experience

A second way we form attitudes is through *direct personal experience*. If we get mugged one Saturday night coming home from a movie, for example, we may change our attitudes toward criminals, the police, personal safety, and a range of other concerns. Or if we have a flat tire and someone stops to help, we may change our attitude about the value of going out of our way to assist others. If our father's business is put in peril because of the dirty tactics of a large corporation, like that of Ida Tarbell's, we would resent such organizations for the rest of our lives. Direct personal experience has the power to create and change attitudes.

Attitudes acquired through direct experience are likely to be strongly held and to affect behavior. People are also more likely to search for information to support such attitudes. For example, people's experience with COVID-19 (e.g., knowing someone who had it) was one of the strongest predictors of whether or not they were willing to get vaccinated against COVID-19 (Kelekar et al., 2021). People are also less likely to be vulnerable to someone trying to persuade them to abandon the attitude. If, for example, your attitude that the environment needs preserving was formed because you lived near a river and observed directly the impact of pollution, you will be less likely to be persuaded even by powerful counterarguments (Wood, 1982).

Direct experience continues to form and shape our attitudes throughout life. One study examined the effects of direct experience with government agencies on younger and older individuals' attitudes toward government (Tyler & Schuller, 1991). The experiences involved, for example, getting a job, job training, unemployment compensation, and medical and hospital care. The older people changed their attitudes following a positive or negative experience as much as, if not more than, the younger people. This finding argues against the impressionable-years model, which assumes that young people are more open to forming new attitudes, and supports the lifelong-openness model, which emphasizes that people can form new attitudes throughout their life. We should note here that in later years, Ida Tarbell came to know John D. Rockefeller's successor, Judge Gary, who caused her to write a more favorable second edition of *The History of the Standard Oil Company*.

Operant and Evaluative Conditioning

Most social psychologists would agree that the bulk of our attitudes are learned. That is, attitudes result from our experiences, not our genetic inheritance. Through *socialization*, individuals learn the attitudes, values, and behaviors of their culture. Important influences in the process include parents, peers, schools, and the mass media.

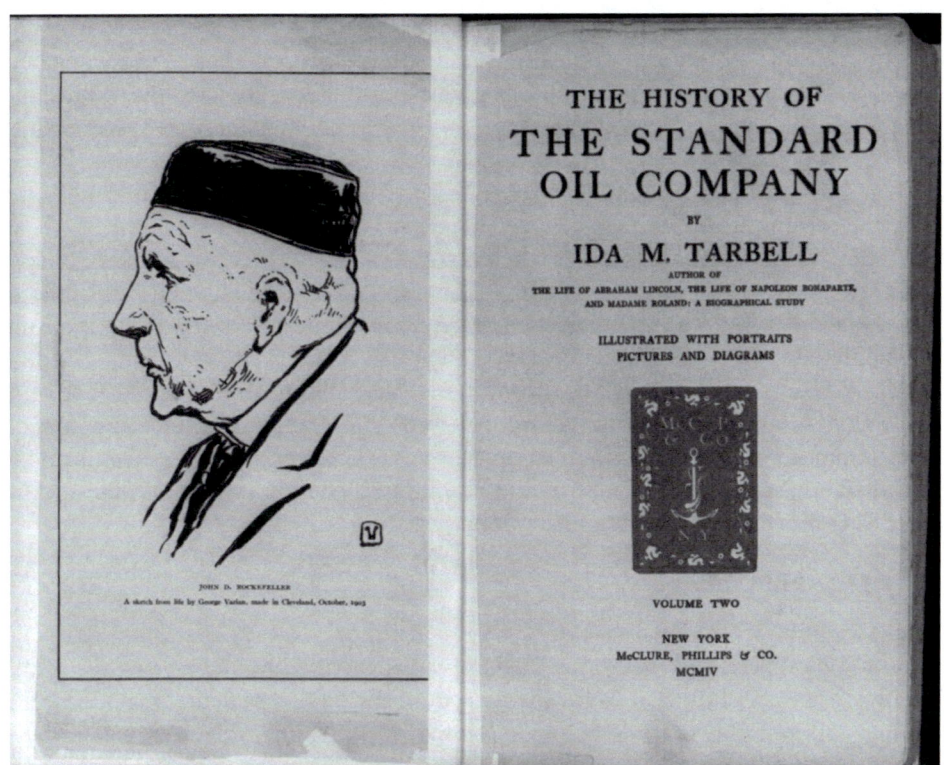

Ida Tarbell's attitudes toward the Standard Oil Company were based on her personal experience of how her father's business was affected by its actions.
Source: Everett Collection/Shutterstock.

As an example, let's look at the formation of attitudes about politics. The formation of some of these attitudes begins early, perhaps at age 6 or 7. In one early study, grade-school students thought that the American system was the best and that "America is the best country in the world" (Hess & Torney, 1967). When children are young, parents exert a major influence on their political attitudes, but later, peers and the mass media have a greater impact. In fact, by the time young adults are seniors in high school, there is a fairly low correlation between the political attitudes of children and those of their parents (Oskamp, 1991). Parents and children may identify with the same political party, but their attitudes about politics are likely to differ.

During the course of socialization, a person's attitudes may be formed through operant and evaluative conditioning, two well-known learning processes. In **operant conditioning**, the individual's behavior is strengthened or weakened by means of reward or punishment. Parents may, for example, reward their daughter with praise when she expresses the attitude that doing math is fun. Each time the child is rewarded, the attitude becomes stronger. Or, parents may punish their son with a verbal rebuke when he expresses that same attitude. In these examples, operant conditioning serves to impart attitudes.

Simply rewarding people for expressing an attitude can affect what they believe. In one study, participants took part in a debate and were randomly assigned to one or the other side of an issue (Scott, 1957). Those debaters who were told, again randomly, that they won were more likely to change their attitudes in the direction of their side of the topic than those who were told that they lost.

In **evaluative conditioning**, we develop an attitude (positive or negative) toward something because a neutral stimulus is associated with a positive or negative stimulus (Walther et al., 2011). If, for example, a new person you meet is associated with something positive (e.g., meeting that person while attending a lively party), you develop a positive attitude toward that new person. On the other hand, if you met that same person in a negative situation (e.g., while having a painful medical procedure), you may develop a negative attitude toward that person. You might recognize this process as being highly similar to the general process of *classical conditioning*. The basic associations formed in evaluative conditioning and classical conditioning are the same: pairing a neutral stimulus (conditioned stimulus) with an emotion-arousing stimulus (unconditioned stimulus). However, there are differences between

operant conditioning
A method by which attitudes are acquired by rewarding a person for a given attitude in the hopes it will be maintained or strengthened.

evaluative conditioning
A process in which you develop an attitude (positive or negative) toward something because a neutral stimulus is associated with a positive or negative stimulus.

Chapter 5 Attitudes

the two. Walther et al. point out, for example, that associations formed via evaluative conditioning are more persistent than classically conditioned responses. That is, evaluatively conditioned associations are more resistant to extinction than classically conditioned responses. This means that a positive (or negative) impression you form of another person via evaluative conditioning will persist even when that person is absent for a long period of time.

How might attitudes be learned through evaluative (classical) conditioning? In one experiment, when an attitude object (a person) was paired with positive or negative stimuli, participants came to associate the person with the positive or negative emotions (Krosnick et al., 1992). Participants were shown nine different slides in which a target person was engaged in various activities, such as walking on a street or getting into a car. Immediately before each slide there were very short exposures (13 milliseconds) of positive slides (e.g., newlyweds, a pair of kittens) or negative slides (e.g., a face on fire, a bloody shark). The participants then reported their impressions of the person. Generally, participants who had seen the person paired with warm, positive stimuli rated the person as having a better personality and as more physically attractive than did those who had seen the person paired with violent, negative stimuli.

Observational Learning

Although we often learn attitudes by getting rewarded or associating stimuli, we can also learn simply by observing. One often hears parents, shocked by the aggressive attitudes and behavior of their child, ask, "Now, where could she have gotten that from?" Research shows that children may learn to act aggressively by watching violent movies or by seeing their friends fight (Bandura, 1977). **Observational learning** occurs when we watch what people do and then model, or imitate, that behavior. For example, a child who hears her mother say, "We should keep that kind of people out of our schools," will very likely express a version of that attitude.

observational learning
Attitude formation learned through watching what people do and whether they are rewarded or punished and then imitating that behavior.

Observational learning does not depend on rewards, but rewards can strengthen the learning. In the preceding example, when the child expresses the attitude she has imitated, the mother might reward her with an approving smile. Furthermore, people are more likely to imitate behavior that is rewarded. Thus, if aggressive behavior seems to be rewarded—if children observe that those who use violence seem to get what they want—it is more likely to be imitated.

When there are discrepancies between what people say and what they do, children tend to imitate the behavior. A parent may verbally instruct a child that violence is a bad way of solving conflicts with other children. However, if the child observes the parent intimidate the newspaper carrier into bringing the paper to the front door rather than dropping it on the driveway, the child has noticed the truth of the matter. The parent thinks she is imparting one attitude toward violence but in fact is conveying another.

Study Break

Our attitudes come from a number of sources, such as mere exposure, direct personal experience, and learning. Before you go on to the next section, answer the following questions:

1. What is the mere exposure effect, and how does it relate to attitude formation?
2. How does direct personal experience contribute to attitude formation?
3. How do operant and evaluative conditioning contribute to attitude formation?
4. What is observational learning, and how does it relate to attitude formation?

The Effect of the Mass Media

Mass media play an important role in our society. For example, media heroes tend to be a very important influence in the development of our attitudes toward all manner of things:

politics, race, gender, violence, crime, love, abortion, and sex. Issues given extensive coverage in the media become foremost in the public's consciousness. For example, the saturation coverage of the 2020 presidential election elevated politics to a level not often considered by the average person.

As we shall see later in this chapter, the news media can play an important role in shaping attitudes. How news outlets frame and present information on a wide range of issues influences people's attitudes about those issues. Is the same true of fictional programming in the media? If, for example, abortion is portrayed in a positive light in a movie, can that affect a person's attitude toward abortion? This was addressed in an experiment by Mulligan and Habel (2011). Mulligan and Habel had participants watch the movie *Cider House Rules*, which presents abortion from a strong pro-choice perspective. Participants then completed a questionnaire that assessed their attitudes toward abortion. Participants in a control group completed the same questionnaire but did not see the movie. Mulligan and Habel found that watching the movie did not change abortion attitudes generally. However, they did find that participants who watched the movie were more in favor of abortion for cases involving incest. Participants who watched the movie were also more likely than control participants to endorse the notion that people should follow their own conscience when making decisions about abortion. Mulligan and Habel refer to the impact of fictional media on attitudes as *fictional framing*.

Mass media can take many forms today, including streaming services, social media applications, Internet-based websites, gaming consoles, and traditional television. With all these choices, our media consumption has slowly risen. In 2019, the average American adult spent a little over 12 hours a day viewing some form of entertainment (Nielsen, 2020). These expanded choices have also led to shifts in how people consume entertainment. Older adults (above age 50) still primarily receive their entertainment via traditional television; however, younger adults (below age 35) spend their time consuming media via apps on their smartphones (Nielsen, 2020). Media use for children follows a pattern simliar to that of adults. Children are watching less traditional television and instead are streaming and using smartphones more than they did in the past. Overall, total media use in children aged 8–18 accounts for about 7½ hours a day on average (Kaiser Family Foundation, 2010).

What do they experience from exposure to media sources? Most get a constant fare of violence. This violence affects the attitudes of at least some children in their interactions with peers, and the more violence they see, the more aggressive their interaction style. This effect is strongest in children in neighborhoods where violence is commonplace; the media violence evidently serves as reinforcement.

In addition to providing aggressive models, many forms of digital entertainment emphasize situations that are linked to violence. People who are exposed to high levels of media violence are likely to overestimate by far the amount of violence and crime that occurs in the world (Jowett & O'Donnell, 1992). As a result, they are more likely to anticipate violence in their own lives. Anderson et al. (2003) studied the effects of songs with violent lyrics on both the listeners' attitudes and their feelings. In a series of five studies, Anderson and his colleagues reported that college students who listened to a violent song felt more hostile and reported an increase in aggressive thoughts compared to another group that heard a similar but nonviolent song (Anderson et al., 2003). Of course, it may not always be the lyrics themselves that cause these changes in attitudes and feelings. Research suggests that tense, pounding musical scores provoke aggressive feelings also (Rubin et al., 2001). In fact, Rubin et al. (2001) reported that college students who preferred heavy metal and rap music expressed more hostile attitudes than those who did not. It's not clear what the line of causality is in this case. It is reasonable to suggest that people prefer rap because they feel hostile in the first place, and thus it is not necessarily the lyrics that cause the attitudes. However, as Anderson et al. (2003) observe, every exposure to a violent media event (TV, music, violent video games, violent movies) is a "learning trial in which one rehearses aggressive thoughts and feelings," and these repetitive events make hostile attitudes quite prominent and easy to recall and access (Anderson et al., 2003, p. 964).

By emphasizing some events and ignoring others, television, movies, and music, along with other mass media, define reality for us. They directly affect how many of us think and feel about the world. In one study, Chinese and Canadian children were asked to imagine that they were an animal and then write a story including themselves as that animal. The results showed that male children selected animals that were dangerous, strong, and wild. On the other hand, female children selected animals that were safe, weak, and tame (Harvey et al., 1997). In another study, Trepanier and Romatowski (1985) analyzed stories written by male and female children for a "young author's" competition. Specifically, they analyzed the stories for portrayals of male and female characters. As one might expect, male authors included more male characters in their stories, and female authors included more female characters. However, overall, male characters outnumbered female characters. Positive attributes were more likely to be attributed to male characters (74%) than to female characters (26%). Both male and female authors assigned fewer occupational roles to female characters than male characters. Additionally, males tended to have a wider variety of interesting roles assigned to them than females. Thus, the themes in children's stories reflect the content of books to which they are exposed. The media have a definite role in shaping a child's worldview of appropriate gender-based roles.

Wells and Twenge (2005) combined 530 studies that studied over a quarter of a million subjects in a "meta-analysis" and discovered not unexpectedly that sexual attitudes and behavior have undergone enormous changes from 1943 to 1999. This analysis showed that the largest changes occurred among girls and young women. Both young men and women became more sexually active over time, as indicated by a younger age of first intercourse, which was lowered from 19 to 15 years among young women, and percentage of sexually active young women, from 13% to 47% in 1999 (Wells & Twenge, 2005). Feelings of sexual guilt decreased for both men and women. Wells and Twenge observe that their data support the idea that culture has a large effect on women's sexuality.

Why the change? Wells and Twenge (2005) note the enormous cultural changes that occurred in the prior 50 years. Changes in sexual attitudes and behaviors are among the most noticeable and striking of these shifts. The authors believe that the mass media had an enormous impact on sexual attitudes and behavior. They note that "television programs and movies regularly mention topics such as teenage pregnancy, abortion, sexually transmitted diseases, and rape, whereas 30 years ago these topics were taboo. This sexual revolution has dramatically altered American culture, especially for women" (Wells & Twenge, 2005, p. 249).

The Role of the Media in Setting the Agenda

How is it that celebrities get more play in the media than, say, the burgeoning national debt? Does it matter? So what if those "reality TV stars" get more space in the media than a discussion of potential changes in the immigration laws? Again, does it matter?

Communication researchers have long argued that the topics most salient in the mass media tend to set the public agenda. This *agenda setting* occurs because the topics most prominent in the news shape the public's cognitions, increasing the focus on certain issues as opposed to others (Kiousis et al., 2005). Agenda setting exists on two levels. In *first-level agenda setting,* the news media determine which stories are important enough to go on page one of the newspaper or end up on social media newsfeeds. Typically, editors select those stories they see as most important to head the news cycle. In *second-level agenda setting,* the news media try to tell us how to think about news-related issues. This is done by presenting stories in a manner that alters our perceptions and emotions about events and people. For example, political candidates may be presented in a positive or negative way in the news, which then alters the perceptions we have of these candidates. In one study, researchers looked at how George Bush and Al Gore were portrayed in the media during the 2000 presidential election (Coleman & Banning, 2006). Coleman and Banning found that Al Gore received more positive and less negative coverage than George Bush. Unsurprisingly, public opinion, which they also measured, showed that the public had a more favorable opinion of Gore than Bush.

There is an important factor that mediates the relationship between how a person or event is portrayed in the news and public perception. Emotion generated by news stories mediates this relationship through a process called *affective framing* (Miller, 2007).

Among the sources of attitudes is the media. Children and adults can learn a wide range of attitudes from watching television.
Source: KaliAntye/Shutterstock.

So, for example, if a candidate is presented in a positive way, then the emotion attached to that candidate will be positive, leading to more positive perceptions and attitudes about that candidate. On the other hand, a negative portrayal leads to negative emotion and a negative attitude toward the candidate.

Some argue that, through the process of agenda setting, various interest groups, policymakers, TV, and other media personalities and outlets, including newspapers and magazines, determine which issues receive the most attention (Scheufele, 2005). Some observers maintain that news outlets show political biases, some leaning left and some leaning right. How a story or a person is portrayed on these different leaning outlets may be influenced by the political bias of the outlet. For example, Hehman et al. (2012) analyzed how former Presidents Barack Obama and George W. Bush were portrayed in photos on conservative (e.g., Fox.com) and liberal (e.g., MSNBC.com) Internet outlets. They evaluated photos of the two presidents for how the sites portrayed their warmth and competence. Their results are shown in Figure 5.2. As you can see, the portrayal of each president was consistent with the political leanings of the news outlet. Presidents who were ideologically consistent with the news source were shown as more competent and warmer than presidents who were ideologically inconsistent with the news source.

What is important about setting the agenda is that it seems to make people more sensitive to the issues contained in a news story. When this happens, the story becomes more salient, and everything about it is more easily retrieved by the individual. People who attend to the most salient topics in the media have strong opinions about those topics and are more likely to identify with others who believe the way they believe. Issues such as abortion, immigration, and others are good examples of this (Kiousis, 2005). Indeed, these issues tend to fracture the public into several, often antagonistic, opinion groups. Finally, you might be wondering whether agenda setting really matters all that much. Does it really have an influence over what people think? A meta-analysis by Luo et al. (2019) analyzing the agenda-setting literature between 1972 and 2015 found a strong relationship between media agenda setting and public attitudes.

The Heritability Factor

Most theories about the formation of attitudes are based on the idea that attitudes are formed primarily through experience. However, some research suggests that attitudes as well as other complex social behaviors may have a genetic component

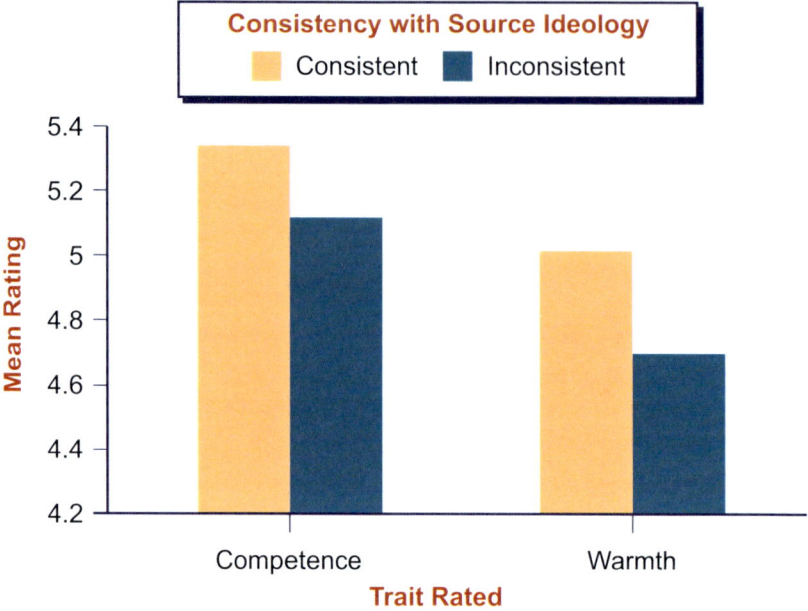

FIGURE 5.2
Competence and warmth ratings of Presidents Obama and Bush by ideological left or right Internet news outlets.
Based on data from Hehman et al. (2012).

(Plomin, 1989). Some attitudes may have a significant genetic component. For example, moral attitudes seem to have an inherited component (Brandt & Wethere, 2012). When studying the origins of a trait or behavior, geneticists try to calculate what proportion of it may be determined by heredity, rather than by learning or other environmental influences involved. **Heritability** refers to the extent to which genetics accounts for differences among people in a given characteristic or behavior. For example, eye color is entirely determined by genetics; there are no environmental or learning influences. If the heritability of a characteristic is less than 100%, then other influences are involved. Height, for example, is about 90% heritable; nutrition also plays a determining role.

Eye color and height are clearly based in one's heredity. But how can complex social structures such as attitudes have a genetic basis? The answer is that genetics may have an indirect effect on our attitudes. That is, characteristics that are biologically based might predispose us to certain behaviors and attitudes. For example, genetic differences in sensory structures, such as hearing and taste, could affect our preferences for certain kinds of music and foods (Tesser, 1993). As another example, consider aggressiveness, which, as research has shown, has a genetic component. Level of aggressiveness can affect a whole range of attitudes and behaviors, from watching violent TV shows and movies, to hostility toward women or members of other groups, to attitudes toward capital punishment (Oskamp, 1991). In this case, a biologically based characteristic affects how one thinks, feels, and acts.

Plomin et al. (1990) were interested in children's attitudes and behaviors related to television viewing. Learning—particularly the influence of parents and friends—certainly plays a role in the formation of TV-viewing attitudes and behaviors. Is it possible that genetics could also play a role? If so, how could we know this? To answer these questions, Plomin studied the TV viewing of adopted children, comparing it to the TV-viewing habits of the children's biological parents and adoptive parents. The question he asked was, would the child's behavior more closely resemble that of the biological parents or that of the adoptive parents? A close resemblance to the habits of the biological parents would argue for a biological interpretation, because the biological parents did not share the child's environment. A close resemblance to the habits of the adoptive parents, on the other hand, would argue for an environmental interpretation. Thus, the study of adoptive children made it possible to calculate the extent to which TV viewing is determined, indirectly, by genetics.

heritability An indicator of the degree to which genetics accounts for differences among people for any given behavior or characteristic.

Plomin's findings were surprising. There was a very high resemblance between the TV viewing of the children and that of the biological parents. Although shared environment influenced the amount of viewing, the genetic component was much higher. This doesn't mean that children whose biological parents watch a lot of TV are doomed to be glued to the TV for the rest of their days. It simply suggests that there is something in our genetic makeup that may incline us to certain behaviors and attitudes.

Attitudes that have a high heritability factor might be expected to differ in certain ways from those that are primarily learned. Specifically, they might be expected to be more strongly held. Is this, in fact, the case? There are at least two indicators of attitude strength: A person responds quickly on encountering the object of that attitude, and the person is unlikely to give in to pressure to change the attitude. Evidence suggests that both these indicators are indeed present with attitudes that have a high heritability factor (Tesser, 1993). However, genes will be expressed differently in different environments, so speed and yielding to pressure are not perfect measures of heritability. Also, attitudes with a high heritability factor tend to be more complex than those with a low heritability factor (Conway et al., 2011). Conway et al. found that the complexity of inherited attitudes could not be adequately accounted for by factors such as attitude strength. They hypothesized that complex, inherited attitudes (especially those relating to social issues) may trigger a biological mechanism that requires more physical and cognitive space in the brain.

Bourgeois (2002) found that members of groups also show greater variability the higher the heritability of the attitude. Thus, if you are against "permissiveness" in everyday life, an attitude with a fairly high heritability factor, the less likely your neighbors will influence you to change your opinion. This explains greater variability in attitudes with high heritability components (Bourgeois, 2002). Usually, groups tend to produce pressures that make people conform, especially on important issues. But those attitudes that have a high heritability loading appear to be much more difficult to change.

SOCIAL PSYCHOLOGY IN ACTION

Toe the Party Line

Although we have so far emphasized the individual in the learning and expression of attitudes, many of our attitudes are learned and reinforced in group settings. Indeed, social psychological research has shown that group influence is the most influential factor in which opinions we express. It should not be surprising that group membership is a powerful influence on our attitudes and their expression. We know that by as early as 12 months of age, we are influenced by the emotional expressions of those around us (Moses et al., 2001).

Geoffrey Cohen (2003), in a series of four clever and interrelated studies, demonstrated that a person's stated attitude toward a public issue was dependent solely on the stated position of the political party with which the person was aligned. This was true no matter what the objective of the policy or the person's own position on that policy. Furthermore, the individuals did not seem to be aware that the group's position was counter to what they personally believed. For example, in one study, Cohen presented two versions of a welfare policy to liberal and conservative college students. One version of the plan had generous benefits, whereas the other version had very limited benefits. Some students read the generous plan, others the stringent plan. In addition, they were given information that the Republicans or the Democrats had taken a stand either in favor of or against the plan. Therefore, some conservative students may have read the generous plan and been told that the Republicans had endorsed that plan. Similarly, some liberal students read the stringent plan and were told that the Democratic Party had endorsed that plan.

The results were striking. Both conservative and liberal participants in this study simply followed the party line. If their party endorsed a policy, so did the liberal and conservative students, no matter their originally expressed beliefs on that issue. So, liberals supported a harsh welfare policy if their party did, and conservatives supported a generous welfare policy if their party did as well. In follow-up studies, it became clear that in the absence of any information about how their party stood on the issues, conservatives preferred the less generous plan, whereas liberals preferred the more generous one. Cohen (2003) also found that the effect of group information influenced both attitudes and behavior.

(continued)

However, there are limits on how much the endorsement of a political party will influence our own attitudes. Bolsen et al. (2014) asked participants to form an opinion about an energy policy being presented in Congress. There were several conditions in the study. In some conditions, the new policy was endorsed by the participant's party. In other conditions, the policy was endorsed by the opposing party of the participant. Additionally, the endorsement was presented as cross-partisan in some conditions. That is, the policy was supported by some members of both the Republican Party and the Democratic Party, but there was not unanimous support in either party. Finally, in addition to manipulating the endorsement of the policy, some participants were also asked to evaluate the policy in an "even-handed way and from various perspectives" (accuracy goal). The researchers replicated previous work and found clear evidence that when your party is in unanimous support of a policy, you are likely to favor it yourself. Also, if an opposing party is in unanimous support of a policy, you are likely to oppose it. However, if the participants were given an accuracy goal, or if the policy had cross-partisan support, there was no effect of party endorsement. The researchers argued that in both of these instances, participants were motivated to think more deeply about the policy and less likely to be influenced by their party's position.

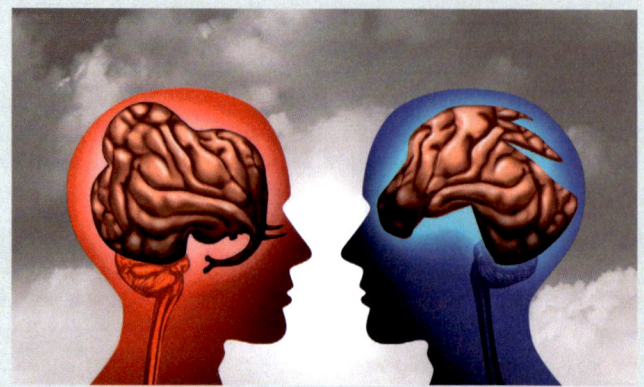

The attitudes we express are typically those endorsed by groups with which we identify. Most people will "toe the party line" and support whatever position is supported by their political party.
Source: Lightspring/Shutterstock.

Discussion Questions

1. How are attitudes learned and reinforced in group settings?
2. Are there limits on how much the endorsement of a political party will influence our own attitudes?

Social Networks

Groups can have an important influence on our evaluation of public issues. What we know, obviously, is that we do not form nor do we keep attitudes in isolation from important groups.

Visser and Mirabile (2004) showed that when you are part of congruent social networks (people with similar views), your attitude becomes more resistant to change because you have strong social support for that attitude. However, if you are embedded in a heterogeneous social network with lots of people who have different views, you are less resistant to change. It appears that when you are with people who think as you do, not surprisingly, you become more certain of your attitudes, and any doubts you may have had are removed (Visser & Mirabile, 2004). Social media sites such as Facebook and Twitter have opened up a whole new world of social network possibilities, allowing people to make connections with large numbers of others. Although there is concern that people will use social media to interact with like-minded others, there is evidence that people using social media do not actively avoid others with whom they disagree (Garrett, 2009). On social media, it appears that individuals are being exposed to a diverse range of opinions on a number of topics. When people are exposed to a point of view with which they disagree, most people (66%) simply ignore the information rather than respond to the post with their own post (28%) or unfriend a person (9%) (Rainie & Smith, 2012). Interestingly, the more time people spend on social media like Facebook or Twitter, the more likely it is that they will experience a diverse network (Lee et al., 2014). Additionally, Lee et al. found that the more time an individual who engaged in political discussions spent on a heterogeneous social network, the more polarized his or her political attitudes were. However, no such relationship was found for individuals who did not take part in many political discussions.

However, the nature of what is being discussed can influence the extent to which social media appears like an echo chamber. Political topics, such as an upcoming election or a State of the Union Address, tend to resemble an echo chamber. Interactions and the exchanges of information for these types of topics tend to occur only among individuals with highly similar ideological preferences. However, events of a nonpolitical nature, such as the Super Bowl or the Olympics, tend to fit the pattern of a "national conversation." For these events, people of all political stripes tend to read and retweet each other's messages. Finally, some events (i.e., school shooting at Sandy Hook Elementary in 2012) can start off like a national conversation and then become politicized and more like an echo chamber (Barberá et al., 2015).

Social psychologists have observed that individuals will adjust, or "tune," their beliefs to the apparent beliefs of other people when they desire to get along with this person. This type of behavior is referred to as the affiliative social tuning hypothesis (Sinclair et al., 2005). Often, we will modify our expressed attitudes so that social interaction in groups is smooth. Therefore, people will modify their expressed, often automatic racial attitudes within groups that contain people of different racial or ethnic groups. Sinclair et al. (2005) have shown that automatic attitudes serve a social regulatory function, That is, they regulate social interactions so as to make them less confrontational and more congenial. Thus, these automatic racial or ethnic attitudes are sensitive to the social demands of interpersonal interactions. Therefore, automatic attitudes are influenced by the desire to get along with others.

Study Break

In addition to the other factors discussed in this chapter, attitudes can also be shaped via the media and biological forces. Before you begin the next section, answer the following questions:

1. How can the media shape attitudes?
2. What are the two types of agenda setting and how do they relate to attitude formation?
3. How do genetic factors relate to one's attitudes?
4. How does group membership influence a person's attitudes?
5. How do social networks operate to influence attitudes?

Attitudes and Behavior

Intuitively, it makes sense that if we know something about a person's attitudes, we should be able to predict his or her behavior. In Allport's definition of attitude given at the beginning of this chapter, attitudes exert a directive influence on the individual's behavior. There is a rationality bias in all of this—a belief that people will act in a manner consistent with their innermost feelings and ideas. Do we, in fact, behave in accordance with our attitudes? Early researchers assumed that a close link did exist between attitudes and behavior. However, a review of attitude-behavior research revealed a quite different picture: Attitudes appeared to be, at best, only weak predictors of behavior (Wicker, 1969).

We begin this section by looking at one early study that appeared to show little correlation between attitudes and behavior. Social psychologists eventually concluded that a relationship exists but is more complex than they suspected. We look at their attempts to unravel the complexities and to thereby show that attitudes can predict behavior. More recently, other social psychologists have argued that our behavior often is nonrational and has nothing to do with our attitudes. We conclude the section by seeing how the rational and nonrational approaches can be reconciled.

An Early Study of Attitudes and Behavior

In one well-known study from the 1930s, a young sociologist traveled around the United States with a young Chinese couple (LaPiere, 1934). They traveled 10,000 miles and visited over 200 places (Oskamp, 1991). The 1930s were a time of relatively overt expression of prejudice against many groups, including Asians. What did LaPiere and the Chinese couple encounter? Interestingly, during their entire trip, they were refused service by only one business. Several months after the trip, LaPiere wrote to every establishment he and his friends had visited and asked the owners if they would object to serving a Chinese couple. About half the establishments answered; of these, only nine said they would offer service, and only under certain conditions.

The visits measured the behavior of the business owners. The follow-up question about offering service was a measure of attitudes. Clearly, the expressed attitudes (primarily negative) and the behavior (primarily positive) were not consistent. This kind of finding led to a great deal of pessimism among attitude researchers concerning the link between attitudes and behavior. But let's consider the inconsistency more closely. Our behavior is determined by many attitudes, not just one. LaPiere measured the owners' attitudes about Asians. He did not measure their attitudes about losing money or creating difficulties for themselves by turning away customers. Furthermore, it is easier to express a negative attitude when you are not face-to-face with the object of that attitude. Think how easy it is to tell the aluminum-siding salesperson over the phone that you never want to hear about aluminum siding again as long as you live. Yet when the person shows up at your door, you are probably less blunt and might even listen to the sales pitch. In the case of LaPiere's study, being prejudiced is easy by letter, harder in person.

To summarize, LaPiere's findings did not mean there is little relationship between attitudes and behavior. They just indicated that the presence of the attitude object (in this case, the Chinese couple) is not always enough to trigger the expression of the attitude. Other factors can come into play.

There are several reasons why attitudes aren't good predictors of behavior. First, research showed that it was when investigators tried to link general attitudes and specific behaviors that the link appeared weak. When researchers looked at a specific attitude, they often were able to find a good relationship between that attitude and behavior. However, when researchers asked people about a general attitude, such as their religious beliefs, and assessed a specific behavior related to that attitude, such as praying before meals, they found only a weak correlation (Eagly, 1992).

Another reason why attitudes and behaviors may not relate strongly is the fact that a behavior may relate to more than one attitude. For example, whether you vote for a particular candidate may depend on how she stands on a range of issues (e.g., abortion, health care, defense spending, civil rights). Measuring any single attitude may not predict very well how you vote. However, if the entire range of attitudes is measured, the relationship between attitudes and behavior improves. Similarly, if only one behavior is measured, your attitude may not relate to that behavior very well. It is much better if a behavioral trend (several behaviors measured over time) is measured. Attitudes tend to relate better to behavioral trends than a single behavior.

Theory of Planned Behavior

theory of planned behavior
A theory that explains attitude-behavior relationships, focusing on the relationship between the strength of our behavioral intentions and our performance of them.

Ajzen and Fishbein (1980) proposed the **theory of planned behavior**. This theory sensibly assumes that the best predictor of how we will behave is the strength of our intentions (Ajzen, 1987). The theory is essentially a three-step process to the prediction of behavior. The likelihood that individuals will carry out a behavior consistent with an attitude they hold depends on the strength of their intention, which is in turn influenced by three factors. By measuring these factors, we can determine the strength of intention, which enables us to predict the likelihood of the behavior.

The first factor that influences behavioral intention is *attitude toward the behavior*. Be careful here: We are talking about the attitude toward the behavior, not toward the object. For example, you might have a positive attitude about exercise, because you believe that it reduces tension. Exercise is the object of the attitude. But you might not like to sweat. In fact, you hate to sweat. Will you exercise? The theory says that the attitude toward the behavior, which includes sweating, is a better predictor of your actions than your attitude about exercise, because it affects your intentions.

According to the theory of planned behavior, engaging in an attitude-relevant behavior depends on one's attitude toward a behavior, subjective norms, perceived behavior control, and forming an intention to engage in the behavior.
Source: vesperstock/Shutterstock.

The second factor, *subjective norms*, refers to how you think your friends and family will evaluate your behavior. For example, you might think, "All my friends exercise, and they will think that it is appropriate that I do the same." In this case, you may exercise despite your distaste for it. Your friends' behavior defines exercise as normative, the standard. Wellness programs that attempt to change dietary and exercise habits rely heavily on normative forces. By getting people into groups, they encourage them to perceive healthy lifestyles as normative (everyone else is involved).

Perceived behavioral control, the third factor, refers to a person's belief that the behavior he or she is considering is easy or hard to accomplish. For example, a person will be more likely to engage in health-related preventive behaviors such as dental hygiene or breast self-examination if he or she believes that they can be easily done (Ronis & Kaiser, 1989).

In summary, the theory of planned behavior emphasizes that behavior follows from attitudes in a reasoned way. If a person thinks that a particular behavior associated with an attitude will lead to positive outcomes, that other people would approve, and that the behavior can be done readily, then the person will engage in the behavior (Eagly, 1992). People essentially ask themselves if they can reasonably expect that the behavior will achieve their individual and social needs.

Let's use the theory of planned behavior to analyze voting behavior. Assume you have a positive attitude about voting (the object). Will you actually vote? Let's say you think that it is the duty of every citizen to vote. Furthermore, your friends are going to vote, and you believe they will think badly of you if you don't (subjective norms). Finally, you feel that you will be able to easily rearrange your schedule on election day (perceived behavioral control). If we know all this about you, we can conclude you have a strong intention to vote and can make a pretty confident prediction that, in keeping with your attitude, you are likely to vote.

The accuracy of behavioral intentions in predicting behavior is evident in the Gallup Poll. The Gallup organization has been conducting voting surveys since 1936, the year Franklin Delano Roosevelt ran against Alf Landon, governor of Kansas. Figure 5.3 shows the record of the Gallup Poll in national elections from 1968 to 2000. In general, the polls are quite accurate. As you might expect, polls are not always accurate in their predictions of the winning presidential candidate. Many polls failed to predict Donald Trump's victory over Hillary Clinton in 2016. A *Washington Post* analysis (Atanasov & Joseph, 2016) showed that a number of polls predicted, with increasing confidence, that Clinton would win the Electoral College vote, right up to Election Day. This prediction failure was most likely a result of overconfidence in Clinton's ability to win the election (Atanasov & Joseph, 2016). Polls also got it wrong in 1948 when the data indicated that Harry Truman did not have much of a chance to win.

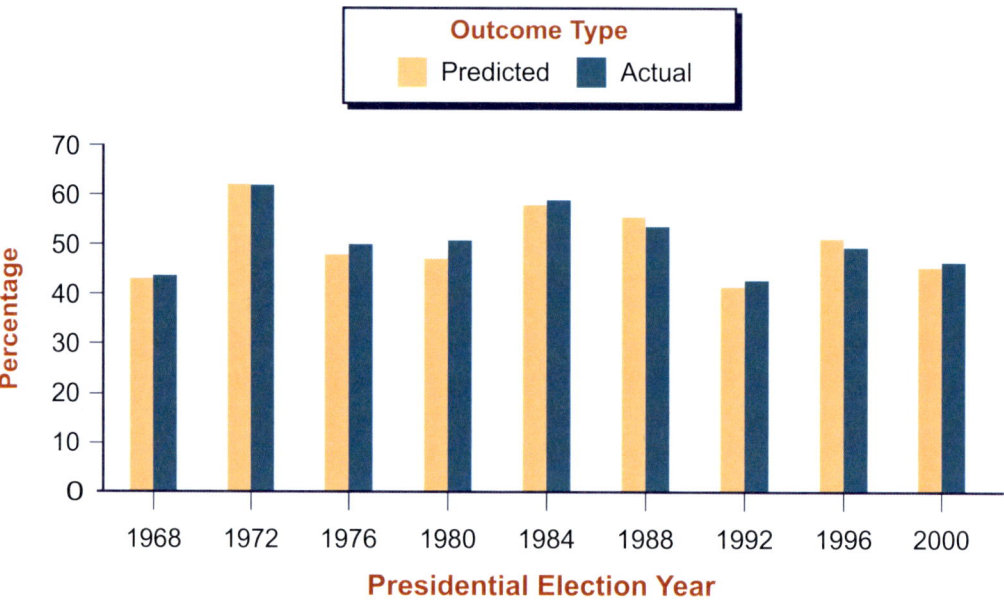

FIGURE 5.3

Gallup Poll data showing predicted and actual outcomes for presidential elections from 1968 to 2000. Gallup Polls are remarkably accurate in predicting not only the winner but also the margin of victory. (Note: Average error = –1.93.)

But rarely in history books do we hear mention of Thomas E. Dewey, the governor of New York who ran against Truman and who was projected as the winner. In this case, the pollsters were wrong primarily because they stopped polling a little too early. They had not yet learned that people have other things on their minds than elections and may not start to pay serious attention to the campaign until a week or so before the actual vote.

Although the question, "For whom will you vote, candidate X or candidate Y?" might appear to be a measure of attitude, it is really a measure of behavioral intention. Voting is a single act and can be measured by a single direct question. These are the circumstances in which consistency between attitude and behavior is likely to be the highest. Pollsters often try to determine the strength of these intentions by asking such questions as: How strongly do you feel about your preferred candidate? How intense are your feelings? Although refinements like these may add to the accuracy of voting surveys in the future, what is needed is a concrete way of measuring behavioral intentions.

Research has reinforced the notion that emotions are crucially involved in turning attitude into behavior. For example, Farley and Stasson (2003) examined the relationship between attitudes and giving blood donations. They found that both donors' behavioral intentions to give blood and their positive emotions about doing so were predictive of actually donating blood.

The Importance of Attitude Strength

So, what we have seen in the previous section is that the importance of some of our attitudes is a crucial determinant of how we act. Some of our attitudes are important to us; others are much less important. One reason researchers underestimated the attitude–behavior link is because they did not focus on attitudes that are important to people (Abelson, 1988). Strong attitudes are central to the person holding them. Examples include attitudes of racial and gender equality, racism and sexism, patriotism, religious fundamentalism, and occultism. Attitudes held with conviction are like possessions (Abelson, 1988). Strong attitudes are hard to change, are stable over time, influence how we think, and shape our behavior. Weak attitudes, on the other hand, are easy to change, and they seldom influence behavior. One function of a strong attitude is that it defines us; it tells people who we are. The person owns his or her attitudes, proudly displaying them to those who would appreciate them and defending them against those who would try to take them away. For example, someone deeply committed to one side or the other of the abortion issue will likely defend his view against the other side and show his solidarity with those on the same side. Such attitudes will be hard to change, as a change would mean a major alteration in the way the person sees the world.

Because strong attitudes are hard to manipulate in a laboratory experiment, researchers tended to stay away from them. As a result, social psychologists overestimated the ease with which attitudes might be changed and underestimated the relationship between attitudes and behavior. If an attitude is important to people, they expect that behavior in agreement with that attitude will help them get what they want. Thus, strong attitudes and behavior tend to be closely linked.

A strong attitude held with conviction is easily accessible. This means that if you discuss with someone a subject about which they feel strongly, they respond quickly and have a lot of ideas about it. Moreover, attitude accessibility—the ease with which one can bring a particular attitude to mind—is increased by constant use and application of that attitude (Doll & Ajzen, 1992). In a study several years ago, researchers measured latencies (speed of response) with respect to questions about women's rights, abortion, and racial integration (Krosnick, 1989). Whatever the issue, people who considered an attitude important responded more quickly than those who considered it unimportant. Important attitudes are more available in memory and are more likely to correspond to behavior. If your stand on abortion, women's rights, gun ownership, or the Dallas Cowboys is important, you are more likely to act in a manner consistent with that attitude.

You can get a sense of how accessible an attitude is by noting how long it takes you to recall it. For example, notice how long it takes you to recall your attitude toward the following: living wills, parent-teacher associations, the death penalty, aisle seats, snakes, water filters, political action committees, the clergy, daylight-savings time, baseball. Some of these notions brought feelings and thoughts to mind quickly; others may not have.

If attitude accessibility indicates the strength of an attitude, we might expect attitudes high in accessibility to be better predictors of behavior than attitudes lower in accessibility. Fazio, who has extensively studied attitude accessibility, investigated this issue in connection with the 1984 presidential election (Fazio & Williams, 1986). The summer before the election, potential voters were asked whether they agreed with each of the following two statements: "A good president for the next 4 years would be Walter Mondale (the then Democratic nominee)," and "A good president for the next 4 years would be Ronald Reagan (the elected Republican)." The respondents had to indicate how strongly they agreed or disagreed by pressing one of five buttons: strongly agree, agree, don't care, disagree, strongly disagree.

The researchers measured the time that passed before respondents pressed the button. The delay interval between the moment you are confronted with an object and the moment you realize your attitude is called the *latency* (Rajecki, 1990). The longer respondents took to hit the button, the less accessible the attitude. Not only were the researchers able to get a reading of the attitude toward the candidates, but also they were able to get a measure of accessibility.

On the day after the election, respondents were asked whether they had voted and, if so, for whom they had voted. Was there a relationship between latency times and voting behavior? That is, did attitude accessibility predict behavior? The answer is, yes, it did. Attitude accessibility measured in June and July 1984 accurately predicted voting behavior in November. Those who had responded quickly for Reagan were more likely to vote for him than those who had taken longer to respond. The same relationship held, although not quite as strongly, for Mondale supporters.

Study Break

The definition offered for attitudes at the beginning of the chapter stated that attitudes should predict behavior. This section explored the connection between attitudes and behavior. Before you begin the next section, answer the following questions:

1. What did the early studies on the attitude-behavior relationship show about this relationship?
2. What were some of the ideas that social psychologists came up with to explain the weak relationship between attitudes and behavior?
3. What is the theory of planned behavior, and what does it say about the attitude-behavior relationship?
4. What is attitude strength, and how does it relate to the attitude-behavior relationship?

The Nonrational Actor

The theories and ideas about attitudes and behavior so far tend to assume a rational, almost calculated approach to behavior. In the theory of planned behavior, if you can get measures of people's attitude toward a behavior, their perception of how important others might approve or disapprove of what they do, and their sense of control over that behavior, then you can predict their intentions and, therefore, their likely behavior. If there is a significant criticism of the theory of planned behavior, it is that when you ask people to tell you about the components of their intentions, they know that their answers should be logical. If you reported that you voted but you had no interest in the candidates and you thought all candidates were crooks, this hardly makes you look like a logical individual.

Some theories have taken the opposite approach: They assume that human beings are **nonrational actors** (Ronis & Kaiser, 1989), and our attitudes may often be totally irrelevant to our behavior. Cigarette smoking, for example, is so habitual as to be automatic, totally divorced from any attitude or behavioral intention the smoker may have. Most of our behaviors are like that (Ronis & Kaiser, 1989). We do them over and over without thought (Gilbert, 1991). You floss your teeth, but your attitude and intentions about dental hygiene are activated only when you run out of floss. Even though you believe flossing is important, and even though you remember that sign in your dentist's office that reads, "No, you don't have to floss all your teeth—only the ones you want to keep," you now have to act on your attitude. Are you willing to get in the car at 11 P.M. and drive to the store to buy more dental floss? Similarly, if your regular aerobics class becomes inconvenient, is your attitude about the importance of exercise strong enough that you will rearrange your whole schedule?

In sum, people usually behave habitually, unthinkingly, even mindlessly. They make active decisions only when they face new situations. Thus, there is a good chance of inconsistencies between our attitudes and our behavior.

nonrational actor A view that humans are not always rational in their behavior and their behavior can be inconsistent with their attitudes.

Mindless Behavior in Everyday Life

Have you ever arrived home after work or school and not been able to recall a single thing about how you got there? In everyday life, we often run on a kind of automatic pilot. Our behavior becomes so routine and automatic that we are hardly aware of what we are doing. We are in a state of mind that Ellen Langer (1989) termed *mindlessness*, one that involves reduced attention and loss of active control in everyday activities. Mindlessness occurs when we're engaging in behaviors that have been overlearned and routinized. In this state, we carry out the behaviors rigidly, according to a preconceived pattern and without thought or appraisal. Mindlessness is fairly common in our everyday interactions. The cashier at a restaurant asks you, "How was everything?" You say that your steak was overcooked, your potato was cold, and the service was terrible. The cashier replies, "Here's your change, have a nice day." In this example, the cashier's question and response were automatic; she really didn't care how you enjoyed your meal.

Langer was interested in studying this state of mind (Langer et al., 1978). She had a researcher approach people waiting to use a copy machine in the library and ask to use it first. The request was phrased in one of several ways: "Excuse me, I have five pages to copy. May I use the machine because I am in a rush?" "Excuse me, I have five pages to copy. May I use the machine?" and "Excuse me, I have five pages to copy. May I use the machine because I have to make copies?" The researcher also asked to make 20 copies in these three different ways. Request 2 offers no reason for using the copier first, and request 3 offers a mindless reason ("because I have to make copies"); only request 1 provides a minimally acceptable reason ("because I am in a rush"). If the participants in this situation were dealing with the request in a mindless fashion, they would fail to distinguish between legitimate and illegitimate (or ridiculous) reasons. As it turns out, any kind of excuse works as long as the request is small. When the request was to make five copies, people apparently did not appraise the quality of the excuse as long as one was offered: Having to make copies was just as good as being in a rush. People snapped out of their mindless state, however, when the request was to make 20 copies. It is clear that when the behavior (the request) had a significant impact, people paid more attention to the difference between bad and good excuses. Although we usually pay close attention to good and bad reasons for people's behavior, it may be that the request to copy five pages isn't worth the effort. When the ante is raised to 20 pages, then we are more mindful.

The fact that we hold a number of attitudes without really thinking about them means there can be some interesting consequences once we are forced to think about them. Thinking about our attitudes and the reasons we hold them can sometimes be disruptive and confusing (Wilson et al., 1989). More generally, the process of introspecting—of looking into our own mind, rather than just behaving—can have this effect.

Timothy Wilson's work showed that thinking about the reasons for our attitudes can often lead us to behave in ways that seem inconsistent with those attitudes (Wilson et al., 1989). For example, if you are forced to think about why you like your romantic partner, you might wind up ending the relationship in the near future. Much depends on the strength of the relationship. If the relationship is not strong, thinking about reasons might weaken it. If it is pretty strong, then reasoning might further strengthen it. The stronger our attitude or belief, the more likely that thinking about it will increase the consistency between it and our behavior (Fazio, 1986).

Why should thinking about reasons for our attitudes sometimes lead to inconsistency between our attitudes and behavior? The basic answer is that if we have never really thought about an attitude before, then thinking about it may cause us to change it (Wilson et al., 1989). If you are forced to count the ways you love your current partner, and it takes you a lot of time to use all the fingers on one hand, you have gotten some insight into how you really think about the relationship.

This explanation was supported by a study in which people were asked their attitudes about social issues, such as the death penalty, abortion, and national health insurance, in two separate telephone surveys conducted a month apart (Wilson & Kraft, 1988). In the first survey, some people were asked to give their reasons for their opinions, whereas others were just asked their opinions. A month later, those people who had been asked to give reasons proved more likely to have changed their opinion. So thinking about reasons seems to lead to change. Why? The full explanation might lie in the biased sample hypothesis, proposed by Wilson and colleagues (1989). It goes like this: If you ask people why they believe something, they are not likely to say, "I don't know." Instead, they will conjure up reasons that seem plausible but may be wrong or incomplete. That is, because people often do not know their true reasons, they sample only part of those reasons. Thus, they present a biased sample of their reasons. People then assume the reasons in the biased sample are their true reasons for holding the belief. If these reasons don't seem compelling, thinking about them may persuade people to change their belief.

The Rational and Nonrational Actors: A Resolution

Sometimes we are rational actors; sometimes we are nonrational actors. Sometimes our behavior is "coupled" to our attitudes; sometimes it is "uncoupled" from them. Isn't this where we began? Let's see if we can now resolve the apparent conflict. It makes sense to see attitudes and behavior as ordinarily linked, with uncoupling occurring primarily under two kinds of circumstances.

Although your existing attitude toward exercising might be weak and lead to sporadic exercise, after finding out that a friend had a heart attack, your attitude might get stronger.
Source: Lisa-S/Shutterstock.

The first circumstance is when an attitude is not particularly important to you. You may not have thought about the attitude object much or have expressed the attitude very often. So in this case, you don't really know what you think. True, capital punishment and national health care are important issues. But many of us may not have thought them through. When you are forced to consider these issues, you may be surprised by what you say. This may make you reconsider your attitude.

The second circumstance is slightly more complicated. Essentially, it is when you don't have a clear sense of your goals and needs. Let's go back to the theory of planned behavior for a moment. The theory says if you expect that a behavior can help you achieve your goals and social needs, you will do it. But people are often not clear about their goals and needs (Hixon & Swann, 1993). When you are not clear about what you want to accomplish, then your behavior will be relatively unpredictable and might well be uncoupled from your attitudes.

For example, we exercise, but only sporadically, because we are mainly concerned about looking good in front of our health-obsessed friends. Our reasons are weak, not clear to us, and therefore our exercising behavior is infrequent and unpredictable. But if we or a friend the same age has a heart attack, we develop a much stronger attitude toward exercise. We now know that our reasons for exercising are to improve cardiovascular function, to enhance our sense of well-being, and, in short, to save our lives. Now we change our schedule around to exercise every day, subscribe to *Runner's World* magazine, invest in better exercise shoes, and so on.

In sum, then, our behavior is more likely to be consistent with our attitudes when the attitudes concern an area that is important to us and when the behavior helps us achieve clear and strong social needs. Attitudes we hold with conviction are not vulnerable to uncoupling because we have expressed those attitudes in a variety of situations and have thought deeply about them.

Study Break

Most research and theory in the area of attitudes assume that people are rational when it comes to their attitudes and behavior. An alternative view is that people are not always rational in these areas. Before you begin the next section, answer the following questions:

1. How do social psychologists define the nonrational actor?
2. What is mindlessness, and how does it relate to everyday behavior?
3. How does mindlessness relate to the attitude-behavior relationship?
4. How have social psychologists resolved the notions of the rational and nonrational actors?

Ideology and How We Feel About Those Who Think Differently from Us

We saw in our previous discussion that general attitudes sometimes are not good predictors of specific behaviors. If we extend our discussion to encompass broader concepts related to attitudes, we may see that the sometimes-elusive relationship between attitudes and behavior gets stronger. In this section, we will explore the concept of ideology and see how it relates to behavior. We also will explore how we perceive and react to others who do not share our ideological perspectives.

Differences in ideology can contribute to political polarization and conflict.
Source: Matt Gush/Shutterstock.

Ideology

Even a cursory search of the Internet turns up a number of definitions for *ideology*. For our purposes, we will define **ideology** as a set of ideas, beliefs, or stances that determine a perspective with which to interpret social and political realities (New World Encyclopedia, 2016). You can think of an ideology as the lens through which a person sees the world, with the lenses for different ideologies being different. For example, if you were to view the world through a pair of sunglasses with green lenses, you would see the world with a given tint. If you changed the sunglasses to ones with amber lenses, the tint would change. In the same way, viewing the world through one ideological perspective will yield different social constructions of reality than viewing through another. Two common, and important, ideologies relating to the world of politics are liberalism and conservatism. *Liberalism* is an ideology emphasizing "an enthusiasm for freedom, toleration, individualism and reason, on the one hand, and a disapproval of power, authority and tradition, on the other" (Alexander, 2015, p. 984). *Conservatism* is an ideology that is more resistant to change than liberalism and roots change in what has worked in the past (Alexander, 2015). Although there are other ideologies (e.g., socialism, communism), we will focus our discussion on liberalism and conservatism because they play a large role in politics and discourse.

ideology A set of ideas, beliefs, or stances that determine a perspective with which to interpret social and political realities.

Ideology and Political Polarization

It is often true that people divide into distinct groups based on political ideology leading to *political polarization*. The news media is always talking about "red states" (American states that lean conservative) and "blue states" (American states that lean liberal), implying that there is a sharp ideological divide in the American population. Although this may be true on the surface, a look at a county-by-county map of the United States shows that these red and blue states are actually a blend of ideologies. People often ask whether political polarization has increased over the past several years. Even a cursory look at American history shows us that political polarization has always existed and that it waxes and wanes over the course of history.

There is increasing evidence that political polarization in the United States is on the rise (Abramowitz, 2013; Abramowitz & Saunders, 2008; Gallup, 2017; McCarty et al., 2006; Pew Research Center, 2014). For example, Gallup has been tracking the job approval of American presidents since the 1950s. Unsurprisingly, partisans tend to give higher approval ratings of presidents who belong to the same party as they do. That is, Democrats think Democratic presidents are doing a better job than do Republicans, and vice versa. However, historically, this gap in approval rarely exceeded 40 points—that is, until the Clinton presidency. Since then, the partisan gap has been widening, and the Trump presidency had the largest gap on record. On average across his time in office, 83% of Republicans thought Trump was doing a good job as president, whereas only about 8% of Democrats thought the same. That is a whopping 75-point gap in approval numbers—one of the most politically polarized in recent history. This trend continued into the first 9 months of the Biden administration with 90% of Democrats and only 6% of Republicans approving of his performance, with an average gap of 84% (Gallup, 2021b) (see Figure 5.4).

Interestingly, although actual polarization has increased, people tend to perceive that polarization has increased even more than it actually has (Westfall et al., 2015). Westfall et al. suggest that three processes are involved in the tendency to perceive more polarization than actually exists. First, the mere process of categorizing people as Republicans or Democrats ("us versus them") enhances the perception that the groups differ more than they actually do. Second, the more strongly an individual identifies with a political party, the more polarization he or she is likely to see. Third, those with extreme personal political attitudes are more likely to exaggerate the degree of political polarization. Finally, the tendency to see more polarization than actually exists appears to have behavioral consequences. Individuals who perceive greater political polarization are more likely to engage in political action than those who see less polarization (Westfall et al., 2015).

Another factor contributing to political polarization is selective exposure to partisan media. Fritz Hippler, the head of the German film industry in Nazi Germany, once noted that people like to hear things that are agreeable. That is, people like to hear and see information that confirms their already existing attitudes. In modern times, it is possible to choose from the myriad of information sources (e.g., cable news, Internet blogs, Twitter) that are in line with one's political attitudes across media types (Stroud, 2008). Stroud (2008) found that during the 2004 election cycle supporters of George W. Bush exposed themselves to media outlets that supported Bush (e.g., Fox News), whereas supporters of John Kerry exposed themselves to outlets that supported Kerry (e.g., MSNBC). Generally, conservatives tend to gravitate to talk radio and Fox News and liberals to PBS and Facebook (Wicks et al., 2014). Does this selective exposure lead to political polarization? Research suggests that it does. People actively seek out information sources that support their political attitudes (Kim, 2015). This relationship is especially strong for people with already extreme political attitudes (Prior, 2013). Interestingly, exposure to information that is different from one's political attitudes can reduce political polarization (Kim, 2015). Finally as discussed earlier in this chapter, social media sites can serve as

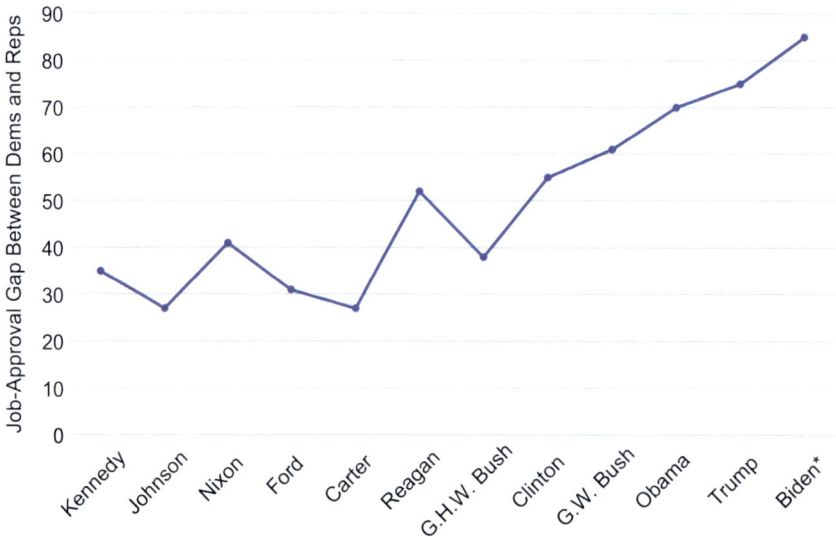

*Ratings for Biden are for only the first 9 months of his presidency

FIGURE 5-4

The gap between the average job-approval rating of Republicans and Democrats for Presidents Kennedy through Biden.
Based on data from Gallup (2017, 2021a,b).

"echo chambers"; particularly in regard to political topics, this tends to lead to increased polarization (Hong & Kim, 2016).

Ideology as Motivated Social Cognition

A person's ideology is also related to how that person thinks and his or her motivations for action. *Motivated social cognition* means that a person adopts a way of thinking (ideology) because it serves some psychological need and relates to a person's needs and motivations (Jost et al., 2003). The initial research in this area focused on conservative ideology and found that conservative thought was correlated with an intolerance of ambiguity, anxiety about death, low openness to new experience, fear of threat and loss, and lowered self-esteem (among others) (Jost et al., 2003).

Based on these findings, some commentators concluded that conservative thinking was less flexible than liberal thinking. However, there was a problem with this conclusion. Research shows that inflexibility and biased thinking are found whenever a person has an extreme ideological position, regardless of whether the person is liberal or conservative (Ditto et al., 2019; van Baar & FeldmanHall, 2021). Additionally, the pattern of thinking identified by Jost et al. among conservatives might also apply to liberals in other domains of issues. That is, the relatively rigid thought patterns observed may be domain specific. For example, conservatives may show rigid thinking for issues such as abortion or gun control but more nuanced thinking for other issues. Similarly, liberals may show nuanced thinking on those issues but rigid thinking on others (e.g., climate change). In a test of this idea, Conway et al. (2016) had conservative and liberal individuals respond to a number of issues (e.g., the death penalty, truth of the bible, censorship, refugees). They found that conservatives showed greater integrative complexity of thinking than liberals on issues such as the death penalty and refugees. Liberals, on the other hand, showed greater integrative complexity on censorship and the truth of the bible. So, whether liberals or conservatives are more dogmatic and close-minded depends on the issue being addressed. Finally, the differences in motivated social cognition between liberals and conservatives may relate to functional and structural brain differences between the two groups (Jost & Amodio, 2012). For example, Jost and Amodio report that compared to liberals, conservatives have a larger right amygdala, which is associated with sensitivity to threat.

Does Ideology Predict Behavior?

Each time an opening occurs on the Supreme Court (or other federal court), an ideological battle ensues. Although such ideological battles date back well into the 1950s, they became more pronounced after the failed nomination of Robert Bork in 1987 (Epstein et al., 2006). Both liberal and conservative senators line up along the ideological divide to oppose nominees from the other side. However, are these battles worth the effort? Does it really matter all that much who sits on the Supreme Court? After all, in a vast majority of cases, the justices on the court agree. Although this is true for most cases, in some cases the ideological leaning of a justice does matter. Most of these cases involve important social issues such as abortion, gun control, and same-sex marriage. In fact, research shows that for these ideologically related cases, one can predict with a high degree of accuracy how a justice will vote based on his or her ideology (Ringhand, 2007). Ringhand analyzed the voting patterns of the Supreme Court justices on the Rehnquist Court. As shown in Figure 5.5, she found a clear pattern of conservative justices (Thomas, Scalia, Rehnquist, O'Connor, and Kennedy) casting votes to invalidate a federal statute in a conservative direction and liberal justices (Ginsburg, Breyer, Souter, and Stevens) in a liberal direction (Ringhand, 2007). It is worth noting that although ideology is a good predictor of a justice's voting, for some justices ideology can shift. Later in her tenure, for example, O'Connor moved to the center and often provided a swing vote on cases. Similarly, Kennedy also showed such an ideological shift. For others, however, ideology remained more fixed. For example, Thomas has remained squarely in the conservative camp, and the late Justice Ginsburg remained squarely in the liberal camp during her tenure on the court. Finally, the relationship between ideology and voting patterns is not limited to Supreme

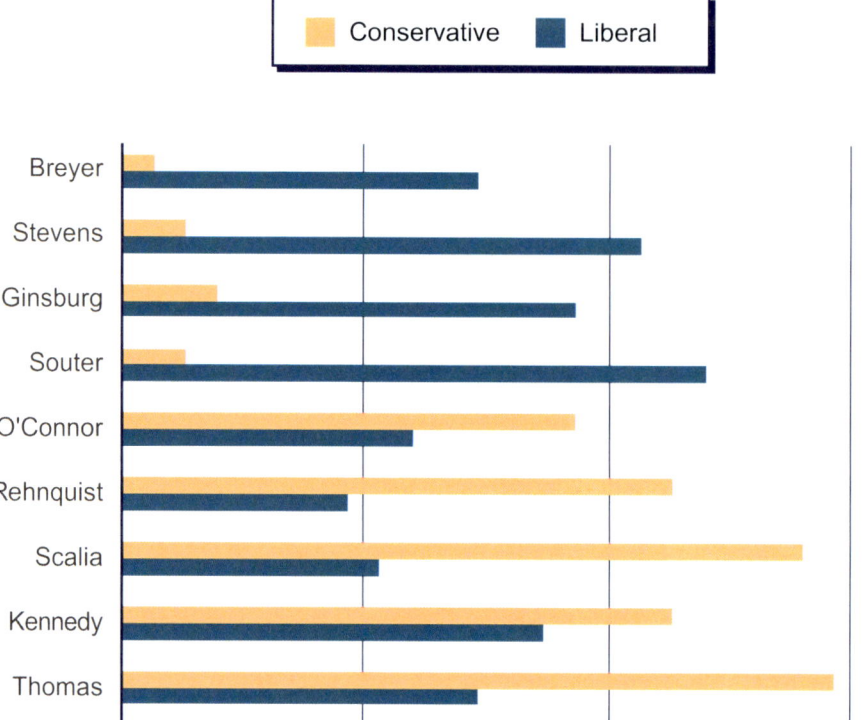

FIGURE 5.5

Voting patterns for Supreme Court justices on the Rehnquist Court.
Based on data from Ringhand (2007).

Court justices. Research also shows that ideology is a strong predictor of how a senator voted on important abortion legislation in the 1980s, with ideologically conservative senators voting consistently against pro-abortion amendments (Chressanthis et al., 1991).

There is a confirmed tendency to question the motives of those who disagree with us, particularly when the topic is of high importance (Reeder & Tramifow, 2005, Malle & Hodges, 2006). One big reason for this observation has to do with the power of what the great Swiss developmentalist Jean Piaget called naïve realism. For Piaget, naïve realism was the last stage of the child's cognitive development before adulthood. It was the last remnant of egocentrism, when our thought processes are concerned first and foremost with ourselves and our own views of the world.

Naïve realism involves three intertwined processes. First is the belief that we are seeing the world objectively, and second, that other people who are rational will also see the world as we do. And finally, if those others don't see the world as we do, then either they do not have the right information or they are not rational and harbor ulterior and bad motives (Reeder et al., 2005). In essence, we are motivated to see ourselves as free of bias and objective, and we have what might fairly be called a *bias blind spot* (Cohen, 2003).

Therefore, if we examine any hotly contested controversial issue in the American political scene, we will see evidence of thinking that has elements of naïve realism. During the COVID-19 pandemic, proponents of harsh antivirus measures (e.g., lockdown, mask wearing) characterized those who opposed such measures as irrational and "anti-science." From their perspective, COVID-19 was seen as a highly infectious disease that threatened the well-being of Americans, thus justifying extreme measures. Those who believed that more flexible measures were in order characterized those on the other side as overly restrictive and even fascist in some cases. For partisans on both sides, anyone who disagreed with them was believed to have motives and thought processes that were not objective. Recall that from the view of the naïve realist, if your opposition had received the right information, they would see the righteousness of your view. In the case

naïve realism The belief that we see the world objectively, while others are biased, and that if others do not see the world as we do, they are not rational.

of COVID-19, anyone who has not been exposed to information about the virus is likely brain-dead and not worthy of a response. Thus, the only explanation left to the naïve realist is to question the rationality and the motive of one's opponents.

Our tendency to ascribe bad motives to our staunch opponents on big issues does not mean that we ignore or dismiss their views. It just means that we think they are wrong for the wrong reasons (irrationality and multiple biases). Eagly and colleagues have challenged the notion that we attend to and select information that we agree with and reject and indeed ignore information that we find uncongenial to our most strongly held beliefs (Eagly et al., 2001). Eagly et al. examined a total of 70 experiments that tested the "congeniality hypothesis" (to wit, that we only examine carefully congenial information and ignore the rest). They found that the assumption was untrue. People do attend to information that disagrees with their strong view. But they examine it in a specific way. What they do is a kind of "skeptical and active scrutiny" as compared to information they agree with, which is approached with a view to confirm the congeniality of that information. Our view of arguments that offend or challenge us is to figure out what the "devil" is saying and devise counterarguments to that view. We know what they are saying, but we will not be convinced by them because that is not the purpose of our examination. We want to know how to beat the heck out of those who would hold such views. At least, some of us see it that way.

Are naïve realism and the bias blind spot related to the cognitive abilities of the individual? That is, are less sophisticated thinkers more prone to the bias blind spot than more sophisticated thinkers? If this were true, it would be comforting because we could convince ourselves that only less capable people show the bias. Unfortunately for us, research does not support this. West et al. (2012) conducted a pair of studies testing the relationship between the level of sophisticated thinking and the bias blind spot. In their first study, West et al. measured the bias blind spot along with a number of measures of cognitive sophistication (e.g., open-minded thinking, SAT scores, ability to solve a complex cognitive problem). West et al. found that cognitive sophistication was not a strong correlate of the likelihood of showing the bias blind spot. In fact, they found that cognitively sophisticated thinkers were *more* likely to show the bias blind spot than less sophisticated thinkers.

Ida Tarbell Revisited

Today, Ida Tarbell is not a well-known historical figure, but she held her attitudes with conviction and expressed them courageously. Although she didn't like being called a muckraker at first, she realized that there was a lot of "muck" in American life that needed to be raked. President Roosevelt and the American public came to agree.

Tarbell followed her beliefs with a powerful sense of purpose. Her early experiences, her family's support, and her own strong education and temperament combined to produce a woman whose attitudes and behavior were consistently in accord. No doubt this is an unusual situation. Ida was a rational actor; the coupling of her attitudes and her life's work was fierce and unshakeable.

Study Break

Social psychologists have investigated the role that ideology plays in thinking and behavior. Before you read the Chapter Review, answer the following questions:

1. What are the definitions of ideology and liberalism and conservatism?
2. How does ideology relate to political polarization?
3. What are the factors that contribute to political polarization?
4. What is motivated social cognition, and how does it relate to ideology?
5. How does ideology relate to behavior?
6. How do we reach to those that disagree with us on an important issue?

Chapter Review

1. **What is an attitude?**

   An attitude is a mental and neural state of readiness, organized through experience, exerting a directive or dynamic influence upon the individual's response to all objects and situations with which it is related.

2. **What is the relationship of attitudes to values?**

   A value is a conception of what is desirable; it is a guideline for a person's actions, a standard for behavior. Our attitudes flow from and express our values. Freedom, equity, and similar concepts are values, and attitudes toward free speech, voting rights, and so on flow from those values.

3. **What are implicit and explicit attitudes?**

   Explicit attitudes operate on a conscious level, so we are aware of them—aware of the cognitive underpinnings of them—and are conscious of how they relate to behavior. They operate via controlled processing and take some cognitive effort to activate. For example, you may know how you feel toward a given political candidate and match your behavior (e.g., voting for him or her) to that attitude. It is these explicit attitudes that we often find having a directive effect on behavior.

   Implicit attitudes affect behaviors automatically, without conscious thought, and below the level of awareness. For example, an individual may have a quick negative reaction toward a member of a minority group, even thought the individual professes positive and tolerant attitudes toward that group. The "gut-level" reaction occurs without thought and is often distasteful to the individual.

4. **How are attitude surveys conducted?**

   The most commonly used techniques for measuring attitudes are attitude surveys. In an attitude survey, the researcher mails a questionnaire to a potential respondent, conducts a face-to-face interview, or asks a series of questions on the telephone. Because respondents report on their own attitudes, an attitude survey is a self-report measure. A respondent indicates his or her attitude by answering a series of questions.

5. **What are the potential sources of bias in a survey?**

   Among the greatest biases in attitude surveys are badly worded questions as well as the lack of a random sample of sufficient size.

6. **What are behavioral measures of attitudes?**

   Behavioral measures are used to overcome some of the problems inherent in attitude (paper-and-pencil) measures. The idea is that an individual's actions are the truest reflection of how he or she feels. For example, rather than asking people how they feel about a new ethnic group moving into their neighborhood, a researcher might use the "lost letter technique," in which stamped envelopes are apparently accidentally lost near mailboxes. The letters have a foreign-sounding name on them, and one compares the proportion of those mailed with other letters having more conventional names on the envelopes.

7. **What is the Implicit Attitude Test (IAT)?**

   The IAT is an online test of implicit attitudes. The IAT measures the relationship of associative strength between positive or negative attitudes and various racial and ethnic groups.

8. **What does the IAT tell us about our prejudices?**

   The results of the millions of tests on IAT Web sites show that a large proportion of the test-takers display unconscious biases against other social, racial, and ethnic groups.

9. **How are attitudes formed?**

   The basic mechanisms of attitude formation are the same as those for the acquisition of other behavior: evaluative (classical) and operant conditioning and observational learning. In addition, the mass media have had a profound effect on our attitudes and behavior. Since its entry into American homes 50 years ago, television has altered our conception of everything from our notions of "the good life" to sexual behavior. Research has also shown that changes in music genres and the advent of video games and cellular telephones have had significant influences on what people consider acceptable behavior.

10. **Can attitudes be inherited?**

    Yes, indirectly. Genetic differences in sensory structures, such as hearing and taste, could affect our preferences for certain kinds of music and foods. Also, aggressiveness, which has a genetic component, can affect a whole range of attitudes and behaviors, from watching violent TV shows and movies, to hostility toward women or members of other groups, to attitudes toward capital punishment.

11. **What is agenda setting?**

    Many researchers suggest that the topics foremost in the mass media tend to set the public agenda.

This *agenda setting* occurs because the topics most prominent in the news shape the public's cognitions, increasing the focus on certain issues as opposed to others.

12. How do groups influence one's attitudes?

Many attitudes are learned and reinforced in group settings. Groups may be the most influential factor in determining which attitudes we express. Research shows that a person's stated attitude toward a public issue was dependent solely on the stated position of the political party with which the person was aligned. Both liberals and conservatives tend to toe the party line even if that line is different from an individual's original attitude. However, there are limits to the extent to which a person will toe the party line. If one's primary goal is accuracy or if a policy has bi-partisan support, then party endorsement does not affect attitudes as much.

13. How do social networks influence a person's attitudes?

When you are part of congruent social networks (people with similar views), your attitude becomes more resistant to change because you have strong social support for that attitude. However, if you are embedded in a heterogeneous social network with lots of people who have different views, individuals are less resistant to change. It appears that when you are with people who think as you do, not surprisingly, you become more certain of your attitudes, and any doubts you may have had are removed. Social media operates as a sort of echo chamber in which like-minded individuals exchange ideas. Individuals will tune their beliefs to match others' beliefs.

14. What is the relationship between attitudes and behavior?

Researchers have found only a modest relationship between attitudes and behavior. One reason is that more than one attitude may be involved in deciding whether to do something or not to do it. Second, while you might like to express a particular attitude in some circumstances, other factors may stop you from doing so. For example, you may think that your best friend made a grave mistake in marrying Jane, but you would have to be an oaf to express that opinion in your wedding toast.

15. What is the notion of the nonrational actor?

Some attitude theorists have criticized the theory of planned behavior because it assumes that individuals are always rational when attitudes are concerned. Other theorists maintain that humans are nonrational actors and that sometimes attitudes are totally irrelevant to our behavior. In many cases, according to this view, people behave habitually, unthinkingly, and even mindlessly in everyday life.

16. How has the controversy over the rational and nonrational actor been resolved?

The short answer is that sometimes we are rational actors, and our attitudes are coupled with our behavior. Other times we are nonrational actors, and our behaviors and attitudes are uncoupled. Uncoupling is likely to occur when an attitude is not particularly important to us or if we don't have a clear sense of our goals and needs.

17. What is ideology, and how does it relate to behavior?

Ideology is a set of ideas, beliefs, or stances that determine a perspective with which to interpret social and political realities. There are two common ideologies. Liberalism, which emphasizes freedom, toleration, individualism, reason, and a rejection of traditional authority. Conservatism is more resistant to change than liberalism and roots change in what has worked in the past. Strong adherence to a political ideology can lead to political polarization. Although research suggests that political polarization has not increased much in the recent past, people perceive that polarization has increased. This is likely due to the tendency to categorize people, a strong identification with a political party, and exaggeration of polarization by individuals with strong ideologies. Polarization also relates to selective exposure to partisan media. People tend to gravitate to news sources that support their ideology. Ideology is a source of motivated social cognition, meaning that ideological thinking is related to a person's motivation for behavior. Ideology has been found to relate to ideologically relevant behavior. For example, voting records of Supreme Court justices show that liberal and conservative justices vote in a manner that is highly consistent with their ideology on certain cases.

18. What is naïve realism, and how does it influence our political attitudes?

Naïve realism involves three intertwined processes. First is the belief that we are seeing the world objectively, and second, that other people who are rational will also see the world as we do. And finally, if those others don't see the world as we do, then either they do not have the right information or they are not rational and harbor ulterior and bad motives.

Key Terms

Attitude (p. 169)
Attitude structure (p. 170)
Attitude survey (p. 173)
Evaluative conditioning (p. 177)
Explicit attitude (p. 172)
Heritability (p. 182)

Ideology (p. 193)
Implicit Association Test (IAT) (p. 174)
Implicit attitude (p. 172)
Mere exposure (p. 175)
Naïve realism (p. 196)

Nonrational actor (p. 190)
Observational learning (p. 178)
Operant conditioning (p. 177)
Theory of planned behavior (p. 186)
Unobtrusive measure (p. 174)
Value (p. 171)

Chapter Quiz

1. Which of the following was *not* listed as one of the components of the attitude structure in your text?
   A. Behavior
   B. Affective responses
   C. The social environment
   D. Cognitions

2. Whereas the _____ component of the attitude structure includes information relevant to the attitude, the _____ component includes the emotional response to an attitude object.
   A. affective; cognitive
   B. cognitive; affective
   C. cognitive; behavioral
   D. affective; behavioral

3. An attitude that operates on a conscious level and of which we are aware is known as a(n)
   A. overt attitude.
   B. concrete attitude.
   C. implicit attitude.
   D. explicit attitude.

4. According to your text, a sample for a survey must be
   A. representative.
   B. large.
   C. small.
   D. homogeneous.

5. You download some new music. The first time you listen to it, you are not sure if you like it. However, as you listen to it more, you come to like it more and more. This is an example of _____ in attitude formation.
   A. direct personal experience
   B. mere exposure
   C. instrumental conditioning
   D. classical conditioning

6. According to your text, the news media helps shape attitudes through
   A. the generalized exposure model.
   B. the mere exposure effect.
   C. making direct personal experience more salient.
   D. agenda setting.

7. According to research, genetics
   A. may have an indirect effect on attitudes.
   B. has a direct effect on attitudes.
   C. is more important than the environment in determining attitudes.
   D. has no effect on attitudes.

8. Michelle is politically very liberal, and she joins and becomes active in the Liberal Campus Coalition at her college. According to research cited in your text, which of the following is likely to occur?
   A. Michelle's liberal attitudes will be more susceptible to change.
   B. Michelle may start to develop some conservative attitudes to distinguish herself from others in the group.
   C. Michelle's attitudes will become more resistant to change.
   D. None of the above

9. Which of the following are true of strongly held attitudes?
   A. They are difficult to change.
   B. They are easily accessible.
   C. They are closely linked with behavior.
   D. All of the above
   E. A and B only

10. Selective exposure to partisan media
    A. does occur but has no effect on political polarization.
    B. does occur and contributes to political polarization.
    C. is limited to people who do not have strong political opinions.
    D. is largely a myth and does not really occur.

Answers can be found in the end-of-book Answers section.

Persuasion and Attitude Change

With reasonable men I will reason; with humane men I will plead; but to tyrants I will give no quarter, nor waste arguments where they will certainly be lost.

—William Lloyd Garrison

CHAPTER 6

Source: Everett Collection/Shutterstock.

Key Questions

As you read this chapter, find the answers to the following questions:

1. What is persuasion?
2. What is the Yale communication model?
3. What factors about the communicator affect persuasion?
4. What message factors mediate persuasion?
5. What is the elaboration likelihood model of persuasion?
6. What is the impact of vividness on persuasion?
7. What are the need for cognition and the need for affect?
8. What is the heuristic and systematic information model of persuasion?
9. What is cognitive dissonance theory, and what are its main ideas?
10. How does cognitive dissonance relate to cult membership?
11. What is self-perception theory?
12. What is self-affirmation theory?
13. What is psychological reactance?
14. What is propaganda?
15. How are the tactics of propaganda used on a mass scale?

Possibly the most important public health issue in 2020–2021 was the COVID-19 pandemic. In 2020, COVID-19 was the third-leading cause of death in the United States, responsible for approximately 375,000 deaths (Centers for Disease Control and Prevention, 2021a). COVID-19 disrupted the world's economy and changed our behaviors (e.g., social distancing and mask wearing) in dramatic ways. The scientific community has responded remarkably well to this novel virus, including improvements in treatments and the development of effective vaccines. Even with all these advancements in medicine, the only way to truly eradicate COVID-19 is to persuade most people to get vaccinated.

Hesitancy to receive the COVID-19 vaccination became one of the biggest public health issues in 2021. Approximately 58% of the total population of the United States was fully vaccinated as of November 2021, and 67% of the total population had received at least one dose (Centers for Disease Control and Prevention, 2021b). This left 33% unvaccinated. There are several factors related to people being reluctant to receive a vaccination, but one of the most prominent is age. Of older Americans (i.e., 65 years or older), 97.8% have received at least one vaccine dose, whereas only 60.3% of younger Americans (i.e., 18–24 years) have been

201

similarly vaccinated (Centers for Disease Control and Prevention, 2021b USA Facts, 2021). It appears that younger Americans' attitudes toward the COVID-19 vaccine are contributing to their low vaccination rate. The three most common attitudes among younger adults associated with not getting vaccinated are (1) concern about possible side effects, (2) lack of trust in the vaccine, and (3) the belief they do not need a vaccine (Centers for Disease Control and Prevention, 2021c).

Although we would like to believe that vaccine hesitancy is a new problem, it has been an issue ever since the creation of vaccines. Widespread smallpox vaccinations began in England in the 1800s. Almost immediately, this vaccine was met with skepticism, and after England made the vaccination mandatory for children under the age of 14, antivaccination leagues began to form (Durbach, 2000). Additionally, these antivaccination groups cropped up around the world whenever a government began to implement a smallpox vaccination program (Wolfe & Sharpe, 2002). Despite early resistance to the smallpox vaccine, people's attitudes eventually became more accepting, and widespread vaccination against smallpox led to the eradication of this disease. People are no longer vaccinated against smallpox because it no longer exists in nature—largely as a result of vaccinations.

In the 1950s, attitudes toward the polio vaccine also had an age gap. Although parents with young children were eager to get them vaccinated, teenagers were very hesitant to receive the vaccination. In 1956, fewer than 1% of teenagers were vaccinated against polio, even though they were, after children, the most at-risk group. Many teenagers didn't want to get vaccinated for the same reasons younger people don't want to get vaccinated for COVID-19 today: they believed they were not at risk or would suffer side effects from the vaccine. How did the United States change the attitudes of these teenagers in the 1950s? The answer was to appeal to a celebrity. In late 1956, a 21-year-old Elvis Presley, at the height of his stardom, received the polio vaccination in front of the press before his appearance on *The Ed Sullivan Show*. After Elvis's famous jab, vaccination rates among teenagers surged to 80% within 6 months. Historians have dubbed this the "Elvis effect" (Hershfield & Brody, 2021).

Although vaccine hesitancy is nothing new, there do seem to be unique factors related to the COVID-19 vaccine. Groups that have not typically been opposed to vaccinations in the past are reluctant to receive a COVID-19 vaccination (Motta et al., 2021). In addition to the young, conservatives, rural populations, and Blacks are particularly resistant to receiving a COVID-19 vaccination. Part of the unique resistance to COVID-19 vaccines may be due to the speed with which they were produced and the fact that they use a new type of vaccination method (involving the use of messenger ribonucleic acid [mRNA]). Note: It appears that the next battle in the pandemic will center on the most effective way to persuade vaccine-hesitant populations to get vaccinated.

In this chapter, we will explore various techniques used to persuade people to change their attitudes and behaviors, such as those concerning getting the COVID-19 vaccination. As in past health crises, interested parties are engaging in campaigns to persuade the public to get the vaccine. Various persuasive techniques were used to convince people that getting the COVID-19 vaccination was not only in their best interest but also in the best interest of society as a whole. Can people be persuaded to overcome their vaccine hesitancy?

What techniques work best to get people to change their attitudes and behaviors? How can persuasion techniques be applied on a mass basis? These are some of the questions that we shall address next.

The Persuasion Process

Public health officials have been using their powers of persuasion to shape the public opinion on vaccinations and other issues pertaining to public health for many years. **Persuasion** is the application of rational and/or emotional arguments to convince others to change their attitudes or behavior. It is a form of social influence used not only for issues of public health but also in every part of daily social life. The persuasion process goes on in the classroom, in religious institutions, in the political arena, and in the media. Persuasive messages are so much a part of our lives that we often are oblivious to the bombardment from billboards, TV, radio, newspapers, parents, peers, the Internet, and public figures.

persuasion A form of social influence that involves changing others' thoughts, attitudes, or behaviors by applying rational and/or emotional arguments to convince them to adopt your position.

Persuasion, then, is a pervasive form of social influence. We are all agents of social influence when we try to convince others to change their attitudes or behavior. We are also targets of social influence when others try to persuade or coerce us to do what they want us to do.

The Yale Communication Model

What is the best way to communicate your ideas to others and persuade them to accept your point of view? An early view suggested that the most effective approach to persuasion was to present logical arguments that showed people how they would benefit from changing their attitudes. This view was formulated by Carl Hovland, who worked for the U.S. government in its propaganda efforts during World War II. After the war, he returned to Yale University, where he gathered a team of 30 coworkers and began to systematically study the process of persuasion. Out of their efforts came the **Yale communication model** (Hovland et al., 1953).

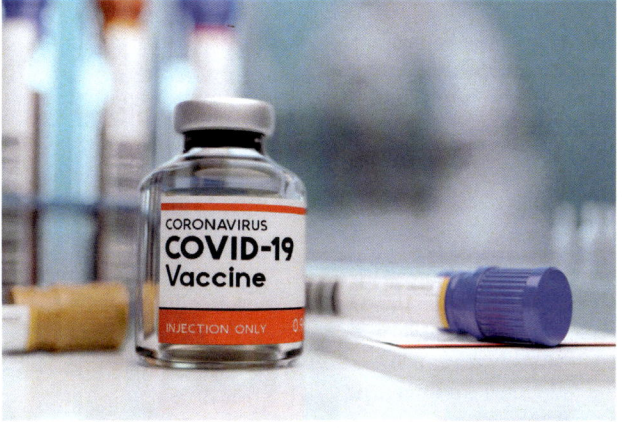

Public health officials used a number of persuasion techniques to encourage people to take the COVID-19 vaccine.
Source: Minerva Studio/Shutterstock.

Yale communication model A model of the persuasion process that stresses the role of the communicator (source of a message), the nature of the message, the audience, and the channel of communication.

According to the Yale communication model, the most important factors comprising the communication process are expressed by the question, Who says what to whom by what means? This question suggests that there are four factors involved in persuasion. The "who" refers to the communicator, the person making the persuasive argument. The "what" refers to the organization and content of the persuasive message. The "whom" is the target of the persuasive message, the audience. Finally, the "means" points to the importance of the channel or medium through which the message is conveyed, such as the Internet, television, radio, or interpersonal face-to-face communication. For each factor, there are several variables that can potentially influence the persuasion process.

A key assumption of the Yale model is that these four factors (which can be manipulated in an experiment) provide input into three internal mediators: the attention, comprehension, and acceptance mediators. Persuasion, according to the Yale model, will occur if the target of a persuasive message first attends to the message, then comprehends (understands) the content of the message, and finally accepts the content of the message. What this means is that the Yale model proposes that persuasion is a function of controlled processing of the message. That is, a person who is persuaded actively attends to the message, makes an effort to understand the content of the message, and finally decides to accept the message.

Finally, the four factors contributing to persuasion are not independent of one another; they interact to create a persuasive effect. In practice, the content and presentation of the message depend on the communicator, the audience, and the channel. Public health officials often tailor their messages in this way. For example, Elvis (the who) was selected specifically to target younger people (the whom) using the most popular media of the time, television (the means). We turn now to a discussion of the four factors, considering selected variables within each component. We also look at how the factors interact with one another.

The Communicator

Have you ever seen a late-night infomercial on TV? These half-hour commercials usually push a "miracle" product, such as the car wax that supposedly can withstand a direct hit from a hydrogen bomb. The car is vaporized but the wax survives. There is an "expert" (usually the inventor) who touts the product's virtues. Do you believe what this person tells you? Many people must, given the large amounts of money made from infomercials. However, many people clearly are not convinced. If you are not persuaded, one thing you may focus on is the communicator. You may find yourself questioning this fellow's integrity (because he will profit by persuading you to buy the atomic car wax) and, consequently, disbelieving his claims. In other words, you question his credibility.

Credibility: Expertise and Trustworthiness

credibility The believability (expertise and trustworthiness) of the communicator of a persuasive message.

Public health officials recognize the importance of **credibility**, which is the believability of the message source. Typically, people view their own doctors as credible sources when it comes to matters of their own health. In addition to elaborate advertising campaigns with celebrities, public health officials have requested that doctors talk with their patients to help alleviate vaccine fears.

expertise A component of communicator credibility that refers to the communicator's credentials and stems from the individual's training and knowledge.

trustworthiness A component of communicator credibility that involves our assessment of the communicator's character and motives for delivering the message.

Although other variables are important, including a communicator's perceived attractiveness and power, credibility is the most critical variable affecting the ability to persuade. Credibility has two components: expertise and trustworthiness. **Expertise** refers to a communicator's credentials and stems from the person's training and knowledge. For example, your doctor has the ability to persuade you on health matters because she has the education and experience that give her words power. **Trustworthiness** refers to the audience's assessment of the communicator's character as well as his or her motives for delivering the message. We ask, "Why is this person trying to convince us?" Trustworthiness may be diminished when we perceive that the communicator has something to gain from persuading us. For example, you might trust a review of a product published in *Consumer Reports* (which accepts no advertising and runs independent tests) more than a similar review based on research conducted by the manufacturer of the product.

Expertise and trustworthiness do not always go together. A communicator may be high in one but low in the other. A research physician speaking about a new drug to treat COVID-19 may have expertise and derive credibility from that expert knowledge. But if we discover that the physician stands to gain something from the sale of this drug, we probably will question her trustworthiness. We wonder about her character and motives and may no longer consider her a credible source.

A political figure with the unfortunate mix of high expertise and low trustworthiness was former President Bill Clinton. He was highly knowledgeable on matters of state but was not perceived as very trustworthy. During the "Monica Lewinsky" scandal, there is the enduring image of President Clinton waving his finger at the TV cameras, saying he never had sexual relations with "that woman." In contrast, a source can be highly trustworthy but low in expertise. This was the case with the late President Ronald Reagan. During speeches he often used unsubstantiated statistics, sending his aides scrambling for sources. However, the public generally saw him as trustworthy. People wanted to believe him. Public opinion surveys showed again and again that a majority of the public viewed President Reagan as personally attractive and likable, and these qualities prime us to accept a persuader's message (Roskos-Ewoldsen & Fazio, 1992). The interesting thing about Presidents Clinton and Reagan is that they were both enormously effective communicators, but for different reasons. It is also worth noting that a communicator's credibility is not carved in stone and can change along with new information. For example, early in the COVID-19 pandemic, Dr. Anthony Fauci was looked to as a trusted, expert source for pandemic-related information. However, after a series of missteps by Fauci and allegations that he was involved in funding research that may have led to the creation of the COVID-19 virus, people's trust in him began to slip. A poll done in May 2021 showed that 42.2% of those polled indicated that their confidence in Dr. Fauci had decreased (The Trafalgar Group, 2021). This drop was highest among Republicans (66.1%) followed by independents (41.7%), and Democrats (20%).

Expertise rests on a communicator's level of education, training, and credentials. Generally, the higher a communicator's expertise, the higher is the ability to persuade. Although a high-expertise communicator will generally be more persuasive than a low-expertise communicator, this may not always be the case. Imagine, for example, that you are watching a low-expertise communicator who expresses a great deal of confidence or certainty in his or her message. Will you be persuaded by this communicator? Research suggests that you will. Karmarkar and Tormala (2010) exposed participants to a high-expertise or low-expertise communicator who expressed high or low certainty in his message. Karmarkar and Tormala found that a low-expertise source who expressed high certainty was more persuasive than one who expressed low certainty. For the high-expertise source, expressing uncertainty actually led to higher persuasion than expressing high certainty. Karmarkar and Tormala found that the interaction between source expertise and certainty related to the degree of involvement participants showed in the message. When a communicator violates our expectations (e.g., a high-expertise source expressing uncertainty), we become more involved in the message than if our expectations (e.g., a high-expertise source expressing certainty) are met. That is, we pay more attention to the message from a source that violates our expectation and are more persuaded than if the communicator meets our expectation.

Trustworthiness is, in part, a judgment about the motives of the communicator. If someone is trying very hard to persuade us, we are likely to question his or her motives (Eagly et al., 1978). We may be more convinced by the communicator's arguments if we don't think he or she is trying to persuade us (Walster [Hatfield] & Festinger, 1962). This is the theory behind the hidden-camera technique used by television advertisers. Presumably, a person touting the virtues of a fabric softener on hidden camera must be telling the truth. The communicator is not trying to convince us; he or she is giving a seemingly unbiased testimonial.

Interestingly, messages coming from a trustworthy or untrustworthy source are processed differently (Preister, 2003). A target of a persuasive appeal from a trustworthy source is less likely to process the content of the message carefully and elaborate it in memory, compared to the same message coming from an untrustworthy source. That is, the arguments made by a trustworthy source are more likely to be accepted on face value than those presented by an untrustworthy source. Further, the difference between an untrustworthy and trustworthy source is greatest when the arguments being presented are weak. When strong arguments are presented, the trustworthy and untrustworthy sources are equally likely to produce attitude change (Priester & Petty, 2003).

A communicator who appears to argue against his or her own best interest is more persuasive than a communicator who takes an expected stance (Eagly et al., 1978). For example, Combs and Keller (2010) found that a political candidate who argued against his own self-interest was rated as more trustworthy than one who argued in his own self-interest. This appears to occur because participants perceive the candidate who argues against his own self-interest as showing unexpected positivity. This unexpected positivity then translates into a greater intention to vote for that candidate (Combs & Keller, 2010).

Limits on Credibility: The Sleeper Effect Does a credible communicator have an advantage over a noncredible one in the long run? Apparently not. Research has shown that there are limits to a credible communicator's influence. The Yale group found that although the credibility of the communicator has a strong effect on attitude change, over

sleeper effect A phenomenon of persuasion that occurs when a communication has more impact on attitude change after a long delay than when it is first heard.

time people forget who said what, so the effects of credibility wear off. Initially, people believe the credible source. But 6 weeks later, they are about as likely to show attitude change from a noncredible source as from a credible source. So, if you read an article in the *National Enquirer*, it probably would have little effect on you right away. But after a few weeks, you might show some change despite the source's low credibility. The phenomenon of a message having more impact on attitude change after a long delay than when it is first heard is known as the **sleeper effect**.

The sleeper effect has been shown in a wide variety of persuasion situations, including political attack advertisements (Lariscy & Tinkham, 1999). In their experiment Lariscy and Tinkham exposed participants to a televised political attack advertisement. Some participants also saw a second political advertisement that called the credibility of the attack ad into question (discounting cue). This defensive advertisement was presented either before or after the attack advertisement. Lariscy and Tinkham measured perceived credibility of the source of the attack advertisement and how certain participants were that they would vote for the candidate who sponsored the attack advertisement. The results showed that the negative advertisement was effective, even though participants indicated they disliked the negativity. Evidence was also found for a sleeper effect. When the defensive advertisement was presented after the attack advertisement, perceptions of the candidate who sponsored the attack ad were negative. However, after a delay, the defensive advertisement lost its power to attenuate the effect of the attack advertisement.

Why does the sleeper effect occur? One possible cause of the sleeper effect may be that the communicator's credibility does not increase the listener's understanding of the message (Kelman & Hovland, 1953). In other words, people understand messages from credible and noncredible communicators equally well. As the effects of credibility wear off over time, listeners are left with two equally understood (or misunderstood) messages (Gruder et al., 1979).

Three factors make it more likely that the sleeper effect will occur (Rajecki, 1990):

1. There is a strong persuasive argument.

2. There is a discounting cue, something that makes the receiver doubt the accuracy of the message, such as lack of communicator credibility or new information that contradicts the original message.

3. Enough time passes that the discounting cue and the message become disassociated, and people forget which source said what.

Communicator efficacy is the effectiveness of a communicator to bring about change. Communicators with high efficacy are more persuasive than those with low efficacy.
Source: BaanTaksinStudio/Shutterstock.

A meta-analysis of the sleeper effect literature (Kumkale & Albarracin, 2004) found that two other factors were also relevant to the occurrence of the sleeper effect. First, the sleeper effect is most likely to occur if both the message and the credibility information are strong. Second, the sleeper effect is stronger for individuals who are motivated to carefully process and think about the message and credibility information. This latter finding suggests that the sleeper effect requires active, controlled processing of the message content and credibility information.

Studies also show that the sleeper effect occurs most reliably when the receivers get the discounting cue after they hear the message rather than before (Kumkale & Albarracin, 2004; Pratkanis et al., 1988). If the discounting cue comes before the message, the receiver doubts the message before it is even conveyed. But if the discounting cue comes after the message, and if the argument is strong, the receiver probably has already been persuaded. Over time, the memory of the discounting cue "decays" faster than the memory of the persuasive message (Pratkanis et al., 1988). Because the message is stored before the discounting cue is received, the message is less likely to be weakened. After a long period has elapsed, all the receiver remembers is the original persuasive message (Figure 6.1).

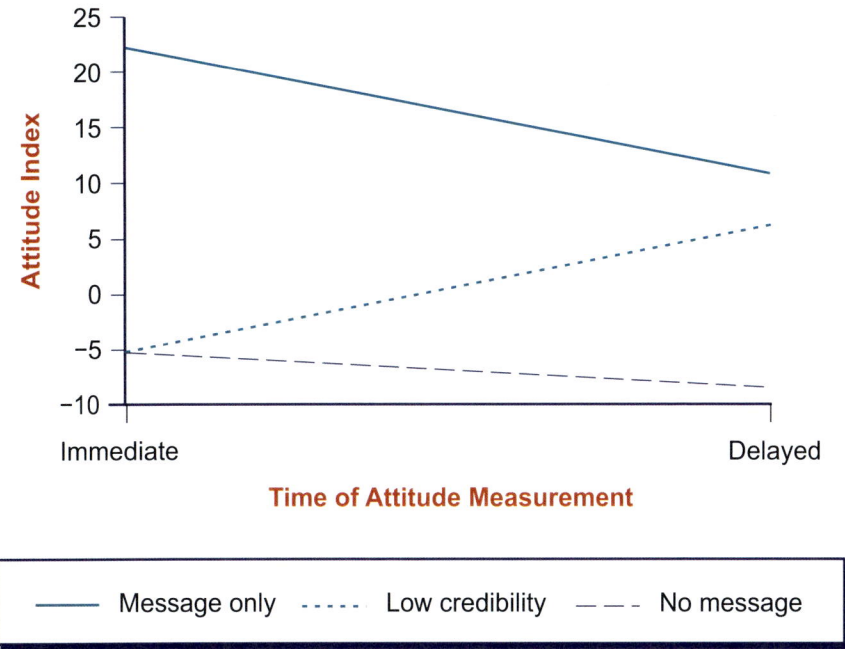

FIGURE 6.1

The sleeper effect in persuasion. When attitudes are measured immediately, a message from a low-credibility communicator is not persuasive. However, after a delay, the low-credibility communicator becomes more persuasive.

From data provided by Gruder et al. (1979).

What can we say happens to a persuasive message after several weeks? When the discounting cue occurs before the message, the effect of the message diminishes. When the discounting cue occurs after the message, the power of the message is reinforced. The lesson for persuaders, then, is that they should attack their adversary before he or she makes a case or conveys a rebuttal.

Communicator Efficacy and Persuasion

Another communicator variable that affects persuasion is the *efficacy* of the communicator. Efficacy refers to the effectiveness of a communicator to bring about change. A high-efficacy communicator is one who has been successful in bringing about attitude and/or behavior change. In contrast, a low-efficacy communicator is one who has been unsuccessful. A communicator can be credible (i.e., we believe him or her) but still not be effective (i.e., we do not take action based on the communicator's message). Research shows that a high-efficacy communicator is more likely to bring about attitude change than a low-efficacy communicator when a person's level of personal involvement is low but not high (Clark et al., 2011). That is, when the message has little relevance to a person, he or she will be impressed by the efficacy of the communicator. However, if the message is relevant to the person, he or she is less impressed with the efficacy of the communicator and bases an attitude more on the quality of the arguments made by the communicator (Clark et al., 2011).

Study Break

The previous sections introduced you to persuasion and the Yale communication model. Before you begin the next section, answer the following questions:

1. What is the definition of persuasion?
2. What is the Yale communication model, and what are the factors that go into persuasion (define each)?

3. What is communicator credibility, and what are its two components (define each)?
4. What is the sleeper effect, and how does it relate to persuasion?
5. What is communicator efficacy, and how does it relate to persuasion?

Gender of the Communicator and Persuasion

Does it matter whether the communicator of a persuasive message is male or female? Unfortunately, there is not a great deal of research on this. Early research produced inconsistent results (Flanagin & Metzger, 2003). Sometimes, males were more persuasive, and sometimes, females were more persuasive. In fact, the relationship between gender of the communicator and persuasion is not simple, as we shall see next.

In one experiment male and female participants evaluated information on a personal Web site attributed to either a male or female author (Flanagin & Metzger, 2003). Participants visited a Web site that was specially designed for the experiment. On the Web site participants read a passage on the harmful effects to pregnant women of radiation exposure during pregnancy. Participants rated the credibility of the source of the message. The results showed that male participants rated the female author as more credible than the male author. Conversely, female participants rated the male source as more credible than the female source.

In another study (Schuller, 2005), male and female participants evaluated expert testimony (simple or complex) that was presented by either a male or female expert witness. The results, shown in Figure 6.2, showed that the male expert witness was more persuasive (resulting in higher dollar awards) than the female expert witness when the evidence was complex. However, the female expert witness was more persuasive when the evidence was less complex. The male expert has an advantage when the content of the message requires more cognitive effort to process, and the female expert has an advantage when the message does not require such effort. Gender, then, is used differently depending on the nature of the cognitive processing required (Schuler et al., 2005).

There is also some evidence for a *gender-domain effect*, meaning that a male communicator may be more persuasive for male-oriented issues, and a female communicator may be more persuasive for female-oriented issues (McKimmie et al., 2004; Schuller

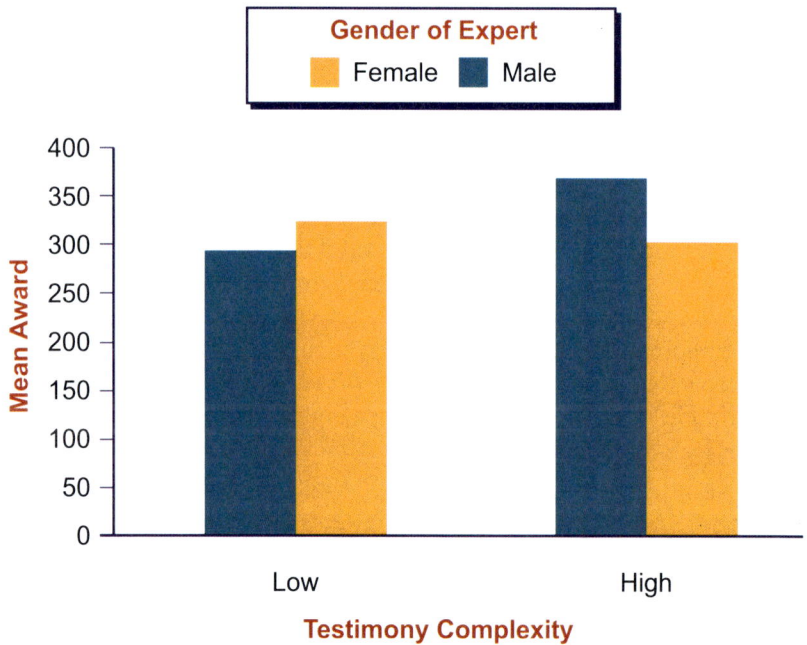

FIGURE 6.2

The relationship between the gender of an expert witness and the complexity of trial testimony.
Based on data from Schuller et al. (2005).

et al., 2001). McKimmie et al. (2004) found that a male expert was more persuasive than a female expert when the case was male-oriented (a case involving an automotive service company). When the case was female-oriented (a case involving a cosmetics company), the female expert was more persuasive. They also found that jurors evaluated the expert witness more favorably when he or she testified about a gender-congruent case.

The Message and the Audience

Thus far, we have seen that the characteristics of the communicator can influence the degree to which we modify our attitudes in response to a persuasive message. But what about the message itself? What characteristics of messages make them more or less persuasive, and how do these elements interact with the characteristics of the audience? We address these questions next.

What Kind of Message Is Most Effective? The Power of Fear

An important quality of the message is whether it is based on rational or emotional appeals. Early research showed that appeal to one emotion in particular—fear—can make a message more effective than can appeal to reason or logic. Psychologists found at first that an appeal containing a mild threat and evoking a low level of fear was more effective than an appeal eliciting very high levels of fear (Hovland et al., 1953). Then research suggested that higher levels of fear may be most effective (Leventhal, 1970). That is, you need enough fear to grab people's attention but not so much you send them running for their lives. If the message is boring, people do not pay attention. If it is too ferocious, they are repelled. There appears to be an inverted-U-shaped relationship between fear intensity and persuasion (see Figure 6.3). That is, increasing levels of fear in a message lead to increasing persuasion, up to a point. After this point, additional fear intensity leads to decreased persuasion (Shen, 2017).

Fear appeals attempt to persuade by arousing emotions such as fear. Fear appeals have been used in health advertisements like ones warning of the dangers of smoking.
Source: Marko Aliaksandr/Shutterstock.

However, persuaders need to do more than make the audience fearful; they also need to provide a possible solution. If the message is that smoking cigarettes results in major health risks, and if the communicator does not offer a method for smokers to quit, then little attitude or behavior change will occur. The smoker will be motivated to change behavior if effective ways of dealing with the threat are offered. This principle is in keeping with the Yale group's notion that people will accept arguments that benefit them.

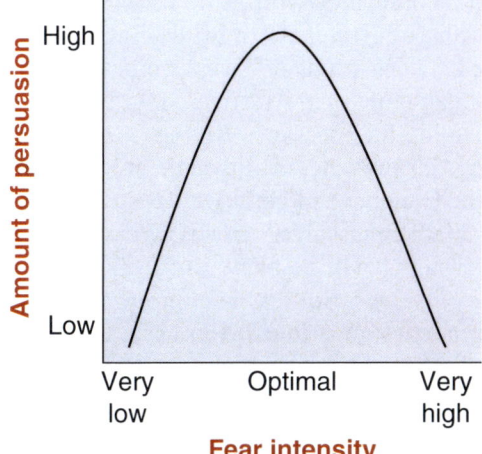

FIGURE 6.3

Inverted-U-shaped relationship between persuasion and fear intensity.

Chapter 6 Persuasion and Attitude Change

Using fear in persuasive messages can be a tricky affair. Sometimes when we are exposed to fear-producing messages, we put up our defenses (van't Riet & Ruiter, 2013). We often avoid messages that make us uncomfortable. This simple fact must be taken into account when determining a persuasion strategy. For example, a strong fear appeal on television is not very effective. The message is there only by our consent; we can always change the channel. This is why the American Cancer Society's most effective antismoking commercial involved a cartoon character named "Johnny Smoke," a long, tall cowboy cigarette. He was repeatedly asked, as he blew smoke away from his gun: "Johnny Smoke, how many men did you shoot today?" That was it: no direct threat, no explicit conclusion about the harm of smoking. The message was low key, and audience members were allowed to draw their own conclusions.

Despite evidence that high-fear messages tend to repulse people, fear appeals are widely used in health education, politics, and advertising. The assumption is that making people afraid persuades them to stop smoking or to vote for a certain candidate or to buy a particular product (Gleicher & Petty, 1992). Does fear work? Sometimes it does.

In one study of the effect of low versus high fear, Gleicher and Petty (1992) had students at Ohio State University listen to one of four different simulated radio news stories about crime on campus. The broadcasts were either moderate in fear (crime was presented as a serious problem) or only mildly fearful (crime was not presented as a serious problem). Besides manipulating fear, the researchers varied whether the appeals had a clear assurance that something could be done about crime (a crime-watch program) or that little could be done (i.e., the crime-watch programs do not work). The researchers also varied the strength of the arguments; some participants heard strong arguments, and others heard weak ones. In other words, some participants heard powerful arguments in favor of the crime-watch program whereas others heard powerful arguments that showed that crime-watch programs did not work. In the weak argument condition, some participants heard not very good arguments in favor of crime-watch programs whereas others heard equally weak arguments against the effectiveness of crime-watch programs. In all these variations of the persuasive message, the speaker was the same person with the same highly credible background.

The researchers found that under low fear conditions, strong persuasive arguments produced more attitude change than weak arguments, regardless of whether the programs were expected to be effective. In other words, if crime did not appear to be a crisis situation, students were not overly upset about the message or the possible outcome (effectiveness of the crime-watch program) and were simply persuaded by the strength of the arguments.

However, people who heard moderately fearful broadcasts focused on solutions to the crime problem. When there was a clear expectation that something could be done about crime on campus, weak and strong arguments were equally persuasive. If students were confident of a favorable outcome, they worried no further and did not thoroughly analyze the messages. But when the effectiveness of crime-fighting programs was in question, students did discriminate between strong and weak arguments. In other words, when there was no clear assurance that something effective could be done, fear motivated the participants to carefully examine the messages, so they tended to be persuaded by strong arguments. Again, concern for the outcome made them evaluate the messages carefully.

What we know from the Gleicher and Petty, (1992) study is that fear initially motivates us to find some easily available, reassuring remedy. We will accept an answer uncritically if it promises us that everything will be okay. But if no such promise is there, then we have to start to think for ourselves. So, fear in combination with the lack of a clear and effective solution (a program to fight crime, in this case) leads us to analyze possible solutions carefully. Note that Petty and Gleicher were not dealing with really high fear. Ethical considerations prevent researchers from creating such a situation in the laboratory. It may be that very high fear shuts off all critical thinking for most of us.

What do we know, then, about the effectiveness of using fear to persuade? The first point is that if we do scare people, it is a good idea to give them some reassurance that they can protect themselves from the threat we have presented. The *protection–motivation* explanation of how fear appeals work argues that intimidation motivates us to think about ways to protect ourselves (Rogers, 1983). We are willing to make the effort to evaluate arguments carefully. But, in keeping with the cognitive miser strategy, if we don't need to analyze the arguments, we won't. Also, according to the *extended parallel process model* (Witte, 1992), we are more likely to act on the fear aroused in a persuasive message if we believe that the response we can make to the fear-arousing stimulus will be effective. So, for example, men are more likely to do a self-examination for testicular cancer if they believe that the exam will be effective in early detection of the cancer (Morman, 2000).

What is the bottom line on the effectiveness of fear appeals? Based on the available research we can conclude that fear appeals are most effective when four conditions are met (Pratkanis & Aronson, 1992):

1. The appeal generates relatively high levels of fear but not too high.
2. The appeal offers a specific recommendation about how to avoid any dire consequences depicted in the appeal.
3. The target of the appeal is provided with an effective way of avoiding the dire consequences depicted in the appeal.
4. The target of the appeal believes that he or she can perform the recommended action to avoid the dire consequences.

The Importance of Timing: Primacy Versus Recency

The effectiveness of any persuasive attempt hinges on the use of an effective strategy, including the timing of the message's delivery. When is it best to deliver your message? If you were given the option of presenting your message before or after your opponent in a debate, which should you choose? Generally, persuasive situations like these are governed by a **law of primacy** (Lawson, 1969). That is, the message presented first has more impact than the message presented second. However, the law of primacy does not always hold true. It depends on the structure of the situation. A primacy effect occurs when the two messages follow one another closely, and there is a delay between the second message and the audience response or assessment. In this situation, the first message has the greater impact. But when there is a delay between the two messages, and a response or assessment is made soon after the second message, we see a *recency effect*—the second message has a greater impact (Figure 6.4).

law of primacy The law of persuasion stating that the first persuasive argument received is more persuasive than later persuasive arguments.

The primacy and recency effects apply most clearly under certain conditions: when both sides have equally strong arguments and when listeners are reasonably motivated to understand them. If one side has a much stronger argument than the other side, listeners are likely to be persuaded by the strong argument, regardless of whether it is presented

Law of Primacy: First message is more persuasive under these conditions.

Law of Recency: Second message is more persuasive under these conditions.

FIGURE 6.4
Conditions that favor either a primacy effect (top) or recency effect (bottom). Primacy or recency depends on when a delay is introduced.

first or last (Haugtvedt & Wegener, 1993). When listeners are very motivated, very interested in the issue, they are more likely to be influenced by the first argument (the primacy effect) than by those they hear later on (Haugtvedt & Wegener, 1993).

Study Break

The previous sections covered additional communicator factors and some message factors that can affect the persuasion process. Before you begin the next section, answer the following questions:

1. How does the gender of the communicator relate to persuasion, and what is the gender-domain effect?
2. What is a fear appeal, and how does fear relate to persuasion?
3. What are the four factors that increase the effectiveness of a fear appeal?
4. What are primacy and recency effects, and how does each relate to persuasion?

Fitting the Message to the Audience

The Yale group also was interested in the construction and presentation of persuasive messages. One of their findings was that messages have to be presented differently to different audiences. For example, an educated or highly involved audience requires a different type of persuasive message than an uneducated or uninvolved audience. Rational arguments are effective with educated or analytical audiences (Cacioppo et al., 1983). Emotional appeals work better with less educated or less analytical groups.

One-Sided Versus Two-Sided Messages

The nature of the audience also influences how a message is structured. For less educated, uninformed audiences, a one-sided message works best. In a one-sided message you present only your side of the issue and draw conclusions for the audience. For a well-educated, well-informed audience, a two-sided message works best. The more educated audience probably is already aware of the other side of the argument. If you attempt to persuade them with a one-sided argument, they may question your motives. Also, well-educated audience members can draw their own conclusions. They probably would resent your drawing conclusions for them. Thus, a more educated audience will be more persuaded by a two-sided argument (Hovland et al., 1953).

One-sided and two-sided appeals also have different effects, depending on the initial attitudes of the audience. Generally, a one-sided message is effective when the audience already agrees with your position. If the audience is against your position, a two-sided message works best. You need to consider both the initial position of audience members and their education level when deciding on an approach. A two-sided appeal is best when your audience is educated, regardless of their initial position. A one-sided appeal works best on an uneducated audience that already agrees with you.

Inoculating the Audience

When presenting a two-sided message, you don't want to accidentally persuade the audience of the other side. Therefore, the best approach is to present that side in a weakened form to "inoculate" the audience against it (McGuire, 1985). When you present a weakened message, listeners will devise their own counterarguments: "Well, that's obviously not true! Any fool can see through that argument! Who do they think they're kidding?" The listeners convince themselves that the argument is wrong. **Inoculation theory** is based on the medical model of inoculation. People are given a weakened version of a bacterium or a virus so that they can develop the antibodies to fight the disease on their own. Similarly, in attempting to persuade people of your side, you give them a weakened version of the opposing argument and let them develop their own defenses against it.

inoculation theory The theory that if a communicator exposes an audience to a weakened version of an opposing argument, the audience will devise counterarguments to that weakened version and avoid persuasion by stronger arguments later.

In a study of the inoculation effect, McGuire and Papageorgis (1961) exposed participants to an attack on their belief that brushing their teeth prevented tooth decay. Obviously, everybody believes that brushing your teeth is beneficial. This is a cultural truism, something we all accept without thinking or questioning. Therefore, we may not have any defenses in place if someone challenges those truisms.

Participants in one group heard an attack on the tooth-brushing truism. A second group received a supportive defense that reinforced the concept that brushing your teeth is good for you. A third group was inoculated, first hearing a mild attack on the truism and then hearing a defense of tooth brushing. A fourth group, the control group, received no messages. Of the three groups who heard a message, the "inoculated" group was most likely to believe tooth brushing was beneficial (Figure 6.5). In fact, people in the inoculated group, who were given a mild rebuttal of the truism, were *more likely* to believe in the benefits of tooth brushing than were the people who heard only a supportive defense of the truism.

Why does inoculation work? The study just reviewed suggests that inoculation motivates people to generate their own counterarguments and makes them more likely to believe the persuader's side of the issue. In this case, forewarned is truly forearmed. Inoculation also appears to operate by increasing attitude accessibility, or the ease with which a person can call an attitude to mind (Pfau et al., 2003). According to Pfau et al., inoculation works by making an attitude more accessible, which increases the strength of that attitude and its resistance to change.

The Role of Discrepancy

Another aspect of the audience a persuader has to consider is their preexisting attitudes in relation to the content of the message the persuader conveys. For instance, imagine you are going to deliver a pro-vaccination message to a roomful of people with strong attitudes against vaccinations. Obviously, your message will be very different from the preexisting attitudes of your audience. This is a high-discrepancy situation. On the other hand, if you are trying to convince a roomful of pro-vaccination individuals, your message will not be very different from preexisting attitudes. This is an example of low discrepancy. In either of these cases, you would not expect much persuasion. In the first case, your message is too discrepant from the one your audience already holds; they will reject your message without giving it much thought. There is even evidence that in a high-discrepancy situation you may get a *boomerang effect* where the audiences' attitude becomes stronger against the position advocated in the message (Zhao & Fink, 2021).

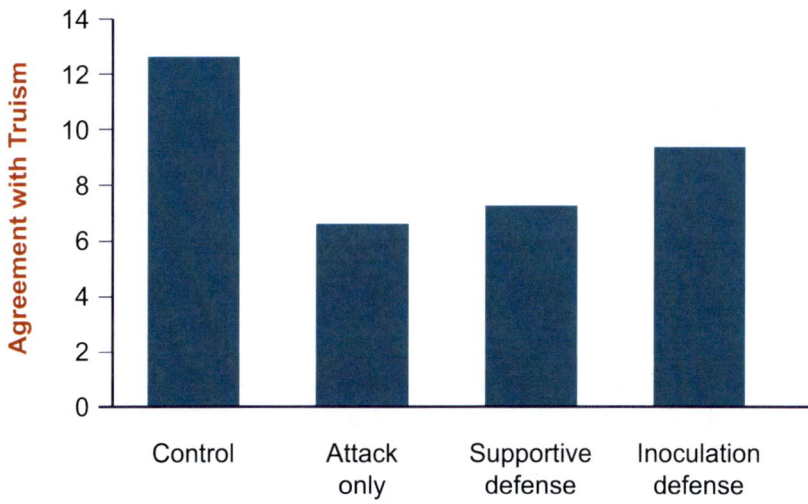

FIGURE 6.5

The inoculation effect. A persuasive attack on a truism caused a decrease in the belief of the validity of the truism unless participants were first "inoculated" with a weakened form of the persuasive message before receiving the attack message.

Based on data from McGuire and Papageorgis (1961).

In the second case, you are basically saying what your audience already believes, so there won't be much persuasive effect or attitude change. Generally, a moderate amount of discrepancy produces the greatest amount of change.

Discrepancy interacts with the characteristics of the communicator. A highly credible communicator can induce change even when a highly discrepant message—one we ordinarily would reject or that contradicts a stereotype—is delivered. In one study, researchers found that Scottish participants had definite stereotypes of male hairdressers and of "skinheads" (Macrae et al., 1992). Male hairdressers were perceived as meek, and skinheads were perceived as aggressive. However, a report from a psychiatrist that stated the contrary—that a particular hairdresser was aggressive or a skinhead was meek—altered the participants' opinions of those two groups. Of course, a credible communicator cannot say just anything and expect people to believe it. An effective communicator must be aware of the audience's likely perception of the message. One of the reasons people in the 1800s were so skeptical of the smallpox vaccine was that it did not fit with their existing ideas of disease transmission. The common belief among the general population at the time was that smallpox was caused and spread by "decaying matter" in the air. They could not reconcile how placing material from a cowpox lesion into their arm could protect them from smallpox; this procedure was too discrepant from their existing beliefs.

In other words, even highly credible communicators have to keep in mind how discrepant their message is from the audience's views.

Social Judgment Theory

How does discrepancy work? Sherif suggested that audience members make social judgments about the difference between the communicator's position and their own attitude on an issue (Sherif & Hovland, 1961; Sherif et al., 1965). This **social judgment theory** argues that the degree of personal involvement in an issue determines how the target will evaluate an attempt at persuasion.

Sherif suggested that an individual's perception of a message falls into one of three judgment categories, or latitudes. The **latitude of acceptance** is the set of positions the audience would find acceptable. The **latitude of rejection** is the set of arguments the audience would not accept. The **latitude of noncommitment** is a neutral zone falling between the other two and including positions audience members do not accept or reject but will consider.

The breadth of the latitudes is affected by how strongly the person feels about the issue, how ego-involved he or she is. As Figure 6.6 shows, as involvement increases, the latitudes of acceptance and noncommitment narrow, but the latitude of rejection increases (Eagly & Telaak, 1972). In other words, the more important an issue is, the less likely you

social judgment theory An attitude theory suggesting that the degree of personal involvement with an issue determines how a target of persuasion will judge an attempt at persuasion.

latitude of acceptance In social judgment theory, the region of an attitude into which messages that one will accept fall.

latitude of rejection In social judgment theory, the region of an attitude into which messages that one will reject fall.

latitude of noncommitment In social judgment theory, the region of an attitude into which messages that one will neither accept nor reject fall.

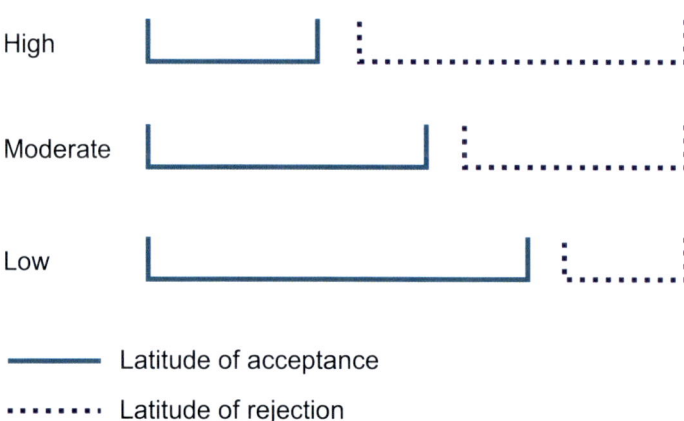

FIGURE 6.6

The effect of involvement with an issue on the size of the latitudes of rejection and acceptance in social judgment theory. High involvement leads to an increased latitude of rejection and a related decreased latitude of acceptance.

are to accept a persuasive message unless it is similar to your position. Only messages that fall within your latitude of acceptance, or perhaps within your latitude of noncommitment, will have a chance of persuading you. As importance of an issue increases, the number of acceptable arguments decreases. Sherif measured the attitudes of Republicans and Democrats in a presidential election and found that very committed Republicans and very committed Democrats rejected almost all of the other side's arguments (Sherif et al., 1965). However, voters who were less extreme in their commitment were open to persuasion. Moderates of both parties usually accepted as many arguments from the opposition as they rejected. Therefore, as Darrow knew, a persuasive message must fall at least within the audience's latitude of noncommitment to be accepted.

The Problem of Multiple Audiences

On January 23, 1968, the USS *Pueblo* was stationed in international waters off the coast of North Korea. The *Pueblo* was a "spy ship" and was gathering intelligence about North Korea. On the morning of January 23, a North Korean subchaser S0-1 approached the *Pueblo* at high speed. At the same time three North Korean torpedo boats were approaching. Eventually, the North Korean ships fired upon the *Pueblo* and eventually boarded her. One member of the *Pueblo* crew was killed and 82 were taken prisoner and held in North Korea. While in captivity, the crew members were beaten, tortured, and starved. The North Koreans wanted them to confess that they were actually in North Korean waters running the spy operation. Propaganda photographs were taken of the crew and were widely distributed. Movies were taken of the crew in staged situations that made crew members appear as though they were cooperating. Some members of the crew decided to send a message home indicating that they were being forced to say and do things. In one example of this, some crew members clearly displayed the "Hawaiian good luck sign" (a.k.a., the finger) against their faces or against their legs. Captain Bucher read statements using a monotone voice so that he sounded drugged.

The dilemma facing the crew of the *Pueblo* was to send two messages to two different audiences. On the one hand, they had to placate their captors by appearing to cooperate. On the other hand, they wanted to communicate to the American public and their families and friends that they did not subscribe to what they were being forced to do and say. This is the **multiple audience problem**—how to send different meanings in the same message to diverse audiences (Fleming et al., 1990; Van Boven et al., 2000).

multiple audience problem In persuasion, the problem that arises when a communicator directs the same message at two different audiences, wishing to communicate different meanings to each.

How do people manage these difficult situations? Researchers interested in this question had communicators send messages to audiences composed of friends and strangers (Fleming et al., 1990). The communicators were motivated to send a message that would convey the truth to their friends but deceive the strangers. Participants in this experiment were quite accurate at figuring out when their friends were lying. Strangers were not so accurate. Recall the fundamental attribution error and the correspondence bias from Chapter 3: We tend to believe that people mean what they say. In general, we are not very good at detecting lies (Ekman, 1985).

Friends also were able to pick up on the communicator's hidden message, because they shared some common knowledge. For example, one communicator said she was going to go to Wales, a country her friends knew she loved, and was going to do her shopping for the trip in a department store her friends knew she hated. The message was clear to those in the know: She is lying. The department store reference was *a private key* that close friends understood. This is the way communicators can convey different meanings in the same message. They use special, private keys that only one audience understands. We often see private keys used in political ads, especially those ads aimed at evoking stereotypes and emotional responses.

Another instance of the multiple-audience problem is when you have to maintain different personas to different people at the same time. For example, if your boss and a potential dating partner are attending a party you are attending, you probably want to project a "professional" persona to your boss and a more "fun-loving" persona to your dating interest. Can we pull this off? Can we, in fact, maintain vastly different personas at the same time and be successful in communicating them to the appropriate target, while concealing the other persona from the person we don't want to see it? The answer appears to be that we can.

In one experiment, Van Boven et al. (2000) had participants project a "party animal" persona to one observer during an interaction session. The same participant then projected a "serious studious" persona to a second observer. In a third interaction session, the participant interacted with both observers simultaneously. The task facing the participant was to maintain the correct persona with the correct observer at the same time. The results showed that the participants were quite successful at the task. In fact, the participants tended to be overconfident in their ability to successfully project the two personas to the appropriate observers.

Study Break

The preceding sections continued the discussion of audience factors that affect persuasion. Before you go on to the next section, answer the following questions:

1. What are one-sided and two-sided messages, and under what conditions would you use each?
2. What is inoculation theory, and how does it relate to persuasion?
3. How does the degree of discrepancy between message content and audience attitude affect persuasion?
4. What is social judgment theory, and what are the three latitudes involved in message acceptance?
5. What is the multiple audience problem, and how can a message be crafted to address different audiences at the same time?

The Cognitive Approach to Persuasion

You may have noted that in the Yale model of persuasion the audience seems to be nothing more than a target for messages. People just sit there and take it, either accepting the message or not. The Yale model also assumes that individuals carefully process a persuasive message and change their attitudes or behavior only if they accept the message. Is it possible that you could be persuaded by a message even if you do not pay close attention to it and do not carefully process the message? For example, when you glance at an online advertisement, can you still be persuaded to purchase the product even if you do not carefully read it? As we shall see in this section, the answer is yes!

Cognitive response approaches to persuasion emphasize the active participation of the audience (Greenwald, 1968). The cognitive approach looks at *why* people react to a message the way they do, why they say that a message is interesting or that a communicator is biased. Cognitively oriented social psychologists emphasize that a persuasive communication may trigger a number of related experiences, memories, feelings, and thoughts that individuals use to process the message. Therefore, both what a person thinks about when she hears the persuasive message and how the person applies those thoughts, feelings, and memories to analyzing the message are critical. We now turn to the individual's cognitive response to the persuasive message.

The Elaboration Likelihood Model

elaboration likelihood model (ELM) A cognitive model of persuasion suggesting that a target's attention, involvement, distraction, motivation, self-esteem, education, and intelligence all influence central and/or peripheral processing of a persuasive message.

One well-known cognitive response model is the **elaboration likelihood model (ELM)**. This model, first proposed by Petty and Cacioppo (1986), makes clear that audiences are not just passive receptacles but are actively involved in the persuasion process. Their attention, involvement, distraction, motivation, self-esteem, education, and intelligence determine the success of persuasive appeals. The elaboration likelihood model owes a lot to the Yale model, incorporating much of the Yale research on the important roles of communicator and message. But its primary emphasis is on the role of the audience, especially their emotions and motivations. According to the ELM, two routes to persuasion exist: a central processing route and a peripheral processing route. Persuasion may be achieved via either of these routes.

Central Route Processing

Central route processing involves elaboration of the message by the listener. This type of processing usually occurs when the person finds the message personally relevant and has preexisting ideas and beliefs about the topic. The individual uses these ideas and beliefs to create a context for the message, expanding and elaborating on the new information. Because the message is relevant, the person is motivated to listen to it carefully and process it in an effortful manner.

During the pandemic, many of us were glued to our screens, watching every day for any new information about COVID-19. People listened intensely to public health officials, like Dr. Anthony Fauci, explain the effectiveness and safety of the new COVID-19 vaccinations and why they should get vaccinated. As they assimilated the messages, they compared the content of the messages to what they already knew and believed. They may have elaborated on Dr. Fauci's argument by recalling times in the past when they received vaccinations for other viruses and were not negatively affected. They may even have recalled the historical effectiveness of the smallpox and polio vaccines in eliminating these diseases. Elaboration of a message does not always lead to acceptance, however. If the message does not make sense or does not fit the person's knowledge and beliefs, elaboration may lead to rejection. For example, a person may hear Dr. Fauci's message and elaborate by recalling news stories about COVID-19 vaccinations potentially being linked to blood clots or heart inflammation. A person who elaborates Dr. Fauci's message by counterarguing with additional negative information is unlikely to be persuaded.

central route processing
In the ELM, information may be processed by effortful, controlled mechanisms involving attention to and understanding and careful processing of the content of a persuasive message.

During the pandemic, many of us were glued to our screens, watching for information about the pandemic. Because they were motivated to do something, many people processed the messages centrally, involving elaborating and expanding the information in the messages.
Source: LightField Studios/Shutterstock.

Central route processors elaborate on the message by filling in the gaps with their own knowledge and beliefs. Messages processed this way are more firmly tied to other attitudes and are therefore more resistant to change. Attitude change that results from central route processing is stable, long-lasting, and difficult to reverse.

Peripheral Route Processing

What if the individual is not motivated, is not able to understand the message, or simply does not like to deal with new or complex information? In these instances, the listener takes another route to persuasion, a peripheral route. In **peripheral route processing**, listeners rely on something other than the message to make their decisions; they are persuaded by cues peripheral or marginal to the message. This is why Elvis's endorsement of the polio vaccine was effective. Elvis was an attractive and popular celebrity at the time. Although his celebrity had nothing to do with vaccines, he was still effective at persuading teens to get their polio shots.

peripheral route processing
In the ELM, information may be processed using cues peripheral or marginal to the content message.

Emotional cues are very effective in persuading peripheral route processors (Petty & Cacioppo, 1986). Recall the experiment on the effects of fear appeals in campus crime newscasts: A strong emotional appeal offering a reassuring solution was accepted regardless of whether the argument itself was strong or weak. Participants were not processing centrally; they paid no attention to the quality of the argument. They simply wanted reassurance, and the existence of a possible solution acted as a peripheral cue, convincing them that the argument must be valid. High or moderate fear makes us accept whatever reassuring solution is presented to us.

Familiar phrases or clichés included in persuasive messages can serve as peripheral cues to persuasion (Howard, 1997). Howard compared familiar (don't put all of your eggs in one basket) and literal (don't risk everything on a single venture) phrases for their

Chapter 6 Persuasion and Attitude Change

ability to persuade via the peripheral route. Howard found that familiar phrases produced more persuasion under conditions of low attitude involvement (peripheral route) than under high involvement (central route). The familiar phrases were also more effective than the literal phrases when the individual was distracted from the message and when the target of the persuasive communication was low in the need for cognition.

Peripheral route processing often leads to attitude change, but because the listener has not elaborated on the message, the change is not very stable and is vulnerable to counter-pressures (Kassin et al., 1990). A person who processes centrally will be firm in his or her conclusions about the COVID-19 vaccine, but peripheral-route processors will be easy targets for the next celebrity to change their minds.

Although we have distinguished between the central and peripheral routes, message processing is not an either/or proposition. In fact, you may process some parts of a message centrally, others peripherally. For example, a person may be interested in and understand the scientific evidence presented about a vaccine and process that information centrally. However, when an economist talks about how high vaccination rates will impact the economy, the person may be bored or may think that people in bow ties are untrustworthy, and then process that message peripherally.

This combined central and peripheral route processing idea was demonstrated in an experiment by SanJosé-Cabezudo et al. (2009). As we stated above, we tend to use central route processing more when we are motivated to process a message carefully. But, just what does "motivation" mean? In some contexts, motivation might relate to a willingness to cognitively process the message. In others, it might mean processing emotional content. In advertising, for example, advertisers often use emotion to persuade, making emotion-based motivation important. SanJosé-Cabezudo et al. have distinguished between cognitive motivation and affective motivation within the context of applying the ELM to online advertising. According to SanJosé-Cabezudo et al., *cognitive motivation* is a person's motivation to search the Internet for information about a product, whereas *affective motivation* involves the search for entertainment on the Internet. They point out that using the Internet often involves cognitive and affective elements operating at the same time. SanJosé-Cabezudo et al. conducted a study to determine if different motivations for using the Internet related to responses to Web sites using different formats. In their study, participants were exposed to either an amusing Web site (affective motivation) or serious Web site (cognitive motivation) for a fictitious travel agency. They measured participants' primary motivation for normally using the Internet (entertainment vs. information). SanJosé-Cabezudo et al. found evidence that high levels of motivation enhanced the impact of a peripheral processing cue (Web page format) and that central and peripheral route processing were both involved in the persuasion process.

The Effect of Mood on Processing

Many speakers try to put their audience in a good mood before making their case. They tell a joke or an amusing story, or they say something designed to make listeners feel positive. Is this a good strategy? Does it make an argument more persuasive? It depends. Good moods bring out many related pleasant feelings and memories. Everything seems rosy. People in good moods tend to not concentrate very well on messages; oftentimes, they do not process information centrally. In one study on the influence of mood, people were put in either a good or a neutral mood and were given either an unlimited or very limited amount of time to listen to a message (Mackie & Worth, 1989). The strength of the persuasive messages also varied: One message contained strong arguments; the other, only weak arguments. The researchers reasoned that for the participants in good moods, strong and weak arguments would be equally effective. As shown in Figure 6.7, this was found to be the case, but only when there was a limited amount of time to study the messages. People in good moods did not distinguish between strong and weak arguments because they were not processing centrally. Mackie and Worth believed that positive moods limited an individual's cognitive capacity. That is, happy people could not process centrally because they lacked the ability to think deeply about an issue.

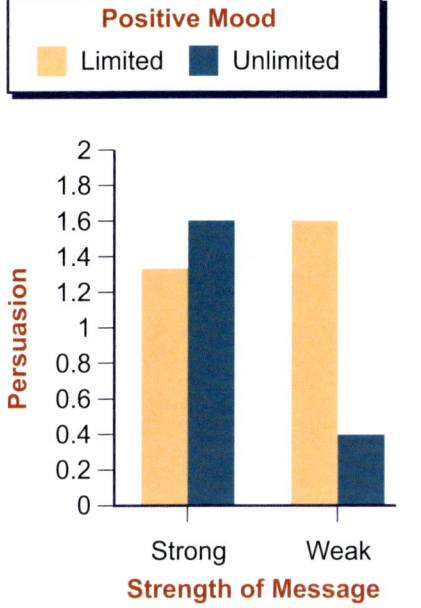
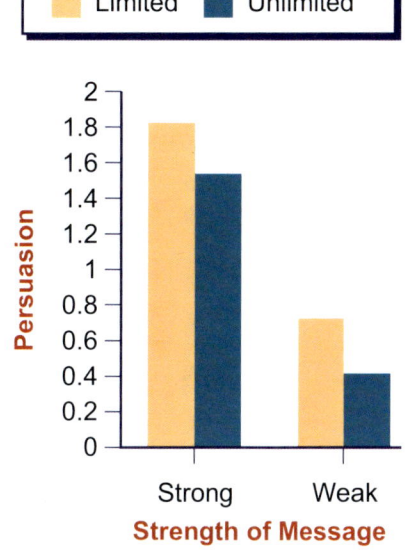

FIGURE 6.7

The effect of mood and processing time on the impact of a persuasive message. When people are in a good mood and have limited time to process the message, there is no effect on argument strength. Given unlimited time, participants are more persuaded by the strong argument. In a neutral mood, participants are more persuaded by strong arguments than weak arguments, regardless of time limitation.

Adapted from Mackie and Worth (1989).

Good feelings do not, however, always prevent central processing. If people in good moods are motivated to carefully evaluate and elaborate on a message, and if they have enough time, they will process centrally. A good mood will not have a direct effect on their attitudes, but it may make them think more positive thoughts about the message, if it is a strong one and they have time to consider it (Petty et al., 1993). The good thoughts then lead to positive attitude change. For those using peripheral route processing, good moods don't lead to more positive thoughts and then to positive attitude change. These people aren't thinking about the message at all and are not elaborating on it. Instead, for them, good mood leads directly to attitude change.

So far we have discussed only the effects of a positive mood on persuasion. How about negative moods? Does being in a negative mood affect how we process a message and ultimately persuasion? Evidence suggests that a negative mood may enhance processing of the content of a persuasive message (Bohner et al., 1992). However, the effect of mood may depend on the motivation of the target of a persuasive message. This was addressed in an experiment by Das et al. (2012). In their experiment, smokers and nonsmokers were exposed to either a strong or weak anti-smoking message while being in either a good or bad mood. Das et al. found that a positive mood increased central processing of the anti-smoking message, but only for smokers. On the other hand, nonsmokers increased central processing when in a negative mood.

The effect of mood on persuasion seems complex. Why do positive moods sometimes increase the processing of persuasive messages, whereas at other times, they decrease processing? The **hedonic contingency model** posits an answer based on our motivation to maintain a positive mood (Wegener et al., 1995). This model argues that people are motivated to maintain positive moods. Furthermore, this hedonic motivation influences the kind of information we are willing to process. When we are in a positive mood, we are motivated to maintain that mood; thus, we are unlikely to *want* to process information that we believe could damage our mood. However, we are likely to process any information or messages that might maintain or enhance our already positive mood. For people in negative moods (e.g., sad), the hedonic contingencies are very different. They are less

hedonic contingency model A model proposing that happy people process tasks that are expected to be pleasant more systematically than tasks that are expected to be unpleasant.

particular about processing information because most information would likely improve mood—or at least not make them feel any worse.

The hedonic contingency model predicts that people in happy moods will process centrally when they believe it will maintain or enhance their mood but will process peripherally when they believe the information will negatively affect their mood. Notice that this theory argues that happy moods alter people's *motivation* to process information, not their *cognitive capacity* to process information. In a study designed to test this model, Wegner et al. (1995) manipulated participants' moods, placing them in either a happy or a sad mood. Then participants were told that they would be reading a message that would be either uplifting or depressing. Additionally, that message contained either strong or weak arguments about a fictitious proposal requiring students to work part-time at the college in exchange for a tuition reduction. Finally, participants' attitudes toward the proposal were measured. When participants were in a happy mood and the message was uplifting, the strong arguments were more persuasive than were the weak arguments. This difference between strong and weak arguments indicates central processing. However, when participants were in a happy mood and the message was depressing, there was no difference in the persuasiveness of the strong and weak arguments. This indicates that participants in this condition were not motivated to process the message.

In addition to increasing or decreasing processing or acting like a peripheral cue, happiness, just like most variables, can also bias the way we process information (see Figure 6.8). Variables that bias the persuasion process still operate when an individual is motivated to process a message centrally (Petty et al., 1998). Petty and Wegener (1993) proposed the **flexible correction model (FCM)** to help us understand how biasing variables influence the persuasion process. According to the FCM, individuals using central route processing (highly motivated) are influenced by biasing variables because they are not aware of the potential impact of the biasing variable (e.g., mood) during a persuasion situation (Petty et al., 1998). Furthermore, correction for biasing conditions, according to the FCM, should take place under the following impact of the biasing conditions (p. 95):

flexible correction model (FCM) A model stating that individuals using central route processing are influenced by biasing variables, because they are not aware of the potential biasing conditions.

1. When an individual is motivated to search for biasing variables.
2. When an individual finds sources of potential bias after a search.

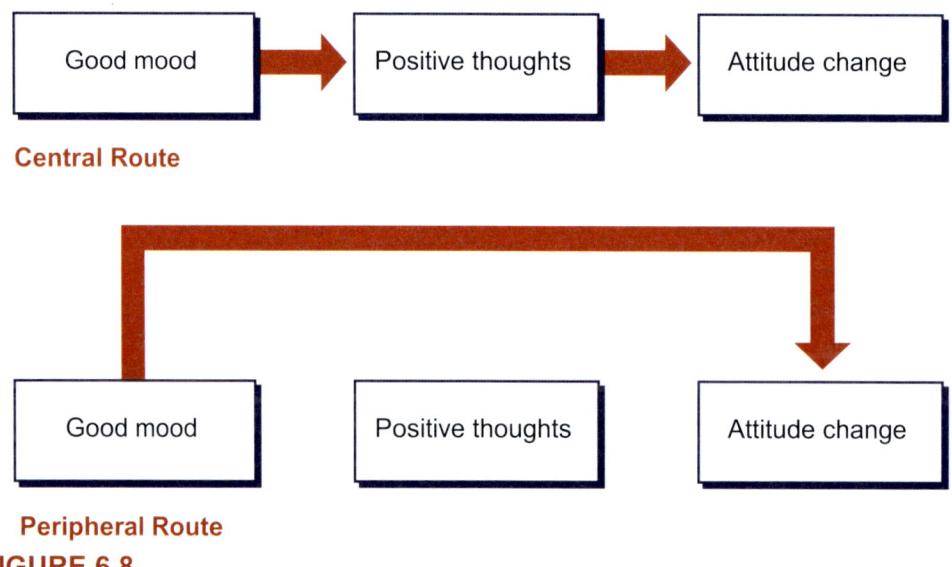

FIGURE 6.8

The effect of mood on central or peripheral route processing. When using central route processing, a good mood leads to the generation of positive thoughts, which affects attitudes. When using peripheral route processing, a good mood directly affects attitudes, bypassing the generation of positive thoughts.

Adapted from Petty et al. (1993).

3. When an individual generates ideas or theories about the nature of the bias.
4. When an individual is motivated and has the ability to make a correction for the biasing variable.

In two experiments, Petty et al. (1998) tested the assumptions made by the FCM. In their first experiment, Petty and colleagues varied the likability of the source of a message (likable and unlikable) along with whether participants received an instruction to correct for the likability information. Petty and colleagues found that when no correction instruction was given, the likable source led to attitude change in the direction of the position advocated in a persuasive message (positive attitude change), whereas the unlikable source led to attitude change in the opposite direction (negative attitude change). This is the usual finding when such variables are manipulated. However, when participants were given an instruction to correct for the likability of the source, the results were just the opposite. The unlikable source produced positive attitude change, whereas the likable source produced negative attitude change. Additionally, there was greater correction for the unlikable source than the likable source.

In their second experiment, Petty and colleagues added a third variable: whether participants used high- or low-elaboration strategies. When participants used low-elaboration strategies and no correction instruction was given, the likable source yielded more persuasion than the unlikable source. However, when a correction instruction was given, the likable and unlikable sources were equally persuasive. The opposite occurred under high-elaboration strategies. Here, in the no-correction condition, the likable and unlikable sources produced the same levels of persuasion, whereas when the correction instruction was given, the unlikable source produced more attitude change than the likable source.

The results of both studies suggest that when individuals become aware of a biasing factor (likability or mood), they will be motivated to correct for the biasing factor under high- or low-elaboration conditions. Thus, when individuals become aware of such biasing factors, they may not influence persuasion more when peripheral route processing is used. Additionally, such factors may not bias the processing of information relevant to the issue contained in a persuasive message when central route processing is used (Petty et al., 1998). It appears as though the mechanisms for correction for biasing factors operate independently from the mechanisms for processing the content of the message (Petty et al., 1998).

Study Break

This section began a discussion of cognitive approaches to persuasion. Before you begin the next section, answer the following questions:

1. What is the elaboration likelihood model, and what does it say about persuasion?
2. What are central and peripheral route processing, and what are the characteristics of each?
3. How does mood relate to the persuasion process?
4. What is the flexible correction model, and how does it relate to the mood-persuasion relationship?

The Effect of Personal Relevance on Processing

Another factor affecting central versus peripheral route processing is personal relevance. If an issue is important to us and affects our well-being, we are more likely to pay attention to the quality of the message. In one study, college students were told that the university chancellor wanted to have all seniors pass a comprehensive examination before they could graduate (Petty et al., 1981). Participants hearing the *high-relevance version* of this message were told the policy would go into effect the following year and, consequently, would affect them. Participants hearing the *low-relevance version* were informed that the policy wouldn't be implemented for several years and therefore would not affect them.

The researchers also varied the quality of the arguments and the expertise of the communicator. Half the participants heard persuasive arguments, and the other half heard weaker arguments. Half were told that the plan was based on a report by a local high school class (low communicator expertise), and the other half were told that the source was the Carnegie Commission on Higher Education (high expertise).

Results indicated that relevance influenced the type of processing participants used (Figure 6.9). Students who thought the change would affect them were persuaded by the strong argument and not by the weak one. In other words, they carefully examined the arguments, using central processing. Students who thought the change wouldn't affect them simply relied on the expertise of the communicator. They were persuaded when they thought the plan was based on the Carnegie Commission report, regardless of whether the arguments were strong or weak. Low relevance, in other words, enhances the influence of communicator credibility and increases the likelihood that listeners will use peripheral processing.

Does high relevance mean that you always will be persuaded by strong and rational arguments? Not at all. An issue may be highly relevant to you because it involves an important personal value. In this case, even a very persuasive argument probably won't change your opinion. In the current abortion debate, for example, an extreme position on either side is based on fundamental values relating to privacy, coercion, and the nature of life. The issue is certainly relevant to individuals with extreme views, but they are unlikely to be persuaded to change their opinions by any argument.

If, however, an issue is highly relevant because of a particular outcome, rather than a value, then a strong, persuasive argument might work (Johnson & Eagly, 1989). If you are strongly opposed to taking a senior comprehensive exam, a persuasive message about the outcome, such as the possibility that passing the exam would increase your chances of getting into graduate school, might well convince you to take it.

The impact of a personally relevant message on central route processing also relates to a process called self-affirmation (which we shall discuss in more detail later in this chapter). In short, self-affirmation means confirming and maintaining one's self-image (Steele, 1988).

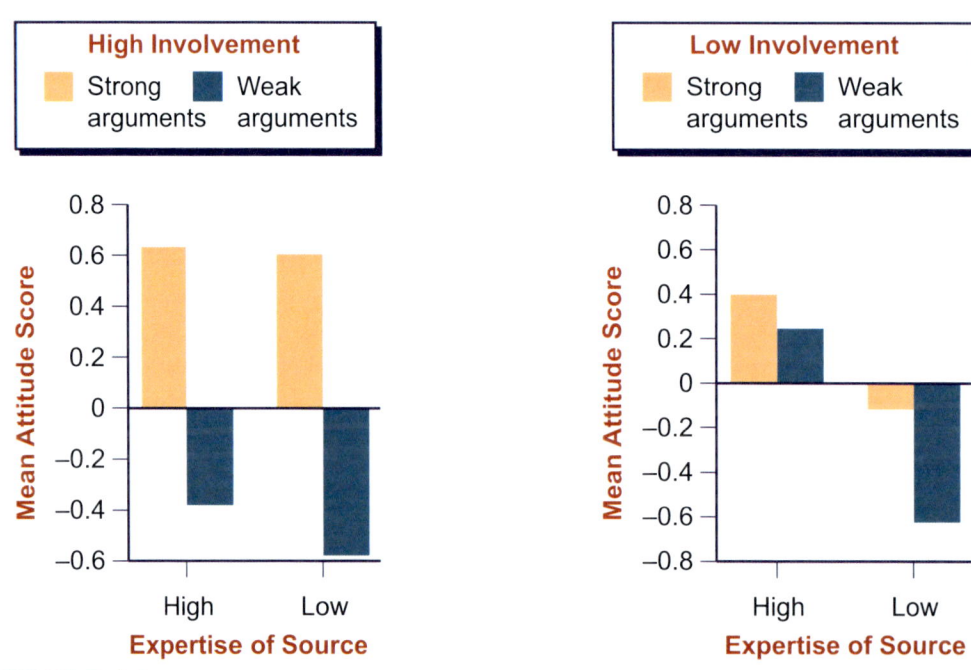

FIGURE 6.9

The effects of audience involvement, expertise of source, and strength of arguments.
From Petty et al. (1981).

Self-affirmation may be especially important when personally relevant information is threatening (Harris & Napper, 2005). According to Harris and Napper, self-affirmation promotes processing of threatening information along the central route. Harris and Napper demonstrated this in an experiment in which college-age women were exposed to a "health promotion leaflet" in which a link was made between alcohol consumption and the risk of breast cancer. Some of the participants wrote an essay describing the values that were most important to them and how they affected their daily lives (self-affirmation condition), whereas other participants wrote about their least important values. Based on their answers on a pre-experimental questionnaire concerning alcohol consumption, the participants were divided into two groups: high-risk women and low-risk women. The results showed that high-risk women who self-affirmed were more likely to accept the content of the message contained in the health leaflet compared to those who did not self-affirm. Further, women in this group reported a perception of higher risk of developing breast cancer, experienced more negative affect while reading the leaflet, and indicated a greater intention to reduce their alcohol consumption. Interestingly, these effects endured over a period of weeks. Thus, self-affirmation can enhance central processing of a threatening, personally relevant message (Harris & Napper, 2005) and better judge the merits of the threatening message (Correll et al. 2004).

Finally, personal relevance may not always increase processing. In a series of studies, Cancela et al. (2021) demonstrated that goals can affect the role of personal relevance in increasing processing. Sometimes when we consume information, we do so to gain accurate knowledge (epistemic goal). We assume that is your primary goal as you read this book. Other times, we consume messages and information with the goal of being distracted or entertained (hedonic goal). Although we hope you find this book somewhat entertaining, we doubt this is your primary goal while reading. Instead, when you read fiction, a hedonic goal is the primary goal. Cancela et al. found that when people held an epistemic goal, personal relevance increased elaboration, leading to people being more persuaded by strong rather than weak arguments. This is the classic finding in attitude research. However, Cancela et al. found that when people hold a hedonic goal orientation, high personal relevance decreased elaboration, leading to no difference in the persuasiveness of strong and weak arguments. Cancela et al. argue that it may just be harder for people to think for fun!

The Impact of Attitude Accessibility on Elaboration

In addition to the relevance of a persuasive message to an individual, processing of a persuasive message is also influenced by *attitude accessibility*. Attitude accessibility refers to the ease with which an attitude can be automatically activated when the correspondent attitude object is encountered (Fabrigar et al., 1998). Attitude accessibility is one dimension along which the strength of an attitude can be measured. Highly accessible attitudes tend to be stronger than less accessible attitudes. Fabrigar and colleagues reasoned that highly accessible attitudes may enhance message elaboration because attitude-relevant information is more readily available than with less accessible attitudes.

Fabrigar and colleagues (1998) conducted two experiments to investigate the role of attitude accessibility in persuasion. In the first experiment, attitude accessibility was measured, and participants' attitudes were classified as low, moderate, or high in accessibility. The researchers manipulated the quality of the arguments made within a persuasive message on nuclear power (high or low quality). The results of the first experiment confirmed that individuals with high-accessibility attitudes were more likely to elaborate the persuasive message than those with low-accessibility attitudes. Specifically, argument quality enhanced attitudes among moderately and highly accessible attitudes but not for low-accessibility attitudes. This effect was strongest for the individuals with highly accessible attitudes. Data from the second experiment confirmed the first.

The bottom line is that attitude accessibility mediates the amount of elaboration that an individual will display when exposed to a persuasive message. High accessibility (high attitude strength) is associated with increased examination of the content of the message (central route processing). When attitude accessibility is low (a weak attitude), an individual is less likely to scrutinize the content of the persuasive message carefully.

Do Vivid Messages Persuade Better Than Nonvivid Messages?

What about the effect of vividness on persuasion? Does it make a difference in our attitudes or behavior? Advertisers and other persuaders certainly believe that vivid messages, presented in eye- or ear-catching terms, are persuasive. Social psychologists interested in this issue stated, "Everybody knows that vividly presented information is impactful and persuasive" (Taylor & Thompson, 1982, p. 155). However, when these researchers surveyed the literature on vividness, they found very weak support for the persuasive power of vivid materials. A more recent meta-analysis of the vividness literature showed a small to moderate effect of vividness on attitudes and behavior intentions (Blondé & Girandola, 2016).

In one study of the *vividness effect,* people were given vivid and nonvivid versions of crime stories in the news (Collins et al., 1988). The vivid versions used colorful language and provided bizarre details. People listened to a vivid or nonvivid story and then rated its quality in terms of emotion, imagery, interest, and so forth as well as its persuasiveness. In a second study, people also had to predict how others would respond to the stories.

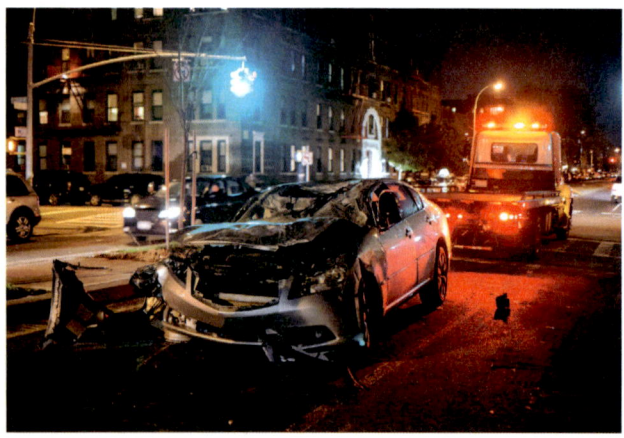

When trying to persuade people on an issue vivid images are sometimes used. In this case using a vivid image of a car crash might be used to dissuade people from drinking and driving. However, research has questioned the effectiveness of vivid messages.

Source: Photo Spirit/Shutterstock.

The studies found no evidence of a vividness effect; vivid messages had about the same persuasive effect as nonvivid messages. However, people believed that vivid messages affected other people. What influenced the participants if vividness did not? Interest: If the message involved a topic that interested them, people felt the message was more effective. Remember the effects of personal relevance in the elaboration likelihood model of persuasion.

On the other hand, some messages, such as political ads, appear to benefit from vividness—perhaps they work because they interest people and force them to pay more attention than they normally might. One study examined the effects of vivid language in a trial concerning a dispute between a contractor and a subcontractor on a building project (Wilson et al., 1989). People playing the role of jurors watched different videotapes of the trial. One version had vivid phrasing; the other, nonvivid language (p. 135):

1. There was a *spiderweb* of cracks through the slab. (vivid)

    There was a *network* of cracks through the slab. (nonvivid)

2. The slab was *jagged* and had to be sanded. (vivid)

    The slab was *rough* and had to be sanded. (nonvivid)

The jurors tended to award the plaintiff more money when they heard vivid phrases. So, is there a vividness effect or not? Based on the evidence, it seems that vivid messages have an initial effect, especially if there is little else to compete with them. In the trial situation, vivid information had a strong impact when the jurors were presented with a lot of evidence that was not directly important for their decision, such as a history of the building project and pictures of the construction site. Then the jurors heard the vivid language ("a spiderweb of cracks through the slab"). Given the background of irrelevant information, they were influenced by the one or two vivid messages they heard.

How can we reconcile the seemingly conflicting results concerning the impact of vividness? One approach suggests that the impact of vividness depends on the number of cognitive resources that are devoted to processing a persuasive message (Meyers-Levy & Peracchio, 1995). According to Meyers-Levy and Peracchio, the impact of vivid information depends on the degree of correspondence between the resources a person has available to process a message and the resources required to adequately process information. Vivid language or illustrations, according to Myers-Levy and Peracchio, should have the greatest impact when a persuasive message requires relatively few resources, and a person is highly motivated to process the message. Conversely, for a highly motivated individual and a persuasive message that requires high levels of resources, vivid content should not have a strong impact. If an individual is not highly motivated to process a message, then vividness will serve as a peripheral cue and have a significant impact on persuasion.

Myers-Levy and Peracchio (1995) conducted two experiments to confirm these predicted relationships. In their first experiment, they found that for highly motivated individuals, a demanding persuasive message (an advertisement of a bicycle) was most effective when vividness was low (a black-and-white photo of the bicycle and model was used). For a less demanding message, a vivid message (a color advertisement) was more effective. In the second experiment, low-motivation and highly motivated individuals were included. They found that for low-motivation individuals, a vivid message was more effective than a less vivid message. For highly motivated individuals, the impact of vividness (color) depended on the level of resources needed to process the message (as described earlier). These results were supported by three experiments by Keller and Block (1997).

Thus, in a situation in which much information already has been made available (low demand), or when the audience is particularly interested in the issue, one vivid message may not have a significant impact. However, when people are not particularly interested, a vivid message may have significant impact. In other words, vividness is a peripheral cue. When individuals find the message interesting and personally relevant, they process centrally, and vividness has little effect. But when the cognitive miser is at work, a vivid message may have a definite influence on attitudes.

The impact of vividness also depends on the nature of the information in a persuasive message presented in a vivid manner. Guadagno et al. (2011) maintained that most research on the vividness effect made relatively unimportant information vivid in a message. They argued that if you made central, important information vivid, you would see a vividness effect. Guadagno et al. exposed participants to a persuasive message on the need for a good night's sleep that made either central, peripheral, or both central and peripheral information in the message vivid. They also included a control condition that did not include vivid information. They measured a number of persuasion-related outcomes. Their results are shown in Figure 6.10. As you can see, when central details were vivid, all persuasion-related measures were higher than if peripheral details were vivid.

The Need for Cognition and Affect

Some people prefer central route processing no matter what the situation or how complex the evidence. These people have a high **need for cognition (NC)**. According to Cacioppo et al. (1983), high-NC people like to deal with difficult and effortful problems. On a scale assessing this cognitive characteristic, they agree with such statements as, "I really enjoy a task that invokes coming up with new solutions to problems," and they disagree with such statements as, "I only think as hard as I have to."

High-NC people are concerned with the validity of the messages they receive, which suggests that they rely mainly on central route processing (Cacioppo et al., 1983). High-NC individuals also organize information in a way that allows them to remember messages and use them later (Lassiter et al., 1991). Those low in need for cognition tend to pay more attention to the physical characteristics of the speaker, indicating peripheral processing (Petty & Cacioppo, 1986).

High-NC individuals are also better able to distinguish the authenticity of persuasive information than low-NC individuals (Engleberg & Sjöberg, 2005). Engleberg and Sjöberg showed high- and low-NC individuals films about the risks of nuclear energy. One of the films was the fictional movie *The China Syndrome,* whereas the other was the film *Chernobyl: The Final Warning* based on a book written by a bone marrow specialist.

need for cognition (NC) An individual difference dimension in persuasion concerning the degree to which individuals prefer effortful processing of information.

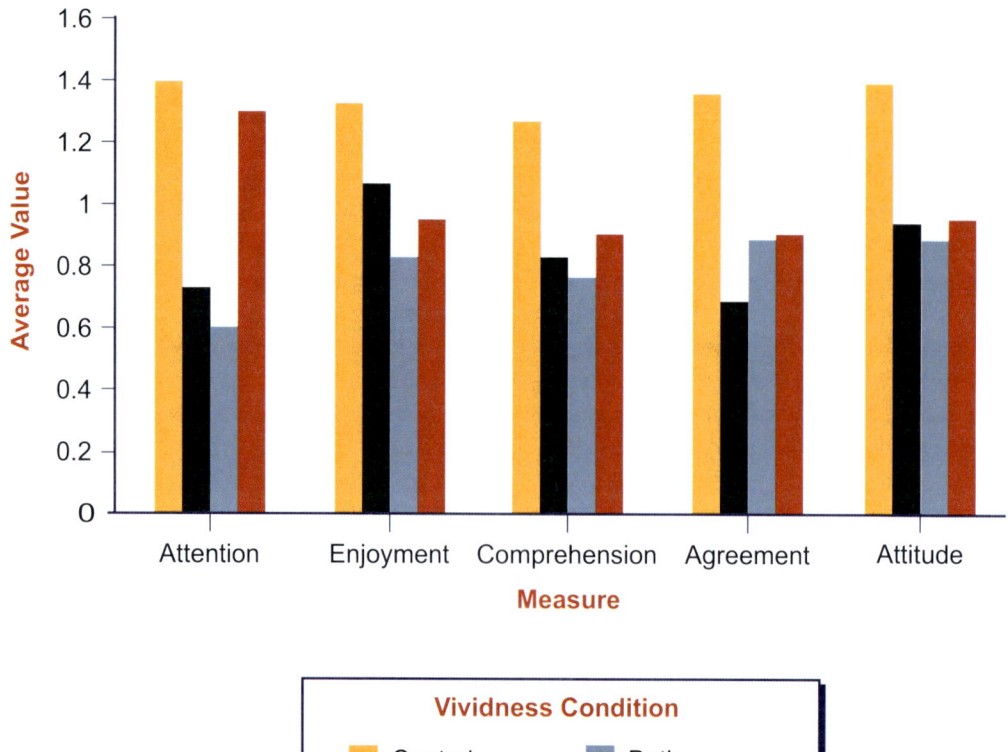

FIGURE 6.10

The effect of detail vividness on persuasion-related measures.
Based on data from Guadagno et al. (2011).

Engleberg and Sjöberg found that high-NC individuals were more likely to identify Chernobyl as an event that actually happened than low-NC individuals. Interestingly, however, both high- and low-NC individuals assessed the risks of nuclear energy at the same levels, regardless of the film they had seen.

Research also shows that high-NC individuals are less likely to switch away from a course of action that has a disappointing outcome than are low-NC individuals (Ratner & Herbst, 2005). Ratner and Herbst report that people tend to shift away from a disappointing strategy because of emotional reactions, rather than focusing on more cognitively based beliefs. Those high in the need for cognition can apparently stay better focused on the cognitive aspects and not be ruled by emotional reactions.

Elaboration likelihood model research shows that people who have a need to process information centrally—high-NC people—accept and resist persuasive arguments in a different way than those low in need for cognition. Because they are processing centrally, they elaborate on the messages they hear. They are influenced by the qualities of the argument or the product advertised rather than by peripheral cues (Haugtvedt et al., 1992). Conversely, low-NC people are more likely to focus on the peripheral aspects of information or an advertisement (Sicilia et al., 2005). Finally, high-NC individuals hold newly formed attitudes longer and are more resistant to counterpersuasion (Haugtvedt & Petty, 1992).

Another individual difference variable that relates to persuasion is the **need for affect (NA)**, which is a person's tendency to approach or avoid emotional situations (Maio & Esses, 2001). As you might expect, NA and NC relate to persuasion differently. Individuals who are high in NA are more persuaded by an emotion-based message than individuals high in NC. Conversely, individuals who are high in NC are more persuaded by a cognitively based message than individuals high in NA (Haddock et al., 2008).

need for affect (NA)
A person's tendency to approach or avoid emotional situations.

Individuals high in NA or NC also evaluate information about their political parties differently (Arceneaux & Vander Wielen, 2013). Arceneaux and Vander Wielen had participants complete online measures of NC, NA, and political party affiliation. Participants were then randomly assigned to read negative factual information about their own party (e.g., Democrat reading negative information about the Democratic Party) or the opposing party (e.g., Republican reading negative information about the Democratic Party). Arceneaux and Vander Wielen found that participants high in NC tended to rate their own party and the other party negatively, regardless of their own party affiliation. However, participants high in NA (regardless of party affiliation) evaluated their own party more positively than the opposing party. So, NC appears to relate to realistic assessments of political parties and NA to less realistic evaluations.

The Heuristic Model of Persuasion

A second cognitive model of persuasion is the **heuristic and systematic information-processing model (HSM)**. Proposed by Chaiken (1987), the HSM has much in common with the ELM. As in the ELM, there are two routes for information processing: the systematic and the heuristic. Systematic processing in the HSM is essentially the same as central processing in the ELM, and heuristic processing is the same as peripheral processing. Heuristics, as you recall from Chapter 3, are simple guides or shortcuts that people use to make decisions when something gets too complicated or when they are just too lazy to process systematically.

The main difference between the two theories lies in the claim of the HSM that reliance on heuristics is more common than is usually thought (Chaiken et al., 1989). If motivation and ability to comprehend are not high, individuals rely on heuristics most of the time. Some of these heuristics might be: "Experts can be trusted." "The majority must be right." "She's from the Midwest; she must be trustworthy." "If it was on the Internet, it must be true."

Heuristic processing can be compared to scanning newsfeed headlines. The information you receive is minimal, and the truth or relevance of the headline will be determined by those simple rules. "COVID-19 vaccines are safe and effective," reads the headline. Your response would be to quickly check the available heuristics that might explain the headline. Here it is: "Trust the science." Next headline, please. The HSM suggests that people are more likely to agree with communicators who are expert and with messages with which most people agree. Again we see the cognitive miser at work.

heuristic and systematic information-processing model (HSM) A cognitive model of persuasion suggesting that of the two routes to persuasion, systematic and heuristic, people choose to use heuristics or peripheral cues more often.

Study Break

The previous sections continued our discussion of the factors that relate to the cognitive processing of persuasive messages. Before you begin the next section, answer the following questions:

1. How does the personal relevance of a message relate to message processing and persuasion?
2. How does attitude accessibility relate to message elaboration?
3. What is the relationship between message vividness and persuasion?
4. What is the need for cognition, and how does it relate to message elaboration and persuasion?
5. What is the heuristic and systematic information processing model (HSM), and how does it account for persuasion?

Cognitive Dissonance Theory: A Model of Self-Persuasion

Direct persuasion by a communicator is not the only route to attitude or behavior change. Attitude change may also occur if we find our existing attitudes in conflict with new information, or if our behavior is inconsistent with our beliefs. Festinger (1957) observed that people try to appear consistent. When we act counter to what we believe or think, we must justify the inconsistency. In other words, if we say one thing and do something else, we need a good reason. Usually, we persuade ourselves that we have a good reason, even if it means changing our previous attitudes. Inconsistency is thus one of the principal motivations for attitude change.

Cognitive Dissonance Theory

cognitive dissonance theory
A theory of attitude change proposing that if inconsistency exists among our attitudes, or between our attitudes and our behavior, we experience an unpleasant state of arousal called cognitive dissonance, which we will be motivated to reduce or eliminate.

Festinger's **cognitive dissonance theory** proposed that if inconsistency exists among our attitudes, or between our attitudes and our behavior, we experience an unpleasant state of arousal called *cognitive dissonance* (Festinger, 1957). The arousal of dissonance motivates us to change something—our attitudes or our behavior—to reduce or eliminate the unpleasant arousal. Reducing the tension helps us achieve *consonance,* a state of psychological balance.

Cognitive dissonance theory is like *homeostatic theory* in biology. Consider what happens when you are hungry: Your brain detects an imbalance in your blood sugar levels, causing a physiological state of hunger. You are motivated to reduce this unpleasant state of arousal by finding and consuming food. Similarly, when cognitive consonance is disrupted, you feel tension and are motivated to reduce it.

The five key assumptions of cognitive dissonance theory can be summarized as follows:

1. Attitudes and behavior can stand in a consonant (consistent) or a dissonant (inconsistent) relationship with one another.
2. Inconsistency between attitudes and behavior gives rise to a negative motivational state known as cognitive dissonance.
3. Because cognitive dissonance is an uncomfortable state, people are motivated to reduce the dissonance.
4. The greater the amount of dissonance, the stronger the motivation to reduce it.
5. Dissonance may be reduced by rationalizing away the inconsistency or by changing an attitude or a behavior.

Does Inconsistency Lead to Cognitive Dissonance?

Given the fact that cognitive dissonance theory gives negative arousal a central role, a legitimate question is whether we can actually show that such arousal occurs and that it is negative. Fortunately for dissonance theory, evidence suggests that inconsistency does lead to negative arousal. For example, in one experiment Croyle and Cooper (1983) put participants into a dissonance-arousing situation or a control situation and obtained physiological measures (e.g., heart rate, skin conductance) as well as attitude measures. They found that participants in the dissonance condition showed greater physiological arousal than those in the control conditions. They also found that participants in the dissonance condition showed more attitude change than those in the control conditions. Other research shows that the arousal of dissonance manifests itself in different activation in the brain than if no dissonance is aroused (van Veen et al., 2009). In their experiment, van Veen et al. found that under conditions of dissonance arousal (compared to control participants), greater activity occurred in the dorsal anterior cingulate cortex and anterior insula and that this arousal was related to more attitude change.

Is the arousal detected actually negative? This question was addressed in research using the *hypocrisy paradigm.*

Cognitive dissonance theory states that when our behavior conflicts with attitudes, a negative motivational state arises that we are motivated to reduce. In this case, cognitive dissonance might be aroused if a person continues to eat unhealthy foods knowing that they are bad for her.
Source: Krakenimages.com/Shutterstock.

The hypocrisy paradigm has a person think about situations in which he or she should have acted in a certain way but did not (Yousaf & Gobet, 2013). In one study, Yousaf and Gobat induced cognitive dissonance in a group of Christian and Muslim students by having them evaluate a list of religiously oriented behaviors (e.g., reading scripture, attending services) and evaluating how often they engaged in those behaviors. A control group did not involve arousing dissonance. Participants evaluated their emotional state on a standard measure of emotions. Yousaf and Gobet found that participants in whom dissonance was aroused experienced more shame and guilt (both negative emotions) than control participants.

Interestingly, dissonance may also be aroused if we see other people experiencing cognitive dissonance (Norton et al., 2003). Norton et al. refer to this as the *vicarious dissonance hypothesis*. In their experiment, Norton et al. had participants listen to a speech from an in-group (student at their college) or out-group (student at another college) member in which the person recording the speech was said to be advocating a position that was contrary to their attitude (advocating a tuition increase). They also measured how much participants identified with their college and their attitude toward raising tuition. The results showed that participants exposed to a speaker from the in-group experiencing dissonance showed attitude change in the direction of advocating the tuition increase. The more a participant identified with his or her college, the greater the attitude change. The opposite was true for those exposed to the out-group speaker. Norton et al. suggest that vicarious dissonance and personal dissonance (dissonance derived from one's own experience of inconsistency) are similar in some ways but different in others. In both types of dissonance, the individual experiences discomfort and reduces the discomfort by changing an attitude. However, they suggest that vicarious dissonance (unlike personal dissonance) is aroused by being exposed to another person experiencing dissonance, rather than direct experience. Additionally, vicarious dissonance may be more difficult to arouse. This was demonstrated by the fact that dissonance-related attitude change occurred only when an in-group member was experiencing dissonance.

How Does Cognitive Dissonance Lead to Attitude Change?

Exactly how does cognitive dissonance change attitudes? To find out, imagine that you have volunteered to be a participant in a social psychological experiment. You are instructed to sit in front of a tray of objects and repeatedly empty and refill the tray for the next hour. Then, to add more excitement to your day, you are asked to turn pegs in holes a little at a time. When your tasks are over, you are asked to tell the next participant how interesting and delightful your tasks were. For doing this, you are paid the grand sum of $1. Unbeknownst to you, other participants go through the same experience and also are asked to tell an incoming participant how interesting the tasks are, but each is paid $20.

When this classic experiment was done in 1959, almost all the participants agreed to misrepresent how much fun the experiment was (Festinger & Carlsmith, 1959). Several weeks later, the participants were contacted by a third party and asked whether they had enjoyed the study. Their responses turned out to depend on how much money they had been paid. You might predict that the participants who got $20 said that they enjoyed their experience more than those who got only $1. Well, that's not what happened. Participants paid $20 said the tasks were boring, and those paid $1 said they had enjoyed the tasks. A third group, the control participants, were given no reward and were not told that anyone else had received one. Like the $20 group, they said the tasks were boring.

Cognitive dissonance theory argues that change occurs when people experience dissonance. Where is the dissonance in this experiment? Being paid $1, a trifling sum even in 1959, was surely insufficient justification for lying. If a $1 participant analyzed the situation logically, it would look like this: "I lied to someone because the experimenter asked me to, and I got paid only a buck." Conclusion: "Either I am a liar or I am stupid." Neither conclusion fits with what we generally think of ourselves. The dissonance is between what we want to think of ourselves and how we have behaved. So, how does the participant resolve the dissonance? The behavior can't be undone, so the participant engages in self-persuasion: "I'm not a liar or stupid, so I must have meant what I said.

I enjoyed the experiment." The $20-participant has an easily available, if not very flattering, justification for the lie: "I needed the money."

The Reverse Incentive Effect

The implications of this study and many more that have replicated the effect over the years are intriguing. One concept that came from the original study is the *reverse-incentive effect*: When people are given a large payment for doing something, they infer that the activity must be difficult, tedious, or risky (Freedman et al., 1992). Thus, professional athletes who once played the game just for fun may now moan about playing the game for $5 million a year. People seem to get suspicious when they are paid large sums for doing something they enjoyed doing in the first place. They feel a little apprehensive and develop a less positive view of the activity (Crano & Sivacek, 1984).

Dissonance theory argues, then, that the less the reward or the less the threatened punishment used to make people behave counter to their attitudes, the more people have to provide their own justifications for their behavior. The more they have to persuade themselves of the rightness of the behavior, the more their attitude is likely to change.

The Importance of Free Choice

An important condition in the arousal of dissonance is whether behavior is freely chosen or coerced. In another study of cognitive dissonance, participants were asked to write an essay arguing a position that ran counter to their real beliefs (Elkin & Leippe, 1986). Furthermore, they did this attitude-inconsistent act when they felt they had freely chosen it. Dissonance theorists call this situation *induced compliance*. The researchers found that when participants wrote an essay counter to their beliefs, they showed greater physiological arousal than if they had written an essay consistent with their beliefs. This finding is compatible with predictions from cognitive dissonance theory, specifically that dissonance increases feelings of tension (physiological arousal).

This study reinforced the finding that people do not experience dissonance if they do not choose the inconsistent behavior (Brehm & Cohen, 1962). If they are forced to do something, the coercion is a sufficient external justification for the attitude-discrepant actions. If they don't have to justify their behavior to themselves, there is no self-persuasion. This suggests that attribution processes may play a role in mediating dissonance arousal and reduction. We explore this possibility later in this chapter.

The importance of free choice was shown in another experiment that investigated whether the arousal of cognitive dissonance affects how a person perceives his or her natural environment (Balcetis & Dunning, 2007). In their experiment, Balcetis and Dunning had participants traverse a distance on a college campus. After agreeing to participate, participants were taken outside and told that the experimenters were interested in how people respond to real-life embarrassing situations. At this point, a participant was handed a "Carmen Miranda" costume to wear. For those of you who do not know who Carmen Miranda was: Carmen Miranda was a 1940s entertainer who was famous for her flamboyant costumes (often involving a skirt, top, and a hat made from fruit). The costume participants wore consisted of a grass skirt, coconut bra, flower lei, and a hat made of fruit. Participants were told that they would have to walk between two points on a busy part of campus wearing the costume. Participants did this under one of three choice conditions. Participants in the high-choice condition were told they could do another (unspecified) task in lieu of the emotion task. Participants in the low-choice condition were told that although other tasks were available, they would have to do the task chosen for them (wearing the costume). Finally, participants in the control condition were not required to wear the embarrassing costume. After walking between the two points on campus, all participants estimated how far they had walked. The results of this experiment are shown in Figure 6.11. As you can see, participants in the low-choice condition estimated the distance to be further than participants in the high-choice and control conditions. According to Balcetis and Dunning, their results show that cognitive motivation in the form of dissonance can distort perceptions of the natural world in addition to motivating individuals to change attitudes.

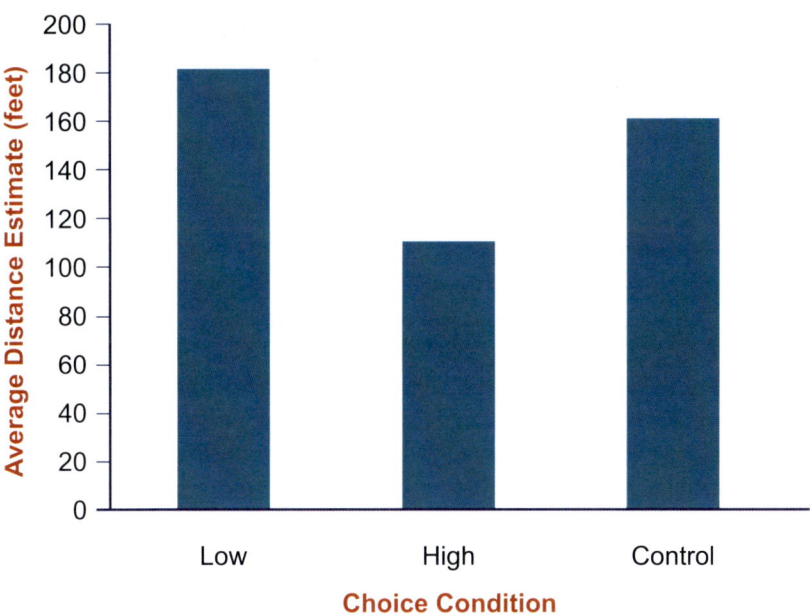

FIGURE 6.11

Average distance estimated between two points as a function of choice condition.
Based on data from Balcetis and Dunning (2010).

Study Break

This section introduced you to cognitive dissonance theory, which is an approach that differs markedly from the Yale model. Before you begin the next section, answer the following questions:

1. What is cognitive dissonance, and how does it relate to attitude change?
2. What evidence exists to demonstrate the relationship between cognitive inconsistency and attitude change?
3. How does cognitive dissonance lead to attitude change?
4. What is the reverse incentive effect, and how does it relate to dissonance and attitude change?
5. How does free choice relate to dissonance and attitude change?

Postdecision Dissonance

Free choice relates to dissonance in another way when you have to choose between two mutually exclusive, equally attractive, but different alternatives (e.g., between two cars or two jobs). After a choice is made, dissonance is experienced. It is important to note that postdecision dissonance is not the same as predecision conflict, where you vacillate between the two alternatives. *Postdecision dissonance* comes *after* your decision.

Here is how it works: Let's say you have enough money to buy a car. There are two cars you are considering that are equally attractive to you. For each car, there is a set of positive cognitions. Once you have made your choice (let's say you picked car 1), all the positive cognitions associated with your chosen alternative are consistent with your choice. However, all the positive cognitions associated with the unchosen alternative are now inconsistent with your choice. Dissonance theory predicts that you will take steps to reduce the dissonance associated with the unchosen alternative. One way to reduce dissonance would be to change your decision (that is, choose car 2). Of course, this won't work, because now all of the cognitions associated with car 1 are inconsistent with your new decision, and the dissonance remains. More likely, you will begin to think of negative things about the unchosen car to reduce dissonance. For example, you may reason

Cognitive dissonance theory shows that we experience dissonance after making a decision between alternative choices. If this man picks the red car, he will probably find flaws with the gray one.

Source: Nestor Rizhniak/Shutterstock.

that the insurance costs would be higher, the color isn't exactly what you wanted, and the warranty is not as good. At the same time, you may also think of more positive things about the chosen car. For example, you may point out how comfortable the seats are, how good the stereo sounds, and how the color fits you perfectly.

The arousal of postdecision dissonance and its subsequent reduction was demonstrated in a classic experiment by Brehm (1956). In this experiment, female participants first rated the desirability of several household products (e.g., a toaster). Brehm then offered the women one of the two products they had rated very closely or they had rated very differently. After the women made their choices, they again rated the products. Brehm found that when the two choice alternatives were close in desirability (a difficult decision), ratings of the chosen alternative became more positive, compared to the original ratings. At the same time, the ratings of the unchosen product became more negative. This effect was less pronounced when the choice was between two products that varied more widely in desirability (easy decision).

Generally, the greater the separation between alternatives, the less dissonance will be produced after a decision. After all, a choice between a highly desirable product and an undesirable product is an easy one. On the other hand, the closer the alternatives are to one another (assuming they are not identical), the more difficult the decision and the more postdecision dissonance will be aroused. Thus, the greatest postdecision dissonance will be realized when you have to choose between two mutually exclusive (you can only have one), equally attractive, but different alternatives.

It is important to understand that postdecision dissonance effects are not limited to product choice situations. For example, Rodriguez and Berry (2009) have shown postdecision dissonance in a simulated jury task. After making a difficult verdict decision in a simulated rape trial, participants reduced postdecision dissonance by adding verdict-consistent thoughts and rating the crime as more severe (thus justifying their decisions) than participants who made an easier decision.

How do we explain these postdecision dissonance effects? Shultz and Lepper (1999) suggested that an analogy can be made between dissonance phenomena and the operation of artificial intelligence neural networks. Networks of cognitions underlie states of consonance and dissonance and are activated by a set of constraints imposed by a problem. For example, in a choice between two cars, you may be constrained by finances, model preference, and color desirability. According to Shultz and Lepper, the decision we make attempts to satisfy as many of the constraints as possible. In short, "the motivation to increase cognitive consonance, and thus to reduce dissonance, results from the various constraints on the beliefs and attitudes that a person holds at a given point in time" (p. 238). Consonance results when similar cognitions are activated and inconsistent cognitions are inhibited. Thus, in the free-choice situation, linkages among positive cognitions associated with an alternative produce consonance. However, for the unchosen alternative, the linkages between inconsistent elements (the unchosen alternative and the positive cognitions associated with it) produce dissonance.

Shultz and Lepper (1996) performed computer simulations of Brehm's (1956) original experiment and produced results that matched quite well with Brehm's results. That is, ratings of the unchosen alternative became more negative, and ratings of the chosen alternative became only slightly more positive. However, Shultz and Lepper pointed out that in Brehm's experiment, participants always made a decision that was both difficult (two products that were rated very similarly) and between two highly desirable products. Shultz and Lepper found that when participants had to choose between two similarly rated but undesirable products, the ratings of the chosen product became much more positive, but the ratings of the unchosen product became only slightly more negative.

An experiment by Shultz et al. (1999) sought to test the results from computer simulations of free-choice experiments against actual behavior of individuals. Participants in this experiment were given the choice between two posters after indicating on a rating scale how much they liked each poster. The choice parameters varied in difficulty. An easy choice was one between two posters—one with a high initial rating and one with a low initial rating. In the "high-difficult" condition, a choice was to be made between two posters that had been rated very positively by participants. Finally, in the "low-difficult" condition, participants had to choose between two posters that had been poorly rated. Following the choice procedure, participants again rated the posters. The results paralleled the computer simulations. In the high-difficult condition, ratings of the unchosen alternative became substantially more negative, whereas ratings of the chosen alternative became only slightly more positive. In the low-difficult condition, the opposite was true; ratings of the chosen alternative became much more positive. However, ratings of the unchosen alternative became only slightly more negative. These results are consistent with Shultz and Lepper's (1996) *consonance constraint satisfaction model*.

The way that postdecision dissonance operates may depend partly on one's culture (Hoshino-Browne et al., 2005; Kitayama et al., 2004). In individualistic cultures (e.g., the United States), *personal dissonance* reduction dominates. This means that when we are selecting between two alternatives for ourselves, we are likely to experience dissonance and resolve it in the manner predicted by dissonance theory. However, in collectivist cultures (e.g., Japan) personal choices do not arouse as much dissonance as they do in individualistic cultures. Instead, *interpersonal dissonance* tends to be more important. Interpersonal dissonance arises when an individual is required to make a choice for someone else. In the Hoshino-Browne et al. (2005) study, for example, European Canadians (i.e., Canadians born in Canada) and Asian Canadians (Canadians born in an Asian country) were asked to rank 10 Chinese cuisine entrees that would be served at an on-campus restaurant. The rankings were done under two conditions. In one condition, participants were instructed to rank the entrees based on their own personal preferences (self-preferences). In the other condition, participants were instructed to rank the entrees according to the preferences of their best friend (other preferences). After completing some other measures, participants were offered two gift certificates for entrees they had ranked (their fifth and sixth choices were offered). Participants had to choose one of the gift certificates for themselves (in the self-preference condition) or their friend (in the other preference condition). The results, as shown in Figure 6.12 showed that when European Canadians were making a choice for themselves, more dissonance reduction was shown than when making

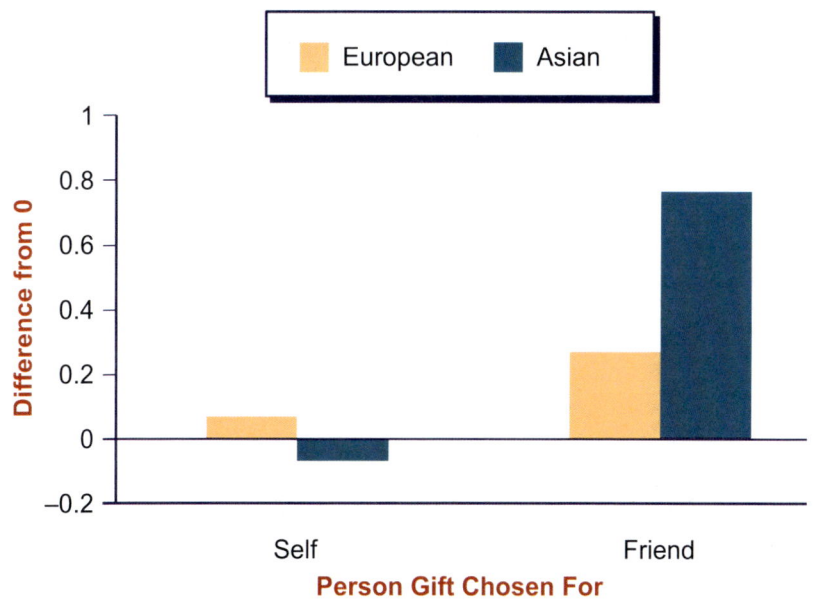

FIGURE 6.12

Dissonance when making a choice for oneself or a friend among Asian and European Canadians.
Based on data from Hoshino-Browne et al. (2005).

a choice for the friend. The opposite was true for the Asian Canadians. They showed more dissonance reduction when making a choice for their friend than for themselves.

Finally, the cognitive processes involved in postdecision dissonance rationalization appear to occur very quickly and without much thought. This was demonstrated in an experiment in which participants chose between names and works of art while in an fMRI scanner (Jarcho et al., 2011). An fMRI scanner gives researchers a real-time picture of brain activity while a person is engaged in some task. Participants were required to choose between names or works of art in rapid succession. The researchers scanned participants' brain activity during this task and looked at brain activity after decisions were made. Jarcho et al. found that certain areas of the brain were highly active during postdecision attitude change (right-inferior frontal gyrus, medial fronto-parietal regions, and ventral striatum), while others were less active (anterior insula). They also found that the brain activity occurred very rapidly, indicating that participants were not engaging in a great deal of thought concerning their choices or attitudes.

Responsibility: Another View of Cognitive Dissonance

Another view suggests that cognitive dissonance occurs only when our actions produce negative consequences (Cooper & Scher, 1992). According to this view, it is not the inconsistency that causes dissonance so much as our feelings of personal responsibility when bad things happen (Cooper & Fazio, 1984).

Let's say, for example, that you wrote a very good essay in favor of something you believed in, such as not raising tuition at your school. You knew that the essay could be presented to the school's board of trustees, the body that determines tuition rates. You then learned that your essay was actually used to convince the board to raise tuition. Or perhaps you were asked to write an essay taking a position you did not believe in—raising tuition. You then learned that the essay convinced the board to raise tuition. How would you feel?

According to this responsibility view, simply doing something counter to your beliefs will not produce dissonance unless there are negative results. If you are opposed to tuition hikes and write an essay in favor of them, but there are no hikes as a result, you do not experience dissonance. In several similar studies, people were asked to write essays advocating a position—raising tuition—that conflicted with their beliefs. When rates were increased and essayists felt responsible for the outcome, they resolved the dissonance by changing their attitude in the direction of the outcome. That is, they began to say they were now more in favor of a fee increase than before they wrote the essay. When students wrote essays in favor of a fee increase, and fees were not increased, they did not experience dissonance and did not change their attitudes. When there is no tension, there is no attitude change.

So, what creates dissonance, inconsistency, or a sense of responsibility? There have been hundreds, perhaps thousands, of experiments that support the basic ideas of cognitive dissonance theory—namely, that inconsistency leads to attitude change. That there are valid alternatives simply means the theory may have to incorporate those ideas and continue to be revised.

Attribution Processes and Dissonance

We noted earlier that dissonance is unlikely to be aroused when a person has a sufficient external justification (attribution) for his or her attitude-discrepant behavior. An experiment by Cooper (1998) highlighted the role of attribution processes in mediating dissonance reactions. Cooper had participants write a counter-attitudinal essay advocating the institution of 7:00 AM classes on campus (something students opposed). They wrote the essays under either a high-choice (participants were asked to write the essay "if you are willing") or a low-choice condition (the "if you are willing" phrase was left out). Participants were also randomly assigned to a misattribution condition (an instruction that inconsistent lighting makes many feel tense and aroused) or a no-misattribution condition (the instruction about the lighting effects was deleted). The main measure was the participants' ratings (positive or negative) about instituting 7:00 AM classes.

Cooper found that greater attitude change occurred under the high-choice condition. This confirms our earlier statement that under conditions of free choice, dissonance is more likely to be aroused and attitude change more likely to occur. Additionally, there was less attitude change in the direction of the essay under the misattribution condition than the no-misattribution condition. Participants in the misattribution condition had an external explanation for their arousal (dissonance), and were consequently less likely to change their attitude. The greatest amount of attitude change in the direction of the essay was realized in the high-choice (participants chose to write the essay)/no-misattribution condition. In a follow-up experiment using a different task, Cooper found that participants who had previously misattributed their arousal to the lighting did not show dissonance-consistent attitude change.

Attribution style also relates to the arousal of dissonance. Stalder and Baron (1998) investigated the relationship between *attributional complexity* (AC) and dissonance-produced attitude change in a series of experiments. Specifically, attributional complexity refers to how complex a person's attributions are for explaining behavior and events. High-AC individuals are those who normally engage in thorough attributional searches for information. Thus, a high-AC person will search long and hard for the source of arousal in a given situation (e.g., a situation that arouses dissonance). A low-AC person is less likely to engage in such a search.

The results from their first experiment confirmed the idea that high-AC individuals show little dissonance-related attitude change, most likely because they are able to generate a wide variety of possible causes for the arousal associated with dissonance (Stalder & Baron, 1998). Having attributed the arousal to something other than the dissonance-arousing situation, the high-AC individual would not be expected to show much attitude change. In their second experiment, Stalder and Baron found that low-AC individuals showed the typical dissonance-related attitude change after dissonance arousal.

The two experiments just discussed suggest strongly that dissonance-related attitude change is mediated by the attributions made about the dissonance situation. If an alternative to dissonance is provided as an explanation for dissonance-related arousal, the typical dissonance result does not occur. Stalder and Baron's study shows us that there are individual differences in attributional style, which correlates with dissonance-related attitude change. Those individuals who are highly motivated to find causes for their arousal are less likely to show dissonance-related attitude change because they settle on an alternative attribution for their arousal, more so than a person who is not so motivated.

Lessons of Cognitive Dissonance Theory

What can we learn about persuasive techniques from cognitive dissonance theory? The first lesson is that cognitive inconsistency often leads to change. Therefore, one persuasive technique is to point out to people how their behavior runs counter to their beliefs. Presumably, if people are aware of their inconsistencies, they will change. Persuasion may also occur if individuals are made aware that their behavior may produce a negative outcome (Cooper & Scher, 1992).

A second lesson is that any time you can induce someone to become publicly committed to a behavior that is counter to their beliefs, attitude change is a likely outcome. One reason for the change is that people use their public behavior as a kind of heuristic, a rule that says people stand by their public acts and bear personal responsibility for them (Baumeister & Tice, 1984; Zimbardo & Leippe, 1992). In other words, the rule is, "If I did it, I meant it."

Although dissonance can produce attitude change, it may not always change the attitude in the desired direction. An ironic effect of dissonance was demonstrated in a study by Nyhan et al. (2014). Nyhan et al. exposed vaccine-hesitant parents to information that debunked the false claim that the measles-mumps-rubella (MMR) vaccine causes autism.

Although dissonance can produce attitude change, it may not always change the attitude in the desired direction. Parents exposed to information debunking anti-vaccine beliefs might actually be more resistant to having their children vaccinated.
Source: fizkes/Shutterstock.

Although this information caused these parents to be less likely to believe the false link between MMR and autism, they were even more likely not to vaccinate their children. It appears that changing their beliefs about the link between the MMR vaccine and autism produced dissonance in anti-vaccination parents. The parents then reduced this dissonance by evoking even more negative beliefs about vaccines, which reduced their overall likelihood to vaccinate their children.

SOCIAL PSYCHOLOGY IN ACTION

Cognitive Dissonance and Cult Membership

Cognitive dissonance plays an important role in the formation and maintenance of cults. Once people make a public commitment to a leader and a movement, it is hard for them to acknowledge their misgivings. Instead, they must throw more and more resources into maintaining their commitment, even when it becomes obvious to others that the loyalty is misplaced. This phenomenon has occurred many times in human history. It happened in 1978 in Guyana, in Jonestown, the "utopian" community of Reverend Jim Jones. On his orders, his followers committed mass suicide by drinking Kool-Aid laced with cyanide. It happened again to the Branch Davidians in Waco, Texas.

In March 1993, a religious cult known as the Branch Davidians came to national attention at the beginning of its standoff with the Bureau of Alcohol, Tobacco, and Firearms (ATF). The cult was led by David Koresh, who claimed to receive orders from God. Koresh created the group's social reality. He separated cult members from the rest of the world, both physically and psychologically. He told them that he was Jesus and that "others" would deny the fact and try to destroy the cult. The Davidians stocked arms, food, and ammunition to prepare for an apocalypse and confrontation with the outside world. Koresh's predictions seemed to come true when ATF agents came to seize the cult's automatic weapons. Guns blazed on both sides, leaving several agents dead and wounded.

A siege of the compound began that lasted nearly 2 months. Federal authorities grew increasingly concerned about the welfare of the many children inside and the lack of progress in the negotiations with Koresh. Finally, assured by experts that the Davidians would not commit mass suicide if threatened, agents pumped tear gas into the compound to force them outside. However, fires erupted inside the buildings, apparently started by the cult. Eighty-six cult members, including 23 children, were incinerated. Apparently, the Davidians chose self-destruction rather than destruction of their reality. Why were members so persuaded by Koresh's outrageous claims? How did they become so committed to the cult?

All cults have many characteristics in common. The primary feature is a charismatic leader. He or she takes

Principles of cognitive dissonance theory play an important role in the formation and maintenance of cult groups. Members must throw more and more resources into maintaining commitment to the group, even when it is obvious that the commitment is misplaced.
Source: Raland/Shutterstock.

on a supernatural aura and persuades group members to devote their lives and fortunes to the cult. Koresh was this type of charismatic individual, able to convince large groups of people through clever arguments and persuasive appeals. For example, he refuted doubters by claiming to possess sole understanding of the scriptures and changed interpretations often to keep cult members constantly uncertain and reliant on him. Koresh used charm and authority to gain control of followers' lives. However, charisma alone is not enough to account for the behavior of the Davidians. We must also look at the cognitive dynamics of the individual members to see how they became so committed to Koresh and his ideals.

Joining the cult was no easy feat. At first, few demands were made, but after a while, members had to give more. In fact, members routinely turned over all of their possessions, including houses, insurance policies, and money. Once in the group, life was quite harsh. Koresh enforced strict (and changeable) rules in every aspect of members' lives, including personally rationing all their food, imposing celibacy on the men while taking women as his wives and concubines, and inflicting physical abuse. In short, residents of the compound had to expend quite a bit of effort to be members.

All the requirements for membership relate directly to what we know about attitudes and behavior from dissonance theory. For example, dissonance research shows that the harder people have to work to get into

(continued)

a group, the more they value that group (Aronson & Mills, 1959). By turning over all of their possessions, members were making an irreversible commitment to the cult. Once such a commitment is made, people are unlikely to abandon positive attitudes toward the group (Festinger et al., 1982). After expending so much effort, questioning commitment would create cognitive dissonance (Osherow, 1988). It is inconsistent to prove devotion to a belief by donating all of your possessions and then to abandon those beliefs. In other words, to a large extent, cult members persuade themselves. Dissonance theory predicts that the Davidians would come to value the group highly and be disinclined to question Koresh. This is, in fact, what happened.

Interestingly, cult members do not lose faith when the situation begins to sour. In fact, there is sometimes an increase in the strength of their commitment. One study investigated a "doomsday" society, a group that predicts the end of the world (Festinger et al., 1982). The study found that when a prophecy failed, members became more committed to the group. There are five conditions that must be met before this effect will occur:

1. The belief must be held with deep conviction and must be reflected in the believer's overt behavior.
2. The believer must have taken a step toward commitment that is difficult to reverse, for example, giving all his or her money to the group.
3. The belief must be specific and well enough related to real-world events that it can be disconfirmed, or proven false—for example, the prediction that the world will end on a specified day.
4. There must be undeniable evidence that the belief is false (the world doesn't end).
5. The individual believer must have social support for the belief after disconfirmation.

Most, perhaps all, five conditions were present in the Waco tragedy. Members were committed to their beliefs and gave everything they had to Koresh. There was evidence that the situation was unstable; several members had left the cult, and some were even talking to federal officials. And when it started to become obvious that Koresh was not invincible, members had each other to turn to for social support. As negotiations deteriorated, Koresh altered his rhetoric to emphasize apocalyptic visions, rationalizing the cult's destruction and self-sacrifice. Cult members probably came to believe it was their destiny to die, if necessary. The power of persuasion can be seen in the tragic results.

Discussion Questions

1. How does cognitive dissonance relate to cult membership?
2. Do cult members abandon their commitment to a cult when core beliefs are found to be invalid?

Study Break

This section continued the discussion of factors that relate to dissonance arousal and attitude change. Before you begin the next section, answer the following questions:

1. What is postdecision commitment, and how does it relate to attitude change?
2. How does responsibility relate to dissonance and attitude change?
3. How do attribution processes affect cognitive dissonance and attitude change?
4. How does cognitive dissonance relate to cult membership, and what are the five factors that lead to increased belief strength after belief disconfirmation?

Alternatives to Cognitive Dissonance Theory

Not all social psychologists believe cognitive dissonance theory is the best way to explain what happens when cognitive inconsistencies occur. Other theories have been proposed to explain how people deal with these discrepancies. In the sections that follow, we explore some alternatives to traditional cognitive dissonance theory.

Self-Perception Theory

Daryl Bem, a student of the great behaviorist psychologist B. F. Skinner, challenged cognitive dissonance theory, because, he asserted, he could explain people's behavior without looking at their inner motives. Bem (1972) proposed **self-perception theory**, which explains attitude-discrepant behavior by simply assuming that people are not self-conscious

self-perception theory
A theory suggesting that we learn about our motivations by evaluating our own behavior, useful especially in the area of attitude change.

processors of information. People observe their own behavior and assume that their attitudes must be consistent with that behavior. If you eat a big dinner, you assume that you must have been hungry. If you take a public stand on an issue, the rule of self-perception theory is, "I said it, so I must have meant it." We don't look at our motives; we just process the information and conclude that there is no inconsistency.

Bem supported his theory with some interesting experiments. In one, he trained people to tell the truth whenever a "truth" (green) light was lit and to lie whenever a "lie" (red) light was lit. When the green light was on, people had to say something about themselves that was true. When the red light was on, people had to lie about themselves. Bem then asked the participants to make further statements that were either true or false under both truth and lie lights. Participants who told lies when the truth light was on came to believe that those false statements were true. Likewise, subjects who made true statements when the lie light was on reported that they lied.

The point of self-perception theory is that we make inferences about our behavior in much the same way an outside observer might. If you were observing the experiment, you would infer, quite reasonably, that whatever anyone said when the light was red was a lie and anything said under the green light was true. The participants assumed the same thing. According to self-perception theory, something does not have to happen "inside" the person for inconsistencies to be resolved—no tension, no motivation to reconcile attitudes and behavior, just information processing.

Rationalization

Imagine a group of cigar smokers sitting around a cigar shop talking about the potential health hazards of their cigar-smoking habit. There is ample evidence that cigarette smoking poses health risks. There is also evidence that cigar smoking may have some health risks as well. How do smokers reconcile the conflict between the health-related risks and continuing to smoke? Cognitive dissonance theory would predict that dissonance would be aroused in this situation. The fact that millions of people smoke is proof that dissonance does not always lead to behavior change. So, how can one continue to smoke, knowing the health risks? The answer is that smokers often engage in rationalization. Smokers convince themselves that: "Nothing will happen to me," "I'll stop when I'm 40," or "My grandfather lived until 95, and he smoked like a chimney." Rationalizations are important in maintaining a coherent self-concept.

An interesting study was conducted by DeSantis (2003) that illustrates this rationalization process. DeSantis, being a cigar smoker himself, was part of a group of regulars who met at a Kentucky cigar store to smoke their cigars and talk sports. DeSantis decided to study the inner workings of this group using a participant observation ethnography method. DeSantis continued his membership and at the same time carefully studied the interactions among the group members (with their knowledge and permission). DeSantis found that members generated five rationalizations to support their continued cigar smoking in the face of evidence of its harmful effects. These rationalizations are listed in Table 6.1, along with a brief explanation of each. Interestingly, these rationalizations were maintained even after one of the members died from heart disease. Rationalization can, indeed, be a powerful thing.

Self-Affirmation Theory

Dissonance may threaten a person's self-concept with negative implications, making the person appear stupid, unethical, or lazy (Steele, 1988). Nonsmokers probably view smokers as being all three. Then why don't people in dissonant situations alter their behavior? In the case of cigarette smoking, a large part of the answer is the highly addictive nature of nicotine. Many people try to quit and fail, or they can't face the prospect of never having another cigarette. So they are stuck with the dissonance. **Self-affirmation theory** suggests that people may not try to reduce dissonance if they can maintain (affirm) their self-concept by proving that they are adequate in other ways: "Yes, I may be a smoker, but I'm also a good mother, a respected professional, and an active citizen in my community."

self-affirmation theory
A theory that individuals may not try to reduce dissonance if they can maintain (affirm) their self-concept by showing they are morally adequate in other ways.

TABLE 6.1 Five Rationalizations Made by Cigar Smokers

Rationalization	Explanation
Things done in moderation won't hurt you.	Participants expressed that smoking in moderation won't be harmful. Some indicated that they cut down or only smoked in certain, limited situations. Some indicated that their physicians said it was OK to smoke cigars in moderation.
There are health benefits to smoking.	Participants pointed to the stress-reducing effect of smoking. Some saw the stress-reducing effect as a legitimate trade-off for any health risks.
Cigars are not as bad as cigarettes.	Participants denied that research on health risks of cigarettes applies to cigars, indicating that one smokes cigars less frequently than cigarettes and that one does not inhale cigars.
Research on health effects of cigar smoking is flawed.	Discounting of research on effects of cigar smoking on the basis that the research is methodologically flawed. Two flaws cited: Lack of adequate research and inconsistent nature of findings.
Life is dangerous.	Relative comparisons made between cigar smoking and other hazards (e.g., air pollution, driving). Dangers of smoking minimized in the light of other hazards.

Based on data in Desantis, 2003

These self-affirmations remove the sting inherent in a dissonance situation (Zimbardo & Leippe, 1992). People cope with a threat to one aspect of the self by affirming an unrelated part of the self (Steele, 1988).

The Action-Based Model

Some research has called into question the applicability of self-affirmation theory to cognitive dissonance (Harmon-Jones, 2000). According to Harmon-Jones, "engaging in self-affirmation following dissonance-evoking behaviors seems subordinate to resolving the specific discrepancy aroused by the behavior" (2000, p. 132). As an alternative, Harmon-Jones suggests that one need not deviate much from the original cognitive dissonance theory to understand discrepancy reduction. Harmon-Jones proposed the **action-based model** of cognitive dissonance reduction. According to this model, "cognitive discrepancy generates dissonance motivation because the cognitive discrepancy has the potential to interfere with effective unconflicted action" (Harmon-Jones et al., p. 69). Anything that enhances the prospect for effective, unconflicted action should, according to the model, enhance cognitive dissonance reduction.

An experiment by Harmon-Jones and Harmon-Jones (2002) demonstrated this clearly. Participants made either a difficult decision (between two equally valued physical exercises they had previously evaluated favorably) or an easy decision (between a highly valued and a lowly valued physical exercise) under one of two mindsets. Half of the participants in each decision condition wrote down seven things that they could do to improve their behavior concerning the chosen alternative (action-oriented mindset). The other half of the participants in each decision condition wrote about seven things they

action-based model A model of cognitive dissonancy stating that cognitive discrepancy generates dissonance motivation because the cognitive discrepancy has the potential to interfere with effective unconflicted action.

do during a normal day (neutral mindset). After making their choices, participants once again evaluated the desirability of the exercises. The researchers predicted that the most dissonance reduction (evidenced by the greatest change in predecision and postdecision evaluation of alternatives) would be when the decision was difficult and an action-oriented mindset was adopted. The results confirmed this prediction. The greatest amount of postdecision spread was found when the decision was difficult and an action-oriented mindset was adopted.

Psychological Reactance

Psychological tension can be reduced in several ways. Sometimes, when people realize they have been coerced into doing or buying something against their wishes, they try to regain or reassert their freedom. This response is called **psychological reactance** (Brehm & Brehm, 1981). The theory of psychological reactance, an offshoot of cognitive dissonance theory, suggests that when some part of our freedom is threatened, we become aroused and motivated to restore that freedom.

> **psychological reactance**
> A psychological state that results when individuals feel that their freedom of action is threatened because other people are forcing them to do or say things, making them less prone to social influence attempts.

The Coca-Cola Company found this out in 1985 when it tried to replace the traditional Coke formula with "New Coke." The company conducted an in-depth marketing study of the new product that included 200,000 taste tests. The tests showed that people really liked New Coke. The company went ahead with plans to retire the old formula and put New Coke in its place. However, the issue was not taste; it was perceived choice. People resented having a choice taken away and reacted by buying the traditional Coke as if it were manna from heaven, never to be seen again. Some people even formed Old Coke clubs. The company got over 1,500 angry calls and letters every day. Coca-Cola had to change its marketing plans, and "Classic Coke" still holds an honored place on the grocery shelves (Oskamp, 1991). Whether consumers liked New Coke did not matter. Their emotional ties to old Coke did matter, as did their freedom to buy it. New Coke just wasn't it for these folks. The life of New Coke was short and within a couple of years of its introduction it disappeared from the market. "Classic" Coca Cola is now simply known as Coca Cola, as it was before the introduction of New Coke.

Although reactance theory has a rich history in attitude research, it has proven to be a difficult concept to measure and conceptualize (Dillard & Shen, 2005). According to reactance theory, the central factor activating reactance is perceived threat to one's freedom of choice or action. Although this may be true, are there other factors that relate to reactance-elicited attitude change? Apparently, there are. Dillard and Shen suggest that one's cognitions concerning the threat to freedom and the arousal of anger over the loss of choice are important factors in the reactance-attitude relationship. In their study, they tested a number of different models that included threat, cognitions about threat, anger, and attitude change. According to Dillard and Shen, an *intertwined model* best accounted for the relationship between threat to freedom and attitudes. In this model, threat gives rise to reactance, which affects attitudes and behavior. The reactance is, in turn, related to threat-related cognitions and anger. That is, it appears that in response to threat to freedom, we experience reactance, which activates thoughts and anger associated with the threat. A meta-analysis of the reactance literature confirmed the validity of the intertwined model (Rains, 2013).

Reactance is yet another attitude-change topic that has been examined regarding vaccine hesitancy. Several studies have demonstrated that attempts to increase vaccination rates through mandatory vaccination programs can elicit reactance, thereby increasing rather than decreasing vaccine hesitancy. The effect of reactance on vaccine hesitancy is strongest for people who already have low intentions of receiving a vaccination (Betsch & Böhm, 2016; Sprengholz & Betsch, 2020; Sprengholz, Betsch, et al., 2021). For these people, a forced mandate is a threat to their freedom of choice. Furthermore, the reactance provoked by mandatory vaccination programs can alter behaviors beyond vaccine compliance. Reactance brought about by possible mandatory vaccine programs is related to resistance to prophylactic measures designed to slow the spread of COVID-19 (e.g., mask wearing and social distancing; Sprengholz, Böhm, et al., 2021).

Study Break

Although considerable evidence supports cognitive dissonance theory, there are alternatives to it. Before you begin the next section, answer the following questions:

1. What is the self-perception explanation for attitude change, and how does it differ from cognitive dissonance theory?
2. How does the rationalization explanation differ from a cognitive dissonance explanation for attitude change?
3. How does the self-affirmation explanation differ from a cognitive dissonance explanation for attitude change?
4. What is the action-based model, and how does it account for dissonance-related attitude change?
5. What is psychological reactance, and how does it account for dissonance-related attitude change?

Persuading the Masses Through Propaganda

As we have discussed throughout this chapter, persuasion techniques are sometimes aimed at changing the attitudes and behavior of large populations. Such mass persuasion can take many forms. Advertisers routinely craft persuasive messages we call advertisements to get you to buy one product rather than another. Various public service persuasive messages attempt to get us to change a wide range of behaviors, including not driving drunk, practicing safe sex, wearing seat belts, avoiding illegal drugs, and of course, receiving life-saving vaccines.

Propaganda: A Definition

Perhaps the most controversial application of mass persuasion techniques is the use of propaganda. **Propaganda** is "a deliberate attempt to persuade people, by any available media, to think in a manner desired by the source" (Taylor, 2003, p. 7). Throughout human history there are many examples of the use of propaganda to shape the attitudes and behaviors of masses of individuals. For example, propaganda was extensively used during the American Revolution to both sell the colonists' cause and demonize the British. It was also used extensively in World War I by both the Germans and Allies. However, perhaps the best example of the application of propaganda was by the Nazis during the years leading up to and throughout World War II. Although it is true that both sides in World War II used propaganda, the Nazis under the guidance of Josef Goebbels raised propaganda to levels never before seen.

There are a few things that you should understand about propaganda before we continue with our discussion. First, it is common to characterize propaganda as a pack of lies used by the enemy to manipulate attitudes and behavior. While it is true that propaganda is often aimed at one's enemy, it is also used extensively to shape the attitudes and behavior of one's own citizens. And, as noted earlier, it is also used by the "good guys." For example, during World War II the U.S. government engaged in propaganda aimed at boosting the war effort at home. Hollywood films such as *Wake Island* (1942) portrayed the Marines on the island holding out to the last man against the Japanese onslaught. In fact, there was no such

propaganda A deliberate attempt to persuade people, by any available media, to think in a manner desired by the source.

Propaganda is a systematic attempt to persuade masses of people. Nazis used propaganda effectively before and during World War II.
Source: Dariush M/Shutterstock.

heroic last stand. Many of the Marines and civilians were captured, and a good number of them were murdered by the Japanese military. The film was intended to provide a much needed boost in morale on the home front, which it in fact did provide. Second, propaganda is not always a "pack of lies." Quite the contrary: modern propaganda attempts to stay as close to the truth as possible (Taylor, 2003). This is not to say that lies are never used; they are. However, a good propagandist knows that his or her credibility is an important commodity. Caught in a lie, this credibility suffers. Finally, propaganda is neither good nor bad. It is simply a means to an end (Taylor, 2003).

Characteristics of Propaganda

Ellul (1965) defines two broad characteristics of propaganda. The *internal characteristics* of propaganda refer to the characteristics of the target of the propaganda. According to Ellul, a good propagandist must know the "psychological terrain" on which he or she is operating. This means that the propagandist must know which attitudes and behaviors can be easily manipulated. Typically, the propagandist stays away from deeply held beliefs and concentrates on those that are more malleable. For example, Communist propaganda in Cold War Poland shied away from attacking the Catholic Church and the Catholic religion. This is because Catholicism and the Catholic Church were extremely important to the Polish people. Conversely, Nazi propaganda exploited already existing anti-Semitism to shape the German population's attitudes about Jews.

The *external characteristics* of propaganda refer to the characteristics of the propaganda itself. One important point that Ellul makes is that in order for propaganda to be effective, it must be *organized and total*. "Organized" means that the propaganda is the product of a concerted effort to shape attitudes and behavior. It is not a hit-or-miss proposition. The good propagandist has a clear plan in mind and uses propaganda to execute that plan. As an example, consider the fact that in 1939, the Nazis spent around a million dollars a day ($19,366,546 in 2021 dollars) on propaganda at the start of World War II. "Total" means that the masses must be immersed in the propaganda. This second characteristic is why propaganda works best in situations where the propagandist can control all of the outlets for propaganda. For example, Josef Goebbels had total control over all of the media outlets of the day: newspapers, radio, and film. Additionally, Nazi propaganda permeated every aspect of life in Germany. The stamps people put on their letters had Nazi images, children's books portrayed Jews in stereotyped ways, museums were full of Nazi art, and pro-Nazi plays filled the theaters. Another external characteristic is the fact that propaganda is directed at the individual in the context of the masses (Ellul, 1965). That is, the propagandist directs propaganda at individuals but uses the masses to help break down individual thought. An individual apart from the masses will offer too much resistance to propaganda (Ellul, 1965). It is for this reason that Nazis held huge rallies (often at night so that one's critical thinking skills were not at their peak). Imagine how difficult it would be for you to counterargue Nazi ideas when you are part of a huge crowd pledging their undying support for those ideas. In short, Nazi propaganda was aimed at making each individual feel as though he or she was a part of something much larger.

A host of other characteristics are typically true of propaganda. These are listed in Table 6.2.

TABLE 6.2 Additional Characteristics of Propaganda

> Takes advantage of emotion
> Prevents critical analysis of issues
> Propagandist has vested interest and some goal
> Attempts to manipulate how we think and act
> Used by just about every society at one time or another (not just the bad guys)

The Aims of Propaganda

As noted, propaganda was extensively used during the American Revolution. For example, Paul Revere made an engraving of the "Boston Massacre" that depicted the event inaccurately (you can find an image of his engraving by doing an Internet search). The British were shown in a military picket line with their commander behind them giving the order to fire. The scene was shown in a wide open area between rows of buildings in clear weather. The colonists were portrayed as passive and peaceful, only to be ruthlessly mowed down by the evil British. There is even a cute little dog shown with the colonists. In fact, the actual event was much different. The colonists were armed and were taunting the British. There was much confusion in the confined space. And, there is evidence that the colonists fired the first shot. In fact, a colonial jury acquitted the British soldiers of any crime in the event. (You can also find a more accurate image of the massacre on the Internet.) Despite the inaccuracies, Revere's engraving was widely distributed throughout the colonies and was successful in its aim of arousing hatred for the British.

Samuel Adams worked for the *Boston Globe* at the time and organized a propaganda team known as the Committee of Correspondence. The committee would gather the news and report back to Adams, who would then send his version of the events out to other newspapers (Jowett & O'Donnell, 1986). Adams had a reputation for being something of a rabble-rouser. However, he did have a clear vision of his cause (separation from England) and how to achieve it. Adams developed five aims of propaganda (Jowett & O'Donnel, 1986). They are as valid today as they were then:

1. The aims of the cause must be justified.
2. The advantages of victory must be made clear and known.
3. The people need to be aroused to action by instilling hatred for the enemy.
4. Logical arguments of the enemy must be negated.
5. All issues must be stated in clear-cut, black-and-white terms.

Propaganda Techniques

The techniques used by propagandists may vary from case to case. However, the goal is the same: Persuade the masses. Common propaganda techniques include the following (Brown, 1967):

- *Use of stereotypes:* Propagandists often take advantage of our natural tendency to stereotype people. Propaganda can eventually lead us to think of a group of people in terms of the stereotype, rather than as individual human beings.
- *Substitution of names:* Propagandists often use derogatory names to refer to disliked groups. Victims of propaganda become dehumanized, and it becomes easier to persecute them.
- *Selection of facts:* Propagandists do not present a balanced view of events. They select specific facts that support their point of view.
- *Downright lying:* Falsehoods are used to persuade others.
- *Repetition:* The same message is repeated over and over. Repeated exposure eventually leads to acceptance of the message.
- *Assertion:* Propagandists are not interested in debating. Instead, they assert their point forcefully.
- *Pinpointing an enemy:* Propaganda is most effective if an enemy can be identified who poses a threat to all. This directs aggression or blame away from the propagandists and strengthens in-group feelings of unity and solidarity. This technique plays on the "us versus them" mentality.

- *Appeals to authority:* Propagandists often make references to or identify their leaders with higher sources of authority. This can mean a higher political authority (e.g., approval from a revered leader) or refer to a higher power (e.g., God). In either case, the propagandists leave the impression that their leader has the support and blessing of the higher authority.

- Using *glittering generalities:* In this technique, the propagandist uses broad, vague, sweeping statements, such as slogans or simple catchphrases. The language use deals with deeply held values and beliefs without providing supporting information or reason (e.g., liberty, freedom), along with attractive, vague words and phrases that say very little of substance (George Mason University, 2008).

Fritz Hippler, the head of the Nazi film industry, captured the essence of successful propaganda. He boiled down propaganda to two main techniques: *simplification and repetition*. All messages used in propaganda should be stated in simple terms so that even the least intelligent members of a society can understand the message. Once the message is formulated, it is then repeated so it becomes familiar to the targets of propaganda.

Hitler's Rise to Power

Looking back at the years between 1924 and 1945 when a darkness descended across Europe, it is obvious to see the outcome of the rise of Nazism and Hitler to power in Germany. However, how could a failed painter, army corporal, and later political prisoner rise to the peak of power in Germany in just nine years? Part of the answer, of course, is the fact that the Nazi Party had a well-organized paramilitary wing that effectively intimidated or eliminated opposition parties such as the Communist Party. However, such street muscle cannot fully explain how a large segment of the German people came to accept and support Hitler and Nazism. To answer this question, we need to look at how the Nazis, through Josef Goebbels, used propaganda to rise to power, consolidate power, and prepare the German people for war and for the extermination of the Jews.

In the years following the end of World War I, the German people and economy were suffering greatly. War reparations were causing widespread economic depression. Inflation ravaged the economy. Within this context, Adolph Hitler would emerge to become the most powerful man in Germany. But it didn't happen right away. On September 9, 1923, Hitler and his followers attempted to overthrow the Bavarian government in Munich. The so-called "Beer Hall Putsch" was a complete failure. The Bavarian government refused to capitulate, and no popular uprising occurred. Instead, Hitler and his followers were imprisoned in Lansberg Prison. This was on April 1, 1924. At this point, the Nazi Party was in a shambles. Its leaders were in prison, the party newspaper was shut down, and the party was declared illegal. During his prison stay, Hitler dictated his manifesto *Mein Kampf* to Rudolph Hess.

On December 24, 1925, Hitler was released from prison. His release provided one of the first propaganda opportunities for his propagandists. The exit from the prison was quite ordinary. So, a photograph was taken at a different location showing an imposing gate and a large black car awaiting the emergence of Hitler. Soon after his release, *Mein Kampf* was published. Still, the party was in dire straits. In fact, on March 9, 1925, the government issued an order prohibiting Hitler from speaking in public. This provided another early propaganda opportunity for the Nazis. A poster was distributed showing Hitler with tape across his mouth. The caption read "He alone among 2,000 million people is forbidden to speak." It would take a while, but the ban was finally lifted in September of 1928. But the party was still not terribly strong, though things were moving along. By 1929 Hitler was the head of the Nazi party. Josef Goebbels gave the party a better image with his skillful application of propaganda. Then on October 29, 1929, the German (and world economy in general) crashed and entered the Great Depression. An already shaky German economy was devastated. People who had secure jobs in the past found themselves unemployed and starving. This gave Hitler and the Nazis their best opportunity to take power. The Nazi message started to sound better and better to many Germans in misery.

The party began to grow and on September 14, 1930, the Nazi Party won 107 seats in the Reichstag (the German Parliament). In April 1932, Hitler lost a runoff election against the immensely popular President Hindenburg, but he did garner 36% of the vote. Despite the overwhelming victory by Hindenburg, political turmoil still existed. With the German government near to collapse and Hitler agitating for power, the 85-year-old Hindenburg reluctantly appointed Hitler to be chancellor of Germany on January 30, 1933. Just a few short weeks later, in March of 1933, Hitler consolidated his power and became the absolute ruler of Germany, the Reichstag was burned, and Germany entered into its darkest period of its history—a history that would include persecution and extermination of Jews and other Eastern Europeans in death camps and the loss of nearly 80 million people in World War II.

The Power of Propaganda in Nazi Germany

Let's turn our attention to how Josef Goebbels used propaganda at various points in the Nazi rise to power and selling of Nazi ideas to the German public and the world. We shall organize our discussion around the techniques of propaganda reviewed earlier. For each technique, we shall explore briefly how Goebbels used propaganda to shape the attitudes and behaviors of the masses. (Examples of Nazi propaganda can be found on several Web sites.)

- *Use of stereotypes:* As noted earlier, propagandists take advantage of the tendency to stereotype people. Propaganda from the Nazi era used this technique to marginalize and demonize the Jews. Various anti-Semitic posters were widely used. Typically these portrayed Jews as hook-nosed evil characters bent upon controlling the German people and the world. For example, one such poster showed a caricature of an evil Jew inciting people into war with the caption "The Jew. The inciter of war, the prolonger of war." Another poster, called "The String Puller," showed a caricature of a Jew as a puppeteer pulling the strings of the German people. German propaganda movies also were used to reinforce negative stereotypes of the Jews and instill fear and loathing of them into the German people. The most infamous of these films was Fritz Hippler's *The Eternal Jew*. In this film Jews were likened to rats and other vermin, and Jewish rituals (e.g., Kosher slaughter of animals) were portrayed in hideous ways. Interestingly, *The Eternal Jew* was neither popular nor effective. However, another propaganda film called *Jude Süss* was a major hit and effective in arousing anti-Semitic attitudes. This film portrayed a duplicitous Jew within a narrative story, which was more effective in reaching audiences. Even children's books were laced with anti-Semitic images and themes. The most famous of these was the series of children's books called *Der Giftpilz* (*The Poison Mushroom*). As in other propaganda materials, Jews were portrayed as crafty, evil, hook-nosed characters, often preying on innocent Germans.

- *Substitution of names:* Nazi propaganda succeeded in characterizing Jews and Eastern Europeans as subhuman. One cartoon that appeared in the Nazi newspaper *Der Sturmer* in February 1930 showed a huge black spider with a Star of David on its torso sucking Germans that were hanging in its web dry, the caption reading "Sucked Dry." Eastern Europeans were often referred to as "untermenchen" (subhuman) in posters that juxtaposed the perfect Aryan against the mongrel-like Eastern European.

- *Selection of facts:* Even when the war was not going well, Goebbels painted a rosy picture of what was happening by selectively releasing information. For example, in a 1943 article Gobbels said:

  > Was there ever a nation that had so favorable a position after five years of war as we do today? The front is unbroken. The homeland is morally and materially able to withstand the bombing terror. A river of war material flows from our factories. A new weapon against the enemy air attacks is being prepared. Countless able hands are working at it day and night. We have a hard test of patience before us, but the reward will come one day. The German farmer is bringing in a good harvest.

What he failed to mention was that the German military industry was being pounded almost around the clock by Allied air forces, the wonder weapons of which he spoke were of little tactical value, and the German military was experiencing defeats on all fronts.

- *Downright lying:* Apparently, Hitler wanted a pretext on which to invade Poland in 1939. So, on August 31, 1939, SS officers took Polish prisoners from a concentration camp, dressed them in Polish army uniforms, and shot them. Their bodies were scattered outside a German radio station and comprised a contrived attack on a German radio station on the Polish border. In fact, Hitler said, *"Polish regular officers fired on our territory. Since 5:45 a.m. we have been returning the fire."* The German invasion of Poland began soon after Hitler's false statement.

- *Repetition:* Nazi propaganda hammered home the same messages and images over and over. For example, several propaganda posters portrayed Hitler as the savior of Germany and a skilled military leader.

- *Assertion:* In 1943, despite the fact that the tide of the war was turning against Germany, Josef Goebbels continued to assert that Germany would win the war. In a New Year's Eve speech in 1943 he stated, "Our war position has indeed become tighter than it was at the end of 1942, but it is more than sufficient to guarantee us a certain final victory." He went on to list the failures of the Allied army and asserted that the facts supported a German victory.

- *Pinpointing an enemy:* Propaganda works best when it comes out against something. An old saying goes that nothing unites people like a common enemy. The enemy becomes the focus of negative thoughts and emotions and serves to deflect criticism from the propagandist's group. Nazi propaganda identified two enemies: the Jews and opposing countries. Of the Jews, Goebbels wrote in 1941, "Every Jew is our enemy in this historic struggle, regardless of whether he vegetates in a Polish ghetto or carries on his parasitic existence in Berlin or Hamburg or blows the trumpets of war in New York or Washington. All Jews by virtue of their birth and their race are part of an international conspiracy against National Socialist Germany." A poster showed a fist smashing the bodies of enemies (one clearly with a British flag on his back) with the caption "Into dust with all enemies of Germany."

- *Appeals to authority:* Even as Hitler rose to power in 1933, he still had an image problem. People, politicians, and military leaders were skeptical of Hitler and his party. So, it was important to show that Hitler had the blessing of someone held in high esteem by the German people. Nazi propagandists went to work giving the German people the idea that Hitler had the support and blessing of the much beloved President Hindenburg. A propaganda poster showed the "Corporal and the Field Marshal" together. In reality, Hindenburg despised Hitler and handed the chancellorship over to him only when he had no other choice. Additionally, Nazi art often showed Hitler in godlike poses and settings, giving the impression that he also had the support of a supreme being.

- *Glittering generalities:* Nazi propaganda made use of glittering generalities when it used language urging Germans to "defend the fatherland" or uphold "racial purity." Ideals such as strength and loyalty were constantly reinforced with slogans and catchphrases.

Study Break

This section introduced you to propaganda, which represents persuasion processes applied to the masses. Before you go on, answer the following questions:

1. What is the definition of propaganda, and what are its characteristics?
2. What are the internal and external characteristics of propaganda?

3. What are the aims of propaganda?
4. List and define each of the techniques used by propagandists, and show how they are used to persuade the masses.
5. How was propaganda used in the rise of Adolph Hitler to power?

COVID-19 Vaccine Hesitancy Revisited

As was the case with past epidemics (e.g., smallpox, polio), public health officials used all available persuasion techniques to raise the rate of COVID-19 vaccination in America. As you have learned in this chapter, it is unlikely that a single campaign or advertising program will be effective for all groups hesitant to receive the vaccine. Instead, the message must be tailored to specific audiences. For example, what might be an effective message for the Black community may not effectively persuade White conservatives. Public health officials also made extensive use of fear appeals when they stated that failing to follow COVID-19 guidelines (e.g., getting vaccinated) could result in the deaths of elderly loved ones. Health officials also used audience-specific channels of communication. As you learned in Chapter 3, younger people are much more likely to consume news and information online than are previous generations. To reach these individuals, public service announcements were made on social media applications such as TikTok and Facebook.

The credibility of the messenger also became an issue during the pandemic. Many of the reasons that people stated for not wanting to receive a vaccine had to do with a lack of trust in its safety. This lack of trust likely stemmed from a decrease of trust in the government in general and certain health officials in particular. Appeals to vaccinate may be more effective if they come from sources outside the government, such as family physicians, whom we tend to trust.

Some persistent vaccine hesitancy may be related to the use of attitude-change techniques that backfired. Attempting to increase vaccine rates using messages that fall into the audience's latitude of rejection or arouse psychological reactance is counterproductive. For example, making vaccines mandatory or requiring university students to get vaccinated before returning to campus could arouse psychological reactance and cause individuals to avoid the COVID-19 vaccination.

Finally, whether one considers public health campaigns as propaganda is debatable. The vaccination campaigns used during the COVID-19 pandemic do share many of the characteristics of propaganda discussed in this chapter. However, remember that propaganda itself is neither good nor evil but, rather, a means to an end. Consequently, questions of whether public health campaigns are propaganda are of less concern. There is no doubt that mass persuasion in the interest of public health can result in reduced infections and deaths, which is an undoubtedly positive outcome.

Chapter Review

1. **What is persuasion?**

   Persuasion is a form of social influence whereby a communicator uses rational and/or emotional arguments to convince others to change their attitudes or behavior.

2. **What is the Yale communication model?**

   The Yale communication model is a theoretical model that guides persuasion tactics. It is based on the assumption that persuasion will occur if a persuader presents a logical argument that clarifies how attitude change is beneficial.

3. **What factors about the communicator affect persuasion?**

   The Yale model focuses on the credibility of the communicator, an important determinant of the likelihood that persuasion will occur. The components of credibility are expertise and trustworthiness. Although an important factor in the persuasiveness of a message, communicator credibility may not have long-lasting effects. Over time, a message from a noncredible source may be as persuasive as one from a credible source, a phenomenon known as the sleeper effect. This is more likely to occur if there is a strong persuasive argument, if a discounting cue is given, and if sufficient time passes that people forget who said what. Other communicator factors that increase persuasion are physical attractiveness, similarity to the target, and a rapid, fluent speech style.

4. **What message factors mediate persuasion?**

Messages that include a mild to moderate appeal to fear seem to be more persuasive than others, provided they offer a solution to the fear-producing situation. The timing of the message is another factor in its persuasiveness, as is the structure of the message and the extent to which the communicator attempts to fit the message to the audience. Research supports inoculation theory, which holds that giving people a weakened version of an opposing argument is an effective approach to persuasion. Good communicators also know their audience well enough not to deliver a highly discrepant message. When this cannot be avoided, as when there is a multiple audience problem, communicators use hidden messages and private keys and codes to get their point across.

Additionally, the amount of discrepancy between the content of a message and the audience members' existing attitudes makes a difference. According to social judgment theory, persuasion relates to the amount of personal involvement an individual has with an issue. A message can fall into a person's latitude of acceptance (positions found to be acceptable), latitude of rejection (positions found to be unacceptable), or latitude of noncommitment (positions neither accepted nor rejected, but to be considered).

5. **What is the elaboration likelihood model of persuasion?**

Cognitive response models focus on the active role of the audience. They assert that people respond to persuasive messages by connecting them with their own knowledge, feelings, and thoughts related to the topic of the message. The elaboration likelihood model (ELM), which examines how individuals respond to the persuasive message, proposes two routes to persuasion. The first, central route processing, is used when people have the capacity and motivation to understand the message and analyze it in a critical and effortful manner. Central route processors elaborate on the message by connecting it to their knowledge and feelings. Sometimes this elaboration will persuade the recipient, depending on the strength of the message. Central route processors tend to experience more durable attitude changes.

The second avenue to persuasion is peripheral route processing. This occurs when individuals do not have the motivation or interest to process effortfully. Instead, they rely on cues other than the merits of the message, such as the attractiveness of the communicator. Whether a person uses central or peripheral route processing depends on a number of factors, including mood, personal relevance, and use of language. The flexible correction model augments the elaboration likelihood model. It suggests that individuals using central route processing are influenced by biasing factors when they are not aware of the potential impact of those factors—for example, when they are in a good mood. Under these conditions, correction for biasing factors takes place.

6. **What is the impact of vividness on persuasion?**

Overall, the effect of vividness of a message on persuasion is not very strong. Studies show, however, that individuals exposed to vivid messages on an issue that was important to them felt the vivid message was effective. Vividness may be beneficial in political ads or in jury trials. For example, jurors awarded more money to a plaintiff when the evidence they heard was vivid as opposed to nonvivid. Vivid information has its greatest impact when a persuasive message requires few resources and a person is highly motivated to process the message. For a message with a highly motivated target that requires many resources, vividness does not have an effect on persuasion.

7. **What are the need for cognition and the need for affect?**

Need for cognition (NC) is an individual difference variable mediating persuasion. Individuals who are high in the need for cognition will process persuasive information along the central route, regardless of the situation or the complexity of the message. Conversely, individuals low in the need for cognition pay more attention to peripheral cues (e.g., physical characteristics of the speaker) and are more likely to use peripheral route processing of a persuasive message. The need for affect (NA) is a person's tendency to approach or avoid emotional situations. Individuals who are high in NA are more persuaded by an emotion-based message than individuals high in NC.

8. **What is the heuristic and systematic information model of persuasion?**

The heuristic and systematic information-processing model (HSM) focuses more heavily on the importance of heuristics or peripheral cues than does the elaboration likelihood model. This model notes that often issues are too complex or too numerous for effortful, systematic processing to be practical.

9. **What is cognitive dissonance theory, and what are its main ideas?**

Cognitive dissonance theory proposes that people feel an uncomfortable tension when their attitudes, or attitude and behavior, are inconsistent. This psychological discomfort is known as cognitive dissonance. According to the theory, people are motivated to reduce this tension, and attitude change is a likely outcome. Dissonance theory suggests that the less reward people receive for a behavior, the more compelled they feel to provide their own justification for it, especially if they believe they have freely chosen it. Similarly, the more they are rewarded, the more they infer that the behavior is suspect. The latter is known as the reverse-incentive effect.

Additionally, cognitive dissonance theory states that an individual will experience dissonance after making a decision between two mutually exclusive, equally attractive alternatives. This is known as postdecision dissonance.

Another, more recent view suggests that cognitive dissonance results not so much from inconsistency as from the feeling of personal responsibility that occurs when inconsistent actions produce negative consequences.

10. **How does cognitive dissonance relate to cult membership?**

Making a public commitment to a cult's leader and a movement makes it hard for individuals to acknowledge any misgivings about the cult after joining it. Instead, cult members may invest more resources into maintaining membership, even if others see those efforts as misplaced. The more effort one must put into joining a cult, the more dissonance is aroused if something happens to cause a member to doubt the decision to join. Cult members must often turn over their money and possessions to the cult, making it difficult to reverse positive attitudes about the cult. Even if the situation turns sour, members are unlikely to reverse their decision. In fact, they may increase their commitment to the cult. This is most likely to occur when five conditions are met: Beliefs are held with deep conviction and relate to behavior, the believer has taken a step toward commitment that is difficult to reverse, the belief must be specific and can be disconfirmed by real events, there is undeniable evidence that the belief is false, and social support exists after belief disconfirmation.

11. **What is self-perception theory?**

One alternative to cognitive dissonance theory is self-perception theory, which argues that behavior and attitude change can be explained without assuming that people are motivated to reduce the tension supposedly produced by inconsistency.

Instead, self-perception assumes that people are not self-conscious processors of information. They simply observe their own behavior and assume that their attitudes must be consistent with that behavior.

12. **What is self-affirmation theory?**

Another alternative to cognitive dissonance, self-affirmation theory explains how people deal with the tension that dissonant thoughts or behaviors provoke. Self-affirmation theory suggests that people may not try to reduce dissonance if they can maintain their self-concept by proving that they are adequate in other ways—that is, by affirming an unrelated and positive part of the self.

13. **What is psychological reactance?**

Individuals may reduce psychological tension in another way as well. When people realize they have been coerced into doing or buying something against their will, they sometimes try to regain or reassert their freedom. This response is called psychological reactance. Reactance operates by activating thoughts related to the threat to freedom and anger.

14. **What is propaganda?**

Propaganda is defined as a deliberate attempt to persuade people, by any available media, to think in a manner desired by the source. The internal characteristics of propaganda refer to the psychological makeup of the targets of propaganda. In order for propaganda to be effective, the propagandist must know which attitudes, sentiments, and behaviors can be easily manipulated. Deeply held beliefs are commonly left alone. The external characteristics of propaganda refer to the characteristics of the propaganda itself. In order for propaganda to be maximally effective, it must be organized and total.

15. **How are the tactics of propaganda used on a mass scale?**

Propagandists use a variety of techniques to persuade the masses. These include use of stereotypes, substitution of names, selection of facts, downright lying, repetition, assertion, pinpointing an enemy, appeals to authority, and glittering generalities.

Key Terms

Action-based model (p. 239)
Central route processing p. 217)
Cognitive dissonance theory (p. 228)
Credibility (p. 204)
Elaboration likelihood model (ELM) (p. 216)
Expertise (p. 204)
Flexible correction model (FCM) (p. 220)
Hedonic contingency model (p. 219)
Heuristic and systematic information-processing model (HSM) (p. 227)
Inoculation theory (p. 212)
Latitude of acceptance (p. 214)
Latitude of noncommitment (p. 214)
Latitude of rejection (p. 214)
Law of primacy (p. 211)
Multiple audience problem (p. 215)

Need for affect (NA) (p. 226)
Need for cognition (NC) (p. 225)
Peripheral route processing (p. 217)
Persuasion (p. 203)
Propaganda (p. 241)
Psychological reactance (p. 240)
Self-affirmation theory (p. 238)
Self-perception theory (p. 237)
Sleeper effect (p. 206)
Social judgment theory (p. 214)
Trustworthiness (p. 204)
Yale communication model (p. 203)

Chapter Quiz

1. The application of rational and/or emotional appeals to change attitudes or behavior is the definition of
   A. propaganda.
   B. social influence.
   C. persuasion.
   D. convincing.

2. According to the Yale communication model, the four factors affecting persuasion
   A. are independent of one another.
   B. interact to produce persuasion.
   C. are not internally mediated but, rather, directly affect behavior.
   D. operate under the control of automatic processing.

3. Communicator credibility comprises which two components?
   A. Similarity and power
   B. Liability and power
   C. Expertise and liability
   D. Expertise and trustworthiness

4. You hear a talk-show host make a statement about the budget deficit but are skeptical about what he said because he has a reputation of being inaccurate. However, 6 weeks later, you use the statement yourself. This is most likely due to which of the following?
   A. Cognitive dissonance reduction
   B. Discrepancy
   C. The sleeper effect
   D. Attitude inoculation
   E. B and C only

5. You are contemplating developing a persuasive message against drunk driving to go along with an alcohol awareness week on campus. You have read that a fear appeal is a good way to persuade people. In order to have its greatest effect, your fear appeal must do which of the following?
   A. Arouse only a little fear so that your audience will not be turned off
   B. Arouse enough fear to get your audience's attention without turning them off
   C. Arouse as much fear as possible, even if you turn off some audience members
   D. None of the above

6. According to your text, recency is most likely to occur when
   A. the communicator has low credibility.
   B. there is a delay between the two messages, and a response or assessment is made soon after the second message.
   C. the two messages follow one another closely, and there is a delay between the second message and the audience response or assessment.
   D. there is a moderate amount of discrepancy between the two messages.

7. Presenting weakened forms of opposing arguments so that your audience can generate counterarguments to them is part of
   A. inoculation theory.
   B. cognitive dissonance theory.
   C. self-perception theory.
   D. the elaboration likelihood model.

8. Which of the following was not listed as a key assumption of cognitive dissonance theory in your text?
   A. Inconsistency between attitudes or between attitudes and behavior leads to a negative motivational state.
   B. The amount of attitude change is unrelated to the magnitude of the dissonance.
   C. Individuals are motivated to reduce dissonance because it is unpleasant.
   D. Both A and B
   E. Both B and C

9. According to your text, disconfirmation of a deeply held belief often results in
   A. decreased commitment to the belief.
   B. increased commitment to the belief.
   C. no change in commitment to the belief.
   D. loss of respect for a cult's leader.

10. According to your text, characteristics of propaganda include which of the following?
    A. It prevents critical analysis of issues.
    B. It makes use of emotion.
    C. It has a vested interest in some goal.
    D. All of the above
    E. B and C only

Answers can be found in the end-of-book Answers section.

Conformity, Compliance, and Obedience

When you think of the long and gloomy history of man, you will find more hideous crimes have been committed in the name of obedience than have ever been committed in the name of rebellion.

—C. P. Snow

CHAPTER 7

Key Questions

As you read this chapter, find the answers to the following questions:

1. What is conformity?
2. What is the source of the pressures that lead to conformity?
3. What research evidence is there for conformity?
4. What factors influence conformity?
5. Do women conform more than men?
6. Can the minority ever influence the majority?
7. How does minority influence work?
8. Why do we sometimes end up doing things we would rather not do?
9. What are compliance techniques, and why do they work?
10. How can the effectiveness of the foot-in-the-door technique be increased for high-cost behaviors?
11. What do social psychologists mean by the term "obedience"?
12. How do social psychologists define evil, and are evil deeds done by evil persons?
13. What research has been done to study obedience?
14. What factors influence obedience?
15. Are there gender differences in obedience?

Source: Minerva Studio/Shutterstock.

Like December 7, 1941, when the Japanese launched their surprise attack against the naval base at Pearl Harbor, January 2020 might go down as another "date that will live in infamy" (Roosevelt, 1941). It was during this fateful month that the first cases of COVID-19 were reported in the United States. What followed was perhaps the worst worldwide virus pandemic since the Spanish Flu pandemic of 1918. As of October 2021, almost 247 million cases had been recorded, with 4.9 million deaths worldwide. In the United States, there were 46 million cases and over 760,000 deaths. Responses to the worsening pandemic varied from country to country and within the United States from state to state. At first, several voluntary measures were put in place, including social distancing, hand washing, business restrictions, and mask wearing. People were asked to maintain at least 6 feet of distance between themselves and others, to wash their hands after touching potentially contaminated surfaces, and to wear masks when around others. The hope was that these measures would slow the spread of the virus and reduce the number of cases and deaths. In short, authorities told the public that such measures would help "flatten the curve" representing cases and deaths.

As the pandemic progressed, it became clear that voluntary compliance with guidelines was not reducing cases. So, many places implemented "mask mandates" that required people to wear masks

251

16. Do Milgram's results apply to other cultures?
17. What criticisms of Milgram's experiments have been offered?
18. How does disobedience occur?

Left on our own, you might not wear a mask in public. However, when with others who are wearing a mask, you are likely to wear one.
Source: View Apart/Shutterstock.

while in public. Signs sprang up like dandelions in the spring stating that masks were required to enter grocery stores, doctor's offices, and just about every other business. Some states issued orders to restaurants that they had to close their doors or cut capacity to as low as 25%. To enforce these mandates, the governors of many states imposed fines and other penalties for those not adhering to the mandates. In some cases, these penalties seemed absurd to many.

Take, for example, the owner of the Mixed Greens Cafe in Gravesend, Brooklyn, New York. The Mixed Greens Cafe was in one of New York City's "red zones," which allowed restaurants to be open only for take-out and delivery. One day, the owner of the cafe left the door to the cafe open. There were no patrons inside the cafe when a city inspector came by and issued the owner a ticket for having the door open. The incredulous owner stated, "You're giving me a ticket because my doors are open, sir? There's nobody sitting in the restaurant. Everything is okay. You're giving me a ticket because my doors are open?" Eventually, Gravesend's district councilmember, Chaim Deutsch, intervened, and the ticket was voided. In Michigan, 13 restaurants were fined by the state health department for COVID-19 mandate violations. In 2020, Los Angeles Mayor Eric Garcetti authorized utilities to be cut off to a house because its owners held a party with a large number of guests. Stories of businesses and individuals being punished for violating mandates became more and more common as the pandemic progressed.

It was not only the government that imposed punishments for violating mandates such as the mask mandate. Another phenomenon quickly emerged called "mask shaming," which involved ordinary citizens shaming others who did not wear a mask. For example, on Staten Island, New York, a woman was chased out of a supermarket because she was not wearing a mask. Five other shoppers screamed at the shopper until she exited the building. Some of the other shoppers even followed her to the door to ensure that she actually left the supermarket (Katwala, 2020). Similar incidents were reported of individuals not wearing a mask being heckled and even beaten (Schwebke & Downey, 2021).

Despite the sometimes-draconian penalties and social pressure to adhere to mandates, there were some who did not go along. For example, on January 3, 2021, protesters who were against wearing masks streamed into a Los Angeles mall without masks. They called themselves "freedom lovers" and claimed that wearing a mask was a form of "control" (Gillespie, 2021). In another example of defiance, the co-owners of the Atilis Gym in Bellmawr, New Jersey, Ian Smith and Frank Trumbetti, defied New Jersey authorities who had ordered them to close their gym. The owners had configured their gym to maintain social distancing, instituted sanitizing protocols, and required patrons to wear masks. However, state and local authorities tried to force them to close, imposing fines totaling $1.2 million (Brown, 2020). Smith and Trumbetti refused to close because the gym was their only source of income. In July 2020, Smith and Trumbetti were even arrested and jailed for refusing to leave their gym. Eventually, the borough council voted 5-1 to revoke the gym's operating license (Duhart, 2020).

However, not all people resisted these mask mandates. In fact, most people obeyed mask mandates. In an observational study conducted in Wisconsin between June and August of 2020, researchers found that prior to the statewide mandate, around 40% of retail customers wore masks. However, after the statewide mandate, the percentage of customers with a mask rose to over 90%.

We are often influenced by what those around us do. For example, when you are seated in a classroom, you will note that most people are behaving similarly: They are taking notes and listening to the professor. In social situations, such as the classroom, the behavior of others often defines the range of appropriate behavior. This is especially true when the situation is new or ambiguous. What if, for example, the fire alarm rang while you were sitting in class? Would you immediately get up and leave, or would you look around to see what others do? Most people insist that they would get up and leave. However, experience teaches us otherwise. If your classmates were just sitting in their seats calmly, you probably would do the same. The social influence processes that operate on you in the classroom situation can also be applied to understanding why most people went along with COVID-19 mandates. In fact, psychologists pointed out that wearing a mask in public sends a powerful social signal that mask wearing is the appropriate behavior (Tuckman, 2020). According to Tuckman, wearing a mask influences the mask-wearing behavior of others.

In this chapter, we explore three types of social influence: conformity, compliance, and obedience. We ask: How does social influence sometimes cause us to do or say things that we don't necessarily like to do, such as wearing a mask? What other factors and types of situations make us more or less likely to conform? When we conform, do we always conform to the majority, or can a minority sometimes lead us to conform to their point of view? Under what conditions do we comply with or agree to a direct request? What factors lead us to obey the orders of a person in a position of authority? And finally, what factors cause some to disobey those in authority, like Smith and Trubetti, the owners of that New Jersey gym? These are some of the questions addressed in this chapter.

Conformity: Going Along with the Crowd

If left on our own, without rules or mandates, we might choose not to wear a mask in public. In fact, research shows that if mask wearing were voluntary, fewer people would express a willingness to wear a mask than if it were mandatory (Capraro & Barcelo, 2020).

conformity A social influence process that involves modifying behavior in response to real or imagined pressure from others.

However, once placed into a social context in which a majority of others are wearing masks, we feel social pressure to follow suit. Responding in this way to what others are doing is what social psychologists call *conformity*. **Conformity** occurs when we modify our behavior in response to real or imagined pressure from others. Even if nobody tells or orders you to wear a mask, the fact that others are will put subtle and not-so-subtle pressure on you to wear your mask as well.

Informational and Normative Social Influence

What is it about the social situation that can cause us to change our behavior, even if we privately feel such a behavior shift is wrong? To adequately address this question, we need to make a distinction between two kinds of social influence: informational and normative (Deutsch & Gerrard, 1955).

informational social influence Social influence that results from a person responding to information provided by others.

Sometimes we modify our behavior in response to information that we receive from others. This is known as **informational social influence**. In many social situations, other people provide important information through their actions and words. In addition to the information coming from others about wearing a mask, there were other sources of information encouraging people to wear masks. Public service announcements popped up on television, the Internet, and social media encouraging people to wear masks in public. Many of these messages contained information on the science behind how masks help prevent the spread of COVID-19. If you modify your behavior based on such new or reinterpreted information, you are responding to informational social influence. The persuasion process discussed in Chapter 6 illustrates informational social influence.

Generally, we are subject to informational social influence because we want to be accurate in our judgments. We use other people's behavior as a source of information by which to test the validity of our own behavior. We conform because we perceive that others have correct information (Campbell & Fairey, 1989). Shifts in behavior based on informational social influence result from the sharing of arguments and factual information (Kaplan & Miller, 1987). Essentially, opinion and behavior change come about via the kind of persuasion processes discussed in Chapter 6.

normative social influence Social influence in which a person changes behavior in response to pressure to conform to a norm.

norm An unwritten social rule existing either on a wide cultural level or on a smaller, situation-specific level that suggests what is appropriate behavior in a situation.

Conformity also comes about as a result of **normative social influence**. In this type of social influence situation, we modify our behavior in response to a **norm**, an unwritten social rule that suggests what constitutes appropriate behavior in a particular situation. Our behavior is guided not only by rational consideration of the issue at hand but also by the discomfort we experience when we are in disagreement with others. We are motivated to conform to norms and to the implicit expectations of others in order to gain social acceptance and to avoid appearing different or being rejected (Campbell & Fairey, 1989).

In a normative social influence situation, at least two factors are relevant. First, the input we obtain from others serves as a cue to the nature of the norm in effect at any given time (Kaplan & Miller, 1987). As noted earlier, seeing others wearing masks in public sends a clear message that wearing a mask is normative. This results in pressure to modify our own behavior to be consistent with the norm. Second, the size and unanimity of the majority convey information about the strength of the norm in effect. As we see later in the chapter, these two variables are important in determining the likelihood and amount of behavior change in a social influence situation.

Although both informational and normative social influence can exert powerful control over our behavior, their effects are different. The changes caused by informational social influence tend to be stronger and more enduring than those caused by normative social influence (Burnstein & Sentis, 1981). This is because changes caused by new information or a new interpretation of existing information may be persuasive and convincing. As we saw in Chapter 6, the opinion changes that result from persuasion are usually based on our accepting information, elaborating on it, and altering our attitudes and behavior accordingly. This type of information processing tends to produce rather stable, long-lasting change.

For normative social influence to occur, we need not be convinced that our opinion is incorrect. We respond to our perception of what we believe others want us to do.

Consequently, a change in opinion, attitude, or behavior brought about by normative pressure is often fragile. Once normative pressure eases up, we are likely to go back to our previous opinions. For example, a juror might go along with the other members of a jury but not really believe they are right. In fact, in one real jury example, a juror actually stated that he would go along with the majority but that he would "never feel right about it."

Because norms play such an important role in our behavior, and because normative social influence is so critical an element in conformity and other forms of social influence, we turn now to a more detailed discussion of these important forces.

Social Norms: The Key to Conformity

Norms play an important role in our everyday lives. These unwritten rules guide much of our social behavior. Humans seem to be predisposed to form norms—and conform to them—even in the most minimal situations. Norms exist on many levels, ranging from broad cultural norms to smaller-scale, situation-specific norms. We have cultural norms for how close we stand to another person when talking, for how men and women interact in business settings, and for the clothing we wear. We have situation-specific norms for how to behave in class or in the courtroom.

Violating norms makes us uncomfortable. We are embarrassed if we show up at a wedding reception in casual dress and find everyone else dressed formally, or if we go to tennis camp in tennis whites only to discover everyone else wearing the camp T-shirt. In general, standing out from the crowd, being the only different one, is something human beings don't like.

To get a better idea of how norms develop and how normative social influence works, imagine that you are taking part in an experiment. You are sitting in a totally dark room waiting for a point of light to appear on the wall across from where you are sitting. After the light is shone, you are asked to judge how far the light moved (in inches). In fact, unknown to you, the light is stationary and only appears to move, a phenomenon called the *autokinetic effect*. If asked to make successive judgments of the amount of movement that you perceive, what will occur? Will your judgments vary widely, or will they show some consistency? If you have to do the same task with two others, will your judgments remain independent or blend with those of the others?

These questions were asked by Sherif (1936, 1972) in his classic studies on norm formation. When participants did the task alone, Sherif found that their judgments eventually reflected some internalized standard that put a limit on their estimates of how far the light moved. That is, rather than being haphazard, individual participants showed evidence of establishing a range and norm to guide their judgments. When these participants were then placed within a group context, the individualized ranges and norms blended into a single group norm.

The results from this experiment showed that subjects who did the task alone showed a wide range of judgments (from 1 inch to 7.5 inches). But after three sessions in which the individuals judged the distance in groups, their judgments converged, producing a funnel-shaped graph. According to Sherif, this convergence shows that the group, without specific instructions to do so, developed a group norm. Interestingly, this group norm was found to persist even when the participants were brought back to do the task again a year later.

Although it is true that norms can powerfully influence behavior, they do not always do so. For example, if you perceive that you have strong social support from others for your behavior, your behavior is not as strongly guided by social norms as it would be if you perceived you had low social support (Cullum et al., 2013). Cullum et al. investigated how college students responded to social norms regarding alcohol consumption. Participants filled out measures of personal support and assessments of social norms for drinking and kept

The behavior of others often affects our behavior. For example, if your friends are all drinking alcohol, you will likely do so as well.
Source: William Perugini/ Shutterstock.

a daily diary of their alcohol consumption. Cullum et al. found that social norms for drinking had their greatest effect when participants perceived that they had low levels of social support. For participants with high levels of perceived social support, their alcohol consumption was unrelated to norms regarding drinking.

Culture also plays a role in how norms relate to behavior. On one hand, there is evidence that although norms may vary across cultures, the predisposition to adhere to social norms is common across different cultures. This is consistent with the view that norms operate in a manner similar to what is viewed within a culture as common sense (Zou et al., 2009). This view is consistent with a *different norms–same adherence* motivation account for the relationship between culture and norms (Savani et al., 2015). On the other hand, there also is a complementary *same norms–different adherence* motivation (Savani et al., 2015). Savani et al. have shown that even when a norm is common across cultures (e.g., American vs. Indian), members of the different cultures act differently with respect to those norms. According to Savani et al., these findings indicate that both the nature and content of a norm *and* a person's individual motivation are important when considering how norms and behavior relate.

Classic Studies in Conformity

The convergence of judgments shown in Sherif's study should not be surprising. The autokinetic effect is misleading, so the task was ambiguous, depending on subjective estimates of the distance traveled by a light. Individual judgments eventually converged on a group norm, demonstrating conformity. But what happens if the task is less ambiguous? Do participants still conform to a group norm? Or do they maintain their independence? These are some of the questions Solomon Asch addressed in a now-classic series of experiments (1951, 1955, 1956).

The Asch Paradigm

Imagine that you have signed up for an experiment investigating perceptual judgments. When you arrive at the lab, you find that several other participants are already present. You take the only remaining seat. You are told that the experiment involves judging the length of lines presented on a card at the front of the room. You are to look at each of three lines and decide which one matches a standard presented to the left (Figure 7.1).

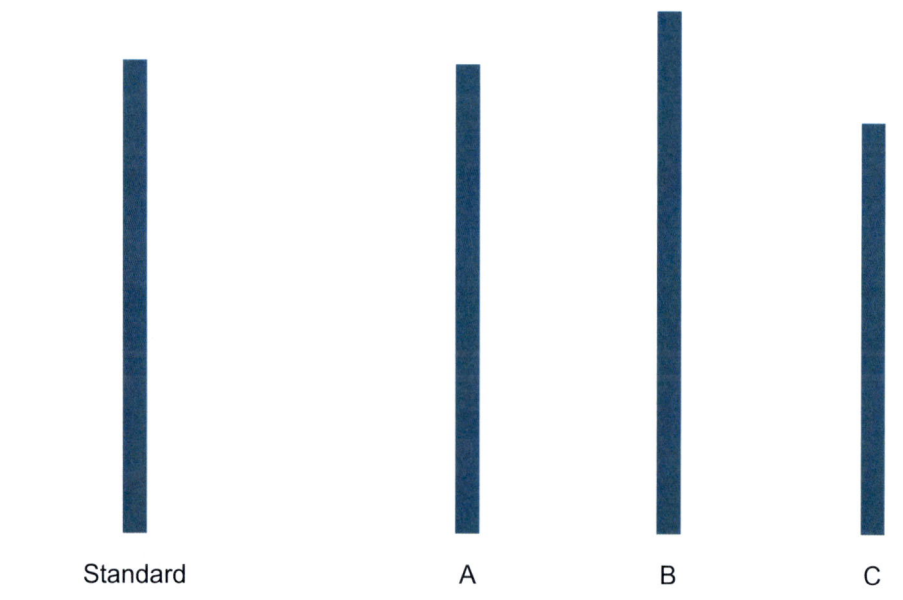

FIGURE 7.1

A line judgment task that might have been used by Asch in his conformity experiments. The participant was required to pick a line from the right that matched the standard line on the left.

The experimenter tells you that each of you will give your judgment orally one after another. Because you are in the last chair, you will give your judgment last. The experiment begins uneventfully. Each member of the group gives what you consider the correct response, and then you give your response. But soon the others begin to give answers you believe to be incorrect, and you must decide what to do. Should you give the correct answer (which is obvious) or go along with the others, who are wrong?

Before we see what happened, let's take a closer look at the Asch paradigm. The "other participants" were not really participants at all. They were confederates of the experimenter who were instructed to give incorrect answers on several "critical trials." Misinformation provided by the incorrect majority places the real participant in a dilemma. On the one hand, he has the evidence of his own senses that tells him what the correct answer is. On the other hand, he has information from the majority concerning what is correct. The participant is placed in a situation in which he must decide between these two competing sources of information. From these competing sources of information, pressure on the participant arises.

Now, when you are faced with a situation like the one created in the Asch experiments, there are two ways you can test reality to determine which line really matches the standard. You can jump up, whip out your pocket measuring tape, rush to the front of the room, and measure the lines. This is directly testing your perceptions against reality. However, you probably won't do this, because it will violate your sense of the operative social norm—how you should act in this situation. The other way is to test the accuracy of your perceptions against those of others through a *social comparison* process (Festinger, 1954). Asch's paradigm strongly favors doing the latter. Given that participants in these experiments probably will not measure the lines, what do they do about the conflict between information from their own senses and information from the majority?

Conformity in the Asch Experiments Asch's experimental paradigm placed the participant's own perceptions into conflict with the opinions of a unanimous majority advocating a clearly incorrect judgment. When confronted with the incorrect majority, Asch's participants made errors in the direction of the incorrect majority on over 33% of the critical trials. Therefore, Asch showed a conformity rate of 33% on his line-judgment task. Almost all participants knew the correct answer. When they did the same task alone, the error rate (mismatching the line with the standard) was 7.4%, one-fourth the error rate when other participants were present. Yet many changed their opinions to be in conformity with the group judgment. So, even with a simple perceptual task, an individual may abandon his or her own judgment and go with the majority. Why would we do this? As we see next, there are different reasons why people conform or remain independent.

Paths to Conformity and Independence Based on his results and interviews with participants, Asch classified them as either yielding (conforming) or independent (nonconforming) (Asch, 1951). Of the yielding participants, some (but relatively few) gave in completely to the majority. These participants experienced *distortion of perception* and saw the majority judgments as correct. They appeared to believe that the incorrect line was actually the correct one. The largest group of yielding participants displayed *distortion of judgment.* These participants yielded because they lacked confidence in their own judgments—"I'm not sure anymore." Without such confidence, they were not able to stick with their own perceptions and remain independent. Finally, some yielding participants experienced *distortion of action.* Here, participants knew that the majority was wrong but conformed so that they did not appear different to the other participants—"I'll go along" (Figure 7.2). Interestingly, there was a remarkable consistency among yielding participants. Once bound to the majority, they stayed on the path of conformity.

Of the independent participants, about 25% remained totally independent, never agreeing with the incorrect majority (Asch, 1955). These participants had a great deal of confidence in their own judgments and withstood the pressure from the majority completely. Other independent participants remained so because they felt a great need to remain

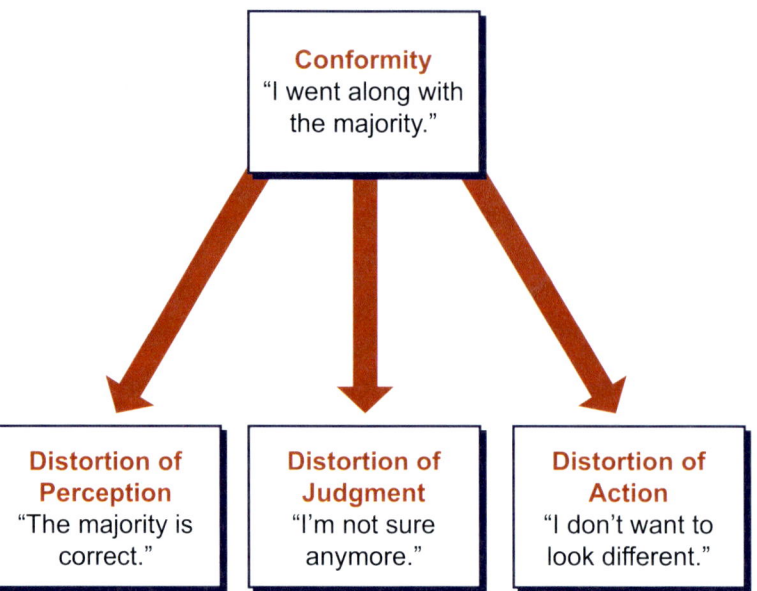

FIGURE 7.2

Based on postexperimental interviews, Asch determined that there was no one path to conformity. Different participants conformed for different reasons.

self-reliant; still others remained independent because they wanted to do well on the task. Individuals who have a strong *need for uniqueness* tend to be highly resistant to majority influence and are unlikely to conform (Imhoff & Erb, 2009).

Asch's interviews tell us that there are many paths to conformity or independence. Some participants remain independent because they trust their own senses, whereas others remain independent because they feel a great need to do so. These latter participants appear to remain independent because of *psychological reactance* (Brehm, 1966). As described in Chapter 6, psychological reactance occurs when individuals feel that their freedom of choice or action is threatened because other people are forcing them to do or say things (Brehm & Brehm, 1981). To reestablish independence, they reject the majority's pressure and go their own way. Even when individuals choose to remain independent, however, they still feel the pressure the incorrect majority exerts. In fact, resisting a majority and remaining independent leads to higher levels of autonomic arousal than conforming (Hatcher et al., 2018). Resisting the pressure of the majority is not easy. Independent participants can withstand that pressure and stick with their own perceptions.

How Does Social Influence Bring About Conformity?

What is it about social influence situations that causes conformity? When your opinion is different from that of a unanimous majority, you are faced with a dilemma. On the one hand, your senses (or belief system) suggest one thing; on the other, the social situation (the majority) suggests something quite different. Placed in such a situation, you experience conflict, which is psychologically uncomfortable (Moscovici, 1985). When you grapple with this conflict, your tendency is to pay attention to the views of the majority. Once the majority influence is removed, however, attention is focused back on the stimulus (e.g., the judgment of lines in the Asch studies). Once majority influence is removed, you will return to your previous judgments (Moscovici, 1985).

The effects of dividing attention between the majority and the stimulus were demonstrated in a study in which participants were asked to judge how similar two noises were in volume (Tesser et al., 1983). Participants performed this task under conditions of high social pressure, when three members of a majority disagreed with the participant's evaluation of the noise, or under conditions of low social pressure, when only one person disagreed. Under high social pressure, participants responded by either attending very little or attending a great deal to the stimulus to be judged. Under low social pressure, participants paid a moderate amount of attention to the stimulus.

Researchers speculated that high social pressure would lead to high levels of arousal. This arousal is due to the competing tendencies to pay attention both to the stimulus and to the source of social influence, other people. The net result is that a person will default to his or her dominant way of behaving. Those who have a strong tendency to conform may resolve the conflict by adopting the view of the majority. Others less prone to the effects of social influence may increase their attention to the stimulus as a way to resolve the conflict. By focusing on the stimulus, they take their minds off the social pressure. Some participants in the Asch studies actually put their hands over their ears or eyes so that they did not hear or see what other people said. This was the only way they could resist conforming.

Another way to approach this question is to examine the effects of consensus, or agreement with others, on our perceptions and behavior. Attitudes and behavior that are in line with those of others are a powerful source of social reinforcement. We like it when our attitudes and behaviors are verified. The perception that our beliefs have social support is related to higher levels of self-esteem (Goodwin et al., 2004). Additionally, we are quicker to express an attitude that has consensual support than one that flies in the face of the majority. This is known as the *minority slowness* effect (Bassili, 2003). The larger the majority, the faster we will be willing to express a view that is in line with that majority (Bassili, 2003). It matters little whether the attitudes are important to us (e.g., political attitudes) or less important (e.g., foods we like); we are slower to express attitudes that deviate from the majority than those that do not (Bassili, 2003).

It is well known that we tend to match our attitudes and behaviors to those of others (Prentice & Miller, 1993). Social norms, once they become popular, take on a life of their own and become "self-replicating" (Conway & Schaller, 2005). Conway and Schaller offer two explanations for the influence of consensus on behavior. First is just plain-old conformity rooted in our desire not to be different from others, as demonstrated by the Asch experiments. Second, the attitudes and behaviors of others provide us with important information about the world and supply "social proof" for the consensually accepted beliefs. In other words, we tend to flock to attitudes and behaviors that are widely accepted. So, not only are we repulsed by being an outcast among our peers, we are attracted to those who hold beliefs with which we agree.

Conformity also relates to the level of confidence expressed by the agent of influence (Goodwin et al., 2013; Horry et al., 2012). Researchers have investigated this using a *memory conformity* task. In the memory conformity task, participants are exposed to a confederate of the experimenter who provides misinformation to the participant. Researchers then measure the degree to which the participant's memory is affected by the incorrect information provided by the confederate. In one experiment, Goodwin et al. had the confederate express either high or low confidence in the misinformation provided. They found that misinformation provided by a highly confident confederate had more influence on a participant's memory than the same misinformation provided by a less confident confederate. Horry et al. found that misinformation from a highly credible confederate had more influence than the same misinformation provided by a low-credibility confederate. The interesting thing about the findings of Horry et al. was that they occurred when participants indicated their responses privately. Although these two studies were not conformity studies in the same sense as Asch's studies, they do suggest that the nature of the source of incorrect information affects judgments.

The perceived competence of the majority also affects conformity. Imagine that you are in a group working on a math problem and the other group members are all experts in math. Would you conform more to this majority than if the other group members were bad at math? Research shows that when you find yourself with a high-competence majority (e.g., math experts), you are more likely to conform than if you find yourself in a low-competence majority, regardless of your own perceived competence (Costanzo et al., 1968). Additionally, if you perceive yourself as highly competent at a task, you conform less than if you perceive yourself as less competent, regardless of the competence of

The ideology of the majority affects conformity. Exposure to views with which you agree from majority members whom you dislike ideologically actually leads to an anti-conformity effect.
Source: Photographee.eu/Shutterstock.

the majority. So, it appears that majority and minority competence operate independently from each other (Costanzo et al., 1968).

In addition to the competence of the majority, the political ideology of the majority also affects conformity. In one experiment, devout Catholics were exposed to either socially conservative or progressive views from other devout Catholics (in-group members) or conservative views from conservative Evangelicals (out-group members). Other participants (control group) were not exposed to the views of others of either ideology. The results showed that the Catholics who were exposed to progressive views from other Catholics expressed similar progressive views later on. However, exposure to conservative views from the Evangelicals that were in line with their own values resulted in the expression of more *progressive* views (Suhay, 2015). So, exposure to views with which you agree from someone you dislike ideologically actually leads to an anticonformity effect!

In an imaginative experiment, Beckner et al. (2016) had participants engage in an Asch-type conformity experiment in which the majority was composed of either other humans or robots (or no majority). The task used was a language conformity task in which the majority used particular morphological forms of verbs. Beckner et al. measured whether participants in the conformity groups used the same forms of the verbs as the members of the majority. Beckner et al. found that the participants conformed only to the human majority, but not the robot majority. Apparently, we don't care what robots think of us!

Finally, recent neuroscience research provides some insight into the mechanisms that underlie conformity. Schnuerch and Gibbons (2014) reviewed a number of studies of the relationship between brain function and conformity. They found that evidence from these studies suggests that conformity is related to activation of the posterior medial frontal cortex and ventral striatum areas of the brain. According to Schnuerch and Gibbons, these areas of the brain are involved in the processes of reinforcement and learning. They suggest that disagreeing with others provides a strong signal that social punishment is coming our way. Conversely, agreement with others signals that social reinforcement or reward is forthcoming. These mechanisms might explain why we don't conform to information provided by robots. We do not expect social rewards to come from machines but do expect them from other humans.

Study Break

The previous sections introduced you to the definition of conformity and the classic research in the area. Before you go on, answer the following questions:

1. What is the definition of conformity?
2. What roles do norms play in bringing about conformity?
3. How did Solomon Asch study conformity, and what did he find?
4. Describe the different pathways to conformity (yielding) and independence.
5. How does social influence bring about conformity?

Different Forms of Conformity

Conformity effects are well established in social psychology. However, some researchers have questioned whether different forms of conformity effects exist (Claidière et al., 2014, 2012). For example, Claidière et al. (2012) define three forms of conformity. *Weak conformity* occurs when a person performs a behavior displayed by a majority that is weaker than the majority's behavior. *Linear conformity* occurs when a person performs a behavior displayed by a majority that is at the same level as the majority's behavior.

Hyper-conformity occurs when a person performs a behavior displayed by a majority that is stronger than the majority's behavior. Which one of these forms of conformity is most prevalent?

In one experiment (Claidière et al., 2012), visitors to a zoo were given the opportunity to comment on an exhibit on index cards. They could do this by answering questions about the exhibit using text (writing an answer) or drawing a picture. At the exhibit was a wall on which others had posted their answers. Claidière et al. manipulated the proportion of the text appearing on the posted cards (0%, 25%, 50%, 75%, 100%). Claidière et al. measured the answers provided by the patrons (text only, drawings only, mainly text, and mainly drawing). The results of this experiment (shown in Figure 7.3) provided evidence for both linear and weak conformity effects. The "text only" results provide support for a strong linear effect. Notice how the bars for "text only" show a marked and consistent increase for text on the card as the percentage of text on the cards on the wall increased. The bars for the "drawing only" condition provide weaker evidence for a weak conformity effect. No evidence was found for a hyper-conformity effect. In a similar experiment (Claidière et al., 2014), evidence was again found for a linear conformity effect. However, some evidence was found for hyper-conformity. It appears, then, that the strongest conformity effect is a linear one with a weaker tendency toward weak conformity or hyper-conformity, depending on the situation.

Factors That Affect Conformity

We have established that the opinions of others can alter our behavior. However, we have not yet explored how variables such as the nature of the task, the size of the majority, and the effect of one other person in agreement work to affect conformity. Next, we explore several variables relating to the amount of conformity observed in social influence situations.

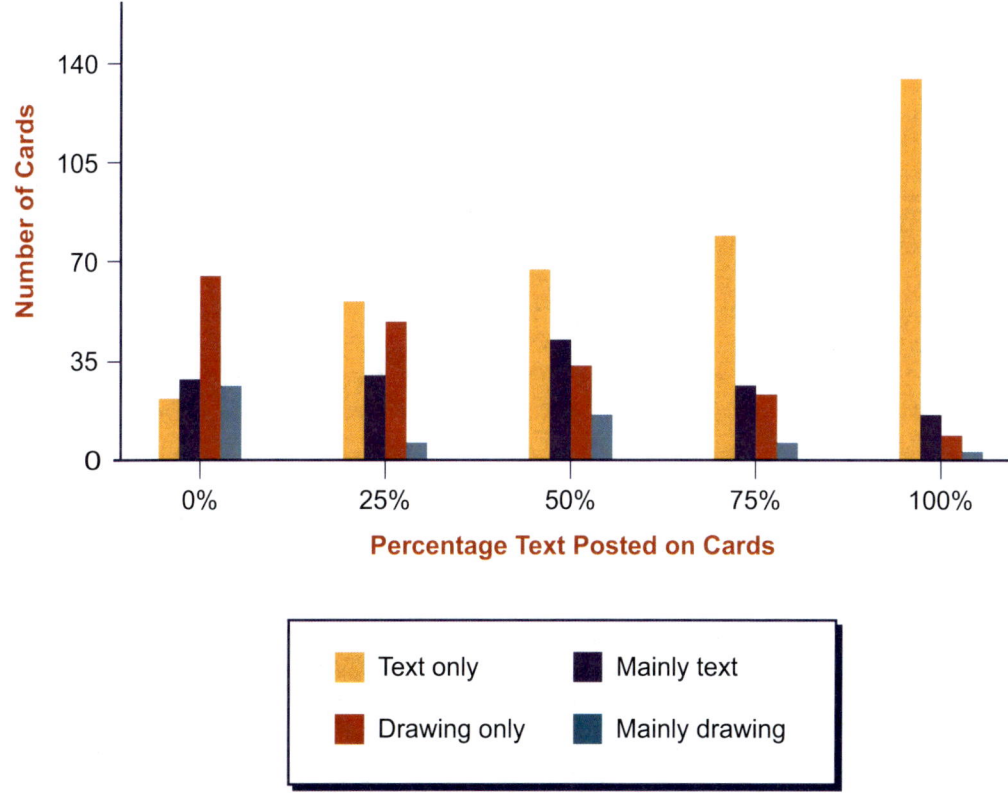

FIGURE 7.3

Results from Claidière et al. (2012) showing the nature of the answers on comment cards.
Based on data from Claidière et al. (2012).

Nature of the Task

The first variable that can affect the amount of conformity observed relates to the task itself. One variable affecting conformity rates is the ambiguity of the task. As the task facing the individual becomes more ambiguous (i.e., less obvious), the amount of conformity increases (Crutchfield, 1955). Asch's task was a simple one, involving the judgment of the length of lines, and produced a conformity rate of about 33%. Conformity research conducted with more ambiguous stimuli shows even higher levels of conformity. For example, Sherif's (1936) experiment on norm formation using the autokinetic effect (an extremely ambiguous task) found conformity rates of about 70%.

Other research involving attitudinal issues with no clear right or wrong answer produced conformity rates similar to Sherif's. In one study, highly independent professionals such as army officers and expert engineers were led to believe that other professionals had answered an opinion item differently than they had (Crutchfield, 1955). For example, colonels in the army were told that other colonels had agreed with the item "I often doubt that I would make a good leader." Now, this is blasphemy for army officers, who are trained to lead. Yet when faced with a false majority, 70% of the officers said they agreed with that item. Privately, they disagreed strongly.

The type of task faced by a group may also determine the type of social influence (informational or normative) that comes into play. For example, informational social influence should be strongest when participants face an *intellective issue,* in which they can use factual information to arrive at a clearly correct answer (Kaplan & Miller, 1987). Normative social influence should be more crucial on a *judgmental issue*. A judgmental issue is based on moral or ethical principles, where there are no clear-cut right or wrong answers. Therefore, resolution of the issue depends on opinion, not fact. In a jury simulation study investigating the use of informational and normative social influence, Kaplan and Miller (1987) impanelled six-person juries to judge a civil lawsuit. The juries were required to award the plaintiff compensatory damages and punitive damages. Compensatory damages are awarded to reimburse the plaintiff for suffering and losses due to the defendant's behavior. Generally, awarding compensatory damages is a fact-based intellective task. If, for example, your lawn mower blows up because the No Pain, No Gain Lawn Mower Company put the gas tank in the wrong place, it is easy for the jury to add up the cost of the mower plus whatever medical costs were incurred. Punitive damages, on the other hand, are awarded to deter the defendant from repeating such actions in the future. The issue of awarding punitive damages is a judgmental task. How much should you punish the manufacturer so that it ceases making mowers that blow up?

The results of the study indicated that juries doing an intellective task (awarding compensatory damages) were more likely to use informational social influence than normative social influence. When the task has a clear standard, then it is the information that majority members can bring forth that convinces other jurors. Juries doing a judgmental task, on the other hand, were more likely to use normative influence. Where there is no clear-cut answer, the jurors in the majority try to convince the minority to agree by pressuring them to conform to the group (majority) decision.

The Size of the Majority

The size of the majority also affects conformity rates. As the size of the majority increases, so does conformity, up to a point (Asch, 1951, 1956; Milgram et al., 1969). Generally, as shown in Figure 7.4, there is a nonlinear relationship between the size of the majority and conformity. That is, majority influence significantly increases until some critical majority size is reached. After that, the addition of more majority members does not significantly increase conformity. For example, Milgram and colleagues (1969) found that increasing the number of individuals (confederates of the experimenter) on a sidewalk who looked upward toward the sky increased conformity (the percentage of passersby looking upward) up to a majority size of five and then leveled off (see Figure 7.4).

There is no absolute critical size of a majority after which addition of majority members does not significantly increase conformity. Milgram and colleagues found that

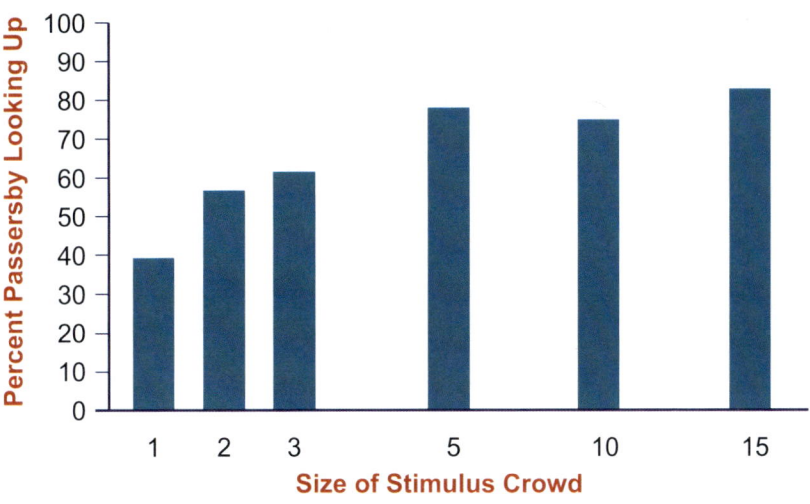

FIGURE 7.4

The effect of majority size on conformity. Conformity initially increases but eventually levels off. Adapted from Milgram et al. (1969).

conformity leveled off after a majority size of five. Asch (1951), using his line-judgment task, found that conformity leveled off after a majority size of three. Regardless of the critical size of the majority, the general nonlinear relationship between majority size and conformity is firmly established.

Why does conformity level off after some critical majority size? Two explanations have been suggested (Baron et al., 1992). First, as majority members are added beyond the critical point, the individual in the conformity situation might suspect that the additional majority members are going along to avoid making trouble in the group. If the individual conformer perceives this to be the motive for joining the majority, the power of the additional majority members is reduced. Second, as the size of the majority grows, each new majority member is probably noticed less. That is, the individual is more likely to notice a third person added to a majority of two than to notice a tenth person added to a majority of nine.

Increases in the size of a majority are most likely to produce increased conformity in normative social influence situations, when the situation causes us to question our perceptions and judgments (Campbell & Fairey, 1989). When a majority is arrayed against us, and we cannot obtain adequate information about the stimuli that we are to judge, we conform. This is exactly what happened in Asch's experiment.

When you know you are right and the rest of the group is wrong, more conformity results when the majority comprises three members than if it comprises only one (Campbell & Fairey, 1989). This makes sense because it is normative influence that is operating in this situation. But what if you are not certain whether the majority is right or wrong? In this case, you search for information that could inform your decision, information that will help you make the right choice. It is informational influence that counts here. Just a few people, perhaps even one person, can convince you through informational social influence if their information is persuasive (Campbell & Fairey, 1989).

Having a True Partner

Often the changes caused by the forces producing conformity are fragile and easily disrupted. This is the case when we find that there is another person who supports our perceptions and

You are less likely to conform when you have a true partner that supports you. For example, you are more likely to dress casually for a formal occasion when another person also dresses casually.
Source: Serge Gorenko/Shutterstock.

actions in a given social situation. Imagine, for example, that you have been invited to a black-tie wedding reception at a posh country club on a Saturday night. When an invitation specifies black-tie, the norm is for men to wear tuxedos and women to wear formal dresses. Now, suppose that you don't want to dress so formally but feel you should because everyone else will (normative social influence). But then suppose that you speak to a friend who is also attending and who also doesn't want to wear a tuxedo or a formal dress. The two of you agree to wear less-formal attire, and you feel comfortable with your decision. The next weekend, you are invited to another black-tie party, but this time your friend is not attending. What will you do this time? You decide to dress formally.

true partner effect
The phenomenon whereby an individual's tendency to conform to a majority position is reduced if there is one other person who supports the nonconforming individual's position.

This example illustrates an important social psychological phenomenon. The **true partner effect** occurs when we perceive that there is someone who supports our position; we are then less likely to conform than if we are alone facing a unanimous majority. This effect was first demonstrated empirically by Asch (1951). In one variation of his experiment, Asch had a true partner emerge at some point during his conformity experiment. On a given trial, the true partner would break with the incorrect majority and support the real participant's judgments. The results of this manipulation were striking: Conformity was cut by nearly 80%! As in the example of the black-tie parties, when we have a true partner, we are better able to withstand the strong forces of normative social influence.

Why does this occur? There are many possible explanations. For example, when we violate a norm by ourselves, we draw attention to ourselves as deviant. Recall that some of Asch's participants conformed because they did not want to appear different. Apparently, it makes us very uncomfortable to be perceived by others as different. When we have a true partner, we can diffuse the pressure by convincing ourselves that we are not the only ones breaking a norm.

Another explanation for the true partner effect draws on the social comparison process (Festinger, 1954; Kruglanski & Mayseless, 1990). As discussed in Chapter 2, social comparison theory proposes that we compare our thoughts, beliefs, and actions with those of others to find out if we are in agreement. When we find that we agree, we feel validated; it is rewarding when we receive such confirmation. Our confidence in our beliefs increases because they are shared with others.

Think back to the second black-tie party. Without a true partner, you bring your behavior into line with the norm in effect: wearing formal attire. Asch (1951) found the very same thing when he had the true partner withdraw his support of the participant. When the participant was abandoned, his conformity went back up to its previous level.

Gender and Conformity

Besides investigating situational forces that affect conformity, social psychologists have investigated how individual characteristics affect conformity. There is some evidence that women conform more than men and that women are less confident in their judgments in the face of a majority (Shiomi & Hagita, 2019). However, there does not appear to be a consistent gender difference. For example, 43% of the studies published before 1970 reported this phenomenon, in contrast to only 21% published after 1970. Did changes in the cultural climate make women less likely to conform? Or did early conformity studies have a male bias, as expressed in male-oriented tasks and a predominantly male environment? Research indicates that the nature of the task was not important in producing the observed gender differences, but the gender of the experimenter was. Generally, larger gender differences are found when a man runs the conformity experiment. No gender differences are found when a woman runs the experiment (Eagly & Carli, 1981).

An analysis of the research also shows that there are conditions under which women are more likely to conform than men and others under which men are more likely to conform than women (Eagly & Chrvala, 1986). For example, women are more likely to conform than men in group pressure situations—that is, under conditions of normative social influence—than in persuasion situations, where informational social influence is being applied (Eagly, 1978; Eagly & Carli, 1981).

Two explanations have been proposed for gender differences in conformity (Eagly, 1987). First, gender may serve as a status variable in newly formed groups. Traditionally, the female gender role is seen as weaker than the male role. In everyday life, males are more likely to hold positions of high status and power than women. Men are more likely to be in the position of "influencer" and women in the position of "influencee." The lower status of the female role may contribute to a greater predisposition to conform on the part of women, especially in group pressure situations. Second, women tend to be more sensitive than men to conformity pressures when their behavior is under surveillance—that is, when they have to state their opinions publicly (Eagly et al., 1981). When women must make their opinions public, they are more likely than men to conform. In the Asch paradigm, participants were required to state their opinions publicly; this favors women conforming more than men.

Increasing use of the Internet for social purposes has led researchers to question whether conformity effects can be demonstrated on the Internet. Research shows that conformity effects do occur in the online environment (Cinnirella & Green, 2007; Rosander & Eriksson, 2012; Wijenayake et al., 2020). Rosander and Eriksson looked at whether men or women conformed more on an Internet conformity task. They found a trend (marginally significant statistically) indicating that men conform more than women in the online environment. Of course, more research is needed before we can be confident that this gender difference is reliable.

Historical and Cultural Differences in Conformity

Asch conducted his classic experiment on conformity during the 1950s in the United States. The sociocultural climate that existed at the time favored conformity. The country was still under the influence of "McCarthyism," which questioned individuals who did not conform to "normal" American ideals. This climate may have contributed in significant ways to the levels of conformity Asch observed (Larsen, 1982; Perrin & Spencer, 1981). Researchers working in England failed to obtain conformity effects as strong as those Asch had obtained (Perrin & Spencer, 1981). This raised a question: Were the Asch findings limited to a particular time and culture?

Unfortunately, this question has no simple answer. Evidence suggests that within the United States, rates of conformity vary with the sociopolitical climate (Larsen, 1974, 1982). The conformity rate in the early 1970s was 62.5% (that is, 62.5% of participants conformed at least once in an Asch-type experiment) compared to a rate of 78.9% during the early 1980s (Larsen, 1982). Compare this to Asch's (1956) rate of 76.5%. Results like these suggest that conformity rates may be tied to the cultural climate in force at the time of a study.

Within the United States, there are regional differences in conformity. Varnum (2012) reviewed 91 conformity studies from 21 states. The states were grouped into five categories: Northeast (e.g., New Jersey and New York), Southeast (e.g., Georgia and Florida), Midwest (e.g., Ohio and Indiana), Southwest (Oklahoma and Texas), and Frontier (e.g., Montana and Oregon). Varnum found that conformity effects were significantly weaker in the Frontier states than in any other region of the country. According to Varnum, the sociocultural climate in the Frontier states has a stronger bias toward nonconformity than in other states, resulting in a weaker predisposition to conform. Varnum found further support for the sociocultural effect on conformity in the fact that conformity effects were stronger in states with a higher rate of popular baby names (especially for girls' names).

The evidence for cross-cultural influences is less clear. A host of studies suggest that conformity is a fairly general phenomenon across cultures. Conformity has been demonstrated in European countries such as Belgium, Holland, and Norway (Doms & Van Avermaet, 1980; Milgram, 1961; Vlaander & van Rooijen, 1985) as well as in non-Western countries such as Japan, China, and some South American countries (Huang & Harris, 1973; Matsuda, 1985; Sistrunk & Clement, 1970). Additionally, some research suggests that there may be cross-cultural differences in conformity when North Americans are compared to non–North Americans (see Furnham, 1984, for a review) and across other non–North American cultures (Milgram, 1961). Differences in conformity in Asian cultures (Korean versus Japanese) have also been found (Park et al., 2003).

What is the bottom line? It is safe to say that the Asch conformity effect is fairly general across cultures. However, some cultural groups may conform at different levels than others. It also seems evident that cultural groups should not be seen as being uniform in conformity. Conformity also appears to fluctuate in size across time within a culture.

Study Break

The previous sections discussed a number of factors that can affect conformity levels. Before you begin the next section, answer the following questions:

1. How does the nature of the task influence conformity?
2. What is the relationship between majority size and conformity?
3. What is the true partner effect, and how does it relate to conformity?
4. What is the relationship between gender and conformity?
5. How do sociopolitical climate and culture relate to conformity?

Minority Influence

In the classic film *Twelve Angry Men,* Henry Fonda portrayed a juror who was firmly convinced that a criminal defendant was not guilty. The only problem was that the other 11 jurors believed the defendant was guilty. As the jurors began to deliberate, Fonda held fast to his belief in the defendant's innocence. As the film progressed, Fonda convinced each of the other 11 jurors that the defendant was innocent. The jury finally returned a verdict of not guilty.

In this fictional portrayal of a group at work, a single unwavering individual not only was able to resist conformity pressure but also convinced the majority that they were wrong. Such an occurrence would be extremely rare in a real trial (Kalven & Zeisel, 1966). With an 11 to 1 split, the jury would almost always go in the direction of the majority (Isenberg, 1986; Kalven & Zeisel, 1966). The film, however, does raise an interesting question: Can a steadfast minority bring about change in the majority? For almost 35 years after Sherif's original experiments on norm formation, this question went unanswered. It was not until 1969 that social psychologists began to investigate the influence of the minority on the majority. This line of investigation has been pursued more by European social psychologists than American social psychologists.

Can a Minority Influence the Majority?

In the first published experiment on minority influence, researchers devised an Asch-like conformity situation. Participants were led to believe that they were taking part in a study on color perception (Moscovici et al., 1969). Participants were shown a series of slides and asked to say the color of the slide aloud. Unbeknownst to the real participants (four, making up the majority), two confederates (comprising the minority) had been instructed to make an error on certain trials—by calling a blue slide green, for example. Researchers found that 8.42% of the judgments made by the real participants were in the direction of the minority, compared to only .025% of the judgments in a control condition in which there was no incorrect minority. In fact, 32% of the participants conformed to the incorrect minority. Thus, a minority can have a surprisingly powerful effect on the majority.

In this experiment, the minority participants were consistent in their judgments. Researchers theorized that consistency of behavior is a strong determinant of the social influence a minority can exert on a majority (Moscovici et al., 1969). An individual in a minority who expresses a deviant opinion consistently may be seen as having a high degree of confidence in his or her judgments. In the color perception experiment, majority participants rated minority members as more confident in their judgments than

A minority in a group is someone whose views differ from the majority. Research shows a minority can influence a majority under the right conditions.
Source: Rawpixel.com/Shutterstock.

themselves. The consistent minority caused the majority to call into question the validity of their own judgments.

What is it about consistency that contributes to the power of a minority to influence a majority? Differing perceptions and attributions made about consistent and inconsistent minorities are important factors. A consistent minority is usually perceived as being more confident and less willing to compromise than an inconsistent minority (Wolf, 1979). A consistent minority may also be perceived as having high levels of competence, especially if it is a relatively large minority (Nemeth, 1986). Generally, we assume that if a number of people share a point of view, it must be correct. As the size of the minority increases, so does perceived competence (Nemeth, 1986).

Although research shows that consistency increases the power of a minority to influence a majority, consistency must be carefully defined. Will a minority that adopts a particular view and remains intransigent be as persuasive as one that is more flexible? Two styles of consistency have been distinguished: rigid and negotiating (Mugny, 1975). In the rigid style, the minority advocates a position that is counter to the norm adopted by the majority but is unwilling to show flexibility. In the negotiating style, the minority, although remaining consistent, shows a willingness to be flexible. Each of these styles contributes to the minority's image in the eyes of the majority (Mugny, 1975). The rigid minority is perceived in a less positive way than a negotiating minority, perhaps leading to perceptions that the rigid minority's goal is to block the majority. Conversely, the negotiating minority may be perceived as having compromise as its goal.

Generally, research suggests that a more flexible minority has more power to influence the majority than a rigid one, as long as the perception of minority consistency remains (Mugny, 1975; Nemeth et al., 1974). The perception of the minority is also partially dependent on the degree to which it is willing to modify its position in response to new information. A minority that adapts to new information is more influential than a minority that holds a position irrespective of any additional information (Nemeth et al., 1974).

A minority also has more power to influence the majority when the majority knows that people have switched to the minority viewpoint. The effect, however, leveled off after three defections from the majority (Clark, 1999). Clark concluded that minority influence depended on the quality of the arguments they made against the majority viewpoint and the number of majority defections. In a later experiment, Clark (2001) employed the "12 angry men paradigm" to further test this effect. In the 12 angry men paradigm, jurors are exposed to arguments opposing a majority verdict by either a single minority juror, or by multiple jurors, some of whom were members of the majority. Clark found that minority influence increased when the original dissenting minority member was joined by a member of the majority.

Another interesting aspect of minority influence is that a minority is more likely to voice a dissenting view when minority members are anonymous (e.g., via computer) compared to face-to-face communication (McLeod et al., 1997). Interestingly, however, a minority has more power to influence a majority in face-to-face communication. Ironically, then, those media that enhance the likelihood of a minority voicing a dissenting opinion also decrease the ability of the minority to influence the majority (McLeod et al., 1997). In another ironic twist, the degree to which a majority will carefully process a persuasive message of the minority is inversely related to the size of the minority. The smaller the minority, the more likely it is that the majority will carefully process the minority's message (Martin et al., 2002). A majority only needs a 50% split to gain compliance from a minority (Martin et al., 2002).

Majority and Minority Influence: Two Processes or One?

Social influence, as we have seen, operates in two directions: from majority to minority and from minority to majority. The discovery of minority influence raised an issue concerning the underlying social psychological processes controlling majority and minority influence. Do two different processes control majority and minority influence, or is there a single process controlling both?

The Two-Process Model

Judgments expressed by a minority may be more likely to make people think about the arguments raised (Moscovici, 1980). This suggests that two different processes operate: majority influence, which occurs almost exclusively on a public level, and minority influence, which seems to operate on a private level. Majority influence, according to the two-process approach, operates through the application of pressure. People agree with a majority because of public pressure, but often they really don't accept the majority's view on a private level. The fact that the majority exerts great psychological pressure is reflected in the finding that people feel very anxious when they find themselves in disagreement with the majority (Asch, 1956; Nemeth, 1986). However, as soon as majority pressure is removed, people return to their original beliefs. Majority influence, in this model, is like normative influence—it does not necessarily have a lasting effect.

Minority influence, according to the two-process approach, operates by making people think more deeply about the minority's position and consider a wider range of options (Nemeth, 1986). In doing so, they evaluate all the aspects of the minority view. This type of thinking is known as divergent thinking. On the other hand, majority influence leads to convergent thinking, where the group narrows its focus and settles on the majority's point of view (Nemeth, 1986). The bottom line is that with minority influence, majority members adopt the minority position because they are converted to its position (Nemeth, 1992). Minority influence is like informational influence. The character played by Henry Fonda in *Twelve Angry Men* convinced the majority members to change their votes through informational social influence. Thus, Fonda changed the minds of the other jurors by applying persuasive informational arguments.

A Single-Process Model: Social Impact Theory

The dual-process model suggests that there are different psychological processes underlying majority and minority influence. A competing view, the single-process approach to social influence, suggests that one psychological process accounts for both majority and minority influence. The first theory designed to explain majority and minority influence with a single underlying process was proposed by Latané (Latané, 1981; Latané & Wolf, 1981). Latané's **social impact theory** suggests that social influence processes are the result of the interaction between the strength, immediacy, and number of influence sources. This model can be summed up by the formula:

$$\text{Influence} = f(SIN)$$

where S represents the strength of the source of the influence, I represents the immediacy (or closeness) of the source of influence, and N represents the number of influence sources.

social impact theory A theory stating that social influence is a function of the combination of the strength, immediacy, and number of influence sources.

Latané (1981) suggested an analogy between the effect of social influence and the effect of light bulbs. If, for example, you have a bulb of a certain strength (e.g., 50 watts) and place it 10 feet from a wall, it will cast light of a given intensity against the wall. If you move the bulb closer to the wall (immediacy), the intensity of the light on the wall increases. Moving it farther from the wall decreases the intensity. Increasing or decreasing the wattage of the bulb (the strength of the source) also changes the intensity of the light cast on the wall. Finally, if you add a second bulb (number), the intensity of light will increase. Similarly, the amount of social influence increases if the strength of a source of influence is increased (e.g., if the source's credibility is enhanced), if the source's immediacy is increased, or if the number of influence sources is increased.

Latané also suggested that there is a nonlinear relationship between the number of sources and the amount of influence. According to Latané, adding a second influence source to a solitary source will have greater impact than adding the 101st source to 100 sources. Social impact theory predicts that influence increases rapidly between zero and three sources and then diminishes beyond that point, which is consistent with the research on the effects of majority size.

Social impact theory can be used to account for both minority and majority influence processes. In a minority influence situation, social influence forces operate on both the minority and majority, pulling each other toward the other's position (Latané, 1981). Latané suggested that minority influence will depend on the strength, immediacy, and number of influence sources in the minority, just as in majority influence. Thus, a minority of two should have greater influence on the majority than a minority of one, a prediction that has received empirical support (Arbuthnot & Wayner, 1982; Moscovici & Lage, 1976).

An experiment by Hart et al. (1999) provides support for the social impact explanation for minority influence. In their experiment, Hart et al. varied the strength of the minority source (high or low) and the physical distance between the minority member and majority (near or far). The results showed that in the "near" condition the high- and low-strength minority had equivalent levels of influence. However, in the "far" condition, the low-strength source had little influence, whereas the high-strength minority had a strong influence. So, two factors included in social impact theory affect the amount of minority influence.

Although there is still a measure of disagreement over the exact mechanisms underlying minority influence, it is fair to say that there is more support for the single-process model. However, there is also evidence supporting the dual-process model.

Study Break

The preceding section discussed how a minority in a group can bring about change in the majority. Before you go on to the next section, answer the following questions:

1. What are the factors that increase the likelihood that a minority will change majority opinion?
2. Describe how the two-process model operates in minority and majority influence.
3. What are divergent and convergent thinking, and how do they relate to minority and majority influence?
4. What is the single-process model, and how does it account for majority and minority influence?

Compliance: Responding to a Direct Request

Compliance occurs when you modify your behavior in response to a direct request from another person. In compliance situations, the person making the request has no power to force you to do as he or she asks. For example, your neighbor can ask that you move your car so that she can back a truck into her driveway. However, assuming your car is legally

compliance Social influence process that involves modifying behavior in response to a direct request.

Salespeople often use compliance techniques like the foot-in-the-door technique to increase the likelihood that you will buy their product.
Source: Yuriy Rudyy/Shutterstock.

parked, she has no legal power to force you to move your car. If you go out and move your car, you have (voluntarily) complied with her request. Early in the COVID-19 pandemic, people were asked to comply voluntarily to requests to social distance and wear a mask. In this section, we explore two compliance strategies: the foot-in-the-door technique and the door-in-the-face technique. We start by looking at the foot-in-the-door technique.

Foot-in-the-Door Technique

Imagine that you are doing some shopping in a mall and a person approaches you. The solicitor asks you to sign a petition condemning drunk driving. Now most people would be happy to sign such a petition. After all, it is for a cause that most people support, and it takes a minimal amount of effort to sign a petition. Imagine further that you agree to this initial request and sign the petition. After you sign the petition, the solicitor then asks you for a $5 donation to PADD (People Against Drunk Driving). You find yourself digging into your wallet for a $5 bill to contribute.

Consider another scenario. You are again in the mall doing some shopping, when a person from PADD approaches you and asks you for a $5 donation to help fight drunk driving. This time, instead of digging out your wallet, you tell the solicitor to hit the road, and you go back to your shopping.

These two scenarios illustrate a common compliance effect: the **foot-in-the-door technique (FITD)**. In the first scenario, you were first asked to do something small and effortless, to sign a petition. Next, you were asked for a donation, a request that was a bit more costly than simply signing a petition. Once you agreed to the first, smaller request, you were more inclined to agree to the second, larger request. This is the essence of the FITD technique. When people agree to a small request before a larger one is made, they are more likely to agree to the larger request than if the larger request were made alone.

In the experiment that first demonstrated the FITD technique (Freedman & Fraser, 1966), participants were contacted in their homes by a representative of a fictitious marketing research company under four separate conditions: (1) Some participants were asked if they would be willing to answer a few simple questions about the soap products used in their households (a request to which most participants agreed). The questions were asked only if the participant agreed. This was called the "performance" condition. (2) Other participants were also asked if they would be willing to answer a few simple questions, but when they agreed, they were told that the company was simply lining up participants for a survey and that they would be contacted later. This was called the "agree-only" condition. (3) Still other participants were contacted, told of the questionnaire, and told that the call

foot-in-the-door technique (FITD) A social influence process in which a small request is made before a larger request, resulting in more compliance to the larger request than if the larger request were made alone.

was merely to familiarize people with the marketing company. This was the "familiarization" condition. (4) A final group of participants was contacted only once. This was the single-contact (control) condition.

Participants in the first three conditions were called again a few days later. This time a larger request was made. The participants were asked if they would allow a team of five or six people to come into their homes for 2 hours and do an inventory of soap products. In the single-contact condition, participants received only this request. The results of the experiment, shown in Figure 7.5, were striking. Notice that over 50% of the participants in the performance condition (which is the FITD technique) agreed to the second, larger request, compared to only about 22% of the participants in the single-contact group. Notice also that simply agreeing to the smaller request or being familiarized with the company was not sufficient to significantly increase compliance with the larger request. The FITD effect occurs only if the smaller task is actually performed. Since this seminal experiment, conducted in 1966, many other studies have verified the FITD effect. It even works in an online environment using Web pages or e-mail to make the small and large requests (Grassini et al., 2013; Guéguen & Jacob, 2001). Researchers quickly turned their attention to investigating the underlying causes for the effect.

Why It Works: Three Hypotheses

One explanation for the FITD effect is provided by self-perception theory (Bem, 1972). Recall from Chapter 6 that we sometimes learn about ourselves from observing our own behavior and making inferences about the causes for that behavior. According to the *self-perception hypothesis*, the FITD works because agreeing to the first request causes changes in our perceptions of ourselves. Once we agree to the smaller, original request, we perceive ourselves as the type of person who gives help in that particular situation, and thus we are more likely to give similar help in the future.

In a direct test of the self-perception explanation, Burger and Caldwell (2003) paid some participants $1 to sign a petition supporting aid to the homeless (the initial request in a FITD procedure). Other participants received a bookmark that said "It's great to see someone who cares about people in need" (self-concept enhancement). Two days later participants received a telephone call asking them to volunteer time to sort items at a food bank to help the homeless. The results showed that participants in the enhancement condition were more likely to agree to the second request than those who were paid $1. Burger and Caldwell explain that those in the enhancement condition showed a shift in

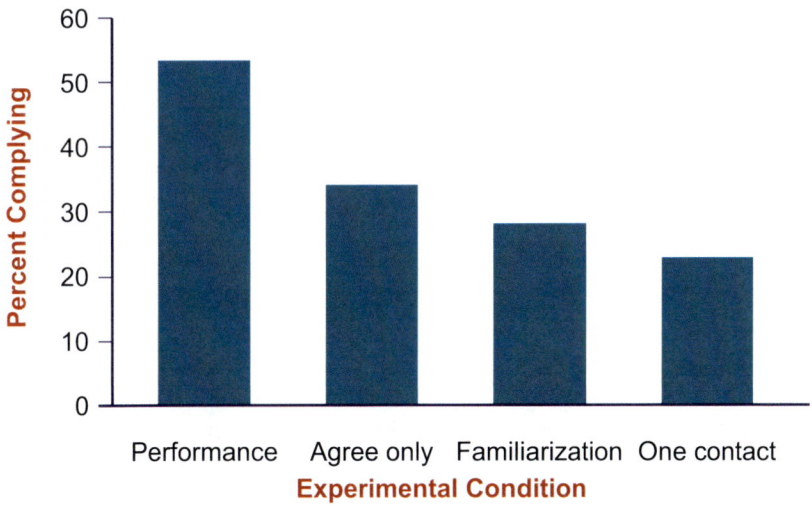

FIGURE 7.5

Compliance to a large request as a function of the nature of an initial, smaller request. The highest level of compliance for a large request was realized after participants performed a smaller request first, illustrating the foot-in-the-door technique.

Based on data from Freedman and Fraser (1966).

their self-perception toward perceiving themselves as helping individuals. Those paid $1 did not show such a shift. Generally, other research has provided support for the self-perception explanation for the FITD technique (Dejong, 1979; Goldman et al., 1982; Snyder & Cunningham, 1975).

Originally it was believed that merely agreeing to any initial request was sufficient to produce the FITD effect. However, we now know differently. The FITD effect works when the initial request is sufficiently large to elicit a commitment from an individual and the individual attributes the commitment to internal, dispositional factors. That is, the person reasons, "I am the type of person who cooperates with people doing a market survey" (or contributes to PADD, or helps in particular types of situations).

Although self-perception theory has been widely accepted as an explanation for the FITD effect, another explanation has also been proposed. This is the *perceptual contrast hypothesis,* which suggests that the FITD effect occurs because the smaller, initial request acts as an "anchor" (a standard of reference) against which other requests are judged (Cantrill & Seibold, 1986). The later request can be either assimilated to or contrasted with the anchor. Theoretically, in the FITD situation, the second, larger request is assimilated to the anchor (the smaller, first request) and is seen as less burdensome than if it were presented alone. That is, the second and larger request is seen as more reasonable because of the first request with which the person has already agreed. Although this hypothesis has generated some interest, there is not as much support for it as there is for the self-perception explanation.

Another explanation for the effectiveness of the FITD effect focuses on the thought processes of its recipients. It was suggested that information about the solicitor's and recipient's behavior affects compliance in the FITD effect (Tybout et al., 1983). According to this view, targets of the FITD technique undergo changes in attitudes and cognitions about the requested behavior. Compliance on a second request depends, in part, on the information available in the participant's memory that relates to the issue (Homik, 1988).

This hypothesis was put to the test in a field experiment involving requests for contributions to the Israeli Cancer Society (ICA; Hornik, 1988). Participants were first asked to fulfill a small request: to distribute ICA pamphlets. Participants agreeing to this request were given a sticker to display on their doors. One version of the sticker touted the participant's continuing involvement in the ICA campaign. A second version suggested that participants had fulfilled their obligation completely. Ten days later participants were contacted again and asked to donate money to the ICA. Additionally, the control group of participants was contacted for the first time.

The results of this study confirmed the power of the FITD technique to produce compliance (compared to the control group). Those participants who received the sticker implying continued commitment to the ICA showed greater compliance with the later request than did either those who had received the sticker showing that an obligation was fulfilled or those in the control group. Participants in the continued-commitment group most likely held attitudes about themselves, had information available, and had self-perceptions suggesting continued commitment. This translated into greater compliance.

As you can see, the FITD technique is a very powerful tool for gaining compliance. Although the effect has been replicated over and over, it has its limits. One important limitation of the FITD technique is that the requests being made must be socially acceptable (Dillard et al., 1984). People do not comply with requests they find objectionable. Additionally, the nature of the first request can affect later compliance. In one experiment (Dolinski, 2012), participants were stopped and asked to answer a couple of marketing questions (typical first request), to help tie shoelaces (unusual first request), or were not stopped for a first request (control). Dolinski found that 46% of participants complied with a second request (watch someone's shopping cart) in the typical request condition, 42% complied in the control condition, and 64% complied in the unusual request condition.

In a typical FITD situation, an individual is asked to *do* something related to a small request. Is it necessary for a person to actually perform a smaller task in order for the FITD technique to work? Apparently not. Cialdini and Sagarin (2005) suggest that merely getting someone to answer questions with a "yes" response may be sufficient to activate the FITD technique. They refer to this as the *four walls* technique. This idea was tested in an experiment in which participants were approached by a confederate of an experimenter and asked a series of questions that would either elicit "yes" or "no" responses (Guéguen et al., 2013). Guéguen et al. found that more participants agreed to a second, larger request if they had been asked the "yes" questions (83.3%) than the "no" questions (60%) or were in a no first request control group (30%).

Characteristics of the person making the request may also affect whether the FITD procedure works. Imagine you are approached by a person who asks you for directions to a building on campus (small request) and then a few moments later drops a bunch of papers on the ground (larger "request"). What do you think you would do if the person who asked you for directions was stinky or smelled nice? Would you be more willing to help the pleasant-smelling person than the stinky-smelling person? This is exactly what was tested in an experiment by Saint-Bauzel and Fointiat (2012). They found that participants were less likely to help the stinky-smelling person than the pleasant-smelling person in picking up the papers.

Finally, the FITD technique does not work equally well on everyone. For example, it works better on individuals who have a stronger need to maintain cognitive consistency than on those who have a weaker need (Cialdini et al., 1995; Guadango et al., 2001). Additionally, individuals who have a clear sense of their self-concepts (high self-concept clarity) were more affected by a FITD manipulation than those low in self-concept clarity (Burger & Guadango, 2003).

SOCIAL PSYCHOLOGY IN ACTION

Using the Foot-in-the-Door Technique to Increase Desired Behavior

Sometimes it is desirable to get people to do things that they really don't want to do. For example, donating blood is a highly desirable behavior that relatively few people engage in. Why is this so? Well, donating blood is a high-cost behavior because it requires a person to go somewhere, give up a significant amount of time, and subject themselves to a potentially painful procedure. Can the FITD technique be used to increase blood donations? In its original form, the FITD technique does not work very well for blood donation (Cialdini & Ascani, 1976; Foss & Dempsey, 1979). Does this mean that the FITD technique cannot be used to increase socially desirable but high-cost behaviors, such as blood donation? Not necessarily. A small modification in the technique may prove effective: adding a moderately strong request between the initial small and final large requests. Adding such an intermediate request increases the power of the FITD technique (Goldman et al., 1981). A gradually increasing, graded series of requests may alter the potential donor's self-perceptions, which are strongly associated with increased compliance in the FITD paradigm. Generally, an FITD technique that uses two initial requests of increasing requirements is more effective than a single-request FITD technique (Souchet & Girandola, 2013).

Interestingly, although the original FTTD technique does not increase blood donations significantly, it can be used to induce people to become organ donors

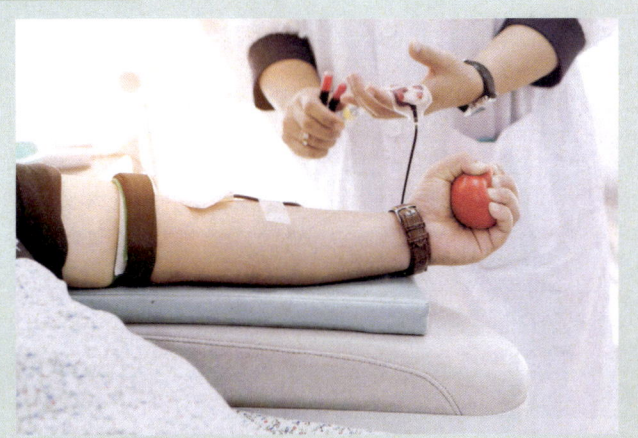

The effectiveness of the foot-in-the-door technique for high-cost behaviors such as blood donation can be increased by adding a moderately strong request between the initial small and final large request.
Source: Happy cake Happy café/Shutterstock.

(Carducci & Deuser, 1984; Carducci et al., 1989). However, there are even some limits here. In an experiment by Girandola (2002), participants were exposed to an FITD procedure under one of four conditions. Some participants received the second request immediately after the first request, and others received it after a delay of 3 days. Half of the participants were presented with the second request (to indicate how willing they were to become an organ donor) by the same person making the initial request or a different person. As shown in Figure 7.6, the FITD procedure was effective in increasing willingness to become an organ donor in

(continued)

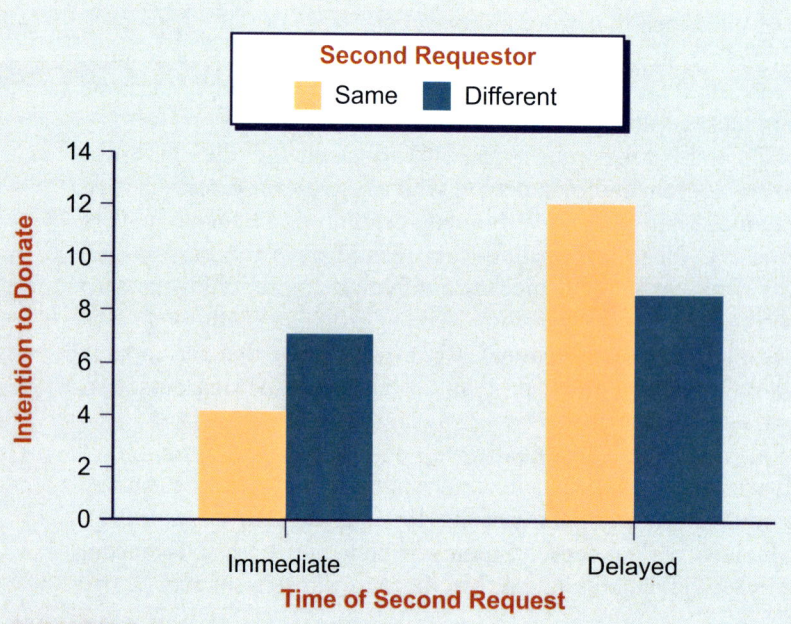

FIGURE 7.6

The relationship between the time of a second request and the identity of the person making the second request on the intention to become an organ donor.
Based on data from Girandola (2002).

all conditions except when the same person who made the first request made the second request immediately.

Why the difference between blood and organ donation? It may be that the two behaviors involve differing levels of commitment. Blood donation takes time and effort and involves some pain and discomfort. Organ donation, which takes place after death, does not. All you have to do is to designate that you are an organ donor on your driver's license. All of the work is done by others after you die! Blood donation requires action; organ donation requires only agreement. It appears that blood donation is seen as a higher-cost behavior than organ donation. Under such high-cost conditions, the FITD technique, in its original form, does not work very well.

Discussion Questions

1. Does the foot-in-the-door (FITD) always work?
2. Can the FITD be modified so that it does work for high-cost behaviors?
3. If the FITD doesn't increase blood donation, then why does it increase organ donation?

Door-in-the-Face Technique

Imagine that you are sitting at home reading when the telephone rings. The caller turns out to be a solicitor for a charity that provides food baskets for needy families at Thanksgiving. The caller describes the charity program and asks if you would be willing to donate $250 to feed a family of 10. To this request you react as many people do: *"What! I can't possibly give that much!"* In response, the caller offers you several other alternatives, each requiring a smaller and smaller donation (e.g., $100, $50, $25, and $10). Each time the caller asks about an alternative, you feel more and more like Ebenezer Scrooge, and finally you agree to provide a $25 food basket.

Notice the tactic used by the solicitor. You were first hit with a large request, which you found unreasonable, and then a smaller one, which you agreed to. The technique the solicitor used was just the opposite of what would take place in the FITD technique (a small request followed by a larger one). In this example you have fallen prey to the **door-in-the-face technique (DITF)**.

After being induced into buying a candy bar from a Boy Scout who used the DITF technique, one researcher decided to investigate the power of this technique to induce compliance (Cialdini, 1993). Participants were approached and asked if they would be willing to escort a group of "juvenile delinquents" to a local zoo (Cialdini et al., 1975).

door-in-the-face technique (DITF) A social influence process in which a large request is made before a smaller request, resulting in more compliance to the smaller request than if the smaller request were made alone.

Not surprisingly, most participants refused this request. But in the DITF condition, this request was preceded by an even larger one, to spend 2 hours per week as a counselor for juvenile delinquents for at least 2 years! It is even less surprising that this request was turned down. However, when the request to escort delinquents to the zoo followed the larger request, commitments for the zoo trip increased dramatically (Figure 7.7). Subsequent studies verified the power of the DITF technique to induce compliance (e.g., Cialdini & Ascani, 1976; Williams & Williams, 1989). As with the FITD technique, the DITF technique also works in an online environment (Guéguen, 2003). Recall from Chapter 1 how a number of findings in social psychology are difficult to replicate. We are happy to report that in the case of the DITF technique, the Cialdini et al. (1975) findings do replicate. Genschow et al. (2021) performed a direct replication of the earlier study and found the same DITF effect!

Some researchers have suggested that the DITF technique works because the target of the influence attempt feels compelled to match the concession (from the first, larger request to the smaller, second request) made by the solicitor (Cialdini et al., 1975). The social psychological mechanism operating here is the norm of reciprocity (Gouldner, 1960). The **norm of reciprocity** states that we should help those who help us. Remember Aesop's fable about the mouse that came across a lion with a thorn in its foot? Despite the obvious danger to itself, the mouse helped the lion by removing the thorn. Later, when the lion came on the mouse in need of help, the lion reciprocated by helping the mouse. This is an illustration of the norm of reciprocity. The norm of reciprocity is apparently a very powerful force in our social lives (Cialdini, 1993).

norm of reciprocity A social norm stating that you should help those who help you.

Implied in this original statement of the norm is the idea that we may feel compelled to reciprocate when we perceive that another person is making a concession to us. This norm helps explain the DITF effect. It goes something like this: When a solicitor first makes a large request and then immediately backs off when we refuse and comes back with a smaller request, we perceive that the solicitor is making a concession. We feel pressure to reciprocate by also making a concession. Our concession is to agree to the smaller request, because refusing the smaller request would threaten our sense of well-being tied to the norm of reciprocity. In the DITF technique, then, our attention becomes focused on the behavior of the solicitor, who appears to have made a concession (Williams & Williams, 1989). If we don't reciprocate, we may later feel guilty or fear that we will appear unreasonable and cheap in the light of the concession the solicitor made.

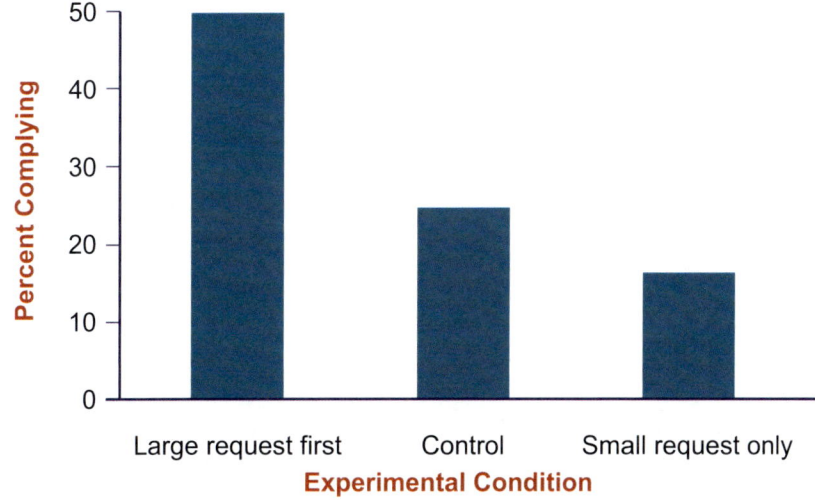

FIGURE 7.7
Compliance to a small request as a function of the nature of an initial request. Participants complied more with a second, smaller request if it followed a larger request, demonstrating the door-in-the-face technique.

Based on data from Cialdini and colleagues (1975).

The power of the norm of reciprocity has been shown in empirical research. For example, one study found that more participants agreed to buy raffle tickets from someone who had previously done them a favor (bought the participant a soft drink) than from someone who had not done them a favor (Regan, 1971). In this study, the norm of reciprocity exerted a greater influence than overall liking for the solicitor. Research has also shown that the norm of reciprocity is central to the DITF effect (Cialdini, 1993; Cialdini et al., 1975; Genschow et al., 2021; Goldman & Creason, 1981). If a solicitor makes more than one concession (when a solicitor reads a list of smaller and smaller requests), compliance is higher than if the solicitor makes only one concession (Goldman & Creason, 1981). This is especially true if the intermediate request is moderate (Goldman et al., 1981).

Although there is support for the role of reciprocity in the DITF effect, some researchers have questioned its validity and have suggested alternative explanations for these situations. One such alternative is the *perceptual contrast hypothesis*. As discussed earlier, this hypothesis focuses on the contrast in size between the first and second requests. Applied to the DITF effect, the perceptual contrast hypothesis suggests that individuals agree to the second (small) request because it appears more reasonable in the light of the first (large) request. The individual may perceive that the second request is less costly than the first. Although there is some evidence against this view of initial commitment to the salesperson, you are likely to follow through on it (Burger & Petty, 1981). There is evidence that commitment to a person (e.g., a salesperson) is more important than commitment to the behavior (e.g., buying a car) in compliance (Burger & Petty, 1981). So, you may not be so inclined to buy the car if you negotiate first with the salesperson and then with the sales manager than if you had continued negotiating with the original salesperson.

Commitment affects our behavior in two ways. First, we typically look for reasons to justify a commitment after making it (Cialdini, 1993). This is consistent with cognitive dissonance theory, as discussed in Chapter 6. Typically, we devise justifications that support our decision to buy the car. Second, we also have a desire to maintain consistency between our thoughts and actions and among our actions (Cialdini, 1993; Festinger, 1957). When the salesperson returns with a higher offer, we may be inclined to accept the offer because refusal would be dissonant with all the cognitions and justifications we developed during the stewing period.

Finally, the *self-presentation* explanation suggests that refusing the first request in the DITF procedure may cause the person making the request to perceive the target as an unhelpful person. In order to avoid this perception, the target agrees to the second request to project a more positive image to the requestor (Pendleton & Batson, 1979). There is some evidence for this explanation. Millar (2002) found that the DITF effect is more powerful when a friend of the target makes the requests than if a stranger makes the requests. Millar also reported that the target of the request was more concerned with self-presentation if the request was made by a friend compared to a stranger. Unfortunately, there is also evidence against the self-presentation explanation (Reeves et al., 1993). So, self-presentation may be involved in the DITF effect, but it may not be the best explanation for the effect.

Compliance Techniques: Summing Up

We described and analyzed two different compliance techniques. Are they all equally effective, or are some more effective than others? Research indicates that the DITF technique elicits more compliance than the FITD technique (Brownstein & Katzev, 1985; Cialdini & Ascani, 1976; Rodafinos et al., 2005). There is also evidence that a combined FITD-DITF strategy elicits greater compliance than either of the techniques alone (Goldman, 1986).

Another two-stage technique called *low-balling* may be more effective for gaining compliance than either the FITD or the DITF techniques (Brownstein & Katzev, 1985). In low-balling an initial request or offer is made that appears too good to be true. Once you agree to this request, a higher request is made. In one experiment, participants were stopped and asked to donate money to a museum fund drive. The request was made under FITD, DITF, low-ball, or a control condition. The average amount of money donated was highest under the low-ball conditions, compared to the FITD, DITF, and control conditions (which did not differ significantly from one another).

TABLE 7.1 Various Compliance Techniques

Compliance Technique	Description
Foot-in-the-door	Small request is followed by a larger request. More likely to agree to the larger request after agreeing to the smaller request.
Door-in-the-face	Large request (refused) is followed by a smaller request. More likely to agree to smaller request after the larger one.
Low-balling	An initial offer is made that is too good to be true (e.g., low price on a car). Later that offer is withdrawn and replaced with a higher one. Person is likely to agree to the higher offer.
That's not all effect	Extras are added to initial offers (e.g., "Buy now and we will include another free product"), which appear to be spontaneous offers of generosity. A person is more likely to buy the original product than if no add-ons are included.
Even a penny will help	After asking for a donation, which is refused, a solicitor may say, "even a penny would help." If the target fails to donate, he or she will feel cheap, so the target donates something.
Four Walls Technique	A series of questions to which a person answers "yes" results in more compliance with a second request than questions eliciting "no" responses (Gueguen et al., 2013).

Although we have focused on two compliance techniques, you should be aware that there are other techniques that are used to induce you into donating money or buying products. Space does not allow a complete discussion of all of these techniques. We have summarized the various compliance techniques in Table 7.1.

All of these compliance techniques have been and will be used to induce people to buy products (some of which they may want and some of which they may not want). The psychological mechanisms of reciprocity, commitment, consistency, and perceptual contrast operate to varying degrees to produce compliance. Because we all share these mechanisms, we all find ourselves on occasion doing something we don't really want to do. Sellers of all types use compliance techniques to sell their products (Cialdini, 2000). The best way to guard ourselves against these techniques is to recognize and understand them when they are used.

Study Break

This section described the two major compliance techniques of the foot-in-the-door and door-in-the-face techniques. Before you begin the next section, answer the following questions:

1. What is compliance, and how does it differ from conformity?
2. What is the foot-in-the-door technique?
3. What are the theories on how the foot-in-the-door technique works?
4. How can the effectiveness of the foot-in-the-door technique be increased for high-cost behaviors?
5. What is the door-in-the-face technique?
6. What are the theories on how the door-in-the-face technique works?

Obedience

In 2003 American soldiers in charge of the Abu Ghraib prison in Iraq subjected inmates to various forms of abuse and humiliation. When the actions of the soldiers came to light in 2004, those directly involved were arrested and subjected to military justice. One soldier, 21-year-old Lynndie England, was one of those arrested. In a now famous photograph, England is shown holding a naked Iraqi prisoner on a dog leash. When asked to explain her actions, England repeatedly said she was following the orders of her superiors. In her words, she was following the directions of "persons in my higher chain of command," and that "I was instructed by persons in higher rank to stand there and hold this leash and look at the camera."

Obedience, which is modifying behavior in response to commands from an authority figure, is an essential part of many organizations such as the military.
Source: KANIN.studio/Shutterstock.

obedience A social influence process involving modification of behavior in response to a command from an authority figure.

When England invoked orders from her superiors to explain her behavior, she was continuing a long tradition of those who have found themselves in similar positions. In fact, high-level Nazis routinely claimed that they were following orders when they perpetrated heinous crimes against Jews, Gypsies, and Eastern Europeans during World War II. The question we shall evaluate in this section is whether an ordinary person can be induced into doing something extraordinary in response to a command from someone in authority.

Defining Obedience

Obedience occurs when we modify our behavior in response to a direct order from someone in authority. Most of the obedience we observe daily is *constructive obedience* because it fosters the operation and well-being of society. Certainly no group, no society, could exist very long if it couldn't make its members obey laws, rules, and customs. Generally, obedience is not a bad thing. Traffic flows much easier when there are motor vehicle laws, for example. But when the rules and norms people are made to obey are negative, obedience is one of the blights of society. This kind of obedience is called *destructive obedience.* Destructive obedience occurs when a person obeys an authority figure and behaves in ways that are counter to accepted standards of moral behavior, ways that conflict with the demands of conscience. It is this latter form of obedience that social psychologists have studied.

Unfortunately, destructive obedience—the form of obedience we are most concerned with in this chapter—is a recurring theme in human history. Throughout human history, there are many instances when individuals carried out orders that resulted in harm or death to others. In addition to the case of Lynndie England just noted, at the Nuremberg trials following World War II, many Nazi leaders responsible for murdering millions of people fell back on the explanation that they were following orders. In another example, in the ethnic violence between Serbs and Bosnians in the former Yugoslavia, Serbian soldiers allegedly received orders to rape Muslim women in captured towns or villages. Islamic tradition condemns women who have been raped or who become pregnant outside marriage; these orders were intended to destroy the fabric of Muslim family life. The Serbian soldiers had been ordered to engage in blatantly immoral and illegal behavior. Additionally, mass murders took place in Kosovo at the behest of the Serbian leadership.

Destructive obedience doesn't only crop up in such large-scale situations. Destructive obedience can also manifest itself so that your everyday activities may be threatened. For example, Tarnow (2000) cites evidence that excessive obedience to the captain's orders may be responsible for up to 25% of all airplane crashes. One form of obedience seems to be particularly problematic: when the nonflying crew member (copilot) does not correctly monitor and subsequently challenge an error made by the pilot. These types of errors are made in 80% of airline accidents (Tarnow, 2000). Tarnow suggests that the atmosphere in the cockpit is one of a captain's absolute authority. The captain is given these powers by law. However, more power flows from the captain's greater flying experience than the copilot (to become a captain, you need at least 1,500 hours of flight time vs. 200 hours for a first officer). The power stemming from the law and greater experience makes it difficult for junior officers to challenge the captain, even in cases where the captain's decision is clearly wrong (Tarnow, 2000). The consequences of this obedience dynamic may be tragic.

Destructive Obedience and the Social Psychology of Evil

There is a tendency to attribute acts of destructive obedience to some abnormal internal characteristics of those who perpetrate such acts. Often we refer to individuals such as Adolph Eichmann (the "architect" of the Holocaust) as "evil." The term *evil* has been widely used historically and in contemporary culture. For example, in his 2002 State of the Union Address, President George Bush identified Iran, Iraq, and North Korea as an "axis of evil" because of their pursuit of nuclear and other weapons of mass destruction. In 1983, the late President Ronald Reagan referred to the former Soviet Union as an "evil empire" and the focus of all evil in the world at the time. And, of course Osama bin Laden was commonly tagged with the "evil" moniker.

What does the term *evil* actually entail? Traditionally, notions of evil have been left to philosophers and theologians. However, social psychologists have given consideration to the concept and have developed social psychological concepts of evil. In contrast to the traditional notion of evil that imbues a person with aberrant internal characteristics, social psychologists favor a view of evil suggesting that evil deeds may be defined in terms of overt behavior or internal characteristics (Burris & Rempel, 2011). On a behavioral level, we are likely to label a behavior as evil if it matches our image of intentional, unjustified harm to others (Burris & Rempel, 2011). We are likely to attribute evil behavior to internal characteristics of the evildoer if we come to believe that a person is chronically predisposed to commit evil acts (Burris & Rempel, 2011). Generally, social psychologists prefer a situational definition of evil focusing on overt behavior. For example, Zimbardo (2004) defines evil as "intentionally behaving, or causing others to act, in ways that demean, dehumanize, harm, destroy or kill innocent people" (p. 22). Under this definition, a wide range of behaviors, including terrorism, genocide, and even corporate misdeeds, could be considered evil (Zimbardo, 2004).

How does a social psychological definition of evil relate to obedience? Obedience to a command from an authority figure can produce evil outcomes. For example, Adolph Eichmann, carrying out orders of his Nazi superiors, was directly responsible for the extermination of millions of innocent human beings. Obedience has the power to transform ordinary people into those who are willing do things they would not ordinarily do (Zimbardo, 2004). Zimbardo has identified 10 principles inherent in obedience that can bring about this transformation. These are shown in Table 7.2.

What are the roots that underlie evil? This question, of course, can be addressed from a number of perspectives, including philosophical and religious. However, we will limit ourselves to a social psychological answer to the question. Baumeister and Vohs (2004) identify four roots of evil deeds. These are:

1. *Instrumentality:* Using violence to achieve a goal or solve a conflict.

2. *Threatened egotism:* Violence as a response to impugned honor or wounded pride.

3. *Idealism:* Evil deeds performed to achieve some higher good.

4. *Sadism:* Enjoying harming others (more likely to be reported by victims than perpetrators).

According to Baumeister and Vohs, the four roots form a causal chain that moves one toward perpetrating evil deeds. A final link between the four roots and the actual evil behavior, however, is a loss of self-control (Baumeister & Vohs, 2004). When one loses normal constraints against carrying out evil deeds (e.g., mass violence), evil is more likely to be the result. When mechanisms of self-control are maintained, evil deeds are less likely.

TABLE 7.2 Ten Principles Inherent in Obedience That Can Bring About Transformation of Obedience to Evil

1. Providing an acceptable reason for the objectionable action.
2. Arranging for a written or verbal contract to perform action.
3. Providing individuals with meaningful roles to play (e.g., prison guard).
4. Developing rules that must be followed, which are then used to justify action.
5. Altering language so that the individual believes he or she is not really hurting a victim.
6. Providing opportunities for passing responsibility on to others (diffusion of responsibility), absolving individual of direct personal responsibility for actions.
7. Beginning the process of obedience with small initial acts and then requiring larger acts later.
8. Increasing the level of harm to the victims incrementally over time.
9. Gradually changing the nature of the authority from reasonable to unreasonable.
10. Making it difficult to suspend obedience and making the costs for disobedience high.

Based on Zimbardo (2004, p. 28).

Staub (1989) suggests three other roots of evil. These are: difficult life conditions, cultural and personal preconditions, and the social-political organization. Staub points out that evil deeds are often perpetrated under difficult life conditions such as economic depression and social disorganization. For example, the dismal economic conditions in Germany after World War I certainly contributed to the rise of the Nazi Party and the subsequent evil perpetrated on Jews and others. Cultural and personal factors are rooted in individual self-concept and traditional in-group/out-group separations in a culture. When one's self-esteem is threatened, that individual will move toward regaining a sense of control and power. This can be accomplished by establishing a sense of superiority of one's in-group over out-groups. This is precisely what happened in Nazi Germany. Finally, certain social-political organization structures are more likely to give rise to evil deeds than others. Totalitarian, authoritarian systems that institutionalize prejudice and discrimination are most likely to lead to evil deeds. Again, this is precisely what existed in Nazi Germany prior to the implementation of the "Final Solution" of the Jewish problem, resulting in the murder of millions.

The Banality of Evil: Eichmann's Fallacy

There is evidence that people believe in the idea of pure evil (Webster & Saucier, 2013). The *belief in pure evil* (BPE) is the belief that evil deeds are perpetrated by individuals with an evil character. Baumeister (1999) identified eight beliefs comprising a BPE:

- Pure evil involves the intentional infliction of harm.
- Pure evil involves inflicting harm purely for enjoyment.
- Pure evil involves intentionally harming innocent victims.
- Evil deeds disrupt normal, peaceful life.
- Outsiders perpetrate evil.
- Pure evil is a stable, internal characteristic.
- Pure evil relates to inflated self-esteem or narcissism.
- Pure evil involves difficulty regulating negative emotions (e.g., anger and rage).

Believing that a person's negative behavior is motivated by BPE is associated with increased aggression directed toward that person (Burris & Rempel, 2011; Webster & Saucier, 2013). Additionally, believing that BPE underlies evil deeds absolves us of the need to try to understand a person's behavior and show tolerance toward that person and automatically justifies any punishment meted out (Webster & Saucier, 2013).

It would be a relief if those carrying out acts of destructive obedience were purely evil individuals predisposed to antisocial behavior. Unfortunately, history tells us that those who perpetrate evil are often quite ordinary. William Calley, who was in command of the platoon that committed a massacre at the Vietnamese village of My Lai, was ordinary before and after My Lai. So too was Mohammad Atta, the leader of the 9/11 hijackers. So was Adolph Eichmann, one of the architects of the Holocaust and the Nazi officer responsible for the delivery of European Jews to concentration camps in World War II.

Eichmann's job was to ensure that the death camps had a steady flow of victims. He secured the railroad cattle cars needed to transport the human cargo. His job was managerial, bureaucratic; often he had to fight with competing German interests to get enough boxcars. When the war was over, Eichmann, a most-wanted war criminal, escaped to Argentina. From 1945 to 1961, he worked as a laborer outside Buenos Aires. His uneventful existence ended in 1961 when he was captured by Israeli secret agents, who spirited him to Israel. There he stood trial for crimes against humanity. After a long trial, Eichmann was found guilty and was later hanged.

ADOLF EICHMANN (1906–1962) was head of the *Judenreferat* (Department for Jewish Affairs) IV B 4 of the *Reichssicherheitshauptamt* (Reich Security Main Office) during the Second World War. He was a leading figure in the mass murder of European Jews. The deportation of Jews to the death camps was centrally organized from his office at Kurfürstenstraße 115/116. Eichmann fled to Argentina after the war. In 1961 his trial in Jerusalem attracted worldwide attention. He was sentenced to death and executed on May 31, 1962.

The idea of the banality of evil suggests that evil deeds are sometimes done by ordinary people. Adolph Eichmann, the architect of the Holocaust, was an ordinary looking man in nonmilitary attire, but more sinister looking in his SS uniform.
Source: meunierd/Shutterstock.

The Israelis constructed a special clear, bulletproof witness box for Eichmann to appear in during the trial. They were afraid that someone in Israel might decide to mete out some personal justice. What did the man in the glass booth look like? Eichmann was a short, bald man whose glasses slipped down his nose now and then. You could walk past him a hundred times on the street and never notice him. During the trial, Eichmann portrayed himself as a man anxious to please his superiors, ambitious for advancement. Killing people was a distasteful but necessary part of his job. Personally, he claimed, he had no real hatred of the Jews. According to him, he was just following orders.

Philosopher and social critic Hannah Arendt observed Eichmann at the trial. She was struck by the wide gap between the ordinariness of the man and the brutal deeds for which he was on trial. In her book, *Eichmann in Jerusalem: A Report on the Banality of Evil* (1963), Arendt essentially accepted Eichmann's defense. Her analysis of Eichmann suggested that evil is often very commonplace. Those who carry out acts of destructive obedience are often ordinary people, rather like you and me.

The contrast between Eichmann as an ordinary person versus an evil person can be reinforced by comparing a photograph of him in street clothes with one of him in his Nazi uniform (see the photograph on this page). In his street clothes, Eichmann looked like anybody's neighbor or uncle. However, he took on a much more sinister look when seen in his uniform, which is a powerful symbol of evil for most people. When a person becomes associated with a recognized evil symbol, we are more likely to label that person as evil (Burris & Rempel, 2011). These evil symbols elicit very powerful negative emotions in most people. Once a person is associated with such an evil symbol, people are likely to perceive that person in very negative ways. For example, Burris and Rempel report that participants exposed to recognized evil symbols are more likely to believe in the *myth of pure evil* (evil deeds are done by evil people), to characterize a negative behavior as evil, and to recommend more severe punishment for a person who performs a seemingly evil behavior.

Eichmann's fallacy
The belief that evil deeds are done only by evil people.

People were shocked by Eichmann and by Arendt's analysis. They had expected a Nazi war criminal to be the epitome of evil. There was a prevailing belief that evil deeds are done by evil people, a belief referred to as **Eichmann's fallacy** (Brown, 1986). Sometimes individuals who perpetrate evil deeds are quite ordinary, as Eichmann apparently was.

As you might expect, not everyone subscribes to the general idea of the banality of evil. For example, Calder (2003) argues that a person can have an "evil character" and still have an ordinary appearance and demeanor. However, Calder admits that it is possible for ordinary individuals to commit acts of evil even in the absence of an evil character. In an interesting distinction, Calder suggests that some people, such as Adolph Hitler, carry out evil deeds on their own, without direction from anyone else (autonomous evil). Calder classifies individuals in this category as *moral monsters*. Moral monsters like Hitler are singled out for special condemnation because of their active roles in initiating and directing evil acts (Calder, 2003). Others, such as Adolph Eichmann, carry out evil at the behest of others (nonautonomous evil). Individuals in this category are *moral idiots*. We may be more inclined to label moral monsters as truly evil rather than as moral idiots. However, it is possible to label the actions of moral idiots as truly evil if those acts are particularly heinous and show a consistent pattern.

If we accept the premise that evil acts are perpetrated by otherwise ordinary people, it raises another question: How does an ordinary person become transformed into an evil person willing to carry out evil deeds? This question is addressed in the book *Becoming Evil: How Ordinary People Commit Genocide and Mass Killing* (Walter, 2002). In this book, James Walter suggests that two levels of influence are involved in "becoming evil." On one level are *ultimate influences* that involve evolutionary factors and human nature. Influences on this level include group-based survival behaviors (e.g., competition, aggression, dominance) passed down from generation to generation that still affect human behavior. On the next level are three *proximate influences*: cultural and worldview causes, intergroup perception causes, and social construction of cruelty causes. Cultural and worldview causes include factors such as cultural collective values, an orientation toward authority, and social dominance views. Intergroup perception causes include a tendency to view the world in "us versus them" terms, blaming victims for negative circumstances, and moral disengagement from victims. Social construction of the causes of cruelty involve professional socialization, identification with a powerful in-group, and social factors that bind a person to the in-group. So, in this view, an ordinary man like Eichmann becomes an evildoer because, at one level, it is human nature to display evil behaviors and because pressures involving the three proximate causes (e.g., becoming oriented toward authority, seeing Jews as a dangerous out-group, and socialization into the role of Nazi bureaucrat) make evil attitudes and behaviors likely.

Zimbardo (2007) has also pondered the forces that lead to the transformation from good to evil. He calls the process the *Lucifer Effect* after the biblical character Lucifer's dramatic transformation from good to evil. Zimbardo points out that a more earthly transformation from good to evil may be a gradual one taking place over a long period of time. Zimbardo suggests that several conditions contribute to the Lucifer Effect. He states that the Lucifer Effect is more likely to occur in novel situations than familiar ones. In familiar situations, we have a wealth of experience and information to draw on to help guide behavior. In novel situations, we are not anchored in that familiarity and are more likely to fall prey to demands (sometimes negative) of that situation. Zimbardo also suggests that the Lucifer Effect is more likely to take place in powerful social situations in which situational forces overwhelm personal characteristics. It is also more likely to occur when a powerful situation overwhelms a person's senses of morality, justice, and compassion. Finally, Zimbardo points to the importance of systemic factors in fostering the transformation from good to evil. According to Zimbardo, the transformation is facilitated in a system (e.g., political) that provides a supportive power structure. In Nazi Germany, for example, Nazi ideology and authority structure allowed for just about anything that achieved the party's goals. Restraints against evil behavior were all but removed, allowing for the emergence of destructive behavior and the transformation of people from good to evil.

Our discussion of the nature of evil leads us to a central question: Are evil deeds the product of an evil character (internal attribution), or are they driven more by aspects of the social situation (external attribution)? This brings us to the main question we shall consider in the sections to follow: Do evil deeds always lead us back to an evil person? Although it might make us feel better if the answer to this question were yes, we see in this chapter that things are not, unfortunately, so simple.

Ultimately, Who Is Responsible for Evil Deeds?

After World War II, the Allies tried many of the high-ranking Nazis who, like Eichmann, claimed innocence. Their principal defense was to shift responsibility to their superiors: They were only following orders. In another case, a former East German border guard, Ingo Heinrich, was brought to trial for his role in preventing East German citizens from escaping to the west during the height of the cold war. Heinrich, along with his fellow border guards, had orders to shoot to kill anyone attempting to escape over the Berlin Wall. Heinrich did just that. But some of his comrades, under the same orders, shot over the heads of escapees. After the fall of the Berlin Wall and the reunification of Germany, Heinrich was arrested and charged with murder. He was eventually convicted and sentenced to 3.5 years in prison.

The cases of Eichmann and Heinrich raise some important issues about responsibility. Is "I was only following orders" a valid defense? Does it erase personal responsibility? Or should individuals be held accountable for their behavior, even if they were following orders? On the surface, it would appear that Eichmann and Heinrich were personally responsible for their behavior. These questions take us back to Lewin's model for social behavior discussed in Chapter 1. Generally, social psychology takes a *situational* perspective on the issue of evil. That is, the focus is on the situational forces that contribute to evil behavior. However, we cannot ignore *dispositional* factors. After all, in Nazi Germany and the old East Germany, thousands of people were exposed to the same situational forces as were Eichmann and Heinrich. Yet, they did not become an Eichmann or Heinrich. Most of Heinrich's colleagues shot over the heads of escapees rather than at them. The lesson is that we must take into account both situational and dispositional factors when trying to explain evil behavior. A deeper examination of authority and its effects on behavior suggests a complex picture, a picture with many aspects. The issues and questions surrounding responsibility for evil behavior served as the catalyst for the famous experiments on obedience.

Study Break

The previous sections introduced you to obedience and how social psychologists approach the relationship between evil and obedience. Before you begin the next section, answer the following questions:

1. What is the definition of obedience, and how do constructive and destructive obedience differ?
2. How do social psychologists define evil, and how does it relate to destructive obedience?
3. What are the roots underlying evil?
4. What is Eichmann's fallacy, and how does it relate to the debate about the origins of evil?
5. How can a good person transform into an evil one, and who is ultimately responsible for evil deeds?

Milgram's Experiments on Obedience

How does one test destructive obedience in a laboratory setting? The late Stanley Milgram devised a simple yet powerful situation. Before we look at it, let's consider the sociohistorical "climate" in the United States at the time. The year was 1962. Vietnam was but a blip on the back pages of the newspapers. The Kennedy assassinations had not yet occurred, nor had the murder of Martin Luther King, Jr., Watergate, or the riots in the streets of Newark, Detroit, and Watts. This was America before the real 1960s began, still holding on to some of the innocence, however illusory, of the 1950s. This context is important to consider because it may have influenced how people behaved in Milgram's experiments.

The Participant's Perspective

Let's begin by considering what these experiments looked like from a participant's perspective (Elms, 1972). Imagine you are living in New Haven, Connecticut. One day you notice an ad in the paper asking for volunteers for an experiment on learning and memory at nearby Yale University. The researchers are clearly seeking a good representation of the general population. The ad piques your curiosity, and you decide to sign up for the experiment.

When you arrive for the experiment, a young man, Mr. Williams, Dr. Milgram's associate, writes out a check to each of you for $4.50. He introduces you to another person who will also be a participant in the experiment. Williams tells you that little is known about the impact of punishment on learning, and that is what this experiment is about. You become a bit concerned when Williams says that one of you will be a learner and the other will be a teacher. Your fears about getting punished soon evaporate when you draw lots to see who will be the learner and you draw the role of the teacher.

Preliminaries out of the way, Williams leads you both into a room past an ominous-looking piece of equipment labeled "Shock Generator, Thorpe ZLB . . . Output 15 volts–450 volts" (Milgram, 1974). The learner, Mr. Wallace, is told to sit in a straight-backed metal chair. Williams coolly tells you to help strap Wallace's arms down to prevent "excessive movement" during the experiment, which you do. Williams then applies a white paste to Wallace's arms, which he says is electrode paste "to avoid blisters and burns." Wallace is now worried, and he asks if there is any danger. Williams says, "Although the shocks can be extremely painful, they cause no permanent tissue damage" (Elms, 1972, p. 114).

In front of the learner is a row of switches that he will use to respond to your questions. Williams tells you that a light panel in the other room will register the learner's responses. If his answers are correct, you, the teacher, tell him so. If incorrect, you deliver an electric shock from the shock generator.

It's time to start the experiment. You leave Wallace strapped to the shock generator and follow Williams into the next room. He places you before a control panel that has 30 levers, each with a little red light and a big purple light above. The lights have signs above them reading 15 volts, 30 volts, 45 volts, and so on, up to 450 volts. There are also printed descriptions of the shock levels above the labels, reading Slight Shock, Moderate Shock, Strong Shock, Intense Shock, Extreme Intense Shock, and finally, over the last few switches, in red, Danger: Severe Shock XXXXX. At this point, you hope that Wallace is brighter than he looks (Elms, 1972).

Before you begin the experiment, Williams gives you a sample shock of 45 volts, which gives you a little jolt. Next, you are told that your task is to teach Wallace several lists of word pairs, such as blue–box, nice–day, wild–duck. You read the entire list of word pairs and then test him, one pair at a time, by providing the first word from each pair.

At first the test is uneventful; Wallace makes no errors. Then he makes his first mistake, and you are required to give him a 15-volt shock. Williams tells you that for every error after that, you are to increase the shock by 15 volts. On subsequent trials Wallace makes frequent errors. When you get to 105 volts, you hear Wallace yell through the wall, "Hey, this really hurts!"

Williams, cool as ever, doesn't seem to notice. You certainly do. At 150 volts, the moaning Wallace yells, "Experimenter, get me out of here! I won't be in the experiment anymore. I refuse to go on!" (Elms, 1972, p. 115). You look at Williams. He says softly but firmly, "Continue."

Williams brings you more word-pair lists. You begin to wonder what you and Wallace have gotten into for $4.50. You are now at 255 volts, Intense Shock. Wallace screams after every shock. Whenever you ask Williams if you can quit, he tells you to continue. At 300 volts, you wonder if Wallace is going to die. "But," you think, "they wouldn't let that happen at Yale . . . or would they?"

"Hey, Mr. Williams," you say, "whose responsibility is this? What if he dies or is seriously injured?" Williams does not bat an eye: "It's my responsibility, not yours, just continue with the experiment." He reminds you that, as he told you before, the labels apply to small animals, not humans.

Finally it is over. There are no more shock switches to throw. You are sweaty, uneasy. Wallace comes in from the other room. He is alive and seems okay. You apologize. He tells you to forget it, he would have done the same if he had been in your shoes. He smiles and rubs his sore wrists, everybody shakes hands, and you and Wallace walk out together.

Predicted Behavior and Results in the Milgram Experiment

How do you think you would behave in Milgram's experiment? Most people think they would refuse to obey the experimenter's orders. Milgram was interested in this question, so he asked a wide range of individuals, both expert (psychiatrists) and nonexpert (college students and noncollege adults), how they thought participants would behave in this situation. They all predicted that they would break off the experiment, defying the experimenter. The psychiatrists predicted that participants would break off when the learner began to protest, at the 150-volt level. So, if you believe that you would defy the experimenter and refuse to inflict pain on another person, you are not alone.

Another study, independent from Milgram's, investigated the role of several variables in predicting obedience in a Milgram-type experiment (Miller et al., 1974). Miller et al. provided participants with verbal descriptions and a slide show depicting Milgram's experiment. Miller et al. looked at two classes of variables: perceiver variables (gender and normative information [some participants were provided with the results of Milgram's baseline experiment and others were not]) and stimulus person variables (gender and physical attractiveness). The dependent variable was the predicted shock level that would be administered in the situation. The results showed that participants believed that males would administer higher shock levels than females and that unattractive individuals would administer higher shock levels than attractive individuals. The latter finding was true mainly for female shock administrators. Interestingly, males showed greater consistency between predictions of another person's obedience behavior than did females. Female participants believed they themselves would administer lower levels of shock than would another person in the same situation.

The underlying assumption of these predictions is that individual characteristics will be more powerful determinants of behavior than situational factors. The predictions of Milgram's participants reflect the notion that moral knowledge predicts moral behavior; in other words, if you know what is right, you will do it. However, the results of Milgram's first "baseline" experiment (in which there was no feedback from the victim) don't support these rosy predictions. A majority of participants (65%) went all the way to 450 volts. In fact, the average shock level delivered by the participants in this first experiment was 405 volts! We can infer from this result that under the right circumstances, most of us probably also would go all the way to 450 volts.

Of course, no electric shock was ever given to Wallace, who was, in fact, a professional actor, playing out a script. However, Milgram's participants did not know that the entire situation was contrived.

Situational Determinants of Obedience

Milgram himself was surprised at the levels of obedience observed in his first experiment. He and others conducted several additional experiments investigating the situational factors that influence levels of obedience. In the following sections, we explore some of these situational factors.

Proximity of the Victim In his first series of experiments, Milgram tested the limits of obedience by varying the proximity, or closeness, between the teacher and the learner (victim). The conditions were:

1. *Remote victim.* The teacher and the learner were in separate rooms. There was no feedback from the victim to the teacher. That is, Wallace didn't speak, moan, or scream.

2. *Voice feedback.* The teacher and the learner were in separate rooms, but Wallace began to protest the shocks as they became more intense. This is the experiment just described. In one version of the voice-feedback condition, Wallace makes it clear that he has a heart condition. After receiving 330 volts he screams, "Let me out of here. Let me out of here. My heart is bothering me" (Milgram, 1974, p. 55).

3. *Proximity.* The teacher and the learner were in the same room, sitting only a few feet apart.

4. *Touch proximity.* The teacher and the learner were in the same room, but the learner received the shock only if his hand was placed on a shock plate. At one point the learner refused to keep his hand on the plate. The teacher was told to hold the learner's hand down while delivering the shock. The teacher often had to hand-wrestle the victim to be sure the hand was properly placed on the shock plate.

These four conditions decrease the physical distance between the teacher and the learner. Milgram found that reducing the distance between the teacher and the learner affected the level of obedience (Figure 7.8). In the remote-victim condition, 65% of the participants obeyed the experimenter and went all the way to 450 volts (the average shock intensity was 405 volts). As you can see from Figure 7.8, obedience was not substantially reduced in the voice-feedback condition. In this condition, obedience dropped only 2.5%, to 62.5%, with an average shock intensity of 368 volts.

Thus, verbal feedback from the learner, even when he indicates his heart is bothering him, is not terribly effective in reducing obedience. Significant drops in the rates of obedience were observed when the distance between the teacher and the learner was

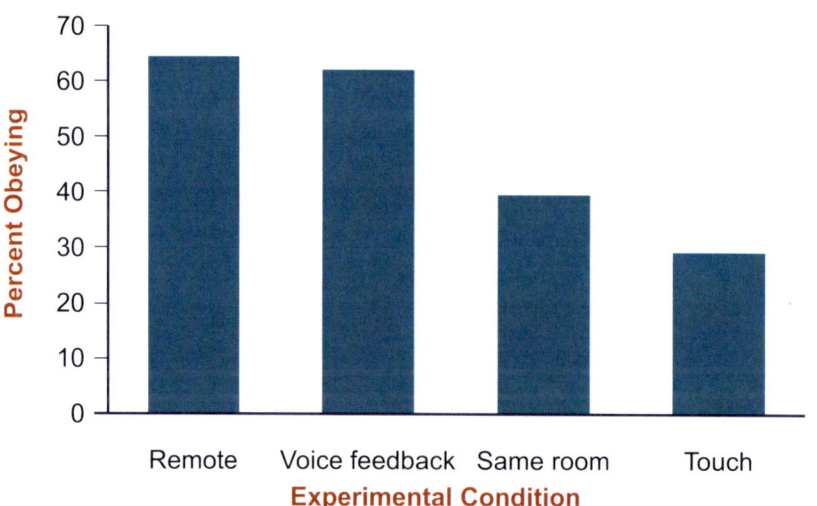

FIGURE 7.8

The effect of moving the learner closer to the teacher. In the remote condition, obedience was highest. Adding voice feedback did not reduce obedience significantly. It was only when the learner and teacher were in the same room that obedience dropped. The lowest level of obedience occurred when the teacher was required to touch the learner in order to administer the electric shock.

Based on data from Milgram (1974).

decreased further. In the proximity condition, where the teacher and the learner were in the same room and only a few feet apart, 39% of the participants went to 450 volts (with an average shock intensity of 312 volts). Finally, when the teacher was required to hold the learner's hand on the shock plate in the touch-proximity condition, only 30% obeyed and went to 450 volts (the average shock intensity was 269 volts). The good news here is that only 30% obeyed the experimenter in the touch proximity condition; the bad news is that 30% of participants obeyed the experimenter. A double-edged sword, indeed!

Why does decreasing the distance between the teacher and the learner affect obedience so dramatically? Milgram (1974) offered several explanations. First, decreasing the distance between the teacher and the learner increases empathic cues from the learner, cues about his suffering, such as screaming or banging on the wall. In the remote-victim condition, the teacher receives no feedback from the learner. There is no way for the teacher to assess the level of suffering of the learner, making it easier on the teacher's conscience to inflict harm. In the feedback conditions, however, the suffering of the learner is undeniable. The teacher has a greater opportunity to observe the learner in voice-feedback, proximity, and touch conditions than in the remote-victim condition. It is interesting to note, however, that even in the touch-proximity condition, a sizable percentage of participants (30%) were willing to fully obey the experimenter. It is apparent that there are some among us who are willing to discount empathic cues and continue to do harm to others in a face-to-face, intimate-contact situation. For example, there was no shortage of Nazis willing to shoot Jews at close range during the early stages of the Holocaust.

Milgram also suggested that in the remote-victim condition a "narrowing of the cognitive field," or *cognitive narrowing,* occurs. That is, the teacher can put the learner out of mind and focus on the learning task instead. As the victim becomes more observable, such narrowing becomes more difficult, and obedience is reduced. These results suggest that it is more difficult to inflict harm on someone you can see, hear, or touch. This is why it is probably easier to drop bombs on a city of 500,000 from 30,000 feet than to strangle one person with your bare hands.

Power of the Situation   A second variable Milgram investigated was the nature of the institution behind the authority. The original studies were conducted at Yale University. To test the possibility that participants were intimidated by the school's power and prestige, Milgram rented a loft in downtown Bridgeport, Connecticut, and conducted the experiment under the name "Research Associates of Bridgeport." He also had the experimenter represent himself as a high school biology teacher. Under these conditions, obedience fell to 47.5%, down from 65% in the original, baseline study. Although this difference of 17.5% does not meet conventional levels of statistical significance, it does suggest that removing some of the trappings of legitimacy from an authority source reduces obedience somewhat.

Presence and Legitimacy of the Authority Figure   What if the authority figure was physically removed from the obedience situation? In another variation on his original experiment, Milgram had the experimenter give orders by telephone, which varied the immediacy of the authority figure, as opposed to varying the immediacy of the victim. He found that when the experimenter is absent or tried to phone in his instructions to give shock, obedience levels dropped sharply, to as little as 20%. The closer the authority figure, the greater the obedience.

After Milgram's original research was publicized, other researchers became interested in the aspects of authority that might influence obedience levels. One line of research pursued the perceived legitimacy of the authority figure. Two different studies examined the effect of a uniform on obedience (Bickman, 1974; Geffner & Gross, 1984). In one study (Geffner & Gross, 1984), experimenters approached participants who were about to cross a street and requested that they cross at another crosswalk. Half the time the experimenter was uniformed as a public works employee, and half the time the experimenter was not in uniform. The researchers found that participants were more likely to obey uniformed than nonuniformed individuals.

Conflicting Messages About Obedience Milgram also investigated the impact of receiving conflicting orders. In two variations, participants received such conflicting messages. In one, the conflicting messages came from the learner and the experimenter. The learner demanded that the teacher continue delivering shocks, whereas the experimenter advocated stopping the experiment. In the second variation, two authority figures delivered the conflicting messages. One urged the teacher to continue whereas the other urged the teacher to stop.

When such a conflict arose, participants chose the path that led to a positive outcome: termination of harm to the learner. When there was conflict between authority sources, or between the learner and the authority source, not one participant went all the way to 450 volts.

Group Effects A fourth variation involved groups of teachers, rather than a single teacher. In this variation, a real participant was led to believe that two others would act as co-teachers. (These other two were confederates of the experimenter.) When the learner began to protest, at 150 volts, one confederate decided not to continue. Defying the experimenter's instructions, he walked away and sat in a chair across the room. At 210 volts, the second confederate followed. Milgram's results showed that having the two confederates defy the experimenter reduced obedience markedly. Only 10% of the participants obeyed to 450 volts (mean shock intensity 305 volts). Thirty-three percent of the participants broke off after the first confederate defied the experimenter but before the second confederate. An additional 33% broke off at the 210-volt level after the second confederate defied the experimenter. Thus, two-thirds of the participants who disobeyed the experimenter did so immediately after the confederates defied the experimenter.

Why does seeing two others disobey the experimenter significantly reduce the participant's obedience? One explanation centers on a phenomenon called *diffusion of responsibility*. Diffusion of responsibility occurs when an individual spreads responsibility for his or her action to other individuals present. In the obedience situation in which there were two other teachers delivering shocks, the participant could tell himself that he was not solely responsible for inflicting pain on the learner. However, when the two confederates broke off, he was left holding the bag; he was now solely responsible for delivering shocks. Generally, when people are in a position where they can diffuse responsibility for harming another person, obedience is higher than if they have to deliver the harm entirely on their own and cannot diffuse responsibility (Kilham & Mann, 1974). In short, having two people defy the experimenter placed the participant in a position of conflict about who was responsible for harming the learner.

There is another explanation for the group effects Milgram observed. When the two confederates broke off from the experiment, a new norm began to form: disobedience. The old norm of obedience to the experimenter is placed into conflict with the new norm of disobedience. The norm of disobedience is more "positive" than the norm of obedience with respect to the harm to the learner. Remember that when participants were given the choice between a positive and a negative command, most chose the positive. The lone participants in the original studies, however, had no such opposing norms and so were more inclined to respond to the norm of obedience. Evidently, having role models who defy authority with impunity emboldens us against authority. Once new norms develop, disobedience to oppressive authority becomes a more viable possibility.

Study Break

Stanley Milgram conducted the major studies of obedience. His studies, along with others, were described in this section. Before you begin the next section, answer the following questions:

1. How did Milgram study obedience, and what was his original finding?

2. What is the relationship between the closeness of the victim and obedience, and why does it affect obedience?
3. How do conflicting messages from authority figures affect the level of obedience?
4. Describe group effects and how they relate to obedience.

The Role of Gender in Obedience

In Milgram's original research, only male participants were used. In a later replication, Milgram also included female participants and found that males and females obeyed at the same levels. However, later research showed that there is a gender difference in obedience. In an experiment conducted in Australia, Kilham and Mann (1974) found that males obeyed more than females. In another study conducted in the United States, Geffner and Gross (1984) found that males obeyed a uniformed authority more than females did. However, a 2006 replication of the Milgram experiment by ABC News (this was not a reenactment, but an actual replication) found that females were more likely to obey the experimenter than males. Blass (2012) found no evidence for a consistent gender effect in obedience experiments done in the United States and other countries. So, there is no clear relationship between gender and obedience.

The relationship between the gender of an authority figure and obedience is complex. Younger, but not older, individuals are more likely to obey a male than female authority figure.
Source: Drop of Light/Shutterstock.

Another way to approach the issue of gender effects in obedience is to determine whether male or female authority figures are more effective in producing obedience. In Geffner and Gross's (1984) experiment, the effects of experimenter gender, participant gender, and participant age on obedience were investigated. The results showed no simple effect of experimenter gender on obedience. Instead, experimenter gender and participant age interacted, as shown in Figure 7.9. Notice that there was no difference between older and younger participants ("younger" participants being under age 30, and "older" participants being over age 50) when the experimenter was female. However, when the experimenter was male, younger participants obeyed the male experimenter more than older participants did.

Obedience or Aggression?

Milgram's experiment used an aggressive response as the index of obedience. Could it be that participants were displaying aggression toward the learner, which had little to do with obedience? Such an interpretation appears unlikely. In situations where participants were allowed to choose the level of shock to deliver to the learner, the average shock delivered was 82.5 volts, with 2.5% obeying completely. This is quite a drop from the 405 volts with 65% obeying completely in the baseline condition (Milgram, 1974).

These results were supported by a replication of Milgram's experiment by other researchers (Mantell, 1971). In one condition of this experiment, participants were allowed to set the level of shock delivered to the learner. Compared to 85% of participants who used the highest level of shock in a replication of Milgram's baseline experiment (no feedback from the learner), only 7% of the participants in the "self-decision" condition did so. These results and others (Kilham & Mann, 1974; Meeus & Raaijmakers, 1986; Shanab & Yahya, 1978) lead us to the conclusion that participants were displaying obedience to the experimenter rather than to their own aggressive impulses.

Obedience Across Culture, Situation, and Time

Milgram's original experiments were conducted in the United States, using a particular research technique. Would his results hold up across cultures and across experimental

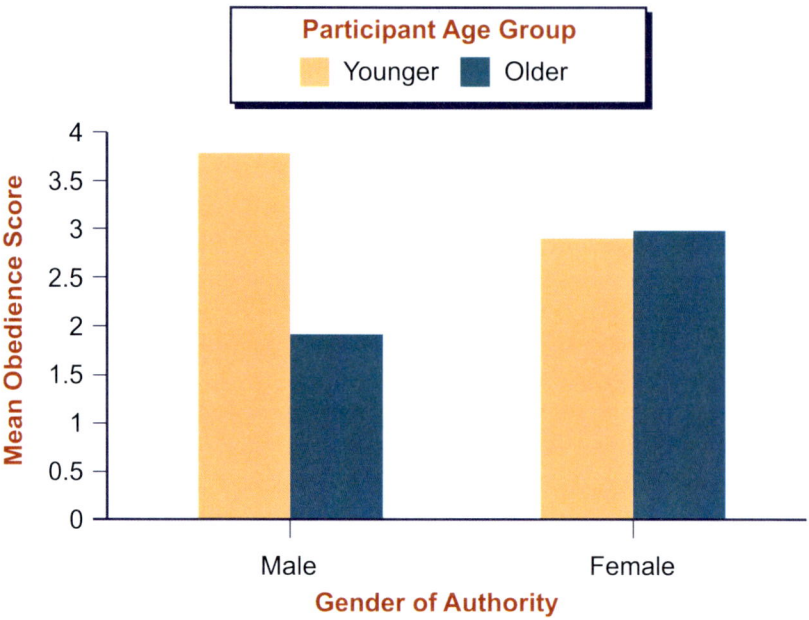

FIGURE 7.9

Obedience as a function of the gender of an authority figure and participant age. Younger participants were more likely to obey a male authority figure than older participants. Younger and older participants obeyed a female authority figure equally.

Based on data from Geffner and Gross (1984).

situations? Generally, they do. Blass (2012) compared obedience rates in Milgram-type obedience experiments across cultures and found fairly consistent obedience rates. Nevertheless, some critics of Milgram's study, Dutch researchers Meeus and Raaijmakers (1986), argued that the type of obedience required in Milgram's experiment—physically hurting another person—was not realistic. Such behavior is rare in everyday life. They argued that people are more often asked to hurt others in more subtle ways. For example, your employer might ask you to do something that makes another employee look bad. Would you obey?

Meeus and Raaijmakers (1986) studied a different form of obedience: *administrative obedience*. Dutch participants were told that the psychology department of a university was commissioned to screen applicants for various state and civic positions and that the department was using this opportunity to test the effects of stress on test achievement. According to instructions, participants made a series of disparaging statements about a person taking a test for a state job. Fifteen statements, each more disruptive than the previous, were used. The mildest statement was, "Your answer to question 9 was wrong"; a moderate statement was, "If you continue like this, you will fail the test"; and the strongest statement was, "According to the test, it would be better for you to apply for lower functions" (p. 323). Understandably, job applicants became increasingly upset with each comment.

Most of the Dutch participants obeyed; 90% read all 15 statements. This resembles the Milgram experiment in which participants had to increase shock in 15 stages as the victim became more upset. In Milgram's terms, they gave the full 450 volts. When questioned about it, they attributed responsibility for the harassment to the experimenter.

In another variation on Milgram's experiment, Australian participants assumed the role of either transmitter of the experimenter's instructions or executor (Kilham & Mann, 1974). In the transmitter condition, participants relayed orders to continue shocking a learner to a confederate of the experimenter who delivered the shocks. In the executor condition, participants received orders indirectly from the experimenter through a confederate of the experimenter. The hypothesis was that there would be greater obedience when the participant was the transmitter rather than the executor of orders, presumably because the participant is not directly responsible for inflicting harm on the victim. Results supported this hypothesis. Participants in the transmitter role showed higher levels of obedience than those in the executor role.

Milgram's obedience effect has been supported by other cross-cultural research. For example, obedience among Jordanian adults was found to be 62.5%—comparable to the 65% rate found by Milgram among Americans—and among Jordanian children, 73% (Shanab & Yahya, 1977). The highest rates of obedience were reported among participants in Germany. In a replication of Milgram's original baseline experiment, 85% of German men obeyed the experimenter (Mantell, 1971). Overall, it appears that obedience is an integral part of human social behavior.

Milgram's findings have withstood the test of time. Blass (2000) evaluated replications of Milgram's experiments conducted over a 22-year period (1963 to 1985) and found that obedience rates varied from a low of 28% to a high of 91%. However, there was no systematic relationship between the time that a study was conducted and the rate of obedience. According to Blass, it does not appear that an *enlightenment effect* has occurred. An enlightenment effect occurs when results of research are disseminated and behavior is altered. If this happened, there should have been reliably less obedience in later studies of obedience than in earlier studies (Blass, 2000).

Further evidence for the durability of Milgram's findings can be found in experiments using a virtual obedience paradigm making use of Immersive Virtual Environment Technology (Dambrun & Vatiné, 2010). In their Immersive Video Milgram Obedience Experiment (IVMOE), Dambrun and Vatiné had people participate in a Milgram-type experiment in which the "learner" was shown on a computer screen reacting in the same way as Milgram's learner. Participants knew that the experiment was a simulation. However, the obedience task was designed to immerse the participant to such an extent that his or her behavior would parallel that of Milgram's participants. Whenever the "learner" made a mistake, Dambrun and Vatiné's participants were told to administer an increasingly strong simulated shock by pressing a red shock button. When Dambrun and Vatiné compared the level of obedience of their participants using the IVMOE procedure with the level of obedience of Milgram's original participants, they found no significant differences. Participants in the "remote" IVMOE condition showed comparable obedience to participants in Milgram's "remote" condition, as did participants in the IVMOE and Milgram's "voice feedback" condition. They also found that the higher the participant's state of anger (i.e., anger related to the obedience situation) and right-wing authoritarianism, the higher was the level of shock administered. One caveat, however, is the fact that Dambrun and Vatiné found that participants who were *more* immersed in the IVMOE task were *less* likely to obey than those who were less immersed in the task. Despite this, it appears then that the IVMOE procedure provides a reasonable, less ethically questionable alternative to a Milgram-type procedure.

In an experiment using the IVMOE, Dambrun and Vatiné manipulated two variables: visibility of the learner (hidden versus visible) and the ethnicity of the learner (White French versus northern African). Dambrun and Vatiné found that more participants obeyed the experimenter in the hidden-victim condition (53%) than in the visible-victim condition (13%). They also found that more participants obeyed the experimenter when the learner was northern African (40%) than White French (25%), although this difference was not statistically significant.

Another study provides additional confirmation of Milgram's findings and extends our understanding of the mechanisms that underlie destructive obedience (Caspar et al., 2016). In their first experiment, female participants delivered electric shocks to another female participant (the victim) in a face-to-face game. In one condition, the person delivering the shock (agent) actively delivered the shock by pressing a key on a computer keyboard (active condition). In a second condition, the experimenter picked up the agent's hand and pressed the key (passive condition). Caspar et al. also varied the role of the authority figure. In one condition the authority figure coerced the agent to deliver a shock (coercion condition), whereas in the second condition the agent did not coerce the agent and allowed the agent to determine whether to deliver the shock (free-choice condition). The way Caspar et al.

conducted the experiment allowed them to time the interval between the beginning of a trial and the delivery of the shock. They had the agents estimate this time interval. Additionally, at some point in the experiment, the agent and victim switched roles. The results showed that even in the free-choice condition, the agents delivered the shock in an average of 52.3% of the trials. They also found that when the victim switched roles and became the agent, she gave more shocks compared to participants in the agent role first. This shows that people who experience being a victim are likely to retaliate against their tormenters when given the chance to deliver punishment to them. Interestingly, Caspar et al. also found that in the coercion condition, agents felt less responsible for the harm inflicted on the victims. In a second experiment, Caspar et al. obtained a physiological measure of brain activity (an EEG). The results showed that when the agents were coerced into delivering a shock, brain activity indicated a reduced pattern of agency. In other words, "the brain may treat consequences of one's actions under coercion as if they were passively triggered" (p. 5).

Reevaluating Milgram's Findings

Milgram sought to describe the dynamics of obedience by comparing obedience rates across different experimental conditions. A wholly different picture of Milgram's findings emerges when a careful analysis of the audiotapes made by Milgram of almost all sessions of his experiment was done (Rochat et al., 2000). Such an analysis by Rochat et al. showed that obedience within an experimental session tended to develop slowly and incrementally through a series of steps. Rochat and colleagues classified participants' behavior as either acquiescence (going along with the experimenter's demands without comment), checks (the participant seeks clarification of a restricted part of the procedure), notifies (the participant provides information to the experimenter that could lead to breaking off of the experiment), questions (the participant overtly expresses doubt or requests additional information about the experimenter's demands), objects (the participant overtly disagrees with the experimenter and brings up some personal reason why he/she should not continue), or refuses (the participant overtly declines to continue the experiment, effectively disobeying the experimenter).

Rochat and colleagues found that the participants' acquiescence to the experimenter was relatively brief. At the 75-volt level (when the learner first indicates he is in pain), 10% of participants exhibited a low-level defiant response (minimum checking). As the experiment progressed, opposition in the form of checking increased. By 150 volts, 49.7% of participants were checking, and by 270 volts, all participants checked. Additionally, 30% of participants questioned, objected to, or refused the experimenter's orders at or before 150 volts, with an additional 35% reaching this high level of opposition between 150 and 330 volts (Rochat et al., 2000). Interestingly, 57% of the participants who eventually refused to continue began to protest before 150 volts, whereas none of the fully obedient participants did so.

Regardless of the path chosen by a participant, he or she experienced a great deal of conflict as the experiment progressed. Participants dealt with the conflict aroused by the demands of the experimenter and the learner by becoming confused and uncertain, and by showing high levels of distress (Rochat et al., 2000). Some participants dealt with the stress of the situation by rationalizing away the suffering of the learner, whereas others rushed through the remaining shock levels. According to Rochat and colleagues, participants resolved their conflict in one of two ways. Some participants completed the task to the 450-volt level in a "resigned or mechanical fashion" (p. 170). Others resolved the conflict by becoming oppositional toward the experimenter by first questioning and/or objecting to the experimenter and then later refusing, despite the pressure put on the participant by the experimenter to continue (Rochat et al., 2000).

Critiques of Milgram's Research

There were aspects of Milgram's experiments and others like them that were never precisely defined but probably influenced levels of obedience. Consider, for example, the gradual, stepwise demands made on the participant. Each 15-volt increment may have "hooked" the participants a little more. This is in keeping with the foot-in-the-door technique. Obeying a small, harmless order (deliver 15 volts) made it likely that they would more easily obey the next small step, and the next, and so on (Gilbert, 1981). Each step made the next step seem not so bad. Imagine if the participant were asked to give 450 volts at the very start. It is likely that many more people would have defied the experimenter.

What about the protests made by many participants? Very few participants went from beginning to end without asking if they should continue or voicing some concern for the victim. But they were always told, "You must continue; you have no choice." Perhaps, as some observers suggest, the experiments are as much a study of ineffectual and indecisive disobedience as of destructive obedience (Ross & Nisbett, 1991). When participants saw others disobey, they suddenly knew how to disobey too, and many of them did so.

Although most participants in Milgram's experiment obeyed the experimenter, many of them experienced significant levels of stress in doing so.
Source: Rawpixel.com/Shutterstock.

There is another, even more subtle factor involved here. The experiments have a kind of unreal, "Alice-in-Wonderland" quality (Ross & Nisbett, 1991). Events do not add up. The participant's job is to give increasing levels of electric shock to a learner in order to study the effects of punishment on learning. The shocks increase as the learner makes errors. Then (in some variations), the learner stops answering. He can't be learning anything now. Why continue to give shocks? Furthermore, the experimenter clearly does not care that the victim is no longer learning.

Some observers suggest that because the situation does not really make sense from the participant's perspective, the participant becomes confused (Ross & Nisbett, 1991). The participant acts indecisively, unwilling or unable to challenge authority. Not knowing what to do, the participant continues, with great anxiety, to act out the role that the experimenter has prescribed.

This analysis suggests that Milgram's experiments were not so much about slavish obedience to authority as they were about the capacity of situational forces to overwhelm people's more positive tendencies. This may, however, be a futile distinction. Either way, the victim would have been hurt if the shock had been real.

Finally, Milgram's research came under fire for violating ethical research practices. Milgram explored the dimensions of obedience in 21 experiments over a 12-year period, and more than a thousand participants participated in these experimental variations. Because Milgram's participants were engaging in behavior that went against accepted moral standards, they were put through an "emotional wringer." Some participants had very unpleasant experiences. They would "sweat, tremble, stutter, bite their lips, groan, dig their fingernails into their flesh" (Milgram, 1963, p. 375). A few had "full-blown uncontrollable seizures" (p. 375). No one enjoyed it.

Milgram's research and its effects on the persons who participated raise an interesting question about the ethics of research. Should we put people through such experiences in the name of science? Was the participants' anguish worth it? Several observers, including Baumrind (1964), criticized Milgram for continuing the research when he saw its effect on his participants. After all, the critics argued, the participants agreed to take part only in an experiment on memory and learning, not on destructive obedience and the limits of people's willingness to hurt others.

But Milgram never doubted the value of his work. He believed it was important to find the conditions that foster destructive obedience. He further believed that his participants learned a great deal from their participation; he knew this because they told him so. Milgram went to great lengths to make sure the teachers knew that Wallace was not harmed and that he held no hard feelings. He also had a psychiatrist interview the participants a year or so after the experiment; the psychiatrist reported that no long-term harm had been done (Aron & Aron, 1989).

Chapter 7 Conformity, Compliance, and Obedience

The current rules for using participants in psychological experiments would make it exceedingly difficult for anyone in the United States to carry out an experiment like Milgram's. All universities require that research proposals be evaluated by institutional review boards (IRBs), which decide if participants might be harmed by the research. A researcher must show the IRB that benefits of research to science or humankind outweigh any adverse effects on the participants. If a researcher were allowed to do an experiment like Milgram's, he or she would be required to ensure that the welfare of the participants was protected. In all likelihood, however, we will not see such research again.

Study Break

The previous sections continued the discussion of factors that affect obedience and also explored some issues relating to Milgram's research. Before you begin the next section, answer the following questions:

1. What is the relationship between gender and obedience?
2. How do culture and changes in social climate relate to obedience?
3. Discuss what research on obedience done after Milgram's shows about the durability of his findings.
4. What does the research re-evaluating Milgram's research tell us about the process of obedience?
5. What are the criticisms of Milgram's research, and do you think they are legitimate?

Disobedience

Although history shows us that obedience can and has become an important norm guiding human behavior, there are also times when disobedience occurs. Recall the disobedience of gym owners Ian Smith and Frank Trumbetti, who defied New Jersey authorities and kept their gym open despite massive fines. Another example of disobedience occurred in 1955 when a Black seamstress named Rosa Parks refused to give up her seat on a Montgomery, Alabama, bus to a White passenger. Her action was in violation of a law that existed at the time. Parks was arrested, convicted, and fined $10 for her refusal. Parks's disobedience served as a catalyst for events that shaped the civil rights movement.

Within 2 days of her arrest, leaflets were distributed in the African American community calling for a 1-day strike against the bus line. Martin Luther King, Jr. and other African American leaders took up her cause. The bus strike that was supposed to last only a day lasted for a year. Eventually, laws requiring African Americans to sit at the back of a bus, or to surrender a seat to a White passenger, were changed. From Rosa Parks's initial act of disobedience flowed a social movement, along with major social change.

Breaking with Authority

Although social psychologists have focused primarily on obedience, research has shown instances where disobedience occurs. For example, Milgram (1974) himself showed conditions under which disobedience takes place (e.g., conflicting authorities, peers disobeying). In one demonstration using a procedure similar to Meeus and Raaijmakers' (1986) administrative obedience procedure, Bocchiaro and Zimbardo (2010) demonstrated relatively high levels of disobedience (70%). When given an opportunity for disobedience (e.g., reporting an authority figure), some people will avail themselves of that opportunity (Bocchiaro et al., 2012). So, there are conditions under which participants are willing to disobey an experimenter's orders. What forces will cause a person to defy an "unjust" authority?

Milgram (1974) suggested that one factor contributing to the maintenance of obedience was that the individual in the obedience situation entered into an **agentic state**,

agentic state In the agentic state, an individual becomes focused on the source of authority, tuning in to the instructions issued.

which involves a person's giving up his or her normal moral and ethical standards in favor of those of the authority figure. In short, the individual becomes an agent or instrument of the authority figure. Milgram suggested further that in this agentic state, a person could experience **role strain** (apprehension about the obedience behavior) that could weaken the agentic state. In an obedience situation, the limits of the role we play are defined for us by the authority source. As long as we are comfortable with, or at least can tolerate, that role, obedience continues. However, if we begin to seriously question the legitimacy of that role, we begin to experience what Milgram called role strain.

In this situation, the individual in the agentic state begins to feel tension, anxiety, and discomfort over his or her role in the obedience situation. In Milgram's (1974) experiment, participants showed considerable signs of role strain in response to the authority figure's behavior. According to Milgram, very few participants were "not at all tense and nervous." Most showed moderate or extreme levels of tension and nervousness. Milgram suggested that this tension arose from several sources:

- The cries of pain from the victim, which can lead the agent to question his or her behavior
- The inflicting of harm on another person, which involves violating established moral and social values
- Potential retaliation from the victim
- Confusion that arises when the learner screams for the teacher to stop while the authority demands that he or she continue
- Harmful behavior, when this behavior contradicts one's self-image

> **role strain** The discomfort one feels in an obedience situation that causes a person to question the legitimacy of the authority figure and weakens the agentic state.

How can the tension be reduced? Participants tried to deny the consequences of their actions by not paying attention to the victim's screams, by dealing only with the task of flipping switches. As mentioned earlier, Milgram (1974) called this method of coping *cognitive narrowing*. Teachers also tried to cheat by subtly helping the learner—that is, by reading the correct answer in a louder voice. These techniques allowed teachers to tolerate doing harm that they wished they did not have to do. Other participants resolved the role strain by breaking the role, by disobeying. This choice was difficult; people felt they had ruined the experiment, which they considered legitimate.

Role strain can, of course, eventually lead to disobedience. However, real-world obedience situations, such as those that occur within military organizations, often involve significant pressures to continue obedience. Nazi soldiers who made up the squads that carried out mass murders *(Einsatzgruppen)* were socialized into obedience and closely allied themselves with their authority sources. When role strain is felt by people in this type of situation, disobedience is difficult, perhaps impossible.

However, this does not necessarily mean that the role strain is ignored. Creative psychological mechanisms may develop to cope with it. A fair number of members of the *Einsatzgruppen* experienced role strain. In his study of Nazi doctors, Robert Lifton (1986) found that many soldiers who murdered Jews firsthand experienced immediate psychological reactions, such as physical symptoms and anxiety. For example, General Erich von dem Bach-Zelewski (one of the Nazis' premier *Einsatzgruppen* generals) was hospitalized for severe stomach problems, physical exhaustion, and hallucinations tied to the shooting of Jews (Lifton, 1986). The conflict soldiers felt was severe: They couldn't disobey, and they couldn't continue. As a result, they removed themselves from the obedience situation by developing psychological problems.

Reassessing the Legitimacy of the Authority

In their book *Crimes of Obedience,* Kelman and Hamilton (1989) pointed out that authority is more often challenged when the individual considers the authority source illegitimate. Recall that when Milgram conducted his experiment in downtown Bridgeport

Disobedience to authority is likely when individuals think that disobedience is possible and are willing to accept the consequences for disobedience.
Source: Isaac Yeung/Shutterstock.

instead of at Yale University, he found a decrease in obedience. When an authority source loses credibility, disobedience becomes possible. Kelman and Hamilton suggested that two kinds of psychological factors precede disobedience. The first comprise *cognitive factors*—the way we think about obedience. In order to disobey, the individual involved in an obedience situation must be aware of alternatives to obedience. For example, Lt. Calley's men in Vietnam were not aware that a soldier may disobey what he has good reason to believe is an illegal order, one that violates the rules of war.

Disobedience is also preceded by *motivational factors*. An individual in the obedience situation must be willing to buck the existing social order (whether in the real world or in the laboratory) and accept the consequences. Milgram's finding supports the importance of this motivation to disobey. Participants who saw another person disobey and suffer no consequences frequently disobeyed.

These same factors could explain the behavior of Lithuanians during the early part of 1990. The Lithuanians declared independence from the Soviet Union, disrupting the long-standing social order. They were willing to accept the consequences: sanctions imposed by the Soviets. Lithuanian disobedience came on the heels of the domino-like toppling of Communist governments in Eastern Europe. Having seen that those people suffered no negative consequences, Lithuanians realized that there was an alternative to being submissive to the Soviets. In this respect, the Lithuanians behaved similarly to Milgram's participants who saw the confederates disobey the experimenter.

According to Kelman and Hamilton (1989), these two psychological factors interact with material resources to produce disobedience. In response, the authority source undoubtedly will apply pressure to restore obedience. Those who have the funds or other material resources will be able to withstand that pressure best. Thus, successful disobedience requires a certain level of resources. As long as individuals perceive that the authority figure has the greater resources (monetary and military), disobedience is unlikely to occur.

Consider the events in Tiananmen Square in China during June 1989. Students occupied the square for several days, demanding more freedom. At first, it appeared that the students had gained the upper hand and had spurred an irreversible trend toward democracy! The government seemed unable to stem the tide of freedom. However, the government's inability to deal with the students was an illusion. Once the Chinese government decided to act, it used its vastly superior resources to quickly and efficiently end the democracy movement. Within hours, Tiananmen Square was cleared. At the cost of hundreds of lives, "social order" was restored.

Navarick (2012) has suggested a three-stage model to describe the process of changing relationships among authority figures and subordinates. Navarick analyzed the behavior of members of Nazi Reserve Police Battalion 101, which was tasked with killing Jews in Poland during World War II. Members of Battalion 101 were individuals who were too old to serve in the German Army. So, they were pressed into service to, at first, guard Jews boarding trains to death camps and then guard the trains taking Jews to death camps. Eventually, however, the battalion was required to actually carry out mass killings, primarily in Józefów, a town in Poland outside of Warsaw. Browning (1992) has estimated that between 10% and 20% of the battalion refused to take part in the killings. Some quit after being ordered to guard Jews in the town square, and others quit after the first mass killing. Navarick suggests that defiant members passed through three stages on the way to disobedience. First is *priming,* involving feelings of distress associated from cues provided by the victims. At this point, battalion members associated their own internal suffering with cues of suffering from the victims. Second is a *decision point,* involving a choice of whether to continue with the obedience behavior or discontinue. Cues based on the immediate situation provide input at the decision point. Third is the *choice,* which may involve immediately refusing to obey (e.g., refusing to shoot Jews) or a delayed refusal (e.g., refusing to shoot Jews in the future).

Strength in Numbers

In Milgram's original experiment, the obedience situation consisted of a one-on-one relationship between the authority figure and the participant. What would happen if that single authority source tried to influence several participants?

In a study of this question, Gamson and his colleagues recruited participants and paid them $10 to take part in a group exercise supposedly sponsored by the Manufacturers' Human Resources Consultants (MHRC) (Gamson et al., 1982). Participants arrived at a hotel and were ushered into a room with a U-shaped table that seated nine persons. In the room were microphones and television cameras. After some introductory remarks, the session coordinator (the experimenter) explained that MHRC was collecting information for use in settling lawsuits. The nine participants were told that the current group would be discussing a case involving the manager of a gas station (Mr. C). Mr. C had been fired by the parent company because he was alleged to be involved in an illicit sexual relationship. The experimenter explained that the courts needed information concerning "community standards" on such an issue to help reach a rational settlement in the case. Participants then signed a "participation agreement," which informed them that their discussions would be videotaped.

Next, they were given the particulars of the case and then were asked to consider the first question: "Would you be concerned if you learned that the manager of your local gas station had a lifestyle like Mr. C's?" (Gamson et al., 1982, p. 46). Before leaving the room, the experimenter conspicuously turned on a videotape recorder to record the group's discussions. A few minutes later, the experimenter came back into the room, turned off the video recorder, and gave the group a second question to consider: "Would you be reluctant to do business with a person like Mr. C because of his lifestyle?" (p. 46). Simultaneously, the experimenter designated certain members of the group to adopt a position against Mr. C, because people were only taking the side of the gas station manager.

He then turned the video recorder back on and left the room. This process was repeated for a third question. Finally, the experimenter came back into the room and asked each person to sign an affidavit stating that the tapes made could be used as evidence in court. The experimenter again left the room, apparently to get his notary public stamp so that the affidavits could be notarized. The measure of obedience was each person's willingness to sign the affidavit.

Let's consider what happened in this study up to this point. Imagine that you are a participant in this study. You are seen on videotape arguing a given position (against Mr. C) that you were told to take. However, because the experimenter turned off the video recorder each time he came into the room, his instructions to adopt your position are not shown. A naive observer—for example, a judge or a juror in a court in which these tapes would be used—would assume that what you say on the tape reflects your actual views. The question for you to evaluate is whether you would sign the affidavit.

Surprisingly, in 16 of the 33 nine-person groups all participants refused to sign. These groups staged what might be considered outright rebellion against the experimenter. Some members even schemed to smuggle the affidavit out of the room so that they would have evidence for future legal action against Mr. C. Disobedience was not a spur-of-the-moment decision, though. Some groups showed signs of reluctance even before the final request was made, such as during break periods between tapings. When the video recorder was off, members of these groups expressed concern about the behavior of the experimenter.

Furthermore, there were nine groups that the researchers termed factional successes. In these groups, most participants refused to sign, although some agreed to sign. Four other groups, called *fizzlers*, included a majority of members who showed signs of rebellion during the early stages of the experiment. However, when it came time to sign the affidavits, these majority members signed them anyway. Finally, four groups, called *tractables,* never showed signs of having a majority of rebellious members. Therefore, in all but four groups, there was a tendency to disobey the experimenter.

What differences are there between the Gamson and Milgram studies? The most important difference is that Gamson's participants were *groups* and Milgram's were *individuals.* The groups could talk, compare interpretations, and agree that this authority was illegitimate. Milgram's participants may have thought the same, but they had no way of confirming their opinions. One important lesson may be that rebellion is a group phenomenon. According to Gamson, people need to work together for disobedience to be effective.

The development of an organized front against authority may occur slowly. A core of committed individuals may mount the resistance, with others falling in later in a *bandwagon effect.* The Chinese student uprising in 1989 is an example. The protest began with a relatively small number of individuals. As events unfolded, more people joined in, until there were hundreds of thousands of protesters.

A second factor is the social climate. Disobedience—often in the form of social movements—occurs within social climates that allow such challenges to authority. Milgram's studies, for example, were conducted mainly between 1963 and 1968. By the time Gamson and his colleagues did theirs, in 1982, the social climate had changed dramatically. Trust in government had fallen sharply after Watergate and the Vietnam War. Furthermore, Gamson's situation involved a large oil company. By 1982, people's trust in the honesty of oil companies had reached a very low level.

Many nonlaboratory examples illustrate the role of social climate in rebellion. Communist governments in Eastern Europe, for example, were overthrown only after major changes in the political system of the Soviet Union that had controlled Eastern Europe since 1945, the end of World War II. Eventually, that climate caught up to the Soviet Union, which disintegrated completely in 1991.

Rebellion against authority may also occur within social climates that do not fully support such rebellion. The resistance movements in France during World War II, for example, helped undermine the German occupation forces, despite the fact that most of France was ruled with an iron fist by the Germans. Within Germany itself, there was some resistance to the Nazi regime (Peukert, 1987). Even the ill-fated student uprising in Tiananmen Square took place within a climate of liberalization that had evolved over several years before the uprising. Unfortunately, the climate reversed rapidly.

Not all acts of disobedience are rebellious in nature. In some instances a group of citizens may advocate and engage in the breaking of laws they see as unjust. This is commonly known as *civil disobedience*. Civil disobedience can take a number of forms, including protests, work stoppages, boycotts, disobeying laws, and violent acts inflicting physical, economic, or property damage. Civil disobedience may be used in response to restrictions of one's basic civil rights or may be ideologically driven when a law is perceived to be unacceptable to one's best interests (Rattner et al., 2001). Finally, the most widely known form of civil disobedience occurs when one person (e.g., Rosa Parks) or a large group of individuals (e.g., protests) engage in direct acts of disobedience. However, a newer channel of civil disobedience is known as *electronic civil disobedience* (Wray, 1999). According to Wray, such acts might include clogging communications channels, physically damaging communication cables, and massive e-mail campaigns designed to shut down government offices and/or services.

Civil disobedience seems to work best when two conditions are met (Dillard, 2002). First, civil disobedience is most effective when it is carried out in a nonviolent and nonthreatening way. So, individuals who engage in peaceful forms of civil disobedience will have the most persuasive power over others. Second, the participants in civil disobedience must be willing to accept the consequences of their disobedience and communicate their suffering to others. Note that Rosa Parks's act of civil disobedience, where she refused to give her seat on a bus up for a White passenger, met both of these conditions.

Civil disobedience occurs when people break laws they feel are unjust and can be effective to bring about change. One form of civil disobedience is electronic civil disobedience, which involves clogging communications channels, physically damaging communication cables, and massive e-mail campaigns designed to shut down government offices and/or services.
Source: Ramji Creations/Shutterstock.

Study Break

Although there is considerable evidence that obedience is pervasive, there are situations in which disobedience occurs. Before you begin the next section, answer the following questions:

1. What are the agentic state and role strain, and how do they relate to obedience and disobedience?
2. What factors contribute to role strain?
3. Describe how cognitive and motivational factors can contribute to the reassessment of authority and disobedience.
4. Describe Navarick's three stages of disobedience, and show how they lead to disobedience.
5. What does Gamson, Fireman, and Rytina's study show us about obedience?
6. What is civil disobedience and under what conditions is it most effective?

To Mask or Not to Mask Revisited

We opened this chapter with a dilemma: how to get people to perform various behaviors to slow the spread of COVID-19. Among these behaviors was wearing a mask in public. Although many people readily adopted this behavior, others did not. What you learned in this chapter should help you understand why this is so. The three forms of social influence we discussed all help us understand why people decided to wear a mask or not. Once a substantial number of people started wearing masks, it conveyed to others that such behavior was normative, putting pressure on others to also wear masks. Social scientists weighed in on how to increase mask wearing, and they fell back on many of the principles we covered in this chapter. They pointed out that "mask shaming" and other forms of punishment would not be the most effective way to increase mask wearing. Instead, many social scientists stressed the importance of "portraying consensus" by showing the population that wearing a mask was normative and represented a consensus (Wall et al., 2020). Of course, conformity to a new norm was not the only social psychological force in play.

Obedience was also involved. A number of states and localities made mask wearing mandatory, with fines for not wearing a mask. Other COVID-related mandates were also enforced through mechanisms of obedience involving fines and other sanctions. As long as people perceived that the authority behind the mandates was legitimate, many were willing to obey. However, a number of others displayed disobedience and defied authority. You might recall that we made the point that when people begin to question the legitimacy of authority, disobedience is more likely. This occurred when many authority figures (e.g., governors) were caught violating their own mandates and rules. Once legitimate authority is undermined, as you have seen, conformity, compliance, and obedience are less likely.

Chapter Review

1. **What is conformity?**

   Conformity is one type of social influence. It occurs when we modify our behavior in response to real or imagined pressure from others. We often find ourselves in situations where we must modify our behavior based on what others do or say. When we modify our attitudes or behavior in such situations, conformity has occurred.

2. **What is the source of the pressures that lead to conformity?**

   The pressure can arise from two sources. We may modify our behavior because we are convinced by information provided by others, which is informational social influence. Or we may modify our behavior because we perceive that a norm, an unwritten social rule, must be followed. This is normative social influence. In the latter case, information provided by others defines the norm we then follow. Norms play a central role in our social lives. The classic research by Sherif making use of the autokinetic effect showed how a norm forms.

3. **What research evidence is there for conformity?**

   Solomon Asch conducted a series of now-classic experiments that showed conformity effects with a relatively clear and simple perceptual line-judgment task. He found that participants conformed to an incorrect majority on 33% of the critical trials where a majority (composed of confederates) made obviously incorrect judgments. In postexperimental interviews, Asch found that there were a variety of reasons why a person would conform (yield) or not conform (remain independent).

4. **What factors influence conformity?**

   Research by Asch and others found several factors that influence conformity. Conformity is more likely to occur when the task is ambiguous than if the task is clear-cut. Additionally, conformity increases as the size of the majority increases, up to a majority size of three. After a majority size of three, conformity does not increase significantly with the addition of more majority members. Finally, Asch found that conformity levels go down if you have another person who stands with you against the majority. This is the true partner effect.

5. **Do women conform more than men?**

   Although early research suggested that women conformed more than men, later research revealed no such simple relationship. Research indicates that the nature of the task was not important in producing the observed sex differences. However, women are more likely to conform if the experimenter is a man. No gender differences are found when a woman runs the experiment. Also, women are more likely to conform than men under conditions of normative social influence than under informational social influence conditions. Two explanations have been offered for gender differences in conformity. First, gender may serve as a status variable in newly formed groups, with men cast in the higher-status roles and women in the lower-status roles. Second, women tend to be more sensitive than men to conformity pressures when they have to state their opinions publicly.

6. **Can the minority ever influence the majority?**

   Generally, American social psychologists have focused their attention on the influence of a majority on the minority. However, in Europe, social psychologists have focused on how minorities can influence majorities. A firm, consistent minority has been found capable of causing change in majority opinion. Generally, a minority that is consistent but flexible and adheres to opinions that fit with the current spirit of the times has a good chance of changing majority opinion. A minority will also be more effective when the majority knows that people have switched to the minority viewpoint, although this effect levels off after three defections. Additionally, a minority has more power in a face-to-face influence situation and, in an ironic twist, is more likely to be taken seriously when the minority is small.

7. How does minority influence work?

Some theorists contend that majority and minority influence represent two distinct processes, with majority influence being primarily normative and minority influence being primarily informational. However, other theorists argue that a single process can account for both majority and minority influence situations. According to Latané's social impact theory, social influence is related to the interaction between the strength of the influence source, the immediacy of the influence source, and the number of influence sources. To date, neither the two- nor the single-process approach can explain all aspects of minority, or majority, influence, but more evidence supports the single-process model.

8. Why do we sometimes end up doing things we would rather not do?

Sometimes we modify our behavior in response to a direct request from someone else. This is known as compliance. Social psychologists have uncovered four main techniques that can induce compliance.

9. What are compliance techniques, and why do they work?

In the foot-in-the-door technique (FITD), a small request is followed by a larger one. Agreeing to the second, larger request is more likely after agreeing to the first, smaller request. This technique appears to work for three reasons. First, according to the self-perception hypothesis, agreeing to the first request may result in shifts in one's self-perception. After agreeing to the smaller request, you come to see yourself as the type of person who helps. Second, the perceptual contrast hypothesis suggests that the second, larger request seems less involved following the smaller, first request. Third, our thought processes may undergo a change after agreeing to the first request. The likelihood of agreeing to the second request depends on the thoughts we developed based on information about the first request.

The door-in-the-face technique (DITF) reverses the foot-in-the-door strategy: A large (seemingly unreasonable) request is followed by a smaller one. Agreement to the second, smaller request is more likely if it follows the larger request than if it is presented alone. The door-in-the-face technique works because the norm of reciprocity is energized when the person making the request makes a "concession." The door-in-the-face technique may also work because we do not want to seem cheap through perceptual contrast or to be perceived as someone who refuses a worthy cause. This latter explanation is the worthy person hypothesis. A final explanation for the DITF technique is self-presentation. According to this explanation, refusing the first request in the DITF procedure may cause the person making the request to perceive the target as an unhelpful person. The target agrees to the second request to avoid this perception.

10. How can the effectiveness of the foot-in-the-door technique be increased for high-cost behaviors?

The original foot-in-the-door technique does not work very well for high-cost behaviors such as blood donation. This is because high-cost behaviors require higher levels of commitment and effort than lower-cost behaviors. A small modification to the FITD involving making a gradually increasing, graded series of demands increases its effectiveness for high-cost behaviors like blood donation. The use of two initial increasing requests is more effective than the original, single-request technique.

11. What do social psychologists mean by the term "obedience"?

Obedience is the social influence process by which a person changes his or her behavior in response to a direct order from someone in authority. The authority figure has the power, which can stem from several sources, to enforce the orders. Generally, obedience is not always bad. Obedience to laws and rules is necessary for the smooth functioning of society. This is called constructive obedience. However, sometimes obedience is taken to an extreme and causes harm to others. This is called destructive obedience.

12. How do social psychologists define evil, and are evil deeds done by evil persons?

From a social psychological perspective, evil has been defined as "intentionally behaving, or causing others to act, in ways that demean, dehumanize, harm, destroy or kill innocent people" (Zimbardo, 2004, p. 22). Under this broad definition, a wide range of deeds could be considered evil. Social psychologists have also analyzed the roots of evil. Baumeister and Vohs (2004) identified four preconditions for evil: instrumentality (using violence to achieve a goal), threatened egotism (perceived challenges to honor), idealism (using violence as a means to a higher goal), and sadism (enjoying harming others). These set the stage for evil to occur, but it is a loss of self-control that directly relates to evil. Staub (1989) also suggests that difficult life conditions, cultural and personal factors, and social-political factors (authoritarian rule) also contribute to evil.

more about how a situation can overwhelm the normal positive aspects of behavior rather than about slavish obedience to authority.

Finally, Milgram's experiments have been criticized for violating ethical standards of research. Participants were placed in a highly stressful situation, one they reacted negatively to. However, Milgram was concerned about the welfare of his participants and took steps to protect them during and after the experiment.

18. How does disobedience occur?

Historically, acts of disobedience have had profound consequences for the direction society takes. When Rosa Parks refused to give up her bus seat, she set a social movement on course. Disobedience has played an important role in the development of social movements and social change. Civil disobedience, or the conscious disobedience of the law, is most effective when it is nonviolent and the individual using it is willing to suffer the consequences.

Disobedience may occur when role strain builds to a point where a person will break the agentic state. If a person in an obedience situation begins to question his or her obedience, role strain (tension and anxiety about the obedience situation) may arise. If this is not dealt with by the individual, he or she may break the agentic state. One way people handle role strain is through cognitive narrowing. Disobedience is likely to occur if an individual is strong enough to break with authority, has the resources to do so, and is willing to accept the consequences. Finally, research on disobedience suggests that there is strength in numbers. When several people challenge authority, disobedience becomes likely.

Key Terms

Agentic state (p. 294)
Compliance (p. 269)
Conformity (p. 254)
Door-in-the-face technique (DITF) (p. 274)
Eichmann's fallacy (p. 282)

Foot-in-the-door technique (FITD) (p. 270)
Informational social influence (p. 254)
Norm (p. 254)
Norm of reciprocity (p. 275)

Normative social influence (p. 254)
Obedience (p. 278)
Role strain (p. 295)
Social impact theory (p. 268)
True partner effect (p. 264)

Chapter Quiz

1. Conformity refers to a change in behavior in response to
   A. a direct order from someone in authority.
   B. real or imagined pressure from others.
   C. a direct request from someone.
   D. internal tension arising from a discrepancy between an attitude and a behavior.

2. Compared to the changes brought about by normative social influence, the changes brought about by informational social influence are
   A. weaker and more susceptible to change.
   B. stronger and more enduring.
   C. as easy to change.
   D. more difficult to bring about.

3. Increases in conformity are shown to occur in which situations?
   A. When the size of the majority decreases
   B. When the task becomes more clear
   C. When minority participants are allowed to write down their responses
   D. When the task becomes more ambiguous
   E. All of the above

4. Research on minority influence shows that a minority
   A. can influence a majority if they are consistent in their judgments.
   B. can influence a majority, but only if they adopt a rigid point of view.
   C. can influence a majority, even if they are inconsistent in their judgments.
   D. cannot influence a majority under any conditions.

5. A salesperson calls on you and asks you to buy an inexpensive product, which you do. Later in the week, she returns and asks you to buy a more expensive product, which you ordinarily would not buy. Again, you buy the product. The social influence technique being used here is the
   A. door-in-the-face technique.
   B. foot-in-the-door technique.
   C. low-ball technique.
   D. that's-not-all technique.

6. According to your text, the effectiveness of the foot-in-the-door technique for high-cost behaviors (e.g., blood donation) can be increased by
   A. using a gradually increasing series of requests before the final request.
   B. eliminating the first request.
   C. making the first request more threatening.
   D. making the target more aware of the importance of the behavior.

7. According to your text, which of the following is true of destructive obedience?
   A. It is rare in history.
   B. It not only occurs in large-scale situations but also in smaller-scale situations that can affect your everyday life.
   C. It only occurs on a large scale and only affects historical events.
   D. It accounts for most of the obedience we experience every day.

8. According to your text, social psychologists favor a view of evil suggesting that evil deeds may be defined in terms of
   A. a person's internal characteristics.
   B. the social environment only.
   C. overt behavior or internal characteristics.
   D. overt behavior only.

9. The results of Milgram's "baseline" experiment
   A. confirmed the predictions individuals made about how others would behave in Milgram's experiment.
   B. lend credibility to the idea that evil deeds are done by evil individuals.
   C. show that under the right circumstances, most ordinary people will obey the experimenter and go all the way to 450 volts.
   D. show that individual characteristics are more important than the situation in determining obedience behavior.

10. Milgram called the psychological tension an individual experiences in an obedience situation
    A. authorization.
    B. role strain.
    C. role tension.
    D. norm strain.

Answers can be found in the end-of-book Answers section.

Group Processes

Never doubt that a small group of thoughtful committed people can change the world: indeed it's the only thing that ever has!

—Margaret Mead

CHAPTER **8**

Source: Rawpixel/Shutterstock.

Key Questions

As you read this chapter, find the answers to the following questions:

1. What is a group?
2. Why do people join groups?
3. How do groups influence their members?
4. What effect does an audience have on performance?
5. What motivational decreases affect performance?
6. What motivational gains occur because of group interaction? What is the Köhler effect?
7. What are the potential negative aspects of groups?
8. With regard to solving problems: Are groups better than individuals, or are individuals better than groups?
9. What are hidden profiles, and what effects do they have on group decision making?
10. What is the effect of different leadership styles on group decision making?
11. How do groups reach decisions?
12. What makes a leader legitimate in the eyes of the group members?
13. What factors affect the decision-making ability and effectiveness of a group?
14. What is group polarization?
15. What is groupthink?

Tuesday, January 28, 1986, was the day all the kids in my (Miller) class had been eagerly awaiting. It was the day the space shuttle *Challenger* was finally going to launch. I was nervous and hoped that the launch would proceed because it had been postponed three times before. I was in the fourth grade, and my teacher, Mrs. Owens, had been telling us since the beginning of the school year that the National Aeronautics and Space Administration (NASA) was going to send a teacher, like her, into space. The teacher, Christa McAuliffe, was selected from over 1,000 applicants, and she would become the first civilian ever to go into space. The *Challenger* mission was an attempt to revive the public's waning interest in the space program, and it did capture the imagination of kids like me. Schools across the United States, including mine, were specially equipped to receive live broadcasts from the *Challenger*. McAuliffe was going to teach us two 15-minute classes from outer space. It was going to be the ultimate field trip. The *Challenger* mission was supposed to be a success, just like the previous 24 U.S. space shuttle flights, but the unthinkable happened as children watched live in classrooms all over the nation. In Mrs. Owen's class, as we counted down and watched the shuttle lift off, our cheers quickly turned to silence. As the *Challenger* began

Space shuttle *Challenger* disaster. 76 seconds into the flight, a reddish-brown cloud enveloped the disintegrating shuttle. Fragments of the shuttle then tumbled into the Atlantic Ocean.
Source: Everett Collection/Shutterstock.

to ascend into the heavens, it suddenly exploded in a huge fireball. Pieces of debris rained down, and the crew cockpit plummeted into the Atlantic Ocean, killing all seven astronauts aboard. Right before Mrs. Owens switched off the television, the two solid rocket boosters spiraled off in different directions, etching the image of the letter *Y* in smoke on the screen. The pattern formed would foreshadow the main question that was on everyone's mind in the days that followed the tragedy: Why?

The answer to this question proved to be complex indeed. The actual physical cause of the explosion was clear. Hot gasses burned through a rubber O-ring that was supposed to seal two segments of the solid rocket booster. Because of the exceptionally cold temperatures on the morning of the launch, the O-rings became brittle and did not fit properly. Hot gasses burned through and ignited the millions of gallons of liquid fuel on top of which *Challenger* sat. The underlying cause of the explosion, relating to the decision-making structure and process at NASA and Morton Thiokol (the maker of the solid rocket booster), took months to disentangle. What emerged was a picture of a flawed decision-making structure that did not foster open communication and free exchange of data. This flawed decision-making structure was the true cause for the *Challenger* explosion. At the top of the decision-making ladder was Jesse Moore, associate administrator for space flight. It was Mr. Moore who made the final decision to launch or not to launch. Also in a top decision-making position was Arnold Aldrich, space shuttle manager at the Johnson Space Center. At the bottom of the ladder were the scientists and engineers at Morton Thiokol. These individuals did not have direct access to Moore. Any information they wished to convey concerning the launch had to be passed along by executives at Morton Thiokol, who would then communicate with NASA officials at the Marshall Space Flight Center. Some people had one set of facts, others had a different set, and sometimes they did not share. The Thiokol scientists and engineers had serious reservations about launching *Challenger*. In fact, one of the engineers later said that he "knew" that the shuttle would explode and felt sick when it happened.

In addition to the communication flaws, the group involved in making the decision suffered from other decision-making deficiencies, including a sense of invulnerability (after all, all other shuttle launches went off safely), negative attitudes toward one another (characterizing the scientists and engineers as overly cautious), and an atmosphere that stifled free expression of ideas (Thiokol engineer Alan McDonald testified before congressional hearings that he felt pressured to give the green light to the launch). What went wrong? Here we had a group of highly intelligent, expert individuals who made a disastrous decision to launch *Challenger* in the cold weather that existed at launch time.

In this chapter, we explore the effects of groups on individuals. We ask, What special characteristics distinguish a group like the *Challenger* decision-making group from a simple gathering of individuals? What forces arise within such groups that change individual behavior? Do groups offer significant advantages over individuals operating on their own? For example, would the launch director at NASA have been better off making a decision by himself rather than assembling and relying on an advisory group? And what are the group dynamics that can lead to such faulty, disastrous decisions? These are some of the questions addressed in this chapter.

What Is a Group?

Groups are critical to our everyday existence. We are born into a group, we play in groups, and we work and learn in groups. We have already learned that we gain much of our self-identity and self-esteem from our group memberships. But what is a *group*? Is it simply a collection of individuals who happen to be at the same place at the same time? If this were the case, the people standing in line outside an Apple store waiting to buy the latest incarnation of the iPhone would be a group. Your social psychology class has many people in it, some of whom may know one another. Some people interact, some do not. Is it a group? Well, it is certainly an *aggregate,* a gathering of people, but it probably does not feel to you like a group.

Groups have special social and psychological characteristics that set them apart from collections or aggregates of individuals. Two major features distinguish groups: In a group, members interact with each other, and group members influence each other through this social interaction. By this definition, the collection of people at the Apple store would not qualify as a group. Although they may influence one another on a basic level (if one person looked up to the sky, others probably would follow suit), they do not truly interact. A true **group** has two or more individuals who mutually influence one another through social interaction (Forsyth, 1990). That is, the influence arises out of the information (verbal and nonverbal) that members exchange. The *Challenger* decision-making group certainly fit this definition. The group members interacted during committee meetings, and they clearly influenced one another.

group An aggregate of two or more individuals who interact with and influence one another.

This definition of a group may seem broad and ambiguous, and in fact, it is often difficult to determine whether an aggregate of individuals qualifies as a group. To refine our definition and to get a closer look at groups, we turn now to a closer look at their characteristics.

Characteristics of Groups

Interaction and mutual influence among people in the group are only two of a number of attributes that characterize a group. What are the others?

First of all, a group typically has a purpose, a reason for existing. Groups serve many functions, but a general distinction can be made between *instrumental groups* and *affiliative groups.* Instrumental groups exist to perform some task or reach some specific goal. The *Challenger* group was an instrumental group, as are most decision-making groups. A jury is also an instrumental group. Its sole purpose is to find the truth of the claims presented in a courtroom and reach a verdict. Once this goal is reached, the jury disperses.

Within a group members may assume formal or informal roles. For example, the leader of the group has specific duties such as setting the agenda and directing group discussion.
Source: fizkes/Shutterstock.

Affiliative groups exist for more general and, often, more social reasons. For example, you might join a fraternity or a sorority simply because you want to be a part of that group—to affiliate with people with whom you would like to be. You may identify closely with the values and ideals of such a group. You derive pleasure, self-esteem, and perhaps even prestige by affiliating with the group.

A second characteristic of a group is that group members share perceptions of how they are to behave. From these shared perceptions emerge **group norms**, or expectations about what is acceptable behavior. As pointed out in Chapter 7, norms can greatly influence individual behavior. For example, the parents of the children on a soccer team might develop into a group on the sidelines of the playing fields. Over the course of the season or several seasons, they learn what kinds of comments they can make to the coach, how much and what kind of interaction is expected among the parents, how to cheer and support the players, what they can call out during a game, what to wear, what to bring for snacks, and so on. A parent who argued with a referee or coach or who used abusive language would quickly be made to realize he or she was not conforming to group norms.

Third, within a true group, each member has a particular job or role to play in the accomplishment of the group's goals. Sometimes, these roles are formally defined; for example, a chairperson of a committee has specific duties. However, roles may also be informal (DeLamater, 1974). Even when no one has been officially appointed leader, for example, one or two people usually emerge to take command or gently guide the group along. Among soccer parents, one person might gradually take on additional responsibilities, such as organizing carpools or distributing information from the coach, and thus come to take on the role of leader.

Fourth, members of a group have affective (emotional) ties to others in the group. These ties are influenced by how well various members live up to group norms and how much other group members like them (DeLamater, 1974). Finally, group members are interdependent. That is, they need each other to meet the group's needs and goals. For example, a fraternity or a sorority will fall apart if members do not follow the rules and adhere to the norms so that members can be comfortable with each other.

What Holds a Group Together?

Once a group is formed, what forces hold it together? **Group cohesiveness**—the strength of the relationships that link the members of the group (Forsyth, 1990)—is essentially what keeps people in the group. Cohesiveness is influenced by several factors:

1. *Group members' mutual attraction.* Groups may be cohesive because the members find one another attractive or friendly. Whatever causes people to like one another increases group cohesiveness (Levine & Moreland, 1990).

2. *Members' propinquity (physical closeness, as when they live or work near each other).* Sometimes, simply being around people regularly is enough to make people feel that they belong to a group. The various departments in an insurance company—marketing, research, sales, and so on—may think of themselves as groups.

3. *Their adherence to group norms.* When members live up to group norms without resistance, the group is more cohesive than when one or two members deviate a lot or when many members deviate a little.

4. *The group's success at moving toward its goals.* Groups that succeed at reaching their goals are obviously more satisfying for their members and, therefore, more cohesive than those that fail. If groups do not achieve what the members wish for the group, they cease to exist or at the very least are reorganized.

5. *Members' identification with the group: group loyalty.* The success of a group will often depend on the degree of loyalty its member have to that group. Van Vugt and Hart (2004) investigated the role of social identity (how strongly the members

---

group norms Expectations concerning the kinds of behaviors required of group members.

group cohesiveness The strength of the relationships that link members of a group.

identified with the group) in developing *group loyalty,* defined as staying in the group when members can obtain better outcomes by leaving their group. In one experiment, high (vs. low) group identifiers expressed a stronger desire to stay in the group even in the presence of an attractive (vs. unattractive) exit option. Other results revealed that high identifiers' group loyalty is explained by an extremely positive impression of their group membership even if other groups might offer more rewards. Social identity seems to act as social glue. It provides stability in groups that might otherwise collapse.

How and Why Do Groups Form?

We know that humans have existed in groups since before the dawn of history. Clearly, then, groups have survival value. Groups form because they meet needs that we cannot satisfy on our own. Let's take a closer look at what these needs are.

Meeting Basic Needs

Groups help us meet a variety of needs. In many cases, these needs, whether biological, psychological, or social, cannot be separated from one another. There are obvious advantages to group membership. Psychology has developed an evolutionary perspective, and evolutionary social psychologists view groups as selecting individual characteristics that make it more probable that an individual can function and survive in groups (Caporael, 1997; Pinker, 2002). Couched in terms of natural selection, evolution would favor those who preferred groups to those who preferred to live in isolation. For example, humans hunting in groups were more successful in bringing down big game than individual hunters. It is not surprising, then, that nature selected for those humans who formed groups in which to hunt.

But groups meet more than biological needs. They also meet psychological needs. Our first experiences occur within the context of the family group. Some people believe that our adult reactions to groups stem from our feelings about our family. That is, we react toward group leaders with much the same feelings we have toward our fathers or mothers (Schultz, 1983). Many recruits to religious cults that demand extreme devotion are searching for a surrogate family (McCauley & Segal, 1987).

Groups also satisfy a variety of social needs, such as social support—the comfort and advice of others—and protection from loneliness. Groups make it easier for people to deal with anxiety and stress. Human beings are social beings; we don't do very well when we are isolated. In fact, research shows that social isolation—the absence of meaningful social contact—is as strongly associated with death as is cigarette smoking or lack of exercise (Brannon & Feist, 1992). This was seen with the social isolation due to the COVID-19 pandemic. A Harvard University study found that 36% of adults reported being lonely frequently or almost all the time. Another 37% reported feeling lonely occasionally. The percentage was even higher (81%) among individuals 18 to 25 years old (Harvard University, 2021). Not coincidentally, 25.5% of 18- to 24-year-olds seriously considered suicide during the pandemic (Centers for Disease Control and Prevention, 2020a).

Groups also satisfy the human need for *social comparison.* We compare our feelings, opinions, and behaviors with those of other people, particularly when we are unsure about how to act or think (Festinger, 1954). We compare ourselves to others who are similar to us to get accurate information about what to do. Those in the groups with which we affiliate often suggest to us the books we read, the movies we see, and the clothes we wear.

Social comparison also helps us obtain comforting information (Taylor & Brown, 1988). Students, for example, may be better able to protect their self-esteem when they know that others in the class also did poorly on an exam. B students compare themselves favorably with C students, and D students compare themselves with those who failed. We are relieved to find out that some others did even worse than we did. This is *downward comparison,* the process of comparing our standing with that of those less fortunate.

As noted earlier, groups play a large role in influencing individual self-esteem. In fact, individuals craft their self-concept from all the groups with which they identify and in which they hold membership, whether the group is a softball team, a sorority, or a street gang.

Of course, groups are also a practical social invention. Group members can pool their resources, draw on the experience of others, and solve problems that they may not be able to solve on their own. Some groups, such as families, form an economic and social whole that functions as a unit in the larger society.

Roles in Groups

Not all members are expected to do the same things or obey precisely the same norms. The group often has different expectations for different group members. These shared expectations help to define individual roles, such as team captain (a formal role) or newcomer (an informal role) (Levine & Moreland, 1990).

Newcomers

Group members can play different roles in accordance with their seniority. Newcomers are expected to obey the group's rules and standards of behavior (its norms) and show that they are committed to being good members (Moreland & Levine, 1989). More-senior members have "idiosyncratic" credit and can occasionally stray from group norms (Hollander, 1985). They have proven their worth to the group and have "banked" that credit. Every now and then, it is all right for them to depart from acceptable behavior and spend that credit. New members have no such credit. The best chance new members have of being accepted by a group is to behave in a passive and anxious way.

Deviates

What happens when the new members find that the group does not meet their hopes or the senior members feel the recruit has not met the group's expectations? The group may try to take some corrective action by putting pressure on the member to conform. Groups will spend much time trying to convince someone who does not live up to group norms to change (Schachter, 1951). If the deviate does not come around, the group then disowns him or her. The deviate, however, usually bows to group pressure and conforms to group norms (Levine, 1989).

Deviates are rejected most when they interfere with the functioning of the group (Kruglanski & Webster, 1991). Imagine an advisor to the launch director at NASA objecting to the launch of *Challenger* after the decision had been made. No matter how persuasive the person's objection to the launch, it is very likely that the deviate would have been told to be silent; he or she would have been interfering with the group's ability to get the job done. Experimental research has verified that when a group member dissents from a group decision close to the group's deadline for solving a problem, the rejector is more likely to be condemned than if the objection is stated earlier (Kruglanski & Webster, 1991).

Study Break

The preceding sections introduced you to the definition of a group and the characteristics that make up a group. Before you begin the next section, answer the following questions:

1. What is a group, and how does it differ from an aggregate?
2. How do instrumental and affiliative groups differ?
3. What roles do group norms, roles, and affective ties play in group functioning?
4. What is cohesiveness, and what factors affect it?
5. How and why do groups form, and what needs do they fulfill?
6. Describe the different roles that may exist in a group.

How Do Groups Influence the Behavior of Individuals?

We have considered why people join groups and what roles individuals play in groups. Now let's consider another question: What effect does being in a group have on individual behavior and performance? Does group membership lead to self-enhancement, as people who join groups seem to believe? Does it have other effects? Some social psychologists have been particularly interested in investigating this question. They have looked not just at the effects of membership in true groups but also at the effects of being evaluated by an audience, of being in an audience, and of being in a crowd. Recall that groups affect the way we think and act even when we only imagine how they are going to respond to us. If you practice a speech, just imagining that large audience in front of you is enough to make you nervous. The actual presence of an audience affects us even more. But how? Let's take a look.

The Effects of an Audience on Performance

Does an audience *always* make you perform better? Or does it *sometimes* make you "choke"? The answer seems to depend, at least in part, on how good you are at what you are doing. The presence of others seems to help when the performer is doing something he or she does well: when the performance is a dominant, well-learned skill, a behavior that is easy or familiar (Zajonc, 1965). If you are a class-A tennis player, for example, your serve may be better when people are watching you. The performance-enhancing effect of an audience on your behavior is known as **social facilitation**. If, however, you are performing a nondominant skill, one that is not very well learned, then the presence of an audience detracts from your performance. This effect is known as **social inhibition**. For example, when you were first learning to parallel park your car (a difficult task), having a group a people on the sidewalk watching you would likely have resulted in you making multiple attempts at the maneuver before being successful.

The social facilitation effect—the strengthening of a dominant response due to the presence of other people—has been demonstrated in a wide range of species, including roaches, ants, chicks, and humans (Zajonc et al., 1969). Humans doing a simple task perform better in the presence of others. On a more difficult task, the presence of others inhibits performance. Interestingly, the facilitating agent does not even need to be real (Gardner & Knowles, 2008). Gardner and Knowles had participants do either a familiar (easy) or unfamiliar (difficult) task in front of either a favorite or nonfavorite TV character. Gardner and Knowles found that participants performed better on the easy task when done in the presence of a favorite character. However, performance was inhibited on the difficult task when performed in front of the favorite character.

Why does this happen? How does an audience cause us to perform better or worse than we do when no one is watching? Psychologists have several alternative explanations.

Increased Arousal

Zajonc (1965) argued that a performer's effort always increases in the presence of others due to increased arousal. Increased arousal increases effort; the consequent increased effort improves performance when the behavior is dominant and impairs performance when the behavior is nondominant. If you are good at tennis, then increased arousal and, therefore, increased effort make you play better. If you are not a good tennis player, the increased arousal and increased effort probably will inhibit your performance (Figure 8.1). Zajonc suggested that the *mere presence* of others—that is, just them being there—is sufficient to produce the facilitation or inhibition effect. The mere presence hypothesis received support from a simple experiment reported by Platania and Moran (2001). Platania and Moran had participants do a simple task that involved assigning numbers to squares of different sizes either alone or with another person in the room to observe the experiment. They found that participants performed the task better with the observer in the room than if they did the task alone.

social facilitation
The performance-enhancing effect of others on behavior; generally, simple, well-learned behavior is facilitated by the presence of others.

social inhibition
The performance-detracting effect of an audience or co-actors on behavior; generally, complex, not well-learned behaviors are inhibited by the presence of others.

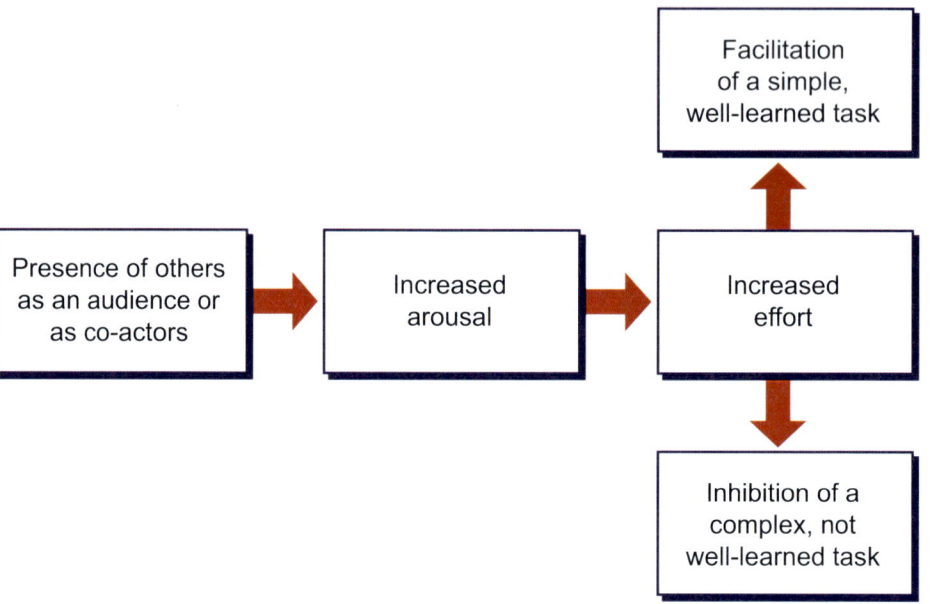

FIGURE 8.1

The arousal model of social facilitation. The presence of others is a source of arousal and increased effort. This increase in arousal and effort facilitates a simple, well-learned task but inhibits a complex, not well-learned task.

Evaluation Apprehension

An alternative explanation for the effects of an audience on performance centers not so much on the increased effort that comes from arousal but on the judgments we perceive others to be making about our performance. A theater audience, for example, does not simply receive a play passively. Instead, audience members sit in judgment of the actors, even if they are only armchair critics. The kind of arousal this situation produces is known as **evaluation apprehension**. Some social scientists believe that evaluation apprehension is what causes differences in performance when an audience is present (Figure 8.2).

evaluation apprehension An explanation for social facilitation suggesting that the presence of others will cause arousal only when they can reward or punish the performer.

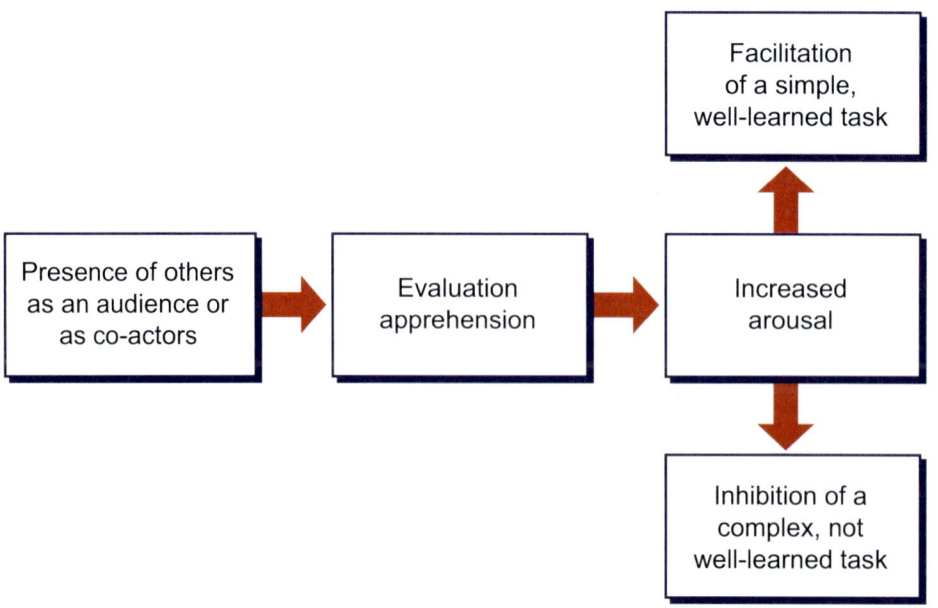

FIGURE 8.2

The evaluation apprehension model of social facilitation. According to this model, audience-related arousal is caused by apprehension about being evaluated.

Chapter 8 Group Processes

Those who favor evaluation apprehension as an explanation of social facilitation and social inhibition suggest that the presence of others will cause arousal only when they can reward or punish the performer (Geen, 1989). The mere presence of others does not seem to be sufficient to account for social facilitation and social inhibition (Cottrell, 1972; Feinberg & Aiello, 2006). In one experiment, when the audience was made up of blindfolded or inattentive persons, social facilitation of performance did not occur. That is, if the audience could not see the performance, or did not care about it, then evaluation apprehension did not occur, nor did social facilitation or social inhibition (Cottrell et al., 1968).

The Distraction-Conflict Effect

Another explanation of the presence-of-others effect is **distraction-conflict theory** (Baron, 1986). According to this theory, arousal results from a conflict between demands for attention from the task and demands for attention from the audience. There are three main points to the theory. First, the presence of other people distracts attention from the task. Our tennis player gets all kinds of attention-demanding cues—rewards and punishments—from those watching him play. He may be aware of his parents, his ex-girlfriend, his tennis coach, an attractive stranger, and his annoying little brother out there in the crowd. This plays havoc with a mediocre serve. Second, distraction leads to conflicts in his attention. Our tennis player has just so much attentional capacity. All of this capacity ought to be focused on throwing the ball in the air and hitting it across the net. But his attention is also focused on those he knows in the crowd. Third, the conflict between these two claims for attention stresses the performer and raises the arousal level (Figure 8.3).

distraction-conflict theory A theory of social facilitation suggesting that the presence of others is a source of distraction that leads to conflicts in attention between an audience and a task that affect performance.

Models of Social Facilitation: Summing Up

Each of the models of social facilitation centers on the role of arousal in social facilitation and inhibition. Each makes the same predictions about the effects of arousal on the performance of well-learned or unfamiliar tasks. Where they differ is on the source of the arousal. The arousal model suggests that the mere presence of others is sufficient to produce arousal and affect performance. The evaluation apprehension model tells us that

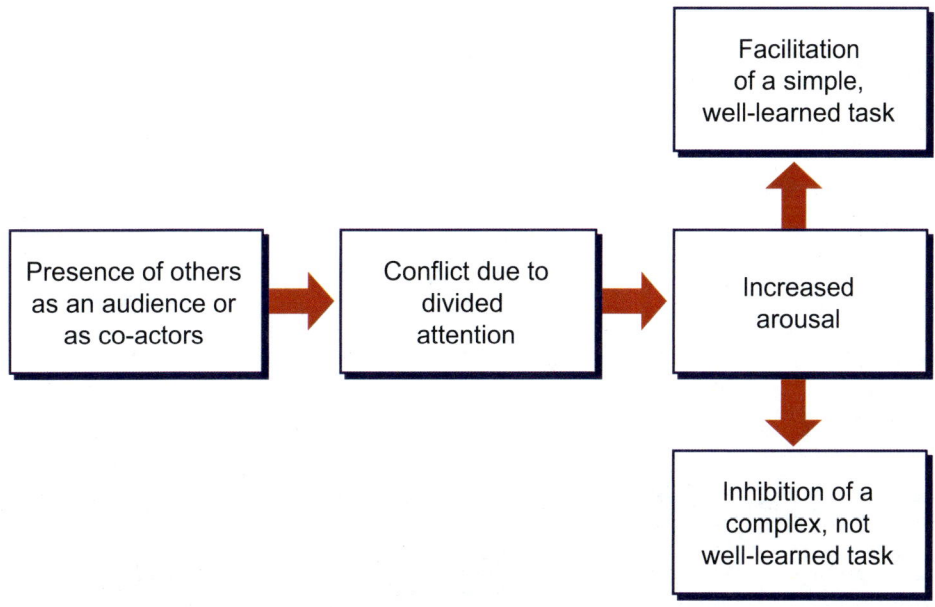

FIGURE 8.3

The distraction-conflict model of social facilitation. According to this model, the source of arousal in a facilitation situation is related to the conflict between paying attention to the task and the audience at the same time.

there is a learned component to the audience-arousal relationship. We learn that others judge us, and this knowledge causes the arousal. The distraction-conflict model posits that a unique form of conflict is the source of arousal. Each of the models informs us about the effects of others on our behavior. When each of the models does best appears to depend on the situation. For example, Feinberg and Aiello (2006) contrasted evaluation apprehension and distraction-conflict in a single experiment. They found that evaluation apprehension was more strongly related to performance on a simple, well-learned task than distraction-conflict. However, on a complex task, a combination of evaluation apprehension and distraction-conflict predicts performance best.

Group Performance: Conditions That Decrease or Increase Motivation of Group Members

We have seen that being watched affects how we perform. Let's take this a step further and examine how being a member of a group affects our performance.

We noted earlier that people who join groups do so largely for self-enhancement: They believe that group membership will improve them in some way. They will become better speakers, better citizens, better soccer players, better dancers or singers; they will meet people and expand their social circle; they will make a contribution to a cause, a political candidate, or society. Does group membership actually lead to improved performance? Or does it detract from individual effort and achievement, giving people the opportunity to underperform? Both effects have been documented.

Enhanced Performance

Imagine that you are a bicycling enthusiast. Three times a week you ride 20 miles, which takes you a little over an hour. One day you happen to come on a group of cyclists and decide to ride along with them. When you look at your time for the 20 miles, you find that your time is less than 1 hour, a full 10 minutes under your best previous time. How can you account for your increased speed? Did the other riders simply act as a windshield for you, allowing you to exert less effort and ride faster? Or is there more to this situation than aerodynamics? Could it be that the mere presence of others somehow affected your behavior?

Performing a task in front of an audience can facilitate or inhibit performance, depending on how familiar we are with the task.
Source: Monkey Business Images/Shutterstock.

This question was asked by Norman Triplett, one of the early figures in social psychology (1898). Triplett, a cycling enthusiast, decided to test a theory that the presence of other people was sufficient to increase performance. He used a laboratory in which alternative explanations for the improvement in cycling time (e.g., other riders being a windshield) could be eliminated. He also conducted what is perhaps the first social psychological experiment. He had children engage in a simulated race on a competition machine he designed. Two fishing reels were attached to a device that allowed Triplett to record how fast the children wound the reels. Children were told to wind fishing reels as fast as they could. Triplett had the children perform the task either alone or in pairs. He found that most of the children who performed the task in the presence of another child wound the reel faster than children who performed the task alone. The improved performance of the children and the cyclist when they participate in a group setting rather than alone gives us some evidence that groups do enhance individual performance.

Decreased Performance: Social Loafing and Free Rides

Is it true that the presence of others is always arousing and that participating in a group always leads to enhanced individual performance? Perhaps not. In fact, the opposite may occur. Sometimes when we are in a group situation, we relax our efforts and rely on others to take up the slack. This effect is called **social loafing**.

Sometimes, people are not more effortful in the presence of others; they, in fact, may loaf when working with others in groups (Harkins & Szymanski, 1987; Latané et al., 1979; Williams & Karau, 1991). In one experiment, participants were informed that they had to shout as loudly as they could to test the effects of sensory feedback on the ability of groups to produce sound. The researchers compared the noise produced by individuals who thought they were shouting or clapping alone to the noise they made when they thought they were in a group. If groups did as well as individuals, then the group production would at least equal the sum of the individual production. But the research findings showed that groups did not produce as much noise as the combined amount of noise individuals made (Latané et al., 1979). Some group members did not do as much as they were capable of doing as individuals: They loafed. In some instances, then, participation of others in the task (e.g., in a tug-of-war game) lowers individual motivation and reduces performance on the task. Simply put, people sometimes exert less effort when working on a task in a group context (Harkins & Petty, 1982).

Why should the group reduce individual performance in some cases and enhance it in others? The nature of the task may encourage social loafing. In a game of tug-of-war, if you do not pull the rope as hard as you can, who will know or care? If you don't shout as loud as you can, what difference does it make? You cannot accurately assess your own contribution, nor can other people evaluate how well you are performing. Also, fatigue increases social loafing. Hoeksema-van Orden and her coworkers had a group of people work for 20 hours continuously, individually or in a group. These researchers found that fatigue increased social loafing in groups, whereas individuals were less likely to loaf even when fatigued (Hoeksema-van Orden et al., 1998). Social loafing tends not to occur in very important tasks. However, many of our everyday tasks are repetitive and dull and are vulnerable to social loafing (Karau & Williams, 1993).

Regardless of the task, some individuals work harder than others in groups (Kerr, 1983). **Free riders** do not do their share of the work. Why not? They are cynical about the other members; they think others may be holding back, so they hold back also. People do not want to be suckers, doing more than their share while others take it easy. Even if they know that their coworkers are doing their share and are competent, individuals may look for a free ride (Williams & Karau, 1991).

The larger the group, the more common are social loafing and free riding. It is harder to determine individual efforts and contributions in big groups. People are likely to feel more responsible for the outcome in smaller groups (Kerr, 1989). Of course, not everyone loafs in groups, nor do people loaf in all group situations.

social loafing The performance-inhibiting effect of working in a group that involves relaxing individual effort based on the belief that others will take up the slack.

free riders Group members who do not do their share of the work in a group.

Motivation Gains in Groups: Social Compensation and the Köhler Effect

While social loafing shows that being in a group may decrease some members' motivation to perform, that is not always the case. What decreases the likelihood of social loafing? It is less likely to occur if individuals feel that it is important to compensate for other, weaker group members (Williams & Karau, 1991). When the task is important and motivation to perform is high, then *social compensation*—working harder to make up for the weakness of others—seems to overcome the tendency toward social loafing and free riding.

Social loafing is also less likely when individual contributions can be clearly identified. Generally, when individuals can be identified and cannot simply blend in with the background of other workers, they are less likely to loaf (Williams et al., 1981). The members of an automobile manufacturing team, for example, are more careful about their tasks and less willing to pass on defective work if they have to sign for each piece they do. If responsibility for defects is clear, if positive effort and contribution are rewarded, and if management punishes free riders, then social loafing will be further diminished (Shepperd, 1993). Similarly, Shepperd and Taylor (1999) showed that if group members perceive a strong relationship between their effort and a favorable outcome for the group, social loafing does not happen, and there are no free riders.

Social loafing is a phenomenon that is very robust and occurs in a variety of situations and cultures (Forgas et al., 2004; Karau & Williams, 1993). It has been found to be more common among men than women and among members of Western as opposed to Eastern cultures. These cultural and gender differences seem to be related to values. Many women and many individuals in Eastern cultures attach more importance to group harmony and group success and satisfaction. Many men, especially in Western cultures, attach more value to individual advancement and rewards and to other people's evaluations. Groups tend to mask individual differences. For this reason, Western men may have less inclination to perform well in group situations. The result is social loafing (Karau & Williams, 1993).

Köhler effect The effect where a less competent group member increases performance in a dyad when group performance depends on combined effort.

Karau and Williams have shown that groups do not necessarily generate conditions that depress some individual members' motivations to perform well. Kerr and his coworkers have rediscovered another motivational gain in groups known as the **Köhler effect** (Kerr & Tindale, 2005; Kerr et al., 2005; Messe et al., 2002). These researchers rediscovered work done by Köhler (1926) in which the researcher reported that a less-capable member of a two-person group (a *dyad*) working together on a task works harder and performs better than expected when the group product is to be a result of the combined (conjunctive) effort of the two members. This seems to be the opposite of social loafing. The weaker member of the group, rather than free riding or loafing, in fact increases his or her effort. For, example, Köhler found that members of a Berlin rowing club worked harder at a physical performance task as part of a two- or three-man crew than when they performed as individuals. Köhler's findings were replicated in a more recent study of student athletes (Osborn et al., 2012). Osborn et al. compared the times of swimmers swimming as individuals or as part of a relay team. They ranked swimmers according to their individual times from slowest to fastest. They found that swimmers with the slowest individual times showed the strongest improvement when they swam as part of a relay team, showing the greatest motivation gain. Swimmers showed progressively less motivation gain as their rank got higher. Hertel et al. (2000) called this a *Köhler motivation gain*. The question then was how this Köhler motivation gain occurs.

It is possible in a small group (and two or three is as small as one can get) that the least-competent member "knows" that her performance is crucial to a good group outcome. Or, conceivably, the weakest member might feel that she is in competition with the other members. These were but two of the possible motivations for the Köhler effect that Kerr et al. (2005) examined in their research. Kerr and his colleagues reasoned that the amount of feedback individuals were given with respect to their performance might be the crucial factor. For example, if you are not as good at the task as the other members, information about how the better members are doing should affect your effort and performance. So Kerr et al. (2005) varied the amount of feedback provided to individuals. The results revealed that knowledge about level of performance (feedback) was not necessary for the Köhler effect (increased performance by the weaker member of the dyad). However, if the group members were anonymous and were given absolutely no feedback about performance, then motivation gain was wiped out. Kerr et al.'s findings regarding feedback were recently replicated by Haugen et al. (2020). They found a Köhler effect for cyclists (increased performance by the weaker member), but only when performance feedback was provided. When participants were given no feedback or were told they were a superior cyclist, no performance gains or losses were detected.

The presence of others affects individual performance in a group. The Köhler effect involves the least competent member of a group performing better in a group than if alone. Köhler found that members of a rowing team will perform better in teams of two or three than alone.
Source: videoTD/Shutterstock.

With no information about the effect of the weakest member's contribution and no possibility for recognition, there is no motivation gain. Well, that's not surprising. So it appears that motivation gains in groups may occur due in part to *social comparison* effects, in which there is some competition between two group members, as well as the personal motivation of the weakest member to see how well that member can perform (Kerr et al., 2005).

Study Break

This section discussed how groups affect individual behavior. Before you begin the next section, answer the following questions:

1. What are social facilitation and inhibition, and under what conditions would you observe each?
2. How do the arousal, evaluation apprehension, and distraction-conflict approaches explain social facilitation and inhibition?
3. Under what conditions would you find social facilitation?
4. What is social loafing, and what factors increase or decrease it?
5. What is the Köhler effect, and how does it relate to member performance within a group?

Groups, Self-Identity, and Intergroup Relationships

Groups not only affect how we perform, but they also influence our individual sense of worth—our self-esteem—which, in turn, has an impact on how one group relates to other groups in a society. In 1971, Tajfel and his colleagues showed that group categorizations, along with in-group identification, are both necessary and sufficient conditions for groups to discriminate against other groups (Rubin & Hewstone, 1998). Recall that in Chapter 4 Tajfel showed that even if people were randomly assigned to a group (minimal group categorization), they tended to favor members of that group when distributing very small rewards (the in-group bias; Tajfel et al., 1971). For example, boys in a minimal group experiment ("you overestimated the number of dots on a screen and, therefore, you are in the overestimator group") gave more money to members of their group (the in-group) than to members of the underestimator group (the out-group). Therefore, even the most minimal group situation appears to be sufficient for an in-group bias (favoring members of your group) to occur.

Tajfel's findings suggested to him that individuals obtain part of their self-concept, their social identity, from their group memberships and that they seek to nourish a positive social (group) identity to heighten their own self-esteem. Groups that are successful and are held in high esteem by society enhance the esteem of their members. The opposite is also true. All of this depends on the social comparison with relevant outgroups on issues that are important to both (Mummendey & Wenzel, 1999). Favorable comparisons enhance the group and its members. Social identity, then, is a definition of the self in terms of group membership (Brewer, 1993; Caporael, 1997). Changes in the fate of the group imply changes in the self-concept of the individual members.

Tajfel's theory is called **self-identity theory (SIT)** and proposes that a number of factors predict one group's reaction to other competing groups in society. It pertains to what may arise from identification with a social category (membership in a social, political, racial, religious group, etc.). It does not say that once we identify with a group, we inevitably will discriminate against other groups. However, SIT does lay out the conditions under which such discrimination may take place. Generally, SIT assumes that the potential that one group will tend to discriminate or downgrade another group will be affected by four factors:

self-identity theory (SIT)
A theory proposing that a number of factors predict one group's reaction to competing groups and concerning what may arise from identification with a social category.

1. How strongly the in-group members identify with their group
2. The importance of the social category that the in-group represents
3. The dimension on which the groups are competing (the more important the dimension, the greater the potential for conflict)
4. The group's relative status and the difference in status between the in-group and the out-group (Oakes et al., 1994)

Therefore, if members strongly identify with the group, if the group represents a crucial identification category—say, race, religion, or more affiliative groups such as a social organization, if the competition occurs on a crucial dimension (jobs, college entrance possibilities, intense sports rivalries), and if the result can be expected to affect the status of the group relative to its competitor, SIT predicts intergroup discrimination. Low or threatened self-esteem will increase intergroup discrimination because of the need to enhance one's social identity (Hogg & Abrams, 1990). Groups that are successful in intergroup discrimination will enhance social identity and self-esteem (Rubin & Hewstone, 1998).

When self-esteem is threatened by group failure, people tend to respond in ways that can maintain their positive identity and sense of reality. For example, Duck and her colleagues examined the response of groups in a hotly contested political campaign. These researchers found that individuals who strongly identified with their political party were more likely to see the media coverage of the campaign as biased and favoring the other side (Duck et al., 1998). This was particularly strong for members of the weaker political party, as SIT would predict, because the weaker party was more threatened. However, when the weaker party won, they were less likely to think that the media were biased, whereas the losing, stronger party began to think the media were biased against them.

A member who threatens the success of a group also threatens the positive image of the group. This leads to the **black-sheep effect**, the observation that whereas an attractive in-group member is rated more highly than an attractive member of an out-group, an unattractive in-group member is perceived more negatively than an unattractive out-group member (Marques & Paez, 1994). The SIT inference is that the unattractive in-group member is a serious threat to the in-group's image (Mummendey & Wenzel, 1999).

black-sheep effect
The phenomenon in which an attractive in-group member is rated more highly than an attractive member of an out-group, and an unattractive in-group member is perceived more negatively than an unattractive out-group member.

The Power of Groups to Punish: Social Ostracism

In 1971, Cadet James Pelosi was taking an exam in one of his classes at West Point. The instructor told the class to put their pencils down, ending the exam. According to the instructor, Pelosi kept on writing in his bluebook, a serious violation of the Academy's honor code. Although Pelosi denied the charge, he had to face the charge in front of a board of officers. The board found insufficient evidence to expel Pelosi and ordered him back to good standing. In most cases like this, the cadet chooses to resign from the academy. Pelosi refused to resign because he felt he had done nothing wrong. A student honor committee decided to impose the harsh punishment of silencing. Other cadets were not to speak to Pelosi, he could not have a roommate, he had to eat alone at a table designed for 10, and he could communicate with others only on official business. Pelosi experienced this treatment for 19 long months, experiencing stress and anxiety. Toward the end of his career at West Point, his fellow cadets began speaking to him because the silencing was unenforceable (Time, 1973). He finally graduated with his class and was commissioned as a second lieutenant in the U.S. Army. Eventually, West Point did away with the harsh treatment of silencing.

Although groups may serve to increase our self-esteem by enhancing our social identity, groups have the power to exact painful, even dreadful, punishment like that experienced by James Pelosi. Baumeister and Leary (1995) observed that there is little in life as frightful as being excluded from groups that are important to us. Most of us spend much of our time in the presence of other people. The presence of others provides us not only with opportunities for positive interactions but also for risks of being ignored, excluded, and rejected. Kipling Williams (Williams et al., 2005; Zadro et al., 2004) provided an innovative approach to the study of the effects of being ignored or rejected by the group. Such behavior is called social **ostracism** and is defined by Williams as the act of excluding or ignoring other individuals or groups. This behavior is widespread and universal. Williams noted that organizations, employers, coworkers, friends, and family all may ignore or disengage from people (the silent treatment) to punish, control, and vent anger. The pervasiveness of ostracism is reflected by a survey conducted by Williams and his coworkers that showed that 67% of the sample surveyed said they had used the silent treatment (deliberately not speaking to a person in their presence) on a loved one, and 75% indicated that they had been a target of the silent treatment by a loved one (Faulkner & Williams, 1995). As you might imagine, the silent treatment is a marker of a relationship that is disintegrating. From the point of view of the victim of this silent treatment, social ostracism is the perception of being ignored by others in the victim's presence (Williams & Zadro, 2001).

ostracism The widespread and universal behavior of excluding or ignoring other individuals or groups.

Williams and Sommer (1997) identified several forms of ostracism. First, they distinguished between social and physical ostracism. Physical ostracism includes solitary confinement, exile, or the time-out room in grade school. Social ostracism is summed up by phrases we all know: the cold shoulder, the silent treatment.

In the social psychological realm, *punitive ostracism* and *defensive ostracism* are among the various guises ostracism may take. Punitive ostracism refers to behaviors (ignoring, shunning) that are perceived by the victim as intended to be deliberate and harmful. Sometimes, Williams and Sommer pointed out, people also engage in defensive ostracism, a kind of preemptive strike when you think someone might feel negatively toward you. Defensive ostracism is intended to shield your ego from potential negative responses from others. As you might expect, people react very negatively to being the targets of ostracism, especially punitive and defensive ostracism (Neziek et al., 2012). In fact, ostracism has recently been shown to have a causal link to suicidal thoughts (Chen et al., 2020).

The purpose of ostracism from the point of view of the ostracizer is clear: controlling the behavior of the victim. Ostracizers also report being rewarded when they see that their tactics are working. Certainly, defensive ostracism, ignoring someone before they can harm you or ignore you, seems to raise the self-esteem of the ostracizer (Sommer et al., 2001).

Ostracism occurs when we are systematically excluded from a group. Ostracism is a very negative experience.
Source: BearFotos/Shutterstock.

Although ostracism may be a tool to control the behavior of others, ostracism has some psychological costs. Researchers have found that ostracizers have more negative moods and feel more disconnected from others as compared to non-ostracizers (Bastian et al., 2013).

Even when people engage in "justified ostracism" (ostracizing for a good reason), they experience negative effects on their psychological health (Legate et al., 2021). Legate and colleagues found that when people ostracized others, even for good reasons, important psychological needs were thwarted, including the need for autonomy and the need for relatedness. Legate and colleagues argue that ostracizers experience negative moods and lower satisfaction because they feel less in control of their behavior (thwarted need for autonomy) and less connected to others (thwarted need for relatedness).

Williams developed a number of creative methods to induce the perception of being ostracized in laboratory experiments. Williams and Sommer (1997) used a ball-tossing game in which two individuals working as confederates of the experimenters either included or socially ostracized a participant during a 5-minute ball-tossing game. Participants who were waiting for a group activity to begin were placed in a waiting room that happened to have a number of objects, including a ball. Three people were involved: the two confederates and the unknowing research participant. All participants were thrown the ball during the first minute, but those in the ostracized condition were not thrown the ball during the remaining 4 minutes. The experimenter then returned to conduct the second part of the study.

After the ball-tossing ended in the Williams and Sommer (1997) experiment, the researchers asked participants to think of as many uses for an object as possible within a specified time limit. They performed this task in the same room either collectively (in which they were told that only the group effort would be recorded) or coactively (in which their own individual performances would be compared to that of the other group members) with the two confederates. Williams and Sommer predicted that ostracized targets—those excluded from the ball tossing—would try to regain a sense of belonging by working comparatively harder on the collective task, thereby contributing to the group's success. Williams and Sommer found support for this hypothesis, but only for female participants. Whether they were ostracized in the ball-tossing task, males displayed social loafing by being less productive when working collectively than when working coactively. Females, however, behaved quite differently, depending on whether they had been ostracized or included. When included, they tended to work about as hard collectively as coactively, but when ostracized, they were actually more productive when working collectively compared to when they worked coactively.

Women also demonstrated that they were interested in regaining a sense of being a valued member of the group by displaying nonverbal commitment (i.e., leaning forward, smiling), whereas males tended to employ face-saving techniques such as combing their hair, looking through their wallets, and manipulating objects, all in the service of being "cool" and showing that they were unaffected by the ostracism. We can conclude that ostracism did threaten sense of belonging for both males and females, but ostracized females tried to regain a sense of belonging, whereas males acted to regain self-esteem (Williams & Sommer, 1997; Williams et al., 2005).

Ostracism is not limited to face-to-face contacts. The power of ostracism is observed even in computer games in which one player is excluded from a ball-tossing (Internet) computer game called *cyberball* (Zadro et al., 2004). At a predetermined point in the game, one of the players is excluded. That is, the other players no longer "throw" the ball to that person. Players that are excluded report a loss of self-esteem. A study by Smith and Williams (2004) also reported that the negative effects of ostracism are not limited to face-to-face contacts. The power of ostracism can also be felt via text messages on cell phones. Smith and Williams (2004) in the text message study devised a three-way interaction via cell phones in which all three people are initially included in the text messaging. However, in one of the conditions of the study, one participant is excluded from the conversation. That person no longer received any direct messages nor did the person see the messages exchanged between the other two text messengers. Those excluded reported feeling lower levels of belonging, control, self-esteem, and "meaningful existence" (Smith & Williams, 2004). Williams and colleagues have also found that ostracism effects can also be demonstrated in immersive virtual environments (IVE). For example, a person who is ostracized by others while playing a complex online interactive game is

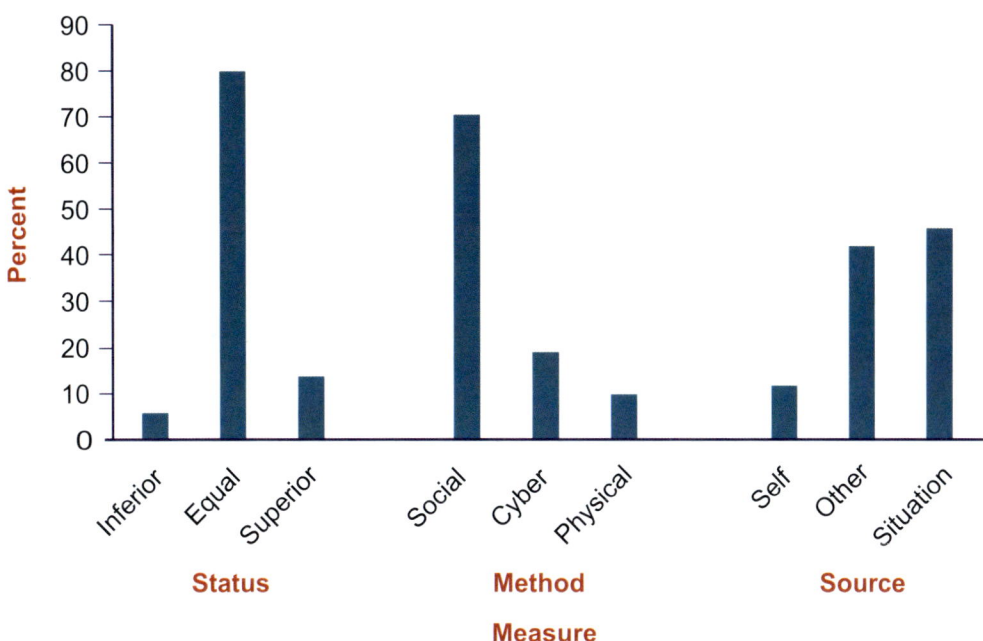

FIGURE 8.4

Ostracism reported by individuals in real-world settings.
Based on data from Nezlek et al. (2012).

likely to feel ostracized and have all of the accompanying negative feelings resulting from the ostracism (Kassner et al., 2012).

How well does what we know from laboratory studies of ostracism apply to the real world of social relationships? This question was addressed in a study by Nezlek et al. (2012). Nezlek et al. had participants keep a diary of their ostracism experiences as they went about their days. Among other measures, Nezlek et al. had participants record the status of the person perpetrating the ostracism, the method of ostracism, and who or what was responsible for the ostracism (source). Participants' responses on these three areas are shown in Figure 8.4. As you can see, most instances of ostracism came from a person of equal status to the participant. Live, social ostracism was the most frequently cited source, and participants attributed most instances of ostracism to others or to the social situation. Participants also reported that most instances of ostracism came from either an acquaintance or a stranger (combined 62%). Ostracism was rarely experienced from a friend or close friend. Emotional responses to ostracism were quite negative. When ostracism happened, participants reported being angry, feeling they lost control, having a lower sense of belonging, and experiencing reduced self-esteem. The results of this study show that in the real world, people react to ostracism in ways that are very similar to how they react in a laboratory.

Deindividuation and Anonymity: The Power of Groups to Do Violence

Although ostracism refers to essentially psychological methods of exclusion from the group, other more dangerous behaviors occur in group settings. We have seen that when certain individuals feel they can't be identified by their actions or achievements, they tend to loaf. This is a common group effect. A decline in individual identity seems to mean a decline in a person's sense of responsibility. Anonymity can alter people's ethical and moral behavior. For example, research indicates that individuals who perpetrate acts of violence (e.g., bombings) often wear disguises to hide their identities and that those who wear disguises engage in more lethal acts of violence (Silke, 2003). Silke content-analyzed stories in publications in Northern Ireland concerning instances of violence and found, as shown in Figure 8.5, that individuals wearing a disguise perpetrated acts that led to more injuries, vandalism, and multiple victims than did perpetrators who did not

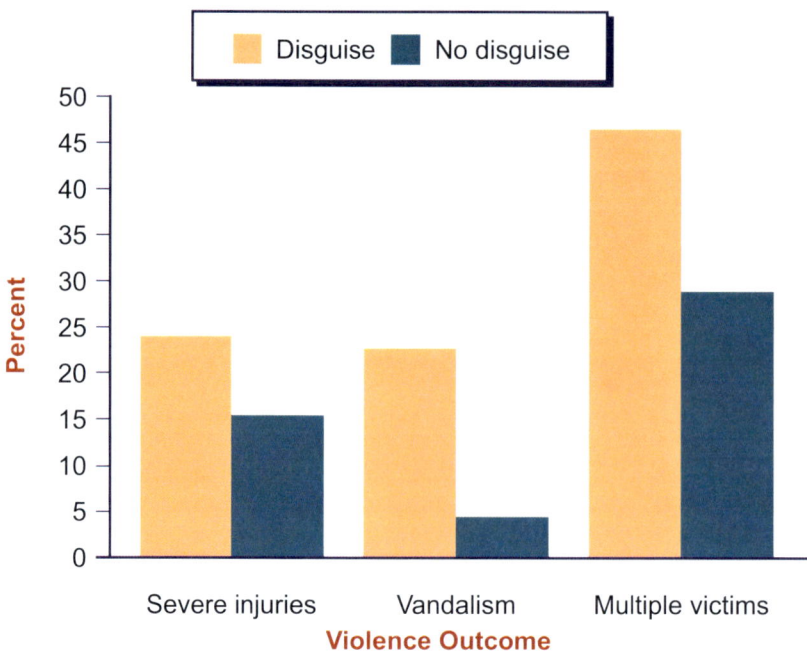

FIGURE 8.5

Severity of violent acts by disguised and nondisguised perpetrators.
Based on data from Silke (2003).

deindividuation
A phenomenon that occurs in large-group (crowd) situations in which individual identity is lost within the anonymity of the large group, perhaps leading to a lowering of inhibitions against negative behaviors.

wear a disguise. This effect was also seen during the COVID-19 pandemic, when wearing a mask in public was required. According to Los Angeles Police Department data, the number of crimes in which the suspect was wearing a mask increased from 200 in 2019 to 1,664 in 2020 (Ward, 2020).

Observers of group behavior have long known that certain kinds of groups have the potential for great mischief. Groups at sporting events have engaged in murder and mayhem when their soccer teams have lost. One element present in such groups is that the individuals are not easily identifiable. People get lost in the mass and seem to lose their self-identity and self-awareness. Social psychologists have called this loss of inhibition while engulfed in a group **deindividuation** (Zimbardo, 1969).

People who are deindividuated seem to become less aware of their own moral standards and are much more likely to respond to violent or aggressive cues (Prentice-Dunn & Rogers, 1989). In fact, deindividuated people are quick to respond to any cues. Research suggests that when people are submerged in a group, they become impulsive, aroused, and wrapped up in the cues of the moment (Spivey & Prentice-Dunn, 1990). Their action is determined by whatever the group does.

Groups and organizations whose primary purpose involves violence often attempt to deindividuate their members. Certainly, the white sheets covering the members of the Ku Klux Klan are a prime example of this. So, too, are the training methods of most military organizations. Uniforms serve to lower a sense of self-awareness and make it easier to respond to aggressive cues.

Hiding one's identity, such as Ku Klux Klan members' hoods, can alter one's ethical and moral identity and cause them to be more likely to perpetrate acts of violence leading to greater injury.
Source: Corrado Baratta/Shutterstock.

In the view of deindividuation theory, being in a group can make the individual feel more anonymous and thus more likely to engage in aggressive nonnormative behavior. These anonymous individuals have less self-awareness and are less concerned with self-evaluation. Another approach to deindividuation emphasizes how identification with a group can interact with anonymity to influence behavior. The *social identity model of deindividuation* (SIDE; Reicher et al., 1995) draws on self-categorization theory and argues that the self can be defined in multiple ways. Sometimes we categorize ourselves at the individual level, and sometimes we categorize ourselves at the group level. The SIDE model argues that when we categorize ourselves at the group level, we do not experience a "loss of self-identity"; rather, we switch from our personal identity to a group level of self-categorization in which the self and others are seen in terms of their group identities. Furthermore, the SIDE model suggests that mindless violence is not the default behavior related to anonymity. Rather, anonymity, when coupled with a salient group identity, will lead to behaviors seen as normative for the group. Thus, if the group is stereotypically aggressive (e.g., hate groups), then anonymity will lead to more aggressive behaviors. However, when the group is stereotypically helpful (e.g., Habitat for Humanity), anonymity will lead to more prosocial behaviors. Deindividuation and SIDE theories have elements of support, and each helps us better understand the relationship between anonymity and deindividuation in groups (Chang, 2008). Deindividuation theory may help us understand anonymity in groups when no salient group identity is present (e.g., random crowds), and the SIDE model offers insight when a group identity is present.

Groups are often used to make decisions. A number of factors such as group composition, size, and leadership style affect how a group functions.
Source: Mangostar/Shutterstock.

Study Break

This section discussed intergroup relations, ostracism, and deindividuation. Before you go on to the next section, answer the following questions:

1. What is self-identity theory, and how does it relate to intergroup relations?
2. What is the black-sheep effect?
3. What is ostracism, and what are its different forms?
4. What are the different sources of ostracism?
5. What are deindividuation and SIDE theories, and how do they relate to behavior?

Group Performance

We have seen how groups can affect individual behavior. Next, we turn our attention to the question of whether groups perform better than individuals on tasks assigned to them. Is the old adage that "two heads are better than one" the case? Or is the alternative adage that "too many cooks spoil the broth" true? In the sections that follow, we will explore how groups combine individual inputs to perform a task.

Individual Decisions and Group Decisions

First of all, let's consider whether group decisions are in fact better than individual decisions. Is it better to have a team of medical personnel decide whether our CAT scan indicates we need surgery, or is that decision better left to a single surgeon? Did the launch director at NASA benefit from the workings of the group, or would he have been wiser to think through the situation on his own?

Does a Group Do Better Than the Average Person?

In general, research shows that groups do outperform individuals—at least the average individual—on many jobs and tasks (Stasser et al., 1989). Three reasons have been proposed for the observed superiority of groups over the average person. First of all, groups do a better job than the average person because they recognize truth—accept the right answer—more quickly. Second, groups are better able to reject error—reject incorrect or implausible answers (Laughlin, 1980; Laughlin et al., 1991; Lorge & Solomon, 1955). Third, groups have a better, more efficient memory system than do individuals. This permits them to process information more effectively.

However, groups do not appear to live up to their potential. That is, their performance seems to be less than the sum of their parts (i.e., the individual members [Kerr & Tindale, 2004]). So let's keep that in mind as we first see what advantages groups have over individuals. Groups may possess what have been called **transactive memory systems (TMSs)**, a shared system for placing events into memory (encoding), storing those memories, and retrieving that information. Wegner (1996) used the example of a directory-sharing computer network to explain the three legs of a TMS:

transactive memory systems (TMSs) Systems within groups that are sets of individual memories that allow group members to learn about each other's expertise and to assign memory tasks on that basis.

1. *Directory updating,* in which people find out what other group members know
2. *Information allocation,* the place where new information is given to the person who knows how to store it
3. *Retrieval coordination,* which refers to how information is recovered when needed to solve a particular problem

Group members learn about each other's expertise and assign memory tasks on that basis. This not only leaves others to concentrate on the memory tasks they do best, it also provides the group with memory aids. Someone in the group may be good in math, for example, so that person is assigned the task of remembering math-related information. When the group wants to recall that information, they go to this expert and use him or her as an external memory aid. Memory thus becomes a transaction, a social event in the group. For some or all of these reasons, groups seem to outperform the average person on many decision-related tasks (Laughlin et al., 2003).

Hollingshead (1998) showed the effectiveness of transactive memory. She studied intimate couples as compared to strangers who worked on problems, some face-to-face and others via a computer-conferencing network. Intimate couples who were able to sit face-to-face and process their partner's verbal and nonverbal cues were able to solve problems better than couples comprised of strangers, because the intimate couples were able to retrieve more information. Intimate couples who worked via a computer-conferencing system did not do as well, again suggesting that the nonverbal cues were important in pooling information.

Transactive memory can be categorized into two types: differentiated and integrated (Gupta & Hollingshead, 2010). In a *differentiated TMS,* different pieces of information are stored by different group members, but all members have access to the information. For example, a team of scientists from different areas will have different information (e.g., chemistry, biology, neurology) that can be accessed by the group. In an *integrated TMS,* the same information is stored by each group member, with all group members having access to it. For example, a group of biologists from the same specialty area have basically the same information available to a group. When Gupta and Hollingshead directly compared the performance of groups with differentiated or integrated memory systems, they found that the groups operated differently. For example, groups with an integrated memory system tended to use more information that members shared in common (shared information), whereas groups with a differentiated memory system used more noncommon information (unshared information). Also, groups with an integrated memory system did better when the groups worked on an intellective task (i.e., one that had a correct answer). They did not find any difference between the two types of groups on a recall task, although other research typically shows that groups with dependent systems do well on recall tasks (Gupta & Hollingshead, 2010).

Are there contextual factors that promote or inhibit TMSs in groups? Do effective leaders help to promote TMSs? Are groups that have a diverse gender composition more or less likely to develop effective TMSs? These questions were addressed in a meta-analysis by Bachrach et al. (2018). Bachrach et al. examined 76 empirical studies and concluded that there are several such contextual factors that influence the development of an effective TMS. First, Bachrach et al. found that groups that operate in volatile environments (environments marked by unpredictable rapid change and uncertainty) are more likely to develop TMSs. They argue that "environmental volatility increases the need for integrating and coordinating knowledge from disparate source and amplifies a team's information processing demands" (Bacharach et al., 2018, p. 472). Second, Bachrach et al. found that effective leadership was positively related to the development of a TMS. Effective leaders can help team members understand "who knows what" on their team. Finally, and counterintuitively, the diversity of a team may negatively affect the development of a TMS. Gender-diverse teams appeared to be less likely to develop TMSs as compared to more gender-homogenous teams. It is possible that gender stereotypes interfere with team members' ability to correctly identify and utilize member expertise. Informationally diverse teams are less likely to develop TMSs. This was the most counterintuitive finding. One might expect that information diversity would be a necessary condition for TMS development. Bachrach et al. speculate that too much diversity may cause members to be unaware of the distribution of expertise or unable to effectively understand and communicate with one another.

Does a Group Do Better Than Its Best Member?

We noted that research shows that groups outperform the average person. But does the group perform better than the best member, the smartest person, the "best and brightest" member of the group?

To test the hypothesis that groups can find correct responses better than individuals, college students were asked to try to discover an arbitrary rule for separating a deck of cards into those that did and did not fit the rule (Laughlin et al., 1991). If the rule was "hearts," for example, then all cards of the hearts suit would fit the rule, and all others would not. Subjects had to guess the rule, and then test it by playing a card. The feedback from the experimenter gave them information on which to base their next guess. The researchers also varied the amount of information that subjects had to process. They presented some subjects with only two arrays of cards, others with three, and others with four: The more arrays, the more difficult the task.

The performance of four-person groups was then compared to the performance of each of the four group members, who had to do a similar task individually. The best individual was able to generate more correct guesses than the group or any other individual member. The group's performance was equal to its second-best member. The third- and fourth-best members were inferior to the group. As the task became more difficult—the arrays increased to four, which made much more information available—the performance of both the best individual and the group fell. The researchers also compared the abilities of groups and their individual members in rejecting implausible hypotheses. The fewer implausible ideas subjects or groups raised, the better they did with respect to rejecting false leads. Groups and the best individual were better at rejecting false leads than were the second-, third-, and fourth-best individuals.

This research suggests that groups in general perform as well as their best or second-best individual member working independently. You might ask, Why not just let the best member do the task? But keep in mind that it is often not possible to identify the group's best member prior to completing the task. This finding tells us that groups tend to perform competently, particularly when the information load is not overwhelming. In addition, it may very well be that the kind of problem that the group has to deal with may influence whether or not a very good individual is or is not better than the group solution.

The Harder the Problem, the Better the Group

Research suggests that we may have underrated the ability of groups to reach solutions, especially to more difficult problems. Crott et al. (1998) argued that their research on group problem solving suggests that difficult tasks provoke creativity in groups. When faced with a problem that required the group to come up with a number of hypotheses to discover the correct answers, groups more than individuals were able to generate a number of novel explanations. Groups were also shown to be less likely to be prone to the confirmation bias than were individuals (Crott et al., 1998).

Similarly, Laughlin et al. (1998) showed that groups were as good as the best individual in solving difficult inductive (proceeding from specific facts to general conclusions) problems and better than all the remaining group members. Groups are especially effective in dealing with information-rich problems because they have more resources (Tindale et al., 1996).

The finding that the best member of a group may outperform the group is also modified by the *size of that group* and by the type of problem. Laughlin and his colleagues studied groups that varied in size from two to five people (Laughlin et al., 2006). The groups had to deal with a complex intellectual problem that required different strategies. The researchers first determined the best, second-best, third-best, and fourth- and fifth-best member of each group. Laughlin et al. then compared the solutions to these complex problems submitted by individual members and those submitted by three-, four-, and five-person groups. These researchers found, contrary to some previous findings, that the groups took significantly less time to solve problems and the quality of the solutions was better than those of the best member of the group. That is, each of the three-, four-, and five-person groups solved the problems more quickly and produced more complex solutions to the problems than the best individual member. And, there were no significant differences between three-, four-, and five-person groups. This is interesting because we might have expected some "motivation loss" due to free riders (see our earlier discussion) as the group got larger.

What about the two-person groups? The two-person groups performed less well than the other groups. Laughlin et al. (2006) concluded that groups of three that are "necessary and sufficient" perform better than the very best individual on *difficult intellective problems*.

We have seen how well groups perform with respect to the abilities of their members. Let's take a closer look at the workings, the dynamics, of how those decisions are made.

How do groups gather and use the information possessed by individual members? How do they reach decisions?

The Group's Use of Information: Hidden Profiles

One advantage groups have over individual decision makers is that a variety of individuals can usually bring to the discussion a great deal more information than can one person. This is usually seen as the great advantage of groups. But does the group make adequate use of that information? Research shows that group members tend to discuss information that they share and avoid discussing information that only one person has (Lu et al., 2012). Research on the insufficient sharing of information that one member of the group may have uses the *hidden profile* paradigm. The hidden profile paradigm refers to a situation in which the group's task is to pick the best alternative, say the best job applicant, but the relevant information to make this choice is distributed among the group members such that no one member has enough information to make the right choice alone (Greitmeyer & Schulz-Hardt, 2003).

In one experiment, each member of a committee received common information about three candidates for student government (Stasser & Titus, 1987). Each also received information about each candidate that none of the others received (unshared information). The committee members met in four-person groups to rank the candidates. The sheer number of facts available to the members varied from one group to the next. When the number of facts was high, the raters ignored information that was unshared. That is, they rated the candidates based solely on the information that they held in common. The information they chose to share tended to support the group decision; they did not share information that would have conflicted with the decision. Because the results of this study indicate that group members try to avoid conflict by selectively withholding information, the researchers concluded that face-to-face, unstructured discussion is not a good way to inform group members of unshared information (Stasser, 1991).

There appear to be at least two reasons for the failure of face-to-face groups to report and use unshared information. The first has to do with the way people think. Whatever is most salient (the shared information) tends to overwhelm that which recedes into the background (the unshared information). In other words, group members hear the shared information and simply neglect to bring up or take into account the unshared information. The second reason is that individuals may be motivated to ignore or forget information (unshared) that they think may cause conflict. Individuals also avoid discussing or disclosing information that goes counter to the group's preferred decision (Greitemeyer & Schulz-Hardt, 2003).

There are various contextual factors that promote information sharing in groups. One factor is the number of group members who have access to the "unshared" information. When information is partially shared, available to more than one group member, it has a greater chance of influencing group discussion (Gigone & Hastie, 1993; Schittekatte, 1996; Schitekatte & Van Hiewl, 1996). Generally, in the hidden profile paradigm, the discussion of both shared and unshared information is dependent on participants' memory. However, in some variations of this paradigm, participants are allowed to take a copy of the information with them into the group discussion. Access to the information during the discussion increases the dissemination of unshared information (Hollingshead, 1996), and in some instances, it actually leads to more concentration on unshared information than shared (Bowman & Wittenbaum, 2012). Finally, another way to increase the likelihood that unshared hidden profiles are brought to the discussion is to suggest to group members that they think in a *counterfactual* way. That is, if you have some information that nobody else has, you might say, "What if this is inaccurate—what would it mean?" With this approach, it seems to be the case that more unshared information sees the light of day (Galinsky & Kray, 2004).

The research of James R. Larson, Jr., showed that access to unshared information is crucial to good group decision making. For example, Larson et al. (1998) examined the decision making of medical teams. Three-person physician teams had to diagnose cases and were given shared information (to all three MDs), whereas the rest of the diagnostic data were divided among the three. Compared with unshared information, the physicians discussed shared information earlier in the discussion. However, the unshared information, when discussed, proved to lead to more accurate (correct diagnosis) outcomes.

In other research, Larson's team reached similar conclusions. Winquist and Larson (1998) gave three-person groups the task of nominating professors for teaching awards. Discussion focused more on shared information, but the quality of the decision was determined by the amount of unshared information that was pooled in the discussion (Henningsen & Henningsen, 2003).

Study Break

This section introduced you to group processes. Before you begin the next section, answer the following questions:

1. Does a group outperform an individual?
2. What is transactive memory, and how does it relate to group performance?
3. What are differentiated and integrated transactive memory systems, and how does each relate to group performance?
4. How does group performance stack up against its best member's performance?
5. How does task difficulty relate to group performance?
6. How do groups handle shared and unshared information?

The Effect of Leadership Style on Group Decision Making

Can leaders influence group members to pool their unshared information? We know that leadership style is important in determining how groups function (Fiedler, 1967). Leaders who encourage group members to share unshared information typically have groups that make better decisions (van Ginkel & van Knippenberg, 2012). In one study (Larson et al., 1998), researchers identified two common styles of leadership. The first, the

participative leader
A leadership style characterized by a leader who shares power with the other members of the group and includes them in the decision making.

directive leader A leadership style involving a leader who gives less value to participation, emphasizes the need for agreement, and tends to prefer his or her own solution.

participative leader, shares power with the other members of the group and includes them in the decision making. Another leadership style, the **directive leader**, gives less value to participation, emphasizes the need for agreement, and tends to prefer his or her own solution.

Directive and Participative Leaders

Research using these leadership styles indicated that participative leaders provoked their groups to discuss more information, both shared and unshared, than did groups with a directive leader (Larson et al., 1998). However, directive leaders were more likely to repeat information that had been pooled, especially unshared information. In other words, directive leaders made unshared information more prominent.

It seems, then, that participative leaders worked to get the group to bring out more information but that directive leaders were more active in managing the information once it was put on the table. What about the quality of the decisions? Interestingly, groups under participative leadership made many more incorrect decisions. This was counter to the researchers' expectations (Larson et al., 1998). If directive leaders have information that favors the best alternative, they use it and bring the group to a good-quality decision. They do this much better than participative leaders. The downside to directive leaders is that they may not be able to get the group members to bring out all the necessary information for good decision making.

Gender and Leadership

Eagly and her colleagues have investigated the possible differences in leadership styles exhibited by men and women. These differences may be important for effective group functioning because the behavior of the leader is critical for group performance (Eagly et al., 2003; Eagly & Karau, 2002). Eagly's analysis is based on social roles theory, which suggests that leaders occupy roles determined both by their position in whatever group they are part of and by the limits imposed by gender-based expectations (Eagly & Karau, 2002). For example, if the leader is a manager of a warehouse, that role is in part determined by the tasks that must be done to keep that warehouse functioning—scheduling workloads, monitoring inventory, dealing with unions. But each manager also has some leeway in carrying out those functions. Eagly points out that there is often an incompatibility between leadership roles and the gendered expectations of women.

transformative leader
A group leader who places emphasis on communicating group goals and expressing optimism about the group's ability to reach those goals.

transactional leader A group leader who rewards positive outcomes but also focus on mistakes made by group members.

Eagly and her colleagues analyzed almost 50 studies that compared the leadership styles of males and females (Eagly et al., 2003). They found that as social roles theory predicted, leadership styles were determined by both gender and demands placed on the leaders. They found significant gender differences with respect to the type of leadership styles men and women exhibited. Women leaders were more *transformative* than were male leaders. **Transformative leaders** tend to focus on communicating the reasons behind the group's mission and to show optimism and excitement about reaching the group's goals. Transformative leaders also tend to mentor their group members and to freely promote new ideas and ways of getting things done.

In contrast, male leaders are more *transactional*. That is, they deal in rewarding positive results but also focus on the mistakes and errors that members have made. Compared to transformative leaders, who may intervene before serious problems occur, **transactional leaders** may wait until problems become severe before intervening. In other words, males are more hands-off leaders, more disengaged, while females seem to be more active.

What do we make of these differences? Do they matter in the functioning of, say, a corporation, or a university? Eagly et al. (2003) point out that the difference between men and women leaders is relatively small. That is, gender accounts for a relatively small part of the variation of leadership styles. That being said, however, the qualities that distinguish women leaders from their male counterparts appear to be directly related to greater group effectiveness. For example, research has demonstrated the difficulty of motivating workers to adopt new safety regulations. Research has shown that hands-on positive leadership, which defines the transformational leader, can be very effective (Kelloway et al., 2006).

The gender of a group's leader also appears to interact with the composition of the group. In one experiment (Grossman et al., 2015), participants played an investment game in either same-gender (all male or all female) or mixed-gender groups. In one-half of the mixed-gender groups, the participants were told of the leader's gender; and in the other half, not informed. Participants had to decide whether to follow the leader's investment decision by investing or not investing their resources. Grossman et al. found that in the mixed-gender groups female leaders performed better when their gender was not made known to the group than if it was. In other words, as long as the female leader's gender was unknown to the mixed group, the female leaders performed well. This outcome was not found to be true of the male leaders in the mixed groups. Female leaders were more comfortable in the all-female groups and in the mixed groups where leader gender was unknown to the group. Grossman et al. suggest that female leaders with male followers (mixed-gender groups) may be hesitant to lead because of gender stereotypes. Female leaders in the mixed groups may have felt that their male followers would not see their leadership as legitimate, causing the female leaders to shy away from the leadership role.

A group leader's gender affects a group's performance and interacts with the composition of the group. Research shows that female leaders appear to be less willing to lead when leading an all-male group because of perceived gender stereotypes.
Source: Jono Erasmus/Shutterstock.

SOCIAL PSYCHOLOGY IN ACTION

Why Group Members Obey Leaders: The Psychology of Legitimacy

Why do group members willingly follow the leader of a group? Tyler (1997) provided insight into when and why groups voluntarily follow their leaders. In order for groups to function, the members have to decide that the leader ought to be obeyed. Although leaders often have access to coercive methods to get members to follow their orders, voluntary compliance is often necessary for a group to successfully achieve its goals.

Tyler was interested in the judgment by group members that they should voluntarily comply with the rules laid down by authorities, regardless of the probability of punishment or reward. Tyler (1997) suggested that the feeling of obligation to obey the leader is best termed *legitimacy*. Following earlier work by French and Raven (1959), Tyler proposed that a leader has legitimate power to influence, and the member has the obligation to obey, when all have accepted (internalized) the central values of the group. Tyler's work suggests that the basis of a leader's legitimacy resides in its psychological foundations. That is, it is not enough for the leader to be successful in getting the group's work done, although clearly, that is quite important.

Among the factors that are crucial for legitimacy are, first, how people are treated by authorities, regardless of how the leaders have evaluated them, and second, whether the members share group membership with the authorities. Finally, Tyler's work indicated that people value the leader's integrity more than they do the leader's competence. This description of legitimacy is called the *relational model*.

Voluntary compliance with the directives of a leader is key to the success of a group. Members will most likely follow a leader if they perceive her as having legitimate authority.
Source: fizkes/Shutterstock.

The relational model emphasizes that individuals are most likely to internalize group values when they are treated with procedural fairness (van den Bos et al., 1998). In fact, people make judgments about authorities when little information is available about them, based on whether the authorities give them dignified, fair treatment (van den Bos et al., 1998). Neidermeier et al. (1999) reported that some groups (juries) may deliberately and willfully disobey the commands of authorities (judges) when they determine that following the authority's instructions would result in an unfair and unjust verdict. People will be more likely to accept a leader when that leader exhibits interpersonal respect, neutrality in judgment, and trustworthiness (Tyler, 1997).

Discussion Questions

1. What is the basis of leader's legitimate power?
2. How do you think the relational model applies in the college classroom?

Again, we should not overlook the importance of instrumental factors in leadership. Getting the group's work done is crucial. It is likely that under some circumstances, relational issues may not be important at all (Fiedler, 1967). If someone has the ability to lead a group out of a burning building, relational issues matter not. But Tyler's earlier work indicated that in judging authorities with whom we have no contact (the U.S. Congress, the Supreme Court), concerns about fairness come into play (Tyler, 1994).

Study Break

This section discussed leadership and how it affects group performance. Before you begin the next section, answer the following questions:

1. What is the difference between participative and directive leaders, and how does each style affect group performance?
2. How does the gender of a leader relate to leadership style? In your answer, define the transactional and transformative leadership styles.
3. Under what conditions do male and female leaders do best?

Factors That Affect the Decision-Making Ability of a Group

What makes a good decision-making group? Is there a particular size that works best? What about the abilities of the group members? What other factors have an impact on the abilities and effectiveness of a group?

Group Composition

Several group investigators emphasize the composition of a group as its most fundamental attribute (Levine & Moreland, 1990). Questions often arise about how to best constitute groups, especially decision-making groups. For example, some people have asked whether random selection of citizens is the best way to put together a jury, especially for a complex trial (Horowitz et al., 1996).

Some researchers have investigated whether groups with high-ability members perform better than groups composed of individuals of lesser abilities. In one study, the composition of three-person battle tank crews was varied (Tziner & Eden, 1985). Some crews had all high-ability members, some had mixtures of high- and low-ability members, and others had all low-ability members. Their results showed that tank groups composed of all high-ability individuals performed more effectively than expected from the sum of their individual talents. Groups composed of all low-ability members did worse than expected.

Psychologist Robert Steinberg believes that every group has its own intelligence level, or "group IQ" (Williams & Steinberg, 1988). The group's IQ is not simply the sum of each member's IQ. Rather, it is the blending of their intellectual abilities with their personalities and social competence. In one study, Steinberg asked volunteers who had been tested on their intelligence and social skills to devise a marketing plan for a new product, an artificial sweetener (Williams & Steinberg, 1988). Other groups had similar tasks, all of which required creative solutions. The decision-making groups that produced the most creative solutions were those that contained at least one person with a high IQ and others who were socially skillful, practical, or creative. In other words, the successful groups had a good mix of people with different talents who brought different points of view to the problem.

This research highlights the fact that everybody in the group must have the skills to make a contribution. If one member of the group is extremely persuasive or extremely good at the task, the other members may not be able to use their abilities to the best effect. According to one study, successful leaders should have IQ scores no more than 10 points higher than the average IQ score of the group (Simonton, 1985). This minimizes the possibility that the most talented person will dominate the group. If this person is more extraordinary, then the collective effort will be hurt by his or her presence (Simonton, 1985).

The gender of group members also influences problem-solving ability (Levine & Moreland, 1990). Research shows that groups composed of all males are generally more effective than all-female groups. However, the success of the groups really depends on the kind of problem they have to solve. Male groups do better when they have to fulfill a specific task, whereas female groups do better at communal activities that involve friendship and social support (Wood, 1987). Additionally, in a study in which participants could allocate a limited, valuable resource, all-male groups were more "generous" (allocated more of the resource) than all-female or mixed-gender groups (Grossman et al., 2015).

Racial Effects on Group Decision Making

One might expect that the racial composition of a group might affect the type and perhaps the quality of decision making of groups. But how and why? As one example, a goal of the judicial system is to ensure that juries be formed from fair cross-sections of the population. This doesn't mean that each jury must represent a fair cross-section but that the group from which the jury is selected is a good representation of the community. Therefore, from a public policy and a constitutional point of view, diverse juries are perceived as a societal "good." But what impact does diversity have on both the process and outcomes of group decision making?

Communication patterns within a group can be affected by the racial makeup of the group. Research shows that mixed-race groups with an equal number of members from each race make better decisions than same-race groups, but the mixed-race groups take longer to make a decision.

Source: sirtravelalot/Shutterstock.

Sommers (2006) studied the effects of the racial composition of one unique group, the jury in criminal trials, on verdicts. Using a "mock jury" paradigm in which participants are asked to play the role of jurors, Sommers constructed juries that were either composed of all Whites or all Blacks, or were racially mixed. Mock jurors were brought to a county courthouse and essentially went through the same procedures any prospective juror would. After being formed into juries, they watched a videotaped trial of a sexual assault case involving an Black defendant and a White victim. Several questions were asked of the jurors before seeing the trial that were designed to make them think about their racial attitudes and to make them salient, uppermost in their minds.

The results suggested that the differences between racially diverse groups and racially homogeneous groups were reflected in jury decision making. For example, Whites in diverse groups were more likely to be lenient toward a Black defendant than were Whites in all-White groups. Whites in diverse juries processed more information and brought out more facts than Whites in homogeneous White groups. Diverse juries took more time to deliberate, and diverse groups discussed more racial issues.

What of verdicts? Diverse groups showed some tendency to hang (i.e., not able to reach a unanimous verdict), and that goes hand in hand with the longer deliberation times. However, only 1 of the 30 six-person juries in the research convicted the defendant. The racial effects in this research are primarily expressed in the quality of the jury process rather than in verdicts, generally.

Research also shows that in mixed-race groups communication patterns differ from those in same-race groups (Aritz & Walker, 2009). Aritz and Walker analyzed the communication patterns in groups made up of all Americans, all East Asian native speakers, or mixed groups of Americans and East Asians. They found that the communication patterns across same-race groups did not differ all that much. That is, the communication patterns in the all American and all East Asian groups were very similar. However, when they analyzed the communication patterns within the mixed groups, some interesting differences emerged. In groups with a majority of East Asians and a minority of Americans, the Americans exhibited communication patterns showing greater involvement in group discussion. Conversely, when Americans were in the majority, the East Asians tended to withdraw from the group discussion. Another study showed that mixed-race groups with an equal number of members from each race (Americans and Chinese) make better decisions than same-race groups (all Americans or Chinese), but the mixed-race groups take longer to reach a decision (Li et al., 2014). However, mixed groups with an imbalance of racial members (e.g., more Chinese than Americans) did not perform as well as balanced mixed-race groups.

Race and gender also affect how "holdouts" are perceived within a group. A holdout is a group member who defies the majority in the group. For example, a juror who continues to vote not guilty when the other 11 jurors vote guilty would be a holdout. A study by Salerno et al. (2019) investigated how a female or a Black holdout expressing a deviant opinion with anger (versus not angry) was perceived by other jurors. Salerno et al. found that a female (but not male) or Black (but not White) juror expressing an opinion with anger was less influential and effective than if the deviant opinion was expressed calmly. Salerno et al. concluded that when a female or Black juror expressed a deviant opinion angrily, it led to that individual being discredited by other jurors.

Group Size

Conventional wisdom tells us that two heads are better than one. If this is so, then why wouldn't three be better than two, four better than three, and so on? Does increasing a group's size also increase its ability to arrive at correct answers, make good decisions, and reach productivity goals?

Increasing the number of members of a group does increase the resources available to the group and therefore the group's potential productivity. On the other hand, increasing group size also leads to more process loss (Steiner, 1972). In other words, the increase in resources due to more group members is counterbalanced by the increased difficulty in arriving at a decision. Large groups generally take more time to reach a decision than small groups (Davis, 1969).

Yet, smaller is not always better. We often misperceive the effect of group size on performance. Researchers interested in testing the common belief that small groups are more effective than large groups gave a number of groups the task of solving social dilemmas, problems that require individuals to sacrifice some of their own gains so that the entire group benefits, such as conserving water during a drought (Kerr, 1989).

Those who participated in the study thought that the size of their group was an important determinant of their ability to satisfactorily resolve social dilemmas. People in larger groups felt there was very little they could do to influence the decisions of the group. They tended to be less active and less aware of what was going on than comparable members of smaller groups. They believed that smaller groups would more effectively solve social dilemmas than larger groups, mainly by cooperating.

In fact, there was no difference in effectiveness between the small and large groups in solving social dilemmas. People enjoyed small groups more than large ones, but the product and the quality of the decisions of both sizes of groups were much the same. Thus, small groups offer only an **illusion of efficacy**. That is, they think they are more effective than larger groups, but the evidence suggests they may not be, based on their actual productivity (Kerr, 1989).

illusion of efficacy
The illusion that members of small groups think they are more effective than larger groups, which may not be the case.

Group Cohesiveness

Does a cohesive group outperform a noncohesive group? When we consider decision-making or problem-solving groups, two types of cohesiveness become important: *task-based cohesiveness* and *interpersonal cohesiveness* (Zaccaro & Lowe, 1988). Groups may be cohesive because the members respect one another's abilities to help obtain the group's goals; this is task-based cohesiveness. Other groups are cohesive because the members find each other to be likable; this is interpersonal cohesiveness.

Each type of cohesiveness influences group performance in a somewhat different way, depending on the type of task facing the group. When a task does not require much interaction among members, task-based cohesiveness increases group productivity, but interpersonal cohesiveness does not (Zaccaro & McCoy, 1988). For example, if a group is working on writing a paper, and each member is responsible for different parts of that paper, then productivity is increased to the extent that the members are committed to doing a good job for the group. The group members do not have to like one another to do the job well.

Now, it is true that when members of the group like one another, their cohesiveness increases the amount of commitment to a task and increases group interaction as well (Zaccaro & Lowe, 1988). However, the time they spend interacting may take away from their individual time on the task, thus offsetting the productivity that results from task-based cohesiveness.

Some tasks require interaction, such as the *Challenger* decision-making group. On these tasks, groups that have high levels of both task-based and interactive cohesiveness perform better than groups that are high on one type but low on the other or that are low on both (Zaccaro & McCoy, 1988).

Cohesiveness can also detract from the successful completion of a task when group members become too concerned with protecting one another's feelings and do not allot enough attention to the actual task. Groups that are highly cohesive have members who are very concerned with one another. This may lead group members to stifle criticism of group decisions.

Members of strongly cohesive groups are less likely to disagree with one another than are members of less cohesive groups, especially if they are under time pressure to come up with a solution. Ultimately, then, very high cohesiveness may prevent a group from reaching a high-quality decision. Cohesiveness is a double-edged sword: It can help or hurt a group, depending on the demands of the task.

Study Break

This section discussed a number of factors that affect group decision making. Before you begin the next section, answer the following questions:

1. How does group composition relate to group decision making?
2. How does the racial make-up of a group affect its performance and decision making?
3. How does group size affect group performance?
4. What are task-based and interpersonal cohesiveness, and how does each relate to group performance?

The Dynamics of Group Decision Making: Decision Rules, Group Polarization, and Groupthink

Now that we have considered various aspects of group decision making, let's consider how the decision-making process works. Although we empower groups to make many important decisions for us, they do not always make good decisions (Janis, 1972). However, the reason we use groups to make important decisions is the assumption that groups are better at it, more accurate than are individual decision makers (Hastie & Kameda, 2005).

Group Decisions: How Groups Blend Individual Choices

A **decision rule** is a rule about how many members must agree before the group can reach a decision. Decision rules set the criteria for how individual choices will be blended into a group product or decision (Pritchard & Watson, 1992). Two common decision rules are *majority rule* (the winning alternative must receive more than half the votes) and *unanimity rule* (consensus, all members must agree).

Groups will find a decision rule that leads to good decisions and stick with that rule throughout the life cycle of the group (Miller, 1989). The majority rule is used in most groups (Davis, 1980). The majority dominates both through informational social

decision rule A rule concerning the number of members of a group who must agree before a group can reach a decision.

influence—controlling the information the group uses (Stasser et al., 1989)—and through normative social influence—exerting the group's will through conformity pressure.

A unanimity rule, or consensus, forces the group to consider the views of the minority more carefully than a majority rule. Group members tend to be more satisfied by a unanimity rule, especially those in the minority, who feel that the majority paid attention and considered their point of view (Hastie et al., 1983).

The decision rule used by a group may depend on what kind of task the group is working on. When the group deals with intellective tasks—problems for which there is a definitive correct answer, such as the solution to an equation—the decision rule is truth wins. In other words, when one member of the group solves the problem, all members (who have mathematical knowledge) recognize the truth of the answer. If the problem has a less definitively correct answer, such as, say, the solution to a word puzzle, then the decision rule is that truth supported wins. When one member comes up with an answer that the others support, that answer wins (Kerr, 1991).

When the group deals with judgmental tasks—tasks that do not have a demonstrably correct answer, such as a jury decision in a complex case—then the decision rule is majority wins (Laughlin & Ellis, 1986). That is, whether the formal decision rule (the one the judge gives to the jury) is unanimity or a 9 out of 12 majority (a rule common in some states), a decision usually is made once the majority rule has been satisfied. Even if the formal rule is unanimity, all jurors tend to go along with the majority once 9 or 10 of the 12 jurors agree.

The Goodness of Decision Rules

Hastie and Kameda (2005) considered a number of group decision rules to determine which are best in reaching an accurate decision under conditions in which the correct answer is uncertain. For example, in the world of political decision making, we may find decision-making rules involving either democratic or dictatorial options. Democratic decision rules may involve a *plurality* rule, in which the winner of an election is the one who gets the most votes when no one has more than 50% of all votes cast, or a *majority* rule in which the one with more than 50% wins. This is contrasted with a dictatorial system (one "best" member decides). In contrast, nondemocratic systems often are, in essence, a "best member" rule; that is, the leader decides. Hastie and Kameda's cogent analysis shows that most of the time the plurality rules give the most adaptive outcomes—that is, the outcomes that best favor the members of the group. In fact, both *majority* rule and *plurality* rule perform quite well most of the time in helping groups determine the most accurate decision (Hastie & Kameda, 2005).

Group Polarization

group polarization
The tendency for individual, prediscussion opinion to become more extreme following group discussion.

A commonplace event observed in group decision making is that groups tend to polarize. **Group polarization** (Moscovici & Zavalloni, 1969; Myers & Lamm, 1976) occurs when the initial-decision tendency of the group becomes more extreme following group discussion. For example, researchers asked French students about their attitudes toward Americans, which prior to group discussion had been negative (Moscovici & Zavalloni, 1969). After group discussion, researchers measured attitudes again and found that group discussion tended to polarize, or pull the attitude to a more extreme position. The initial negative attitudes became even more negative after discussion.

In another study, researchers found that if a jury initially was leaning in the direction of innocence, group discussion led to a shift to leniency. If, on the other hand, the jury was initially leaning in the direction of guilt, there was a shift to severity (Myers & Lamm, 1976). Group polarization can also be recognized in some of the uglier events in the real world. Groups of terrorists become more extreme, more violent, over time (McCauley & Segal, 1987). Extremity shifts, as we have seen, appear to be a normal aspect of group decision making (Blascovich & Ginsburg, 1974).

Why does group polarization occur? First, one of the necessary conditions for group polarization is a majority opinion. That is, a majority of the group must initially (before group discussion) support or oppose a position. The majority then influences others during discussion, producing more extreme opinions. If opinions are initially evenly split (no clear majority), group polarization does not tend to occur. Researchers have focused on two processes in group discussion: *social comparison* and *persuasive arguments*. Group discussion, as we have seen, provides opportunities for social comparison. We cannot compare how we think with how everyone else thinks. We might have thought that our private decision favored a daring choice, but then we find that other people took even riskier stands. This causes us to redefine our idea of riskiness and shift our opinion toward more extreme choices.

The second cause of group polarization is persuasive arguments (Burnstein, 1982; Burnstein & Vinokur, 1977). We already have seen that people tend to share information they hold in common. This means that the arguments put forth and supported are those that the majority of group members support. The majority can often persuade others to accept those arguments (Myers & Lamm, 1975).

As you may recall from Chapter 6, there are two routes to persuasion, a peripheral route and a central route. The two processes involved in group polarization (social comparison and persuasive arguments) appear to map well to these routes of persuasion. Sieber and Ziegler (2019) tested the idea that *social comparison* processes produce group polarization via the peripheral route, whereas *persuasive arguments* produce group polarization via the central route. Results from three experiments indicate that social comparison information (how many people supported a policy) produced group polarization only when participants were either low in motivation to process the information or they lacked the ability to process the information (distracted by an additional task). Thus, when we can't or won't think deeply about an issue, group polarization occurs because social comparison persuades us heuristically (e.g., "Everyone else thinks it is a good idea; I should too"). However, when we are motivated to process information more deeply, the number of people who support an issue is not persuasive. Instead, we are motivated to process the information via the central route, and as a result, we are more persuaded by the strength of the arguments presented by group members.

Research supports the idea that discussion polarizes groups. In one early study on group polarization, group meetings were set up under several conditions (Wallach & Kogan, 1965). In some groups, members merely exchanged information about their views by passing notes; there was no discussion, just information exchange. In others, individuals discussed their views face-to-face. In some of the discussion groups, members were required to reach consensus; in others, they were not. The researchers found that group discussion, with or without reaching consensus, was the only necessary and sufficient condition required to produce group polarization. The mere exchange of information without discussion was not enough, and forcing consensus was not necessary (Wallach & Kogan, 1965).

Groupthink

The late Irving Janis (1972, 1982) carried out several post hoc (after-the-fact) analyses of what he termed historical fiascos. Janis found common threads running through these decision failures. He called this phenomenon **groupthink**, "a mode of thinking that people engage in when they are deeply involved in a cohesive in-group, when the members' striving for unanimity overrides their motivation to realistically appraise alternative courses of actions" (Janis, 1982, p. 9). Groupthink is a breakdown in the rational decision-making abilities of members of a cohesive group. As we have seen, members of a highly cohesive group become motivated to reach unanimity and protect the feelings of other group members and are less concerned with reaching the best decision.

groupthink A group-process phenomenon that may lead to faulty decision making by highly cohesive group members more concerned with reaching consensus than with carefully considering alternative courses of action.

In examining poor decisions and fiascos, we have to acknowledge the benefits we gain from hindsight. From our privileged point of view here in the present, we can see what we believe to be the fatal flaws of many decisions of the past, especially those with disastrous outcomes. This is obviously dangerous from a scientific perspective (a danger that Janis recognized). It can lead us to overstate the power of groupthink processes. What would have happened, for example, if the *Challenger* launch had been a rousing success and Christa McAulif had delivered her lessons from space? How many historical decisions had all the markings of groupthink but led to good outcomes? It is important to keep a sense of perspective as we apply concepts such as groupthink to both historical and contemporary events.

Source: Boris15/Shutterstock.

Conditions That Favor Groupthink

Social psychologist Clark McCauley (1989) identified three conditions that he believed are always involved when groupthink occurs:

1. *Group insulation.* The decision-making group does not seek analysis and information from sources outside the group.
2. *Promotional leadership.* The leader presents his or her preferred solution to the problem before the group can evaluate all the evidence.
3. *Group homogeneity.* Groups that are made up of people of similar background and opinions are prone to have similar views.

These three antecedents, according to McCauley, lead the group to a premature consensus.

Symptoms of Groupthink

Groups that suffer from groupthink show a fairly predictable set of symptoms. Unlike the antecedent conditions just discussed, which increase the likelihood of groupthink, the symptoms protect the group against negative feelings and anxieties during the decision process. Janis (1972) defined several major symptoms of groupthink.

1. *The illusion of invulnerability.* Group members believe that nothing can hurt them. For example, officials at NASA suffered from this illusion. In the 24 space shuttle flights before *Challenger* exploded, not one astronaut was lost in a space-launch mission. Even when there was a near disaster aboard *Apollo 13*, NASA personnel were able to pull the flight out of the fire and bring the three astronauts home safely. This track record of extraordinary success contributed to a belief that NASA could do no wrong. Another example of this illusion can be seen in the decision on how to defend Pearl Harbor, in Honolulu, Hawaii. Prior to the Japanese attack on Pearl Harbor in 1941, advisors to the U.S. commander believed that Pearl Harbor was invincible. Typically, this illusion leads to excessive optimism: The group believes that anything it does will turn out for the better.
2. *Rationalization.* Group members tend not to realistically evaluate information presented to them. Instead, they engage in collective efforts to rationalize away damaging information. For example, prior to the space shuttle *Challenger* exploding in 1986, officials apparently rationalized away information about the O-rings,

whose failure caused the explosion. Negative information about the O-rings dating back as far as 1985 was available but ignored. Six months before the disaster, a NASA budget analyst warned that the O-rings were a serious problem. His warning was labeled an "overstatement."

3. *Stereotyped views of the enemy.* If group members see the enemy as too weak, evil, or stupid to do anything about the group's decision, they are displaying a stereotyped view of that enemy. An enemy need not be a military or other such foe. The enemy is any person or group that poses a threat to a group's emerging decision. The enemy in the *Challenger* decision was the group of Thiokol scientists and engineers who recommended against the launch. These individuals were characterized as being too concerned with the scientific end of things. In fact, one engineer was told to take off his engineer's hat and put on his management hat. The implication here is that engineers are too limited in their scope.

4. *Conformity pressures.* We have seen that majority influences can operate within a group to change the opinions of dissenting members. Strong conformity pressures are at work when groupthink emerges. That is, group members who raise objections are pressured to change their views. One of the engineers involved in the *Challenger* launching was initially opposed to the launch. Under extreme pressure from others, he changed his vote.

5. *Self-censorship.* Once it appears that anyone who disagrees with the group's view will be pressured to conform, members of the group who have dissenting opinions do not speak up because of the consequences. This leads to self-censorship. After the initial opposition to the *Challenger* launching was rejected rather harshly, for example, other engineers were less likely to express doubts.

6. *The illusion of unanimity.* Because of the strong atmosphere of conformity and the self-censorship of those members who have doubts about the group decision, the group harbors the illusion that everyone is in agreement. In the *Challenger* decision, a poll was taken of management personnel (only), who generally favored the launch. The engineers were present but were not allowed to vote. What emerged was a unanimous vote to launch, even though the engineers strongly disagreed. It looked as if everyone agreed to the launch.

7. *Emergence of self-appointed mindguards.* In much the same way as a person can hire a bodyguard to protect him or her, group members emerge to protect the group from damaging information. In the *Challenger* decision, managers at Morton Thiokol emerged in this role. A high-ranking Thiokol manager did not tell Arnold Aldrich about the dissension in the ranks at Thiokol. Thus, Jesse Moore was never made aware of the concerns of the Thiokol engineers.

Study Break

The preceding sections introduced the dynamics of group decision making, including decision rules, group polarization, and groupthink. Before you read the Chapter Review, answer the following questions:

1. What are group decision rules, and how do they relate to group decision making?
2. What is the group polarization effect?
3. How do social comparison and persuasive arguments relate to group polarization?
4. What is the definition of groupthink, and how does it relate to group decision making?
5. What are the conditions that lead to groupthink?
6. What are the symptoms of groupthink (define each)?

The *Challenger* Explosion Revisited

The space program had never had an in-flight disaster. Astronauts had been killed before, but in training missions, and very early in the program's development. Despite the patently dangerous nature of space travel, the possibility of disaster had been dismissed because it simply hadn't happened. In fact, it was deemed so safe that an untrained civilian, a school teacher, was chosen to be a crew member on the *Challenger*.

When the leaders of groups have a preferred outcome and are under pressure to make decisions quickly, it becomes highly likely that information that does not conform to the favored point of view will be ignored by decision-making groups. Understanding how groups interact and influence their members is crucial to designing procedures that will provide for rational decision-making processes.

Chapter Review

1. **What is a group?**

   A group is an assemblage of two or more individuals who influence one another through social interaction. Group members share perceptions of what constitutes appropriate behavior (group norms), and they have formal and informal roles. Group members are interdependent; that is, they depend on one another to meet group goals, and they have emotional (affective) ties with one another. Groups can be either instrumental (existing to perform a task or reach a goal) or affiliative (existing for more general, usually social, reasons). Groups vary in cohesiveness, the strength of the relationships that link the members of the group. Groups may be cohesive because the members like one another (interpersonal cohesiveness), because they are physically close to one another (propinquity), because they adhere to group norms, or because they help each other do a good job and, therefore, attain group goals (task-based cohesiveness).

2. **Why do people join groups?**

   Groups help people meet their biological, psychological, and social needs. Groups were certainly useful in the evolutionary history of humans, aiding the species in its survival. Among the basic needs groups meet are social support, protection from loneliness, and social comparison—the process by which we compare our feelings, opinions, and behaviors with those of others in order to get accurate information about ourselves. People join groups to fulfill these needs and to enhance themselves.

3. **How do groups influence their members?**

   In addition to fulfilling members' needs, groups also influence members' individual senses of worth and self-esteem, which, in turn, has an impact on how one group relates to other groups in a society. Self-identity theory suggests that much of our self-esteem derives from the status of the groups to which we belong or with which we identify.

   Members who threaten the success of a group also threaten the positive image of the group. This leads to the black-sheep effect, the observation that whereas an attractive in-group member is rated more highly than an attractive member of an out-group, an unattractive in-group member is perceived more negatively than an unattractive out-group member.

4. **What effect does an audience have on performance?**

   The presence of other people or audiences may enhance our performance, a process known as social facilitation. Other times, the presence of a critical audience or an audience with high expectations decreases performance ("choking"). Research has shown that the presence of others helps when people perform a dominant, well-learned response but diminishes performance when they perform a skill not very well learned or novel (social inhibition). This may be due to increased effort as a result of increased arousal; or it may be due to anxiety about being judged (evaluation apprehension), which increases arousal; or, according to distraction-conflict theory, it may be due to conflicts for attention.

5. **What motivational decreases affect performance?**

   Sometimes, being in a group enhances performance. Other times, individuals performing in groups display social loafing, a tendency not to perform to capacity. This seems to occur when the task is not that important or when individual output cannot be evaluated. When people become free riders, others often work harder to make up for their lack of effort, a process known as social compensation.

6. **What motivational gains occur because of group interaction? What is the Köhler effect?**

   Kerr and his colleagues rediscovered work done by Köhler (1926) in which the researcher reported that a less-capable member of a two-person group (a dyad) working together on a task works harder and performs

Chapter 8 Group Processes

better than expected when the group product is to be a result of the combined (conjunctive) effort of the two members. This seems to be the opposite of social loafing. The weaker member of the group, rather than free riding or loafing, in fact increases his or her effort. Why does this occur? It seems that motivation gains in groups may occur due in part to social comparison effects, in which there is some competition between two group members, as well as the personal motivation of the weakest member to see how well that member can perform.

7. **What are the potential negative aspects of groups?**

When members of a crowd cannot be identified individually, and therefore feel they have become anonymous, they may experience deindividuation, a loss of self-identity. Their sense of personal responsibility diminishes, and they tend to lose their inhibitions. This is more likely to happen if the crowd is large or is physically distant from a victim. Deindividuation can be a factor in mob violence. Loss of personal identity can also be positive, such as when group members act without thinking to save others' lives.

Although groups may serve to increase our self-esteem by enhancing our social identity, they also have the power to exact painful, even dreadful, punishment. Kipling Williams has studied the effects of being ignored or rejected by the group. Such behavior is called social ostracism and is defined by Williams as the act of excluding or ignoring other individuals or groups. This behavior is widespread and universal. Williams noted that organizations, employers, coworkers, friends, and family all may ignore or disengage from people (the silent treatment) to punish, control, and vent anger. The pervasiveness of ostracism is reflected by a survey conducted by Williams and his coworkers that showed that 67% of the sample surveyed said they had used the silent treatment (deliberately not speaking to a person in their presence) on a loved one, and 75% indicated that they had been a target of the silent treatment by a loved one. From the point of view of the victim of this silent treatment, social ostracism is the perception of being ignored by others in the victim's presence.

8. **With regard to solving problems: Are groups better than individuals, or are individuals better than groups?**

Groups are more effective in processing information than are the individual members of the group, perhaps because they use transactive memory systems, by which each member may recall different things so that the group can produce a more complete memory then any one member can. Groups do not usually perform better than their very best individual member, but recent work has shown that groups may be superior when dealing with complex problems, because they have more resources and can be more creative than can individuals. In one study, three-, four-, and five-person groups solved the problems more quickly and produced more complex solutions to the problems than the best individual member. So, when problems are really intellectually challenging, groups do better than the best member working alone.

9. **What are hidden profiles, and what effects do they have on group decision making?**

"Hidden profiles" are when a group's task is to pick the best alternative—say, the best job applicant—but the relevant information to make this choice is distributed among the group members such that no one member has enough information to make the right choice alone. It appears that group members try to avoid conflict by selectively withholding information; the researchers concluded that face-to-face, unstructured discussion is not a good way to inform group members of unshared information.

10. **What is the effect of different leadership styles on group decision making?**

Leadership is also a factor in group effectiveness. Research has identified two common styles of leadership. The first, the participative leader, is someone who shares power with the other members of the group and includes them in the decision making. Another leadership style, the directive leader, gives less value to participation, emphasizes the need for agreement, and prefers his or her solution. Groups under participative leadership made many more incorrect decisions. Participative leaders can get members to bring out more unshared information, and that is important because it is usually unshared information that leads to the most accurate decisions. However, a directive leader makes the group focus more on unshared information and therefore tends to produce fewer mistakes than do participative leaders.

Gender accounts for a relatively small part of the variation among leadership styles. However, some research indicates that the qualities that distinguish women leaders from their male counterparts appear to be directly related to greater group effectiveness. Research has shown that hands-on positive leadership, which defines the transformational leader (the preferred style of women), can be effective.

11. **What makes a leader legitimate in the eyes of the group members?**

Two factors that are crucial for legitimacy are, first, how people are treated by authorities, regardless of how the leaders have evaluated them, and second, whether the members share group membership with the authorities. Finally, research shows that people value the leader's integrity more than they do the leader's competence.

12. **What factors affect the decision-making ability and effectiveness of a group?**

    Group composition is important to the decision-making ability of a group. Groups of high-ability individuals seem to perform better than groups of low-ability individuals, but members' abilities blend and mix in unexpected ways to produce a group IQ. Groups seem to perform better when members have complementary skills but when no single member is much more talented than the others.

    Group size also affects group productivity. Although increasing group size increases the resources available to the group, there is also more process loss; that is, it becomes harder to reach a decision. As more people are added to the group, the number of people who actually make a contribution—the group's functional size—does not increase.

    Research has shown differences between racially diverse groups and racially homogeneous groups in jury decision making. For example, Whites in diverse groups were more likely to be lenient toward a Black defendant than were Whites in all-White groups. Whites in diverse juries processed more information and brought out more facts than Whites in homogeneous White groups. Diverse juries took more time to deliberate, and diverse groups discussed more racial issues. However, racial composition did not affect verdicts.

    Some groups and group processes offer an illusion of efficacy; people think they are more effective than they are. This is true of small groups, which many people erroneously think are better at solving social dilemmas than are larger groups.

    Another factor in group effectiveness is group cohesiveness. When a task does not require much interaction among members, task-based cohesiveness—cohesiveness based on respect for each other's abilities—increases group productivity, but interpersonal cohesiveness—cohesiveness based on liking for each other—does not. Sometimes, interpersonal cohesiveness can impede the decision-making abilities of the group, because people are afraid of hurting each other's feelings.

13. **How do groups reach decisions?**

    Decision-making groups need to develop decision rules—rules about how many people must agree—in order to blend individual choices into a group outcome. Two common decision rules are majority and unanimity (consensus). Generally, majority wins is the dominant decision rule, but the selection of a decision rule often depends on the group task.

14. **What is group polarization?**

    Group decision making often results in group polarization—that is, the initial decision tendency of the group becomes more extreme following group discussion. It seems that the group discussion pulls the members' attitudes toward more extreme positions as a result of both social comparison and persuasive arguments.

15. **What is groupthink?**

    Groups often make bad decisions when they become more concerned with keeping up their members' morale than with reaching a realistic decision. This lack of critical thinking can lead to groupthink, a breakdown in the rational decision-making abilities of members of a cohesive group. The group becomes driven by consensus seeking; members do not want to rock the boat.

    Three conditions favor the emergence of groupthink: group insulation (failure to seek information from outside sources), promotional leadership (the leader making his or her preferred solution known), and group homogeneity (the group made up of similar people). There are seven symptoms of groupthink: The illusion of invulnerability, rationalization, stereotyped views of the enemy, conformity pressures, self-censorship, the illusion of unanimity, and the emergence of self-appointed mindguards.

Key Terms

Black-sheep effect (p. 318)
Decision rule (p. 333)
Deindividuation (p.322)
Directive leader (p. 328)
Distraction-conflict theory (p. 313)
Evaluation apprehension (p. 312)
Free riders (p. 315)
Group (p. 307)

Group cohesiveness (p. 308)
Group norms (p. 308)
Group polarization (p. 334)
Groupthink (p. 335)
Illusion of efficacy (p. 332)
Köhler effect (p. 316)
Ostracism (p. 319)
Participative leader (p. 328)

Self-identity theory (SIT) (p. 318)
Social facilitation (p. 311)
Social inhibition (p. 311)
Social loafing (p. 315)
Transactive memory systems (p. 324)
Transformative leader (p. 328)
Transactional leader (p. 328)

Chapter Quiz

1. According to the definition offered in your text, which of the following would be a group?
   A. Students passing between classes in a hallway
   B. People waiting on a subway platform for a train
   C. Patients in a doctor's waiting room
   D. Four friends debating politics at a party
   E. All of the above

2. _____ is the strength of the relationships among group members that link them together.
   A. A norm
   B. A role expectation
   C. Group cohesiveness
   D. Attachment

3. According to your text, social needs that are satisfied by membership in a group include which of the following?
   A. Relief of anxiety and stress
   B. Receiving social support
   C. Protection from loneliness
   D. All of the above
   E. Both A and B

4. Chandra is a novice tennis player on her college tennis team. She is playing for the first time in front of an audience. What effect would you expect the audience to have on her performance?
   A. The presence of an audience should facilitate her performance.
   B. The presence of an audience should inhibit her performance.
   C. The presence of an audience will at first facilitate performance but eventually inhibit it.
   D. The presence of an audience will have no effect on her performance.

5. Amy is a factory worker who allows defects in her work to slip by because nobody will know that she is the one doing the shoddy work. Which principle of group dynamics best explains Amy's behavior?
   A. Social loafing
   B. Group polarization
   C. Deindividuation
   D. Social facilitation

6. Which of the following is listed in your text as an explanation for the Köhler motivation gain?
   A. The least competent member's knowledge that his or her contribution is essential to the group
   B. The least competent member feeling like he or she is in competition with others
   C. Social comparison processes
   D. All of the above
   E. Both A and B

7. The black-sheep effect is the phenomenon in which
   A. an attractive out-group member is rated more positively than an attractive in-group member.
   B. an attractive in-group member is rated more positively than an attractive member of the out-group.
   C. an unattractive in-group member is rated more negatively than an unattractive out-group member.
   D. an unattractive in-group member is rated more positively than an attractive out-group member.
   E. both B and C

8. Marcus attends a meeting of his fraternity. He has been told that another member of the fraternity does not like him very much. Consequently, Marcus avoids and ignores this member. According to your text, Marcus is employing
   A. physical ostracism.
   B. social ostracism.
   C. punitive ostracism.
   D. defensive ostracism.

9. Three environmental engineers work together to determine the best place to build a new wind farm. According to your text, in this situation, the group would benefit from a(n) _____ transactive memory system.
   A. differentiated
   B. aggregated
   C. associated
   D. integrated

10. _____ occurs when members of a group become more concerned with reaching consensus than rationally assessing alternative courses of action.
    A. Groupthink
    B. Group polarization
    C. The risky shift effect
    D. Rationalization
    E. None of the above

Answers can be found in the end-of-book Answers section.

Interpersonal Attraction and Close Relationships

CHAPTER 9

Intimate relationships cannot substitute for a life plan. But to have any meaning or viability at all, a life plan must include intimate relationships.

—Harriet Lerner

Source: Nebojsa Tatomirov/Shutterstock.

Key Questions

As you read this chapter, find the answers to the following questions:

1. What is a close relationship?
2. What are the roots of interpersonal attraction and close relationships?
3. What are loneliness and social anxiety?
4. What are the components and dynamics of love?
5. How does attachment relate to interpersonal relationships?
6. How does interpersonal attraction develop?
7. What does evolutionary theory have to say about mate selection?
8. How can one attract a mate?
9. How do close relationships form and evolve?
10. How are relationships evaluated?
11. What is a communal relationship?
12. How do relationships change over time?
13. What are the strategies couples use in response to conflict in a relationship?
14. What are the four horsemen of the apocalypse?
15. What is the nature of friendships?

Both Gertrude Stein and Alice B. Toklas were born in California and lived in the San Francisco Bay area. Both eventually left the United States to live in Paris. The first visit between these two people on September 8, 1907, who would be lifelong friends and lovers, did not begin well. They had become acquainted the previous night at a Paris restaurant and had arranged an appointment for the next afternoon at Gertrude's apartment. Perhaps anxious about the meeting, Gertrude was in a rage when her guest arrived a half hour later than the appointed time. But soon she recovered her good humor, and the two went walking in the streets of Paris. They found that each loved walking, and they would share their thoughts and feelings on these strolls for the rest of their lives together.

On that first afternoon, they stopped for ices and cakes in a little shop that Gertrude knew well because it reminded her of San Francisco. The day went so well that Gertrude suggested dinner at her apartment the following evening. Thus began a relationship that would last for nearly 40 years.

The one was small and dark, the other large—over two hundred pounds—with short hair and a striking Roman face. Neither was physically attractive. Each loved art and literature and opera, for which they were in the right place. The Paris in which they met in the 1920s was the home to great painters (Picasso and Matisse) and enormously talented writers (Ernest Hemingway, F. Scott Fitzgerald). Gertrude knew them all. They began to live together in Gertrude's apartment, for she was the one who had a steady supply of money. Gertrude, who had dropped out of medical school in her final year, had decided to write novels. Soon, they grew closer, their walks longer, and their talks more intimate. They traveled to Italy, and it was there, outside Florence, that Gertrude proposed marriage. Both knew the answer to the proposal, and they spent the night in a 6th-century palace. They shared each other's lives fully, enduring two wars together. In 1946, Gertrude, then 70, displayed the first signs of the tumor that would soon kill her. Gertrude handled this crisis in character, forcefully refusing any medical treatment. Not even her lifelong companion could convince her to do otherwise. When Gertrude eventually collapsed, she was rushed to a hospital in Paris. In her hospital room before surgery, Gertrude grasped her companion's small hand and asked, "What is the answer?" Tears streamed down Alice Toklas's face, "I don't know, Lovey." The hospital attendants put Gertrude Stein on a cot and rolled her toward the operating room. Alice murmured words of affection. Gertrude commanded the attendants to stop, and she turned to Alice and said, "If you don't know the answer, then what is the question?" Gertrude settled back on the cot and chuckled softly. It was the last time they saw each other (Burnett, 1972; Simon, 1977; Toklas, 1963).

We have briefly recounted what was perhaps the most famous literary friendship of the last century, the relationship between Gertrude Stein and Alice B. Toklas. Stein and Toklas were not officially married. They did not flaunt their sexual relationship, for the times in which they lived were not particularly accommodating to what Stein called their "singular" preferences. Yet their partnership involved all the essential elements of a close relationship: intimacy, friendship, love, and sharing. Philosophers have commented that a friend multiplies one's joys and divides one's sorrows. This, too, was characteristic of their relationship.

In this chapter we ask a number of questions that most of us, at least, do not have the answers for. What draws two people together into a close relationship, whether a friendship or a more intimate love relationship? What influences attractiveness and attraction? How do close relationships develop and evolve, and how do they stand up to conflict and destructive impulses? What are the components of love relationships? And finally, what are friendships, and how do they differ from love?

The Roots of Interpersonal Attraction and Close Relationships

It is a basic human characteristic to be attracted to others, to desire to build close relationships with friends and lovers. In this section, we explore two needs that underlie attraction and relationships: affiliation and intimacy. Not everyone has the social skills or resources necessary to initiate and maintain close relationships. Therefore, we also look at the emotions of social anxiety and loneliness.

Affiliation and Intimacy

Although each of us can endure and even value periods of solitude, for most of us extended solitude is aversive. After a time, we begin to crave the company of others. People have a **need for affiliation**, a need to establish and maintain relationships with others (Wong & Csikzentmihalyi, 1991). Contact with friends and acquaintances provides us with emotional support, attention, and the opportunity to evaluate the appropriateness of our opinions and behavior through the process of social comparison. The need for affiliation is the fundamental factor underlying our interpersonal relationships.

People who are high in the need for affiliation wish to be with friends and others more than do people who are low in the need for affiliation, and they tend to act accordingly. For example, in one study, college men who had a high need for affiliation picked living situations that increased the chances for social interaction. They were likely to have more housemates or to be more willing to share a room than were men with a lower need for affiliation (Switzer & Taylor, 1983). Men and women show some differences in the need for affiliation. Teenage girls, for example, spend more time with friends and less often wish to be alone than do teenage boys (Wong & Csikzentmihalyi, 1991). This is in keeping with other findings that women show a higher need for affiliation than do men.

There is evidence that the affiliation motive operates on an implicit and an explicit level (Köllner & Schultheiss, 2014). The explicit need for affiliation is tied to more cognitive elements of affiliation, including self-concept and one's values, beliefs, and goals. The implicit system is more strongly related to the emotional aspect of affiliation (Köllner & Schultheiss, 2014). Köllner and Schultheiss conducted a meta-analysis of the literature on the explicit and implicit needs for affiliation and found a very small correlation between the two systems. This means that the two systems, like other implicit and explicit systems, are independent from one another and are related to different types of behavior. Additionally, they reported that the relationship between the explicit and implicit needs for affiliation is weaker for women than for men.

Although this research shows that the need for affiliation is generally a positive social motive fostering social relationships, there is also a darker side. Individuals with a high implicit need for affiliation show sensitivity to being rejected by others (Wang & Jing, 2018). This sensitivity to potential rejection was shown in a study by Wang and Jing. Wang and Jing showed participants pictures depicting positive, neutral, and negative social interactions. They found that participants with a high implicit need for affiliation showed a greater physiological response to the negative pictures than those lower in the implicit need for affiliation. Apparently, participants with a high need for affiliation found the negative images more disturbing than those lower in the need for affiliation. The explicit need for affiliation is associated with anxiety (Byrne, 1961). Donn Byrne randomly assigned participants to one of two conditions. In the experimental condition, participants were told that they would be carefully observed while they completed a task for how popular they were with other participants, their level of attractiveness to the opposite sex, and how likable they appeared to be. For participants in the control condition, no mention was made of such observations. Participants then completed a measure of anxiety and need for affiliation (1 week later). Byrne found that being observed led to higher levels of anxiety for participants high in the need for affiliation than those low in the need for affiliation. The levels of anxiety for participants with both high and low needs for affiliation did not differ in the control group.

But merely being with others is often not enough to satisfy our social needs. We also have a **need for intimacy**, a need for close and affectionate relationships (McAdams, 1982, 1989). Intimacy with friends or lovers involves sharing and disclosing personal information. Individuals with a high need for intimacy tend to be warm and affectionate

need for affiliation
A motivation that underlies our desire to establish and maintain rewarding interpersonal relationships.

The needs for affiliation and intimacy motivate us to form and sustain relationships and close, affectionate relationships.
Source: Rido/Shutterstock.

need for intimacy
A motivation for close and affectionate relationships.

Chapter 9 Interpersonal Attraction and Close Relationships and to show concern about other people. Most theorists agree that intimacy is an essential component of many different interpersonal relationships (Laurenceau et al., 1998).

Intimacy has several dimensions, according to Baumeister and Bratslavsky (1999). One is mutual disclosure that is sympathetic and understanding. Intimate disclosure involves verbal communication but also refers to shared experiences. Another dimension of intimacy includes having a favorable attitude toward the other person that is expressed in warm feelings and positive acts such that the person is aware of how much the other cares.

The need for affiliation and intimacy gives us positive social motivation to approach other people. They are the roots of **interpersonal attraction**, which is defined as the desire to start and maintain relationships with others. But there are also emotions that may stand in the way of our fulfilling affiliation and intimacy needs and forming relationships. We look at these emotions next.

interpersonal attraction The desire to start and maintain relationships with others.

Loneliness and Social Anxiety

Loneliness and social anxiety are two related conditions that have implications for one's social relationships. Whereas the needs for affiliation and intimacy are positive motives that foster interpersonal relationships, loneliness and social anxiety can be seen as negative motivational states that interfere with the formation of meaningful relationships. In this section we shall explore loneliness and social anxiety.

Loneliness

loneliness A psychological state that results when we perceive that there is an inadequacy or a deprivation in our social relationships.

Loneliness is a psychological state that results when we perceive an inadequacy in our relationships—a discrepancy between the way we want our relationships to be and the way they actually are (Peplau & Perlman, 1982). When we are lonely, we lack the high-quality intimate relationships that we need. Loneliness may occur within the framework of a relationship. For example, women often expect more intimacy than they experience in marriage, and that lack of intimacy can be a cause of loneliness (Tornstam, 1992).

Loneliness is common during adolescence and young adulthood, times of life when old friendships fade and new ones must be formed. For example, consider an 18-year-old going off to college. As she watches her parents drive away, she is likely to feel, along with considerable excitement, a sense of loneliness or even abandonment. New college students often believe that they will not be able to form friendships and that no one at school cares about them. The friendships they make don't seem as intimate as their high school friendships were. These students often don't realize that everybody else is pretty much in the same boat emotionally, and loneliness is often a significant factor when a student drops out of school.

Loneliness is a subjective experience and is not dependent on the number of people we have surrounding us (Peplau & Perlman, 1982). We can be alone and yet not be lonely; sometimes we want and need solitude. On the other hand, we can be surrounded by people and feel desperately lonely. Our feelings of loneliness are strongly influenced by how we evaluate our personal relationships (Peplau & Perlman, 1982). We need close relationships with a few people to buffer ourselves against feeling lonely.

Culture is also related to perception of loneliness. There is evidence that loneliness is a cross-cultural phenomenon (DiTommaso et al., 2005). However, the way loneliness is experienced differs across cultures. For example, DiTommaso et al. found that Chinese students living in Canada reported higher levels of three types of loneliness than did Canadians. Additionally, Rokach and Neto (2005) compared Canadian and Portuguese individuals of varying ages on several dimensions relating to loneliness. They found that Canadians were more likely to point to their own shortcomings to explain their loneliness than were Portuguese individuals. Rokach and Neto suggest that this might be due to a greater disposition of North Americans to view loneliness as a form of social failure and to different family values and structures between the two cultures. Finally, cultural expectations about relationships can also affect the experience of loneliness. For example, in Western culture, greater importance is attached to romantic relationships than in non-Western cultures (Seepersad et al., 2008). Consequently, when not in a romantic relationship, members of a Western culture (Americans) experience more romantic loneliness than those in a non-Western culture (Koreans) (Seepersad et al., 2008).

One way in which culture is important in the experience of loneliness is in the process of how migrants adjust to their new country. Heritage cultures (the cultures from which migrants come) differ in how much they encourage and support the formation of relationships. Migrants from cultures in which it is normative to form new relationships may be better insulated against the loneliness that accompanies attempting to establish oneself in a new country and thus be insulated from the experience of loneliness (Heu et al., 2020). Heu et al. hypothesized that individuals from heritage cultures with high "relational mobility" would experience less loneliness in a new cultural context than those from heritage cultures with low relational mobility. Heu et al. define *relational mobility* as "the extent to which a socioecological environment provides individuals with opportunities to meet new others and, as such, how much choice with respect to social relationships they have" (p. 141). Heu et al. studied German (higher-relational-mobility culture) and Chinese (lower-relational-mobility culture) migrant students in the Netherlands who had spent equivalent amounts of time in their heritage cultures. Participants from both cultures completed a questionnaire measuring how much loneliness they experienced in their new cultural environment. Heu et al. found that participants from the high-relational-mobility culture experienced less loneliness than those from the low-relational-mobility culture. They also found that for German students, low levels of freedom of choice in forming relationships were associated with higher levels of loneliness. Freedom of choice for German students was a more important predictor of loneliness than opportunities to meet new people. This effect was not present for Chinese students. Heu et al. concluded that individual choice in forming new relationships may be more important in individualistic cultures (Germany) than in collective cultures (China).

Loneliness occurs when we perceive an inadequacy or deprivation in our social relationships. It can result from social anxiety and lead to depression.
Source: evrymmnt/Shutterstock.

As suggested earlier, loneliness can be associated with certain relationships or certain times of life. There are, however, individuals for whom loneliness is a lifelong experience. Such individuals have difficulty in forming relationships with others, and consequently, they go through life with few or no close relationships. What is the source of their difficulty? The problem for at least some of these people may be that they lack the basic social skills needed to form and maintain relationships. Experiences of awkward social interactions intensify these individuals' uneasiness in social settings. Lacking confidence, they become increasingly anxious about their interactions with others. Often, because of their strained social interactions, lonely people may be further excluded from social interaction, thereby increasing feelings of depression and social anxiety (Leary & Kowalski, 1995).

Beyond the psychological effects of loneliness, there are also physical and health effects. Within families, loneliness is associated with an increase in self-reported health problems and a higher rate of self-reported physical ailments (Segrin et al., 2012). Hawkley et al. (2003) report that lonely individuals are more likely to show elevated total peripheral resistance (a suspected precursor to hypertension) and lower cardiac output than nonlonely individuals. Loneliness is also associated with a higher risk for a heart condition in the elderly (Sorkin et al., 2002). Loneliness and social isolation are also associated with higher levels of depression in older males (Alpass & Neville, 2003) and among male and female college students (Segrin et al., 2003). In the Segrin et al. study, the relationship between loneliness and depression was related to relationship satisfaction. Individuals who are dissatisfied with their relationships tend to be lonely and, in turn, are more likely to experience depression. Lonely individuals get poorer-quality sleep (i.e., awaken more after falling asleep and show poor sleep efficiency) compared to nonlonely individuals (Cacioppo et al., 2002). This latter finding suggests that lonely people may be less resilient and more prone to physical problems (Cacioppo et al., 2002). Finally, loneliness among older adults has been found to be a significant predictor of an early death over a six-year period (Luo et al., 2012).

Chapter 9 Interpersonal Attraction and Close Relationships

Social Anxiety

social anxiety Anxiety tied to interpersonal relationships that occurs because of an individual's anticipation of negative encounters with others.

Social anxiety is one of the most widely diagnosed anxiety disorders. Social anxiety (sometimes referred to as social phobia) arises from a person's expectation of negative encounters with others (Leary, 1983a, 1983b). Socially anxious people anticipate negative interactions and think that other people will not like them very much. These negative expectations then translate into anxiety in a social situation, using "safety behaviors" (e.g., avoiding eye contact and closely monitoring one's behavior) and underestimating the quality of the impressions made on others (Hirsch et al., 2004). Socially anxious individuals tend to see ambiguous social situations more negatively than individuals without social anxiety (Huppert et al., 2003). Additionally, socially anxious individuals tend to dwell on negative aspects of social interactions more than individuals who are low in social anxiety and also recall more negative information about the social interaction (Edwards et al., 2003). According to Edwards et al., this pattern of findings is consistent with the idea that socially anxious individuals perform a negatively biased "postmortem" of social events.

There is a cluster of characteristics that define those with social anxiety. People who suffer from social anxiety tend to display some of the following interrelated traits (Nichols, 1974):

- A sensitivity to and fearfulness of disapproval and criticism.
- A strong tendency to perceive and respond to criticism that does not exist.
- Low self-evaluation.
- Rigid ideas about what constitutes "appropriate" social behavior.
- A tendency to foresee negative outcomes to anticipated social interactions, which arouses anxiety.
- An increased awareness and fear of being evaluated by others.
- Fear of situations in which withdrawal would be difficult or embarrassing.
- The tendency to overestimate one's reaction to social situations (e.g., believing that you are blushing when you are not).
- An inordinate fear of the anxiety itself.
- A fear of being perceived as losing control.

Interestingly, many of these perceptions and fears are either wrong or unfounded. The research of Christensen and Kashy (1998) shows that lonely people view their own behavior more negatively than do other people. Other research shows that socially anxious individuals tend to process disturbing social events negatively immediately after they occur and a day after the event (Lundh & Sperling, 2002). Social anxiety relates directly to this *post-event rumination*. However, social anxiety also operates through negative self-evaluation of social behavior and the inordinately high amount of attention that people with social anxiety focus on their negative self-image (Chen et al., 2013). In other words, individuals with social anxiety tend to see their own social interactions with others as very negative and spend time reinforcing their image of themselves as socially inept.

Of course, real events and real hurts may be the source of much social anxiety. Leary and his colleagues examined the effects of having our feelings hurt in a variety of ways, ranging from sexual infidelity, to unreturned phone calls, to being teased (Leary et al., 1998). The basic cause of the hurt feelings and consequent anxiety is what Leary calls *relational devaluation*, the perception that the other person does not regard the relationship as being as important as you do. Perhaps the major source of social anxiety is the feeling that you are being excluded from valued social relations (Baumeister & Tice, 1990). Having one's feelings hurt, however, leads to more than anxiety. People experience a complex sense of being distressed, upset, angry, guilty, and wounded. Leary and colleagues (1998) examined the stories written by people who had been emotionally hurt. They found that unlike the old saying about "sticks and stones," words or even gestures or looks elicit hurt feelings, last for a long time, and do not heal as readily as broken bones. Teasing is one example of what appeared to be an innocent event—at least from the teaser's point of view—that in reality imprints long-lasting hurt feelings for many victims. The males and females in the study did not differ much in their reactions to hurt feelings or to teasing.

The people who do these nasty deeds do not realize the depth of the damage that they cause, nor do they realize how much the victims come to dislike them. Perpetrators often say that they meant no harm. No harm, indeed.

Study Break

The preceding sections introduced you to the definition of interpersonal attraction and the factors that can facilitate or inhibit relationship formation. Before you go on, answer the following questions:

1. What is the need for affiliation?
2. What is the need for intimacy, and how does it differ from the need for affiliation?
3. What is loneliness, and how does it relate to the number of friends a person has?
4. How can social anxiety interfere with the formation of relationships?
5. What are the characteristics of social anxiety?

Love and Close Relationships

Psychologists and other behavioral scientists long thought that love was simply too mysterious a topic to study scientifically (Thompson & Borrello, 1992). However, psychologists have become more adventuresome, and love has become a topic of increasing interest (Hendrick & Hendrick, 1987). This is only right, because love is among the most intense of human emotions.

Love's Triangle

Robert Sternberg (1986, 1988) proposed a **triangular theory of love**, based on the idea that love has three components: passion, intimacy, and commitment. As shown in Figure 9.1, the theory represents love as a triangle, with each component defining a vertex.

triangular theory of love
A theory suggesting that love has three components—passion, intimacy, and commitment—each of which is conceptualized as a leg of a triangle that can vary.

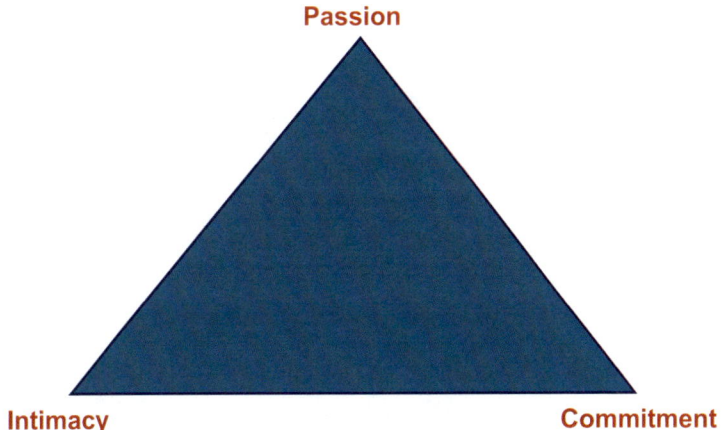

FIGURE 9.1

Robert Sternberg's triangular theory of love. Each leg of the triangle represents one of the three components of love: passion, intimacy, and commitment.
From Sternberg (1986).

Passion is the emotional component of love. The "aching" in the pit of your stomach when you think about your love partner is a manifestation of this component. Passion is "a state of intense longing for union with the other" (Hatfield & Walster, 1981, p. 13). Passion tends to be strongest in the early stages of a romantic relationship. It is sexual desire that initially drives the relationship. Defining passion simply as sexual desire does not do justice to this complicated emotion. It is not improbable that people may love passionately without sexual contact or in the absence of the ability to have sexual contact. However, as a rough measure, sexual desire serves to define passion (Baumeister & Bratslavsky, 1999).

Intimacy is the component that includes self-disclosure—the sharing of our innermost thoughts—as well as shared activities. Intimate couples look out for each other's welfare, experience happiness by being in each other's company, are able to count on each other when times are tough, and give each other emotional support and understanding (Sternberg & Gracek, 1984).

The third vertex of the triangle, *commitment*, is the long-term determination to maintain love over time. It is different from the decision people make, often in the heat of passion, that they are in love. Commitment does not necessarily go along with a couple's decision that they are in love. Sternberg defined various kinds of love, based on the presence or absence of intimacy, passion, and commitment. Table 9.1 shows each of these kinds of love and the component or components with which it is associated.

According to Sternberg (1986), the components of love need not occur in a fixed order. There is a tendency for passion to dominate at the start, for intimacy to follow as a result of self-disclosure prompted by passion, and for commitment to take the longest to fully develop. However, in an arranged marriage, for example, commitment occurs before intimacy, and passion may be the laggard.

Baumeister and Bratslavsky (1999) studied the relationship between passion and intimacy and suggested that one may be a function of the other. These scholars argued that rising intimacy at any point in the relationship will create a strong sense of passion. If intimacy is stable, and that means it may be high or low, then passion will be low. But when intimacy rises, so does passion. Passion, then, is a function of change in intimacy over time (Baumeister & Bratslavsky, 1999). Research generally shows that passion declines steadily in long-term relationships, particularly among women, but intimacy does not and may increase in the late stages of the relationship (Acker & Davis, 1992). Positive changes in the amount of intimacy—self-disclosures, shared experiences—lead to increases in passion at any stage of a relationship. Finally, the relationship between relationship length and the components of love's triangle can be complex. For example,

TABLE 9.1 Triangular Theory and Different Love Types

Kind of Love	Love Component		
	Intimacy	Passion	Commitment
Non-love	No	No	No
Liking	Yes	No	No
Infatuated love	No	Yes	No
Empty love	No	No	Yes
Romantic love	Yes	Yes	No
Companionate love	Yes	No	Yes
Fatuous love	No	Yes	Yes
Consummate love	Yes	Yes	Yes

couples who are casually dating report lower levels of passion and intimacy than engaged couples. However, married couples report lower levels of passion and intimacy than engaged couples. Commitment, on the other hand, increases with relationship length (Lemieux & Hale, 2002).

Levels of passion, intimacy, and commitment are also related to relationship satisfaction (Madey & Rodgers, 2009). Madey and Rogers found strong positive correlations between all three components and overall relationship satisfaction. They also found that intimacy and commitment showed the strongest correlations with relationship satisfaction. Additionally, they reported that individuals with a secure attachment experience higher levels of passion, intimacy, and commitment than those with a less secure attachment. Finally, intimacy and commitment mediate the relationship between attachment security and relationship satisfaction. That is, a secure attachment is related to higher levels of intimacy and commitment. In turn, these higher levels of intimacy and commitment are related to higher relationship satisfaction.

Types of Love

What, then, are Sternberg's types of love? Probably the most fascinating is **romantic love**, which involves passion and intimacy but not commitment. Romantic love is reflected in that electrifying yet conditional statement, "I am in love with you." Compare this with the expression reflecting consummate love, "I love you." Romantic love can be found around the world and throughout history. It is most likely to be first experienced by members of diverse ethnic groups in late adolescence or early adulthood (Regan et al., 2004). Additionally, concepts of romantic love are almost universally positive with characteristics such as trust and fulfilling emotional needs. One of the only negative characteristics that emerged as a "peripheral characteristic" was jealousy (Regan et al., 1998).

romantic love Love involving strong emotion and having the components of passion and intimacy but not commitment.

In some cultures, such as in India, some marriages are arranged in which commitment comes first followed by romance.
Source: IVASHstudio/Shutterstock.

Romantic love varies somewhat across cultures. Some elements of romantic love may be common across cultures, but some are not (de Munck et al., 2011). Research by de Munck et al. found, for example, that intrusive thinking, happiness, passion, altruism, and improved well-being of partner were common elements to the concept of romantic love among Americans, Russians, and Lithuanians. On the other hand, there were some differences. Americans included the elements of friendship and comfort love as important to romantic love for the U.S. sample, but Russians and Lithuanians did not. Russians and Lithuanians said that romantic love was temporary, unreal, and a fairytale. Romantic love is still an alien idea in most cultures and romance have little to do with the choice of a spouse. In fact, there are still some cultures (e.g., some Indian sects) that practice arranged marriages in which commitment comes first, followed by romance. Interestingly, these arranged marriages appear to be just as satisfying as love-based marriages (Reagan et al., 2012). Even in U.S. culture, the appeal of marrying for love seems to have increased among women across time, perhaps because women's roles have changed, and they no longer have so great a need to find a "good provider" (Berscheid et al., 1989).

The importance of passion in romantic love is clear. Romantic lovers live in a pool of emotions, both positive and negative—sexual desire, fear, exultation, anger—all experienced in a state of high arousal. Intense sexual desire and physical arousal are the prime forces driving romantic love (Berscheid, 1988). One study confirms the physical arousal aspect of romantic love (Enzo et al., 2006). In this study individuals who had recently fallen in love were compared to single individuals and individuals in a long-term relationship. Enzo et al. found that the "in-love" participants showed higher levels of nerve growth factor (NGF) in their blood than single individuals or those involved in a long-term relationship. Interestingly, those "in-love" couples showed a drop in NGF if they remained together for 12 to 14 months. In fact, their blood levels of NGF were comparable to those who were in long-term relationships—perhaps providing evidence for the old adage that romance (passion) burns hot, but burns fast.

As noted, romantic love and sexual desire are likely to be seen as going together and being inseparable. This may be true in some cases. However, there is evidence that romantic love and sexual desire are two separate entities that can be experienced separately (Diamond, 2004). It is possible to experience the passion of romantic love without experiencing sexual desire. There may even be different physiological underpinnings to the two experiences (Diamond, 2004). For example, hormones associated with strong sexual desire have nothing to do with the intense bond experienced in romantic love (Diamond, 2003). Additionally, higher levels of norepinephrine and dopamine are more associated with sexual lust (i.e., the desire for sex with a willing partner without love) than with romantic love (Dundon & Rellini, 2012). Physiological mechanisms underlying the formation of strong attachments are more closely associated with activity involving naturally occurring opioids in the brain (Diamond, 2004).

Tennov (1979) distinguished a particular type of romantic love, which she called *limerence* and characterized it as occurring when "you suddenly feel a sparkle (a lovely word) of interest in someone else, an interest fed by the image of returned feeling" (p. 27). Limerence is not driven solely or even primarily by sexual desire. It occurs when a person anxious for intimacy finds someone who seems able to fulfill all of his or her needs and desires. For limerent lovers, all the happiness one could ever hope for is embodied in the loved one. Indeed, one emotional consequence of limerent love is a terror that all hope will be lost if the lover leaves us (Brehm, 1988).

consummate love Love that includes all three components: passion, intimacy, and commitment.

Consummate love combines all three vertices of love's triangle: passion, intimacy, and commitment. These couples have it all; they are able to maintain their passion and intimacy along with a commitment to a lifetime together.

Although we may fantasize about romantic love and view consummate love as a long-term ideal, other types of love can also bring happiness. Many couples are perfectly happy with *companionate love*, which has little or no passion but is infused with intimacy and commitment. Such partners are "friends for life" and generally have great trust in and tolerance for each other. Although they may regret the lack of passion, they are pragmatic and are able to live happily within the rules or limits of the relationship (Duck, 1983).

Unrequited Love

unrequited love Love expressed by one person that is rejected and not returned by the other.

A special and very painful kind of infatuated love is love that is unfulfilled. **Unrequited love** occurs when we fall deeply and passionately in love and that love is rejected. Almost all of us have had some experience with unrequited love. In one study, 98% of the subjects had been rejected by someone they loved intensely (Baumeister et al., 1993). The emotional responses to unrequited love are generally negative. This is true for heterosexuals (Baumeister et al., 1993) and gay men (Manalastas, 2011).

What makes unrequited love so painful is that both individuals feel victimized (Aron et al., 1998). Very often, unrequited love ostensibly starts as a platonic friendship, but then one of the individuals admits that it was never just friendship, that he or she was always secretly in love with the other (Baumeister et al., 1993). In many cases, the object of the unrequited love is often unable to express lack of interest in terms that are sufficiently discouraging. The unrequited lover takes anything as encouragement, sustains hope, and then finds the final rejection devastating. The object of unwanted love, after the initial boost to the ego, feels bewildered, guilty, and angry.

In a typical case of spurned love, a college woman took pity on a young man whom no one liked, and one night invited him to join her and some friends in a game of Parcheesi. He thought the invitation signaled something more than she intended. Much to her horror, he began to follow her around and told her how much he loved her. She wanted this to stop, but she was unable to tell him how upset she was, because she was afraid of hurting his feelings. He interpreted her silence as encouragement and persisted (Baumeister et al., 1993).

Men are more likely than women to experience unrequited love (Aron et al., 1998). This is because men are more beguiled by physical attractiveness than are women. Men tend to fall in love with someone more desirable than they are. Interestingly, people report that they have been the object of unrequited love twice as many times as they have been rejected by another. We prefer to believe that we have been loved in vain rather than having loved in vain.

Unrequited love is viewed differently depending on one's perspective: pursuer or pursued. In one study those being pursued reported being the recipients of more unwanted courtship tactics, both violent and nonviolent, than they say they used as a pursuer (Sinclair & Frieze, 2005). Some interesting gender differences emerged in this study. For example, men tended to overestimate the extent to which their romantic advances were reciprocated. Women, on the other hand, were more likely than men to report multiple attempts to clearly reject unwanted advances.

Secret Love

If unrequited love is the most painful kind of love, then *secret love* may be the most exciting. In this form of love, individuals have strong passion for one another, but cannot or will not make those feelings publicly known. Secrecy seems to increase the attraction of a relationship. Researchers have found that people continued to think more about past relationships that had been secret than about those that had been open (Wegner et al., 1994). In fact, many individuals were still very much preoccupied with long-past secret relationships. In a study of secrecy and attraction, subjects paired as couples were induced to play "footsie" under the table while they were involved in a card game with another couple (Wegner et al., 1994). The researchers found that when the under-the-table game was played in secret, participants reported greater attraction for the other person than when it was not played in secret.

Why does secrecy create this strong attraction? Perhaps it is because individuals involved in a secret relationship think constantly and obsessively about each other. After all, they have to expend a lot of energy in maintaining the relationship. They have to figure out how to meet, how to call each other so that others won't know, and how to act neutrally in public to disguise their true relationship. Secrecy creates strong bonds between individuals; it can also be the downfall of ongoing relationships. The sudden revelation of a secret infidelity will often crush an ongoing relationship and further enhance the secret one (Wegner et al., 1994).

The Formation of Intimate Relationships

The habits of the heart may be shaped by our earliest relationships. Developmental psychologists have noted that infants form attachments with their parents or primary caregivers based on the kinds of interactions they have (Ainsworth, 1992). These patterns of attachment, or attachment styles, evolve into **working models**, mental representations of what the individual expects to happen in close relationships (Shaver et al., 1988). Working models are carried forth from relationship to relationship (Brumbaugh & Fraley, 2006). So, attachment patterns we use in one relationship are likely to be transferred to subsequent relationships. Attachment theory suggests that attachment styles developed in early childhood govern the way individuals form and maintain close relationships in adulthood. Three attachment styles have been identified: secure, anxious/ambivalent, and avoidant. Statements describing each style are shown in Table 9.2.

working model Mental representations of what an individual expects to happen in close relationships.

Attachment styles relate to how relationships are perceived and how successful they are. According to research, people who identified their attachment style as secure characterized their lovers as happy, friendly, and trusting and said that they and their partner were tolerant of each other's faults (Shaver et al., 1988). Avoidant lovers were afraid of intimacy, experienced roller-coaster emotional swings, and were constantly jealous. Anxious/ambivalent lovers experienced extreme sexual attraction coupled with extreme jealousy. Love is very intense for anxious lovers, because they strive to merge totally with their mate; anything less increases their anxiety. This experience of love for anxious

TABLE 9.2 Attachment Styles

Answers and Percentages	Newspaper Sample	University Sample
Secure I find it relatively easy to get close to others and am comfortable depending on them and having them depend on me. I don't worry about being abandoned or about someone getting too close to me.	56%	56%
Avoidant I am somewhat uncomfortable being close to others; I find it difficult to trust them completely, difficult to allow myself to depend on them. I am nervous when anyone gets too close, and often, love partners want me to be more intimate than I feel comfortable about.	25%	23%
Anxious/Ambivalent I find that others are reluctant to get as close as I would like. I often worry that my partner doesn't really love me or won't want to stay with me. I want to merge completely with another person, and this desire sometimes scares people away.	19%	20%

From Shaver et al. (1988).

lovers is a strong desire for union and a powerful intensity of sexual attraction and jealousy. It is no accident that anxious lovers, more than any other style, report love at first sight (Shaver et al., 1988). Interestingly, the relationship between attachment style and relationship quality found with White samples applies to Spanish individuals as well (Monteoliva et al., 2005). In this study, a secure attachment was associated with positive relationship experiences. Anxious and avoidant attachments were associated with more negative relationship outcomes.

Given the working model of a partner and the expectations that anxious lovers have, it will not come as a surprise to you that individuals with this style tend to have rather turbulent relationships (Simpson et al., 1999). Research shows that anxious/ambivalents have relationships that are filled with strong conflicts. One reason for this, apparently, is that anxious/ambivalent individuals have *empathic accuracy,* the ability to correctly infer their partner's thoughts and feelings. Because of this ability, they are more threatened than are other individuals and feel much more anxious (Simpson et al., 1999). This is a case of knowing too much or, at least, placing too much emphasis on their partners' present moods and feelings that may or may not tell where the relationship is going. As you might imagine, Simpson and colleagues found that of all the couples they studied, the highly anxious/ambivalent partners were much more likely to have broken up within months. Finally, males and females with an anxious attachment react to hypothetical transgressions of their partners quite negatively. Typical responses included high levels of emotional stress, attribution patterns that are damaging to the relationship, and behaviors that escalate conflict (Collins et al., 2006).

Attachment Styles and Adult Love Relationships

Fraley and Shaver (1998) showed that the ways in which we respond to our earliest caregivers may indeed last a lifetime and are used when we enter adult romantic relationships. Where better to observe how adult individuals respond to the potential loss of attachment than at an airport? The researchers had observers take careful notes on the behavior of couples when one of the members was departing. After the departure, the remaining member of the couple was asked to complete a questionnaire determining his or her attachment style.

Those with an anxious working model showed the greatest distress at the impending separation and tended to engage in actions designed to delay or stop the departure, although in reality that was not going to happen. The anxious individuals would hold on to, follow, and search for their partner, not unlike a child would for a parent under similar circumstances. So attachment styles tend to be engaged particularly when there is threat (departure in this case) to the relationship. The effects seemed stronger for women than for men (Fraley & Shaver, 1998).

It is quite likely that the behavior of those airport visitors with an anxious working model was determined in great part by the level of trust they had in their partners. Mikulincer (1998) examined the association between adult attachment style and feelings of trust in close relationships. The results of this research suggest that those with a secure working model showed and felt more trust in their partners, and even when trust was violated, secure individuals found a constructive way to deal with it. For secure individuals, the main goal of the relationship was to maintain or increase intimacy.

In contrast, anxious working model individuals, although also desiring greater intimacy, were very concerned with achieving a greater sense of security in their relationships. Avoidant individuals wanted more control. But clearly, level of trust differs significantly among the three types of attachment styles. Anxious-style individuals continually have their sense of trust undermined, because they tend to fail at relationships. Sometimes, these individuals try to start relationships that are bound to fail. As you might suspect, the likelihood of someone falling in love with another who does not love them in return is dependent on one's attachment style. Arthur and Elaine Aron found that individuals with an anxious attachment style were more likely to have experienced unreciprocated love (Aron et al., 1998). Secure individuals had been successful in the past in establishing relationships, and avoidants were unlikely to fall in love at all. Anxious individuals place great value in establishing a relationship with someone who is very desirable but are unlikely to be able to do so. They tend to fail at close relationships and, therefore, they should experience more incidents of unrequited love; indeed, that is exactly what the research findings show (Aron et al., 1998). Finally, compared to individuals with a secure or avoidant attachment, individuals with an anxious attachment are more likely to engage in negative thoughts known as rumination (Reynolds et al., 2014). Rumination is "a maladaptive process of self-reflection, featuring a hyper-focus on internal distress and the possible causes and consequences of these cognitive-affective experiences" (Reynolds et al., 2014, para 8). Reynolds et al. also found that individuals showing a higher level of rumination also report more anxiety associated with intimate relationships.

Are attachment styles a factor in long-term relationships? A study of 322 young married couples, all under age 30, found a tendency for those with similar attachment styles to marry one another (Senchak & Leonard, 1992). Attachment style is not destiny, however, as shown by the observation that people may display different attachment styles in different relationships (Bartholomew & Horowitz, 1991). None of these findings, however, come from long-term studies on the effects of attachment styles beyond childhood. Longitudinal research that follows individuals from infancy at least until early adulthood would give us more definitive information about whether early attachment styles really influence the way we respond in adult love relationships.

Study Break

This section introduced you to love relationships and different types of love. Before you begin the next section, answer the following questions:

1. What are the three legs of the triangular theory of love, and how do they relate to one another?
2. What is romantic love, and how does culture relate to its experience?
3. What is consummate love, and what are its components?
4. What are unrequited and secret love, and how do people react when they happen?

5. What is a working model, and how does it relate to relationship formation?
6. How do different attachment styles relate to adult relationships?

Determinants of Interpersonal Attraction

What determines why we are attracted to some individuals but not others? Social psychologists have developed a number of models addressing this question. Some specific factors identified by these models that play a role in attraction are physical proximity, similarity, and physical attractiveness.

Physical Proximity: Being in the Right Place

How did you and your best friend first meet? Most likely, you met because you happened to be physically close to each other at some point in your life. For example, you might have been neighbors or sat next to each other in elementary school. The idea that you are most likely to become friends with another person you happened to be physically close to suggests that those with whom you form friendships is more happenstance (chance) than providence. Confirmation for this idea was found in a study by Back et al. (2008). Back et al. randomly assigned freshman students to seats in a classroom at the beginning of the school year. Then the students rated each other one at a time. A year later, students were given photographs of the other students and were asked to rate the strength of their friendship with each student. Back et al. found that students who sat next to another indicated stronger friendships than those who sat in the same row or had no physical relation to each other. As this and other studies show, physical proximity, or physical immediacy, is an important determinant of attraction, especially at the beginning of a relationship.

The importance of the **physical proximity effect** in the formation of friendships was also shown in a study of the friendship patterns that developed among students living in on-campus residences for married students (Festinger et al., 1959). As the distance between units increased, the number of friendships decreased. Students living close to one another were more likely to become friends than were those living far apart.

Physical proximity is such a powerful determinant of attraction that it may even overshadow other, seemingly more important, factors. One study looked at friendship choices among police recruits in a police academy class (Segal, 1974). Recruits were assigned to seats alphabetically, and the single best predictor of interpersonal attraction turned out to be the letter with which a person's last name began. Simply put, those whose names were close in the alphabet and were thus seated near each other were more likely to become friends than those whose names were not close in the alphabet and were thus seated apart. The proximity effect proved more important than such variables as common interests and religion.

Why is proximity so important at the beginning stages of a friendship? The answer seems to have two parts: familiarity and the opportunity for interaction. To understand the role of familiarity, think about this common experience. You download some new music, but when you first listen to it, you are lukewarm about it. However, after repeated exposure, it "grows on you." That is, exposure to the new music seems to increase your appreciation of it. A similar effect occurs with people we encounter. These are examples of the *mere exposure effect*, in which repeated exposure to a neutral stimulus enhances one's positive feeling toward that stimulus. Since it was first identified in 1968 by Robert Zajonc, there have been over 200 studies of the mere exposure effect (Bornstein, 1989). These studies used a wide range of stimuli, and in virtually every instance, repeated exposure to a stimulus produced liking.

Physical proximity, in addition to exposing us to other people, also increases the chances that we will interact with them. That is, proximity also promotes liking, because it gives us an opportunity to find out about each other. Physical proximity and the nature of the interaction combine to determine liking (Schiffenbauer & Schavio, 1976). If we discover that the other person has similar interests and attitudes, we are encouraged to pursue the interaction.

physical proximity effect
The fact that we are more likely to form a relationship with someone who is physically close to us; proximity affects interpersonal attraction, mostly at the beginning of a relationship.

SOCIAL PSYCHOLOGY IN ACTION

Internet Relationships

Traditional social psychological research on the proximity effect focused on the role of *physical closeness* in interpersonal attraction and relationship formation. However, evidence shows that more and more of us are using the Internet as a way to meet others (Rosenfeld & Thomas, 2012), which means that we must reevaluate the role of physical proximity in the attraction process. The Internet allows for the formation of relationships over great distances. One need no longer be in the same class, work at the same place, or live on the same block with another person to form a relationship. The Internet effectively reduces the *psychological distance* between people, even when the physical distance between them is great.

There is evidence that people use the Internet to form relationships. In a Pew Research Organization survey (2015), 57% of teens aged 13 to 17 reported making new friends online. The survey also found that male teens were more likely to report making a friend online (61%) than female teens (52%). Older teens (15–17) were more likely to make an online friend (60%) than younger teens (13–14; 51%). Social media sites are the most common means of meeting friends online (64%), with gaming being far behind social media (36%). Female teens are more likely to use social media to form friendships (78%) than male teens (52%). However, male teens are more likely to meet a new friend while gaming online (57%) than female teens (13%). So, although males and females may differ in some aspects, the Internet appears to be an important vehicle for making friends. In another study, 88.3% of male and 69.3% of female research participants reported using the Internet to form "casual or friendly" relationships with others. The study also found that 11.8% of men and 30.8% of women used the Internet to form intimate relationships (McCown et al., 2001). In yet another study, 40% of college students reported using the Internet to form friendships. One of the main reasons for using the Internet in this capacity was to avoid the anxiety normally associated with meeting people and forming friendships. Finally, there was no gender difference in how the Internet was used to form intimate relationships (Knox et al., 2001).

Is using the Internet to form form friendships changing or even harming the entire concept of a friendship? The answer to this question appears to be "no." Although the Internet provides a different way to communicate with friends than face-to-face contact, it does not appear to be changing the core qualities that define friendship, such as self-disclosure, closeness,

People are increasingly using the Internet to form and maintain friendships. Research shows that Internet friendships are important to people and are not harming the concept of friendship.
Source: giuseppelombardo/Shutterstock.

and even conflict (Yau & Reich, 2018). In fact, the use of the Internet appears to be improving social relationships in some ways (Amichai-Hamburger et al., 2013). For example, Amichai-Hamburger et al. suggest that getting social support from friends is enhanced with the Internet because it is more easily accessed than in an offline friendship. If anything the use of the Internet for social relationships appears to be stimulating the quantity and quality of the interactions among people and increasing relationship intimacy (Valkenburg & Peter, 2011). The Internet provides greater opportunity to seek out others who share our interests and attitudes (Amichai-Hamburger & Hayat, 2011), which is another important factor contributing to interpersonal attraction.

How do relationships formed via the Internet stack up against relationships formed the old-fashioned way? Apparently, they stack up quite well. McKenna et al. (2002) found that relationships formed on the Internet were important in the lives of those who formed them. This parallels what we know about relationships formed in a face-to-face situation. Further, they found that online relationships became integrated into the participants' lives, just as face-to-face relationships do. The Internet relationships formed were stable and tended to last over a 2-year period. Once again, this parallels more traditional relationships. Finally, McKenna et al. found that women found their relationships to be more intimate than men.

There are some differences between Internet relationships and offline relationships. Chan and Cheng (2004), using a sample of participants from Hong Kong, had participants describe the quality of one

(continued)

Internet relationship and one traditional, offline relationship. Their results showed that offline relationship descriptions tended to show that these relationships were more interdependent, involved more commitment, and had greater breadth and depth than Internet relationships. However, both types of relationships tended to improve over time, and fewer differences between the two types of friendships were noted as the relationship matured. Online friendships appear to be of lower quality than offline friendships (Antheunis et al., 2012; Glüer & Lohaus, 2016). Glüer and Lohaus compared preadolescent online and offline friendships and found that online friendships had lower overall quality than offline friendships. Preadolescents were more likely to discuss personal problems with offline than online friends. However, online friendships that eventually extend to offline interactions (mixed-mode friendship) are equal in quality to traditional offline friendships (Antheunis et al., 2012). Another study found that romantic relationships (e.g., dating and marital) formed offline lasted longer than those formed online (Paul, 2014). Paul also found that a smaller percentage of couples who met online went on to get married (32%) than those who met offline (67%).

So, it seems clear that the Internet is serving as a medium for the formation of meaningful interpersonal relationships. Is there any downside to this method of relationship formation? The answer is yes. One other finding reported by McKenna et al. (2002) was that individuals who felt that the "real me" was represented on the Internet were most likely to form Internet relationships. These individuals also tend to be socially anxious and lonely. It is these anxious and lonely individuals who are most likely to turn to the Internet as a way to form relationships that they find threatening offline. However, the relationships that socially anxious individuals form online may not be high quality. Tian (2013) found that compared to individuals with low levels of social anxiety, socially anxious individuals formed fewer new friendships, interacted with fewer existing friends, and had lower quality relationships with existing friends on the Internet. However, they did have higher quality relationships with new friends they made on the Internet. So, is lonely people's use of the Internet to form relationships a bad thing? It depends on what one means by loneliness. Weiss (1973) suggested that there are actually two types of loneliness. *Social loneliness* consists of the negative affect associated with not having friends and meaningful relationships. *Emotional loneliness*

Although research shows that physical proximity is a strong predictor of relationship formation, more people are using the Internet for this purpose. The Internet reduces psychological distance, but not physical distance.
Source: insta_photos/Shutterstock.

refers to an empty feeling tied to the lack of intimate relationships (Moody, 2001). A study conducted by Moody (2001) evaluated how face-to-face and Internet relationships related to these two forms of loneliness. Moody found that face-to-face relationships were associated with low levels of both social and emotional loneliness. However, Internet relationships were associated with lower levels of social loneliness, but higher levels of emotional loneliness. In Moody's words: "the Internet can decrease social well-being, even though it is often used as a communication tool" (p. 393). So, while Internet relationships can fulfill one's need for social contact, they may still leave a sense of emotional emptiness. Additionally, shyness has also been found to correlate with a condition called *Internet addiction*. The shyer the person, the more likely he or she is to become addicted to the Internet (Chak & Leung, 2004). Shyness is related to loneliness, with shy individuals being more likely to also be lonely (Jackson et al., 2002). So, even though the Internet can help shy, lonely people establish relationships, it comes with an emotional and behavioral cost.

Discussion Questions

1. How does using the Internet to form relationships relate to the physical proximity effect?
2. Is using the Internet to form relationships changing or harming the concept of friendship?
3. Is there a downside to Internet friendships?

Similarity

Similarity between ourselves and others is another important factor in friendship formation. Similarity in attitudes, beliefs, interests, personality, and even physical appearance strongly influence the likelihood of interpersonal attraction. An interesting study conducted by Byrne et al. (2004) demonstrated the effects of similarity and physical attractiveness on attraction. This study used a computer dating situation in which participants were given a 50-item questionnaire assessing personality characteristics and attitudes. Students were then paired. Some students were paired with a similar other and others with a dissimilar other. The pairs were then sent on a 30-minute date, after which they reported back to the experimenter to have their date assessed. Byrne et al. found that similarity and physical attractiveness, as expected, positively related to interpersonal attraction.

Clearly, there are many possible points of similarity between people. Attitude similarity, for example, might mean that two people are both Democrats, are both Catholics, and in addition to their political and religious beliefs, have like views on a wide range of other issues. However, it is not the absolute number of similar attitudes between individuals that influences the likelihood and strength of attraction. Far more critical are the proportion and importance of similar attitudes. It does little good if someone agrees with you on everything except for the one attitude that is central to your life (Byrne & Nelson, 1965).

What about the notion that in romantic relationships, opposites attract? This idea is essentially what Newcomb called *complementarity*. Researchers have found little evidence for complementarity (Duck, 1988). Instead, a **matching principle** seems to apply in romantic relationships. People tend to become involved with a partner with whom they are usually closely matched in terms of physical attributes or social status (Schoen & Wooldredge, 1989).

matching principle
A principle that applies in romantic relationships, suggesting that individuals become involved with a partner with whom they are closely matched socially and physically.

Different kinds of similarity may have different implications for attraction. If you and someone else are similar in interests, then liking results. Similarity in attitudes, on the other hand, leads to respect for the other person. In a study of college freshmen, similarity in personality was found to be the critical factor determining the degree of satisfaction in friendships (Carli et al., 1991). This study found similarity in physical attractiveness to have some positive effect on friendships but not a large one.

The attitude similarity effect encompasses political ideology as well. Most singles (54%) want a dating partner who shares their political ideology. Additionally, 67% of Gen-Z and 60% Millennials say that a dating partner must support their social justice views (Match, 2021). In the age of COVID-19 vaccination status also matters. A majority of singles (54%) say they would not consider a relationship with an unvaccinated person. However, this willingness factor differs according to generation with 84% of Baby Boomers, 52% of Gen-Xers, and 24% of young singles saying they would not date someone that is not vaccinated (Match, 2021).

Why does similarity promote attraction? Attitude similarity promotes attraction in part because of our need to verify the "correctness" of our beliefs. Through the process of social comparison, we test the validity of our beliefs by comparing them to those of our friends and acquaintances (Hill, 1987). When we find that other people believe as we do, we can be more confident that our attitudes are valid. It is rewarding to know that someone we like thinks the way we do; it shows how smart we both are. Similarity may also promote attraction because we believe we can predict how a similar person will behave (Hatfield et al., 1978).

Limits of the Similarity-Attraction Relationship

The similarity-attraction relationship is one of the most powerful and consistent effects found in social psychology. This, however, does not mean that similarity and attraction relate to one another positively in all situations and relationships. Similarity is most important for relationships that are important to us and that we are committed to (Amodio & Showers, 2005). For less committed relationships, dissimilarity was actually more strongly related to liking and maintaining a relationship over time (Amodio & Showers, 2005). Also, in supervisor-subordinate relationships within organizations, dissimilarity is associated with greater liking on the part of the subordinate for the supervisor (Glomb & Welch, 2005). In organizations, dissimilarity is most likely to translate into positive interpersonal relationships when there is a commitment to diversity (Hobman et al., 2004).

One also has to wonder if the increased emphasis on diversity in education, housing, and employment will erode the strength of the similarity effect. A majority of Americans of all ethnic groups see diversity as a positive force. A Pew Research Organization poll (2019a) found that 55% of Whites, 59% of Blacks, and 60% of Hispanics said that racial diversity was very good for the country. Similar majorities of Whites, Blacks, and Hispanics agreed that diversity has a positive effect on the country's culture. Does this mean that people will start forming more friendships with others who are different from themselves? It appears so. In another Pew poll (2018), 60% of teenagers said that they had a close friend of a different gender, race, or ethnicity. Positive attitudes about diversity are important in the formation of diverse friendships. A study by Angela Bahns (2019) found that valuing diversity was a significant predictor of forming diverse friendships. Individuals who value diversity were more likely to have a friend of a different race, religion, or sexual orientation than those who did not value diversity. Additionally, 7 in 10 singles indicate that they are willing to date someone of a different race or ethnicity from themselves (Match, 2021).

Recall from Chapter 4 how contact with members of an out-group can increase positive feelings toward them. Will the same thing occur as we come into contact with others in diverse environments? The answer to this question is "yes." Physical proximity with diverse others, such as in a workplace, increases the likelihood of forming diverse relationships (Kokkonen et al., 2015). Kokkonen et al. analyzed data from the European Social Survey to explore the formation of interethnic friendship formation. They found that individuals working in a diverse workplace were more likely to form diverse friendships than those who did not. Living in a diverse neighborhood also increased the likelihood of forming diverse friendships. However, the effect of workplace diversity was twice as strong as that for living in a diverse neighborhood. These studies show that valuing diversity and increasing contact with diverse others foster the formation of diverse friendships. It suggests that the similarity effect may become weaker as time goes on and we have increasing contact with those who are different from ourselves.

Although it is true that diverse friendships appear to be becoming more frequent, same-race friendships are still more common than cross-race friendships. Cross-race friendships also get less common as children get older (Aboud et al. 2003). There is also evidence that such friendships may lack stability. For example, a study by Jugert et al. (2013) found that among 10-year-old children, cross-ethnic friendships were less stable than same-ethnicity friendships, a finding confirming other research. For example, cross-race friendships are less stable than same-race friendships (Rude & Herda, 2010). Why might this be the case? Diverse friendships have lower levels of similarity between friends and are of lower quality than less diverse friendships (Rude & Herda, 2010). Also, Jugert et al. found that when there are lower levels of empathy in a cross-ethnic friendship, stability decreases. Jugert et al. suggest that relationship stability is a good indicator of the depth of a friendship. If this is the case, then diverse friendships may lack the depth of intimacy characterized by less diverse friendships.

According to the matching principle, similar people are more likely to form a relationship than dissimilar people. Matching takes place with personality, attitudes, and physical attractiveness.
Source: Antonio Guillem/Shutterstock.

Along the same lines, Rosenbaum (1986) argued that it is not so much that we are attracted to similar others as that we are repulsed by people who are dissimilar. Further examination of this idea that dissimilarity breeds repulsion suggests that dissimilarity serves as an initial filter in the formation of relationships. Once a relationship begins to form, however, similarity becomes the fundamental determinant of attraction (Byrne et al. 1986; Smeaton et al., 1989). Thus, the effect of similarity on attraction may be a two-stage process, with dissimilarity and other negative information leading us to make the initial "cuts," and similarity and other positive information then determining with whom we become close.

There also appears to be a difference between relationships formed in laboratory studies and real-life relationships with respect to the impact of similarity. Researchers have made a distinction between perceived similarity and actual similarity. *Perceived similarity* is how much similarity you believe exists between you and another person. *Actual similarity* is the actual amount of similarity that exists. A meta-analysis of the similarity-attraction literature showed that perceived similarity is a strong predictor of attraction in both the laboratory and real-life relationships. However, actual similarity predicts attraction in laboratory studies, but not in real-life relationships (Montoya et al., 2008). In an interesting study, Ilmarinen et al. (2016) explored the relationship between personality similarity and friendship formation in a group of Finnish military cadets. The cadets completed measures of the big-five personality model (extraversion, agreeableness, conscientiousness, neuroticism, and openness to experience) and two "dark personality traits" (manipulativeness and egotism). They also rated the likeableness of their fellow cadets. Ilmarinen et al. found that similarity only predicted liking for the dark traits, especially at the low end of these dimensions. A person who scores on the low end of the manipulativeness (representing honesty) and egotism (non-egotist) scales is attracted to others with the same levels of these traits. Ilmarinen et al. suggest that this shows that people value the trait honesty when deciding whom to like.

Study Break

This section discussed some of the factors relating to interpersonal attraction. Before you go on to the next section, answer the following questions:

1. How and why does physical proximity relate to interpersonal attraction?
2. How do Internet relationships compare to more traditional relationships?
3. How does similarity relate to interpersonal attraction?
4. What is the matching principle, and why is it important in attraction?
5. What are the limits of the similarity effect?

Physical Attractiveness

Physical attractiveness is an important factor in the early stages of a relationship. Research shows, not surprisingly, that we find physically attractive people more appealing than unattractive people, at least on initial contact (Eagly et al., 1991). Moreover, our society values physical attractiveness, so a relationship with an attractive person is socially rewarding to us.

In their now classic study of the effects of physical attractiveness on dating, Elaine Hatfield and her colleagues led college students to believe that they had been paired at a dance based on their responses to a personality test, but in fact, the researchers had paired the students randomly (Hatfield et al., 1966). At the end of the evening, the couples evaluated each other and indicated how much they would like to date again. For both males and females, the desire to date again was best predicted by the physical attractiveness of the partner. This is not particularly surprising, perhaps, because after only one brief date, the partners probably had little other information to go on.

Physical attractiveness affects not only our attitudes toward others but also our interactions with them. A study of couples who had recently met found that, regardless of gender, when one person was physically attractive, the other tried to intensify the interaction (Garcia et al., 1991). Men were eager to initiate and maintain a conversation, no matter how little reinforcement they got. Women tried to quickly establish an intimate and exclusive relationship by finding things they had in common and by avoiding talk about other people.

There are, however, gender differences in the importance of physical attractiveness. Generally, women are less impressed by attractive males than are men by attractive females (Buss, 1988a). Women are more likely than men to report that attributes other than physical attractiveness, such as a sense of humor, are important to them.

Despite the premium placed on physical attractiveness in Western culture, there is evidence that individuals tend to match for physical attractiveness in much the same way that they match on personality and attitudinal dimensions. You can demonstrate this for yourself. Look at the engagement announcements accompanied by photographs of the engaged couples. You will find remarkable evidence for matching. Beyond such anecdotal evidence, there is research evidence for matching for physical attractiveness. Shafer and Keith (2001) found that married couples (especially younger and older couples) matched for weight.

What accounts for this matching for physical attractiveness? It turns out that physically attractive people tend to have higher standards for what they consider another person's level of attractiveness to be. For example, in one study, participants of varying levels of objective attractiveness (as rated by others) rated the attractiveness of several target individuals. The results showed that more physically attractive participants rated the target individuals lower in attractiveness than less attractive participants (Montoya, 2008). Further, more attractive participants expected less satisfaction in a relationship with targets they rated as less attractive. Additionally, attractive participants showed less fear of rejection from an attractive other than less attractive participants and saw a relationship with a target person of similar attractiveness more probable. So, people may match for attractiveness because they expect a satisfying relationship with others of similar attractiveness, have less fear of being rejected, and view a relationship with an attractive potential mate as likely to happen (Montoya, 2008).

Dimensions of Physical Attractiveness

What specific physical characteristics make someone attractive? Facial appearance has been shown to strongly affect our perceptions of attractiveness through much of our life span (McArthur, 1982; Zebrowitz et al., 1993). Moreover, various aspects of facial appearance have specific effects. One group of researchers suspected that people find symmetrical faces more attractive than asymmetrical faces (Cardenas & Harris, 2006; Thornhill & Gangestad, 1994). Cardenas and Harris had participants examine pairs of faces, asking them to indicate which was more attractive. They found that more symmetrical faces were chosen over less symmetrical faces. Interestingly, when the researchers added asymmetrical makeup decoration to a symmetrical face, it reduced the perceived attractiveness of the symmetrical face. Similarly, Thornhill and Gangestad took photographs of males and females, fed those photos into a computer, created computer versions of the faces, and made precise measurements of the symmetry of the faces. They then asked subjects to rate the computer-generated images for attractiveness. They found that people do judge symmetrical faces to be more attractive than asymmetrical ones. Thornhill and Gangestad also asked the photographed students to fill out questionnaires about their sex and social lives. Those with symmetrical faces reported that they were sexually active earlier than others and had more friends and lovers. Finally, Mealey et al. (1999) report that between identical twins, the twin with the more symmetrical face is judged to be more physically attractive.

Why should symmetry and facial features in general be so important? The answer may lie more in our biology than in our psychology, an issue we explore later in the chapter.

There is a body of research that suggests that people's facial appearance plays a role in how others perceive and treat them (Berry, 1991; Noor & Evans, 2003; Zebrowitz et al. 1998; Zebrowitz & Lee, 1999). Zebrowitz and her coworkers (1998) noted that there is a **physical attractiveness bias**, a "halo," whereby individuals who are physically attractive are thought to also have other positive attributes. One cultural stereotype is that what is beautiful is good. That is, we tend to believe that physically attractive individuals possess a wide range of desirable characteristics and that they are generally happier than unattractive individuals (Dion et al. 1972) Not only do we find attractive individuals more appealing physically, but we also confer on them a number of psychological and social advantages. We think that they are more competent and socially appealing than the average-appearing person. Attractive people are also more likely to join and be invited to join social organizations, especially early in adulthood (Palmer & Peterson, 2021). This is important

physical attractiveness bias
The tendency to confer a number of psychological and social advantages to physically attractive individuals.

because it allows attractive people to build social capital that could not be established without joining such organizations (Palmer & Peterson, 2021). You can think of social capital as analogous to putting money into a savings account. When you need it, you can draw some out. Similarly, attractive people build savings accounts of social capital that they can draw upon in certain situations, giving them an advantage over less attractive individuals. Moreover, unattractive individuals may experience discrimination because of their appearance. A study by Noor and Evans (2003) confirms this. They found that an asymmetrical face was perceived to be more neurotic, less open, less agreeable, and less attractive than a symmetrical face. So, individuals with symmetrical faces are associated with more positive personality characteristics than those with asymmetrical faces.

Much of this attractiveness bias is probably learned. However, there is some evidence that the attractiveness bias may have a biological component as well. In one experiment, infants 2 or 3 months old were exposed to pairs of adult faces and their preferences were recorded (Langlois et al., 1987). Preference was inferred from a measure known as *fixation time*, or the amount of time spent looking at one face or the other. If the infant prefers one over the other, the infant should look at that face longer. As shown in Figure 9.2, when attractive faces were paired with unattractive faces, infants displayed a preference for the attractive faces. It is therefore quite unlikely that infants learned these preferences.

Furthermore, a number of distinctly different cultures seem to have the same biases. This doesn't necessarily mean that these biases aren't learned; various cultures may simply value the same characteristics. Studies comparing judgments of physical attractiveness in Korea and in the United States found agreement on whether a face was attractive and whether the face conveyed a sense of power. In both countries, for example, faces with broad chins, thin lips, and receding hairlines were judged to convey dominance (Triandis, 1994).

Zebrowitz and her coworkers showed that appearances of both attractive people and people with baby faces (round faces, large eyes, small nose and chin, high eyebrows) affect how others treat them (Zebrowitz & Lee, 1999; Zebrowitz et al., 1998). Whereas attractive people are thought to be highly competent both physically and intellectually, baby-faced individuals are viewed as weak, submissive, warm, and naive. What happens when baby-faced individuals do not conform to the stereotype that they are harmless? In a study of delinquent adolescent boys, Zebrowitz and Lee (1999) showed that baby-faced boys, in contrast to more mature-looking delinquents, were punished much more severely. This is a contrast effect: Innocent-looking people who commit antisocial actions violate our expectations.

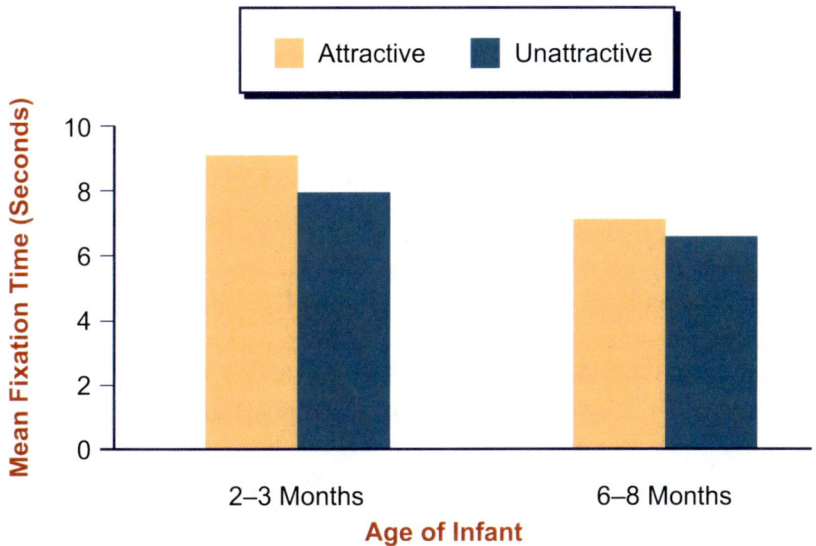

FIGURE 9.2

Infant fixation time as a function of the attractiveness of a stimulus face. Infants as young as 2 or 3 months old showed a preference for an attractive face over an unattractive face.
From Langlois et al. (1987).

Although attractiveness and baby-facedness may have a downside when these individuals run afoul of expectations, the upside is, as you might expect, that the positive expectations and responses of other people shape the personalities of attractive individuals across their life (Zebrowitz et al., 1998). This is self-fulfilling prophecy, whereby attractive men who are treated positively because of their appearance become more socially secure as they get older. Similarly, Zebrowitz found that a man who had an "honest" face in his youth tended to be more honest as he got older.

For baby-faced individuals, the effect over time was somewhat different. These individuals become more assertive and aggressive over time, probably as a way of compensating for the stereotype of a baby-faced individual as submissive and weak.

However, Zebrowitz and colleagues (1998) did not observe such a self-fulfilling prophecy for women. That is, attractive young women do not become more attractive and competent socially as they age. Zebrowitz suggested further that less-attractive women may learn to compensate by becoming more socially able to counteract the negative image held of less-attractive women. This would explain the lack of significant differences in socially valued personality attributes between younger attractive and less-attractive women as they age into their fifties. Interestingly, women who had an attractive personality in their youth developed high attractiveness in their fifties, suggesting, according to Zebrowitz, that women manipulated their appearance and presentation (makeup, etc.) more than men did. It may be that this is due to women's greater motivation to present an attractive appearance because they have less power to achieve their social goals in other ways (Zebrowitz et al., 1998).

Physique and the Attractiveness Bias

Physique also profoundly affects our perceptions of attractiveness. Buss (1994) observed that the importance of physical attractiveness has increased in the United States in every decade since the 1930s. This is true for both men and women, although men rate physical attractiveness as much more important than do women. Western society has widely shared notions of which bodily attributes are attractive. We have positive perceptions of people who fit these notions and negative perceptions of those who do not. We sometimes even display discriminatory behavior against those who deviate too far from cultural standards.

People can be categorized by body type into *ectomorphs* (thin, perhaps underweight), *mesomorphs* (athletic build), and *endomorphs* (overweight). Positive personality traits tend to be attributed to mesomorphs and negative ones to people with the other body types (Ryckman et al., 1991). There is some ambivalence about ectomorphs, especially as societal attitudes toward thinness seem to shift, influenced by such factors as an increasing health consciousness. Perceptions of endomorphs, in contrast, remain consistently negative. Of course, some people are more intensely attuned to physical appearance than are others. It appears that those people who are most conscious of their own appearance are the most likely to stereotype others on the basis of physique.

Certainly this is the case with regard to overweight individuals. Research confirms that obese individuals are stigmatized and are the target of negative stereotypes in our society. For example, in one experiment in which participants evaluated overweight or average-weight targets, overweight individual were found to be less attractive, less happy, less popular, less successful, and less outgoing than average-weight individuals (Grant et al., 2016). This bias cuts across genders. Obese men and women are likely to be stigmatized (Hebl & Turchin, 2005). These negative stereotypes exist on both the implicit and explicit level (Waller et al., 2012; Wang et al. 2004). In one study (Harris, 1990), subjects judged a stimulus person who was depicted as either normal weight or (with the help of extra clothing) obese. They evaluated "Chris," the stimulus person, along several dimensions including the likelihood that Chris was dating or married, her self-esteem, and her ideal romantic partner. The results, almost without exception, reflected negative stereotyping of an obese Chris compared to a normal-weight Chris. Subjects judged that the obese Chris was less likely to be dating or married compared to the normal-weight Chris. They also rated the obese Chris as having lower self-esteem than the normal-weight Chris and felt that her ideal love partner should also be obese.

Studies also show the practical consequences of these attitudes. For example, it has been shown that overweight college students are less likely than other students to get financial help from home (Crandall, 1991). This effect was especially strong with respect to female students and was true regardless of the resources the student's family had, the number of children in the family, or other factors that could affect parents' willingness to provide financial help. The researchers suggested that the finding might be largely explained by parents' negative attitudes toward their overweight children and consequent lack of optimism about their future. In a related domain, there is evidence that businesspeople sacrifice $1,000 in annual salary for every pound they are overweight (Kolata, 1992). Weight can also affect evaluations of employability (Grant & Mizzi, 2014). Grant and Mizzi found that an overweight potential job applicant was rated as less employable than a normal weight applicant. They also found that stereotypes about overweight people did not mediate the relationship between weight and employability ratings. They did find, however, that a "rational bias" (e.g., customers would feel uncomfortable with the overweight employee) mediated the relationship.

Interestingly, the bias against overweight people is shown by children. Children between the ages of 2 and 5 were shown two line drawings of children. One of the drawings showed a child who was 23% larger than the other. The children were asked to ascribe various characteristics to the figures in the drawing. The results showed that the children were more likely to ascribe negative qualities to the larger figure (Turnbull et al., 2000). This finding should not be surprising since these stereotypic images of body image are portrayed in children's literature and movies (Herbozo et al., 2004). Just think, for example, about the Disney film *The Little Mermaid*, in which the mermaid Ariel is depicted as a slim, beautiful, young woman and the sea witch (the villain) is depicted as an obese, unattractive woman.

The bias against overweight people even extends into the world of health care. For example, Waller et al. (2012) found a stronger implicit bias against overweight people in a medical than nonmedical context. In another study, an implicit prejudice and implicit stereotypes were shown toward overweight people by health care workers, a majority of whom were doctors (Teachman & Brownell, 2001). There was, however, little evidence for an explicit prejudice. In another study, doctors showed more negative attitudes toward hypothetical obese patients than average-weight patients and that they would spend less time with an obese patient (Hebl & Xu, 2001). Physicians indicated that they would be more likely to refer obese patients for mental health care. The good news was, however, that doctors seemed to follow an appropriate course of action with respect to weight-unrelated tests.

The bias against obese people may be culturally related. Western culture seems to place a great deal of emphasis on body image (just take a look at the models [male and female] used in advertisements). One cross-cultural study using British and Ugandan participants showed that the Ugandan participants rated a drawing of an obese figure more positively than British participants (Furnham & Baguma, 2004). Another study conducted in New Zealand found that obese job applicants were evaluated more negatively than nonobese applicants (Ding & Stillman, 2005). The bias may also have a racial component as well. One study found that Black males stigmatized an obese person less than White males and that obese Black males are less likely to be stigmatized than obese White males (Hebl & Turchin, 2005).

One reason obese individuals are vilified is that we believe that their weight problem stems from laziness and a lack of discipline. If we know that an individual's weight problem is the result of biology and thus beyond his or her control, we are less likely to make negative judgments of that individual (DeJong, 1980; Linn & Stutts, 2020). What we fail to realize is that most obese people cannot control their weight. There is a genetic component in obesity, and this tendency can be exacerbated by social and cultural factors, such as lack of information and an unhealthy lifestyle.

Attractiveness judgments and stereotyping in everyday life may not be as strong as they are in some laboratory studies. In these studies, we make pure attraction judgments: We see only a face or a physique. When we deal with people, we evaluate an entire package even if much of what we see initially is only the wrapping. The entire package includes many attributes. A person may be overweight but may also have a mellifluous voice and a powerful personality. In a laboratory study in which subjects were exposed to a person's face and voice, the perception of the person's physical attractiveness was affected by judgments about that person's vocal attractiveness and vice versa (Zuckerman et al., 1991). Gertrude Stein was a woman many people found attractive even though she weighed over 200 pounds. Her striking face and her powerful personality were the main attributes that people remembered after meeting her.

Beauty and the View from Evolutionary Psychology

It is obvious that we learn to associate attractiveness with positive virtues and unattractiveness with vice, even wickedness. Children's books and movies often portray the good characters as beautiful and the villains as ugly. As noted, in the Walt Disney movie *The Little Mermaid*, the slender, beautiful mermaid, Ariel, and the evil, obese sea witch are cases in point. Such portrayals are not limited to works for children. The hunchback of Notre Dame, the phantom of the opera, and Freddy Kruger are all physically unattractive evildoers.

Evolutionary psychologists suggest that perhaps beauty is more than skin deep. Recall the research on the attractiveness of symmetrical faces. It seems that it is not only humans who value symmetry but also a variety of other species. For example, Watson and Thornhill (1994) reported that female scorpion flies can detect and prefer as mates males with symmetrical wings. Male elks with the most symmetrical racks host the largest harems.

Mate Selection: Good Genes or Good Guys? Proponents of evolutionary psychology, a subfield of both psychology and biology, employ the principles of evolution to explain human behavior and believe that symmetry is reflective of underlying genetic quality. Lack of symmetry is thought to be caused by various stresses, such as poor maternal nutrition, late maternal age, attacks by predators, or disease, and may therefore reflect bad health or poor genetic quality. Thus, the preference for symmetry in potential mates, whether human or animal, may be instinctive (Watson & Thornhill, 1994). Indeed, even small differences matter. Twins with lower levels of symmetry are reliably rated as less attractive than their slightly more symmetrical counterpart (Mealey et al., 1999).

The degree to which biology may control human mating preferences can be underscored by the finding that the type of face a woman finds attractive varies with her menstrual cycle. Perret and Penton-Voak (1999) reported a study that showed that when a woman is ovulating, she is more likely to prefer men with highly masculine features. In contrast, during other times, men with softer, feminine features are preferred. The researchers had numerous women from various countries—Japan, Scotland, England—judge male faces during different parts of their menstrual cycles. The researchers believe that these results are explained by the observation that masculine looks, in all of the animal kingdom, denote virility and the increased likelihood for healthy offspring. In a related finding, Gangestad and Thornhill (1998) reported a study that showed that females preferred the smell of a "sweaty" T-shirt worn by the most symmetrical males but only if the women were ovulating.

Of course, it is likely that more choice is involved in mate selection than would be indicated by these studies. In any event, most people do rebel against the notion that decisions about sex, marriage, and parenthood are determined by nothing more than body odor (Berreby, 1998).

Certainly we would expect those with symmetrical appearances to become aware of their advantages in sexual competition. For example, consider the following study by Simpson and his coworkers. Heterosexual men and women were told that they would be competing with another same-sex person for a date with an attractive person of the opposite sex. The experimenters videotaped and analyzed the interactions among the two competitors and the potential date. Men who had symmetrical faces used direct competition tactics. That is, when trying to get a date with the attractive woman, symmetrical men simply and baldly compared their attractiveness (favorably) with the competitor. Less-attractive (read as less-symmetrical-faced) men used indirect competitive methods, such as emphasizing their positive personality qualities (Simpson et al., 1999).

Gangestad and Thornhill (1998) have argued that physical appearance marked by high symmetrical precision reveals to potential mates that the individual has good genes and is, therefore, for both men and women, a highly desirable choice. These individuals, especially men, should have fared very well in sexual competition during evolutionary history. Why? Research suggests that greater symmetry is associated with higher survival rates as well as higher reproductive rates in many species (Simpson et al., 1999). In men, it seems that certain secondary sexual attributes that are controlled by higher levels of testosterone, such as enlarged jaws, chins, and so forth, may project greater health and survival capability (Mealey et al., 1999). Indeed, symmetrical men and women report more sexual partners and have sex earlier in life than less symmetrical individuals. The more symmetrical the individual—again, especially males—the more probable the person will have the opportunity for short-term sexual encounters, and the more likely, as Simpson and colleagues (1999) found, they will use direct competitive strategies to win sexual competitions.

Of course, good genes are not enough. Raising human offspring is a complicated, long-term—some might say never-ending—affair, and having a good partner willing to invest in parenthood is important. Indeed, theorists have developed what are called "good provider" models of mate selection that emphasize the potential mate's commitment to the relationship and ability to provide resources necessary for the long-term health of that relationship (Gangestad & Thornhill, 1997; Trivers, 1972).

How to Attract a Mate David Buss, a prominent evolutionary social psychologist, suggested that to find and retain a reproductively valuable mate, humans engage in love acts—behaviors with near-term goals, such as display of resources the other sex finds enticing. The ultimate purpose of these acts is to increase reproductive success (Buss, 1988a, 1988b). Human sexual behavior thus can be viewed in much the same way as the sexual behavior of other animal species.

Subjects in one study (Buss, 1988b) listed some specific behaviors they used to keep their partner from getting involved with someone else. Buss found that males tended to use display of resources (money, cars, clothes, sometimes even brains), whereas females tried to look more attractive and threatened to be unfaithful if the males didn't shape up. Buss argued that these findings support an evolutionary interpretation of mate retention: The tactics of females focus on their value as a reproductive mate and on arousing the jealousy of the male, who needs to ensure they are not impregnated by a rival.

Jealousy is evoked when a threat or loss occurs to a valued relationship due to the partner's real or imagined attention to a rival (Dijkstra & Buunk, 1998). Men and women respond differently to infidelity, according to evolutionary psychologists, due to the fact that women bear higher reproductive costs than do men (Harris & Christenfeld, 1996). Women are concerned with having a safe environment for potential offspring, so it would follow that sexual infidelity would not be as threatening as emotional infidelity, which could signal the male's withdrawal from the relationship. Men, however, should be most concerned with ensuring the prolongation of their genes and avoiding investing energy in safeguarding some other male's offspring. Therefore, males are most threatened by acts of sexual infidelity and less so by emotional ones. Thus, males become most jealous when their mates are sexually unfaithful, whereas women are most jealous when their mates are emotionally involved with a rival (Buss, 1994; Harris & Christenfeld, 1996).

According to the evolutionary psychology view, males ought to be threatened by a rival's dominance, the ability to provide resources (money, status, power) to the female in question, whereas women ought to be most threatened by a rival who is physically attractive, because that attribute signals the potential for viable offspring. Indeed, a clever experiment by Dijkstra and Buunk (1998), in which participants judged scenarios in which the participant's real or imagined mate was flirting with a person of the opposite sex, showed that dominance in a male rival and attractiveness in a female rival elicited the greatest amount of jealousy for men and women, respectively.

Although physical attractiveness and earning potential are important to men and women in mate selection, women are more likely to pay attention to earning potential more than men. Men pay more attention to physical attractiveness than women. This is consistent with an evolutionary psychology explanation for mate selection.

Source: Sisacorn/Shutterstock.

Many of Buss's findings about human mating behavior are disturbing because both men and women in pursuit of their sexual goals cheat and frustrate their mates and derogate their rivals. However, some of his findings are kinder to our species. For example, he points out that the most effective tactics for men who wish to keep their mates are to provide love and kindness, to show affection, and to tell their mates of their love. That sounds rather romantic.

Indeed, evidence suggests that women are driven, at least in long-term mate selection strategies, by behavior and traits represented by the good provider models. Although men are strongly influenced by traits such as youth and attractiveness, women tend to select partners on the basis of attributes such as social status and industriousness (Ben Hamida et al., 1998). Note the intriguing differences between traits that men find attractive in women and those that women find attractive in men. The obvious one is that men seem to be driven by the "good genes" model, whereas women's preferences seem to follow the good provider models. This preference appears across a range of cultures. One study by Shackelford et al. (2005) had males and females evaluate several characteristics that could define a potential mate. The participants were drawn from 37 cultures (including African, Asian, and European). Their results confirmed that, across cultures, women valued social status more than men, and men valued physical attractiveness more than women.

The other difference, however, is that traits that make women attractive are in essence uncontrollable: Either you are young or you are not; either you are attractive or you are not. Modern science can help, but not much. Therefore, a woman who desires to increase her value has the problem of enhancing attributes that are really not under her control (Ben Hamida et al., 1998). Male-related attributes—status, achievement—are all, to a greater or lesser extent, under some control and may be gained with effort and motivation. Ben Hamida and his colleagues argue that the uncontrollability of the factors that affect a woman's fate in the sexual marketplace may have long-term negative emotional consequences.

Before we conclude that there is an unbridgeable difference between men and women and that men follow only the good genes model and women only the good provider model, we need to take into account a recent meta-analysis showing that physical attractiveness and good earning potential mediate mate preferences for both men and women (Eastwick et al., 2014). We should also consider the possibility that what one wants in the sexual marketplace depends on what one's goals are and what one can reasonably expect to get. In fact, it appears that when looking for a casual sexual partner, both men and women emphasize attractiveness, and when searching for a long-term relationship, both look for a mate with good interpersonal skills, an individual who is attentive to the partner's needs, has a good sense of humor, and is easygoing (Regan, 1998). In fact, Miller (2000), an evolutionary psychologist, argued that the most outstanding features of the human mind—consciousness, morality, sense of humor, creativity—were shaped not so much by natural selection but rather by sexual selection. Miller suggested that being funny and friendly and a good conversationalist serves the same purpose for humans as an attractive tail serves peacocks: It helps attract mates. This is reinforced by the Singles in America survey (Match, 2021) indicating that 80% of singles or more indicated they valued in a dating partner traits such as someone they could confide in, with emotional maturity, that can make them laugh, and whom is open-minded.

Regan (1998) reported that women were less willing to compromise on their standards. For example, although women wanted an attractive partner for casual sex, they also wanted a male who was older and more interpersonally responsive. Men wanted attractiveness and would compromise on everything else. In fact, a woman's attractiveness seems to overcome a male potential partner's common sense as well. Agocha and Cooper (1999) reported that when men knew a potential partner's sexual history and also knew that she was physically attractive, they weighed attractiveness as much more important in the decision to engage in intercourse than the probability of contracting a sexually transmitted disease as suggested by that sexual history. However, women and men are less willing to compromise when it comes to long-term relationships. The results conform to the idea that casual sex affords men a chance to advertise their sexual prowess and gain favor with their peer group but that long-term relationships are driven by quite different needs (Regan, 1998).

Finally, students often ask about any differences between heterosexual and same-sex orientation mate preferences. The available research suggests that mate selection preferences between these groups may not differ all that much (Over & Phillips, 1997). For example, a study of personal advertisements placed by heterosexual and same-sex orientation males and females was conducted by Kenrick et al. (1995). Kenrick et al. found that mate selection patterns for heterosexual and same-sex orientation men were highly similar and showed similar patterns of change with age. Both groups of men preferred younger mates, and this preference grew stronger with age. This finding was replicated in a similar study of personal ads conducted by Burrows (2013). She found that gay men advertised for partners who were on average 13 years younger than themselves (heterosexuals advertised for someone 14 years younger). Kenrick et al. found a slight difference between same-sex orientation and heterosexual women. Younger women in both groups expressed interest in same-aged mates. However, with age, same-sex orientation women were more likely than heterosexual women to desire a younger partner. In another study of personal advertisements placed by same-sex orientation men and women, Hatala and Prehodka (1996) found that men expressed a greater interest in physically attractive partners than women. Women showed more interest in the personality traits of potential partners than men. This finding parallels what is found for heterosexual men and women. In another study, same-sex orientation women were found to be more interested in visual sexual stimulation and less in partner status than heterosexual women. There are some differences between gay men and lesbians in their dating preferences. Gay men express a greater interest than lesbians in long-term relationships. However, lesbians express more interest than gay men in monogamous relationships (Potârcă et al., 2015).

Study Break

This section explored how physical attractiveness affects interpersonal attraction. Before you begin the next section, answer the following questions:

1. Overall, how and why is physical attractiveness important in attraction?
2. What characteristics of faces contribute to the perception of facial attractiveness?
3. What is the physical attractiveness bias, and what are some of its components?
4. How and why does a person's weight relate to perceptions of attractiveness and behavior?
5. How do evolutionary psychologists explain the effects of physical attractiveness on attraction?
6. What are the factors relevant to human mate selection, and how can one attract a mate?

Dynamics of Close Relationships

We have discussed why people form close relationships and why they form them with the people they do. We turn now to the dynamics of close relationships—how they develop and are kept going, and how in some cases conflict can lead to their dissolution. But what exactly are close relationships? What psychological factors define them?

There appear to be three crucial factors, all of which we saw in the relationship between Gertrude Stein and Alice Toklas. The first factor is emotional involvement, feelings of love or warmth and fondness for the other person. The second is sharing, including sharing of feelings and experiences. The third is interdependence, which means that one's well-being is tied up with that of the other (Kelley et al., 1983). As is clear from this definition, a close relationship can be between spouses, lovers, or friends. Note that even when research focuses on one type of close relationship, it is usually also applicable to the others.

Relationship Development

Models of how relationships develop emphasize a predictable sequence of events. This is true of both models we examine in this section, the stage model of relationship development and social penetration theory. According to the stage model of relationship development, proposed by Levinger and Snoek (1972), relationships evolve through the following stages:

Stage 0, no relationship. This is a person's status with respect to virtually all other people in the world.

Stage 1, awareness. We become conscious of another's presence and feel the beginning of interest. When Stein and Toklas first met in the company of friends, their conversation suggested to each of them that they might have much in common.

Stage 2, surface contact. Interaction begins but is limited to topics such as the weather, politics, and mutual likes and dislikes. Although the contact is superficial, each person is forming impressions of the other. Stein and Toklas moved into this stage the day after their first meeting and soon moved beyond it.

Stage 3, mutuality. The relationship moves, in substages, from lesser to greater interdependence. The first substage is that of involvement, which is characterized by a growing number of shared activities (Levinger, 1988). A subsequent substage is commitment, characterized by feelings of responsibility and obligation each to the other. Although not all close relationships involve commitment (Sternberg, 1988), those that have a serious long-term influence on one's life generally do. We noted how Stein and Toklas began by sharing activities, then feelings, and then an increasing commitment to each other.

The first stages of Levinger and Snoek's model give us insight into the early stages of a relationship where people first meet. However, it does not tell us anything about *how* people meet each other, giving them a chance to form a relationship. Surprisingly, there has not been all that much research on this issue. One exception is a comprehensive study of relationship formation by Rosenfeld and Thomas (2012). In their study, Rosenfeld and Thomas studied how people meet each other and how methods of meeting others have changed over time. Figure 9.3 shows some of the ways that heterosexual and same-sex couples meet (based on data from Rosenfeld, 2010). As you can see, there are different ways that couples meet, and for some methods, there are striking differences between heterosexual and same-sex couples. Heterosexual couples are more likely to meet through family members and friends. On the other hand, same-sex couples are more likely to meet via the Internet. Rosenfeld and Thomas report that some methods of meeting have shown a decline over the past decades, and some have shown an increase. For example, there has been a decline in couples (both heterosexual and same-sex) meeting via friends from 1980 to 2010. However, there has been a sharp increase in the percentage of couples who meet via the Internet from the late 1990s through 2010, especially for same-sex couples. Further, the gap between Internet use by heterosexuals and same-sex orientation individuals is even greater when you consider only couples who have met in the past 10 years of the study (Rosenfeld & Thomas, 2012). One reason why same-sex orientation individuals use the Internet more than heterosexuals is that the more traditional ways of meeting one's partner (e.g., family, friends, and church) have never been very useful for gays and lesbians. Consequently, they are likely to turn to the Internet because it represents the best possibility of meeting other

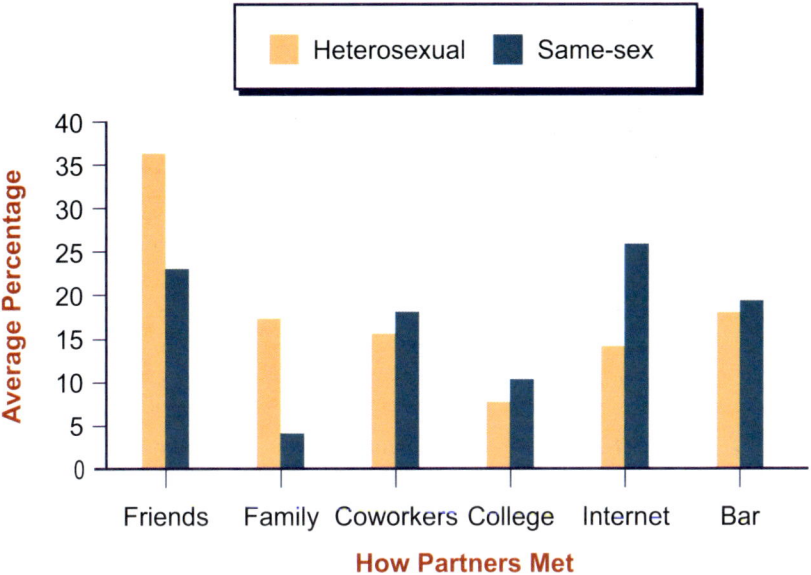

FIGURE 9.3

How couple's partners meet each other (average percent across relationship types). Based on data from Rosenfeld (2010).

gay or lesbian partners (Rosenfeld & Thomas, 2012). Interestingly, how couples meet is not related to whether or not they stay together (Rosenfeld & Thomas, 2012).

Once couples meet, their relationship progresses in terms of the communication patterns they show. A second model of relationship development, **social penetration theory**, developed by Altman and Taylor (1973), centers on the idea that relationships change over time in both breadth (the range of topics people discuss and activities they engage in together) and depth (the extent to which they share their inner thoughts and feelings). Relationships progress in a predictable way from slight and superficial contact to greater and deeper involvement. First the breadth of a relationship increases. Then there is an increase in its depth, and breadth may actually decrease. Casual friends may talk about topics ranging from sports to the news to the latest rumors at work. But they will not, as will more intimate friends, talk about their feelings and hopes. Close friends allow each other to enter their lives—social penetration—and share on a deeper, more intimate level, even as the range of topics they discuss may decrease.

Evidence in support of social penetration theory comes from a study in which college students filled out questionnaires about their friendships several times over the course of a semester and then again 3 months later (Hays, 1985). Over 60% of the affiliations tracked in the study developed into close relationships by the end of the semester. More important, the interaction patterns changed as the relationships developed. As predicted by social penetration theory, interactions of individuals who eventually became close friends were characterized by an initial increase in breadth followed by a decrease in breadth and an increase in intimacy, or depth.

An important contributor to increasing social penetration—or to the mutuality stage of relationship development—is *self-disclosure*, the ability and willingness to share intimate areas of one's life. College students who kept diaries of their interactions with friends reported that casual friends provided as much fun and intellectual stimulation as close friends but that close friends provided more emotional support (Hays, 1988b). Relationship development is fostered by self-disclosure simply because we often respond to intimate revelations with self-disclosures of our own (Jourard, 1971).

social penetration theory
A theory that relationships vary in breadth, the extent of interaction, and depth, suggesting they progress in an orderly fashion from slight and superficial contact to greater and deeper involvement.

Dating Scripts and Relationship Formation

Once people meet one another and enter into a relationship, what ideas do they carry into their relationships? Research on how people perceive relationships has focused on

A dating script includes ideas about what a date should be like. Men and women have somewhat different dating scripts.

Source: Jacob Lund/Shutterstock.

dating scripts. Cognitive psychologists define a *script* as our knowledge and memories of how events occur. For example, you may have a script concerning a basketball game in which 10 large, athletic individuals come onto a court and try to get a round ball through a hoop. A *dating script* is your concept of how a date should progress. That is, we have an idea about what we expect to happen on a date (for example, a "first date"). These scripts will guide our actions when we find ourselves in a dating situation and are derived from cultural and personal experiences (Rose & Frieze, 1989). Research shows that first-date scripts for men and women have many similarities but some important differences (Bartoli & Clark, 2006). Women, for example, have first-date scripts that are focused on the social interactions during the date. Men's first-date scripts are more action-oriented, which includes things like deciding what to do and when to initiate physical contact (Rose & Frieze, 1989). Generally, men's first-date scripts are proactive, and women's are reactive (Rose & Frieze, 1993). Additionally, men's dating scripts tend to place more emphasis on expecting sexual activity, whereas women's scripts are more likely to emphasize limiting such activity (Bartoli & Clark, 2006).

Recent research reveals some interesting things about dating scripts. First, dating scripts that conform to dominant gender-role stereotypes are seen more positively than those that do not (McCarty & Kelly, 2015). McCarty and Kelly had male and female participants rate a stereotypic (e.g., the man picks up the woman, holds the door open, etc.), counter-stereotypic (the female engaged in the behaviors depicted in the stereotypic date), or an egalitarian (none of the behaviors mentioned) date. McCarty and Kelly found that the stereotypic date was rated most positively. Additionally, the male in the stereotypic date was rated more positively (e.g., warmer, more appropriate) than in the other dating scenarios. Second, dating scripts of deaf individuals show some differences from traditional dating scripts of hearing individuals (Gilbert et al., 2012). Gilbert et al. compared the dating scripts of deaf individuals with those of hearing individuals (established in other studies) and found that a sexual outcome was not as strongly expressed among the deaf than among the hearing. In other aspects, however, the dating scripts of the deaf and hearing are very similar.

Culture provides a pretty clear set of scripts concerning heterosexual dating. There are countless movies, books, plays, and other sources of information providing a clear road map for heterosexual dating. The same does not appear to be true for dating scripts for same-sex relationships. There are differences in the dating scripts of gay men and lesbian women. The scripts of gay men tend to be more oriented toward sexual behavior and less toward emotion and intimacy. On the other hand, scripts of lesbians tend to be more oriented toward emotions (Klinkenberg & Rose, 1994). This difference parallels differences seen in heterosexual relationships, where men stress sexual and physical aspects of a date and women stress intimacy and emotion (Goldberg, 2010).

When we move from the realm of first dates and dating in general to more committed relationships, we again see that there are similarities and differences between same-sex and heterosexual couples. We must start this discussion with the fact that there are many more similarities than differences between same-sex and heterosexual couples in committed relationships (Roisman et al., 2008). However, Roisman et al. report that lesbian partners work together better than partners in other relationships. Additionally, same-sex relationships tend to be more egalitarian than mixed-sex relationships (Shechory & Ziv, 2007). That is, in same-sex relationships, there is more equal distribution of household tasks and more liberal attitudes toward gender roles than in mixed-sex relationships.

Generally, women in mixed-sex relationships feel less equitably treated in their relationships than women in same-sex relationships do (Shechory & Ziv, 2007). Additionally, partners in lesbian couples report a higher level of relationship quality than partners in either gay or heterosexual relationships (Kurdek, 2008). As a relationship progresses, partners in gay and lesbian couples show little change in reported relationship quality, whereas partners in heterosexual relationships show a decline in relationship quality that eventually levels off (Kurdek, 2008). Interestingly, partners in heterosexual relationships with children show two periods of declining relationship quality (Kurdek, 2008). Finally, couples in same-sex relationships are more likely to keep a romantic secret from their partners than couples in heterosexual relationships (Easterling et al., 2012).

Study Break

This section discussed how relationships form. Before you begin the next section, answer the following questions:

1. What are the stages of Levinger and Snoek's model of relationship formation, and what happens at each stage?
2. How do people tend to meet one another?
3. What dimensions underlie social penetration theory, and how do they relate to relationship formation?
4. How does self-disclosure relate to relationship formation?
5. What is a dating script, and how do scripts differ among people?

Evaluating Relationships

Periodically we evaluate the state of our relationships, especially when something is going wrong or some emotional episode occurs. Berscheid (1985) observed that emotion occurs in a close relationship when there is an interruption in a well-learned sequence of behavior. Any long-term dating or marital relationship develops sequences of behavior—Berscheid called these *interchain sequences*—that depend on the partners coordinating their actions. For example, couples develop hints and signals that show their interest in lovemaking. The couple's lovemaking becomes organized, and the response of one partner helps coordinate the response of the other. A change in the frequency or pattern of this behavior will bring about a reaction, positive or negative, from the partner. The more intertwined the couples are, the stronger are their interchain sequences; the more they depend on each other, the greater the impact of interruptions of these sequences.

Exchange Theories

One perspective on how we evaluate relationships is provided by **social exchange theory** (Thibaut & Kelley, 1959), which suggests that people make assessments according to rewards and costs, which correspond to all of the positive and all of the negative factors derived from a relationship. Generally, rewards are high if a person gets a great deal of gratification from the relationship, whereas costs are high if the person either must exert a great deal of effort to maintain the relationship or experiences anxiety about the relationship. According to this economic model of relationships, the outcome is decided by subtracting costs from rewards. If the rewards are greater than the costs, the outcome is positive; if the costs are greater than the rewards, the outcome is negative.

This doesn't necessarily mean that if the outcome is positive, we will stay in the relationship, or that if the outcome is negative, we will leave it. We also evaluate outcomes against *comparison levels*. One type of comparison level is our expectation of what we will obtain from the relationship. That is, we compare the outcome with what we think the relationship should be giving us. A second type is a *comparison level of alternatives*, in which we compare the outcome of the relationship we are presently in with the expected

social exchange theory
A theory of how relationships are evaluated, suggesting that people make assessments according to the rewards (positive things derived from a relationship) and costs (negative things derived from a relationship).

outcomes of possible alternative relationships. If we judge that the alternative outcomes would not be better, or even worse, than the outcome of our present relationship, we will be less inclined to make a change. If, on the other hand, we perceive that an alternative relationship promises a better outcome, we are more likely to make a change.

A theory related to social exchange theory—*equity theory*—says that we evaluate our relationships based on their rewards and costs, but it also focuses on our perception of equity, or balance, in relationships (Hatfield et al., 1985). Equity in a relationship occurs when the following equation holds:

$$\frac{\text{Person A's Benefits (rewards } - \text{ costs)}}{\text{B's Contributions}} = \frac{\text{Person B's Benefits (rewards } - \text{ costs)}}{\text{A's Contributions}}$$

Rewards may include, but are not limited to, companionship, sex, and social support. Costs may include loss of independence and increases in financial obligations. The contributions made to the relationship include earning power or high social status. The rule of equity is simply that person A's benefits should equal person B's if their contributions are equal. However, fairness requires that if A's contributions are greater than B's, A's benefits should also be greater.

Thus, under equity theory, the way people judge the fairness of the benefits depends on their understanding of what each brings to the relationship. For example, the spouse who earns more may be perceived as bringing more to the marriage and, therefore, as entitled to higher benefits. The other spouse may, as a result, increase her costs, perhaps by taking on more of the household chores.

In actual relationships, of course, people differ, often vigorously, on what counts as contributions and on how specific contributions ought to be weighed. For example, in business settings, many individuals believe that race or gender should count as a contribution when hiring. Others disagree strongly with that position.

When evaluating a relationship people often weigh each partner's benefits and costs to find equity in a relationship. However, inequities may still exist based on cultural expectations. For example, husbands tend to have more control over financial matters than wives.
Source: WAYHOME studio/Shutterstock.

Has the fact that most women now work outside the home altered the relationship between wives and husbands as equity theory would predict? It appears, in keeping with equity theory, that the spouse who earns more, regardless of gender, often has fewer childcare responsibilities than the spouse who earns less (Steil & Weltman, 1991, 1992).

However, it also appears that cultural expectations lead to some inequity. Husbands tend to have more control over financial matters than wives do, regardless of income (Biernat & Wortman, 1991). Moreover, a study of professional married couples in which the partners earned relatively equal amounts found that although the wives were satisfied with their husbands' participation in household chores and childrearing, in reality there was considerable inequity (Biernat & Wortman, 1991). Women were invariably the primary caregivers for the children. Men spent time with their children and did many of the household chores, but they were not the primary caregivers. This may reflect a lack of equity in these relationships, or it may mean that women simply do not fully trust their husbands to do a competent job of taking care of the children.

What happens when people perceive inequity in a relationship? As a rule, they will attempt to correct the inequity and restore equity. If you realize that your partner is dissatisfied with the state of the relationship, you might try, for example, to pay more attention to your partner and in this way increase the rewards he or she experiences. If equity is not restored, your partner might become angry or withdraw from the relationship. Inequitable relationships are relationships in trouble.

In one study, researchers measured the level of perceived equity in relationships by means of the following question and scale (Hatfield et al., 1978, p. 121):

Comparing what you get out of this relationship with what your partner gets out of it, how would you say the relationship stacks up?

+3 I am getting a much better deal than my partner.

+2 I am getting a somewhat better deal.

+1 I am getting a slightly better deal.

  0 We are both getting an equally good—or bad—deal.

−1 My partner is getting a slightly better deal.

−2 My partner is getting a somewhat better deal.

−3 My partner is getting a much better deal than I am.

Respondents were grouped into three categories: those who felt that their relationship was equitable, those who felt that they got more out of the relationship than their partners and therefore were overbenefited, and those who felt that they got less than their partners and therefore were underbenefited.

The researchers then surveyed 2,000 people and found, as expected, that those individuals who felt underbenefited were much more likely to engage in extramarital sex than those who thought that their relationship was equitable or felt overbenefited (Hatfield et al., 1978). Generally, couples who feel that they are in an equitable relationship are more likely to maintain the relationship than those who are less equitably matched (Hill et al., 1976).

Communal Relationships

Although the research just reviewed suggests that people make rather cold-blooded, marketplace judgments about the quality of their relationships, it is likely that they also have other ways of evaluating relationships. For example, a distinction has been made between relationships governed by exchange principles—in which, as we have seen, people benefit each other with the expectation of receiving a benefit in return—and relationships governed by communal principles—in which individuals benefit each other in response to the other's needs (Clark, 1986). In **communal relationships**, if one partner can put more into the relationship than the other, so be it. That is, people may deliberately underbenefit themselves for the sake of the relationship.

Love relationships are often governed by communal principles. Clark and Grote (1998) reviewed the research concerning how couples evaluate their relationships, and although some of the results show that costs are negatively related to satisfaction as exchange theories would predict, sometimes, however, costs are positively related to satisfaction. That is, Clark and Grote found evidence that, sometimes, the more costs a partner incurs, the higher the satisfaction. How might we explain this? Well, if we consider the communal norm as one that rewards behavior that meets the needs of one's partner, then we might understand how costs could define a warm, close, and affectionate relationship. As Clark and Grote noted, it may be admirable, and one may feel good about oneself if, having helped one's partner, one has also lived up to the communal ideal. By doing so, the helping partner gains the gratitude of the other, feels good about oneself, and these positive feelings then become associated with the relationship.

One way to reconcile the different findings concerning the relationship between costs and satisfaction is to note that the costs one bears in a communal relationship are qualitatively different than those we bear in a purely exchange relationship that may be deteriorating. For example, consider the following costs borne in an exchange relationship: "She told me I was dumb." This is an intentional insult (and cost) that suggests a relationship that may be going badly. Compare this to a communal cost: "I listened carefully to what he said when a problem arose, even though I was quite busy and had other things to get done." This communal cost served to strengthen the relationship (Clark & Grote, 1998). To state the obvious, there are costs and then there are costs.

communal relationship An interpersonal relationship in which individuals benefit each other in response to each other's needs.

Love over Time

We have talked about how relationships get started and how the partners evaluate how that relationship is going. Now let's consider what happens to relationships over time. What factors keep them together and what drives them apart? Sprecher (1999) studied partners in romantic relationships over a period of several years. The measures of love, commitment, and satisfaction taken several times over the period of the research show that couples who maintained their relationship increased on all measures of relationship satisfaction. Couples who broke up showed a decrease in measures of relationship health just before the breakup. The collapse of the relationship did not mean that love was lost. In fact, the splintered partners continued to love each other, but everything else had gone wrong.

Sprecher's work as well as that of others suggests that intact relationships are perceived by the partners in idealistic ways and that the partners truly feel that their love and commitment grows stronger as time goes on. Intact, long-term couples are very supportive of each other and that makes it easier for them to weather difficult personal or financial problems (Gottman et al., 1998). For example, couples who support each other during times of stress are much better able to survive periods of economic pressure that tend to cause much emotional distress in a relationship (Conger et al., 1999).

Some individuals are especially idealistic and affirm a belief that they have met the person that destiny provided. Knee (1998) examined the relationships of those romantic partners who believed in romantic destiny and those who did not. He found that he could predict the longevity of the relationship by two factors: One was belief in romantic destiny and the other was whether the initial interaction was very positive. As Figure 9.4 shows, individuals who believed in romantic destiny and had that confirmed by initial satisfaction tended to have longer relationships than those who did not believe in destiny. But if things don't go quite so well at first, those who believe in destiny tend to bail out quite quickly and do not give the relationship a chance (Knee, 1998).

FIGURE 9.4

Relationship longevity as a function of belief in destiny and initial satisfaction with a relationship. Individuals who believed in romantic destiny and had initial satisfaction with the relationship tended to have longer relationships than those who did not. However, when initial satisfaction was low, individuals who believed in destiny tended not to give the relationship a chance and exited the relationship after a short time.

From Knee (1998).

Sculpting a Relationship

So we see that strong relationships are idealized and are able to withstand stresses because the partners support each other rather than work at cross-purposes. How do such relationships develop? Drigotas et al. (1999) and his coexperimenters found that successful couples have an obliging interdependence in which each, in essence, sculpts the other, much as Michelangelo carved David out of the embryonic stone. This Drigotas aptly called the *Michelangelo phenomenon* (Drigotas et al., 1999). In a series of four studies, these researchers showed that each partner tended to become more like the ideal self that their partner envisioned for them. In other words, each partner supports the other's attempts to change. This partner affirmation of each other is strongly associated with ongoing, well-functioning couples.

Of course, one reason that successful couples have similar views of each other is that individuals tend to search for people who are similar to them. There are two types of similarity that are relevant to relationship sculpting: actual similarity and ideal similarity. Actual similarity refers to the degree to which partners possess similar traits. For example, Klohnen and Mendelsohn (1998) reported research that showed that individuals pair up with partners of approximately equal value and attributes. Note that this is in line with exchange theories discussed earlier. Therefore, people with positive self-images tend to have more positive descriptions of their ideal partner as compared to those with lesser self-images. Ideal similarity refers to "the extent to which a partner possesses attributes and traits that are part of *(a)* one's ideal self standards, or *(b)* one's ideal partner standards" (Rusbult et al. 2009, p. 62). Klohnen and Mendelsohn (1998) reported a significant similarity between one partner's description of the ideal self and his or her description of the partner. In fact, individuals tended to bias their views of their partner in the direction of the ideal self-concepts. Rusbult et al. evaluated the contributions of actual and ideal similarity to relationship sculpting and found that both were involved. However, each contributed independently to relationship sculpting. That is, ideal similarity accounted for sculpting processing over and above that accounted for by actual similarity. Additionally, Rusbult et al. found that the level of ideal similarity in a relationship relates to the longevity of the relationship. Relationships with lower levels of ideal similarity were more likely to end than those with a higher level.

It appears then that successful relationships require that each partner work to affirm his or her beliefs about the other partner. What happens when one partner, say, gets a nasty surprise and learns that her spouse, a competent individual in social situations with people he does not know, is an awkward mutterer with close family members? Certainly, she may be upset and disillusioned. Past research by Swann (1996) has shown that when individuals confront evidence that goes against their firmly held views of themselves, they work very hard to refute or downgrade that evidence. Similarly, De La Ronde and Swann (1998) found that partners work hard to verify their views of their spouses. As Drigotas and colleagues (1999) suggested, we often enter into relationships with people who view us as we view ourselves. Therefore, we and our partners are motivated to preserve these impressions. Therefore, our surprised spouse will be motivated to see her husband as competent in social situations, as he sees himself, by suggesting perhaps that there is something about family gatherings that makes him act out of character.

There seems, then, to be a kind of unspoken conspiracy among many intact couples to protect and conserve the social world that the couple inhabits. The downside of this, of course, is when one of the partners changes in a way that violates the expectations of the other partner. For example, as De La Ronde and Swann (1998) suggested, if one partner, because of low self-esteem goes into therapy and comes out with a more positive self-image, the spouse holding the other in low regard in the first place is motivated, according to the notion of partner verification, to maintain that original negative image. Clearly, that does not bode well for the relationship.

Of course, having negative views of one's partner, as you might expect, is associated with decreased relationship well-being (Ruvolo & Rotondo, 1998). In fact, some people have a strong belief that people can change and, to go back to the example used here, that someone with a negative self-image can change for the better. Ruvolo and Rotondo (1998) measured the extent to which people involved in relationships believed that people can change. They found that when individuals had strong beliefs that individuals can change, then the views that they had of their partner were less likely to be related to the current well-being of the relationship. This means that if you saw that your partner had a negative self-image, but you were convinced that he or she could change for the better, that current image was not crucial to how you viewed the status of the relationship. However, for those individuals who did not feel that it was possible for people to change, the views of their partners were crucial to how they evaluated their relationships. So, if you believed that your partner's attributes and feelings were forever fixed, it makes sense that those views would be crucial to how you felt about the relationship. But, if things could change, probably for the better, well then these negative views won't last forever. Therefore, many successful couples behave in a manner that verifies initial images of each other.

Study Break

This section discussed a number of ways that people evaluate their relationships and how relationships change over time. Before you begin the next section, answer the following questions:

1. How do exchange theories maintain that people evaluate relationships?
2. How does equity theory account for relationship evaluation, and what happens if a relationship is inequitable?
3. What is a communal relationship, and how does this approach differ from the exchange theory approach?
4. How do relationships change over time?
5. How do people go about sculpting a relationship? In your answer, describe the Michelangelo Effect.

Responses to Conflict

When relationships are deemed to be unfair, or inequitable, the result almost inevitably will be conflict. Conflict also can occur when a partner behaves badly, and everyone behaves badly at one time or another. The mere passage of time also makes conflict more likely. Couples are usually more affectionate and happier as newlyweds than they are 2 years later (Huston & Vangelisti, 1991). What happens, then, when conflicts arise? How do people in a relationship respond to conflicts? In this section we shall look at three responses to conflict: developing stories to explain conflict, accommodation, and forgiveness.

Developing Stories

Satisfied couples bias their impressions of their partner in ways that cause idealization of the partner and increase satisfaction in the relationship (McGregor & Holmes, 1999). Researchers have discovered that when satisfied couples confront a threat in the marriage due to something the partner has done (say, had a drink with another man or woman on the sly), individuals devise stories that work to diminish that threat. They construct a story to explain the event in a way that takes the blame away from their partner. The story puts the partner in the best light possible. McGregor and Holmes (1999) suggested that the process of devising a story to explain a behavior convinces the storyteller of the truth of that story. Constructing the motives of the characters in the story (the partner and others) and making the story come to a desired conclusion—all of this cognitive work is convincing to the story's author, who comes to believe in its conclusions.

When reality is complicated, a story that is charitable, apparently, can go far in soothing both the offending partner and the storytelling partner (McGregor & Holmes, 1999).

Sometimes, instead of escalating the conflict, couples find ways to accommodate each other, even when one or both have acted in a negative or destructive manner (Rusbult et al., 1991). Typically, our initial impulse in response to a negative act such as our partner embarrassing us in front of other people is to be hurtful in return. That is, we tend toward the primitive response of returning the hurt in kind.

Then other factors come into play. That initial impulse gets moderated by second thoughts: If I react this way, I'm going to hurt the relationship and I will suffer. What should I do? Should I lash back, or should I try to be constructive? Do I satisfy the demands of my ego, or do I accommodate for the good of the relationship?

Conflict in a relationship is inevitable. How couples handle conflict can determine whether the relationship continues or ends.
Source: Goncharov_Artem/Shutterstock.

Accommodation

These second thoughts, therefore, might lead to an **accommodation process**, which means that in interactions in which there is conflict, a partner does things that maintain and enhance the relationship (Rusbult et al., 1991). Whether a partner decides to accommodate will depend largely on the nature of the relationship. To accommodate, a person must value the relationship above his or her wounded pride. If the relationship is happy, if the partners are committed to each other, then they will be more likely to accommodate. People are also more likely to accommodate when they have no alternatives to the relationship. Interestingly, accommodation may occur spontaneously and very quickly after a negative event. In one study (Häfner & IJzerman, 2011), participants were shown a picture of either their partner's or a stranger's face showing a happy or angry expression. Participants' facial responses to the pictures were recorded. Häfner and IJzerman found that participants responded to the angry face of their partners with a smile within a second of seeing the picture. This finding was limited to participants who indicated that their relationship was strongly communal. An angry face of a stranger elicited an angry response.

accommodation process Interacting in such a way that, despite conflict, a relationship is maintained and enhanced.

Willingness to accommodate also relates to how hopeful people are about the ultimate success of the relationship. *Hope* has two components: pathways and agency (Snyder, 2002). *Pathways* refers to the number of ways a person can think of to achieve a goal. So, if you find yourself in conflict with your partner, you may think of a number of ways of approaching the problem or resolving the conflict. The more pathways, the better. *Agency* refers to one's motivation to use those pathways. Some people are more hopeful than others. That is, they possess more *dispositional hope* than others. Hope can also be seen as specific to certain situations, such as relationships. Hope relating to specific relationships is called *relationship-specific hope* (Merolla, 2014). High levels of hope relate to an increase in relationship-maintaining behaviors, such as having more pro-relationship goals and problem-solving strategies. Conversely, low hope is associated with increased negativity in relationships, such as personal attacks, withdrawal, and negative affect (Merolla, 2014). Merolla found that high levels of dispositional hope related to increased pro-relationship conflict goals (e.g., having a constructive conversation) and fewer destructive conflict management strategies. Relationship-specific hope predicted positive strategies over and above those predicted by dispositional hope alone. In another study, relationship-specific hope related to increased use of accommodation in relationship conflict. Relationship-specific hope was more important in predicting accommodation than more general dispositional hope (Merolla & Harman, 2018).

Accommodation does not always mean being positive. Consistently reacting to a partner's negative behavior in positive ways may lessen the power that constructive comments can have under really serious circumstances. At times, it may be better to say nothing at all than to respond in a positive way. More important than being positive and agreeing with one's partner is to avoid being unduly negative (Montgomery, 1988). The health of a relationship depends less on taking good, constructive actions than on carefully avoiding insulting, destructive actions (Rusbult et al., 1991).

The way people in a committed relationship handle conflict, in short, is an excellent predictor of the health of the relationship. Relationship health correlates with handling conflict through accommodation, rather than ignoring conflict or focusing on negatives. Research shows a positive association between happiness in a relationship and a couple's commitment to discuss and not ignore conflicts (Crohan, 1992). Those couples who ignore conflicts report less happiness in their relationship.

Couples who tend to focus on negatives when dealing with conflict are more likely to end their relationship. An initial study showed that couples whose relationship was in difficulty tended to express negative feelings, sometimes even in anticipation of an interaction, and to display high levels of physiological arousal, whereas couples whose relationship was not in difficulty expected interactions to be constructive and were able to control their emotions (Levenson & Gottman, 1983). A follow-up study of most of the couples revealed that those couples who had recorded high physiological arousal were likely to have separated or ended the relationship (Gottman & Levenson, 1986).

As should be clear, conflict is not the cause of relationship breakup, nor is the lack of overt conflict a sign that a relationship is well. Rather, it is the way couples handle conflict that counts. Mark Twain mused that people may think of perhaps 80,000 words a day but only a few will get them into trouble. So it is with relationships. Just a few "zingers"—contemptuous negative comments—will cause great harm (Notarius & Markman, 1993). Consider the husband who thinks of himself as an elegant dresser, a person with impeccable taste in clothes. If, one day, his wife informs him during a heated exchange that she finds his clothing vulgar and is often embarrassed to be seen with him, she has struck a sensitive nerve. Her comment, perhaps aimed at damaging his self-esteem, may provoke an even more hurtful response and lead to growing ill will between the two—or to defensiveness and withdrawal. One zinger like this can undo a whole week's worth of loving and supportive interchanges.

Forgiveness

It is relatively easy to see how accommodation can solve conflict in certain situations. For example, if there is a disagreement over whether to buy a new Corvette or how to discipline the children, accommodation would be the most effective method of dealing with the conflict. However, there are events that occur in a relationship that might not be fixed by accommodation by itself. For example, an incident of infidelity may call for more than reaching an accommodation. Clinically speaking, infidelity presents one of the most serious challenges in a relationship and is one of the most difficult to handle in therapy (Gordon et al., 2005). Infidelity is particularly damaging to an ongoing relationship when the transgressor is caught in the act or is discovered through an unsolicited third-party account (Afifi et al., 2001).

Given the potentially damaging impact of infidelity on a relationship, how can a relationship be repaired following such an event? One possibility is forgiveness, which makes conflict resolution and accommodation easier to achieve (Fincham et al., 2004). In a case of infidelity the harmed partner will need to forgive the offender in order to begin the process of healing the relationship through conflict resolution and accommodation.

Most of us have some sense of what is meant by forgiveness. However, in order to study a concept like forgiveness empirically, we need a scientific definition. McCullough et al. (1997) define **interpersonal forgiveness** as changes involving a harmed individual showing decreased motivation to retaliate against one's relationship partner, a reduced tendency to maintain distance from the partner, and an increased tendency to express conciliation and goodwill toward the partner (pp. 321–322). McCullough et al. characterize forgiveness as the transition from negative motivational states (e.g., desire for revenge) to positive motivational states (e.g., conciliation) that help preserve a relationship. There are several ways in which interpersonal forgiveness can be expressed (see Table 9.3).

interpersonal forgiveness
A harmed individual's decreased motivation to retaliate against and a reduced tendency to maintain distance from one's relationship partner, and an increased willingness to express conciliation and goodwill toward the partner.

TABLE 9.3 Different Methods That Can Be Used to Give Forgiveness

Forgiveness method	Description
Nonverbal	Using a nonverbal gesture to express forgiveness (e.g., a hug)
Conditional	Making forgiveness contingent on a change in behavior (e.g., I will forgive you if you don't see her any more)
Minimizing	Forgiving by minimizing the severity of the transgression (e.g., It really isn't that big of a deal that you stay out late)
Discussion-based	Changing the rules of a relationship, talking about the transgression or expressing emotions
Explicit	Overtly expressing forgiveness (e.g., stating "I forgive you")

Source: Sheldon et al. (2014).

Which method is used may depend on the nature of the relationship (e.g., married or dating) and the severity of the transgression (Sheldon et al., 2014).

As you might expect, a wronged partner's likelihood of forgiving his or her transgressing partner relates to the severity of the transgression. The more severe the transgression, the less likely forgiveness will be given (Apostolou et al., 2020; Fincham et al., 2005). The more severe the transgression, the less likely it is that the nonverbal and minimizing methods of forgiveness will be used (Sheldon et al., 2014). Forgiveness is more likely if the infidelity is a one-time occurrence rather than a pattern of behavior and if an apology is offered for the infidelity (Gunderson & Ferrari, 2008). Older individuals who had experienced infidelity in a previous relationship were more likely to forgive a cheating partner than younger ones who had not experienced infidelity before (Apostolou et al., 2020). There is also a gender difference in how men and women respond to infidelity. Men, for example, are less likely to forgive sexual infidelity (e.g., your partner engaging in a passionate sexual relationship with another person) than emotional infidelity (e.g., your partner forming an intimate bond with another person) and would be more likely to terminate a relationship after sexual infidelity than after emotional infidelity (Shackelford et al., 2002). Conversely, women would be less likely to forgive an emotional infidelity than a sexual one and would be more likely to break up with a partner who engages in emotional infidelity. Forgiveness is also more likely to occur if there is a high-quality relationship between partners before the infidelity occurs (McCullough et al., 1998).

What are the psychological factors that mediate forgiveness for infidelity? Forgiveness is related to whether empathy for the transgressing partner is aroused (McCullough et al., 1997). McCullough et al. report that when a transgressing partner apologizes, it activates feelings of empathy for the transgressor and leads to forgiveness. Additionally, the type of attribution made for infidelity is important. For partners in a pre-transgression relationship that is of high quality, attributions for a transgression like infidelity are likely to be "benign" and arouse empathy, which will lead to forgiveness (Fincham et al., 2002).

Love in the Lab

John Gottman has studied marriages in a systematic and scientific manner by using a variety of instruments to observe volunteer couples who agree to live in an apartment that is wired and to have their behavior observed and recorded. Results of research from what is known as the "love lab" suggest that there are three kinds of stable marriages (Gottman, 1995). The first type is the *conflict avoiding couple,* who survive by accentuating the positive and simply ignoring the negative; the second type is the *volatile couple,* who are passionate in everything they do, even fighting. Last is the *validating couple,* who listen carefully to each other, compromise, and reconcile differences (Gottman, 1995). All these styles work because the bottom line is that each style promotes behavior that most of the time is positive. What happens if partners in a relationship are mismatched for their styles? For example, what would happen if one person has a volatile style and the other an avoiding style? When mismatches occur, it does not bode well for the relationship, especially if one partner is volatile and the other is avoiding (Busby & Hollman, 2009). With this type of mismatch, partners are less satisfied with their relationship, experience more conflict, and are more likely to experience stonewalling (see next paragraph) than are matched or other mismatched couples (Busby & Hollman, 2009). Gottman and Levenson (2002) have also found that the manner in which emotion is expressed in a marriage relates to how long a marriage lasts before divorce. Marriages with high levels of unregulated, volatile expressions of emotion (positive or negative) are shorter than those in which emotion is more neutral.

Gottman has been able to predict with uncanny accuracy the couples that are headed for divorce. He has identified four factors he refers to as the **four horsemen of the apocalypse**. These four factors are: complaining/criticizing, contempt, defensiveness, and withdrawal from social interaction (stonewalling). The last factor is the most destructive to a relationship and is a very reliable predictor of which couples divorce. There is no answer to stonewalling, but it means that communication has ceased and one partner is in the process of ostracizing the other by refusing to talk. Gottman suggested that there is a cascading relationship between the four horsemen of the apocalypse. Criticism may lead to contempt, which may lead to defensiveness and finally to stonewalling. The seeds of trouble in a marriage may be present very early in the marriage. Carrère and Gottman (1999) had newlywed couples discuss an instance of conflict that occurred in their marriages. They videotaped and analyzed how the couples interacted concerning the conflict. Carrère and Gottman found that couples who expressed negative emotion in the first three minutes of their conversation were more likely to divorce six years later than those who expressed positive emotion.

Most happy couples do not refuse to talk. Indeed, Gottman's observations in the love lab suggest that these partners make lots of attempts to repair a dispute to make sure the argument does not spiral out of control. These repair attempts, reaching out to the other, also include humor that works to defuse anger. Gottman (1995) noted that most marital problems are not easy to resolve. But happy couples realize that their relationship is more important than satisfying their own preferences and idiosyncrasies. For example, one spouse may be a "morning" person and the other is not. So when this couple goes on trips, they compromise. The "morning" person is willing to wait a bit later to start the day, and the "night" person is willing to wake up a bit earlier.

four horsemen of the apocalypse Four factors identified as important in relationship dissolution: complaining/criticizing, contempt, defensiveness, and withdrawal from social interaction (stonewalling).

Study Break

This section introduced conflict in relationships and how conflict can be handled when it occurs. Before you begin the next section, answer the following questions:

1. How do couples use stories to handle conflict?
2. What is the accommodation process, and when is it most likely to be successful in reducing conflict?
3. How is interpersonal forgiveness used in cases of relationship infidelity, and when is it most likely to be successful?
4. What are the marriage styles described by Gottman, and how do they relate to the success or failure of a marriage?
5. What are the four horsemen of the apocalypse, and how do they relate to divorce?

Friendships

According to Sternberg's definition mentioned earlier, liking involves intimacy without passion. Given that liking involves intimacy, does liking lead to romantic loving? The answer to this question appears to be no. Liking evidently leads only to liking. It is as if the two states—liking and loving—are on different tracks (Berscheid, 1988). People may be fond of each other and may go out together for a long time without their affection ever quite ripening into romantic love. Can we say, then, that liking and loving are basically different?

Rubin (1970, 1973) thought that liking and loving were indeed essentially different. He constructed two separate measures, a liking scale and a loving scale, to explore the issue systematically. He found that although both friends and lovers were rated high on the liking scale, only lovers were rated high on the loving scale. Moreover, separate observations revealed that dating couples who gave each other high scores on the loving scale tended more than others to engage in such loving actions as gazing into each other's eyes and holding hands. A follow-up study found that these couples were more likely to have maintained the relationship than were those whose ratings on the loving scale were lower. Therefore, according to Rubin, we may like our lovers, but we do not generally love those we like, at least with the passion we feel toward our lovers.

However, even if liking and (romantic) loving are conceptually different, this does not necessarily mean that friendship does not involve love or that some of the same motives that drive romantic relationships are absent in long-term friendships. The friendships that we form during our lives can be loving and intimate and passionate. Baumeister and Bratslavsky (1999) suggested that passion can be just as strong in friendships except that the sexual component may be absent for a variety of reasons, the most obvious one being that the gender of the friend is not consistent with his or her sexual orientation. The history of a friendship ought not to differ very much from that of a romantic relationship. When two individuals become friends, they experience attraction and affection and share disclosures and experiences. This rising intimacy leads to an increase in the passion of the friends, absent the sexual component (Baumeister & Bratslavsky, 1999).

Friendships can be either same-sex or cross-sex. Cross-sex friendships, of course, comprise a male and female friend. Although many people maintain both types of friendships, for most people same-sex friendships are more numerous than cross-sex friendships (O'Meara, 2006). O'Meara also found that men and women report having about the same number of cross-sex friends. Both same-sex and cross-sex relationships have their challenges. However, cross-sex relationships pose challenges not present in same-sex friendships. Cross-sex friendships may be fraught with sexual tension not present in same-sex friendships. Additionally, in American culture cross-sex friendships may not be seen as "normative," causing the friends to have to defend the relationship to others (O'Meara, 1989). O'Meara lists four challenges facing those in cross-sex friendships: determining the nature of the emotional bonds in the relationship, dealing with sexual tension, dealing with gender inequality within the relationship, and managing how the friendship looks to others. The good news is, however, that most people in cross-sex friendships successfully manage these problems and they become major issues in only a small percentage of cross-sex friendships (Monsour et al., 1994). Another problem confronting those in cross-sex relationships is that others may perceive that a sexual relationship exists, even if it does not. How do individuals in cross-sex friendships conceptualize and describe these friendships to others? Research shows that men and women overlay their cross-sex friendships with different descriptions. Women are likely to describe these friendships as being like "a brother," whereas men describe them as being "just friends" (Reeder, 2017). Reeder reported that women and men who conceptualized their cross-sex friendships in these ways were more satisfied with those friendships than those who described them as romantic.

Gender Differences in Friendships

Female same-sex friendships and male same-sex friendships show somewhat different patterns (Brehm, 1985). Males tend to engage in activities together, whereas females tend to share their emotional lives. Richard and Don may play basketball twice a week, and while playing, they may talk about their problems and feelings, but that is not their purpose in getting together. Karen and Teri may have lunch twice a week with the express purpose of sharing their problems and feelings. Men live their friendships side by side; women live them face to face (Hendrick 1988; Wright, 1982).

The degree of this difference may be diminishing. In the last few decades, there has been a marked increase in the importance both men and women assign to personal intimacy as a source of fulfillment (McAdams, 1989). In fact, both men and women see self-disclosure as an important component in an intimate friendship. It is just that men may be less likely to express intimacy via self-disclosure (Fehr, 2004). Some research suggests that men and women self-disclose with equal frequency and perhaps intensity (Prager et al., 1989). Additionally, both males and females place greater weight on the "communal" nature of friendship (i.e., friendship involving interpersonal closeness, intimacy, and trust) over the "agentic" nature (e.g., enhancing social status) of friendship (Zarbatany et al., 2004).

Men and women report having about the same number of close friends. Women tend to view their close friends as more important than men do, but men's close friendships may last longer than women's (Fiebert & Wright, 1989). Men typically distinguish between same-sex and cross-sex friendships. For men, cross-sex bonds offer the opportunity for more self-disclosure and emotional attachment. Men generally obtain more acceptance and intimacy from their female friends than from their male friends (Duck, 1988). However, for heterosexual men, cross-sex relationships are often permeated with sexual tension (Rawlins, 1992).

Women, in comparison, do not sharply distinguish among their friendships with males and females. They also see differences in their feelings for the various men in their lives. Some of their relationships with men are full of sexual tension, whereas other men may be liked, even loved, but sexual tension may be absent in those relationships.

Greater levels of interaction with females are associated with fewer episodes of loneliness for both men and women. Why? Interactions with women are infused with disclosure, intimacy, and satisfaction, and all these act as buffers against loneliness (Wheeler et al., 1983). Women seem to make better friends than men do. It is telling that married men, when asked to name their best friend, are likely to name their wives. The expectations women have for friendship are often not satisfied by their spouse, and they tend to have at least one female friend in whom they confide (Oliker, 1989).

Anyone who has been in a relationship, intimate or a friendship, knows that conflict is inevitable. Sooner or later, one person will make the other mad over something. Do men and women differ in how they respond to transgressions committed in friendships? This and other related questions were addressed in a study by Mary Grace Antony and Pavica Sheldon (2019). Antony and Sheldon had male and female participants complete a survey covering transgressions and forgiveness in their friendships. A gender difference emerged in the causes of conflict. For males, arguments concerning encroaching on one's romantic partner were mentioned, as were conflicts over unpaid debts and theft of money or personal property. For females, betrayal of trust was mentioned, as was bringing up unpleasant truths within the friendship. Another source of conflict in female friendships was one friend trying to break up the other's romantic relationship. There were also gender differences in how forgiveness was used to repair a conflict. Women were more likely than men to use nonverbal (a shrug), conditional (change behavior and I'll forgive you), explicit (saying "I forgive you"), and discussion (acknowledging a transgression and talking about it) strategies than men. Men were more likely than women to use a minimizing strategy ("It was no big deal").

Friendships over the Life Cycle

Friendships are important throughout the life cycle. Younger people have a higher proportion of intimate friends than older people. However, older people have more satisfying relationships with their friends than younger people. Across the life span, individuals with intimate friends report less loneliness than those lacking such friends (Nicolaisen & Thorsen, 2017). Moreover, placing a high value on friendships relates to better health and happiness across the life span. However, this relationship is strongest for older adults (Chopik, 2017). Friendships also change somewhat in relation to the stage of the life cycle and to factors in the individual's life. Sharing and intimacy begin to characterize friendships in early adolescence, as a result of an increasing ability to understand the thoughts and feelings of others. Girls have more intimate friendships in their early adolescent years than boys do, and this tends to remain true throughout life (Rawlins, 1992).

Why are boys less intimate than girls with same-sex friends? The reason might be that girls trust their friends more than boys do (Berndt, 1992). Girls tend to listen to their friends and protect their friends' feelings, whereas boys tend to tease or embarrass their friends when the opportunity arises. The more intimate the adolescent friendships, the more loyal and supportive they are. However, disloyalty and lack of support can sometimes result from pressure to conform to the peer group. Of course, these issues are not unique to adolescent friendships. Conflicts between intimacy and social pressure simply take on different forms as people get older (Berndt, 1992).

As individuals move into early and middle adulthood, the end of a marriage or other long-term intimate relationship can profoundly affect the pattern of a couple's friendships. When a woman experiences the breakup of a relationship, her friends rally around and support her (Oliker, 1989). Often, the couple's close friends will have already guessed that the relationship was in trouble. When the breakup occurs, they tend to choose one partner or the other, or to simply drift away, unable to deal with the new situation.

In later adulthood, retirement affects our friendships. We no longer have daily contact with coworkers, and thus lose a source of potential friends. With increasing age, new issues arise. The death of a spouse affects friendships perhaps as much as the breakup of a marriage. People who are recently widowed can often feel like "fifth wheels" (Rawlins, 1992). The physical problems often associated with old age can lead to a conflict between a need for independence and a need for help (Rawlins, 1992). As a result, older friends might have to renegotiate their relationships to ensure that both needs are met. Whatever the problems, friendships among the elderly are often uplifting and vital. This is well illustrated by the following statement from a 79-year-old widower: "I don't know how anyone would ever live without friends, because to me, they're next to good health, and all your life depends on friendship" (quoted in Rawlins, 1992).

Although friendships are important throughout the lifespan, they do change across stages of the life cycle due to individual life factors. For example, individuals in middle adulthood may have friendship changes due to divorce. In later adulthood friendships may be affected by retirement or death of a spouse.
Source: Diego Cervo/Shutterstock.

Study Break

This section introduced different types of friendships and how they change over time. Before you read the Chapter Review, answer the following questions:

1. How do friendships differ from romantic relationships?
2. What are the rewards and challenges of same-sex and cross-sex friendships?
3. How does gender relate to friendships?
4. How do friendships change over the course of the life cycle?

Gertrude and Alice Revisited

Stein and Toklas are important because of their role in the vibrant literary world of Paris just after the end of World War I, a period that lasted well into the 1930s. However, aside from their historical importance, the relationship of these two individuals reflects and exemplifies the basic characteristics of close relationships. We saw how the need for intimacy overcame Alice's very strong feelings of social anxiety. Their relationship changed over time, of course, ending, finally, in a companionate one. However, they touched all the vertices of Sternberg's triangle of love: intimacy, passion, and commitment.

Chapter Review

1. **What is a close relationship?**

   The essence of a close relationship is intimacy, friendship, sharing, and love between two people.

2. **What are the roots of interpersonal attraction and close relationships?**

   Human beings possess positive social motives—the need for affiliation (the desire to establish and maintain rewarding interpersonal relationships) and the need for intimacy (the desire for close and affectionate relationships)—which influence us to seek fulfilling relationships. There are, however, motives that may inhibit the formation of social relationships, particularly loneliness and social anxiety, which arise because of a person's expectation of negative encounters with and evaluations from others. Another important factor in interpersonal attraction and close relationships is our earliest interaction with our primary caregiver, which shapes our particular attachment style. Attachment styles are patterns of interacting and relating that influence how we develop affectional ties with others later in life. Each of these styles evolves into a working model, a mental representation of what we as individuals expect to happen in a close relationship.

3. **What are loneliness and social anxiety?**

   Loneliness is a psychological state that results when we perceive an inadequacy in our relationships. It arises when there is a discrepancy between the way we want our relationships to be and the way they actually are. It is not related to the number of relationships we have. The way loneliness is experienced varies across cultures and across age levels. Loneliness has been found to have psychological effects (e.g., feelings of social exclusion and depression) and physical effects (e.g., precursors to hypertension and heart ailments).

   Social anxiety arises from a person's expectation of negative encounters with others. A person with social anxiety anticipates negative interactions with others, overestimates the negativity of social interactions, and dwells on the negative aspects of social interaction. Many of these negative assessments are not valid, however. Social exclusion and teasing are major factors in a person developing social anxiety.

4. **What are the components and dynamics of love?**

   In Sternberg's triangular theory of love, love has three components: passion, intimacy, and commitment. Passion is the emotional component involving strong emotions. Intimacy involves a willingness to disclose important personal information. Commitment is the cognitive component of love involving a decision to maintain love long term.

   Different mixes of these three components define different types of love. Romantic love, for example, has passion and intimacy; it involves strong emotion and sexual desire. Companionate love has intimacy and commitment; it is based more on mutual respect and caring than on strong emotion. Consummate love has all three components. Limerence is an exaggerated form of romantic love that occurs when a person anxious for intimacy finds someone who seems able to fulfill all of his or her needs. Unrequited love—love that is not returned—is the most painful kind of love. Secret love seems to have a special quality. Secrecy makes a partner more attractive and creates a bond between individuals.

5. **How does attachment relate to interpersonal relationships?**

   During infancy, humans form attachments to their primary caregivers. These early attachments evolve into working models, which are ideas about what is expected to happen in a relationship. Working models transfer from relationship to relationship. Individuals with a secure attachment style characterized their lovers as happy, friendly, and trusting and said that they and their partner were tolerant of each other's faults. Those with an avoidant attachment style were afraid of intimacy, experienced roller-coaster emotional swings, and were constantly jealous. An anxious-ambivalent style is associated with extreme sexual attraction coupled with extreme jealousy. The ways in which we respond to our earliest caregivers may indeed last a lifetime and are used when we enter adult romantic relationships.

6. **How does interpersonal attraction develop?**

   Several factors influence the development of interpersonal attraction. The physical proximity effect is an initially important determinant of potential attraction. The importance of proximity can be partly accounted for by the mere exposure effect, which suggests that repeated exposure to a person increases familiarity, which in turn increases attraction. Proximity is also important because it increases opportunities for interaction, which may increase liking. The advent of the Internet as a communication tool has led to a reevaluation of the proximity effect. Individuals who live far apart can now easily contact each other and form relationships. Research shows that Internet relationships are similar to face-to-face relationships: They are important to the individuals involved, they are incorporated into everyday lives, and they are stable over time. However, face-to-face relationships tended to be more interdependent, involved more commitment, and had greater breadth and depth than Internet relationships. On the downside, individuals who use the Internet to form relationships tend to be socially anxious and lonely. These lonely individuals may still experience negative affect, despite having formed relationships over the Internet.

Another factor affecting attraction is the similarity effect. We are attracted to those we perceive to be like us in interests, attitudes, personality, and physical attractiveness. We tend to seek out partners who are at the same level of attractiveness as we are, which is known as the matching principle. Matching becomes more important as a relationship progresses. Similarity is most important for relationships that are important to us and that we are committed to. One hypothesis says that we are repulsed by dissimilar others, rather than being attracted to similar others. In fact, dissimilarity serves as an initial filter in the formation of relationships. Once a relationship begins to form, however, similarity becomes the fundamental determinant of attraction.

We also tend to be more attracted to people who are physically attractive, which is a third factor in interpersonal attraction. Generally, males are more overwhelmed by physical attractiveness than are females. Facial appearance, body appearance, and the quality of one's voice contribute to the perception of physical attractiveness. We tend to ascribe positive qualities to physically attractive people.

The downside to the physical attractiveness bias is that we tend to stigmatize those who are unattractive and ascribe negative qualities to them. In our society, obese people are particularly stigmatized and are portrayed negatively in art, literature, and films.

There is research evidence that the physical attractiveness bias is rooted in our biology: Even at 2 months, infants attend more to an attractive than an unattractive face. A new theory suggests that attractiveness, in the form of facial and body symmetry, may reflect genetic soundness. The physical attractiveness bias would thus have survival value for the species.

7. **What does evolutionary theory have to say about mate selection?**

Evolutionary theory suggests that symmetry (physical attractiveness) is reflective of underlying genetic quality. The preference for symmetry in potential mates may be instinctive. Physical appearance marked by high symmetry reveals to potential mates that the individual has good genes and is therefore, for both men and women, a highly desirable choice. Of course, good genes are not enough in a relationship. Successful relationships are long-term. "Good provider" models of mate selection emphasize the potential mate's commitment to the relationship and ability to provide resources necessary for the long-term health of that relationship.

8. **How can one attract a mate?**

Evolutionary theorists suggest that to attract a mate humans have developed love acts—behaviors, such as display of resources the other sex finds enticing, to attract a mate. Males tended to use displays of resources, whereas females tried to look more attractive and threatened to be unfaithful to arouse jealousy. Jealousy is evoked when a threat or loss occurs to a valued relationship due to the partner's attention to a rival. Men and women react differently to infidelity. Men are more concerned with sexual infidelity, and women are more concerned with emotional infidelity. Even though men and women use different criteria for selecting a long-term mate (women look for resources, men for physical attractiveness), they have similar strategies for short-term relationships. When looking for a casual sexual partner, both men and women emphasize attractiveness.

9. **How do close relationships form and evolve?**

Models of how relationships develop emphasize a predictable sequence of events. One such model suggests that relationships develop across a series of stages involving an initial increase in shared activities followed by an increase in mutuality. That is, friends or lovers begin to share more intimate thoughts and feelings and become more and more interdependent.

Social penetration theory emphasizes that relationships change over time in both breadth (the range of topics people discuss and activities they engage in together) and depth (the extent to which they share their inner thoughts and feelings). Relationships progress in a predictable way from slight and superficial contact to greater and deeper involvement. An important contributor to increasing social penetration is self-disclosure, the ability and willingness to share intimate areas of one's life.

10. **How are relationships evaluated?**

We periodically evaluate the status of our intimate relationships. Any interruption in the normal sequence of events in a relationship sends up a red flag. Social exchange theory suggests that relationships are evaluated according to the rewards and costs derived from a relationship. As long as rewards outweigh costs, a relationship is likely to continue. However, even if rewards outweigh costs, we may not continue the relationship. We use comparison levels to evaluate the outcomes we derive from a relationship. One comparison level is our expectation of what we will obtain from the relationship. Another comparison level involves comparing the outcomes of the relationship we are presently in with the expected outcomes of possible alternative relationships. If we conclude that alternative relationships would not be better or may even be worse than a current relationship, we will likely stay in our relationship. However, if we believe that an alternative relationship holds out the promise of better outcomes, we may end a current relationship.

Another theory is equity theory, which says that we evaluate our relationships based on their rewards and costs, but it also focuses on our perception of equity, or balance, in relationships. An equitable relationship is likely to be stable, whereas an inequitable one is likely to be unstable. Inequity leads people to try to restore equity to the relationship.

11. What is a communal relationship?

A communal relationship is a relationship governed more by communal principles than principles of exchange or equity. In a communal relationship, individuals benefit each other in response to the other's needs. In such a relationship, partners tolerate inequity. Love relationships are often governed by communal principles. In such relationships, high costs are often associated with relationship satisfaction. Making sacrifices for the sake of a relationship can strengthen the relationship.

12. How do relationships change over time?

Research shows that couples who maintained their relationship showed increased relationship satisfaction. Couples who broke up showed a decrease in relationship health just before the breakup. Long-term couples are very supportive of each other, and that makes it easier to overcome hardship. A belief in romantic destiny (i.e., that partners were made for each other) is positively related to relationship duration. In a sense, successful relationships involve partners sculpting a relationship by inducing changes in each other. Successful couples work hard at protecting the social structures that support their relationships.

13. What are the strategies couples use in response to conflict in a relationship?

One strategy for handling conflict is to construct a story to explain the event in a way that takes the blame away from their partner, showing the partner in the best possible light. This strategy, however, may just go so far to reduce conflict. Couples can also engage in an accommodation process, which means a partner focuses on positive things that maintain and enhance the relationship in the face of conflict. Accommodation is most likely in important relationships and when no potential alternative relationships exist. Couples who handle conflict via accommodation tend to have successful relationships. Dwelling on negativity harms a relationship.

There may be situations where accommodation is difficult to accomplish. For example, in a case of infidelity, accommodation may not solve a problem. In such cases couples may engage in interpersonal forgiveness. Forgiveness involves a decrease in the use of retaliation along with an increase in conciliation. Forgiveness involves a transition from a negative motivational state to a positive one. Forgiveness is made more difficult as the seriousness of a transgression increases.

14. What are the four horsemen of the apocalypse?

The four horsemen of the apocalypse are four steps identified by Gottman that can lead to the breakup of a relationship. They are complaining/criticizing, contempt, defensiveness, and withdrawal from social interaction (stonewalling). The last factor is the most damaging to a relationship and is highly predictive of marital divorce. There is a cascading relationship between the four horsemen: Criticism can lead to contempt. Contempt can lead to defensiveness, which can lead to withdrawal. Gottman has observed that successful couples take steps to repair a dispute to make sure the argument does not spiral out of control.

15. What is the nature of friendships?

According to Sternberg, friendships are characterized by liking and involve intimacy but not passion or commitment. Friendships are based on an ongoing interdependence between people. There are some gender differences in friendships, although these differences may have decreased in recent years. Both males and females need the intimacy offered by friendships. However, females still seem to view friends as more important than males do, and females make better friends. Interactions with females are more likely to be characterized by disclosure, intimacy, and satisfaction, all of which act as buffers against loneliness. Friendships can be same-sex or cross-sex. Each type of friendship has its own rewards and challenges. Cross-sex relationships may involve sexual tension that must be dealt with.

Key Terms

Accommodation process (p. 379)
Communal relationship (p. 375)
Consummate love (p. 352)
Four horsemen
　of the apocalypse (p. 382)
Interpersonal attraction (p. 346)
Interpersonal forgiveness (p. 380)

Loneliness (p. 346)
Matching principle (p. 359)
Need for affiliation (p. 345)
Need for intimacy (p. 345)
Physical attractiveness bias (p. 362)
Physical proximity effect (p. 356)
Romantic love (p. 351)

Social anxiety (p. 348)
Social exchange theory (p. 373)
Social penetration theory (p. 371)
Triangular theory of love (p. 349)
Unrequited love (p. 352)
Working model (p. 353)

Chapter Quiz

1. According to your text, the need for affiliation is
   A. only weakly related to our interpersonal relationships.
   B. often subordinate to our desire to be alone.
   C. the fundamental factor underlying our interpersonal relationships.
   D. not involved in our interpersonal relationships.

2. Which of the following statements about loneliness is true?
   A. It is a subjective experience and not related to the number of people we have around us.
   B. It is more dependent on the number of people we have around us than any subjective experience.
   C. It is unhealthy to desire solitude.
   D. Loneliness is always temporary.

3. Which is true according to Sternberg's triangular theory of love?
   A. We strive for balance in our love relationships.
   B. A culture must support the idea of love before we can experience it.
   C. Love consists of three components: passion, intimacy, and commitment.
   D. Passionate love is the "ideal" that just about everyone strives for.

4. Andrea loves Robert. She thinks about him constantly and tells him intimate things about herself. However, she doesn't think the relationship will last very long. Andrea is experiencing _____ love.
   A. romantic
   B. consummate
   C. companionate
   D. empty

5. Which of the following is true of unrequited love?
   A. Women are more likely than men to experience it.
   B. Men are more likely than women to experience it.
   C. People report that they have experienced unrequited love twice as much as they have been the object of unrequited love.
   D. Both B and C are true.

6. Research has shown that individuals with a(n) _____ working model trust their partners and respond to problems in a constructive way.
   A. anxious
   B. secure
   C. bipolar
   D. avoidant

7. According to your text, a downside to forming relationships on the Internet is that
   A. Internet relationships are less stable than traditional relationships.
   B. Internet relationships cannot fulfill the need for intimacy.
   C. people often lie about themselves on the Internet.
   D. socially anxious, lonely individuals tend to use the Internet to form relationships.

8. The tendency for people to become involved with a partner with whom they closely match (e.g., physical attributes or social status) is known as the
   A. matching principle.
   B. complementarity principle.
   C. similarity principle.
   D. reciprocity principle.
   E. physicality principle.

9. Research suggests that obese individuals are viewed negatively because
   A. they deviate from what most people consider to be "normal."
   B. there is a tendency to believe that the weight problem stems from laziness or a lack of discipline.
   C. there is a tendency to believe that the weight problem stems from biological factors.
   D. weight is such an obvious characteristic.

10. According to research cited in your text, same-sex couples are more likely than heterosexual couples to meet
    A. on the Internet.
    B. in a bar.
    C. through family and friends.
    D. through coworkers.

Answers can be found in the end-of-book Answers section.

Interpersonal Aggression

To live without killing is a thought which could electrify the world, if men were only capable of staying awake long enough to let the idea soak in.

—Henry Miller

CHAPTER 10

Source: vchal/Shutterstock.

Early in the morning in May of 2021, 57-year-old Samuel Cassidy left his house and headed to his place of employment: Valley Transportation Authority (VTA) in San Jose, California. Cassidy had worked at VTA as an electromechanic since around 2012. Before getting into his car, Cassidy rigged a timing device to ensure that his house caught on fire after he left. The house was packed with explosives and a stockpile of guns and ammunition. You see, Cassidy wasn't just leaving for a normal workday. He had something else in mind. He arrived at VTA at around 6:30 AM, where there were over 100 workers on-site. None had any idea what lay in store for them as Cassidy entered.

Cassidy began shooting at his fellow employees as soon as he entered the building. Witnesses reported that Cassidy did not shoot randomly. Instead, he appeared to select his victims while letting others go. Surveillance video showed that Cassidy did not limit his shooting spree to a single location. The recordings showed Cassidy exiting one building and entering another, where he selected and shot more victims (Hollyfield et al., 2021). Cassidy was armed with three handguns with 32 high-capacity magazines. He had come well prepared to carry out his deed. In all, he fired 39 times in the two buildings. Later, police found the makings of bombs (explosive material and detonator cords) in Cassidy's locker inside VTA.

Key Questions

As you read this chapter, find the answers to the following questions:

1. How do social psychologists define aggression?
2. What are the different types of aggression?
3. What are the gender differences in aggression?
4. How can we explain aggression?
5. What are the ethological, sociobiological, and genetic explanations for aggression?
6. What role do brain mechanisms play in aggression?
7. How does alcohol consumption relate to aggression?
8. What is the frustration-aggression hypothesis?
9. How does anger relate to frustration and aggression, and what factors contribute to anger?
10. How does social learning theory explain aggression?
11. What are aggressive scripts, and how do they relate to aggression?
12. How does the family socialize a child into aggression?
13. What is the role of culture in aggression?
14. What role do the media play in aggression?

391

15. How does social media use relate to aggression?
16. What are the effects of playing violent video games on aggressive behavior?
17. What is the link between sexual violence portrayed in the media and sexual aggression toward women?
18. How can aggression be reduced?

The sheriff's office received a call about the shooting at around 6:34 AM, and officers were on the scene quickly. A deputy immediately entered the building. As he entered, he could still hear Cassidy shooting his victims. Eventually, the shooting stopped. However, the sheriff's deputies had not fired their weapons. Cassidy had turned his gun on himself.

Ironically, VTA employees had recently completed active-shooter training at VTA. Police were able to rescue 40 employees; 9 VTA employees were not so lucky. One of Cassidy's victims was Taptejdeep Singh, a 36-year-old light rail train driver who had worked at VTA for 9 years. In addition to Singh, the other victims were Paul Delacruz Megia, 42; Adrian Balleza, 29; Jose Dejesus Hernandez, 35; Timothy Michael Romo, 49; Michael Joseph Rudometkin, 40; Abdolvahab Alaghmandan, 63; and Lars Kepler Lane, 63 (Glecker & Mendoza, 2021).

Who was Samuel Cassidy, and why did he kill nine of his coworkers? His ex-wife, Cecilia Nelms, told authorities that Samuel had a bad temper and had told her years before of his desire to kill his fellow coworkers. He had also expressed frustration and anger over his work at VTA. She said that as he talked, his anger got worse and worse. Apparently, Cassidy was the type of person who did not let things go and would dwell on perceived wrongs against him (Glecker & Mendoza, 2021). She also said that Cassidy had been treated for depression, and his father said that Cassidy was bipolar. Cassidy had also had an encounter with authorities in the past. In 2016, Cassidy was stopped by U.S. Customs officials as he returned from a trip to the Philippines. Cassidy had in his possession books on terrorism and a notebook filled with writing about how much he hated VTA. However, he told authorities at the time that he did not have any problems with his coworkers. The authorities never released this information. Cassidy had also been arrested in 1983 for misdemeanor obstruction and resisting a peace officer (Har & Dazio, 2021).

What possessed Samuel Cassidy to murder nine innocent, unsuspecting people? Was he a disturbed individual, or was he a product of his environment? Was he frustrated with his work and coworkers? Were alcohol or drugs involved? Had he somehow learned that violence was an acceptable way to solve one's problems?

Aggression occurs whenever we intentionally harm another person. There are many types of aggression, including hostile and instrumental aggression.
Source: Monkey Business Images/Shutterstock.

The VTA mass-shooting case also raises other important questions. For example, what can be done to lessen the use of violence and aggression as a form of conflict resolution? What steps can individuals and society as a whole take to prevent such a tragic event from occurring again? These are some of the questions addressed in this chapter.

What Is Aggression?

What exactly is aggression? The term tends to generate a certain amount of confusion because a layperson's concept of aggression differs somewhat from what social psychologists study. In day-to-day life we hear about the aggressive salesperson who will not take no for an answer and the aggressive businessperson who stops at nothing to win a promotion. These usages convey forceful, overbearing, or overly assertive behavior.

Social psychologists, however, define **aggression** as any behavior that is intended to inflict harm (whether psychological or physical) on another organism or object. There are several important things to note about this definition. First, a crucial element of the definition is intent: A person must have intended to harm in order for the act to be classified as aggressive. If someone deliberately hits a neighbor with a baseball bat during an argument, it is considered aggressive. If the person accidentally hits the neighbor with a baseball bat while playing ball in the yard, it is not considered aggressive.

Note, too, that the harm intended by an aggressive act need not be physical. A navy commander who continually sexually harasses a female subordinate, causing stress, anxiety, and depression, may not be doing her any overt physical harm; he is, however, causing her psychological harm. Third, aggression is not limited to actions directed toward living organisms. Aggression also can be directed toward inanimate objects. A person who smashes the window of a neighbor's car in retaliation for some real or imagined conflict with that neighbor is behaving aggressively.

This broad definition covers a great deal of ground, but it requires further elaboration. Using this definition, we would be tempted to liken the actions of a police officer who kills an armed murder suspect in the line of duty with those of a paid assassin who kills for profit. Because such a wide range of behavior can be called aggressive, psychologists have defined several different types of aggression, which we look at next.

aggression Any behavior intended to inflict either psychological or physical harm on another organism or object.

Levels and Types of Aggression

Clearly, aggression exists on many different levels and is made up of several types of behavior. All aggression, for example, does not stem from the same underlying motives and intentions. Some, referred to as **hostile aggression**, stems from angry and hostile impulses (Feshbach, 1964), and its primary goal is to inflict injury on some person or object. This appears to be the type of aggression perpetrated by Samuel Cassidy at VTA. He had clearly expressed anger and a desire to hurt his coworkers. Acts of aggression that stem from such emotional states are examples of hostile aggression. **Instrumental aggression** stems from the desire to achieve a goal. Terrorism often has some instrumental goal behind it. For example, a terrorist may be acting to remove foreign troops from his or her homeland.

Hostile aggression and instrumental aggression are not mutually exclusive. One can commit an aggressive act having both underlying motives. In 1994, when Baruch Goldstein killed over 30 Palestinians in a mosque in Hebron, he had two motives. He was motivated by intense hatred of Palestinians, whom he perceived as trying to take away land that rightfully belonged to Jews. He also was motivated by the hope of derailing the fragile peace talks between the Palestine Liberation Organization and the Israeli government. His act, thus, had a hostile component (hatred) and an instrumental component (derailing the peace talks).

Another distinction can be made between direct aggression and indirect aggression. (The origin of these terms is difficult to trace, so we shall not attempt to specifically identify who coined these terms. Suffice it to say that this is a distinction made by a variety

hostile aggression Aggressive behavior stemming from angry or hostile impulses, with a primary goal to inflict injury on some person or object.

instrumental aggression Aggressive behavior stemming from a desire to achieve a goal.

direct aggression Overt forms of aggression such as physical aggression (hitting, punching, kicking, etc.) and verbal aggression (name calling, denigration, etc.).

indirect aggression Aggression that is social in nature, such as social ostracism and deliberate social exclusion.

relational aggression Aggression using aspects of a relationship to cause harm to another person that has elements of both direct and indirect aggression.

symbolic aggression Aggressive behavior that interferes with a victim's advancement toward a goal.

sanctioned aggression Aggressive behavior that society accepts or encourages.

bullying Aggression that is intentional, repetitive, and directed toward an individual of lower power.

of aggression researchers.) **Direct aggression** refers to overt forms of aggression such as physical aggression (hitting, punching, kicking, etc.) and verbal aggression (name calling, denigration, etc.). **Indirect aggression** is aggression that is social in nature (social ostracism, deliberate social exclusion).

Relational aggression uses aspects of a relationship to cause harm to another person and has elements of both direct and indirect aggression (Archer, 2004). This form of aggression involves using social ostracism and rejection (indirect aggression), but can also be directly confrontational (direct aggression). An example of the direct aspect of relational aggression occurs when a child tells another child that she will stop liking her unless the other child does what she wants (Archer, 2004).

In some forms of aggression the target is harmed verbally through gossip, character assassination, damage to the victim's property (Moyer, 1987), or interference with the victim's advancement toward a goal. This form of aggression is called **symbolic aggression**. For example, if a person spreads rumors about a coworker in order to keep her from being promoted, the person has used symbolic aggression. Although no physical harm was done, the coworker was blocked from achieving a goal.

The forms of aggression just noted can be either hostile or instrumental. The office worker may have spread rumors because she was angry at her coworker—a case of hostile aggression. Alternatively, she may have spread rumors to secure the promotion for herself at her coworker's expense—a case of instrumental aggression.

Yet another form of aggression is **sanctioned aggression**. A soldier taking aim and killing an enemy soldier in battle engages in sanctioned aggression. Self-defense, which occurs when a person uses aggression to protect himself or herself or others from harm, is another example of sanctioned aggression. Society declares that in certain situations, aggression is acceptable, even mandatory. A soldier who refuses to engage in aggressive behavior may be subject to disciplinary action or even have his or her military service abruptly ended. Predatory aggression would also fall into the sanctioned aggression category. A lioness that hunts and kills an antelope in Africa is killing to survive. The lioness has no particular animus toward the antelope. So, typically, sanctioned aggression is instrumental in nature. Soldiers kill each other to save their own lives, to follow orders, to help win a war. There need not be anger among enemy soldiers for them to try to kill one another.

Another type of aggression that is in the news more and more is bullying. **Bullying** is aggression that is intentional, repetitive, and directed toward an individual of lower power (Görzig & Frumkin, 2013). According to the Bureau of Justice Statistics (2019), around 20% of students between 12 and 18 in the United States reported being the victim of bullying in school, with more females than males reporting being bullied. Among those who reported being bullied, 46.9% were White, 31.8% were Black, and 33.3% were Hispanic. Another form of bullying is *cyberbullying*, which is when bullying takes place via an electronic device such as a smartphone or on the computer via the Internet (we will explore this form of bullying in more depth later in this chapter). Approximately 12% of public school students report being the victim of cyberbullying. Once again, more females than males report being victims of cyberbullying (Bureau of Justice Statistics, 2019). The rate of cyberbullying is even higher among adolescents in Europe (21.4%) (Tsitsika et al., 2015) and among college students in the United States (27%) (Selkie et al., 2015). Being the target of bullying or cyberbullying has consistently been associated with higher levels of psychological problems such as depression (Selkie et al., 2014) and stress and suicidal ideation (Kowalski et al., 2014).

Gender Differences in Aggression

One of the most striking features of aggression is the difference in its expression by males and females. Certainly females can be aggressive, but males show higher levels of physical aggression (Archer et al., 1988). This is true among humans (Eagly & Steffen, 1986) as well as animals (Vallortigara, 1992). A meta-analysis by John Archer (2004) on studies investigating "real-world aggression" (i.e., self-reported aggression, peer ratings of aggression, and observational methods) confirmed that males are more aggressive than females, especially for direct aggression (e.g., physical aggression). This gender difference was consistent across age and peaked between 20 and 30 years of age. The gender difference was also consistent across cultures. Archer also found that females used more indirect aggression (e.g., social ostracism), but only during late childhood and adolescence and when an observational method was used.

A form of aggression in which males and females differ is appetitive aggression. *Appetitive aggression* is aggression that brings fascination and pleasure (Meyer-Parlapanis et al., 2016; Elbert et al., 2010). Appetitive aggression is expressed in behaviors such as hunting (Elbert et al., 2010) and may also manifest itself during combat (Meyer-Parlapanis, 2015). Meyer-Parlapanis et al. studied appetitive aggression among civilians and military personnel in Burundi. They found that men showed more appetitive aggression among the civilian participants, but not among combat veterans. Given the chance, men and women may be equally likely to engage in aggression that brings pleasure (Meyer-Parlapanis et al., 2016).

That males use more direct, physical forms of aggression is clear. However, the role of gender in the use of indirect, relational aggression is still an open question. A meta-analysis of the literature in this area revealed the typical gender difference for direct aggression (i.e., males more aggressive than females), but showed little or no gender differences for indirect aggression (Card et al., 2008). As noted earlier, greater female use of indirect aggression has been shown only for a limited age range of females. Another study suggests that the difference between males and females in the use of indirect aggression is small (Salmivalli & Kaukiainan, 2004). In only one subgroup of females was indirect aggression predominant: highly aggressive females. In a study using an observational method (that is, children were observed during free-play situations and aggression was measured), preschool-aged females showed more indirect aggression than males (Ostrove & Keating, 2004).

Males and females did not differ on the levels of anger underlying aggression. Additionally, males tend to favor aggression, verbal or physical, as a method of conflict resolution (Bell & Forde, 1999; Reinisch & Sanders, 1986). They also are more likely to be the target of physical aggression (Archer et al., 1988). Finally, males are more motivated to use aggression for revenge than females (Wilkowski et al., 2012). In a series of studies, Wilkowski et al. found that a desire for revenge mediated the relationship between gender and aggression. However, anger alone did not.

There are further gender differences in the cognitive aspects of using aggression. Females report more guilt over using aggression than do males and are more concerned about the harm their aggression may inflict on others (Eagly & Steffen, 1986). This difference is especially pronounced when physical aggression is used.

Both boys and girls are encouraged to engage in gender-typed activities, and activities deemed appropriate for boys are more aggressive than those for girls.
Sources: sirtravelalot/Shutterstock (left); AlesiaKan/Shutterstock (right)

Why do these differences exist? Possible causes fall into two major areas: biological factors and social factors. Biological factors include both brain mechanisms and hormones. Most research in this area centers on the male hormone testosterone. Higher levels of this hormone are associated with heightened aggression in both humans and animals. There is also evidence that there is a gender difference in brain neurochemistry related to aggression (Suarez & Krishnan, 2006). Suarez and Krishnan found that for both males and females, the predisposition of expressing anger verbally was related to higher levels of "free plasma tryptophan" (TRP), which is a precursor to a serotonin-related neurotransmitter. However, elevated levels of TRP were associated with a greater predisposition toward hostility and an outward expression of anger among females, but not males.

Despite hormonal and other physiological differences between males and females, differences in aggressive tendencies and expression may relate more closely to gender roles than to biology (Eagly & Steffen, 1986). Both boys and girls are encouraged to engage in gender-typed activities, and activities deemed appropriate for boys are more aggressive than those for girls (Lytton & Romney, 1991). For example, parents, especially fathers, encourage their sons to play with war toys such as GI Joe figures and their daughters to play with Barbie dolls. Socialization experiences probably further reinforce the inborn male push toward being more aggressive.

Yet another possible reason for the observed differences in aggression between males and females is that females tend to be more sympathetic and empathic (Carlo et al., 1999). Carlo and colleagues studied the relationship between sympathy, parental involvement, and aggression (Carlo et al., 1999). They found that individuals with high levels of sympathy and empathy were less likely to be aggressive. Males scored lower on these dimensions but higher on aggressiveness. Additionally, if an individual perceived that his or her parents were highly involved in childrearing, aggression was lower for both males and females. Thus, prosocial motives (on which females tend to outscore males) and level of parental involvement are important mediators of physical aggression.

Finally, gender differences in aggression might relate to how males and females react to emotional signals from others. Generally, females are better at reading emotions in others than males. However, males seem to be more attuned to threatening emotions and cues from others (Kret & De Gelder, 2012). According to Kret and De Gelder, males respond to threatening cues with higher levels of brain activity and physiological activity than females. This heightened sensitivity to threat cues, resulting in more physiological arousal, may translate into higher levels of physical aggression among males than females. Finally, women appear to be more sensitive to emotional cues than men, which mediates aggressive behavior (Arriaga & Aguiar, 2019). Arriaga and Aguiar found that during an aggressive game, women, but not men, showed a reduction in aggression in response to a sad or angry cue from the opponent.

It is important to note that although social psychological research (both in the laboratory and in the field) shows a consistent difference between males and females in aggression, this difference is very small (Eagly & Steffen, 1986; Hyde, 1984). Further, gender differences in aggression appear to be situation dependent. Males are more aggressive than females when they are unprovoked, but males and females show equivalent levels of aggression when provoked (Bettencourt & Miller, 1996). Males and females also respond differently to different types of provocation. Bettencourt and Miller (1996) report a large gender difference when different forms of provocation are used. If provocation involves an attack on one's intellectual ability, then males are much more aggressive than females. However, if provocation takes the form of a physical attack or a negative evaluation of one's work, males and females respond similarly. In other words, although males and females differ in levels of aggression, we should not conclude that gender is the only—or even a predominant—factor in aggression. It is evident that the relationship between gender and aggression is more complex than meets the eye.

Nevertheless, we must also note that there are relatively large gender differences in real-life expressions of aggression. Statistics for violent crimes show that males are far more likely to commit violent offenses than females. According to Uniform Crime Statistics compiled by the FBI, in 2011, 87.6% of individuals arrested for murder were male.

Similarly, 77.8% of arrestees for aggravated assault were male. With respect to murder, the gap between males and females has widened over the years. In 2020, for example, men committed 77.2% of murders, and women committed only 1.3% (Statista, 2021). So, even though the difference between the genders in measurable acts of aggressiveness is small, in any specific real-world situation, this difference is magnified and elaborated.

Study Break

This section introduced you to the definition of aggression in its various forms and the relationship between gender and aggression. Before you go on, answer the following questions:

1. What is the social psychological definition for aggression?
2. What are hostile and instrumental aggression? Give an example of each.
3. What is the difference between direct and indirect aggression? Give an example of each.
4. What are relational aggression, symbolic aggression, sanctioned aggression, and bullying? Give an example of each.
5. What is the relationship between gender and aggression?

Biological Explanations for Aggression

Biological explanations for aggression occur on two levels, the macro and the micro. On the macro level, aggression is considered for its evolutionary significance, its role in the survival of the species. On the micro level, aggression is investigated as a function of brain and hormonal activity. We consider here two theories of aggression on the macro level—the ethological and sociobiological approaches—and then turn to the physiology and genetics of aggression. We also consider the effects of alcohol on aggression.

Ethology

Ethology is the study of the evolution and functions of animal behavior (Drickamer & Vessey, 1986). Ethological theory views behavior in the context of survival; it emphasizes the role of instincts and genetic forces in shaping how animals behave (Lorenz, 1963). From an ethological perspective, aggression is seen as behavior that evolved to help a species adapt to its environment. Aggression is governed by innate, instinctual motivations and triggered by specific stimuli in the environment. Aggressive behavior helps establish and maintain social organization within a species.

ethology A theoretical perspective that views behavior within the context of survival and emphasizes the role of instincts and genetic forces.

For example, many species mark and defend their territories, the space they need to hunt or forage. If they didn't do this, they wouldn't survive. Territorial defense occurs when one member of a species attacks another for crossing territorial boundaries. The intruder is driven off by aggressive displays or overt physical attacks—or loses his territory to the intruder. Aggression also is used to establish dominance hierarchies within groups of animals. Within a troop of baboons, for example, the dominant males enjoy special status, ascending to their positions of power by exercising physical aggression.

Although animals use aggression against each other, few species possess the power to kill a rival with a single blow (Lorenz, 1963). In most species, furthermore, there are biological inhibitions against killing another member. When a combatant makes a conciliatory gesture, such as rolling over and exposing its neck, the aggressive impulse in the other animal is automatically checked. Thus, aggression may involve merely exchanging a few violent actions; the fight soon ends with no major harm done. This is known as *sham aggression*.

How does ethological theory relate to the human animal? First of all, humans display territorial behavior just as animals do. Konrad Lorenz, the foremost ethologist of the 20th century, believed that aggression had little to do with murderous intent and a lot to

Ethologists view aggression as a behavior designed to help organisms survive. Of the many behaviors relating to this is territoriality where members of a species mark and defend territories. Ethologists see aggression among gang members as a way of protecting their territories.
Source: Orangedrink/Shutterstock.

do with territory (Lorenz, 1963). Ethologists, for example, see aggressive behaviors among gang members as a matter of protecting one's turf, such as when members of urban street gangs physically attack members of rival gangs who cross territorial boundaries (Johnson, 1972). Urban gang territories start out as relatively small areas that then expand. The territories of rival gangs eventually form into identifiable boundaries that become the focus of conflict between the rival gangs (Brantingham et al., 2012). Brantingham et al. studied the distribution of violence between rival gangs in a Los Angeles neighborhood and found that, as one might expect, the majority of intergang violent crimes took place along the territorial borders of the gangs.

Second, there is evidence that aggression plays a role in the organization of dominance hierarchies in human groups just as it does among animals. In one study, researchers organized first- and third-grade children into play groups and observed the development of dominance hierarchies within those groups (Pettit et al., 1986). Aggression was found to play a significant role in establishing dominance within both groups. Interestingly, however, among the older children, another variable emerged as important in establishing dominance: leadership skills. Leaders did not always have to use aggression to control the group.

Finally, ethological theory points out that humans still possess the instinct to fight. Unlike most animals, however, humans can make the first blow the last. Technology has given us the power to make a single-blow kill (Lorenz, 1963). According to Lorenz (1963), human technological evolution has outpaced biological evolution. We have diminished the importance of conciliatory cues; bombs dropped from 30,000 feet cannot respond to a conciliatory gesture.

Sociobiology

sociobiology A theoretical perspective that views social behavior as helping groups of organisms within a species survive.

Like ethology, **sociobiology** is the study of the biological basis of behavior. Sociobiologists, however, focus on the evolution and function of social behavior (Drickamer & Vessey, 1986; Reiss, 1984). Like ethological theory, sociobiology emphasizes the biological origins and causes of behavior and views aggression as a behavior with survival value for members of a species. For sociobiologists, aggression, like many other behaviors, plays a natural role in the intricate balance that keeps species alive and growing.

Sociobiologist E. O. Wilson (1975) suggested that the principal function of aggression within and between species is to resolve disputes over a common limited resource. Competition can be divided into two categories: sexual competition and resource competition. Sexual competition occurs when males compete for females at mating time. The stronger male drives the weaker male off and then mates with the female. As a result, the species becomes stronger. Resource competition occurs when animals must vie for environmental resources such as food, water, and shelter. Again, the stronger animals are able to win these competitive situations with the use of aggression.

Aggression, then, is one of many behaviors that are genetically programmed into a species and passed along from generation to generation, according to sociobiologists. Patterns of aggression (often mere displays of pseudoaggression) steer the course of natural selection. Also programmed into a species are behaviors and gestures of submission. An animal can choose not to fight or to withdraw from a competitive situation. There is, thus, a natural constraint on aggression within a species. It is kept at an "optimal level," allowing the species to secure food and shelter and to resolve disputes over mating partners. Aggression, a potentially destructive behavior, actually contributes to the biological health of a species, according to sociobiologists (Wilson, 1975).

In both ethology and sociobiology, then, aggression is viewed as a genetically programmed behavior with evolutionary significance. Human beings display aggression under various circumstances because it is part of their biological heritage. However, as noted earlier, biology plays another role in aggression. We next consider another biological approach to aggression that focuses on physiological forces within the individual that cause aggressive behavior.

Genetics and Aggression

Later in this chapter we shall discuss extensively the social learning explanation for aggression. Briefly, this approach suggests that aggression is a behavior that is learned during childhood primarily through the mechanism of observational learning. The social learning approach places a great deal of emphasis on the role of various aspects of the environment (e.g., parents, peers, media sources) in the formation of aggressive behaviors. However, it does not leave much room for the possibility that genetics also may influence aggressive behavior. In this section we shall explore the role of genetics in aggressive behavior.

Genetic factors are related to individual differences in aggression. The heritability (the degree to which individual differences can be accounted for by genetics) is around 50% (Odintsova et al., 2019). The 50% score suggests that the environment is also involved. In fact, research on genetic influences on aggressive behavior suggests that there is a genetic component to aggression that operates along with epigenetics and the environment (e.g., poverty, exposure to violent media, family stress). For example, a meta-analysis by Miles and Carey (1997) found that both genetics and common environment (e.g., aspects of the social environment shared by siblings) account for individual differences in aggressive behavior. They also reported that genetic factors were slightly more important for males than females and that genetic factors were less powerful among younger subjects. In a study comparing monozygotic twins (twins that develop from a single egg and share genetic material) and dizygotic twins (twins that develop from two separate eggs and share less genetic material), Hines and Saudino (2004) found that "intimate partner aggression" (physical and psychological) has a genetic component. Hines and Saudino concluded that "familial resemblance in psychological aggression arises because members share the genes that influence this behavior" (p. 714). They suggest that children inherit genes from their parents that predispose the children for aggression. Interestingly, Hines and Saudino suggest that whether the aggressive behavior is expressed overtly may be more strongly related to affiliation with aggressive peer groups than parental use of partner aggression.

In addition to the two studies just discussed, other studies also support the idea that aggression is at least partially determined by one's genetic makeup (e.g., Vierikko et al., 2003). However, we need to be cautious when interpreting the results from these studies, for a number of reasons. First, the number of studies establishing the genetic-aggression link is relatively small. Clearly, more research is needed in this area. Second, the degree of contribution of genetics depends on the methodology used. For example, observational studies tend to show stronger links between heredity and aggression than do laboratory studies (Miles & Carey, 1997). Finally, we must underscore that it is important to keep results that show a genetic influence in their proper perspective. There is little evidence that genetics has a direct effect on aggression. Instead, genetics appears to influence characteristics (e.g., personality characteristics) that predispose a person to aggression. Just because someone has a genetic predisposition toward aggression does not mean that the person will behave aggressively. Finally, recent advances in the field of epigenetics show that environmental factors can affect how one's genetic code is expressed (Champagne & Mashoodh, 2009). Scientists have discovered that there is an epigenetic code that can affect whether a gene is switched on or off and that this epigenetic code can be influenced by the environment throughout life (Champagne & Mashoodh, 2009).

The Physiology of Aggression

The brain and endocrine systems of humans and animals play an intricate role in mediating aggression. Research on the physiology of aggression has focused on two areas: brain mechanisms and hormonal influences. The sections that follow explore each of these.

Brain Mechanisms

Research on brain mechanisms has focused on the brain structures that mediate aggressive behavior. Researchers have found, for example, that aggressive behavior is elicited when parts of the **hypothalamus** are stimulated. The hypothalamus is part of the limbic system, a group of brain structures especially concerned with motivation and emotion. Stimulation of different parts of the hypothalamus (called nuclei) produces different forms of aggressive behavior.

In one study, researchers implanted electrodes in the brains of cats in various parts of the hypothalamus (Edwards & Flynn, 1972). A small electric current was then passed through these structures. When one part of the hypothalamus was stimulated, the cats displayed the characteristic signs of anger and hostile aggression: arched back, hissing and spitting, fluffed tail. This reaction was nondiscriminating; the cats attacked anything placed in their cage, whether a sponge or a live mouse. When another part of the hypothalamus was stimulated, the cats displayed selective predatory aggression. They went through the motions of hunting; with eyes wide open, they stalked and pounced on a live animal, but they ignored the sponge.

Recent evidence shows that other parts of the brain, such as the amygdala, are also involved in aggression (Carré et al., 2013). The amygdala is a tiny structure buried deep within the brain that reacts to emotions. Carré et al. report that activity in the amygdala

hypothalamus A structure in the limbic system of the brain associated with aggressive behavior.

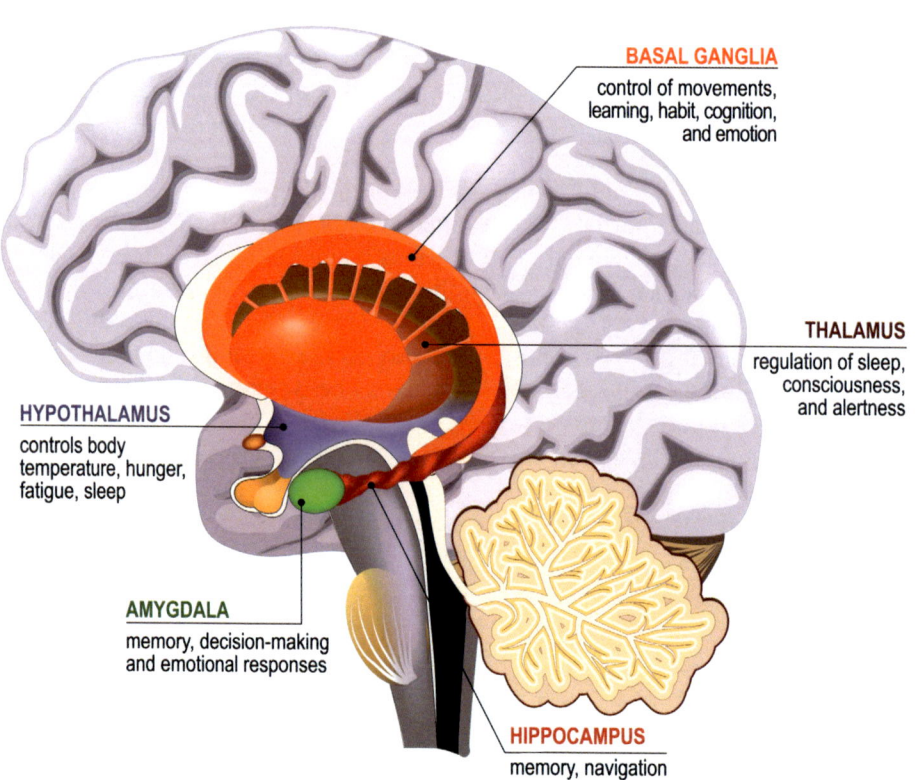

Among the brain structures mediating aggression is the limbic system, which is a collection of structures involved in motivation and emotion. The amygdala is one structure in the limbic system that plays a role in aggressive behavior.
Source: Designua/Shutterstock.

related to a threatening face was associated with aggression, especially for men. In these types of situations, the amygdala appears to be activated by heightened levels of testosterone (Derntl et al., 2009), which we shall see later is related to aggressive behavior.

The gender difference in aggression discussed earlier in the chapter also relates to differential activation of the areas of the brain in males and females (Repple et al., 2018; Visser et al., 2014). Repple et al. had participants engage in an aggression-inducing game (against a computer) while undergoing functional magnetic resonance imaging (fMRI). Repple et al. varied the degree of provocation experienced by participants between high (lose 80–90 cents) and low (lose 0–20 cents). No differences between male and female participants were found for general brain activation. However, under high provocation, compared with women, men showed more activation in the left amygdala (a brain structure associated with emotion and aggression), as well as in the anterior cingulate gyrus and the orbitofrontal cortex. There was a significant correlation between the degree of trait aggressiveness and activation of the left amygdala in males but not females.

The bottom line is that there is no one structure in the brain that "controls" aggression. Rather, there is a neural circuit in the brain, including parts of the limbic system and the cortex, that organizes aggressive behavior. Furthermore, brain stimulation does not inevitably lead to aggression. In one study, brain stimulation led to an aggressive response if a monkey was restrained in a chair (Delgado, 1969). But if the monkey was placed in a cage with another docile monkey, the same brain stimulation produced a different behavior: The monkey ran across the cage making repeated high-pitched vocalizations. The expression of aggressive behavior also depended on a monkey's status within a group. If a more dominant monkey was present, brain stimulation did not lead to aggression. If a less dominant monkey was present, stimulating the same part of the brain did lead to aggression. Thus, even with brain stimulation, aggressive behavior occurred only under the "right" social conditions.

Hormonal Influences

Researchers also have investigated the role of hormones in aggressive behavior. As mentioned earlier, high levels of the male hormone testosterone are generally associated with increased aggression (Christiansen & Knussmann, 1987). Testosterone is not the only hormone that affects aggression. According to the *dual hormone hypothesis* (Montoya et al., 2012), in addition to testosterone, cortisol (a stress hormone) is also involved in regulating aggression (Montoya et al., 2012). In fact, testosterone and cortisol appear to operate together in affecting aggression levels. Research shows that a high testosterone-to-cortisol ratio is related to a person having a "socially aggressive" behavioral style (Montoya et al., 2012). The interactive effect of testosterone and cortisol on aggression has also been found to be true for females (Denson et al., 2013).

The influence of testosterone on aggressive behavior—like the effect of brain stimulation—is complex. Hormones come into play twice during the normal course of development in humans: first, during prenatal development, and later, at puberty. Prenatally, testosterone influences the sex organs and characteristics of the unborn child. Testosterone levels are higher for a genetic male than for a genetic female. The hormone permeates the entire body, including the brain, making it possible that the male brain is "wired" for greater aggression. Early in life, testosterone exposure serves an *organization function*, influencing the course of brain development. Later in life, it serves an *activation function* (Carlson, 1991), activating behavior patterns, such as aggression, that are related to testosterone levels. These two effects were shown clearly in an experiment conducted by Conner and Levine (1969). Conner and Levine castrated rats either neonatally (immediately after birth) or as weanlings (about 3 weeks after birth). (In rats, the critical period for exposure to testosterone is within a day or so after birth. Castrating males immediately after birth effectively prevents exposure to the necessary levels of testosterone for normal masculinization. The rats castrated as weanlings were exposed to the early necessary levels of testosterone and were masculinized normally.) Other rats were not castrated. Later, as adults, the castrated rats were exposed either to testosterone or to a placebo.

The experiment showed that for the rats castrated neonatally, the levels of aggression displayed after exposure to testosterone as adults did not differ significantly from the levels displayed after exposure to a placebo. For the weanling rats, exposure to testosterone as adults increased the level of aggression compared to that of the rats receiving the placebo. The levels of aggression after exposure to the testosterone or placebo did not differ for noncastrated rats.

This study showed that early exposure to male hormones is necessary in order for later exposure to a male hormone to increase aggression. Those rats castrated at birth missed the "organizing function" of the male hormone; the normal process of masculinization of the brain did not occur. Later injections of testosterone (activation function) thus had little effect. Rats castrated as weanlings were subjected to the organization function of the male hormone. Their brains were normally masculinized and more receptive to the activation function of the testosterone injections received later in life. We can conclude that high testosterone levels are effective in elevating levels of aggression only if there is normal exposure to male hormones early in life.

Another experiment demonstrated that hormonal influences interact with social influences to affect aggression. In this experiment, male rats were castrated and then implanted with a capsule (Albert et al., 1989a). For some rats the capsule was empty; for others it contained testosterone. These rats were then housed with another rat under one of two conditions. Half the rats were housed with a single feeding tube, requiring the animals to compete for food. The other half were housed with two feeding tubes, so no competition was necessary. The treated rats were then tested for aggression. The results were striking. Testosterone increased aggression only if the rats competed for food. If the rats were not required to compete, the levels of aggression were quite low, about the same as those for the rats implanted with the empty capsule.

Another example of how situational factors can affect testosterone levels and aggression is provided by Kleinsmith et al. (2006), who conducted an experiment to see if handling a gun would increase testosterone levels and aggression. Kleinsmith et al. informed male participants that they would be taking part in an experiment on how taste sensitivity is affected by attention to detail. Kleinsmith et al. obtained a saliva sample as soon as participants arrived at the lab. Testosterone levels were measured with the saliva sample. Then participants were led into another room where they would perform an attention task. Some participants were given a pellet gun that was a model of a Desert Eagle semiautomatic pistol. Other participants were given the child's game *Mousetrap*. Both groups of participants were instructed to write a set of instructions on how to assemble or disassemble the gun or game. Following this task another saliva sample was obtained. Next, participants were given a cup of water that had a drop of hot sauce in it. Participants were told that a previous participant had prepared the sample. After drinking the water sample, participants rated the sample. Finally, participants were told to prepare a water sample for the next participant. They were provided with a small cup of water and a bottle of hot sauce and told to add as much hot sauce to the water as they wished. The results of the experiment showed that participants who handled the gun showed a large increase in testosterone level when pre- and post-manipulation saliva samples were analyzed (average change was 62 pg/ml). Participants who handled the game showed a negligible increase (average change was .68 pg/ml). Additionally, participants who handled the gun added far more hot sauce to the water (average was 13.61 grams) than participants who handled the game (average was 4.23 grams).

Female aggression is also mediated by hormones. In another study, the ovaries were removed from some female rats but not from others (Albert et al., 1989b). The rats were then housed with a sterile yet sexually active male rat. Weekly, the male rat was removed and an unfamiliar female rat was introduced into the cage. Female rats whose ovaries had been removed displayed less aggression toward the unfamiliar female than those whose ovaries had not been removed, suggesting a role of female hormones in aggression among female rats.

Most of the research we just reviewed was conducted with animal subjects. This research establishes a link between testosterone and aggression. How about human beings? Does the same link exist? A recent meta-analysis by Geniole et al. (2020) found a relatively weak but significant relationship between human testosterone levels and aggression. These researchers found that the relationship was stronger for males than for females. Like the previously cited animal studies, Geniole et al. reported that testosterone interacts with a number of environmental factors to affect aggression.

Alcohol and Aggression

Our final topic relating physiology and aggression is to explore the relationship between alcohol (a powerful drug affecting the nervous system) and aggression. There is ample evidence showing a connection between alcohol consumption and aggression (Bushman & Cooper, 1990; Quigley & Leonard, 1999). What is it about alcohol that increases violent behavior? Is there something about the drug effects of alcohol, or is it a function of the social situations in which alcohol is used?

There is no question that alcohol has pharmacological (drug-related) effects on the body, especially on the brain. Alcohol becomes concentrated in organs with a high water content, and the brain is one such organ. Alcohol lowers reaction time, impairs judgment, and weakens sensory perception and motor coordination. Under the influence of alcohol, people focus more on external cues, such as people or events in the situation that seem to encourage them to take action, and less on internal ones, such as thoughts about risks and consequences.

Although alcohol is a central nervous system depressant, it initially seems to act as a stimulant. People who are drinking at first become more sociable and assertive. This is because alcohol depresses inhibitory brain centers (Insel & Roth, 1994). As more alcohol is consumed, however, the effects change. Drinkers often become irritable and are easily angered. Levels of hostility and aggressiveness increase. Considering all the effects of alcohol, it is not surprising that it is a major factor not only in automobile crashes and fatal accidents of other kinds (such as drownings, falls, and fires) but also in homicides, suicides, assaults, and rapes.

Research confirms that levels of direct and indirect aggression increase with the amount of alcohol consumed (Kreutzer et al., 1984; Pihl & Zacchia, 1986; Sheehan et al., 2016; Shuntich & Taylor, 1972). In one study, participants who consumed 1.32 g/kg of 95% alcohol were more aggressive than participants receiving a placebo (nonalcoholic) drink or no drink at all (Pihl & Zacchia, 1986). The type of beverage consumed affects aggression as well (Gustafson, 1999; Pihl et al., 1984). As shown in Figure 10.1, participants who consumed a distilled beverage gave more severe shocks to a target than those who consumed wine or beer (Gustafson, 1999). Gustafson also found that longer shocks were given after consuming a distilled beverage compared to wine and beer. In another study, participants in a bar were approached and asked a series of annoying questions. In this natural setting, bar patrons drinking distilled beverages displayed more verbal aggression toward the interviewer than those drinking beer (Murdoch & Pihl, 1988). There is also evidence that drinking a caffeinated alcoholic beverage (e.g., Red Bull and vodka) leads to more aggression than a noncaffeinated drink (Miller et al., 2016; Sheehan et al., 2016).

Although we often have a good time when drinking alcohol, alcohol consumption also increases aggression.
Source: Studio Romantic/Shutterstock.

There is also evidence that alcohol can magnify one's prejudices and increase aggression toward out-group members (Parrott & Lisco, 2015). Parrot and Lisco measured heterosexual men's levels of prejudice against gays and lesbians. Participants then drank either an alcoholic or a nonalcoholic beverage. After consuming the beverage, participants played a competitive game against a fictitious opponent in which a participant received an electric shock. The gender of the fictitious opponent was varied (male or female), as was

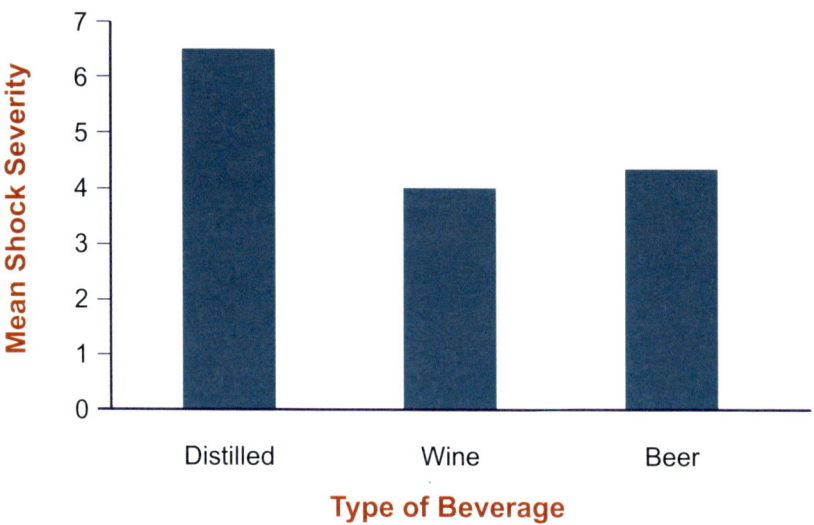

FIGURE 10.1

Mean shock severity as a function of type of alcoholic beverage consumed.
Based on data from Gustafson (1999).

the sexual orientation of the opponent (heterosexual or same-sex orientation). The measure of aggression was the intensity of the shock level the participant chose to deliver to the fictitious opponent. Parrott and Lisco found that consuming alcohol did not increase aggression against the gay male target for participants low in prejudice against gays and lesbians. However, for participants who were higher in this prejudice, alcohol consumption significantly increased aggression toward the gay male. This effect was not shown for a heterosexual male, heterosexual female, or lesbian female target.

How does alcohol increase aggression? Most likely, alcohol has an indirect effect on aggression by reducing a person's ability to inhibit behaviors that are normally suppressed by fear, such as aggression (Pihl et al., 1993). Although the precise brain mechanisms that are involved in this process are not fully known, there is evidence that alcohol is associated with a significant drop in the amount of brain serotonin (a neurotransmitter), which makes individuals more likely to engage in aggression in response to external stimuli (Badaway, 1998; Pihl & Lemarquand, 1998) and to be more impulsive (Montoya et al., 2012). Serotonin, when it is operating normally, inhibits antisocial behaviors such as aggression through the arousal of anxiety under threatening conditions (Pihl & Peterson, 1993). When serotonin levels are reduced, anxiety no longer has its inhibitory effects, but intense emotional arousal remains, resulting in increased aggression under conditions of threat (Pihl & Peterson, 1993).

Alcohol has also been found to influence the functioning of the prefrontal cortex of the brain (Denson et al., 2018), disrupting executive cognitive functioning (ECF), or functions that help one use higher cognitive processes such as attention, planning, and self-monitoring (Hoaken et al., 1998; Pihl et al., 2003). These executive functions play a major role in one's ability to effectively regulate goal-directed behavior (Hoaken et al., 1998). In individuals with low-functioning ECF, aggression is more likely than among individuals with high-functioning ECF, regardless of alcohol consumption (Hoaken et al., 1998). If the ECF remains active after alcohol consumption, alcohol-related aggression is lower than if the ECF is inhibited (Giancola, 2004). In addition to reducing activity in the prefrontal cortex, it also reduces activity in the caudate and ventral striatum (both involved in motivation and emotion). At the same time, alcohol increases activity in the hippocampus. This pattern of activation has been found to be related to increased aggression (Denson et al., 2018). Denson et al. concluded that alterations in the function of the prefrontal cortex contribute to aggression among intoxicated individuals. Alcohol also impairs the connection between the amygdala and the frontal lobes (Gorka et al., 2013). Gorka et al. also found that alcohol reduced activity in the amygdala in response to anger and fear facial expressions (but not to a happy face). This suggests that alcohol dulls the ability of a person to process information about the emotions of others and transmit that information to the frontal lobes. This may prevent an intoxicated person from responding appropriately to others. It is apparent, then, that the inhibitory effect of alcohol on ECF and the connections between other parts of the brain involved in interpreting emotions are factors contributing to increased aggression after alcohol consumption.

When in an intoxicated state, one can override the effects of alcohol if properly motivated (Hoaken et al., 1998). Hoaken and his associates (1998) placed intoxicated and sober individuals into a situation where they could deliver electric shocks to another person. Half the participants in each group received an incentive to deliver low levels of shocks (the promise of money). The results showed that intoxicated participants were just as able as their sober counterparts to reduce the severity of shocks delivered when the incentive was provided. However, when no incentive was provided, intoxicated participants delivered higher shock levels than the sober participants.

Although the amount and type of alcohol consumed affect aggression, research shows that one's expectations about the effects of alcohol also have an impact on aggression (Lang et al., 1975; Leonard et al., 2003; Kreutzer et al., 1984; Rohsenow & Bachorowski, 1984). Generally, participants in experiments who believe they are drinking alcohol display elevated levels of aggression, even if in reality they are drinking a nonalcoholic placebo. The mere belief that one has consumed alcohol is enough to enhance aggression. In fact, even the experimenter's knowledge of who has consumed alcohol can affect the level of aggression observed in experiments like this. An analysis of the literature shows that the effects of alcohol on aggression are smaller when the experimenter is blind to the conditions of the experiment (Bushman & Cooper, 1990). This relationship also holds outside the laboratory. Leonard et al. (2003) conducted a study in which male participants were asked about aggressive events that happened to them in bars. Leonard et al. measured several personality and situational variables. They found that a belief that alcohol was the cause for aggression was related to the occurrence (but not severity) of an aggressive encounter in a bar.

Expectations cannot account for the entire effect of alcohol, however. The pharmacological effects of alcohol are more powerful than expectations in mediating aggression (Stappenbeck & Fromme, 2013). In some cases even when there is an expectation that alcohol may lead to aggression, such an expectation does not increase aggression, whereas actual alcohol consumption does (Quigley & Leonard, 1999). Social cues, expectations, and attitudes play some part in mediating alcohol-induced aggression. However, the pharmacological effects of alcohol on the body and brain are real. Probably through a combination of reducing inhibitions and increasing irritability and hostility on the one hand, and giving the drinker "permission" to act out in social situations on the other, alcohol has the net effect of enhancing aggressive behavior.

Finally, the alcohol-aggression link is mediated by individual characteristics and the social situation. Individuals, especially men, who are high on a characteristic known as *dispositional empathy* (an emotion associated with helping behavior) are less likely to behave aggressively after alcohol consumption than those low on this characteristic (Giancola, 2003). Cheong and Nagoshi (1999) had participants engage in a competitive game with a bogus participant. The game was played under one of three conditions. In one condition, the real participant was told that his opponent could deliver a loud noise in an attempt to disrupt his performance (aggression). In the second condition, the real participant was told that his opponent would use the loud noise to keep the real participant alert during the boring task (altruism). In the third condition, the real participant was given ambiguous information about his opponent's motives (maybe aggression or maybe altruism). Furthermore, before engaging in the task, participants consumed either alcoholic drinks or a placebo. One-half of the placebo participants were told they were consuming an alcoholic beverage (expectancy for alcohol), and the other half were told their drinks were placebos. Finally, participants completed a personality measure of their impulsiveness and sensation-seeking tendencies.

The results of this experiment showed that alcohol-mediated aggression depended on the nature of the situation (aggression vs. altruism), personality, and alcohol consumption.

Specifically, participants who scored highly on the measure of impulsiveness/sensation-seeking were the most aggressive after consuming alcohol, but only when they believed their opponent was using the loud noise aggressively. When the opponent's motive was either altruistic or ambiguous, this effect did not occur. Thus, whether an individual behaves aggressively after consuming alcohol depends on the nature of the situation and one's predisposition toward impulsive behavior or sensation-seeking.

An individual's approval of the use of aggression also interacts with alcohol to increase aggression. Cheri Levinson et al. (2011) measured participants' approval of aggression and then had them do a task in which they could receive or deliver electric shocks to a fictitious opponent in a competitive game. Participants played the game after drinking either an alcoholic beverage or a nonalcoholic placebo beverage. Levinson et al. found that intoxicated participants who were high in approval of the use of aggression showed more aggression than nonintoxicated participants. Aggression was not affected by alcohol consumption for participants low in aggression approval.

Physiology and Aggression: Summing Up

What can we learn from this research on the physiological aspects of aggression in animals? How much of it can be applied to human beings? Not many people would attribute Samuel Cassidy's murderous behavior to an overabundance of testosterone or abnormal brain circuitry. Research with animals supports the general conclusion that aggression does have a physiological component. However, in humans, biological forces cannot account for all, or even most, instances in which aggression is displayed (Huesmann & Eron, 1984). The human being is a profoundly cultural animal. Although aggression is a basic human drive, the expression of that drive depends on forces operating in a particular society at a particular time. Samuel Cassidy's behavior was the product not only of his biology but also of his social world. Laws and social and cultural norms serve as powerful factors that can inhibit or facilitate aggressive behavior.

Study Break

This section introduced you to biological explanations for aggression. Before you begin the next section, answer the following questions:

1. How do ethologists and sociobiologists explain the causes of aggression?
2. What is the relationship between genetics and aggression?
3. What are the brain mechanisms involved in aggression?
4. How do hormones relate to aggression?
5. What are the pharmacological effects of alcohol on aggression?
6. How do the expectations about the effects of alcohol relate to aggression?

The Frustration-Aggression Link

Imagine for a moment that you are standing in front of a snack machine. You dig into your pocket and come up with your last dollar. You breathe a sigh of relief. You are very hungry and have just enough money to get a bag of chips. You put your money into the machine and press the button. You watch and wait for the mechanism to operate and drop your bag of chips. Instead, the mechanism grinds away and your bag of chips gets hung up in the machine. You mutter a few choice words, kick the machine, and walk away in a huff.

Analysis of this incident gives us some insight into a factor that social psychologists believe instigates aggression. In the example, a goal you wished to obtain—satisfying your hunger—was blocked. This produced an emotional state that led to aggression (kicking the vending machine). Your reaction to such a situation illustrates the general principles of a classic formulation known as the **frustration-aggression hypothesis** (Dollard et al., 1939).

frustration-aggression hypothesis A hypothesis that frustration and aggression are strongly related, suggesting that aggression is always the consequence of frustration and frustration leads to aggression.

In its original form, the frustration-aggression hypothesis stated that "aggression is always a consequence of frustration, the occurrence of aggressive behavior always presupposes the existence of frustration and, contrariwise . . . the existence of frustration leads to some form of aggression" (Dollard et al., 1939, p. 1). In other words, according to the frustration-aggression hypothesis, when we are frustrated, we behave aggressively.

Components of the Frustration-Aggression Sequence

What are the components of the frustration-aggression sequence? An assumption of the frustration-aggression hypothesis is that emotional arousal occurs when goal-directed behavior is blocked. Frustration occurs, then, when two conditions are met. First, we expect to perform certain behaviors, and second, those behaviors are blocked (Dollard et al., 1939).

Frustration can vary in strength, depending on three factors (Dollard et al., 1939). The first is the strength of the original drive. If you are very hungry, for example, and are deprived of a snack, your frustration will be greater than if you are only slightly hungry. The second factor is the degree to which the goal-directed behavior is thwarted. If your kicking of the machine dislodged a smaller snack, for example, you would be less frustrated than if you received no snack at all. The third factor is the number of frustrated responses. If your thwarted attempt to get a snack came on the heels of another frustrating event, your frustration would be greater.

Once we are frustrated, what do we choose as a target? Our first choice is the source of our frustration (Dollard et al., 1939)—the vending machine, in our example. But sometimes aggression against the source of frustration is not possible. The source may be a person in a position of power over us, such as our boss. When direct aggression against the source of aggression is blocked, we may choose to vent our frustration against another safer target—a pet, perhaps. If we have a bad day at work or school, we may take it out on an innocent roommate or family member when we get home. This process is called *displaced aggression* (Dollard et al., 1939). Displaced aggression is influenced by the following factors (Marcus-Newhall et al., 2000):

1. Intensity of the original provocation. The higher the intensity, the less the displacement.

2. Similarity between the original and displaced target. The higher the similarity, the greater the displacement.

3. The negativity of the interaction between the individual and original target. The more negative the interaction, the greater the displacement.

Another type of displaced aggression is *triggered displaced aggression*. Triggered displaced aggression occurs when a second provocation occurs after an initial provocation (Miller et al., 2003). For example, imagine that your boss frustrated you all day at work and you came home and displaced aggression by kicking your dog. That would be displaced aggression. Now, imagine that when you open the door, your dog barks loudly at you. You might kick your dog a bit harder than in the first scenario. This is an example of triggered displaced aggression because your dog's loud barking serves as a second provoking event (Miller et al., 2003). Research shows that adding a second, even minor, provoking event (e.g., your dog barking) to an initial provocation (e.g., your boss frustrating you) leads to stronger aggression than either of the provoking events by itself (Pedersen et al., 2000). Triggered displaced aggression is increased if you are given an opportunity to ruminate, or stew, over the initial provocation before the second provocation, especially if the provocation occurs in public (Vasquez et al., 2013). So, if you have a long drive home from work, allowing you to stew over your boss's behavior, before encountering your barking dog, your aggressive response to your dog will be more intense than if you had a short drive. And, if you stop for a couple of drinks on your way home, the alcohol will enhance the effects of the second provocation (your poor barking dog!) (Aviles et al., 2005).

Although the original frustration-aggression hypothesis stated categorically that frustration always leads to aggression, acts of frustration-based aggression can be inhibited (Dollard et al., 1939). If there is a strong possibility that your aggressive behavior will be punished, you may not react aggressively to frustration. If a campus security guard were standing beside the vending machine, for example, you probably wouldn't kick it for fear of being arrested.

Factors Mediating the Frustration-Aggression Link

The frustration-aggression hypothesis stirred controversy from the moment it was proposed. Some theorists questioned whether frustration inevitably led to aggression (Miller, 1941). Others suggested that frustration leads to aggression only under specific circumstances, such as when the blocked response is important to the individual (Blanchard & Blanchard, 1984).

As criticisms of the original theory mounted, modifications were made. For example, Berkowitz (1989) proposed that frustration is connected to aggression by negative affect, such as anger. If, as shown in Figure 10.2, the frustration of goal-directed behavior leads to anger, then aggression will occur. If no anger is aroused, no aggression will result. If anger mediates frustration, we must specify which frustrating conditions lead to anger. Theoretically, if the blocking of goal-directed behavior does not arouse anger, then the frustrated individual should not behave aggressively. Let's consider other factors that mediate the frustration-aggression link.

Attributions About Intent

Recall from Chapter 3 that we are always interpreting people's behavior, deciding that they did something because they meant it (an internal attribution) or because of some outside situational factor (an external attribution). The type of attribution made about a source of frustration is one important factor contributing to aggression. If someone's behavior frustrates us and we make an internal attribution, we are more likely to respond with aggression than if we make an external attribution.

Research shows that the intent behind an aggressive act is more important in determining the degree of retaliation than the actual harm done (Ohbuchi & Kambara, 1985). Individuals who infer negative intent on the part of another person are most likely to retaliate. The actual harm done is not so important as the intent behind the aggressor's act (Ohbuchi & Kambara, 1985).

There is additional evidence about the importance of attributions for aggression. Research shows that if we are provided with a reasonable explanation for the behavior of someone who is frustrating us, we will react less aggressively than if no explanation is given (Johnson & Rule, 1986; Kremer & Stephens, 1983). Moreover, if we believe that aggression directed against us is typical for the situation in which it occurs, we are likely

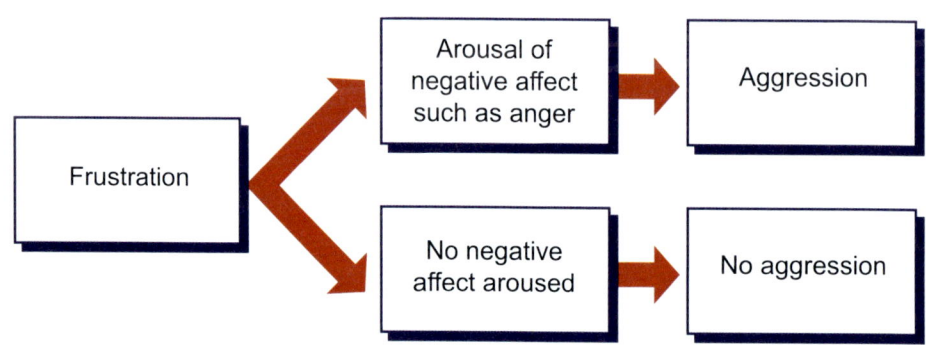

FIGURE 10.2

The relationship among frustration, anger, and aggression. Frustration leads to aggression only if it arouses negative affect, such as anger.

to attribute our attacker's actions to external factors. Thus, we will retaliate less than if we believe the attacker was choosing atypical levels of aggression (Dyck & Rule, 1978). In this case, we would be more likely to attribute the attacker's aggression to internal forces and to retaliate in kind if given the opportunity.

What happens if someone does something to frustrate and anger us and then indicates it was all a mistake? This question was addressed in an experiment reported by Krieglmeyer et al. (2009). Participants in this experiment were told that they were participating in an experiment on virtual communication and would be working with another person via email. Participants were asked to generate six names for a new energy drink. The names were then evaluated by the participant's partner. In one condition (unintentional frustration), the partner gave the participant a low rating and then subsequently sent a message that he misunderstood the rating scale and changed his rating to a higher one. In another condition (intentional frustration), the partner gave the low ratings but did not change them. Krieglmeyer et al. found that aggression toward the partner was lower in the unintentional frustration than the intentional frustration condition. Interestingly, participants in the unintentional frustration condition remained angry, even though the partner apologized for the error. However, that anger was not translated into aggression.

Perceived Injustice and Inequity

Another factor that can contribute to anger and ultimately to aggression is the perception that we have been treated unjustly. The following account of a violent sports incident illustrates the power of perceived injustice to incite aggression (Mark et al., 1983, pp. 83–84):

> In November 1963, a riot occurred at Roosevelt Raceway, a harness racing track in the New York metropolitan area. Several hundred fans swarmed onto the track. The crowd attacked the judges' booth, smashed the tote board, set fires in program booths, broke windows, and damaged cars parked in an adjacent lot. Several hundred police officers were called to the scene. Fifteen fans were arrested, 15 others hospitalized.

What incited this riot? The sixth race was the first half of a daily double, in which bettors attempt to select the winners of successive races, with potentially high payoffs. During the sixth race, six of the eight horses were involved in an accident and did not finish the race. In accordance with New York racing rules, the race was declared official. All wagers placed on the six nonfinishing horses were lost, including the daily double bets. Many fans apparently felt that they were unjustly treated, that the race should have been declared no contest.

This incident is not unique. Frequently, we read about fans at a soccer match who riot over a "bad call" or fans at a football game who pelt officials with snowballs or beer cans following a call against a home team. In each case, the fans are reacting to what they perceive to be an injustice done to the home team. We see similar reactions after events that are not sports related. For example, the riots in Minneapolis following the death of George Floyd in 2020 were undoubtedly a response to perceived injustice.

Aggression is often seen as a way of restoring justice and equity in a situation. The perceived inequity in a frustrating situation, as opposed to the frustration itself, leads to aggression (Sulthana, 1987). For example, a study of juvenile offenders found a positive correlation between an individual's degree of perceived injustice in encounters with the police and the likelihood of aggressive behavior (Zapolski et al., 2018). Zapolski et al. also measured participants' degree of moral disengagement, which involves justifying amoral behavior, minimizing

One source of anger that can mediate between frustration and aggression is injustice. Riots often occur when a group perceives that group members have been treated unjustly.
Source: Studio Romantic/Shutterstock.

one's role in maladaptive behavior, and a host of other cognitive adjustments to justify bad behavior. Zapolski et al. found that higher levels of moral disengagement positively correlated with higher levels of aggression. Interestingly, individuals who are both morally disengaged and perceive injustice are most likely to behave aggressively.

Of course, not all perceived injustice leads to aggression. Not everyone rioted at the New York race track, and most sports fans do not assault referees for bad calls. There may be more of a tendency to use aggression to restore equity when the recipient of the inequity feels particularly powerless (Richardson et al., 1986). In one study, participants with lower status than their opponents chose higher shock levels than did participants with equal or higher status than their opponents (Richardson et al., 1986). We can begin to understand from these findings why groups who believe themselves to be unjustly treated, who have low status and feel powerless, resort to aggressive tactics, especially when frustrated, to remedy their situation. Riots and terrorism are often the weapons of choice used to respond to perceived injustice by those with little power. In fact, the "ground floor" of the *staircase model of terrorism* includes a response by potential terrorists to perceived injustice (Moghaddam, 2005).

In addition to the moral disengagement, a myriad of cognitive factors may mediate the relationship between perceived injustice and aggression (Beugré, 2005). Beugré suggests that factors such as a person's values, types of attributions made about the injustice, likelihood of negative consequences for aggression, potential rewards to be gained by the aggression, and the availability of an opportunity to engage in aggression will affect a person's response to injustice.

The Heat Effect

heat effect The observation that aggression is more likely when people are hot than when they are cool.

For centuries it has been the belief that aggression is more likely to occur when it is hot than when it is cool. The **heat effect** refers to the observation that aggression is more likely when people are hot than when they are cool (Anderson, 1989, 2001). For example, as shown in Table 10.1, most major riots in the United States have occurred during months when the weather is hot. A similar effect was reported for civil unrest in African cities (Yeeles, 2015). However, Yeeles found that the heat effect was relatively small and got smaller when he took into account whether other unrest had occurred in the recent past.

TABLE 10.1 Riots in the United States and Heat

State	Dates	City
New York	July 24–26, 1964	Rochester
New Jersey	August 2, 11, 12, 1964	Jersey City, Patterson, Elizabeth
Pennsylvania	August 28–30, 1964	Philadelphia
Illinois	August 16–17, 1964	Dixmoor riot, Chicago
California	August 11–17, 1965	Los Angeles
Michigan	July 23–24, 1967	12th St. Riot, Detroit
New Jersey	July 12–16, 1967	Newark
Washington, DC	April 4–7, 1968	Washington (MLK death)
Illinois	August 26–29, 1968	Chicago (Democratic Convention)
New York	June 27, 1969	Stonewall
New York	September 9, 1971	Attica Prison
California	April 29–30, 1992	Los Angeles (R. King)

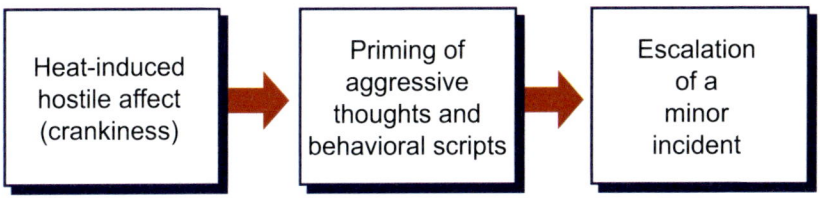

FIGURE 10.3

GAM model explanation for heat effect.

If there was another incident of civil unrest in the recent past, the heat effect disappeared. Yeeles concluded that heat does not directly cause civil unrest but serves to supplement aggression triggered by other factors. Larrick et al. (2011) investigated the frequency with which baseball batters were hit by pitches in relation to temperature. They found that increasing temperature alone did not account for an increase in hit batters. Instead, heat increased the likelihood that a batter would be hit by a pitch, especially if the pitcher's teammate was hit by an opposing pitcher. In another demonstration of the heat effect, incidents of homicides, assaults, rapes, and family disturbances all peak during summer months, especially during the month of July (Anderson, 1989). Anderson (2001) has reviewed the research (field and laboratory) and has concluded that the heat effect is real and is most likely due to the fact that when it is hot, people get more cranky (Berkowitz, 1993). According to Berkowitz, heat distorts assessments of social interactions so that what might ordinarily be passed off as a minor incident gets blown out of proportion and becomes a cause for aggression. Anderson and his colleagues (2000) have proposed the *General Aggression Model (GAM)* that draws on this idea to account for the effects of heat on aggression. As shown in Figure 10.3, heat-induced negative affect (crankiness) primes aggressive thoughts and perceptions, which then cause the escalation of a minor incident.

Study Break

This section discussed the frustration-aggression hypothesis and the factors that mediate between frustration and aggression. Before you go on to the next section, answer the following questions:

1. What is the frustration-aggression hypothesis, and what conditions relate to the arousal of frustration?
2. What is displaced aggression, and how does it relate to the frustration-aggression hypothesis?
3. How does anger relate to the link between frustration and aggression?
4. What is the relationship between attributions about intent, anger, and aggression?
5. How does perceived injustice relate to anger and aggression?
6. What is the heat effect, and what explanation has been offered to account for it?

The Social Learning Explanation for Aggression

The frustration-aggression hypothesis focuses on the responses of individuals in particular, frustrating situations. But clearly, not all people respond in the same ways to frustrating stimuli. Some respond with aggression, whereas others respond with renewed determination to overcome their frustration. It appears that some people are more predisposed to aggression than others. How can we account for these differences?

Although there are genetically based, biological differences in aggressiveness among individuals, social psychologists are more interested in the role of socialization in the development of aggressive behavior (Huesmann, 1988; Huesmann & Malamuth, 1986). Socialization, as mentioned earlier, is the process by which children learn the behaviors, attitudes, and values of their culture. Socialization is the work of many agents, including parents, siblings, schools, religious institutions, and the media. Through the socialization process, children learn many of the behavior patterns, both good and bad, that will stay with them into adulthood.

Aggression is one behavior that is developed early in life via socialization and persists into adulthood (Huesmann et al., 1984). In fact, a long-term study of aggressive behavior found that children who were rated by their peers as aggressive at age 8 were likely to be aggressive as adults, as measured by self-ratings, ratings by participants' spouses, and citations for criminal and traffic offenses (Huesmann et al., 1984).

The stability of aggression over time applies to both males and females (Pulkkinen & Pitkanen, 1993). However, the age at which early aggressiveness predicts later aggressive behavior differs for males and females. In one study, researchers investigated the relationship between Swedish children's aggressiveness (measured by teacher ratings) at two ages (10 and 13) and crime rates through age 26 (Stattin & Magnusson, 1989). For males, aggressiveness ratings at both age levels were significant predictors of serious crimes committed later in life. However, for females, only aggressiveness ratings at age 13 predicted later criminal behavior. For males and females, early aggressiveness was most closely related to crimes of the "acting out" type, such as violent crimes against property and other people, rather than drug offenses, traffic offenses, or crimes committed for personal gain (Stattin & Magnusson, 1989).

Taken together, these studies show a clear pattern of early aggression being significantly related to aggression later in life (as measured by crime statistics). Although there is some difference between males and females (at least in terms of the age at which the relationship between early aggression and later aggression begins), it is clear that the relationship between childhood aggression and adulthood aggression is true for both males and females.

What happens during these early years to increase aggression among some children? In the sections that follow, we look at how socialization relates to the development of aggressive behavior patterns.

The Socialization of Aggression

social learning theory
A theory that social behavior is acquired through direct reinforcement or punishment of behavior and observational learning.

observational learning
Learning through watching what people do and whether they are rewarded or punished and then imitating that behavior.

Unlike the biological approaches to aggression, Albert Bandura's (1973) **social learning theory** maintains that aggression is learned, much like any other human behavior. Aggression can be learned through two general processes: direct reinforcement and punishment, and **observational learning** or learning by watching others. Often, individuals who commit violent acts grew up in a neighborhood where violence was commonplace. These individuals saw that aggression was a method of getting one's way. They probably even tried it for themselves and obtained some goal. If aggression pays off, one is then more likely to use aggressive behavior again, learning through the process of direct reinforcement. If the aggression fails, or one is punished for using aggression, aggression is less likely to be used in the future.

Although the processes of direct reinforcement and punishment are important, social learning theory maintains that its primary channel is through observational learning, or modeling. This occurs when, for example, a young man standing in a playground sees a person get money by beating up another person. People quickly learn that aggression can be effective. By watching others, they learn new behaviors, or they have existing behaviors encouraged or inhibited.

Bandura and his colleagues (Bandura et al., 1963) provided powerful evidence in support of the transmission of aggression through observational learning. They showed that children who watch an aggressive model can learn new patterns of behavior and will display them when given the opportunity to do so. Bandura and his colleagues designed an ingenious experiment to test this central principle of social learning theory.

In this experiment, children were exposed to a model who behaved aggressively against a "Bobo doll," a large, inflatable, plastic punching doll. The model engaged in some specific behavior, such as kicking and punching the doll while screaming, "Sock him in the nose" (Bandura et al., 1961). After the child observed the model engage in this behavior, he or she was taken to a room with several toys. After a few minutes, the experimenter went in and told the child that he or she could not play with the toys because they were being saved for another child (this was to frustrate the child). The child was then taken to another room with several other toys, including the Bobo doll.

Bandura performed a number of variations on this basic situation. In one experiment, for example, the children saw the model being rewarded, being punished, or receiving no consequences for batting around the Bobo doll (Bandura, 1965). In another, children observed a live model, a filmed model, or a cartoon model (Bandura et al., 1963). In all the variations, the dependent variable was the same—the number of times the child imitated the aggressive behaviors the model displayed.

Bandura found that when the children saw aggression being rewarded, they showed more imitative responses than when it was punished. Live models evoked the most imitative responses, followed by film models and then cartoon models, but any aggressive model increased imitative responses over the nonaggressive or no-model conditions. Exposure to the aggressive model elicited other aggressive responses that the child had not seen from the model (Bandura et al., 1963). Apparently, an aggressive model can motivate a child to behave aggressively in new, unmodeled ways.

Bandura (1973) concluded that observational learning can have the following effects. First, a child can learn totally new patterns of behavior. Second, a child's behavior can be inhibited (if the model is punished) or disinhibited (if the model is rewarded). Disinhibition in this context means that a child already knows how to perform a socially unacceptable behavior (such as hitting or kicking) but is not doing it for a reason. Seeing a model rewarded removes inhibitions against performing the behavior. Bandura calls this process vicarious reinforcement. And third, a socially desirable behavior can be enhanced by observing models engaged in prosocial activities.

Bandura's findings have been observed across cultures. McHan (1985) replicated Bandura's basic experiment in Lebanon. Children were exposed either to a film showing a child playing aggressively with a Bobo doll or to a film showing a boy playing nonaggressively with some toys. McHan found that the children who were exposed to the aggressive film were more aggressive in a subsequent play situation. They also exhibited more novel aggressive behaviors than children who had seen the nonaggressive film. These results exactly replicate Bandura's original findings and offer additional support for the social learning approach to aggression.

We have established that exposing children to filmed aggressive models contributes to increased physical aggression. Is there any evidence that exposure to violence in naturalistic settings relates to levels of aggression? According to a study by Gorman-Smith and Tolan (1998), the answer to this question is yes. Gorman-Smith and Tolan investigated the relationship between exposure to community violence and aggression in a sample of minority males growing up in high-crime neighborhoods. Their results showed that exposure to violence in the community was related to an increase in aggression and feelings of depression. They also reported that the increase in aggression is specific to exposure to violence in the neighborhood and not to general levels of stress. Finally, Gorman-Smith and Tolan reported that the number of people who are exposed to community violence does not relate significantly to parental discipline practices but may relate more strongly to peer influences and other community-related factors.

Social learning theory says that children learn aggression like any other behavior. One mechanism they stress is observational learning. If a child sees an aggressive model rewarded for aggression, the child is likely to show aggression. If an aggressive model is punished, the child will likely inhibit aggression.
Source: Lopolo/Shutterstock.

Aggressive Scripts: Why and How They Develop

aggressive script
An internalized representation of an event that leads to increased aggression and the tendency to interpret social interactions aggressively.

One mechanism believed to underlie the relationship between observation and aggression is the formation of **aggressive scripts** during the socialization process. Scripts are internalized representations of how an event should occur. Another term for a script is *event schema*. You may, for example, have a script about what goes on at a college basketball game: You go to the arena, sit in your seat, and cheer for your team. Such scripts influence how people behave in a given social situation.

Exposing a child to aggressive models—parents, peers, television characters, video games—during socialization contributes to the development of aggressive scripts (Huesmann, 1986; Huesmann & Malamuth, 1986). These scripts, in turn, lead to increased aggression and a tendency to interpret social interactions aggressively. And they can persist, greatly influencing levels of aggression in adulthood.

Aggressive scripts develop through three phases (Huesmann & Malamuth, 1986). During the acquisition and *encoding phase*, the script is first learned and placed into the child's memory. Much like a video camera, a child who sees violence—or is reinforced directly for violence—records the violent scenes into memory. A script will be most easily encoded into memory if the child believes the script-related behavior is socially acceptable (Huesmann, 1988). When one grows up in a violent neighborhood, for example, one will undoubtedly acquire and encode an aggressive script based on one's experiences.

The stored script is strengthened and elaborated on during the *maintenance phase*. Strengthening and elaboration occur each time a child thinks about an aggressive event, watches an aggressive television show, plays aggressively, or is exposed to violence from other sources (Huesmann, 1988; Huesmann & Malamuth, 1986). Research shows, for example, that children who are exposed to high levels of violence in their communities tend to develop aggressive behaviors (Gorman-Smith & Tolan, 1998).

Initially, during the *retrieval and emission phase*, the internalized script guides the child's behavior whenever a situation similar to the one in the script occurs. If the child has watched too many Clint Eastwood movies, for example, competition with another child for a toy may lead to a "make my day" scenario. The script may suggest to young Clint that competition is best resolved using aggression. Often aggressive behavior certainly fits with this model. Those who are exposed to violence on a day-to-day basis and feel threatened may turn to violence as a way to resolve conflicts. Aggressive scripts are played out to their bloody conclusions.

The Role of the Family in Developing Aggressive Behaviors

Although children are exposed to many models, the family provides the most immediate environment and is the most influential agent of socialization. It makes sense, then, that aggressive behavior is closely linked with family dynamics. In Chapter 9, we discussed three parenting styles (indulgent, authoritative, and authoritarian) in relation to interpersonal relationships. These parenting styles also relate to aggressive behavior (Martínez-Ferrer et al., 2016). Belén Martínez-Ferrer et al. conducted a study of the relationship between parenting style and cyberbullying among adolescents. They found that adolescents with authoritarian parents were more likely to cyberbully (direct and indirect) others than those with authoritative or indulgent parents.

social-interactional model
A model suggesting that antisocial behavior arises early in life and is the result of poor parenting, leading a child to develop conduct problems that affect peer relations and academic performance.

One developmental model proposed to explain the evolution of aggressive behavior is the **social-interactional model** (Patterson et al., 1989). According to this model, antisocial behavior (such as aggression) arises early in life as a result of poor parenting, such as harsh, inconsistent discipline and poor monitoring of children. Poor parenting leads to a child's behavior problems, which in turn contribute to rejection by peers and academic problems in school. Such children often become associated with deviant peer groups in late childhood and adolescence. In many cases, delinquency results.

Aggressive Parenting

Key to the social-interactional model is the disciplinary style adopted by parents and the parent-child interaction style that results. Some parents have an antisocial parenting style,

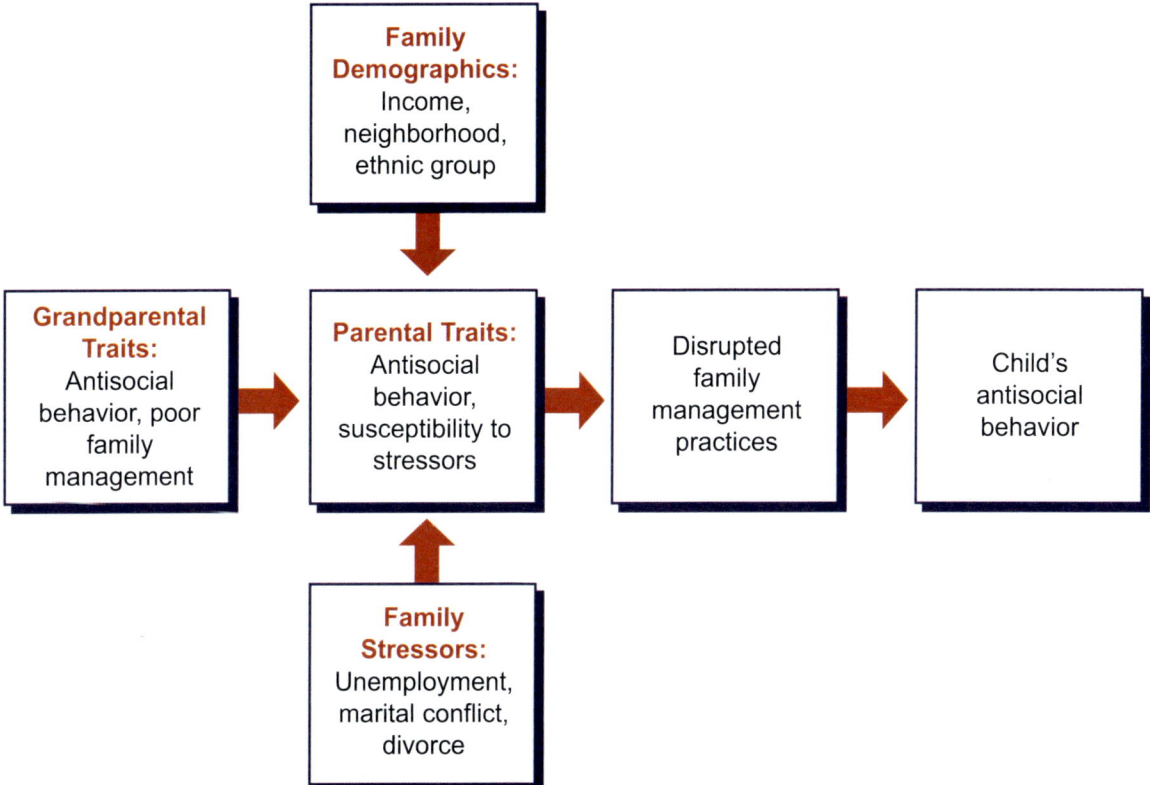

FIGURE 10.4

The social-interactional model of antisocial behavior. According to this model, antisocial parenting gives rise to disrupted family management and an increase in a child's antisocial behavior. Antisocial parenting relates to three factors: family demographics, grandparental traits, and family stressors.

From Patterson et al. (1989).

according to the model. Several factors contribute to such parental behavior. As shown in Figure 10.4, these factors include antisocial behavior and poor family management by their own parents, family demographics, and family stressors. Parents' antisocial behavior contributes to disruptions in their family management practices and, ultimately, to antisocial behavior from the child.

Parents who fall into a harmful cycle of parenting generally rely heavily on the use of power or harsh measures designed to control the child's behavior. They also use physical and/or verbal punishment. Do these techniques encourage children to act aggressively themselves? The answer is a firm yes! Although parents use power assertion and punishment with their children to make them comply, research shows that it actually reduces children's compliance (Crockenberg & Litman, 1986). This noncompliance may, in turn, cause parents to adopt an even more coercive disciplinary style.

What does this increased antisocial behavior resulting from poor parenting mean for the child? Research shows that aggressive (antisocial behavior) children are more likely to be rejected by their peers (Kereteš & Milanovi, 2006). Interestingly, rejection by others is more negative and leads to more aggression than merely being disliked by others (DeBono & Muraven, 2014). Rejection by peers, in turn, is associated with poor academic performance (DeRosier & Mercer, 2009) and the child falling in with a negative peer group (Light & Dishion, 2007). Further, children who are rejected and ostracized by peers react with anger, especially if the child feels that the ostracism was unfair (Chow et al., 2008). There is a significant association between peer ostracism and the likelihood of being involved in a school shooting (Leary et al., 2003). Leary et al. found that in all but 2 of 15 school shootings, ostracism or some other form of rejection (e.g., teasing or bullying) was a factor. They also found that ostracism combines with other factors

Chapter 10 Interpersonal Aggression

(e.g., psychological problems, fascination with death, and obsession with guns and explosives) to increase the risk of being a perpetrator of a school shooting.

Sometimes parents find it necessary to discipline a child using physical punishment, most notably *spanking*. Spanking is a form of punishment that is (1) physically noninjurious, (2) intended to modify behavior, and (3) administered with an open hand to the extremities or buttocks (Friedman & Schonberg, 1996, p. 853). Attitudes toward spanking have changed over the past decades, but a majority of survey respondents (66%) agreed with the statement that "it is sometimes necessary to discipline a child with a good, hard spanking" (General Social Survey, 2021). In another survey, 35% of adults agreed that it is sometimes necessary to "smack" a child. More people 55 or older agreed with smacking (46%) than younger (16–34; 24%) or middle-aged (35–54; 34%) individuals (Government Social Research, 2019). These numbers are lower than the almost 90% of U.S. parents of children aged 3 to 4 who reported using some form of physical punishment in the past (Straus, 1991). Straus found that the rate of physical punishment declined slowly after age 4 but remained at a relatively high level—60% or above—until the child was 13 years old. Despite this decline, physical punishment as a parenting technique remains popular in society. But does it work? Research suggests that it does. Physical punishment, in the form of spanking, does work in the sense that it can be an effective means to get a child to stop engaging in a given behavior (Gershoff, 2002; Kazdin & Benjet, 2003).

Although physical punishment can be effective, it does have a downside. Parental use of spanking is associated with negative outcomes for children (Gershoff & Grogan-Kaylor, 2016). For example, adolescents whose parents used physical punishment have more conduct problems and show more depression than those whose parents did not (Wang et al., 2014). Additionally, Straus (1991) found that as the frequency of physical punishment used during socialization increased, so did the rate of physical aggression used outside the family later on in adulthood. More ominously, as the frequency of physical punishment increased, so did homicide rates.

The negative effects of punishment apply to other cultures as well. One study conducted in Singapore found that parental use of physical punishment (caning or slapping) was related to higher levels of aggression among preschool-aged children (Sim & Ong, 2005). Other results from this study showed that caning by fathers increased aggression among both male and female children. However, there was a cross-sex relationship for fathers and mothers who slapped their children. Father slapping had the greatest effect on female children, whereas mother slapping had the greatest effect on male children. Finally, physical punishment is significantly associated with a variety of negative outcomes, including aggressive behavior, lower levels of moral internalization of behavior, degraded parent-child relationships, and poorer mental health (Gershoff, 2002). The only positive behavior associated with physical punishment is immediate compliance on the part of the child (Gershoff, 2002).

Physical punishment is not the only form of parental behavior associated with heightened aggression. Parents also subject their children to verbal and symbolic aggression, which can include these behaviors (Vissing et al. 1991, p. 228):

- Insulting or swearing at the child.
- Sulking or refusing to talk about a problem.
- Stomping out of the room or house.
- Doing or saying something to spite the child.
- Threatening to throw something at or hit the child.
- Throwing, smashing, hitting, or kicking something.

Like physical aggression, verbal or symbolic aggression is commonly directed at children and can contribute to "problems with aggression, delinquency, and interpersonal relationships" on the part of the children (Vissing et al., 1991, p. 231). This relationship holds even when the effects of other variables—such as physical aggression, age and gender of the child, socioeconomic status, and psychosocial problems of the child—are held constant. Moreover, parents' use of verbal or symbolic aggression as part of their parenting style is more highly associated with aggression in children than is physical aggression. One possible explanation for the pernicious effects of verbal aggression on children is that name calling and similar parental behaviors have implications for the child's self-esteem, with children experiencing verbal aggression showing lower levels of self-esteem (Ruth & Francoise, 1999).

Supporting evidence comes from a 22-year study of the relationship between the parental behaviors of rejection, punishment, and low identification with their children and aggression in children (Eron et al.,1991). This study suggests that parental rejection and punitiveness are significantly correlated with aggression in childhood and later in adulthood. Children whose parents rejected them at age 8, for example, showed a greater tendency toward aggression as adults than nonrejected children, and harsh parental punishment, particularly for girls, led to increased aggression. Generally, parental rejection and punitiveness were found to have their most enduring relationship with aggression if the rejection and punitiveness began before age 6. Similar effects were reported with a sample of Dutch adolescents (Hale et al., 2005). Hale et al. also found that parental rejection operates through depression to produce aggression. That is, parental rejection contributes to adolescent depression, which relates to elevated levels of aggression. The picture, however, is quite complex. For example, rejected children tend to behave in ways that lead parents to reject them (Eron et al., 1991). So, parental rejection that is related to aggression later in life may be partly caused by the child's behavior—a vicious cycle.

Exposure to high levels of family aggression also relates to aggression, as well as a number of other negative outcomes (Chermack & Walton, 1999; Khaleque, 2017; Murphy & Blumenthal, 2000). For example, Chermack and Walton (1999) studied the relationship between family aggression (parent-to-parent aggression, parent-to-child aggression) and the use of aggression in several types of relationships (dating, marital, etc.). They found that if participants saw their parents behaving aggressively toward each other and were the recipients of parental aggression themselves, the participants were more likely to use aggression in their own dating relationships. Interestingly, general aggression related positively only to being the actual target of parental aggression. Additionally, seeing one's parents behave aggressively also contributes to heightened feelings of psychological stress among both men and women (Julian et al., 1999). However, the psychological stress was most likely to be transformed into verbal or physical aggression among men as opposed to women (Julian et al., 1999). Thus, exposure to aggression in the family appears to influence adult aggression through the arousal of negative psychological symptoms. In any event, the evidence is clear: Exposure to family violence as a child contributes significantly to aggression later in life.

Role Modeling of Aggressive Behavior

What is the link between parental aggression and child aggression? The most likely explanation is role modeling. Whenever parents use physical or verbal aggression, they are modeling that behavior for their children. This is a special case of observational learning. Children observe their parents behaving aggressively; they also see that the aggressive behavior works because ultimately the children are controlled by it. Because the behavior is reinforced, both parents and children are more likely to use aggression again. The message sent to the child is loud and clear: You can get your way by using physical or verbal aggression. Through these processes of learning, children develop aggressive scripts (Eron et al., 1991), which organize and direct their aggressive behavior in childhood and in adulthood.

Child Abuse and Neglect

Parental discipline style is not the only family-related factor related to increases in aggression. Child abuse is associated with high levels of clinically significant aggression in children (Holmes et al., 2015). Child abuse has also been linked to aggressive behavior

Child abuse and neglect are two family factors that can contribute to aggression in children. Research shows that abused and neglected children are more likely to be arrested for juvenile and adult violent criminal behavior compared to non-abused, non-neglected adolescents.

Source: Gorodenkoff/Shutterstock.

later in life, especially among children who also have intrinsic vulnerabilities, such as cognitive, psychiatric, and neurological impairments (Lewis et al.,1989). Research shows that being abused or witnessing abuse is strongly related to highly violent behavior patterns. But physical abuse is not the only kind of abuse that contributes to increased aggressive behavior. Abused and neglected children are more likely to be arrested for juvenile (26%) and adult (28.6%) violent criminal behavior compared to a nonabused, nonneglected control group (16.8% and 21.1% arrest rates for juvenile and adult violent crime, respectively; Widom, 1992). Children who were only neglected had a higher arrest rate for violent crime (12.5%) than nonneglected children had (7.9%). A more recent study confirms this relationship between child abuse and criminal behavior (Lantos et al., 2019). Lantos et al. report that abused children were more likely than nonabused children to commit nonviolent and violent offenses. They also found that this relationship was stronger for males than for females.

Being the victim of child abuse has another pernicious effect. Exposure to abusive situations desensitizes one to the suffering of others. In one study (Main & George, 1985), for example, abused and nonabused children were exposed to a peer showing distress. Nonabused children showed concern and empathy for the distressed peer. Abused children showed a very different pattern. These children did not respond with concern or empathy but rather with anger, including physical aggression. Thus, child abuse and neglect are major contributors not only to aggressive behavior later in life but also to an attitude of less caring for another person's suffering.

There is some good news with respect to child abuse and neglect. Not all abused or neglected children show increased levels of aggression. Some factors increase a child's resiliency in the face of child abuse, which moderate the effects of abuse on aggression (Holmes et al., 2015). Abused children who show prosocial behaviors show fewer signs of psychological problems (e.g., depression, somatic problems), have caregivers with fewer problems (e.g., depression, alcoholism), and show lower levels of clinically significant aggression than abused children who do not show this pattern.

Family Disruption

Yet another family factor that contributes to aggressive behavior patterns is family disruption—for example, disruption caused by an acrimonious divorce. Research shows that disruption of the family is significantly related to higher rates of crime (Mednick et al., 1990; Sampson, 1987). One study investigated the relationship between several family variables, such as family income, male employment, and family disruption (defined as a female-headed household with children under age 18), and homicide and robbery rates among Blacks and Whites (Sampson, 1987). The study found that the single best predictor of African American homicide was family disruption.

A similar pattern emerged for robbery committed by Blacks and Whites. Family disruption, which was strongly related to living under economically deprived conditions, was found to have its greatest effect on juvenile crime, as opposed to adult crime. It was found that, at least for robbery, the effects of family disruption cut across racial boundaries. Family disruption was equally harmful to Blacks and Whites.

Another study looked at family disruption from a different perspective: the impact of divorce on children's criminal behavior (Mednick et al., 1990). The study examined Danish families that had divorced but were stable after the divorce (the divorce solved interpersonal problems between the parents); divorced but unstable after the divorce (the divorce failed to resolve interpersonal problems between the parents); and not divorced. The study showed the highest crime rates among adolescents and young adults who came from a disruptive family situation. The crime rate for those whose families divorced but still had significant conflict was substantially higher (65%) than for those whose families divorced but were stable afterward (42%) or for families that did not divorce (28%).

Clearly, an important contributor to aggression is the climate and structure of the family in which a child grows up. Inept parenting, in the form of overreliance on physical or verbal punishment, increases aggression. Child abuse and neglect, as well as family disruption, also play a role in the development of aggressive behavior patterns. Children learn their aggressive behavior patterns early as a result of being in a family environment that supports aggression. And, as we have seen, these early aggressive behavior patterns are likely to continue into adolescence and adulthood.

Study Break

This section introduced you to the social learning explanation for aggression. Before you begin the next section, answer the following questions:

1. What is social learning theory, and what is the main mechanism for learning aggression according to the theory?
2. What are aggressive scripts, how do they develop, and how do they relate to aggression?
3. What is the social interactional model of aggression, and how does it explain the origins of aggression?
4. How does aggressive parenting contribute to aggression?
5. How do punishment and modeling aggression relate to the development of aggressive behavior?
6. How do child abuse and family disruption relate to aggression?

The Role of Culture in Violent Behavior

In addition to the influence of the immediate family on the socialization of aggression, social psychologists have also investigated the role that culture plays. Cross-cultural research (Bergeron & Schneider, 2005) suggests that aggression is less likely to be seen in cultures that show the following characteristics:

1. Collectivist values
2. High levels of moral discipline
3. Egalitarian values
4. Low levels of avoiding uncertainty
5. Confucian values

There are also cultural differences with respect to the expression of verbal aggression through the use of different invectives (De Raad et al., 2005). De Raad et al. found that invectives referring to social relationships (e.g., "son of a whore," "good for nothing") were most common among Spanish participants. Participants from the Netherlands seem to prefer invectives relating to the genital region (e.g., "prick," "scrotum cleaner"), and participants from Germany prefer invectives targeting the anal region (e.g., "asshole") and social inadequacy (e.g., "spastic"). Participants from all three countries used references to abnormality to insult others.

Another cultural difference can be seen among different segments of culture in the United States. Nisbett and his colleagues have been studying this issue by comparing southern and northern regions of the United States. In a series of studies that include examining homicide statistics (Nisbett, 1993), field experiments (Nisbett et al., 1995), and laboratory experiments (Cohen, 1998), a clear trend toward greater violence among southern than northern Americans emerges.

To what can we attribute the regional differences in violence? Nisbett (1993) suggested that there are a variety of explanations for regional differences. These include traditional explanations suggesting that the South has more poverty, higher temperatures, and a history of slavery, as well as the possibility that Whites have imitated aggressive behavior seen among the Black population. Nisbett suggested that there is another more plausible explanation for the regional differences observed. He hypothesized that in the South (and to some extent in the frontier West) a **culture of honor** has evolved in which violence is both more widely accepted and practiced than in the North, where no such culture exists. Nisbett suggested that this culture of honor arose because of the different peoples who settled in the North and South in the 17th and 18th centuries.

culture of honor An evolved culture in the southern and western United States in which violence is more widely accepted and practiced than in the northern and eastern United States, where no such culture exists.

The South was largely settled by people who came from herding economies in Europe, most notably from borderlands of Scotland and Ireland (Nisbett, 1993). The North, in contrast, was settled by Puritans, Quakers, and Dutch farmers, who developed a more agriculturally based economy (Nisbett, 1993). According to Nisbett, violence is more endemic to herding cultures because it is important to be constantly vigilant against theft of one's livestock. It was important in these herding economies to respond to any threat to one's herd or grazing lands with sufficient force to drive away intruders or potential thieves. Nisbett maintains that from this herding economy arose the culture of honor that persists in the South to this day. This culture of honor primes southern individuals for greater violence than their northern counterparts.

Is there any evidence to support the supposition that individuals from a herding economy are more predisposed to honor-related aggression than those from other economies? One study provides some support for this relationship (Figueredo et al., 2004). Figueredo et al. looked at whether herding and farming populations differ in their adherence to a culture of honor, using participant samples from Mexico and other Central American countries. Consistent with the hypothesis stated by Nesbitt and his colleagues, individuals from herding populations were more likely to adhere to the culture of honor (e.g., more likely to endorse revenge) than those making up farming communities.

What evidence do we have that such a culture of honor exists and that it affects violence levels in the South? Nisbett (1993) reported that when southern and northern cities of equal size and demographic makeup are compared, there is a higher homicide rate among southern White males than among northern White males. This difference is only true for argument-related homicides, not for homicides resulting from other felonies (e.g., robbery; Cohen et al., 1996). Interestingly, this regional difference holds only for White males and not Black males (Nisbett et al., 1995). Additionally, Nisbett found a greater acceptance of violence to solve interpersonal conflicts and to respond to a perceived insult among southern than among northern White males. The differences between southern and northern White males are most pronounced for behaviors that receive moderate to low support from the general public (Hayes & Lee, 2005). Hayes and Lee found that differences emerged between northern and southern White males on the following behaviors (p. 613):

1. If an adult male stranger hit a man's child after accidentally damaging the stranger's car
2. If a drunk adult male stranger bumped into a man and his wife on the street
3. If an adult male stranger was encountered by a man at a protest rally showing opposition to the man's views

No difference was found between northerners and southerners for behaviors receiving more widespread approval. For example, no difference was found for a scenario involving an adult male punching a woman.

Findings, based on homicide rates, were verified by Nisbett and his colleagues in a series of experiments. In a field experiment (Cohen & Nisbett, 1997), employers in various parts of the United States were sent a letter from a potential job applicant who committed either an honor-based homicide (killing someone who was having an affair with his fiancé) or an auto theft. Each response was analyzed for whether an application was sent to the potential employee and the tone of the return letter. Cohen and Nisbett found that more southern-based companies sent a job application to the employee convicted of manslaughter than did northern-based companies. However, there was no difference between southern and northern companies in the rate of compliance to the employee who stole a car. Additionally, the tone of the letters coming from southern companies was warmer and more understanding of the homicide than was the tone of the letters from northern companies. Again, there was no difference in warmth or understanding between northern and southern companies for the theft letter.

Regional differences in violence between the North and South have been well documented. But is the culture of honor responsible? Are southern males more likely to react negatively to insults than northern males? In a series of interesting laboratory experiments (Cohen et al., 1996), southern and northern White males were insulted or not insulted by a male confederate of the experimenter. In one experiment, Cohen and colleagues (1996) were interested in whether there was a difference between southerners and northerners in their physiological responses to the insult. Participants were told that they were going to take part in an experiment that required monitoring of blood sugar levels. Saliva samples were obtained from participants before and after the insult (or no insult). The saliva samples were analyzed for cortisol and testosterone levels. (Cortisol is a stress-related hormone that increases when one is aroused or under stress.)

The results from this experiment are shown in Figure 10.5 (testosterone levels) and Figure 10.6 (cortisol levels). As you can see, there was no difference between insulted and noninsulted northern participants for both cortisol and testosterone levels. However, for southern participants, there was a significant rise in both cortisol and testosterone levels for insulted southern participants (compared to the noninsulted southerners). Thus, in response to an insult, southern White males are more "primed" physiologically for aggression than their northern counterparts (Cohen et al., 1996). In another experiment, Cohen and colleagues (1996) found that after being publicly insulted (compared to being privately insulted or not insulted), southern White males were more likely to experience a drop in perceived masculinity. No such difference was found for northern White males.

Cohen (1998) investigated those aspects of southern and western culture that relate most closely to the acceptance and use of violence. Cohen looked at the role of community and family stability in explaining honor-based violence. Cohen hypothesized that among

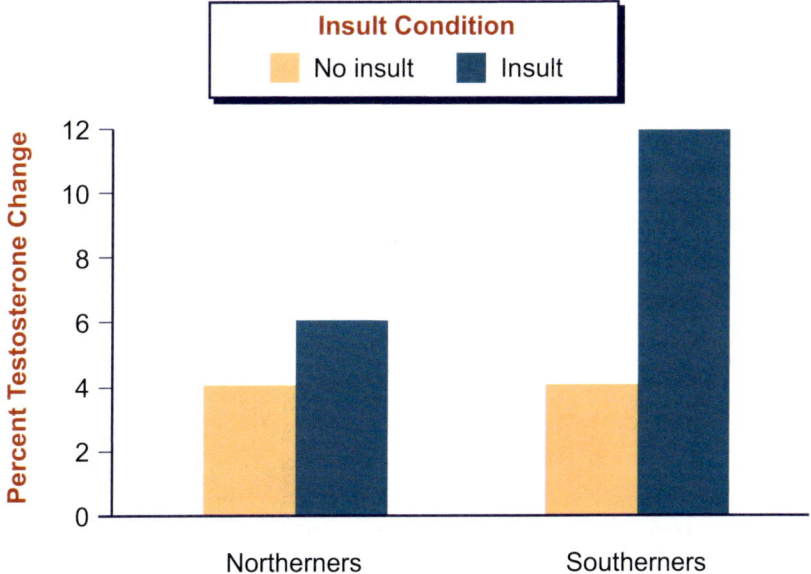

FIGURE 10.5

Percentage testosterone change as a function of culture and insult. Northerners did not show a significant increase in testosterone levels after being insulted. Southerners, on the other hand, showed substantial increases in testosterone levels after being insulted.

Based on data from Cohen et al. (1996).

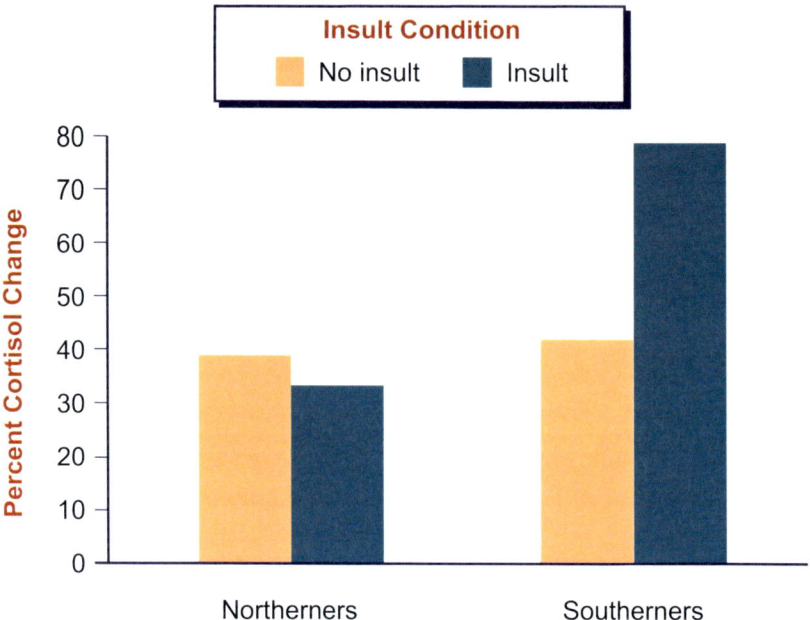

FIGURE 10.6

Percentage cortisol change as a function of culture and insult. Northerners did not show a significant increase in cortisol levels after being insulted. In contrast, southerners showed an increase in cortisol levels after being insulted.

Based on data from Cohen et al. (1996).

more stable communities, reputations and honor would have more meaning than in less stable communities. As a consequence, more honor-based violence was expected in stable than in unstable communities. Homicide rates among stable and unstable communities in the North, South, and West were compared. Cohen found a higher honor-based homicide rate among stable southern and western communities than among unstable southern and western communities. No such difference existed for stable and unstable northern communities. Cohen also found that the rate of felony-related homicides (not related to honor) was lower among stable than among unstable communities in the South and West, but not in the North. Additionally, Cohen found that honor-related homicides were higher among communities in the South and West in which traditional families (i.e., intact nuclear families) were more common than less common. The opposite was true for northern communities. Thus, the manner in which cultures evolve, with respect to stability and adherence to traditional family structures, relates closely to patterns of violence. In the South and West, evolution toward community stability (in which honor and reputation in the South and West are important) and adherence to more traditional family structures give rise to higher levels of violence. Such is not the case for northerners, for whom honor and reputation appear to be less important.

Further evidence for a unique southern culture of honor is provided in another study by Cohen (1996). Cohen compared northern and southern (and western) states with respect to gun-control laws, self-defense laws, treatment of violence used in defense of one's property, laws concerning corporal punishment, capital punishment laws, and stances taken by legislators on using military responses to threats to U.S. national interests. Cohen found that compared to northern states, southern (and western) states had more lax gun-control laws, more lenient laws concerning using violence for self-defense and protection of property, more lenient laws for domestic violence offenders (where disciplining one's wife is used as a justification for male perpetrators of domestic violence), and a greater tolerance for the use of corporal punishment. Southern states were more likely to execute condemned prisoners than northern or western states. Southern legislators were more likely to endorse the use of military force than northern (or western) states. Finally, among Whites in culture-of-honor states (but not Blacks), there is a greater preference for using firearms in suicides than in non-honor states (Brown et al., 2014). These findings support the conclusion that cultural differences, embodied in regional laws, exist between the North and South (and to a lesser extent between the West and the North). More lenient laws in the South tend to sanction and support the use of violence.

There is also a link between the culture of honor and school shootings. Argument-related school shootings are more frequent in culture-of-honor states. Seventy-five percent of school shootings have taken place in American states with relatively strong cultures of honor (Brown et al., 2009). The frequency of school shootings is higher in states that allow corporal punishment in schools and where corporal punishment is used in the home (both features of the culture of honor) (Arcus, 2002). High school students in culture-of-honor states are more likely to bring a gun to school than students in non-culture-of-honor states (Brown et al., 2009). Brown et al. suggest that threats to honor (e.g., bullying and humiliation) may have special meaning to males in culture-of-honor states that increases school shootings.

Interestingly, the culture of honor may not be unique to American culture. One study compared Polish and German young adults' views concerning using aggression to defend one's reputation (Szmajke & Kubica, 2003). Szmajke and Kubica found that Polish young adults were more favorably inclined toward using aggression in response to a social offense and expected their children to react aggressively toward provocation from other children. Additionally, the acceptance of aggression related to threatened family honor differs across cultures. In one study, 40% of male and 20% of school-aged children in Jordan indicated that it was justified to kill a female (e.g., wife, daughter) who dishonored a family (Eisner & Ghuneim, 2013). Turkish individuals who endorse honor-related values are more likely to use aggression to retaliate against a perceived threat to family honor than Americans (Uskul et al., 2015). In another study, Turkish participants indicated a greater willingness to behave aggressively after an insult than Dutch participants. This difference was more strongly related to notions of family honor among the Turkish participants than notions of masculine honor, which have been shown to be important in explaining culture-of-honor violence in the West (van Osch et al., 2013).

Study Break

This section discussed the relationship between culture and aggression. Before you begin the next section, answer the following questions:

1. Generally, how do various aspects of culture relate to aggression?
2. What is the culture of honor, and what evidence is there for its effects on aggression?
3. What are the cultural differences between the northern and southern states in the United States that relate to the culture of honor?
4. How does the culture of honor relate to school shootings?
5. What evidence is there that the culture of honor exists outside the United States?

Exposure to Media Violence and Aggression

In addition to family and culture, exposure to media violence is another factor that can contribute to aggression (Huesmann et al., 1984). As you shall see next, research shows a consistent but sometimes small relationship between exposure to media violence and aggression. In the sections that follow, we will explore three forms of media that can contribute to aggression: television, video games, and pornography. Remember, however, that despite media influences, interpersonal aggression probably can best be explained with a multiprocess model, one that includes media violence and a wide range of other influences (Huesmann et al., 1984). In all likelihood, media violence interacts with other variables in complex ways to produce aggression.

The Role of Television in Teaching Aggression

Although parents play the major role in the socialization of children and probably contribute most heavily to the development of aggressive scripts, children are exposed to other models as well. Over the years, considerable attention has focused on the role of television in socializing aggressive behaviors. Generally, most research on this topic suggests that there is a link (though not necessarily a causal link) between exposure to television violence and aggressive behavior (Coyne et al., 2019; Huesmann, 1988; Huesmann et al., 1984; Josephson, 1987). Evidence also suggests that the link between watching violent programming and aggression persists from childhood through adolescence into adulthood (Huesmann et al., 2003).

A meta-analysis conducted by Hogben (1998) revealed the following significant relationships:

1. Viewing "justified" televised violence leads to more aggression.

2. Viewing violence with "inaccurate" consequences leads to more violence.

3. Viewing "plausible" violence leads to more aggression.

4. The effect of televised violence is stronger for studies conducted outside the United States than those conducted in the United States.

5. The size of the effect of television violence on aggression is small.

Hogben estimates that if violence were eliminated from television, the overall amount of aggression we see in our culture would go down by around 10%.

We should note at this point that research in this area has traditionally focused on the effect of violent television content and direct, physical aggression. However, research has shown that there may also be an effect of depictions of indirect aggression on indirect aggressive behavior. Indirect aggression is portrayed on television and is shown more frequently (50.6%) than physical (17.8%) or verbal aggression (31.6%) (Coyne & Archer, 2004). This study also revealed that female characters on television were more likely to engage in indirect aggression than male characters. Research shows a link between viewing indirect aggression and the use of indirect aggression (Coyne & Archer, 2005; Coyne et al., 2004). For example, a study by Coyne and Archer (2005) found that girls who were exposed to media portrayals of indirect aggression tended to show higher levels of that form of aggression. Finally, there is also evidence that viewing relational aggression on television increases this type of aggression among adolescents (Coyne, 2016). In another study, Sarah Coyne and her colleagues examined this relationship by looking at the content of text messages sent by adolescents. They found that adolescents who watched television with higher levels of relational aggression were more likely to show relational aggression in text messages than those who did not. This relationship was only significant for female adolescents.

An increasingly popular genre of television is "reality television." These shows purportedly depict people in real-life situations, often depicting social forms of aggression. Is there a relationship between watching these programs and various forms of indirect aggression? Research shows that watching reality television shows can affect an individual's view of the world and acceptance of indirect aggression (e.g., gossiping about another person). For example, a national survey conducted by the Girl Scouts of America (2011) found that compared to girls who did not watch much reality television, those who did believed that gossiping is a normal part of girls' relationships (78% versus 54%, respectively), it is in a girl's nature to be catty and competitive with others (68% versus 50%), and that it is hard to trust others (63% versus 50%). Research shows that viewing reality television shows with socially aggressive content is positively correlated with self-reported frequency of social aggression (Ward & Carlson, 2013). Additionally, college-aged women who perceive reality television as real are more likely to subscribe to gender-stereotyped sex roles and view social aggression as rewarding than those who did not see reality television as real (Behm-Morawitz et al., 2016).

Some early research in the area showed that males are more influenced than females by violent television (Liebert & Baron, 1972). Other research suggests that gender may not be important in understanding the relationship between exposure to televised violence and aggression (Huesmann et al., 1984). The correlations between watching television violence and aggression are about the same for male and female children. However, one interesting gender difference exists. Children, especially males, who identify with television characters (that is, want to be like them) are most influenced by television violence.

Watching television violence may also have some subtle effects. People who watch a lot of violence on television tend to become desensitized to the suffering of others, as we saw was the case with abused children (Rule & Ferguson, 1986). Furthermore, children who watch a lot of violent television generally have a more favorable attitude toward aggressive behavior than do children who watch less.

Even sanctioned aggression can increase the incidence of aggressive behavior among those who view it on television. The impact on aggression of well-publicized heavyweight championship fights has been documented (Phillips, 1983). Among adults, homicide rates were found to increase for 3 days after these boxing matches (Miller et al., 1991). When a White person loses the match, homicides of Whites increase; when an African American loses the match, homicides of African Americans increase. A similar effect can be seen with suicide rates. The number of suicides increases during the month in which a suicide is reported in the media compared to the month before the report appears (Phillips, 1986). Interestingly, the rate remains high (again compared to the month before the report) a month after the report.

Television is one source of aggressive models for children. Research shows that the more violent television programming a child watches, the more aggressive behavior they will show. This is especially true for children already predisposed to aggressive behavior.
Source: Jack Frog/Shutterstock.

Although most studies support the general conclusion that there is a relationship between watching media portrayals of violence and aggression, a few words of caution are appropriate (Freedman, 1984):

1. The relationship may not be strong. Correlational studies report relatively low correlations between watching media violence and aggression, and experimental studies typically show weak effects.

2. Although watching violence on television is associated with increased aggression, there is evidence that watching television is also associated with socially appropriate behavior, such as cooperative play or helping another child (Gadow & Sprafkin, 1987; Mares & Woodard, 2005).

3. Other variables, such as parental aggressiveness and socioeconomic status, also correlate significantly with aggression (Huesmann et al., 1984). One 3-year study conducted in the Netherlands found that the small correlation between violent television viewing and aggression ($r = .23$ and $.29$ for boys and girls, respectively) virtually disappeared when children's preexisting levels of aggression and intelligence were taken into account (Wiegman et al., 1992).

4. Many studies of media violence and aggression are correlational and, as explained in Chapter 1, cannot be used to establish a causal relationship between these two variables. Other variables, such as parental aggressiveness, may contribute causally to both violent television viewing and aggression in children.

Individual personality characteristics and social conditions mediate the relationship between exposure to violent content and aggressive behavior. For example, Haridakis (2002) found that "disinhibition" (nonconformity to social norms) and "locus of control" (perception of the degree to which one is controlled by external events or internal motives) were significant predictors of media-related aggression. Generally, individuals with higher levels of disinhibition and have an external locus of control showed the most aggression. Children who identify with TV characters and perceive TV violence to be realistic are most affected by TV violence (Huesmann et al., 2003). Finally, violent media have a greater effect on adolescents who feel alienated from school and victimized by their peers (Slater et al., 2004).

With the connection between exposure to televised violence and aggressive behavior established, researchers have turned their attention to explaining why the relationship exists. One explanation for this relationship is that exposure to violence on television and movies contributes to the development of aggressive scripts (see our previous discussion on this topic). Another possible explanation is that exposure to aggressive media content may prime aggressive thoughts, making them more accessible (Chory-Assad, 2004). There is some evidence for this. Chory-Assad found that after watching sitcoms with high levels of verbal aggression, participants produced high numbers of verbally aggressive thoughts characterized by attacks on a person's character and competence. So, it appears that exposure to aggressive programming increases aggressive thinking patterns.

SOCIAL PSYCHOLOGY IN ACTION

Social Media and Aggression

Although there are many positives to social media, one negative consequence of its use is cyberbullying. Being the recipient of hurtful social media posts or text messages has negative consequences.
Source: Daisy Daisy/Shutterstock.

In addition to more traditional forms of media (e.g., television and video games), social media has emerged as another form of media that provides a fertile platform for aggression. Of course, we will not be talking about direct, physical aggression in the discussion that follows. However, as you learned earlier in the chapter, there are other forms of aggression that can be and are perpetrated on social media. These are more indirect forms of aggression, including verbal and relational aggression.

Social media use, to say the least, has exploded over the past decade and a half. A 2021 Pew Research Center poll showed that in 2005, 5% of U.S. adults reported using at least one social media site. In 2020, that number stood at 72%. With the growth of social media has come a new outlet for aggression (Craig et al., 2020). Craig et al. report that cyberbullying can be found across many countries. They also found that when a gender difference exists in a country, females who show signs of problematic social media use (e.g., being obsessed with using social media, complaining about not having enough screen time) are more likely to perpetrate cyberbullying than males. For intense users (those who use social media a great deal but not in a problematic way), females were more likely than males to be the victim of cyberbullying. Finally, being a victim of cyberbullying increases the likelihood of actually being a cyberbully (Whittaker et al., 2015).

People use social media for a variety of reasons. Some use it to gain information (e.g., newsfeeds), whereas others use it to form and sustain relationships (e.g., romantic relationships, friendships). Does the motivation for using social media relate to aggression? Apparently, it does. Rachel Young and her colleagues (2017) surveyed adolescents concerning their social media use and online aggression. They found that those who used social media for romantic and social belongingness reasons and for social comparison were more likely to be the victims of online aggression than those who used social media for informational and entertainment purposes.

What happens when someone is the victim of cyberbullying or another form of online aggression? In one study (Whittaker et al., 2015), participants were asked how others on social media responded to their being cyberbullied. The largest percentage (25%) said that others did nothing about it. Another 15.9% said that others urged the person doing the bullying to stop, 11.4% indicated that they bullied back, and 13.6%

(continued)

said others acted in some unspecified way to stop the cyberbullying. In some instances, victims of online aggression and their peers will retaliate with like aggression against the perpetrator. A study by Kim Sylwander et al. (2020) investigated how Swedish social media users responded to someone calling another user a "whore." They found that targets of the slur and the target's peers responded with their own sexualized and aggressive responses against the perpetrator. Another study (Chen, 2015) found that even moderately face-threatening comments elicited retaliatory aggression. Chen found that such face-threatening comments generated negative affect, which then acted to increase retaliatory aggression.

How people react to cyberbullying varies from person to person. Some people exist in what is called a *social media identity bubble*. Individuals who live in such bubbles carefully filter out and delete any posts or comments that disturb them. What results is a sanitized social media environment relatively free of threatening information and comments. Do people who live in social media bubbles respond more negatively to cyberbullying than those who do not? The answer to this question appears to be yes. Atte Oksanen et al. (2020) studied Finnish workers' reactions to workplace cyberbullying. They investigated the extent to which the participants existed in a social media bubble and how they reacted to cyberbullying. They found that cyberbullying most frequently occurred via social exclusion and aggressive/threatening messages. They also found that cyberbullying was related to increased workplace exhaustion, psychological distress, and technostress (stress related to having to use social media). Workers who existed in social media bubbles reported higher levels of stress resulting from cyberbullying than those who did not.

Can anything be done to reduce online cyberbullying and aggression? One strategy is to have people reflect on the consequences of posting hurtful material. An experiment by Kathleen Van Royen et al. (2017) tested the effectiveness of three "reflective messages" on participants' intentions to post a hurtful message. After reading a scenario in which one person uses a sexual slur toward another, participants indicated how willing they were to post such a message. Those who were willing were then exposed to one of three reflective messages. One message stated that the participant's parents and the target's parents would see the comment. A second message indicated that some bystanders would see the message. The third message reminded participants how hurtful the message would be to the target. Van Royen et al. found that all three messages were effective in reducing the intention to post the hurtful message. However, not all participants were equally affected by the messages. Participants with a low ability to inhibit their behavior were not as affected as those higher in this characteristic.

Cyberbullying (as well as offline bullying) can also be reduced by exposing students to specialized training programs. One such training program is called "Safe Surfing." The eight-session school program addresses issues such as defining cyberbullying, developing personal responsibility, and self-monitoring comments before posting them and focuses on the implications of cyberbullying (Aizenkot & Kashy-Rosenbaum, 2020). Aizenkot and Kashy-Rosenbaum found a significant reduction in offline bullying and cyberbullying after children were exposed to the Safe Surfing program. Programs could also focus on increasing empathy toward others. Research shows that adolescents low in empathy are more likely to be cyberbullies than those higher in empathy (Ang & Goh, 2010). Efforts to increase empathy would then be expected to reduce cyberbullying.

Discussion Questions

1. Can using social media lead to an increase in aggression?
2. How do people react to being cyberbullied?
3. Can anything be done to reduce online cyberbullying and aggression?

Violent Video Games and Aggression

Video games have come a long way from the original "Pong" game (a rather crude tennis game) to today's highly realistic games. Many modern video games involve elaborate stories and scenarios designed to involve the player. These story lines are quite successful in immersing the player in the game, maintaining interest and arousal (Schneider et al., 2004). Additionally, many popular games involve moderate to high levels of violence. The popularity of video games containing highly realistic violent content has raised concerns about the effects of such games on children's behavior. A major concern is that exposure to these realistic, violent games can cause children and adults to behave aggressively. In recent years social scientists have addressed this concern. In this section we shall explore the relationship between playing violent video games and overt aggression.

Social learning theory states that we learn aggression from a number of sources, such as playing violent video games.
Source: Blackregis/Shutterstock.

The main question we need to address is whether exposure to violent video games increases aggression. The answer to this question is that it can (Addo et al., 2021; Anderson & Bushman, 2001). Anderson and Bushman conducted a meta-analysis of the literature and concluded that playing violent video games increased aggression among both males and females. This was the case regardless of whether the study reported was experimental or correlational. Additionally, playing violent video games increases physiological arousal and aggressive thoughts and emotions. Violent video games were also associated with a short-term decrease in prosocial behavior. Generally, research suggests that there is a link between playing violent video games and aggression, and that link is quite strong (Anderson & Bushman, 2001; Anderson & Dill, 2000). However, the effect of playing violent video games on aggression is probably not as strong as the effect of televised violence on aggression (Sherry, 2001). Playing violent video games does not appear to increase aggression for all players (Zheng & Zhang, 2016). Jia-Kun Zheng and Qian Zhang found that male gamers and those higher in trait aggression were most likely to show aggressive behavior after playing a violent video game. Playing violent video games has also been found to increase an individual's immediate level of "state hostility." That is, playing a violent video game increases hostility while the person is playing the game (Arriaga et al., 2006).

There is evidence that playing violent video games increases aggressive thoughts and reduces feelings of empathy. These two outcomes then operate to increase aggression (Addo et al., 2021). Exposure to violent video games also affects attitudes about violence and increases aggressive behavior (Anderson, 2006; Bartholow et al., 2005). The content of violent video games tends to be realistically, graphically violent, which may affect attitudes concerning aggression (Bartholow et al., 2003). Bartholow et al. (2005) had college students play violent video games and compared them to other students who played nonviolent video games. These researchers then took short- and moderately long-term measures of the effect of playing these games. The results show that those who play violent video games become less empathetic and more hostile concerning other people and are more likely to feel and act aggressively. Playing violent video games also increases aggression-related thoughts and emotions (Anderson & Carnagey, 2009). It appears that playing these games affects the players' attitudes, thoughts, and emotions concerning violence. They become less upset by violence; it becomes more acceptable to them. Like watching violent television programming, playing violent video games desensitizes players to violence.

One explanation for the heightened aggressive attitudes of video game players is that the violent games bring forth a "hostile expectation bias" (Bushman & Anderson, 2002). This bias suggests that violent game players come to expect that other people will respond to potential conflicts by responding violently. In other words, the games condition them to expect that others will also act violently. Bushman and Anderson use the General Aggression Model (GAM) to explain these findings. The GAM model suggests that playing a violent video game promotes thinking about violence, increases the players' level of arousal, and creates angry feelings (Bushman & Anderson, 2002).

Interestingly, playing a violent video game activates parts of the brain that are commonly associated with aggressive thoughts and behavior. In a study conducted by Weber et al. (2006), participants played a video game that had violent and nonviolent sequences while undergoing a functional MRI (fMRI) scan. Weber et al. found that while playing the violent segments of the game, there was activation in the dorsal anterior cingulate cortex (normally associated with aggression) and suppression of the anterior cingulate cortex and amygdala. Weber et al. suggest that this pattern of brain activity indicates that areas of the brain associated with emotions such as empathy are suppressed, allowing the game player to engage in the violent activities needed for the game.

How about gender effects? Anderson and Bushman's (2001) meta-analysis showed that both males and females are affected by playing violent video games. Research confirms that females are affected by violent video games (Anderson & Murphy, 2003). However, one experiment suggests that the effect of violent video games is more pronounced for men than for women (Bartholow & Anderson, 2002). These researchers found that males delivered more intense punishment on another person after playing a violent video game (compared to a nonviolent video game) than females under the same conditions. Research on whether the gender of the main character a person controls affects aggression is mixed. One study found that females are most affected by violent video games when they controlled a female character in the game (Anderson & Murphy, 2003). However, another study found that both males and females showed more aggression after playing a violent video game with a male avatar than with a female avatar (Yang et al., 2014).

Although there is a large body of research suggesting that playing violent video games is related to increased aggression, there is an emerging body of research suggesting that video games may not be all that bad with respect to aggression. For example, Christopher Ferguson (2013) has questioned the validity of much of the research in this area. Ferguson points out that there is research showing that violent video games have far less impact on aggression than claimed by researchers and that there are even studies suggesting a decrease in aggression after playing a violent video game. Ferguson himself has published a study showing that playing violent video games had little effect on dating violence (Ferguson et al., 2012). Additionally, one must keep in mind that most violent video games are competitive. There is research showing that it may be the competitive nature of the games, and not the violent content, that relates to increased aggression (Adachi & Willoughby, 2013). Adachi and Willoughby found that competitive gambling games were just as strongly related to aggression as were violent video games. There is also evidence suggesting that frustration over losing a video game may account for some of the increased aggression after playing a violent video game. The negative emotion resulting from losing appears to be related to the increased aggression (Breuer et al., 2015). Further, not everyone is affected by violent video games. Long-term playing of violent video games is associated with increased aggression most strongly among people with aggressive personalities (Anderson & Dill, 2000). Among these individuals, exposure to high levels of video game violence produces high levels of aggression. Individuals with less aggressive personalities are less affected by video game violence. Based on their experimental and correlational studies, Anderson and Dill suggest that playing violent video games increases real-life aggression (delinquent behavior) and aggression under controlled conditions. They suggest that playing violent video games primes a person for aggression by increasing aggressive thoughts.

Study Break

This section discussed the relationship between watching violent television and playing violent video games on aggression. Before you begin the next section, answer the following questions:

1. What are the significant factors discussed by Hogben (1998) relating to the relationship between violent television and aggressions, and how do social psychologists explain the relationship between watching violent television and aggression?
2. What are some of the variables studied by social psychologists that relate to the relationship between watching violent television and aggression?
3. What are the four "cautions" about the relationship between watching violent television and aggression?
4. How does social media use relate to aggression?
5. What is the relationship between playing violent video games and aggression?
6. What are the effects of playing violent video games on attitudes about aggression and on the brain?
7. Why should we be cautious about concluding that playing violent video games causes aggression?

Viewing Sexual Violence: The Impact on Aggression

Television and video games are not the only media that have come under fire for depicting violence. Many groups have protested the depiction of violence against women in pornographic magazines, movies, and on the Internet. These groups claim that such sexually explicit materials influence the expression of violence, particularly sexual violence, against women in real life.

In the debate about pornographic materials, researchers have made a distinction between sexually explicit and sexually violent materials (Linz et al., 1987). Sexually explicit materials are those specifically created to produce sexual arousal. A scene in a movie depicting two nude people engaging in various forms of consensual sex is sexually explicit. Interestingly, college-aged men seem to incorporate behaviors they see in sexually explicit videos into their sexual scripts. Sun et al. (2014) found that the more pornography men watched, the more likely it was that they would use what they saw on the video during sex with their partners, request specific pornographic sexual acts from their partners, and use pornographic imagery during sex to maintain arousal. Sexually violent material includes scenes of violence within a sexual context that are degrading to women. These scenes need not necessarily be sexually explicit (e.g., showing nudity). A rape scene (with or without nudity) is sexually violent. Of course, materials can be both sexually explicit and sexually violent.

Although the causes of rape are complex (Groth, 1979; Malamuth, 1986), some researchers and observers have focused on pornography as a factor that contributes to the social climate in which sexual violence against women is tolerated. However, not all forms of pornography are associated with sexual violence. Exposure to sexually violent materials does relate to increased sexual violence (Malamuth & Check, 1983). However, mild, nonviolent forms of erotica, such as pictures found on Web sites on the Internet or scenes of sex between consenting couples, may inhibit sexual violence against women (Donnerstein et al., 1975).

In a study reported by Donnelly and Fraser (1998), 320 college students responded to a questionnaire concerning arousal to sadomasochistic fantasies and acts. The results showed that males were significantly more likely than females to be aroused by fantasizing about and engaging in sadomasochistic sexual acts. Specifically, males scored higher than females on measures of being dominant during sex, participating in bondage and discipline, being restrained, and being spanked. In terms of arousal to behaviors, males scored higher than females on watching bondage and discipline, being dominant during sex, and taking part in discipline and bondage.

Of course, sexual arousal does not usually lead to aggression. Most males can easily control their sexual and aggressive impulses. A wide range of social norms, personal ethics, and moral beliefs act to moderate the expression of violence toward women, even when conditions exist that, according to research, lead to increased violence.

As you might expect, most research on the link between viewing pornography and sexual violence has focused on males and on physical aggression. After all, males view pornography more than females. However, women do view pornography as well, and physical aggression is not the only form of sexual violence. Psychological aggression and coercion also qualify as sexual violence as well. A 2015 poll, for example, found that 31% of women reported viewing porn every week or so, with another 30% indicating they view porn a few times a month (Mirror, 2015). There is some evidence that women who view pornography are more likely than those who do not to engage in sexual coercion (Kernsmith & Kernsmith, 2009). Kernsmith and Kernsmith reported that the relationship between viewing pornography and engaging in sexual coercion was relatively strong.

When a person is exposed to pornographic materials also affects its relationship with sexual violence. In a study by Mancini et al. (2012), data were collected on participants in an ongoing longitudinal study on when they were exposed to pornography (adolescence, early adulthood, or just before a sex crime). Mancini et al. found that although exposure to pornography during adolescence was not significantly related to the likelihood of committing a sex crime, it was related to the amount of humiliation of the victim during a sex crime. Adolescent exposure to pornography related to increased levels of victim humiliation. Interestingly, exposure to pornography just before a sex crime is committed was related to a reduced amount of violence in the sex crime and less victim injury. There was no relationship between watching pornography as an adult and sexual violence.

The Impact of Sexually Violent Material on Attitudes

Besides increasing violence against women, exposure to sexually violent material has another damaging effect. It fosters attitudes, especially among males, that tacitly allow rape to continue. There is a pervasive rape myth in U.S. society, which fosters such beliefs as "only bad girls get raped," "if a woman gets raped, she must have asked for it," "women 'cry rape' only when they've been jilted or have something to cover up," and "when a woman says no, she really means yes" (Burt, 1980, p. 217; Groth, 1979). Men are more likely than women to accept the rape myth (Muir et al., 1996). Additionally, such beliefs are most common among men who believe in stereotyped sex roles, hold adversarial sexual beliefs, and find interpersonal aggression an acceptable form of behavior. Thus, the rape myth is integrally tied to a whole set of related attitudes (Burt, 1980). Interestingly, research shows that the rape myth may be stronger in U.S. culture than in other cultures. Muir et al. (1996) compared U.S. and Scottish individuals for acceptance of the rape myth. They found that the rape myth was more pervasive among Americans than Scots.

Do media portrayals of sexual violence contribute to rape myths and attitudes? Research suggests that they do. For example, in a survey of male fraternity members, Foubert et al. (2011) found a small but statistically significant positive correlation between viewing sadomasochistic or rape pornography and acceptance of the rape myth. They also found that viewing such pornography was also positively correlated with the likelihood (self-reported) of committing a sexually violent crime. In other studies (Malamuth & Check, 1981, 1985), viewing sexually explicit, violent films increased male (but not female) participants' acceptance of violence against women. Such portrayals also tended to reinforce rape myths. Media portrayals of a woman enjoying sexual violence had their strongest impact on males who were already predisposed to violence against women (Malamuth & Check, 1985). Men who are likely to commit rape also have beliefs that support the rape myth, such as a belief that rape is justified and the perception that the victim enjoyed the rape (Linz et al., 1987; Malamuth & Check, 1981).

Malamuth and Check, for example, had some participants watch films widely distributed in mainstream movie theaters that depicted sexual violence against women (e.g., *The Getaway*). In these films, the sexual violence was portrayed as justified and having positive consequences. Other participants watched films with no sexual violence (e.g., *Hooper*). After viewing the films, participants (both male and female) completed measures of rape-myth acceptance and acceptance of interpersonal violence. The results showed that for male participants, exposure to the films with sexual violence against women increased acceptance of the rape myth and acceptance of interpersonal violence against women. Female participants showed no such increase in acceptance of the rape myth or in violence against women. In fact, there was a slight trend in the opposite direction for female participants.

These "softer" portrayals of sexual violence with unrealistic outcomes in films and on television (e.g., the raped woman marrying her rapist) may have a more pernicious effect than hard-core pornography. Because they are widely available, many individuals see these materials and may be affected by them. The appetite for such films has not subsided since Malamuth and Check's 1981 experiment, and films depicting violence against women are still made and widely distributed.

Finally, one need not view sexually explicit or violent materials in order for one's attitudes toward women and sexual violence to be altered. McKay and Covell (1997) reported that male students who looked at magazine advertisements with sexual images (compared to those who saw more "progressive" images) expressed attitudes that showed greater acceptance of interpersonal violence and the rape myth. They were also more likely to express adversarial sexual attitudes and less acceptance of the women's movement.

Men Prone to Sexual Aggression: Psychological Characteristics

We have seen that male college students are aroused by depictions of rape and can be instigated to aggression against women through exposure to sexually explicit, violent materials. Does this mean that all, or at least most, males have a great potential for sexual aggression, given the appropriate circumstances? No, apparently not. Research shows that men predisposed to sexual violence are most most likely to show sexual aggression after viewing pornography (Seto et al., 2001). Psychological characteristics play a part in a man's inclination to express sexual aggression against women (Malamuth, 1986).

In one study, six variables were investigated to see how they related to self-reported sexual aggression. The six predictor variables were:

1. Dominance as a motive for sexual behavior
2. Hostility toward women
3. Accepting attitudes toward sexual aggression
4. Antisocial characteristics or psychoticism
5. Sexual experience
6. Physiological arousal to depictions of rape

Participants' sexual aggression was assessed by a test that measured whether pressure, coercion, force, and so on were used in sexual relationships. Positive correlations were found between five of the six predictor variables and sexual aggression directed against women. Psychoticism was the only variable that did not correlate significantly with aggression. However, the presence of any one predictor alone was not likely to result in sexual aggression. Instead, the predictor variables tended to interact to influence sexual aggression. For example, arousal to depictions of rape is not likely to translate into sexual aggression unless other variables are present. So, just because a man is aroused by depictions of rape, he will not necessarily be sexually violent with women. In other words, several variables interact to predispose a man toward sexual aggression. Lackie and de Man (1997) investigated the relationship between several variables, including sex-role attitudes, physical aggression, hostility toward women, alcohol use, and fraternity affiliation, and sexual aggression. Their findings showed that sexually aggressive males tended to be physically aggressive in general. Furthermore, they found that stereotyped sex-role beliefs, acceptance of interpersonal violence, masculinity, and fraternity membership were positively related to self-reported sexual aggression. They also found that the most important predictors of sexual aggression were the use of physical aggression, stereotyped sex-role beliefs, and fraternity membership. In another study, Carr and VanDeusen (2004) found a similar pattern of results. Carr and VanDeusen found that four variables significantly related to sexual violence. These were alcohol use, exposure to pornography, sexual conservatism, and acceptance of interpersonal violence. Those prone to sexual violence used alcohol and pornography to a greater extent, were more sexually conservative, and were more accepting of interpersonal violence than those less prone to sexual violence.

So, whether an individual will be sexually aggressive is mediated by other factors. For example, Dean and Malamuth (1997) found that males who are at risk for sexual violence against women were most likely to behave in a sexually aggressive way if they were also self-centered. A high-risk male who is not self-centered but rather is sensitive to the needs of others is not likely to behave in a sexually aggressive way. However, regardless of whether a high-risk male is self-centered, he is likely to fantasize about sexual violence (Dean & Malamuth, 1997). Additionally, feelings of empathy also appear to mediate sexual aggression. Malamuth, Heavey, and Linz (1993) found that males who are high in empathy are less likely to show arousal to scenes of sexual violence than males who are low in empathy (cited in Dean & Malamuth, 1997).

What do we know, then, about the effects of exposure to sexual violence on aggression? The research suggests the following conclusions:

1. Exposure to mild forms of nonviolent erotica tends to decrease sexual aggression against women.
2. Exposure to explicit or sexually violent erotica tends to increase sexual aggression against women but not against men.
3. Individuals who are angry are more likely to be more aggressive after viewing sexually explicit or violent materials than are individuals who are not angry.
4. Male college students are aroused by depictions of rape. However, men who show a greater predisposition to rape are more aroused, especially if the woman is portrayed as being aroused.
5. Exposure to media portrayals of sexual aggression against women increases acceptance of such acts and contributes to the rape myth. Thus, sexually explicit, violent materials contribute to a social climate that tolerates rape.
6. No single psychological characteristic predisposes a man to sexual aggression. Instead, several characteristics interact to increase the likelihood that a man will be sexually aggressive toward women.

Reducing Aggression

We have seen that interpersonal aggression comes in many different forms, including murder, rioting, and sexual violence. We also have seen that many different factors can contribute to aggression, including innate biological impulses, situational factors such as frustration, situational cues such as the presence of weapons, and aggressive scripts internalized through the process of socialization. We turn now to a more practical question: What can be done to reduce aggression? Although aggression can be addressed on a societal level, such as through laws regulating violent television programming and pornography, the best approach is to undermine aggression in childhood, before it becomes a life script.

Reducing Aggression in the Family

According to the social-interactional model described earlier in this chapter, antisocial behavior begins early in life and results from poor parenting. The time to target aggression, then, is during early childhood, when the socialization process is just under way.

Teachers, health workers, and police need to look for signs of abuse and neglect and intervene as soon as possible (Widom, 1992). Waiting until an aggressive child is older is not the best course of action (Patterson et al., 1989). Intervention attempts with adolescents produce only temporary reductions in aggression, at best.

One way to counter the development of aggression is to give parents guidance with their parenting. Parents who show tendencies toward inept parenting can be identified, perhaps through child-welfare agencies or schools, and offered training programs in productive parenting skills. Such training programs have been shown to be effective in reducing noncompliant and aggressive behavior in children (Forehand & Long, 1991). Children whose parents received training in productive parenting skills were also less likely to show aggressive behavior as adolescents.

What types of parenting techniques are most effective in minimizing aggression? Parents should avoid techniques that provide children with aggressive role models. Recommended techniques include positive reinforcement of desired behaviors and time-outs (separating a child from activities for a time) for undesired behaviors. Also, parenting that involves inductive techniques, or giving age-relevant explanations for discipline, is related to lowered levels of juvenile crime (Shaw & Scott, 1991). Parents can also encourage prosocial behaviors that involve helping, cooperating, and sharing. It is a simple fact that prosocial behavior is incompatible with aggression. If a child learns to be empathic and altruistic in his or her social interactions, aggression is less likely to occur. To support the development of prosocial behaviors, parents can take four specific steps (Bee, 1992, pp. 331–443):

One way that aggression can be reduced is to provide parents with guidance for their parenting, especially for parents who show patterns of inept parenting. Parents should be taught to avoid parenting practices that provide children with aggressive role models.
Source: Monkey Business Images/Shutterstock.

1. Set clear rules and explain to children why certain behaviors are unacceptable. For example, tell a child that if he or she hits another child, that other child will be hurt.

2. Provide children with age-appropriate opportunities to help others, such as setting the table, cooking dinner, and teaching younger siblings.

3. Attribute prosocial behavior to the child's internal characteristics; for example, tell the child how helpful he or she is.

4. Provide children with prosocial role models who demonstrate caring, empathy, helping, and other positive traits.

Reducing Aggression with Cognitive Intervention and Therapy

Reducing aggression through better parenting is a long-term, global solution to the problem. Another more direct approach to aggression in specific individuals makes use of cognitive intervention. We have seen that children who are exposed to violence develop aggressive scripts. These scripts increase the likelihood that a child will interpret social situations in an aggressive way. Dodge (1986) suggested that aggression is mediated by the way we process information about our social world. According to this **social information-processing view of aggression**, there are five important steps involved in instigating aggression (as well as other forms of social interaction). These are (as cited in Kendall et al., 1991):

social information-processing view of aggression A view stating that how a person processes social information mediates aggression.

1. We perceive and decode cues from our social environment.

2. We develop expectations of others' behavior based on our attribution of intent.

3. We look for possible responses.

4. We decide which response is most appropriate.
5. We carry out the chosen response.

Individuals with aggressive tendencies see their own feelings reflected in the world. They are likely to interpret and make attributions about the behaviors of others that center on aggressive intent. This leads them to respond aggressively to the perceived threat. Generally, aggressive individuals interpret the world as a hostile place, choose aggression as a desired way to solve conflict, and enact those aggressive behaviors to solve problems (Kendall et al., 1991).

Programs to assess and treat aggressive children have been developed using cognitive intervention techniques. Some programs use behavior management strategies (teaching individuals to effectively manage their social behavior) to establish and enforce rules in a nonconfrontational way (Kendall et al., 1991). Aggressive children (and adults) can be exposed to positive role models and taught to consider nonaggressive solutions to problems. Finally, interventions in the schools can also be effective in reducing aggression. In a study conducted with Israeli elementary and junior high school students, both interventions aimed at changing the classroom environment (e.g., fostering a nonaggressive climate, developing aggression-related norms) and interventions addressing an individual child's behavior in the classroom were effective in reducing aggression (Shechtman & Ifargan, 2009). Children can also be trained to think differently about situations that may give rise to aggressive behavior. In one study (Romero-López et al., 2021), a group of preschool children was enrolled in a 16-session training program designed to teach children to exercise cognitive and emotional control in aggression situations. For example, the children were read a story in which a child behaved aggressively toward another because she could not be first in line. Children then thought about a similar situation they were in and were taught different emotional and impulse-control techniques. Other children were not enrolled in the program (control group). Romero-López et al. found that compared with children in the control group, children enrolled in the training program showed better cognitive and emotional control as well as less aggressive behavior. They showed a better ability to control their emotions, resist impulses toward aggression, and avoid engaging in inappropriate behavior than did children in the control group.

Other programs focus more specifically on teaching aggressive individuals new information-processing and social skills that they can use to solve interpersonal problems (Pepler et al., 1991; Sukhodolsky et al., 2005). Individuals are taught to listen to what others say and, more importantly, think about what they are saying. They are also taught how to correctly interpret others' behaviors, thoughts, and feelings, and how to select nonaggressive behaviors to solve interpersonal problems. These skills are practiced in role-playing sessions where various scenarios that could lead to aggression are acted out and analyzed. In essence, the aggressive child (or adult) is taught to reinterpret social situations in a less-threatening, less-hostile way. Cognitively based interventions may also be effective with high-risk individuals. LeSure-Lester (2002) contrasted a cognitive intervention program that included anger recognition, self-talk, and alternatives to aggression with a more traditional intervention with a sample of abused African American adolescents. LeSure-Lester found that the cognitive intervention resulted in greater reductions in aggressive behavior than the more traditional intervention.

As you can see, cognitively based therapy techniques have produced some encouraging results. It appears that they can be effective in changing an individual's perceptions of social events and in reducing aggression. However, the jury is still out on these programs. It may be best to view them as just one technique among many to help reduce aggression.

Other therapeutic techniques might also be effective in reducing aggression. In one study conducted in Israel, group-based "bibliotherapy" involving both the mother and child was most successful in reducing children's aggression (Schectman & Birani-Nasaraladen, 2006). Among schoolchildren, using a system that reinforced nonaggressive behavior on the playground (a straight behavioral intervention) also is effective in reducing aggression (Roderick et al., 1997). Finally, a strategy called leadership implementation training (LIT) incorporates training on leadership skills into anger management group interventions

(Burt et al., 2013). The goal in LIT is to have aggressive children develop leadership skills that can be used in schools to create more positive impressions on other students and teachers. This may, in turn, result in reduced anger and aggression for these children. Burt et al. report some initial success with LIT.

Study Break

The preceding sections discussed the relationship between exposure to sexually violent materials and aggression and how aggression can be reduced. Before you read the Chapter Review, answer the following questions:

1. How do sexually explicit and sexually violent materials differ, and what are the effects of each on sexual violence?
2. How does exposure to sexually violent material affect attitudes about sexual violence?
3. What are the characteristics of men prone to sexual violence, and what conclusions can you draw about their relationship to sexual violence?
4. What steps can be taken within the family to reduce aggression?
5. What cognitive and therapeutic interventions can be used to reduce aggression?

The Valley Transportation Authority Case Revisited

The fate that befell the victims of the Valley Transportation Authority (VTA) mass shooting was the result of naked aggression directed against them. We would classify the type of aggression displayed by Samuel Cassidy as hostile aggression. Cassidy had clearly expressed anger toward his co-workers, as reported by his former wife. Apparently, he acted on those hostile emotions on the day of the shooting.

Although it would be difficult to pinpoint an exact cause for Cassidy's killing his coworkers, it is fairly clear that there were no direct physiological causes for the aggression (e.g., no damage to the prefrontal cortex of his brain). The best explanation for Cassidy's murderous behavior may lie in the frustration-aggression hypothesis. Recall that he was reported to have been frustrated and angry over his job at VTA. We have seen how frustration, mediated by anger, can provoke aggressive behavior. Recall also that Cassidy was reported to have had a short temper. His former wife described him as the type of person who let things fester and to dwell on things until he exploded in anger. It may have been that some unknown factors at work drove Cassidy over the edge until he exploded in a fit of violence. Of course Samuel Cassidy's exact motives are difficult to determine. However, many of the principles we covered in this chapter can help explain why Cassidy murdered his coworkers that day.

Chapter Review

1. **How do social psychologists define aggression?**

   For social psychologists, the term *aggression* carries a very specific meaning, which differs from a layperson's definition. For social psychologists, aggression is any behavior intended to inflict harm (whether psychological or physical) on another organism or object. Key to this definition are the notions of intent and the fact that harm need not be limited to physical harm but can also include psychological harm.

2. **What are the different types of aggression?**

   Social psychologists distinguish different types of aggression, including hostile aggression (aggression stemming from emotions such as anger or hatred) and instrumental aggression (aggression used to achieve a goal). Direct aggression refers to overt forms of aggression such as physical aggression and verbal aggression. Indirect aggression is aggression that is social in nature. Another type of aggression, called relational aggression (using social ostracism, rejection, and direct confrontation), has elements of both direct and indirect aggression. Symbolic aggression involves doing things that block another person's goals. Sanctioned aggression is aggression that society approves, such as a soldier killing in war or a police officer shooting a suspect in the line of duty.

3. **What are the gender differences in aggression?**

   Research has established that there are, in fact, differences in aggression between males and females. One of the most reliable differences between males and females is the male's greater predisposition toward direct, physical aggression, most evident among children. However, the role of gender in the use of indirect, relational aggression is still an open question. Males tend to favor physical aggression as a way to settle a dispute and are more likely than females to be the target of aggression. Females, however, tend to use verbal aggression more than males. Males and females also think differently about aggression. Females tend to feel guiltier than males about using aggression and show more concern for the harm done by aggression. The observed gender differences are most likely a result of the interaction between biological and social forces.

   Laboratory research on gender differences in aggression suggests that the difference between males and females is reliable but quite small. However, crime statistics bear out the commonly held belief that males are more aggressive than females. Across three major categories of violent crime (murder, robbery, and assault), males commit far more violent crimes than females.

4. **How can we explain aggression?**

   As is typical of most complex behaviors, aggression has multiple causes. Several explanations for aggression can be offered, including both biological and social factors.

5. **What are the ethological, sociobiological, and genetic explanations for aggression?**

   Biological explanations include attempts by ethologists and sociobiologists to explain aggression as a behavior with survival value for individuals and for groups of organisms. Ethology theory suggests that aggression is related to the biological survival and evolution of an organism. This theory emphasizes the roles of instincts and genetics. Sociobiology, like ethology, looks at aggression as having survival value and resulting from competition among members of a species. Aggression is seen as one behavior biologically programmed into an organism. There is also a genetic component for aggression, especially for males. Research has found that genetics and the common environment combine to influence aggression. Most likely, genetics operates by resulting in characteristics that predispose a person to behave aggressively. However, just because a person has a genetic predisposition for aggression does not guarantee that the person will behave aggressively.

6. **What role do brain mechanisms play in aggression?**

   The roles of brain mechanisms and hormonal influences in aggression have also been studied. Stimulation of certain parts of the brain elicits aggressive behavior. The hypothalamus is one part of the brain that has been implicated in aggression. Stimulation of one part of the hypothalamus in a cat leads to emotional aggression, whereas stimulation of another elicits predatory aggression. Interacting with social factors, these neurological factors increase or decrease the likelihood of aggression. The male hormone testosterone has also been linked to aggressive behavior. Higher concentrations of testosterone are associated with more aggression. Like brain mechanisms, hormonal influences interact with the social environment to influence aggression.

7. **How does alcohol consumption relate to aggression?**

   Although alcohol is considered a sedative, it tends to increase aggression. Research shows that individuals who are intoxicated behave more aggressively than those who are not. Furthermore, it is not only the pharmacological effects of alcohol that increase aggression. An individual's expectations about the effects of alcohol also can increase aggression after consuming a beverage believed to be alcoholic. Alcohol appears to operate on the brain to reduce levels of the neurotransmitter serotonin. This reduction in serotonin is related to increased aggression. Furthermore, alcohol tends to suppress the executive cognitive functions that normally operate to mediate aggressive responses. The alcohol-aggression link is mediated by individual characteristics and the social situation. Individuals, especially men, who are high on a characteristic known as *dispositional empathy* are less likely to behave aggressively. It appears that alcohol interacts with individual characteristics and the social situation to influence aggression.

8. **What is the frustration-aggression hypothesis?**

   The frustration-aggression hypothesis suggests that aggression is caused by frustration resulting from blocked goals. This hypothesis has raised much controversy. Once frustrated, we choose a target for aggression. Our first choice is the source of the frustration, but if the source is an inappropriate target, we may vent our frustration against another target. This is called displaced aggression. Whether aggression is displaced depends on three factors: the intensity of the original frustration, the similarity between the original and displaced target, and the negativity of the interaction between the individual and original target.

9. **How does anger relate to frustration and aggression, and what factors contribute to anger?**

   A modified version of the frustration-aggression hypothesis suggests that frustration does not lead to aggression unless a negative emotion such as anger is aroused. Anger may be aroused under several conditions. Cognitive mediators, such as attributions about intent, have been found to play a role in the frustration-aggression link as well. If we believe that another person intends to harm us, we are more likely to react aggressively. If we are given a good reason for why another person has frustrated us, we are less likely to react aggressively.

   Another social psychological mechanism operating to cause aggression is perceived injustice. Aggression can be used to restore a sense of justice and equity in such situations. Research suggests that a perceived inequity in a frustrating situation is a stronger cause for aggression than frustration itself.

   High temperature also relates to frustration-related aggression. Research shows that under conditions of high temperature, aggression is likely to occur. One explanation for this is that heat makes people cranky and more likely to interpret situations as aggressive, calling for an aggressive response.

10. **How does social learning theory explain aggression?**

    According to social learning theory, aggression is learned, much like any other human behavior. The primary means of learning for social learning theorists is observational learning, or modeling. By watching others, we learn new behaviors or have preexisting behaviors inhibited or disinhibited. Research confirms the role of early experience in the development of aggressive behavior. Additionally, there is continuity between childhood aggression and adult aggression.

11. **What are aggressive scripts, and how do they relate to aggression?**

    One mechanism believed to underlie the relationship between observation and aggression is the formation of an aggressive script during the socialization process. These aggressive scripts lead a person to behave more aggressively and to interpret social situations in aggressive terms. During the socialization process, children develop aggressive scripts and behavior patterns because they are exposed to acts of aggression, both within the family and in the media.

12. **How does the family socialize a child into aggression?**

    Research shows that aggressive behavior patterns develop early in life.

    According to the social-interactional model, antisocial behavior such as aggression results from inept parenting. Parental use of physical or verbal aggression is related to heightened aggressiveness among children, a finding that extends across cultures. Physical punishment is significantly associated with a variety of negative outcomes, including aggressive behavior, lower levels of moral internalization of behavior, degraded parent-child relationships, and poorer mental health. Other research shows that verbal aggression directed at children by parents is particularly problematic. Verbal aggression may signal parental rejection, which has been associated with a host of negative outcomes, including aggression.

    Child abuse and neglect also have been found to be related to increases in aggression (as measured by violent crime). In addition, child abuse leads to a desensitization to the suffering of others. An abused child is likely to respond to an agemate in distress with anger and physical abuse, rather than concern or empathy (as would a nonabused child). Child abuse, then, leads to a callous attitude toward others as well as to increases in aggression.

    Finally, family disruption also relates to increases in aggression. Children from disrupted homes have been found to engage in more criminal behavior as adults than children from nondisrupted homes.

13. **What is the role of culture in aggression?**

    An individual's level of aggressiveness relates to the cultural environment within which he or she is reared. Cross-cultural research shows that aggression is less likely to occur in cultures that have collectivist values, high levels of moral discipline, egalitarian values, low levels of avoiding uncertainty, and Confucian values.

    Research comparing individuals from the American South with the American North has shown differences in attitudes toward using aggression. Generally, individuals from the South are more favorable toward using aggression than individuals from the North. One explanation for this is that a culture of honor has developed in the South (and the West) because different people settled these regions during the 17th and 18th centuries. The South was settled by people from herding economies, and these people were predisposed to be constantly vigilant for theft of their stock and react with force to drive intruders away to protect their property. From this the culture of honor emerged, which is related to increased honor-related aggression.

14. **What role do the media play in aggression?**

    One important application of social learning theory to the problem of aggression is the relationship between media portrayals of aggression and aggressive behavior. Research suggests that children who watch aggressive television programs tend to be more aggressive. Although some early research suggested that males were more affected by television violence than were females, more recent research suggests that there is no reliable, general difference between males and females. One gender difference that does emerge is that children, especially males, who identify with television characters are most affected by television violence. Additionally, heavy doses of television violence desensitize individuals to violence. A meta-analysis has shown that televised violence is most likely to lead to overt aggression when the violence shown on television is justified, is shown as having inaccurate consequences, and is plausible.

Although many studies have established a link between watching media violence and aggression, the observed effects are small. Additionally, televised violence does not affect everyone in the same way. Some individuals are more prone to be affected by televised violence than others.

15. How does social media use relate to aggression?

Social media can contribute to aggression, especially indirect forms of aggression, including verbal and relational aggression. With the growth of social media has come a new outlet for aggression: cyberbullying. Females who show problematic social media use are more likely to cyberbully others than are males. Being a victim of cyberbullying increases the likelihood of being a cyberbully. Additionally, those who use social media for romantic and social belongingness reasons and for social comparison are more likely to be the victims of online aggression than those who use social media for informational and entertainment purposes. How individuals respond to being cyberbullied varies from person to person. Individuals who live in a social identity bubble carefully filter out and delete any posts that are offensive to them. People who live in such bubbles report higher levels of stress resulting from cyberbullying than those who do not. Cyberbullying can be reduced by having people reflect on the consequences of posting hurtful material. It can also be reduced by exposing students to specialized training programs. Such programs can be effective if they address issues such as defining cyberbullying, developing personal responsibility, and self-monitoring comments before posting them and focus on the implications of cyberbullying.

16. What are the effects of playing violent video games on aggressive behavior?

Research shows that playing violent video games increases aggression and positive attitudes toward aggression among both males and females. Additionally, playing violent video games increases physiological arousal, aggressive thoughts and emotions, and state hostility. Violent video games are also associated with a short-term decrease in prosocial behavior. Playing a violent video game activates parts of the brain that are commonly associated with aggressive thoughts and behavior, while suppressing parts of the brain associated with empathy. Finally, playing violent video games does not affect everyone equally. Long-term playing of violent video games is associated with increased aggression most strongly among people with aggressive personalities.

17. What is the link between sexual violence portrayed in the media and sexual aggression directed toward women?

The research on the link between violent sexual media portrayals and violence directed at women leads to six conclusions: (1) Exposure to mild forms of erotica tends to decrease sexual violence against women. (2) Exposure to explicit or sexually violent erotica increases aggression against women but not against men. (3) Individuals who are angry are more likely to be more aggressive after viewing sexually explicit or violent materials than individuals who are not angry. (4) Male college students are aroused by depictions of rape. However, individuals who show a greater predisposition to rape are more aroused, especially if the victim is shown being aroused by sexual violence. (5) Exposure to media portrayals of sexual violence increases acceptance of violence against women and contributes to the rape myth. Thus, sexually explicit, violent pornography contributes to a social climate that tolerates rape. (6) There is no single psychological characteristic that predisposes a man to sexual violence. Instead, several characteristics interact to increase the likelihood that a man will be sexually violent.

18. How can aggression be reduced?

Many factors contribute to aggression, including biological predispositions, frustration, the presence of aggressive cues, the media, and family factors. The most fruitful approach to reducing aggression is to target family factors that contribute to aggression. Aggression can be reduced if parents change inept parenting styles, do not abuse or neglect their children, and minimize family disruption. Parents should reduce or eliminate their use of physical and verbal aggression directed at children. Positive reinforcement for desired behavior and time-out techniques should be used more often. Socializing children to be altruistic and caring can also help reduce aggression.

According to the cognitive approach, children are encouraged to reinterpret situations as nonaggressive. The social information-processing view of aggression maintains that there are five important steps involved in the instigation to aggression: We perceive and decode cues from our social environment, we develop expectations of others' behavior based on our attribution of intent, we look for possible responses, we decide which response is most appropriate, and we carry out the chosen response. The cognitive approach suggests that aggressive individuals need to change their view of the world as a hostile place, to manage their aggressive impulses, and to learn new social skills for managing their interpersonal problems.

Key Terms

Aggression (p. 393)
Aggressive script (p. 414)
Bullying (p. 394)
Culture of honor (p. 420)
Direct aggression (p. 394)
Ethology (p. 397)
Frustration-aggression hypothesis (p. 406)
Heat effect (p. 410)
Hostile aggression (p. 393)
Hypothalamus (p. 400)
Indirect aggression (p. 394)
Instrumental aggression (p. 393)
Observational learning (p. 412)
Relational aggression (p. 394)
Sanctioned aggression (p. 394)
Social information-processing view of aggression (p. 434)
Social-interactional model (p. 414)
Social learning theory (p. 412)
Sociobiology (p. 398)
Symbolic aggression (p. 394)

Chapter Quiz

1. "Any behavior that is intended to inflict harm on another person or object" is the definition offered in your text for which term?
   A. Violence
   B. Hostility
   C. Aggression
   D. None of the above

2. Jeff's father tells him that he cannot go to a Halloween party. Jeff becomes angry, stomps upstairs, and breaks a window. This is an example of
   A. hostile aggression.
   B. instrumental aggression.
   C. symbolic aggression.
   D. sanctioned aggression.

3. With respect to gender differences in physical aggression,
   A. women generally display higher levels of physical aggression than men.
   B. men generally display higher levels of physical aggression than women.
   C. both men and women display equally high levels of physical aggression.
   D. both men and women display equally low levels of physical aggression.

4. Sociobiologists argue that aggression serves to
   A. satisfy instinctive pressures toward aggression.
   B. reduce frustration.
   C. relieve frustration.
   D. resolve disputes over common limited resources.

5. Research on the role of brain mechanisms in aggression has shown that the _____ plays an important role in aggression.
   A. cerebellum
   B. brainstem
   C. hypothalamus
   D. thalamus

6. Increases in aggression have been associated with drops in the levels of which neurotransmitter?
   A. Dopamine
   B. Serotonin
   C. Acetylcholine
   D. Melatonin
   E. All of the above

7. According to the frustration-aggression hypothesis, which is a cause of aggression?
   A. Elevated levels of testosterone
   B. Frustration resulting from blocked goals
   C. Frustration resulting from watching others behave aggressively
   D. None of the above

8. In social learning theory, the principal channel of learning is
   A. direct reinforcement of aggressive behavior.
   B. direct punishment of aggressive behavior.
   C. observational learning.
   D. classical conditioning.

9. According to your text, individuals who live in a(n) _____ are most likely to react negatively to cyberbullying.
   A. social media bubble
   B. collectivist culture
   C. individualistic culture
   D. southern or western region of the United States

10. Playing violent video games has been found to increase _____ and reduce _____.
    A. hostile thoughts; empathy
    B. hostile thoughts; aggressive behavior
    C. empathy; aggressive behavior
    D. empathy; hostile thoughts

Answers can be found in the end-of-book Answers section.

Prosocial Behavior and Altruism

Whoever destroys a single life is as guilty as though he had destroyed the entire world; and whoever rescues a single life earns as much merit as though he had rescued the entire world.

—The Talmud

CHAPTER 11

Source: Rawpixel.com/Shutterstock.

Key Questions

As you read this chapter, find the answers to the following questions:

1. What is altruism, and how is it different from helping behavior? Why is the difference important?
2. What are empathy and egoism, and how do they relate to altruism?
3. What about the idea that we may help to avoid guilt or shame?
4. What is pathological altruism, and what types of maladaptive behavior can it contribute to?
5. What role does biology play in altruism?
6. How do social psychologists explain helping in an emergency situation?
7. What factors affect the decision to help?
8. If you need help, how can you increase your chances of receiving help?
9. Other than traditional helping in emergency situations, what other forms of helping are there?
10. How do personality characteristics relate to helping?
11. What situational and personality variables played a role in the decision to help Jews in Nazi-occupied Europe?

When Irene Gut Opdyke was growing up in Poland during the 1930s, she could never have imagined the fate that the future had in store for her. Irene was born in a small village in Poland on May 5, 1922. Early in her life she decided to enter a profession that involved helping others, so she enrolled in nursing school. However, Irene had to flee her home when the Nazis invaded Poland in 1939. Irene eventually joined a Polish underground unit but was beaten and raped by a group of Russian soldiers who found her group in the woods.

Next, Irene decided to try to find her family and began making her way back home. She was captured in a church by the Germans and forced to work in a munitions plant. The work was physically demanding, and one day Irene collapsed under the burden of her work. Because of her youth, Aryan appearance, and good looks, Irene caught the eye of a German major named Eduard Rugemer. Rugemer arranged for Irene to work in a local hotel that catered to German army and SS officers. Her primary duties involved serving the officers their meals.

It was during her period of employment at the hotel that she first noticed what was happening to Jews. She saw firsthand the treatment the Jews endured in the ghetto behind the hotel. She saw a baby flung into the air and shot by a Nazi. She then decided that she had to do something. One of her first helping acts was to save table scraps and

441

12. What factors contribute to a person's developing an altruistic personality?
13. What is the interactionist view of altruism?
14. How does long-term helping relate to models of emergency helping?
15. What factors influence a person's likelihood of seeking and receiving help?
16. What reactions do people show to receiving help?

leave them for the starving dwellers of the ghetto. As the war progressed, the Germans were forced to move their munitions plant to Ternopol, Poland. Here Irene resumed her duties serving meals. Major Rugemer also put Irene in charge of the laundry, where she met a family of Jews and befriended them. Irene started helping them by giving them food and blankets. Around this time Major Rugemer also made Irene his personal housekeeper. One day while serving a meal to the German officers, she overheard a conversation indicating that more and more Jews were to be rounded up and killed. Her friends in the laundry were clearly in danger. So, Irene made a momentous decision. She decided to hide the Jews to save them from extermination.

At first she hid the group behind a false wall in the laundry area. Then she hid them in a heating duct in Major Rugemer's apartment. When Major Rugemer moved to a large villa with servant's quarters in the cellar and a bunker beneath the house, Irene took her charges and hid them in the cellar of Major Rugemer's villa.

One day Irene was at the marketplace in town when the Gestapo herded everyone into the town center. There a Polish family was hanged along with the Jewish family they were hiding. Usually when Irene returned home, she locked the door and left the key turned in the lock so nobody could come in unexpectedly. Irene was so shaken by what she had witnessed that she locked the door, but pulled the key out of the lock. Two members of the Jewish family, Fanka Silberman and Ida Bauer, came out of the cellar to help Irene with her chores. The three were in the kitchen when Major Rugemer came home unexpectedly and found them. Irene had been caught, and the Jews were in danger. Major Rugemer, visibly angry, retreated to his study. Irene followed him and made a plea for her Jewish friends. Major Rugemer agreed to let the Jews stay, but at a cost. Irene would have to become his mistress.

Eventually, Ternopol was liberated by the advancing Russian army. Irene and her charges fled into the woods to await liberation. Irene Opdyke's courageous acts were directly responsible for saving Fanka Silberman, Henry Weinbaum, Moses Steiner, Marian Wilner, Joseph Weiss, Alex Rosen, David Rosen, Lazar Haller, Clara Bauer, Thomas Bauer, Abram Klinger, Miriam Morris, Hermann Morris, Herschel Morris, and Pola Morris. Without Irene's help they all surely would have ended up in labor and/or death camps. After the war Irene's story was verified, and she was designated a *righteous rescuer* by the state of Israel.

What motivated Irene Opdyke? Why did she risk her relatively secure position with Major Rugemer for people she had only recently befriended? And, what about Major Rugemer's decision to allow Irene to continue hiding the Jews at his villa? Was his action altruistic, or did he have another reason for his behavior? Why do we care about the fate of other people? Indeed, do we care at all? These are fundamental questions about human nature. Theologians, philosophers, evolutionary biologists, and novelists all have suggested answers. Social psychologists have suggested answers, too, contributing their empirical findings to the discussion.

Irene Opdyke's behavior was clearly out of the ordinary. Very few Poles were willing to risk their lives to save Jews. A notable aspect of Irene's behavior was that she expected nothing in return, neither material nor psychological rewards. In fact, rescuers such as Irene Opdyke typically shy away from the hero status awarded them. In her mind, she did what had to be done—end of story. Regardless, her actions were purely altruistic. So Irene was an unusual human being—but not unique. Others, albeit few, have performed equally selfless acts.

In this chapter we consider why people help others, when they help, and what kinds of people help. We ask, what lies behind behavior such as Irene Opdyke's? Does it spring from compassion for her fellow human beings? Does it come from a need to be able to sleep at night, to live with ourselves? Or is there some other motivation? What circumstances led Opdyke to offer the help she did, and what process did she go through to arrive at this decision? Or was her decision more a function of her character, her personal traits? Was she perhaps an example of an altruistic personality? And what about the people Irene Opdyke saved? How did receiving her help affect them? What factors determined how they responded to that help? These are some of the questions addressed in this chapter.

Why Do People Help?

There are two types of motives for behaviors such as Irene Opdyke's. Sometimes we help because we want to relieve a person's suffering. Behavior motivated by the desire to relieve a victim's suffering is called **altruism**. Other times we help because we hope to gain something from it for ourselves. We may give to a charity to get a tax deduction, for example, or we may give because we think it makes us look good. Often, we experience personal satisfaction and increased self-esteem after helping. When we give help with an eye on the reward we will get, our behavior is not really altruistic. It falls into the category of behaviors known simply as *helping behavior*.

altruism Helping behavior motivated purely by the desire to relieve a victim's suffering and not by the anticipation of reward.

Notice that the distinction between altruism and helping behavior lies in the motivation for performing the behavior, not the outcome. A person who is motivated purely by the need to relieve the suffering of the victim may receive a reward for his or her actions. However, he or she didn't perform the actions with the expectation of receiving that reward. This marks the behavior as altruistic.

The distinction between altruism and helping behavior may seem artificial because the outcome in both cases is that someone in need receives help. Does it matter what motivates the behavior? Yes, it does. The quality of the help given may vary according to the motivation behind the behavior. For example, there were others besides Irene Opdyke who helped rescue Jews, but some of them were paid for their efforts. The Jews who paid their helpers were not necessarily treated very well. In fact, Christians in Nazi-occupied Europe who helped hide Jews for pay did not extend the same level of care as those who were not paid. Jews hidden by "paid helpers" were more likely to be mistreated, abused, and turned in than were those hidden by the more altruistic "rescuers" (Tec, 1986). Additionally, the motivation behind the helping relates to how long a person is willing to help. For example, individuals who helped victims (e.g., by donating money) after the September 11, 2001, terrorist attacks expressed a number of motivations for helping, including making oneself feel better and helping victims. In the short term, a number of these motives correlated with helping. However, after a year, only a desire to relieve the suffering of others was important in determining helping (Piferi et al., 2006). So, people focused on helping victims are most likely to sustain helping over a long period of time.

The question posed by social psychologists about all of these acts is: What motivates people to help? Is there really such a thing as altruism, or are people always hoping for some personal reward when they help others? Researchers have proposed a number of hypotheses to answer this question.

Empathy is the capacity to vicariously experience the suffering of others and is positively related to altruism.
Source: Monkey Business Images/Shutterstock.

Empathy: Helping in Order to Relieve Another's Suffering

Social psychologist C. Daniel Batson (1987, 1990a, 1990b) suggested that we may help others because we truly care about them and their suffering. This caring occurs because humans have strong feelings of *empathy*—compassionate understanding of how the person in need feels. Feelings of empathy encompass sympathy, pity, and sorrow (Eisenberg & Miller, 1987).

What cognitive and/or emotional experience underlies empathy? Batson et al. (1997) suggested that *perspective taking* is at the heart of helping acts. According to Batson and colleagues, there are two perspectives that are relevant to helping situations: *imagine other* and *imagine self*. An imagine-other perspective operates when you think about how the person in need of help perceives the helping situation and the feelings that are aroused in that situation. An imagine-self perspective operates when you imagine how you would think and feel if you were in the victim's situation. Batson and colleagues predicted that the perspective taken affects the arousal of empathy or personal distress.

Batson and colleagues (1997) conducted an experiment in which participants were told to adopt one of three perspectives while listening to a story about a person in need (Katie). In the *objective-perspective* condition, participants were instructed to be as objective as possible and not to imagine what the person had been through. In the *imagine-other* condition, participants were instructed to try to imagine how the person in need felt about what had happened. In the *imagine-self* condition, participants were told to imagine how they themselves would feel in the situation. Batson and colleagues measured the extent to which the manipulation produced feelings of empathy or personal distress.

Batson and colleagues (1997) found that participants in both imagine conditions felt more empathy for Katie than did those in the objective condition. Furthermore, they found that participants in the imagine-other condition felt more empathy than did those in the imagine-self condition. Participants in the imagine-self condition were more likely to experience personal distress than empathy. Thus, two emotional experiences were produced, depending on which perspective a person took.

How does empathy relate to altruism? Although attempts to answer this question have been somewhat controversial, it appears that empathy, once aroused, increases the likelihood of an altruistic act. This is exactly what is predicted from Batson and colleagues' (1997) **empathy-altruism hypothesis**. Psychologists, however, have never been comfortable with the idea that people may do selfless acts. The idea of a truly altruistic act runs contrary to the behaviorist tradition in psychology. According to this view, behavior is under control of overt reinforcers and punishers. Behavior develops and is maintained if it is reinforced. Thus, the very idea of a selfless, nonrewarded act seems farfetched.

empathy-altruism hypothesis An explanation suggesting that the arousal of empathy leads to altruistic acts.

Empathy and Egoism: Two Paths to Helping

When we see or hear about someone in need, we often experience personal distress. Now, distress is an unpleasant emotion, and we try to avoid it. After all, most of us do not like to see others suffer. Therefore, we may give help not out of feelings of empathy for victims but in order to relieve our own personal distress. This motive for helping is called *egoism*. For example, if you saw the suffering after Hurricane Katrina and thought, "If I don't do something, I'll feel terrible all day," you would be focused on your own distress rather than on the distress of the victims. Generally, egoistic motives are more self-centered and selfish than empathic motives (Batson et al., 1987). Thus, there are different paths to helping, one involving empathy and the other personal distress. Along the "egoism" path, after seeing someone suffering, it arouses feelings of our own personal distress. The distress can lead to a number of behaviors, one of which being helping. However, along this path, helping is not guaranteed. A person could choose to flee the situation to reduce the personal distress. So, you could turn off the television so you no longer see the victims of Katrina suffering. Along the second path, the suffering of others arouses empathy. The only way to reduce the empathic motivation is to help the victims. So, rather than turning off the television, you may pick up the telephone and donate to a victim's relief organization.

How can we know which of these two paths better explains helping behavior? Note that when the motivation is to reduce personal distress, helping is only one solution. Another is to remove ourselves from the situation. But when the motivation is altruistic, only one solution is effective: helping the victim. The egoist, motivated by reducing personal distress, is more likely to respond to someone in need by escaping the situation if possible. The altruist, motivated by empathy for the victim, is not.

Batson designed some experiments to test the relative merits of the personal distress versus the empathy-altruism explanations by varying the ease with which participants could avoid contact with the person in need. In one study, participants watched someone (apparently) experiencing pain in response to a series of electric shocks (Batson, 1990a). Some participants were told that they would see more of the shock series—the difficult-escape condition. Others were told that they would see no more of the shock series, although the victim would still get shocked—the easy-escape condition.

The personal distress reduction explanation predicts that everyone will behave the same in this situation. When escape is easy, everyone will avoid helping—we all want to relieve our feelings of personal distress. When escape is difficult, everyone will help— again, we all want to relieve our feelings of personal distress. The empathy-altruism explanation, on the other hand, predicts that people will behave differently, depending on their motivation. This will be particularly apparent when it is easy to escape. Under these conditions, those motivated by egoistic concerns will escape. Those motivated by empathy will help even though they easily could have escaped.

Batson's research confirmed the empathy hypothesis, which predicts that empathic feelings matter very much. Some people chose to help even when escape was easy, indicating that it was their caring about the victim, not their own discomfort, that drove their behavior (Figure 11.1). In a replication of Batson's original experiment employing all female participants, the same pattern of results was found (Bierhoff & Rohmann, 2004). When escape was easy, empathic individuals were more likely to help than egoistic

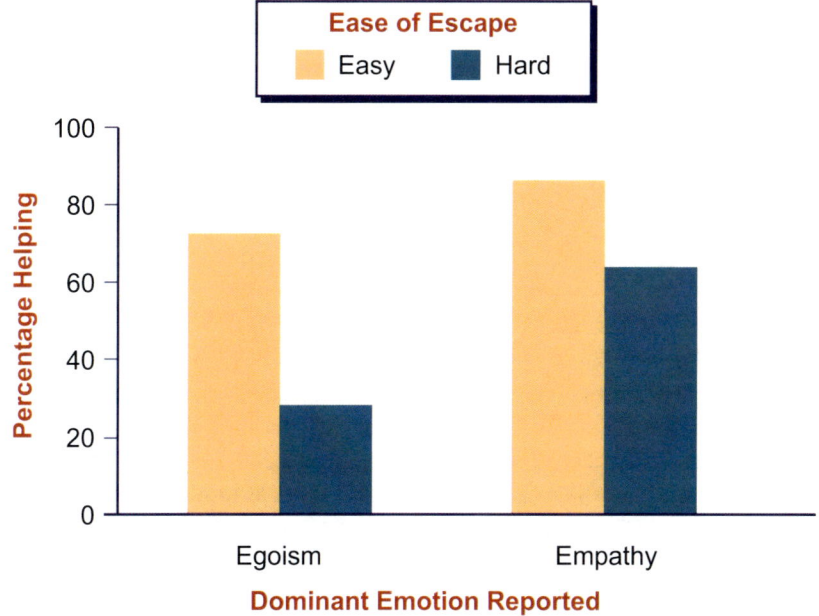

FIGURE 11.1

The relationship between the emotion experienced, ease of escape, and helping.
Based on data from Batson et al. (1988).

individuals. No such difference emerged for the difficult escape condition. Other research shows that it is the helper's empathic feelings for the person in need that are the prime motivators for helping (Dovidio et al., 1990).

In a different test of the empathy-altruism hypothesis, Batson and Weeks (1996) reasoned that if a person aroused to empathy tries to help a person in distress and fails, there should be a substantial change in the helper's state of mind to a negative mood. They reasoned further that less negative mood change would result when little or no empathy was aroused. The results of their experiment confirmed this. Participants in the high-empathy condition experienced greater negative mood shifts after failed help than participants in the low-empathy condition.

Interestingly, empathy does not always lead to an increase in altruism. Batson and colleagues (1999) demonstrated that both egoism and empathy can lead to reduced helping or, what they called a "threat to the common good." Batson and colleagues gave participants the opportunity to divide resources among a group or keep them for themselves (egoism). In one group-allocation condition, one of the group members aroused the empathy of the participants. In a second group-allocation condition, there was no group member who aroused empathy. In both group conditions, participants could choose to allocate resources to the group as a whole or to an individual member of the group. Batson and colleagues found that when a participant's allocation scheme was private, he or she allocated fewer resources to the group than the self. This was true regardless of whether the empathy-arousing victim was present. Conversely, when allocation strategies were public, participants allocated fewer resources to the group as a whole only when the empathy-arousing victim was present. The research from Batson and colleagues suggests that both egoism and empathy can threaten the common good. However, potential evaluation by others (the public condition) strongly inhibits those motivated by egoism but not empathy.

Empathy appears to be a powerful emotion that can lead to helping even when the altruistic individual has been treated badly by another. In an imaginative experiment by Batson and Ahmad (2001), female participants took part in a game involving an exchange of raffle tickets. The participant was given three tickets worth +5, +5 and –5. The participant was told that her partner in the game (there was no partner; the partner's behavior was determined by the experimenter) had the same tickets (+5, +5, and –5). Batson and Ahmad aroused high empathy for the partner for some participants and low empathy for others. On the first exchange the "partner" gave the participant the –5 raffle ticket, meaning that the partner was in effect trying to keep as many tickets as possible. The measure of altruism was the number of participants who would give a +5 ticket to the partner. The empathy-altruism hypothesis predicts that participants experiencing high empathy for the partner should be willing to give the partner positive raffle tickets, despite the defection by the partner. The results were consistent with this prediction: 45% of the high-empathy participants gave the defecting partner the +5 ticket, whereas only 10% of the low-empathy participants gave the +5 ticket.

Finally, empathy is an emotion that is not directed equally to all individuals in need. Empathy has been found to be a stronger predictor of helping when an in-group member needs help than if an out-group member needs help (Sturmer et al., 2005).

Challenging the Empathy-Altruism Hypothesis

Everett Sanderson was standing on a subway platform one day when a woman fell onto the tracks. Sanderson leapt down onto the tracks and pulled the woman to safety just moments before a train rushed into the station. When asked why he went to a stranger's aid, he replied that he would not have been able to live with himself had he not helped. Perhaps people help because not helping would violate their view of themselves as moral and altruistic and would make them feel guilty. Or, perhaps they are concerned with what others may think if they do not help, and they would experience shame. The notion that people may help because of the shame and guilt they will feel if they do not help—known as the **empathy-punishment hypothesis**—presents a challenge to the empathy-altruism hypothesis.

Batson accepted the challenge of this hypothesis. He thought that people who help to avoid guilt or shame should help less when provided with a good justification for not helping. After all, if you can plausibly justify not helping to other people (avoid shame)

empathy-punishment hypothesis A hypothesis suggesting that helping occurs because individuals are motivated to avoid the guilt or shame brought about by failure to help.

and to yourself (avoid guilt), then no punishment occurs. If, however, your motive for helping is purely altruistic, then reduction of the victim's distress is the issue, not good rationalizations for not helping.

Batson and his colleagues (1988) designed research to pit the empathy-altruism hypothesis against the empathy-punishment explanation. There were two variables in this experiment: the participant's level of empathy for the victim (high or low) and the strength of the justification for not helping (strong or weak). Participants listened to a simulated news interview in which a college senior (Katie) was interviewed about her parents' and sister's recent deaths in an automobile accident and her current role as sole supporter of her younger brother and sister. Empathy was manipulated by instructing participants either to pay attention to the "technical aspects" of the news program (low empathy) or to "try to imagine how the person who is being interviewed feels" (Batson et al., 1988, p. 61).

After hearing the news program, the participants read two letters left by the professor in charge of the experiment. The first letter thanked the participants for participating and indicated that it occurred to him that some participants might want to help Katie. The second letter was from Katie herself, outlining ways that the participants could help her (e.g., babysitting, helping around the house, helping with fundraising projects). Participants indicated their willingness to help on a response form that was used for the justification manipulation. The response form had eight spaces for individuals to indicate whether they would help Katie. In all cases, seven of the eight spaces were already filled in with fictitious names. In the low justification for not helping condition, five of the seven individuals on the list had agreed to help Katie. In the high justification for not helping condition, only two of the seven agreed to help.

The empathy-punishment explanation predicts that when there is a strong justification for not helping, the amount of empathy aroused won't matter. The empathy-altruism hypothesis predicts that empathic motivation matters most when justification for not helping and empathy are high. Only when people fail to empathize with the person in need does high justification for not helping have an effect on helping. The results of the research support the empathy-altruism hypothesis (Batson, 1990a; Batson et al., 1988). If a person has empathic feelings and truly cares about the person in need, rationalizations, however strong, do not stop him or her from helping.

Yet another challenge to the empathy-altruism hypothesis comes from research by Cialdini and his colleagues. Cialdini suggested that the data supporting the empathy-altruism hypothesis can be reinterpreted with changes in one's sense of self that occur in empathy situations. Cialdini and colleagues argued that in addition to arousing empathic concern about a person in distress, helping situations also arouse a greater sense of self-other overlap. Specifically, the helper sees more of himself or herself in the person in need (Cialdini et al., 1997). When this occurs, the helper may engage in helping because of a greater sense of closeness with the victim than with the arousal of empathic concern alone.

Cialdini and colleagues (1997) conducted three experiments to test the self-other-oneness hypothesis. They found that when the self-other-oneness dimension was considered along with empathy arousal, the relationship between empathy and altruism was weakened substantially. Furthermore, they found that empathy increases altruism only if it results in an increase in self-other oneness. According to Cialdini and colleagues, empathic concern for a victim serves as an emotional cue for the increase in self-other oneness. Additionally, as suggested by Neuberg and colleagues, because empathy is an emotion, it may only be important in deciding between not helping or providing minimal or superficial help (Newberg et al., 1997).

However, the matter was not resolved because Batson (1997) pointed out that the methods used by Cialdini and colleagues were questionable. In fact, Batson and colleagues (1997) found that when more careful procedures were used, there was little evidence that self-other oneness was critical in mediating the empathy-altruism link. As to whether empathy arousal leads only to superficial helping, Batson pointed out that the empathy-altruism hypothesis only states that empathy arousal is often associated with an altruistic act and does not specify the depth of the act. Batson, however, does acknowledge that there may be limits to the empathy-altruism relationship.

Where do we stand currently on these hypotheses about helping? Although the research of Batson and others supports the empathy-altruism hypothesis (Batson et al., 1988; Dovidio et al., 1990), other research does not. For example, a strong relationship has been found between feeling and giving help, a finding that does not support the empathy-altruism hypothesis (Cialdini & Fultz, 1990). If we give help when we feel sad, it seems more likely that we are helping to relieve personal distress than out of pure altruism.

It is apparent that the empathy-altruism hypothesis remains a point of controversy in social psychology. Batson (1997) suggested that the controversy exists mainly over whether there is enough clear evidence to justify acceptance of the empathy-altruism hypothesis. There is agreement, according to Batson, that empathy can be a factor in altruistic behavior. At this point, it is probably best to adopt a position between the competing hypotheses. People may be motivated by empathic altruism, but they seem to need to know that the victim benefited from their help (Smith et al., 1989). This allows them to experience *empathic joy* for helping the victim. Empathic joy simply means that helpers feel good about the fact that their efforts helped someone and that there was a positive outcome for that person. Helpers get a reward: the knowledge that someone they helped benefited. Additionally, helping situations may arouse a greater sense of closeness or oneness with the helper and the victim. In any event, empathy does appear to be an important emotion involved in altruism.

SOCIAL PSYCHOLOGY IN ACTION

When a Good Thing Is Taken too Far

Traditionally, empathy and altruism have been presented in a positive way. That is, we normally think of these two concepts as something desirable, which is largely true. However, like many things in life, empathy and altruism can become a problem if they are carried too far. According to Oakley (2014), empathy and altruism can both backfire and become harmful. She refers to this situation as pathological altruism. *Pathological altruism* is behavior or a personal tendency intended to promote the welfare of others, but has unreasonable negative consequences to others or oneself (Oakley, 2014). Oakley points out that pathological altruism can lead to behavior that is self-serving, self-defeating, and even narcissistic. For example, imagine a person who has a partner who is an alcoholic. Attempts to "help" the person may reach a point at which the person is making excuses for the partner's behavior and may even be enabling the negative behavior. Although the person's intentions are good (i.e., to help the partner), excessive empathy and helping can actually make the situation worse. This notion is embodied in the old saying "the road to hell is paved with good intentions." Pathological altruism relates to a wide range of psychological and social psychological situations including psychopathology, eating disorders, victimhood, addiction, and even foreign aid (see Oakely et al., 2012).

There is evidence linking feelings of guilt, empathy, and altruism. For example, O'Connor et al. (2012) found the usual link between empathy and altruism. However, they also found that feelings of guilt were also positively

Pathological altruism is behavior or a personal tendency intended to promote the welfare of others but that has unreasonable negative consequences to others or oneself. Research shows that pathological altruism can contribute to maladaptive behavior such as eating disorders.
Source: Vgstockstudio/Shutterstock.

correlated with empathy, altruism, and psychological inhibitions. In turn, psychological inhibitions were positively correlated with empathic distress and neuroticism. O'Connor et al. suggest that their pattern of findings reinforce the idea pathological altruism is related to feelings of guilt over not being able to help others enough, which may interfere with a person's normal functioning. Of course, these findings are correlational and do not support a conclusion that guilt causes pathological altruism and diminished psychological functioning. Experimental research on the topic is necessary to establish such a causal relationship.

(continued)

There appears to be a relationship between pathological altruism and eating disorders such as anorexia nervosa and bulimia nervosa (Bachner-Melman, 2012). According to Rachel Bachner-Melman, those with eating disorders often derive great pleasure preparing and serving others food, all the while depriving themselves of food. Bachner-Melman suggests that this may be a manifestation of pathological altruism. The giving and pleasing of others rises to the level of pathological because the pleasing behavior is motivated by a desire to gain the approval of others and avoid rejection and criticism. It also enhances the individual's sense of self-worth resulting from extreme self-sacrifice (Bachner-Melman, 2012). Of course, Bachner-Melman is not saying that pathological altruism is the only, or even major, cause for eating disorders. In fact, eating disorders arise from a complex interaction of biological and social factors.

Our opening vignette to this chapter focused on the altruistic behavior of Irene Opdyke who risked her life to save a group of Jews who were initially strangers to her. Her behavior was certainly very risky. If she were caught by the authorities, she could have been sent to a death camp or executed immediately. One might argue that her behavior had a pathological component to it due to its extreme risk. How do we separate *heroic altruism* such as Opdyke's from pathological altruism? Robert Homant and Daniel Kennedy (2012) suggested four factors that might separate heroic from pathological altruism:

- Pathological altruism is likely to be unneeded or uncalled for in the sense that the victim's suffering is not sufficient to warrant the altruistic behavior.
- In pathological altruism the helper complains about the impact of the altruism on him- or herself, yet continues the behavior.
- With pathological altruism the internal motives of the individual engaging in the altruistic act are irrational or relate to a psychological disorder.
- In pathological altruism, the supposedly altruistic act is of no real benefit; a fact that just about anyone could see.

Homant and Kennedy admit that these factors, especially the last one, are highly subjective. They also pointed out that for pathological altruism to exist, all of the factors need not be present. Irene Opdyke's altruistic behavior had none of the four characteristics. Therefore, we can safely conclude that hers was heroic and not pathological altruism.

Discussion Questions

1. Are empathy and altruism always a good thing?
2. Is there a relationship between pathological altruism and psychopathology?
3. How does pathological altruism relate to acts of heroism?

Biological Explanations: Helping in Order to Preserve Our Own Genes

As mentioned earlier, some psychologists have been skeptical about the existence of purely altruistic behavior because they believe behavior is shaped and regulated by rewards and punishments. But there is another reason psychologists have been skeptical about the existence of pure altruism, and that reason is biological: People or animals that engage in altruism involving personal danger to its logical conclusion will sometimes die. Because self-preservation, or at least the preservation of one's genes (i.e., one's children or relatives), is a fundamental rule of evolutionary biology, pure altruism stands on some shaky grounds (Wilson, 1978). Self-sacrificing behavior is very rare. When it occurs, we reward it extravagantly. The Medal of Honor, for example, is given for extraordinary bravery, behavior that goes beyond the call of duty.

Evolutionary biologists find altruistic behavior fascinating because it presents a biological paradox: In light of the principle of survival of the fittest, how can a behavior have evolved that puts the individual at risk and makes survival less likely (Wilson, 1975)? The principle of natural selection favors selfish behavior. Those animals that take care of themselves and do not expend energy on helping others are more likely to survive and reproduce their genes. The basic measure of biological fitness is the relative number of an individual's offspring that survive and reproduce (Wilson, 1975).

The evolutionary biologist's answer to the paradox is to suggest that there are no examples of purely altruistic, totally selfless behavior in nature. Instead, there is behavior that may have the effect of helping others but also serves some selfish purpose. For example, consider the white-fronted bee eater, a bird living in eastern and southern Africa. These birds live in complex colonies consisting of 15 to 25 extended families. Family units consist of about four overlapping generations. When breeding time arrives, some family members do not breed. Instead, they serve as helpers who devote themselves to constructing nests, feeding females, and defending the young (Emlen & Wrege, 1988). This helping is called *alloparenting,* or cooperative breeding.

How could such behavior have evolved? The bee eaters who do not breed lose the opportunity to pass on their genes to offspring. However, their behavior does help to ensure the survival of the whole colony and, specifically, the family members with whom they share genes. This conclusion is supported by the fact that the bee eater helpers provide cooperative help only to their closest relatives. Birds that could have provided help, but do not, turn out to be "in-laws"—birds that have no genetic connection with the mating pairs (Emlen & Wrege, 1988). Although the helping behavior does not further the survival of the individual's genes, it serves to preserve the individual's gene pool.

Do humans differ significantly from animals when it comes to altruism? According to sociobiologists, human social behavior is governed by the same rules that order all animal behavior. A central problem of sociobiology is to explain how altruism can exist even though such behavior endangers individual fitness and survival (Wilson, 1975, 1978). However, there is ample evidence that altruism among humans flourishes and endures. There is also evidence that good deeds (altruism) may serve a sexual selection function for males. That is, human males appear to perform good deeds as a way to impress and attract females (Van Vugt & Iredale, 2013). Van Vugt and Iredale gave male and female participants an opportunity to help another person in front of either a male or female observer. They found that men, but not women, helped more when in front of a member of the opposite sex. They also found that the more attractive the males perceived the observer to be, the more they helped.

One possible resolution to this apparent paradox lies in the idea that human survival, dating to the beginnings of human society, depends on cooperation. Human beings, smaller, slower, and weaker than many other animal species, needed to form cooperative groups to survive. In such groups *reciprocal altruism* may be more important than *kin altruism.* In reciprocal altruism, the costs of behaving altruistically are weighed against the benefits. If there is greater benefit than cost, an altruistic response will occur. Also, reciprocal altruism involves a kind of tit-for-tat mentality: You help me, and I'll help you.

Cooperation and reciprocal altruism (helping one another) would have been selected for, genetically, because they increase the survival of human beings (Hoffman, 1981). Unlike animals, humans do not restrict their helping to close genetic relatives. Instead, humans can maintain the gene pool by helping those who share common characteristics, even if they are not close kin (Glassman et al., 1986). Helping nonkin may help one preserve one's distinguishing characteristics in the gene pool in a manner analogous to helping kin.

Social psychologists acknowledge that biology plays a role in altruistic behavior. Altruism does not occur as often or as naturally as aggression, but it does occur. However, social psychology also points out that altruistic behavior in humans is determined by more than the biological dimension of our nature.

Study Break

The preceding sections introduced the definition of altruism and explored the relationship between empathy and altruism. Before you go on, answer the following questions:

1. What are the social psychological definitions for helping behavior and altruism, and how does the motivation behind helping affect helping behavior?
2. What is empathy?
3. What is the empathy-altruism hypothesis, and what roles do empathy and egoism play in altruistic behavior?
4. What are the limits of the empathy-altruism hypothesis?
5. What is pathological altruism, and what types of maladaptive behavior can it contribute to?
6. How do biological factors relate to altruism?

Helping in Emergencies: A Five-Stage Decision Model

Irene Opdyke's decision to help the Jews in Ternopol is an example of helping involving a long-term commitment to a course of action. We refer to this as *long-term helping*. Opdyke's help involved a commitment that was extended over a period of months and required a great investment of effort and resources. However, there are many other situations that require quick action involving a short-term commitment to helping. For example, if you saw a child fall into a pond, you probably would rescue that child. We refer to this type of helping as *situation-specific helping*. For example, in May of 2021, a female San Francisco police officer was attacked by a homeless man. The man wrestled the officer to the ground, got behind her, and began choking her. Within seconds, multiple bystanders came to her aid, pulling the man off. The quick action of the bystanders might have saved the officer's life (Aaro, 2021). This helping, most likely in response to an emergency, does not require a long-term investment of effort and resources.

If you saw a child drowning in a pool or pond you would likely try to save the child. This type of help is known as situation-specific helping.
Source: Irik Bik/Shutterstock.

Emergency situations in which bystanders give help occur quite often. But there are also many instances in which bystanders remain passive and do not intervene. Nowadays, it seems that bystanders are much more interested in getting an incident on video than aiding a person in need. This is true even when a victim is in clear need of help. One such incident captured the attention not only of the public but also of social psychologists: the tragic death of Kitty Genovese on March 13, 1964.

Genovese, a 24-year-old waitress, was coming home from work in Queens, New York, late one night. As she walked to her apartment building, a man wielding a knife attacked her. She screamed for help; 38 of her neighbors took notice from their apartments. It should be noted that not all of the 38 had the same level of knowledge of what was happening. It is not that each of the 38 witnesses was sitting at a window looking directly at what was happening to Kitty. One neighbor who *did* see what was happening yelled for the man to stop. The attacker ran off, only to return when it was obvious that nobody was coming to her aid. He stabbed Genovese repeatedly, eventually killing her. The attack lasted 40 minutes. When the police were called, they responded within 2 minutes. More than 40 years later, this tragedy continues to raise questions about why her neighbors did not respond to her cries for help.

The Genovese tragedy and similar incidents that occur all too frequently have raised many questions among the public and among social scientists. Dissatisfied with explanations that blamed life in the big city ("urban apathy"), social psychologists Darley and Latané began to devise some explanations about why the witnesses to Genovese's murder did nothing to intervene. Darley and Latané sketched out a social psychological model to explain the bystanders' behavior.

The model proposed that there are five stages a bystander must pass through, each representing an important decision, before he or she will help a person in need (Latané, & Darley, 1968). In their original formulation of the model, Latané and Darley (1968) suggested that a bystander must notice the situation, label the situation correctly as an emergency, and assume responsibility for helping. Darley and Latané proposed that there is a factor even beyond assuming responsibility: The individual must decide how to help. Help, according to these researchers, could take the form of direct intervention (Irene Opdyke's behavior) or indirect intervention (calling the police). The general model proposed by Latané and Darley (1968; Darley & Latané, 1968), along with an additional stage, is shown in Figure 11.2.

At each stage of the model, the individual must assess the situation and make a "yes" or "no" decision. At any point in the decision process, a "no" decision will lead to failure to help. A "yes" decision itself does not guarantee intervention; it simply allows the person

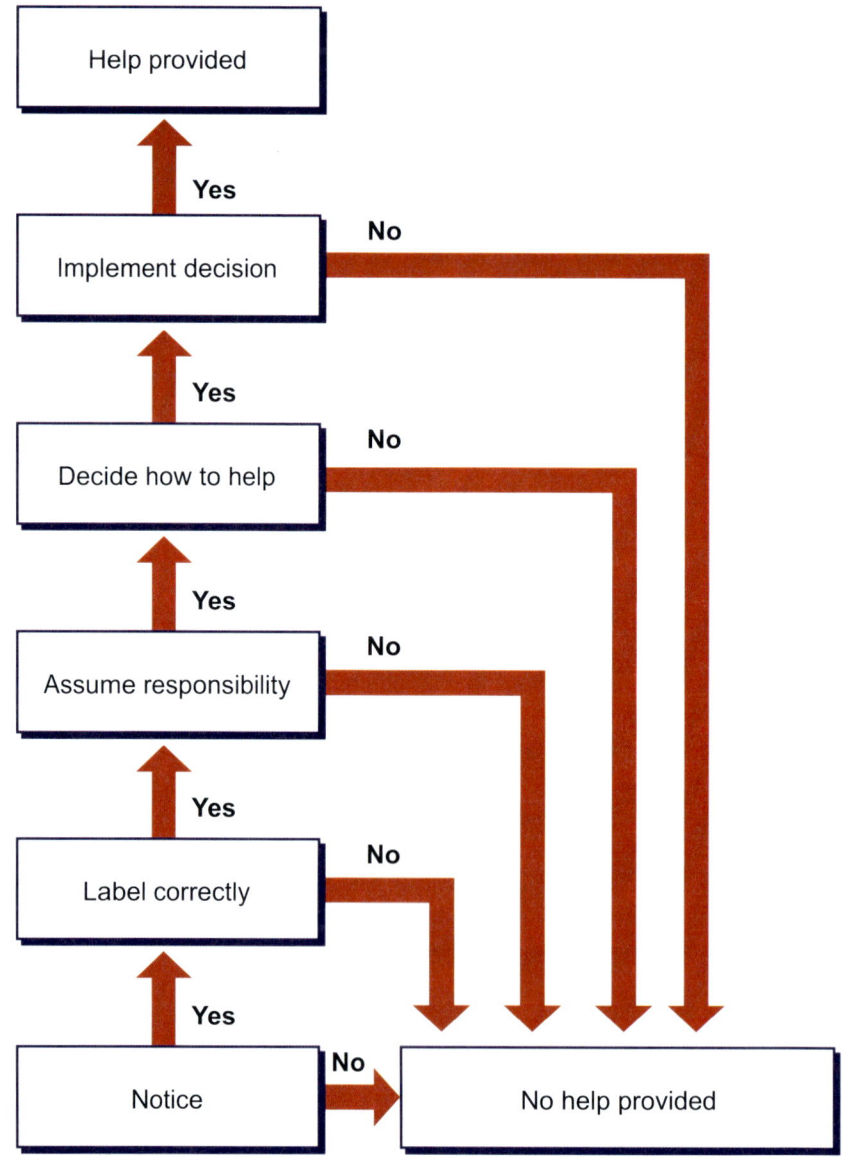

FIGURE 11.2

The five-stage model of helping. The path to helping begins with noticing an emergency situation. Next, a potential helper must label the situation correctly as an emergency and then assume responsibility for helping. A negative decision at any point will lead to nonhelping.

Based on Darley and Latané (1968) and Latané and Darley (1968).

to move to the next stage of the model. According to the model, help will be given only if a "yes" decision is made at each stage. Let's consider each of the five stages.

Stage 1: Noticing the Situation

Before we can expect a person to intervene in a situation, that person must have noticed that an emergency exists. If for example, the police officer attacked by the homeless man had been attacked on a desolate, rural road, those who came to her aid could not be expected to help because they would not have been aware of the attack. Before one can act, one must be aware that something has occurred. For example, at least some of Kitty Genovese's neighbors were aware of what was happening to Kitty. For them, noticing was not a problem.

Noticing is purely a sensory/perceptual phenomenon. If the emergency situation catches our attention, we will notice the situation. As such, noticing involves the basic laws of perception, such as the figure-ground relationship. This fundamental relationship is manifested when a stimulus stands out against a background. For example, when you go to a museum and look at a painting hanging on the gallery wall, the painting is the figure and the gallery wall is the background. We pay most attention to the figure (so when you tell a friend about your trip to the museum, you will describe the painting and not the gallery wall). In general, we are particularly likely to notice a stimulus that is brightly colored, noisy, or somehow stands out against a background. This is also true when noticing an emergency. Our chances of noticing an emergency increase if it stands out against the background of everyday life. For example, we are more likely to notice an automobile accident if there is a loud crash than if there is little or no sound. Anything that makes the emergency more conspicuous will increase the probability that we will attend to it.

Stage 2: Labeling the Situation as an Emergency

If a person notices the situation, the next step is to correctly label it as one that requires intervention. One very important factor at this stage is whether there is ambiguity or uncertainty about what has happened. For example, imagine that you look out the window of your second-floor apartment one day and notice immediately below the window a car with its driver's side door open and a person laying half in and half out of the car. Has the person collapsed, perhaps of a heart attack or a stroke? Or is the person changing a fuse under the dashboard or fixing the radio? If you decide on the latter explanation, you will turn away and not give it another thought. You have made a "no" decision in the labeling stage of the model.

Recognizing an emergency can be highly ambiguous because there is often more than one interpretation for a situation. Correctly labeling a situation as an emergency may depend on whether you can tell the difference between an emergency and a more benign situation. For example, often in active shooter situations, the victims report that they initially believed that the shots were firecrackers going off. When walking in a mall or sitting in a classroom, people do not expect to hear gunshots and thus misinterpret them as harmless. Most people do not know how to distinguish gunshots from the sound of firecrackers, further complicating the labeling process. Many emergencies have this quality:

Is the woman upstairs beating her child or merely disciplining her? Is the man staggering down the street sick or drunk? Is that person slumped in the doorway injured or a drunken derelict? These questions must be resolved if we are to correctly label a situation as an emergency requiring our intervention.

When two 10-year-old boys abducted a 2-year-old from a shopping center in Liverpool, England, in 1993 and subsequently killed him, they walked together for two miles along a busy road congested with traffic. Thirty-eight people remembered seeing the three children, and some said later that the toddler was being dragged or appeared to be crying. Apparently, the situation was ambiguous enough—were they his older brothers, trying to get him home for dinner?—that no one stopped. A driver of a dry-cleaning van said he saw one of the older boys aim a kick at the toddler, but it looked like a "persuading" kind of kick such as one might use on a 2-year-old (Morrison, 1994). The driver failed to label the situation correctly.

The first stage of the five-stage model of helping is noticing an emergency. Before you can provide help, you must first notice the emergency. Anything that makes the emergency more conspicuous increases the chances that others will notice the situation.
Source: Dmytro Zinkevych/Shutterstock.

The Ambiguity of the Situation

Research confirms that situational ambiguity is an important factor in people correctly labeling a situation as an emergency. In one study, participants were seated in a room and asked to fill out a questionnaire (Yakimovich & Salz, 1971). Outside the room, a confederate of the experimenter was washing windows. When the experimenter signaled, the confederate knocked over his ladder and pail, fell to the pavement, and grabbed his ankle. In one condition (the verbalization condition), the confederate screamed and cried for help. In the other condition (the no-verbalization condition), the confederate moaned but didn't cry for help.

In both conditions, participants jumped up and went to the window when they heard the sound of the crash. Therefore, all participants noticed the emergency. In the verbalization condition, 81% (13 of 16) tried to help the victim. In the no-verbalization condition, however, only 29% (5 of 17) tried to help. The clear cry for help, then, increased the probability that people would help. Without it, it wasn't clear that the man needed help.

Note also that the potential helpers had all seen the victim before his accident. He was a real person to them. Recall in the Genovese case that the witnesses had not seen her before she was stabbed. Given this fact and that the murder took place in the fog of the early morning hours, ambiguity must have existed, at least for some witnesses.

The Presence of Others

The presence of other bystanders also may affect the labeling process. Reactions of other bystanders often determine the response to the situation. If bystanders show little concern over the emergency, individuals will be less likely to help. When we are placed in a social situation (especially an ambiguous one), we look around us to see what others are doing (the process of social comparison). If others are not concerned, we may not define the situation as an emergency, and we probably will not offer to help.

In one study, increasing or decreasing the availability of cues from another bystander affected helping (Darley et al., 1973). Participants were tested either alone or in groups of two. Those participating in groups were either facing each other across a table (face-to-face condition) or seated back-to-back (not-facing condition). An emergency was staged (a fall) while the participants worked on their tasks. More participants who were alone helped (90%) than participants who were in groups. However, whether participants were facing each other made a big difference. Participants who were facing each other were significantly more likely to help (80%) than participants not facing each other (20%). Consider what happens when you sit across from someone and you both hear a cry for help. You look at her, she looks at you. If she then goes back to her work, you probably will not define the situation as an emergency. If she says, "Did you hear that?" you are more likely to go investigate.

Generally, we rely on cues from other bystanders more and more as the ambiguity of the situation increases. Thus, in highly ambiguous emergency situations, we might expect the presence of others who are passive to suppress helping. The fact that the witnesses to Genovese's murder were in their separate apartments and did not know what others were doing and thinking operated to suppress intervention.

Stage 3: Assuming Responsibility to Help: The Bystander Effect

Noticing and correctly labeling a situation as an emergency are not enough to guarantee that a bystander will intervene. It is certain that many of the 38 witnesses to Genovese's murder noticed, to one degree or another, the incident and probably labeled it as an emergency. What they did not do is conclude that they had a responsibility to help. Darley and Latané (1968), puzzled by the lack of intervention on the part of the witnesses, thought that the presence of others might inhibit rather than increase helping. They designed a simple yet elegant experiment to test for the effects of multiple bystanders on helping. Their experiment demonstrated the power of the **bystander effect**, in which a person in need of help is less likely to receive help as the number of bystanders increases.

Participants in this experiment were told it was a study of interpersonal communication. They were asked to participate in a group discussion of their current problems. To ensure anonymity, the discussion took place over intercoms. In reality, there was no group. The experimenter played a tape of a discussion to lead the participant to believe that other group members existed.

bystander effect The social phenomenon that helping behavior is less likely to occur as the number of witnesses to an emergency increases.

Darley and Latané (1968) varied the size of the group. In one condition, the participant was told that there was one other person in the group (so the group consisted of the participant and the victim); in a second condition, there was one other person (participant, victim, and one other). In another condition the participant believed there were four additional participants. The discussion went along uneventfully until it was the victim's turn to speak. The actor who played the role of the victim on the tape simulated a seizure. Darley and Latané noted the number of participants who tried to help and how long it took them to try to help.

The study produced two major findings. First, the size of the group had an effect on the percentage of participants helping. When the participant believed that he or she was alone in the experiment with the victim, 85% of the participants helped. The percentage of participants offering help declined when the participant believed there was one other bystander (62%) or four other bystanders (31%). In other words, as the number of bystanders increased, the likelihood of the participant helping the victim decreased.

The second major finding was that the size of the group had an effect on time between the onset of the seizure and the offering of help. When the participant believed he or she was alone, help occurred more quickly than when the participant believed other bystanders were present. In essence, the participants who believed they were members of a larger group became "frozen in time" by the presence of others. They had not decided to help or not to help. They were distressed but could not act.

A crucial stage of the helping process is assuming responsibility to help. In Kitty Genovese's case, her neighbors were isolated from one another in their own apartments. Many may have assumed that someone else would or already had helped. This diffusion of responsibility reduces helping.
Source: Anastasios71/Shutterstock.

Interestingly, the "other bystanders" need not be physically present in order for the bystander effect to occur. In one experiment conducted by Garcia et al. (2002), participants were asked to imagine that they had won a dinner for either themselves and 30 friends, 10 friends, or just for themselves (alone condition). Later, participants were asked to indicate how much money they would be willing to donate to charity after they graduated college. Garcia et al. found that participants indicated the lowest level of donations in the 30 friends condition, and the most in the alone condition (the 10-friends condition fell between these two groups). This effect extends to computer chat rooms (Markey, 2000). Markey found that as the number of participants in a chat room increased, the time it took to receive requested help also increased. Interestingly, the chat room bystander effect was eliminated when the person making the request personalized the request by singling someone out by name.

Why Does the Bystander Effect Occur?

The best explanation offered for the bystander effect is **diffusion of responsibility** (Darley & Latané, 1968). According to this explanation, each bystander assumes that another bystander will take action. If all the bystanders think that way, no help will be offered. This explanation fits quite well with Darley and Latané's findings in which the bystanders could not see each other, as was the case in the Genovese killing. Under these conditions, it is easy to see how a bystander (unaware of how other bystanders are acting) might assume that someone else has already taken or will take action.

diffusion of responsibility
An explanation suggesting that each bystander assumes another person will take responsibility to help.

What about emergency situations in which bystanders can see one another? In this case, the bystanders could actually see that others were not helping. Diffusion of responsibility under these conditions may not explain bystander inaction (Latané & Darley, 1968). Another explanation has been offered for the bystander effect that centers on *pluralistic ignorance*, which occurs when a group of individuals acts in the same manner despite the fact that each person has different perceptions of an event (Miller & McFarland, 1987). In the bystander effect, pluralistic ignorance operates when the bystanders in an ambiguous emergency situation look around and see each other doing nothing; they assume that the others are thinking that the situation is not an emergency (Miller & McFarland, 1987). In essence, the collective inaction of the bystanders leads to a redefinition of the situation as a nonemergency.

Whether you intervene in an emergency, such as finding a collapsed person, depends on noticing the emergency, labeling it correctly, assuming responsibility to help, knowing how to help, and implementing your decision to help.
Source: Lisa-S/Shutterstock.

social category relationship
A relationship in which bystanders assume that the parties involved belong together in some way.

Latané and Darley (1968) provided evidence for this explanation. Participants filled out a questionnaire alone in a room, with two passive bystanders (confederates of the experimenter) or with two other actual participants. While the participants were filling out the questionnaire, smoke was introduced into the room through a vent. The results showed that when participants were alone in the room, 75% of the participants reported the smoke, many within 2 minutes of first noticing it. In the condition in which the participant was in the room with two passive bystanders, only 10% reported the smoke. In the last condition, in which the participant was with two other participants, 38% reported the smoke. Thus, the presence of bystanders once again suppressed helping. This occurred despite the fact that participants in the bystander conditions denied that the other people in the room had any effect on them.

In post-experimental interviews, Latané and Darley (1968) searched for the underlying cause for the observed results. They found that participants who reported the smoke felt that the smoke was unusual enough to report, although they didn't feel that the smoke was dangerous. Participants who failed to report the smoke, which was most likely to occur in the two-bystander condition, developed a set of creative reasons why the smoke should not be reported. For example, some participants believed that the smoke was smog piped into the room to simulate an urban environment, or that the smoke was truth gas designed to make them answer the questionnaire truthfully. Whatever reasons these participants came up with, the situation was redefined as a nonemergency.

Is diffusion of responsibility, dependent on the number of bystanders present, *always* the underlying cause for the bystander effect? Although diffusion of responsibility is the most widely accepted explanation, it is not the only explanation. Levine (1999) suggests that there are situations in which diffusion of responsibility based on the presence of bystanders cannot explain nonintervention. Instead, Levine suggests that if a bystander assumes that a **social category relationship** exists between parties in a potential helping situation, intervention is unlikely. A social category relationship is one in which bystanders assume that the parties involved belong together in some way. For example, a spousal relationship would fit this definition because the two individuals are seen as belonging together in the relationship. Levine argues that when we are confronted with a situation in which a social category relationship exists or is assumed, a social norm of nonintervention is activated. In short, we are socialized to keep our noses out of family matters. In fact, there is research that shows that bystanders are less willing to intervene in an emergency situation when a social category relationship exists (Shotland & Straw, 1976). Shotland and Straw, for example, found that 65% of participants were willing to intervene in an argument between a male and female who were strangers, but only 19% were willing to intervene when the male and female were said to be married.

Levine (1999) provides further evidence for this effect. He analyzed the trial transcript of the trial of two 10-year-old boys who murdered a 2-year-old child in London in 1993 (we briefly described this crime earlier in this chapter). The two older boys, Jon Thompson and Robert Venables, abducted James Bulger and walked Bulger around London for over 2 hours. During this time, the trio of boys encountered 38 witnesses. Some witnesses were alone, whereas others were with other bystanders. In a situation reminiscent of the Kitty Genovese murder, none of the 38 witnesses intervened. Based on his analysis of the trial transcript, Levine concluded that the nonintervention had little or nothing to do with the number of bystanders present, or diffusion of responsibility. Instead, statements of witnesses during trial testimony indicated that the witnesses assumed (or were told by the older boys) that the older boys were Bulger's brothers taking him home. According to Levine, the assumption that a social category relationship existed among the boys was the best explanation for why the 38 witnesses did not intervene.

We need to understand that category relationships can extend beyond social categories. We may assume that a relationship exists between people and objects. For example, imagine you are going to your car after work and see another car parked next to yours. You see that the hood is open and there is someone tinkering with something under the hood. What would you think is going on? Most likely you would assume that the person tinkering under the hood owns the car and is fixing something. You would then be surprised to learn the next day that the car was stolen and the man tinkering under the hood was a thief! Assuming that such relationships exist can be a powerful suppressant to intervention.

Finally, there is evidence that the presence of bystanders in an emergency situation changes brain functioning related to helping (Hortensius & de Gelder, 2014). Hortensius and de Gelder had participants perform a color naming task and scanned their brain activity using fMRI. In this task, three colored dots were projected on to a screen. In the background a video was played showing a person collapsing to the floor. The number of passersby in the video varied between one and four. Hortensius and de Gelder found reduced brain activity associated with preparation for quick action as the number of bystanders in the video increased. They also found an increase in activity in brain areas associated with visual attention as the number of bystanders increased. These results suggest that the presence of bystanders increases visual attention to an emergency, while it suppresses the likelihood that a person will take quick action.

Limits to the Bystander Effect

Increasing the number of bystanders does not always suppress helping; there are exceptions to the bystander effect. There is evidence for a *positive bystander effect* when the intervention required is dangerous. That is, in a dangerous situation the presence of others increases helping compared to if a helper is alone. This is what occurred in the example of the San Francisco police officer helped by bystanders we discussed earlier. In a meta-analysis of the literature, Fischer et al. (2011) found that the bystander effect was reduced for helping in dangerous situations. They also found that if the consequences to the helper were physical, the bystander effect was also reduced. In one illustrative experiment, Fischer et al. (2006) had participants watch what they believed was a live interaction between a male and female (actually the participants viewed a prerecorded videotape). In the high-potential-danger condition, the male was shown to be a large, "thug-like" individual who made progressively more aggressive sexual advances toward the female, culminating in sexually aggressive touching of the female and the female crying for help. At that point the tape went blank. In the low-potential-danger condition, the male was shown as a thin, short male who engaged in the same sexually aggressive behavior with the same victim reactions. Half of the participants watched the interaction alone (no bystander), and the other half watched it in the presence of a confederate of the experimenter (bystander). The experimenters measured whether the participant tried to help the female in distress. As shown in Figure 11.3, the bystander effect was replicated in the low-danger situation: Fewer participants attempt to help when a bystander is present than when the participant is alone. In the high-danger situation, however, the bystander effect was not evident. A similar effect was found using a staged bicycle theft situation (Fischer & Greitemeyer, 2013).

In another experiment, a reversal of the typical bystander effect was shown with a potentially dangerous helping situation. One group of researchers staged a rape on a college campus and measured how many participants intervened (Harari et al., 1985). The participants had three options in the experimental situation: fleeing without helping, giving indirect help (alerting a police officer who is out of view of the rape), or giving direct help (intervening directly in the rape).

Male participants were tested as they walked either alone or in groups. (The groups in this experiment were simply participants who happened to be walking together and not interacting with one another.) As the participants approached a certain point, two actors staged the rape. The woman screamed, "Help! Help! Please help me! You bastard! Rape! Rape!" (Harari et al., 1985, p. 656). The results of this experiment did not support the

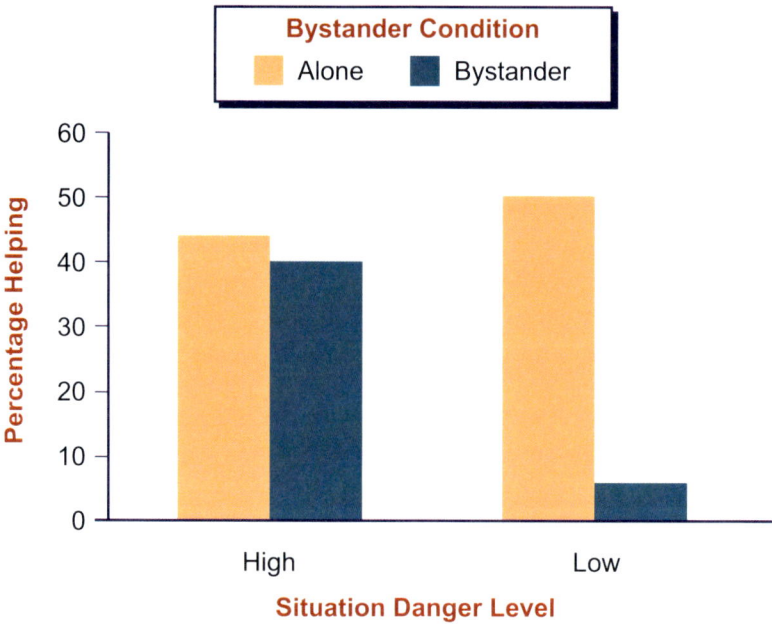

FIGURE 11.3

Bystanders who are alone are likely to help in high and low danger situations. The presence of another bystander increased helping in the high danger but not low danger situation; a clear reversal of the usual bystander effect.

Based on data from Fischer et al. (2006).

bystander effect. Participants walking in groups were more likely to help (85%) than participants walking alone (65%). In this situation—a victim is clearly in need and the helping situation is dangerous—it seems that bystanders in groups are more likely to help than solitary bystanders (Clark & Word, 1974; Harari et al., 1985). A similar effect was found by Katz et al. (2015). In this study, female participants expressed more willingness to intervene in a party rape scenario when the scenario placed the participant in a group than alone. They also found that the female participants expressed a greater willingness to help a female than male victim. Unwillingness to help the male victim was related to greater perceived danger and a perception that the victim might be gay. Additionally, if surveillance is added to an emergency situation, the bystander effect is reduced (van Bommel et al., 2014). In their experiment, van Bommel et al. put participants into a bystander effect situation. In one condition, there was a surveillance camera in the room with the participant and in the other there was no camera. They found that the bystander effect was reduced in the camera condition compared to the no camera condition.

Finally, the bystander effect is less likely to occur when the helping situation confronting us involves a clear violation of a social norm that we personally care about. Imagine, for example, you see a person throw an empty bottle into the bushes at a public park. In such a situation you may engage in *social control* behaviors (e.g., confront the offender, complain to your partner). Contrast this with a situation where private property is involved (e.g., painting graffiti in an elevator in a building owned by a large corporation). You may be less likely to engage in social control behaviors. Chekroun and Brauer (2001) wondered if the bystander effect would operate differently in these two situations. They hypothesized that the bystander effect would hold for situations involving low personal implications (e.g., graffiti in the elevator), but not in situations involving high personal implications (e.g., littering in a public park). In the low-personal-implication condition a confederate of the experimenters entered an elevator in a shopping center parking lot. As soon as the door closed, the confederate began scrawling graffiti on the wall with a magic marker. This was done under two conditions: a participant alone in the elevator with the confederate (no bystanders) or two or three naïve individuals in the elevator with the confederate. In the high-personal-implications condition a confederate of

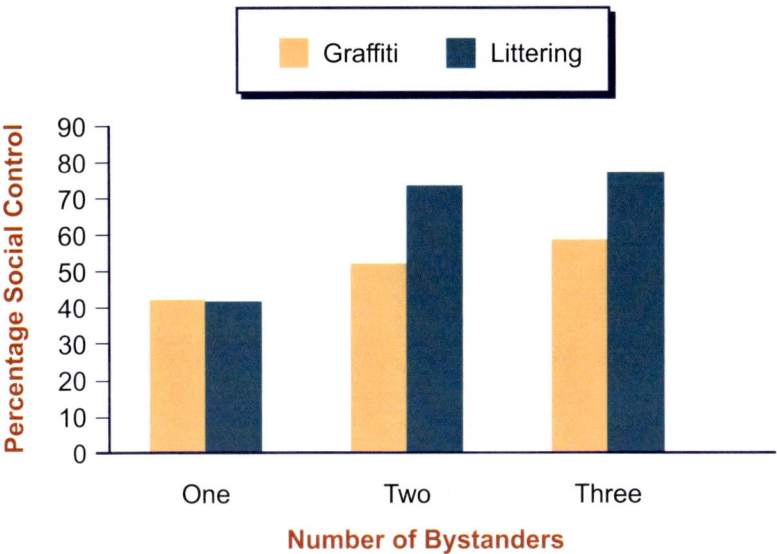

FIGURE 11.4

Social control behaviors are more likely with bystanders present if a behavior has high personal implications (littering in a public park) than if the behavior has low personal implications (graffiti in a privately owned elevator).

Based on data from Checkroun and Brauer (2002).

the experimenters threw an empty plastic bottle into some bushes in a public park in front of one participant or a group of two or three participants. In both situations the reaction of the participant(s) was recorded on a scale ranging from no social control to an audible negative comment. As you can see in Figure 11.4, social control was most likely to occur when other bystanders were present in the park-littering situation (high personal implications). Less social control was shown by the groups of participants in the graffiti situation (low personal implications).

Study Break

This section introduced you to Darley and Latané's five-stage model of helping in emergency situations. Before you begin the next section, answer the following questions:

1. What factors affect whether a person notices an emergency?
2. What factors affect correct labeling of an emergency?
3. What factors affect assuming responsibility for helping?
4. What is the bystander effect, and why does it occur?
5. What are the limits of the bystander effect?

Stage 4: Deciding How to Help

The fourth stage of the five-stage model of helping is deciding how to help. In the staged rape study, for example, participants had a choice of directly intervening to stop the rape or aiding the victim by notifying the police (Harari et al., 1985). What influences decisions like this?

There is considerable support for the notion that people who feel competent, who have the necessary skills, are more likely to help than those who feel they lack such competence. In a study in which participants were exposed to a staged arterial bleeding emergency, the likelihood of providing effective help was determined only by the expertise of the participants (some had Red Cross training) (Shotland & Heinhold, 1985).

There are two reasons why greater competence may lead to more helping. First, feelings of competence increase confidence in one's ability to help and to know what ought to be done (Cramer et al., 1988). Second, feelings of competence increase sensitivity to the needs of others and empathy toward victims (Barnett et al., 1985). People who feel like leaders are probably also more likely to help because they feel more confident about being able to help successfully.

Many emergencies, however, do not require any special training or competence. Irene Opdyke had no more competence in rescuing Jews than anyone else in Ternopol. In the Genovese case, a simple telephone call to the police was all that was needed. Clearly, no special competence was required.

Stage 5: Implementing the Decision to Help

Having passed through these four stages, a person may still choose not to intervene. To understand why, imagine that as you drive to campus, you see a fellow student standing next to his obviously disabled car. Do you stop and offer to help? Perhaps you are late for your next class and feel that you do not have the time. Perhaps you are not sure it is safe to stop on the side of the highway. Or perhaps the student strikes you as somehow undeserving of help (Bickman & Kamzan, 1973). Or perhaps the place where the help is needed is noisy (Moser, 1988). These and other considerations influence your decision whether to help.

Assessing Rewards and Costs for Helping

Social psychologists have found that people's evaluation of the rewards and costs involved in helping affect their decision to help or not to help. There are potential rewards for helping (gratitude from the victim, monetary reward, recognition by peers) and for not helping (avoiding potential danger, arriving for an appointment on time). Similarly, there are costs for helping (possible injury, embarrassment, inconvenience) and for not helping (loss of self-esteem). Generally, research indicates that the greater the cost of helping, the less likely people are to help (Batson et al., 1983; Darley & Batson, 1973; Piliavin & Piliavin, 1972; Piliavin et al., 1975). Conversely, the greater the potential reward for helping, the more likely it is that a person will help.

In a study of the relationship between potential cost for helping and actual helping, Darley and Batson (1973) told seminarians taking part in an experiment at Princeton University that a high school group was visiting the campus and had requested a seminarian speaker. Half the participants were told they had little time to get across campus to speak to the high school group, and the other half were told they had plenty of time. Additionally, some participants were asked to speak about the meaning of the parable of the Good Samaritan. The seminarians then left the building to give their talk, and lo and behold, while walking down a narrow lane, they saw a young man collapse in front of them. What did they do?

Now, do you recall the story of the Good Samaritan? A traveler is set upon by robbers and left by the side of the road. A priest and a Levite, people holding important positions in the clergy of the time, walked by swiftly without helping. But a Samaritan, passing along the same road, stopped and helped. We might say that, for whatever reasons, helping was too costly for the priest and the Levite but not too costly for the Samaritan.

What about the seminarians? The "costly" condition in this experiment was the tight schedule: Stopping to help would make them late for their talk. Was helping too costly for them? Yes, it was. Participants who were in a hurry, even if they were thinking about the story of the Good Samaritan, were less likely to stop and help than were participants who were not in a hurry.

In an attempt to "capture" the effects of various costs for helping and nonhelping, Fritzsche et al. (2000) had participants evaluate scenarios containing three costs for helping (time required to help, the discomfort involved in helping, and the urgency of the help) and three costs for not helping (victim responsibility, ability to diffuse responsibility, and victim deservingness). Participants read the scenarios in which these six variables were manipulated and were instructed to play the role of the individual receiving the request for help. For each scenario, the participant indicated his or her likelihood of helping the person making the request for help.

Fritzsche et al. (2000) found confirmation for the effects of cost on helping. In the scenarios where costs for helping were high, participants expressed lower willingness to help. Fritzsche et al. evaluated the importance of each of the six variables in determining willingness to give help. They found that the cues varied in importance with respect to helping. There was no significant gender difference in how the variables affected willingness to help. The following list shows the importance of the six variables (in order starting with the most important one):

1. Victim responsibility
2. Urgency of the help
3. Time required for help
4. Diffusion of responsibility
5. Discomfort involved in helping
6. Victim's deservingness

As is the case in decision-making research, there was a discrepancy between what participants believed would be important in determining helping and what actually turned out to be important. Participants believed that victim deservingness, time required to render help, and ability to diffuse responsibility would be the most important factors driving willingness to help. However, as you can see from the previous list, only one of those factors was near the top of the list (time required for help). Finally, there was a gender difference in this finding. Males were more accurate than females in identifying the importance of the variables.

How Seeing Others Help Affects Helping

Another factor that can affect whether we implement a decision to help is if we see someone else helping. It is well known that seeing another person helping increases the likelihood that we ourselves will also help. This was demonstrated in a classic study by Bryan and Test (1967). In one of their experiments, Bryan and Test placed a disabled car (a flat tire) on a residential street. In one condition, only the disabled car was present. In another condition, a male confederate was helping the female confederate change the tire (model condition). A quarter-mile down the road was another car with a flat tire. There was also a female confederate leaning against the car, apparently in need of help. The dependent variable was the number of cars that stopped to offer help to the female next to the second car. The results showed that more passersby stopped to help the female confederate when they had just seen another woman receiving help. The presence of a helping model, then, significantly increased the frequency of helping. Since this early study, other studies have verified the positive effect of seeing a helping model on helping behavior. A meta-analysis of 88 studies of the effects of prosocial models on helping behavior showed that exposure to a prosocial model had a moderate effect on helping. The effect held up across a number of different individuals needing help and different types of helping (Jung et al., 2020).

The effect of a prosocial model on behavior starts early in life. It can be seen in children as young as 16 months of age (Schumacher et al., 2019). In one study, Schumacher et al. exposed 16-month-old children to either a prosocial model or no model. In the prosocial model condition, the children saw an adult helping another child perform a task (e.g., stacking containers). In the no-model control condition, the adult was present but did not help the other child. During the test phase, the adult model left the room, and another adult came in (who did not know which model condition had just been run) and gave the child an opportunity to help on the task on which they had just seen the model give help to another child. Schumacher et al. found that more children helped the second

Individuals in a good mood are more likely to help others than those in a bad mood. Evidence also suggests that if another person smiles at you, then you will be more likely to help someone than if you were not smiled at.

Source: fizkes/Shutterstock.

adult after seeing the prosocial model help another child (47%) than after seeing the control model (13%). A similar prosocial modeling effect has been found for 2-year-old children (Williamson et al., 2014).

What is it about seeing someone else helping that causes us to help? One explanation offered is that seeing another person acting in an altruistic manner elicits a unique emotion in us called *elevation* (Schnall & Roper, 2012). Schnall and Roper tested the effect of elevation on helping by having participants watch one of three videos in an experiment ostensibly on episodic memory. In the *elevation* video, participants saw a musician thanking a mentor for rescuing him from gang life. In the *mirth* condition, participants saw a video of a British comedy (this condition was included to elicit a positive emotion not related to helping). In the *control* condition, participants watched a video of a nature show. After watching the videos, participants were asked if they would voluntarily agree to fill out an additional questionnaire. The number of minutes the participants spent on the additional questionnaire was the measure of helping. The results showed that participants spent more time filling out the additional questionnaire in the elevation condition than in the mirth or control conditions (which did not differ). It was only those participants who witnessed someone thanking another for helping who were moved to help the experimenter on the additional questionnaire.

The Effect of Mood on Helping

Likelihood of helping can even be affected by the bystander's mood. The research of Isen (1987) and her coworkers has shown that adults and children who are in a positive mood are more likely to help others than people who are not. People who had found a dime in a phone booth in a shopping mall were more likely to pick up papers dropped by a stranger than people who had not found a coin. Students who had gotten free cookies in the library were more likely to volunteer to help someone and were less likely to volunteer to annoy somebody else when asked to do so as part of an experiment. Evidence also shows that people who are smiled at by another person report a more positive mood and are more willing to help another person than people who are not smiled at (Vrugt & Vet, 2009). People are even more likely to help on a sunny day than on a cloudy day, presumably because the sun puts them in a better mood (Guéguen & Lamy, 2013a, 2013b)!

Although positive mood is related to an increase in helping, it does not lead to more helping if the person thinks that helping will destroy the good mood (Isen & Simmonds, 1978). Good moods seem to generate good thoughts about people, and this increases helping. People in good moods also are less concerned with themselves and more likely to be sensitive to other people, making them more aware of other people's needs and therefore more likely to help (Isen, 1987).

Music, it is said, can soothe the wild beast. Can it also make you more likely to help? North et al. (2004) investigated this question. Participants in a gym were exposed to either soothing or annoying music during their workout periods. After the workout, participants were asked to help in a low-cost (sign a petition) or high-cost (help distribute leaflets) situation. North et al. found that when the soothing music had been played during the workout, participants were more likely to help in the high-cost situation than if the annoying music had been played. There was no difference between the two types of music for the low-cost helping situation.

Gratitude and Helping

Another factor that can affect helping is whether an individual received help when he or she needed help. Gratitude is an emotional state that has three functions relating to prosocial behavior (McCullough et al., 2001). First, gratitude acts as a sort of "moral barometer," indicating a change in one's state of mind after receiving help. Second, gratitude can function as a "moral motivator," impelling the recipient of help to reciprocate to his or her benefactor or strangers. Third, gratitude can serve as a "moral reinforcer." When someone expresses gratitude after receiving help, it increases the likelihood that the recipient of the gratitude will engage in prosocial behavior in the future. Taken together, these three functions suggest that gratitude will increase helping. But does it?

The answer to this question is yes. A feeling of gratitude tends to enhance helping (Bartlett & DeSteno, 2006; Tsang, 2006). In Bartlett and DeSteno's experiment, participants were led to believe that they would be performing a group task with another participant. Actually, the "other participant" was a confederate of the experimenter. The real participant and confederate performed tasks on separate computers. In the "gratitude" condition, after completing a task and while waiting for scores to be displayed, the confederate surreptitiously kicked the real participant's monitor plug out of a power strip. The confederate then "helped" the participant by finding and fixing the problem. In the "amusement" condition, participants watched a brief, amusing video clip (to induce positive affect unrelated to gratitude) after completing the task (the confederate did not kick out the plug or offer help). In the "neutral" condition the confederate did not kick the plug out and only carried on a brief conversation with the real participant. Sometime later the confederate approached the participant and asked the participant to complete a long and tedious problem-solving survey. As shown in Figure 11.5, Bartlett and DeSteno found that participants were more willing to help in the gratitude condition than in either the amusement or neutral conditions. Thus, it was the gratitude itself and not just positive feelings that might be generated by receiving help that increased helping. Bartlett and DeSteno conducted some follow-up studies to determine if gratitude merely activates the norm of reciprocity (you should help those who help you), thus leading to an increase in helping. Based on their results, Bartlett and DeSteno concluded that it was, in fact, the feeling of gratitude experienced by the real participants that increased helping, and not the norm of reciprocity.

So, gratitude appears to be an important factor in increasing helping behavior. In real-life situations, it may behoove us to take steps to increase the expression of gratitude to increase helping behavior. Katina Sawyer and her colleagues (2021) point out, however, that in many situations (e.g., at work), there simply isn't time for the expression of gratitude. In such situations, they add, people tend to focus on their own needs and wants

FIGURE 11.5

Gratitude and not just positive emotions increase helping. Gratitude seems to have special qualities that increase helping.

Based on data from Bartlett and DeSteno (2006).

(self-centric view) rather than on those of others. In short, people may simply not think to express gratitude because of the hectic nature of life. They suggest that if we can get people to pause and take time to express gratitude and see things from another's point of view, we can increase the chances that people will help others when needed. Sawyer et al. conducted a series of studies to test these possibilities. In one study, participants were randomly assigned to one of two conditions. In one condition, participants were assigned to a "mindfulness intervention," which involved having them listen to a mindfulness meditation tape encouraging them to "connect with any present-moment experiences in a nonjudgmental way (e.g., thoughts, emotions, or sensations)" (p. 6). In the inactive control condition, participants did not listen to the tape. They were then asked to list as many things as possible in their lives for which they felt grateful. Sawyer et al. found that those in the mindful condition listed more such things than those in the control condition. In a second study, they found that making gratitude mindful led to a greater willingness to help compared with a control condition. After a series of studies, Sawyer et al. concluded that making gratitude mindful increased positive affect and the tendency to take the perspectives of others. These two factors enhanced gratitude, which directly affected helping behavior.

What is the psychological mechanism underlying the effect of gratitude on helping? One thing that receiving gratitude does for us is increase our sense of self-worth, which then relates to an increase in the likelihood of helping others (Adam & Gino, 2010). In a series of experiments, Adam and Gino tested the role of self-worth against self-efficacy (a belief that our behavior will be effective in helping others), another psychological mechanism that might flow from gratitude. The results of all of their experiments confirmed that increased self-worth was a more powerful predictor of helping than self-efficacy.

Characteristics of the Victim

A decision to help (or not to help) also is affected by the victim's characteristics. For example, males are more likely to help females than to help other males (Eagly & Crowley, 1986; West et al., 1975). Females, on the other hand, are equally likely to help male and female victims (Eagly & Crowley, 1986). Physically attractive people are more likely to receive help than unattractive people (Benson et al., 1976). In one study, a pregnant woman, whether alone or with another woman, received more help than a non-pregnant woman or a facially disfigured woman (Walton et al., 1988).

Potential helpers also make judgments about whether a victim deserves help. If we perceive that a person got into a situation through his or her own negligence and is therefore responsible for his or her own fate, we tend to generate "just-world" thinking (Lerner & Simmons, 1966). According to the **just-world hypothesis**, we believe that people get what they deserve and deserve what they get. This type of thinking often leads us to devalue a person whom we think caused his or her own misfortune (Lerner & Simmons, 1966). Generally, we give less help to victims we perceive to have contributed to their own fate than to those we perceive as needy through no fault of their own (Berkowitz, 1969; Schopler & Matthews, 1965).

just-world hypothesis
A hypothesis that we believe people get what they deserve and deserve what they get.

However, we may relax this exacting standard if we perceive that the person in need is highly dependent on our help. In one experiment, participants received telephone calls at home in which the caller mistook them for the owner of "Ralph's Garage" and told them that her car had broken down (Gruder et al., 1978). The caller says either that she meant to have the car serviced but forgot (help needed due to victim's negligence) or that the car was just serviced (no negligence). In one condition, after the participant informs the caller that she has not reached Ralph's Garage, the caller says that she has no more change to make another call (high dependency). In another condition, no mention is made of being out of change. In all conditions the caller asks the participant to call Ralph's Garage for her. The researchers found that participants were more likely to help the negligent victim who had no more change than the negligent victim who presumably had other ways to get help (Figure 11.6). It seems that high dependence mediates just-world thinking. Regardless of whether the victim deserves what she gets, we can't help but take pity on her.

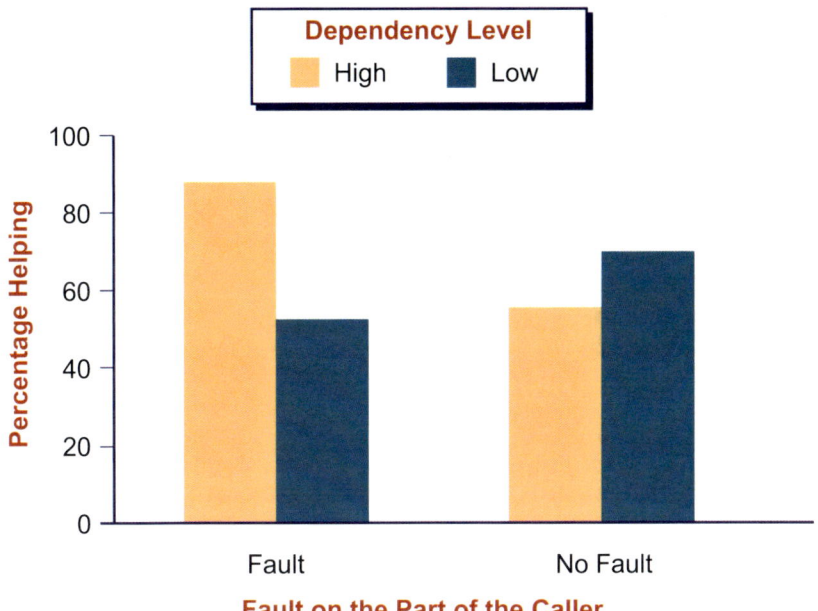

FIGURE 11.6

The effect of dependency and victim fault on helping. In Gruder's "Ralph's Garage" experiment, participants were more likely to help a victim high in dependency who was at fault for his predicament.
Based on data from Gruder, Romer, and Kroth (1974).

Just-world thinking also comes into play when we consider the degree to which a victim contributed to his or her own predicament. If you, as a helper, attribute a victim's suffering to his or her own actions (i.e., make an internal attribution), you will be less likely to help than if you attribute the suffering to some external cause (Schmidt & Weiner, 1988). When making judgments about individuals in need of help, we take into account the degree to which the victim had control over his or her fate (Schmidt & Weiner, 1988). For example, Greg Schmidt and Bernard Weiner (1988) found that participants expressed less willingness to help a student in need of class notes if he needed the notes because he went to the beach instead of class (a controllable situation) than if he had medically related vision problems that prevented him from taking notes (uncontrollable situation).

Why do perceptions of controllability matter? Schmidt and Weiner (1988) reported that the emotions aroused are important factors in one's reaction to a person in need. If a victim's situation arouses anger, as in the controllable situation, we are less likely to give help than if the victim's situation arouses sympathy (as in the uncontrollable situation). Apparently, we are quite harsh when it comes to a victim whom we perceive as having contributed to his or her own plight. We reserve our sympathy for those victims who had little or no control over their own fates.

In an interesting application of this effect, Weiner and his colleagues (Graham et al., 1993; Weiner, 1993; Weiner et al., 1988) applied this analysis to victims of various illnesses. Participants tended to react with pity (and less anger) toward victims of conditions over which the victims had little control (Alzheimer's disease, cancer). Conversely, participants tended to react with anger (and less pity) for victims of supposedly controllable conditions (AIDS, obesity) (Weiner, 1993; Weiner et al., 1988). The emotion tied to the victim's situation (pity versus anger) mediated willingness to help. Participants indicated less willingness to help victims with controllable problems than those with uncontrollable problems (Weiner et al., 1988). Additionally, participants assigned greater responsibility to a person with a disease (AIDS) if the victim's behavior was perceived to have contributed to his or her disease than if the victim's behavior was not perceived to have contributed. For example, if a person with AIDS contracted the disease via a blood transfusion, less responsibility was assigned to the victim than if the person contracted the disease via a sexual route (Graham et al., 1993).

Does this concept of the deserving versus the nondeserving victim hold across cultures? In an interesting study conducted by Mullen and Skitka (2009), U.S. and Ukranian participants were compared. Participants read profiles about individuals who needed organ transplants. Half the individuals were portrayed as having contributed to their own problems (practicing poor health behaviors), whereas the other half were said to have their condition because of a genetic disorder. Two other variables were manipulated. One was the degree to which the individual needing the transplant contributed to society (high or low), and the other was the degree of need for the new organ (i.e., 95% versus 80% chance of dying if a transplant was not performed). Mullen and Skitka found clear evidence for a cultural difference in the variables that mediate helping. U.S. participants mainly based their helping decisions on the degree to which an individual contributed to his or her own problems. That is, less help is likely to be given to the person who practiced poor health habits than to the person who suffers from a genetic disorder. Ukranian participants, on the other hand, placed more weight on one's contributions to society than on the other factors. However, both American and Ukranian participants were influenced by the other variables. U.S. participants were influenced by contribution to society and need, in that order, following personal responsibility. Ukranian participants also were influenced by personal responsibility and need, in that order, after contributions to society.

There is evidence that characteristics of the helper may interact with perceived controllability in determining affective responses to victims and helping behavior. In an analysis of reactions to individuals living in poverty, Zucker and Weiner (1993) found that politically conservative individuals were likely to blame the victim for being in poverty, attributing poverty to characteristics of the victim. Consequently, these individuals tend to react with anger and are less willing to help. On the other hand, more liberal individuals see poverty as driven by societal forces, not under control of the victim, and react with pity and are more willing to help.

Finally, social categorization also affects one's decision to help (Levine & Thompson, 2004; Levine et al., 2002; Levine et al., 2005; Sturmer et al., 2005). That is, we are more likely to help someone in need who is from our "in-group" as opposed to someone from an "out-group." In one study that demonstrated this effect, Levine and Thompson (2004) had participants read two scenarios depicting natural disasters (a flood and an earthquake). The scenarios depicted disasters of equal severity and elicited similar helping responses. Each disaster was said to have occurred either in Europe or South America. Participants were British students enrolled at Lancaster University in England. Levine and Thompson manipulated the "social identity" of the participants. Some participants were induced into adopting a "British social identity" and others a more general "European social identity." After reading the scenarios, participants were asked the extent to which they would be willing to help the victims of the natural disasters. Consistent with the notion that we are more likely to help members of an in-group, participants who were induced into a European social identity expressed a greater willingness to help European victims of either disaster than those who adopted the British social identity. Less help was extended to victims of a South American disaster, regardless of the identity induced. Thus, members of an out-group were least likely to be helped. In another experiment Levine et al. (2005) found that soccer fans were more likely to help someone in need who was wearing their team's jersey than someone wearing a rival team's jersey.

Race and Helping Behavior

Another characteristic of the victim investigated by social psychologists is race. Are Blacks more or less likely than Whites to receive help when they need it? If you base your answer on stories on television and in the newspapers, you might think that Blacks and Whites in our society never help each other. But this is simply not true. Many Blacks risked their lives to save Whites during the Los Angeles riots in 1992. A group of African American residents of south central Los Angeles helped get Reginald Denny to the hospital, saving his life. Interracial helping does occur. What does the social psychological research say about this issue?

A meta-analysis of the literature in this area (Saucier et al., 2005) found that race and helping present a rather complex picture. According to Saucier et al., the meta-analysis did not show any overall, universal bias against Black victims in need of help. Black and White victims, given the same helping situation, are equally likely to receive help. However, racial bias did emerge when specific variables were examined. Most specifically, variables relating to aversive racism (see Chapter 4) did show bias. Saucier et al. found that Blacks are less likely to receive help than Whites under the following conditions:

1. When the help required longer commitments of time
2. When the help was more risky
3. When the help was more difficult
4. When the distance between the helper and victim increased
5. When a White helper could rationalize away nonhelp

There have been numerous studies conducted to investigate aspects of interracial helping (Kunstman & Plant, 2008; Benson et al., 1976; Dovidio & Gaertner, 1981; Gaertner et al., 1982). In the Kunstman and Plant study, White participants were given the opportunity to help either a White or Black victim who fell backward out of a chair and was either mildly injured (low-level emergency) or more severely injured (high-level injury). Kunstman and Plant found that in the high-level emergency condition, the White participants were more likely to help the White than Black victim and were quicker to offer help to the White victim. Further, the White participants expressed more aversion (e.g., more disgusted, uneasy, and irritated) toward the Black victim in the high- than low-level emergency condition (aversion toward the White victim did not differ across emergency levels). In a second study, Kunstman and Plant found that in a high-level emergency with a Black victim, White participants perceived the emergency as less severe and felt less responsibility for helping than if the victim was White. Time pressure enhances the race difference in helping. In an experiment using an immersive virtual environment, participants were less likely to help a Black than White victim when they were told to exit the environment as quickly as possible than if a fire broke out or in a control condition (Gamberini et al., 2015). When help was offered to the Black victim, it was slower than if the victim were White.

In another study, White participants, assessed as either high or low in prejudice, were given an opportunity to help either a Black or a White victim (Gaertner et al., 1982). The participants were either alone (participant and victim) or with four others (three bystanders and the victim). The researchers recorded the amount of time participants took to give the victim aid. Their results showed that White victims were helped more quickly than Black victims, especially by prejudiced participants, when bystanders were present. Blacks and Whites were helped equally quickly when no bystanders were present. Thus, the bystander effect is stronger for Black than for White victims (Gaertner & Dovidio, 1977; Gaertner et al., 1982).

Given the opportunity to diffuse responsibility, bystanders will avail themselves of the opportunity more with Black than with White victims (Gaertner & Dovidio, 1977). This may occur because when multiple bystanders are present, a Black victim is seen as less severely injured than a White victim (Gaertner, 1975). When there is a single bystander, there is no such differential assessment of injury severity (Gaertner, 1975).

Other factors also influence the help given to Black versus White victims. In another study, White participants were given an opportunity to help either a Black or White male (Dovidio & Gaertner, 1981). This person was introduced as the participant's "supervisor" or "subordinate" and was said to be of either higher or lower cognitive ability than the participant. When given an opportunity to help, White participants helped the Black subordinate (lower status) more than the Black supervisor (higher status), regardless of the ability level. However, African American participants gave help based more on ability than on status. According to this study, status is relevant in Whites' decision to help Blacks, with more help given to lower-status Blacks (Dovidio & Gaertner, 1981). Ability is more relevant in Blacks' decision to help Whites, with more help given to high-ability than low-ability Whites.

The relationship between race and helping behavior is complex and involves numerous situational factors as well as racial attitudes. A review of the literature by Crosby, Bromley, and Saxe (1980) found mixed results. These researchers drew three conclusions:

1. Bias exists against Black victims, but the bias is not extreme. Clear discrimination against Black victims was reported in 44% of the studies reviewed; 56% showed no discrimination, or Blacks were helped more quickly than Whites.

2. Whites and Blacks discriminate against the opposite race at about the same level.

3. Whites discriminate against Black victims more under remote conditions (over the telephone) than in face-to-face situations.

In another study, researchers investigated race differences in the level of help given to elderly individuals who lived at home (Morrow-Howell et al., 1990). They analyzed a program in which volunteers were assigned to help elderly clients shop and provide them with transportation, counseling, and telephone social support. This study found very few differences between Black and White volunteers. For example, both Black and White volunteers attended training sessions at equal rates and were evaluated equally by their supervisors.

There was, however, one interesting difference between Black and White volunteers when the race of the client was considered. According to client reports, volunteers who were of a different race than the client spent less time with clients than did volunteers of the same race. Additionally, when the volunteer and client were of the same race, the client reported that there were more home visits and that the volunteer was more helpful than if the volunteer and client differed in race.

A few cautions are in order here, however. There was no independent measure of the amount of time volunteers spent with clients or the quality of service rendered. The data on the volunteers' performance were based on client reports. It could be that same-race clients were simply more inclined to rate their volunteers positively than were different-race clients. Nevertheless, the study documented a program of helping in which altruistic tendencies transcended racial barriers.

Sexual Orientation and Helping

The sexual orientation of a person in need influences willingness to help (Gabriel et al., 2001; Gore et al., 1997; Shaw et al., 1994). For example, Gore and colleagues (1997) had either a male or female victim make a telephone call to participants. When the participant answered, the victim made it clear that he or she had dialed the wrong number. Implied sexual orientation was manipulated by having the victim tell the participant that he or she was trying to reach his or her boyfriend or girlfriend. They also told the participant that they had either used their last quarter (high urgency) or were down to their last quarter (low urgency). Participants were asked to call a number to report the emergency (which was actually the experimenter's number). The proportion of participants who returned the victim's call to the experimenter within 60 seconds was the measure of helping. The results showed that heterosexuals were more likely to get help (80%) than same-sex orientation individuals (48%). Additionally, even when same-sex orientation individuals were helped, it took longer for the participants to call back than when the victim was heterosexual. In a field experiment, Hendren and Blank (2009) found that a male or female in need of money for parking was less likely to be helped if he or she were wearing a pro-gay/lesbian t-shirt than a neutral t-shirt.

Increasing the Chances of Receiving Help

We have been looking at helping behavior from the point of view of the potential helper. But what about the person in need of help? Is there anything a victim can do to increase the chances of being helped? Given all the obstacles along the path of helping, it may seem a small miracle that anyone ever receives any help. If you are in a position of needing help, however, there are some things you can do.

First, make your plea for help as loud as possible. Yelling and waving your arms increase the likelihood that others will notice your plight. Make your plea as clear as possible. You do not want to leave any room for doubt that you need help. This will help bystanders correctly label the situation as an emergency.

Next, you want to increase the chances that a bystander will assume responsibility for helping you. Don't count on this happening by itself. Anything you can do to increase a bystander's personal responsibility for helping will increase your chances of getting help. Making eye contact is one way to do this; making a direct request is another.

The effectiveness of the direct-request approach was graphically illustrated in a field experiment in which a confederate of the experimenter approached participants on a beach (Moriarty, 1975). In one condition, the confederate asked the participant to watch his things (a blanket and a radio) while the confederate went to the boardwalk for a minute (the participant is given responsibility for helping). In another condition, the confederate simply asked the participant for a match (social contact, but no responsibility). A short time after the confederate left, a second confederate came along and took the radio and ran off. More participants helped in the personal-responsibility condition (some actually ran the second confederate down) than in the nonresponsibility condition. Thus, making someone personally responsible for helping increases helping.

Study Break

The preceding sections continued the discussion of the five-stage model of helping. Before you go on to the next section, answer the following questions:

1. What factors affect the decision on how to help in an emergency?
2. What factors affect a person's decision to implement his or her decision to intervene in an emergency?
3. How does gratitude relate to helping?
4. How do characteristics of the victim affect helping?
5. How do race and sexual orientation relate to helping?
6. How can you increase your chances of receiving help?

Courageous Resistance and Heroism

A vast majority of research on altruism in social psychology has focused on helping in emergency situations. Typically, this type of help requires an immediate decision to a specific situation. However, not all helping falls into this category. There are helping situations that may involve nonemergencies (e.g., volunteering in a hospital) and may require a more deliberative decision than is required in an emergency situation. For example, if you are trying to decide whether to volunteer your time for a certain cause, you may take time to consider all aspects of your decision. One category of such helping is called **courageous resistance** (Shepela et al., 1999). According to Shepela et al., courageous resistance is "selfless behavior in which there is a high risk/cost to the actor, and possibly to the actor's family or associates, where the behavior must be sustained over time, is most often deliberative, and often where the actor is responding to a moral calling" (p. 789).

Courageous resistors can be found in a wide range of situations. For example, William Lawless was put in charge of waste disposal at the Savannah River reactor, even though he

courageous resistance Selfless behavior involving risk to a helper (and/or family) that is sustained over time, is a product of a deliberative process, and involves a moral calling.

had little experience in radioactive waste disposal. He became aware that liquid radioactive wastes were being dumped into shallow trenches. When he started asking questions, he was told to keep quiet about it. Instead, Lawless went public, and as a result, massive cleanup efforts were undertaken to remove radioactive waste disposed of improperly. From the political world is Nelson Mandela, founder of the African National Congress in South Africa. Mandela took a stand against apartheid (the system in South Africa that separated Whites and Blacks socially, economically, and linguistically). For his efforts he spent 28 years in prison. Eventually, he was released and went on to become the leader of that country.

Sometimes the individuals who arise as courageous resistors surprise us. Two examples are John Rabe and Albert Goering. Rabe was a Nazi businessman in Nanking, China. After the Japanese invaded Nanking in 1937 and began murdering Chinese civilians, Rabe used his Nazi credentials and connections to save nearly 250,000 Chinese by protecting them in a German compound, often facing down armed Japanese soldiers only with his Nazi credentials. Albert Goering, the half-brother of Hermann Goering (the second highest official in Nazi Germany), is credited with saving hundreds of persecuted Jews during World War II. He would forge his brother's name on transit documents and use his brother's influence if he got caught. Despite having grown up in the same house as his brother Hermann, Albert emerged as a much different person, dedicated to helping persecuted Jews escape those his brother sent to persecute them.

heroism Helping that involves significant risk above what is normally expected and serves some socially valued goal.

A concept closely related to courageous resistance is heroism. **Heroism** is any helping act that involves significant risk above what is normally expected and serves some socially valued goal (Becker & Eagly, 2004). The two elements of this definition require some elaboration. There are many jobs that require considerable risk, such as police officer and firefighter. We expect individuals in these roles to accept a degree of risk. So, for example, we expect a firefighter to enter a burning building to save victims. Such behavior is not necessarily heroic because it is expected of firefighters. However, if a firefighter goes back several times into a building on the verge of collapse to rescue victims, that would qualify as heroic. The second requirement of a heroic act is that it serves some valued goal. Saving lives is certainly a valued goal, as is putting one's job on the line to expose a wrong.

The definition of an act as heroic or a person as a hero is complicated by the fact that the designation is applied in situations that might raise questions about whether a behavior is truly heroic. Consider, for example, the designation of doctors and nurses as heroes during the COVID-19 pandemic. It was fairly common to see signs proclaiming "heroes work here" outside of hospitals. P. D. Hopkins (2021) raised a number of questions concerning designating doctors and nurses as heroes because they were involved in behavior we see as part of their jobs: treating sick people who sometimes have contagious and deadly diseases.

A form of helping that is different from helping in emergency involves courageous resistance involving selfless behavior that can result in serious risk or harm to the actor or his or her family. Nelson Mandela fought against Apartheid in South Africa and spend years in prison as a result. His act of courageous resistance helped end apartheid.
Source: Alessia Pierdomenico/Shutterstock.

Hopkins suggests that designating doctors and nurses as heroes raises three questions concerning the medical profession. First, if it is true that heroism involves going well beyond what is called for by professional expectations, then is treating diseased people no longer part of the traditional duties of doctors and nurses? Second, should people in other jobs who put themselves at risk (e.g., grocery store and restaurant workers) also be considered heroes? Third, what does it mean to be in a profession that does or does not regularly call for risky behavior?

You might be thinking at this point: "What is the harm in labeling doctors and nurses heroes?" Well, there might be subtle negative effects of designating doctors and nurses as heroes (Cox, 2020). Caitríona Cox points out that doing so may stifle discussion of the limits that are actually involved in a doctor's or nurse's duty to treat. She also suggests that it can affect the psychological well-being of those involved by implying that all doctors and nurses must act heroically. Raising these issues is not intended to diminish the behavior of doctors and nurses (and anyone else who was put at risk in the pandemic). Rather, these questions are relevant to the issue of what is considered heroic behavior. Unfortunately, there are no easy answers to these questions.

Franco et al. (2011) have extended thinking on heroism by suggesting that heroism is a more complex behavior than meets the eye. They maintain that heroism is a culturally driven concept and that what is heroic in one era may be seen negatively in another. For example, in the years after the battle at Little Bighorn, Lieutenant Colonel George Armstrong Custer was hailed as a military hero. More recently, historians have suggested that his actions prior to the battle were reckless and led to the unnecessary sacrifice of his men. In some Middle Eastern countries, suicide bombers are venerated as heroes. Their pictures are prominently displayed and their families provided for. In the West, these suicide bombers are viewed as evil.

Heroism is helping that involves significant risk above what is normally expected and serves some socially valued goal. Physical danger is an important dimension underlying what we see as heroism.
Source: Gorodenkoff/Shutterstock.

Franco et al. distinguish between *military heroes*, *civil heroes*, and *social heroes*. Military heroes act under a code of conduct carrying with it expectations of bravery. Military heroes also have specific training related to the situations in which they may display heroism. Civil heroes have no such code of conduct, nor are they trained. For both military and civil heroes, Franco et al. point out that heroic acts are dangerous and put the hero at great risk. Social heroes, on the other hand, do not face peril of life or limb. Socially heroic acts still carry with them substantial risks, such as financial risks, potential ostracism, and possible health risks. An example of a social hero would be a whistleblower who comes forward with knowledge of corporate or government wrongdoing. Based on these three categories of heroic acts, Franco et al. came up with a list of 12 hero types. In a study of how the public perceives these 12 types of heroic acts, Franco et al. found that physical risk was a crucial defining quality for heroism. This ran contrary to what they had expected but confirms Becker and Eagly's 2004 ideas about heroism. Additionally, participants were more likely to see military and civil heroism as more heroic than social heroism. In the category of civil heroism, a civilian fire rescue, wrestling a gun away from someone, and a criminal risking his life to protect another were seen as much more heroic than altruistic. Interestingly, a vigilante who helps catch criminals was seen as neither heroic nor altruistic. So a shady character such as a criminal can be seen as heroic, whereas an otherwise upstanding citizen (the vigilante) is not. On the military side, a soldier dying so others can escape, a soldier saving a buddy, and a soldier refusing to give information to an enemy were all seen as much more heroic than altruistic.

When faced with a situation requiring help, how does the heroic person act? Daniel Kahnamen (2013) has distinguished between slow and fast thinking. Slow thinking involves deliberation and reflection before action is taken. Fast thinking is more intuitive and does not involve deliberation or careful consideration of the situation. Heroes, when faced with a dangerous helping situation, show fast thinking and act intuitively (Rand & Epstein, 2014). Rand and Epstein obtained copies of interviews with recipients of the Carnegie Hero Medal done soon after their heroic act. Raters then evaluated the heroes' responses to determine whether the action they took was intuitive or deliberative. Rand and Epstein found that the medal recipients' statements indicated that they acted more out of intuition than deliberation. Where does this disposition toward rapid action come from? Are heroes born or made? It appears as though they are made. In another study, McNamee and Wesolik (2014) interviewed Carnegie Hero Medal recipients to determine the factors that contributed to their heroism. They found that the medal recipients indicated that they had parents who encouraged and expected them to help others. They also indicated that they felt a great need to help others, even if it meant risking their lives. Non-medal-recipients rarely made such statements (McNamee & Wesolik, 2014).

Heroism and courageous resistance have common elements. They have one important difference: A heroic act need not involve an extended commitment. A heroic act can be a one-shot occurrence involving a quick decision made on the spot. For example, Rick Rescorla (head of security for a firm at the World Trade Center), who reentered the World Trade Center to help stragglers get out and died when one of the towers collapsed, would be considered heroic. His behavior clearly involved risk and served the higher goal. It did not, however, involve the deliberative process over time and the long-term commitment to a course of action. So, one can be heroic without being a courageous resistor.

A heroic act need not always be motivated by empathy for a victim. There can be a number of motives for a heroic act. For example, a firefighter might act in a heroic way to gain recognition and secure a promotion. His or her egoistic motivations do not diminish the heroic nature of any act he or she performs.

In this section of the chapter we shall focus on one particular example of courageous resistance and heroism: Ordinary people who, under extraordinary circumstances, helped rescue Jews from the Nazis during World War II. You should keep in mind that what these individuals did was exceedingly dangerous. Anyone caught helping Jews was dealt with harshly, including being sent to death camps or summarily hanged. Because of prevailing anti-Jewish attitudes and the threat of punishment, engaging in rescue activity was relatively rare, especially in Eastern Europe. However, there were those who risked their lives to help others, in some cases for years.

Before we begin our discussion of rescuers, it is important to note that the relationship between altruism and courageous resistance may, at times, be tenuous. Not all altruistic individuals are courageous. For example, undoubtedly there were many Christians who deplored what the Nazis were doing to Jews and felt empathy for the Jews. However, because of fear of being caught and executed, many of these individuals did not translate their empathic concern into tangible action to help. Likewise, not all courageous people are altruistic. For example, Tec (1986) reports that some people who helped the Jews were "paid helpers" who helped Jews primarily for the money. These individuals were not motivated by empathy or altruism. As a result, the quality of care received by Jews helped by paid helpers was far lower than those helped by rescuers (Tec, 1986).

Explaining Courageous Resistance and Heroism: The Role of Personality

Much of the research on helping behavior that we have discussed suggests that whether people help depends on situational factors. For example, research shows that the costs of helping, the degree of responsibility for helping, the assumed characteristics of the victim, and the dangerousness of the situation all affect helping behavior. None of these factors are under the control of the potential helper; they are part of the situation.

Situational factors seem to be crucial in situations that require spontaneous helping (Clary & Orenstein, 1991). The situations created in the laboratory, or for that matter in the field, are analogous to looking at a single frame in a motion picture. Recall the seminarians. They were in a hurry, and although thinking of the parable of the Good Samaritan, they practically leapt over the slumped body of a person in need of their help. Is this unexpected event a fair and representative sample of their behavior? It was for that particular situation. But, unless we look at what comes before and after, we cannot make judgments about how they would behave in other situations. Looking at these single-frame glimpses of helping can lead us to overlook personality variables.

Researchers have also looked at how people with different characteristics emerge in different helping roles. For example, Walker and Frimer (2007) looked at personality differences between brave and caring people. Brave people are those who have put their lives on the line to save others (such as Irene Opdyke). Caring people are those who have extraordinary long-term commitment to helping others (e.g., Mother Teresa). Walker and Frimer wanted to know if moral judgment (caring) was sufficient to account for moral action (bravery). Walker and Frimer had individuals who had either won the Canadian Medal of Bravery or received the Caring Canadian Award complete a number of personality measures and provide a narrative of an actual moral conflict they had experienced. Walker and Frimer found that there was considerable similarity in the personalities of brave and caring individuals. However, there were also some differences. Caring individuals were higher on the dimensions of nurturance, affiliation/intimacy, generativity (concern for providing for the next generation), communion (e.g., love/friendship), affective tone (optimism/pessimism), sensitivity to the needs of others, and quality of attachments to others. Walker and Frimer suggest that the personality profile of the caring person led them to engage in extended acts of kindness to others. On the other hand, brave individuals, who engaged in a single act of bravery, showed a different cluster of characteristics.

Although personality factors come into play in all forms of altruism, they may be more likely to come to the fore in long-term helping situations. Helping on a long-term basis, whether it involves volunteering at a hospital or Albert Goering helping Jews, requires a degree of planning. This planning might take place before the help begins. Or it may occur after help begins. For example, rescuers of Jews in Nazi-occupied Europe often did not plan their initial helping acts (Tec, 1986). However, their continued helping required thought and planning. During planning, helpers assess risks, costs, and priorities, and they match personal morals and abilities with victims' needs.

History teaches us that in times of great need, a select few individuals emerge to offer long-term help. What is it about these people that sets them apart from others who remain on the sidelines? Midlarsky et al. (2005) compared rescuers and nonrescuers on a number of personality dimensions. They found that the rescuers possessed a cluster of personality characteristics that distinguished them from nonrescuers. These characteristics were: "locus of control, autonomy, risk taking, social responsibility, empathic concern, and altruistic moral reasoning" (p. 918). Rescuers, compared to nonrescuers, were more internally motivated, were more independent, were more likely to take risks, showed higher levels of social responsibility, had more empathic concern for others, and were more likely to be driven by internal moral/altruistic values. Further, they found that altruistic moral reasoning was the strongest correlate of rescue activity.

So, there is evidence for an **altruistic personality**, or a cluster of personality traits, including empathy, that predisposes individuals to great acts of altruism. However, we also must remain mindful that situational forces still may be important, even in long-term helping situations. In the sections that follow, we explore how situational factors and personality factors combine to influence altruism. We begin by considering the factors that influenced a relatively small number of individuals to help rescue Jews from the Nazis during their World War II occupation of Europe.

altruistic personality
A cluster of personality traits that predisposes a person to acts of altruism.

Study Break

This section introduced you to courageous resistance and heroism. Before you begin the next section, answer the following questions:

1. What is courageous resistance, and how does it differ from helping in emergencies?
2. What is heroism, and what are the two main components of its definition?
3. What are the different types of heroism presented, and what dimensions define them?
4. How does a heroic person react to a situation requiring help, and what motivates a heroic act?
5. How does personality relate to courageous resistance and heroism?
6. What is the altruistic personality, and what evidence is there that it exists?

Righteous Rescuers in Nazi-Occupied Europe

As Hitler's final solution (the systematic extermination of European Jews) progressed, life for Jews in Europe became harder and more dangerous. Although most of Eastern Europe's and many of Western Europe's Jews were murdered, some did survive. Some

righteous rescuer The designation bestowed by Israel on non-Jews who helped save Jews from the Nazis during World War II.

survived on their own by passing as Christians or leaving their homes ahead of the Nazis. Many, however, survived with the help of non-Jews who risked their lives to help them. The state of Israel recognizes a select group of those who helped Jews for their heroism and designates them as **righteous rescuers** (Tec, 1986).

Sadly, not as many individuals emerged as rescuers as one might wish. The number of rescuers is estimated to have been between 50,000 and 500,000, a small percentage of those living under Nazi rule (Oliner & Oliner, 1988). In short, only a minority of people were willing to risk their lives to help others.

It should not be too surprising that the majority did not help the Jews. Those caught helping Jews, even in the smallest way, were subjected to punishment, death in an extermination camp, or summary execution. In other cases, especially in Poland, rescuing Jews amounted to flying in the face of centuries of anti-Semitic attitudes and religious doctrine that identified Jews as the killers of Jesus Christ (Oliner & Oliner, 1988; Tec, 1986). The special problems facing Polish rescuers are illustrated in the following quotation from one: "My husband hated Jews. . . . Anti-Semitism was ingrained in him. Not only was he willing to burn every Jew but even the earth on which they stood. Many Poles feel the way he did. I had to be careful of the Poles" (Tec, 1986, p. 54).

autonomous altruism Selfless altruism that society does not support or might even discourage.

Because Polish rescuers violated such powerful social norms, some social psychologists have suggested that their behavior is an example of **autonomous altruism**, selfless help that society does not reinforce (Tec, 1986). In fact, such altruism may be discouraged by society. Rescuers in countries outside Poland may have been operating from a different motive. Most rescuers in Western Europe, although acting out of empathy for the Jews, may have had a *normocentric motivation* for their first act of helping (Oliner & Oliner, 1988). A normocentric motivation for helping is oriented more toward a group (perhaps society) with whom an individual identifies than toward the individual in need. In small towns in southern France, for example, rescuing Jews became normative, the accepted and expected thing to do. This type of altruism is known as **normative altruism**, altruism that society supports and encourages (Tec, 1986).

normative altruism Altruism that society supports and encourages.

Finally, it is important to understand that not only were general attitudes throughout Europe related to the frequency and type of rescue activity, but so were specific cultural and social forces within specific regions of Europe. For example, Buckser (2001) points out that the large-scale rescue of Danish Jews is best understood within the cultural context of Denmark and its relationship to its Jewish population. Buckser points out that in many areas the Danish population did not resist German occupation. However, when it came to the Jewish population, Danes came together to save all but a few Danish Jews. Buckser believes that Danes rose up to help the Jews because of *Grundtvigian Nationalism,* which essentially placed Danish national and cultural identity above differences among people. In Denmark, Jews had successfully assimilated into the larger Danish culture. So, when the Germans invaded and tried to portray the Jews as threatening outsiders, it didn't work well. Instead, the German characterization of the Jews activated the unique Danish nationalism, and Danes who otherwise acquiesced to the Germans actively took part in the large-scale evacuation of Danish Jews to Sweden.

Although there were many who aided the Nazis in the extermination of Jews during World War II, a relatively small number of others risked their lives to help Jews hide or escape from the Nazis. Among these rescuers was Oskar Schindler who saved 1,200 Jews by employing them in his factory.
Source: Gerardo C. Lerner/Shutterstock.

The Oliners and the Altruistic Personality Project

One family victimized by the Nazis in Poland was that of Samuel Oliner. One day in 1942, when Samuel was 12 years old and living in the village of Bobawa, he was roused by the sound of soldiers' boots cracking the predawn silence. He escaped to the roof and hid there in his pajamas until they left. When he dared to come down from his rooftop perch, the Jews of Bobawa lay buried in a mass grave. The village was empty.

Two years earlier, Samuel's entire family had been killed by the Nazis. Now he gathered some clothes and walked for 48 hours until he reached the farm of Balwina Piecuch, a peasant woman who had been friendly to his family in the past. The 12-year-old orphan knocked at her door. When Piecuch saw Samuel, she gathered him into her house. There she harbored him against the Nazis, teaching him what he needed to know of the Christian religion to pass as a Polish stable boy.

Oliner survived the war, immigrated to the United States, and went on to teach at Humboldt State University in Arcata, California. One of his courses was on the Holocaust. In it, he examined the fate of the millions of Jews, Gypsies, and other Europeans who were systematically murdered by the Nazis between 1939 and 1945. In 1978, one of his students, a German woman, became distraught, saying she couldn't bear the guilt over what her people had done.

At this point, Oliner realized that the history of the war, a story of murder, mayhem, and sadism, had left out a small but important aspect: the accomplishments of the many altruistic people who acted to help Jews and did so without expectation of external rewards (Goldman, 1988; Oliner & Oliner, 1988). Oliner and his wife, Pearl, established the Altruistic Personality Project to study the character and motivations of those altruists, whom the Oliners rightly call heroes.

Situational Factors Involved in Becoming a Rescuer

Oliner and Oliner (1988) and Tec (1986) investigated the situational forces that influence individuals to become rescuers. These situational factors can be captured in the five questions for which the Oliners wanted to find answers:

1. Did rescuers know more about the difficulties the Jews faced than nonrescuers?
2. Were rescuers better off financially and therefore better able to help?
3. Did rescuers have social support for their efforts?
4. Did rescuers adequately evaluate the risks, the costs of helping?
5. Were rescuers asked to help, or did they initiate helping on their own?

The Oliners interviewed rescuers and a matched sample of nonrescuers over the course of a 5-year study and compared the two groups. The Oliners used a 66-page questionnaire, translated into Polish, German, French, Dutch, Italian, and Norwegian and used 28 bilingual interviews. Results indicate that the situational differences between rescuers and nonrescuers were not as significant as expected. For example, rescuers were not wealthier than nonrescuers. Tec (1986) reported that the greatest number of Polish helpers came from the peasant class, not the upper class of Poles. Additionally, rescuers and nonrescuers alike knew about the persecution of the Jews and knew the risks involved in going to their aid (Oliner & Oliner, 1988).

Only two situational variables were relevant to the decision to rescue. First, family support was important for the rescue effort (Tec, 1986). Sixty percent of the rescuers in Tec's sample reported that their families supported the rescue effort, compared to only 12% who said that their families opposed rescue efforts, a finding mirrored in Oliner and Oliner's study. Evidence suggests that rescue was made more likely by the rescuers' being affiliated with a group that supported the rescue effort (Baron, 1986). We can conclude that support from some outside agency, be it the family or another support group, made rescue more likely.

The second situational factor was how the rescuer first began his or her efforts. In most cases (68%), rescuers helped in response to a specific request to help; only 32% initiated help on their own (Oliner & Oliner, 1988). Tec reported a similar result. For most rescuers the first act of help was unplanned. But once a rescuer agreed to help that first time, he or she was likely to help again. Help was refused in a minority of instances (about 15%), but such refusal was related to specific risks involved in giving help. Most rescuers (61%) helped for 6 months or more (Tec, 1986). And 90% of the people rescuers helped were strangers (Goldman, 1988).

These situational factors—the costs of helping, a request for help, and the support of other bystanders in a group of which the rescuer was a member—also have been identified in research as important in influencing the decision to help.

Personality Factors Involved in Becoming a Rescuer

The results of the work by Oliner and Oliner (1988) suggest that rescuers and nonrescuers differed from each other less by circumstances than by their upbringing and personalities. The Oliners found that rescuers exhibited a strong feeling of personal responsibility for the welfare of other people and a compelling need to act on that felt responsibility. They were moved by the pain of the innocent victims, by their sadness, helplessness, and desperation. Empathy for the victim was an important factor driving this form of altruism. Interestingly, rescuers and nonrescuers did not differ significantly on general measures of empathy. However, they did differ on a particular type of empathy called *emotional empathy*, which centers on one's sensitivity to the pain and suffering of others (Oliner & Oliner, 1988). According to the Oliners, this empathy, coupled with a sense of social responsibility, increased the likelihood that an individual would make and keep a commitment to help.

Beyond empathy, rescuers shared several other characteristics (Tec, 1986). First, they showed an inability to blend in with others in the environment. That is, they tended to be socially marginal, not fitting in very well with others. Second, rescuers exhibited a high level of independence and self-reliance. They were likely to pursue their personal goals even if those goals conflicted with social norms. Third, rescuers had an enduring commitment to helping those in need long before the war began. The war did not make these people altruists; rather, it allowed these individuals to remain altruists in a new situation.

Fourth, rescuers had (and maintained while alive) a matter-of-fact attitude about their rescue efforts. During and after the war, rescuers denied that they were heroes, instead saying that they did the only thing they could do. Finally, rescuers had a universalistic view of the needy. That is, rescuers were able to put aside the religion or other characteristics of those they helped. Interestingly, some rescuers harbored anti-Semitic attitudes (Tec, 1986). But they were able to put those prejudices aside and help a person in need. These characteristics, along with high levels of empathy, contributed to the rescuers' decision to help the Jews.

The research on rescuers clearly shows that they differed in significant ways from those who were nonrescuers (Oliner & Oliner, 1988) or paid helpers (Tec, 1986). How can we account for these differences? To answer this question, we must look at the family environments in which rescuers were socialized.

Altruism as a Function of Childrearing Style

In Chapter 10, we established that inept parenting contributes to the development of antisocial behaviors such as aggression. Oliner and Oliner (1988) found that the childrearing styles used by parents of rescuers contributed to the development of prosocial attitudes and behaviors. The techniques used by parents of rescuers fostered empathy in the rescuers. Generally, a child who has parents who provide a supportive environment, use authoritative parenting, and use a less restrictive parenting style shows higher levels of prosocial moral reasoning than parents who do not show these parenting characteristics (Janssens & Dekovic, 1997).

Research shows that a parental or adult model who behaves altruistically is more likely to influence children to help than are verbal exhortations to be generous (Bryan & Walbek, 1970). Additionally, verbal reinforcement has a different effect on children's helping, depending on whether a model behaves in a charitable or selfish manner (Midlarsky et al., 1973). Verbal social approval from a selfish model does not increase children's donations. However, social approval from a charitable model does.

Models obviously have a powerful effect on both aggressive and prosocial behaviors. Why, however, do you think that a prosocial model has more effect on younger children than older children? What factors can you think of to explain the fact that a model's behavior is more important than what the model says? Based on what you know about the effect of prosocial models on children's altruism, if you were given the opportunity to design a television character to communicate prosocial ideals, what would that character be like? What would the character say and do to foster prosocial behavior in children? Similarly, what types of models should we be exposing adults to in order to increase helping? Parents of rescuers provided role models for their children that allowed them to develop the positive qualities needed to become rescuers later in life. For example, rescuers (more than nonrescuers) came from families that stressed the universal similarity of all people, despite superficial differences among them (Oliner & Oliner, 1988). Families stressed the aspect of religion that encouraged caring for those in need. Additionally, families of rescuers did not discuss negative stereotypes of Jews, which was more common among families of nonrescuers. As children, then, rescuers were exposed to role models that instilled in them many positive qualities.

It is not enough for parents simply to embrace altruistic values and provide positive role models (Staub, 1985); they must also exert firm control over their children. Parents who raise altruistic children coach them to be helpful and firmly teach them how to be helpful (Goleman, 1991; Staub, 1985). Parents who are warm and nurturing and use reasoning with the child as a discipline technique are more likely to produce an altruistic child than cold, uncaring, punitive parents (Eisenberg & Mussen, 1989). A meta-analysis of the literature on the relationship between parenting style and prosocial behavior in children shows that such behavior relates to parents using an authoritative parenting style (using warmth, sensitivity, and setting limits). Conversely, an authoritarian style (low warmth and nurturing and more punitive) is associated with lower levels of prosocial behavior (Wong et al., 2021). This was certainly true of families of rescuers. Parents of rescuers tended to avoid using physical punishment, using an inductive style that focused on verbal reasoning and explanation.

As important as the family is in the socialization of altruism, it cannot alone account for a child growing up to be an altruistic individual. Recall that Albert and Hermann Goering grew up in the same household yet went down very different paths in adulthood. The child's cognitive development, or his or her capacity to understand the world, also plays a role.

Altruism as a Function of Cognitive Development

As children grow, their ability to think about and understand other people and the world changes. The cognitive perspective focuses on how altruistic behavior develops as a result of changes in the child's thinking skills. Generally, a child's prosocial behavior undergoes changes, moving from more simple forms of helping to more sophisticated ones. For example, a study conducted by Svetlova et al. (2010) looked at two forms of helping among 18- to 30-month-old toddlers. *Instrumental helping* involves helping another person accomplish something (e.g., get something off a shelf). Children are capable of this form of helping at a young age (12 to 14 months). *Empathic helping* is emotion-based helping focused on the well-being of another person. This form of helping develops later. Svetlova et al. gave toddlers several opportunities to help an adult, some of which were instrumental and some empathic. Svetlova et al. found that the 18-month-old toddlers showed stronger instrumental than empathic helping. The 30-month-olds showed equally strong instrumental and empathic helping. Svetlova et al. point out that the older children's helping was more autonomous and represented a higher level of social understanding than the younger children's helping.

In another study, Nancy Eisenberg presented children with several moral dilemmas that pit one person's welfare against another person's welfare. Here is one example: Bob, a young man who was very good at swimming, was asked to help young crippled children who could not walk to learn to swim so that they could strengthen their legs for walking. Bob was the only one in his town who could do this job well because only he had both life-saving and teaching experiences. But helping crippled children took much of Bob's free time left after work and school, and Bob wanted to practice hard as often as possible for an upcoming series of important swimming contests. If Bob did not practice swimming in all his free time, his chances of winning the contests and receiving a paid college education or sum of money would be greatly lessened (Eisenberg & Mussen, 1989, p. 124).

The dilemma pits Bob's needs against those of other people. The children in Eisenberg's study were asked several questions about what Bob should do. For example, "Should Bob agree to teach the crippled children? Why?" Based on their responses, children were classified according to Eisenberg's levels of prosocial reasoning. Eisenberg's findings show that as children get older, they are more likely to understand the needs of other people and are less focused on their own selfish concerns. The research suggests that this is a continual process and that people's altruistic thinking and behavior can change throughout life.

The idea that the development of altruism is a lifelong process is supported by the fact that rescuers did not magically become caring and empathic at the outset of the war. Instead, the ethic of caring grew out of their personalities and interpersonal styles, which had developed over the course of their lives. Rescuers were altruistic long before the war (Huneke, 1986; Oliner & Oliner, 1988; Tec, 1986) and tended to remain more altruistic than nonrescuers after the war (Oliner & Oliner, 1988).

Study Break

This section introduced research on rescuers of Jews from the Nazis during World War II. Before you begin the next section, answer the following questions:

1. What is a righteous rescuer, and how do the ideas of autonomous and normative altruism relate to rescue behavior?
2. What situational factors relate to rescue activity?
3. What personality characteristics relate to rescue activity?
4. How does childrearing style relate to the development of altruism?
5. How does cognitive development relate to the development of altruism?

Becoming an Altruistic Person

Altruism requires something more than empathy and compassionate values (Staub, 1985). It requires the psychological and practical competence to carry those intentions into action (Goleman, 1991). Goodness, like evil, begins slowly, in small steps. Recall from the Chapter 7 discussion on social influence that we are often eased into behaviors in small steps (i.e., through the foot-in-the-door technique). In a similar manner, many rescuers gradually eased themselves into their roles as rescuers. People responded to a first request for help and hid someone for a day or two. Once they took that first step, they began to see themselves differently, as the kind of people who rescued the desperate. Altruistic actions changed their self-concept: Because I helped, I must be an altruistic person. As we saw in Chapter 2, one way we gain self-knowledge is through observation of our own behavior. We then apply that knowledge to our self-concept.

This is how Swedish diplomat Raoul Wallenberg got involved in rescuing Hungarian Jews during World War II (Staub, 1985). The first person he rescued was a business partner who happened to be a Hungarian Jew. Wallenberg then became more involved and more daring. He began to manufacture passes for Jews, saying that they were citizens of Sweden. He even handed out passes to Jews who were being put in the cattle cars that would take them to the death camps. Wallenberg disappeared soon after, and his fate is still unknown. Apparently, there is a unique type of person who is likely to take that very first step to help and to continue helping until the end (Goleman, 1991). Wallenberg and the other rescuers were such people.

Gender and Rescue

Research suggests that a small majority of the rescuers were women (Becker & Eagly, 2004). For example, in Poland 57% of rescuers were women. In France 55.6% were women. And in the Netherlands, 52.5% were women (Becker & Eagly, 2004). Becker and Eagly report that women rescuers who were not part of a couple (e.g., husband-wife team) significantly exceeded the number of such women in the general population. Further, the motivation underlying male and female rescue differed. Women were more likely to be motivated by interpersonal caring and a relationship orientation than men (Anderson, 1993).

Anderson (1993) content analyzed the questionnaire and interview data collected by Sam and Pearl Oliner (1988). Anderson evaluated information on socialization experiences, the family histories, and self-concepts of male and female rescuers. Anderson found very different socialization experiences for male and female rescuers. She found that men tended to be socialized toward civic life, had at least a high school education, and were socialized to be autonomous. Women were more likely to be socialized to be family oriented, were less likely to have had an education, and were socialized for altruism. Anderson points out that these different socialization experiences related to different forms of rescue activity for men and women. Men, reflecting their socialization toward autonomy, were more likely to work alone, rescuing large numbers of people, one at a time. Male rescue was also more likely to be brief and repetitive (e.g., smuggling people out of dangerous areas). Female rescuers, on the other hand, were more likely to work with others in helping networks and help the same people over a longer period of time. Anderson also found that women tended to be motivated by guilt and expressed depression and doubts about their ability to help. Men were more motivated to protect the innocent and were less socially connected than women.

A Synthesis: Situational and Personality Factors in Altruism

We have seen that both situational and personality factors influence the development and course of altruism. How do these factors work together to produce altruistic behavior? Two approaches provide some answers: the interactionist view and the application of the five-stage decision model to long-term helping situations.

The Interactionist View

The **interactionist view of altruism** argues that an individual's internal motives (whether altruistic or selfish) interact with situational factors to determine if a person will help (Callero, 1986). Romer and his colleagues (Romer et al., 1986) identified four altruistic orientations based on the individual's degree of nurturance (the need to give help) and of succorance (the need to receive help):

1. *Altruistic*—Those who are motivated to help others but not to receive help in return
2. *Receptive giving*—Those who help to obtain something in return
3. *Selfish*—Those who are primarily motivated to receive help but not give it
4. *Inner-sustaining*—Those who are not motivated to give or receive help

In their study, Romer and colleagues (1986) led people to believe that they either would or would not be compensated for their help. On the basis of the four orientations just described, these researchers predicted that individuals with an altruistic orientation would help even if compensation was not expected; receptive givers would be willing to help only if they stood to gain something in return; selfish people would not be oriented toward helping, regardless of compensation; and those described as inner-sustaining would neither give nor receive, no matter what the compensation.

Romer's (1986) results confirmed this hypothesis. Figure 11.7 shows the results on two indexes of helping: the percentage of participants who agree to help and the number of hours volunteered. Notice that altruistic people were less likely to help when compensation was offered. This is in keeping with the reverse incentive effect described in Chapter 6. When people are internally motivated to do something, giving them an external reward decreases their motivation and their liking for the activity. There is also evidence that personality and the situation interact in a way that can reduce the bystander effect. In one study, researchers categorized participants as either "esteem oriented" or

interactionist view of altruism The view that an individual's altruistic or selfish internal motives interact with situational factors to determine whether a person will help.

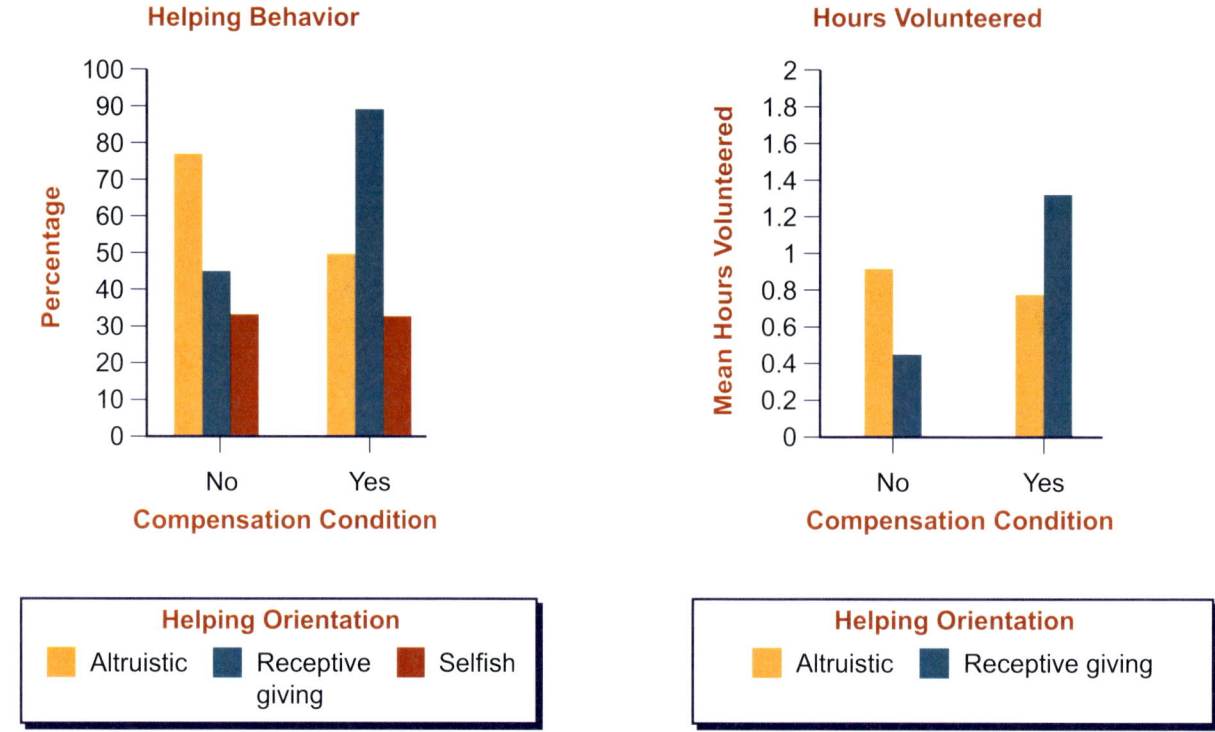

FIGURE 11.7

Helping behavior and hours volunteered as a function of helping orientation and compensation. Participants whose orientation was receptive giving were more likely to help when they received compensation. Altruistic participants were willing to help regardless of whether they were compensated.

From Romer et al. (1986).

"safety oriented" (Wilson, 1976). Esteem-oriented individuals are motivated by a strong sense of personal competency rather than by what others do. Safety-oriented individuals are more dependent on what others do. Participants were exposed to a staged emergency (a simulated explosion that supposedly hurt the experimenter), either while alone, in the presence of a passive bystander (who makes no effort to help), or in the presence of a helping bystander (who goes to the aid of the experimenter).

The study showed that esteem-oriented participants were more likely to help than safety-oriented participants in all cases (Figure 11.8). Of most interest, however, is the fact that the esteem-oriented participants were more likely to help when a passive bystander was present than were the safety-oriented participants. Thus, participants who are motivated internally (esteem oriented) are not just more likely to help than those who are externally motivated (safety oriented); they are also less likely to fall prey to the influence of a passive bystander. This suggests that individuals who helped in the classic experiments on the bystander effect may possess personality characteristics that allow them to overcome the help-depressing effects of bystanders.

We might also expect that the individual's personality will interact with the costs of giving help. Some individuals help even though the cost of helping is high. For example, some participants in Batson's (1990a) research described earlier in this chapter helped by offering to change places with someone receiving electric shocks even though they could have escaped the situation easily. And rescuers helped despite the fact that getting caught helping Jews meant death. In contrast, there are those who will not help even if helping requires minimal effort.

The degree to which the personality of the helper affects helping may depend on the perceived costs involved in giving aid. In relatively low-cost situations, personality will be less important than the situation. However, in high-cost situations, personality will be more important than the situation. As the perceived cost of helping increases, personality exerts a stronger effect on the decision to help. This is represented in Figure 11.9.

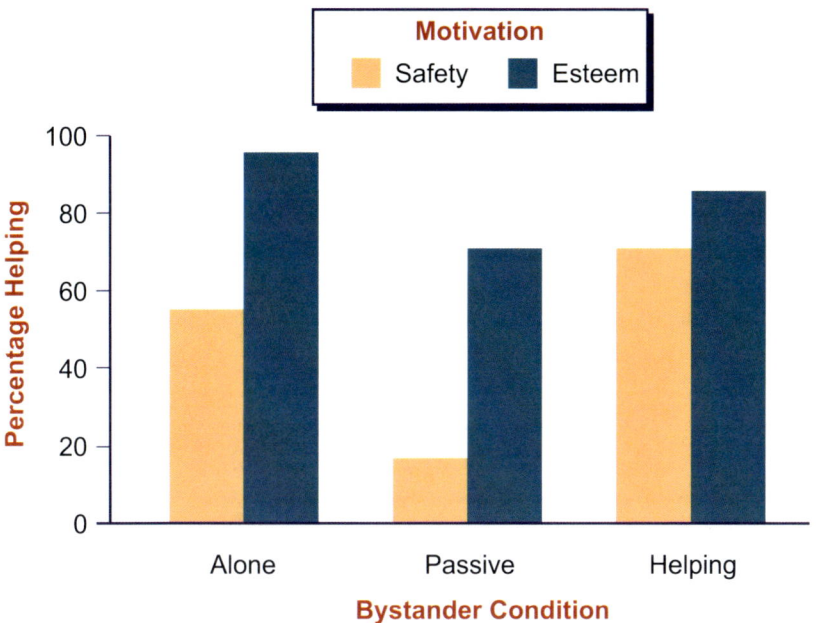

FIGURE 11.8

The relationship between personality characteristics, presence, and type of bystander on the likelihood of helping. Esteem-oriented participants were most likely to help, regardless of bystander condition. Safety-oriented participants were most likely to help if they were alone or if there was a helping bystander present.

Based on data from Wilson (1976).

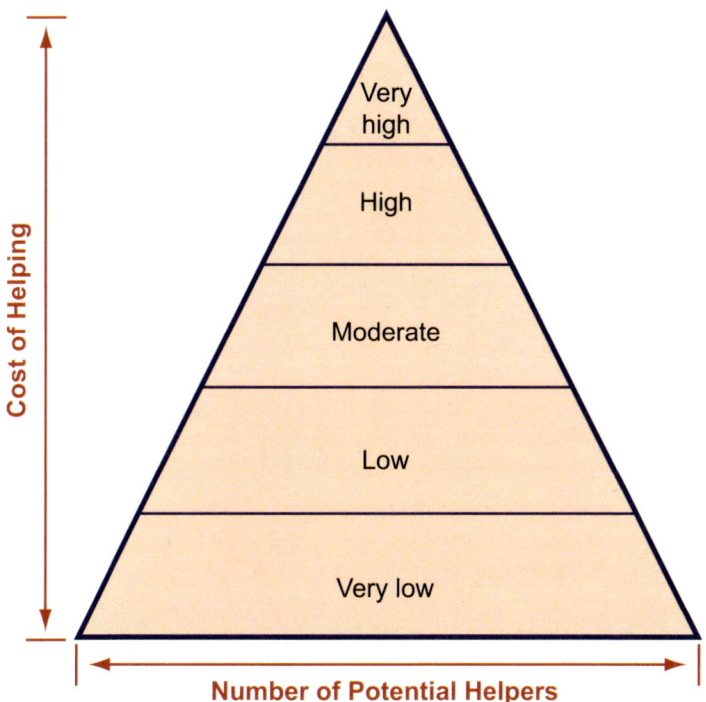

FIGURE 11.9

The relationship between personality and likeliness of helping in different helping situations. Nearly everyone would help if costs were very low. As the cost of the helping act increases, fewer and fewer individuals are expected to help. Only the most altruistic individuals are expected to help in very high-cost situations.

The base of the triangle represents very low-cost behaviors. As you move up the triangle, the cost of helping increases. The relative size of each division of the triangle represents the number of people who would be willing to help another in distress.

An extremely low-cost request (e.g., giving a stranger directions to the campus library) would result in most people's helping. People's personalities matter little when it costs almost nothing to help. In fact, probably more effort is spent on saying no than on directing the passerby to the library. When the cost of helping becomes high, even prohibitive, as in the case of rescuing Jews from the Nazis, fewer people help. However, there are those who successfully overcome the situational forces working against helping, perhaps due to their altruistic personalities, and offer help.

Applying the Five-Stage Decision Model to Long-Term Helping

Earlier in this chapter we described a five-stage decision model of helping. That model has been applied exclusively to the description and explanation of helping in spontaneous emergencies. Now that we have explored some other aspects of helping, we can consider whether that model may be applied to long-term and situation-specific spontaneous helping. Let's consider how each stage applies to the actions of those who rescued Jews from the Nazis.

Noticing the Situation   For many rescuers, seeing the Nazis taking Jews away provoked awareness. One rescuer, Irene Opdyke, first became aware of the plight of the Jews when she happened to look through a hotel window and saw Jews being rounded up and taken away (Opdyke, 1992). Oliner and Oliner (1988) reported that rescuers were motivated to action when they witnessed some external event such as the one Opdyke witnessed. Of course, however, many nonrescuers also saw the same events yet did not help.

Labeling the Situation as an Emergency   A critical factor in the decision to rescue Jews was to label the situation as one serious enough to require intervention. Here, the differences between rescuers and nonrescuers became important. Apparently, rescuers were more likely to see the persecution of the Jews as something serious that required intervention. The persecutions appeared to insult the sensibilities of the rescuers. Nonrescuers often decided that Jews must truly have done something to deserve their awful fate. They tended to blame the victim and by so doing relieved themselves of any responsibility for helping.

Rescuers also had social support to help because they belonged to groups that valued such action. This is consistent with the notion that encouragement from others may make it easier to label a situation as one requiring intervention (Dozier & Miceli, 1985).

Assuming Responsibility to Help   The next step in the process is for the rescuer to assume responsibility to help. For rescuers, the universalistic view of the needy, ethics of justice and caring, and generally high levels of empathy made assuming responsibility probable. In fact, many rescuers suggested that after they noticed the persecution of Jews, they had to do something. Their upbringing and view of the world made assumption of responsibility almost a given rather than a decision. The main difference between the rescuers and the nonrescuers who witnessed the same events was that the rescuers interpreted the events as a call to action (Oliner & Oliner, 1988). For the rescuers, the witnessed event connected with their principles of caring (Oliner & Oliner, 1988) and led them to assume responsibility.

Another factor may have come into play when the rescuers (or a bystander to an emergency situation) assumed responsibility. Witnessing maltreatment of the Jews may have activated the *norm of social responsibility* in these individuals. This norm involves the notion that we should help others without regard to receiving help or a reward in exchange (Berkowitz, 1972; Schwartz, 1975).

Deciding How to Help   Rescuers helped in a variety of ways (Oliner & Oliner, 1988). They had to assess the alternatives available and decide which was most appropriate. Alternatives included donating money to help Jews, providing false papers, and hiding

Jews. It appears that, at least sometimes, perceived costs were not an issue. For example, Opdyke hid several Jews in the basement of a German major's house in which she was the housekeeper, even after she witnessed a Polish family and the family of Jews they were hiding hanged by the Nazis in the town marketplace.

Implementing the Decision to Help The final stage, implementing the decision to help, includes assessing rewards and costs for helping and potential outcomes of helping versus not helping. When Everett Sanderson rescued someone who had fallen onto the subway tracks, he said he could not have lived with himself if he had not helped. This is an assessment of outcomes. For Sanderson, the cost for not helping outweighed the cost for helping, despite the risks.

It is quite probable that the altruistic personalities we have been studying made similar assessments. Because of their upbringing and the events of their lives that defined them as altruistic people, they decided that helping was less costly to them than not helping. Most of them engaged in long-term helping. This suggests that they assessed the outcome of their initial decision to help and decided that it was correct. This was certainly true of Balwina Piecuch. It was also true of the Polish woman in the following example, which illustrates the interactionist nature of helping—the interplay of situational and personality factors and the combination of spontaneous and long-term events:

A woman and her child were being led through Kracow, Poland, with other Jews to a concentration station. The woman ran up to a bystander and pleaded, "Please, please save my child." A Polish woman took the young boy to her apartment, where neighbors became suspicious of this sudden appearance of a child and called the police. The captain of the police department asked the woman if she knew the penalty for harboring a Jewish child. The young woman said, with some heat, "You call yourself a Pole, a gentleman, a man of the human race?" She continued her persuasive act, claiming that one of the police in the room had actually fathered the child "and stooped so low as to be willing to have the child killed" (Goldman, 1988, p. 8). Both the woman and the young boy survived the war.

Study Break

This section continued the discussion of rescue behavior and showed how the five-stage model of emergency helping applies. Before you begin the next section, answer the following questions:

1. How does one become an altruistic person?
2. What is the relationship between gender and gender roles and rescue activity?
3. What is the interactionist view of altruism?
4. How do situational and personality characteristics interact to produce altruistic behavior?
5. How does the five-stage model of helping apply to long-term helping? Give an example for each stage.

Altruistic Behavior from the Perspective of the Recipient

Our discussion of altruism to this point has centered on the helper. But helping situations, of course, involve another person: the recipient. Social psychologists have asked two broad questions that relate to the recipient of helping behavior: What influences an individual's decision to seek help? What reactions do individuals have to receiving help?

Seeking Help from Others

The earlier discussion of helping in emergencies may have suggested that helping behavior occurs when someone happens to stumble across a situation in which help is needed. Although this does happen, there are also many situations in which an individual actively seeks out help from another. Many Jews in Nazi-occupied Europe approached potential helpers and asked for help. And today, we see many examples of people seeking help: refugees seeking entrance to other countries, the homeless seeking shelter, individuals seeking treatment for mental health issues.

Seeking help has both positive and negative aspects. On the positive side, the help a person needs will often be forthcoming. For example, medical care may be given for a life-threatening condition. On the negative side, a person may feel threatened or suffer loss of self-esteem by asking for help (Fisher et al., 1982). In Western society, a great premium is placed on being self-sufficient and taking care of oneself. There is a social stigma attached to seeking help, along with potential feelings of failure. One manifestation of this is the relationship between gender role concepts and seeking help. In one study, male college students who adhered closely to masculine gender role concepts were less willing to seek academic help than men with more liberal gender role concepts (Wimer & Levant, 2011). Apparently, the negative consequences of violating one's sense of self-reliance and dominance overrode the need for academic help (Wimer & Levant, 2011). Culture and ethnicity can also affect one's predisposition toward seeking help. For example, Freitas-Murrell and Swift (2015) studied attitudes toward seeking psychological therapy among a sample of Native Alaskans. Freitas-Murrell and Swift found, consistent with the above, that the more stigma attached to seeking help, the less favorable the attitude toward actually seeking help. They also found that participants who more strongly identified with Caucasian culture (versus native Alaskan culture), the more positive the attitudes toward seeking help. In other studies, members from Asian and Hispanic cultures have more negative attitudes toward seeking help than Caucasians. For example, Asians and Hispanics are less likely than Whites to seek help for mental health issues (National Institute of Mental Health, 2017). Why is this so? Members of Asian and Hispanic cultures attach greater stigma to seeking help than do Caucasians (Nam et al., 2010; Shim et al., 2009). Generally, seeking help generates costs, as does helping (DePaulo & Fisher, 1980).

Whether you seek help and are grateful for receiving help depends on a number of factors.
Source: Prostock-studio Shutterstock.

Factors Influencing the Decision to Seek Help

Clearly, the decision to seek help is just as complex as the decision to give help. What factors come into play when a person is deciding whether to seek help?

For one, individuals may be more likely to ask for help when their need is low than when it is high (Krishan, 1988). This could be related to the perceived "power" relationship between the helper and the recipient. When need is low, people may perceive themselves to be on more common footing with the helper. Additionally, when need is low, there is less cost to the helper. People may be less likely to seek help if the cost to the helper is high (DePaulo & Fisher, 1980).

Another variable in this decision-making process is the person from whom the help is sought. Are people more willing to seek help from a friend or from a stranger? In one study, the relationship between the helper and the recipient (friends or strangers) and the cost to the helper (high or low) were manipulated (Shapiro, 1980). Generally, participants were more likely to seek help from a friend than from a stranger (Figure 11.10). When help was sought from a friend, the potential cost to the helper was not important. When the helper was a stranger, participants were reluctant to ask when the cost was high.

There are several possible reasons for this. First, people may feel more comfortable and less threatened asking a friend rather than a stranger for costly help. Second, the norm of reciprocity (see Chapter 7) may come into play in a more meaningful way with friends (Gouldner, 1960). People may reason that they would do it for their friends if they needed it. Thus, the expectation of reciprocity may make it easier to ask for high-cost help from

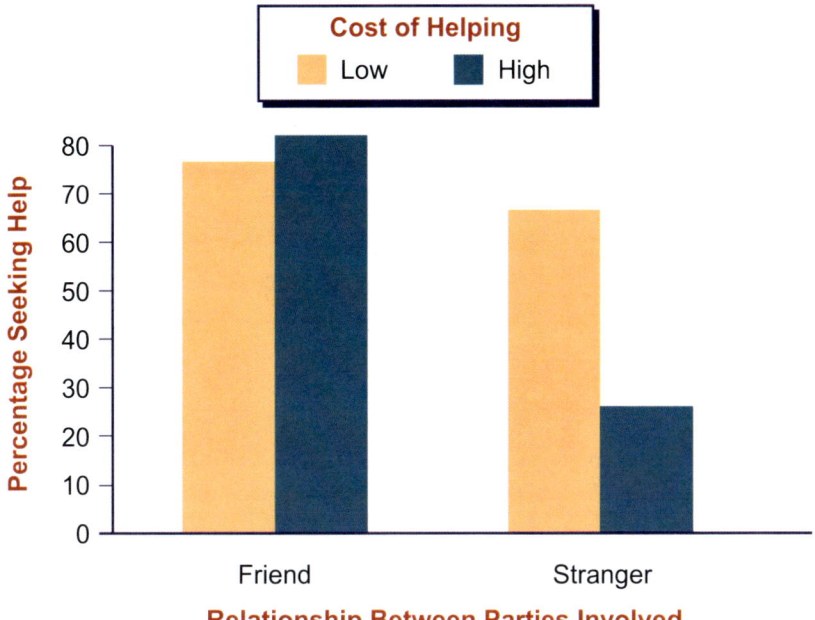

FIGURE 11.10

Help seeking as a function of the cost of help and the nature of the potential helper. Participants were likely to seek help from a friend in both low-cost and high-cost helping situations. However, help was more likely to be sought from a stranger if the cost of help was low.

Based on data from Shapiro (1980).

a friend. Third, people may perceive that they will have more opportunities to reciprocate a friend's help. They may never see a stranger again.

A final variable that comes into play in deciding to seek help is the type of task on which the help is needed. If someone is doing something easy (but needs help), the person is less likely to seek help than if the task is hard (DePaulo & Fisher, 1980). And if the task is something in which the person has ego involvement, he or she is also less likely to seek help. So, for example, accountants would be unlikely to seek help preparing their own taxes, even if they needed the help.

Reacting to Help When It Is Given

When we help someone, or we see someone receiving help, it is natural to expect that the person receiving the help will show gratitude. However, there are times when received help is not appreciated or when victims complain about the help that was received. After Hurricane Katrina, for example, many displaced New Orleans residents complained about the living accommodations and other support provided weeks after the hurricane struck. Why do people who receive help not always react positively toward that help? We shall explore this topic in this section.

Receiving help is a double-edged sword. On the one hand, people are grateful for receiving help. On the other hand, they may experience negative feelings when they are helped, feelings of guilt, lowered self-esteem, and indebtedness. Jews who were hidden by rescuers, for example, probably were concerned about the safety of their benefactors; they also may have been disturbed by the thought that they could never reciprocate the help they received.

Generally, there are four potentially negative outcomes of receiving help. First, an inequitable relationship may be created. Second, those who are helped may experience psychological reactance; that is, they may feel their freedom is threatened by receiving help. Third, those who receive help may make negative attributions about the intent of those who have helped them. Fourth, those who receive help may suffer a loss of self-esteem (Fisher et al., 1982). Let's look at two of these outcomes: inequity and threats to self-esteem.

The Creation of an Inequitable Relationship

Recall from Chapter 9 that we strive to maintain equity in our relationships with others. When inequity occurs, we feel distress and are motivated to restore equity. Helping someone creates inequity in a relationship (Fisher et al., 1982) because the recipient feels indebted to the helper (Leventhal et al., 1969). The higher the cost to the helper, the greater the inequity and the greater the negative feelings (Gergen, 1974).

Inequity can be reversed when the help is reciprocated. Generally, a recipient reacts more negatively to help and likes the helper less if he or she does not have the ability to reciprocate (Castro, 1974). Recipients are also less likely to seek help in the future when they have not been able to reciprocate, especially if the cost to the helper was high.

The relationship between degree of indebtedness and need to reciprocate is a complex one. For example, if someone helps you voluntarily, you will reciprocate more than if someone is obliged to help you as part of a job (Goranson & Berkowitz, 1966). You also are likely to reciprocate when the cost to the donor is high (Pruitt, 1968). Interestingly, the absolute amount of help given is less important than the cost incurred by the helper (Aikwa, 1990; Pruitt, 1968). For example, if a person who makes $100,000 per year gave you $1,000 (1% of the income), you would feel less indebted to that person than if you received the same $1,000 from someone who makes $10,000 per year (10% of the income).

Finally, we need to distinguish between the obligation and sense of gratitude a person receiving help might experience and how that relates to reciprocity. Obligation is a feeling of "owing" someone something. So, if I help you with a difficult task, you might feel that you owe it to me to reciprocate the favor to restore equity. Gratitude is an expression of appreciation. So, if I help you with that difficult task, you may express your appreciation by reciprocating the favor. In an interesting study by Goei and Boster (2005), obligation and gratitude were found to be conceptually different and affected reciprocity differently. Goei and Boster found that doing a favor for someone, especially a high-cost favor, increased gratitude but not obligation. In response to increased gratitude, participants were then willing to comply with a request for help. So, it may be a response to a feeling of gratitude that drives the restoration of equity after receiving help.

Threats to Self-Esteem

Perhaps the strongest explanation for the negative impact of receiving help centers on threats to self-esteem. When people become dependent on others, especially in Western society, their self-esteem and self-worth come into question (Fisher et al., 1982). Under these conditions, receiving help may be a threatening experience.

There is considerable support for the **threat to self-esteem model**. In one study, participants who received aid on an analogy task showed greater decrements in situational self-esteem (self-esteem tied to a specific situation) than participants not receiving help (Balls & Eisenberg, 1986). In another study, researchers artificially manipulated participants' situational self-esteem by providing them with either positive or negative information about themselves (Nadler et al., 1979). The researchers then created a situation in which the individual either received or did not receive aid. Participants who received self-enhancing information (positive self-information) showed more negative affect when aid was offered than when no aid was offered. Participants who received negative self-information showed positive affect when they were helped.

Thus, participants who had positive thoughts about themselves were more negatively affected by help than those who had negative thoughts about themselves. The offer of help was a greater threat to those with high self-esteem than to those with low self-esteem. In other words, not only does receiving help threaten self-esteem but also the higher a person's self-esteem is, the more threatened that person is by offers of help. For example, if you consider yourself the world's best brain surgeon, asking for assistance on a case would be more disturbing to you than if you saw yourself as an average brain surgeon.

threat to self-esteem model A model explaining the reactions of victims to receiving help, suggesting that they might refuse help because accepting it is a threat to their self-esteem.

When someone with high self-esteem fails at a task, that failure is inconsistent with his or her positive self-image (Nadler et al., 1976). Help offered in this situation is perceived as threatening, especially if it comes from someone who is similar (Fisher & Nadler, 1974; Nadler et al., 1979). Receiving help from someone similar may be seen as a sign of relative inferiority and dependency (Nadler et al., 1979).

Conversely, when a person with high self-esteem receives help from a dissimilar person, he or she experiences an increase in situational self-esteem and self-confidence. When a person with low self-esteem receives help from a similar other, that help is more consistent with the individual's self-image. For these individuals, help from a similar other is seen as an expression of concern, and they respond positively (Nadler et al., 1979).

A model to explain the complex relationship between self-esteem and receiving help was developed by Nadler et al. (1983). The model suggests that help from a friend is more psychologically significant than help from a stranger. This greater significance is translated into negative affect if failure occurs on something that is ego involving (e.g., losing a job). Here, help from a friend is seen as a threat to one's self-esteem, and a negative reaction follows.

Receiving help can be particularly threatening when it is unsolicited and imposed by someone (Deelstra et al., 2003). Deelstra et al. had participants work on a task that did not present a problem, a task that involved a solvable problem, and a task that presented an unsolvable problem. In each condition, a confederate either did or did not provide unsolicited help. The results showed that participants had the strongest negative reaction to the help imposed when they perceived that no problem existed or that a solvable problem existed. There was also a significant change in the participant's heart rate that paralleled this finding. Participants showed the most heart rate increase when help was imposed in the no-problem or solvable-problem conditions. Apparently, receiving unwanted help is not only psychologically threatening, but it is also physiologically arousing!

A study conducted in France investigated how a recipient's age (young, middle, or older adult) and degree of control over a situation affected reactions to receiving help (Raynaud-Maintier & Alaphillippe, 2001). Participants worked on an anagram task and received varying amounts of help. The researchers found that, consistent with the threat to self-esteem model, receiving help was threatening, especially when the help was offered by an older adult or a helper with high self-esteem. The more control participants had over the situation, the less threatening the help was, and the older the participant, the lower the threat of receiving help.

One's self-esteem may be more threatened if help comes from an out-group member. In a study conducted in Israel (Halabi et al., 2011), Arab students received help from either another Arab student (in-group) or from a Jewish helper (out-group) or received no help. The Arab students were led to believe that the problem they were working on was easy, hard, or they received no information on the difficulty of the task. After completing the task, participants filled out a questionnaire that assessed a number of variables (e.g., self-esteem, emotions). Halabi et al. found that the Arab students reacted much more negatively to the help from a Jewish helper than another Arab helper. Halabi et al. also found that receiving help from the Jewish helper led to lower levels of collective self-esteem and situational self-worth than receiving no help at all. So, receiving help from an out-group member appears to be a threat to one's self-esteem.

There are also gender differences in how people react to receiving help. In one study, males and females were paired with fictitious partners of comparable, superior, or inferior ability and were offered help by that partner (Balls & Eisenberg, 1986). Females paired with a partner of similar ability showed greater reductions in situational self-esteem than males paired with a similar partner. Thus, females perceived help as more threatening to self-esteem than did males. Females, however, were more satisfied than males with the help they received. Females were also more likely than males to express a need for help.

Reactions to receiving help, then, are influenced by several factors, including the ability to reciprocate, the similarity or dissimilarity of the helper, self-esteem, and gender. Other factors can play a role as well. For example, if the helper has positive attributes and is seen as having good motives, the person receiving help is more likely to feel positive about the experience. A positive outcome is also more likely if the help is offered rather than requested, if the help is given on an ego-relevant task, and if the help does not compromise the recipient's freedom (e.g., with a very high obligation to repay the helper). Overall, we see that an individual's reaction to receiving help is influenced by an interaction between situational variables (for example, the helper's characteristics) and personality variables (Fisher et al., 1982).

Study Break

This section discussed factors relating to receiving help. Before you read the Chapter Review, answer the following questions:

1. What are the positives and negatives involved in seeking help, and who is more or less likely to seek help?
2. What three questions are involved in the decision to ask for help, and what factors affect the answer to each?
3. What factors influence the decision to seek help?
4. How does the concept of equity affect a person's reaction to receiving help?
5. What factors contribute to threatening one's self-esteem as a result of receiving help?

Irene Opdyke Revisited

Irene Opdyke offered help to people she hardly knew and put her life at great risk. Opdyke was undoubtedly an empathic person who felt the suffering of the Jews. In deciding to help, she almost surely went through something similar to the process described in this chapter. She noticed the situation requiring help when she heard about the liquidation of the ghetto. She labeled the situation as one that required help, and she assumed responsibility for helping. She knew what she had to do to help: find a place to hide the Jews. Finally, she implemented her decision to help. Irene Opdyke's behavior fits quite well with the five-stage decision model for helping.

Opdyke's decision was also similar to the decisions made by hundreds of other rescuers of Jews. Opdyke and the other rescuers put their lives on the line to save others. We know something about Irene Opdyke and her commitment to helping people. After all, she was studying to be a nurse before the war. It is obvious that Irene Opdyke had empathy for those in need and was able to translate that empathy into tangible action. Irene Opdyke provides us with an inspiring example of an altruistic person who put the welfare of others above her own.

Chapter Review

1. **What is altruism, and how is it different from helping behavior? Why is the difference important?**

    Altruism is behavior that helps a person in need, that is focused on the victim, and that is motivated purely by the desire to help the other person. Other, similar behaviors may be motivated by relieving one's personal distress or to gain some reward. These behaviors are categorized as helping behavior. The motivation underlying an act of help is important because it may affect the quality of the help given.

2. **What are empathy and egoism, and how do they relate to altruism?**

    Empathy refers to compassionate understanding of how a person in need feels. Some acts of helping are focused on and motivated by our desire to relieve the suffering of the victim rather than our own discomfort. Empathy for a person in need is rooted in perspective taking. A person who focuses on how a person in distress feels is more likely to experience empathy. The empathy-altruism hypothesis proposes that arousal of empathy increases the likelihood of altruism. This hypothesis has received research support, but it remains controversial. In contrast, egoism refers to a motive for helping that is focused on relieving our own discomfort rather than on relieving the victim's suffering.

3. **What about the idea that we may help to avoid guilt or shame?**

This has been raised as a possibility in the empathy-punishment hypothesis, which states that people help to avoid the guilt and shame associated with not helping. Research pitting this hypothesis against the empathy-altruism hypothesis has fallen on the side of empathy-altruism. However, the book is still open on the validity of the empathy-altruism hypothesis.

4. **What is pathological altruism, and what types of maladaptive behavior can it contribute to?**

Pathological altruism is behavior or a personal tendency intended to promote the welfare of others but that has unreasonable negative consequences to others or oneself. Pathological altruism can lead to behavior that is self-serving, self-defeating, and even narcissistic. There is a relationship between pathological altruism and eating disorders such as anorexia nervosa and bulimia nervosa. People with anorexia, for example, often derive pleasure in preparing and serving food to others while avoiding food themselves. This wish to please others is motivated by the need for the approval of others and can give rise to pathological altruism.

5. **What role does biology play in altruism?**

There is evidence that helping has biological roots, as suggested by sociobiologists. According to this view, helping is biologically adaptive and helps a species survive. The focus of this explanation is on survival of the gene pool of a species rather than on survival of any one member of a species. According to evolutionary biologists, animals are more likely to help members of their own family through alloparenting. For humans, a similar effect occurs: We are more likely to help others who are like us and who thus share genetic material.

Although this idea has some merit, it cannot account for the complexity of animal or human altruism. We might have predicted, based on the biological explanation, that Irene Opdyke would not have been motivated to help the Jews in Ternopol because they were not related and were members of different ethnic and religious groups.

6. **How do social psychologists explain helping in an emergency situation?**

To explain helping (or nonhelping) in emergencies, social psychologists Darley and Latané developed a decision model with five stages: noticing the emergency, labeling the emergency correctly, assuming responsibility to help, knowing what to do, and implementing the decision to help. At each stage, many variables influence an individual's decision to help.

At the noticing stage, anything that makes the emergency stand out increases the likelihood of help being offered. However, interpreting a situation as an emergency can be ambiguous, and we may mislabel it, in which case we do not give help.

Next, we must assume personal responsibility for helping. This is known as the bystander effect. Three reasons for this failure to help when bystanders are present are diffusion of responsibility (assuming that someone else will help), pluralistic ignorance (responding to the inaction of others), and assuming a social category relationship (assuming that parties in a situation belong together). Although the bystander effect is a powerful, reliable phenomenon, there are exceptions to it. Research shows that when help requires potentially dangerous intervention, people are more likely to help when in groups than when alone. The bystander effect is less likely to occur when the helping situation confronting us involves a clear violation of a social norm that we personally care about.

Even if we assume responsibility, we may not help because we do not know what to do or lack skills, or we may think that someone else is more qualified to help. Finally, we may fail to help because the costs of helping are seen as too high. Costs are increased when we might be injured or otherwise inconvenienced by stopping to help.

7. **What factors affect the decision to help?**

Mood makes a difference. Bystanders who are in a positive (good) mood are more likely to help others. However, people may not help if they think helping will spoil their good mood. Characteristics of the victim also play a role. Females are more likely to be helped if the helper is male. Physically attractive people are more likely to be helped than unattractive people. We also take into account whether we feel that the victim deserves help. If we believe the victim contributed to his or her own problems, we are less likely to help than if we believe the victim did not contribute. This fits with the just-world hypothesis, the idea that people get what they deserve and deserve what they get. We may relax this standard if we believe the victim strongly needs our help.

Race and sexual orientation can also affect helping. Under certain conditions White helpers are less likely to help a Black victim than a White victim. Individuals with a same-sex orientation receive less help than heterosexuals.

8. **If you need help, how can you increase your chances of receiving help?**

You need to help people come to the right decision at each stage of the decision model. To ensure that you get noticed, make any plea for help as loud and as clear as possible. This will also help bystanders correctly label your situation as an emergency. To get someone to assume responsibility, make eye contact with a bystander. Better yet, make a direct request of a particular bystander for help. Research shows that making such a request increases a bystander's sense of responsibility for helping you and increases the likelihood of helping.

9. **Other than traditional helping in emergency situations, what other forms of helping are there?**

Although social psychologists have historically focused on helping in relatively benign emergency situations, there are other forms of help that involve risk. Courageous resistance is one such form of helping. Courageous resistance is a form of helping that involves significant risk to the helper (or the helper's family), requires a long-term commitment, and occurs after a deliberative process. Courageous resistors include whistleblowers, political activists, and rescuers of Jews during the Holocaust. Heroism is another form of helping that is closely related to courageous resistance. In both cases there is substantial risk to the helper. However, heroism need not involve a long-term commitment and may not require a deliberative process to decide to help.

10. **How do personality characteristics relate to helping?**

Although situational factors play an important role in helping, especially spontaneous helping, they may not give us a true picture of the helper and how he or she might behave across helping situations. Personality characteristics may become more relevant when nonspontaneous, long-term helping is considered. In this case, more planning and thought are required. Some individuals might possess an altruistic personality, or a cluster of traits, including empathy, that predisposes a person to helping.

Research on rescuers of Jews in Nazi-occupied Europe—who have been designated righteous rescuers by Israel—provides evidence for the existence of an altruistic personality. Rescuers from Eastern Europe (especially Poland) displayed autonomous altruism, altruism that is not supported by social norms. Rescuers from Western Europe were more likely to display normative altruism, altruism that society supports and recognizes.

11. **What situational and personality variables played a role in the decision to help Jews in Nazi-occupied Europe?**

Although situational factors did not exert as strong an influence on the decision to help as one might expect, two have been found to be significant: the presence of family or group support and the initiation of rescue efforts as a result of a specific request for help. After rescuers began helping, they were likely to continue helping.

There were also personality variables that related to the decision to become a rescuer. Compared to nonrescuers, rescuers were higher in emotional empathy (sensitivity to the suffering of others) and had a strong sense of social responsibility. Other characteristics of rescuers included an inability to blend with others, a high level of independence and self-reliance, a commitment to helping before the war, a matter-of-fact attitude about their helping, and a universalistic view of the needy.

12. **What factors contribute to a person's developing an altruistic personality?**

Oliner and Oliner found that families of rescuers of Jews in Nazi-occupied Europe and families of nonrescuers differed in their styles. Families of rescuers provided role models for helping and stressed the universal nature of all people. They emphasized aspects of religion that focus on caring for others, and they were less likely to discuss negative stereotypes of Jews. Parents of altruistic individuals tended to be warm and nurturing in their parenting style. Parents of rescuers used less physical punishment than parents of nonrescuers, relying instead on induction.

Cognitive development also contributes to the development of an altruistic personality. As children get older, they are more likely to understand the needs of others. This development is a lifelong process.

Rescuers did not magically become altruists when World War II broke out. Instead, they tended to be helpers long before the war. Becoming a rescuer involved a series of small steps. In many cases, rescuers started with a small act and then moved to larger ones.

13. **What is the interactionist view of altruism?**

According to the interactionist view of altruism, personality and situational factors interact to influence helping. Research has identified four altruistic orientations: altruistic (those who are motivated to help others but not to receive help in return), receptive giving (those who help to obtain something in return), selfish (those who are primarily motivated to receive help but not give it), and inner sustaining (those who are not motivated to give or receive help).

Research shows that individuals with an altruistic orientation are less likely to help if compensation is offered. There is also evidence that personality factors can help a person overcome the bystander effect. Esteem-oriented individuals (who are motivated internally) are more likely to help than safety-oriented individuals (who are externally motivated) when a passive bystander is present. Additionally, personality and cost of help might interact. For low-cost behaviors, we would expect personality factors to be less important than for high-cost behaviors.

14. How does long-term helping relate to models of emergency helping?

With slight modification, Latané and Darley's five-stage model applies to long-term helping. Noticing, labeling, accepting responsibility, deciding how to help, and implementing the decision to help are all relevant to acts of long-term help. Additionally, at the assuming responsibility stage, the norm of social responsibility may have been activated. This norm suggests that we should help those in need without regard to reward.

15. What factors influence a person's likelihood of seeking and receiving help?

Seeking help from others is a double-edged sword: The person in need is more likely to receive help but also incurs a cost. Helping also involves costs for the helper. A person in need of help weighs these costs when deciding whether to ask for help, progressing through a multistage process. A person is more likely to seek help when his or her needs are low, and to seek help from a friend, especially if the cost to the helper is high. A person is less likely to seek help with something easy than with something hard.

16. What reactions do people show to receiving help?

Receiving help is also a double-edged sword. The help relieves the situation but leads to negative side effects, including feelings of guilt, lowered self-esteem, and indebtedness to the helper. Generally, there are four negative reactions to receiving aid: the creation of inequity between the helper and the recipient, psychological reactance, negative attributions about the helper, and threats to one's self-esteem. There is considerable support for the threat to self-esteem model of reactions to receiving help. How much a person's self-esteem is threatened depends on several factors, including the type of task and the source of the help. Males and females differ in their responses to receiving help. Females react more negatively to receiving help but are more satisfied than males with the help they receive.

Key Terms

Altruism (p. 443)
Altruistic personality (p. 473)
Autonomous altruism (p. 474)
Bystander effect (p. 454)
Courageous resistance (p. 469)
Diffusion of responsibility (p. 455)
Empathy-altruism hypothesis (p. 444)
Empathy-punishment hypothesis (p. 446)
Heroism (p. 470)
Interactionist view of altruism (p. 479)
Just-world hypothesis (p. 464)
Normative altruism (p. 474)
Righteous rescuer (p. 474)
Social category relationship (p. 456)
Threat to self-esteem model (p. 486)

Chapter Quiz

1. _____ is a type of behavior that helps a person in need and is motivated purely by the desire to reduce that person's suffering.
   A. Altruism
   B. Helping behavior
   C. Prosocial behavior
   D. Bystander intervention

2. According to the _____, the arousal of empathy is an important factor in altruism.
   A. empathy-punishment hypothesis
   B. empathy-altruism hypothesis
   C. empathy-helping hypothesis
   D. perspective-taking hypothesis

3. _____ altruism is behavior or a personal tendency intended to promote the welfare of others but that has unreasonable negative consequences to others or oneself.
   A. Maladaptive
   B. Pathological
   C. Abnormal
   D. Aberrant

4. Which of the following is *not* one of the stages in the five-stage model of helping outlined in your text?
   A. Noticing a situation
   B. Labeling a situation appropriately
   C. Arousal of empathy or egoism
   D. Assuming responsibility to help
   E. All of the above *are* stages in the model.

5. You are more likely to receive help on a lightly traveled street than on a busy highway. This illustrates
   A. bystander apathy.
   B. the bystander effect.
   C. the empathy-punishment hypothesis.
   D. pluralistic ignorance.

6. The idea that nonresponsive bystanders define a situation as a nonemergency for others is which explanation for the bystander effect?
   A. Bystander apathy
   B. Diffusion of responsibility
   C. Egoism
   D. Pluralistic ignorance
   E. None of the above

7. According to your text, which effect is observed when a social category relationship is assumed?
   A. Bystanders are less likely to notice an emergency.
   B. Bystanders are more likely to assume responsibility for helping.
   C. Pluralistic ignorance is more likely to occur.
   D. Bystanders are less likely to intervene in an emergency.

8. You find out that an acquaintance of yours contracted AIDS because he received tainted blood before blood was routinely tested. According to Weiner's attributional analysis of helping, you will probably feel
   A. anger.
   B. egoism.
   C. pity.
   D. fear.

9. According to your text, with respect to race and helping, the bystander effect
   A. does not hold for White victims.
   B. does not hold for Black victims.
   C. is stronger for Black victims compared with White victims.
   D. applies equally to Black and White victims.

10. _____ is helping that involves significant risk above what is normally expected and serves some socially valued goal.
    A. Heroism
    B. Courageous resistance
    C. Empathic altruism
    D. Normative altruism

Answers can be found in the end-of-book Answers section.

Applying Social Psychology: Law, Business, and Health

CHAPTER 12

The purpose of life is not to be happy. It is to be useful, to be honorable, to be compassionate, to have it make some difference that you have lived and lived well.

—Ralph Waldo Emerson

Source: sdecoret/Shutterstock.

In the early hours of July 28, 1984, a man broke into Jennifer Thompson's apartment, put a knife to her throat, and raped her. Jennifer was a bright 22-year-old college student at the time. While she was being attacked, Jennifer studied the face and body of her attacker, trying to remember distinctive facial features or scars. She also tried to turn on lights in the apartment, hoping to get a better view of her attacker's face. At one point during the attack, Jennifer persuaded her attacker to let her go to the kitchen to get a glass of water, and was able to escape through the back door.

Jennifer arrived at the hospital and learned that a second rape victim was being examined just a few stalls away—a victim of the same man who had raped her. Jennifer was given a rape kit, then taken to a police station where she assisted with putting together a sketch of her assailant. Three days after she was raped, Jennifer was given a photo lineup by the police and asked if she could identify any of the men in the photos as her attacker. She selected a photo and days later was brought in for a physical lineup. Jennifer wanted to get it right. She wanted to make sure that the person who raped her and the other woman that night would pay for his actions. Jennifer identified one of the men from the lineup— the same man she had selected from the photos. That man was Ronald Cotton, a 22-year-old local man with a criminal history.

Key Questions

As you read this chapter, find the answers to the following questions:

1. What influence do eyewitnesses have on a jury?
2. What is the difference between estimator and system variables?
3. Why does the weapon focus effect occur?
4. How do stress or strong emotions affect eyewitness testimony?
5. How accurate is eyewitness memory?
6. Why would someone give a false confession?
7. What are the steps involved in personnel selection?
8. What types of measures can be used for a performance appraisal?
9. What factors influence work motivation?
10. How is stress defined?
11. How does coping relate to stress?
12. What is the effect of perceived control on stress?
13. Does social support affect health?
14. How does optimism relate to health?
15. How does social support relate to positive health outcomes?

493

16. What factors relate to happiness?
17. How can social psychological principles be applied to improving the health of individuals?

In two separate trials, Ronald Cotton was convicted of rape and burglary and sentenced to life in prison. Jennifer Thompson was a convincing eyewitness. She was absolutely certain that Ronald Cotton was the man who had attacked her. Even in the second trial, when an alternate suspect, who would later turn out to be the actual rapist, was presented, Jennifer still pointed to Ronald as the man who raped her. In her mind, Ronald Cotton would always be the man who hurt her.

While in prison, Ronald Cotton wrote countless letters professing his innocence. With the help of a law professor and advances in DNA testing, Cotton's DNA was tested against evidence from the crime scenes. Eleven years after his conviction, Ronald Cotton was released. DNA evidence exonerated him and implicated a serial rapist named Bobby Poole. In the years after being released from prison, Ronald Cotton entered the workforce, purchased a home, got married, and had a child.

What makes this case extraordinary is the relationship between Jennifer Thompson and Ronald Cotton. Years after Jennifer learned of Ronald's release and the DNA evidence, Jennifer asked to meet with Ronald. That first meeting was emotional for both Jennifer and Ronald. They have written a book together about their experience and the power of forgiveness.

So how do social psychological principles, theories, and methods apply to legal cases such as Ronald Cotton's? Ronald Cotton was a young Black man with a criminal record, while Jennifer Thompson was a petite, blonde White college student at the time of the crime. How might stereotypes and prejudice influence public response to the crime, police decisions, jury decision-making processes, and sentencing of the defendant? Jennifer was also persuasive as an eyewitness because of her confidence in Ronald's guilt. How might confidence influence judges and juries, and how does confidence relate to accuracy? Finally, how are witnesses, victims, and juries presented with information? Social psychological research on individual and group decision making can offer insights into reducing bias in legal cases.

In this chapter we consider, along with two other topics (business and health), how social psychology applies to the law and how it can help us understand events like the wrongful conviction of Ronald Cotton.

Social Psychology and the Law

For more than half a century, social psychologists have been studying the American legal system and applying social psychology. After all, the law ultimately rests on assumptions about how people will behave. In fact, law and psychology are both concerned with the prediction and control of human behavior. Through its findings in such areas of inquiry as social perception, prejudice and stereotyping, attitudes, group processes and dynamics, persuasion, and conformity, social psychology can clarify some of the assumptions that the law routinely makes about human beings.

Eyewitness Testimony

During a trial, many types of evidence can be presented. Police officers and expert witnesses may testify about details of the crime and crime scene. Expert witnesses may testify about the defendant's state of mind. The defendant may testify in his or her own defense. However, there is one type of evidence that is of paramount importance to the jury: the eyewitness. An **eyewitness** is a person who observed the crime and can relate the events to the jury in court. Eyewitnesses are crucial to the outcome of criminal trials (Loftus, 1979a), and eyewitness testimony is frequently the primary or sole evidence against a defendant (Wells et al., 1998). According to practicing attorneys, eyewitness evidence ranks as the second most common type of evidence (after crime scene photographs) in homicide cases (Schweitzer & Nuñez, 2018). The presence of an eyewitness markedly increases conviction rates. Because of the eyewitness's crucial role and the fact that many social psychological variables influence perception, there is a vast body of research on the performance of eyewitnesses.

Two classes of variables can influence the accuracy of an eyewitness: estimator variables and system variables (Wells, 1978). **Estimator variables** are related directly to the eyewitness and the conditions under which the eyewitness viewed the crime. They include lighting, exposure time, the presence of a weapon, and personal biases of the eyewitness. **System variables** are variables that are under control of the criminal justice system. They include the time that elapses between the crime and the questioning of a witness, the manner in which a lineup is conducted, and the way that questions are asked of eyewitnesses. Both classes of variables influence the accuracy of eyewitness perceptions, memories, and reports. We turn now to some variables that affect eyewitness accuracy.

eyewitness A person who observed a crime and can relate the events to the jury in court.

estimator variables Variables directly related to the eyewitness and the conditions under which the eyewitness viewed the crime (e.g., presence of a weapon).

system variables Variables that are under the control of the criminal justice system (e.g., how a lineup is conducted).

Weapon Focus

One important estimator variable is whether a weapon is present during the commission of a crime. Weapons command our attention and change our perceptual world. When a gun is pointed at us, we are less able to pay attention to other details of a situation. This phenomenon is called **weapon focus** (Loftus, 1979b). As you might expect, the presence of a weapon reduces eyewitness accuracy.

Weapon focus is a function of attention. When we view a scene, we don't pay equal attention to all details. Instead, we select out the most salient details, the features that stand out; these are the details we remember best later. In a study that demonstrated the importance of detail salience, participants were shown a 2-minute-long movie depicting

weapon focus The phenomenon by which eyewitness accuracy is reduced when a weapon is present.

A number of factors relating to an event witnessed and the witness him- or herself can affect how accurately an eyewitness remembers a crime or accident.
Source: Photographee.eu/ Shutterstock.

an automobile striking a pedestrian in a supermarket parking lot (Marshall et al., 1971). Prior to the experiment the film was pretested to determine the salience of the various details depicted. This was done by counting the number of times particular details were mentioned by participants who had viewed the film. Some details were mentioned often (high salience) and others rarely (low salience). After viewing the film, the participants were asked what they could recall about the film. Researchers measured two factors: the accuracy of their perceptions (proportion of details correctly reported) and the completeness of their perceptions (the proportion of details mentioned).

High-salience details were more likely to be included than low-salience details. However, even very low-salience items were recalled quite accurately (an accuracy score of near 70 out of 100). Detail salience is most critical for the completeness of a witness's report. In this case, the higher the salience of an item, the more complete the report of that detail. Thus, details that stand out, such as a weapon, are most likely to be remembered and reported by an eyewitness to a crime.

A weapon is clearly a salient detail, as shown in research. In a meta-analysis of 28 studies on weapon focus, Fawcett et al. (2013) not only found evidence for a moderate effect of weapon presence, they also found that retention interval, threat, and exposure duration all had significant effects on memory performance. Interestingly, who holds the weapon might matter. Keri Pickel (2009) reasoned that the weapon focus effect might be stronger if a female perpetrator was holding a weapon during a crime than a male perpetrator. Because weapons are more associated with men than women, Pickel hypothesized that the weapon would stand out more with the female perpetrator and have a greater effect on eyewitness accuracy. In her experiment she had either a male or female perpetrator shown in a film hold either a weapon (a gun) or neutral object (a music CD) while robbing a victim. Pickel found that the weapon focus effect was stronger when the female used the gun to commit the crime. Eyewitnesses recalled fewer accurate facts and more inaccurate facts for the armed female perpetrator than the male perpetrator. Stereotypical expectations also apply to Black perpetrators. Compared with a White perpetrator, a Black perpetrator with a weapon produces a weaker weapon focus effect. As is the case for men, guns are more stereotypically associated with Blacks than Whites, weakening the weapon focus effect. (Pickel & Sneyd, 2018). The weapon focus effect is also weaker if a perpetrator with a weapon has a distinctive facial feature (e.g., a tattoo) than if the perpetrator does not have a distinctive feature (Carlson & Carlson, 2012). Most likely this occurs because the feature competes for the witness's attention with the weapon. Finally, the weapon focus effect occurs with children as well as adults (Pickel et al., 2008).

Why does the weapon focus effect occur? One explanation, as we have seen, is that a weapon is a salient detail that captures attention. But once it captures our attention, why does the weapon affect memory so much? Is it because it is an unusual object, one we do not see all that often in real life? Or is it that the weapon increases the perceived threat of the situation? After all, a gun or knife in the hands of a criminal can harm us the way other objects cannot. An experiment by Mansour et al. (2019) investigated the underlying causes of the weapon focus effect. In their experiment, they varied the object a perpetrator was holding in a simulated crime (knife, gun, flamingo, or a binder), as well as the complexity of the crime situation (simple or complex), the duration of the crime (short or long), the type of lineup the witness viewed (target present or target absent), and whether the individual in the lineup was holding the object or not holding the object. After watching a video of the crime, participants completed several measures of memory and viewed a lineup to identify the perpetrator. Mansour et al. found that participants remembered less when the perpetrator was holding a threatening object (the gun or knife) than a nonthreatening object (the flamingo or binder). They also found that participants remembered more when the perpetrator was holding a common item (the binder) than an unusual object (the flamingo, gun, or knife). However, memory was worse when the perpetrator was holding the gun or knife than if he was holding the flamingo. Participants were less accurate in identifying the perpetrator in a lineup if he held a gun or knife compared with the other objects. The results showed a clear weapon focus effect and that it is the threatening nature of the weapon, more than its unusual nature, that contributes to the weapon focus effect.

Emotional Experience of the Eyewitness

Yet another important variable that affects eyewitness accuracy is the emotional experience of the eyewitness. When a crime is violent, eyewitnesses experience more negative emotion and are generally less accurate than when a crime is nonviolent (Clifford & Scott, 1978).

A violent crime is a highly stressful event that may impair an eyewitness's ability to accurately recognize the perpetrator of a crime (Morgan et al., 2004, 2007). However, the relationship between emotional arousal (stress) and eyewitness accuracy may not be as simple as it once appeared. Stress may interact with other variables, such as the type of event (emotional or neutral) and the type of detail to be recalled (high or low salience) in eyewitness-memory situations (Christianson, 1992).

In two experiments on the effect of emotion on eyewitness memory, researchers examined participants' ability to recall and recognize details about the perpetrator of a crime (Houston et al., 2013). Participants were randomly assigned to view a video of a man mugging an older woman and running off with her purse (emotional condition) or a video of a man picking up an older woman's purse (neutral condition). As shown in Figure 12.1, participants viewing the emotional event provided a more complete description of the perpetrator compared to neutral participants. This finding indicates that participants in the emotional condition might have been paying more attention to central features of the event, such as the perpetrator, than those in the neutral condition. When it came to completeness of recall about environmental information (e.g., details about the event), participants in the neutral condition performed better than those in the emotional condition (see Figure 12.1), supporting the idea that negative emotions might improve memory for central aspects of a crime and impair memory for more peripheral aspects. However, there were no differences in levels of accuracy between the two groups; both emotional and neutral participants were highly accurate in their descriptions of the perpetrator and the environment. In a separate experiment, participants were shown a photographic line-up and asked to identify the perpetrator from the video. Consistent with past research on

Eyewitnesses focus on the most salient details of an event. If a weapon is present it can dominate the eyewitnesses' attention and they do not pay attention to other important details. This is known as the weapon focus effect.

Source: rbkomar/Shutterstock.

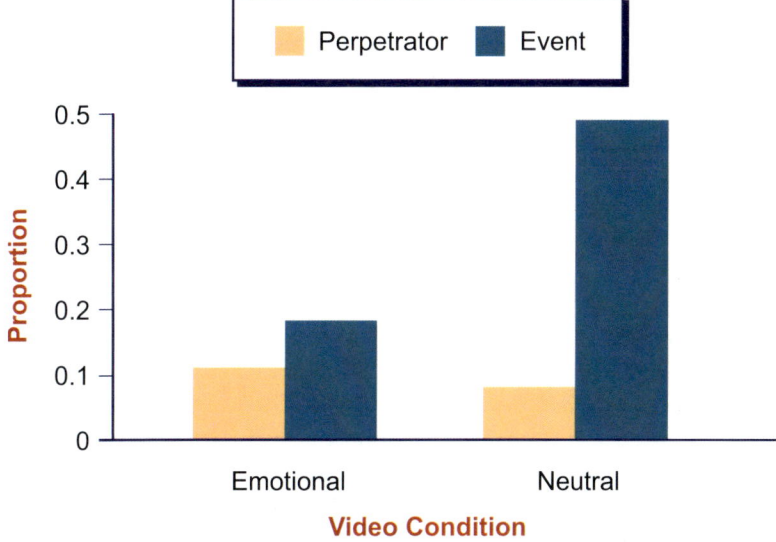

FIGURE 12.1

Completeness of eyewitness recall in the emotional and neutral videotape conditions. Participants in the emotional condition provided a more complete description of the perpetrator than those in the neutral condition. The opposite was true for memory for the event itself.

Based on data from Houston et al. (2013).

the effect of stress on eyewitness accuracy, emotional participants were less accurate in identifying the perpetrator compared to neutral participants.

The implications of this study are fairly significant for law enforcement officials. The same eyewitness who is able to produce a complete and accurate description of a perpetrator may not be able to accurately recognize that individual in a lineup. Remember Jennifer Thompson's first interview with police after her rape? She was able to provide a detailed description of her assailant, working to create a fairly accurate sketch of the suspect. However, this degree of accuracy did not hold up during the photographic or physical lineup.

The study by Houston et al. (2013) investigated one aspect of eyewitness memory: memory for specific details of a crime. However, eyewitnesses also have to remember information concerning *binding factors*, who did what in a crime (Earles et al., 2016). That is, an eyewitness might have to recall which of multiple perpetrators held a gun on victims and which stole money. This is all in addition to having to recall specific details (e.g., the race of a perpetrator or type of gun). How does emotion affect memory for binding factors? Earles et al. had participants view either a positive, negative, or neutral event and then recall specific details and binding factors. Earles et al. found that emotion enhanced memory for the specific details, but not for binding factors. They also found that this effect was strongest for older compared to younger witnesses.

Eyewitness accuracy is a complex phenomenon involving memory processes that may be affected either positively or negatively by emotional arousal. Later, we'll discuss some of the techniques that psychologists have developed that might be helpful in improving the accuracy of eyewitness recall.

Eyewitness Memory

Human memory tends to be more frail and subject to outside influence than we are willing to admit. In our day-to-day lives we have memory failures all the time. We forget where we parked our cars, where we put our notebooks, and where we left our cell phones. These everyday failures amount to very little. Eventually, we locate our cars or find our cell phones. However, when an eyewitness fails to recall something accurately, it may mean that an innocent person goes to prison.

One view of human memory is that it works much like the video recorder on your phone. When we want to record something, we press record. When we want to remember something, we press play. Out comes the information just as it went in. Basically, this is the view taken of human memory by the court system. Unfortunately, human memory does not work that way. Our memories are stored in a dynamic way. That is, we tend to store details of events, and during recall we reconstruct the original event (Bartlett, 1932) through a process known as **reconstructive memory**. The dynamic nature of human memory suggests that information in memory can be influenced by a variety of factors. For example, what we decide to encode into memory is affected by information already in memory. Further, information already in memory can be affected by postevent information—new information that we encounter after witnessing an event (Loftus, 1979a).

reconstructive memory The idea that human memory is a reconstruction of the original event, and not an exact playback of that event.

Postevent information in a variety of forms has been found to influence what eyewitnesses have in memory and what they report about a crime (Dodson & Reisberg, 1991; Lindsay & Johnson, 1989; Loftus, 1979a, 1979b; McCloskey & Zaragoza, 1985; Tversky & Tuchin, 1989). When a piece of information that was not part of the original event becomes part of the witness's memory of the event, it is known as the **misinformation effect** (Loftus et al., 1985). For example, suppose a witness originally describes a suspect as clean shaven. Later that night she reads that another witness has described the suspect as having a mustache. If the first eyewitness now reports that the suspect had a mustache, her memory has been distorted by postevent information. The mustache has become a new element in the witness's memory.

misinformation effect When a piece of information that was not part of the original event becomes part of the witness's memory of the event.

The misinformation effect can also occur when misleading information is encountered *before* the event. In one study, participants who were exposed to misleading information before a slide show were vulnerable to the misinformation effect (Lindsay & Johnson, 1989). In this context, misleading information may bias a witness by setting up an expectation that certain information will be encountered. Misleading information need not even be specific to the event witnessed to produce a biasing effect. In another study, participants' attributions of responsibility to individuals involved in a traffic accident were found to be affected by misleading information that didn't relate directly to the incident (Köhnken & Brockmann, 1987).

Although the existence of the misinformation effect has been demonstrated quite frequently, some controversy exists over exactly what causes it. The debate raises age-old controversies about the nature of human memory. Some believe that conflictual postevent information actually alters the original memory trace and makes it unavailable to the eyewitness (Loftus, 1979a, 1979b). Others dispute the idea that the original memory trace is altered (McCloskey & Zaragoza, 1985). Still others argue that the misinformation effect relates to retrieval-induced forgetting (MacLeod & Saunders, 2005). According to this view, the misleading information leads to inhibition of recall of accurate information. This leaves only the misleading information available for retrieval.

At this point it is not possible to specify exactly the mechanism underlying the misinformation effect. It is safe, however, to conclude that if a witness is exposed to misleading postevent information, the witness's *report* of what was experienced may be influenced in the direction of the misleading information. Regardless of the reason for the distortion, the bottom line is that what the witness says may not be an accurate reflection of the original memory and new elements may have been added based on exposure to postevent information.

Is there anything that can be done to reduce the misinformation effect? It turns out that the misinformation effect can be reversed under certain circumstances (Crozier & Strange, 2019; Oeberst & Blank, 2012). Oeberst and Blank created a misinformation effect by having participants watch a film clip from the movie *The World According to Garp*. After viewing the clip, participants were exposed to inaccurate postevent information on a number of critical items (misled items) via an audiotape. A memory test established that the misinformation effect was successfully established by comparing memory for the misled items with control items on which participants were not misled. Then, participants were exposed to an "enlightenment" procedure during which they were told about the exposure to the misleading information and urged to rely solely on their own memories of the video clip. After this enlightenment procedure, memory was assessed with a second test (again comparing misled items with control items). The results of this experiment are shown in Figure 12.2. As you can see, before enlightenment

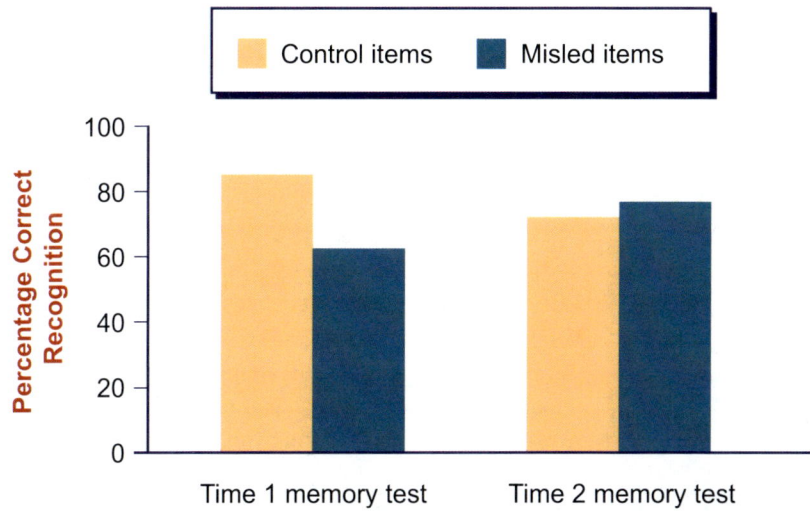

FIGURE 12.2

The effect of enlightenment on the misinformation effect. Enlightenment about the presence of misleading information reduced the misinformation effect.

Based on data from Oeberst and Blank (2012).

(Time 1 memory test) memory performance on the misled items was poorer than on the control items, indicating a misinformation effect. After the enlightenment procedure (Time 2 memory test) performance on misled and control items was equivalent, indicating that the misinformation effect was removed. A meta-analysis of 25 studies on post-memory warnings about misinformation supports these findings (Blank & Launay, 2014). Blank and Launay found that a post-memory warning reduced the misinformation effect by 43%. They also found that enlightenment warnings are the most effective way to reduce the misinformation effect. The implications of these studies for real-world eyewitness situations are quite clear. It might be a good idea to inform eyewitnesses of the misinformation effect and encourage them to make an effort to rely only on their true memories of the event they witnessed. However, it is important to keep in mind that post-memory warnings may *reduce* the misinformation effect but may not *eliminate* it completely.

The Jury's Use of Eyewitness Testimony

Generally, the side that presents eyewitness testimony wins the trial, even if the other side has objective evidence to counterbalance the eyewitness testimony (Minshull & Sussman, 1979). There are few events as powerful as an eyewitness taking the stand, pointing to the defendant, and saying: "That's him. I'll never forget that face." An eyewitness making such a statement using fluent, powerful language (i.e., devoid of hesitations, pauses, and fillers such as "um" and "ah") is likely to be highly persuasive (Clancy & Bull, 2015).

This is what happened to Ronald Cotton. Jennifer Thompson made a positive identification of him and he was convicted. Interestingly, the power of the eyewitness remains intact even when other types of evidence, such as DNA evidence, are presented (O'Neill et al., 2011). O'Neill et al. found that when the prosecution presents a credible eyewitness, conviction rates are high. The addition of credible DNA evidence from the prosecutor does not overshadow the impact of the credible eyewitness. This strongly suggests that the impact of eyewitness testimony remains strong regardless of other types of evidence presented.

Eyewitnesses typically appear highly confident about their testimony, undoubtedly because they have told their story so many times by the time the trial begins. Juries often confuse a witness's confidence for accuracy, and they act on their belief in the eyewitness's confidence (Wells et al., 1981). The greater the eyewitness's confidence, the greater the probability of conviction. However, a great deal of research shows that there is virtually no relationship between confidence and accuracy (Deffenbacher, 1980). There is evidence, however, that eyewitness confidence and accuracy may be higher for the initial identification made by an eyewitness soon after a crime was witnessed (Penrod & Cutler, 1995; Wixted et al., 2015). The tendency to rely too heavily on an eyewitness's confidence is not reduced with traditional legal remedies such as judicial instructions and cross-examination. However, having an expert testify about factors affecting eyewitness memory can reduce overreliance on eyewitness confidence (Penrod & Cutler, 1995). Regardless of the actual confidence-accuracy relationship, jurors appear to misinterpret eyewitness statements of confidence, especially if the witness adds a justification for his or her confidence (e.g., pointing to a specific facial feature) (Dodson & Dobolyi, 2015). Jurors have difficulty discriminating between inaccurate and accurate eyewitnesses (Lindsay et al., 1989), convicting the defendant at about the same rate in both situations.

Further, it is difficult (although not impossible) to discredit the eyewitness. In one study, simulated jurors were exposed to testimony from an eyewitness identifying the defendant as the person who had committed the crime (Loftus, 1979a). In one condition (the discredited eyewitness condition), the jurors were told that the eyewitness was not wearing his glasses and that his vision was 20/400 without his glasses. In another condition (the nondiscredited eyewitness condition), nothing was said

An eyewitness pointing out the defendant in court is powerful testimony that can sway a jury, especially if it is made using powerful, fluent language. The power of an eyewitness may not be harmed by the presence of other contrary evidence such as DNA evidence.
Source: Junial Enterprises/Shutterstock.

about the eyewitness's vision. Finally, in a control condition no eyewitness was present. The results showed that even when the eyewitness was discredited, simulated jurors still convicted the defendant at a high rate. On the other hand, other researchers have shown that discredited eyewitness testimony has less impact on jurors than nondiscredited testimony (Sigler & Couch, 2002). Interestingly, it doesn't take much to enhance the credibility of an eyewitness. If an eyewitness testifies that he or she remembers some trivial detail, unrelated to the crime itself, the witness's credibility and ability to persuade the jury are increased (Bell & Loftus, 1988, 1989).

Can Eyewitness Testimony Be Improved? Educating Jurors about Eyewitness Testimony

Jurors tend to be woefully ignorant of the potential flaws of eyewitness identifications and testimony (Cutler et al., 1988). A typical juror typically is not familiar with how a number of factors can affect the accuracy of an eyewitness (Durham & Dane, 1999). As a consequence, wrongful convictions often occur because jurors overbelieve faulty eyewitness testimony. Of course, this leads to a lot of guilty defendants being convicted. However, it can also lead to wrongful convictions. According to the Innocence Project (2020), 69% of individuals convicted of crimes but later cleared by DNA evidence were initially convicted based on wrongful eyewitness testimony.

It may be that jurors are simply not aware of problems associated with eyewitness testimony, identification, and memory. In fact, jurors seem to know some things about eyewitness testimony, but not others (Houston et al., 2013). As shown in Figure 12.3, jurors showed knowledge that was reasonably consistent with what experts say for witness intoxication and exposure time to the crime. However, juror knowledge was lower for the weapon focus effect and the eyewitness confidence-accuracy relationship. Knowledge for system variables ranged from approximately 61% to 67%. So, it appears that juror knowledge of variables affecting eyewitness identification may be a problem.

One solution to this problem is to have a social psychologist provide expert testimony about the potential pitfalls of eyewitness testimony. The expert can "educate" the jurors about such issues as the weapon focus and other variables that influence perception and memory of a crime. In fact, such expert testimony has been allowed and used in criminal trials. However, not all social psychologists agree with this practice (McCloskey & Egeth, 1983). Two major issues arise when considering the role of expert witnesses: First, are jurors already aware of the problems associated with eyewitness testimony? Second, will an expert make jurors overly skeptical and lead them to reject all eyewitness testimony?

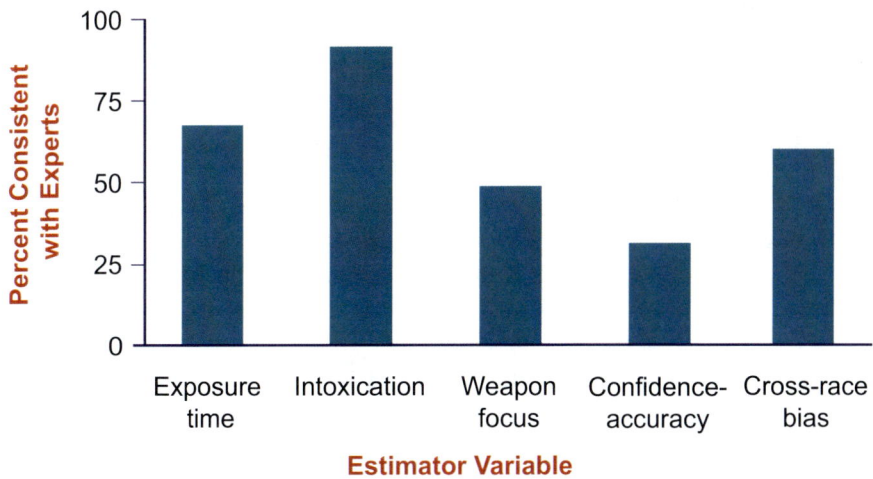

FIGURE 12.3

Percentage of juror knowledge that is consistent with expert opinion for estimator variables. Jurors have little knowledge of weapon focus, the confidence-accuracy relationship, and the cross-race bias.
Based on data from Houston et al. (2013).

Research indicates that an expert can make jurors more sensitive to the factors that affect eyewitness identification (Cutler et al., 1989; Penrod & Cutler, 1995; Safer et al., 2016). For example, Cutler et al. point out that jurors are not generally aware of the weapon focus, and an expert can increase juror knowledge in this area. In general, an expert increases juror's knowledge of the factors that can affect eyewitness identification, reduces the juror's reliance on the confidence of the eyewitness, and helps the juror make correct inferences about the credibility of an eyewitness (Cutler et al., 1989). Cutler et al. also found that expert witnesses raise a juror's knowledge and sensitivity without significantly increasing skepticism. Overall, the benefits gained by having an expert present outweigh any potential negative side effects.

Study Break

The preceding sections introduced you to the role of the eyewitness in the law and some factors relating to eyewitness identification and testimony. Before you go on, answer the following questions:

1. What are estimator and system variables, and how do they relate to eyewitness testimony?
2. What is weapon focus, and what factors affect it?
3. How do emotion and the misinformation effect relate to eyewitness memory?
4. How does the jury use eyewitness testimony?
5. How can eyewitness accuracy and testimony be improved?

Juries: Group Processes in Action

A typical criminal trial is played out in three acts, each with a number of scenes. The first act involves selecting a jury. A panel of citizens, known as the venire, is drawn from the community. From the venire the jury is selected. The second act is the trial itself. During the trial the lawyers make opening and closing statements, witnesses are presented, and the judge issues instructions to the jurors. If there were eyewitnesses to the crime, they often form the centerpiece of this part of the process. The third and final act is played out behind closed doors. After hearing all the evidence and arguments, the jury retires to deliberate (discuss the evidence) and reach a verdict. The climax of act three is reached when the jury announces its verdict in open court. Of course, after this three-act play ends, there is an encore: A guilty defendant must be sentenced.

Once the jury is selected, jury members sit as individuals and hear all the evidence in the case. They are not permitted to discuss the case with each other or anyone else. After the evidence is presented, the judge instructs the jury about the law applicable to the case. Jury members then retire to a jury room and by their own devices deliberate and come to a verdict.

Once the jury members retire to the jury room, they become a group. They must discuss the case and arrive at a verdict. How do the individual opinions of jurors get forged into a jury decision? What social psychological variables affect the jury's decision? And how do group dynamics affect the whole process?

The first act in a jury trial is jury selection. The venire is selected from the community using various lists. From the venire the jury members are selected.

Source: sirtravelalot/Shutterstock.

Conformity Pressure as a Function of Jury Size

When a juror deviates from an emerging majority consensus, pressure is exerted on the deviant juror to accept the majority view. A major side effect of the shift from 12-person to 6-person juries is the potential for different conformity effects.

Because fewer people are involved, minorities are less likely to be represented on a small jury. Now, minority in this sense does not refer only to race, sex, or ethnic origin. It also refers to dissenting opinions. In a 6-person jury, the odds are that there will be only 1 juror with a dissenting opinion, whereas in the 12-person jury, 2 minority views are more likely. Thus, in the 6-person jury, there will be a 5:1 split, and in the 12-person jury, there will be a 10:2 split.

In a 1971 decision, the Supreme Court reasoned in *Williams v. Florida* that the 5:1 split was equivalent to the 10:2 split. But two social psychological findings argue against this logic (Asch, 1951). First, a person with a "true partner" is more likely to hold out against the majority than a lone dissenter. Thus, the two-member minority is in a better position to withstand conformity pressure than the one-member minority in the six-person group. Second, there is a nonlinear relationship between majority size and conformity. Conformity increases up to a group size of about four. Therefore, it does not really matter if there are 5 or 10 members of the majority. The conformity pressure exerted by these disparate majorities will not differ significantly. Five against one, however, is more powerful than 10 against 2 because the single outlier has no social support.

Arriving at a Decision

During the **deliberation** process, the decisions of the individual jurors must be blended into a single, unanimous (in most cases) group decision. Jury deliberation is dominated by discussions of the evidence and statements in support of jurors' verdicts (Tanford & Penrod, 1986). Generally, the predeliberation distribution of individual verdicts is a good predictor of the final verdict of the jury (Kalven & Zeisel, 1966; Tanford & Penrod, 1986). That is, if there is an 11:1 (guilty: not guilty) predeliberation distribution, the jury will convict in 99% of the cases (Kalven & Zeisel, 1966). A reversal such as the one depicted in the film Twelve Angry Men, in which the character played by Henry Fonda systematically convinces the other 11 jurors to vote not guilty, is extremely rare.

deliberation The process by which the decisions of individual jury members must be blended into a single group decision.

As the majority-minority split becomes more even, the probability of conviction (or acquittal) drops accordingly (Kalven & Zeisel, 1966; Tanford & Penrod, 1986). It appears that juries operate under a simple decision rule: If there is a two-thirds majority, the likelihood is that the jury will find in the direction of the majority. If the majority is less than two thirds, but more than one half, then the likelihood is that the jury will hang (Davis et al., 1975). In cases where the split is even or almost even, juries often default to acquittal (Tanford & Penrod, 1986).

Social Influence in the Jury Room

Individual decisions translate into a final verdict via two social psychological mechanisms: informational social influence and normative social influence (Tanford & Penrod, 1986). Recall from Chapter 7 that informational social influence involves a person changing his or her view based on the content of the deliberations and that normative social influence involves a person changing based on perceived pressure to conform.

Individual verdicts influence the verdict indirectly, working through the deliberation process (Tanford & Penrod, 1986). One could say that each juror contributes information to the deliberation that is consistent with his or her judgment of guilt. When this information is made known to the other jurors, opinion change takes place. Normative social influence is a function of the initial distribution of verdicts within the jury and has a direct effect on the final verdict (Tanford & Penrod, 1986). For example, if the jury takes a pre-deliberation ballot and there is an 11:1 split for conviction, social pressure is exerted on the deviant member to conform to the group, and the jury is very likely to convict. It is unlikely that this one person will hold out for acquittal, even if he or she holds a strong belief that the defendant should be found not guilty.

Informational social influence also operates in a jury. During the deliberation process, jurors attempt to influence each other through the exchange of information about the evidence. Recall that Tanford and Penrod (1986) found that during deliberation, jurors focus on the evidence and make statements in support of their positions. These are both indicators of informational influence. Jurors will also express emotions during deliberation while trying to influence each other. Interestingly, how emotion is interpreted by jurors depends on the gender of the juror expressing emotion (Salerno & Peter-Hagene, 2015). Salerno and Peter-Hagene found that a male hold-out juror who expressed anger had more

After hearing the evidence, the jury will retire to a jury room to privately discuss the case during the deliberation process and reach a verdict. Research shows that jury deliberations are dominated by discussion of the evidence and statements supporting the jurors' positions.

Source: Alexander Oganezov/Shutterstock.

influence on other jurors' confidence in their own verdicts than a female hold-out juror expressing anger and making the same arguments during deliberation. In fact, the angry female hold-out juror was less influential than a non-angry female juror making the same arguments. This effect also occurs for Black holdout jurors expressing anger. A Black holdout expressing anger is less persuasive than a White holdout making the same arguments (Salerno, et al., 2019). A juror's social status (defined by social class) also relates to social influence in the jury room. In post-trial surveys of actual jurors, jurors indicated that high-status jurors were more influential than low-status jurors. This difference was mainly due to the fact that high-status jurors are perceived to be more competent than low-status jurors, regardless of race or gender (York & Cornwell, 2006).

We know that individual juror sentiments are pretty good predictors of the final jury decision. What seems to happen is that juries (about 90% of them) wind up in the direction they were going in the first place (Myers & Kaplan, 1976). Jury deliberation seems to polarize the jury. That is, the jury's initial direction is enhanced or intensified by deliberation, as in any decision-making group (i.e., group polarization occurs), as discussed in Chapter 8. If 9 out of 12 jurors vote initially for conviction, the group is polarized in that direction. Through the group processes of persuasion and conformity, the minority three will likely, although not always, come to agree with the majority nine.

Intergroup Bias in Court

Most people would agree that the outcome of a trial should depend on the evidence presented, but social psychological research indicates that the race of the defendant can also influence the outcome.

Generally, cross-race eyewitness identifications are more difficult to make than same-race identifications (Lindsay et al., 1991; Malpass & Kravitz, 1969; Smith et al., 2004). Therefore, a White eyewitness will be less accurate identifying a Black suspect than identifying a White suspect, and the same will be true for a Black eyewitness and a White suspect. The general phenomenon is called the *other-race effect*, and studies show that the bias exists in Whites and Blacks alike (Bothwell et al., 1989). It is important to note that the other-race effect is not limited to Black-White cross-race identifications. For example, both White and Native Canadian ("First Nation") individuals have more difficulty making cross-race than same-race identifications (Jackiw et al., 2008).

Why are cross-racial identifications more difficult than same-race identifications? There are several explanations that have been offered. One explanation is that through experience, we develop perceptual expertise for the faces of members of our own race (Thorup et al., 2018). This perceptual expertise gives us a greater sensitivity to the features and the configuration of faces from our own race, making them easier to identify than faces from other races. If this is the case, then members of a race who have a great deal of experience with faces from another race should show a reduced other-race bias compared with members of that same race with less experience. Research supports the hypothesis (Thorup et al., 2018). Thorup et al. had Asians living in Asia and Asian Americans complete a face-recognition task for Asian and Caucasian faces. They found that Asians living in Asia showed the own-race effect. However, Asian Americans, who have greater perceptual expertise with White faces, did not show the bias. In fact, they showed a reversal of the effect. These results suggest that perceptual experience with faces of another race moderates or eliminates the other-race effect.

There is also a difference in how own-race and other-race faces are processed perceptually. Two types of processing of faces are holistic and configural and component feature processing. *Holistic processing* involves processing all features (e.g., eyes, nose, and mouth) together at the same time. *Configural and component feature processing* involves processing facial features independently. Configural and component feature processing is how we process most objects we perceive (Hayward et al., 2013). According to Hayward et al., holistic and configural and feature processing of other-race faces are not as robust as processing for own-race faces. They concluded that it is likely there is an advantage in many types of facial information processing for own-race faces rather than simply an advantage in holistic processing.

Another implication is that making a cross-racial identification affects the clarity of eyewitnesses' memory and their confidence that they can make an accurate identification (Smith et al., 2004). Smith et al. found that eyewitnesses reported that their memories of a videotaped crime that they viewed were less clear when making a cross-racial identification, especially among those who actually made a choice in a lineup. Eyewitnesses also said that they had less confidence that their cross-racial identifications were accurate. It appeared that eyewitnesses making a cross-racial identification were aware of their difficulties in making an identification because they expressed more concern over the ultimate consequences of their decisions.

Research shows that eyewitness identification can be especially problematic when the witness must identify someone of a different race from his or her own.
Source: Frame Stock Footage/Shutterstock.

The other-race effect also relates to how information is processed in memory. Evidence exists showing that the other-race effect relates to face processing in long-term memory (Meissner & Brigham, 2001). There is a growing body of evidence that the bias relates to differences in how same- and other-race faces are processed in short-term memory, especially visual working memory (Stelter & Degner, 2018).

Finally, the other-race effect influences how other identification cues are used. Victoria Lawson and Jennifer Dysart (2014) had White participants attempt to identify either a White or Black suspect in a show-up (presenting only one target to identify); the suspect was wearing either the same clothes that a perpetrator wore in a simulated crime or different clothes. They found that when making an own-race identification, participants took longer to make a decision when the target's clothes in the show-up were different from those worn by the actual perpetrator. The opposite was true when making other-race identifications. Lawson and Dysart suggest that this means that the clothing cue was used differently when making an other-race rather than a same-race identification.

Study Break

This section introduced you to how juries reach a decision through deliberation. Before you go on, answer the following questions.

1. How do conformity pressures affect jury functioning?
2. What is the deliberation process and how does it relate to jury verdicts?
3. How do informational and normative social influence operate in jury deliberations?
4. How do intergroup biases affect jury decisions and eyewitness accuracy?

Confessions: Are They Always What They Seem?

In the criminal justice system, confession evidence is persuasive. When a suspect confesses to a crime, both investigative insiders and outsiders might be tempted to think of the case as closed. However, not all confessions are true, and the reasons behind different type of false confessions vary from case to case. Kassin and Wrightsman (1985) categorize false confessions as falling into one of three categories: voluntary, compliant, and internalized. **Voluntary false confessions** are situations where an individual claims responsibility for a crime without police influence. John Mark Karr confessed to killing JonBenet Ramsey, but DNA evidence failed to link him to the crime, and other evidence indicated that he was most likely in another state during the time of the murder. **Compliant false confessions** are characterized by suspects confessing in order to escape a stressful police interrogation or to avoid punishment. In such situations, the suspect publicly complies during the interview, but his or her internal beliefs remain unchanged. Suspects in

voluntary false confessions
Situation where an individual falsely claims responsibility for a crime without police influence.

compliant false confessions
A situation where an individual falsely confesses to a crime, typically under police influence. Privately, the individual knows they are not guilty.

internalized false confessions
A situation where an individual falsely confesses to a crime, typically under police influence. Privately, the individual comes to believe they are guilty of crime.

these cases know that they are innocent but confess, oftentimes under duress. Laypersons often have a difficult time understanding why someone who is innocent would confess to a crime that he or she did not commit, making discounting of such information difficult. Finally, **internalized false confessions** occur when suspects not only confess to a crime they did not commit, but often through the use of suggestion, come to believe they are guilty.

How frequent are false confessions? One study showed that 32% of confessions from German prison inmates were false, a percentage in line with other research (Gubi-Kelm et al., 2020). Under what conditions are people more likely to provide a false confession? One tactic that is frequently used in interrogations is the introduction of false evidence or misinformation. In a study on the effect of misinformation on false confessions, participants typing either quickly or slowly on a keyboard were accused of crashing the computer and thus ruining the study because they pressed a key they had previously been instructed to avoid (Kassin & Kiechel, 1996). The experimenter asked the participants to sign a confession, even though all participants were innocent. Still, nearly half of the participants signed a confession. In a second condition of the study, a confederate told the experimenter that she had seen the participant tap the forbidden key. In this condition, nearly all of the participants signed a written confession and when presented with the confederate's testimony, participants were more likely to believe they were guilty (see Figure 12.4). This study illustrates the powerful effect false evidence can have on confessions. Another factor that can lead to a false confession is sleep deprivation. In one study, using a procedure similar to the one just described, sleep-deprived participants were 4.5 times more likely to falsely confess to pressing a forbidden key than rested participants (Frenda et al., 2016). Sleep deprivation may be a problem if interrogations last for several hours. In fact, in verified cases of false confessions, 39% lasted between 12 and 24 hours and 34% between 6 and 12 hours (Drizen & Leo, 2004).

As you might expect, a false confession can have a tremendous impact on the outcome of a case. When a confession is made (whether it is false or not), the outcome is more likely than not a conviction (Leo & Davis, 2010). Of course, a false confession results in a wrongful conviction. According to Leo and Davis, between 14 and 60 percent of wrongful convictions relate to false confessions. Leo and Davis suggest that false confessions bias a criminal case because of seven psychological factors, many relating to social psychological phenomena discussed in earlier chapters (see Table 12.1). In addition to those factors listed in Table 12.1, another reason a false confession can lead to conviction is that

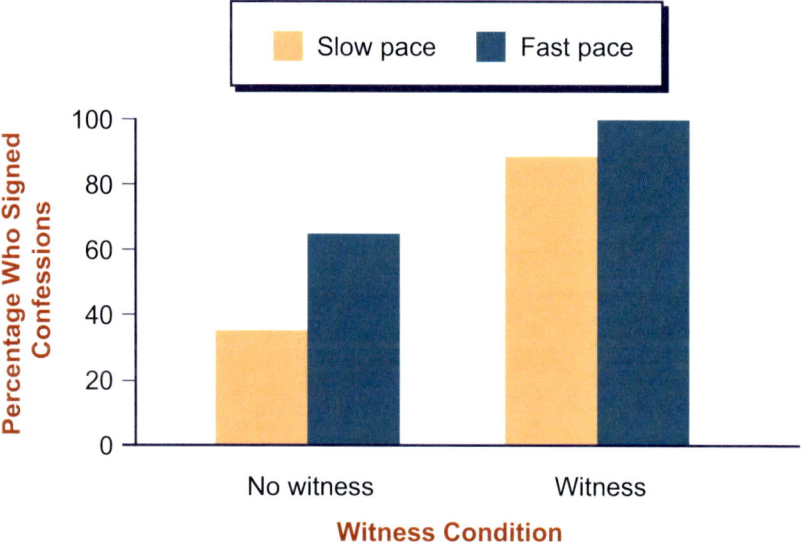

FIGURE 12.4

The difference between having a "witness" to a transgression and signing a false confession. When a witness claimed to have seen a transgression, more people signed a confession than if there was no witness.

Based on data from Kassin and Kiechel (1996).

TABLE 12.1 Seven psychological reasons why false confessions lead to wrongful conviction.

1. **The information in the confession itself.** The confessor appears to have special knowledge of the crime, often supplied by the interrogator.
2. **Tunnel vision and the confirmation bias.** Once a confession is obtained, investigators narrow their search for further information and look for evidence to confirm the confession.
3. **Motivational bias.** Once a confession is obtained, the goals of investigators and prosecutors can change from finding the truth to obtaining a conviction. This can contribute to the second factor when the search for information becomes narrowed to information confirming the confession.
4. **Escalating commitment to the idea of the suspect's guilt.** As the case progresses investigators and prosecutors show an increasing commitment to the suspect's guilt, resulting in acceptance of confession-consistent information and rejection of confession-inconsistent information.
5. **Emotion.** Confessions, including false ones, take place in the context of strong emotion. For example, strong fear of dire consequences can motivate a suspect to confess to reduce possible punishment.
6. **Institutional considerations.** Institutional factors, such as financial considerations, may motivate investigators to elicit a confession in order to streamline the course of a case.
7. **Inadequate context for evaluating evidence.** Police and investigators may deny the reality of false confessions or lack knowledge about them and press ahead with efforts to obtain a confession at all costs.

alibi witnesses are likely to abandon a suspect once the witness finds out that the suspect has confessed. In one simulation study, only 45% of alibi witnesses continued to support a suspect after a confession. This number dropped to 20% if the alibi witness believed that he or she would be implicated in the crime if support was continued (Marion et al., 2016). The absence of the alibi witness will undoubtedly increase the likelihood that the suspect will be convicted in court.

How do jurors evaluate the voluntariness of a confession? Which police tactics do they perceive as inappropriate? These questions were addressed in a study by Hall et al. (2020). They had participants evaluate 18 interrogation tactics, with some being coercive (e.g., physical abuse or sleep deprivation), and others being psychologically manipulative (e.g., lying about evidence). The results showed that participants believed that coercive tactics were inappropriate. The tactics viewed as least appropriate were physical abuse, degrading the suspect, excessive force, depriving suspects of a basic need (e.g., sleep), and questioning suspects while they were intoxicated. Participants generally viewed psychologically manipulative tactics as appropriate, except for lying about evidence. In a second study, Hall et al. investigated whether the perceived appropriateness of a tactic related to two other factors: the strength of the evidence and the severity of the crime. When a crime was more severe, participants viewed coercive tactics as more appropriate than for a less severe crime. Crime severity did not significantly affect appropriateness ratings for psychological manipulation tactics. When the evidence police had was weak, coercive tactics were rated as less appropriate compared with if the evidence was strong. The opposite was found for psychological manipulation tactics. When the evidence was weak, manipulation tactics were seen as more appropriate compared with if the evidence was strong. Finally, in a third study, Hall et al. found that the perceived appropriateness of a tactic was affected by the outcome of the interrogation. If the interrogation yielded a clear confession of guilt, coercive tactics were viewed as more appropriate than psychological manipulation compared with if the outcome was not clear. Overall, how individuals view interrogation tactics depends on other factors, such as crime severity and interrogation outcome.

Summary of This Section

As is evident from this brief overview, social psychological research has implications for many aspects of the legal system: from the initial crime event, to the police interrogation of a suspect or witness, and finally, to the judge and jury's deliberation of a crime. Social psychological research can also be applied to understanding the factors that might influence an individual's decision to engage in criminal behavior and the effectiveness of deterrents of crime. For example, Tittle et al. (2011) found that disapproval and loss of respect from family and friends had stronger deterrent effects on crime than formal punishment, such as jail time. Basic social psychological principles, such as conformity, social influence, and stereotypes, are useful tools for understanding law-related processes.

Study Break

This section covered juries and how they make decisions. Before you begin the next section, answer the following questions:

1. What are the different types of false confessions?
2. What factors affect the likelihood of a false confession?
3. How do confessions, real and false, affect the outcome of a case?
4. How do jurors evaluate the voluntariness of a confession?

The Social Psychology of Work: Industrial Organizational Psychology

The previous section illustrated how social psychology can help explain and clarify human behavior in the court room. The next section of the chapter will demonstrate that the principles and theories of social psychology are also useful in explaining and clarifying behaviors in the workplace. Employers routinely must decide who to hire, how to evaluate employee performance, and how to motivate employees to perform at their best. As you will see in the next section, findings in the areas of social perception, persuasion, social influence, and group processes can help improve the accuracy of these decisions, and help employers avoid potential biases and errors.

Personnel Selection

How do organizations decide which applicant to hire? Ideally, organizations would rely on evidence and research to help select one job candidate over another. Industrial/organizational (I/O) psychologists who specialize in personnel psychology can assist organizations in areas such as employee selection, recruitment, and performance reviews. Traditionally, personnel selection is a three step-process: job analysis, employee recruitment, and employee screening (see Figure 12.5).

job analysis The systematic study of a job's tasks, duties, and responsibilities and the knowledge, skills, and abilities needed to perform the job.

The first step requires an organization to describe the job. **Job analysis** is the systematic study of a job's tasks, duties, and responsibilities, and the knowledge, skills, and abilities needed to perform the job. An I/O psychologist might use research methods such as observation, surveys, job diaries, or interviews to get a better sense of what a particular job entails and how to measure job performance.

FIGURE 12.5

Three steps of the personnel selection process.

Employee recruitment is the process of attracting potential workers to apply for jobs. Organizations might use advertisements, college recruitment programs, employment agencies, online job sites, and even Facebook to attract applicants. It is in the best interest of the organization to attract a large pool of applicants, and past research has found that initial recruiting strategies have a significant effect on the size of the applicant pool (Boudreau & Rynes, 1985). Organizations are looking for the best qualified applicants, but at the same time, applicants are looking for organizations with positive qualities. Jones et al. (2006) applied the elaboration likelihood model (Petty & Cacioppo, 1986) discussed in Chapter 6 to understanding the factors that might influence attitudes toward a written job advertisement. Participants were presented with several job advertisements, some with high-quality information (central cues) about the job, such as information about promotion opportunities or benefits. The peripheral cues used in the job ads were features such as the size of the font used and the use of a company logo within the ad. Participants who were able to carefully review all of the job ads preferred ads with more high-quality information compared to participants who were only allowed to skim the ads. The results suggest that organizations carefully consider the type of information to put into a job advertisement and the medium by which the information is presented. The extent to which central and peripheral cues in a job advertisement affect attitudes about a potential employer also depends on the job seeker's experience (Walker et al., 2008). Walker et al. found that information about an organization (central cue) had more effect on experienced than inexperienced job seekers. Conversely, the attractiveness of the advertisement (a peripheral cue) affected inexperienced more than experienced job seekers. These results suggest that if an organization is posting an ad on monster.com, which contains thousands of job postings, it might want to include peripheral cues to get its advertisement noticed, especially if it is targeting entry-level recruits. For job seekers who have the employment experience and the motivation and ability to process the information included in a job advertisement, more high-quality information about the job and the organization can help make the ad more attractive.

employee recruitment
The process of attracting potential workers to apply for jobs.

Employee recruitment is the process of attracting potential workers to apply for jobs. Once applicants are attracted, employee screening takes place, which is the process of reviewing information about applicants. Employee screening may involve job-relevant tests.
Source: fizkes/Shutterstock.

Like many other aspects of our lives, the rapid growth of the Internet has affected employee recruitment. There are two primary ways the Internet has been utilized for recruitment: job boards or job-search Web sites (e.g., monster.com or careerbuiler.com) and social networking sites (e.g., LinkedIn or Facebook). Job boards and job-search sites have a longer history with employee recruitment and have been widely used since the late 1990s. These job boards are quite popular with job seekers. They offer job seekers a centralized location from which to search a large database of potential jobs. These boards also hold advantages for recruiters, giving them access to an ever-expanding pool of applicants, usually for some nominal fee.

Despite the popularity of job boards, research shows that most generalized job boards (e.g., monster.com or indeed.com) often produce low-quality recruits compared to industry-specific job boards (e.g., healthcareJobsite.com for people in the health care industry; Jattuso & Sinar, 2003). Nevertheless, likely because of their extensive history, job seekers tend to use job boards more frequently, and they see them as more effective as compared to social networking sites (Nikolaou, 2014). Social networking sites can be divided into two broad categories. There are professionally oriented sites, like LinkedIn, and there are social network sites that are primarily used to connect with family and friends, such as Facebook. Job seekers tend to find the more professional sites more effective (Nikolaou, 2014). However, job recruiters are increasingly using social networking sites such as Facebook as a screening tool. Before checking references, employers may first examine a potential applicant's social network profiles, and what they find could mean the difference between landing an interview and your résumé ending up in the trash can (Chang & Madera, 2012; McCarthy et al., 2017; Roulin & Bangerter, 2013).

employee screening
The process of reviewing information about job applicants.

Employee screening is the process of reviewing information about job applicants. Organizations might start with a review of written materials, such as applications, resumes, and cover letters. The second step in screening could be employee testing to ensure that the job applicant has the skills necessary to perform the job. Any screening test or method must demonstrate that it is a reliable and valid predictor of job performance. Screening tests must have high content validity, or whether the test content adequately measures the knowledge, skills, and abilities required by the job, and criterion related validity, or the relationship between screening test scores and some criterion of job success.

Employee screening tests vary widely and can include cognitive ability tests, mechanical ability tests, motor and sensory ability tests, job skills and knowledge tests, personality tests, and polygraphs. Although standardized tests can be powerful and effective tools at predicting job performance, the burden of demonstrating this relationship is on the employer.

For example, in the 1950s, Duke Power Company employed both Black and White workers. However, the Black workers were only allowed to work in a low-status and low-wage department, not in other departments. After the Civil Rights Act of 1964, Duke Power allowed Black workers to apply for jobs in other, higher-paying divisions. However, one of the screening requirements for such jobs was a high school diploma. Black applicants were much less likely to have a high school diploma compared to White applicants and were therefore hired at a much lower rate compared to Whites. In 1971 the Supreme Court decided that such a requirement had an **adverse impact** on Black applicants. Adverse impact means that employment practices that can appear neutral, but have a discriminatory effect on a protected group. The court also found that Duke Power had failed to show how a high school diploma was related to job performance.

adverse impact Employment practices that can appear neutral, but have a discriminatory effect on a protected group.

The Civil Rights Act of 1964 and its 1967 amendment prohibit discrimination based on race, religion, color, national origin, or sex. And as we learned earlier, if an employment practice adversely affects one of these groups, the practice is illegal. Does this mean that a clothing manufacturer that sells only men's clothing would be required to hire both male and female models when advertising? Of course not! The law actually allows employers to discriminate against employees on the basis of religion, sex, or national origin in instances where the religion, sex, or national origin of the employee is a *bona fide occupational qualification* (BFOQ). BFOQs are qualities of employees that are related to essential job duties. Thus, being male would be a BFOQ for a job that involves modeling male clothing options. There are several examples of BFOQs that have been held up in court. For example, Catholic schools may require their faculty to be Catholic because in this instance, religion would be a BFOQ. Furthermore, mandatory retirement ages for occupations such as police officers or pilots have also passed the BFOQ test.

Although some employers have been able to successfully defend claims of adverse impact in their hiring decisions, arguing that the discrimination is based on a BFOQ, this is not an easy task. The restaurant chain Hooters, famous for its scantily clad female servers, has been sued multiple times since the mid-1990s. These cases hinged on the fact that Hooters only hired female servers, and the servers tended to make more money than the cooks, who tended to be male. Hooters defended these hiring practices, claiming that the sex appeal of the servers was part of the theme of the restaurant and thus a BFOQ. Hooters has never actually defended this argument in court and has settled all lawsuits outside of court. As part of its settlements, Hooters still continues to hire only women for its server positions, but it has agreed to create other gender-neutral positions, such as that of bartender.

Performance Appraisals

performance appraisals
Tools or measures to assess worker performance in comparison to some standards.

Employees need to know how they are doing in their job. **Performance appraisals** assess worker performance in comparison to some standards and provide valuable information to the worker and the organization. Performance appraisals are usually tied to pay increases and promotions, and ideally, they should help to improve employee performance.

The first issue to address when looking at performance appraisals has to do with the source of the performance information. Although an employee's supervisor provides appraisals in most organizations, other sources of information such as self-appraisals, peer-appraisals, and customer appraisals can be used. Another model of feedback is called multi-rater feedback or 360-degree feedback. In a 360-degree feedback model, information is gathered from different levels of an organization; supervisors, subordinates, peers, and customers all provide information that can be used in performance appraisals. Such models are complex, and research is still providing information about the conditions under which 360-degree feedback is valuable and can lead to behavior change (Bracken & Rose, 2011).

In addition to different models of performance appraisals, there are also different types of measures or tools that can be used to evaluate an employee. Supervisors may choose to compose a written narrative of the worker's performance or complete a checklist of the worker's performance on different tasks. On **trait-based scales**, workers are evaluated on their personality and job-related traits, such as leadership and initiative. **Behavior-based scales**, such as the behavioral observation scale (BOS), require raters to recall how frequently an employee has engaged in specific job-related behaviors. Tziner and Kopelman (2002) argue that BOS-based evaluations have advantages over other measures because of the focus on directly observable behaviors. BOS feedback should facilitate clear goals, acceptance of these goals, and increased commitment to these goals (Tziner & Kopelman, 2002, p. 483).

trait-based scales Scales used in performance appraisals, where workers are evaluated on their personality and job-related traits, such as leadership and initiative.

behavior-based scales Scales used in performance appraisals, where workers are evaluated on observable job-related behavior.

Regardless of the type of information used in a performance appraisal, it is important that an employee view the appraisal process as one that is fair and credible. Factors such as (a) selecting raters who have sufficient opportunity to observe the ratee, (b) training the rater, and (c) using an appraisal instrument that is clear and has face validity can all influence perceptions of fairness and legitimacy of the appraisal process (Bracken & Rose, 2011). Salleh et al. (2013) found that employees' perceptions of fairness in performance appraisals were positively related to satisfaction with the process and organizational commitment.

Employee perceptions and expectations about performance appraisals also depend on the gender of the supervisor doing the appraisals. Might women expect more leniency from a female supervisor than a male supervisor? Similarly, might men expect more leniency from a male supervisor than a female supervisor? These questions were addressed in an experiment conducted by Maas and Torres-González (2011). In this experiment, male and female participants read a description of a company and its performance evaluation procedures in which the likelihood of being evaluated by a female supervisor was manipulated (10%, 50%, or 90%) along with the nature of the evaluation (objective or subjective). The results showed that female participants expected to receive an above-average bonus and saw the company as more attractive when there was a 90% chance of being evaluated subjectively by a female supervisor. The opposite was true for being evaluated objectively by a female supervisor. On the other hand, expectations of males were not significantly affected by the likelihood of being evaluated by a female supervisor. This study reinforces the complexity of job performance evaluations and that a number of variables can affect how employees perceive them.

What are some of the potential problems with performance appraisals? Just as previous research has found that attractive individuals are evaluated more positively on a number of different dimensions (Dion et al., 1972), the **halo effect** can also occur in performance appraisals. Raters might use positive information they have about the worker in one area and rate the worker more positively across all areas. For example, if you have information that your employee, Sharon, is very good at working with difficult customers, you might assume that Sharon is also good at working with her colleagues or writing reports, which may or may not be true. Results from two large studies demonstrated that public employees required to rate the work achievements of a fictional subordinate were influenced by halo effects (Bellé et al., 2017). Results from two large studies demonstrated that public employees required to rate the work achievements of a fictional subordinate were influenced by halo effects (Bellé et al., 2017). Proper training of raters and an emphasis on accountability can help to minimize or alleviate the halo effect (Palmer & Feldman, 2005).

halo effect A bias in which one's impression of a person's ability in one domain is influenced by one's impression of a person's ability in another domain, even when these two domains might be unrelated.

Chapter 12 Applying Social Psychology: Law, Business, and Health

Study Break

This section covered employment and performance evaluations. Before reading further, answer the following questions.

1. What factors affect job analysis and employee recruitment?
2. How is job screening done, and what is the idea of adverse impact?
3. How are trait-based and performance-based scales used in performance appraisals?
4. What factors affect employee perceptions of fairness and legitimacy of performance appraisals?
5. What is a halo effect and how can it affect performance appraisals?

Motivation at Work

Why do some people work hard at their jobs while other people don't? What would motivate someone to spend hours at night and on the weekend on job-related activities without monetary compensation such as overtime pay? The area of work motivation focuses on understanding the personal, situational, and structural factors that contribute to work-related behaviors.

The basis for most motivational theories is the concept of needs, with the idea being that individuals are motivated to satisfy physiological and psychological **needs**. According to McClelland (1961), people are motivated by three needs: achievement, power, and affiliation. Most individuals will be motivated by one need more strongly than the other two. For example, a worker who has a strong need for achievement will be motivated by possibilities for success in the workplace and to avoid failures (Fisher, 2009).

Another well-known need theory is Maslow's (1943) hierarchy of needs. At the base of Maslow's hierarchy are basic physiological needs, such as food, water, and sleep. This level is followed by safety needs (e.g., having a place to live) and social needs (e.g., relationships with friends and family). The next level includes esteem needs, or the need to be admired and respected by others. The highest level of the hierarchy is self-actualization, or the need to reach one's highest potential (see Figure 12.6).

How might we apply Maslow's hierarchy of needs to the workplace? Let's imagine Sam is a mid-level manager in a bank. He makes more than enough money to pay for food and rent. As Sam's manager, you might try to figure out if Sam's social needs are being met. Is he connected with other co-workers and customers? If his social needs at the job are being met, then you might try and motivate Sam by satisfying his esteem needs, through the development of an employee recognition program (e.g., "Employee of the Month").

When we are considering the relationship between worker needs and job motivation, it is important to understand that not all needs relate to one's job motivation. For example, Maslow's need for self-actualization may have nothing to do with one's motivation as an auto worker. When assessing the relationship between needs and job motivation, we must consider the salience of the needs with respect to the job (Sahoo et al., 2011). A salient need is one that is closely associated with one's job. Sahoo et al. studied the relationship between need salience and job motivation in four studies of workers in India. They found that only salient needs correlated significantly with job motivation. Nonsalient needs were not related to job motivation. Sahoo et al. also addressed the issue of how well Maslow's need hierarchy applies to cultures beyond

needs A psychological or physiological feature that arouses an individual to action toward a goal, giving purpose and direction to behavior.

An employee's job-salient needs, goals and personality relate to how well he or she performs his or her job.
Source: Lichtmeister/Shutterstock.

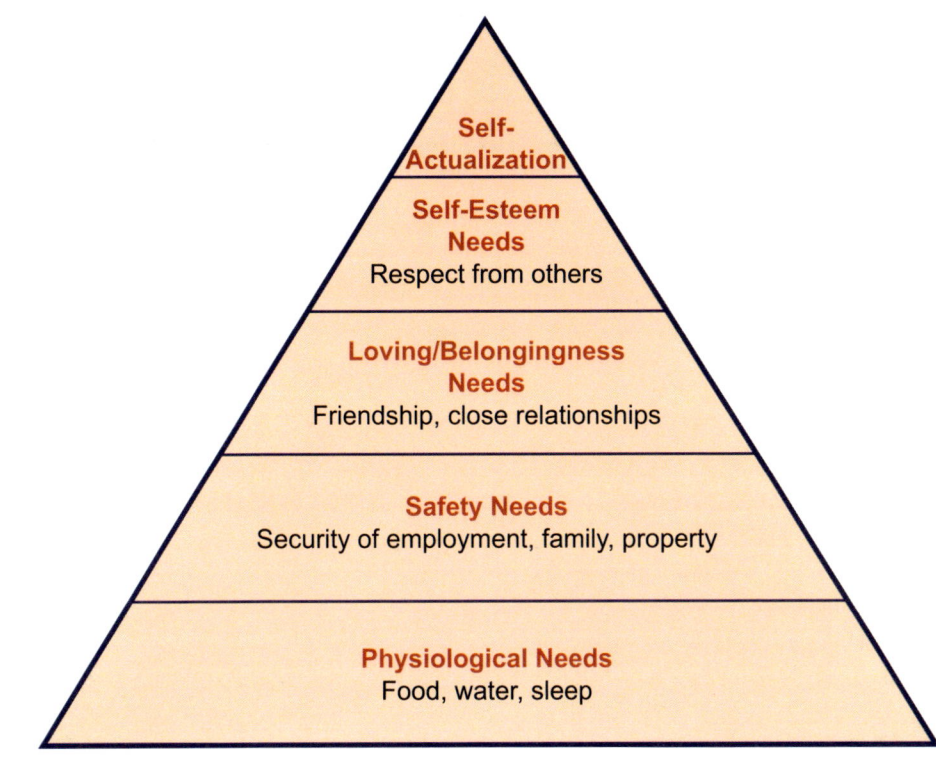

FIGURE 12.6

Maslow's hierarchy of needs.

Western cultures. They suggest that Maslow's model may not apply well to non-Western cultures. That is, across cultures, workers may not be strongly motivated by individualistic needs such as the need for self-esteem or self-actualization. They suggest that for different cultures different needs, salient to the job itself, may motivate workers.

I/O psychologists often look at personality traits as a way of understanding differences in work motivation among individuals. Personality is a strong predictor of one's job choice and job satisfaction. In a recent meta-analysis of the research on personality and job satisfaction, researchers found both neuroticism and conscientiousness to be significantly associated with job satisfaction—the former negatively and the latter positively (Bruk-Lee et al., 2009).

For a more behaviorally based approach to understanding work motivation, we can turn to goal-setting theory (Locke & Latham, 2002). Goal-setting theory suggests that an individual's conscious goals and intentions are the primary determinants of behavior. A goal is the object or aim of an action, usually within a specified time limit. For goals to be most effective, they must be specific and difficult. Meta-analytic findings indicate that the most difficult goals produce the highest levels of effort and performance (Locke & Latham, 1990). Also, setting a specific goal (e.g., call five customers by the end of the day) leads to better performance compared to a "do your best" or more general goal.

For goals to be effective, they must be clear and individuals must be committed to them (Peralta et al., 2015). How personally interested is an individual in reaching this goal? Individuals tend to be more committed to goals that are important to them and more committed when self-efficacy is high. Individuals need to believe that they can actually achieve the goal. Organizations can facilitate self-efficacy by providing workers with skills training and mentors. They can also provide workers with feedback about performance, which can increase motivation toward the goal. Feedback allows for individuals to make changes to their strategies and adjust their future behaviors. For example, in many sales jobs, salespersons are required to make connections with new potential clients. If an organization sets a goal of 10 new client interactions each week, then salespersons can decide on a particular strategy for the week and make adjustments mid-week if they

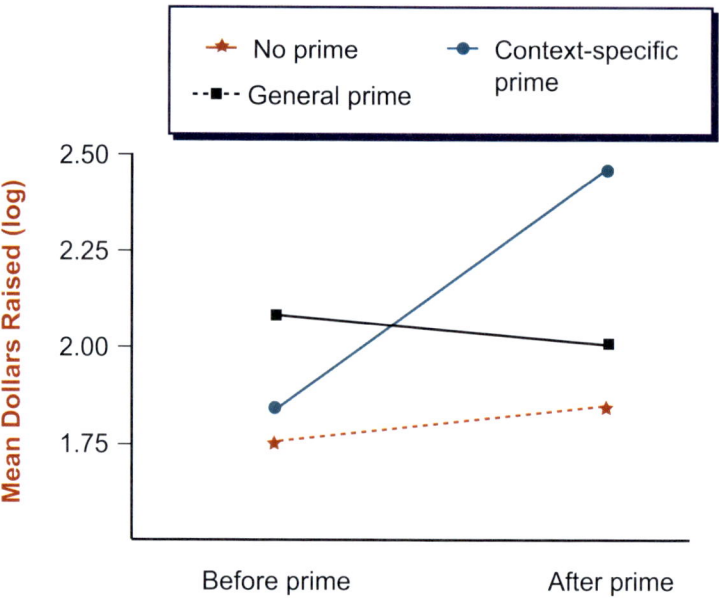

FIGURE 12.7

The relationship between priming and work performance. A context-specific prime (photo of employees at their jobs) was most effective in improving job performance.
Based on data from Latham and Piccolo (2012).

find they are not meeting the goal. They might start out trying to make new connections through existing clients and then move on to using social media tools.

What are the mechanisms by which goal setting works? According to Locke and Latham (1990), goals serve a directive function; they direct attention and effort toward goal-relevant activities and away from goal-irrelevant activities. Second, goals have an energizing function; difficult goals lead to increased effort, with both physical and cognitive tasks. Third, goals influence persistence; hard goals prolong effort. Fourth, goals lead to the arousal, discovery, and/or use of task-relevant knowledge and strategies. If the task for which a goal is assigned is new to people, they will engage in deliberate planning to develop strategies that will enable them to attain their goals (Smith et al., 1990).

In addition to conscious goal setting, goals can also be primed subconsciously. Latham and Piccolo (2012) randomly assigned participants, university call-center employees, to one of two prime conditions. The job of the call-center employees was to raise funds for the university. In the general achievement condition, participants were shown a picture of a female runner winning a race. In the context-specific prime condition, participants viewed a picture of three call-center employees wearing headsets, engaged in their work. The researchers then measured how many donors pledged dollars to the university and the monetary value of the pledges. The results indicate that participants in the context-specific prime condition raised more money than those in either the general achievement condition or a control condition (see Figure 12.7). The results highlight the effect that goal setting can have on actual performance and that this effect can be somewhat effortless. Perhaps the future of office artwork is photographs of people simply doing their jobs.

Organizational Citizenship Behaviors

Beyond just being motivated to perform the duties required for a particular job, more organizations and organizational psychologists are becoming interested in citizenship in the workplace. According to Organ (1988), **organizational citizenship behaviors** are those that promote the efficient and effective functioning of the organization, typically without any formal reward tied to them. Organizational citizenship behaviors can fall into one of several categories: altruism, conscientiousness, sportsmanship, courtesy, and civic virtue (Organ, 1988). If you've worked in an organization, it's likely that you've witnessed

organizational citizenship behaviors Behaviors that promote the efficient and effective functioning of the organization, typically without any formal reward tied to them.

co-workers who are high or low in different types of organizational citizenship behaviors. Think about the co-worker who offers to stay late so that you can get home in time to celebrate a family member's birthday. Or, the co-worker who offers to help you finish an important presentation with a looming deadline. Even somewhat trivial gestures, like the office-mate who asks if you are OK with her choice of music playing in the background, can affect the work climate.

So, what factors increase organizational citizenship behaviors? In Chapter 8, we discussed different leadership styles and how they relate to group decision making. One of the components of transformational leadership is charisma, described as the ability to influence others. Research has found that higher levels of charisma in a leader is positively related to organizational citizenship behaviors (Babcock-Robertson & Strickland, 2010). But, this relationship was mediated by work engagement. That is, charismatic leaders are more likely to have workers who are engaged in and enthusiastic about their work, and this, in turn, is related to more organizational citizenship behaviors. A good example of a charismatic leader was the late co-founder and chairman of Apple Corporation, Steve Jobs. His innovative and visionary leadership style has been credited for the innovations that occurred within Apple Corporation during his tenure. Employees' perceptions of their companies' values and fairness can influence organizational citizenship behaviors as well (Sharma, 2018). When employees perceive that an organization is treating them unfairly, or when they perceive that their company's values are immoral, they are much less likely to engage in organizational citizenship behaviors.

Study Break

The preceding sections introduced you to industrial and organizational psychology. Before you go on to the next section, answer the following questions:

1. How do worker needs and goals relate to worker performance?
2. How does Maslow's need hierarchy relate to work motivation?
3. How does need salience relate to work motivation and performance?
4. What does it mean to prime work goals?
5. What are organizational citizenship behaviors, and what affects them?

Social Psychology and Health

Health in the United States and other Western countries has changed dramatically in the past century. Whereas in past generations, infectious diseases such as influenza and tuberculosis were a major cause of death, today we see chronic, mostly preventable diseases as the leading causes of death. According to the Centers for Disease Control and Prevention (2020b), 60% of adults in the United States have a chronic disease. Almost 50% of deaths each year in the United States are from chronic diseases such as heart disease, cancer, and stroke (see Figure 12.8). And today, 42% of American adults are obese (Centers for Disease Control, 2020c), a condition that is linked to several diseases, including heart disease and diabetes.

According to Spiro (2007), health is a lifelong process that starts in utero and ends at death. Health is affected by current behaviors and practices, but also by one's history of choices and genetic factors. The study of health is also pluralistic, in that it requires conversations between biomedical and behavioral sciences. Psychologists can help people make better health-related decisions, but they need good medical evidence to help them

Organizational citizenship behaviors are those that promote the efficient and effective functioning of the organization, typically without any formal reward tied to them. Such behaviors include helping fellow coworkers. Charismatic leadership and employee perceptions of employer fairness can increase organizational citizenship behaviors.

Source: fizkes/Shutterstock.

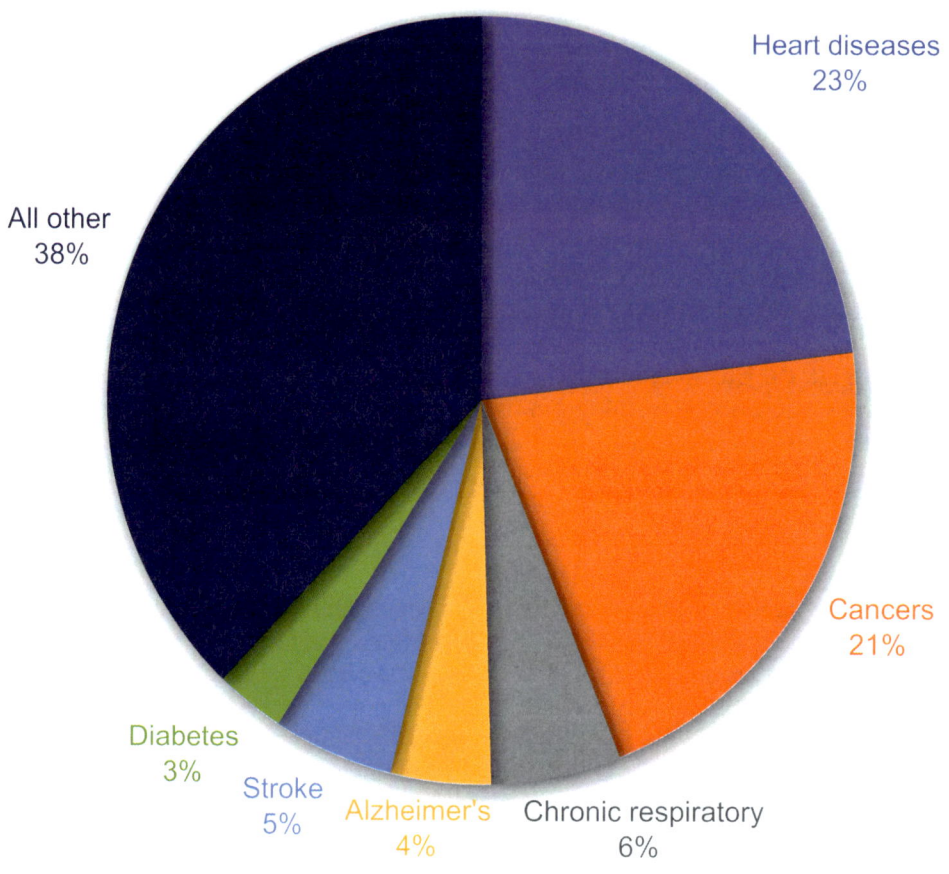

FIGURE 12.8

Deaths by chronic disease.
Based on data from the CDC (2020b).

identify what behaviors and activities lead to positive health-related outcomes. Spiro (2007) advocates for understanding and studying health in a cultural, socioeconomic, and historical context. And finally, he emphasizes the importance of recognizing individual differences in health—both within and between individuals. People have different experiences with the same disease and use different coping mechanisms.

How can psychologists help to improve the health of others? Psychologists are in a unique position to work in the area of health because their goal is to understand and predict behavior. And because many of the conditions that have an adverse effect on health are conditions that have behavioral components, psychologists can use theory and research to help people make healthier decisions across their lifespan. In the current section, we examine some of the factors that influence health and well-being.

Perceived Stress and Health

Unmanaged stress and other lifestyle factors also have an effect on the immune system, as verified by substantial scientific evidence. Studies have shown that negative moods and feelings, such as depression, anxiety, fear, and anger are associated with a decline in immune functioning, at least temporarily (Graham et al., 2006; Herbert & Cohen, 1993; Segerstrom et al., 1998). The connections take place through a complex communication system involving the brain, the endocrine system (glands and hormones), and the immune system. The immune system is the body's first line of defense against illness. When it breaks down, the body becomes vulnerable to disease and death.

There are several ways of defining and thinking about stress (Bishop, 1994). One way, referred to as the stimulus definition of stress, focuses on the stimuli that produce stress. Stress is defined in terms of what is happening in the environment. According to this way

FIGURE 12.9

Three stages of the general adaptation syndrome.

of looking at stress, different people respond pretty much the same way to given events. Any individual who experienced a great deal of work-related stress, for example, would probably become ill, in this view.

A second way of defining stress, the response definition of stress, focuses on how people react, both physiologically and psychologically, when they are in stressful situations. The response of the body in stressful situations was studied extensively by Hans Selye (1975), a pioneer in the area of stress and physiology. Selye proposed a three-step model called the **general adaptation syndrome** describing the reaction of the body to a stressor—any event or situation that requires that a person make an adjustment (see Figure 12.9). Stage 1 of this model is the **alarm stage**, in which the body reacts to the stressor with an instinctive, automatic response. A branch of the autonomic nervous system (a part of the nervous system that operates independently of conscious thought) releases hormones into the bloodstream that prepare the body for fight or flight. Heart rate accelerates, bronchi dilate to allow more air into the lungs, the liver releases sugar for extra energy, digestion halts, perspiration increases to cool the skin, hearing and vision become more acute, and endorphins are released to provide pain relief in case of injury (Insel & Roth, 1994).

The body resists such dramatic change, however, and as soon as possible it initiates the adjustments needed to restore balance. Stage 2 is the **resistance stage**, in which the alarm reaction is halted and the body attempts to restore normal functioning. However, if the stressful situation persists, or if there is a series of such events, the body has difficulty returning to normal. Both the alarm reaction and the resistance stage require a considerable amount of energy. If these stages go on for too long, reserve stores of energy are depleted and the third stage, the **exhaustion stage**, sets in. This is not the everyday kind of exhaustion; rather it is a profound, life-threatening physiological exhaustion that may be accompanied by such symptoms as distorted thinking and perceptions (Insel & Roth, 1994). At this point the person becomes vulnerable to disease or death (Spacapan, 1988).

A third definition of stress, the one used in social psychology, focuses on the observation that stress is a transaction between the individual and the environment. In this perspective, the most critical aspect of stress is the way in which the individual perceives and responds to the stressful event (Bishop, 1994). The experience of stress is mediated by individuals' appraisal of the situation and their ability to cope with that situation. Implied in this definition is the idea that the experience of stress is subjective. Stress is in the eye of the beholder. If individuals perceive that the demands made of them exceed their ability to cope with those demands, then the situation is stressful for them (Cohen et al., 1993). If individual resources exceed the demands of the situation, however great those demands may be, then the situation will not be perceived or experienced as stressful.

Appraisals of Stress

The third definition of stress defined in the previous paragraph is exemplified by the *transactional model of stress and coping* (Antonovsky & Kats, 1967; Cohen, 1984; Lazarus & Cohen, 1977). The effect of an external stressor on a person is mediated first by the person's appraisal (primary appraisal) of the stressor and second on the resources available to deal with the stressor (secondary appraisal). Primary appraisals involve an individual making an assessment of what is happening in a situation. Is this stressful situation harmful or involve loss? Is this situation challenging or threatening? Secondary appraisals address what one can do about the situation, and can be classified as either **problem-focused coping** or **emotion-focused coping**. Problem-focused coping strategies work to

general adaptation syndrome (GAS) A three-step model describing the reaction of the body to a stressor.

alarm stage Stage 1 of the GAS, in which the body reacts to the stressor with an instinctive, automatic response.

resistance stage Stage 2 of the GAS, in which the alarm reaction is halted and the body attempts to restore normal functioning.

exhaustion stage Stage 3 of the GAS, characterized by profound, life-threatening physiological exhaustion that may be accompanied by such symptoms as distorted thinking and perceptions.

problem-focused coping Coping strategies that work to manage the external demands of a situation, often through the development of plans and goals.

emotion-focused coping Coping strategies that involve attempts to manage one's internal emotions or feelings.

Social psychologists have found a link between life stressors and health. Even positive events, like getting married, can be a significant source of life stress.

Source: Wedding and lifestyle/Shutterstock.

manage the external demands of a situation. Emotion-focused coping involves attempts to manage one's internal emotions or feelings.

Imagine it's the end of the semester and you thinking about your final exams. Your career goal is to become a physician, and one of your most difficult classes this semester has been organic chemistry. You have done well all semester, but you still need a high score on the final exam to get an "A" in the course, which would look great on your applications to medical school next year. What is your primary appraisal of your chemistry final exam? Because you have done well all semester and an "A" is within your reach, you might be more likely to view this situation as a challenge. If you had done poorly all semester and there was a strong possibility that you could fail, then you might be more likely to see this situation as a threat. What is your secondary appraisal of the situation? You might use problem-focused coping, such as planning your study sessions for the exam or forming a study group. You might cut down on your hours at work that week, giving you more time to review the material for the final exam. Or, you might use emotion-focused coping, such as talking to your best friend about how stressed you feel about this exam. You might also minimize the importance of your performance on this exam, telling yourself that medical schools are going to look at more than just your grade in one class.

In most cases, individuals will engage in *both* problem-focused and emotion-focused coping strategies (Folkman & Lazarus, 1980). However, previous research has found that challenge appraisals are more likely to be followed up by problem-focused coping strategies than threat appraisals (Franks & Roesch, 2006). When you view the stressful situation as an outcome, then you are less likely to think there is anything you can do to change that situation. In such cases (e.g., the loss of a loved one, a terminal illness), individuals focus on making themselves feel better about the situation (emotion-focused coping). However, when you view the stressful situation as one that is still malleable (e.g., a future exam, pre-diabetic diagnosis), then you are more likely to try and make the situation better (problem-focused coping).

Life Stressors and Illness

In the early 1960s, two physicians working at the naval air base in San Diego began to notice that many of the sailors who visited the infirmary had undergone stressful life events in the previous few months (Holmes & Rahe, 1967). The two doctors began to keep track of the events—they called them life stressors—that appeared to affect the health of the sailors. Many of these stressors were marital and sexual problems, but others were successes, such as promotions; failures, such as being passed over for a promotion; worries over mortgages and rents; parking tickets; and other stuff of daily life.

To study the relationship between stress and health, the two physicians devised a questionnaire called the schedule of recent events, which was later modified and published as the *social readjustment rating scale* (SRRS) (Holmes & Rahe, 1967). Holmes and Rahe told their participants to use marriage as their base and to assume that it was worth 50 (stress) points. They then asked participants to rate the other life events on the list in comparison to marriage. They found that the more points sailors accumulated in one year, the more likely they were to get sick. Accumulating 300 points or more was virtually a guarantee of illness. The relationship between life stressors and health issues has withstood the test of time and research scrutiny. For example, Thorsteinsson and Brown (2009) found significant positive correlations between exposure to stressful life events and fatigue. The more life stressors participants were exposed to, the more fatigue they experienced.

Now, there are two things to note about the list of life events. First, both good and bad events are considered stressful; getting married is almost as stressful as going to jail. Second, it may not be that the stressful event causes illness; a person may already be getting sick and therefore be experiencing some of these difficulties. People who do not feel well may be more likely to have sexual problems, for example, or to get low grades in school, or to experience problems at work. Therefore, although there may not always be a causal relationship between stressful life events and disease, it is not surprising that scores on the SRRS correlate with subsequent illness.

Sleep, Stress, and Health

Do you often become ill (e.g., flu, head cold) at the beginning of winter break? If you do, it is not surprising. A study of first-year medical students found that these students had poorer immune function and increased self-reported symptoms of illness after exams (Glaser et al., 1987). Final exams can be the "perfect storm" for the development of an illness. The lack of sleep and the stress of exams can suppress immune functioning. The relationship between sleep, stress, and health is a complex one. Sleep and stress appear to have bidirectional effects (Burg et al., 2016). When we are under stress, it can lead to poor sleep quality (Valerio et al., 2016). You are probably already aware of this. I am sure there have been nights where the stress of an upcoming event (e.g., an exam) may have made it hard for you to sleep. In addition to stress causing poor sleep, poor sleep can lead to increased stress. When sleep is restricted to just 4 to 5 hours per night, people report significant increases in negative mood and stress (Dinges et al., 1997). Although sleep and stress influence each other, they also appear to have independent effects on health. Benham and Charak (2019) found that both sleep and stress predict health status independently. That is, models that include both sleep and stress together are better at predicting health outcomes than are models that omit one of these variables.

Although stress can lead to physical and psychological illness, many people develop effective coping strategies to deal with the stress they experience. Coping mechanisms can help a person deal with the causes and effects of stress.
Source: fizkes/Shutterstock.

Study Break

This section introduced you to the application of psychology to health. Before you go on to the next section, answer the following questions:

1. How, generally, does psychology relate to health?
2. What are the stages of the general adaptation syndrome, and how does it relate stress to health?
3. What is the transactional model of stress and coping?
4. What are problem-focused and emotion-focused coping strategies, and how are they used to cope with stress?
5. What is a life stressor, and how does it relate to one's health?
6. How does sleep relate to stress and health?

Coping with Stress

Although stress has been associated with many physical and psychological disorders, not everyone who experiences stress is afflicted. Some people develop effective mechanisms to cope with the stress that they experience. These coping mechanisms help individuals lessen and manage both the causes and the effects of stress (Baum et al., 1982). In this section we look at the mechanisms people use to cope with stress.

Resilience

How do people cope with stress, either in the form of single events or chronic, everyday stressors? There is a range of responses that individuals have to stress; some of those responses are negative, such as drug and alcohol use, while other responses are more positive, such as exercise and reliance on social support. Psychologists are interested in the

resilience An individual's ability to cope with stress and adversity.

individual difference variables and socio-structural and situational factors that influence responses to both acute and chronic stress. Research on **resilience** offers insights into how individuals not only respond to stress, but thrive in the conditions of adversity. Resilience has three components. The first is *recovery*, defined as a return to baseline function following a major stressor. The second component is *sustainability*, which is the capacity to continue forward during stressors. Finally, *growth* is indicated by enhanced adaptation beyond original levels of functioning (Zautra et al., 2010).

resilience resources Different tools or characteristics that individuals might use to help them cope with stress and adversity (e.g., social support).

In a review of the research on resilience, Dunkel Schetter and Dolbier (2011) identified categories of **resilience resources** that individuals use to help them adapt to high levels of chronic stress. The six categories are (1) personality, or individual resources; (2) self and ego-related resources; (3) interpersonal and social resources; (4) world views and culturally based beliefs and values; (5) behavior and cognitive skills; (6) other resources, such as level of education, health practices, and past experiences with adversity. When individuals are able to call upon these resources, they increase the likelihood that they can achieve healthy physical and psychological functioning, in spite of stress or other negative events.

Perceived Control and Self-Efficacy Beliefs

A person's ability to cope with stress depends to a large extent on the degree of control the individual thinks he or she has over the stress-producing events. Perceived control is important to any coping response; it indicates that people believe they have power over what happens in their life. When the life events on the Holmes and Rahe scale are broken down into controllable and uncontrollable, only the uncontrollable events correlate highly with future illness (Thompson et al., 1988). Even the trivial everyday hassles that drive us crazy are those that have an uncontrollable quality to them, such as the painter who says he will be at your house on Tuesday at 9 a.m. and doesn't show up until Wednesday at noon. As we all know, these relatively minor uncontrollable events can take a toll on us.

self-efficacy The belief in one's ability to succeed in specific situations.

People who believe that they have some degree of control over what happens to them also feel that they can effectively cope with stressful or threatening events (Affleck et al., 1987). These individuals usually express feelings of **self-efficacy**, the notion that one can do what one sets out to do (Bandura, 1986). People who have strong feelings of self-efficacy are likely to respond to stress by throwing more effort and resources into coping with the threat.

Another study of the effects of perceived control and self-efficacy beliefs on health status was conducted with patients in a nursing home as participants (Langer & Rodin, 1976). Typically, when people enter nursing homes, they are expected to allow the home's staff to run their lives. Meals are planned and scheduled, as are visiting hours. All rooms are furnished exactly alike. In fact, families expect that when they place a relative in a nursing home, all the person's needs will be met.

In this study, patients on one floor of a high-quality nursing home were given a modest increase in control over their lives. They were told they could arrange their rooms the way they liked, choose how to spend their spare time, and decide when or if they watched TV, listened to the radio, or engaged in other activities. This was the experimental group. Patients on the other floors of the nursing home—the control groups—were told that the staff would arrange for all their needs. Since patients were randomly assigned to different floors, there was no reason to believe that any floor had healthier or unhealthier individuals.

Eighteen months later, the mortality rates of the two groups were compared. The researchers found that 15% of the patients on the experimental floor had died and 30% of the patients on the other floors had died. Why the difference? The researchers suggest that those patients who perceived that they had some control over their environment were more positive, more sociable, and generally happier than other patients. This translated into better health and lower mortality rates.

There is a link between *coping self-efficacy*, which is a belief that one can manage reactions to potentially traumatic events (Bosmans & van der Velden, 2015), and long-term reactions to stress. Bosmans and van der Velden conducted a longitudinal study of the relationship between exposure to traumatic events and symptoms of post-traumatic stress disorder (PTSD). They found that individuals who had higher levels of coping self-efficacy showed lower levels of PTSD symptoms. Why would self-efficacy relate to coping with stress?

According to Skinner and Zimmer-Gembeck (2011), when individuals have confidence and high self-efficacy, they are more likely to approach a stressful situation as a challenge, as opposed to a threat. They stay focused on solutions to a problem and break tasks into manageable parts. These processes are more likely to be successful when dealing with stressful situations and may even reduce the likelihood of future stressful situations. Individuals who feel they have less control are more likely to see a situation as threatening and give up quickly. Instead of focusing on how to solve the problem, these individuals are preoccupied with fear and worry.

Optimism and Health

As you most likely know, some people are more optimistic than others. These individuals are higher on a personality trait known as **dispositional optimism**, which is the tendency to see things from an optimistic perspective (Rius-Ottenheim et al., 2012; Scheier et al., 1994). It is fair to say that optimists and pessimists see the world quite differently. Optimists focus on good things and expect them to happen, whereas pessimists are focused on negative elements and tend to expect bad outcomes. In a very clever experiment, Isaacowitz (2005) used eye tracking to test the idea that pessimists pay more attention to negative stimuli than optimists. College students were asked to track visual stimuli (skin cancers, matched schematic drawings, and neutral faces). The experimenter measured the amount of fixation time—the time students spent tracking the stimuli. Optimists showed "selective *inattention*" to the skin cancers. Optimists averted their gaze from the negative stimuli, so optimists may, in fact, wear "rose-colored glasses," or rather, they may take their glasses off when negative stimuli are in their field of vision.

We know that optimism is sometimes extraordinarily helpful in human affairs. Compared with a pessimistic coping style, an optimistic coping style appears to help individuals recover more rapidly and more effectively from coronary bypass surgery. Research demonstrates that optimistic bypass patients had fewer problems after surgery than pessimistic patients (Scheier et al., 1986). Following their surgery, the optimists reported more positive family, sexual, recreational, and health-related activities than did pessimistic patients. Optimistic patients with traumatic brain injuries (TBIs) also fare better than their less optimistic counterparts (Ramanathan et al., 2011). Ramanathan et al. found that people who scored higher on a measure of dispositional optimism showed less stress after TBI than those scoring lower. They also found that the relationship between dispositional optimism and cognitive ability after TBI was mediated by stress. This means that more optimistic TBI patients do better cognitively because they experience less stress after their head injuries.

Optimism can even help military personnel adjust to life after traumatic experiences. In one longitudinal study of repatriated Vietnam War prisoners of war, optimism was found to be the strongest predictor of positive physical and psychological health (Segovia et al., 2015). We have already seen that self-efficacy can serve as a buffer against PTSD, and optimism functions in a similar fashion. In one study, optimistic Iraq war combat veterans showed fewer symptoms of PTSD than did less optimistic veterans. Optimistic combat veterans also showed fewer symptoms of depression and less work impairment than did less optimistic veterans (Thomas et al., 2011).

Why would optimism contribute to better health outcomes after a traumatic event such as bypass surgery or TBI? One explanation is that optimistic individuals are more likely to see positive outcomes from adversity (Prati & Pietrantoni, 2009). Another reason is that optimism allows a person to apply more flexible coping strategies than does pessimism (Prati & Pietrantoni, 2009). Additionally, optimistic people react to threatening events by developing **positive illusions**, which are beliefs that include unrealistically

> **dispositional optimism** The tendency to see things from an optimistic perspective.

> **positive illusions** Beliefs that include unrealistically optimistic notions about individuals' ability to handle a threat and create a positive outcome.

optimistic notions about their ability to handle the threat and create a positive outcome (Taylor, 1989). These positive illusions are adaptive in the sense that ill people who are optimistic will be persistent and creative in their attempts to cope with the psychological and physical threat of disease. The tendency to display positive illusions has been shown in individuals who have tested positive for the HIV virus but have not yet displayed any symptoms (Taylor et al., 1992). These individuals often expressed the belief that they had developed immunity to the virus and that they could "flush" the virus from their systems. They acted on this belief by paying close attention to nutrition and physical fitness.

Can You Improve Your Level of Optimism?

As we pointed out earlier, some people show higher levels of dispositional optimism than others. Does this mean that we are born with a level of optimism that we carry with us for our entire lives? Or can we do things to change our outlooks to be more optimistic? Given the relationships between cognitive optimism and health, it may behoove us to try to adopt a more optimist worldview. Research suggests that it is possible to raise your level of optimism. For example, Meevissen et al. (2011) had people imagine their "best possible self" or their daily activities for a 2-week period. They found that individuals who imagined their best possible selves showed a sharper increase in optimism than those who had imagined their daily activities. Optimism can also be increased by imagining a positive future (Blackwell et al., 2012; Peters et al., 2010). Keep in mind that in these studies, short-term increases in optimism were measured. It may be possible to increase situational optimism in the short run by thinking and imagining happy thoughts. However, these strategies may not be effective in increasing long-term dispositional optimism.

Study Break

This section covered issues relating to life stress and how it relates to health and how people cope with stress. Before you continue, answer the following questions:

1. What is resilience, and how does it relate to coping with stress?
2. What are resilience resources, and how do they affect coping with stress?
3. How do perceived control and self-efficacy relate to coping with stress?
4. How does optimism relate to coping with stress?
5. How can you increase your level of optimism?

The Effects of Positive Mood

Positive moods also affect the way both sick and healthy people deal with stress. In one study, researchers made groups of ill or healthy participants feel sad, happy, or neutral (Salovey & Birnbaum, 1989). Participants who were sad reported more general aches and pain than did happy participants. A positive mood increased participants' belief that they could lessen their symptoms and cope so that they could carry on daily activities. Mood may also influence the course of illness (Salovey & Birnbaum, 1989). A sad, depressed mood often leads to feelings of fatigue and weakness. People may tend to interpret these symptoms as part of their physical illness. Such a misinterpretation of symptoms may slow recovery.

Some researchers argue that there is a disease-prone personality, in which a persistent depressed mood plays an important role (Friedman & Booth-Kewley, 1987). A good mood is often expressed in laughter. The German philosopher Friedrich Nietzsche observed about humans that the most acutely suffering animal on earth invented laughter. Research shows that laughter may play a role in altering the course of some types of illnesses. In one study, researchers looked at the effects of laughter and relaxation on the ability of participants to withstand the discomfort produced by the inflation of a blood-pressure cuff (Cogan et al., 1987). Participants listened to one of three audiotapes: a humorous tape that induced laughter, a relaxation tape, or an informative narrative. A fourth group, the control group, did not hear a tape. Participants who heard a humorous tape were able to withstand the most discomfort, followed by the relaxation group. The other two groups were able to withstand the least discomfort.

Much of the research into the effects of positive mood on health was inspired by former magazine publisher Norman Cousins (1979, 1989). Cousins was stricken with a severe inflammation of the spine and joints, and his physicians told him that the disorder would leave him disabled. Cousins would not accept this prognosis. Day after day he watched Marx brothers movies from his hospital bed. He found that 10 minutes of solid laughter gave him 2 hours of pain-free sleep. Cousins eventually left the hospital free of pain and other symptoms.

Although laughter was good medicine, Cousins and the scientists who support his ideas do not claim that you can actually laugh your way out of serious disease. Cousins used laughter as a metaphor, a figure of speech, for all those emotions involved in hope, faith, and determination that may affect people's perception of stress and their ability to cope (Cassileth et al., 1985). Note that the technique Cousins used permitted him to feel he had control over his illness and could be effective in doing something about it.

Cousins's account of his use of laughter in his recovery has led to some interesting developments. Some hospitals have equipped the rooms of cancer patients with TVs and stereos so that they see or hear their own equivalent of the Marx brothers. The Duke University Comprehensive Cancer Center uses humor, art, music, literature, and anything related to the patient's interests as part of the treatment, including a laugh wagon stocked with humorous tapes and books, which is as important as the pill wagon in the treatment scheme (Cousins, 1989).

Another aspect of positive mood and its relationship to coping with stress is one's expectations about the ability to regulate negative moods. This is known as *negative mood regulation expectancies,* or NMRE (Catanzaro et al., 2014). In addition to being related to the ability to regulate negative moods, NMRE also relates to a person's ability to generate positive moods when he or she is experiencing a negative mood. Catanzaro et al. found that higher levels of NMRE were related to better ability to cope with the emotional stress related to depression. Higher levels of NMRE were also related to higher levels of negative symptom change.

Positive emotions not only seem to help us fight disease, but some evidence suggests that these positive emotions may forestall the onset of certain diseases. Richman and her colleagues (2005) studied the effects of *hope* and *curiosity* on hypertension, diabetes mellitus, and respiratory infections. They reasoned that if negative emotions negatively affected disease outcomes, then positive ones may be helpful. As is well known, high levels of anxiety are related to a much higher risk of hypertension (high blood pressure). This research studied 5,500 patients, ages 55 to 69. All patients were given scales that measured "hope" and "curiosity." Independently of other factors that affected the health of the patients, positive emotions appeared to have a preventative effect on disease. The authors hypothesized that the experience of positive emotions bolsters the immune system. Also, it is reasonable to assume that people with hope, curiosity, and other positive emotions may very well take steps to protect their health (Richman et al., 2005). One way of looking at these studies is to observe that happy people are resilient. They take steps to protect their health, and they respond in a positive manner to threats and disappointments.

Social Support

Social support is defined as the experience that one is loved and cared for by others and is part of a social network (Taylor, 2011). In a review of the literature, Taylor

Social support is related to better adjustment to stress and diseases such as cancer and diabetes. However, not all social support is equal. Research shows that wives give more social support to husbands than they receive in return. It is not enough to merely have social support in times of need.
Source: ABO PHOTOGRAPHY/Shutterstock.

(2011) notes that social support is linked to a number of positive health outcomes, including better adjustment to stress and diseases, such as cancer, diabetes, and rheumatoid arthritis. Social support can even influence how long people live. In a study with terminally ill patients, those who received social support from volunteers lived an average of 80 days longer than those who did not have such support (Herbst-Damm & Kulik, 2005). Although this may not seem like a substantial amount of time, this study was conducted with hospice patients, who by definition, are not expected to live more than 6 months. Other longitudinal research has found that social support can increase one's life expectancy by more than 2 years (Berkman & Syme, 1979).

You might think that one of the best and most readily available sources of social support would be one's spouse. However, some research has shown that although spouses can be positive sources of social support during an illness, they can also undermine their partner through criticism and blame. Vinokur and Vinokur-Kaplan (1990) looked at older married couples. Half of the wives in the study were breast cancer survivors. Wives reported giving more social support to their husbands than receiving. Reports from husbands tended to agree with this finding; they reported receiving more support from their wives than giving. Higher levels of social support were related to lower levels of depression and better emotional functioning in wives. However, wives' reports of being undermined by the husbands were related to more depression and diminished emotional functioning in wives. Clearly, it is not enough to have a close friend or family member nearby during a time of illness.

SOCIAL PSYCHOLOGY IN ACTION

What Makes Us Happy?

Happiness and optimism have powerful positive effects on our health. But what factors account for happiness? Could it be the usual suspects: money and sex? Edward Diener's longtime research concerning happiness suggests that subjective factors (feeling in control, feeling positive about oneself) are more important than objective factors such as wealth (Diener et al., 1999). Yes, wealth counts, but not as much as one would think. For example, one of Diener's studies showed that Americans earning millions of dollars are only slightly happier than those who are less fortunate. In fact, increases in wealth above a modestly low baseline are not related to increases in happiness (Diener & Biswas-Diener, 2002; Kahneman & Deaton, 2010).

Would winning the lottery bring you happiness? Although winning the lottery can lead to a boost in subjective well-being soon after the win (Gardner & Oswald, 2001), it may not guarantee long-term happiness. Studies show that winners of a substantial lottery jackpot are no happier than nonwinners in the long run (Brickman et al., 1978; Kuhn et al., 2008). According to a study by Lau and Kramer (cited in Lutter, 2007), the initial euphoria of winning the jackpot is powerful and lasts for a while, but it eventually wears off, and many lottery winners long to return to their old lives.

Interestingly, how we spend our money might be more related to happiness than having the money. In one experiment, participants who spent money on others were happier than those who spent money on themselves, regardless of whether they earned the money or received it in a windfall (Geenen et al., 2014). Furthermore, research has indicated that spending your money on experiences (e.g., vacations) instead of objects (e.g., a new car) can lead to higher levels of happiness (Carter & Gilovich, 2010). However, these effects do not appear to be universal. It appears that there are individual differences, and spending money on experiences and on others will not increase happiness for everyone (Hill & Howell, 2014). It seems that spending needs to be matched with personality. Matz et al. (2016) found that people whose spending better matched their personality reported higher levels of happiness.

If money doesn't buy happiness, how about sex? Economists have reported that money and sex may be partially exchangeable commodities (Blanchflower

(continued)

& Oswald, 2004). These researchers found that if you are having sex only once a month and you get lucky and increase it to twice a week, it is as good as making an extra $50,000 a year. Similar results were obtained from a more recent study using a sample drawn from China (Cheng & Smyth, 2015). These researchers found that increased sex was related to increased happiness and that better-quality sex was also related to increased happiness. However, both of these studies are correlational—could the key to happiness just be to increase the amount of sex you have with your partner? An experimental study by Loewenstein et al. (2015) suggests it is not that simple. In their experiment, they randomly assigned couples to either engage in their normal levels of sexual intercourse or to double the amount of sex they had per month. They found that when sex was experimentally induced, it actually had a weak (but significant) negative impact on happiness. The authors suggest that it is possible that being told to have sex by the experimenters (extrinsic motivation) may have actually made the sex less enjoyable (intrinsic motivation) and more like a job.

The research on the relationship between money, sex, and happiness reveals a curious aspect of happiness. We don't seem to quite know what will make us happy or how happy something will make us feel. We think that increased wealth will bring us happiness, but it does not. The same seems to be true for sex.

What makes us happy? Research shows that money or winning the lottery may bring temporary happiness, but it soon wears off. Spending money on vacations brings more happiness than spending money on objects such as a new car.
Source: Photobank gallery/Shutterstock.

Discussion Questions

1. What is the relationship between wealth and happiness? Is it surprising to you? Why or why not?
2. What is the relationship between sex and happiness? Is it surprising to you? Why or why not?

Prevention: Promoting Healthier Behavior

Social psychological principles can be used to understand health outcomes and disease and also in prevention strategies. One of the most pressing health issues facing America is the obesity epidemic, with exercise and healthy eating habits being the two main strategies for preventing and reducing obesity. Both of these strategies require individuals to make choices and modify their behavior. So, how do we help people make healthy choices? What tools or strategies lead to behavioral changes?

One of the most prominent frameworks for predicted and influencing behavior, including health-related behavior, is the theory of planned behavior (TPB; Ajzen, 2002) discussed in Chapter 5. According to TPB, behaviors can be predicted by a behavioral intention. For example, if I have a general goal of exercising more often, the best predictor of my exercise behavior is a specific intention to exercise (e.g., "I intend to walk for 30 minutes at lunchtime every Monday"). Behavioral intentions are influenced by attitudes toward the behavior and subjective norms. If I have a positive attitude toward walking and I believe that most other people walk for exercise and approve of such behavior, then I should have a fairly strong intention to walk for exercise. Perceived behavioral control also influences behavioral intention—how difficult will it be for me to walk for 30 minutes at lunchtime? In support of TPB, meta-analytic findings indicate that attitudes toward exercise predicted exercise intentions and those intentions, in turn, were strongly related to exercise behavior (Hausenblas et al., 1997). In one study with Korean adults, Chang-Ik and Hee Sun (2015) examined how the various components of the TPB related to the intention to exercise. They found that attitudes toward exercising were related to the intention to keep exercising, especially for sports played with others (versus those played alone). They also found that subjective norms (how others view exercising) were related to an intention to play sports alone (versus with others).

Given that behavioral intentions are predictors of actual behavior, how can we strengthen such intentions? One of the ways to strengthen behavioral intentions is to reframe the effort required to engage in a behavior. Peetz et al. (2011) examined behavioral intentions in a sample of undergraduate students who stated they had health improvement goals. Participants were asked about their willingness to engage in walking and meditation programs. Participants in the control condition were given instructions on how to carry out the programs and informed that the programs would each take either 2 hours twice a week (walking) or 2 hours once a week (meditation). Participants in the daily reframing condition were given the same information, except they were also given information about the daily time commitment of each program, either 34 minutes per day (walking) or 17 minutes per day (meditation). Participants in the daily reframing condition reported feeling that the time required to complete the programs was shorter compared to those in the control condition. They also had stronger intentions to try the walking and meditation programs (see Figure 12.10).

In addition to reframing the behavior, self-efficacy can also contribute to the strength of behavioral intentions to exercise. For example, in one study, researchers randomly assigned participants to read an article about factors influencing individual levels of physical activity (Beauchamp et al., 2010). Participants in the genetically primed condition read about the strong link between genetic factors and inactivity, and how scientists had identified particular genes that lead to inactivity, implying that activity levels were really out of one's control. In the experientially primed condition, participants read about how one's social environment, and not genetic factors, strongly influences levels of activity, implying that activity levels could be changed. The researchers found that participants in the experiential condition had higher exercise self-efficacy and greater intentions to exercise compared to those in the genetically primed or control conditions.

Self-efficacy is also an important construct for other health-related behaviors, such as prevention of HIV/AIDs and sexually transmitted disease. French and Holland (2013)

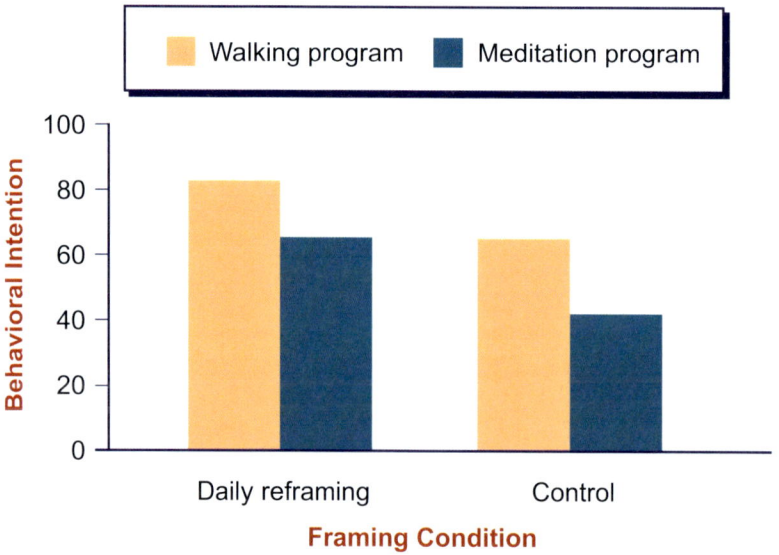

FIGURE 12.10

The relationship between the strength of the intention to exercise, exercise framing, and behavioral intention to exercise. Reframing the time required for exercise increased the intention to exercise.

Based on data from Peetz et al. (2011).

found that condom use self-efficacy was a positive predictor of consistent condom use and also a positive predictor of several different condom use influence strategies. Participants who felt confident that they could use a condom and talk to their partner about using a condom were more likely to have strong behavioral intentions to use a condom.

Clearly, psychologists have a role in framing health messages and providing information to the public in a way that increases self-efficacy.

Study Break

This section discussed how mood and social support relate to health. Before you read the Chapter Review, answer the following questions:

1. How does a positive mood relate to health? Can laughter be the best medicine?
2. What are negative mood regulation expectancies, and how do they relate to health?
3. How does social support relate to health outcomes?
4. How can the theory of planned behavior be applied to improving health behaviors?
5. How does self-efficacy contribute to improving health?

Chapter Review

1. **What influence do eyewitnesses have on a jury?**

   Eyewitnesses have a significant effect on decisions made by a jury and eyewitness testimony is frequently the primary evidence against a defendant.

2. **What is the difference between estimator and system variables?**

   Estimator and system variables are related to eyewitness testimony. Estimator variables, such as features of the crime location and individual characteristics of the eyewitness are fixed and out of the control of the criminal justice system. System variables, such as the types of questions asked of an eyewitness or the manner in which questions are presented, are under the control of the criminal justice system. Both types of variables influence eyewitness accuracy.

3. **What is weapon focus and why does it occur?**

   Weapon focus occurs when an eyewitness's attention is focused on a weapon and not other details of a crime situation. It causes poorer memory for those details. One explanation for the weapon focus effect is a shift in attention resources. When a weapon is present, a target is more likely to focus on the weapon as opposed to less salient details about the perpetrator or the setting of the event. Factors such as retention interval, threat, and exposure duration also moderate the weapon focus effect.

4. **How do stress or strong emotions affect eyewitness testimony?**

   Most research has shown that eyewitnesses who feel stress or strong emotions during an event are less accurate in their ability to identify the perpetrator compared to eyewitnesses who do not feel strong emotions.

5. **How accurate is eyewitness memory?**

   Eyewitness memory is subject to several factors that influence its accuracy and reliability. Memory is reconstructed from stored details; it is not like a tape-recorder and therefore is often inaccurate. Sometimes, unrelated information that is presented either before or after an event becomes incorporated into the memory for an event, referred to as the misinformation effect. Eyewitnesses are often confident in their memory for an event, although research shows that there is not a strong relationship between confidence and accuracy.

6. **Why would someone give a false confession?**

   There are several reasons why someone might give a false confession. In some cases, an individual might claim responsibility for a crime as a way to gain attention and respect. Other individuals might confess to a crime because they feel pressured by the police to do so and often given misinformation about the consequences or rewards of confessing. In some rare cases, suspects who confess to a crime they did not commit become confused and actually come to believe, based on the information being told to them, that they are guilty of a crime.

7. **What are the steps involved in personnel selection?**

   The three steps involved are job analysis, employee recruitment, and employee screening. An organization must first determine what a particular job entails and how to best measure performance. Then, organizations develop and implement a process for attracting applicants for the position. Finally, employees are screened, typically through an application and interview process. Organizations must be mindful to comply with anti-discrimination employment laws during the personnel selection process.

8. **What types of measures can be used for a performance appraisal?**

   Workers can be evaluated on their traits or characteristics, such as leadership and conscientiousness. They can also be evaluated on how frequently they perform specific job-related behaviors.

9. **What factors influence work motivation?**

   Generally, one's individual needs and goals influence work motivation. Performance tends to be best when an individual sets a specific and challenging goal.

10. **How is stress defined?**

    Stress can be defined and examined in multiple ways. We can look at the causes of stress within one's environment. We can look at how people respond to stress, both physiologically and psychologically. We can look at how individual differences, such as personality traits, interact with the environment to produce a stress response.

11. **How does coping relate to stress?**

    Depending on the particular coping strategy used in a particular situation, coping can help to reduce stress. For example, if you are presented with a stressful situation that you can change, then developing and implementing a plan to reduce that stress will lead to a greater chance of reducing the stress compared to a situation where you take no action.

12. **What is the effect of perceived control on stress?**

    Whether real or imagined, perceived control can often lead to reduced levels of stress. The perception of uncontrollable events has been shown to be related to future illness and reduced well-being. Similar to the previous question, if you believe you have control over your outcomes, you are more likely to feel able to cope with difficult situations.

13. **Does social support affect health?**

    Social support is related to a wide range of positive health outcomes, including increased life expectancy. However, some research shows that social support is more than simply having people around you. Positive social support is associated with positive health outcomes, while negative social support, such as criticism, has been linked to negative health outcomes.

14. **How does optimism relate to health?**

    More optimistic people show better health than less optimistic people. Some people are higher on a personality dimension known as *dispositional optimism*, or a tendency to see things from an optimistic perspective. Optimistic people show better outcomes after traumatic events such as bypass surgery and traumatic brain injury. One explanation for this is that optimistic people are more likely to see positive outcomes from adversity. Optimism allows a person to apply more flexible coping strategies than pessimism, and optimistic individuals react to threatening events by developing positive illusions, which are beliefs that include unrealistically optimistic notions about their ability to handle the threat and create a positive outcome.

15. **How does social support relate to positive health outcomes?**

    Social support is linked to a number of positive health outcomes, including better adjustment to stress and diseases, such as cancer, diabetes, and rheumatoid arthritis. It also relates positively to longevity. Although it would seem that social support from one's spouse would be important, research shows that spouses can also be a source of criticism and blame. Husbands of breast cancer patients often receive more social support than they provide.

16. **What factors relate to happiness?**

    Research shows that money doesn't always make people happy. Rather, subjective factors, such as feeling in control and positive about oneself, are more important determinants of happiness than money. Also, millionaires are not significantly happier than those with less money. Winning the lottery may initially make one happy, but in the long run, winners are no happier than those who do not win. How one spends his or her money affects happiness. Some research has found that those who spend money on others or on experiences (e.g., a vacation) are happier than those who spend money on themselves or on objects (e.g., a new car). However, this is not universally true; it appears that happiness is greatest when our spending matches our personalities. Correlational research suggests that couples that have more frequent sex are happier than couples that engage in less frequent sex. However, when the frequency of sex is experimentally manipulated, an opposite pattern emerges. Couples that were asked to double their amount of sex actually reported decreased happiness. However, we don't seem to quite know what will make us happy or how happy something will make us feel. We think that increased wealth will bring us happiness, but it does not. The same seems to be true for sex.

17. How can social psychological principles be applied to improving the health of individuals?

Social psychological principles such as persuasion, attitude change, and social norms have all been used to increase positive health-related behaviors. For example, by increasing self-efficacy in regard to both exercise and condom usage, social psychologists have demonstrated increased behavioral intentions to engage in such actions.

Key Terms

Adverse impact (p. 510)
Alarm stage (p. 517)
Behavior-based scales (p. 511)
Compliant false confessions (p. 505)
Deliberation (p. 503)
Dispositional optimism (p. 521)
Emotion-focused coping (p. 517)
Employee recruitment (p. 509)
Employee screening (p. 510)
Estimator variables (p. 495)
Exhaustion stage (p. 517)

Eyewitness (p. 495)
General adaptation syndrome (GAS) (p. 517)
Halo effect (p. 511)
Internalized false confessions (p. 506)
Job analysis (p. 508)
Misinformation effect (p. 498)
Needs (p. 512)
Organizational citizenship behaviors (p. 514)
Performance appraisals (p. 510)

Positive illusions (p. 521)
Problem-focused coping (p. 517)
Reconstructive memory (p. 498)
Resilience (p. 520)
Resilience resources (p. 520)
Resistance stage (p. 517)
Self-efficacy (p. 520)
System variables (p. 495)
Trait-based scales (p. 511)
Voluntary false confessions (p. 505)
Weapon focus (p. 495)

Chapter Quiz

1. _____ are related directly to the eyewitness, whereas _____ are related to the criminal justice system.
   A. System variables; estimator variables
   B. Estimator variables; system variables
   C. Person variables; justice variables
   D. Justice variables; person variables

2. For which reason is the weapon focus effect weaker when a perpetrator with a gun has a distinctive facial feature?
   A. Witnesses are surprised by the distinctive facial feature.
   B. The distinctive facial feature causes a witness to shut his or her eyes.
   C. The distinctive feature competes for the witnesses' attention with the weapon.
   D. All of the above

3. Human memory is _____ in nature.
   A. reconstructive
   B. reproductive
   C. restructuring
   D. reflective

4. Research by Tanford and Penrod (1986) shows that during deliberation, jurors focus on
   A. characteristics of the defendant.
   B. jurors' personal interpretations of the evidence.
   C. the evidence and statements in support of jurors' verdicts.
   D. prosecution witnesses more than defense witnesses.

5. The three steps of personnel selection are
   A. job analysis, employee screening, and employee training.
   B. job analysis, employee recruitment, and employee screening.
   C. job posting, interviews, and selection.
   D. job posing, phone interviews, and face-to-face interviews.

6. McClelland proposed which of the following three needs?
   A. Achievement, power, and affiliation
   B. Water, food, and sleep
   C. Money, power, and love
   D. Success, safety, and affiliation

Chapter 12 Applying Social Psychology: Law, Business, and Health

7. Organizations can facilitate self-efficacy by providing workers with
   A. mentors, but not skills training.
   B. clear and simple goals.
   C. skills training, but not mentors.
   D. skills training and mentors.

8. Which personality traits have been found to be significantly associated with job satisfaction?
   A. Extraversion and neuroticism
   B. Neuroticism and conscientiousness
   C. Conscientiousness and openness
   D. Agreeableness and extraversion

9. What are the stages of the general adaptation syndrome?
   A. Alarm, resistance, and exhaustion
   B. Arousal, retreat, and recovery
   C. Cognition, behavior, and affect
   D. Stress, resistance, and response

10. Individuals with high confidence and self-efficacy are likely to approach a stressful situation as
    A. a tragedy.
    B. insurmountable.
    C. a threat.
    D. a challenge.

Answers can be found in the end-of-book Answers section.

Answers to Discussion Questions, Social Psychology in Action Boxes

Chapter 1: Distinguishing Science from Pseudoscience

1. **What is pseudoscience and what are its characteristics?**

   Pseudoscience means false science and is defined as a set of ideas based on theories put forth as scientific when they are not scientific. There are several defining characteristics (listed in Table 1.2) including: disconfirmed ideas are not adjusted based on new information, claims are based on anecdotal evidence, the use of impressive-sounding jargon, and shifting the burden of proof to critics.

2. **Why is it important to learn about pseudoscience?**

   There are two reasons to learn about pseudoscience, theoretical and practical. The theoretical reason is that learning about pseudoscience helps us better understand the philosophy of science. The practical reason is that it can help you avoid falling prey to false claims about the effectiveness of products and services, saving you money.

Chapter 2: The Internet Self

1. **What is the Internet self?**

   The Internet self is an expression of the self that appears on social media such as Facebook. It is an alternate self that exists in cyberspace or in a virtual world. It may include personal information, photos, and self-disclosure information posted online.

2. **Do people express aspects of the Internet self in the same was as they do in face-to-face situations?**

   It appears that people express the Internet self differently from how they express their offline self. Generally, people disclose more information about themselves online than in face-to-face situations, especially extraverted (outgoing) people. People are most likely to self-disclose online if they believe that followers will respond to those disclosures.

3. **Do all people express the Internet self in the same way?**

   No. Women are more likely to use carefully chosen self-promotional pictures to present themselves, whereas men are more likely to use verbal descriptions and present self-promotional information. Self-disclosure on social media presents a particular problem for members of the LGBTQ community. Often they maintain different selves online and offline. Members of different cultures also express themselves differently on social media.

Chapter 3: Body Art and Impressions

1. **Can body art affect another person's first impressions of another person?**

   Yes. Individuals with either a body piercing or a tattoo were evaluated less favorably than those without a piercing or tattoo. Larger tattoos and those on the face were perceived more negatively than smaller ones and ones elsewhere on the body.

2. **Is body art always perceived negatively?**

   No. Body art is viewed more negatively for people with some jobs compared with others. For customer-facing jobs, a person with no facial piercings or tattoos is rated as more hireable than a person with a piercing or a tattoo. Also, tattoos are seen as less appropriate for so called white-collar professions (e.g., bank loan officer, accountant, stockbroker) and health care professionals (dentist and nurse) than for blue-collar workers.

Chapter 4: The Disarming of Racism in the U.S. Army

1. **What did the U.S. Army do to address racism within its ranks?**

   The army adopted several strategies to reduce racism. It created a level playing field by treating all members the same and instituted a remedial program for those with leadership skills but little education. The army also adopted a strict nondiscrimination policy in which those expressing prejudice were punished or jeopardized their careers. Nondiscrimination policies were supported by the rank hierarchy, making any social barriers based on rank and not on race.

2. **What can we learn from the U.S. Army's experience?**

   First, a fair implementation of the contact hypothesis is a good starting point for reducing prejudice. Second, the implementation of no-discrimination policies must be clear, and any policy violations must be met with consequences. Third, race relations can be addressed and improved by strengthening positive social norms.

Chapter 5: Toe the Party Line

1. **How are attitudes learned and reinforced in group settings?**

   Social psychological research has shown that group influence is the most influential factor in determining which opinions we express. Consequently, groups exert a great deal of influence over people's attitudes and how they are expressed. This is demonstrated by the fact that individuals often adopt positions favored by the political party with which they identify.

2. **Are there limits on how much the endorsement of a political party will influence our own attitudes?**

   Yes. If there is bipartisan support for a position, then party endorsement does not affect individual attitudes. Similarly, party endorsement of a position is less powerful if people adopt the goal of being accurate rather than one of being consistent with the party line.

Chapter 6: Cognitive Dissonance and Cult Membership

1. **How does cognitive dissonance relate to cult membership?**

   Cognitive dissonance is involved in cult membership through cult members' commitment. People often make a strong commitment to a movement and its leader. These individuals will expend a great deal of effort to maintain that commitment, even after it becomes obvious that such commitment is misplaced. To do otherwise would generate unpleasant cognitive dissonance. Cults often make increasingly stringent demands on members, requiring more and more commitment. Cognitive dissonance research shows that the harder individuals work to be in a group, the more they value that group.

2. **Do cult members abandon their commitment to a cult when core beliefs are found to be invalid?**

   Unfortunately, no. In fact, the opposite often happens—people become more committed to the cult. This will occur when five conditions are met. First, beliefs must be held with deep conviction and be reflected in the member's behavior. Second, the member must have taken steps toward commitment that are difficult to undo. Third, the belief must be specific so that it can be disconfirmed by evidence. Fourth, there must be undeniable evidence that the belief is false. Fifth, there must be social support for the member after disconfirmation.

Chapter 7: Using the Foot-in-the-Door Technique to Increase Desired Behavior

1. **Does the foot-in-the-door (FITD) always work?**

   No. Although the FITD is a powerful compliance technique, it does not work well for high-cost behaviors. For example, research shows that the FITD in its original form is not effective in increasing blood donations, a high-cost (in terms of time and effort) behavior.

2. **Can the FITD be modified so that it does work for high-cost behaviors?**

   Yes. A small modification to the FITD involving making a gradually increasing, graded series of demands increases its effectiveness for high-cost behaviors like blood donation. The use of two initial increasing requests is more effective than the original, single-request technique.

3. **If the FITD doesn't increase blood donation, then why does it increase organ donation?**

   Ironically, organ donation is a lower-cost behavior than blood donation. Blood donation requires a significant investment of time and effort, and it can be painful. Organ donation takes place after death and has none of these qualities. All of the work is done by others after you die, whereas blood donation requires action on the part of the donor.

Chapter 8: Why Group Members Obey Leaders

1. **What have been your experiences with leaders? Have you had experiences with legitimate and illegitimate leaders?**

   Tyler's work suggests that the basis of a leader's legitimacy resides in its psychological foundations. Two psychological factors are crucial. First, how people are treated by leaders. Leaders need to treat subordinates with fairness and respect in order to be seen as legitimate.

Second, when the leader and the subordinates share group membership, the leader is usually seen as more legitimate.

2. **How do you think the relational model applies in the college classroom? What can a professor do to make sure students comply with requests, such as a request to come to class prepared?**

The relational model implies that when students believe their professor is treating them fairly and with respect, the students will be more likely to comply with a professor's requests to come to class prepared. Students may note various behaviors of professors that they view as respectful, such as responding to emails, or fair, such as clearly establishing grading criteria.

Chapter 9: Internet Relationships

1. **How does the use of the Internet to form relationships relate to the physical proximity effect?**

A powerful determinant of interpersonal relationships in offline situations is the physical distance between individuals. In short, you are more likely to form a friendship with someone with whom you are physically close (e.g., in the same class) than someone more distant. The Internet allows you to form relationships over great distances. You no longer need to be physically close to another person to exchange information. Instead, you could meet in an online chat room or video game. The Internet effectively reduces the *psychological distance* between people, even when the physical distance between them is great. People are increasingly using the Internet to form relationships with others.

2. **Is the use of the Internet to form relationships changing or harming the concept of friendship?**

This does not appear to be the case. The Internet can actually stimulate the quality and quantity of interactions between people and increase intimacy. Research shows that Internet friendships compare quite well with traditional offline friendships. For example, like traditional friendships, Internet friendships are important in our lives, become integrated into our lives, and are stable. However, there are some differences between Internet and traditional friendships. Offline relationship descriptions tend to show that these relationships are more interdependent, involve more commitment, and have greater breadth and depth than Internet relationships.

3. **Is there a downside to Internet friendships?**

Yes, there is a downside. Socially anxious, lonely people tend to use the Internet to form friendships. Research shows that these online relationships are of lower quality than those formed by less anxious people. There are two types of loneliness that relate differently to Internet friendships. *Social loneliness* means not having friends and meaningful relationships, whereas *emotional loneliness* refers to lacking intimate relationships. Internet relationships can fulfill one's need for social contact, but they may still leave a sense of emotional emptiness.

Chapter 10: Social Media and Aggression

1. **Can using social media lead to an increase in aggression?**

Yes, at least for indirect forms of aggression, including verbal and relational aggression. With the growth of social media has come a new outlet for aggression: cyberbullying. Females who show problematic social media use are more likely to cyberbully others than are males. And being a victim of cyberbullying increases the likelihood of being a cyberbully. Additionally, those who use social media for romantic and social belongingness reasons and for social comparison are more likely to be the victims of online aggression than those who use social media for informational and entertainment purposes.

2. **How do people react to being cyberbullied?**

Responses vary from person to person. Individuals who live in a social identity bubble carefully filter out and delete any posts that are offensive to them. People who live in such bubbles report higher levels of stress resulting from cyberbullying than those who do not.

3. **Can anything be done to reduce online cyberbullying and aggression?**

One strategy is to have people reflect on the consequences of posting hurtful material. Cyberbullying can also be reduced by exposing students to specialized training programs. Such programs can be effective if they address issues such as defining cyberbullying, developing personal responsibility, and self-monitoring comments before posting them and focus on the implications of cyberbullying.

Chapter 11: When a Good Thing Is Taken Too Far

1. **Are empathy and altruism always a good thing?**

Although we would like to think so, sometimes empathy and altruism can be taken too far and become a problem. Pathological altruism is behavior or a personal tendency intended to promote the welfare of others but that has unreasonable negative consequences to others or oneself. Pathological altruism can lead to behavior that is self-serving, self-defeating, and even narcissistic. Additionally, there is evidence linking feelings of guilt, empathy, and altruism.

2. **Is there a relationship between pathological altruism and psychopathology?**

   Yes. There appears to be a relationship between pathological altruism and eating disorders such as anorexia nervosa and bulimia nervosa. People with anorexia, for example, often derive pleasure in preparing and serving food to others while avoiding food themselves. This wish to please others is motivated by the need for the approval of others and can give rise to pathological altruism.

3. **How does pathological altruism relate to acts of heroism?**

   Acts of heroism, such as risking your life to save others, may appear to have things in common with pathological altruism. However, there are factors that separate heroism from pathological altruism. Homant and Kennedy (2012) point out that pathological altruism may not be warranted given the victim's level of suffering. In pathological altruism, the helpers often complain about the impact of the altruism on their own lives, yet continue the behavior. With pathological altruism, the internal motives of the individual engaging in the altruistic act are irrational or relate to a psychological disorder. Finally, in pathological altruism, the supposedly altruistic act is of no real benefit. Truly heroic acts do not have these characteristics.

Chapter 12: What Makes Us Happy?

1. **What is the relationship between wealth and happiness? Is it surprising to you? Why or why not?**

   Research shows that money doesn't always make people happy. Millionaires are not significantly happier than those with less money. Winning the lottery may initially make one happy, but in the long run, winners are no happier than those who do not win. How one spends his or her money affects happiness. Some research has found that those who spend money on others or on experiences (e.g., a vacation) are happier than those who spend money on themselves or on objects (e.g., a new car). However, this is not universally true; it appears that happiness is greatest when our spending matches our personalities.

2. **What is the relationship between sex and happiness? Is it surprising to you? Why or why not?**

   Correlational research suggests that couples that have more frequent sex are happier than couples that engage in less frequent sex. However, when the frequency of sex is experimentally manipulated, an opposite pattern emerges. Couples that were asked to double their amount of sex actually reported decreased happiness.

Answers to Chapter Quiz Questions

Chapter 1
1. A
2. C
3. D
4. A
5. D
6. B
7. C
8. C
9. B
10. D

Chapter 2
1. A
2. B
3. D
4. B
5. C
6. A
7. C
8. B
9. B
10. D

Chapter 3
1. A
2. B
3. B
4. A
5. C
6. B
7. A
8. C
9. D
10. C

Chapter 4
1. D
2. A
3. B
4. D
5. A
6. A
7. C
8. B
9. A
10. D

Chapter 5
1. C
2. B
3. D
4. A
5. B
6. D
7. A
8. C
9. D
10. B

Chapter 6
1. C
2. B
3. D
4. C
5. B
6. B
7. A
8. B
9. B
10. D

Chapter 7
1. B
2. B
3. D
4. A
5. B
6. A
7. B
8. C
9. C
10. B

Chapter 8
1. D
2. C
3. D
4. B
5. A
6. D
7. E
8. D
9. D
10. A

Chapter 9
1. C
2. A
3. C
4. A
5. B
6. B
7. D
8. A
9. B
10. A

Chapter 10
1. C
2. A
3. B
4. D
5. C
6. B
7. B
8. C
9. A
10. A

Chapter 11

1. A
2. B
3. B
4. C
5. B
6. D
7. D
8. C
9. C
10. A

Chapter 12

1. B
2. C
3. A
4. C
5. B
6. A
7. D
8. B
9. A
10. D

Glossary

A

accommodation process Interacting in such a way that, despite conflict, a relationship is maintained and enhanced.

action-based model A model of cognitive dissonance stating that cognitive discrepancy generates dissonance motivation because the cognitive discrepancy has the potential to interfere with effective unconflicted action.

actor-observer bias An attribution bias showing that we prefer external attributions for our own behavior, especially if outcomes are negative, whereas observers tend to make internal attributions for the same behavior performed by others.

actual self A person's current self-concept.

adverse impact Employment practices that can appear neutral, but have a discriminatory effect on a protected group.

agentic state In the agentic state, an individual becomes focused on the source of authority, tuning in to the instructions issued.

aggression Any behavior intended to inflict either psychological or physical harm on another organism or object.

aggressive script An internalized representation of an event that leads to increased aggression and the tendency to interpret social interactions aggressively.

alarm stage Stage 1 of the general adaptation syndrome, in which the body reacts to the stressor with an instinctive, automatic response.

altruism Helping behavior motivated purely by the desire to relieve a victim's suffering and not the anticipation of reward.

altruistic personality A cluster of personality traits that predisposes a person to acts of altruism.

applied research Research that has a principal aim to address a real-world problem.

attitude A mental and neural state of readiness, organized through experience, exerting a directive or dynamic influence on the individual's response to all objects and situations with which it is related.

attitude structure The fact that attitudes comprise a cognitive, affective, and behavioral component in their basic structure.

attitude survey A self-report method of measuring attitudes that involves a researcher's mailing a questionnaire to a potential respondent, conducting a face-to-face interview, or asking a series of questions on the telephone or on the Internet.

attribution The process of assigning causes of behavior, both your own and that of others.

authoritarian personality A personality dimension characterized by submissive feelings toward authority, rigid and unchangeable beliefs, and a tendency toward prejudicial attitudes.

authoritarianism A personality characteristic that relates to a person's unquestioned acceptance of and respect for authority.

autobiographical memory Memory for information relating to the self that plays a powerful role in recall of events.

automatic processing Any type of information processing that primarily occurs without conscious intention or control.

autonomous altruism Selfless altruism that society does not support or might even discourage.

availability heuristic A shortcut used to estimate the frequency or likelihood of an event based on how quickly examples of it come to mind.

aversive racism Racism involving a person who believes he or she is unprejudiced, but feels uneasy and uncomfortable in the presence of someone from a different racial group.

B

basic research Research that has the principal aim of empirically testing a theory or a model.

behavior-based scales Scales used in performance appraisals, where workers are evaluated on observable job-related behavior.

behavioral confirmation A tendency for perceivers to behave as if their expectations are correct and the targets then to respond in ways that confirm the perceivers' beliefs.

belief perseverance The tendency for initial impressions to persist despite later conflicting information, accounting for much of the power of first impressions.

black-sheep effect The phenomenon in which an attractive in-group member is rated more highly than an attractive member of an out-group, and an unattractive in-group member is perceived more negatively than an unattractive out-group member.

bullying Aggression that is intentional, repetitive, and directed toward an individual of lower power.

bystander effect The social phenomenon that helping behavior is less likely to occur as the number of witnesses to an emergency increases.

C

central route processing In the elaboration likelihood model (ELM), information may be processed by effortful, controlled mechanisms involving attention to and understanding and careful processing of the content of a persuasive message.

cognitive dissonance theory A theory of attitude change proposing that if inconsistency exists among our attitudes, or between our attitudes and our behavior, we experience an unpleasant state of arousal called cognitive dissonance, which we will be motivated to reduce or eliminate.

cognitive miser The idea suggesting that because humans have a limited capacity to understand information, we deal only with small amounts of social information and prefer the least effortful means of processing it.

collective self The part of our self-concept that comes from our membership in groups.

collective threat The awareness that the poor performance of a member of one's group may be evaluated with a stereotype and may be generalized into a negative judgment of one's entire group.

communal relationship An interpersonal relationship in which individuals benefit each other in response to each others' needs.

compliance Social influence process that involves modifying behavior in response to a direct request.

compliant false confessions A situation where an individual falsely confesses to a crime, typically under police influence. Privately, the individual knows he or she is not guilty.

confirmation bias A tendency to engage in a search strategy that confirms rather than disconfirms our hypothesis.

conformity A social influence process that involves modifying behavior in response to real or imagined pressure from others.

confounding variable An extraneous variable in an experiment that varies systematically with the independent variable, making it difficult or impossible to establish a causal connection between the independent and dependent variables.

consummate love Love that includes all three components: passion, intimacy, and commitment.

contact hypothesis A hypothesis that contact between groups will reduce hostility, which is most effective when members of different groups have equal status and a mutual goal.

control group A group in an experiment comprised of participants who do not receive the experimental treatment.

controlled processing Processing involving conscious awareness, attention to the thinking process, and effort.

correlation coefficient A statistical technique used to determine the direction and strength of a relationship between two variables.

correlational research Research that measures two or more dependent variables and looks for a relationship between them; causal relationships among variables cannot be established.

correspondent inference An inference that occurs when we conclude that a person's overt behavior is caused by or corresponds to the person's internal characteristics or beliefs.

correspondent inference theory A theory to explain how internal attributions are made about others.

counterfactual thinking The tendency to create positive alternatives to a negative outcome that actually occurred, especially when we can easily imagine a more positive outcome.

courageous resistance Selfless behavior involving risk to a helper (and/or family) that is sustained over time, is a product of a deliberative process, and involves a moral calling.

covariation principle The rule that if a response is present when a situation (person, object, or event) is present and absent when that same situation is absent, the situation is presumed to be the cause of the response.

credibility The believability (expertise and trustworthiness) of the communicator of a persuasive message.

culture of honor An evolved culture in the southern and western United States in which violence is more widely accepted and practiced than in the northern and eastern United States, where no such culture exists.

D

decision rule A rule concerning the number of members of a group who must agree before a group can reach a decision.

deindividuation A phenomenon that occurs in large-group (crowd) situations in which individual identity is lost within the anonymity of the large group, perhaps leading to a lowering of inhibitions against negative behaviors.

deliberation The process by which the decisions of individual jury members must be blended into a single group decision.

dependent variable The measure the researcher assesses to determine the influence of the independent variable on the participants' behavior.

diffusion of responsibility An explanation for the bystander effect suggesting that each bystander assumes another person will take responsibility to help.

direct aggression Overt forms of aggression, such as physical aggression (hitting, punching, kicking, etc.) and verbal aggression (name calling, denigration, etc.).

directive leader A leadership style involving a leader who gives less value to participation, emphasizes the need for agreement, and tends to prefer his or her own solution.

discrimination Overt behavior—often negatively directed toward a particular group and often tied to prejudicial attitudes—which involves behaving in different ways toward members of different groups.

dispositional optimism The tendency to see things from an optimistic perspective.

distinctiveness theory The theory suggesting that individuals think of themselves in terms of those attributes or dimensions that make them different—rather than in terms of attributes they have in common with others.

distraction-conflict theory A theory of social facilitation suggesting that the presence of others is a source of distraction that leads to conflicts in attention between an audience and a task that affects performance.

door-in-the-face technique (DITF) A social influence process in which a large request is made before a smaller request, resulting in more compliance to the smaller request than if the smaller request were made alone.

E

ego depletion The loss of self-energy that occurs when a person has to contend with a difficult cognitive or emotional situation.

egotistical bias The tendency to present yourself as responsible for success, whether you are or not, and the tendency to believe these positive presentations.

Eichmann's fallacy The belief that evil deeds are done only by evil people.

elaboration likelihood model (ELM) A cognitive model of persuasion suggesting that a target's attention, involvement, distraction, motivation, self-esteem, education, and intelligence all influence central and/or peripheral reception to a persuasive attempt.

emotional intelligence A person's ability to perceive, use, understand, and manage emotions.

emotion-focused coping Coping strategies that involve attempts to manage one's internal emotions or feelings.

empathy-altruism hypothesis An explanation suggesting that the arousal of empathy leads to altruistic acts.

empathy-punishment hypothesis A hypothesis suggesting that helping occurs because individuals are motivated to avoid the guilt or shame brought about by failure to help.

employee recruitment The process of attracting potential workers to apply for jobs.

employee screening The process of reviewing information about job applicants.

estimator variables Variables directly related to the eyewitness and the conditions under which the eyewitness viewed the crime (e.g., presence of a weapon).

ethology A theoretical perspective that views behavior within the context of survival and emphasizes the role of instincts and genetic forces.

evaluation apprehension An explanation for social facilitation suggesting that the presence of others will cause arousal only when they can reward or punish the performer.

evaluative conditioning A process in which you develop an attitude (positive or negative) toward something because a neutral stimulus is associated with a positive or negative stimulus.

everyday prejudice Prejudice that comprises recurrent and familiar events considered to be commonplace.

exhaustion stage Stage 3 of the general adaptation syndrome, characterized by profound, life-threatening physiological exhaustion that may be accompanied by such symptoms as distorted thinking and perceptions.

experimental group A group comprised of participants who receive the experimental treatment in an experiment.

experimental research Research involving manipulating a variable suspected of influencing behavior to see how that change affects behavior; results show causal relationships among variables.

expertise A component of communicator credibility that refers to the communicator's credentials and stems from the individual's training and knowledge.

explicit attitude An attitude that operates on a conscious level via controlled processing.

explicit self-esteem Self-esteem that arises primarily from the interaction with people in our everyday life.

external attribution The process of assigning the cause of behavior to some situation or event outside a person's control, rather than to some internal characteristic.

extraneous variable Any variable not controlled by the researcher that could affect the results of a study.

eyewitness A person who observed a crime and can relate the events to the jury in court.

F

factorial experiment An experimental design in which two or more independent variables are manipulated.

false consensus bias The tendency to believe that our own feelings and behavior are shared by everyone else.

field experiment A research setting in which the researcher manipulates one or more independent variables and measures behavior in the participant's natural environment.

field study A descriptive research strategy in which the researcher makes unobtrusive observations of the participants without making direct contact or interfering in any way.

field survey A descriptive research strategy in which the researcher directly approaches participants and asks them questions.

flexible correction model (FCM) A model stating that individuals using central route processing are influenced by biasing variables, because they are not aware of the potential biasing conditions.

foot-in-the-door technique (FITD) A social influence process in which a small request is made before a larger request, resulting in more compliance to the larger request than if the larger request were made alone.

four horsemen of the apocalypse Four factors identified as important in relationship dissolution: complaining-criticizing, contempt, defensiveness, and withdrawal from social interaction (stonewalling).

free riders Group members who do not do their share of the work in a group.

frustration-aggression hypothesis A hypothesis that frustration and aggression are strongly related, suggesting that aggression is always the consequence of frustration and that frustration leads to aggression.

fundamental attribution error The tendency to automatically attribute the causes for another person's behavior to internal rather than situational forces.

G

general adaptation syndrome (GAS) A three-step model describing the reaction of the body to a stressor.

group An aggregate of individuals who interact with and influence one another.

group cohesiveness The strength of the relationships that link members of a group.

group norms Expectations concerning the kinds of behaviors required of group members.

group polarization The tendency for individual, prediscussion opinion to become more extreme following group discussion.

groupthink A group-process phenomenon that may lead to faulty decision making by highly cohesive group members more concerned with reaching consensus than with carefully considering alternative courses of action.

H

halo effect A bias in which one's impression of a person's ability in one domain is influenced by one's impression of a person's ability in another domain, even when these two domains might be unrelated.

heat effect The observation that aggression is more likely when people are hot than when they are cool.

hedonic contingency model A model proposing that happy people process tasks expected to be pleasant more systematically than tasks expected to be unpleasant.

heritability An indicator of the degree to which genetics account for differences among people for any given behavior or characteristic.

heroism Helping that involves significant risk above what is normally expected and serves some socially valued goal.

heuristic and systematic information processing model (HSM) A cognitive model of persuasion suggesting that of the two routes to persuasion, systematic and heuristic, people choose to use heuristics or peripheral cues most often.

heuristics Handy rules of thumb that serve as shortcuts to organizing and perceiving social reality automatically.

hindsight bias Also known as the "I-knew-it-all-along" phenomenon; shows that with the benefit of hindsight, everything looks obvious.

hostile aggression Aggressive behavior stemming from angry or hostile impulses, with a primary goal to inflict injury on some person or object.

hypothalamus A structure in the limbic system of the brain associated with aggressive behavior.

hypothesis A tentative and testable statement about the relationship between variables.

I

ideal self The mental representation of what a person would like to be or what a significant other would like him or her to be.

ideology A set of ideas, beliefs, or a stance that determines a perspective with which to interpret social and political realities.

illusion of efficacy The illusion that members of small groups think they are more effective than larger groups, which may not be the case.

illusion of transparency The belief that observers can read our private thoughts and feelings because they somehow leak out.

illusory correlation An error in judgment about the relationship between two variables in which two unrelated events are believed to covary.

Implicit Association Test The most widely known measure of implicit attitudes.

implicit attitude An attitude that affects behavior automatically, without conscious thought and below the level of awareness, via automatic processing.

implicit personality theory A common person-schema belief that certain personality traits are linked together and may help us make a quick impression of someone, but there is no guarantee that initial impression will be correct.

implicit self-esteem An efficient system of self-evaluation that is below our conscious awareness.

imposter phenomenon The feeling that one lacks the skills and abilities to succeed.

impression formation The process by which we make judgments about others.

independent variable The variable that the researcher manipulates in an experiment.

indirect aggression Aggression that is social in nature, such as social ostracism and deliberate social exclusion.

individual self The part of the self that refers to our self-knowledge, including our private thoughts and evaluations of who and what we are.

informational social influence Social influence that results from a person responding to information provided by others.

informed consent An ethical research requirement that participants must be informed of the nature of the study, the requirements for participation, any risks or benefits associated with participating in the study, and the right to decline or withdraw from participation with no penalty.

in-group bias The powerful tendency of humans to favor in-group members over out-group members.

inoculation theory The theory that if a communicator exposes an audience to a weakened version of an opposing argument, the audience will devise counterarguments to that weakened version and avoid persuasion by stronger arguments later.

instrumental aggression Aggressive behavior stemming from a desire to achieve a goal.

interaction When the effect of one independent variable in a factorial experiment changes over levels of a second, indicating a complex relationship between independent variables.

interactionist view of altruism The view that an individual's altruistic or selfish internal motives interact with situational factors to determine whether a person will help.

internal attribution The process of assigning the cause of behavior to some internal characteristic rather than to outside forces.

internalized false confessions A situation where an individual falsely confesses to a crime, typically under police influence. Privately, the individual comes to believe that he or she is guilty of the crime.

interpersonal attraction The desire to start and maintain relationships with others.

interpersonal forgiveness A harmed individual's decreased motivation to retaliate against and a reduced tendency to maintain distance from one's relationship partner, and an increased willingness to express conciliation and goodwill toward the partner.

introspection The act of examining our own thoughts and feelings to understand ourselves, which may yield a somewhat biased picture of our own internal state.

J

job analysis The systematic study of a job's tasks, duties, and responsibilities and the knowledge, skills, and abilities needed to perform the job.

just-world hypothesis A hypothesis that we believe people get what they deserve and deserve what they get.

K

Köhler effect The effect where a less competent group member increases performance in a dyad when group performance depends on combined effort.

L

latitude of acceptance In social judgment theory, the region of an attitude into which messages that one will accept fall.

latitude of noncommitment In social judgment theory, the region of an attitude into which messages that one will neither accept nor reject fall.

latitude of rejection In social judgment theory, the region of an attitude into which messages that one will reject fall.

law of primacy The law of persuasion stating that the first persuasive argument received is more persuasive than later persuasive arguments.

legitimacy A group member's feeling of obligation to obey the group's leader.

loneliness A psychological state that results when we perceive that there is an inadequacy or a deprivation in our social relationships.

M

matching principle A principle that applies in romantic relationships, suggesting that individuals become involved with a partner with whom they are closely matched socially and physically.

mere exposure The phenomenon that being exposed to a stimulus increases one's feelings, usually positive, toward that object; repeated exposure can lead to positive attitudes.

misinformation effect When a piece of information that was not part of the original event becomes part of a witness's memory of an event.

modern racism Subtle racial prejudice, expressed in a less open manner than is traditional overt racial prejudice and characterized by an uncertainty in feeling and action toward minorities.

multiple audience problem In persuasion, the problem that arises when a communicator directs the same message at two different audiences, wishing to communicate different meanings to each.

N

näive realism The belief that we see the world objectively while others are biased, and that if others do not see the world as we do, they are not rational.

need for affect (NA) A person's tendency to approach or avoid emotional situations.

need for affiliation A motivation that underlies our desire to establish and maintain rewarding interpersonal relationships.

need for cognition (NC) An individual difference dimension in persuasion concerning the degree to which individuals prefer effortful processing of information.

need for intimacy A motivation for close and affectionate relationships.

needs A psychological or physiological feature that arouses an individual to action toward a goal, giving purpose and direction to behavior.

negative correlation The direction of a correlation in which the value of one variable increases whereas the value of a second decreases.

Next Generation Science Standards An approach to science setting out eight practices for science and engineering to guide scientific research.

nonrational actor A view that humans are not always rational in their behavior and their behavior can be inconsistent with their attitudes.

norm An unwritten social rule existing either on a wide cultural level or on a smaller, situation-specific level that suggests what is appropriate behavior in a situation.

norm of reciprocity A social norm stating that you should help those who help you.

normative altruism Altruism that society supports and encourages.

normative social influence Social influence in which a person changes behavior in response to pressure to conform to a norm.

O

obedience A social influence process involving modification of behavior in response to a command from an authority figure.

observational learning Attitude formation learned through watching what people do and whether they are rewarded or punished and then imitating that behavior.

operant conditioning A method by which attitudes are acquired by rewarding a person for a given attitude in the hopes it will be maintained or strengthened.

organizational citizenship behaviors Behaviors that promote the efficient and effective functioning of the organization, typically without any formal reward tied to them.

ostracism The widespread and universal behavior of excluding or ignoring other individuals or groups.

ought self The mental representation of what a person believes he or she should be.

out-group homogeneity bias The predisposition to see members of an out-group as having similar characteristics or being all alike.

P

participative leader A leadership style characterized by a leader who shares power with the other members of the group and includes them in the decision making.

performance appraisals Tools or measures to assess worker performance in comparison to some standards.

peripheral route processing In the elaboration likelihood model (ELM), information may be processed using cues peripheral or marginal to the content message.

personal attributes An aspect of the self-concept involving the attributes we believe we have.

persuasion A form of social influence that involves changing others' thoughts, attitudes, or behaviors by applying rational and/or emotional arguments to convince them to adopt your position.

physical attractiveness bias The tendency to confer a number of psychological and social advantages to physically attractive individuals.

physical proximity effect The fact that we are more likely to form a relationship with someone who is physically close to us; proximity affects interpersonal attraction, mostly at the beginning of a relationship.

positive correlation The direction of a correlation in which the values of two variables increase or decrease in the same direction.

positive illusions Beliefs that include unrealistically optimistic notions about individuals' ability to handle a threat and create a positive outcome.

prejudice A biased, often negative, but sometimes positive attitude toward a group of people.

primacy effect The observation that information encountered early in the impression formation process plays a powerful role in our eventual impression of an individual.

primary compensation A method by targets of prejudice that reduces threats posed by using coping strategies that allow the targets of prejudice to achieve their goals.

problem-focused coping Coping strategies that work to manage the external demands of a situation, often through the development of plans and goals.

process loss The loss of group efficiency that results from increased group size and generally leads to a decrement in productivity.

propaganda A deliberate attempt to persuade people, by any available media, to think in a manner desired by the source.

psychological reactance A psychological state that results when individuals feel that their freedom of action is threatened because other people are forcing them to do or say things, making them less prone to social influence attempts.

R

random assignment A method of assigning participants to groups in an experiment that involves each participant's having an equal chance of being in the experimental or control group.

reconstructive memory The idea that human memory is a reconstruction of the original event, and not an exact playback of that event.

reflected self-appraisal A source of social information involving our view of how other people react to us.

relational aggression Aggression using aspects of a relationship to cause harm to another person that has elements of both direct and indirect aggression.

representativeness heuristic A rule used to judge the probability of an event or a person falling into a category based on how representative it or the person is of the category.

resilience An individual's ability to cope with stress and adversity.

resilience resources Different tools or characteristics that individuals might use to help them cope with stress and adversity (e.g., social support).

resistance stage Stage 2 of the general adaptation syndrome, in which the alarm reaction is halted and the body attempts to restore normal functioning.

righteous rescuer The designation bestowed by Israel on non-Jews who helped save Jews from the Nazis during World War II.

role strain The discomfort one feels in an obedience situation that causes a person to question the legitimacy of the authority figure and weakens the agentic state.

romantic love Love involving strong emotion and having the components of passion and intimacy but not commitment.

S

sanctioned aggression Aggressive behavior that society accepts or encourages.

schema A set of organized cognitions that help us interpret, evaluate, and remember a wide range of social stimuli, including events, persons, and ourselves.

science A set of activities designed to generate a systematic, reliable body of knowledge and generating explanations for social behavior.

secondary compensation A method of handling prejudice involving attempts to change one's mode of thinking about situations to psychologically protect oneself against the outcomes of prejudice.

self-affirmation theory A theory that individuals may not try to reduce dissonance if they can maintain (affirm) their self-concept by showing they are morally adequate in other ways.

self-categorization theory A theory suggesting people need to reduce uncertainty about whether their perceptions of the world are "correct" and seek affirmation of their beliefs from fellow group members.

self-concept All the ideas, thoughts, and information we have about ourselves.

self-control A form of self-regulation involving the conscious and effortful suppression of a dominant behavior.

self-efficacy The belief in one's ability to succeed in specific situations.

self-esteem An individual's evaluation of the self, which can be positive or negative.

self-evaluation maintenance (SEM) theory A theory explaining how the behavior of other people affects how you feel about yourself, especially when they perform some behavior that is important to your self-conception.

self-focus The extent to which one has a heightened awareness of oneself in certain situations (e.g., when a minority within a group).

self-fulfilling prophecy A tendency to expect ourselves to behave in ways that lead to confirmation of our original expectation.

self-handicapping Self-defeating behavior engaged in when you are uncertain about your success or failure at a task to protect your self-esteem in the face of failure.

self-identity theory (SIT) A theory proposing that a number of factors predict one group's reaction to competing groups and concerning what may arise from identification with a social category.

self-monitoring The degree, ranging from low to high, to which a person focuses on his or her behavior when in a given social situation.

self-perception theory A theory suggesting that we learn about our motivations by evaluating our own behavior, useful especially in the area of attitude change.

self-regulation A critical control mechanism used by individuals to match behavior to internal standards of the self or to the expectations of others.

self-schemas Self-conceptions that guide us in ordering and directing our behavior involving how we represent our thoughts and feelings about our experiences in a particular area of life.

self-serving bias Our tendency to attribute positive outcomes of our own behavior to internal, dispositional factors and negative outcomes to external, situational forces.

self-verification A method of supporting and confirming your self-identity.

sexual self-schema How we think about the sexual aspects of the self, derived from past sexual knowledge and experience, and which guides future sexual activity.

sleeper effect A phenomenon of persuasion that occurs when a communication has more impact on attitude change after a long delay than when it is first heard.

social anxiety Anxiety tied to interpersonal relationships that occurs because of an individual's anticipation of negative encounters with others.

social category relationship A relationship in which bystanders assume that the parties involved belong together in some way.

social cognition The general process we use to make sense out of social events, which may or may not include other people.

social comparison process A source of social knowledge involving how we compare our reactions, abilities, and attributes to others.

social dominance orientation Desire to have one's in-group in a position of dominance or superiority to out-groups. High social dominance orientation is correlated with higher levels of prejudice.

social exchange theory A theory of how relationships are evaluated, suggesting that people make assessments according to the rewards (positive things derived from a relationship) and costs (negative things derived from a relationship).

social facilitation The performance-enhancing effect of others on behavior; generally, simple, well-learned behavior is facilitated by the presence of others.

social identity theory An assumption that we all need to have a positive self-concept, part of which is conferred on us through identification with certain groups.

social impact theory A theory stating that social influence is a function of the combination of the strength, immediacy, and number of influence sources.

social information-processing view of aggression A view stating that how a person processes social information mediates aggression.

social inhibition The performance-detracting effect of an audience or co-actors on behavior; generally, complex, not-well-learned behaviors are inhibited by the presence of others.

social-interactional model A model suggesting that antisocial behavior arises early in life and is the result of poor parenting, leading a child to develop conduct problems that affect peer relations and academic performance.

social judgment theory An attitude theory suggesting that the degree of personal involvement with an issue determines how a target of persuasion will judge an attempt at persuasion.

social learning theory A theory that social behavior is acquired through direct reinforcement or punishment of behavior and observational learning.

social loafing The performance-inhibiting effect of working in a group that involves relaxing individual effort based on the belief that others will take up the slack.

social penetration theory A theory that relationships vary in breadth, the extent of interaction, and depth, suggesting they progress in an orderly fashion from slight and superficial contact to greater and deeper involvement.

social perception The social processes by which we come to comprehend the behavior, words, and actions, of other people.

social psychology The scientific study of how individuals think about, interact with, and influence each other.

sociobiology A theoretical perspective that views social behavior as helping groups of organisms within a species survive.

spotlight effect A phenomenon occurring when we overestimate the ability of others to read our overt behavior, how we act and dress, suggesting that we think others notice and pay attention to whatever we do.

stereotype A set of beliefs, positive or negative, about the characteristics or attributes of a group, resulting in rigid and overgeneralized images of members of that group.

stereotype threat The condition that exists when a person is asked to perform a task for which there is a negative stereotype attached to the person's group and performs poorly because the task is threatening.

symbolic aggression Aggressive behavior that interferes with a victim's advancement toward a goal.

system justification theory A theory stating that prejudice can occur when members of groups justify the existence of social arrangements at the expense of interpersonal and group interests.

system variables Variables that are under the control of the criminal justice system (e.g., how a lineup is conducted).

T

theory A set of interrelated propositions concerning the causes for a social behavior that helps organize research results, make predictions about the influence of certain variables, and give direction to future social research.

theory of planned behavior A theory that explains attitude-behavior relationships, focusing on the relationship between the strength of our behavioral intentions and our performance of them.

threat to self-esteem model A model explaining the reactions of victims to receiving help, suggesting that they might refuse help because accepting it is a threat to their self-esteem.

trait-based scales Scales used in performance appraisals, where workers are evaluated on their personality and job-related traits, such as leadership and initiative.

transactional leader A group leader who rewards positive outcomes but also focuses on mistakes made by group members.

transformative leader A group leader who places emphasis on communicating group goals and expressing optimism about the group's ability to reach those goals.

transactive memory systems Systems within groups that are sets of individual memories that allow group members to learn about each other's expertise and to assign memory tasks on that basis.

triangular theory of love A theory suggesting that love has three components—passion, intimacy, and commitment—each of which is conceptualized as a leg of a triangle that can vary.

true partner effect The phenomenon whereby an individual's tendency to conform with a majority position is reduced if there is one other person who supports the nonconforming individual's position.

trustworthiness A component of communicator credibility that involves our assessment of the communicator's character and motives for delivering the message.

U

ultimate attribution error The tendency to give in-group, but not out-group, members the benefit of the doubt for negative behaviors.

unobtrusive measure A method of assessing attitudes such that the individuals whose attitudes you are measuring are not aware of your interest in them.

unrequited love Love expressed by one person that is rejected and not returned by the other.

V

value A concept closely related to an attitude that is a standard of what is desirable for one's actions.

voluntary false confessions Situation where an individual falsely claims responsibility for a crime without police influence.

W

weapon focus The phenomenon by which eyewitness accuracy is reduced when a weapon is present.

working model Mental representations of what an individual expects to happen in close relationships.

Y

Yale communication model A model of the persuasion process that stresses the role of the communicator (source of a message), the nature of the message, the audience, and the channel of communication.

References

A

Aaro, D. (2021, May 31). *San Francisco cop rescued by bystanders after brazen attack caught on video.* https://www.foxnews.com/us/san-francisco-police-officer-rescued-by-bystanders-after-violent-attack-by-apparent-homeless-man-video-shows

ABC News (Producer). *Primetime live, 1/03/07, P070103–51: Basic instincts, part 5.* Available from ABCnewsstore.com.

Abelson, R. P. (1986). Beliefs are like possessions. *Journal for the Theory of Social Behavior, 16,* 223–250.

Abelson, R. P. (1988). Conviction. *American Psychologist, 43,* 267–275.

Abelson, R. P., & Prentice, D. A. (1989). Beliefs as possessions: A functionalized perspective. In A. Pratkanis, S. Breckler, & A. G. Greenwald (Eds.), *Attitude structure and function* (pp. 361–381). Erlbaum.

Aboud, F. E., Mendelson, M. J., & Purdy, K. T. (2003). Cross-race peer relations and friendship quality. *International Journal of Behavioral Development, 27,* 165–173.

Abramowitz, A. I. (2013). The electoral roots of America's dysfunctional government. *Presidential Studies Quarterly, 43,* 709–731.

Abramowitz, A. I., & Saunders, K. L. (2008). Is polarization a myth? *Journal of Politics, 70,* 542–555.

Acker, M., & Davis, M. H. (1992). Intimacy, passion and commitment in adult romantic relationships: A test of the triangular theory of love. *Journal of Social and Personal Relationships, 9,* 21–50.

Acor, A. (2001, January). Employers' perceptions of persons with body art and an experimental test regarding eyebrow piercing. *Dissertation Abstracts International, 61.*

Adachi, P. C., & Willoughby, T. (2013, April 18). Demolishing the competition: The longitudinal link between competitive video games, competitive gambling, and aggression. *Journal of Youth and Adolescence 42,* 1090–1104.

Adam M. G., & Gino, F. (2010). A little thanks goes a long way: Explaining why gratitude expressions motivate prosocial behavior. *Journal of Personality and Social Psychology, 98,* 946–955.

Adams, J., & Roscigno, V. J. (2005). White supremacists, oppositional culture and the World Wide Web. *Social Forces, 84,* 759–778.

Addo, P. C., Fang, J., Kulbo, N. B., Gumah, B., Dagadu, J. C., & Li, L. (2021). Violent video games and aggression among young adults: The moderating effects of adverse environmental factors. *Cyberpsychology, Behavior and Social Networking, 24,* 17–23.

Adorno, T. W., Frenkel-Brunswik, E., Levison, D. J., & Sanford, R. N. (1950). *The authoritarian personality.* Harper.

Affleck, G., Tennen, H., Pfeiffer, C., & Fifield, J. (1987). Appraisals of control and predictability in adapting to a chronic disease. *Journal of Personality and Social Psychology, 53,* 273–279.

Afifi, W., & Faulkner, S. L. (2000). On being "just friends": The frequency and impact of sexual activity in cross-sex friendships. *Journal of Social and Personal Relationships, 17,* 205–222.

Afifi, W. A., Falato, W. L., & Weiner, J. L. (2001). Identity concerns after a severe relational transgression: The role of discovery method for the relational outcomes of infidelity. *Journal of Social and Personal Relationships, 18,* 291–308.

Agocha, V. B., & Cooper, M. L. (1999). Risk perceptions and safer-sex intention: Does a partner's physical attractiveness undermine the use of risk-relevant information? *Personality and Social Psychology Bulletin, 25,* 756–759.

Aikwa, A. (1990). Determinants of the magnitude of indebtedness in Japan: A comparison of relative weight of the recipient's benefits and the donor's costs. *Journal of Psychology, 124,* 523–533.

Ainsworth, M. D. S. (1992). Epilogue. In D. Cicchetti, M. M. Greenberg, & M. Cummings (Eds.), *Attachment in the preschool years* (pp. 463–488). University of Chicago Press.

Aizenkot, D., & Kashy-Rosenbaum, G. (2020). The effectiveness of safe surfing, an anti-cyberbullying intervention program in reducing online and offline bullying and improving perceived popularity and self-esteem. *Cyberpsychology, 14,* 1–23.

Ajzen, I. (1985). From actions to intentions: A theory of planned behavior. In J. Kuhl & J. Beckman (Eds.), *Action control: From cognition to behavior* (pp. 11–39). Springer-Verlag.

Ajzen, I. (1987). Attitudes, traits, and actions: Dispositional prediction of behavior in personality and social psychology. In L. Berkowitz (Ed.), *Advances in experimental social psychology* (Vol. 20, pp. 1–64). Academic Press.

Ajzen, I. (1989). Attitude structure and behavior. In A. R. Pratkanis, S. J. Breckler, & A. G. Greenwald (Eds.), *Attitude structure and function* (pp. 241–274). Erlbaum.

Ajzen, I. (1991). The theory of planned behavior. *Organizational Behavior and Human Decision Processes, 50*, 179–211.

Ajzen, I. (2002). Perceived behavioral control, self-efficacy, locus of control, and the theory of planned behavior. *Journal of Applied Social Psychology, 32*, 665–683.

Ajzen, I., & Fishbein, M. (1980). *Understanding attitudes and predicting human behavior.* Prentice-Hall.

Albert, D. J., Petrovic, D. M., & Walsh, M. L. (1989a). Competitive experience activates testosterone-dependent social aggression toward unfamiliar males. *Physiology and Behavior, 45*, 723–727.

Albert, D. J., Petrovic, D. M., & Walsh, M. L. (1989b). Ovariectomy attenuates aggression by female rats cohabiting with sexually active sterile males. *Physiology and Behavior, 45*, 225–228.

Albright, L., Kenny, D. A., & Malloy, T. E. (1988). Consensus in personality judgments at zero acquaintance. *Journal of Personality and Social Psychology, 55*, 387–395.

Alexander, J. (2015). The major ideologies of liberalism, socialism and conservatism. *Political Studies, 63*, 980–994.

Allen, K. M., Blascovich, J., Tomaka, J., & Kelsey, R. M. (1991). Presence of human friends and pet dogs as moderators of autonomic responses to stress in women. *Journal of Personality and Social Psychology, 61*, 582–589.

Allport, G. W. (1935). Attitudes. In C. Murchison (Ed.), *Handbook of social psychology* (pp. 173–210). Clark University Press.

Allport, G. W. (1954a). *The nature of prejudice.* Addison-Wesley.

Allport, G. W. (1954b). Historical background of modern social psychology. In G. Lindzey (Ed.), *Handbook of social psychology* (Vol. 1, pp. 3–56). Addison-Wesley.

Alpass, F. M., & Neville, S. (2003). Loneliness, health and depression in older males. *Aging and Mental Health, 7*, 212–216.

Altemeyer, B. (1981). *Right-wing authoritarianism.* University of Manitoba Press.

Altemeyer, B. (1996). *The authoritarian specter.* Harvard University Press.

Altemeyer, B. (1998). The other "authoritarian personality." *Advances in Experimental Social Psychology, 30*, 41–92.

Altemeyer, B. (2004). Highly dominating, highly authoritarian personalities. *Journal of Social Psychology, 144*, 421–447.

Altman, I., & Taylor, D. A. (1973). *Social penetration: The development of interpersonal relationships.* Holt, Rinehart & Winston.

Ambady, N. (2010). The perils of pondering: Intuition and thin slice judgments. *Psychological Inquiry, 21*, 271–278.

American Psychological Association (APA). (1992). Ethical principles of psychologists. *American Psychologist, 45*, 1597–1611.

American Psychological Association (APA). (1998). *Psychology examines the issues: Hate crimes today: An age-old foe in modern dress*. American Psychological Association. http://www2.hawaii.edu/~jamess/hate-ap2.htm

Ames, D. R., Kammrath, L. K., Suppes, A., & Bolger, N. (2010). Not so fast: The (not-quite-complete) dissociation between accuracy and confidence in thin-slice impressions. *Personality and Social Psychology Bulletin, 36*, 264–277.

Amichai-Hamburger, Y., & Hayat, Z. (2011). The impact of the Internet on the social lives of users: A representative sample from 13 countries. *Computers in Human Behavior, 27*, 585–589.

Amichai-Hamburger, Y., Kingsbury, M., & Schneider, B. H. (2013). Friendship: An old concept with a new meaning? *Computers in Human Behavior, 29*, 33–39.

Amodio, D. M., & Showers, C. J. (2005). "Similarity breeds liking" revisited: The moderating role of commitment. *Journal of Social and Personal Relationships, 22*, 817–836.

Andersen, B. L., Cyranowski, J. M., & Espindle, D. (1999). Men's sexual self-schema scale. *Journal of Personality and Social Psychology, 76*, 645–661.

Anderson, C. A. (1989). Temperature and aggression: Ubiquitous effects of heat on human violence. *Psychological Bulletin, 106*, 74–96.

Anderson, C. A. (1999). Attributional style, depression, and loneliness: A cross-cultural comparison of American and Chinese students. *Personality and Social Psychology Bulletin, 25*, 482–499.

Anderson, C. A. (2001). Heat and violence. *Current Directions in Psychological Science, 10*, 33–38.

Anderson, C. A., Anderson, K. B., Dorr, N., DeNeve, K. M., & Flanagan, M. (2000). Temperature and aggression. In M. P. Zanna (Ed.), *Advances in experimental social psychology* (pp. 63–133). Academic Press.

Anderson, C. A., & Bushman, B. J. (2001). Effects of violent video games on aggressive behavior, aggressive cognition, aggressive affect, physiological arousal, and prosocial behavior: A meta-analytic review of the scientific literature. *Psychological Science, 12*, 353–359.

Anderson, C. A., & Carnagey, N. L. (2009). Causal effects of violent sports video games on aggression: Is it competitiveness or violent content? *Journal of Experimental Social Psychology, 45*, 731–739.

Anderson, C. A., Carnagey, N. L., & Eubanks, J. (2003). Exposure to violent media: The effects of songs with violent lyrics on aggressive thoughts and feelings. *Journal of Personality and Social Psychology, 84*, 960–971.

Anderson, C. A., Carnagey, N. L., Flanagan, M., Benjamin, A. J., Eubanks, J., & Valentine, J. C. (2004). Violent video games: Specific effects of violent content on aggressive thoughts and behavior. *Advances in Experimental Social Psychology, 36,* 199–249.

Anderson, C. A., & Dill, K. E. (2000). Video games and aggressive thoughts, feelings, and behavior in the laboratory and in life. *Journal of Personality and Social Psychology, 78,* 772–790.

Anderson, C. A., & Murphy, C. R. (2003). Violent video games and aggressive behavior in young women. *Aggressive Behavior, 29,* 423–429.

Anderson, D. E., Ansfield, M. E., & DePaulo, B. M. (1998). Love's best habit: Deception in the context of relationships. In P. Phiipott, R. S. Feldman, & E. J. Coats (Eds.), *The social context of nonverbal behavior* (pp. 372–409). Cambridge University Press.

Anderson, V. L. (1993). Gender differences in altruism among Holocaust rescuers. *Journal of Social Behavior and Personality, 8,* 43–58.

Ang, R. P., & Goh, D. H. (2010). Cyberbullying among adolescents: The role of affective and cognitive empathy, and gender. *Child Psychiatry & Human Development, 41,* 387–397.

Ansen, D., & Kuflik, A. (1993). Spielberg's obsession [Cover story]. *Newsweek, 122*(25), 112.

Antheunis, M. L., & Schouten, A. P. (2011). The effects of other-generated and system-generated cues on adolescents' perceived attractiveness on social network sites. *Journal of Computer-Mediated Communication, 16,* 391–406.

Antheunis, M. L., Valkenburg, P. M., & Peter, J. (2012). The quality of online, offline, and mixed-mode friendships among users of a social networking site. *Cyberpsychology, 6,* 1–11.

Antonovsky, A., & Kats, R. (1967). The life crisis history as a tool in epidemiologic research. *Journal of Health and Social Behavior, 8,* 15–20.

Antony, M. G., & Sheldon, P. (2019). "Is the friendship worth keeping": Gender differences in communicating forgiveness in friendships. *Communication Quarterly, 67,* 291–311.

Apostolou, M., Aristidou, A., & Eraclide, C. (2019). Reactions to and forgiveness of infidelity: Exploring severity, length of relationship, sex, and previous experience effects. *Adaptive Human Behavior and Physiology, 5,* 317–330.

Arbuthnot, J., & Wayner, M. (1982). Minority influence: Effects of size, conversion and sex. *Journal of Psychology, 111,* 285–295.

Arceneaux, K., & Vander Wielen, R. J. (2013). The effects of need for cognition and need for affect on partisan evaluations. *Political Psychology, 34,* 23–42.

Archer, J. (2004). Sex differences in aggression in real world settings: A meta-analytic review. *Review of General Psychology, 8,* 291–322.

Archer, J., Person, N. A., & Westeman, K. E. (1988). Aggressive behaviour of children aged 6–11: Gender differences and their magnitude. *British Journal of Social Psychology, 27,* 371–384.

Arcus, D. (2002). School shooting fatalities and school corporal punishment: A look at the states. *Aggressive Behavior, 28,* 173–183.

Arendt, H. (1963). *Eichmann in Jerusalem: A report on the banality of evil.* Viking.

Aritz, J., & Walker, R. C. (2009). Group composition and communication styles: An analysis of multicultural teams in decision-making meetings. *Journal of Intercultural Communication Research, 38,* 99–114.

Aron, A., & Aron, E. N. (1989). *The heart of social psychology* (2nd ed.). Lexington Books.

Aron A., Aron, E. N., & Allen, J. (1998). Motivations for unrequited love. *Personality and Social Psychology Bulletin, 21,* 787–796.

Aronson, E., Blaney, N., Stephan, C., Sikes, J., & Snapp, M. (1978). *The jigsaw classroom.* Sage.

Aronson, E., & Mills, J. (1959). The effects of severity of initiation on liking for a group. *Journal of Abnormal and Social Psychology, 59,* 177–181.

Aronson, E., Turner, J., & Carlsmith, J. M. (1963). Communication credibility and communication discrepancy as determinants of opinion change. *Journal of Abnormal and Social Psychology, 67,* 31–36.

Aronson, J., Lustina, M. J., & Good, C. (1999). When White men can't do math: Necessary and sufficient factors in stereotype threat. *Journal of Experimental Social Psychology, 35,* 29–46.

Aronson, J., Quinn, D. M., & Spencer, S. J. (1998). Stereotype threat and the academic underperformance of minorities and women. In J. K. Swim & C. Stangor (Eds.), *Prejudice: The target's perspective* (pp. 85–103). Academic Press.

Arriaga, P., & Aguiar, C. (2019). Gender differences in aggression: The role of displaying facial emotional cues in a competitive situation. *Scandinavian Journal of Psychology, 60,* 421–429.

Arriaga, P., Esteves, F., Carniero, P., & Montiero, M. (2006). Violent computer games and their effects on state hostility and physiological arousal. *Aggressive Behavior, 32,* 146–158.

Arrington, L. J., & Bitton, D. (1980). *The Mormon experience.* Vintage Books.

Asch, S. E. (1946). Forming impressions of personality. *Journal of Abnormal and Social Psychology, 41,* 1230–1240.

Asch, S. E. (1951). Effects of group pressure on the modification and distortion of judgments. In H. Guetzkow (Ed.), *Groups, leadership and men* (pp. 177–190). Carnegie Press.

Asch, S. E. (1955). Opinions and social pressures. *Scientific American, 193,* 31–35.

Asch, S. E. (1956). Studies of independence and conformity: A minority of one against a unanimous majority. *Psychological Monographs: General and Applied, 70,* 1–70.

Ashton, M. C., & Esses, V. M. (1999). Stereotype accuracy: Estimating the academic performance of ethnic groups. *Personality and Social Psychology Bulletin, 25,* 225–236.

Atanasov, P., & Joseph, R. (2016, November 30). Which election forecast was the most accurate? Or rather: The least wrong? https://www.washingtonpost.com/news/monkey-cage/wp/2016/11/30/which-election-forecast-was-the-most-accurate-or-rather-the-least-wrong/

Aviles, F., Earleywine, M., Pollock, V., Stratton, J., & Miller, N. (2005). Alcohol's effect on triggered displaced aggression. *Psychology of Addictive Behaviors, 19,* 108–111.

B

Babcock-Roberson, M. E., & Strickland, O. J. (2010). Leadership, work engagement, and organizational citizenship behaviors. *The Journal of Psychology, 144,* 313–326.

Bachner-Melman, R. (2012). The relevance of pathological altruism to eating disorders. In B. Oakley, A. Knafo, G. Madhavan, & D. S. Wilson (Eds.), *Pathological altruism* (pp. 94–106). Oxford University Press.

Bachrach, D. G., Lewis, K., Kim, Y., Patel, P. C., Campion, M. C., & Thatcher, S. (2019). Transactive memory systems in context: A meta-analytic examination of contextual factors in transactive memory systems development and team performance. *Journal of Applied Psychology, 104,* 464–493.

Back, M. D., Schmukle, S. C., & Egloff, B. (2008). Becoming friends by chance. *Psychological Science, 19,* 439–440.

Back, M. D., Stopfer, J. M., Vazire, S., Gaddis, S., Schmukle, S. C., Egloff, B., & Gosling, S. D. (2010). Facebook profiles reflect actual personality, not self-idealization. *Psychological Science, 21,* 372–374.

Badaway, A. (1998). Alcohol, aggression and serotonin: Metabolic aspects. *Alcohol and Alcoholism, 33,* 66–72.

Badawy, R. L., Gazdag, B. A., Bentley, J. R., & Brouer, R. L. (2018). Are all impostors created equal? Exploring gender differences in the impostor phenomenon-performance link. *Personality and Individual Differences, 131,* 156–163.

Bahns, A. J. (2019). Preference, opportunity, and choice: A multilevel analysis of diverse friendship formation. *Group Processes & Intergroup Relations, 22,* 233–252.

Baker, J. G., & Fishbein, H. D. (1998). The development of prejudice towards gays and lesbians by adolescents. *Journal of Homosexuality, 36,* 89–100.

Balcetis, E., & Dunning, D. (2007). Cognitive dissonance and the perception of natural environments. *Psychological Science, 18,* 917–921.

Ball-Rokeach, S., Rokeach, M., & Grube, J. W. (1984). *The great American values test.* Free Press.

Balls, P., & Eisenberg, N. (1986). Sex differences in recipients reactions to aid. *Sex Roles, 14,* 69–79.

Banaji, M. R., Hardin, C., & Rothman, A. J. (1993). Implicit stereotyping in person judgment. *Journal of Personality and Social Psychology, 65,* 272–281.

Banaji, M. R., & Steele, C. M. (1989). The social cognition of alcohol use. *Social Cognition, 7,* 137–151.

Bandura, A. (1965). Influence of models' reinforcement contingencies on the acquisition of imitative responses. *Journal of Personality and Social Psychology, 1,* 589–595.

Bandura, A. (1973). *Aggression: A social learning analysis.* Prentice-Hall.

Bandura, A. (1977). *Social learning theory.* Prentice-Hall.

Bandura, A. (2004). Health promotion by social cognitive means. *Health Education & Behavior: The Official Publication of the Society for Public Health Education, 31,* 143–164.

Bandura, A., & Jourden, F. J. (1991). Self-regulatory mechanisms governing the impact of social comparison on complex decision making. *Journal of Personality and Social Psychology, 60,* 941–951.

Bandura, A., Ross, D., & Ross, S. A. (1961). Transmission of aggression through imitation of aggressive models. *Journal of Abnormal and Social Psychology, 63,* 575–582.

Bandura, A., Ross, D., & Ross, S. A. (1963). Imitation of film-mediated aggressive models. *Journal of Abnormal and Social Psychology, 67,* 601–607.

Bar-Anan, Y., & Nosek, B. A. (2012). *A comparative investigation of seven implicit measures of social cognition.* https://papers.ssrn.com/sol3/papers.cfm?abstract_id=2074556

Barber, N. (2013). *Do lie detectors work?* https://www.psychologytoday.com/us/blog/the-human-beast/201303/do-lie-detectors-work

Barberá, P., Jost, J. T., Nagler, J., Tucker, J. A., & Bonneau, R. (2015). Tweeting from left to right: Is online political communication more than an echo chamber? *Psychological Science, 26,* 1531–1542.

Bargh, J. A., & Chartrand, T. L. (1999). The unbearable automaticity of being. *American Psychologist, 54,* 462–479.

Bargh, J. A., & Thein, R. D. (1985). Individual construct accessibility, person memory, and recall-judgment link: The case of information overload. *Journal of Personality and Social Psychology, 49,* 1129–1146.

Barkow, J. H. (1980). Sociobiology. In A. Montagu (Ed.), *Sociobiology examined* (pp. 171–192). Oxford University Press.

Barnett, M. A., Thompson, M., & Pfiefer, J. R. (1985). Perceived competence to help and the arousal of empathy. *Journal of Social Psychology, 125,* 679–680.

Baron, L. (1986). The Holocaust and human decency: A review of research on the rescue of Jews in Nazi-occupied Europe. *Humboldt Journal of Social Relations, 13,* 237–251.

Baron, R. S. (1986). Distraction-conflict theory: Progress and problems. In L. Berkowitz (Ed.), *Advances in Experimental Social Psychology* (Vol. 19, pp. 1–40). Academic Press.

Baron, R. S., Kerr, N. L., & Miller, N. (1992). *Group process, group decision, group action.* Brooks/Cole.

Bartholomew, K., & Horowitz, L. M. (1991). Attachment styles among young adults: A test of a four category model. *Journal of Personality and Social Psychology, 61,* 226–244.

Bartholow, B. D., & Anderson, C. A. (2002). Effects of violent video games on aggressive behavior: Potential sex differences. *Journal of Experimental Social Psychology, 38,* 283–290.

Bartholow, B. D., Dill, K. E., Anderson, K. B., & Lindsay, J. J. (2003). The proliferation of media violence and its economic underpinnings. In D. A. Gentile (Ed.), *Media violence and children* (pp. 1–18). Praeger.

Bartholow, B. D., Sestir, M. A., & Davis, E. B. (2005). Correlates and consequences of exposure to video game violence: Hostile personality, empathy, and aggressive behavior. *Personality & Social Psychology Bulletin, 31,* 1573–1586.

Bartlett, F. C. (1932). *Remembering.* Cambridge University Press.

Bartlett, M. Y., & DeSteno, D. (2006). Gratitude and prosocial behavior: Helping when it costs you. *Psychological Science, 17,* 319–325.

Bartoli, A. M., & Clark, M. (2006). The dating game: Similarities and differences in dating scripts among college students. *Sexuality & Culture, 10,* 54–80.

Bassili, J. N. (2003). The minority slowness effect: Subtle inhibitions in the expression of views not shared by others. *Journal of Personality and Social Psychology, 84,* 261–276.

Bastian, B., Jetten, J., Chen, H., Radke, H. R., Harding, J. F., & Fasoli, F. (2013). Losing our humanity: The self-dehumanizing consequences of social ostracism. *Personality and Social Psychology Bulletin, 39,* 156–169.

Batson, C. D. (1987). Prosocial motivation: Is it ever truly altruistic? In L. Berkowitz (Ed.), *Advances in experimental social psychology* (Vol. 20, pp. 65–122). Academic Press.

Batson, C. D. (1990a). How social an animal: The human capacity for caring. *American Psychologist, 45,* 336–346.

Batson, C. D. (1990b). Good Samaritans—or priests of Levites? *Personality and Social Psychology Bulletin, 16,* 758–768.

Batson, C. D. (1997). Self-other merging and the empathy-altruism hypothesis: Reply to Neuberg et al. (1997). *Journal of Personality and Social Psychology, 73,* 517–522.

Batson, C. D., & Ahmad, N. (2001). Empathy-induced altruism in a prisoner's dilemma II: What if the target of empathy has defected? *European Journal of Social Psychology, 31,* 25–36.

Batson, C. D., Dyck, J. L., Brandt, J. R., Batson, J. G., Powell, A. L., McMaster, M. R., & Griffitt, C. (1988). Five studies testing two egoistic alternatives to the empathy-altruism hypothesis. *Journal of Personality and Social Psychology, 55,* 52–77.

Batson, C. D., Early, S., & Salvarani, G. (1997). Perspective taking: Imagining how another feels versus imagining how you would feel. *Personality and Social Psychology Bulletin, 23,* 751–758.

Batson, C. D., Fultz, J., & Schoenrade, P. A. (1987). Distress and empathy: Two qualitatively distinct vicarious emotions with different motivational consequences. *Journal of Personality, 55,* 19–39.

Batson, C. D., Nadia, A., Jodi, Y., Bedell, S. I., & Johnson, J. W. (1999). Two threats to the common good: Self-interest and empathy and empathy-induced altruism. *Personality and Social Psychology Bulletin, 25,* 3–16.

Batson, C. D., O'Quin, K., Fultz, J., & Vanderplas, M. (1983). Influence of self-reported distress and empathy on egoistic versus altruistic motivation to help. *Journal of Personality and Social Psychology, 45,* 706–718.

Batson, C. D., Sager, K., Garst, E., Kang, M., Rubchinsky, K., & Dawson, K. (1997). Is empathy-induced helping due to self-other merging? *Journal of Personality and Social Psychology, 73,* 495–509.

Batson, C. D., & Weeks, J. L. (1996). Mood effects of unsuccessful helping: Another test of the empathy-altruism hypothesis. *Personality and Social Psychology Bulletin, 22,* 148–157.

Baucom, D. H., Sayers, S. L., & Duhe, A. (1989). Attributional style and attributional patterns among married couples. *Journal of Personality and Social Psychology, 56,* 596–607.

Baum, A., Grunberg, N. E., & Singer, J. E. (1982). The use of psychological and neuroendocrinological measurements in the study of stress. *Health Psychology, 1,* 217–236.

Baumeister, R. F. (1984). Choking under pressure: Self-consciousness and paradoxical effects of incentives on skillful performance. *Journal of Personality and Social Psychology, 46,* 610–620.

Baumeister, R. F. (1990). Suicide as escape from the self. *Psychological Review, 97,* 90–113.

Baumeister, R. F. (1999). *Evil: Inside human violence and cruelty.* Henry Holt and Co.

Baumeister, R. F. (2001, April). Violent pride: Do people turn violent because of self-hate, or self-love? *Scientific American, 284,* 96–101.

Baumeister, R. F., & Bratslavsky, E. (1999). Passion, intimacy, and time: Passionate love as a function of change of intimacy over time. *Personality and Social Psychology Review, 3,* 49–67.

Baumeister, R. F., Bratslavsky, E., Muraven, M., & Tice, D. M. (1998). Ego depletion: Is the active self a limited resource? *Journal of Personality and Social Psychology, 74,* 1252–1265.

Baumeister, R. F., Campbell, J. D., Krueger, J. I., & Vohs, K. D. (2003). Does high self-esteem cause better performance, interpersonal success, happiness, or healthier lifestyles? *Psychological Science in the Public Interest, 4,* 1–44.

Baumeister, R. F., & Leary, M. R. (1995). The need to belong: Desire for interpersonal attachments as a fundamental human motivation. *Psychological Bulletin, 117,* 497–529.

Baumeister, R. F., & Sher, S. J. (1988). Self-defeating behavior patterns among normal individuals: Review and analysis of common self-destructive tendencies. *Psychological Bulletin, 104,* 2–22.

Baumeister, R. F., & Tice, D. (1984). Role of self-presentation and choice in cognitive dissonance under forced compliance: Necessary or sufficient causes? *Journal of Personality and Social Psychology, 46,* 5–13.

Baumeister, R. F., & Tice, D. (1990). Anxiety and social exclusion. *Journal of Social and Clinical Psychology, 9,* 165–195.

Baumeister, R. F., & Vohs, K. D. (2004). Four roots of evil. In A. G. Miller (Ed.), *The social psychology of good and evil* (pp. 87–101). Guilford Press.

Baumeister, R. F., Wotman, S., & Stillwell, A. M. (1993). Unrequited love: On heartbreak, anger, guilt, scriptlessness and humiliation. *Journal of Personality and Social Psychology, 64,* 377–394.

Baumgardner, A. H. (1990). To know oneself is to like oneself: Self certainty and self-affect. *Journal of Personality and Social Psychology, 58,* 1062–1072.

Baumrind, D. (1964). Some thoughts on ethics of research: After reading Milgram's "behavioral study of obedience." *American Psychologist, 19,* 421–423.

Beauchamp, M. R., Rhodes, R. E., Kreutzer, C., & Rupert, J. L. (2011). Experiential versus genetic accounts of inactivity: Implications for inactive individuals' self-efficacy beliefs and intentions to exercise. *Behavioral Medicine, 37,* 8–14.

Becker, S. W., & Eagly, A. H. (2004). The heroism of men and women. *American Psychologist, 59,* 163–168.

Beckner, C., Rácz, P., Hay, J., Brandstetter, J., & Bartneck, C. (2016). Participants conform to humans but not to humanoid robots in an English past tense formation task. *Journal of Language & Social Psychology, 35,* 158–179.

Bee, H. (1992). *The developing child* (6th ed.). HarperCollins.

Behm-Morawitz, E., Lewallen, J., & Miller, B. (2016, April 20). Real mean girls? Reality television viewing, social aggression, and gender-related beliefs among female emerging adults. *Psychology of Popular Media Culture, 5,* 1–16.

Bell, B. E., & Loftus, E. F. (1988). Degree of detail of eyewitness testimony and mock juror judgments. *Journal of Applied Social Psychology, 18,* 1171–1192.

Bell, B. E., & Loftus, E. F. (1989). Trivial persuasion in the courtroom: The power of (a few) minor details. *Journal of Personality and Social Psychology, 56,* 669–679.

Bell, M. L., & Forde, D. R. (1999). A factorial survey of interpersonal conflict resolution. *Journal of Social Psychology, 139,* 369–377.

Bellé, N., Cantarelli, P., & Belardinelli, P. (2017). Cognitive biases in performance appraisal: Experimental evidence on anchoring and halo effects with public sector managers and employees. *Review of Public Personnel Administration, 37,* 275–294.

Bem D. J. (1966). Inducing belief in false confessions. *Journal of Personality and Social Psychology, 3,* 707–710.

Bem, D. J. (1967). Self-perception: An alternative interpretation of cognitive dissonance phenomena. *Psychological Review, 74,* 183–200.

Bem, D. J. (1972). Self-perception theory. In L. Berkowitz (Ed.), *Advances in experimental social psychology* (Vol. 6, pp. 1–62). Academic Press.

Benham, G., & Charak, R. (2019). Stress and sleep remain significant predictors of health after controlling for negative affect. *Stress and Health, 35,* 59–68.

Ben Hamida, S., Mineka, S., & Bailey, J. M. (1998). Sex differences in perceived controllability of mate value: An evolutionary perspective. *Journal of Personality and Social Psychology, 75,* 963–966.

Bennett, T. L., Silver, R. C., & Ellard, J. H. (1991). Coping with an abusive relationship: How and why do women stay? *Journal of Marriage and the Family, 13,* 118–122.

Benson, P. L., Karabenick, S. A., & Lerner, R. M. (1976). Pretty pleases: The effects of physical attractiveness, race and sex on receiving help. *Journal of Experimental Social Psychology, 12,* 409–415.

Ben Zeev, T., Fein, S., & Inzlicht, M. (2005). Arousal and stereotype threat. *Journal of Experimental Social Psychology, 41,* 174–181.

Bergeron, N., & Schneider, B. H. (2005). Explaining cross-national differences in peer-directed aggression: A quantitative synthesis. *Aggressive Behavior, 31,* 116–137.

Berglas, S., & Jones, E. E. (1978). Drug choice as a self-handicapping strategy in response to noncontingent success. *Journal of Personality and Social Psychology, 36,* 405–417.

Berkman, L. F., & Syme, S. (1979). Social networks, host resistance, and mortality: A nine-year follow-up study of Alameda County residents. *American Journal of Epidemiology, 109,* 186–204.

Berkowitz, L. (1969). Resistance to improper dependency relationships. *Journal of Experimental Social Psychology, 5,* 283–294.

Berkowitz, L. (1972). Social norms, feelings, and other factors affecting altruism. In L. Berkowitz (Ed.), *Advances in experimental social psychology* (pp. 63–108). Academic Press.

Berkowitz, L. (1988). Introduction. In L. Berkowitz (Ed.), *Advances in experimental social psychology* (Vol. 21, pp. 1–16). Academic Press.

Berkowitz, L. (1989). Frustration-aggression hypothesis: Examination and reformation. *Psychological Bulletin, 106,* 59–73.

Berkowitz, L. (1993). *Aggression: Its causes, consequences, and control.* McGraw Hill.

Bernard, D. L., Jones, S. C. T., & Volpe, V. V. (2020). Impostor phenomenon and psychological well-being: The moderating roles of John Henryism and school racial composition among Black college students. *Journal of Black Psychology, 46*, 195–227.

Bernard, D. L., Lige, Q. M., Willis, H. A., Sosoo, E. E., & Neblett, E. W. (2017). Impostor phenomenon and mental health: The influence of racial discrimination and gender. *Journal of Counseling Psychology, 64*, 155–166.

Berndt, T. J. (1992). Friendship and friends' influence in adolescence. *Current Directions in Psychological Sciences, 1*, 156–159.

Bernieri, F. J., Gillis, J. S., Davis, J. M., & Grahe, J. E. (1996). Dyad rapport and the accuracy of its judgment across situations: A lens model analysis. *Journal of Personality and Social Psychology, 71*, 110–129.

Bernstein, M. J., Young, S. G., & Claypool, H. M. (2010). Is Obama's win a gain for Blacks?: Changes in implicit racial prejudice following the 2008 election. *Social Psychology, 41*, 147–151.

Berreby, D. (1998, June 9). Studies explore love and the sweaty t-shirt. *New York Times,* B14.

Berry, D. (1991). Attractive faces are not all created equal: Joint effects of facial babyishness and attractiveness on social perception. *Personality and Social Psychology Bulletin, 17*, 523–528.

Berscheid, E. (1985). Compatibility, interdependence, and emotion. In W. Ickes (Ed.), *Compatible and incompatible relationships* (pp. 143–161). Springer-Verlag.

Berscheid, E. (1988). Some comments on the anatomy of love: Or what ever happened to old fashioned lust? In R. J. Steinberg & M. L. Barnes (Eds.), *The psychology of love* (pp. 359– 374). Yale University Press.

Berscheid, E., Snyder, M., & Omoto, A. M. (1989). The relationship closeness inventory: Assessing the closeness of interpersonal relationships. *Journal of Personality and Social Psychology 57*, 792–807.

Betsch, C., & Böhm, R. (2016). Detrimental effects of introducing partial compulsory vaccination: Experimental evidence. *European Journal of Public Health, 26*, 378–381.

Bettencourt, B. A., & Miller, N. (1996). Gender differences in aggression as a function of provocation: A meta-analysis. *Psychological Bulletin, 119*, 422–447.

Beugré, C. D. (2005). Understanding injustice-related aggression in organizations: A cognitive model. *International Journal of Human Resource Management, 16*, 1120–1136.

Bickman, L. (1974). The social power of a uniform. *Journal of Applied Social Psychology 4*, 47–61.

Bickman, L., & Kamzan, M. (1973). The effect of race and need on helping behavior. *Journal of Social Psychology, 89*, 73–77.

Bierhoff, H-W., & Rohmann, E. (2004). Altruistic personality in the context of the empathy-altruism hypothesis. *European Journal of Social Psychology, 18*, 361–365.

Biernat, M., & Wortman, C. (1991). Sharing of home responsibilities between professionally employed women and their husbands. *Journal of Personality and Social Psychology, 60*, 844–860.

Billig, M. (1992, January 27). The baseline of intergroup prejudice. *Current Contents, 4.*

Bishop, G. D. (1994). *Health psychology: Integrating mind and body*. Allyn & Bacon.

Blackwell, S. E., Rius-Ottenheim, N., Schulte-van Maaren, Y. M., Carlier, I. E., Middelkoop, V. D., Zitman, F. G., Spinhoven, P., Holmes, E. A. & Giltay, E. J. (2012). Optimism and mental imagery: A possible cognitive marker to promote wellbeing? *Psychiatry Research, 206*, 56–61.

Blaine, B., Crocker, J., & Major, B. (1995). The unintended negative consequences of sympathy for the stigmatized. *Journal of Applied Social Psychology, 25*, 889–905.

Blanchard, D. C., & Blanchard, R. J. (1984). Affect and aggression: An animal model applied to human behavior. In R. J. Blanchard & D. C. Blanchard (Eds.), *Advances in the study of aggression* (Vol. 1, pp. 1–62). Academic Press.

Blanchard, F. A., Lilly, T, & Vaughn, L. A. (1991). Reducing the expression of racial prejudice. *Psychological Science, 2*, 101–105.

Blanchflower, D. G., & Oswald, A. J. (2004). Money, sex and happiness: An empirical study. *Scandinavian Journal of Economics, 106*, 393.

Blank, H., & Launay, C. (2014). How to protect eyewitness memory against the misinformation effect: A meta-analysis of post-warning studies. *Journal of Applied Research in Memory and Cognition, 3*, 77–88.

Blascovich, J., & Ginsburg, G. P. (1974). Emergent norms and choice shifts involving risks. *Sociometry, 37*, 274–276.

Blass, T. (2000). The Milgram paradigm after 35 years: Some things we now know about obedience to authority. In T. Blass (Ed.), *Obedience to authority: Current perspectives on the Milgram paradigm* (pp. 35–59). Lawrence Erlbaum Publishers.

Blass, T. (2012). A cross-cultural comparison of studies of obedience using the Milgram paradigm: A review. *Social and Personality Psychology Compass, 6,* 196–205.

Blondé, J., & Girandola, F. (2016). Revealing the elusive effects of vividness: A meta-analysis of empirical evidences assessing the effect of vividness on persuasion. *Social Influence, 11*, 111–129.

Bocchiaro, P., & Zimbardo, P. G. (2010). Defying unjust authority: An exploratory study. *Current Psychology, 29*, 155–170.

Bocchiaro, P., Zimbardo, P. G., & Van Lange, P. M. (2012). To defy or not to defy: An experimental study of the dynamics of disobedience and whistle-blowing. *Social Influence, 7*, 35–50.

Bodenhausen, G. V. (1990). Stereotypes as judgmental heuristics: Evidence of circadian variations in discrimination. *Psychological Science, 1*, 319–322.

Bodenhausen, G. V. (1993). Emotion, arousal, and stereotypic judgment: A heuristic model of affect and stereotyping. In D. Mackie & D. Hamilton (Eds.), *Affect, cognition, and stereotyping: Interactive processes in group perception* (pp. 13–37). Academic Press.

Bodenhausen, G. V., & Lichtenstein, M. (1987). Social stereotypes and information-processing strategies: The impact of task complexity. *Journal of Personality and Social Psychology, 52,* 871–880.

Bodenhausen, G. V., & Wyer, R. S. (1985). Effects of stereotypes on decision making and information processing strategies: The impact of task complexity. *Journal of Personality and Social Psychology, 48,* 267–282.

Bohner, G., Crow, K., Erb, H-P., & Schwartz, N. (1992). Affect and persuasion: Mood effects on the processing of message content and context cues and on subsequent behavior. *European Journal of Social Psychology, 22,* 511–530.

Bolsen, T., Druckman, J. N., & Cook, F. L. (2014). The influence of partisan motivated reasoning on public opinion. *Political Behavior, 36,* 235–262.

Bonanno, G. A., Rennicke, C., & Dekel, S. (2005). Self-enhancement among high exposure survivors of the September 11th terrorist attack: Resilience or maladjustment? *Journal of Personality and Social Psychology, 88,* 984–998.

Bond Jr., C. F., & DePaulo, B. M. (2006). Accuracy of deception judgments. *Personality and Social Psychology Review, 10,* 214–234.

Bordens, K. S., & Abbott, B. B. (2021). *Research design and methods: A process approach* (11th ed.). McGraw Hill.

Bornstein, R. F. (1989). Exposure and affect: Overview and meta-analysis of research, 1968–1987. *Psychological Bulletin, 106,* 265–289.

Bosmans, M. G., & van der Velden, P. G. (2015). Longitudinal interplay between posttraumatic stress symptoms and coping self-efficacy: A four-wave prospective study. *Social Science & Medicine, 134,* 23–29.

Bothwell, R. K., Brigham, J. C., & Malpass, R. S. (1989). Cross-racial identification. *Personality and Social Psychology Bulletin, 15,* 19–25.

Bouchey, H. A., & Harter, S. (2005). Reflected appraisals, academic self-perceptions, and math/science performance during early adolescence. *Journal of Educational Psychology, 97,* 673–686.

Boudreau, J. W., & Rynes, S. L. (1985). Role of recruitment in staffing utility analysis. *Journal of Applied Psychology, 70,* 354–366.

Bourgeois, M. J. (2002). Heritability of attitudes constrains dynamic social impact. *Personality and Social Psychology Bulletin, 28,* 1063–1072.

Bowman, J. M., & Wittenbaum, G. M. (2012). Time pressure affects process and performance in hidden-profile groups. *Small Group Research, 43,* 295–314.

Bracken, D. W., & Rose, D. S. (2011). When does 360-degree feedback create behavior change? And how would we know it when it does? *Journal of Business and Psychology, 26,* 183–192.

Brandt, M. J., Reyna, C., Chambers, J. R., Crawford, J. T., & Wetherell, G. (2014). The ideological-conflict hypothesis: Intolerance among both liberals and conservatives. *Current Directions in Psychological Science, 23,* 27–34.

Brandt, M. J., & Wethere, G. A. (2012). What attitudes are moral attitudes? The case of attitude heritability. *Social Psychological and Personality Science, 3,* 172–179.

Brannon, J., & Feist, J. (1992). *Health psychology* (2nd ed.). Wadsworth.

Brantingham, P. J., Tita, G. E., Short, M. B., & Reid, S. E. (2012). The ecology of gang territorial boundaries. *Criminology, 50,* 851–885.

Breckler, S. J., & Wiggins, E. C. (1989). On defining attitude and attitude theory: Once more with feeling. In A. R. Pratkanis, S. J. Breckler, & A. G. Greenwald (Eds.), *Attitudes structure and function* (pp. 407–428). Erlbaum.

Brehm, J. W. (1956). Post-decision changes in the desirability of alternatives. *Journal of Abnormal and Social Psychology, 52,* 384–389.

Brehm, J. W. (1966). *A theory of psychological reactance.* Academic Press.

Brehm, J. W., & Cohen, A. R. (1962). *Explorations in cognitive dissonance.* Wiley.

Brehm, S. S. (1985). *Intimate relations.* Random House.

Brehm, S. S. (1988). Passionate love. In R. J. Steinberg & M. L. Barnes (Eds.), *The psychology of love* (pp. 232–263). Yale University Press.

Brehm, S. S., & Brehm, J. W. (1981). *Psychological reactance: A theory of freedom and control.* Academic Press.

Breuer, J., Scharkow, M., & Quandt, T. (2015). Sore losers? A reexamination of the frustration–aggression hypothesis for colocated video game play. *Psychology of Popular Media Culture, 4,* 126–137.

Brewer, M. B. (1988). A dual process model of impression formation. In T. K. Srull & R. S. Wyer (Eds.), *Advances in social cognition* (pp. 1–36). Erlbaum.

Brewer, M. B. (1993, August). The social self inclusion and distinctiveness. Address to the American Psychological Convention, Toronto, Canada.

Brickman, P., Coates, D., & Janoff-Bulman, R. (1978). Lottery winners and accident victims: Is happiness relative? *Journal of Personality and Social Psychology, 36,* 917–927.

Bridges, J. S., & McGrail, C. A. (1989). Attributions of responsibility for date and stranger rape. *Sex Roles, 21,* 273–286.

Brown, J. A. C. (1967). *Techniques of persuasion: From propaganda to brainwashing.* Pelican Books.

Brown, K. T. (1998). Consequences of skin tone bias for African Americans: Resource attainment, and psychological and social functioning. *African American Research Perspectives, 4,* 55–60.

Brown, L. (2020, December, 14). *NJ gym famed for defying COVID-19 lockdown orders fined more than $1.2 million.* https://nypost.com/2020/12/14/nj-gym-that-defied-covid-19-lockdown-fined-more-than-1-2m/

Brown, R. (1986). *Social psychology* (2nd ed.). Free Press.

Brown, R. P., Imura, M., & Osterman, L. L. (2014). Gun culture: Mapping a peculiar preference for firearms in the commission of suicide. *Basic & Applied Social Psychology, 36*, 164–175.

Brown, R. P., & Josephs, R. A. (1999). A burden of proof: Stereotype relevance and gender differences in math performance. *Journal of Personality and Social Psychology, 76*, 246–257.

Brown, R. P., Osterman, L. L., & Barnes, C. D. (2009). School violence and the culture of honor. *Psychological Science, 20*, 1400–1405.

Browning, C. R. (1992). *Ordinary men: Reserve police battalion 101 and the final solution in Poland*. HarperCollins.

Brownstein, R. J., & Katzev, R. D. (1985). The relative effectiveness of three compliance techniques in eliciting donations to a cultural organization. *Journal of Applied Social Psychology, 15*, 564–574.

Bruk-Lee, V., Khoury, H. A., Nixon, A. E., Goh, A., & Spector, P. E. (2009). Replicating and extending past personality/job satisfaction meta-analyses. *Human Performance, 22*, 156–189.

Brumbaugh, C. C., & Fraley, R. C. (2006). Transference and attachment: How do attachment patterns get carried forward from one relationship to the next? *Personality and Social Psychology Bulletin, 32*, 552–560.

Brunner, H. H., Nelon, M., Breakefield, X. O., Ropers, H., & van Oost, B. A. (1993). Abnormal behavior associated with a point mutation in the structural gene for monoamine oxidase. *Science, 262*, 578–580.

Brush, S. G. (1991). Women in engineering and science. *American Scientist, 79*, 404–419.

Bryan, J. H., & Test, M. (1967). Models and helping: Naturalistic studies in aiding behavior. *Journal of Personality and Social Psychology, 6*, 400–407.

Bryan, J. H., & Walbek, N. (1970). Preaching and practicing self-sacrifice: Children's actions and reactions. *Child Development, 41*, 329–353.

Buckser, A. (2001). Rescue and cultural context during the Holocaust: Grundtvigian Nationalism and the rescue of the Danish Jews. *Shofar: An Interdisciplinary Journal of Jewish Studies, 19*, 1–25.

Bureau of Justice Statistics. (2019). *School Crime Supplement (SCS) to the National Crime Victimization Survey, selected years, 2005 through 2019*. https://bjs.ojp.gov/content/pub/pdf/iscs18.pdf

Burg, M. M., King, R. B., Stoney, C. M., & Troxel, W. M. (2016). Insights from the OppNet initiatives on psychosocial stress and sleep: Themes for multidisciplinary team science research. *Sleep Health, 2*, 8–11.

Burger, J. M., & Caldwell, D. F. (2003). The effects of monetary incentives and labeling on the foot-in-the-door technique: Evidence for a self-perception process. *Basic and Applied Social Psychology, 25*, 235–241.

Burger, J. M., & Guadango, R. E. (2003). Self-concept clarity and the foot-in-the-door procedure. *Basic and Applied Social Psychology, 25*, 75–86.

Burger, J. M., & Petty, R. E. (1981). The low-ball compliance technique: Task or person commitment? *Journal of Personality and Social Psychology, 40*, 492–500.

Burnett, A. (1972). *Gertrude Stein*. Atheneum.

Burnstein, E. (1982). Persuasion as argument processing. In H. Brandstatter, J. H. Davis, & G. Stocker-Kreichgauer (Eds.), *Group decision making* (pp. 103–124). Academic Press.

Burnstein, E., & Sentis, K. (1981). Attitude polarization in groups. In R. E. Petty, T. M. Ostrom, & T. C. Brock (Eds.), *Cognitive responses in persuasion* (pp. 197–216). Erlbaum.

Burnstein, E., & Vinokur, A. (1977). Persuasive argumentation and social comparison as determinants of attitude polarization. *Journal of Experimental Social Psychology, 13*, 315–332.

Burris, C. T., & Rempel, J. K. (2011). "Just look at him": Punitive responses cued by "evil" symbols. *Basic & Applied Social Psychology, 33*, 69–80.

Burrows, K. (2013). Age preferences in dating advertisements by homosexuals and heterosexuals: From sociobiological to sociological explanations. *Archives of Sexual Behavior, 42*, 203–211.

Burt, I., Patel, S. H., Butler, S. K., & Gonzalez, T. (2013). Integrating leadership skills into anger management groups to reduce aggressive behaviors: The LIT Model. *Journal of Mental Health Counseling, 35*, 124–141.

Burt, M. (1980). Cultural myths and supports for rape. *Journal of Personality and Social Psychology, 38*, 217–230.

Busby, D. M., & Holman, T. B. (2009). Perceived match or mismatch on the Gottman conflict styles: Associations with relationship outcome variables. *Family Process, 48*, 531–545.

Bushman, B. J., & Anderson, C. A. (2002). Violent video games and hostile expectations: A test of the General Aggression Model. *Personality and Social Psychology Bulletin, 28*, 1679–1686.

Bushman, B. J., & Cooper, H. M. (1990). Effects of alcohol on human aggression: An integrative research review. *Psychological Bulletin, 107*, 341–354.

Buss, A., Booker, A., & Buss, E. (1972). Firing a weapon and aggression. *Journal of Personality and Social Psychology, 22*, 296–302.

Buss, D. M. (1988a). Love acts: The evolutionary biology of love. In R. J. Steinberg & M. L. Barnes (Eds.), *The psychology of love* (pp. 100–118). Yale University Press.

Buss, D. M. (1988b). From vigilance to violence: Tactics of mate retention in American undergraduates. *Ethology and Sociobiology, 9*, 291–317.

Buss, D. M. (1994). *The evolution of desire: Strategies of human mating*. Basic Books.

Byrne, D. (1961). Anxiety and the experimental arousal of affiliation need. *Journal of Abnormal and Social Psychology, 63*, 660–662.

Byrne, D., Clore, G. L., & Smeaton, G. (1986). The attraction hypothesis: Do similar attitudes affect anything? *Journal of Personality and Social Psychology, 51*, 1167–1170.

Byrne, D., Ervin, C. R., & Lamberth, J. (2004). Continuity between the experimental study of attraction and real-life computer dating. In H. T. Reis & C. E. Rusbult (Eds.), *Close relationships: Key readings* (pp. 81–88). Taylor & Francis.

Byrne, D., & Nelson, D. (1965). Attraction as a linear function of proportion of positive reinforcements. *Journal of Personality and Social Psychology, 1*, 659–663.

C

Cacioppo, J. T., Hawkley, L. C., Berntson, G. G., Ernst, J. M., Gibbs, A. C., Stickgold, R., & Hobson, J. A. (2002). Do lonely days invade the night? Potential social modulation of sleep efficiency. *Psychological Science, 13*, 384–387.

Cacioppo, J. T., Petty, R. E., & Morris, K. (1983). Effects of need for cognition on message evaluation, recall, and persuasion. *Journal of Personality and Social Psychology, 45*, 805–818.

Cadinu, M., Maass, A., Rosabianca, A., & Kiesner, J. (2005). Why do women underperform under stereotype threat? Evidence for the role of negative thinking. *Psychological Science, 16*, 572–578.

Calder, T. (2003). The apparent banality of evil: The relationship between evil acts and evil character. *Journal of Social Philosophy, 34*, 364–376.

Callero, P. L. (1986). Putting the social in prosocial behavior: An interactionist approach to altruism. *Humboldt Journal of Social Relations, 13*, 15–32.

Campbell, J. T., & Fairey, P. J. (1989). Informational and normative routes to conformity: The effect of faction size as a function of norm extremity and attention to the stimulus. *Journal of Personality and Social Psychology, 57*, 457–468.

Cancela, A., Briñol, P., & Petty, R. E. (2021). Hedonic vs. epistemic goals in processing persuasive communications: Revisiting the role of personal involvement. *Motivation and Emotion, 45*, 280–298.

Cantrill, J. G., & Siebold, D. R. (1986). The perceptual contrast explanation of sequential request strategy effectiveness. *Human Communication Research, 13*, 253–267.

Caporael, L. R. (1997). The evolution of a truly social cognition: The core configurations model. *Personality and Social Psychology Review, 1*, 276–298.

Capraro, V., & Barcelo, H. (2020, May 11). *The effect of messaging and gender on intentions to wear a face covering to slow down COVID-19 transmission.* https://psyarxiv.com/tg7vz/

Card, N. A., Stucky, B. D., Sawalani, G. M., & Little, T. D. (2008). Direct and indirect aggression during childhood and adolescence: A meta-analytic review of gender differences, intercorrelations, and relations to maladjustment. *Child Development, 79*, 1185–1229.

Cardenas, R. A., & Harris, L. J. (2006). Symmetrical decorations enhance the attractiveness of faces and abstract designs. *Evolution and Human Behavior, 27*, 1–18.

Carducci, B. J., & Deuser, P. S. (1984). The foot-in-the-door technique: Initial request and organ donation. *Basic and Applied Social Psychology, 5*, 75–82.

Carducci, B. J., Deuser, P. S., Bauer, A., Large, M., & Ramaekers, M. (1989). An application of the foot in the door technique to organ donation. *Journal of Business & Psychology, 4*, 245–249.

Carli, L. L., Ganley, R., & Pierce-Otay, A. (1991). Similarity and satisfaction in roommate relationships. *Personality and Social Psychology Bulletin, 17*, 419–427.

Carlo, G., Raffaelli, M., Laible, D. J., & Meyer, K. A. (1999). Why are girls less physically aggressive than boys: Personality and parenting mediators of physical aggression. *Sex Roles, 40*, 711–729.

Carlson, C. A., & Carlson, M. A. (2012). A distinctiveness-driven reversal of the weapon-focus effect. *Applied Psychology in Criminal Justice, 8*, 36–53.

Carlson, N. R. (1991). *Physiology of behavior* (4th ed.). Allyn & Bacon.

Carr, J. L., & VanDeusen, K. M. (2004). Risk factors for male sexual aggression on college campuses. *Journal of Family Violence, 19*, 279–289.

Carré, J. M., Murphy, K. R., & Hariri, A. R. (2013). What lies beneath the face of aggression? *Social Cognitive & Affective Neuroscience, 8*, 224–229.

Carrère, S., & Gottman, J. M. (1999). Predicting divorce among newlyweds from the first three minutes of a marital conflict discussion. *Family Process, 38*, 293–301.

Carroll, R. T. (2006). *Pseudoscience*. http://skepdic.com/pseudosc.html

Carter, T. J., & Gilovich, T. (2010). The relative relativity of material and experiential purchases. *Journal of Personality & Social Psychology, 98*, 146–159.

Carver, C. S. (1975). Physical aggression as a function of objective self-awareness and attitudes toward punishment. *Journal of Personality and Social Psychology, 11*, 510–519.

Caspar, E. A., Christensen, J. F., Cleeremans, A., & Haggard, P. (2016). Coercion changes the sense of agency in the human brain. *Current Biology, 26*, 1–8.

Cassileth, B., Lusk, E. J., Miller, D. S., Brown, L. L., & Miller, C. (1985). Psychosocial correlates of survival in advanced malignant disease? *The New England Journal of Medicine, 312*, 1551–1555.

Castro, M. A. C. (1974). Reactions to receiving aid as a function of cost to donor and opportunity to aid. *Journal of Applied Social Psychology, 4*, 194–209.

Catanzaro, S. J., Backenstrass, M., Miller, S. A., Mearns, J., Pfeiffer, N., & Brendalen, S. (2014). Prediction of symptoms of emotional distress by mood regulation expectancies and affective traits. *International Journal of Psychology, 49*, 471–479.

Centers for Disease Control and Prevention. (2020a). *Mental health, substance use, and suicidal ideation during the COVID-19 pandemic—United States*. https://www.cdc.gov/mmwr/volumes/69/wr/mm6932a1.htm

Centers for Disease Control and Prevention. (2020b). *Mortality in the United States, 2018* (NCHS Data Brief No. 355). https://www.cdc.gov/nchs/products/databriefs/db355.htm

Centers for Disease Control and Prevention. (2020c). *Prevalence of obesity and severe obesity among adults: United States, 2017–2018* (NCHS Data Brief No. 360). https://www.cdc.gov/nchs/products/databriefs/db360.htm

Centers for Disease Control and Prevention. (2021a). Provisional mortality data—United States, 2020. *Morbidity and Mortality Weekly Report (MMWR), 70,* 519–522.

Centers for Disease Control and Prevention. (2021b). *COVID-19 vaccinations in the United States*. https://covid.cdc.gov/covid-data-tracker/#vaccinations

Centers for Disease Control and Prevention. (2021c). COVID-19 vaccination coverage and intent among adults aged 18–39 years—United States, March–May 2020. *Morbidity and Mortality Weekly Report (MMWR), 70,* 928–933.

Chaiken, S. (1987). The heuristic model of persuasion. In M. P. Zanna, J. M. Olson, & C. P Herman (Eds.), *Social influence: The Ontario symposium* (Vol. 5, pp. 3–39). Erlbaum.

Chaiken, S., Liberman, A., & Eagly, A. (1989). Heuristic versus systematic information processing within and beyond the persuasion context. In J. S. Uleman & J. A. Bargh (Eds.), *Unintended thought* (pp. 212–252). Guilford.

Chaiken, S., & Trope, Y. (Eds.). (1999). *Dual process theories in social psychology*. Guilford.

Chak, K., & Leung, L. (2004). Shyness and locus of control as predictors of Internet addiction and Internet use. *CyberPsychology and Behavior, 7,* 559–570.

Chambers, J. R., Schlenker, B. R., & Collisson, B. (2013). Ideology and prejudice: The role of value conflicts. *Psychological Science, 24,* 140–149.

Champagne, F. A., & Mashoodh, R. (2009). Genes in context: Gene–environment interplay and the origins of individual differences in behavior. *Current Directions in Psychological Science, 18,* 127–131.

Chan, D. K-S., & Cheng, G. H-L. (2004). A comparison of offline and online friendship qualities at different stages of relationship development. *Journal of Social and Personal Relationships, 21,* 305–320.

Chang, J. (2008). The role of anonymity in deindividuated behavior: A comparison of deindividuation theory and the social identity model of deindividuation effect. *The Pulse, 6,* 2–8.

Chang, W., & Madera, J. M. (2012). Using social network sites for selection purposes: An investigation of hospitality recruiters. *Journal of Human Resources in Hospitality & Tourism, 11,* 183–196.

Chang-Ik S., & Hee Sun, P. (2015). Testing intention to continue exercising at fitness and sports centers with the theory of planned behavior. *Social Behavior & Personality: An International Journal, 43,* 641–648.

Chapman, L. L., & Chapman, J. (1967). Genesis of popular but erroneous psychodiagnostic observations. *Journal of Abnormal Psychology, 72,* 193–204.

Chau, M., & Xu, J. (2007). Mining communities and their relationships in blogs: A study of online hate groups. *International Journal of Human-Computer Studies, 65,* 57–70.

Chekroun, P., & Brauer, M. (2001). The bystander effect and social control behavior: The effect of the presence of others on people's reactions to norm violations. *European Journal of Social Psychology, 32,* 853–867.

Chen, B., & Marcus, J. (2012). Students' self-presentation on Facebook: An examination of personality and self-construal factors. *Computers in Human Behavior, 28,* 2091–2099.

Chen, G. M. (2015). Losing face on social media: Threats to positive face lead to an indirect effect on retaliatory aggression through negative affect. *Communication Research, 42,* 819–838.

Chen, H., Yates, B. T., & McGinnies, E. (1988). Effects of involvement on observers' estimates of consensus, distinctiveness, and consistency. *Personality and Social Psychology Bulletin, 14,* 468–478.

Chen, J., Rapee, R. M., & Abbott, M. (2013). Mediators of the relationship between social anxiety and post-event rumination, *Journal of Anxiety Disorders, 27,* 1–8.

Chen, J. M., & Francis-Tan, A. (2021). Setting the tone: An investigation of skin color bias in Asia. *Race and Social Problems*. https://doi.org/10.1007/s12552-021-09329-0

Chen, Z., Poon, K. T., DeWall, C. N., & Jiang, T. (2020). Life lacks meaning without acceptance: Ostracism triggers suicidal thoughts. *Journal of Personality and Social Psychology, 119,* 1423–1443.

Cheng, Z., & Smyth, R. (2015). Sex and happiness. *Journal of Economic Behavior & Organization, 112,* 26–32.

Cheong, J., & Nagoshi C. T. (1999). Effects of sensation seeking, instruction set, and alcohol placebo administration on aggressive behavior. *Alcohol, 17,* 81–86.

Chermack, S. T., & Walton, M, A. (1999). The relationship between family aggression history and expressed aggression among college males. *Aggressive Behavior, 25,* 255–267.

Chester, M. R., Sinnard, M. T., Rochlen, A. B., Nadeau, M. M., Balsan, M. J., & Provence, M. M. (2016). Gay men's experiences coming out online: A qualitative study. *Journal of Gay & Lesbian Social Services, 28,* 317–335.

Chopik, W. J. (2017). Associations among relational values, support, health, and well-being across the adult lifespan. *Personal Relationships, 24,* 408–422.

Chory-Assad, R. M. (2004). Effects of television sitcom exposure on the accessibility of verbally aggressive thoughts. *Western Journal of Communication, 68,* 431–453.

Chow, R. M., Tiedens, L. Z., & Govan, C. L. (2008). Excluded emotions: The role of anger in antisocial responses to ostracism. *Journal of Experimental Social Psychology, 44,* 896–903.

Chressanthis, G. A., Gilbert, K. S., & Grimes, P. W. (1991). Ideology, constituent interests, and senatorial voting: The case of abortion. *Social Science Quarterly, 72,* 588–600.

Christensen, P. N., & Kashy, D. (1998). Perceptions of and by lonely people in initial social interaction. *Personality and Social Psychology Bulletin, 24,* 322–329.

Christiansen, K., & Knussmann, R. (1987). Androgen levels and components of aggressive behavior in men. *Hormones and Behavior, 21,* 170–180.

Christianson, S. A. (1992). Emotional stress and eyewitness memory: A critical review. *Psychological Bulletin, 112,* 284–309.

Chung, B. G., Ehrhart, M. G., Holcombe Ehrhart, K., Hattrup, K., & Solamon, J. (2010). Stereotype threat, state anxiety, and specific self-efficacy as predictors of promotion exam performance. *Group & Organization Management, 35,* 77–107.

Cialdini, R. B. (1993). *Influence: Science and practice* (3rd ed.). HarperCollins.

Cialdini, R. B., & Ascani, K. (1976). Test of a concession procedure for inducing verbal, behavioral, and further compliance with a request to give blood. *Journal of Applied Psychology, 61,* 295–300.

Cialdini, R. B., Borden, R. J., Thorne, A., Walker, M. R., Freeman, S., & Sloan, L. R. (1976). Basking in reflected glory: Three (football) field studies. *Journal of Personality & Social Psychology, 34,* 366–375.

Cialdini, R. B., Brown, S. L., Lewis, B. P., Luce, C., & Neuberg, S. L. (1997). Reinterpreting the empathy-altruism relationship: When one into one equals oneness. *Journal of Personality and Social Psychology, 73,* 481–494.

Cialdini, R. B., & Fultz, J. (1990). Interpreting the negative mood-helping literature via "mega"-analysis: A contrary view. *Psychological Bulletin, 107,* 210–214.

Cialdini, R. B., & Sagarin, B. J. (2005). Interpersonal influence. In T. Brock & M. Green (Eds.), *Persuasion: Psychological insights and perspectives* (pp. 143–169). Sage.

Cialdini, R. B., Trost, M. R., & Newsom, J. T. (1995). Preference for consistency: The development of a valid measure and the discovery of surprising behavior implications. *Journal of Personality and Social Psychology, 69,* 318–328.

Cialdini, R. B., Vincent, J. E., Lewis, S. K., Catalan, J., Wheeler, D., & Darby, B. L. (1975). Reciprocal concessions procedure for inducing compliance: The door-in-the-face technique. *Journal of Personality and Social Psychology, 31,* 206–215.

Cinnirella, M., & Green, B. (2007). Does "cyber-conformity" vary cross-culturally? Exploring the effect of culture and communication medium on social conformity. *Computers in Human Behavior, 23,* 2011–2025.

Claidière, N., Bowler, M., Brookes, S., Brown, R., & Whiten, A. (2014). Frequency of behavior witnessed and conformity in an everyday social context. *Plos ONE, 9,* 1–10.

Claidière, N., Bowler, M., & Whiten, A. (2012). Evidence for weak or linear conformity but not for hyper-conformity in an everyday social learning context. *Plos ONE, 7,* 1–8.

Clance, P. R., & Imes, S. A. (1978). The imposter phenomenon in high achieving women: Dynamics and therapeutic intervention. *Psychotherapy: Theory, Research & Practice, 15,* 241–247.

Clancy, D., & Bull, R. (2015). The effect on mock-juror decision-making of power-of-speech within eyewitness testimony and types of scientific evidence. *Psychiatry, Psychology and Law, 22,* 425–435.

Clark, J. K., Evans, A. T., & Wegener, D. T. (2011). Perceptions of source efficacy and persuasion: Multiple mechanisms for source effects on attitudes. *European Journal of Social Psychology, 41,* 596–607.

Clark, M. S. (1986). Evidence for the effectiveness of manipulations of desire for communal versus exchange relationships. *Personality and Social Psychology Bulletin, 12,* 414–425.

Clark, M. S., & Grote, N. K. (1998). Why aren't indices of relationship costs always negatively related to indices of relationship quality? *Personality and Social Psychology Review, 2,* 2–17.

Clark, R. D., & Word, L. E. (1974). What is the apathetic bystander?: Situational characteristics of the emergency. *Journal of Personality and Social Psychology, 29,* 279–287.

Clark, R. D., III (1999). Effect of number of majority defectors on minority influence. *Group Dynamics: Theory, Research and Practice, 3,* 1–10.

Clark, R. D., III (2001). Effect of majority defections and multiple minority sources on minority influence. *Group Dynamics: Theory, Research and Practice, 5,* 57–62.

Clary, E. G., & Orenstein, L. (1991). The amount and effectiveness of help: The relationship of motives and abilities to helping behavior. *Personality and Social Psychology Bulletin, 17,* 58–64.

Clifford, B. R., & Scott, J. (1978). Individual and situational factors in eyewitness testimony. *Journal of Applied Psychology, 63,* 352–359.

Clifford, C. (2020). *Nancy Pelosi visits San Francisco's Chinatown to encourage people amid fears of coronavirus.* https://www.kron4.com/news/bay-area/nancy-pelosi-visits-san-franciscos-chinatown-to-encourage-people-amid-fears-of-coronavirus/

Cogan, R., Cogan, D., Waltz, W., & McCue, M. (1987). Effects of laughter and relaxation on discomfort thresholds. *Journal of Behavioral Medicine, 10,* 139–144.

Cohen, D. (1996). Law, social policy, and violence: The impact of regional cultures. *Journal of Personality and Social Psychology, 70,* 961–978.

Cohen, D. (1998). Culture, social organization and patterns of violence. *Journal of Personality and Social Psychology, 75,* 408–419.

Cohen, D., & Nisbett, R. E. (1997). Field experiments examining the culture of honor: The role of institutions in perpetuating norms. *Personality and Social Psychology Bulletin, 23,* 1188–1199.

Cohen, D., Nisbett, R. E., Bowdle, B. F., & Schwartz, N. (1996). Insult, aggression, and the southern culture of honor: An "experimental ethnography." *Journal of Personality and Social Psychology, 70,* 945–960.

Cohen, F. (1984). Coping. In J. D. Matarazzo, S. M. Weiss, J. A. Herd, N. E. Miller & S. M. Weiss (Eds.), *Behavioral health: A handbook of health enhancement and disease prevention* (pp. 261–274). Wiley.

Cohen, G. L. (2003). Party over policy: The dominating impact of group influence on political beliefs? *Journal of Personality and Social Psychology, 85,* 800–822.

Cohen, G. L., & Garcia, J. (2005). "I am us": Negative stereotypes as collective threats. *Journal of Personality and Social Psychology, 89,* 566–582.

Cohen, S., Tyrrell, D. A., & Smith, A. P. (1993). Negative life events, perceived stress, negative affect, and susceptibility to the common cold. *Journal of Personality and Social Psychology, 64,* 131–140.

Cokley, K., Awad, G., Smith, L., Jackson, S., Awosogba, O., Hurst, & . . . Roberts, D. (2015). The roles of gender stigma consciousness, impostor phenomenon and academic self-concept in the academic outcomes of women and men. *Sex Roles: A Journal of Research, 73,* 414–426.

Coleman, L. T., Jussim, L., & Isaac, J. L. (1991). Black students' reactions to feedback conveyed by White and Black teachers. *Journal of Applied Social Psychology, 21,* 460–481.

Coleman, M. (2011). Emotion and the self-serving bias. *Current Psychology*, 30, 345–354.

Coleman, R., & Banning, S. (2006). Network TV news' affective framing of the presidential candidates: Evidence for a second-level agenda setting effect through visual framing. *Journalism & Mass Communication Quarterly, 83,* 313–328.

Collins, N. L., Ford, M. B., Guichard, A., & Allard, L. M. (2006). Working models of attachment and attribution processes in intimate relationships. *Personality and Social Psychology Bulletin, 32,* 201–219.

Collins, R. L., Taylor, S. E., Wood, J. V., & Thompson, S. C. (1988). The vividness effect: Elusive or illusory? *Journal of Experimental Social Psychology, 24,* 1–18.

Colvin, C. R., & Funder, D. C. (1991). Predicting personality and behavior: A boundary acquaintance effect. *Journal of Personality and Social Psychology 60,* 884–894.

Combs, D. Y., & Keller, P. S. (2010). Politicians and trustworthiness: Acting contrary to self-interest enhances trustworthiness. *Basic & Applied Social Psychology, 32,* 328–339.

Conger, R. D., Rueter, M. A., & Elder, G. H., Jr. (1999). Couple resilience to economic pressure. *Journal of Personality and Social Psychology, 76,* 54–71.

Conner, R. L., & Levine, S. (1969). Hormonal influences on aggressive behavior. In S. Garattini & E. B. Sigg (Eds.), *Aggressive behavior* (pp. 150–163). Wiley.

Conway, L. G., III, Gornick, L. J., Houck, S. C., Anderson, C., Stockert, J., Sessoms, D., & McCue, K. (2016). Are conservatives really more simple-minded than liberals? The domain specificity of complex thinking. *Political Psychology, 37,* 777–798.

Conway, L. G., III, Dodds, D. P., Towgood, K., McClure, S., & Olson, J. M. (2011). The biological roots of complex thinking: Are heritable attitudes more complex? *Journal of Personality, 79,* 101–134.

Conway, L. G., III, Houck, S. C., Gornick, L. J., & Repke, M. A. (2018). Finding the Loch Ness monster: Left-wing authoritarianism in the United States. *Political Psychology, 39,* 1049–1067.

Conway, L. G., III, & Schaller, M. (2005). When authorities' commands backfire: Attributions about consensus and effects on deviant decision making. *Journal of Applied Psychology, 89,* 311–326.

Cook, S. W. (1984). Cooperative interaction in multiethnic contexts. In N. Miller & M. B. Brewer (Eds.), *Groups in contact: The psychology of desegregation* (pp. 155–185). Academic Press.

Cooley, C. H. (1902). *Human nature and the social order.* Scribner.

Cooper, J. (1998). Unlearning cognitive dissonance: Toward an understanding of the development of dissonance. *Journal of Experimental Social Psychology, 34,* 562–565.

Cooper, J., & Scher, S. J. (1992). Actions and attitudes: The role of responsibility and aversive consequences in persuasion. In T. Brock & S. Shavitt (Eds.), *The psychology of persuasion* (pp. 63–79). Freeman.

Cooper, L., & Fazio, R. H. (1984). A new look at cognitive dissonance theory. In L. Berkowitz (Ed.), *Advances in experimental social psychology* (Vol. 17, pp. 229–267). Academic Press.

Corker, R. (2001). *Distinguishing science from pseudoscience.* https://hep.physics.utoronto.ca/~orr/wwwroot/JPH441/Pseudoscience.pdf

Correll, J., Park, B., Judd, C. M., & Wittenbrink, B. (2002). The police officer's dilemma: Using ethnicity to disambiguate potentially threatening individuals. *Journal of Personality and Social Psychology, 83,* 1314–1329.

Correll, J., Spencer, S. J., & Zanna, M. P. (2004). An affirmed self and an open mind: Self-affirmation and sensitivity to argument strength. *Journal of Experimental Social Psychology, 40,* 350–356.

Costanzo, P. R., Reitan, H. T., & Shaw, M. E. (1968). Conformity as a function of experimentally induced minority and majority competence. *Psychonomic Science, 10,* 320–330.

Cottrell, C. A., & Neuberg, S. L. (2005). Different emotional responses to different groups: A sociofunctional, threat-based approach to "prejudice." *Journal of Personality and Social Psychology, 88,* 770–789.

Cottrell, N. B. (1972). Social facilitation. In C. G. McClintock (Ed.), *Experimental social psychology* (pp. 185–236). Holt, Rinehart & Winston.

Cottrell, N. B., Wack, D. L., Sekerak, G. J., & Rittle, R. M. (1968). Social facilitation of dominant responses by the presence of an audience and the mere presence of others. *Journal of Personality and Social Psychology, 9,* 245–250.

Cousins, N. (1979). *Anatomy of an illness*. Bantam.

Cousins, N. (1989). *Head first: The biology of hope*. E.P. Dutton.

Cox, C. L. (2020). "Healthcare heroes": Problems with media focus on heroism from healthcare workers during the COVID-19 pandemic. *Journal of Medical Ethics, 46,* 510–513.

Coyne, S. M. (2016). Effects of viewing relational aggression on television on aggressive behavior in adolescents: A three-year longitudinal study. *Developmental Psychology, 52,* 284–295.

Coyne, S. M., & Archer, J. (2004). Indirect aggression in the media: A content analysis of British television programs. *Aggressive Behavior, 30,* 254–271.

Coyne, S. M., & Archer, J. (2005). The relationship between *indirect* and physical a*ggression* on television and in real life. *Social Development, 14,* 324–338.

Coyne, S. M., Archer, J., & Eslea, M. (2004). Cruel intentions on television and in real life: Can viewing indirect aggression increase viewers' subsequent indirect aggression? *Journal of Experimental Child Psychology, 88,* 234–253.

Coyne, S. M., Ehrenreich, S. E., Holmgren, H. G., & Underwood, M. K. (2019). "We're not gonna be friends anymore": Associations between viewing relational aggression on television and relational aggression in text messaging during adolescence. *Aggressive Behavior, 45,* 319–326.

Coyne, S. M., Stockdale, L., Linder, J., Nelson, D., Collier, K., Essig, L., & . . . Essig, L. W. (2017). Pow! Boom! Kablam! Effects of viewing superhero programs on aggressive, prosocial, and defending behaviors in preschool children. *Journal of Abnormal Child Psychology, 45,* 1523–1535.

Craig, W., Boniel-Nissim, M., King, N., Walsh, S. D., Boer, M., Donnelly, P. D., & . . . Pickett, W. (2020). Social media use and cyber-bullying: A cross-national analysis of young people in 42 countries. *Journal of Adolescent Health, 66,* S100–S108.

Cramer, R. E., McMaster, M. R., Bartell, P. A., & Dragna, M. (1988). Subject competence and minimization of the bystander effect. *Journal of Applied Social Psychology 18,* 1133–1148.

Crandall, C. E., Eshleman, A., & O'Brien, L. (2002). Social norms and the expression and suppression of prejudice: The struggle for internalization. *Journal of Personality and Social Psychology, 82,* 359–378.

Crandall, C. S. (1991). Do heavyweight students have more difficulty paying for college? *Personality and Social Psychology Bulletin, 17,* 606–611.

Crandall, C. S. (1994). Prejudice against fat people: Ideology and self-interest. *Journal of Personality and Social Psychology, 66,* 882–894.

Crano, W. P., & Sivacek, J. (1984). The influence of incentive-aroused ambivalence on overjustification effects in attitude change. *Journal of Experimental Social Psychology, 20,* 137–158.

Crisp, R. J., & Turner, R. N. (2009). Can imagined interactions produce positive perceptions?: Reducing prejudice through simulated social contact. *American Psychologist, 64,* 231–240.

Crockenberg, S., & Litman, C. (1986). Autonomy as competence in 2-year-olds: Maternal correlates of child defiance, compliance and self-assertion. *Developmental Psychology 26,* 961–971.

Crocker, J., & Major, B. (1989). Social stigma and self-esteem: The self-protective properties of stigma. *Psychological Review, 96,* 608–630.

Crocker, J., & Park, L. E. (2004). The costly pursuit of self-esteem. *Psychological Bulletin*, *130,* 392–414.

Crocker, J., Voelkl, K., Testa, M., & Major, B. (1991). Social stigma: The affective consequences of attributional ambiguity. *Journal of Personality and Social Psychology, 60,* 218–228.

Crohan, S. E. (1992). Marital happiness and spousal consensus on beliefs about marital conflict: A longitudinal investigation. *Journal of Social and Personal Relationships, 9,* 89–102.

Crosby, F., Bromley, S., & Saxe, L. (1980). Recent unobtrusive studies of Black and White discrimination and prejudice: A literature review. *Psychological Bulletin, 87,* 546–563.

Crosby, J. R., King, M., & Savitsky, K. (2014). The minority spotlight effect. *Social Psychological and Personality Science, 5,* 743–750.

Crott, H., Giesel, M., & Hoffman, C. (1998). The process of inductive inference in groups: The use of positive or negative hypothesis and target testing in sequential rule-discovery tasks. *Journal of Personality and Social Psychology, 75,* 938–954.

Croyle, R. T., & Cooper, J. (1983). Dissonance arousal: Physiological evidence. *Journal of Personality and Social Psychology, 45,* 782–791.

Crozier, W. E., & Strange, D. (2019). Correcting the misinformation effect. *Applied Cognitive Psychology, 33,* 585–595.

Crutchfield, R. S. (1955). Conformity and character. *American Psychologist, 10,* 191–198.

Cullum, J., O'Grady, M., Sandoval, P., Armeli, S., & Tennen, H. (2013). Ignoring norms with a little help from my friends: Social support reduces normative influence on drinking behavior. *Journal of Social and Clinical Psychology, 32,* 17–33.

Cutler, B. L., Penrod, S. D., & Dexter, H. R. (1989). The eyewitness, the expert psychologist, and the jury. *Law and Human Behavior, 13,* 311–332.

Cutler, B. L., Penrod, S. D., & Stuve, T. E. (1988). Juror decision making in eyewitness identification cases. *Law and Human Behavior, 12,* 41–55.

Cyranowski, J. M., & Andersen, B. L. (1998). Schemas, sexuality, and romantic attachment. *Journal of Personality and Social Psychology, 74,* 1364–1379.

D

Dambrun, M., Duarte, S., & Guimond, S. (2004). Why are men more likely to support group-based dominance than women? The mediating role of gender identification. *British Journal of Social Psychology, 43,* 287–297.

Dambrun, M., & Vatiné, E. (2010). Reopening the study of extreme social behaviors: Obedience to authority within an immersive video environment. *European Journal of Social Psychology, 40,* 760–773.

Darley, J. M., & Batson, C. D. (1973). "From Jerusalem to Jericho": A study of situational and dispositional variables in helping behavior. *Journal of Personality and Social Psychology, 27,* 100–108.

Darley, J. M., & Gross, P. H. (1983). A hypothesis confirming bias in labeling effects. *Journal of Personality and Social Psychology, 44,* 20–33.

Darley, J. M., & Latané, B. (1968). Bystander intervention in emergencies: Diffusion of responsibility. *Journal of Personality and Social Psychology, 8,* 377–383.

Darley, J. M., Teger, A. I., & Lewis, L. D. (1973). Do groups always inhibit individuals' response to potential emergencies? *Journal of Personality and Social Psychology, 26,* 395–399.

Das, E., Vonkeman, C., & Hartmann, T. (2012). Mood as a resource in dealing with health recommendations: How mood affects information processing and acceptance of quit-smoking messages. *Psychology & Health, 27,* 116–127.

Dasgupta, N., & Asgari, S. (2004). Seeing is believing: Exposure to counterstereotypic women leaders and its effect on the malleability of automatic gender stereotyping. *Journal of Experimental Social Psychology, 40,* 642–658.

Davis, J. H. (1969). *Group performance.* Addison-Wesley.

Davis, J. H. (1973). Group decision and social interaction: A theory of social decision schemes. *Psychological Review, 80,* 97–125.

Davis, J. H. (1980). Group decision and procedural justice. In M. Fishbein (Ed.), *Progress in social psychology* (Vol. 1, pp. 234–278). Erlbaum.

Davis, J. H., Kerr, N. L., Atkin, R. S., Holt, R., & Meek, D. (1975). The decision processes of 6- and 12-person mock juries assigned unanimous and two-thirds majority rules. *Journal of Personality and Social Psychology, 32,* 1–14.

Davis, M., Markus, K. A., Walters, S. B., Vorus, N., & Connors, B. (2005). Behavioral cues to deception vs. topic incriminating potential in criminal confessions. *Law and Human Behavior, 29,* 683–704.

Dean, D. H. (2010). Consumer perceptions of visible tattoos on service personnel. *Managing Service Quality, 20,* 294–308.

Dean, K. E., & Malamuth, N. M. (1997). Characteristics of men who aggress sexually and men who imagine aggressing: Risk and moderating variables. *Journal of Personality and Social Psychology, 72,* 449–455.

DeAndrea, D. C., Shaw, A. S., & Levine, T. R. (2010). Online language: The role of culture in self-expression and self-construal on Facebook. *Journal of Language and Social Psychology, 29,* 425–442.

DeBono, A., & Muraven, M. (2014). Rejection perceptions: Feeling disrespected leads to greater aggression than feeling disliked. *Journal of Experimental Social Psychology, 55,* 43–52.

De Cadenet, A. (2015). *More women watch (and enjoy) porn than you ever realized: A Marie Claire study.* https://www.marieclaire.com/sex-love/a16474/women-porn-habits-study/

Deelstra, J. T., Peeters, M. C. W., Schaufeli, W. B., Stroebe, W., Zijlstra, F. R. H., & van Doornen, L. P. (2003). Receiving instrumental support at work: When help is not wanted. *Journal of Applied Psychology, 88,* 324–331.

Deffenbacher, K. A. (1980). Eyewitness accuracy and confidence: Can we infer anything about their relationship? *Law and Human Behavior, 4,* 243–260.

DeHart, T., Pelham, B. W., & Tennen, H. (2006). What lies beneath: Parenting style and implicit self-esteem. *Journal of Experimental Social Psychology, 42,* 1–18.

DeJong, M. (1980). The stigma of obesity: The consequence of naive assumptions concerning the causes of physical deviance. *Journal of Health and Social Behavior, 21,* 75–87.

DeJong, W. (1979). An examination of self-perception mediation of the foot-in-the-door effect. *Journal of Personality and Social Psychology, 37,* 2171–2180.

DeLamater, J. (1974). A definition of "group." *Small Group Behavior, 5,* 30–44.

De La Ronde, C., & Swann, W. B., Jr. (1998). Partner verification: Restoring the shattered images of our intimates. *Journal of Personality and Social Psychology, 75,* 374–382.

Del Barrio, V., Aluja, A., & García, L. F. (2004). Relationship between empathy and the Big Five personality traits in a sample of Spanish adolescents. *Social Behavior & Personality: An International Journal, 32,* 677–682.

Delgado, J. M. R. (1969). Offensive-defensive behaviour in free monkeys and chimpanzees induced by radio stimulation of the brain. In S. Garattini & E. B. Sigg (Eds.), *Aggressive behavior* (pp. 109–119). Wiley.

de Munck, V. C., Korotayev, A., de Munck, J., & Kaltourina, D. (2011). Cross-cultural analysis of models of romantic love among U.S. residents, Russians, and Lithuanians. *Cross-Cultural Research, 45,* 128–154.

De Raad, B., Van Oudenhoven, J. P., & Hofstede, M. (2005). Personality terms of abuse in three cultures: Type nouns between description and insult. *European Journal of Personality, 19,* 153–165.

Dennis, A. R., Valacich, J. S., & Nunamaker, J. F. (1990). An experimental investigation of the effects of group size in an electronic meeting environment. *IEEE Transactions on Systems, Man, and Cybernetics, 25,* 1049–1057.

Denrell, J. (2005). Why most people disapprove of me: Experience sampling in impression formation. *Psychological Review, 112,* 951–978.

Denson, T. F., Blundell, K. A., Schofield, T. P., Schira, M. M., & Krämer, U. M. (2018). The neural correlates of alcohol-related aggression. *Cognitive, Affective & Behavioral Neuroscience, 18,* 203–215.

Denson, T. F., Mehta, P. H., & Ho Tan, D. (2013). Endogenous testosterone and cortisol jointly influence reactive aggression in women. *Psychoneuroendocrinology, 38,* 416–424.

DePaulo, B. M., Charlton, K., Cooper, H., Lindsay, J. J., & Muhlenbruck, L. (1997). The accuracy-confidence correlation in detection of deception. *Personality and Social Psychology Review, 4,* 346–357.

DePaulo, B. M., & Fisher, J. D. (1980). The costs of asking for help. *Basic and Applied Social Psychology, 1,* 23–35.

DePaulo, B. M., & Kashy, D. (1999). Everyday lies in close and casual relationships. *Journal of Personality and Social Psychology, 74,* 63–79.

DePaulo, B. M., Kenny, D. A., Hoover, C., Webb, W., & Oliver, P. V. (1987). Accuracy of person perception: Do people know what kinds of impressions they convey? *Journal of Personality and Social Psychology, 52,* 303–315.

DePaulo, B. M., Lindsay, J. J., Malone, B. E., Muhlenbruck, L., Charlton, K., & Cooper, H. (2003). Cues to deception. *Psychological Bulletin, 129,* 74–118.

Derlega, V. J., Winstead, B. A., & Jones, W. H. (1991). *Personality: Contemporary theory and research.* Nelson-Hall.

Derman, K. H., & George, W. H. (1989). Alcohol expectancy and the relationship between drinking and physical aggression. *Journal of Psychology, 123,* 153–161.

Derntl, B., Windischberger, C., Robinson, S., Kryspin-Exner, I., Gur, R. C., Moser, E., & Habel, U. (2009). Amygdala activity to fear and anger in healthy young males is associated with testosterone. *Psychoneuroendocrinology, 34,* 687–693.

DeRosier, M. E., & Mercer, S. H. (2009). Perceived behavioral atypicality as a predictor of social rejection and peer victimization: Implications for emotional adjustment and academic achievement. *Psychology in the Schools, 46,* 375–387.

Des Pres, T. (1976). *The survivor.* Oxford University Press.

DeSantis, A. D. (2003). A couple of White guys sitting around talking: The collective rationalizations of cigar smokers. *Journal of Contemporary Ethnography, 32,* 432–466.

Desdentado, L., Cebolla, A., Miragall, M., Llorens, R., Navarro, M. D., & Baños, R. M. (2021). Exploring the role of explicit and implicit self-esteem and self-compassion in anxious and depressive symptomatology following acquired brain injury. *Mindfulness, 12,* 899–910.

Desforges, D., Lord, C. G., Ramsey, S. L., Mason, J. A., Van Leeuwen, H. M., West, S. C., & Lepper, M. R. (1991). Effects of structured cooperative contact on changing negative attitudes towards stigmatized social groups. *Journal of Personality and Social Psychology, 60,* 531–544.

Deutsch, M., & Gerrard, H. B. (1955). A study of normative and informational social influence upon individual judgment. *Journal of Abnormal and Social Psychology, 51,* 629–636.

Devine, P. G. (1989). Stereotypes and prejudice: Their automatic and controlled components. *Journal of Personality and Social Psychology, 56,* 5–18

Devine, P. G., Monteith, M. J., Zuwerink, J. R., & Elliot, A. J. (1991). Prejudice with and without compunction. *Journal of Personality and Social Psychology, 60,* 817–830.

Dhont, K., & Van Hiel, A. (2012). Intergroup contact buffers against the intergenerational transmission of authoritarianism and racial prejudice. *Journal of Research in Personality, 46,* 231–234.

Diamond, L. M. (2003). What does sexual orientation orient? A biobehavioral model distinguishing romantic love and sexual desire. *Psychological Review, 110,* 173–192.

Diamond, L. M. (2004). Emerging perspectives on distinctions between romantic love and sexual desire. *Current Directions in Psychological Science, 13,* 116–119.

Diekman, A. B., Eagly, A. H., & Kulesa, P. (2002). Accuracy and bias in stereotypes about the social and political attitudes of women and men. *Journal of Experimental Social Psychology, 38,* 268–282.

Diener, E., & Biswas-Diener, R. (2002). Will money increase subjective well-being? *Social Indicators Research, 57,* 119–169.

Diener, E., & Diener, C. (1996). Most people are happy. *Psychological Science, 7,* 181–185.

Diener, E., Suh, E. M., Lucas, R. E., & Smith, H. L. (1999). Subjective well-being: Three decades of progress. *Psychological Bulletin, 125,* 276–302.

Dijksterhuis, A., & Knippenberg, A. V. (2000). Behavioral indecision: Effects of self-focus on automatic behavior. *Social Cognition, 18,* 55–74.

Dijkstra, P., & Buunk, B. (1998). Jealousy as a function of rival characteristics: An evolutionary perspective. *Personality and Social Psychology Bulletin, 42,* 1158–1166.

Dillard, C. L. (2002). Civil disobedience: A case study in factors of effectiveness. *Society & Animals, 10,* 47–62.

Dillard, J. P., Hunter, J. E., & Burgoon, M. (1984). Sequential-request persuasive strategies: Meta analysis of foot-in-the-door and door-in-the-face. *Human Communication Research, 10,* 461–488.

Dillard, J. P., & Shen, L. (2005). On the nature of reactance and its role in persuasive health communication. *Communication Monographs, 72,* 144–168.

Ding, V. J., & Stillman, J. A. (2005). An empirical investigation of discrimination against overweight female job applicants in New Zealand. *New Zealand Journal of Psychology, 39,* 139–148.

Dinges, D. F., Pack, F., Williams, K., Gillen, K. A., Powell, J. W., Ott, G. E., & . . . Pack, A. I. (1997). Cumulative sleepiness, mood disturbance, and psychomotor vigilance performance decrements during a week of sleep restricted to 4–5 hours per night. *Sleep, 20,* 267–277.

Dion, K., Berscheid, E., & Walster, E. (1972). What is beautiful is good. *Journal of Personality and Social Psychology, 24,* 285–290.

Dion, K. L., & Earn, B. M. (1975). The phenomenology of being a target of prejudice. *Journal of Personality and Social Psychology, 32,* 944–950.

DiTommaso, E., Brannen, C., & Burgess, M. (2005). The universality of relationship characteristics: A cross-cultural comparison of different types of attachment and loneliness in Canadian and visiting Chinese students. *Social Behavior and Personality, 33,* 57–68.

Ditto, P. H., Liu, B. S., Clark, C. J., Wojcik, S. P., Chen, E. E., Grady, R. H., & . . . Zinger, J. F. (2019). At least bias is bipartisan: A meta-analytic comparison of partisan bias in liberals and conservatives. *Perspectives on Psychological Science, 14,* 273–291.

Dodge, K. A. (1986). A social information processing model of social competence in children. In M. Perlmutter (Ed.), *Minnesota symposium on child psychology* (Vol. 18 pp. 77–126.). Erlbaum.

Dodson, C., & Reisberg, D. (1991). Post-event misinformation has no impact on implicit memory. *Bulletin of the Psychonomic Society, 29,* 333–336.

Dodson, C. S., & Dobolyi, D. G. (2015). Misinterpreting eyewitness expressions of confidence: The featural justification effect. *Law & Human Behavior, 39,* 266–280.

Dolinoy, D. C., Weidman, J. R., Waterman, R. A., & Jirtle, R. L. (2006). Maternal genistein alters coat color and protects Avy mouse offspring from obesity by modifying the fetal epigenome. *Environmental Health Perspectives, 114,* 567–572.

Dolinski, D. (2012). The nature of the first small request as a decisive factor in the effectiveness of the foot-in-the-door technique. *Applied Psychology: An International Review, 61,* 437–453.

Doll, J., & Ajzen, I. (1992). Accessibility and stability of predictors in the theory of planned behavior. *Journal of Personality and Social Psychology, 63,* 754–765.

Dollard, J., Doob, L., Miller, N., Mowrer, O., & Sears, R. (1939). *Frustration and aggression.* Yale University Press.

Doms, M., & Van Avermaet, E. (1980). Majority influence and conversion behavior: A replication. *Journal of Experimental Social Psychology, 16,* 283–292.

Donnelly, D., & Fraser, J. (1998). Gender differences in sadomasochistic arousal among college students. *Sex Roles, 39,* 391–407.

Donnerstein, E., & Donnerstein, M. (1973). Variables in interracial aggression: Potential in-group censure. *Journal of Personality and Social Psychology, 27,* 143–150.

Donnerstein, E., Donnerstein, M., & Evans, R. (1975). Erotic stimuli and aggression: Facilitation or inhibition. *Journal of Personality and Social Psychology, 32,* 237–244.

Douglas, K. M., McGarty, C., Bliuc, A. M., & Lala, G. (2005). Understanding cyberhate: Social competition and social creativity in online White supremacist groups. *Social Science Computer Review, 23,* 68–76.

Dovidio, J. F., Allen, J. L., & Schroeder, D. A. (1990). Specificity of empathy-induced helping: Evidence for altruistic motivation. *Journal of Personality and Social Psychology, 59,* 249–260.

Dovidio, J. F., & Gaertner, S. L. (1981). The effects of race, status, and ability on helping behavior. *Social Psychology Quarterly, 44,* 192–203.

Dovidio, J. F., & Gaertner, S. L. (2000). Aversive racism and selection decisions: 1989 and 1999. *Psychological Science, 11,* 315–319.

Dovidio, J. F., Kawakami, K., Johnson, C., Johnson, B., & Howard, A. (1997). On the nature of prejudice: Automatic and controlled processes. *Journal of Experimental Social Psychology, 33,* 510–540.

Dozier, J. B., & Miceli, M. P. (1985). Potential predictors of whistle-blowing: A prosocial perspective. *Academy of Management Review, 10,* 820–836.

Drickamer, L. C., & Vessey, S. H. (1986). *Animal behavior: Concepts, processes and methods* (2nd ed.). Prindle, Weber, & Schmidt.

Drigotas, S. M., Rusbult, C. E., Wieselquist, J., & Whitton, S. (1999). Close partner as sculptor of the ideal self: Behavioral affirmation and the Michelangelo phenomenon. *Journal of Personality and Social Psychology, 77,* 293–324.

Drizen, S. A., & Leo, R. A. (2004). The problem of false confessions in the post-DNA world. *North Carolina Law Review, 82,* 891–1005.

Duck, J., Terry, D. J., & Hogg, M. A. (1998). Perceptions of a media campaign: The role of social identity and the changing intergroup context. *Personality and Social Psychology Bulletin, 24,* 3–16.

Duck, S. W. (1982). A topography of relationship disengagement and dissolution. In S. W. Duck (Ed.), *Personal relationships 4: Dissolving personal relationships* (pp. 1–30). Academic Press.

Duck, S. W. (1988). *Handbook of personal relationships.* Wiley.

Duhart, B. (2020, August 12). *Town votes to rescind license of N.J. gym whose owners repeatedly defied coronavirus restrictions.* https://www.nj.com/coronavirus/2020/08/town-votes-to-rescind-license-of-nj-gym-whose-owners-repeatedly-defied-coronavirus-restrictions.html

Dunbar, E. (1995). The prejudiced personality, racism and anti-Semitism: The PR scale forty years later. *Journal of Personality Assessment, 65,* 270–277.

Dunbar, R. I. M. (1987). Sociobiological explanations and the evolution of ethnocentrism. In V. Reynolds, V. Falger, & I. Vine (Eds.), *The sociobiology of ethnocentrism* (pp. 404–405). University of Georgia Press.

Duncan, L. E., Peterson, B. E., & Winter, D. G. (1997). Authoritarianism and gender roles: Toward a psychological analysis of hegemonic relationships. *Personality and Social Psychology Bulletin, 23,* 41–49.

Dundon, C. M., & Rellini, A. H. (2012). Emotional states of love moderate the association between catecholamines and female sexual responses in the laboratory. *Journal of Sexual Medicine, 9,* 2617–2630.

Dunkel Schetter, C., & Dolbier, C. (2011). Resilience in the context of chronic stress and health in adults. *Social and Personality Psychology Compass, 5,* 634–652.

Dunning, D., Griffin, D. W., Milojkovic, J. D., & Ross, L. (1990). The overconfidence effect in social prediction. *Journal of Personality and Social Psychology 58,* 568–581.

Durante, F., Tablante, C. B., & Fiske, S. T. (2017). Poor but warm, rich but cold (and competent): Social classes in the stereotype content model. *Journal of Social Issues, 73,* 138–157.

Durbach, N. (2000). "They might as well brand us": Working-class resistance to compulsory vaccination in Victorian England. *Social History of Medicine, 13,* 45–63.

Durham, M., & Dane, F. (1999). Juror knowledge of eyewitness behavior: evidence for the necessity of expert testimony. *Journal of Social Behavior & Personality, 14,* 299–308.

Dyck, R. J., & Rule, B. G. (1978). Effect on retaliation of causal attributions concerning attack. *Journal of Personality and Social Psychology, 36,* 521–529.

E

Eagly, A. H. (1978). Sex differences in influenceability. *Psychological Bulletin, 85,* 86–116.

Eagly, A. H. (1987). *Sex differences in social behavior: A social role interpretation.* Erlbaum.

Eagly, A. H. (1992). Uneven progress: Social psychology and the study of attitudes. *Journal of Personality and Social Psychology, 63,* 693–710.

Eagly, A. H., Ashmore, R. D., Makhijani, M. G., & Longo, L. C. (1991). What is beautiful is good, but . . .: A metaanalytic review of research on the physical attractiveness stereotype. *Psychological Bulletin, 110,* 109–128.

Eagly, A. H., & Carli, L. L. (1981). Sex of researchers and sex-typed communications as determinants of sex differences in influenceability: A meta-analysis of social influence studies. *Psychological Bulletin, 90,* 1–20.

Eagly, A. H., & Chrvala, C. (1986). Sex differences in conformity: Status and gender role interpretations. *Sex Roles, 10,* 203–220.

Eagly, A. H., & Crowley, M. (1986). Gender and helping behavior: A meta-analytic review of the social psychological literature. *Psychological Bulletin, 100,* 309–330.

Eagly, A. H., Johannesen-Schmidt, M. C., & van Engen, M. (2003). Transformational, transactional, and laissez-faire leadership styles: A meta-analysis comparing women and men. *Psychological Bulletin, 129,* 569–591.

Eagly, A. H., & Johnson, B. T. (1990). Gender and leadership style. *Psychological Bulletin, 108,* 233–256.

Eagly, A. H., & Karau, S. L. (1991). Gender and the emergence of leaders: A meta-analysis. *Journal of Personality and Social Psychology, 60,* 685–710.

Eagly, A. H., & Karau, S. J. (2002). Role congruity theory of prejudice toward female leaders. *Psychological Review, 109,* 573–598.

Eagly, A. H., Kulesa, P., Chen, S., & Chaiken, S. (2001). Do attitudes affect memory? Tests of the congeniality hypothesis. *Current Directions in Psychological Sciences, 10,* 5–9.

Eagly, A. H., & Steffen, V. J. (1986). Gender and aggressive behavior: A meta-analytic review of the social psychological literature. *Psychological Bulletin, 100,* 309–330.

Eagly, A. H., & Telaak, K. (1972). Width of the latitude of acceptance as a determinant of attitude change. *Journal of Personality and Social Psychology, 23,* 388–397.

Eagly, A. H., Wood, W., & Chaiken, S. (1978). Causal inferences about communicators and their effect on opinion change. *Journal of Personality and Social Psychology, 36,* 424–435.

Eagly, A. H., Wood, W., & Fishbaugh, L. (1981). Sex differences in conformity: Surveillance by the group as a determinant of male nonconformity. *Journal of Personality and Social Psychology, 40,* 384–394.

Earles, J. L., Kersten, A. W., Vernon, L. L., & Starkings, R. (2016). Memory for positive, negative and neutral events in younger and older adults: Does emotion influence binding in event memory? *Cognition and Emotion, 30,* 378–388.

Earp, B. D., & Trafimow, D. (2015). Replication, falsification, and the crisis of confidence in social psychology. *Frontiers in Psychology, 6,* 1–11.

Easterling, B., Knox, D., & Brackett, A. (2012). Secrets in romantic relationships: Does sexual orientation matter? *Journal of GLBT Family Studies, 8,* 196–208.

Eastwick, P. W., Luchies, L. B., Finkel, E. J., & Hunt, L. L. (2014). The predictive validity of ideal partner preferences: A review and meta-analysis. *Psychological Bulletin, 140,* 623–665.

Edwards, J. A., Weary, G., von Hippel, W., & Jacobson, J. A. (1999). The effects of depression on impression formation: The role of trait and category diagnosticity. *Personality and Social Psychology Bulletin, 25,* 1350–1363.

Edwards, S. B., & Flynn, J. P. (1972). Corticospinal control of striking in centrally elicited attack behavior. *Brain Research, 41,* 51–65.

Edwards, S. L., Rapee, R. M., & Franklin, J. (2003). Postevent rumination and recall bias for a social performance event in high and low socially anxious individuals. *Cognitive Therapy and Research, 27,* 603–617.

Ehrlich, G. A., & Gramzow, R. H. (2015). The politics of affirmation theory: When group-affirmation leads to greater ingroup bias. *Personality & Social Psychology Bulletin, 41,* 1110–1122.

Eisenberg, N., & Miller, P. A. (1987). The relation of empathy to prosocial and related behaviors. *Psychological Bulletin, 101,* 91–119.

Eisenberg, N., & Mussen, P. (1989). *The roots of prosocial behavior in children.* Cambridge University Press.

Eisner, M., & Ghuneim, L. (2013). Honor killing attitudes amongst adolescents in Amman, Jordan. *Aggressive Behavior, 39,* 405–417.

Eitzen, D. S. (1973). Two minorities: The Jews of Poland and the Chinese of the Philippines. In D. E. Gelfand & R. D. Lee (Eds.), *Ethnic conflicts and power: A cross-national perspective* (pp. 140–156). Wiley.

Ekehammar, B., & Akrami, N. (2003). The relation between personality and prejudice: A variable-and person-centered approach. *European Journal of Personality, 17,* 449–464.

Ekehammar, B., Akrami, N., Gylje, M., & Zakrisson, I. (2004). What matters most to prejudice: Big five personality, social dominance orientation, or right-wing authoritarianism? *European Journal of Personality, 18,* 463–482.

Ekman, P. (1985). *Telling lies: Clues to deceit in the marketplace, politics, and marriage.* Norton.

Ekman, P., O'Sullivan, M. O., Frank, M. G. (1999). A few can catch a liar. *Psychological Science, 10,* 263–266.

Elbert, T., Weierstall, R., & Schauer, M. (2010). Fascination violence: On mind and brain of man hunters. *European Archives of Psychiatry and Clinical Neuroscience, 260*(Suppl. 2), S100–S105.

Elder, W. B., Morrow, S. L., & Brooks, G. R. (2015). Sexual self-schemas of gay men: A qualitative investigation. *Counseling Psychologist, 43,* 942–969.

Elkin, R. A., & Leippe, M. R. (1986). Physiological arousal, dissonance, and attitude change: Evidence for a dissonance-arousal link and a "don't remind me" effect. *Journal of Personality and Social Psychology, 51,* 55–65.

Ellul, J. (1965). *Propaganda: The formation of men's attitudes.* Vintage.

Elms, A. (1972). *Social psychology and social relevance.* Little Brown.

Elms, A., & Milgram, S. (1966). Personality characteristics associated with obedience and defiance toward authoritative command. *Journal of Experimental Research in Personality, 1,* 282–289.

Emlen, S. T., & Wrege, P. H. (1988). The role of kinship in helping decisions among white-fronted bee-eaters. *Behavioral Ecology and Sociobiology, 23,* 305–315.

Engleberg, E., & Sjöberg, L. (2005). Perceived validity of visually mediated hazards and beliefs about risk. *Applied Cognitive Psychology, 19,* 899–912.

Ensari, N., Christian, J., Kuriyama, D., & Miller, N. (2012). The personalization model revisited: An experimental investigation of the role of five personalization-based strategies on prejudice reduction. *Group Processes & Intergroup Relations, 15,* 503–522.

Enzo, E., Politi, P., Bianchi, M., Minoretti, P., Bertona, M., & Geroldi, D. (2006). Raised plasma nerve growth factors associated with early stage romantic love. *Psychoneuroendocrinology, 31,* 288–294.

Epstein, L., Lindstädt, R., Segal, J. A., & Westerland, C. (2006). The changing dynamics of senate voting on supreme court nominees. *Journal of Politics, 68,* 296–307.

Eron, L. D., Huesmann, L. R., & Zelli, A. (1991). The role of parental variables in the learning of aggression. In D. J. Pepler & K. H. Rubin (Eds.), *The development and treatment of childhood aggression* (pp. 169–188). Erlbaum.

Essien, I., Calanchini, J., & Degner, J. (2021). Moderators of intergroup evaluation in disadvantaged groups: A comprehensive test of predictions from system justification theory. *Journal of Personality and Social Psychology, 120,* 1204–1230.

Etcoff, N. L., Ekman, P., & Frank, M. G. (2000, May 11). Lie detection and language loss. *Nature, 405,* 139–140.

F

Fabrigar, L. R., Priester, J. R., Petty, R. E., & Wegener, D. T. (1998). The impact of attitude accessibility on elaboration of persuasive messages. *Personality and Social Psychology Bulletin, 24,* 339–352.

Farley, S. D., & Stasson, M. D. (2003). Relative influences of affect and behavior on behavior: Are feelings or beliefs more closely related to blood donation intentions? *Experimental Psychology, 50,* 55–62.

Faulkner, S. L., & Williams, K. D. (1995, May). The causes and consequences of social ostracism: A qualitative analysis. Paper presented at the Midwestern Psychological Association, Chicago, IL.

Fawcett, J. M., Russell, E. J., Peace, K. A., & Christie, J. (2013). Of guns and geese: A meta-analytic review of the "weapon focus" literature. *Psychology, Crime & Law, 19,* 35–66.

Fazio, R. H. (1986). How do attitudes guide behavior? In R. M. Sorrentino & E. T. Higgins (Eds.), *Handbook of motivation and cognition: Foundations of social behavior* (pp. 204–243). Guilford.

Fazio, R. H., & Williams, C. J. (1986). Attitude accessibility as a moderator of the attitude-perception and attitude-behavior relationships. *Journal of Personality and Social Psychology, 51,* 505–514.

Fehr, B. (2004). Intimacy expectations in same-sex friendships: A prototype interaction-pattern model. *Journal of Personality and Social Psychology, 86,* 265–284.

Feinberg, J. M., & Aiello, J. R. (2006). Social facilitation: A test of competing theories. *Journal of Applied Social Psychology, 36,* 1087–1109.

Ferguson, C. J. (2013). Violent video games and the Supreme Court: Lessons for the scientific community in the wake of *Brown v. Entertainment Merchants Association. American Psychologist, 68,* 57–74.

Ferguson, C. J., San Miguel, C., Garza, A., & Jerabeck, J. M. (2012). A longitudinal test of video game violence influences on dating and aggression: A 3-year longitudinal study of adolescents. *Journal of Psychiatric Research, 46,* 141–146.

Feshbach, S. (1964). The function of aggression and the regulation of aggressive drive. *Psychological Bulletin, 71,* 257–272.

Festinger, L. (1954). A theory of social comparison processes. *Human Relations, 7,* 117–140.

Festinger, L. (1957). *A theory of cognitive dissonance.* Stanford University Press.

Festinger, L., & Carlsmith, J. M. (1959). Cognitive consequences of forced compliance. *Journal of Abnormal and Social Psychology, 58,* 203–210.

Festinger, L., Riecken, H. W., & Schachter, S. (1982). When prophecy fails. In A. Pines & C. Maslach (Eds.), *Experiencing social psychology: Readings and projects* (pp. 69–75). Knopf.

Festinger, L., Schachter, S., & Back, K. W. (1959). *Social pressures in informal groups: A study of human factors in housing.* Harper & Row.

Fiebert, M. S., & Wright, K. S. (1989). Midlife friendships in an American faculty sample. *Psychological Reports, 64,* 1127–1130.

Fiedler, F. W. (1967). *A theory of leadership effectiveness.* McGraw Hill.

Figueredo, A. J., Tal, I. R., McNeill, P., & Guillen, A. (2004). Farmers, herders, and fishers: The ecology of revenge. *Evolution and Human Behavior, 25,* 336–353.

Fincham, F. D., Beach, S. R. H., & Davila, J. (2004). Forgiveness and conflict resolution in marriage. *Journal of Family Psychology, 18,* 72–81.

Fincham, F. D., Jackson, H., & Beach, S. R. H. (2005). Transgression severity and forgiveness: Different moderators for objective and subjective severity. *Journal of Social and Clinical Psychology, 24,* 860–875.

Fincham, F. D., Paleari, F. G., & Regalia, C. (2002). Forgiveness in marriage: The role of relationship quality, attributions, and empathy. *Personal Relationships, 9,* 27–37.

Finez, L., Berjot, S., Rosnet, E., Cleveland, C., & Tice, D. M. (2012). Trait self-esteem and claimed self-handicapping motives in sports situations. *Journal of Sports Sciences, 30,* 1757–1765.

Fischer, P., Greitemeir, T., Pollozek, F., & Frey, D. (2006). The unresponsive bystander: Are bystanders more responsive in dangerous emergencies? *European Journal of Social Psychology, 36,* 267–278.

Fischer, P., Krueger, J. I., Greitemeyer, T., Vogrincic, C., Kastenmüller, A., Frey, D., & . . . Kainbacher, M. (2011). The bystander-effect: A meta-analytic review on bystander intervention in dangerous and non-dangerous emergencies. *Psychological Bulletin, 137,* 517–537.

Fishbein, M., & Ajzen, I. (1975). *Belief attitude, intention, and behavior: An introduction to theory and research.* Addison-Wesley.

Fisher, E. (2009). Motivation and leadership in social work management: A review of theories and related studies. *Administration in Social Work, 33,* 347–367.

Fisher, H. (1992). *Anatomy of love.* Norton.

Fisher, J. D., & Nadler, A. (1974). The effect of similarity between donor and recipient on recipient's reactions to aid. *Journal of Experimental Social Psychology, 4,* 230–243.

Fisher, J. D., Nadler, A., & Whitcher-Algana, S. (1982). Recipient reactions to aid. *Psychological Bulletin, 91,* 27–54.

Fischer, P., & Greitemeyer, T. (2013). The positive bystander effect: Passive bystanders increase helping in situations with high expected negative consequences for the helper. *Journal of Social Psychology, 153,* 1–5.

Fiske, S. T. (1982). Schema-triggered affect: Applications to social perception: In M. S. Clark & S. T. Fiske (Eds.), *Affect and cognition: The 17th annual Carnegie Symposium on Cognition* (pp. 55–78). Erlbaum.

Fiske, S. T. (1992). Thinking is for doing: Portraits of social cognition from daguerreotype to laser photo. *Journal of Personality and Social Psychology, 63,* 877–889.

Fiske, S. T. (1993). Social cognition and social perception. In M. R. Rosenzweig & L. W. Porter (Eds.), *Annual review of psychology* (Vol. 44, pp. 155–194). Annual Reviews.

Fiske, S. T. (2012). Warmth and competence: Stereotype content issues for clinicians and researchers. *Canadian Psychology, 53,* 14–20.

Fiske, S. T., Cuddy, A. J. C., Glick, P., & Xu, J. (2002). A model of (often mixed) stereotype content: Competence and warmth respectively follow from perceived status and competition. *Journal of Personality and Social Psychology, 82,* 878–902.

Fiske, S. T., & Neuberg, S. L. (1990). A continuum of impression formation, from category based to individuating processes: Influence of information and motivation attention and interpretation. In M. Zanna (Ed.), *Advances in experimental social psychology* (Vol. 23, pp. 1–74). Academic Press.

Fiske, S. T., & Taylor, S. E. (1984). *Social cognition.* Addison-Wesley.

Fiske, S. T., & Taylor, S. E. (1991). *Social cognition* (2nd ed.). McGraw Hill.

FitzGerald, C., & Hurst, S. (2017). Implicit bias in healthcare professionals: A systematic review. *BMC Medical Ethics, 18,* 1–18.

Fitzgerald, F. S. (1925). *The great Gatsby.* Collier.

Flanagin, A. J., & Metzger, M. J. (2003). The perceived credibility of personal Web page information as influenced by the sex of the source. *Computers in Human Behavior, 19,* 683–701.

Fleming, A. (1986). *Ida Tarbell.* Bantam.

Fleming, J. H., & Darley, J. M. (1990). The purposeful-action sequence and the illusion of control. *Personality and Social Psychology Bulletin, 16,* 346–357.

Fleming, J. H., Darley, J. M., Hilton, J. L., & Kojetin, B. A. (1990). Multiple audience problem: A strategic communication perspective on social perception. *Journal of Personality and Social Psychology, 58,* 593–609.

Flohr, H. (1987). Biological bases of social prejudices. In V. Reynolds, V. Falger, & I. Vine (Eds.), *The sociobiology of ethnocentrism.* University of Georgia Press.

Flynn, F. J. (2005). Having an open mind: The impact of openness to experience on interracial attitudes and impression formation. *Journal of Personality and Social Psychology, 88,* 816–826.

Flynn, F. J., & Wiltermuth, S. S. (2010). Who's with me? False consensus, brokerage, and ethical decision making in organizations. *Academy of Management Journal, 53,* 1074–1089.

Folkman, S., & Lazarus, R. S. (1980). An analysis of coping in a middle-aged community sample. *Journal of Health and Social Behavior, 21,* 219–239.

Ford, T. E., Wentzel, E. R., & Lorion, J. (2001). Effects of exposure to sexist humor on perceptions of normative tolerance of sexism. *European Journal of Social Psychology, 31,* 677–691.

Forehand, R., & Long, N. (1991). Prevention of aggression and other behavior problems in the early adolescent years. In D. J. Pepler & K. H. Rubin (Eds.), *The development and treatment of childhood aggression* (pp. 317–330). Erlbaum.

Forgas, J. P (1998). On being happy and mistaken: Mood effects on the fundamental attribution error. *Journal of Personality and Social Psychology, 75,* 318–331.

Forgas, J. P., Furnham, A., & Frey, D. (1990). Cross-national differences in attributions of wealth and economic success. *The Journal of Social Psychology, 129,* 643–657.

Forgas, J. P., Williams, K. D., & von Hippel, W. (2004). *Social motivation: Conscious and unconscious processes.* Cambridge University Press.

Forsyth, D. (1990). *Group dynamics* (2nd ed.). Brooks/Cole.

Foss, R. D., & Dempsey, C. B. (1979). Blood donation and the foot-in-the-door technique. *Journal of Personality and Social Psychology, 37,* 580–590.

Foubert, J. D., Brosi, M. W., & Bannon, R. (2011). Pornography viewing among fraternity men: Effects on bystander intervention, rape myth acceptance and behavioral intent to commit sexual assault. *Sexual Addiction & Compulsivity, 18,* 212–231.

Frable, D. E. S., Platt, L., & Hoey, S. (1998). Concealable stigmas and positive self-perceptions: Feeling better around similar others. *Journal of Personality and Social Psychology, 74,* 909–922.

Fraley, R. C., & Shaver, P. R. (1998). Airport separations: A naturalistic study of adult attachment dynamics in separating couples. *Journal of Personality and Social Psychology, 75,* 1198–1212.

Franco, Z. E., Blau, K., & Zimbardo, P. G. (2011). Heroism: A conceptual analysis and differentiation between heroic action and altruism. *Review of General Psychology, 15,* 99–113.

Franks, H. M., & Roesch, S. C. (2006). Appraisals and coping in people living with cancer: A meta-analysis. *Psycho-oncology, 15,* 1027–1037.

Freedman, J. L. (1984). Effect of television violence on aggressiveness. *Psychological Bulletin, 96,* 227–246.

Freedman, J. L., Cunningham, J. A., & Krismer, K. (1992). Inferred values and the reverse-incentive effect in induced compliance. *Journal of Personality and Social Psychology, 62,* 357–368.

Freedman, J. L., & Fraser, S. C. (1966). Compliance without pressure: The foot-in-the-door technique. *Journal of Personality and Social Psychology, 4,* 195–202.

Freitas-Murrell, B., & Swift, J. K. (2015). Precicting attitudes toward seeking professional psychological help among Alaska natives. *American Indian & Alaska Native Mental Health Research: The Journal of the National Center, 22,* 21–35.

French, J. R. P., Jr., & Raven, B. H. (1959). The bases of social power. In D. Cartwright (Ed.), *Studies in social power* (pp. 150–167). University of Michigan.

French, J. R. P, Jr., & Raven, B. H. (1968). The bases of social power. In D. Cartwright & A. Zander (Eds.), *Group dynamics: Research and theory* (pp. 259–269). Harper and Row.

French, S. E., & Holland, K. J. (2013). Condom negotiation strategies as a mediator of the relationship between self-efficacy and condom use. *Journal of Sex Research, 50,* 48–59.

Frenda, S. J., Berkowitz, S. R., Loftus, E. F., & Fenn, K. M. (2016). Sleep deprivation and false confessions. *Proceedings of the National Academy of Sciences of the United States of America, 113,* 2047–2050.

Fried, M., Kaplan, K. J., & Klein, K. W. (1975). Juror selection: An analysis of *voir dire*. In R. J. Simon (Ed.), *The jury system in America* (pp. 49–66). Sage.

Friedman, H. S., & Booth-Kewley, S. (1987). The "disease-prone personality": A meta-analytic view of the construct. *American Psychologist, 42,* 539–555.

Friedman, S. B., & Schonberg, S. K. (Eds.). (1996). The short- and long-term consequences of corporal punishment [Supplement]. *Pediatrics, 98*(4, Pt. 2), i–vi.

Fritzsche, B. A., Finkelstein, M. A., & Penner, L. A. (2000). To help or not to help: Capturing individuals' decision policies. *Social Behavior and Personality, 28,* 561–578.

Furnham, A. (1984). Studies of cross-cultural conformity: A brief critical review. *Psychologia: An International Journal of Psychology, 27,* 65–72.

Furnham, A., & Baguma, P. (2004). Cultural differences in the evaluation of male and female body shapes. *International Journal of Eating Disorders, 15,* 81–89.

G

Gabriel, U., Beyeler, G., Däniker, N., Fey, W., Gutweniger, K., Lienhart, M., & Gerber, B. L. (2001). Perceived sexual orientation and helping behaviour: The wrong number technique, a Swiss replication. *Journal of Cross-Cultural Psychology, 32,* 743–749.

Gadow, K. P., & Sprafkin, J. (1987). Effects of viewing high versus low aggression cartoons on emotionally disturbed children. *Journal of Pediatric Psychology, 12,* 413–427.

Gaertner, L., Sedikides, C., & Graetz, K. (1999). In search of self-definition: Motivational primacy of the collective self, or contextual primacy? *Journal of Personality and Social Psychology, 76,* 5–18.

Gaertner, S. L. (1975). The role of racial attitudes in helping behavior. *Journal of Social Psychology, 35,* 95–101.

Gaertner, S. L., & Dovidio, J. F. (1977). The subtlety of White racism, arousal, and helping behavior. *Journal of Personality and Social Psychology, 35,* 691–707.

Gaertner, S. L., & Dovidio, J. F. (1986). The aversive form of racism. In J. F. Dovidio & S. L. Gaertner (Eds.), *Prejudice, discrimination, and racism* (pp. 1–34). Academic Press.

Gaertner, S. L., Dovidio, J. F., & Johnson, G. (1982). Race of victim, nonresponsive bystander, and helping behavior. *Journal of Social Psychology, 117,* 69–77.

Galinsky, A. D., & Kray, L. J. (2004). From thinking about what might have been to sharing what we know: The effects of counterfactual mind-sets on information sharing in groups. *Journal of Experimental Social Psychology, 40,* 606–618.

Gallup. (2017). *Obama job approval ratings most politically polarized by far.* https://news.gallup.com/poll/203006/obama-job-approval-ratings-politically-polarized-far.aspx

Gallup. (2021a). *Presidential approval ratings—Donald Trump.* https://news.gallup.com/poll/203198/presidential-approval-ratings-donald-trump.aspx

Gallup. (2021b). *Presidential approval ratings—Joe Biden.* https://news.gallup.com/poll/329384/presidential-approval-ratings-joe-biden.aspx

Gallup. (2021c). *Ratings of Black-White relations at new low.* https://news.gallup.com/poll/352457/ratings-black-white-relations-new-low.aspx

Gamberini, L., Chittaro, L., Spagnolli, A., & Carlesso, C. (2015). Psychological response to an emergency in virtual reality: Effects of victim ethnicity and emergency type on helping behavior and navigation. *Computers in Human Behavior, 48,* 104–113.

Gamson, W. A., Fireman, B., & Rytina, S. (1982). *Encounters with unjust authority.* Dorsey.

Gangestad, S. W., & Thornhill, R. (1997). Human sexual selection and developmental instability. In J. A. Simpson & D. T. Kenrick (Eds.), *Evolutionary social psychology* (pp. 169–195). Erlbaum.

Gangestad, S. W., & Thornhill R. (1998, May 22). Menstrual cycle variation in women's preferences for the scent of symmetrical men. *Proceedings of the Royal Society of London, 265,* 927.

Garcia, S., Stinson, L., Ickes, W., Bissonette, W., & Briggs, S. R. (1991). Shyness and physical attractiveness in mixed-sex dyads. *Journal of Personality and Social Psychology, 61,* 35–49.

Garcia, S. M., Weaver, K., Moskowitz, G. D., & Darley, J. M. (2002). Crowded minds: The implicit bystander effect. *Journal of Personality and Social Psychology, 83,* 843–853.

Gardner, J., & Oswald, A. (2001). *Does money buy happiness? A longitudinal study using data on windfalls.* https://www2.warwick.ac.uk/fac/soc/economics/staff/ajoswald/marchwindfallsgo.pdf

Gardner, W. L., Gabriel, S., & Lee, A. Y. (1999). "I" value freedom, but "we" value relationships: Self-construal priming mirrors cultural differences in judgment. *Psychological Science, 10,* 321–326.

Gardner, W. L., & Knowles, M. L. (2008). Love makes you real: Favorite television characters are perceived as "real" in a social facilitation paradigm. *Social Cognition, 26,* 156–168.

Garrett, R. K. (2009). Politically motivated reinforcement seeking: Reframing the selective exposure debate. *Journal of Communication, 59,* 676–699.

Gavanski, I., & Wells, G. L. (1989). Counterfactual processing of normal and exceptional events. *Journal of Experimental Social Psychology, 25,* 314–325.

Gawronski, B., Bodenhausen, G. V., & Banse, R. (2005). We are, therefore they aren't: Ingroup construal as a standard of comparison for outgroup judgments. *Journal of Experimental Social Psychology, 41,* 515–526.

Gazzard Kerr, L., Borenstein-Laurie, J., & Human, L. (2020). Are some first dates easier to read than others? The role of target well-being in distinctively accurate first impressions. *Journal of Research in Personality, 88,* 1–8.

Geen, R. G. (1989). Alternative conceptions of social facilitation. In P. B. Paulus (Ed.), *Psychology of group influence* (2nd ed., pp. 15–52). Erlbaum.

Geenen, N. R., Hohelüchter, M., Langholf, V., & Walther, E. (2014). The beneficial effects of prosocial spending on happiness: Work hard, make money, and spend it on others? *Journal of Positive Psychology, 9,* 204–208.

Geffner, R., & Gross, M. M. (1984). Sex role behavior and obedience to authority: A field study. *Sex Roles, 10,* 973–985.

General Social Survey. (1999). http://www.icpsr.umich.edulGSS99/home.htm

General Social Survey. (2021). *Agree or disagree that sometimes necessary to spank child.* https://gssdataexplorer.norc.org/trends/Gender%20&%20Marriage?measure=spanking

Geniole, S. N., Bird, B. M., McVittie, J. S., Purcell, R. B., Archer, J., & Carré, J. M. (2020). Is testosterone linked to human aggression? A meta-analytic examination of the relationship between baseline, dynamic, and manipulated testosterone on human aggression. *Hormones and Behavior, 123.* https://doi.org/10.1016/j.yhbeh.2019.104644

Genschow, O., Westfal, M., Crusius, J., Bartosch, L., Feikes, K. I., Pallasch, N., & Wozniak, M. (2021). Does social psychology persist over half a century? A direct replication of Cialdini et al.'s (1975) classic door-in-the-face technique. *Journal of Personality & Social Psychology, 120,* e1–e7.

Gentile, A., Servidio, R., Caci, B., & Boca, S. (2021). Social stigma and self-esteem as mediators of the relationship between body mass index and internet addiction disorder: An exploratory study. *Current Psychology: A Journal for Diverse Perspectives on Diverse Psychological Issues, 40,* 1262–1270.

Gentile, B., Twenge, J. M., & Campbell, W. K. (2010). Birth cohort differences in self-esteem, 1988–2008: A cross-temporal meta-analysis. *Review of General Psychology, 14,* 261–268.

Gentry, C. S. (1987). Social distance regarding male and female homosexuals. *Journal of Social Psychology, 127,* 199–208.

George Mason University. (2008). *Glittering generalities.* http://www.sourcewatch.org/index.php/Glittering_generalities

Gergen, K. J., Gergen, M., & Barton H. (1973, October). Deviance in the dark. *Psychology Today,* 129–130.

Gerow, J., & Bordens, K. S. (2015). *Psychology: An introduction* (5th ed.). Pearson.

Gershoff, E. T. (2002). Corporal punishment by parents and associated child behaviors and experiences: A meta-analytic and theoretical review. *Psychological Bulletin, 128,* 539–579.

Gershoff, E. T., & Grogan-Kaylor, A. (2016). Spanking and child outcomes: Old controversies and new meta-analyses. *Journal of Family Psychology, 30,* 453–469.

Giancola, P. R. (2003). The moderating effects of dispositional empathy on alcohol-related aggression in men and women. *Journal of Abnormal Psychology, 112,* 275–281.

Giancola, P. R. (2004). Executive functioning and alcohol-related aggression. *Journal of Abnormal Psychology, 113,* 541–555.

Giarndola, F. (2002). Sequential requests and organ donation. *Journal of Social Psychology, 142,* 171–178.

Gibbons, F. X. (1990). Self-attention and behavior: A review and theoretical update. In M. P. Zanna (Ed.), *Advances in experimental social psychology* (Vol. 12, pp. 249–303). Academic Press.

Gigone, D., & Hastie, R. (1993). The common knowledge effect: Information sharing and group judgment. *Journal of Personality and Social Psychology, 65,* 959–974.

Gilbert, D. T. (1989). Thinking lightly about others: Automatic components of the social inference process. In J. Uleman & J. A. Bargh (Eds.), *Unintended thought* (pp. 189–211). Guilford.

Gilbert, D. T. (1991). How mental systems believe. *American Psychologist, 46,* 107–119.

Gilbert, D. T., & Hixon, G. J. (1991). The trouble of thinking: Activation and application of stereotypic beliefs. *Journal of Personality and Social Psychology, 60,* 509–517.

Gilbert, D. T., & Krull, D. S. (1988). Seeing less is knowing more: The benefits of perceptual ignorance. *Journal of Personality and Social Psychology, 54,* 193–202.

Gilbert, D. T., & Malone, P. S. (1995). The correspondence bias. *Psychological Bulletin, 117,* 21–38.

Gilbert, D. T., McNulty, S. F., Guiliano, T. A., & Benson, J. E. (1992). Blurry words and fuzzy deeds: Attribution of obscure behavior. *Journal of Personality and Social Psychology, 62,* 18–25.

Gilbert, G., Clark, M., & Anderson, M. (2012). Do deaf individuals' dating scripts follow the traditional sexual script? *Sexuality & Culture, 16,* 90–99.

Gilbert, S. J. (1981). Another look at the Milgram obedience studies: The role of the graduated series of shocks. *Personality and Social Psychology Bulletin, 7,* 600–695.

Gill, M. J., Swann, W. B., Jr., & Silvera, D. H. (1998). On the genesis of confidence. *Journal of Personality and Social Psychology, 75,* 1101–1114.

Gillespie, C. (2021, January 5). *Why do some people refuse to wear a face mask in public?* https://www.health.com/condition/infectious-diseases/coronavirus/face-mask-refuse-to-wear-one-but-why

Gillis, J., Bernieri, F. J., & Wooten, E. (1995). The effects of stimulus medium and feedback on judgment of rapport. *Organizational Behavior and Human Decision Processes, 63,* 33–45.

Gilovich, T. (1991). *How we know what isn't so: The fallibility of human reason in everyday life.* Free Press.

Gilovich, T., Medvec, V. H., & Savitsky, K. (2000). The spotlight effect in social judgment: An egocentric bias in estimates of the salience of one's own actions and appearance. *Journal of Personality and Social Psychology, 78,* 211–222.

Gilovich, T., Savitsky, K., & Medvec, V. H. (1998). The illusion of transparency: Biased assessments of others' ability to read one's emotional state. *Journal of Personality and Social Psychology, 75,* 332–346.

Girl Scouts of America. (2011). *Real to me: Girls and reality TV.* https://www.girlscouts.org/content/dam/girlscouts-gsusa/forms-and-documents/about-girl-scouts/research/real_to_me_factsheet.pdf

Glaser, R., Rice, J., Sheridan, J., Fertel, R., Stout, J., Speicher, C., & . . . Kiecolt-Glaser, J. (1987). Stress-related immune suppression: Health implications. *Brain, Behavior, and Immunity, 1,* 7–20.

Glassman, R. B., Packel, E. W., & Brown, D. L. (1986). Green-beards and kindred spirits: A preliminary mathematical model of altruism toward nonkin who bear similarities to the giver. *Ethology and Sociobiology, 7,* 107–115.

Glecker, J., & Mendoza, M. (2021, May 26). *Authorities identify 8 victims of California railyard shooting.* https://www.usnews.com/news/us/articles/2021-05-26/official-gunfire-erupts-at-san-jose-railyard-several-hurt

Gleicher, F., & Petty, R. E. (1992). Expectations of reassurance influence the nature of fear-stimulated attitude change. *Journal of Experimental Social Psychology, 28,* 86–100.

Glomb, T. M., & Welch, E. T. (2005). Can opposites attract? Personality heterogeneity in supervisor-subordinate dyads as a predictor of subordinate outcomes. *Journal of Applied Psychology, 90*, 749–757.

Glüer, M., & Lohaus, A. (2016). Participation in social network sites: Associations with the quality of offline and online friendships in German preadolescents and adolescents. *Cyberpsychology, 10*, 21–36.

Goei, R., & Boster, F. J. (2005). The roles of obligation and gratitude in explaining the effects of favors on compliance. *Communication Monographs, 72*, 284–300.

Goldberg, A. E. (2010). *Lesbian and gay parents and their children: Research on the family life cycle.* American Psychological Association.

Goldman, M. (1986). Compliance employing a combined foot-in-the-door and door-in-the-face procedure. *Journal of Social Psychology, 126*, 111–116.

Goldman, M. (1988, January). The fate of Europe's Jews under Nazi rule. *Toledo Jewish News,* 6–14.

Goldman, M., & Creason, C. R. (1981). Inducing compliance by a two-door-in-the-face procedure and a self-determination request. *Journal of Social Psychology, 114*, 229–235.

Goldman, M., Creason, C. R., & McCall, C. G. (1981). Compliance employing a two-feet-in-the-door procedure. *Journal of Social Psychology, 114*, 259–265.

Goldman, M., Seever, M., & Seever, M. (1982). Social labeling and the foot-in-the-door effect. *Journal of Social Psychology, 117*, 19–23.

Goleman, D. (1991). *Psychology updates.* HarperCollins.

Goleman, D. (1993, February 9). Poets know how spurned lovers suffer: Science finds pain on the other side, too. *New York Times,* B1.

Goodwin, K. A., Kukucka, J. P., & Hawks, I. M. (2013). Co-witness confidence, conformity, and eyewitness memory: An examination of normative and informational social influences. *Applied Cognitive Psychology, 27*, 91–100.

Goodwin, R., Costa, P., & Adonu, J. (2004). Social support and its consequences: "Positive" and "deficiency" values and their implications for support and self-esteem. *British Journal of Social Psychology, 43*, 465–474.

Goranson, R. E., & Berkowitz, L. (1966). Reciprocity and responsibility reactions to prior help. *Journal of Personality and Social Psychology, 3*, 227–232.

Gordon, K. C., Baucom, D. H., & Snyder, D. K. (2005). Treating couples recovering from infidelity: An integrative approach. *Journal of Clinical Psychology, 61*, 1393–1405.

Gore, K. Y., Tobiasen, M. A., & Kayson, W. A. (1997). Effects of sex of caller, implied sexual orientation, and urgency on altruistic response using the wrong number technique. *Psychological Reports, 80*, 927–930.

Gorka, S., Fitzgerald, D., King, A., & Phan, K. (2013). Alcohol attenuates amygdala-frontal connectivity during processing social signals in heavy social drinkers. *Psychopharmacology, 229*, 141–154.

Gorman-Smith, D., & Tolan, P. (1998). The role of exposure to community violence and developmental problems among inner-city youth. *Development and Psychopathology, 10*, 101–116.

Görzig, A., & Frumkin, L. A. (2013). Cyberbullying experiences on-the-go: When social media can become distressing. *Cyberpsychology, 7*, 11–22.

Gosling, S. D., Augustine, A. A., & Vazire, S. (2011). Manifestations of personality in online social networks: Self-reported Facebook-related behaviors and observable profile information. *Cyberpsychology, Behavior, and Social Networks, 14*, 483–488.

Gosselin, P. (2005). Le décodage de l'expression faciale des émotions au cours de l'enfance. *Canadian Psychology, 46*, 126–138.

Gottman, J. M. (1995). *Why marriages fail or succeed.* Fireside.

Gottman, J. M., Coan, J., Carrère, S., & Swanson, C. (1998). Predicting marital happiness and stability from newlywed interactions. *Journal of Marriage and the Family, 60*, 5–22.

Gottman, J. M., & Levenson, R. W. (1986). Assessing the role of emotion in marriage. *Behavioral Assessment, 8*, 31–48.

Gottman, J. M., & Levenson, R. W. (2002). A two-factor model for predicting when a couple will divorce: Exploratory analyses using 14-year longitudinal data. *Family Process, 41*, 83–96.

Gough, H. G. (1951). Studies of social intolerance I: Psychological and sociological correlates of anti-Semitism. *Journal of Social Psychology, 33*, 237–246.

Gouldner, A. W. (1960). The norm of reciprocity: A preliminary statement. *American Sociological Review, 25*, 161–178.

Government Social Research. (2019). *Public attitudes to physical punishment of children: Baseline survey, 2018.* https://gov.wales/public-attitudes-physical-punishment-children-baseline-survey-2018

Graham, J. E., Christian, L. M., & Kiecolt-Glaser, J. K. (2006). Stress, age, and immune function: Toward a lifespan approach. *Journal of Behavioral Medicine, 29*, 389–400.

Graham, S., Weiner, B., Giuliano, T., & Williams, E. (1993). An attributional analysis of reactions to Magic Johnson. *Journal of Applied Social Psychology, 23*, 996–1010.

Grant, S., & Mizzi, T. (2014). Body weight bias in hiring decisions: Identifying explanatory mechanisms. *Social Behavior and Personality, 42*, 353–370.

Grant, S. L., Mizzi, T., & Anglim, J. (2016). "Fat, four-eyed and female" 30 years later: A replication of Harris, Harris, and Bochner's (1982) early study of obesity stereotypes. *Australian Journal of Psychology, 68*, 290–300.

Grassini, A., Pascual, A., & Guéguen, N. (2013). The effect of the foot-in-the-door technique on sales in a computer-mediated field setting. *Communication Research Reports, 30*, 63–67.

Greenwald, A. G. (1968). Cognitive learning, cognitive response to persuasion, and attitude change. In A. G. Greenwald, T. C. Brock, & T. M. Ostrom (Eds.), *Psychological foundations of attitudes* (pp. 147–170). Academic Press.

Greenwald, A. G. (1980). The totalitarian ego: Fabrication and revision of personal history. *American Psychologist, 35,* 603–612.

Greenwald, A. G., & Banaji, M. R. (1989). The self as a memory system: Powerful but ordinary. *Journal of Personality and Social Psychology, 57,* 41–54.

Greenwald, A. G., & Banaji, M. R. (1995). Implicit social cognition: Attitudes, self-esteem, and stereotypes. *Psychological Review, 102,* 4–27.

Greenwald, A. G., Poehlman, T. A., Uhlmann, E. L., & Banaji, M. R. (2009). Understanding and using the Implicit Association Test: III. Meta-analysis of predictive validity. *Journal of Personality and Social Psychology, 97,* 17–41.

Greenwald, A. G., & Pratkanis, A. R. (1984). The self. In R. S. Wyer & T. K. Srull (Eds.), *Handbook of social cognition* (pp. 129–178). Erlbaum.

Greenwald, A. G., McGhee, D. E., & Schwartz, J-L. K. (1998). Measuring individual differences in implicit cognition: The implicit association test. *Journal of Personality and Social Psychology, 74,* 1464–1480.

Greenwood, D., & Isbell, L. M. (2002). Ambivalent sexism and the dumb blonde: Men's and women's reactions to sexist jokes. *Psychology of Women Quarterly, 26,* 341–350.

Greitemeyer, T., & Schulz–Hardt, S. (2003). Preference–consistent evaluation information in hidden profile paradigm beyond group–level explanations for dominance of shared information in group decisions. *Journal of Personality and Social Psychology, 84,* 322–339.

Grieve, P. G., & Hogg, M. A. (1999). Subjective uncertainty and intergroup discrimination in the minimal group situation. *Personality and Social Psychology Bulletin, 25,* 926–940.

Grossman, P. J., Komai, M., & Jensen, J. E. (2015). Leadership and gender in groups: An experiment. *Canadian Journal of Economics, 48,* 368–388.

Groth, A. N. (1979). *Men who rape: The psychology of the offender.* Plenum.

Gruder, C. L., Cook, T. D., Hennigan, K. M., Flay, B. R., Alessis, C., & Halamaji, J. (1979). Empirical tests of the absolute sleeper effect predicted from the discounting cue hypothesis. *Journal of Personality and Social Psychology, 36,* 1061–1074.

Gruder, C. L., Romer, D., & Korth, B. (1978). Dependency and fault as determinants of helping. *Journal of Experimental Social Psychology, 14,* 227–235.

Grysman, A., & Hudson, J. A. (2011). The self in autobiographical memory: Effects of self-salience on narrative content and structure. *Memory, 19,* 501–513.

Guadagno, R. E., Rhoads, K. L., & Sagarin, B. J. (2011). Figural vividness and persuasion: Capturing the "elusive" vividness effect. *Personality and Social Psychology Bulletin, 37,* 626–638.

Gubi-Kelm, S., Grolig, T., Strobel, B., Ohlig, S., & Schmidt, A. F. (2020). When do false accusations lead to false confessions? Preliminary evidence for a potentially overlooked alternative explanation. *Journal of Forensic Psychology Research and Practice, 20,* 114–133.

Guéguen, N. (2003). Fund raising on the web: The effect of an electronic door-in-the-face technique on compliance to a request. *CyberPsychology and Behavior, 6,* 189–192.

Guéguen, N. (2015). Women's hairstyle and men's behavior: A field experiment. *Scandinavian Journal of Psychology, 56,* 637–640.

Guéguen, N., & Jacob, C. (2001). Fund raising on the web: The effect of an electronic foot-in-the-door on donation. *CyberPsychology and Behavior, 4,* 705–709.

Guéguen, N., Joule, R-V., Courbet, D., Halimi-Falkowicz, S., & Marchand, M. (2013). Repeating "yes" in a first request and compliance with a later request: The four walls technique. *Social Behavior & Personality, 41,* 199–202.

Guéguen, N., & Lamy, L. (2013a). Weather and helping: Additional evidence of the effect of the sunshine samaritan. *Journal of Social Psychology, 153,* 123–126.

Guéguen, N., & Stefan, J. (2013b). Hitchhiking and the "Sunshine Driver": Further effects of weather conditions on helping behavior. *Psychological Reports, 113,* 994–1000.

Guion Peoples, D. T. (2017). Nothing compares to you: Prince and the theory of optimal distinctiveness. *Journal of African American Studies, 21,* 443–460.

Gunderson, P. R., & Ferrari, J. R. (2008). Forgiveness of sexual cheating in romantic relationships: Effects of discovery method, frequency of offense, and presence of apology. *North American Journal of Psychology, 10,* 1–14.

Günsoy, C., Cross, S. E., Sarıbay, A., Olcaysoy Ökten, I., & Kurutaş, M. (2015). Would you post that picture and let your dad see it? Culture, honor, and Facebook. *European Journal of Social Psychology, 45,* 323–335.

Gupta, N., & Hollingshead, A. B. (2010). Differentiated versus integrated transactive memory effectiveness: It depends on the task. *Group Dynamics: Theory, Research, and Practice, 14,* 384–398.

Gupta, S., & Bonanno, G. A. (2010). Trait self-enhancement as a buffer against potentially traumatic events: A prospective study. *Psychological Trauma: Theory, Research, Practice, and Policy, 2,* 83–92.

Gustafson, R. (1999). Male alcohol-related aggression as a function of type of drink. *Aggressive Behavior, 25,* 401–408.

H

Haddock, G., Maio, G. R., Arnold, K., & Huskinson, T. (2008). Should persuasion be affective or cognitive? The moderating effects of need for affect and need for cognition. *Personality and Social Psychology Bulletin, 34,* 769–778.

Häfner, M., & IJzerman, H. (2011). The face of love: Spontaneous accommodation as social emotion regulation. *Personality and Social Psychology Bulletin, 37,* 1551–1563.

Haischer, M. H., Beilfuss, R., Hart, M. R., Opielinski, L., Wrucke, D., Zirgaitis, G., & . . . Hunter, S. K. (2020). Who is wearing a mask? Gender-, age-, and location-related differences during the COVID-19 pandemic. *PloS ONE, 15,* e0240785.

Halabi, S., Nadler, A., & Dovidio, J. F. (2011). Reactions to receiving assumptive help: The moderating effects of group membership and perceived need for help. *Journal of Applied Social Psychology, 41,* 2793–2815.

Hale, W. W., III, Van Der Valk, I., Engels, R., & Meeus, W. (2005). Does perceived parental rejection make adolescents sad and mad? The association of perceived parental rejection with adolescent depression and aggression. *Journal of Adolescent Health, 36,* 466–474.

Hall, J. A., Pennington, N., & Lueders, A. (2014). Impression management and formation on Facebook: A lens model approach. *New Media & Society, 16,* 958–982.

Hall, V., Eastwood, J., & Clow, K. A. (2020). An exploration of laypeople's perceptions of confession evidence and interrogation tactics. *Canadian Journal of Behavioural Science/Revue Canadienne Des Sciences Du Comportement, 52,* 299–313.

Halpern, D. F., Straight, C. A., & Stephenson, C. L. (2011). Beliefs about cognitive gender differences: Accurate for direction, underestimated for size. *Sex Roles, 64,* 336–347.

Hamamura, T., & Septarini, B. G. (2017). Culture and self-esteem over time: A cross-temporal meta-analysis among Australians, 1978–2014. *Social Psychological and Personality Science, 8,* 904–909.

Hamilton, D. L., & Sherman, S. J. (1989). Illusory correlations: Implications for stereotype theory. In D. Bar-Tal, C. F. Graumann, A. W. Kruglanski, & W. Stroebe (Eds.), *Stereotypes and prejudice* (pp. 59–82). Springer-Verlag.

Hannagan, R. J., & Larimer, C. W. (2010). Does gender composition affect group decision outcomes? Evidence from a laboratory experiment. *Political Behavior, 32,* 51–67.

Hansen, C. H., & Hansen, R. D. (1988). Finding the face in the crowd: An anger superiority effect. *Journal of Personality and Social Psychology, 54,* 917–924.

Hansson, S. O. (2017). *Science and pseudo-science.* https://plato.stanford.edu/archives/sum2017/entries/pseudo-science/

Har, J., & Dazio, S. (2021, May 28). *Sheriff: Rail yard shooter stockpiled guns, ammo at his home.* https://abcnews.go.com/US/wireStory/horror-heroism-mark-deadly-shooting-california-rail-yard-77956892

Harari, H., Harari, O., & White, R. V. (1985). The reaction to rape by American male bystanders. *Journal of Social Psychology, 125,* 653–668.

Harber, K. (2005). Self-esteem and affect as information. *Personality and Social Psychology Bulletin, 31,* 276–288.

Haridakis, P. M. (2002). Viewer characteristics, exposure to television violence, and aggression. *Media Psychology, 4,* 323–352.

Harkins, S. G., & Petty, R. E. (1982). Effects of task difficulty and task uniqueness on social loafing. *Journal of Personality and Social Psychology, 43,* 1214–1229.

Harkins, S. G., & Szymanski, K. (1987). Social loafing and social facilitation: New wine in old bottles. In C. Hendrick (Ed.), *Review of personality and social psychology* (Vol. 9, pp. 167–188). Sage.

Harmon-Jones, E. (2000). An update on cognitive dissonance theory, with a focus on the self. In A. Tesser, R. B. Felson, & J. M. Suls (Eds.), *Psychological perspectives on self and identity* (pp. 119–144). American Psychological Association.

Harmon-Jones, E., & Harmon-Jones, C. (2002). Testing the action-based model of cognitive dissonance: The effect of action orientation on postdecisional attitudes. *Personality and Social Psychology Bulletin, 28,* 711–723.

Harmon-Jones, E., Peterson, H., & Vaughn, K. (2003). The dissonance-inducing effects of inconsistency between experienced empathy and knowledge of past failures to help: Support for the action-based model of dissonance. *Basic and Applied Social Psychology, 25,* 69–78.

Harris, C. R., & Christenfeld, N. (1996). Gender, jealousy, and reason. *Psychological Science, 7,* 364–366.

Harris, M. B. (1990). Is love seen as different for the obese? *Journal of Applied Social Psychology, 20,* 1209–1224.

Harris, P. R., & Napper, L. (2005). Self-affirmation and the biased processing of threatening health-risk information. *Personality and Social Psychology Bulletin, 39,* 1250–1263.

Hart, J. W., Stasson, M. F., & Karau, S. J. (1999). The effects of source strength and physical distance on minority influence. *Group Dynamics: Theory, Research and Practice, 3,* 81–92.

Harvard University. (2021). *Loneliness in America: How the pandemic has deepened an epidemic of loneliness and what we can do about it.* https://static1.squarespace.com/static/5b7c56e255b02c683659fe43/t/6021776bdd04957c4557c212/1612805995893/Loneliness+in+America+2021_02_08_FINAL.pdf

Harvey, C. B., Ollila, L., Baxter, K., & Guo, S. Z. (1997). Gender-related and grade-related differences in writing topics in Chinese and Canadian children. *Journal of Research and Development in Education. 31,* 1–6.

Harvey, J. H., & Weary, G. (1981). *Perspectives on attributional processes.* W. C. Brown.

Haslam, S. A., Oakes, P. J., Reynolds, K. I., & Turner, J. C. (1999). Social identity salience and the emergence of stereotype consensus. *Personality and Social Psychology Bulletin, 25,* 809–818.

Hass, R. G., Katz, I., Rizzo, N., Bailey, J., & Eisenstadt, D. (1991). Cross-racial appraisals as related to attitude ambivalence and cognitive complexity. *Personality and Social Psychology Bulletin, 17,* 83–92.

Hastie, R., & Kameda, T. (2005). The robust beauty of majority rules in group decisions. *Psychological Review, 112,* 494–508.

Hastie, R., Penrod, S., & Pennington, N. (1983). *Inside the jury.* Harvard University Press.

Hatala, M. N., & Prehodka, J. (1996). Content analysis of gay male and lesbian personal advertisements. *Psychological Reports, 78,* 371–374.

Hatcher, J. W., Cares, S., Detrie, R., Dillenbeck, T., Goral, E., Troisi, K., & Whirry-Achten, A. M. (2018). Conformity, arousal, and the effect of arbitrary information. *Group Processes & Intergroup Relations, 21,* 631–645.

Hatfield, E., & Walster, G. W. (1981). *A new look at love.* Addison-Wesley.

Hatfield, E., Traupmann, J., Sprecher, S., Utne, M., & Hay, J. (1985). Equity and intimate relationships: Recent research. In W. Ickes (Ed.), *Compatible and incompatible relationships* (pp. 91–117). Springer-Verlag.

Hatfield, E. H., Walster, G. W., & Berscheid, E. (1978). *Equity theory and research.* Allyn & Bacon.

Hatfield, E. H., Walster, G. W., & Traupmann, J. (1978). Equity and premarital sex. *Journal of Personality and Social Psychology, 36,* 82–92.

Haugen, T., Pels, F., Gysland, T. S., Hartvigsen, F. K., & Høigaard, R. (2020). Racing with superior and inferior team-members: An experimental test of effort changes in a cycling team sprint. *International Journal of Sport and Exercise Psychology.* Advance online publication. https://doi.org/10.1080/1612197X.2020.1827001

Haugtvedt, C. P., & Petty, R. E. (1992). Personality and persuasion: Need for cognition moderates the persistence and resistance of attitude change. *Journal of Personality and Social Psychology, 63,* 308–319.

Haugtvedt, C. P., & Wegener, D. T. (1993, May 1). Need for cognition and message order effects in persuasion. Paper presented at the sixty-fifth annual meeting of the Midwestern Psychological Association, Chicago.

Haugtvedt, C. P., Petty, R. E., & Cacioppo, J. T. (1992). Need for cognition and advertising: Understanding the role of personality in consumer behavior. *Journal of Consumer Psychology 1,* 239–260.

Hausenblas, H. A., Carron, A. V., & Mack, D. E. (1997). Application of the theories of reasoned action and planned behavior to exercise behavior: A meta-analysis. *Journal of Sport & Exercise Psychology, 19,* 36–51.

Hawkley, L. C., Burleson, M. H., Berntson, G. G., & Cacioppo, J. T. (2003). Loneliness in everyday life: Cardiovascular activity, psychosocial context, and health behaviors. *Journal of Personality and Social Psychology, 85,* 105–120.

Hayes, T. C., & Lee, M. R. (2005). The southern culture of honor and violent attitudes. *Sociological Spectrum, 25,* 593–617.

Hays, R. B. (1985). A longitudinal study of friendship development. *Journal of Personality and Social Psychology 48,* 261–273.

Hays, R. B. (1988). The day-to-day functioning of casual versus close friendships. *Journal of Social and Personal Relationships, 5,* 261–273.

Hayward, W. G., Crookes, K., & Rhodes, G. (2013). The other-race effect: Holistic coding differences and beyond. *Visual Cognition, 21,* 1224–1247.

Heaton, A. W., & Sigall, H. (1991). Self-consciousness, self-presentation, and performance: Who chokes, and when? *Journal of Applied Social Psychology, 21,* 175–188.

Hebb, D. O., & Thompson, W. R. (1968). The social significance of animal studies. In G. Lindzey & E. Aronson (Eds.), *The handbook of social psychology* (2nd ed., Vol. 2, pp. 729–774). Addison-Wesley.

Hebl, M. R., & Turchin, J. M. (2005). The stigma of obesity: What about men? *Basic and Applied Social Psychology, 27,* 267–275.

Hebl, M. R., & Xu, J. (2001). Weighing the care: Physicians' reaction to the size of a patient. *International Journal of Obesity, 25,* 1246–1252.

Hehman, E., Graber, E. C., Hoffman, L. H., & Gaertner, S. L. (2012). Warmth and competence: A content analysis of photographs depicting American presidents. *Psychology of Popular Media Culture, 1,* 46–52.

Heider, F. (1944). Social perception and phenomenal causality. *Psychological Review, 51,* 258–374.

Heider, F. (1958). *The psychology of interpersonal relations.* Wiley.

Heine, S. J., & Lehman, D. R. (1999). Culture, self-discrepancies, and self-satisfaction. *Personality and Social Psychology Bulletin, 25,* 915–925.

Hendren, A., & Blank, H. (2009). Prejudiced behavior toward lesbians and gay men: A field experiment on everyday helping. *Social Psychology, 40,* 234–238.

Hendrick, C. (1988). Roles and gender in relationships. In S. Duck (Ed.), *Handbook of personal relationships* (pp. 429–448). Wiley.

Hendrick, S. S., & Hendrick, C. (1987). Love and sex attitudes: A close relationship. *Journal of Social and Clinical Psychology, 5,* 391–398.

Henningsen, D. D., & Henningsen, M. L. M. (2003). Examining social influence in information-sharing contexts. *Small Group Research, 34,* 391–412.

Henningsen, D. D., & Miller, M. L. (2004). The effect of individual variables on information sharing in decision groups. *Human Communication Research, 30,* 540–555.

Herbert, T. B., & Cohen, S. (1993). Depression and immunity: A meta-analytic review. *Psychological Bulletin, 113,* 472–486.

Herbozo, S., Tantleff-Dunn, S., Gokee-Larose, J., & Thompson, J. K. (2004). Beauty and thinness messages in children's media: A content analysis. *Eating Disorders, 12,* 21–34.

Herbst-Damm, K. L., & Kulik, J. A. (2005). Volunteer support, marital status, and the survival times of terminally ill patients. *Health Psychology, 24,* 225–229.

Hershfield, H., & Brody, I. (2021, January). How Elvis got Americans to accept the polio vaccine. *Scientific American.* https://www.scientificamerican.com/article/how-elvis-got-americans-to-accept-the-polio-vaccine/

Hertel, G., Kerr, N. L., & Messe, L. A. (2000). Motivation gains in performance groups: Paradigmatic and theoretical developments in the Kohler effect. *Journal of Personality and Social Psychology, 79,* 580–601.

Hess R. D., & Torney, J. V. (1967). *The development of political attitudes in children.* Aldine.

Heu, L. C., van Zomeren, M., & Hansen, N. (2020). Far away from home and (not) lonely: Relational mobility in migrants' heritage culture as a potential protection from loneliness. *International Journal of Intercultural Relations, 77,* 140–150.

Hewstone, M., Hantzi, A., & Johnston, L. (1991). Social categorization and person memory: The pervasiveness of race as an organizing principle. *European Journal of Social Psychology, 21,* 517–528.

Hicks, J. A., & King, L. A. (2011). Subliminal mere exposure and explicit and implicit positive affective responses. *Cognition and Emotion, 25,* 726–729.

Higgins, E. T. (1989). Self-discrepancy theory: What patterns of self-beliefs cause people to suffer? In L. Berkowitz (Ed.), *Advances in experimental social psychology* (Vol. 22, pp. 93–136). Academic Press.

Higgins, E. T. (1998). Promotion and prevention: Regulatory focus as a motivational principle. In M. P. Zanna (Ed.), *Advances in experimental social psychology* (Vol. 30, pp. 1–46). Academic Press.

Higgins, E. T., Shah, J., & Friedman, R. (1997). Emotional responses to goal attainment: Strengths of regulatory focus as a moderator. *Journal of Personality and Social Psychology, 72,* 515–525.

Higgins, E. T., & Stangor, C. (1988). Context-driven social judgment and memory when "behavior engulfs the field" in reconstructive memory. In D. Bar-Tal & A.W. Kruglanski (Eds.), *The social psychology of knowledge* (pp. 262–298). Cambridge University Press.

Higgins, E. T., & Tykocinsky, O. (1992). Self-discrepancies and biographical memory: Personality and cognition at the level of psychological situation. *Personality and Social Psychological Bulletin, 18,* 527–535.

Hill, C. A. (1987). Affiliation motivation: People who need people. . . but in different ways. *Journal of Personality and Social Psychology, 52,* 1008–1018.

Hill, C. T., Rubin, Z., & Peplau, L. A. (1976). Breakups before marriage: The end of 103 affairs. *Journal of Social Issues, 32,* 147–168.

Hill, D. B. (2007). Differences and similarities in men's and women's sexual self-schemas. *Journal of Sex Research, 44,* 135–144.

Hill, G., & Howell, R. T. (2014). Moderators and mediators of pro-social spending and well-being: The influence of values and psychological need satisfaction. *Personality and Individual Differences, 69,* 69–74.

Hines, D. A., & Saudino, K. J. (2004). Genetic and environmental influences on intimate partner aggression: A preliminary study. *Violence and Victims, 19,* 701–718.

Hirsch, C., Meynen, T., & Clark, D. M. (2004). Negative self-imagery in social anxiety contaminates social interactions. *Memory, 12,* 496–506.

Hirt, E. R., McCrea, S. M., & Boris, H. I. (2003). "I know you self-handicapped last exam": Gender differences in reactions to self-handicapping. *Journal of Personality and Social Psychology, 84,* 177–193.

Hixon, J. G., & Swann, W. B., Jr. (1993). When does introspection bear fruit? Self-reflection, self-insight, and interpersonal choice. *Journal of Personality and Social Psychology, 64,* 35–43.

Hoaken, P. N. S., Assaad, J., & Pihl, R. O. (1998). Cognitive functioning and the inhibition of alcohol-induced aggression. *Journal of Studies on Alcohol, 59,* 599–607.

Hoaken, P. N. S., Giancola, P. R., & Pihl, R. O. (1998). Executive cognitive functions as mediators of alcohol-related aggression. *Alcohol and Alcoholism, 33,* 47–54.

Hobman, E. V., Bordia, P., & Gallois, C. (2004). Perceived dissimilarity and work group involvement: The moderating effects of group openness to diversity. *Group & Organization Management, 29,* 560–587.

Hodson, G., Hogg, S. M., & MacInnis, C. C. (2009). The role of "dark personalities" (narcissism, Machiavellianism, psychopathy), Big Five personality factors, and ideology in explaining prejudice. *Journal of Research in Personality, 43,* 686–690.

Hoeksema-van Orden, C. Y. D., Gaillard, A. W. K., & Buunk, B. (1998). Social loafing under fatigue. *Journal of Personality and Social Psychology, 75,* 1179–1190.

Hoffman, M. L. (1981). Is altruism part of human nature? *Journal of Personality and Social Psychology, 40,* 121–137.

Hogan, D. E., & Mallott, M. (2005). Changing racial prejudice through diversity education. *Journal of College Student Development, 46,* 115–125.

Hogben, M. (1998). Factors moderating the effect of televised aggression on viewer behavior. *Communication Research, 25,* 220–247.

Hogg, M. A., & Abrams, D. (1990). Social motivation, self-esteem, and social identity. In D. Abrams & M. A. Hogg (Eds.), *Social identity theory: Constructive and critical advances* (pp. 28–47). Springer-Verlag.

Hogg, M. A., & Mullin, B. A. (1999). Joining groups to reduce uncertainty: Subjective uncertainty reduction and group identification. In D. Abrams & M. A. Hogg (Eds.), *Social identity and social cognition* (pp. 249–279). Blackwell.

Hollander, E. P. (1985). Leadership and power. In C. Lindzey & E. Aronson (Eds.), *Handbook of social psychology* (Vol. 2, pp. 485–537). Random House.

Hollingshead, A. B. (1996). The rank-order effect in group decision making. *Organizational Behavior & Human Decision Processes, 68,* 181–193.

Hollingshead, A. B. (1998). Retrieval processes in transactive memory systems. *Journal of Personality and Social Psychology, 74,* 659–671.

Hollyfield, A., Martichoux, A., Noyes, D., Sierra, S., del Castillo, A., & Barnard, C. (2021). Surveillance video shows VTA gunman walking between buildings during mass shooting. https://abc7news.com/san-jose-shooting-vta-bay-area-victims/10702158/

Holmes, M. R., Yoon, S., Voith, L. A., Kobulsky, J. M., & Steigerwald, S. (2015). Resilience in physically abused children: Protective factors for aggression. *Behavioral Sciences (2076–328X), 5,* 176–189.

Holmes, T. H., & Rahe, R. H. (1967). The social readjustment rating scale. *Journal of Psychosomatic Research, 11,* 213–218.

Homant, R. J., & Kennedy, D. B. (2012). Does no good deed go unpunished? The victimology of altruism. In B. Oakley, A. Knafo, G. Madhavan, & D. S. Wilson (Eds.), *Pathological altruism* (pp. 193–206). Oxford University Press.

Hong, S., & Kim, S. H. (2016). Political polarization on Twitter: Implications for the use of social media in digital governments. *Government Information Quarterly, 33,* 777–782.

Hopkins, P. D. (2021). Viral heroism: What the rhetoric of heroes in the COVID-19 pandemic tells us about medicine and professional identity. *HEC Forum: An Interdisciplinary Journal on Hospitals' Ethical and Legal Issues, 33,* 109–124.

Hornik, J. (1988). Cognitive thoughts mediating compliance in multiple request situations. *Journal of Economic Psychology, 9,* 69–79.

Horowitz, I. A., & Bordens, K. S. (1990). An experimental investigation of procedural issues in toxic tort trials. *Law and Human Behavior, 14,* 269–286.

Horowitz, I. A., ForsterLee, L., & Brolly, L. (1996). The effects of trial complexity on decision making. *Journal of Applied Psychology, 81,* 757–768.

Horry, R., Palmer, M. A., Sexton, M. L., & Brewer, N. (2012). Memory conformity for confidently recognized items: The power of social influence on memory reports. *Journal of Experimental Social Psychology, 48,* 783–786.

Hortensius, R., & de Gelder, B. (2014). The neural basis of the bystander effect—The influence of group size on neural activity when witnessing an emergency. *Neuroimage, 93*(Pt.1), 53–58.

Horwitz, M., & Rabbie, J. M. (1989). Stereotype of groups, group members, and individuals in categories: A differential analysis. In D. Bar-Tal., C. E Graumann, A.W. Kruglanski, & W. Stoebe (Eds.), *Stereotyping and prejudice* (pp. 105–129). Springer-Verlag.

Hoshino-Browne, E., Zanna, A. S., Spencer, S. J., Zanna, M. P., Kitayama, S., & Lackenbauer, S. (2005). On the cultural guises of cognitive dissonance: The case of easterners and westerners. *Journal of Personality and Social Psychology, 89,* 294–310.

Hostetter, A. B., & Potthoff, A. L. (2012). Effects of personality and social situation on representational gesture production. *Gesture, 12,* 62–83.

Houston, K. A., Clifford, B. R., Phillips, L. H., & Memon, A. (2013). The emotional eyewitness: The effects of emotion on specific aspects of eyewitness recall and recognition performance. *Emotion, 13,* 118–128.

Houston, K. A., Hope, L., Memon, A., & Don Read, J. (2013). Expert testimony on eyewitness evidence: In search of common sense. *Behavioral Sciences & the Law, 31,* 637–651.

Hovland, C. I., Janis, I. L., & Kelley, H. H. (1953). *Persuasion and communication.* Yale University Press.

Howard, D. J. (1997). Familiar phrases as peripheral persuasion cues. *Journal of Experimental Social Psychology, 33,* 241–243.

Hoxter, A. L., & Lester, D. (1994). Gender differences in prejudice. *Perceptual and Motor Skills, 79,* 1666.

Huang, L., & Harris, M. (1973). Conformity in Chinese and Americans: A field experiment. *Journal of Cross-Cultural Psychology, 4,* 427–434.

Huesmann, L. R. (1986). Psychological processes promoting the relationship between exposure to media violence and aggressive behavior by the viewer. *Journal of Social Issues, 42,* 125–139.

Huesmann, L. R. (1988). An information processing model for the development of aggression. *Aggressive Behavior, 14,* 13–24.

Huesmann, L. R., & Eron, L. D. (1984). Cognitive processes and the persistence of aggressive behavior. *Aggressive Behavior, 10,* 243–251.

Huesmann, L. R., Eron, L. D., Lefkowitz, M. M., & Walder, L. O. (1984). Stability of aggression over time and generations. *Developmental Psychology, 20,* 1120–1134.

Huesmann, L. R., Lagerspetz, K., & Eron, L. D. (1984). Intervening variables in the TV violence-aggression relation: Evidence from two countries. *Developmental Psychology, 20,* 746–775.

Huesmann, L. R., & Malamuth, N. M. (1986). Media violence and antisocial behavior: An overview. *Journal of Social Issues, 42,* 1–6.

Huesmann, L. R., Moise-Titus, J., Podolski, C.-L., & Eron, L. D. (2003). Longitudinal relations between children's exposure to TV violence and their aggressive and violent behavior in young adulthood: 1977–1992. *Developmental Psychology, 39,* 201–221.

Hugenberg, K., Blusiewicz, R. L., & Sacco, D. F. (2010). On malleable and immalleable subtypes: Stereotype malleability in one subtype does not spill over to other prominent subtypes. *Social Psychology, 41,* 124–130.

Human, L. J., & Biesanz, J. C. (2011). Through the looking glass clearly: Accuracy and assumed similarity in well-adjusted individuals' first impressions. *Journal of Personality and Social Psychology, 100,* 349–364.

Huneke, D. K. (1986). The lessons of Herman Graebe's life: The origins of a moral person. *Humboldt Journal of Social Relations, 13,* 320–332.

Huppert, J. D., Foa, E. B., Furr, J. M., Filip, J. C., & Matthews, A. (2003). Interpretation bias in social anxiety: A dimensional perspective. *Cognitive Therapy and Research, 27,* 569–577.

Huston, T. L., & Vangelisti, A. L. (1991). Socioemotional behavior and satisfaction in marital relationships: A longitudinal study. *Journal of Personality and Social Psychology, 61,* 721–733.

Hyde, J. S. (1984). How large are gender differences in aggression? A developmental meta-analysis. *Developmental Psychology, 20,* 722–736.

Hymowitz, C., & Weismann, M. (1984). *A history of women in America.* Bantam.

I

Ike, B. W. (1987). Man's limited sympathy as a consequence of his evolution in small kin groups. In V. Reynolds, V. Falger, & I. Vine (Eds.), *The sociobiology of ethnocentrism* (pp. 216–234). University of Georgia Press.

Ilmarinen, V., Lönnqvist, J., & Paunonen, S. (2016). Similarity-attraction effects in friendship formation: Honest platoon-mates prefer each other but dishonest do not. *Personality & Individual Differences, 92,* 153–158.

Imhoff, R., & Erb, H. (2009). What motivates nonconformity? Uniqueness seeking blocks majority influence. *Personality and Social Psychology Bulletin, 35,* 309–320.

Inbar, Y., & Lammers, J. (2012). Political diversity in social and personality psychology. *Perspectives on Psychological Science, 7,* 496–503.

Innocence Project. (2020). *How eyewitness misidentification can send innocent people to prison.* https://innocenceproject.org/how-eyewitness-misidentification-can-send-innocent-people-to-prison/+

Insel, P. M., & Roth, W. T. (1985). *Core concepts in health* (4th ed.). Mayfield.

Insel, P. M., & Roth, W. T. (1994). *Core concepts in health* (7th ed.). Mayfield.

Ionnidis, J. P. A. (2005). Why most published research findings are false. *PLoS Medicine, 2,* 696–701.

Irwin, C. J. (1987). A study in the evolution of ethnocentrism. In V. Reynolds, V. Falger, & I. Vine (Eds.), *The sociobiology of ethnocentrism* (pp. 131–156). University of Georgia Press.

Isaacowitz, D. M. (2005). The gaze of the optimist. *Personality and Social Psychology Bulletin, 31,* 407–415.

Isen, A. M. (1987). Positive affect, cognitive processes and social behavior. In L. Berkowitz (Ed.), *Advances in social psychology* (Vol. 20, pp. 203–253). Academic Press.

Isen, A. M., & Simmonds, S. F. (1978). The effect of feeling good on helping: Cookies and kindness. *Social Psychology, 41,* 346–349.

Isenberg, D. J. (1986). Group polarization: A critical review and meta-analysis. *Journal of Personality and Social Psychology, 50,* 1141–1151.

J

Jackiw, L. B., Arbuthnott, K. D., Pfeifer, J. E., Marcon, J. L., & Meissner, C. A. (2008). Examining the cross-race effect in lineup identification using Caucasian and First Nations samples. *Canadian Journal of Behavioural Science/Revue Canadienne Des Sciences Du Comportement, 40,* 52–57.

Jackson, T., Fritch, A., Nagasaka, T., & Gunderson, J. (2002). Toward explaining the relationship between shyness and loneliness: A path analysis with American college students. *Social Behavior and Personality, 30,* 263–270.

James, L., Vila, B., & Daratha, K. (2013). Results from experimental trials testing participant responses to White, Hispanic and Black suspects in high-fidelity deadly force judgment and decision-making simulations. *Journal of Experimental Criminology, 9,* 189–212.

James, W. (1890). *The principles of psychology.* Dover.

Janis, I. L. (1972). *Victims of groupthink.* Houghton Mifflin.

Janis, I. L. (1982). *Groupthink* (2nd ed.). Houghton Mifflin.

Janssens, J. M., & Dekovic, M. (1997). Child rearing, prosocial moral reasoning, and prosocial behaviour. *International Journal of Behavioral Development, 20,* 509–527.

Jarcho, J. M., Berkman, E. T., & Lieberman, M. D. (2011). The neural basis of rationalization: Cognitive dissonance reduction during decision-making. *Social Cognitive & Affective Neuroscience, 6,* 460–467.

Jattuso, M. L., & Sinar, E. F. (2003). Source effects in Internet-based screening procedures. *International Journal of Selection and Assessment, 11,* 137–140.

Jenkins, M. J., & Dambrot, F. H. (1987). The attribution of date rape: Observer's attitudes and sexual experiences and the dating situation. *Journal of Applied Social Psychology, 17,* 875–895.

Jiang, T., Chen, Z., & Sedikides, C. (2020). Self-concept clarity lays the foundation for self-continuity: The restorative function of autobiographical memory. *Journal of Personality and Social Psychology, 119,* 945–959.

Joanisse, M., Gagnon, S., & Voloaca, M. (2013). The impact of stereotype threat on the simulated driving performance of older drivers. *Accident Analysis and Prevention, 50,* 530–538.

Johnson, B. T., & Eagly, A. H. (1989). Effects of involvement on persuasion: A meta-analysis. *Psychological Bulletin, 106,* 290–314.

Johnson, J. D., & Lecci, L. (2003). Assessing anti-White attitudes and predicting perceived racism: The Johnson-Lecci scale. *Personality and Social Psychology Bulletin, 29,* 299–312.

Johnson, R. N. (1972). *Aggression in man and animals.* Saunders.

Johnson, T. E., & Rule, B. G. (1986). Mitigating circumstances, information, censure, and aggression. *Journal of Personality and Social Psychology, 50,* 537–542.

Jones, C., & Aronson, E. (1973). Attribution of fault of a rape victim as a function of respectability of the victim. *Journal of Personality and Social Psychology, 26,* 415–419.

Jones, D. A., Shultz, J. W., & Chapman, D. S. (2006). Recruiting through job advertisements: The effects of cognitive elaboration on decision making. *International Journal of Selection and Assessment, 14,* 167–179.

Jones, E. E. (1990). *Interpersonal perception.* Freeman.

Jones, E. E., & Davis, K. E. (1965). From acts to dispositions: The attribution process in person perception. In L. Berkowitz (Ed.), *Advances in experimental social psychology* (Vol. 2, pp. 219–266). Academic Press.

Jones, E. E., & Gerard, H. B. (1967). *Foundations of social psychology.* Wiley.

Jones, E. E., & Harris, V. A. (1967). The attribution of attitudes. *Journal of Experimental Social Psychology, 3,* 1–24.

Jones, E. E., Rock, L., Shaver, K. G., Goethals, G. R., & Ward, L. M (1968). Pattern of performance and ability attribution: An unexpected primacy affect. *Journal of Personality and Social Psychology, 10,* 317–340.

Jordan, C. H., Spencer, S. J., & Zanna, M. P. (2005). Types of high self-esteem and prejudice: How implicit self-esteem relates to racial discrimination among high explicit self-esteem individuals. *Personality and Social Psychology Bulletin, 31,* 693–702.

Joseph, T. D. (2003). Overshooting the fundamental attribution error: Caribbean immigrants living in the United States. *Dissertation Abstracts International: Section B: The Sciences and Engineering, 64,* 2985.

Josephson, W. L. (1987). Television violence and children's aggression: Testing the priming, social script, and disinhibition predictions. *Journal of Personality and Social Psychology, 53,* 882–890.

Jost, J., & Amodio, D. (2012). Political ideology as motivated social cognition: Behavioral and neuroscientific evidence. *Motivation & Emotion, 36,* 55–64.

Jost, J. T., Banaji, M. R., & Nosek, B. A. (2004). A decade of system justification theory: Accumulated evidence of conscious and unconscious bolstering of the status quo. *Political Psychology, 25,* 881–919.

Jost, J. T., Glaser, J., Kruglanski, A. W., & Sulloway, F. J. (2003). Political conservatism as motivated social cognition. *Psychological Bulletin, 129,* 339–375.

Jost, J. T., Kivetz, Y., Rubini, M., Guermandi, G., & Mosso, C. (2005). System-justifying functions of complementary regional and ethnic stereotypes: Cross-national evidence. *Social Justice Research, 18,* 305–333.

Jourard, S. M. (1971). *Self-disclosure: An experimental analysis of the transparent self.* Wiley.

Jowett, G. S., & O'Donnell, V. (1992). *Propaganda and persuasion* (2nd ed.). Sage.

Judd, C. M., & Park, B. (1993). Definition and assessment of accuracy in social stereotypes. *Psychological Review, 100,* 109–128.

Jugert, P., Noack, P., & Rutland, A. (2013). Children's cross-ethnic friendships: Why are they less stable than same-ethnic friendships? *European Journal of Developmental Psychology, 10,* 649–662.

Julian, T. W., McKenry, P. C., Gavazzi, S. M., & Law, J. C. (1999). Test of family of origin structural models of male verbal and physical aggression. *Journal of Family Issues, 20,* 397–423.

Jung, H., Seo, E., Han, E., Henderson, M. D., & Patall, E. A. (2020). Prosocial modeling: A meta-analytic review and synthesis. *Psychological Bulletin, 146,* 635–663.

Jussim, L. (1986). Self-fulfilling prophecies: A theoretical and integrative review. *Psychological Review, 93,* 429–445.

Jussim, L. (1991). Social perception and social reality: A reflection-construction model. *Psychological Review, 98,* 54–73.

Jussim, L., Crawford, J. T., & Rubinstein, R. S. (2015). Stereotype (in)accuracy in perceptions of groups and individuals. *Current Directions in Psychological Science, 24,* 490–497.

Jussim, L., & Eccles, J. S. (1992). Teacher expectations II: Construction and reflection of student achievement. *Journal of Personality and Social Psychology, 63,* 947–961.

Jussim, L., Harber, K. D., Crawford, J. T., Cain, T. R., & Cohen, F. (2005). Social reality makes the social mind: Self-fulfilling prophecy, stereotypes, bias, and accuracy. *Interaction Studies: Social Behaviour and Communication in Biological and Artificial Systems, 6,* 85–102.

Jussim, L., Nelson, T. E., Manis, M., & Soffin, S. (1995). Prejudice, stereotypes, and labeling effects: Sources of bias in person perception. *Journal of Personality and Social Psychology, 68,* 228–246.

K

Kahneman, D. (2013). *Thinking, fast and slow.* Farrar, Straus and Giroux.

Kahneman, D., & Deaton, A. (2010). High income improves evaluation of life but not emotional well-being. *Proceedings of the National Academy of Sciences of the United States of America, 107,* 16489–16493.

Kahneman, D., Slovic, P., & Tversky, A. (1982). *Judgment under uncertainty: Heuristics and biases.* Cambridge University Press.

Kahneman, D., & Tversky, A. (1982). The simulation heuristic. In D. Kahneman, P. Slovic, & A. Tversky (Eds.), *Judgment under uncertainty: Heuristics and biases* (pp. 201–208). Cambridge University Press.

Kaiser, C. R., & Miller, C. T. (2004). A stress and coping perspective on confronting sexism. *Psychology of Women Quarterly, 28,* 168–178.

Kaiser Family Foundation. (2010). *Generation M². Media in the lives of 8- to 18-year-olds.* https://www.kff.org/wp-content/uploads/2013/01/8010.pdf

Kalven, H., & Zeisel, H. (1966). *The American jury.* Little, Brown.

Kaplan, M. F., & Miller, C. E. (1987). Group decision making and normative and informational social influence: Effects of type of issue and assigned decision rule. *Journal of Personality and Social Psychology, 53,* 306–313.

Karau, S. J., & Williams, K. D. (1993). Social loafing: A meta-analytic review and theoretical integration. *Journal of Personality and Social Psychology, 65,* 681–706.

Karmarkar, U. R., & Tormala, Z. L. (2010). Believe me, I have no Idea what I'm talking about: The effects of source certainty on consumer involvement and persuasion. *Journal of Consumer Research, 36*, 1033–1049.

Kashima, Y., Kokubo, T., Kashima, E. S., Boxall, D., Yamaguchi, S., & Macrae, K. (2004). Culture and self: Are there within-culture differences in self between metropolitan areas and regional cities? *Personality and Social Psychology Bulletin, 30*, 816–823.

Kassin, S. M., & Kiechel, K. L. (1996). The social psychology of false confessions: Compliance, internalization, and confabulation. *Psychological Science, 7*, 125–128.

Kassin, S. M., Reddy, M. E., & Tulloch, W. F. (1990). Juror interpretations of ambiguous evidence: The need for cognition, presentation order, and persuasion. *Law and Human Behavior, 14*, 43–56.

Kassin, S. M., & Wrightsman, L. S. (1985). Confession evidence. In S. M. Kassin & L. S. Wrightsman (Eds.), *The psychology of evidence and trial procedure* (pp. 67–94). Sage.

Kassner, M. P., Messelmann, E. D., Law, A. T., & Williams, K. D. (2012). Virtually ostracized: Studying ostracism in Immersive Virtual Environments. *CyberPsychology, Behavior & Social Networking, 15*, 399–403.

Katwala, A. (2020, May 27). *The rise of mask shaming reveals the tricky science of social change.* https://www.wired.co.uk/article/mask-shaming

Katz, I., Wakenhut, J., & Hass, R. G. (1986). Racial ambivalence, value duality and behavior. In J. F. Dovidio & S. L. Gaertner (Eds.), *Prejudice, discrimination and racism* (pp. 35–59). Academic Press.

Katz, J., Colbert, S., & Colangelo, L. (2015). Effects of group status and victim sex on female bystanders' responses to a potential party rape. *Violence and Victims, 30*, 265–277.

Kawakami, K., Dovidio, J. F., Moll, J., Hermsen, S., & Russin, A. (2000). Just say no (to stereotyping): Effects of training in negation of stereotypic associations on stereotype activation. *Journal of Personality and Social Psychology, 78*, 871–888.

Kawakami, K., Dovidio, J. F., & van Kamp, S. (2005). Kicking the habit: Effects of nonstereotypic association training and correction processes on hiring decisions. *Journal of Experimental Social Psychology, 41*, 68–75.

Kawakami, K., Phills, C. E., Greenwald, A. G., Simard, D., Pontiero, J., Brnjas, A., & . . . Dovidio, J. F. (2012). In perfect harmony: Synchronizing the self to activated social categories. *Journal of Personality and Social Psychology, 102*, 562–575.

Kazdin, A. E., & Benjet, C. (2003). Spanking children: Evidence and issues. *Current Directions in Psychological Science, 12*, 99–103.

Kelekar, A. K., Lucia, V. C., Afonso, N. M., & Mascarenhas, A. K. (2021). COVID-19 vaccine acceptance and hesitancy among dental and medical students. *Journal of the American Dental Association, 152*, 596–603.

Keller, J., & Bless, H. (2005). When negative expectancies turn into negative performance: The role of ease of retrieval. *Journal of Experimental Social Psychology, 41*, 535–541.

Keller, P. A., & Block, L. G. (1997). Vividness effects: A resource-matching perspective. *Journal of Consumer Research, 24*, 295–304.

Kelley, H. H. (1967). Attribution theory in social psychology. *Nebraska Symposium on Motivation, 14*, 192–241.

Kelley, H. H. (1971). Attribution theory in social interaction. In E. E. Jones, D. Kanouse, & H. H. Kelley (Eds.), *Attribution: Perceiving the causes of behavior* (pp. 1–26). General Learning Press.

Kelley, H. H., Berscheid, E., Christensen, A., Harvey, J. H., Huston, T. L., Levinger, G., & . . . Peterson, D. R. (1983). *Close relationships.* Freeman.

Kelloway, E. K., Mullen, J., & Francis, L. (2006). Divergent effects of transformational and passive leadership on employee safety. *Journal of Occupational Health Psychology, 11*, 76–86.

Kelman, H. C., & Hamilton, V. L. (1989). *Crimes of obedience: Toward a social psychology of authority and responsibility.* Yale University Press.

Kelman, H. C., & Hovland, C. I. (1953). "Reinstatement" of the communicator in delayed measurement of opinion change. *Journal of Abnormal and Social Psychology, 48*, 327–335.

Kemmelmeier, M. (2005). The effects of race and social dominance orientation in simulated juror decision making. *Journal of Applied Social Psychology, 35*, 1030–1045.

Kendall, P. C., Ronan, K. R., & Epps, J. (1991). Aggression in children/adolescents: Cognitive-behavioral treatment perspectives. In D. J. Pepler & K. H. Rubin (Eds.), *The development and treatment of childhood aggression* (pp. 341–360). Erlbaum.

Kennedy, P. H. (1987). *The rise and fall of the great powers: Economic change and military conflict from 1500 to 2000.* Random House.

Kenny, D., & Albright, L. (1987). Accuracy in interpersonal perception: A social relations analysis. *Psychological Bulletin, 102*, 390–402.

Kenrick, D. T., Keefe, R. C., Bryan, A., Barr, A., & Brown, S. (1995). Age preferences and mate choice among homosexuals and heterosexuals: A case for modular psychological mechanisms. *Journal of Personality and Social Psychology, 69*, 1169–1172.

Kereteš, G., & Milanovi, A. (2006). Relations between different types of children's aggressive behavior and sociometric status among peers of the same and opposite gender. *Scandinavian Journal of Psychology, 47*, 477–483.

Kernsmith, P., & Kernsmith, R. (2009). Female pornography use and sexual coercion perpetration. *Deviant Behavior, 30*, 589–610.

Kerr, N. L. (1983). Motivation losses in small groups: A social dilemma analysis. *Journal of Personality and Social Psychology, 45*, 819–828.

Kerr, N. L. (1989). Illusions of efficacy: The effects of group size on perceived efficacy in social dilemmas. *Journal of Experimental Social Psychology, 25,* 287–313.

Kerr, N. L. (1991). Issue importance and group decision making. In S. Worchel, W. Wood, & J. A. Simpson (Eds.), *Group process and productivity* (pp. 68–88). Sage.

Kerr, N. L., Messé, L. M., Park, E. S., & Sambolec, E. (2005). Identifiably, performance feedback and the Köhler effect. *Group Processes and Intergroup Relations, 8,* 375–390.

Kerr, N. L., & Tindale, R. S. (2004). Group performance and decision making. *Annual Review of Psychology, 55,* 623–655.

Kessler, T., & Hollback, S. (2005). Group-based emotions as determinants of ingroup identification. *Journal of Experimental Social Psychology, 41,* 677–685.

Khaleque, A. (2017). Perceived parental hostility and aggression, and children's psychological maladjustment, and negative personality dispositions: A meta-analysis. *Journal of Child & Family Studies, 26,* 977–988.

Kilham, W., & Mann, L. (1974). Level of destructive obedience as a function of transmitter and executive roles in the Milgram obedience paradigm. *Journal of Personality and Social Psychology, 29,* 696–702.

Kim, K., Lee, Y., Kim, H., & Lee, J. (2019). Detecting deception: Effect of auditory and visual stimuli on pupil dilation. *Social Behavior & Personality: An International Journal, 47,* 1–10.

Kim, Y. (2015). Does disagreement mitigate polarization? How selective exposure and disagreement affect political polarization. *Journalism & Mass Communication Quarterly, 92,* 915–937.

King, L. A. (1998). Ambivalence over emotional expression and reading emotions in situations and faces. *Journal of Personality and Social Psychology, 74,* 753–762.

Kiousis, S. (2005). Compelling arguments and attitude strength: Exploring the impact of second-level agenda setting on public opinion of presidential candidate images. *Harvard International Journal of Press/Politics, 10,* 3–27.

Kiousis, S., McDevitt, N., & Wu, X. (2005). The genesis of civic awareness: Agenda setting in political socialization. *Journal of Communication, 55,* 630–643.

Kitayama, S., Snibbe, A. C., Markus, H. R., & Suzuki, T. (2004). Is there any "free" choice? Self and dissonance in two cultures. *Psychological Science, 15,* 527–533.

Kite, M. E. (1984). Sex differences in attitudes toward homosexuality: A meta-analysis. *Journal of Homosexuality, 10,* 69–81.

Kite, M. E., & Whitley, B. E., Jr. (1998). Do heterosexual women and men differ in their attitudes toward homosexuality? In G. M. Herek (Ed.), *Stigma and sexual orientation* (pp. 39–61). Sage.

Klein, S. B., Loftus, J., & Plog, A. (1992). Trait judgments about the self: Evidence from encoding specificity paradigm. *Personality and Social Psychology Bulletin, 18,* 730–735.

Kleinsmith, J., Kasser, T., & McAndrew, F. T. (2006). Guns, testosterone and aggression: An experimental test of a mediational hypothesis. *Psychological Science, 17,* 568–571.

Klinkenberg, D., & Rose, S. (1994). Dating scripts of gay men and lesbians. *Journal of Homosexuality, 26,* 23–35.

Klohnen, E. C., & Mendelsohn, G. A. (1998). Partner selection for personality characteristics: A couple-centered approach. *Personality and Social Psychology Bulletin, 24,* 268–278.

Knee, C. R. (1998). Implicit theories of relationship: Assessment and prediction of romantic initiation, coping, and longevity. *Journal of Personality and Social Psychology, 74,* 360–370.

Knox, D., Daniels, V., Sturdivant, L., & Zusman, M. E. (2001). College student use of the Internet for mate selection. *College Student Journal, 35,* 158–161.

Köhler, O. (1926). Kraftleistungen bei Einzel und Gruppenabeit [Physical performance in individual and group situations]. *Industrielle Psychotechnik, 3,* 274–282.

Köhnken, G., & Brockmann, C. (1987). Unspecific postevent information, attribution of responsibility, and eyewitness performance. *Applied Cognitive Psychology, 1,* 197–207.

Kokkonen, A., Esaiasson, P., & Gilljam, M. (2015). Diverse workplaces and interethnic friendship formation—a multilevel comparison across 21 OECD countries. *Journal of Ethnic & Migration Studies, 41,* 284–305.

Kolata, G. (1992, November 24). After kinship and marriage, anthropology discovers love. *New York Times,* p. B9.

Köllner, M. G., & Schultheiss, O. C. (2014). Meta-analytic evidence of low convergence between implicit and explicit measures of the needs for achievement, affiliation, and power. *Frontiers in Psychology, 5*(Article 826), 1–20.

Kowalski, R. M., Giumetti, G. W., Schroeder, A. N., & Lattanner, M. R. (2014). Bullying in the digital age: A critical review and meta-analysis of cyberbullying research among youth. *Psychological Bulletin, 140,* 1073–1137.

Kravitz, D. A., & Martin, B. (1986). Ringelmann rediscovered: The original article. *Journal of Personality and Social Psychology, 50,* 936–941.

Kremer, J. F., & Stephens, L. (1983). Attributions and arousal as mediators of mitigation's effect on retaliation. *Journal of Personality and Social Psychology, 45,* 335–343.

Kret, M. E., & De Gelder, B. B. (2012). A review on sex differences in processing emotional signals. *Neuropsychologia, 50,* 1211–1221.

Kreutzer, J. S., Schneider, H. G., & Myatt, C. R. (1984). Alcohol, aggression, and assertiveness in men: Dosage and expectancy effects. *Journal of Studies on Alcohol, 45,* 275–278.

Krieglmeyer, R., Wittstadt, D., & Strack, F. (2009). How attribution influences aggression: Answers to an old question by using an implicit measure of anger. *Journal of Experimental Social Psychology, 45,* 379–385.

Krishan, L. (1988). Recipient need and anticipation of reciprocity in prosocial exchange. *Journal of Social Psychology, 128,* 223–231.

Kristiansen, C. M., & Zanna, M. P. (1988). Justifying attitudes by appealing to values: A functional perspective. *British Journal of Social Psychology, 27,* 247–256.

Krosnick, J. (1989). Attitude importance and attitude accessibility. *Personality and Social Psychology Bulletin, 15,* 297–308.

Krosnick, J. A., Betz, A. L., Jussim, L. J., & Lynn, A. R. (1992). Subliminal conditioning of attitudes. *Personality and Social Psychology Bulletin, 18,* 152–163.

Kruglanski, A. W., & Mayseless, O. (1990). Classic and current comparison research: Expanding the perspective. *Psychological Bulletin, 108,* 195–208.

Kruglanski, A. W., & Webster, D. M. (1991). Group members' reactions to opinion deviates and conformists at varying degrees of proximity to decision deadline and of environmental noise. *Journal of Personality and Social Psychology, 61,* 212–225.

Krull, D. S., Loy, M., Lin, J., Wang, C., Chen, S., & Zhao, X. (1999). The fundamental fundamental attribution error: Correspondence bias in individualist and collectivist cultures. *Personality and Social Psychology Bulletin, 25,* 1208–1219.

Kuhn, P., Kooreman, P., Soetevent, A. R., & Kapteyn, A. (2008). *The own and social effects of an unexpected income shock: Evidence from the Dutch postcode lottery.* http://escholarship.org/uc/item/07k895v4#page-2

Kukulj, S., & Keresteš, G. (2019). Sexual self-schemas of Croatian university students: Gender differences and links with sexual activity. *Sexuality & Culture: An Interdisciplinary Quarterly, 23,* 848–861.

Kumkale, G. T., & Albarracin, D. (2004). The sleeper effect in persuasion: A meta-analytic review. *Psychological Bulletin, 130,* 143–172.

Kunda, Z. (1999). *Social cognition.* MIT Press.

Kunstman, J. W., & Plant, E. A. (2008). Racing to help: Racial bias in high emergency helping situations. *Journal of Personality and Social Psychology, 95,* 1499–1510.

Kuo, F., Tseng, C., Tseng, F., & Lin, C. S. (2013). A study of social information control affordances and gender difference in Facebook self-presentation. *Cyberpsychology, Behavior & Social Networking, 16,* 635–644.

Kurdek, L. A. (2008). Change in relationship quality for partners from lesbian, gay male, and heterosexual couples. *Journal of Family Psychology, 22,* 701–711.

Kurdi, B., Seitchik, A. E., Axt, J. R., Carroll, T. J., Karapetyan, A., Kaushik, N., & . . . Banaji, M. R. (2019). Relationship between the Implicit Association Test and intergroup behavior: A meta-analysis. *American Psychologist, 74,* 569.

L

Lackie, L., & de Man, A. F. (1997). Correlates of sexual aggression among male university students. *Sex Roles, 5/6,* 451–457.

LaFrance, M., & Woodzicka, J. A. (1998). No laughing matter: Women's verbal and nonverbal reactions to sexist humor. In J. K. Swim & C. Stangor (Eds.), *Prejudice: The target's perspective* (pp. 62–80). Academic Press.

Lagerspetz, K. M., Bjorkqvist, K., & Peltonen, T. (1988). Is indirect aggression typical of females? Gender differences in aggressiveness in 11- to 12-year-old children. *Aggressive Behavior, 14,* 403–414.

Lang, A. R., Goeckner, D. J., Adesso, V. J., & Marlatt, G. A. (1975). Effects of alcohol on aggression in male social drinkers. *Journal of Abnormal Psychology, 84,* 508–518.

Langer, E. J. (1989). *Mindfulness.* Addison-Wesley.

Langer, E. J., Blank, A., & Chanowitz, B. (1978). The mindlessness of ostensibly thoughtful action: The role of placebic information in interpersonal interaction. *Journal of Personality and Social Psychology, 36,* 886–893.

Langer, E. J., & Rodin, J. (1976). The effects of choice and enhanced personal responsibility for the aged: A field experiment in an institutional setting. *Journal of Personality and Social Psychology, 34,* 191–198.

Langlois, J. H., Roggman, L. A., Casey, R. I., Riesner-Danner, L. A., & Jenkins, V. Y. (1987). Infant preferences for attractive faces: Rudiments of a stereotype? *Developmental Psychology, 23,* 363–369.

Lantos, H., Wilkinson, A., Winslow, H., & McDaniel, T. (2019). Describing associations between child maltreatment frequency and the frequency and timing of subsequent delinquent or criminal behaviors across development: Variation by sex, sexual orientation, and race. *BMC Public Health, 19,* 1–12.

LaPiere, R. T. (1934). Attitudes vs. actions. *Social Forces, 13,* 230–237.

Lariscy, R. A. W., & Tinkham, S. F. (1999). The sleeper effect and negative political advertising. *Journal of Advertising, 28,* 13–30.

Larrick, R. P., Timmerman, T. A., Carton, A. M., & Abrevaya, J. (2011). Temper, temperature, and temptation: Heat-related retaliation in baseball. *Psychological Science, 22,* 423–428.

Larsen, K. (1974). Conformity in the Asch experiment. *Journal of Social Psychology, 94,* 303–304.

Larsen, K. (1982). Cultural conditions and conformity: The Asch effect. *Bulletin of the British Psychological Society, 35,* 347.

Larson, J. R., Jr., Foster-Fishman, P. G., & Franz, T. M. (1998). Leadership style and the discussion of shared and unshared information in decision-making groups. *Personality and Social Psychology Bulletin, 24,* 482–495.

Lassiter, G. D., Briggs, M. A., & Bowman, R. E. (1991). Need for cognition and the perception of ongoing behavior. *Personality and Social Psychology Bulletin, 17,* 156–160.

Latané, B. (1981). The psychology of social impact. *American Psychologist, 36,* 343–356.

Latané, B., & Darley, J. M. (1968). Group inhibition of bystander intervention in emergencies. *Journal of Personality and Social Psychology, 10,* 215–221.

Latané, B., Williams, K. D., & Harkins, S. G. (1979). Many hands make light the work: The causes and consequences of social loafing. *Journal of Personality and Social Psychology, 37,* 822–832.

Latané, B., & Wolf, S. (1981). The social impact of majorities and minorities. *Psychological Review, 88,* 438–453.

Latham, G. P., & Piccolo, R. F. (2012). The effect of context-specific versus nonspecific subconscious goals on employee performance. *Human Resource Management, 51,* 511–523.

Laughlin, P. R. (1980). Social combination processes of cooperative problem-solving groups on verbal intellective tasks. In M. Fishbein (Ed.), *Progress in social psychology* (Vol. 1, pp. 127–156). Erlbaum.

Laughlin, P. R., Bonner, B. L., & Altermatt, T. W. (1998). Collective versus individual induction with single versus multiple hypotheses. *Journal of Personality and Social Psychology, 75,* 1481–1489.

Laughlin, P. R., & Ellis, A. L. (1986). Demonstrability and social combination processes on mathematical intellective tasks. *Journal of Experimental Social Psychology, 22,* 177–189.

Laughlin, P. R., Hatch, E. C., Silver, J. S., & Boh, L. (2006). Groups perform better than the best individuals on letters-to-numbers problems: Effects of group size. *Journal of Personality and Social Psychology, 90,* 644–651.

Laughlin, P. R., VanderStoep, S. W., & Hollingshead, A. D. (1991). Collective versus individual induction: Recognition of truth, rejection of error, and collective information processing. *Journal of Personality and Social Psychology, 61,* 50–67.

Laughlin, P. R., Zander, M. L., Knievel, E. M., & Tan, T. K. (2003). Groups perform better than the best individuals on letters-to-numbers problems: Informative equations and effective strategies. *Journal of Personality and Social Psychology, 85,* 684–694.

Laurenceau, J. P., Barrett, L. F., & Pietromanaco, P. R. (1998). Intimacy as an interpersonal process: The importance of self-disclosure, partner disclosure, and perceived partner responsiveness in interpersonal exchanges. *Journal of Personality and Social Psychology, 74,* 1238–1251.

Laurens, S., Hanzo, F., & Morchain, P. (2016). A research note on delegation of responsibility in the observation of a situation of obedience to authority. *Imagination, Cognition & Personality, 36,* 116–127.

LaVasseur, J. B. (1997). Authoritarianism and political orientation: Validation of a left-wing authoritarianism scale. *Dissertation Abstracts International.*

Lawson, R. G. (1969). The law of primacy in the criminal courtroom. *Journal of Social Psychology, 77,* 121–131.

Lawson, V. Z., & Dysart, J. E. (2014). The showup identification procedure: An exploration of systematic biases. *Legal & Criminological Psychology, 19,* 54–68.

Lazarus, R. S., & Cohen, J. B. (1977). Environmental stress. In I. Altman & J. F. Wohlwill (Eds.), *Human behavior and environment* (Vol. 2, pp. 89–127). Plenum.

Leary, M. R. (1983a). *Understanding social anxiety: Social, personality, and clinical perspectives* (Vol. 153, Sage Library of Social Research). Sage.

Leary, M. R. (1983b). Social anxiousness: The construct and its measurement. *Journal of Personality Assessment, 47,* 66–75.

Leary, M. R., & Kowalski, R. M. (1995). *Social anxiety.* Guilford.

Leary, M. R., Kowalski, R. M., Smith, L., & Phillips, S. (2003). Teasing, rejection, and violence: Case studies of the school shootings. *Aggressive Behavior, 29,* 202–214.

Leary, M. R., Springer, C., Negel, L., Ansell, E., & Evans, K. (1998). The causes, phenomenology, and consequences of hurt feelings. *Journal of Personality and Social Psychology, 74,* 1225–1237.

Lee, F., Hallahan, M., & Herzog, T. (1996). Explaining real life events: How culture and domain shape attributions. *Personality and Social Psychology Bulletin, 22,* 732–741.

Lee, J. K., Choi, J., Kim, C., & Kim, Y. (2014). Social media, network heterogeneity, and opinion polarization. *Journal of Communication, 64,* 702–722.

Legate, N., Weinstein, N., & Ryan, R. M. (2021). Ostracism in real life: Evidence that ostracizing others has costs, even when it feels justified. *Basic and Applied Social Psychology, 43,* 226–238.

Lemiuex, R., & Hale, J. L. (2002). Cross-sectional analysis of intimacy, passion, and commitment: Testing the assumptions of the triangular theory of love. *Psychological Reports, 90,* 1009–1014.

Lenton, A. P., Bruder, M., & Sedikides, C. (2009). A meta-analysis on the malleability of automatic gender stereotypes. *Psychology of Women Quarterly, 33,* 183–196.

Leo, R. A., & Davis, D. (2010). From false confession to wrongful conviction: Seven psychological processes. *Journal of Psychiatry & Law, 38,* 9–56.

Leonard, K. E., Collins, R. L., & Quigley, B. M. (2003). Alcohol consumption and the occurrence and severity of aggression: An event-based analysis of male to male barroom violence. *Aggressive Behavior, 29,* 346–365.

Leonardelli, G. J., Pickett, C. L., & Brewer, M. B. (2010). Optimal distinctiveness theory: A framework for social identity, social cognition, and intergroup relations. In M. P. Zanna & J. M. Olson (Eds.), *Advances in experimental social psychology* (Vol. 43, pp. 63–113). Academic Press.

Lerner, M. J., & Simmons, C. H. (1966). Observers' reactions to the "innocent victim": Compassion or rejection? *Journal of Personality and Social Psychology, 4,* 203–210.

LeSure-Lester, G. E. (2002). An application of cognitive-behavior principles in the reduction of aggression among abused African American adolescents. *Journal of Interpersonal Violence, 17,* 394–402.

Letzring, T. D., & Noftle, E. E. (2010). Predicting relationship quality from self-verification of broad personality traits among romantic couples. *Journal of Research in Personality, 44,* 353–362.

Levenson, R. W., & Gottman, J. M. (1983). Marital interaction: Physiological linkage and affective exchange. *Journal of Personality and Social Psychology, 45,* 587–597.

Leventhal, G. S., Allen, J., & Kemelgor, B. (1969). Reducing inequity by reallocating rewards. *Psychonomic Science, 14,* 295–296.

Leventhal, H. (1970). Findings and theory in the study of fear communication. In L. Berkowitz (Ed.), *Advances in experimental social psychology* (Vol. 5, pp. 119–186). Academic Press.

Levin, S. (2004). Perceived group status differences and the effects of gender, ethnicity, and religion on social dominance orientation. *Political Psychology, 25,* 31–48.

Levine, J. M. (1989). Reaction to opinion deviance in small groups. In P. Paulus (Ed.), *The psychology of group influence* (2nd ed., pp. 187–232). Erlbaum.

Levine, J. M., & Moreland, R. L. (1990). Progress in small group research. *Annual Review of Psychology, 41,* 585–634.

Levine, M. (1999). Rethinking bystander nonintervention: Social categorization and the evidence of witnesses at the James Bulger murder trial. *Human Relations, 52,* 1133–1155.

Levine, M., Cassidy, C., Brazier, G., & Reicher, S. (2002). Self-categorization and bystander non-intervention: Two experimental studies. *Journal of Applied Social Psychology, 32,* 1452–1463.

Levine, M., Prosser, A., Evans, D., & Reicher, S. (2005). Identity and emergency intervention: How social group membership and inclusiveness of group boundaries shape helping behavior. *Personality and Social Psychology Bulletin, 31,* 443–453.

Levine, M., & Thompson, K. (2004). Identity, place, and bystander intervention: Social categories and helping after natural disasters. *Journal of Social Psychology, 144,* 229–245.

Levinger, C., & Snoek, J. D. (1972). *Attraction in relationships: A new look at interpersonal attraction.* General Learning Press.

Levinger, G. (1988). Can we picture "love"? In R. J. Sternberg & M. L. Barnes (Eds.), *The psychology of love* (pp. 139–158). Yale University Press.

Levinson, C. A., Giancola, P. R., & Parrott, D. J. (2011). Beliefs about aggression moderate alcohol's effects on aggression. *Experimental and Clinical Psychopharmacology, 19,* 64–74.

Levy, S. R., Stroessner, S. J., & Dweck, C. (1998). Stereotype formation and endorsement: The role of implicit theories. *Journal of Personality and Social Psychology, 74,* 1421–1436.

Lewin, K. (1936). *A dynamic theory of personality.* McGraw Hill.

Lewis, D. O., Lovely, R., Yeager, C., & Della Femina, D. (1989). Toward a theory of the genesis of violence: A follow-up study of delinquents. *Journal of the American Academy of Child and Adolescent Psychiatry, 28,* 431–437.

Leyens, J-P., Paladino, P. M., Rodriguez-Torres, R., Vaes, J., Demoulin, S., Rodriguez-Perez, A., & Gaunt, R. (2000). The emotional side of prejudice: The attribution of secondary emotions to ingroups and outgroups. *Personality and Social Psychology Review, 4,* 186–197.

Li, H., Rau, P. P., & Salvendy, G. (2014). The effect of mixed American–Chinese group composition on computer-mediated group decision making. *Human Factors and Ergonomics in Manufacturing & Service Industries, 24,* 428–443.

Li, Y., Johnson, K. A., Cohen, A. B., Williams, M. J., Knowles, E. D., & Chen, Z. (2012). Fundamental(ist) attribution error: Protestants are dispositionally focused. *Journal of Personality & Social Psychology, 102,* 281–290.

Libby, L. K., & Eibach, R. P. (2002). Looking back in time: Self-concept change affects individual perspective in autobiographical memory. *Journal of Personality and Social Psychology, 82,* 167–179.

Liebert, R. M., & Baron, R. A. (1972). Some immediate effects of televised violence on children's behavior. *Developmental Psychology, 6,* 469–475.

Lifton, R. J. (1986). *The Nazi doctors: Medical killing and the psychology of genocide.* Basic Books.

Light, J. M., & Dishion, T. J. (2007). Early adolescent antisocial behavior and peer rejection: A dynamic test of a developmental process. *New Directions for Child & Adolescent Development, 118,* 77–89.

Likert, R. (1932). A technique for the measurement of attitudes. *Archives of Psychology, 140,* 43–55.

Lilienfeld, S. O. (2005). The 10 commandments of helping students distinguish science from pseudoscience in psychology. *APS Observer, 18.* https://www.psychologicalscience.org/observer/the-10-commandments-of-helping-students-distinguish-science-from-pseudoscience-in-psychology

Lin, S., & Stutts, L. A. (2020). Impact of exposure to counter stereotypic causality of obesity on beliefs about weight controllability and obesity bias. *Psychology, Health & Medicine, 25,* 730–741.

Lindner, C., Nagy, G., Ramos Arhuis, W. A., & Retelsdorf, J. (2017). A new perspective on the interplay between self-control and cognitive performance: Modeling progressive depletion patterns. *PLoS ONE, 12,* 1–22.

Lindsay, D. S., Jack, P. C., & Christian, M. A. (1991). Other-race face perception. *Journal of Applied Psychology, 76,* 587–589.

Lindsay, D. S., & Johnson, M. K. (1989). The eyewitness suggestibility effect and memory for source. *Memory & Cognition, 17,* 349–358.

Lindsay, R. C. L., Wells, G. L., & O'Connor, F. J. (1989). Mock-juror belief of accurate and inaccurate eyewitnesses: A replication and extension. *Law and Human Behavior, 13,* 333–339.

Linville, P. (1985). Self-complexity and affective extremity. Don't put all your eggs in one cognitive basket. *Social Cognition, 3*, 92–120.

Linville, P. (1987). Self-complexity as a cognitive buffer against stress related illnesses and depression. *Journal of Personality and Social Psychology, 52*, 663–676.

Linville, P. W., Fischer, G. W., & Salovey, P. (1989). Perceived distributions of the characteristics of in-group and out-group members: Empirical evidence and computer simulation. *Journal of Personality and Social Psychology 57*, 165–188.

Linz, D., Penrod, S., & Donnerstein, E. (1987, Fall). The attorney general's commission on pornography: The gaps between "findings" and facts. *American Bar Foundation Research Journal*, 713–736.

Lippmann, W. (1922). *Public opinion.* Harcourt, Brace & World.

Lips, H. (1993). *Sex and gender.* Mayfield.

Litchblau, E. (2004). *Cracker Barrel agrees to plan to address reports of bias*. https://www.nytimes.com/2004/05/04/us/cracker-barrel-agrees-to-plan-to-address-reports-of-bias.html#:~:text=Cracker%20Barrel%20restaurants%20agreed%20Monday,diners%20in%20about%2050%20locations.

Locke, E. A., & Latham, G. P. (2002). Building a practically useful theory of goal setting and task motivation: A 35-year odyssey. *American Psychologist, 57*, 705–717.

Locke, K. D., & Horowitz, L. M. (1990). Satisfaction in interpersonal interactions as a function of similarity in level of dysphoria. *Journal of Personality and Social Psychology, 58*, 823–831.

Loewenstein, G., Krishnamurti, T., Kopsic, J., & McDonald, D. (2015). Does increased sexual frequency enhance happiness? *Journal of Economic Behavior & Organization, 116*, 206–218.

Loftus, E. F. (1979a). *Eyewitness testimony.* Harvard University Press.

Loftus, E. F. (1979b). The malleability of human memory. *American Scientist, 67*, 312–320.

Loftus, E. F., Schooler, J. W., & Wagenaar, W. A. (1985). The fate of memory: Comment on McCloskey and Zaragoza. *Journal of Experimental Psychology: General, 114*, 375–380.

Lopes, P. N., Salovey, P., Cote, S., & Beers, M. (2005). Emotion regulation abilities and the quality of social interaction. *Emotion, 5*, 113–118.

Lorenz, K. (1963). *On aggression.* Methuen.

Lorenzo, G. L., Biesanz, J. C., & Human, L. J. (2010). What is beautiful is good and more accurately understood: Physical attractiveness and accuracy in first impressions of personality. *Psychological Science, 21*, 1777–1782.

Lorge, I., & Solomon, H. (1955). Two models of group behavior in the solution of Eureka-type problems. *Psychometrika, 20*, 139–148.

Lu, L., Yuan, Y., & McLeod, P. (2012). Twenty-five years of hidden profiles in group decision making: A meta-analysis. *Personality and Social Psychology Review, 16*, 54–75.

Luginbuhl, J., & Palmer, T. (1991). Impression management aspects of self-handicapping: Positive and negative effects. *Personality and Social Psychology Bulletin, 17*, 655–662.

Lundh, L.-G., & Sperling, M. (2002). Social anxiety and the post-event processing of distressing social events. *Cognitive Behaviour Therapy, 31*, 129–134.

Luo, Y., Burley, H., Moe, A., & Sui, M. (2019). A meta-analysis of news media's public agenda-setting effects, 1972–2015. *Journalism & Mass Communication Quarterly, 96*, 150–172.

Lutter, M. (2007). Book review: Winning a lottery brings no happiness! *Journal of Happiness Studies: An Interdisciplinary Forum on Subjective Well-Being, 8*, 155–160.

Luzsa, R., & Mayr, S. (2021). False consensus in the echo chamber: Exposure to favorably biased social media news feeds leads to increased perception of public support for own opinions. *Cyberpsychology: Journal of Psychosocial Research on Cyberspace, 15*. https://doi.org/10.5817/CP2021-1-3

Lytton, H., & Romney, D. M. (1991). Parents' differential socialization of boys and girls: A meta-analysis. *Psychological Bulletin, 109*, 267–296.

Lyubomirsky, S., Caldwell, N. D., & Nolen-Hoeksema, S. (1998). Effects of ruminative and distracting responses to depressed mood on retrieval of autobiographical memories. *Journal of Personality and Social Psychology, 75*, 166–177.

M

Maas, V. V., & Torres-González, R. (2011). Subjective performance evaluation and gender discrimination. *Journal of Business Ethics, 101*, 667–681.

MacInnis, C. C., & Hodson, G. (2015). Why are heterosexual men (vs. women) particularly prejudiced toward gay men? A social dominance theory explanation. *Psychology & Sexuality, 6*, 275–294.

Mackie, D. M., Allison, S. T., Worth, L. T., & Asuncion, A. C. (1992). The impact of outcome biases on counterstereotypic inferences about groups. *Personality and Social Psychology Bulletin, 18*, 4–51.

Mackie, D. M., & Worth, L. T. (1989). Processing deficits and the mediation of positive affect in persuasion. *Journal of Personality and Social Psychology, 57*, 27–40.

MacLeod, M. D., & Saunders, J. (2005). The role of inhibitory control in the production of misinformation effects. *Journal of Experimental Psychology: Learning, Memory, and Cognition, 31*, 964–979.

Macrae, C. N., Hewstone, M., & Griffiths, R. J. (1993). Processing load and memory for stereotype-based information. *European Journal of Social Psychology, 23*, 77–87.

Macrae, C. N., Mime, A. B., & Bodenhausen, G. V. (1994). Stereotypes as energy saving devices: A peek inside the cognitive toolbox. *Journal of Personality and Social Psychology, 66*, 37–47.

Macrae, C. N., Quinn, K. A., Mason, M. F., & Quadflieg, S. (2005). Understanding others: The face and person construal. *Journal of Personality and Social Psychology, 89*, 686–695.

Macrae, C. N., Shepherd, J. W., & Milne, A. B. (1992). The effects of source credibility on the dilution of stereotype-based judgments. *Personality and Social Psychology Bulletin, 18,* 765–775.

Maddox, K. B. (2004). Perspectives on racial phenotypicality bias. *Personality and Social Psychology Review, 8,* 383–401.

Maddox, K. B., & Gray, S. A. (2002). Cognitive representations of Black Americans: Reexploring the role of skin tone. *Personality and Social Psychology Bulletin, 28,* 250–259.

Madey, S. F., & Rodgers, L. (2009). The effect of attachment and Sternberg's triangular theory of love on relationship satisfaction. *Individual Differences Research, 7,* 76–84.

Mae, L., & Carlston, D. E. (2005). Hoist on your own petard: When prejudiced remarks are recognized and backfire on speakers. *Journal of Experimental Social Psychology, 41,* 240–255.

Main, M., & George, C. (1985). Responses of abused and disadvantaged toddlers to distress in age mates: A study in the day care setting. *Developmental Psychology, 21,* 407–412.

Maio, G. R., & Esses, V. M. (2001). The need for affect: Individual differences in the motivation to approach or avoid emotions. *Journal of Personality, 69,* 583–615.

Major, B. (1980). Information acquisition and attribution processes. *Journal of Personality and Social Psychology, 39,* 1010–1024.

Malamuth, N. M. (1986). Predictors of naturalistic sexual aggression. *Journal of Personality and Social Psychology, 50,* 953–962.

Malamuth, N. M., & Check, J. V. P. (1980). Sexual arousal to rape and consenting depictions: The importance of the woman's arousal. *Journal of Abnormal Psychology, 89,* 763–766.

Malamuth, N. M., & Check, J. V. P. (1981). The effects of mass media exposure on acceptance of violence against women: A field experiment. *Journal of Research in Personality, 15,* 436–446.

Malamuth, N. M., & Check, J. V. P. (1983). Sexual arousal to rape depictions: Individual differences. *Journal of Abnormal Psychology, 92,* 55–67.

Malamuth, N. M., & Check, J. V. P. (1985). The effects of aggressive pornography on beliefs in rape myths: Individual differences. *Journal of Research in Personality, 19,* 299–320.

Malamuth, N. M., Heavey, C. L., & Linz, D. (1993). *Predicting men's antisocial behavior against women: The interaction model of sexual aggression.* Taylor & Francis.

Malle, B. F. (1999). How people explain behavior. A new theoretical framework. *Personality and Social Psychology Review, 3,* 23–48.

Malle, B. F. (2006). Intentionality, Morality, and Their Relationship in Human Judgment. *Journal of Cognition & Culture, 6,* 87–112.

Malle, B. F., & Hodges, S. (Eds.). (2006). *Other minds: How humans bridge the divide between self and others* (pp. 98–115). Guilford Press.

Malpass, R. S., & Kravitz, J. (1969). Recognition for faces of own and other race. *Journal of Personality and Social Psychology, 13,* 330–334.

Manalastas, E. J. (2011). Unrequired love among young Filipino gay men: Subjective experiences of unreciprocated lovers. *Social Science Diliman, 7,* 63–81.

Mancini, C., Reckdenwald, A., & Beauregard, E. (2012). Pornographic exposure over the life course and the severity of sexual offenses: Imitation and cathartic effects. *Journal of Criminal Justice, 40,* 21–30.

Mansour, J. K., Hamilton, C. M., & Gibson, M. T. (2019). Understanding the weapon focus effect: The role of threat, unusualness, exposure duration, and scene complexity. *Applied Cognitive Psychology, 33,* 991–1007.

Mantell, D. M. (1971). The potential for violence in Germany. *Journal of Social Issues, 27,* 101–112.

Marcus, B., Machilek, F., & Schütz, A. (2006). Personality in cyberspace: Personal websites as media for personality expressions and impressions. *Journal of Personality and Social Psychology, 90,* 1014–1031.

Marcus-Newhall, A., Pederson, W. C., Carlson, M., & Miller, N. (2000). Displaced aggression is alive and well: A meta-analytic review. *Journal of Personality and Social Psychology, 78,* 670–689.

Mares, M.-L., & Woodard, E. (2005). Positive effects of television on children's social interactions: A meta-analysis. *Media Psychology, 7,* 301–322.

Marion, S. B., Kukucka, J., Collins, C., Kassin, S. M., & Burke, T. M. (2016). Lost proof of innocence: The impact of confessions on alibi witnesses. *Law and Human Behavior, 40,* 65–71.

Mark, M. M., Bryant, F. B., & Lehman, D. R. (1983). Perceived injustice and sports violence. In J. G. Goldstein (Ed.), *Sports violence* (pp. 83–110). Springer-Verlag.

Markey, P. M. (2000). Bystander intervention in computer-mediated communication. *Computers in Human Behavior, 16,* 183–188.

Markus, H. (1977). Self-schemata and processing information about the self. *Journal of Personality and Social Psychology, 35,* 63–78.

Markus, H., & Kitayama, S. (1991). Culture and self: Implications for cognition, emotion, and motivation. *Psychological Review, 98,* 224–253.

Markus, H., & Kunda, Z. (1986). Stability and malleability of the self-concept. *Journal of Personality and Social Psychology, 51,* 858–866.

Markus, H., & Zajonc, R. B. (1985). The cognitive perspective in social psychology. In G. Lindzey & E. Aronson (Eds.), *The handbook of social psychology: Vol. 1. Theory and method* (pp. 137–230). Random House.

Marques, J. M., & Paez, D. (1994). The "black sheep effect": Social categorization, rejection of ingroup deviates, and perception of group variability. In W. Stroebe & M. Hewstone (Eds.), *European review of social psychology* (Vol. 5, pp. 37–68). Wiley.

Marshall, J., Marquis, K. H., & Oskamp, S. E. (1971). Effects of kind of question and atmosphere of interrogation on accuracy and completeness of testimony. *Harvard Law Review, 84,* 1620–1644.

Martin, R., Gardikiotis, A., & Hewstone, M. (2002). Levels of consensus in majority and minority influence. *European Journal of Social Psychology, 32,* 645–665.

Martínez-Ferrer, B., León-Moreno, C., Musitu-Ferrer, D., Romero-Abrio, A., Callejas-Jerónimo, J. E., & Musitu-Ochoa, G. (2019). Parental socialization, school adjustment and cyber-aggression among adolescents. *International Journal of Environmental Research and Public Health, 16,* 1–14.

Maslow, A. H. (1943). A theory of human motivation. *Psychological Review, 50,* 370–396.

Mastrangelo, D. (2020). *Pelosi encouraged public gatherings in late February, weeks after Trump's China travel ban.* https://www.washingtonexaminer.com/news/pelosi-encouraged-public-gatherings-in-late-february-weeks-after-trumps-china-travel-ban

Match. (2021). *Singles in America.* https://www.singlesinamerica.com/

Matsuda, N. (1985). Strong, quasi-and weak conformity among Japanese in the modified Asch procedure. *Journal of Cross-Cultural Psychology, 16,* 83–97.

Matz, S. C., Gladstone, J. J., & Stillwell, D. (2016). Money buys happiness when spending fits our personality. *Psychological Science, 27,* 715–725.

McAdams, D. P. (1982). Intimacy motivation. In A. J. Stewart (Ed.), *Motivation and society.* Jossey-Bass.

McAdams, D. P. (1989). *Intimacy.* Doubleday.

McArthur, L. Z. (1972). The how and what of why: Some determinants and consequences of causal attribution. *Journal of Personality and Social Psychology, 22,* 171–193.

McArthur, L. Z. (1982). Judging a book by its cover: A cognitive analysis of the relationship between physical appearance and stereotyping. In A. Hastorf & A. Isen (Eds.), *Cognitive social psychology* (pp. 149–211). Elsevier/North Holland.

McCarthy, J. M., Bauer, T. N., Truxillo, D. M., Anderson, N. R., Costa, A. C., & Ahmed, S. M. (2017). Applicant perspectives during selection: A review addressing "So what?," "What's new?," and "Where to next?" *Journal of Management, 43,* 1693–1725.

McCarty, M. K., & Kelly, J. R. (2015). Perceptions of dating behavior: The role of ambivalent sexism. *Sex Roles, 72,* 237–251.

McCarty, N., Poole, K. T., & Rosenthal, H. (2006). *Polarized America: The dance of ideology and unequal riches.* MIT Press.

McCauley, C., & Segal, M. E. (1987). Social psychology of terrorist groups. In C. Hendrick (Ed.), *Group processes and intergroup relations* (pp. 231–256). Sage.

McClelland, D. C. (1961). *The achieving society.* D. Van Nostrand.

McCloskey, M., & Egeth, H. E. (1983). Eyewitness identification: What can a psychologist tell a jury? *American Psychologist, 38,* 550–563.

McCloskey, M., & Zaragoza, M. (1985). Misleading postevent information and memory for events: Arguments and evidence against memory impairment hypotheses. *Journal of Experimental Psychology: General, 114,* 3–18.

McConahay, J. G. (1986). Modern racism, ambivalence, and the modern racist scale. In J. F. Dovidio & S. L. Gaertner (Eds.), *Prejudice, discrimination, and racism* (pp. 91–125). Academic Press.

McConnell, E., Néray, B., Hogan, B., Korpak, A., Clifford, A., & Birkett, M. (2018). "Everybody puts their whole life on Facebook": Identity management and the online social networks of LGBTQ youth. *International Journal of Environmental Research and Public Health, 15.* https://doi.org/10.3390/ijerph15061078

McCown, J. A., Fischer, D., Page, R., & Homant, M. (2001). Internet relationships: People who meet people. *CyberPsychology and Behavior, 4,* 593–596.

McCrae, R. R., & Costa, P. (1987). Validation of the five-factor model of personality across instruments and observers. *Journal of Personality and Social Psychology, 52,* 81–90.

McCullough, M. E., Exline, J. J., & Baumeister, R. F. (1998). An annotated bibliography of research on forgiveness and related concepts. In E. L. Worthington (Ed.), *Dimensions of forgiveness: Psychological research and theological perspectives* (pp. 193–317). Templeton Press.

McCullough, M. E., Kilpatrick, S. D., Emmons, R. A., & Larson, D. B. (2001). Is gratitude a moral affect? *Psychological Bulletin, 127,* 249–266.

McCullough, M. E., Worthington, E. L., Jr., & Rachal, K. C. (1997). Interpersonal forgiving in close relationships. *Journal of Personality and Social Psychology, 73,* 321–336.

McFarland, C., & Buehler, R. (1998). The impact of negative affect on autobiographical memories: The role of self-focused attention to moods. *Journal of Personality and Social Psychology, 75,* 1424–1440.

McGregor, I., & Holmes, I. G. (1999). How storytelling shapes memory and impressions of relationships over time. *Journal of Personality and Social Psychology, 76,* 406–419.

McGregor, L., Gee, D. E., & Posey, K. E. (2008). I feel like a fraud and it depresses me: The relation between the imposter phenomenon and depression. *Social Behavior and Personality: An International Journal, 36,* 43–48.

McGuire, W. J. (1973). The yin and yang of progress in social psychology. *Journal of Personality and Social Psychology, 26,* 46–456.

McGuire, W. J. (1985). Attitudes and attitude change. In G. Lindzey & E. Aronson (Eds.), *The handbook of social psychology* (3rd ed., Vol. 2, pp. 233–346). Random House.

McGuire, W. J., & McGuire, C. V. (1988). Content and process in the experience of self. In L. Berkowitz (Ed.), *Advances in experimental social psychology* (Vol. 21, pp. 97–144). Academic Press.

McGuire, W. J., & Papageorgis, D. (1961). The relative efficacy of various types of prior belief-defense in producing immunity against persuasion. *Journal of Abnormal and Social Psychology, 62,* 327–337.

McHan, E. (1985). Imitation of aggression by Lebanese children. *Journal of Social Psychology, 125,* 613–617.

McKay, N. J., & Covell, K. (1997). The impact of women in advertisements on attitudes toward women. *Sex Roles, 9/10,* 573–583.

McKenna, K., Green, A., & Gleason, M. (2002). Relationship formation on the Internet: What's the big attraction? *Journal of Social Issues, 58,* 9–31.

McKimmie, B., Newton, C. J., Terry, D., & Schuller, R. A. (2004). Jurors' responses to expert testimony: The effects of gender stereotypes. *Group Processes and Intergroup Relations, 7,* 131–143.

McLeod, P. L., Baron, R. S., Marti, M. W., & Yoon, K. (1997). The eyes have it: Minority influence in face-to-face and computer-mediated group discussion. *Journal of Applied Psychology, 82,* 706–718.

McNamee, L. G., Peterson, B. L., & Peña, J. (2010). A call to educate, participate, invoke and indict: Understanding the communication of online hate groups. *Communication Monographs, 77,* 257–280.

McNamee, S., & Wesolik, F. (2014). Heroic behavior of Carnegie Medal heroes: Parental influence and expectations. *Peace and Conflict: Journal of Peace Psychology, 20,* 171–173.

McNeill, W. H. (1982). *The pursuit of power: Technology, armed force, and society since A.D. 1000.* University of Chicago Press.

Mead, N. L., Baumeister, R. F., Gino, F., Schweitzer, M. E., & Ariely, D. (2009). Too tired to tell the truth: Self-control resource depletion and dishonesty. *Journal of Experimental Social Psychology, 45,* 594–597.

Mealey, L., Bridstock, R., & Townsend, G. C. (1999). Symmetry and perceived facial attractiveness: A monozygotic twin comparison. *Journal of Personality and Social Psychology, 76,* 151–158.

Mednick, B. R., Baker, R. L., & Carothers, L. E. (1990). Patterns of family disruption and crime: The association of timing of the family's disruption with subsequent adolescent and young adult criminality. *Journal of Youth and Violence, 19,* 201–220.

Meeus, W., & Raaijmakers, Q. (1986). Administrative obedience: Carrying out orders to use psychological-administrative violence. *European Journal of Social Psychology, 16,* 311–324.

Meevissen, Y. C., Peters, M. L., & Alberts, H. M. (2011). Become more optimistic by imagining a best possible self: Effects of a two week intervention. *Journal of Behavior Therapy and Experimental Psychiatry, 42,* 371–378.

Mehdizadeh, S. (2010). Self-presentation 2.0: Narcissism and self-esteem on Facebook. *Cyberpsychology: Behavior and Social Networking, 13,* 357–364.

Meissner, C. A., & Brigham, J. C. (2001). Thirty years of investigating the own-race bias in memory for faces: A meta-analytic review. *Psychology, Public Policy, and Law, 7,* 3–35.

Meissner, F., Grigutsch, L. A., Koranyi, N., Müller, F., & Rothermund, K. (2019). Predicting behavior with implicit measures: Disillusioning findings, reasonable explanations, and sophisticated solutions. *Frontiers in Psychology, 10.* https://doi.org/10.3389/fpsyg.2019.02483

Merolla, A. J. (2014). The role of hope in conflict management and relational maintenance. *Personal Relationships, 21,* 365–386.

Merolla, A. J., & Harman, J. J. (2016). Relationship-specific hope and constructive conflict management in adult romantic relationships: Testing an accommodation framework. *Communication Research, 45,* 339–364.

Messe, L. A., Hertel, G., Kerr, N. L., Lount, P., & Park, E. S. (2002). Knowledge of partner's ability as a moderator of group motivation gains: An exploration of the Koehler discrepancy effect. *Journal of Personality and Social Psychology, 82,* 935–946.

Meyer-Parlapanis, D., Weierstall, R., Nandi, C., Bambonyé, M., Elbert, T., & Crombach, A. (2016). Appetitive aggression in women: Comparing male and female war combatants. *Frontiers in Psychology, 6,* 1–8.

Meyers-Levy, J., & Peracchio, L. A. (1995). Understanding the effects of color: How the correspondence between available and required resources affects attitudes. *Journal of Consumer Research, 22,* 121–138.

Micevski, M., Diamantopoulos, A., & Erdbrügger, J. (2021). From country stereotypes to country emotions to intentions to visit a country: Implications for a country as a destination brand. *Journal of Product & Brand Management, 30,* 118–131.

Midlarsky, E., Bryan, J. H., & Brickman, P. (1973). Aversion approval: Interactive effects of modeling and reinforcement on altruistic behavior. *Child Development, 44,* 321–328.

Midlarsky, E., Fagin Jones, S., & Corley, R. P. (2005). Personality correlates of heroic rescue during the Holocaust. *Journal of Personality, 73,* 907–934.

Mikulincer, M. (1998). Attachment working models and the sense of trust: An exploration of interaction goals and affect regulation. *Journal of Personality and Social Psychology, 74,* 1209–1224.

Miles, D. R., & Carey, G. (1997). Genetic and environmental architecture of human aggression. *Journal of Personality and Social Psychology, 72,* 207–217.

Milgram, S. (1961). Nationality and conformity. *Scientific American, 205,* 45–51.

Milgram, S. (1963). Behavioral study of obedience. *Journal of Abnormal Psychology, 67,* 371–378.

Milgram, S. (1974). *Obedience to authority.* Harper.

Milgram, S., Bickman, L., & Berkowitz, L. (1969). Note on the drawing power of crowds of different size. *Journal of Personality and Social Psychology, 13,* 79–82.

Milgram, S. L., Mann, L., & Hartner, S. (1965). The lost letter technique: A tool of social science research. *Public Opinion Quarterly, 29,* 437–438.

Millar, M. G. (2002). The effectiveness of the door-in-the-face compliance strategy on friends and strangers. *Journal of Social Psychology, 142,* 295–304.

Miller, A. G., Gillen, B., Scheker, C., & Radlove, S. (1974). The prediction and perception of obedience to authority. *Journal of Personality, 42,* 23–42.

Miller, C. E. (1989). The social psychological effects of group decision rules. In P. Paulus (Ed.), *Psychology of group influence* (2nd ed., pp. 327–355). Erlbaum.

Miller, C. T., & Downey, K. T. (1999). A meta-analysis of heavyweight and self-esteem. *Personality and Social Psychology Review, 3,* 68–84.

Miller, C. T., & Myers, A. M. (1998). Compensating for prejudice: How heavyweight people (and others) control outcomes despite prejudice. In J. K. Swim & C. Stangor (Eds.), *Prejudice: The target's perspective* (pp. 191–218). Academic Press.

Miller, D. A., Bordens, K. S., & Lochbihler, S. L. (2012, January). Left-wing radicalism and prejudice. Poster presented at the Annual Meeting of the Society for Personality and Social Psychology, San Diego, CA.

Miller, D. A., Smith, E. R., & Mackie, D. M. (2004). Effects of intergroup contact and political predispositions on prejudice: Role of intergroup emotions. *Group Processes & Intergroup Relations, 7,* 221–237.

Miller, D. A., Tobin, E., Roth, Z. C., Jackson, M., & Noble, S. (2013, May). When multicultural activities backfire: The case of "Archie Bunker's Neighborhood" and system justification. Poster presented at the Annual Meeting of the Midwestern Psychological Association, Chicago, IL.

Miller, D. T., & McFarland, C. (1987). Pluralistic ignorance: When similarity is interpreted as dissimilarity. *Journal of Personality and Social Psychology, 53,* 298–305.

Miller, D. T., Turnbull, W., & McFarland, C. (1989). When a coincidence is suspicious: The role of mental simulation. *Journal of Personality and Social Psychology, 57,* 581–589.

Miller, G. (2000). Evolution of human music through sexual selection. In N. L. Wallin, B. Merker, & S. Brown (Eds.), *The origins of music* (pp. 329–360). MIT Press.

Miller, J. M. (2007). Examining the mediators of agenda setting: A new experimental paradigm reveals the role of emotions. *Political Psychology, 28,* 689–717.

Miller, K. E., Quigley, B. M., Eliseo, A. R. K., & Ball, N. J. (2016). Alcohol mixed with energy drink use as an event-level predictor of physical and verbal aggression in bar conflicts. *Alcoholism: Clinical and Experimental Research, 40,* 161–169.

Miller, N., & Brewer, M. B. (1984). The social psychology of desegregation: An introduction. In N. Miller & M. B. Brewer (Eds.), *Groups in contact: The psychology of desegregation* (pp. 1–9). Academic Press.

Miller, N., Pedersen, W. C., Earleywine, M., & Pollock, V. E. (2003). A theoretical model of triggered displaced aggression. *Personality and Social Psychology Review, 7,* 75–97.

Miller, N. E. (1941). The frustration-aggression hypothesis. *Psychological Review, 48,* 337–342.

Miller, S. L., & Maner, J. K. (2009). Sex differences in response to sexual versus emotional infidelity: The moderating role of individual differences. *Personality and Individual Differences, 46,* 287–291.

Miller, T. Q., Heath, L., Molcan, I. R., & Dugoni, B. L. (1991). Imitative violence in the real world. *Aggressive Behavior, 17,* 121–134.

Minshull, M., & Sussman, M. (1979). Strength of eyewitness testimony vs. strength of objective evidence in influencing jury decisions. Paper presented at the annual meeting of the Midwestern Psychological Association, Chicago, IL.

Mirror. (2015, October 21). *One in three women admit to watching porn regularly in sex survey.* https://www.mirror.co.uk/news/world-news/one-three-women-admit-watching-6673573

Mischel, W. (1998). Metacognition at the hyphen of social-cognitive psychology. *Personality and Social Psychology Review, 2,* 84–86.

Moberg, S. P., Krysan, M., & Christianson, D. (2019). The polls-trends: Racial attitudes in America. *Public Opinion Quarterly, 83,* 450–471.

Moghaddam, F. M. (2005). The staircase to terrorism: A psychological exploration. *American Psychologist, 60,* 161–169.

Monahan, J. L., Murphy, S. T., & Zajonc, R. B. (2000). Subliminal mere exposure: Specific, general, and diffuse effects. *Psychological Science, 11,* 462–466.

Monsour, M., Harris, B., Kurzweil, N., & Beard, C. (1994). Challenges confronting cross-sex friendships: "Much ado about nothing?" *Sex Roles, 31,* 55–77.

Monteith, M. J., Devine, P. G., & Zuwernik, J. R. (1993). Self-directed versus other-directed affect as a consequence of prejudice-related discrepancies. *Journal of Personality and Social Psychology, 64,* 198–210.

Monteith, M. J., & Spicer, C. V. (2000). Contents and correlates of Whites' and Blacks' racial attitudes. *Journal of Experimental Social Psychology, 36,* 125–154.

Monteoliva, A., & Garcia-Martinez, J. M. A. (2005). Adult attachment style and its effect on the quality of romantic relationships in Spanish students. *Journal of Social Psychology, 145,* 745–747.

Montgomery, B. M. (1988). Quality communication in personal relationships. In S. Duck, D. F. Hay, S. E. Hobfoll, W. Ickes, B. M. Montgomery (Eds.), *Handbook of personal relationships: Theory, research and interventions* (pp. 343–359). Wiley.

Montoya, E., Terburg, D., Bos, P., & Honk, J. (2012). Testosterone, cortisol, and serotonin as key regulators of social aggression: A review and theoretical perspective. *Motivation & Emotion, 36,* 65–73.

Montoya, R. M. (2008). I'm hot, so I'd say you're not: The influence of objective physical attractiveness on mate selection. *Personality and Social Psychology Bulletin, 34,* 1315–1331.

Montoya, R. M., Horton, R. S., & Kirchner, J. (2008). Is actual similarity necessary for attraction? A meta-analysis of actual and perceived similarity. *Journal of Social and Personal Relationships, 25,* 889–922.

Montoya, R. M., Horton, R. S., Vevea, J. L., Citkowicz, M., & Lauber, E. A. (2017). A re-examination of the mere exposure effect: The influence of repeated exposure on recognition, familiarity, and liking. *Psychological Bulletin, 143,* 459–498.

Moody, E. J. (2001). Internet use and its relationship to loneliness. *CyberPsychology and Behavior, 4,* 393–401.

Moreland, R. L., & Levine, J. M. (1989). Newcomers and old-timers in small groups. In P. Paulus (Ed.), *The psychology of group influence* (2nd ed., pp. 143–186). Erlbaum.

Morgan, C. A., III, Hazlett, G., Baranoski, M., Doran, A., Southwick, S., & Loftus, E. F. (2007). Accuracy of eyewitness identification is significantly associated with performance on a standardized test of face recognition. *International Journal of Law and Psychiatry, 30,* 213–223.

Morgan, C. A., III, Hazlett, G., Doran, A., Garrett, S., Hoyt, G., Thomas, P., Southwick, S. M. (2004). Accuracy of eyewitness memory for persons encountered during exposure to highly intense stress. *International Journal of Law and Psychiatry, 27,* 265–279.

Moriarty, T. (1975). Crime, commitment, and the unresponsive bystander: Two field experiments. *Journal of Personality and Social Psychology, 31,* 370–376.

Morman, M. T. (2000). The influence of fear appeals, message design, and masculinity on men's motivation to perform the testicular self-exam. *Journal of Applied Communication Research, 28,* 91–116.

Morrison, B. (1994, February 14). Letter from Liverpool: Children of circumstance. *The New Yorker,* 48–60.

Morrow-Howell, N., Lott, L., & Ozawa, M. (1990). The impact of race on volunteer helping relationships among the elderly. *Social Work, 35,* 395–403.

Morton, T. L. (1978). Intimacy and reciprocity of exchange: A comparison of spouses and strangers. *Journal of Personality and Social Psychology, 36,* 72–81.

Moscovici, S. (1980). Toward a theory of conversion behavior. In L. Berkowitz (Ed.), *Advances in experimental social psychology* (Vol. 13, pp. 209–239). Academic Press.

Moscovici, S. (1985). Social influence and conformity. In G. Lindzey & E. Aronson (Eds.), *Handbook of social psychology* (3rd ed., pp. 347–412). Erlbaum.

Moscovici, S., & Lage, E. (1976). Studies in social influence III: Majority versus minority influence in a group. *European Journal of Social Psychology, 6,* 149–174.

Moscovici, S., Lage, E., & Naffrechoux, M. (1969). Influence of a consistent minority on the responses of a majority in a color perception task. *Sociometry, 32,* 365–369.

Moscovici, S., & Zavalloni, M. (1969). The group as a polarizer of attitudes. *Journal of Personality and Social Psychology, 12,* 124–135.

Moser, G. (1988). Urban stress and helping behavior: Effects of environmental overload and noise on behavior. *Journal of Environmental Psychology, 8,* 287–298.

Moses, L. J., Baldwin, D. A., Rosicky, J. G., & Tidball, G. (2001). Evidence for referential understanding in the emotions domain at twelve and eighteen months. *Child Development, 72,* 718–735.

Moskos, C. (1990). *A call to civic service.* Free Press.

Moskos, C. (1991, August 5). How do they do it? *The New Republic,* 16–21.

Moskowitz, G. B., Stone, J., & Childs, A. (2012). Implicit stereotyping and medical decisions: Unconscious stereotype activation in practitioners' thoughts about African Americans. *American Journal of Public Health, 102,* 996–1001.

Motta, M., Sylvester, S., Callaghan, T., & Lunz-Trujillo, K. (2021, January 28). Encouraging COVID-19 vaccine uptake through effective health communication. *Frontiers in Political Science, 3,* 1–12.

Moyer, K. E. (1987). *Violence and aggression.* Paragon House.

Mugny, G. (1975). Negotiations, image of the other and the process of minority influence. *European Journal of Social Psychology, 5,* 209–228.

Muir, G., Lonsway, K. A., & Payne, D. L. (1996). Rape myth acceptance among Scottish and American students. *Journal of Social Psychology, 136,* 261–262.

Mullen, B. (1986). Atrocity as a function of lynch mob composition: A self-attention perspective. *Personality and Social Psychology Bulletin, 12,* 187–197.

Mullen, B., & Riordan, C. A. (1988). Self-serving attributions for performance in naturalistic settings: A metaanalytic review. *Journal of Applied Social Psychology, 18,* 3–22.

Mullen, E., & Skitka, L. J. (2009). Comparing Americans' and Ukrainians' allocations of public assistance: The role of affective reactions in helping behavior. *Journal of Cross-Cultural Psychology, 40,* 301–318.

Mulligan, K., & Habel, P. (2011). An experimental test of the effects of fictional framing on attitudes. *Social Science Quarterly, 92,* 79–99.

Mummendey, A., Kessler, T., Klink, A., & Mielke, R. (1999). Strategies to cope with negative social identity: Predictions by social identity theory and relative deprivation theory. *Journal of Personality and Social Psychology, 76,* 229–245.

Mummendey, A., & Wenzel, M. (1999). Social discrimination and tolerance in intergroup relations: Reactions to intergroup differences. *Personality and Social Psychology Review, 3,* 158–174.

Muraven, M., Tice, D. M., & Baumeister, R. F. (1998). Self-control as limited resource: Regulatory depletion patterns. *Journal of Personality and Social Psychology, 74,* 774–789.

Murdoch, D. D., & Pihl, R. O. (1988). The influence of beverage type on aggression in males in the natural setting. *Aggressive Behavior, 14,* 325–335.

Murphy, C. M., & Blumenthal, D. R. (2000). The mediating influence of interpersonal problems on the intergenerational transmission of relationship aggression. *Personal Relationships, 7,* 203–218.

Myers, D. G., & Kaplan, M. F. (1976). Group-induced polarization in simulated juries. *Personality and Social Psychology Bulletin, 2,* 63–66.

Myers, D. G., & Lamm, H. (1975). The polarizing effect of group discussion. *American Scientist, 63,* 297–303.

Myers, D. G., & Lamm, H. (1976). The group polarization phenomenon. *Psychological Bulletin, 83,* 602–303.

Myrdal, G. (1962). *An American dilemma: The Negro problem in American democracy.* Harper & Row.

N

Nadler, A., Altman, A., & Fisher, J. D. (1979). Helping is not enough: Recipient's reactions to aid as a function of positive and negative information about the self. *Journal of Personality, 47,* 615–628.

Nadler, A., Fisher, J. D., & Ben Itchak, S. (1983). With a little help from my friend: Effect of single or multiple act aid as a function of donor and task characteristics. *Journal of Personality and Social Psychology, 44,* 310–321.

Nadler, A., Fisher, J. D., & Streufert, S. (1976). When helping hurts: Effects of donor-recipient similarity and recipient self-esteem on reactions to aid. *Journal of Personality, 44,* 392–409.

Nagoshi, J., Adams, K., Terrell, H., Hill, E., Brzuzy, S., & Nagoshi, C. (2008). Gender differences in correlates of homophobia and transphobia. *Sex Roles, 59,* 521–531.

Nam, S. K., Chu, H. J., Lee, M. K., Lee, J. H., Kim, N., & Lee, S. M. (2010). A meta-analysis of gender differences in attitudes toward seeking professional psychological help. *Journal of American College Health, 59,* 110–116.

Nario-Redmond, M. R., Noel, J. G., & Fern, E. (2013). Redefining disability, re-imagining the self: Disability identification predicts self-esteem and strategic responses to stigma. *Self & Identity, 12,* 468–488.

National Institute of Mental Health. (2017). *Mental illness.* https://www.nimh.nih.gov/health/statistics/mental-illness

National Oceanic and Atmospheric Administration. (2021). *What is a rip current?* https://oceanservice.noaa.gov/facts/ripcurrent.html

National Science Teaching Association. (2014). *Science and engineering practices.* https://ngss.nsta.org/PracticesFull.aspx

Navarick, D. J. (2012). Historical psychology and the Milgram paradigm: Test of an experimentally derived model of defiance using accounts of massacres by Nazi Reserve Police Battalion 101. *The Psychological Record, 62,* 133–154.

Neimeyer, G. J., & Rareshide, M. B. (1991). Personal memories and personal identity: The impact of ego identity development on autobiographical memory recall. *Journal of Personality and Social Psychology, 60,* 562–569.

Neisser, U. (1976). *Cognition and reality: Principles and implications of cognitive psychology.* W. H. Freeman.

Nelson, T. D. (2002). *The psychology of prejudice.* Allyn and Bacon.

Nemeth, C. (1986). Differential contributions of majority and minority influence. *Psychological Review, 93,* 23–32.

Nemeth, C. (1991). Minority dissent as a stimulant to group performance. In S. Worchel, W. Wood, & J. A. Simpson (Eds.), *Group process and productivity* (pp. 95–111). Sage.

Nemeth, C., Swedlund, M., & Kanki, B. (1974). Patterning of the minority's responses and their influence on the majority. *European Journal of Social Psychology, 4,* 428–450.

Neuberg, S. L., Cialdini, R. B., Brown, S. L., Luce, C., & Sagarin, B. J. (1997). Does empathy lead to anything more than superficial helping? Comment on Batson et al., 1997. *Journal of Personality and Social Psychology, 73,* 510–516.

Newcomb, T. M. (1961). *The acquaintance process.* Holt, Rinehart & Winston.

Newseum Institute. (2015). *Survey: Americans say that it's ok to take down "that" flag.* https://www.freedomforuminstitute.org/2015/07/09/survey-americans-say-its-ok-to-take-down-that-flag/

New World Encyclopedia. (2016). *Ideology.* http://www.newworldencyclopedia.org/entry/Ideology

Neziek, J. B., Wesselmann, E. D., Wheeler, L., & Williams, K. D. (2012). Ostracism in everyday life. *Group Dynamics: Theory, Research, and Practice, 16,* 91–104.

Nichols, K. A. (1974). Severe social anxiety. *British Journal of Medical Psychology, 74,* 301–306.

Nicolaisen, M., & Thorsen, K. (2017). What are friends for? Friendships and loneliness over the lifespan—from 18 to 79 years. *International Journal of Aging & Human Development, 84,* 126–158.

Nielsen. (2020). *The Nielsen total audience report.* https://www.nielsen.com/us/en/insights/report/2020/the-nielsen-total-audience-report-august-2020/

Nikolaou, I. (2014). Social networking Web sites in job search and employee recruitment. *International Journal of Selection and Assessment, 22*, 179–189.

Nisbett, R. E. (1993). Violence and U.S. regional culture. *American Psychologist, 48*, 441–449.

Nisbett, R. E., Polly, G., & Lang, S. (1995). Homicide and U.S. regional culture. In R. B. Ruback & N. A. Weiner (Eds.), *Interpersonal violent behaviors* (pp. 133–151). Springer-Verlag.

Noor, F., & Evans, D. C. (2003). The effect of facial symmetry on perceptions of personality and attractiveness. *Journal of Research in Personality, 37*, 339–347.

North, A. C., Tarrent, M., & Hargreaves, D. J. (2004). The effects of music on helping behavior: A field study. *Environment and Behavior, 36*, 266–275.

Norton, M. I., Monin, B., Cooper, J., & Hogg, M. A. (2003). Vicarious dissonance: Attitude change from the inconsistency of others. *Journal of Personality and Social Psychology, 85*, 47–62.

Nosek, B. A. (2007). Implicit–explicit relations. *Current Directions in Psychological Science, 16*, 65–69.

Nosek, B. A., & Banaji, M. R. (2001). The go/no-go association task. *Social Cognition, 19*, 625–666.

Nosek, B. A., & Smyth, F. L. (2007). A multitrait-multimethod validation of the Implicit Association Test. *Experimental Psychology, 54*, 14–29.

Notarius, C., & Markman, H. (1993). *We can work it out: Making sense out of marital conflict.* Putnam.

NYC. (2020). *Mayor de Blasio, Speaker Johnson and Queens Chamber of Commerce encourage New Yorkers to visit Asian-American owned small businesses.* https://www1.nyc.gov/office-of-the-mayor/news/079-20/mayor-de-blasio-speaker-johnson-queens-chamber-commerce-encourage-new-yorkers-visit#/0

Nyhan, B., Reifler, J., Richey, S., & Freed, G. L. (2014). Effective messages in vaccine promotion: A randomized trial. *Pediatrics, 133*, e835–e842.

O

O'Connell, R. L. (1989). *Of arms and men: A history of war, weapons and aggression.* Oxford University Press.

O'Connor, L. E., Berry, J. W., Stiver, D. J., & Rangan, R. K. (2012). Depression, guilt, and Tibetan Buddhism. *Psychology, 3*, 805–809.

O'Meara, D. J. (1989). Cross-sex friendship: Four basic challenges of an ignored relationship. *Sex Roles, 21*, 525–543.

O'Meara, D. J. (2006). Cross-sex friendships: Who has more? *Sex Roles, 54*, 809–820.

O'Neill Shermer, L., Rose, K. C., & Hoffman, A. (2011). Perceptions and credibility: Understanding the nuances of eyewitness testimony. *Journal of Contemporary Criminal Justice, 27*, 183–203.

Oakley, B. (2014). Empathy in academe: On the origins of pathological altruism. *Academic Questions, 27*, 48–64.

Oakley B., Knafo, A., Madhavan, G., & Wilson, D. S. (Eds.). (2012). *Pathological altruism.* Oxford University Press.

Odintsova, V. V., Roetman, P. J., Ip, H. F., Pool, R., Van der Laan, C. M., Tona, K.-D., & . . . Boomsma, D. I. (2019). Genomics of human aggression: Current state of genome-wide studies and an automated systematic review tool. *Psychiatric Genetics, 29*, 170–190.

Oeberst, A., & Blank, H. (2012). Undoing suggestive influence on memory: The reversibility of the eyewitness misinformation effect. *Cognition, 125*, 141–159.

Ohbuchi, K. (1981). A study of attack patterns: Equity or recency? *Japanese Psychological Research, 23*, 191–195.

Ohbuchi, K., & Kambara, T. (1985). Attackers' intent and awareness of outcome, impression management, and retaliation. *Journal of Experimental Social Psychology, 21*, 321–330.

Oksanen, A., Oksa, R., Savela, N., Kaakinen, M., & Ellonen, N. (2020). Cyberbullying victimization at work: Social media identity bubble approach. *Computers in Human Behavior, 109*. https://doi.org/10.1016/j.chb.2020.106363

Oliker, S. J. (1989). *Best friends and marriage: Exchange among women.* University of California Press.

Oliner, S. P., & Oliner, P. M. (1988). *The altruistic personality: Rescuers of Jews in Nazi Europe.* Free Press.

Olweus, D. (1984). Development of stable reaction patterns. In R. J. Blanchard and D. C. Blanchard (Eds.), *Advances in the study of aggression* (Vol. 1, pp. 103–138). Academic Press.

Öner, S., & Gülgöz, S. (2018). Autobiographical remembering regulates emotions: A functional perspective. *Memory, 26*, 15–28.

Opdyke, I. G. (1992). *Into the flames: The life story of a righteous gentile.* Borgo Press.

Open Science Collaboration (OSC). (2015). Estimating the reproducibility of psychological science. *Science, 349*, 1–8.

Organ, D. W. (1988). *Organizational citizenship behavior: The good soldier syndrome.* Lexington Books.

Osborn, K. A., Irwin, B. C., Skogsberg, N. J., & Feltz, D. L. (2012). The Köhler effect: Motivation gains and losses in real sports groups. *Sport, Exercise, and Performance Psychology, 1*, 242–253.

Osherow, N. (1988). Making sense of the nonsensical: An analysis of Jonestown. In E. Aronson (Ed.), *Readings about the social animal* (5th ed., pp. 68–86). Freeman.

Oskamp, S. (1991). *Attitudes and opinions* (2nd ed.). Prentice-Hall.

Ostrove, J. M., & Keating, C. F. (2004). Gender differences in preschool aggression during free play and structured interactions: An observational study. *Social Development, 13*, 255–277.

Oswald, F. L., Mitchell, G., Blanton, H., Jaccard, J., & Tetlock, P. E. (2013). Predicting ethnic and racial discrimination: A meta-analysis of IAT criterion studies. *Journal of Personality and Social Psychology, 105,* 171–192.

Oswald, P. A. (2002). The interactive effects of affective demeanor, cognitive processes, and perspective-taking focus on helping behavior. *Journal of Social Psychology, 142,* 120–132.

Ouellette, J. A., Hessling, R., Gibbons, F. X., Reis-Bergan, M., & Gerrard, M. (2005). Using images to increase exercise behavior: Prototypes versus possible selves. *Personality and Social Psychology Bulletin, 31,* 610–620.

Over, R., & Phillips, G. (1997). Differences between men and women in age preferences for a same-sex partner. *Behavioral and Brain Sciences, 20,* 138–140.

P

Palmer, C. L., & Peterson, R. D. (2021). Physical attractiveness, halo effects, and social joining. *Social Science Quarterly, 102,* 552–566.

Palmer, J. K., & Feldman, J. M. (2005). Accountability and need for cognition effects on contrast, halo, and accuracy in performance ratings. *The Journal of Psychology, 139,* 119–137.

Paluck, E. (2009). Reducing intergroup prejudice and conflict using the media: A field experiment in Rwanda. *Journal of Personality and Social Psychology, 96,* 574–587.

Park, Y., Killen, M., Crystal, D. S., & Wantanabe, H. (2003). Korean, Japanese, and U.S. students' judgments about peer exclusion: Evidence for diversity. *International Journal of Behavior Development, 27,* 555–565.

Parrott, D. J., & Lisco, C. G. (2015). Effects of alcohol and sexual prejudice on aggression toward sexual minorities. *Psychology of Violence, 5,* 256–265.

Patterson, G. R., DeBaryshe, B. D., & Ramsey, E. (1989). A developmental perspective on antisocial behavior. *American Psychologist, 44,* 329–335.

Paul, A. (2014). Is online better than offline for meeting partners? Depends: Are you looking to marry or to date? *Cyberpsychology, Behavior & Social Networking, 17,* 664–667.

Paulhus, D. L., & Reid, D. B. (1991). Enhancement and denial in socially desirable responding. *Journal of Personality and Social Psychology, 60,* 307–317.

Payne, B. K., Cheng, C. M., Govorun, O., & Stewart, B. D. (2005). An inkblot for attitudes: Affect misattribution as implicit measurement. *Journal of Personality and Social Psychology, 89,* 277–293.

Pedersen, W. C., Gonzales, C., & Miller, N. (2000). The moderating effect of trivial triggering provocation on displaced aggression. *Journal of Personality and Social Psychology, 78,* 913–927.

Peetz, J., Buehler, R., & Britten, K. (2011). Only minutes a day: Reframing exercise duration affects exercise intentions and behavior. *Basic and Applied Social Psychology, 33,* 118–127.

Peixoto, M. M., & Nobre, P. (2015). Cognitive schemas activated in sexual context: A comparative study with homosexual and heterosexual men and women, with and without sexual problems. *Cognitive Therapy Research, 39,* 390–402.

Pelham, B. (1991). On confidence and consequence: The certainty and importance of self-knowledge. *Journal of Personality and Social Psychology, 60,* 18–20.

Pelham, B., & Swann, W. B., Jr. (1989). From self-conceptions to self-worth: On sources and structure of global self-esteem. *Journal of Personality and Social Psychology, 57,* 672–680.

Pelosi, N. (2020). *Pelosi statement on the Lunar New Year.* https://www.speaker.gov/newsroom/12520

Pendleton, M., & Batson, D. (1979). Self-presentation and the door-in-the-face technique for inducing compliance. *Personality and Social Psychology Bulletin, 5,* 77–81.

Pennebaker, J. W. (1989). Confession, inhibition, and disease. In L. Berkowitz (Ed.), *Advances in experimental social psychology* (Vol. 22, pp. 211–244). Academic Press.

Pennington, C. R., Heim, D., Levy, A. R., & Larkin, D. T. (2016). Twenty years of stereotype threat research: A review of psychological mediators. *PloS ONE, 11,* e0146487.

Pennisi, E. (2001). Behind the scenes of gene expression. *Science, 293,* 1064–1068.

Penrod, S., & Cutler, B. (1995). Witness confidence and witness accuracy: Assessing their forensic relation. *Psychology, Public Policy, and Law, 1,* 817–845.

Peplau, L. A., & Perlman, D. (1982). Perspectives on loneliness. In L. A. Peplau & D. Perlman (Eds.), *Loneliness: A source-book of current theory research, and therapy* (pp. 1–18). Wiley.

Pepler, D. J., King, G., & Byrd, W. (1991). A social-cognitively based social skills training program for aggressive children. In D. J. Pepler & K. H. Rubin (Eds.), *The development and treatment of childhood aggression* (pp. 361–379). Erlbaum.

Peralta, C. F., Lopes, P. N., Gilson, L. L., Lourenço, P. R., & Pais, L. (2015). Innovation processes and team effectiveness: The role of goal clarity and commitment, and team affective tone. *Journal of Occupational & Organizational Psychology, 88,* 80–107.

Perdue, C. W., Dovidio, J. F., Gurtman, M. B., & Tyler, R. B. (1990). Us and them: Social categorization and the process of intergroup bias. *Journal of Personality and Social Psychology, 59,* 475–486.

Perlman, D., & Oskamp, S. (1971). The effects of picture content and exposure frequency on evaluations of Negroes and Whites. *Journal of Experimental Social Psychology, 7,* 503–514.

Perrin, S., & Spencer, C. (1981). The Asch effect—A child of its time? *Bulletin of the British Psychological Society, 33,* 405–406.

Peters, M. L., Flink, I. K., Boersma, K., & Linton, S. J. (2010). Manipulating optimism: Can imagining a best possible self be used to increase positive future expectancies? *Journal of Positive Psychology, 5,* 204–211.

Pettigrew, T. E. (1979). The ultimate attribution error: Extending Allport's cognitive analysis of prejudice. *Personality and Social Psychology Bulletin, 5,* 461–476.

Pettit, G. S., Bakshi, A., Dodge, K. A., & Coie, J. D. (1986). The emergence of social dominance in young boys' play groups: Developmental differences and behavioral correlates. *Developmental Psychology, 26,* 1017–1025.

Petty, R. E., & Cacioppo, J. T. (1986). *Communication and persuasion: Central and peripheral routes to attitude change.* Springer-Verlag.

Petty, R. E., Cacioppo, J. T., & Goldman, R. (1981). Personal involvement as a determinant of argument-based persuasion. *Journal of Social Behavior and Personality, 41,* 847–855.

Petty, R. E., Schumann, D. W., Richman, S. A., & Strathman, A. J. (1993). Positive mood and persuasion: Different roles for affect under high and low elaboration conditions. *Journal of Personality and Social Psychology, 64,* 5–20.

Petty, R. E., & Wegener, D. T. (1993). Flexible correction processes in social judgment: Correcting for context-induced contrast. *Journal of Experimental Social Psychology, 29,* 137–165.

Petty, R. E., Wegener, D. T., & White, P. H. (1998). Flexible correction in social judgment: Implications for persuasion. *Social Cognition, 16,* 93–113.

Peukert, D. (1987). *Inside Nazi Germany: Conformity, opposition, and racism in everyday life.* Yale University Press.

Pew Research Center. (2014). *Public strongly backs affirmative action programs on campus.* http://www.pewresearch.org/fact-tank/2014/04/22/public-strongly-backs-affirmative-action-programs-on-campus/

Pew Research Center. (2020). *Social media fact sheet.* https://www.pewresearch.org/internet/fact-sheet/social-media/#which-social-media-platforms-are-most-common

Pew Research Center. (2021). *Social media fact sheet.* https://www.pewresearch.org/internet/fact-sheet/social-media/

Pew Research Organization. (2015). *Teens, technology and friendships.* https://www.pewresearch.org/internet/2015/08/06/teens-technology-and-friendships/

Pew Research Organization. (2018). *Teens' social media habits and experiences.* https://www.pewresearch.org/internet/2018/11/28/teens-social-media-habits-and-experiences/

Pew Research Organization. (2019a). *Americans see advantages and challenges in country's growing racial and ethnic diversity.* https://www.pewresearch.org/social-trends/2019/05/08/americans-see-advantages-and-challenges-in-countrys-growing-racial-and-ethnic-diversity/

Pew Research Organization. (2019b). *Race in America 2019.* https://www.pewresearch.org/social-trends/2019/04/09/race-in-america-2019/

Pfau, M., Roskos-Ewoldsen, D., Wood, M., Yin, S., Cho, J., Lu, K.-H., & Shen, L. (2003). Attitude accessibility as an alternative explanation for how inoculation confers resistance. *Communication Monographs, 70,* 39–51.

Phillips, A. G., & Silvia, P. J. (2005). Self-awareness and emotional consequences of self-discrepancies. *Personality and Social Psychology Bulletin, 3,* 703–713.

Phillips, D. P. (1983). The impact of mass media violence on U.S. homicides. *American Sociological Review, 48,* 560–568.

Phillips, D. P. (1986). Natural experiments on the effects of mass media violence on fatal aggression: Strengths and weaknesses of a new approach. In L. Berkowitz (Ed.), *Advances in experimental social psychology* (Vol. 19, pp. 207–250). Academic Press.

Pickel, K. L. (2009). The weapon focus effect on memory for female versus male perpetrators. *Memory, 17,* 664–678.

Pickel, K. L., Narter, D. B., Jameson, M. M., & Lenhardt, T. T. (2008). The weapon focus effect in child eyewitnesses. *Psychology, Crime & Law, 14,* 61–72.

Pickel, K. L., & Sneyd, D. E. (2018). The weapon focus effect is weaker with Black versus White male perpetrators. *Memory, 26,* 29–41.

Piferi, R. L., Jobe, R. L., & Jones, W. H. (2006). Giving to others during national tragedy: The effects of altruistic and egoistic motivations on long-term giving. *Journal of Social and Personal Relationships, 23,* 171–184.

Pihl, R. O., Assad, J. M., & Hoaken, P. N. S. (2003). The alcohol-aggression relationship and differential sensitivity to alcohol. *Aggressive Behavior, 29,* 302–315.

Pihl, R. O., & Lemarquand, D. (1998). Serotonin and aggression and the alcohol-aggression relationship. *Alcohol and Alcoholism, 33,* 55–65.

Pihl, R. O., & Peterson, J. B. (1993). Alcohol, serotonin and aggression. *Alcohol Health and Research World, 17,* 113–116.

Pihl, R. O., Peterson, J. B., & Lau, M. A. (1993). A biosocial model of the alcohol-aggression relationship. *Journal of Studies on Alcohol, 11,* 128–139.

Pihl, R. O., Smith, M., & Farrell, B. (1984). Alcohol and aggression in men: A comparison of brewed and distilled beverages. *Journal of Studies on Alcohol, 45,* 278–282.

Pihl, R. O., & Zaccia, C. (1986). Alcohol and aggression: A test of the affect-arousal hypothesis. *Aggressive Behavior, 12,* 367–375.

Pila, E., Sabiston, C. M., Brunet, J., Castonguay, A. L., & O'Loughlin, J. (2015). Do body-related shame and guilt mediate the association between weight status and self-esteem? *Journal of Health Psychology, 20,* 659–669.

Piliavin, I. M., Piliavin, J. A., & Rodin, J. (1975). Costs, diffusion, and the stigmatized victim. *Journal of Personality and Social Psychology, 32,* 429–438.

Piliavin, J. A., & Piliavin, I. M. (1972). Effects of blood on reactions to a victim. *Journal of Personality and Social Psychology, 8,* 353–361.

Pinker, S. (2002). *The blank slate*. Viking.

Plant, E. A., & Devine, P. G. (2003). The antecedents and implications of interracial anxiety. *Personality and Social Psychology Bulletin, 29,* 790–800.

Plant, E. A., & Peruche, B. M. (2005). The consequences of race for police officers' response to criminal suspects. *Psychological Science, 16,* 180–183.

Platania, J., & Moran, G. P. (2001). Social facilitation as a function of the mere presence of others. *Journal of Social Psychology, 141,* 190–197.

Plomin, R. (1989). *Nature and nurture: An introduction to human behavioral genetics*. Brooks/Cole.

Plomin, R., Corley, R., DeFries, J. C., & Fulker, D. W. (1990). Individual differences in television viewing in early childhood: Nature as well as nurture. *Psychological Science, 1,* 371–377.

Plous, S. (2016). *The psychology of prejudice: An overview*. http://www.understandingprejudice.org/apa/english/page2.htm

Postmes, T., Spears, R., Lee, A. T., & Novak, R. J. (2005). Individuality and social influence in groups: Inductive and deductive routes to group identity. *Journal of Personality and Social Psychology, 89,* 747–763.

Potârcă, G., Mills, M., & Neberich, W. (2015). Relationship preferences among gay and lesbian online daters: Individual and contextual influences. *Journal of Marriage and Family, 77,* 523–541.

Prati, G., & Pietrantoni, L. (2009). Optimism, social support, and coping strategies as factors contributing to posttraumatic growth: A meta-analysis. *Journal of Loss and Trauma, 14,* 364–388.

Pratkanis, A. R., & Aronson, E. (1992). *The age of propaganda*. Freeman.

Pratkanis, A. R., Greenwald, A. G., Leippe, M. R., & Baumgardner, M. H. (1988). In search of reliable persuasion effects. III. The sleeper effect is dead. Long live the sleeper effect. *Journal of Personality and Social Psychology, 54,* 203–218.

Pratto, F., & Bargh, J. H. (1991). Stereotyping based on apparently individuating information: Trait and global components of sex stereotypes under attention overload. *Journal of Experimental Social Psychology, 27,* 26–47.

Pratto, F., & John, O. (1991). Automatic vigilance: The attention-grabbing power of negative social information. *Journal of Personality and Social Psychology, 51,* 380–391.

Pratto, F., Sidanius, J., Stallworth, L. M., & Malle, B. F. (1994). Social dominance orientation: A personality variable predicting social and political attitudes. *Journal of Personality and Social Psychology, 67,* 741–763.

Prentice, D. A., & Miller, D. T. (1993). Pluralistic ignorance and alcohol use on campus: Some consequences of misperceiving the social norm. *Journal of Personality and Social Psychology, 64,* 243–256.

Prentice-Dunn, S., & Rogers, R. W. (1989). Deindividuation and the self-regulation of behavior. In P. B. Paulus (Ed.), *Psychology of group influence* (2nd ed., pp. 87–110). Erlbaum.

Priester, J. R., & Petty, R. E. (2003). The influence of spokesperson trustworthiness on message elaboration, attitude strength, and advertising effectiveness. *Journal of Consumer Psychology, 13,* 408–421.

Prior, M. (2013). Media and political polarization. *Annual Review of Political Science, 16,* 101–127.

Pritchard, R. D., & Watson, M. D. (1991). Understanding and measuring group productivity. In S. Worchel, W. Wood, & J. A. Simpson (Eds.), *Group process and productivity* (pp. 251–275). Sage.

Pruitt, D. G. (1968). Reciprocity and credit building in a laboratory dyad. *Journal of Personality and Social Psychology, 8,* 143–147.

Pulkkinen, L., & Pikanen, T. (1993). Continuities in aggressive behavior from childhood to adulthood. *Aggressive Behavior, 19,* 249–263.

Pyszczynski, T., Greenberg, J., Solomon, S., Arndt, J., & Schimel, J. (2004). Why do people need self-esteem? A theoretical and empirical review. *Psychological Bulletin, 130,* 435–468.

Q

QuanIei, Y., Jianwen, C., Qiuying, Z., & Shenghua, J. (2015). Implicit and explicit self-esteem: The moderating effect of individualism. *Social Behavior & Personality: An International Journal, 43,* 519–528.

Quattrociocchi, W., Scala, A., & Sunstein, C. R. (2016). *Echo chambers on Facebook*. https://papers.ssrn.com/sol3/papers.cfm?abstract_id=2795110

Quattrone, G. A., & Jones, E. E. (1980). The perception of variability within in-groups and out-groups. *Journal of Personality and Social Psychology, 38,* 141–152.

Quigley, B. M., & Leonard, K. E. (1999). Husband alcohol expectancies, drinking and marital-conflict styles as predictors of severe marital violence among newlywed couples. *Psychology of Addictive Behaviors, 13,* 49–59.

Quinton, W. J., Cowan, G., & Watson, B. D. (1996). Personality and attitudinal predictors of support of proposition 187—California's anti-illegal immigrant initiative. *Journal of Applied Social Psychology, 26,* 2204–2223.

R

Rainie, L., & Smith, A. (2012). *Social networking sites and politics*. http://www.pewinternet.org/2012/03/12/social-networking-sites-and-politics/

Rains, S. A. (2013). The nature of psychological reactance revisited: A meta-analytic review. *Human Communication Research, 39*, 47–73.

Rajecki, D. W. (1990). *Attitudes* (2nd ed.). Sinauer.

Ramanathan, D. M., Wardecker, B. M., Slocomb, J. E., & Hillary, F. G. (2011). Dispositional optimism and outcome following traumatic brain injury. *Brain Injury, 25*, 328–337.

Rand, D. G., & Epstein, Z. G. (2014). Risking your life without a second thought: Intuitive decision-making and extreme altruism. *Plos ONE, 9*, 1–6.

Rast, D. E., Gaffney, A. M., & Yang, F. (2018). The effect of stereotype content on intergroup uncertainty and interactions. *Journal of Social Psychology, 158*, 711–720.

Ratner, R. K., & Herbst, K. C. (2005). When good decisions have bad outcomes: The impact of affect on switching behavior. *Organizational Behavior and Human Decision Processes, 96*, 23–37.

Rattner, A., Yagil, D., & Pedahzur, A. (2001). Not bound by the law: Legal disobedience in Israeli society. *Behavioral Sciences and the Law, 19*, 265–283.

Rawlins, W. K. (1992). *Friendship matters: Communication, dialectics, and life course.* Aldine De Gruyter.

Raynaud–Maintier, C., & Alaphillippe, D. (2001). The effects of help on self-esteem according to age. English abstract, *PsycInfo,* Accession Number 2001-17468-001.

Reagan, P. C., Lakhanpal, S., & Anguiano, C. (2012). Relationship outcomes in Indian-American love-based and arranged marriages. *Psychological Reports, 110*, 915–924.

Reed, P. J., Spiro, E. S., & Butts, C. T. (2016). Thumbs up for privacy? Differences in online self-disclosure behavior across national cultures. *Social Science Research, 59*, 155–170.

Reeder, G. D., Pryor, J. B., Wohl, M. J. A., & Griswell, M. L. (2005). On attributing negative motives to others who disagree with our opinions. *Personality and Social Psychology Bulletin, 31*, 1498–1510.

Reeder, G. D., & Trafimow, D. (2005). Attributing motives to other people. In B. F. Malle and S. D. Hodges (Eds.), *Other minds: How humans bridge the divide between self and others* (pp. 106–123). Guilford Publications, Inc.

Reeder, H. (2017). "He's like a brother": The social construction of satisfying cross-sex friendship roles. *Sexuality & Culture, 21*, 142–162.

Reeves, R., Baker, G., Boyd, J., & Cialdini, R. (1991). The door-in-the-face technique: Reciprocal concessions vs. self-presentational explanations. *Journal of Social Behavior and Personality, 6*, 545–558.

Regan, D. T. (1971). Effects of a favor and liking on compliance. *Journal of Experimental Social Psychology, 7*, 627–639.

Regan, P. (1998). What if you can't get what you want? Willingness to compromise ideal mate selection standards as a function of sex, mate value, and relationship context. *Personality and Social Psychology, 24*, 1294–1303.

Regan, P. C., Durvasula, R., Howell, L., Ureno, O., & Rea, M. (2004). Gender, ethnicity, and the timing of first sexual and romantic experiences. *Social Behavior and Personality, 32*, 667–676.

Regan, P. C., Kocan, E. R., & Whitlock, T. (1998). Ain't love grand: A prototype analysis of the concept of romantic love. *Journal of Social and Personal Relationships, 15*, 411–420.

Reicher, S. D., Spears, R., & Postmes, T. (1995). A social identity model of deindividuation phenomena. *European Review of Social Psychology, 6*, 161–198.

Reinisch, J. M., & Sanders, S. A. (1986). A test of sex differences in aggressive response to hypothetical conflict situations. *Journal of Personality and Social Psychology, 50*, 1045–1049.

Reis, H. T., & Shaver, P. (1988). Intimacy as an interpersonal process. In S. Duck, D. F. Hay, S. E. Hobfall, W. Ickes, & B. M. Montgomery (Eds.), *Handbook of personal relationships* (pp. 367–389). Wiley and Sons.

Reiss, M. J. (1984). Human sociobiology. *Zygon, 19*, 117–140.

Repple, J., Habel, U., Wagels, L., Pawliczek, C. M., Schneider, F., & Kohn, N. (2018). Sex differences in the neural correlates of aggression. *Brain Structure & Function, 223*, 4115–4124.

Resenhoeft, A., Villa, J., & Wiseman, D. (2008). Tattoos can harm perceptions: A study and suggestions. *Journal of American College Health, 56,* 593–596.

Reynolds, S., Searight, H. R., & Ratwik, S. (2014). Adult attachment style and rumination in the context of intimate relationships. *North American Journal of Psychology, 16*, 495–506.

Reynolds, V., Falger, V., & Vine, I. (1987). *The sociobiology of ethnocentrism.* University of Georgia Press.

Rhodewalt, F. T., Morf, C., Hazlett, S., & Fairfield, M. (1991). Self-handicapping: The role of discounting and augmentation in the preservation of self-esteem. *Journal of Personality and Social Psychology, 61*, 122–131.

Richards, Z., & Hewstone, M. (2001). Subtyping and subgrouping: Processes for the prevention and promotion of stereotype change. *Personality and Social Psychology Review, 5*, 52–73.

Richardson, D. R., Vandenberg, R. J., & Humphries, S. A. (1986). Effect of power to harm on retaliative aggression among males and females. *Journal of Research in Personality, 20*, 402–419.

Richman, L. S., Kubzansky, L., Maselko, J., Kawachi, I., Choo, P., & Bauer, M. (2005). Positive emotion and health: Going beyond the negative. *Health Psychology, 24*, 422–429.

Ringhand, L. A. (2007). Judicial activism: An empirical examination of voting behavior on the Rehnquist natural court. *Constitutional Commentary, 24*, 43–102.

Rios, K. (2013). Right-wing authoritarianism predicts prejudice against "homosexuals" but not "gay men and lesbians." *Journal of Experimental Social Psychology, 49*, 1177–1183.

Risen, J. L., Gilovich, T., & Dunning, D. (2007). One-shot illusory correlations and stereotype formation. *Personality and Social Psychology Bulletin, 33*, 1492–1502.

Rius-Ottenheim, N., Kromhout, D., van der Mast, R. C., Zitman, F. G., Geleijnse, J. M., & Giltay, E. J. (2012). Dispositional optimism and loneliness in older men. *International Journal of Geriatric Psychiatry, 27*, 151–159.

Rochat, F., Maggioni, O., & Modgiliani, A. (2000). The dynamics of obeying and opposing authority: A mathematical model. In T. Blass (Ed.), *Obedience to authority: Current perspectives on the Milgram paradigm* (pp. 161–192). Lawrence Erlbaum Publishers.

Rodafinos, A., Vucevic, A., & Sideridis, G. D. (2005). The effectiveness of compliance techniques: Foot in the door versus door in the face. *Journal of Social Psychology, 145*, 237–239.

Roderick, C., Pitchford, M., & Miller, A. (1997). Reducing aggressive playground behaviour by means of a school-wide raffle. *Educational Psychology in Practice, 13*, 57–63.

Rodriguez, D. N., & Berry, M. A. (2009). Dissonance reduction in jurors' post-verdict decisions. *American Journal of Forensic Psychology, 27*, 5–17.

Rodríguez-García, J., & Wagner, U. (2009). Learning to be prejudiced: A test of unidirectional and bidirectional models of parent–offspring socialization. *International Journal of Intercultural Relations, 33*, 516–523.

Roese, N. J., & Olson, J. M. (1997). Counterfactual thinking: The intersection of affect and function. In M. P. Zanna (Ed.), *Advances in experimental social psychology* (Vol. 29, pp. 1–59). Academic Press.

Rogers, R. W. (1983). Cognitive and physiological processes in fear appeals and attitude change: A revised theory of protection motivation. In J. T. Cacioppo & R. E. Petty (Eds.), *Social psychophysiology* (pp. 153–177). Guilford.

Rohsenow, D. J., & Bachorowski, J. (1984). Effects of alcohol and expectancies on verbal aggression in men and women. *Journal of Abnormal Psychology, 93*, 418–432.

Roisman, G. I., Clausell, E., Holland, A., Fortuna, K., & Elieff, C. (2007). Adult romantic relationships as contexts of human development: A multimethod comparison of same-sex couples with opposite-sex dating, engaged, and married dyads. *Developmental Psychology, 44*, 91–101.

Rokach, A., & Neto, F. (2005). Age, culture and the antecedents of loneliness. *Social Behavior and Personality, 33*, 477–494.

Rokeach, M. (1973). *The nature of human values*. Free Press.

Rokeach, M. (1979). *Understanding human values: Individual and social*. Free Press.

Romer, D., Gruder, C. L., & Lizzadro, T. (1986). A person-situation approach to altruistic behavior. *Journal of Personality and Social Psychology 51*, 1001–1012.

Romero-López, M., Pichardo, M. C., Justicia-Arráez, A., & Bembibre-Serrano, J. (2021). Reducing aggression by developing emotional and inhibitory control. *International Journal of Environmental Research and Public Health, 18*. https://doi.org/10.3390/ijerph18105263

Ronis, D. L., & Kaiser, M. K. (1989). Correlates of breast cancer self-examinations in a sample of college women: Analysis of linear structural variations. *Journal of Applied Social Psychology, 19*, 1068–1085.

Roosevelt, F. D. (1941, December 8). *Address to the Congress asking that a state of war be declared between the United States and Japan*. https://www.loc.gov/resource/afc1986022.afc1986022_ms2201/?st=text&r=0.065,-0.028,0.5,0.459,0

Rosander, M., & Eriksson, O. (2012). Conformity on the Internet—the role of task difficulty and gender differences. *Computers in Human Behavior, 28*, 1587–1595.

Rose, S., & Frieze, I. H. (1989). Young singles' scripts for a first date. *Gender & Society, 3*, 258–268.

Rose, S., & Frieze, I. H. (1993). Young singles' contemporary dating scripts. *Sex Roles, 28*, 499–509.

Rosenbaum, M. E. (1986). The repulsion hypothesis: On the nondevelopment of relationships. *Journal of Personality and Social Psychology, 51*, 1156–1166.

Rosenfeld, M. J. (2010). *Meeting online: The rise of the Internet as a social intermediary*. https://web.stanford.edu/~mrosenfe/Rosenfeld_How_Couples_Meet_PAA_updated.pdf

Rosenfeld, M. J., & Thomas, R. J. (2012). Searching for a mate: The rise of the Internet as a social intermediary. *American Sociological Review, 77*, 523–547.

Rosenthal, R., & Jacobson, L. (1968). *Pygmalion in the classroom: Teacher expectation and pupil's intellectual development*. Holt.

Roskos-Ewoldsen, D., & Fazio, R. H. (1992). On the orienting value of attitudes: Attitude accessibility as a determinant of an object's attraction of visual attention. *Journal of Personality and Social Psychology, 63*, 198–211.

Ross, L., Amabile, T., & Steinmetz, J. L. (1977). Social roles, social control, and biases in social perception process. *Journal of Personality and Social Psychology, 35*, 484–494.

Ross, L., & Nisbett, R. E. (1991). *The person and the situation*. McGraw Hill.

Roulin, N., & Bangerter, A. (2013). Social networking websites in personnel selection. *Journal of Personnel Psychology, 12*, 143–151.

Rubin, A. M., West, D. V., & Mitchell, W. S. (2001). Differences in aggression, attitudes toward women, and distrust as reflected in popular music preferences. *Media Psychology, 3*, 25–42.

Rubin, M., & Hewstone, M. (1998). Social identity theory's self-esteem hypothesis: A review and some suggestions for clarification. *Personality and Social Psychology Review, 2,* 40–62.

Rubin, Z. (1970). Measurement and romantic love. *Journal of Personality and Social Psychology, 16,* 265–273.

Rubin, Z. (1973). *Liking and loving: An invitation to social psychology.* Holt, Rinehart & Winston.

Rude, J., & Herda, D. (2010). Best friends forever? Race and the stability of adolescent friendships. *Social Forces, 89,* 585–607.

Rudman, L. A., Ashmore, R. D., & Gary, M. L. (2001). "Unlearning" automatic biases: The malleability of implicit prejudice and stereotypes. *Journal of Personality and Social Psychology, 81,* 856–868.

Ruiter, R. C., Kessels, L. E., Peters, G. Y., & Kok, G. (2014). Sixty years of fear appeal research: Current state of the evidence. *International Journal of Psychology, 49,* 63–70.

Rule, B. G., & Ferguson, T. J. (1986). The effects of media violence on attitudes, emotions, and cognitions. *Journal of Social Issues, 42,* 29–50.

Rusbult, C. E., Kumashiro, M., Kubacka, K. E., & Finkel, E. J. (2009). "The part of me that you bring out": Ideal similarity and the Michelangelo phenomenon. *Journal of Personality and Social Psychology, 96,* 61–82.

Rusbult, C. E., Verette, J., Whitney, G. A., Slovik, L. F., & Lipkus, I. (1991). Accommodation processes in close relationships: Theory and preliminary empirical evidence. *Journal of Personality and Social Psychology 61,* 641–647.

Ruth, S. C., & Francoise, S. (1999). Effects of parental verbal aggression on children's self-esteem and school marks. *Child Abuse and Neglect, 23,* 339–351.

Ruvolo, A. P., & Rotondo, J. L. (1998). Diamonds in the rough: Implicit personality theories and views of partner and self. *Personality and Social Psychology Bulletin, 24,* 750–758.

Ryan, K. M., & Kanjorski, J. (1998). The enjoyment of sexist humor, rape attitudes, and relationship aggression in college students. *Sex Roles, 38,* 743–756.

Ryckman, R. M., Robbins, M. A., Thornton, B., Kaaczor, L. M., Gayton, S. L., & Anderson, C. V. (1991). Public self-consciousness and physique stereotyping. *Personality and Social Psychology Bulletin, 18,* 400–405.

S

Sadler, M. S., Meagor, E. L., & Kaye, K. E. (2012). Stereotypes of mental disorders differ in competence and warmth. *Social Science & Medicine, 74,* 915–922.

Safer, M. A., Murphy, R. P., Wise, R. A., Bussey, L., Millett, C., & Holfeld, B. (2016). Educating jurors about eyewitness testimony in criminal cases with circumstantial and forensic evidence. *International Journal of Law and Psychiatry, 47,* 86–92.

Sahoo, F. M., Sahoo, K., & Das, N. (2011). Need saliency and management of employee motivation: Test of an indigenous model. *Vilakshan: The XIMB Journal of Management, 7,* 21–36.

Saint-Bauzel, R., & Fointiat, V. (2012). The sweet smell of the requester: Vanilla, camphor and the foot-in-the-door. *Social Behavior & Personality: An International Journal, 40,* 369–374.

Sakulku, J., & Alexander, J. (2011). The impostor phenomenon. *Journal of Behavioral Science, 6,* 75–97.

Salerno, J. M., & Peter-Hagene, L. C. (2015). One angry woman: Anger expression increases influence for men, but decreases influence for women, during group deliberation. *Law and Human Behavior, 39,* 581–592.

Salerno, J. M., Peter-Hagene, L. C., & Jay, A. C. V. (2019). Women and African Americans are less influential when they express anger during group decision making. *Group Processes & Intergroup Relations, 21,* 57–79.

Salleh, M., Amin, A., Muda, S., & Halim, M. A. S. A. (2013). Fairness of performance appraisal and organizational commitment. *Asian Social Science, 9,* 121–129.

Salmivalli, C., & Kaukiainan, A. (2004). "Female aggression" revisited: Variable- and person-centered approaches to studying gender differences in different types of aggression. *Aggressive Behavior, 30,* 158–163.

Salovey, P., & Birnbaum, D. (1989). Influence of mood on health-relevant cognitions. *Journal of Personality and Social Psychology, 57,* 539–551.

Salovey, P., & Grewal, D. (2005). The science of emotional intelligence. *Current Directions in Psychological Science, 14,* 281–285.

Sampson, R. J. (1987). Urban Black violence: The effect of male joblessness and family disruption. *American Journal of Sociology 93,* 348–382.

Sanbonmatsu, D. M., Akimoto, S. A., & Biggs, E. (1993). Overestimating causality: Attributional effects of confirmatory processing. *Journal of Personality and Social Psychology 65,* 892–903.

SanJosé-Cabezudo, R., Gutiérrez-Arranz, A. M., & Gutiérrez-Cillán, J. (2009). The combined influence of central and peripheral routes in the online persuasion process. *Cyberpsychology & Behavior, 12,* 299–308.

Sassenberg, K., & Moskowtiz, G. B. (2005). Don't stereotype, think different! Overcoming automatic stereotype activation by mindset priming. *Journal of Experimental Social Psychology, 41,* 506–514.

Saucier, D. A., Miller, C. T., & Doucet, N. (2005). Differences in helping Whites and Blacks: A meta-analysis. *Personality and Social Psychology Review, 9,* 2–16.

Savani, K., Wadhwa, M., Uchida, Y., Ding, Y., & Naidu, N. (2015). When norms loom larger than the self: Susceptibility of preference–choice consistency to normative influence across cultures. *Organizational Behavior and Human Decision Processes, 12,* 970–979.

Sawyer, K. B., Thoroughgood, C. N., Stillwell, E. E., Duffy, M. K., Scott, K. L., & Adair, E. A. (2021). Being present and thankful: A multi-study investigation of mindfulness, gratitude, and employee helping behavior. *Journal of Applied Psychology*. Advance online publication. https://doi.org/10.1037/apl0000903

Scalabrini, A., Xu, J., & Northoff, G. (2021). What COVID-19 tells us about the self: The deep intersubjective and cultural layers of our brain. *Psychiatry & Clinical Neurosciences, 75,* 37–45.

Schachter, S. (1951). Deviation, rejection and communication. *Journal of Abnormal and Social Psychology, 46,* 189–207.

Schachter, S., & Singer, J. E. (1962). Cognitive, social, and physiological determinants of emotional state. *Psychological Review, 69,* 379–399.

Schaeffer, K. (2021). *How Americans feel about "cancel culture" and offensive speech in 6 charts*. https://www.pewresearch.org/fact-tank/2021/08/17/how-americans-feel-about-cancel-culture-and-offensive-speech-in-6-charts/

Schaller, M. (1991). Social categorization and the formation of group stereotypes: Further evidence for biased processing in the perception of group-behavior correlations. *European Journal of Social Psychology, 21,* 25–35.

Schectman, Z., & Birani-Nasaraladen, D. (2006). Treating mothers of aggressive children: A research study. *International Journal of Group Psychotherapy, 56,* 93–112.

Scheier, M. F., & Carver, C. S. (1987). Dispositional optimism and physical well-being: The influence of generalized outcome expectancies on health. *Journal of Personality 55,* 172–210.

Scheier, M. F., & Carver, C. S. (1988). A model of behavioral self-regulation: Translating intention into action. In L. Berkowitz (Ed.), *Advances in experimental social psychology* (Vol. 21, pp. 303–346). Academic Press.

Scheier, M. F., Carver, C. S., & Bridges, M. W. (1994). Distinguishing optimism from neuroticism (and trait anxiety, self-mastery, and self-esteem): A reevaluation of the Life Orientation Test. *Journal of Personality and Social Psychology, 67,* 1063–1078.

Scheier, M. F., Matthews, K. A., Owens, J., Abbott, A., Lebfevre, C., & Carver, C. S. (1986). Optimism and bypass surgery. Unpublished manuscript, Carnegie-Mellon University, Pittsburgh, PA.

Scheufele, D. A. (2005). Setting the agenda. *Mass Communication & Society, 8,* 387–390.

Schiffenbauer, A., & Schavio, S. R. (1976). Physical distance and attraction: An intensification effect. *Journal of Experimental Social Psychology 12,* 274–282.

Schimmack, U. (2020). A meta-psychological perspective on the decade of replication failures in social psychology. *Canadian Psychology, 63,* 364–376.

Schimmack, U. (2021). The Implicit Association Test: A method in search of a construct. *Perspectives on Psychological Science, 16,* 396–414.

Schittekatte, M. (1996). Facilitating information exchange in small decision-making groups. *European Journal of Social Psychology, 26,* 537–556.

Schittekatte, M., & Van Hiel, A. (1996). Effects of partially shared information and awareness of unshared information on information sampling. *Small Group Research, 27,* 431–449.

Schlenker, B. R. (1987). Threats to identity: Self-identification and social stress. In C. R. Snyder & C. Ford (Eds.), *Coping with negative life events: Clinical and social psychological perspectives* (pp. 273–321). Academic Press.

Schlenker, B. R., Soraci, S., Jr., & McCarthy, B. (1976). Self-esteem and group performance as determinants of egocentric perceptions in cooperative groups. *Human Relations, 29,* 1163–1176.

Schlenker, B. R., Weigold, M. F., & Hallam, J. R. (1990). Self-serving attributions in social context: Effects of self-esteem and social pressure. *Journal of Personality and Social Psychology, 58,* 855–863.

Schmader, T., & Johns, M. (2003). Converging evidence that stereotype threat reduces working memory capacity. *Journal of Personality and Social Psychology, 85,* 440–452.

Schmidt, G., & Weiner, B. (1988). An attribution-affectaction theory of behavior: Replications of judgments of help giving. *Personality and Social Psychology Bulletin, 14,* 610–621.

Schmitt, D. P., & Allik, J. (2005). Simultaneous administration of the Rosenberg self-esteem scale in 53 nations: Exploring the universal and culture specific features of global self-esteem. *Journal of Personality and Social Psychology, 89,* 623–642.

Schnall, S., & Roper, J. (2012). Elevation puts moral values into action. *Social Psychological and Personality Science, 3,* 373–378.

Schneider, E. F., Lang, A., Shin, M., & Bradley, S. D. (2004). Death with a story: How story affects emotional, motivational, and physiological responses to first-person shooter video games. *Human Communication Research, 30,* 361–375.

Schnuerch, R., & Gibbons, H. (2014). A review of neurocognitive mechanisms of social conformity. *Social Psychology, 45,* 466–478.

Schoen, R., & Wooldredge, J. (1989). Marriage choices in North Carolina and Virginia, 1969–71 and 1979–81. *Journal of Marriage and the Family, 51,* 465–481.

Schopler, J., & Matthews, M. (1965). The influence of perceived causal locus of partner's dependence on the use of interpersonal power. *Journal of Personality and Social Psychology 2,* 609–612.

Schuhmacher, N., Köster, M., & Kärtner, J. (2019). Modeling prosocial behavior increases helping in 16-month-olds. *Child Development, 90,* 1789–1801.

Schuller, R. A., Terry, D., & McKimmie, B. (2005). The impact of expert testimony on jurors' decisions: Gender of the expert and testimony complexity. *Journal of Applied Social Psychology, 35,* 1266–1280.

Schultz, W. (1983). A theory of small groups. In H. H. Blumberg, A. P. Hare, V. Kent, & M. F. Davis (Eds.), *Small groups and social interaction* (Vol. 2, pp. 479–486). Wiley.

Schwartz, S. H. (1975). The justice of need and the activation of humanitarian norms. *Journal of Social Issues, 31,* 111–136.

Schwarz, N. (1999). Self-reports: How the questions shape the answers. *American Psychologist, 54,* 93–105.

Schwebke, S., & Downey, D. (2020, May 13). Mask shaming erupts as latest public battle over coronavirus restrictions. *Orange County Register.* https://www.ocregister.com/2020/05/13/mask-shaming-erupts-as-latest-public-battle-over-coronavirus-restrictions/

Schweder, R. A., Much, N. C., Mahapatra, M., & Park, L. (1997). The "big three" of morality and the "big three" explanations for suffering. In A. Brandt & P. Rozin (Eds.), *Moralization* (pp. 119–169). Rutledge.

Schweitzer, K., & Nuñez, N. (2018). What evidence matters to jurors? The prevalence and importance of different homicide trial evidence to mock jurors. *Psychiatry, Psychology and Law, 25,* 437–451.

Schwinger, M., Wirthwein, L., Lemmer, G., & Steinmayr, R. (2014). Academic self-handicapping and achievement: A meta-analysis. *Journal of Educational Psychology, 106,* 744–761.

Scopelliti, I., Min, H. L., McCormick, E., Kassam, K. S., & Morewedge, C. K. (2018). Individual differences in correspondence bias: Measurement, consequences, and correction of biased interpersonal attributions. *Management Science, 64,* 1879–1910.

Scott, W. A. (1957). Attitude change through reward of verbal behavior. *Journal of Abnormal and Social Psychology, 55,* 72–75.

Sedikides, C., Campbell, W. K., Reeder, G. D., & Eliot, A. D. (1998). The self-serving bias in relational context. *Journal of Personality and Social Psychology, 74,* 378–386.

Seepersad, S., Mi-Kyung, C., & Nana, S. (2008). How does culture influence the degree of romantic loneliness and closeness. *Journal of Psychology, 142,* 209–220.

Segal, M. W. (1974). Alphabet and attraction: An unobtrusive measure of the effect of propinquity in a field setting. *Journal of Personality and Social Psychology, 30,* 654–657.

Segerstrom, S. C., Taylor, S. E., Kemeny, M. E., & Fahey, J. L. (1998). Optimism is associated with mood, coping, and immune change in response to stress. *Journal of Personality and Social Psychology, 74,* 1646–1655.

Segovia, F., Moore, J. L., Linnville, S. E., & Hoyt, R. E. (2015). Optimism predicts positive health in repatriated prisoners of war. *Psychological Trauma: Theory, Research, Practice, and Policy, 7,* 222–228.

Segrin, C., Burke, T., & Dunivan, M. (2012). Loneliness and poor health within families. *Journal of Social and Personal Relationships, 29,* 597–611.

Segrin, C., Powell, H., Givertz, M., & Brackin, A. (2003). Symptoms of depression, relational quality, and loneliness in dating relationships. *Personal Relationships, 10,* 25–36.

Selensky, J. C., & Carels, R. A. (2021). Weight stigma and media: An examination of the effect of advertising campaigns on weight bias, internalized weight bias, self-esteem, body image, and affect. *Body Image, 36,* 95–106.

Selkie, E. M., Kota, R., Chan, Y., & Moreno, M. (2015). Cyberbullying, depression, and problem alcohol use in female college students: A multisite study. *Cyberpsychology, Behavior & Social Networking, 18,* 79–86.

Selye, H. (1975). Implications of stress concept. *New York State Journal of Medicine, 75,* 2139–2145.

Senchak, M., & Leonard, K. E. (1992). Attachment styles and marital adjustment among newlywed couples. *Journal of Social and Personal Relationships, 9,* 221–238.

Seto, M. C., Maric, A., & Barbaree, H. E. (2001). The role of pornography in the etiology of sexual aggression. *Aggression and Violent Behavior, 6,* 35–53.

Shackelford, T. P., Schmitt, D. P., & Buss, D. M. (2005). Universal dimensions of human mate preferences. *Personality and Individual Differences, 39,* 447–458.

Shafer, R. B., & Keith, P. M. (2001). Matching by weight in married couples: A life cycle perspective. *Journal of Social Psychology, 130,* 657–664.

Shanab, M. E., & Yahya, K. A. (1977). A behavioral study of obedience in children. *Journal of Personality and Social Psychology, 35,* 530–536.

Shanab, M. E., & Yahya, K. A. (1978). A cross-cultural study of obedience. *Bulletin of the Psychonomic Society, 11,* 267–269.

Shapiro, E. G. (1980). Is seeking help from a friend like seeking help from a stranger? *Social Psychology Quarterly, 43,* 259–263.

Sharma, D. (2018). When fairness is not enough: Impact of corporate ethical values on organizational citizenship behaviors and worker alienation. *Journal of Business Ethics, 150,* 57–68.

Shaver, P., Hazan, C., & Bradshaw, D. (1988). Love as attachment: The integration of three behavioral systems. In R. Sternberg & M. Barnes (Eds.), *The psychology of love* (pp. 68–99). Yale University Press.

Shaw, J. I., Borough, H. W., & Fink, M. I. (1994). Perceived sexual orientation and helping behavior by males and females: The wrong number technique. *Journal of Psychology and Human Sexuality, 6,* 73–81.

Shaw, J. M., & Scott, W. A. (1991). Influence of parent discipline style on delinquent behavior: The mediating role of control orientation. *Australian Journal of Psychology, 43,* 61–67.

Shechory, M., & Ziv, R. (2007). Relationships between gender role attitudes, role division, and perception of equity among heterosexual, gay and lesbian couples. *Sex Roles, 56,* 629–638.

Shechtman, Z., & Ifargan, M. (2009). School-based integrated and segregated interventions to reduce aggression. *Aggressive Behavior, 35,* 342–356.

Sheehan, B. E., Linden-Carmichael, A. N., & Lau-Barraco, C. (2016). Caffeinated and non-caffeinated alcohol use and indirect aggression: The impact of self-regulation. *Addictive Behaviors, 58,* 53–59.

Sheets, T. L., & Bushardt, S. C. (1994). Effects of the applicant's gender-appropriateness and qualifications and rater self-monitoring propensities on hiring decisions. *Public Personnel Management, 23,* 373–382.

Sheldon, P., Gilchrist-Petty, E., & Lessley, J. A. (2014). You did what? The relationship between forgiveness tendency, communication of forgiveness, and relationship satisfaction in married and dating couples. *Communication Reports, 27,* 78–90.

Shelton, N. J., Richeson, J. A., & Salvatore, J. (2005). Expecting to be the target of prejudice: Implications for interethnic interactions. *Personality and Social Psychology Bulletin, 31,* 1189–1202.

Shen, L. (2017). Putting the fear back again (and within individuals): Revisiting the role of fear in persuasion. *Health Communication, 32,* 1331–1341.

Shepela, S. T., Cook, J., Horlitz, E., Leal, R., Luciano, S., Lufty, E., & ... Worden, E. (1999). Courageous resistance: A special case of altruism. *Theory & Psychology, 9,* 787–805.

Shepperd, J. A. (1993). Productivity loss in performance groups: A motivation analysis. *Psychological Bulletin, 113,* 67–81.

Shepperd, J. A., & Taylor, K. M. (1999). Social loafing and value-expectancy theory. *Personality and Social Psychology Bulletin, 25,* 1147–1158.

Sherif, C. W., Sherif, M., & Nebergall, R. E. (1965). *Attitude and attitude change: The social judgment-involvement approach.* Saunders.

Sherif, M. (1936). *The psychology of social norms.* Harper & Row.

Sherif, M. (1972). Experiments on norm formation. In E. P. Hollander & R. G. Hunt (Eds.), *Classic contributions to social psychology,* Oxford University Press.

Sherif, M., Harvey, O. J., White, B. J., Hood, W. E., & Sherif, C. (1961). *Intergroup conflict and cooperation: The robbers cave experiment.* University of Oklahoma Book Exchange.

Sherif, M., & Hovland, C. I. (1961). *Social judgment.* Yale University Press.

Sherman, S. L., Hamilton, D. K., & Roskos-Ewoldsen, D. R. (1989). Attenuation of illusory correlation. *Personality and Social Psychology Bulletin, 15,* 559–571.

Sherry, P. (2001). The effects of violent video games on aggression: A meta-analysis. *Human Communication Research, 27,* 409–431.

Shim, R. S., Compton, M. T., Rust, G., Druss, B. G., & Kaslow, N. J. (2009). Race-ethnicity as a predictor of attitudes toward mental health treatment seeking. *Psychiatric Services, 60,* 1336–1341.

Shiomi, M., & Hagita, N. (2019). Do the number of robots and the participant's gender influence conformity effect from multiple robots? *Advanced Robotics, 33,* 756–763.

Shotland, R. L., & Heinhold, W. D. (1985). Bystander response to arterial bleeding: Helping skills, the decision-making process, and differentiating the helping response. *Journal of Personality and Social Psychology, 49,* 347–356.

Shotland, R. L., & Straw, M. K. (1976). Bystander response to an assault: When a man attacks a woman. *Journal of Personality and Social Psychology, 34,* 990–994.

Showers, C. (1992). Evaluatively integrative thinking about characteristics of the self. *Personality and Social Psychology Bulletin, 18,* 719–729.

Shultz, T. R., & Lepper, M. R. (1996). Cognitive dissonance reduction as constraint satisfaction. *Psychological Bulletin, 103,* 219–240.

Shultz, T. R., & Lepper, M. R. (1999). Computer simulation of cognitive dissonance reduction. In E. Harmon-Jones & J. Mills (Eds.), *Cognitive dissonance: Progress on a pivotal theory in social psychology* (pp. 235–265). American Psychological Association.

Shultz, T. R., Leveille, F., & Lepper, M. R. (1999). Free choice and cognitive dissonance revisited: Choosing "lesser evils" versus "greater goods." *Personality and Social Psychology Bulletin, 25,* 40–48.

Shuntich, R. J., & Taylor, S. P. (1972). The effects of alcohol on human physical aggression. *Journal of Experimental Research in Personality, 6,* 34–38.

Sibicky, M., & Dovidio, J. F. (1986). Stigma of psychological therapy: Stereotypes, interpersonal reactions, and the self-fulfilling prophecy. *Journal of Counseling Psychology, 33,* 148–154.

Sicilia, M., Ruiz, S., & Munuera, J. L. (2005). Effects of interactivity in a web site: The moderating effect of need for cognition. *Journal of Advertising, 34,* 31–45.

Sieber, J., & Ziegler, R. (2019). Group polarization revisited: A processing effort account. *Personality and Social Psychology Bulletin, 45,* 1482–1498.

Sigler, J. N., & Couch, J. V. (2002). Eyewitness testimony and the jury verdict. *North American Journal of Psychology, 4,* 143–148.

Silke, A. (2003). Deindividuation, anonymity, and violence: Findings from Northern Ireland. *Journal of Social Psychology, 143,* 493–499.

Sim, J. J., Correll, J., & Sadler, M. S. (2013). Understanding police and expert performance: When training attenuates (vs. exacerbates) stereotypic bias in the decision to shoot. *Personality and Social Psychology Bulletin, 39,* 291–304.

Sim, J. J., Goyle, A., McKedy, W., Eidelman, S., & Correll, J. (2014). How social identity shapes the working self-concept. *Journal of Experimental Social Psychology, 55,* 271–277.

Sim, T. N., & Ong, L. P. (2005). Parent physical punishment and child aggression in a Singapore Chinese preschool sample. *Journal of Marriage and the Family, 67,* 85–99.

Simmons, A. (2020, October 26). *A group of teens on their surfboards saved two swimmers from drowning.* https://www.rd.com/article/surfer-dudes-to-the-rescue/

Simmons, J. P., Nelson, L. D., & Simonsohn, U. (2011). False-positive psychology: Undisclosed flexibility in data collection and analysis allows presenting anything as significant. *Psychological Science, 22,* 1359–1366.

Simon, L. (1977). *The biography of Alice B. Toklas.* Doubleday.

Simonton, D. K. (1985). Intelligence and personal influence in groups: Four nonlinear models. *Psychological Review, 92,* 532–547.

Simpson, J. A., Gangestad, S. W., Christensen, P. N., & Leck, K. (1999). Fluctuating symmetry, sociosexuality, and intrasexual competition. *Journal of Personality and Social Psychology, 76,* 159–172.

Simpson, J. A., Ickes, W., & Grich, J. (1999). When accuracy hurts: Reactions of anxious-ambivalent dating partners to a relationship-determining situation. *Journal of Personality and Social Psychology, 76,* 754–769.

Sinclair, H. C., & Frieze, I. H. (2005). When courtship persistence becomes intrusive pursuit: Comparing rejecter and pursuer perspectives of unrequited attraction. *Sex Roles, 52,* 839–852.

Sinclair, S., Dunn, E., & Lowery, B. S. (2005). The relationship between parental racial attitudes and children's implicit prejudice. *Journal of Experimental Social Psychology, 41,* 283–289.

Sinclair, S., Lowery, B. S., Hardin, C. D., & Colangelo, A. (2005). Social tuning of automatic racial attitudes: The role of affiliative motivation. *Journal of Personality and Social Psychology, 89,* 583–592.

Singal, J. (2017, May 30). How the self-esteem craze took over America and why the hype was irresistible. *The Cut.* https://www.thecut.com/2017/05/self-esteem-grit-do-they-really-help.html

Singh, B., Axt, J., Hudson, S. M., Mellinger, C. L., Wittenbrink, B., & Correll, J. (2020). When practice fails to reduce racial bias in the decision to shoot: The case of cognitive load. *Social Cognition, 38,* 555–570.

Sistrunk, F., & Clement, D. (1970). Cross-cultural comparisons of the conformity behavior of college students. *Journal of Social Psychology, 82,* 273–274.

Skinner, E. A., & Zimmer-Gembeck, M. J. (2011). Perceived control and the development of coping. In S. Folkman (Ed.) & P. E. Nathan (Series Editor), *The Oxford handbook of health, stress and coping* (pp. 35–62). Oxford University Press.

Skowronski, J. J., Betz, A. L., Thompson, C. P., & Shannon, L. (1991). Social memory in everyday life: Recall of self-events and other-events. *Journal of Personality and Social Psychology, 60,* 831–843.

Slater, M. D., Henry, K. L., Swaim, R. C., & Cardador, J. M. (2004). Vulnerable teens, vulnerable times: How sensation seeking, alienation, and victimization moderate violent media content-aggressiveness relationship. *Communication Research, 31,* 642–668.

Slovic, P., & Fischoff, B. (1977). On the psychology of experimental surprise. *Journal of Experimental Psychology: Human Perception and Performance, 3,* 544–551.

Smeaton, G., Byrne, D., & Murnen, S. K. (1989). The repulsion hypothesis revisited: Similarity irrelevance or dissimilarity bias. *Journal of Personality and Social Psychology, 56,* 4–59.

Smith, A., & Williams, K. D. (2004). RU there? Effects of ostracism by cell phone messages. *Group Dynamics: Theory, Research, & Practice, 8,* 291–304.

Smith, K. D., Keating, J. P., & Stotland, E. (1989). Altruism reconsidered: The effect of denying feedback on a victim's status to empathetic witnesses. *Journal of Personality and Social Psychology, 57,* 641–650.

Smith, K. G., Locke, E. A., & Barry, D. (1990). Goal setting, planning, and organizational performance: An experimental simulation. *Organizational Behavior and Human Decision Processes, 46,* 118–134.

Smith, S. M., Stinson, V., & Prosser, M. A. (2004). Do they all look alike? An exploration of decision-making strategies in cross-race facial identifications. *Canadian Journal of Behavioural Science, 36,* 146–154.

Sniderman, P. M., & Piazza, T. (1994). *The scar of race.* Harvard University Press.

Snowden, F. M., Jr. (1983). *Before color prejudice: The ancient view of Blacks.* Harvard University Press.

Snyder, K. E., Malin, J. L., Dent, A. L., & Linnenbrink-Garcia, L. (2014). The message matters: The role of implicit beliefs about giftedness and failure experiences in academic self-handicapping. *Journal of Educational Psychology, 106,* 230–241.

Snyder, M. (1987). *Public appearances as private realities: The psychology of self-monitoring.* Freeman.

Snyder, M. (1992). Motivational foundations of behavioral confirmation. In M. P. Zanna (Ed.), *Advances in experimental social psychology* (Vol. 25, pp. 67–114). Academic Press.

Snyder, M., Bersheid, E., & Glick, P. (1985). Focusing on the interior and exterior. Two investigations of the initiation of personal relationships. *Journal of Personality and Social Psychology, 48,* 147–149.

Snyder, M., & Cunningham, M. (1975). To comply or not to comply: Testing the self-perception explanation of the foot-in-the-door phenomenon. *Journal of Personality and Social Psychology, 31,* 64–67.

Snyder, M., & Gangestad, S. (1986). On the nature of self-monitoring: Matters of assessment, matters of validity. *Journal of Personality and Social Psychology, 51,* 125–139.

Snyder, M., & Swann, W. B., Jr. (1978). Hypothesis-testing processes in social interaction. *Journal of Personality and Social Psychology, 36,* 1201–1212.

Snyder, M., Tanke, E. D., & Berscheid, E. (1977). Social perception and interpersonal behavior: On the self-fulfilling nature of social stereotypes. *Journal of Personality and Social Psychology, 35,* 656–666.

Sommer, K. L., Williams, K. D., Ciarocco, N. J., & Baumeister, R. F. (2001). When silence speaks louder than words: Explorations into interpersonal and intrapsychic consequences of social ostracism. *Basic and Applied Social Psychology, 23,* 225–243.

Sommers, S. R. (2006). On racial diversity and group decision-making: Informational and motivational effects of racial composition on jury deliberations. *Journal of Personality and Social Psychology, 90,* 597–612.

Sorkin, D., Rook, K. S., & Lu, J. L. (2002). Loneliness, lack of emotional support, lack of companionship, and likelihood of having a heart condition in an elderly sample. *Annals of Behavior Medicine, 24,* 290–298.

Souchet, L., & Girandola, F. (2013). Double foot-in-the-door, social representations, and environment: Application for energy savings. *Journal of Applied Social Psychology, 43,* 306–315.

Spacapan, S. (1988). Psychosocial mediators of health status: An introduction. In S. Spacapan & S. Oskamp (Eds.), *The social psychology of health* (pp. 17–29). Sage.

Spanos, S., Vartanian, L. R., Herman, C. P., & Polivy, J. (2015). Personality, perceived appropriateness, and acknowledgement of social influences on food intake. *Personality and Individual Differences, 87,* 110–115.

Spiro, A. III. (2007). The relevance of a lifespan developmental approach to health. In C. M. Aldwin, C. L. Park, & A. Spiro III (Eds.), *Handbook of health psychology and aging* (pp. 75–93). Guilford Press.

Spivey, C. B., & Prentice-Dunn, S. (1990). Assessing the directionality of deindividuated behavior: Effects of deindividuation, modeling, and private self-consciousness on aggressive and prosocial responses. *Basic and Applied Social Psychology, 11,* 387–403.

Sprecher, S. (1999). "I love you more today than yesterday": Romantic partners' perceptions of changes in love and related affect over time. *Journal of Personality and Social Psychology, 76,* 46–53.

Sprecher, S., Fehr, B., & Zimmerman, C. (2007). Expectations for mood enhancement as a result of helping: The effects of gender and compassionate love. *Sex Roles: A Journal of Research, 56,* 543–549.

Sprengholz, P., & Betsch, C. (2020). Herd immunity communication counters detrimental effects of selective vaccination mandates: Experimental evidence. *eClinicalMedicine, 22,* Article 100352.

Sprengholz, P., Betsch, C., & Böhm, R. (2021). Reactance revisited: Consequences of mandatory and scarce vaccination in the case of COVID-19. *Applied Psychology: Health and Well-Being*. Advance online publication. https://doi.org/10.1111/aphw.12285

Sprengholz, P., Böhm, R., & Betsch, C. (2021). *Vaccination policy reactance: Predictors, consequences, and countermeasures*. https://doi.org/10.31234/osf.io/98e4t

Stalder, D. R., & Baron, R. S. (1998). Attributional complexity as a moderator of dissonance-produced attitude change. *Journal of Personality and Social Psychology, 75,* 449–455.

Stangor, C., Carr, C., & Kiang, L. (1998). Activating stereotypes undermines task performance expectations. *Journal of Personality and Social Psychology, 74,* 1191–1197.

Stangor, C., & Lange, J. E. (1994). Mental representations of social groups: Advances in understanding stereotypes and stereotyping. In M. P. Zanna (Ed.), *Advances in experimental social psychology* (Vol. 26, pp. 357–416). Academic Press.

Stanton, A. M., Boyd, R. L., Pulverman, C. S., & Meston, C. M. (2015). Determining women's sexual self-schemas through advanced computerized text analysis. *Child Abuse & Neglect, 46,* 78–88.

Stappenbeck, C. A., & Fromme, K. (2013, April 15). The effects of alcohol, emotion regulation, and emotional arousal on the dating aggression intentions of men and women. *Psychology of Addictive Behaviors*.

Stasser, G. (1991). Pooling of shared and unshared information during group discussions. In S. Worchel, W. Wood, & J. A. Simpson (Eds.), *Group process and productivity* (pp. 48–67). Sage.

Stasser, G., Kerr, N. L., & Davis, J. H. (1989). Influence processes and consensus models in decision-making groups. In P. Paulus (Ed.), *Psychology of group influence* (2nd ed., pp. 279–326). Erlbaum.

Stasser, G., Taylor, L. A., & Hanna, C. (1989). Information sampling and unstructured discussions of three-and six-person groups. *Journal of Personality and Social Psychology, 57,* 67–78.

Stasser, G., & Titus, W. (1987). Effects of information load and percentage of shared information on dissemination of unshared information during group discussion. *Journal of Personality and Social Psychology, 53,* 81–93.

Statista. (2021). *Number of murder offenders in the United States in 2020, by gender*. https://www.statista.com/statistics/251886/murder-offenders-in-the-us-by-gender/

Stattin, H., & Magnusson, D. (1989). The role of early aggressive behavior in the frequency, seriousness, and types of later crime. *Journal of Consulting and Clinical Psychology, 57,* 710–718.

Staub, E. (1985). *The roots of evil: The origins of genocide and other group violence.* Cambridge University Press.

Steele, C. M. (1988). The psychology of self-affirmation: Sustaining the integrity of the self. In L. Berkowitz (Ed.), *Advances in experimental social psychology* (Vol. 21, pp. 261–302). Academic Press.

Steele, C. M., & Aronson, J. (1995). Stereotype threat and the intellectual test performance of African Americans. *Journal of Personality and Social Psychology, 69,* 797–811.

Steil, J. M., & Weltman, K. (1991). Marital inequality: The importance of resources, personal attributes, and social norms on career valuing and the allocation of domestic responsibilities. *Sex Roles, 24,* 161–179.

Steil, J. M., & Weltman, K. (1992). Influence strategies at home and at work: A study of sixty dual-career couples. *Journal of Social and Personal Relationships, 9,* 65–88.

Steiner, I. D. (1972). *Group process and productivity.* Academic Press.

Stelter, M., & Degner, J. (2018). Investigating the other-race effect in working memory. *British Journal of Psychology, 109,* 777–798.

Stephan, W. G., Boniecki, K. A., Ybarra, O., Bettencourt, A., Ervin, K. S., Jackson, L. A., et al. (2002). The role of threats in the racial attitudes of Blacks and Whites. *Personality and Social Psychology Bulletin, 28,* 1242–1254.

Sternberg, R. J. (1986). A triangular theory of love. *Psychological Review, 93,* 119–135.

Sternberg, R. J. (1988). Triangulating love. In R. J. Sternberg & M. L. Barnes (Eds.), *The psychology of love* (pp. 119–138). Yale University Press.

Sternberg, R. J., & Gracek, S. (1984). The nature of love. *Journal of Personality and Social Psychology, 47,* 312–329.

Stewart, T. L., LaDuke, J. R., Bracht, C., Sweet, B. A. M., & Gamarel, K. E. (2003). Do the "eyes" have it? A program evaluation of Jane Elliott's "blue-eyes/brown-eyes" diversity training exercise. *Journal of Applied Social Psychology, 33,* 1898–1921.

Still, W. (1968). *The underground railroad.* Arno Press. (Originally published 1872.)

Stone, J., Lynch, C. I., Sjomeling, M., & Darley, J. M. (1999). Stereotype threat effects on Black and White athletic performance. *Journal of Personality and Social Psychology, 77,* 1213–1227.

Storms, M. D. (1973). Videotape and the attribution process: Reversing actors' and observers' points of view. *Journal of Personality and Social Psychology, 27,* 165–175.

Straus, M. A. (1991). Discipline and deviance: Physical punishment of children and violence and other crime in adulthood. *Social Problems, 38,* 133–152.

Stroud, N. (2008). Media use and political predispositions: Revisiting the concept of selective exposure. *Political Behavior, 30,* 341–366.

Suarez. E. C., & Krishnan, K. R. R. (2006). The relation of free plasma tryptophan to anger, hostility, and aggression in a nonpatient sample of adult men and women. *Annals of Behavioral Medicine, 31,* 254–260.

Suhay, E. (2015). Explaining group influence: The role of identity and emotion in political conformity and polarization. *Political Behavior, 37,* 221–251.

Sukheja, B. (2019, November 19). *Four teen surfers rescue drowning swimmers in northern California ocean.* https://www.republicworld.com/world-news/us-news/teen-surfers-rescue-drowning-swimmers-in-northern-california-ocean.html

Sukhodolsky, D. G., Golub, A., Stone, E. C., & Orban, L. (2005). Dismantling anger control training for children: A randomized pilot study of social problem-solving versus social skills training components. *Behavior Therapy, 36,* 15–23.

Sulthana, P. (1987). The effect of frustration and inequity on the displacement of aggression. *Asian Journal of Psychology and Education, 19,* 26–33.

Sun, C., Bridges, A., Johnason, J., & Ezzell, M. (2014). Pornography and the male sexual script: An analysis of consumption and sexual relations. *Archives of Sexual Behavior, 45,* 983–994.

Svetlova, M., Nichols, S. R., & Brownell, C. A. (2010). Toddlers' prosocial behavior: From instrumental to empathic to altruistic helping. *Child Development, 81,* 1814–1827.

Swami, V., & Furnham, A. (2007). Unattractive, promiscuous and heavy drinkers: Perceptions of women with tattoos. *Body Image, 4,* 343–352.

Swann, W. B., Jr. (1996). *Self-traps: The elusive quest for higher self-esteem.* Freeman.

Swann, W. B., Jr., & Gill, M. J. (1997). Confidence and accuracy in person perception: Do we know what we think we know about relationship partners? *Journal of Personality and Social Psychology, 73,* 747–757.

Swann, W. B., Jr., Hixon, J. G., & De La Ronde, C. (1992). Embracing the bitter truth: Negative self-concepts and marital commitment. *Psychological Science, 3,* 118–121.

Swann, W. B., Jr., Pelham, B. W., & Krull, D. S. (1989). Agreeable fancy or disagreeable truth? Reconciling self-enhancement and self-verification. *Journal of Personality and Social Psychology, 57,* 782–791.

Swann, W. B., Jr., Stein-Seroussi, A., & Giesler, K. B. (1992). Why people self-verify. *Journal of Personality and Social Psychology, 62,* 392–410.

Swann, W. B., Jr., Stein-Seroussi, A., & McNulty, S. (1992). Outcasts in a white-lie society: The enigmatic worlds of people with negative self-conceptions. *Journal of Personality and Social Psychology, 62,* 618–624.

Swann, W. B., Jr., Wenzlaff, R. M., Krull, D. S., & Pelham, B. W. (1992). The allure of negative feedback: Self-verification strivings among depressed persons. *Journal of Abnormal Psychology, 101,* 293–306.

Swim, J. K., Cohen, L. F., & Hyers, L. L. (1998). Experiencing everyday prejudice and discrimination. In J. K. Swim & C. Stangor (Eds.), *Prejudice: The target's perspective* (pp. 37–60). Academic Press.

Swim, J. K., & Hyers, L. L. (1999). Excuse me—What did you just say? Women's public and private responses to sexist remarks. *Journal of Experimental Social Psychology, 35,* 68–88.

Switzer, R., & Taylor, R. B. (1983). Sociability versus privacy of residential choice: Impacts of personality and local social ties. *Basic and Applied Social Psychology, 4,* 123–136.

Sykes, C. J. (1992). *A nation of victims.* St. Martins Press.

Sylwander, K. R., & Gottzén, L. (2020). Whore! Affect, sexualized aggression and resistance in young social media users' interaction. *Sexualities, 23,* 971–986.

Szmajke, A., & Kubica, M. (2003). Geographically close—culturally distant: The values of culture of honor in the mentality of young Poles and Germans. *Polish Psychological Bulletin, 34,* 153–159.

T

Tajfel, H. (1981). *Human groups and social categories.* Cambridge University Press.

Tajfel, H. (1982). *Social identity and group relations.* Cambridge University Press.

Tajfel, H., Billig, M., Bundy, R., & Flament, C. (1971). Social categorization and intergroup behavior. *European Journal of Social Psychology, 1,* 149–178.

Tanford, S., & Penrod, S. (1986). Jury deliberations: Discussion content and influence processes in jury decision making. *Journal of Applied Social Psychology, 16,* 322–347.

Tarnow, E. (2000). Self-destructive obedience in the airplane cockpit and the concept of obedience optimization. In T. Blass (Ed.), *Obedience to authority: Current perspectives on the Milgram paradigm* (pp. 111–123). Lawrence Erlbaum Publishers.

Tausch, N., & Hewstone, M. (2010). Social dominance orientation attenuates stereotype change in the face of disconfirming information. *Social Psychology, 41,* 169–176.

Taylor, P. (2003). *Munitions of the mind: A history of propaganda from the ancient world to the present day.* Manchester University Press.

Taylor, S. E. (1981). The interface of cognitive and social psychology. In J. H. Harvey (Ed.), *Cognition, social behavior, and the environment.* Erlbaum.

Taylor, S. E. (1989). *Positive illusions: Creative self-deception and the healthy mind.* Basic Books.

Taylor, S. E. (2011). Social support: A review. In H. S. Friedman (Ed.), *The Oxford handbook of health psychology* (pp. 189–214). Oxford University Press.

Taylor, S. E., & Brown, J. D. (1988). Illusion and wellbeing: A social psychological perspective on mental health. *Psychological Bulletin, 103,* 193–210.

Taylor, S. E., Kemeny, M. E., Aspinwall, L. G., & Schneider, S. G. (1992). Optimism, coping, psychological distress, and high-risk sexual behavior among men at risk for acquired immunodeficiency syndrome (AIDS). *Journal of Personality and Social Psychology, 63,* 460–473.

Taylor, S. E., & Thompson, S. C. (1982). Stalking the elusive vividness effect. *Psychological Review, 89,* 166–181.

Teachman, B. A., & Brownell, K. D. (2001). Implicit anti-fat bias among health professionals: Is anyone immune? *International Journal of Obesity, 25,* 1525–1531.

Tebbe, E. N., & Moradi, B. (2012). Anti-transgender prejudice: A structural equation model of associated constructs. *Journal of Counseling Psychology, 59,* 251–261.

Tec, N. (1986). *When light pierced the darkness: Christian rescue of Jews in Nazi-occupied Poland.* Oxford University Press.

Tennen, H., & Affleck, G. (1987). The costs and benefits of optimistic explanations and dispositional optimism. *Journal of Personality, 55,* 377–393.

Tennov, D. (1979). *Love and limerence: The experience of being in love.* Stein & Day.

Tesser, A. (1988). Toward a self-evaluation maintenance model of social behavior. In L. Berkowitz (Ed.), *Advances in experimental social psychology* (Vol. 21, pp. 181–228). Academic Press.

Tesser, A. (1993). The importance of heritability in psychological research: The case of attitudes. *Psychological Review, 100,* 129–142.

Tesser, A., Campbell, I., & Mickler, S. (1983). The role of social pressure, attention to the stimulus, and self-doubt in conformity. *European Journal of Social Psychology, 13,* 217–233.

Tesser, A., & Collins, J. E. (1988). Emotion in social eflection and comparison situations: Intuitive, systematic, and exploratory approaches. *Journal of Personality and Social Psychology, 55,* 695–709.

Testone, G. (2004). *GLAAD to provide resources for journalists covering Beenie Man's hate lyrics.* http://www.glaad.org/publications/archive_detail.php?id=3703

Tetlock, P. E. (1985). Accountability: A social check on the fundamental attribution error. *Social Psychology Quarterly, 48,* 227–236.

Tetlock, P. E. (1986). Is categorization theory the solution to the level-of-analysis problem? *British Journal of Social Psychology, 25,* 255–256.

Tetlock, P. E., & Levi, A. (1982). Attribution bias: On the inconsistencies of the cognition-motivation debate. *Journal of Experimental Social Psychology, 18,* 68–88.

The 9/11 Commission Report. (2004). *Foresight—and hindsight.* https://govinfo.library.unt.edu/911/report/911Report_Ch11.pdf

The Press Democrat. (2019, November. 19). *How 4 teen surfers rescued drowning swimmers from a rip current.* https://www.pressdemocrat.com/article/news/how-4-teen-surfers-rescued-drowning-swimmers-from-a-rip-current/

The Trafalgar Group. (2021). *Nationwide issues survey May 2021.* https://thetrafalgargroup.org/COSA-National-Fauci-Full-Report.pdf

Thibaut, J. W., & Kelley, H. H. (1959). *The social psychology of groups.* Wiley.

Thomas, C., & Esses, V. M. (2004). Individual differences in reactions to sexist humor. *Group Processes and Intergroup Relations, 7,* 89–100.

Thomas, J. L., Britt, T. W., Odle-Dusseau, H., & Bliese, P. D. (2011). Dispositional optimism buffers combat veterans from the negative effects of warzone stress on mental health symptoms and work impairment. *Journal of Clinical Psychology, 67,* 866–880.

Thompson, B., & Borrello, C. M. (1992). Different views of love: Deductive and inductive lines of inquiry. *Psychological Science, 1,* 154–155.

Thompson, S. C., Cheek, P. R., & Graham, M. A. (1988). The other side of perceived control: Disadvantages and negative effects. In S. Spacapan & S. Oskamp (Eds.), *The social psychology of health* (pp. 69–93). Sage.

Thornhill, R., & Gangestad, S. W. (1994). Human fluctuating asymmetry and sexual behavior. *Psychological Science, 5,* 297–302.

Thorsteinsson, E. B., & Brown, R. F. (2009). Mediators and moderators of the stressor-fatigue relationship in nonclinical samples. *Journal of Psychosomatic Research, 66,* 21–29.

Thorup, B., Crookes, K., Burton, N., Pond, S., Rhodes, G., Chang, P. P. W., Li, T. K., & Hsiao, J. (2018). Perceptual experience shapes our ability to categorize faces by national origin: A new other-race effect. *British Journal of Psychology, 109,* 583–603.

Tian, Q. (2013). Social anxiety, motivation, self-disclosure, and computer-mediated friendship: A path analysis of the social interaction in the blogosphere. *Communication Research, 40,* 237–260.

Time. (1973). An end to silence. *Time, 101*(25).

Timming, A. R. (2015). Visible tattoos in the service sector: A new challenge to recruitment and selection. *Work, Employment and Society, 29,* 60–78.

Timming, A. R., Nickson, D., Re, D., & Perrett, D. (2017). What do you think of my ink? Assessing the effects of body art on employment chances. *Human Resource Management, 56,* 133–149.

Tindale, R. S., Smith, C. M., Thomas, L. S., Filkins, J., & Sheffey, S. (1996). Shared representations and asymmetric social influence processes in small groups. In F. Witte & J. Davis (Eds.), *Understanding group behavior* (Vol. 1, pp. 81–104). Erlbaum.

Tittle, C. R., Botchkovar, E. V., & Antonaccio, O. (2010). Criminal contemplation, national context, and deterrence. *Journal of Quantitative Criminology, 27,* 225–249.

Toklas, A. B. (1963). *What is remembered.* Holt, Rinehart & Winston.

Tong, S. T., Van Der Heide, B., & Langwell, L. (2008) Too much of a good thing? The relationship between number of friends and interpersonal impressions on Facebook. *Journal of Computer-Mediated Communication, 13,* 531–549.

Tonnesmann, W. (1987). Group identification and political socialization. In V. Reynolds, V. Falger, & I. Vine (Eds.), *The sociobiology of ethnocentrism.* University of Georgia Press.

Tornstam, L. (1992). Loneliness in marriage. *Journal of Social and Personal Relationships, 9,* 197–217.

Trautwein, U., Lüdtke, O., Marsh, H. W., & Nagy, G. (2009). Within-school social comparison: How students perceive the standing of their class predicts academic self-concept. *Journal of Educational Psychology, 101,* 853–866.

Tremblay, R. E. (2010). Developmental origins of disruptive behaviour problems: The prevention. *Journal of Child Psychology & Psychiatry, 51,* 341–367.

Trepanier, M. L., & Romatowski, J. A. (1985). Attributes and roles assigned to characters in children's writing: Sex differences and sex-role perceptions. *Sex Roles, 13,* 263–272.

Trepte, S., Masur, P. K., & Scharkow, M. (2018). Mutual friends' social support and self-disclosure in face-to-face and instant messenger communication. *Journal of Social Psychology, 158,* 430–445.

Triandis, H. C. (1994). *Culture and social behavior.* McGraw Hill.

Triplett, N. (1898). Dynamogenic factors in pacemaking and competition. *American Psychologist, 9,* 507–533.

Trivers, R. (1972). *Social evolution.* Benjamin/Cummings.

Trope, Y. (1986). Identification and inference processes in disposition attribution. *Psychological Review, 93,* 239–257.

Trope, Y., & Alfieri, T. (1997). Effortfulness and flexibility of dispositional judgment processes. *Journal of Personality and Social Psychology, 73,* 703–718.

Trope, Y., Cohen, O., & Alfieri, T. (1991). Behavior identification as the mediator of dispositional inference. *Journal of Personality and Social Psychology, 61,* 873–883.

Tropp, L. R., & Pettigrew, T. F. (2005a). Relationships between intergroup contact and prejudice among majority and minority status groups. *Psychological Science, 16,* 951–957.

Tropp, L. R., & Pettigrew, T. F. (2005b). Differential relationships between intergroup contact and affective and cognitive dimensions of prejudice. *Personality and Social Psychology Bulletin, 31,* 1145–1158.

Tsang, J. (2006). Gratitude and prosocial behaviour: An experimental test of gratitude. *Cognition and Emotion, 20,* 138–148.

Tsitsika, A., Janikian, M., Wójcik, S., Makaruk, K., Tzavela, E., Tzavara, C., & . . . Richardson, C. (2015). Cyberbullying victimization prevalence and associations with internalizing and externalizing problems among adolescents in six European countries. *Computers in Human Behavior, 51*(Pt. A), 1–7.

Tuckman, A. (2020, July 8). The social influence of wearing a mask (or not). *Psychology Today.* https://www.psychologytoday.com/us/blog/sex-matters/202007/the-social-influence-wearing-mask-or-not

Turnbull, J., Heaslip, S., & McLeod, H. A. (2000). Preschool children's attitudes to fat and normal male and female stimulus figures. *International Journal of Obesity, 24,* 705–706.

Turner, J. C. (1987). *Rediscovering the social group: A self-categorization theory.* Basil Blackwell.

Tversky, A., & Kahneman, D. (1973). Availability: A heuristic for judgment frequency and probability. *Cognitive Psychology, 5,* 207–232.

Tversky, B., & Tuchin, M. (1989). A reconciliation of the evidence on eyewitness testimony: Comments on McCloskey and Zaragoza (1985). *Journal of Experimental Psychology: General, 118,* 86–91.

Twist, M. L. C., Bergdall, M. K., Belous, C. K., & Maier, C. A. (2017). Electronic visibility management of lesbian, gay, and bisexual identities and relationships in young adulthood. *Journal of Couple & Relationship Therapy, 16,* 271–285.

Tybout, A. M., Sternthal, B., & Calder, B. (1983). Information availability as a determinant of multiple request effectiveness. *Journal of Marketing Research, 20,* 280–290.

Tyler, T., & Schuller, R. A. (1991). Aging and attitude change. *Journal of Personality and Social Psychology, 61,* 689–697.

Tyler, T. R. (1994). Governing amid diversity: Can fair decision-making procedures bridge competing public interests and values? *Law and Society Review, 28,* 701–722.

Tyler, T. R. (1997). The psychology of legitimacy: A relational perspective on voluntary deference to authorities. *Personality and Social Psychology Review, 1,* 323–345.

Tziner, A., & Eden, D. (1985). Effects of crew composition on crew performance: Does the whole equal the sum of its parts? *Journal of Applied Psychology, 70,* 85–93.

Tziner, A., & Kopelman, R. E. (2002). Is there a preferred performance rating format? A non-psychometric perspective. *Applied Psychology, 51,* 479–503.

U

Uniform Crime Statistics. (2011). *Crime in the United States, table 66.* https://www.fbi.gov/about-us/cjis/ucr/crime-in-the.u.s/2011/crime-in-the.u.s.-2011/tables/table_66_arrests_suburban_areas_by_sex_2011.xls

Unkelbach, C., Forgas, J. P., & Denson, T. F. (2008). The turban effect: The influence of Muslim headgear and induced affect on aggressive responses in the shooter bias paradigm. *Journal of Experimental Social Psychology, 44,* 1409–1413.

USA Facts. (2021). *US coronavirus vaccine tracker.* https://usafacts.org/visualizations/covid-vaccine-tracker-states/

Uskul, A. K., Cross, S. E., Günsoy, C., Gerçek-Swing, B., Alözkan, C., Ataca, B., & . . . Alözkan, C. (2015). A price to pay: Turkish and Northern American retaliation for threats to personal and family honor. *Aggressive Behavior, 41,* 594–607.

V

Valerio, T. D., Kim, M. J., & Sexton-Radek, K. (2016). Association of stress, general health, and alcohol use with poor sleep quality among U.S. college students. *American Journal of Health Education, 47,* 17–23.

Valkenburg, P. M., & Peter, J. (2007). Preadolescents' and adolescents' online communication and their closeness to friends. *Developmental Psychology, 43,* 267–277.

van Baar, J. M., & FeldmanHall, O. (2021). The polarized mind in context: Interdisciplinary approaches to the psychology of political polarization. *American Psychologist.* Advance online publication. https://doi.org/10.1037/amp0000814

van Bommel, M., van Prooijen, J., Elffers, H., & van Lange, P. M. (2014). Intervene to be seen: The power of a camera in attenuating the bystander effect. *Social Psychological and Personality Science, 5,* 459–466.

Van Boven, L., Kruger, J., Savitsky, K., & Gilovich, T. (2000). When social worlds collide: Overconfidence in the multiple audience problem. *Personality and Social Psychology Bulletin, 26,* 619–628.

Vandello, J. A., & Cohen, D. (1999). Patterns of individualism and collectivism across the United States. *Journal of Personality and Social Psychology, 77,* 279–292.

Van den Bos, K., Wilke, H. A. M., & Lund, E. A. (1998). When do we need procedural fairness? The role of trust in authority. *Journal of Personality and Social Psychology, 75,* 1449–1458.

Van Gilder, B. J. (2019). Sexual orientation stigmatization and identity work for gays, lesbians, and bisexuals in the US military. *Journal of Homosexuality, 66*, 1949–1973.

van Ginkel, W. P., & van Knippenberg, D. (2012). Group leadership and shared task representations in decision making groups. *The Leadership Quarterly, 23*, 94–106.

Van Laar, C., Levin, S., Sinclair, S., & Sidanius, J. (2005). The effect of university roommate contact on ethnic attitudes and behavior. *Journal of Experimental Social Psychology, 41*, 329–345.

van Osch, Y., Breugelmans, S. M., Zeelenberg, M., & Bölük, P. (2013). A different kind of honor culture: Family honor and aggression in Turks. *Group Processes & Intergroup Relations, 16*, 334–344.

Van Royen, K., Poels, K., Vandebosch, H., & Adam, P. (2017). "Thinking before posting?" Reducing cyber harassment on social networking sites through a reflective message. *Computers in Human Behavior, 66*, 345–352.

van Tuijl, L. A., Bennik, E. C., Penninx, B. W. J. H., Spinhoven, P., & de Jong, P. J. (2020). Predictive value of implicit and explicit self-esteem for the recurrence of depression and anxiety disorders: A 3-year follow-up study. *Journal of Abnormal Psychology, 129*, 788–798.

Vallortigara, G. (1992). Affiliation and aggression as related to gender in domestic chicks. *Journal of Comparative Psychology, 106*, 53–58.

vanDellen, M. R., Hoyle, R. H., & Miller, R. (2012). The regulatory easy street: Self-regulation below the self-control threshold does not consume regulatory resources. *Personality and Individual Differences, 52*, 898–902.

van't Riet, J., & Ruiter, R. A. (2013). Defensive reactions to health-promoting information: An overview and implications for future research. *Health Psychology Review, 7*(Suppl. 1), S104–S136.

van Veen, V., Krug, M. K., Schooler, J. W., & Carter, C. S. (2009). Neural activity predicts attitude change in cognitive dissonance. *Nature Neuroscience, 12*, 1469–1474.

Van Vugt, M., & Hart, C. M. (2004). Social identity as social glue: The origins of group loyalty. *Journal of Personality and Social Psychology, 86*, 585–598.

van Vugt, M., & Iredale, W. (2013). Men behaving nicely: Public goods as peacock tails. *British Journal of Psychology, 104*, 3–13.

Varnum, M. E. W. (2012). Conformity effect sizes are smaller on the frontier. *Journal of Cognition and Culture, 12*, 359–364.

Vasquez, E. A., Pedersen, W. C., Bushman, B. J., Kelley, N. J., Demeestere, P., & Miller, N. (2013). Lashing out after stewing over public insults: The effects of public provocation, provocation intensity, and rumination on triggered displaced aggression. *Aggressive Behavior, 39*, 13–29.

Vierikko, E., Pulkkinen, L., Kaprio, J., Viken, R., & Rose, R. J. (2003). Sex differences in genetic and environmental effects on aggression. *Aggressive Behavior, 29*, 55–68.

Vinokur, A. D., & Vinokur-Kaplan, D. (1990). "In sickness and in health": Patterns of social support and undermining in older married couples. *Journal of Aging and Health, 2*, 215–241.

Visser, P. S., & Mirabile, R. R. (2004). Attitudes in the social context: The impact of social network composition on individual-level attitude strength. *Journal of Personality and Social Psychology, 87*, 779–795.

Visser, T. A. W., Ohan, J. L., Whittle, S., Yücel, M., Simmons, J. G., & Allen, N. B. (2014). Sex differences in structural brain asymmetry predict overt aggression in early adolescents. *Social Cognitive and Affective Neuroscience, 9*, 553–560.

Vissing, Y. M., Straus, M. A., Gelles, R. I., & Harrop, J. W. (1991). Verbal aggression by parents and psychosocial problems of children. *Child Abuse and Neglect, 15*, 223–238.

Vlaander, G. P. J., & van Rooijen, L. (1985). Independence and conformity in Holland: Asch's experiment three decades later. *Tijdschmrmft Voor Psychtologie, 13*, 49–55.

Vrugt, A., & Vet, C. (2009). Effects of a smile on mood and helping behavior. *Social Behavior & Personality: An International Journal, 37*, 1251–1257.

Vonk, R. (1999). Effects of outcome dependency on correspondence bias. *Personality and Social Psychology Bulletin, 25*, 382–389.

W

Walker, B. H., Sinclair, H. C., & MacArthur, J. (2015). Social norms versus social motives: The effects of social influence and motivation to control prejudiced reactions on the expression of prejudice. *Social Influence, 10*, 55–67.

Walker, H. J., Feild, H. S., Giles, W. F., & Bernerth, J. B. (2008). The interactive effects of job advertisement characteristics and applicant experience on reactions to recruitment messages. *Journal of Occupational & Organizational Psychology, 81*, 619–638.

Walker, L. J., & Frimer, J. A. (2007). Moral personality of brave and caring exemplars. *Journal of Personality and Social Psychology, 93*, 845–860.

Wall, H., Balani, A., & Larkin, D. (2020, December 10). How the psychology of mask wearing can encourage mask use. https://www.socialsciencespace.com/2020/12/what-the-psychology-of-mask-wearing-can-encourage-their-use/

Wallach, M. A., & Kogan, N. (1965). The roles of information, discussion and consensus in group risk taking. *Journal of Experimental Social Psychology, 1*, 1–19.

Waller, T., Lampman, C., & Lupfer-Johnson, G. (2012). Assessing bias against overweight individuals among nursing and psychology students: An implicit association test. *Journal of Clinical Nursing, 21*, 3504–3512.

Walsh, R. M., Forest, A. L., & Orehek, E. (2020). Self-disclosure on social media: The role of perceived network responsiveness. *Computers in Human Behavior, 104*, 1–12.

Walster, E. Aronson, V., Abrahams, D., & Rottman, L. (1966). Importance of physical attractiveness in dating behavior. *Journal of Personality and Social Psychology, 4,* 508–516.

Walster (Hatfield), E., & Festinger, L. (1962). The effectiveness of overheard conversations. *Journal of Abnormal and Social Psychology, 65,* 395–402.

Walter, J. (2002). *Becoming evil: How ordinary people commit genocide and mass killing.* Oxford University Press.

Walther, E., Weil, R., & Düsing, J. (2011). The role of evaluative conditioning in attitude formation. *Current Directions in Psychological Science, 20,* 192–196.

Walton, M. D., Sachs, D., Ellington, R., Hazlewood, A., Grilfiti, S., & Bass, D. (1988). Physical stigma and the pregnancy role: Receiving help from strangers. *Sex Roles, 18,* 323–331.

Wang, J., Wu, Y., & Jing, L. (2018). Implicit need for affiliation and processing of emotional images: Event-related potential correlates. *Social Behavior and Personality: An International Journal, 46,* 273–280.

Wang, M.-T., & Kenny, S. (2014). Parental physical punishment and adolescent adjustment: Bidirectionality and the moderation effects of child ethnicity and parental warmth. *Journal of Abnormal Child Psychology, 42,* 717–730.

Wang, S. S., Brownell, K. D., & Wadden, T. A. (2004). The influence of the stigma of obesity on overweight individuals. *International Journal of Obesity, 28,* 1333–1337.

Ward, E. (2020, November 23). *A spate of mask-wearing criminals.* https://xtown.la/2020/11/23/criminals-wear-masks-covid/

Ward, L. M., & Carlson, C. (2013). Modeling meanness: Associations between reality TV consumption, perceived realism, and adolescents' social aggression. *Media Psychology, 16,* 371–389.

Watson, P. W., & Thornhill, P. (1994). Fluctuating asymmetry and sexual selection. *Trends in Ecology and Evolution, 9,* 21–25.

Watt, S. E., & Larkin, C. (2010). Prejudiced people perceive more community support for their views: The role of own, media, and peer attitudes in perceived consensus. *Journal of Applied Social Psychology, 40,* 710–731.

Weary, C., & Edwards, I. A. (1994). Social cognition and clinical psychology: Anxiety, depression, and the processing of information about others. In P. S. Wyer & T. K. Srull (Eds.), *Handbook of social cognition* (2nd ed., Vol. 2, pp. 89–338). Erlbaum.

Webb, E. J., Campbell, D. T., Schwartz, R. D., Sechrist, L., & Grove, J. (1981). *Nonreactive measures in the social sciences* (2nd ed). Houghton Mifflin.

Weber, R., Ritterfield, U., & Mathiak, K. (2006). Does playing violent video games induce aggression? Empirical evidence of a functional magnetic resonance imaging study. *Media Psychology, 8,* 39–60.

Webster, R. J., & Saucier, D. A. (2013). Angels and demons are among us: Assessing individual differences in belief in pure evil and belief in pure good. *Personality & Social Psychology Bulletin, 39,* 1455–1470.

Wegener, D. T., Petty, R. E., & Smith, S. M. (1995). Positive mood can increase or decrease message scrutiny: The hedonic contingency view of mood and message processing. *Journal of Personality and Social Psychology, 69,* 5–15.

Wegner, D. M. (1989). *White bears and unwanted thoughts.* Viking/Penguin.

Wegner, D. M. (1993). Thought suppression. In M. Zanna (Ed.), *Advances in experimental social psychology* (Vol. 25, pp. 193–225). Academic Press.

Wegner, D. M. (1996). A computer network model of human transactive memory. *Social Cognition, 13,* 319–339.

Wegner, D. M., Lane, J. D., & Dimitri, S. (1994). The allure of secret relationships. *Journal of Personality and Social Psychology, 66,* 287–300.

Wegner, D. M., & Pennebaker, J. W. (Eds.). (1993). *Handbook of mental control.* Prentice-Hall.

Wehde, W., & Nowlin, M. C. (2021). Public attribution of responsibility for disaster preparedness across three levels of government and the public: Lessons from a survey of residents of the U.S. south Atlantic and Gulf coast. *Publius: The Journal of Federalism, 51,* 212–237.

Weinberg, A., & Weinberg, L. (Eds.).(1961). *The muckrakers.* Capricorn Books.

Weiner, B. (1986). *An attributional theory of motivation and emotion.* Springer-Verlag.

Weiner, B. (1993). On sin versus sickness: A theory of perceived responsibility and social motivation. *American Psychologist, 48,* 957–965.

Weiner, B., Osborne, D., & Rudolph, U. (2011). An attributional analysis of reactions to poverty: The political ideology of the giver and the perceived morality of the receiver. *Personality and Social Psychology Review, 15,* 199–213.

Weiner, B., Perry, R. P., & Magnusson, J. (1988). An attributional analysis of reactions to stigmas. *Journal of Personality and Social Psychology, 55,* 738–748.

Weisman, A. D. (1991). Bereavement and companion animals. *Omega: Journal of Death and Dying, 22,* 241–248.

Weiss, R. (1973). *Loneliness: The experience of emotional and social isolation.* The MIT Press.

Wells, B. E., & Twenge, J. M. (2005). Changes in young people's sexual behavior and attitudes, 1943–1999: A cross-temporal meta-analysis. *Review of General Psychology, 9,* 249–261.

Wells, G. L. (1978). Applied eyewitness-testimony research: System variables and estimator variables. *Journal of Personality and Social Psychology, 36,* 1546–1557.

Wells, G. L. (1995). Scientific study of witness memory: Implications for public and legal policy. *Psychology, Law, and Public Policy, 1*, 726–731.

Wells, G. L., Ferguson, T. J., & Lindsay, R. C. (1981). The tractability of eyewitness confidence and its implications for triers of fact. *Journal of Applied Psychology, 66*, 688–696.

Wells, G. L., & Gavanski, I. (1989). Mental simulation of causality. *Journal of Personality and Social Psychology, 56*, 161–169.

Wells, G. L., Small, M., Penrod, S., Malpass, R. S., Fulero, S. M., & Brimacombe, C. A. E. (1998). Eyewitness identification procedures: Recommendations for lineups and photospreads. *Law and Human Behavior, 22*, 603–647.

West, K., & Hewstone, M. (2012). Culture and contact in the promotion and reduction of anti-gay prejudice: Evidence from Jamaica and Britain. *Journal of Homosexuality, 59*, 44–66.

West, K., Holmes, E., & Hewstone, M. (2011). Enhancing imagined contact to reduce prejudice against people with schizophrenia. *Group Processes & Intergroup Relations, 14*, 407–428.

West, R. F., Meserve, R. J., & Stanovich, K. E. (2012). Cognitive sophistication does not attenuate the bias blind spot. *Journal of Personality and Social Psychology, 103*, 506–519.

West, S. G., Whitney, G., & Schnedler, R. (1975). Helping a motorist in distress: The effects of sex, race, and neighborhood. *Journal of Personality and Social Psychology, 31*, 691–698.

Westfall, J., Van Boven, L., Chambers, J. R., & Judd, C. M. (2015). Perceiving political polarization in the United States: Party identity strength and attitude extremity exacerbate the perceived partisan divide. *Perspectives on Psychological Science, 10*, 145–158.

Weststrate, N. M., & McLean, K. C. (2010). The rise and fall of gay: A cultural-historical approach to gay identity development. *Memory, 18*, 225–240.

Wheeler, L., Reis, H., & Nezlek, J. (1983). Loneliness, social interaction, and sex roles. *Journal of Personality and Social Psychology, 45*, 943–953.

White, C. M., Cutello, C. A., Gummerum, M., & Hanoch, Y. (2018). A cross-cultural study of risky online self-presentation. *Cyberpsychology, Behavior and Social Networking, 21*, 25–31.

White-Means, S., Zhiyong, D., Hufstader, M., & Brown, L. T. (2009). Cultural competency, race, and skin tone bias among pharmacy, nursing, and medical students: Implications for addressing health disparities. *Medical Care Research & Review, 66*, 436–455.

Whitley, B. E. (1999). Right-wing authoritarianism, social dominance orientation, and prejudice. *Journal of Personality and Social Psychology, 77*, 126–134.

Whitley, B. E., Jr., & Lee, S. E. (2000). The relationship of authoritarianism and related constructs to attitudes toward homosexuality. *Journal of Applied Social Psychology, 30*, 144–170.

Whittaker, E., & Kowalski, R. M. (2015). Cyberbullying via social media. *Journal of School Violence, 14*, 11–29.

Wicker, A. W. (1969). Attitudes versus actions: The relationship of verbal and overt behavioral responses to attitude objects. *Journal of Social Issues, 25*, 41–78.

Wicklund, R. A. (1975). Objective self-awareness. In L. Berkowitz (Ed.), *Advances in experimental social psychology*, (Vol. 8, pp. 319–342). Academic Press.

Wicks, R. H., Wicks, J. L., & Morimoto, S. A. (2014). Partisan media selective exposure during the 2012 presidential election. *American Behavioral Scientist, 58*, 1131–1143.

Widom, C. S. (1992). *The cycle of violence*. https://www.ojp.gov/pdffiles1/nij/136607.pdf

Wiegman, O., Kuttschreuter, M., & Baarda, B. (1992). A longitudinal study of the effects of television viewing on aggressive and prosocial behaviors. *British Journal of Social Psychology, 31*, 147–164.

Wihbey, J. (2014). *White racial attitudes over time: Data from the General Social Survey*. https://journalistsresource.org/criminal-justice/white-racial-attitudes-over-time-data-general-social-survey/

Wijenayake, S., van Berkel, N., Kostakos, V., & Goncalves, J. (2020). Impact of contextual and personal determinants on online social conformity. *Computers in Human Behavior, 108*, Article 106302.

Wilder, D. A. (1986). Social categorization: implications for creation and reduction of intergroup bias. In L. Berkowitz (Ed.), *Advances in experimental psychology* (Vol. 19, pp. 293–355). Academic Press.

Wilder, D. A., & Shapiro, P. (1984). The role of outgroup salience in determining social identity. *Journal of Personality and Social Psychology, 47*, 177–194.

Wilder, D. A., & Shapiro, P. (1991). Facilitation of outgroup stereotypes by enhanced ingroup identity. *Journal of Experimental Social Psychology, 27*, 431–452.

Wilford, J. N. (1992, February 11). Nubian treasures reflect Black influence on Egypt. *New York Times*, PCI.

Wilkowski, B. M., Hartung, C. M., Crowe, S. E., & Chai, C. A. (2012). Men don't just get mad; they get even: Revenge but not anger mediates gender differences in physical aggression. *Journal of Research in Personality, 46*, 546–555.

Williams, K. D. (1994). The relations between intentions to vote and actual voting behavior. Unpublished manuscript, University of Toledo.

Williams, K. D. (2001). *Ostracism: The power of silence*. Guilford Press.

Williams, K. D., Forgas, J. P., & von Hippel, W. (Eds.). (2005). *The social outcast: Ostracism, social exclusion, rejection, and bullying*. The Psychology Press.

Williams, K. D., Harkins, S. G., & Latané, B. (1981). Identifiability as a deterrent to social loafing: Two cheering experiments. *Journal of Personality and Social Psychology, 40*, 303–311.

Williams, K. D., & Karau, S. I. (1991). Social loafing and social compensation: The effects of expectations of co-worker performance. *Journal of Personality and Social Psychology, 61,* 570–581.

Williams, K. D., & Sommer, K. L. (1997). Social ostracism by one's coworkers: Does rejection lead to loafing or compensation? *Personality and Social Psychology Bulletin, 23,* 693–706.

Williams, K. D., & Williams, K. B. (1989). Impact of source strength on two compliance techniques. *Basic and Applied Social Psychology, 10,* 149–160.

Williams, K. D., & Zadro, L. (2001). Ostracism: On being ignored, excluded and rejected. In M. Leary (Ed.), *Rejection* (pp. 21–53). Oxford University Press.

Williams, W. M., & Steinberg, R. J. (1988). Group intelligence: Why some groups are better than others. *Intelligence, 12,* 351–357.

Williams v. Florida. (1970). 399 U.S. 78.

Williamson, R. A., Donohue, M. R., & Tully, E. C. (2013). Learning how to help others: Two-year-olds' social learning of a prosocial act. *Journal of Experimental Child Psychology, 114,* 543–550.

Wilson, E. O. (1975). *Sociobiology: The new synthesis.* Harvard University Press.

Wilson, E. O. (1978). *On human nature.* Harvard University Press.

Wilson, I. P. (1976). Motivation, modeling, and altruism: A person × situation analysis. *Journal of Personality and Social Psychology, 34,* 1078–1086.

Wilson, M. G., Northcraft, G. B., & Neale M. A. (1989). Information competition and vividness effects in on-line judgments. *Organizational Behavior and Human Decision Processes, 44,* 132–139.

Wilson, T. D., Lindsey, S., & Schooler, T. Y. (2000). A model of dual attitudes. *Psychological Review, 107,* 101–126.

Wilson, T. D., Dunn, U. S., Kraft. D., & Lisle, D. L. (1989). Introspection, attitude change, and attitude behavior consistency: The disruptive effects of explaining why we feel the way we do. In L. Berkowitz (Ed.), *Advances in experimental social psychology* (Vol. 22, pp. 287–344). Academic Press.

Wilson, T. D., & Kraft, D. (1988). The effects of analyzing reasons on affectively-versus cognitively-based attitudes. Unpublished raw data. Cited in Wilson, T. D., Dunn, D. S., Kraft, D., & Lisle, D. L. (1989), Introspection, attitude change, and attitude behavior consistency: The disruptive effects of explaining why we feel the way we do. In L. Berkowitz (Ed.), *Advances* in *experimental social psychology* (Vol. 22, pp. 287–344). Academic Press.

Wimer, D. J., & Levant, R. F. (2011). The relation of masculinity and help-seeking style with the academic help-seeking behavior of college men. *Journal of Men's Studies, 19,* 256–274.

Winquist, J. R., & Larson, J. R., Jr. (1998). Information pooling: When it impacts group decision-making. *Journal of Personality and Social Psychology, 74,* 371–377.

Wiseman, D. B. (2010). Perceptions of a tattooed college instructor. *Psychological Reports, 106,* 845–850.

Witte, K. (1992). Putting the fear back into fear appeals: The extended parallel process model. *Communication Monographs, 59,* 329–349.

Wixted, J. T., Mickes, L., Clark, S. E., Gronlund, S. D., & Roediger III, H. L. (2015). Initial eyewitness confidence reliably predicts eyewitness identification accuracy. *American Psychologist, 70,* 515–526.

Woike, B., Gershkovich, I., Piorkowski, R., & Polo, M. (1999). The role of motives in the content and structure of autobiographical memory. *Journal of Personality and Social Psychology, 76,* 600–612.

Wolf, S. (1979). Behavioral style and group cohesiveness as sources of minority influence. *European Journal of Social Psychology, 9,* 381–395.

Wolf, T., & Demiray, B. (2019). The mood-enhancement function of autobiographical memories: Comparisons with other functions in terms of emotional valence. *Consciousness and Cognition: An International Journal, 70,* 88–100.

Wolfe, R. M., & Sharp, L. K. (2002). Anti-vaccinationists past and present. *British Medical Journal, 325,* 430–432.

Wong, M. Mei-ha, & Csikzentmihalyi, M. (1991). Affiliation motivation and daily experience. *Journal of Personality and Social Psychology, 60,* 154–164.

Wong, T. K. Y., Konishi, C., & Kong, X. (2021). Parenting and prosocial behaviors: A meta-analysis. *Social Development, 30,* 343–373.

Wong, W. (2020, September, 21). S*ingle plane passenger infected 15 people with Covid-19, study finds.* https://www.nbcnews.com/news/us-news/single-plane-passenger-infected-15-others-covid-19-cdc-says-n1240607

Wood, C. (1978). The I-knew-it-all-along effect. *Journal of Experimental Psychology: Human Perception and Performance, 4,* 345–353.

Wood, W. (1982). Retrieval of attitude relevant information from memory: Effects on susceptibility to persuasion and on intrinsic motivation. *Journal of Personality and Social Psychology, 42,* 798–810.

Wood, W. (1987). Meta-analytic review of sex differences in competence. *Psychological Bulletin, 102,* 53–71.

Wray, S. (1999). On electronic civil disobedience. *Peace Review, 11,* 107–111.

Wright, P. H. (1982). Men's friendships, women's friendships and the alleged inferiority of the latter. Sex *Roles, 8,* 1–21.

Wrightsman, L. S. (1969). Wallace supporters and adherence to "law and order." *Journal of Personality and Social Psychology, 13,* 17–22.

Wu, S., Peng, M., Mei, H., & Shang, X. (2019). Unwilling but not unable to control: Ego depletion increases effortful dishonesty with material rewards. *Scandinavian Journal of Psychology, 60,* 189–194.

Wyer, R. S., Jr., & Srull, T. K. (1986). Human cognition in its social context. *Psychological Review, 93,* 322–359.

Y

Yakimovich, D., & Salz, E. (1971). Helping behavior: 'The cry for help. *Psychonomic Science, 23,* 427–428.

Yancy, G. (2010). Who has religious prejudice? Differing sources of anti-religious animosity in the United States. *Review of Religious Research, 52,* 159–171.

Yang, G. S., Huesmann, L. R., & Bushman, B. J. (2014). Effects of playing a violent video game as male versus female avatar on subsequent aggression in male and female players. *Aggressive Behavior, 40,* 537–541.

Yao, E., & Siegel, J. T. (2021). The influence of perceptions of intentionality and controllability on perceived responsibility: Applying attribution theory to people's responses to social transgression in the COVID-19 pandemic. *Motivation Science, 7,* 199–206.

Yau, J. C., & Reich, S. M. (2018). Are the qualities of adolescents' offline friendships present in digital interactions? *Adolescent Research Review, 3,* 339–355.

Yeeles, A. (2015). Weathering unrest: The ecology of urban social disturbances in Africa and Asia. *Journal of Peace Research, 52,* 158–170.

York, E., & Cornwell, B. (2006). Status on trial: Social characteristics and influence in the jury room. *Social Forces, 85,* 455–477.

Young, R., Len-Ríos, M., & Young, H. (2017). Romantic motivations for social media use, social comparison, and online aggression among adolescents. *Computers in Human Behavior, 75,* 385–395.

Yousaf, O., & Gobet, F. (2013). The emotional and attitudinal consequences of religious hypocrisy: Experimental evidence using a cognitive dissonance paradigm. *Journal of Social Psychology, 153,* 667–686.

Z

Zaccaro, S. J., & Lowe, C. A. (1988). Cohesiveness and performance on an additive task: Evidence for multidimensionality. *Journal of Social Psychology, 128,* 547–558.

Zaccaro, S. J., & McCoy, M. C. (1988). The effects of task and interpersonal cohesiveness on performance of a disjunctive group task. *Journal of Applied Social Psychology, 18,* 837–851.

Zadro, L., Williams, K. D., & Richardson, R. (2004). How low can you go? Ostracism by a computer lowers belonging, control, self-esteem and meaningful existence. *Journal of Experimental Social Psychology, 40,* 560–567.

Zajonc, R. B. (1960). The process of cognitive tuning in communication. *Journal of Abnormal and Social Psychology, 61,* 159–167.

Zajonc, R. B. (1965). Social facilitation. *Science, 149,* 269–274.

Zajonc, R. B. (1968). Attitudinal effects of mere exposure. *Journal of Personality and Social Psychology, 9,* 1–27.

Zajonc, R. B., Heingartner, A., & Herman, F. M. (1969). Social enhancement and impairment of performance in the cockroach. *Journal of Personality and Social Psychology, 13,* 83–92.

Zajonc, R. B., & Rajecki, D. W. (1969). Exposure and affect: A field experiment. *Psychonomic Science, 17,* 216–217.

Zanna, M. P., & Rempel, J. K. (1988). Attitudes: A new look at an old concept. In D. Bar-Tal & A. Kruglanski (Eds.), *The social psychology of knowledge* (pp. 315–334). Cambridge University Press.

Zapolski, T. C. B., Banks, D. E., Lau, K. S. L., & Aalsma, M. C. (2018). Perceived police injustice, moral disengagement, and aggression among juvenile offenders: Utilizing the general strain theory model. *Child Psychiatry and Human Development, 49,* 290–297.

Zarbatany, L., Conley, R., & Pepper, S. (2004). Personality and gender differences in friendship needs and experiences in preadolescence and young adulthood. *International Journal of Behavioral Development, 28,* 299–310.

Zautra, A. J., Arewasikporn, A., & Davis, M. C. (2010). Resilience: Promoting well-being through recovery, sustainability, and growth. *Research in Human Development, 7,* 221–238.

Zebrowitz, L. A., Collins, M. A., & Dutta, R. (1998). The relationship between appearance and personality across life-span. *Personality and Social Psychology Bulletin, 24,* 736–749.

Zebrowitz, L. A., & Lee, S. Y. (1999). Appearance, stereotype-incongruent behavior, and social relationships. *Personality and Social Psychology, 25,* 569–584.

Zebrowitz, L. A., Olson, K., & Hoffman, K. (1993). Stability of babyfaceness and attractiveness across the lifespan. *Journal of Personality and Social Psychology, 64,* 453–466.

Zhang, J. W., Howell, R. T., Caprariello, P. A., & Guevarra, D. A. (2014). Damned if they do, damned if they don't: Material buyers are not happier from material or experiential consumption. *Journal of Research in Personality, 50,* 71–83.

Zhang, X., & Peng, C. (2020). Ego-depletion and increased stereotyping of the older adults as forgetful in the Chinese culture. *Journal of Psychology in Africa, 30,* 427–432.

Zhao, X., & Fink, E. L. (2021). Proattitudinal versus counterattitudinal messages: Message discrepancy, reactance, and the boomerang effect. *Communication Monographs, 88,* 286–305.

Zheng, J-K., & Zhang, Q. (2016). Priming effect of computer game violence on children's aggression levels. *Social Behavior & Personality: An International Journal, 44,* 1747–1759.

Zimbardo, P. G. (1969). The human choice. In W. J. Arnold and G. Levine (Eds.), *Nebraska symposium on motivation* (Vol. 17, pp. 237–307). University of Nebraska.

Zimbardo, P. G. (2004). A situationist perspective on the psychology of evil: Understanding how good people are transformed into perpetrators. In A. G. Miller (Ed.), *The social psychology of good and evil* (pp. 21–50). Guilford Press.

Zimbardo, P. G. (2007). *The Lucifer Effect: Understanding how good people turn evil.* Random House.

Zimbardo, P. G., & Leippe, M. R. (1992). *The psychology of attitude change and social influence.* McGraw Hill.

Zitek, E. M., & Hebl, M. R. (2007). The role of social norm clarity in the influenced expression of prejudice over time. *Journal of Experimental Social Psychology, 43,* 867–876.

Zucker, G. S., & Weiner, B. (1993). Conservatism and perceptions of poverty: An attributional analysis. *Journal of Applied Social Psychology, 23,* 925–943.

Zuckerman, M., Keiffer, S. C., & Knee, C. R. (1998). Consequences of self-handicapping: Effects on coping, academic performance, and adjustment. *Journal of Personality and Social Psychology, 74,* 1619–1628.

Zuckerman, M., Mann, R. W., & Bernieri, F. J. (1982). Determinants of consensus estimates: Attribution, salience, and representativeness. *Journal of Personality and Social Psychology, 42,* 839–852.

Zuckerman, M., Miyake, K., & Hodgins, H. S. (1991). Cross-channel effects of vocal and physical attractiveness and their implications for interpersonal perception. *Journal of Personality and Social Psychology, 60,* 545–554.

Name Index

A

Aaro, D., 451
Abbott, B. B., 10, 11, 12, 24
Abelson, R. P., 188
Aboud, F. E., 360
Abramowitz, A. I., 193
Abrams, D., 318
Acker, M., 350
Acor, A., 78
Adachi, P. C., 429
Adam, M., 464
Adams, J., 133
Adams, Samuel, 243
Addo, P. C., 428
Adorno, T. W., 120–121
Affleck, G., 520
Afifi, W. A., 380
Agocha, V. B., 368
Aguiar, C., 396
Ahmad, N., 446
Aiello, J. R., 313, 314
Aikwa, A., 486
Ainsworth, M. D. S., 353
Aizenkot, D., 427
Ajzen, I., 170, 186, 189, 525
Akrami, N., 123–124
Alaphillippe, D., 487
Albarracin, D., 206
Albert, D. J., 402
Albright, L., 65
Aldrich, Arnold, 306, 337
Alexander, J., 34, 193
Alfieri, T., 89
Allik, J., 53
Allport, G., 135, 145, 146, 152, 154, 155, 156, 169, 175, 185
Alpass, F. M., 347
Altemeyer, B., 122, 123, 124
Altman, I., 371
American Psychological Association, 25
Ames, D. R., 80
Amichai-Hamburger, Y., 357
Amodio, D. M., 195, 359
Andersen, B. L., 43–45, 46, 47
Anderson, C. A., 179, 410, 411, 428, 429, 479
Anderson, D. E., 82
Anderson, K. B., 428
Ang, R. P., 427
Antheunis, M. L., 80, 358
Anthony, L., 391
Antonovsky, A., 517

Antony, M. G., 384
Apostolou, M., 381
Arbuthnot, J., 269
Arceneaux, K., 227
Archer, J., 394, 395, 424
Arendt, Hannah, 281
Aritz, J., 331
Aron, A., 290, 352, 353, 355
Aron, E. N., 293, 355
Aronson, E., 4, 156, 211, 237
Aronson, J., 147, 148, 150, 156
Arriaga, P., 396, 428
Arrington, L. J., 106
Ascani, K., 273, 275, 276
Asch, S., 256–260, 262–266, 268, 503
Asgari, S., 117
Ashton M. C., 116
Atanasov, P., 187
Atta, Mohammad, 281
Aviles, F., 407

B

Babcock-Robertson, M. E., 515
Bach-Zelewski, Erich von dem, 295
Bachner-Melman, R., 449
Bachorowski, J., 405
Bachrach, D. G., 325
Back, M. D., 80, 356
Badaway, A., 404
Baguma, P., 365
Bahns, A. J., 360
Baker, J. G., 125
Balcetis, E., 230, 231
Ball-Rokeach, S., 171
Balls, P., 486, 487
Banaji, M. R., 36, 107, 112, 113, 174
Bandura, A., 178, 412, 413, 520
Bangerter, A., 509
Banning, S., 180
Bar-Anan, Y., 174
Barber, N., 12
Barberá, P., 185
Barcelo, H., 253
Bargh, J. A., 57, 97
Bargh, J. H., 157
Barkow, J. H., 137
Barnett, M. A., 460
Baron, L., 313, 475
Baron, R. A., 425
Baron, R. S., 235, 263
Bartholomew, K., 355

Bartholow, B. D., 428, 429
Bartlett, F. C., 498
Bartlett, M. Y., 463
Bartoli, A. M., 372
Bassili, J. N., 259
Bastian, B., 319
Batson, C. D., 444, 445, 446, 447, 448, 460
Batson, D., 276
Bauer, Clara, 442
Bauer, Ida, 442
Bauer, Thomas, 442
Baum, A., 519
Baumeister, R. F., 53, 57, 61, 64, 137, 235, 279–280, 319, 346, 348, 350, 352, 383
Baumgardner, A. H., 61
Baumrind, D., 293
Beauchamp, M. R., 526
Becker, S. W., 470, 471, 478
Beckner, C., 260
Bee, H., 434
Beenie Man, 157
Behm-Morawitz, E., 424
Bell, B. E., 501
Bell, M. L., 395
Bellé, N., 511
Bem, D. J., 34, 237, 238, 271
Ben Hamida, S., 368
Ben Zeev, T., 149
Benham, G., 519
Benson, P. L., 464, 467
Bergeron, N., 419
Berglas, S., 63, 64
Berkman, L. F., 524
Berkowitz, L., 49, 408, 411, 464, 482, 486
Bernard, D. L., 35
Berndt, T. J., 385
Bernieri, F. J., 77
Bernstein, M. J., 116
Berreby, D., 366
Berry, D., 362
Berry, M. A., 232
Berscheid, E., 351, 373, 383
Betsch, C., 240
Bettencourt, B. A., 396
Beugré, C. D., 410
Bickman, L., 287, 460
Bierhoff, H-W., 445
Biernat, M., 374
Biesanz, J. C., 75
Billig, M., 135
bin Laden, Osama, 279
Birani-Nasaraladen, D., 435

I-1

Birnbaum, D., 522
Bishop, G. D., 516, 517
Bitton, D., 106
Blaine, B., 152
Blanchard, D. C., 408
Blanchard, F. A., 157
Blanchard, R. J., 408
Blank, H., 20, 468, 499, 500
Blascovich, J., 334
Blass, T., 289, 290, 291
Block, L. G., 225
Blondé, J., 224
Blumenthal, D. R., 417
Bocchiaro, P., 294
Bodenhausen, G. V., 134, 157
Boggs, Lilburn W., 106
Böhm, R., 240
Bohner, G., 219
Bolsen, T., 184
Bonanno, G. A., 50–51
Bond, C. F., 81
Booth-Kewley, S., 522
Bordens, K. S., 10, 11, 12, 21, 24, 124
Bork, Robert, 195
Bornstein, R. F., 175, 176, 356
Borrello, C. E., 349
Bosmans, M. G., 520, 521
Boster, F. J., 486
Bothwell, R. K., 504
Bouchey, H. A., 33
Boudreau, J. W., 509
Bourgeois, M. J., 183
Bowman, J. M., 327
Bracken, D. W., 511
Brandt, M. J., 122, 182
Brannon, J., 309
Brantingham, P. J., 398
Bratslavsky, E., 346, 350, 383
Brauer, M., 458, 459
Breckler, S. J., 170
Brehm, J. W., 230, 232, 240, 258, 352, 383
Brehm, S. S., 240, 258
Breuer, J., 429
Brewer, M. B., 134, 156, 318
Brigham, J. C., 505
Brockmann, C., 499
Brody, I., 202
Bromley, S., 468
Brown, J. A. C., 243
Brown, J. D., 309
Brown, K. T., 109
Brown, L., 253
Brown, R., 135, 282
Brown, R. F., 518
Brown, R. P., 148, 423
Brownell, K. D., 365
Browning, C. R., 296
Brownstein, R. J., 276
Bruk-Lee, V., 513
Brumbaugh, C. C., 353
Brunner, H. H., 8
Bryan, J. H., 461, 476
Buckser, A., 474
Buehler, R., 38, 39

Bulger, James, 456
Bull, R., 500
Bureau of Justice Statistics, 394
Bureau of Justice Statistics., 394
Burg, M. M., 519
Burger, J. M., 271, 273, 276
Burnett, A., 344
Burnstein, E., 254, 335
Burris, C. T., 279, 281
Burrows, K., 369
Burt, I., 436
Burt, M., 431
Busby, D. M., 382
Bush, George, 22, 180–181, 194, 279
Bush, George W., 180–181, 194
Bushardt, S. C., 63
Bushman, B. J., 403, 405, 428, 429
Buss, D. M., 361, 364, 367, 368
Buunk, B., 367
Byrne, D., 345, 359, 360

C

Cacioppo, J. T., 212, 216, 217, 225, 347, 509
Cadinu, M., 150
Calder, T., 282
Caldwell, D. F., 271
Callero, P. L., 479
Calley, William, 281
Campbell, J. T., 254, 263
Cancela, A., 223
Cantril, J. G., 272
Caporael, L. R., 309, 318
Capraro, V., 253
Card, N. A., 395
Cardenas, R. A., 362
Carducci, B. J., 273
Carels, R. A., 52
Carey, G., 399
Carli, L. L., 264, 359
Carlo, G., 396
Carlsmith, 229
Carlson, C., 424
Carlson, David, 71–72
Carlson, M. A., 496
Carlson, N. R., 401
Carlston, D. E., 144
Carnagey, N. L., 428
Carnegie Commission on Higher Education, 222
Carr, C., 148
Carr, J. L., 433
Carré, J. M., 400
Carrère, S., 382
Carter, T. J., 524
Caspar, E. A., 291–292
Cassidy, Samuel, 391–393, 406, 436
Cassileth, B., 523
Castro, M. A. C., 486
Catanzaro, S. J., 523
Centers for Disease Control and Prevention, 201–202, 309, 515
Chaiken, S., 88, 227
Chak, K., 358

Chambers, J. R., 123
Champagne, F. A., 399
Chan, D. K-S., 357
Chang-Ik, S., 525
Chapman, J., 140
Chapman, L. L., 140
Charak, R., 519
Chau, M., 133
Check, J. V. P., 430, 431, 432
Chekroun, P., 458
Chen, B., 41
Chen, G. M., 427
Chen, J., 87, 348
Chen, J. M., 109
Chen, Z., 319
Cheng, G. H-L., 357
Cheng, Z., 525
Cheong, J., 405
Chermack, S. T., 417
Chester, M. R., 42
Chopik, W. J., 384
Chory-Assad, R. M., 426
Chow, R. M., 415
Chressanthis, G. A., 196
Christenfeld, N., 367
Christensen, P. N., 348
Christiansen, K., 401
Christianson, S. A., 497
Chung, B. G., 150
Cialdini, R. B., 136, 272, 273, 274, 275, 276–277, 447, 448
Cinnirella, M., 265
Claidière, N., 260–261
Clance, P. R., 34
Clancy, D., 500
Clark, Grote, 372
Clark, J. K., 207
Clark, M., 372
Clark, M. S., 458
Clark, R. D, 267, 458
Clary, E. G., 472
Clement, D., 265
Clifford, B. R., 497
Clinton, Bill, 204
Cogan, R., 523
Cohen, A. R., 230
Cohen, D., 40, 419, 420–422
Cohen, G. L., 150–151, 196
Cohen, Geoffrey, 183
Cohen, J. B., 517
Cohen, L. F., 150, 151
Cohen, S., 516, 517
Cokley, K., 35
Coleman, L. T., 152
Coleman, M., 59
Coleman, R., 180
Collins, J. E., 49, 50
Collins, N. L., 354
Collins, R. L., 224
Colvin, C. R., 65
Combs, D. Y., 205
Conger, R. D., 376
Conner, R. L., 401
Conway, L. G., 123, 183, 195, 259

Cook, S., 157
Cooley, C. H., 33
Cooper, H. M., 403, 405
Cooper, J., 228, 234, 235
Cooper, M. L., 368
Cornwell, B., 504
Correl, J., 113, 223
Costa, P., 124
Costa, P. T., Jr., 124
Costanzo, P. R., 259–260
Cotton, Ronald, 493, 494, 500
Cottrell, C. A., 107
Cottrell, N. B., 313
Couch, J. V., 501
Cousins, Norman, 523
Covell, K., 432
Cox, C. L., 470
Coyne, S. M., 424
Craig, W., 426
Cramer, R. E., 460
Crandall, C. E., 133
Crandall, C. S., 122, 365
Crano, W. P., 230
Creason, C. R., 276
Crisp, R. J., 156
Crockenberg, S., 415
Crocker, J., 53, 142, 152
Crohan, S. E., 380
Crosby, F., 468
Crosby, J. R., 66
Crott, H., 325, 326
Crowley, M., 464
Croyle, R. T., 228
Crozier, W. E., 499
Crutchfield, R. S., 262
Csikzentmihalyi, M., 345
Cullum, J., 255, 256
Cunningham, M., 272
Custer, George Armstrong, 471
Cutler, B. L., 500, 501, 502
Cyranowski, J. M., 45, 46

D

Dambrun, M., 125, 291
Dane, F., 501
Darley, J. M., 140, 451, 452, 454, 455, 456, 460
Darrow, Clarence, 208
Das, E., 219
Dasgupta, N., 117
Davenport, Lindsay, 32
Davis, D., 506
Davis, J. H., 332, 333, 503
Davis, Keith, 85
Davis, M., 83
Davis, N. H., 350
Dazio, S., 392
de Gelder, B., 457
de Gelder, B. B., 396
De La Ronde, C., 377
de Man, A. F., 432
de Munck, V. C., 351
De Raad, B., 419

Dean, D. H., 79
Dean, K. E., 433
DeAndrea, D. C., 42
DeBono, A., 415
Deelstra, J. T., 487
Deffenbacher, K. A., 500
Degner, J., 505
DeHart, T., 54
DeJong, M., 272
DeJong, W., 365
Dekovic, M., 476
Del Barrio, V., 18–19, 19
DeLamater, J., 308
Delgado, J. M. R., 401
Demiray, B., 39
Dempsey, C. B., 273
Denny, Reginald, 466
Denrell, J., 79
Denson, T. F., 401, 404
DePaulo, B. M., 65, 81, 82, 83, 484, 485
Derlega, V. J., 9
Derntl, B., 401
DeRosier, M. E., 415
DeSantis, A. D., 238
Desdentado, L., 54
Desforges, D., 155
DeSteno, D., 463
Deuser, P. S., 273
Deutsch, Chaim., 252
Devine, P. G., 80, 143–144
Dhont, K., 155
Diamond, L. M., 352
Diekman, A. B., 116
Dijksterhuis, A., 61
Dijkstra, P., 367
Dill, K. E., 428, 429
Dillard, C. L., 298
Dillard, J. P., 240, 272
Ding, V. J., 365
Dinges, D. F., 519
Dion, K., 362, 511
Dion, K. L., 145
DiTommaso, E., 346
Dobolyi, D. G., 500
Dodge, K. A., 434
Dodson, C., 498, 500
Dolbier, C., 520
Dolinoy, D. C., 8
Dolinski, D., 272
Doll, J., 189
Dollard, J., 406, 407, 408
Doms, M., 265
Donnelly, D., 430
Donnerstein, E., 131, 430
Donnerstein, M., 131
Douglas, K. M., 133
Douglass, Frederick, 126
Dovidio, J. F., 113, 128, 130, 142, 446, 448, 467, 468
Downey, D., 252
Downey, K. T., 52
Dozier, J. B., 482
Drickamer, L. C., 397, 398
Drigotas, S. M., 377

Drizen, S. A., 506
Duck, J., 318
Duck, S. W., 352, 359, 384
Duhart, B., 253
Dunbar, R. I. M., 121, 124
Duncan, L. E., 122
Dundon, C. M., 352
Dunkel Schetter, C., 520
Dunning, D., 230, 231
Durante, F., 111
Durbach, N., 202
Durham, M., 501
Dyck, R. J., 409
Dysart, J. E., 505

E

Eagly, A. H., 186, 187, 197, 205, 214, 222, 264–265, 328, 464, 470, 471, 478
Earles, J. L., 498
Earn, B. M., 145
Earp, B. D., 23
Easterling, B., 373
Eastwick, P. W., 368
Eccles, J. S., 98
The Ed Sullivan Show, 202
Eden, D., 330
Edwards, I. A., 75–76
Edwards, S. B., 400
Edwards, S. L., 348
Egeth, H. E., 501
Ehrlich, G. A., 136
Eibach, R. P., 39
Eichmann, Adolph, 279–283
Eisenberg, N., 444, 477, 478, 486, 487
Eisner, M., 423
Eitzen, D. S., 137
Ekehammar, B., 123–124
Ekman, P., 81, 82, 215
Elbert, T., 395
Elder, W. B., 47, 48
Elkin, R. A., 230
Ellis, A. L., 334
Ellul, J., 242
Elms, A., 284
England, Lynndie, 278
Engleberg, E., 225–226
Ensari, N., 157
Enzo, E., 351
Epstein, L., 195
Epstein, Z. G., 471
Erb, H., 258
Eriksson, O., 265
Esses, V. M., 116, 146, 226
Essien, I., 140
Etcoff, N. L., 82
Evans, D. C., 362, 363
Evans, K., 362–363

F

Fabrigar, L. R., 223
Fairey, P. J., 254, 263
Farley, S. D., 188

Name Index   **I-3**

Faulkner, Williams, 319
Fawcett, J. M., 496
Fazio, R. H., 34, 189, 191, 204, 234
Fehr, B., 384
Feinberg, J. M., 313, 314
Feist, J., 309
Feldman, J. M., 511
FeldmanHall, O., 195
Ferguson, C. J., 429
Ferguson, T. J., 425
Ferrari, J. R., 381
Feshbach, S., 393
Festinger, L., 34, 205, 228, 229, 237, 257, 264, 276, 309
Fiebert, M. S., 384
Fiedler, F. W., 327, 330
Figueredo, A. J., 420
Fincham, F. D., 380, 381
Finez, L., 64, 65
Fink, E. L., 213
Fischer, P., 457, 458
Fischoff, B., 22
Fishbein, H. D., 125
Fishbein, M., 186
Fisher, E., 512
Fisher, J. D., 484, 485, 486, 487, 488
Fiske, A. P., 97
Fiske, S. T., 58, 73, 94, 95, 97, 111, 134, 143, 156, 157
Flanagin, A. J., 208
Fleming, A., 167, 168
Fleming, J. H., 215
Flohr, H., 75, 137
Flynn, F. J., 96, 124
Flynn, J. P., 400
Fointiat, V., 273
Folkman, S., 518
Fonda, Henry, 266, 268
Ford, T. E., 146
Forde, D. R., 395
Forehand, R., 434
Forgas, J. P., 93, 94, 316
Forsyth, D., 307, 308
Foss, R. D., 273
Frable, D. E. S., 51, 52
Fraley, R. C., 353, 354, 355
Francis-Tan, A., 109–110
Franco, Z. E., 471
Francoise, S., 417
Franks, H. M., 518
Fraser, J., 430
Fraser, S. C., 270, 271
Freedman, J. L., 230, 270, 271, 425
Freitas-Murrell, B., 484
French, S. E., 329, 526
Frenda, S. J., 506
Friedman, H. S., 522
Friedman, S. B., 416
Frieze, I. H., 353, 372
Frimer, J. A., 472, 473
Fritzsche, B. A., 460, 461
Fromme, K., 405
Frumkin, L. A., 394
Fultz, J., 448

Funder, D. C., 65
Furnham, A., 79, 265, 365

G

Gabriel, U., 468
Gadow, K. P., 425
Gaertner, L., 40, 41
Gaertner, S. L., 128, 130, 467, 468
Galinsky, A. D., 327
Gallup, 129, 187, 193, 194
Gamberini, L., 467
Gamson, W. A., 297–298
Gangestad, S. W., 362, 366, 367
Garcia, J., 150–151
Garcia, S., 361
Garcia, S. M., 455
Gardner, W. L., 43, 311
Garrett, R. K., 184
Garrison, William Lloyd, 201
Gavanski, I., 100
Gawronski, B., 135
Gazzard Kerr, L., 76
Geen, R. G., 313
Geffner, R., 287, 289, 290
General Social Survey, 128
Geniole, S. N., 403
Genovese, Kitty, 451, 454, 455–456, 460
Genschow, O., 275, 276
Gentile, A., 52
Gentile, B., 53
Gentry, C. S., 125
George, C., 418
George Mason University, 244
Gerard, H. B., 33
Gergen, K. J., 486
Gerow, J., 124
Gerrard, H. B., 254
Gershoff, E. T., 416
Ghuneim, L., 423
Giancola, P. R., 404, 405
Gibbons, F. X., 61
Gibbons, H., 260
Gigone, D., 327
Gilbert, D. S., 93
Gilbert, D. T., 88, 89, 110, 190
Gilbert, G., 372
Gilbert, S. J., 293
Gill, M. J., 77
Gillespie, C., 253
Gillis, J., 82
Gilovich, T., 65–66, 97, 524
Gino, F., 464
Ginsburg, G. P., 334
Girandola, F., 224, 273
Glaser, R., 519
Glassman, R. B., 450
Glecker, J., 392
Gleicher, F., 210
Glomb, T. M., 360
Glüer, M., 358
Gobet, F., 229
Goebbels, Josef, 241, 242, 244–246
Goei, R., 486

Goering, Albert, 470, 473
Goering, Hermann, 470, 477
Goh, D. H., 427
Goldberg, A. E., 372
Goldman, M., 272, 273, 276, 475, 483
Goldstein, Baruch, 393
Goleman, D., 127, 173, 477, 478
Goodall, Jane, 19
Goodwin, K. A., 259
Goodwin, R., 259
Goranson, R. E., 486
Gordon, K. C., 380
Gore, Al, 180
Gore, K. Y., 468
Gorka, S., 404
Gorman-Smith, D., 413, 414
Gosling, S. D., 80
Gosselin, P., 81
Gottman, J. M., 376, 380–82
Gough, H. G., 124
Gouldner, A. W., 275, 484
Government Social Research, 416
Gracek, S., 350
Graham, J. E., 516
Graham, M. A., 516
Graham, S., 465, 466
Gramzow, R. H., 136
Grant, S., 364, 365
Grassini, A., 271
Gray, S. A., 109
Green, B., 265
Greenwald, A. G., 36, 37, 40, 107, 172, 174, 216
Greenwood, D., 146, 147
Greitemeyer, T., 327, 457
Grewal, D., 49
Grieve, P. G., 136, 137
Grogan-Kaylor, A., 416
Gross, M. M., 287, 289, 290
Gross, P. H., 140
Grossman, P. J., 328, 329, 331
Groth, A. N., 430, 431
Gruder, C. L., 206, 207, 464, 465
Grysman, A., 36
Goading, R. E., 225
Goring, A., 394
Gubi-Kelm, S., 506
Guéguen, N., 14–15, 271, 273, 275, 277, 462
Gülgöz, S., 38
Gunderson, J., 381
Gunderson, P. R., 381
Günsoy, C., 43
Gupta, N., 324
Gupta, S., 51
Gustafson, R., 403, 404

H

Habel, P., 179
Haddock, G., 226
Häfner, M., 379
Hagita, N., 264
Halabi, S., 487
Hale, J. L., 351
Hale, Matt, 121

Hale, W. W., 417
Hall, J. A., 80
Hall, V., 507
Haller, Lazar, 442
Halpern, D. F., 116
Hamamura, T., 53
Hamilton, D. K., 140
Hamilton, L., 295–296
Hansen, C. H., 141
Hansen, R. D., 141
Hansson, S. O., 12
Har, J., 392
Harari, H., 457–459
Harari, O., 458, 459
Harber, K., 49
Harkins, S. G., 315
Harmon-Jones, E., 239
Harris, C. R., 367
Harris, L. J., 362
Harris, M., 265
Harris, M. B., 364
Harris, P. R., 223
Harris, V. A., 85
Hart, C., M., 308
Hart, J. W., 269
Harter, S., 33
Harvard University, 51, 309
Harvey, C. B., 180
Harvey, J. H., 95
Haslam, S. A., 136
Hass, R. G., 131
Hastie, R., 327, 333, 334
Hatala, M. N., 369
Hatcher, J. W., 258
Hatfield, E. H., 350, 359, 361, 374, 375
Haugen, T., 317
Haugtvedt, C. P., 212, 226
Hausenblas, H. A., 525
Hawkley, L. C., 347
Hayat, Z., 357
Hayes, T. C., 420
Hays, R. B., 371
Hayward, W. G., 505
Heaton, A. W., 61
Hebb, D. O., 9
Hebl, M. R., 133, 364, 365
Hee Sun, P., 525
Hehman, E., 181
Heider, F., 84–86, 93
Heine, S. J., 55
Heinhold, W. D., 459
Heinrich, Ingo, 283
Hendren, A., 20, 468
Hendrick, C., 349, 383
Hendrick, S. S., 349
Henningsen, D. D., 327
Henningsen, M. L. M., 327
Herbert, T. B., 516
Herbozo, S., 365
Herbst, K. C., 226
Herbst-Damm, K. L., 524
Herda, D., 360
Hershfield, H., 202
Hertel, G., 316
Hess, R. D., 177

Hess, Rudolph, 244
Heu, L. C., 347
Hewstone, M., 116, 117, 123, 154, 317
Hicks, J. A., 175
Higgins, E. T., 54, 55, 97
Higgins, F. T., 56
Hill, C. A., 359
Hill, C. T., 375
Hines, D. A., 399
Hippler, Fritz, 194, 244, 245
Hirsch, C., 348
Hirt, E. R., 65
Hitler, Adolf, 244–246, 282, 473
Hixon, G. J., 89, 110
Hixon, J. G., 192
Hoaken, P. N. S., 404, 405
Hobman, E. V., 360
Hodges, S., 196
Hodson, G., 124–125
Hoeksema-van Orden, C. Y. D., 315
Hoffman, M. L., 450
Hogan, D. E., 159
Hogben, M., 424
Hogg, M. A., 136, 137, 318
Holland, K. J., 526
Hollander, E. P., 310
Hollbach, S., 135
Hollingshead, A. B., 324, 327
Hollman, T. B., 382
Holmes, I. G., 374, 379
Holmes, M. R., 417, 418
Holmes, T. H., 518, 520
Homant, R. J., 449
Homik, J., 272
Hong, S., 195
Hopkins, P. D., 470
Horowitz, I. A., 21, 330
Horowitz, L. M., 355
Horry, R., 259
Hortensius, R., 457
Horwitz, M., 156
Hoshino-Browne, E., 233
Hostetter, A. B., 4
Houston, K. A., 497, 498, 501
Hovland, C. I., 203, 206, 209, 212, 214
Howard, B. K., 78
Howard, D. J., 217–218
Hoxter, A. L., 126
Huang, L., 265
Hudson, J. A., 36
Huesmann, L. R., 406, 412, 414, 423, 424, 425, 429
Hugenberg, K., 117
Human, L. J., 75
Huneke, D. K., 478
Huppert, J. D., 348
Huston, T. L., 378
Hyde, J. S., 396
Hyers, L. L., 153
Hymowitz, C., 167

I

Ifargan, M., 435
IJzerman, H., 379

Ike, B. W., 141
Ilmarinen, V., 361
Imes, S. A., 34
Imhoff, R., 258
Innocence Project, 501
Insel, P. M., 403, 517
Iredale, W., 450
Irwin, C. J., 137
Isbell, L. M., 146, 147
Isen, A. M., 462
Isenberg, D. J., 266

J

Jackiw, L. B., 504
Jackson, H., 358
Jackson, T., 358
Jacobson, J. A., 72
Jacobson, L., 97
James, L., 113
James, William, 39
Janssens, J. M., 476
Jarcho, J. M., 234
Jattuso, M. L., 509
Jiang, T., 37
Joanisse, M., 147
Jobs, Steve, 515
John, O., 141
Johns, M., 150
Johnson, B., 109
Johnson, B. T., 222
Johnson, C., 109
Johnson, J. D., 109
Johnson, M. K., 498, 499
Johnson, R. N., 398
Johnson, T. E., 408
Jones, D. A., 509
Jones, E. E., 33, 60, 63, 64, 74, 77, 85, 86, 87, 143
Jones, Jim, 236
Jordan, C. H., 54
Joseph, R., 187
Joseph, T. D., 93
Josephs, R. A., 148
Jost, J. T., 139–140, 195
Jourard, S. M., 371
Jowett, G. S., 179, 243
Judd, C. M., 110, 116
Jugert, P., 360
Julian, T. W., 417
Jussim, L., 73, 97, 98, 116, 118

K

Kahneman, D., 95, 100, 471, 524
Kaiser, C. R., 153
Kaiser, M. K., 187, 190
Kaiser Family Foundation, 179
Kalven, H., 266, 503
Kambara, T., 408
Kameda, T., 333, 334
Kamzan, M., 460
Kanjorski, J., 145
Kaplan, M. F., 254, 262, 504
Karau, S. L., 315, 316, 328

Karmarkar, U. R., 205
Karr, John Mark, 505
Kashima, Y., 40
Kashy, D., 82, 348
Kashy-Rosenbaum, G., 427
Kassin, S. M., 218, 505–506
Kassner, M. P., 321
Kats, R., 517
Katwala, A., 252
Katz, I., 127
Katz, J., 458
Katzev, R. D., 276
Kaukiainan, A., 395
Kawakami, K., 36, 158, 159
Keillor, Garrison, 58
Keith, P. M., 362
Kelekar, A. K., 176
Keller, P. A., 225
Keller, P. S., 205
Kelley, H. H., 370, 373
Kelley, Harold, 85–86
Kelloway, E. K., 328
Kelly, J. R., 372
Kelman, H. C., 206, 295–296
Kemmelmeier, M., 123
Kendall, P. C., 434, 435
Kennedy, D. B., 449
Kennedy, P. H., 9
Kenny, D. A., 65
Kenrick, D. T., 369
Keresteš, G., 47, 415
Kernsmith, P., 431
Kernsmith, R., 431
Kerr, N. L., 315, 316, 317, 324, 332, 334
Kerry, John, 194
Kessler, T., 135
Khaleque, A., 417
Kiang, L., 148
Kiechel, K. L., 506
Kim, C., 180
Kim, K., 83
Kim, S. H., 195
Kim, Y., 195
King, L. A., 75, 175
King, Martin Luther Jr., 284, 294
Kiousis, S., 180, 181
Kitayama, S., 40, 233
Kite, M. E., 125
Klein, S. B., 37
Kleinsmith, J., 402
Klinger, Abram, 442
Klinkenberg, Rose, 372
Klohnen, E. C., 377
Knee, C. R., 376
Knippenberg, A. V., 61
Knowles, M. L., 311
Knox, D., 357
Knussmann, R., 401
Kogan, N., 335
Köhler, W., 316–317
Köhnken, G., 499
Kokkonen, A., 360
Kolata, G., 365
Köllner, M. G., 345

Kopelman, R. E., 511
Koresh, David, 236–237
Kowalski, R. M., 347, 394
Kraft, D., 191
Kravitz, J., 504
Kray, L. J., 327
Kremer, J. F., 408
Kret, M. E., 396
Kreutzer, J. S., 403, 405
Krieglmeyer, R., 409
Krishan, L., 484
Krishnan, K. R. R., 396
Kristiansen, C. M., 171
Krosnick, J. A., 176, 178, 189
Kruglanski, A. W., 264, 310
Krull, D. S., 88, 93
Kubica, M., 423
Kukulj, S., 47
Kulik, J. A., 524
Kumkale, G. T., 206
Kunda, Z., 36
Kunstman, J. W., 467
Kuo, F., 42
Kurdek, L. A., 373
Kurdi, B., 129

L

Lackie, L., 432
LaFrance, M., 145
Lage, E., 269
Lamm, H., 334, 335
Lamy, L., 462
Landon, Alf, 187
Lang, A. R., 405
Lange, J. E., 110, 116
Langer, E. J., 191, 520
Langlois, J. H., 363
Lantos, H., 418
LaPiere, R. T., 185, 186
Lariscy, R. A. W., 206
Larrick, R. P., 411
Larsen, K., 265
Larson, J. R., 327, 328
Lassiter, G. D., 225
Latané, B., 268–269, 315, 451, 452, 454, 455, 456
Latham, G. P., 513, 514
Laughlin, P. R., 324, 325, 326, 334
Launay, C., 500
Laurenceau, J. P., 346
LaVasseur, J. B., 122–123
Lawless, William, 469, 470
Lawson, R. G., 211
Lawson, V. Z., 505
Lazarus, R. S., 517, 518
Leary, M. R., 319, 347, 348, 415
Leci, L., 109
Lee, F., 93
Lee, J. K., 184
Lee, M. R., 420
Lee, S. E., 122
Lee, S. Y., 362, 363
Legate, N., 320
Lehman, D. R., 55

Leippe, M. R., 170, 230, 235, 239
Lemarquand, D., 404
Lenton, A. P., 117
Leo, R. A., 506
Leonard, K. E., 355, 403, 405
Leonardeli, G. J., 35
Lepper, M. R., 232, 233
Lerner, Harriet, 343
Lerner, M. J., 464
Lester, D., 126
LeSure-Lester, G. E., 435
Letzring, T. D., 59
Leung, L., 358
Levant, R. F., 484
Levenson, R. W., 380, 382
Leventhal, G. S., 486
Leventhal, H., 209
Levi, A., 58
Levin, S., 123
Levine, J. M., 308, 310, 330, 331
Levine, M., 456, 466
Levine, S., 401
Levinger, C., 370
Levinger, G., 370
Levinson, C. A., 406
Levy, S. R., 117–118
Lewin, Kurt, 4, 6
Lewinsky, Monica, 204
Lewis, D. O., 418
Leyens, J.-P., 135
Li, H., 332
Libby, L. K., 39
Lichtenstein, M., 134
Liebert, R. M., 425
Lifton, Robert, 295
Lilienfeld, S. O., 12
Lincoln, Abraham, 126
Lindner, C., 58
Lindsay, D. S., 498, 499, 500
Lindsay, R. C. L., 504
Linn, S., 365
Linville, P. W., 48, 143
Linz, D., 430, 431, 433
Lippmann, W., 110
Lips, H., 108
Lisco, C. G., 403, 404
Litchblau, E., 133
Litman, C., 415
Locke, E. A., 513, 514
Loewenstein, G., 525
Loftus, E. F., 495, 498, 499, 500, 501
Lohaus, A., 358
Long, N., 434
Lopes, P. N., 49
Lorenz, K., 397, 398
Lorenzo, G. L., 76
Lorge, I., 324
Lowe, C. A., 332, 333
Lu, L., 326
Luginbuhl, J., 63
Lundh, L.-G., 348
Luo, Y., 347
Lutter, M., 524
Luzsa, R., 96

Lytton, H., 396
Lyubomirsky, S., 39

M

Maas, V. V., 511
Macci, Rick, 32
MacInnis, C. C., 125
Mackie, D. M., 154, 218
MacLeod, M. D., 499
Macrae, C. N., 80, 81, 110, 117, 134, 214
Maddox, K. B., 109
Madey, S. F., 351
Mae, L., 144
Magnusson, D., 412
Main, M., 418
Maio, G. R., 226
Major, B., 142, 152
Malamuth, N. M., 412, 414, 430, 432, 433
Malle, B. F., 89–90, 196
Mallott, M., 159
Malone, P. S., 93
Malpass, R. S., 504
Manalastas, E. J., 352
Mancini, C., 431
Mandela, Nelson, 33, 470
Maner, J. K., 5
Manilow, Barry, 66
Mann, L., 288–290
Mansour, J. K., 496
Mantell, D. M., 289, 291
Marcus, B., 80
Marcus, J., 41
Marcus-Newhall, A., 407
Mares, M.-L., 425
Marion, S. B., 507
Mark, M. M., 409
Markey, P. M., 455
Markman, H., 380
Markus, H., 36, 40, 45
Marques, J. M., 318
Marshall, J., 496
Martin, R., 268
Martínez-Ferrer, B., 414
Mashoodh, R., 399
Maslow, A., 512, 513
Match, 359, 360, 368
Matsuda, N., 265
Matthews, M., 464
Matz, S. C., 524
Mayr, S., 96
Mayseless, O., 264
McAdams, D. P., 345, 385
McArthur, L. Z., 88, 362
McAuliffe, Christa, 305
McCarthy, J. M., 509
McCarty, M. K., 372
McCarty, N., 196
McCauley, C., 309, 334, 336
McClelland, D. C., 512
McCloskey, M., 498, 499, 501
McConahay, J. G., 130–131
McConnell, E., 42
McCown, J. A., 357

McCoy, M. C., 332, 333
McCrae, R. R., 124
McCullough, M. E., 380, 381, 463
McDonald, Alan, 306
McFarland, C., 38, 39, 455
McGregor, I., 378, 379
McGregor, L., 35
McGuire, C. V., 35
McGuire, W. J., 35, 212–213
McHan, E., 413
McKay, N. J., 432
McKenna, K., 357–358
McKimmie, B., 208–209
McLean, K. C., 44
McLeod, P. L., 268
McNamee, L. G., 133
McNamee, S., 471
McNeill, W. H., 10
Mead, Margaret, 305
Mead, N. L., 58
Mealey, L., 362, 366, 367
Mednick, B. R., 418
Meeus, W., 289–290, 294
Mehdizadeh, S., 42
Meissner, C. A., 129, 505
Mendelsohn, G. A., 377
Mendoza, M., 392
Mercer, S. H., 415
Merolla, A. J., 379
Messe, L. A., 316
Metzger, M. J., 208
Meyer-Parlapanis, D., 395
Meyers-Levy, J., 224
Miceli, M. P., 482
Micevski, M., 112
Midlarsky, E., 473, 476
Mikulincer, M., 355
Milanovi, A., 415
Miles, D. R., 399
Milgram, S., 6, 24, 174, 262–263, 265–266, 283–298
Millar, M. G., 276
Miller, A. G., 285
Miller, B., 425
Miller, C. E., 254, 262, 333
Miller, C. T., 52, 153, 156
Miller, D. A., 123, 159
Miller, D. T., 100, 259, 455
Miller, G., 368
Miller, J. M., 180
Miller, K., 403
Miller, N., 156, 396, 407
Miller, N. E., 408
Miller, P. A., 444
Miller, R., 52
Miller, S. L., 5
Miller, T. Q., 425
Mills, J., 237
Minshull, M., 500
Mirabile, R. R., 184
Miranda, Carmen, 230
Mirror, 431
Mischel, W., 73
Mizz, T., 365

Moberg, S. P., 128
Moghaddam, F. M., 410
Monahan, J. L., 175
Mondale, Walter, 189
Monsour, M., 383
Monteith, M. J., 109, 144
Monteoliva, A., 354
Montgomery, B. M., 380
Montieth, M. J., 109
Montoya, E., 401, 404
Montoya, R. M., 176, 361, 362
Moody, E. J., 358
Moore, Jesse, 306, 337
Moradi, B., 125
Moran, G. P., 311
Moreland, R. L., 308, 310, 330, 331
Morgan, C. A., 497
Moriarty, T., 469
Morman, M. T., 211
Morris, Hermann, 442
Morris, Herschel, 442
Morris, Miriam, 442
Morris, Pola, 442
Morrison, B., 453
Morrow-Howell, N., 468
Moscovici, S., 258, 266, 268, 269, 334
Moser, G., 460
Moses, L. J., 183
Moskos, C., 160
Moskowitz, G. B., 113, 114
Motta, M., 202
Moyer, K. E., 394
Much, N. C., 34
Mugny, G., 267
Muir, G., 431
Mullen, B., 58, 60, 466
Mulligan, K., 179
Mullin, B. A., 136
Mummenday, A., 136
Muraven, M., 58, 415
Murdoch, D. D., 403
Murphy, C. M., 429
Murphy, C. R., 429
Murphy, K. R., 417
Mussen, P., 477, 478
Myers, A. M., 153
Myers, D. G., 334, 335, 504
Myrdal, G., 137

N

NAACP, 133
Nadler, A., 486, 487
Nagoshi, C. T., 405
Nagoshi, J., 125
Nam, S. K., 484
Napper, L., 223
Nario-Redmond, M. R., 52
National Institute of Mental Health, 484
National Oceanic and Atmospheric Administration, 1
National Science Teaching Association, 11
Navarick, D. J., 296
Neidermeier, K. E., 329

Neimeyer, G. J., 37, 45
Neisser, U., 96
Nelson, D., 359
Nelson, T. D., 107
Nemeth, C., 267, 268
Neto, F., 346
Neuberg, S. L., 107, 143, 156, 157, 447
Neville, S., 347
New World Encyclopedia, 193
Newberg, S. L., 447
Newseum Institute, 128
Neziek, J. B., 319
Nichols, K. A., 348
Nicolaisen, M., 384
Nielsen., 179
Nikolaou, I., 509
The 9/11 Commission Report, 22
Nisbett, R. E., 4, 40, 141, 142, 293, 419, 420, 421
Nobre, P., 47
Noftle, E. E., 59
Noor, F., 362, 363
North, A. C., 462
Norton, M. I., 229
Nosek, B. A., 172, 174
Notarius, C., 380
Nowlin, M. C., 90
Nuñez, N., 495

O

Oakes, P. J., 318
Oakley, B., 448
Obama, Barack, 116, 181
O'Connell, R. L., 9
O'Connor, L. E., 448
Odintsova, V. V., 399
O'Donnell, V., 23, 179
Oeberst, A., 499
Ohbuchi, K., 408
Oksanen, A., 427
Oliker, S. J., 384, 385
Oliner, P. M., 474–479, 482
Oliner, S. P., 474–479, 482
Olson, J. M., 100
Olweus, D., 9
O'Meara, D. J., 383
Öner, S., 38
Ong, L. P., 416
Opdyke, Irene Gut, 441–443, 449, 460, 472, 482–483, 488
Open Science Collaboration (OSC), 24
Orenstein, L., 472
Organ, D. W., 514
Ortiz-Beck, Taj, 1, 2, 4
Osborn, K. A., 316
Osherow, N., 237
Oskamp, S., 175, 176, 177, 182, 186
Ostrove, J. M., 395
Oswald, F. L., 129
Oswald, Patricia, 15, 16
Ouellette, J. A., 56
Over, R., 369

P

Paez, D., 318
Palmer, C. L., 362, 363
Palmer, J. K., 511
Palmer, T., 63
Paluck, E., 157
Papageorgis, D., 213
Park, B., 110, 116
Park, L. E., 53
Park, Y., 266
Parks, Rosa, 294, 298
Parrott, D. J., 403, 404
Partridge, Edward, 106
Patterson G. R., 414, 415, 434
Paul, A., 358
Paulhus, D. L., 174
Payne, B. K., 174
Pedersen, W. C., 407
Peetz, J., 526
Peixoto, M. M., 47
Pelham, B. W., 55, 61
Pelosi, James, 318–319
Pelosi, N., 318–319
Pendleton, M., 276
Peng, C., 134
Pennebaker, J. W., 74
Pennebaker, Jamie, 22
Pennington, C. R., 150
Pennisi, E., 8
Penrod, S., 500, 502, 503
Penton-Voak, I., 366
Peplau, L. A., 346
Pepler, D. J., 435
Peracchio, L. A., 224–225
Peralta, C. F., 513
Perdue, C. W., 138
Perlman, D., 176, 346
Perret, D. L., 366
Perrin, S., 265
Peruche, B. M., 114–115
Peter, J., 357
Peter-Hagene, L. C., 503, 504
Peterson, J. B., 404
Peterson, R. D., 362
Pettigrew, T. E., 143, 156
Pettit, G. S., 398
Petty, R. E., 205, 210, 216, 217, 219, 220, 221, 225, 226, 315, 509
Peukert, D., 298
Pew Research Center, 127, 128, 158
Pew Research Organization, 127, 357, 360
Pfau, M., 213
Philips, A. G., 56
Phillips, D. P., 425
Phillips, G., 369
Phillips, S., 425
Piaget, Jean, 196
Piazza, T., 132, 139
Piccolo, R. F., 514
Pickel, K. L., 496
Piecuch, Balwina, 475, 483
Piferi, R. L., 443
Pihl, R. O., 403, 404
Pila, E., 52
Piliavin, I. M., 460
Piliavin, J. A., 460
Pinker, S., 309
Pitkanen, T., 412
Plant, E. A., 80, 114–115, 467
Platania, J., 311
Plomin, R., 182–183
Plous, S., 118
Poole, Bobby, 494
Potârcă, G., 369
Potthoff, A. L., 4
Powell, Colin, 160
Prager, K., 384
Pratkanis, A. R., 4, 40, 206, 211
Pratto, F., 123, 125, 141, 157
Prehodka, J., 369
Preister, J. R., 205
Prentice, D. A., 259
Prentice-Dunn, S., 322
Presley, Elvis, 202
The Press Democrat, 1
Priester, J. R., 205
Prior, M., 194
Pritchard, R. D., 333
Pruitt, D. G., 486
Pulkkinen, L., 412
Pyszczynski, T., 54

Q

QuanIei, Y., 54
Quattrociocchi, W., 96
Quattrone, G. A., 143
Quigley, B. M., 403, 405
Quinton, W. J., 122

R

Raaijmakers, Q., 289–290, 294
Rabbie, J. M., 156
Rabe, John, 470
Rahe, 518, 520
Rainie, L., 184
Rains, S. A., 240
Rajecki, D. W., 170, 175, 189, 206
Ramsey, JonBenet, 505
Rand, D. G., 471
Rareshide, M. B., 37, 45
Rast, D. E., 111
Ratner, R. K., 226
Rattner, A., 298
Raven, B. H., 329
Rawlins, W. K., 384, 385
Raynaud-Maintier, C., 487
Reagan, P. C., 351
Reagan, Ronald, 82, 167, 189, 204, 279
Reed, P. J., 43
Reeder, G. D., 196
Reeder, H., 383
Reeves, R., 276
Regan, D. T., 276
Regan, P. C., 351, 368, 369
Reich, S. M., 357

Reicher, S. D., 323
Reid, D. B., 174
Reinisch, J. M., 395
Reis, H. T., 41
Reisberg, D., 498
Reiss, M. J., 398
Rellini, A. H., 352
Rempel, J. K., 171, 279, 281
Repple, J., 401
Rescorla, Rick, 472
Resenhoeft, A., 78
Revere, Paul, 243
Reynolds, S., 355
Rhodewalt, F. T., 64
Richards, Z., 116–117
Richardson, D. R., 410
Ringhand, L. A., 195
Riordan, C. A., 58
Rios, K., 122
Risen, J. L., 141
Rochat, F., 292
Rockefeller, John D., 167, 168, 176
Rodafinos, A., 276
Roderick, C., 435
Rodgers, L., 351
Rodin, J., 520
Rodriguez, D. N., 232
Rodríguez-García, J., 154
Roesch, S. C., 518
Roese, N. J., 100
Rogers, Henry, 168
Rogers, R. W., 211, 322
Rogers, Will, 71–72
Rohmann, E., 445
Rohsenow, D. J., 405
Roisman, G. I., 372
Rokach, A., 346
Rokeach, M., 171
Romatowski, J. A., 180
Romer, D., 479, 480
Romero-López, M., 435
Romney, D. M., 396
Ronis, D. L., 187, 190
Roosevelt, F. D., 187, 251
Roosevelt, Teddy, 167, 197
Roper, J., 462
Rosander, M., 265
Roscigno, V. J., 133
Rose, D. S., 511
Rose, S., 372
Rosen, Alex, 442
Rosen, David, 442
Rosenbaum, M. E., 360
Rosenfeld, Thomas, 357, 370, 371
Rosenthal, R., 97
Roskos-Ewoldsen, D., 204
Ross, L., 4, 40, 92, 95, 141, 293
Roth, W. T., 403, 517
Rotondo, J. L., 377, 378
Roulin, N., 509
Rubin, A. M., 179
Rubin, M., 317–318
Rubin, Z., 383

Rude, J., 360
Rudman, L. A., 117
Rugemer, Eduard, 441–442
Ruiter, R. A., 210
Rule, B. G., 408, 409, 425
Rusbult, C. E., 377, 379, 380
Ruth, S. C., 417
Ruvolo, A. P., 377, 378
Ryan, K. M., 145
Ryckman, R. M., 364
Rynes, S. L., 509

S

Sacks, Oliver, 82
Sadler, M. S., 111
Safer, M. A., 502
Sagarin, B. J., 272
Sahoo, F. M., 512
Saint-Bauzel, R., 273
Sakulku, J., 34
Salerno, J. M., 332, 503, 504
Salleh, M., 511
Salmivalli, C., 395
Salovey, P., 49, 522
Salz, E., 453
Sampson, R. J., 418
Sanbonmatsu, D. M., 99
Sanders, S. A., 395
SanJosé-Cabezudo, R., 218
Sassenberg, K., 114
Saucier, D. A., 467
Saudino, K. J., 399
Saunders, J., 499
Saunders, K. L., 193
Savani, K., 256
Sawyer, K. B., 463–464
Saxe, L., 468
Scalabrini, A., 43
Scalia, Antonin, 195
Schachter, S., 91, 310
Schaller, M., 140, 259
Schavio, S. R., 356
Schectman, Z., 435
Scheier, M. F., 45, 60
Scher, S. J., 64, 234, 235
Scheufele, D. A., 181
Schiffenbauer, A., 356
Schimmack, U., 24, 129
Schittekatte, M., 327
Schlenker, B. R., 33, 62
Schmader, T., 150
Schmidt, G., 465
Schmitt, D. P., 53
Schnall, S., 462
Schneider, B. H., 419
Schneider, E. F., 427
Schneider, H. G., 419
Schnuerch, R., 260
Schoen, R., 359
Schonberg, 416
Schopler, J., 464
Schouten, A. P., 80

Schuller, R. A., 208
Schultheiss, O. C., 345
Schultz, W., 309
Schulz-Hardt, S., 326, 327
Schwartz, S. H., 482
Schwarz, N., 173
Schwebke, S., 252
Schweder, R. A., 33
Schweitzer, K., 495
Schwinger, M., 65
Scopelliti, I., 94
Scott, J., 497
Scott, W. A., 177, 434
Sedikides, C., 59
Seepersad, S., 346–347
Segal, M. E., 309, 334
Segal, M. W., 356
Segerstrom, S. C., 516
Segrin, C., 347
Seibold, D. R., 272
Selensky, J. C., 52
Seles, Monica, 32
Selkie, E. M., 394
Selye, Hans, 517
Senchak, M., 355
Sentis, K., 254
Seto, M. C., 432
Shackelford, T. P., 368, 381
Shafer, R. B., 362
Shakespeare, William, S., 83
Shanab, M. E., 289, 291
Shapiro, E. G., 484, 485
Shapiro, P., 136
Sharma, D., 515
Shaver, P., 41, 353, 354
Shaver, P. R., 355
Shaw, J. I., 468
Shaw, J. M., 434
Shechory, M., 372, 373
Shechtman, Z., 435
Sheehan, B. E., 403
Sheets, T. L., 63
Sheldon, P., 381, 384
Shelton, N. J., 151
Shen, L., 209, 240
Shepela, S. T., 469
Shepperd, J. A., 316
Sherif, C. W., 155, 214, 215
Sherif, M., 155, 214, 255, 256, 262, 266
Sherman, S. L., 114, 140
Sherry, P., 428
Shim, R. S., 484
Shiomi, M., 264
Shotland, R. L., 456, 459
Showers, C., 56
Showers, C. J., 359
Shultz, T. R., 232, 233
Shuntich, R. J., 403
Sibicky, M., 142
Sicilia, M., 226
Sidanius, J., 123
Sieber, J., 335
Siegel, J. T., 89

Sigall, H., 61
Sigler, J. N., 501
Silberman, Fanka, 442
Silke, A., 321, 322
Silvia, P. J., 56
Sim, J. J., 36
Sim, T. N., 416
Simmonds, S. F., 462
Simmons, A., 1–2
Simmons, C. H., 464
Simmons, J. P., 23
Simon, L., 344
Simonton, D. K., 330
Simpson, J. A., 354, 366, 367
Sinar, E. F., 509
Sinclair, H. C., 353
Sinclair, S., 121, 185
Singal, J., 53
Singer, J. E., 91
Sistrunk, F., 265
Sivacek, J., 230
Sjöberg, L., 225–226
Skinner, B. F., 237
Skinner, E. A., 521
Skowronski, J. J., 37
Slater, M. D., 426
Slovic, P., 22
Smeaton, G., 360
Smith, A., 184, 320
Smith, A. P., 514
Smith, Benjamin, 121
Smith, Joseph, 105
Smith, K. D., 448
Smith, S. M., 504, 505
Smyth, R., 525
Sneyd, D. E., 496
Sniderman, P. M., 132, 139
Snoek, J. D., 370
Snow, C. P., 251
Snowden, F. M., 120
Snyder, D. K., 379
Snyder, K. E., 63
Snyder, M., 62, 63, 97, 98, 272
Solomon, H., 324
Sommer, K. L., 319–320
Sommers, S. R., 331
Sorkin, D., 347
Souchet, L., 273
Spacapan, S., 517
Spanos, S., 6
Spencer, C., 265
Spencer, S. J., 148
Sperling, M., 348
Spicer, C. V., 109
Spielberg, Steven, 142
Spiro, A., 515
Spivey, C. B., 322
Sprafkin, J., 425
Sprecher, S., 376
Sprengholz, P., 240
Stalder, D. R., 235
Stangor, C., 97, 110, 116, 148
Stanton, Amelia, 47

Stappenbeck, C. A., 405
Stasser, G., 323, 326, 334
Stasson, M. D., 188
Statista, 397
Stattin, H., 412
Staub, E., 280, 477, 478
Steele, C. M., 147, 148, 222, 238–239
Steffen, V. J., 394, 395, 396
Steil, J. M., 374
Stein, Gertrude, 343–344, 366, 369
Steinberg, R. J., 330
Steiner, I. D., 332
Steiner, Moses, 442
Stelter, M., 505
Stephan, W. G., 109
Stephens, L., 408
Sternberg, R. J., 349, 350, 370
Stewart, T. L., 159
Stillman, J. A., 365
Stone, J., 150
Storms, M. D., 94
Strange, D., 499
Stratton, Spenser, 1, 2, 4
Straus, M. A., 416
Straw, M. K., 456
Strickland, O. J., 515
Stroud, N., 194
Sturmer, S., 446, 466
Stutts, L. A., 365
Suarez, E. C., 396
Suhay, E., 260
Sukheja, B., 2
Sukhodolsky, D. G., 435
Sulthana, P., 409
Sun, C., 430
Sussman, M., 500
Svetlova, M., 477
Swami, V., 79
Swann, W. B., 59, 60, 61, 66, 77, 97, 192, 377
Swim, J. K., 145, 152, 153
Switzer, R., 345
Sykes, C. J., 132
Sylwander, K. R., 427
Syme, S., 524
Szmajke, A., 423
Szymanski, K., 315

T

Tajfel, H., 135, 136, 137, 156, 317–318
Tanford, S., 503
Tarbell, Frank, 167
Tarbell, Ida, 167–171, 176–177, 197
Tarnow, E., 278–279
Tausch, N., 123
Taylor, D. A., 371
Taylor, P., 241, 242
Taylor, R. B., 345
Taylor, S. E., 224, 309, 522, 523
Taylor, S. L., 58, 73, 94, 95, 134
Taylor, S. P., 403
Teachman, B. A., 365
Tebbe, E. N., 125

Tec, N., 443, 472, 473, 474, 475, 476, 478
Telaak, K., 214
Tennov, D., 352
Tesser, A., 49, 50, 170, 182–183, 258
Test, M., 461
Testone, C., 157
Tetlock, P. E., 58, 94, 132
Thein, R. D., 97
Thibaut, J. W., 373
Thomas, C., 146
Thompson, B., 349
Thompson, Jennifer, 493–494, 498, 500
Thompson, Jon, 456
Thompson, K., 466
Thompson, S. C., 224, 520
Thompson, W. R., 9
Thornhill, P., 366
Thornhill, R., 362, 366, 367
Thorsen, K., 384
Thorsteinsson, E. B., 518
Thorup, B., 504
Tian, Q., 358
Tice, D., 137, 235, 348
Timming, A. R., 78–79
Tindale, R. S., 316, 324, 326
Tinkham, S. F., 206
Tittle, C. R., 508
Titus, W., 326
Toklas, Alice B., 343, 344, 369–370, 385
Tolan, P., 413, 414
Tong, S. T., 80
Tonnesmann, W., 137
Tormala, Z. L., 205
Torney, J. V., 177
Tornstam, L., 346
Torres-González, R., 511
Trafimow, D., 23, 196
Trautwein, U., 34
Trebek, Alex, 92
Tremblay, R. E., 8
Trepainer, M. L., 180
Trepte, S., 42
Triandis, H. C., 363
Triplett, Norman, 315
Trivers, R., 367
Trope, Y., 88, 89, 143
Tropp, L. R., 156
Truman, Harry, 187
Tsang, J., 463
Tsitsika, A., 394
Tuchin, M., 498
Tuckman, A., 253
Turchin, J. M., 364, 365
Turnbull, J., 365
Turner, J. C., 135, 136
Turner, R. N., 156
Tversky, A., 99, 100
Tversky, B., 498
Twain, Mark, 380
Twenge, J. M., 180
Twist, M. L. C., 42
Tybout, A. M., 272
Tykocinsky, O., 56

Tyler, T. R., 329, 330
Tziner, A., 330, 511

U

Unkelbach, C., 113
USA Facts, 202
Uskul, A. K., 423

V

Valerio, T. D., 519
Valkenburg, P. M., 357
Van Avermaet, E., 265
van Baar, J. M., 195
van Bommel, M., 458
Van Boven, L., 215–216
van den Bos, K., 329
van der Velden, P. G., 520, 521
Van Gilder, B. J., 44
van Ginkel, W. P., 327
van Heil, A., 155
van Knippenberg, D., 327
Van Laar, C., 154
van Osch, Y., 423
van Rooijen, L., 265
Van Royen, K., 427
van Tuijl, L. A., 54
van Veen, V., 228
Van Vugt, M., 308, 450
vanDellen, M. R., 55, 58
Vandello, J. A., 40
Vander Wielen, R. J., 227
VanDeusen, K. M., 433
Vangelisti, A. L., 378
van't Riet, J., 210
Varnum, M. W., 265
Vasquez, E. A., 407
Vatiné, E., 291
Venables, Robert, 456
Vessey, S. H., 397, 398
Vet, C., 462
Vierikko, E., 399
Vinokur, A., 335, 524
Vinokur-Kaplan, D., 524
Visser, P. S., 184
Visser, T. A. W., 184
Vissing, Y. M., 416
Vlaander, G. P. J., 265
Vohs, K. D., 279
Vonk, R., 84
Vrugt, A., 462

W

Wagner, U., 154
Walbek, N., 476
Walker, B. H., 133
Walker, H. J., 509
Walker, L. J., 472, 473
Walker, R. C., 331
Wall, H., 299
Wallach, M. A., 335

Wallenberg, Raoul, 478
Waller, T., 364, 365
Walsh, R. M., 42
Walster, G. W., 350
Walster (Hatfield), E., 205
Walter, James, 282
Walther, E., 177–178
Walton, M. A., 417
Walton, M. D., 464
Wang, J., 345
Wang, M.-T., 416
Wang, S. S., 364
Ward, L. M., 424
Watson, M. D., 333
Watson, P. W., 366
Watt, S. E., 95
Wayner, M., 269
Weary, C., 75
Weary, G., 95
Webb, E. J., 174
Weber, R., 429
Webster, D. M., 310
Weeks, J. L., 446
Wegener, D. T., 212, 219, 220
Wegner, D. M., 58, 74, 324, 353
Wehde, W., 90
Weibel, Narayan, 1, 2, 4
Weinbaum, Henry, 442
Weinberg, A., 168
Weinberg, L., 168
Weiner, B., 58, 465, 466
Weisman, A. D., 119
Weiss, Joseph, 442
Weiss, R., 358
Weissman, M., 167
Welch, E. T., 360
Wells, B. E., 180
Wells, G. L., 77, 100, 495, 500
Weltman, K., 374
Wenzel, M., 136, 318
Wesolik, F., 471
West, K., 154
West, R. F., 197
West, S. G., 464
Westfall, J., 194
Weststrate, N. M., 44
Wethere, G. A., 182
Wheeler, L., 384
White, C. M., 42
White-Means, S., 109
Whitley, B. E., 122, 124, 125
Whittaker, E., 426
Wicker, A. W., 185
Wicklund, R. A., 60
Wicks, R. H., 194
Widom, C. S., 418, 434
Wiegman, O., 425
Wiggins, E. C., 170
Wihbey, J., 127
Wijenayake, S., 265
Wilder, D. A., 136, 143
Wilford, J. N., 120

Wilkowski, B. M., 395
Williams, C. J., 189
Williams, K. B., 275
Williams, K. D., 174, 275, 315, 316, 319, 320
Williams, Oracene, 32
Williams, Richard, 32
Williams, Serena, 31–33, 67
Williams, Venus, 32–33
Williams, W. M., 330
Williamson, G. M., 462
Williamson, R. A., 462
Willoughby, T., 429
Wilner, Marian, 442
Wilson, E. O., 398, 449, 450
Wilson, I. P., 449–450, 480
Wilson, M. G., 224
Wilson, T. D., 34, 172, 191
Wiltermuth, S. S., 96
Wimer, D. J., 484
Winquist, J. R., 327
Wiseman, D., 79
Wiseman, D. B., 79
Witte, K., 211
Wittenbaum, G. M., 327
Wixted, J. T., 500
Woike, B., 36
Wolf, S., 267, 268
Wolf, T., 39
Wong, M., 345
Wong, T. K. Y., 477
Wong, W., 89
Wood, C., 22, 331
Wood, W., 176
Woodard, E., 425
Woodzicka, J. A., 145
Wooldredge, J., 359
Word, L. E., 458
Worth, L. T., 218
Wortman, C., 374
Wray, S., 298
Wright, K. S., 383, 384
Wright, P. H., 383, 384
Wrightsman, L. S., 174, 505
Wu, S., 58
Wyer, R. S., 117, 134

X

Xu, J., 133, 365

Y

Yahya, K. A., 289, 291
Yakimovich, D., 453
Yancy, G., 122
Yang, G. S., 429
Yao, E., 89
Yau, J. C., 357
Yeeles, A., 410–411
York, Adrian, 1
York, E., 504
Young, R., 426
Yousaf, O., 229

Z

Zaccaro, S. J., 332, 333
Zacchia, C., 403
Zadro, L., 319, 320
Zajonc, R. B., 45, 175, 311, 356
Zanna, M. P., 171
Zapolski, T. C. B., 409–410
Zaragoza, M., 498, 499
Zarbatany, L., 384
Zautra, A. J., 520
Zavalloni, M., 334
Zebrowitz, L. A., 362, 363, 364
Zeisel, 266, 503
Zhang, Q., 428
Zhang, X., 134
Zhao, X., 213
Zheng, J-K., 428
Ziegler, R., 335
Zimbardo, P. G., 170, 235, 239, 279–280, 282, 294, 322
Zimmer-Gembeck, M. J., 521
Zitek, E. M., 133
Ziv, R., 372, 373
Zou, X., 256
Zucker, G. S., 466
Zuckerman, M., 65, 95, 366

Subject Index

A

Abu Ghraib prison, 278
Abuse, child, aggression and, 417–418
Academics, self-handicapping in, 65
Acceptance, latitude of, in social judgment theory, 214
Accommodation process, 379–380
Action, distortion of, conformity and, 257
Action-based model, cognitive dissonance, 239–240
Actor-observer attribution bias, 94–95
Actual self, 54
Actual similarity, 361
Adams, Samuel, 243
Administrative obedience, 290
Adverse impact, 510
Affective framing, 180
Affective motivations, 218
Affiliation, need for, 345
Affiliative groups, 307–308
African Americans
    prejudice against, 119–120, 126–133, 140, 152
    racism and, 128–133, 157–158, 160
Agenda setting, 180–181
Agentic state, 294
Aggression, 393–436
    aggressive scripts, 414
    alcohol and, 403–406
    biological explanation for, 397–406
    bullying, 394
    child abuse/neglect and, 417–418
    culture and, 419–423
    definition of, 393
    direct, 394
    displaced, 407
    ethological theory of, 397–398
    factors contributing to, 394–397
    family disruption and, 418–419
    family in development of, 414–417
    frustration-aggression hypothesis and, 406–411
    gender differences in, 394–397
    genetics and, 399
    heat effect, 410–411
    hormonal influences on, 401–403
    hostile, 393
    indirect, 394
    instrumental, 393
    intent and, 408–409
    levels of, 393–394
    media violence and, 423–433
    obedience or, 289
    parenting style and, 414–417
    perceived injustice and inequity and, 409–410
    physiology of, 400–403
    reducing, 433–436
    relational, 394
    role modeling and, 417
    sanctioned, 394
    sexual, men prone to, psychological characteristics of, 432–433
    sexually violent material and, 431–432
    social information-processing view of, 434
    social-interactional model and, 414–417
    social learning theory and, 411–423
    social media and, 426–427
    socialization of, 412–413
    sociobiology and, 398–399
    symbolic, 394
    television and, 424–426
    types of, 393–394
    viewing sexual violence and, 430–433
    violent video games and, 427–429
    See also Violence
Aggressive behavior
    in adolescents, 9
    culture and, 419–423
    role modeling of, 417
Aggressive script, 414
Agreeableness, prejudice and, 124
Alarm stage, 517
Alcohol, aggression and, 403–406
Alloparenting, 450
Alternative explanation, 15
Altruism, 441–488
    autonomous, 474
    biological explanations of, 449–450
    childrearing style and, 476–477
    cognitive development and, 477–478
    definition of, 443
    development of, 478
    egoism and, 444–448
    empathy-altruism hypothesis and, 444
    empathy and, 444–448
    interactionist view of, 479–482
    kin, 450
    motivation for, 443–450
    normative, 474
    pathological, 448–449
    recipient of, 483–488
    reciprocal, 450
Altruistic personality, 473
Altruistic Personality Project, 474–475
Ambiguity, helping behavior and, 453–454
American Revolution, and propaganda, 241, 243
Amygdala, involvement in aggression, 400
Anonymity, group violence and, 321–323
Anthropology, social psychology and, 8
Antilocution, prejudice and, 145
Anxiety
    social, 348–349
    stranger, 9
Applied research, 21
Arousal model, of social facilitation, 311–312
Asch paradigm, 256–257
Attachment styles, adult love relationships and, 354–355
Attitude(s), 167–197
    accessibility of, message elaboration and, 223–224
    Allport's model of, 169–170
    behavior and, 185–192
        importance of attitude strength and, 188–189
        mindless behavior in everyday life and, 190–192
        nonrational actor and, 190–192
        theory of planned behavior and, 186–188
    change in, cognitive dissonance and, 229–230
    definition of, 169
    explicit, 172
    as expression of values, 171–172
    formation of, 175–185
        direct personal experience in, 176
        evaluative conditioning in, 176–178
        heritability factor in, 181–183
        mass media in, 178–181
        mere exposure in, 175–176
        observational learning in, 178
        operant conditioning in, 176–178
        social networks and, 184–185
    ideology and, 192–197
        behavior prediction, 195–197
        motivated social cognition, 195
        political polarization and ideology, 193–195
    implicit, 172
    measurement of, 173–175
        attitude survey in, 173–174
        behavioral measures in, 174
        implicit measures in, 174–175
        Implicit Association Test (IAT), 174
    naïve realism and, 196–197
    sexually violent material and, 431–432
    structure of, 170–171
Attitude strength, importance of, 188–189
Attitude survey, 173–174
    potential biases in, 173–174

Attractiveness, physical dimensions of, 362–364
    in interpersonal attraction, 361–366
Attributional ambiguity, 152
Attributional complexity, 235
Attribution processes, dissonance and, 234–235
Attribution(s), 84–91
    actor-observer, 94–95
    biases in, 91–96
    correspondent inference theory of, 85
    covariation theory of, 85–88
    definition of, 84
    discriminatory stereotypes and, 141–142
        reasons for/correction of, 93–94
        misattributions as, 91–92
        ultimate attribution error as, 143
    dual-process models of, 88–89
    external, 84
    false consensus, 95–96
    fundamental attribution error as, 92–94
    Heider's early work on, 84–85
    intentionality and, 89
    internal, 84
    misdirected, 91
    person, 86
    situational, 86
Audience(s)
    effects on performance, 311–314
    fitting message to, 212
    inoculating of, against message, 212–213
    multiple, persuasion of, 215–216
    view of, discrepancy of message from, 213–215
Authoritarianism, 120
Authoritarian personality, 120–123
Authoritarian Personality, The (Adorno et al.), 121
Authority
    breaking with, 294–295
    legitimacy of, reassessing, 295–297
Autobiographical memory, 36
    emotions and, 38–39
    levels of, 36
Autokinetic effect, 255
Automatic processing, 73
Autonomous altruism, 474
Availability heuristics, 99
Aversive racism, 130
Avoidance, prejudice as, 145
Awareness, intentionality and, 89–90

B

Bandwagon effect, 298
Base-rate data, 100
Base-rate fallacy, definition of, 100
Basic research, 21
Bask in the reflected glory (BIRG) behaviors, 50, 135
Beauty, evolutionary psychology and, 366
Becoming Evil: How Ordinary People Commit Genocide and Mass Killing (Walter), 282
Behavior(s)
    in attitude structures, 170–171
    attitudes and, 185–192. *See also* Attitude(s), behavior and
    in everyday life, 190–191
    group influence on, 311–317
    helping. *See* Helping behavior
    mindless, ideology and, 195–197
    planned, theory of, 186–188
    prosocial, in reducing aggression, 434
    schemas and, 97–99
    social, 1–25. *See also* Social behavior
Behavior, changing, smoking and, 238
Behavioral confirmation, 98
Behavioral control, perceived, behavioral intention and, 187
Behavior-based scales, 511
Belief, intentionality and, 89
Belief perseverance, in impression-formation process, 77
Belief in pure evil (BPE), 280–281
Benevolent sexism, 146, 147
Bias(es)
    attribution, 91–96
        bias blind spot, 196
        egotistical, 62
        hindsight, 22
        self-serving, 58
    confirmation, 99, 507
        stereotypes and, 142–143
    IAT and, 174
    in-group, 135–136
        biological perspective on, 137
        role of language in maintaining, 137–138
    intergroup, 504–505
    motivational, 507
    out-group homogeneity, 143
    in persuasion process, 220
    physical attractiveness, 364–366
        physique and, 364–366
    potential, in attitude survey, 173–174
Big five personality dimensions, prejudice and, 124
Biology/biological perspective
    aggression and, 397–406
    altruism and, 449–450
    homeostatic theory, 228
    in-group bias and, 137
    social psychology and, 8–9
Black sheep effect, 318
Bona fide occupational qualification (BFOQ), 510
Book of Mormon, 105
Boston Globe, 243
Boston Massacre, and propaganda, 243
Bottom-up perspective, 10
Brain mechanisms, of aggression, 400–401
Branch Davidians, 236–237
Brown v. Board of Education, 126
Bullying, 394
Bystander effect, 454–459

C

Calley, William, 281, 296
Carnegie Hero Medal recipients, 471
Cassidy, Samuel, 391–393, 406, 436
Catholic Church, and propaganda, 242
Central route processing
    in message elaboration, 217
    mood and, 218–221
Challenger tragedy, 305–306, 307, 310, 333, 335–338
Chernobyl: The Final Warning, film, 225
Child abuse/neglect, aggression and, 417–418
Childrearing style, altruism as function of, 476–477
China Syndrome, The, film, 225
Choice, disobedience and, 296–297
Christianity, prejudice and, 105–106, 141, 160–161
Cider House Rules, film, 179
Civil disobedience, 298
Civil War, U.S., 126
Classical conditioning, 177
Clinton, Bill, trustworthiness and, 204
Coca-Cola Company, 240
Cognition(s)
    in attitude structures, 170–171
    motivated social, 195
    need for, 225–227
    self-serving, 58–59
    social, definition of, 5
Cognitive approach, to persuasion, 216–227
    attitude accessibility and elaboration in, 223–224
    effect of mood on processing in, 218–221
    effect of personal relevance on processing in, 221–223
    elaboration likelihood model in, 216–218
    heuristic model of persuasion in, 227
    need for cognition and affect in, 225–227
    vividness of message in, 224–225
Cognitive development, altruism as function of, 477–478
Cognitive dissonance theory, 227–240
    alternatives to, 237–240
    attitude change and, 229–230
    attribution processes and, 234–235
    cult membership and, 236–237
    free choice and, 230
    inconsistency and, 228–236
    lessons of, 235–236
    postdecision dissonance and, 231–234
    responsibility and, 234
    reverse incentive effect and, 230
Cognitive intervention, in reducing aggression, 434–436
Cognitive miser, 73
Cognitive motivation, 218
Cognitive narrowing, obedience and, 287, 295
Cognitive optimism, 522
Cohen, Geoffrey, 183
Cohesiveness, of groups
    definition of, 308
    group decision-making ability and, 333
    interpersonal, 332
    task-based, 332–333
Collective self, 40
Collective threat, 150–151
Commitment, love and, 349–350
Committee of Correspondence, 243
Communal relationships, 375
Communicator
    in Yale communication model, 203–216

I-14 Subject Index

credibility of, 204–207
credibility of, limits on, 205–207
efficacy of, 207–209
expertise of, 204–205
gender of, 209–210
trustworthiness of, 204–205
Communists, and propaganda, 242, 244
Companionate love, 352
Comparison
downward, 309
levels, relationship evaluation, 373
social, need for, groups satisfying, 309
Compensation
primary, 153
secondary, 153
social, in groups, 316–317
Complementarity, in interpersonal attraction, 359
Compliance, 269–277
door-in-the-face technique of, 274–276
foot-in-the-door technique of, 270–274
induced, 230
low-ball technique of, 276, 277
Compliant false confessions, 505
Conditioning
evaluative, in attitude formation, 176–178
operant, in attitude formation, 176–178
Confederate flag battle, 128
Confessions, 505–507
compliant false, 505
how false confessions lead to wrongful convictions, 507
internalized false, 506
voluntary false, 505
Confidence, impression formation and, 76–77
Confirmation, behavioral, 98
Confirmation bias, 99
stereotypes and, 142–143
Conflict avoiding couple, 380
Conflict in relationships, 378–381
Conformity, 253–266
in Asch experiments, 257
Asch paradigm and, 256–257
classic studies in, 256–257
cultural differences in, 265–266
definition of, 254
factors affecting, 261–266
forms of, 260–261
gender and, 264–265
historical differences in, 265–266
minority influence in, 266–269
nature of task and, 262
paths to, 257–258
pressure as a function of jury size, 502–503
pressures for, groupthink and, 337
size of majority and, 262–263
social influence and, 258–260
true partner and, 263–264
Confounding variable, 15
Consensus information, 86
Conservatism, 193
Consistency information, 87
Consonance, 228
Consonance constraint satisfaction model, 233
Constructive obedience, 278
Consummate love, 352

Contact hypothesis, on reducing prejudice, 154–156
Context of question, attitude survey bias and, 173–174
Control group, 14
Controlled processing, 74
Coping self-efficacy, 520
Correlation(s)
illusory, stereotypes and, 140–142
negative, 17
positive, 17
Correlational research, 17–19
Correlation coefficient, 18
Correspondent inference theory, of attribution, 85
Co-schematic, 45
Cotton, Ronald, 493–494
Counterfactual thinking, 100
Courageous resistance, 469–483
defined, 469
personality and, 472–473
righteous rescuers, 473–479
situational and personal factors in, 479–483
Covariation principle, 86
Covariation theory, of attribution, 85–88
COVID-19 pandemic, 201–205, 217–218, 247, 251–254, 270, 299
Credibility, of communicator, 204–205
limits on, 205–207
Cross-race identification, 504–505
Cult membership, cognitive dissonance and, 236–237
Culture
conformity and, 265–266
expression of self and, 43–44
of honor, violence and, 419–423
influence of, on self-concept, 43–44
influence of, on self-esteem, 53
obedience and, 289–292
violent behavior and, 419–423
Cut off reflected failure (CORF) behaviors, 135
Cyberbullying, 394, 427

D

Darrow, Clarence, 215
Dating script, 371–373
Deception, detection of, 81–83
Decision making, group, 323–330
dynamics of, 333–337
factors affecting, 330–333
group composition and, 330–332
group size and, 332–333
individual decision making versus, 323–325
leadership style and, 327–330
racial effects and, 331–332
group cohesiveness and, 308
Decision point, disobedience and, 296
Decision rules, 333
Defensive ostracism, 319
Deindividuation, 321–323
Deliberation process in court, 503
Dependent variable, 14
Desire, intentionality and, 89
Destructive obedience, 279–283
Devaluation, relational, 348

Different norms–same adherence motivation, 256
Differentiated transactive memory system, 324
Diffusion of responsibility, 288, 455
Direct aggression, 394
Directive leaders, 328
Discrimination, 118
definition of, 118
prejudice and, 145
self-categorization theory and, 136–137
See also Prejudice; Racism; Sexism; Stereotypes
Disinhibition, observational learning and, 413
Disobedience, 294–299
breaking with authority and, 294–295
civil disobedience, 298
group's effect on, 297–298
reassessment of legitimacy of authority, 295–297
role strain and, 295
social climate and, 298
See also Obedience
Displaced aggression, 407
Dispositional empathy, 5
Dispositional optimism, 521
Distinctive accuracy, 75
Distinctiveness information, 86
Distinctiveness theory, 35
Distraction-conflict effect, on social facilitation, 313
Distortion of judgment, 257
Distortion of perception, 257
Divergent thinking, 268
Divorce
aggression and, 418–419
predicting, 382
Door-in-the-face technique, of compliance, 274–276
Douglass, Frederick, 126
Downward comparison, 309
Dual hormone hypothesis, 401–403

E

Ectomorphs, 364
Efficacy, communicator, persuasion and, 207–209
Ego-depletion, definition of, 57
Egoism, empathy versus, 444–448
Egotistical bias, 62
Eichmann, Adolph, 279–283
Eichmann in Jerusalem: A Report on the Banality of Evil (Arendt), 281
Eichmann's fallacy, 279–283
Elaboration likelihood model, 216–218
Electronic civil disobedience, 298
Elevation, effect of on helping, 462
Emancipation Proclamation, 126
Emotional empathy, becoming rescuer and, 476
Emotional intelligence
defined, 49
self-esteem and, 48–49
Emotional loneliness, 358
Emotion-focused coping, 517
Emotions
autobiographical memory and, 38–39
eyewitness testimony and, 497–498

Subject Index I-15

Empathic accuracy, 354
Empathic helping, 477
Empathic joy, 448
Empathy
    definition of, 444
    dispositional, 5
    egoism versus, 444–448
    emotional, becoming rescuer and, 476
Empathy-altruism hypothesis, 444
    challenging, 446–448
Empathy-punishment hypothesis, 446
Employee recruitment, 509
Employee screening, 508, 510
Encoding phase, aggressive scripts, 414
Endomorphs, 364
England, Lynndie, 278
Enlightenment effect, 291
Entity theories, of implicit stereotypes, 117
Equity theory, 374
Estimator variables, 495
Eternal Jew, The (Hippler), 245
Ethics, social psychological research and, 24–25
Ethnocentrism, 121
Ethological theory, of aggression, 397–398
Evaluation apprehension, social facilitation/inhibition and, 312–313
Evaluative conditioning, in attitude formation, 176–178
Event schema, 414
Everyday prejudice, 145
Evil
    banality of, 280–283
    definition of, 279
    obedience and, 279–283
    responsibility for, 283
    roots of, 279
    transformation to, 282
Evolutionary psychology
    beauty and, 366
Exchange theories, 373–375
Exhaustion stage, 517
Experience, direct personal, in attitude formation, 176
Experiment(s)
    evaluating, 17
    factorial, 15–17
    field, 20
Experimental group, definition of, 14
Experimental research, 13–17
    controlling extraneous variables, 15
    definition of, 14
    equivalence of groups in, 14–15
    experiment evaluation, 17
    factorial experiments, 15–17
    manipulating variables in, 14
Expertise, of communicator, 204–207
Explicit attitudes, 172
Explicit prejudice, 107, 129
Explicit self-esteem, 54
Explicit stereotypes, 112–115
Exposure, mere, in attitude formation, 175–176
Extended parallel process model, 211
Extermination, prejudice and, 145
External attribution, 84
External validity, 15

Extraneous variable(s)
    controlling, 15
    definition of, 15
Eyewitness testimony, 494–502
    cross-race identifications, 504–505
    eyewitness, defined, 495
    improving, 501–502
    inaccuracy of, 494–498
    jury's use of, 500–501
    other race effect, 504–505
    variables that affect accuracy, 494–498
        emotional experience of eyewitness, 497–498
        memory of eyewitness, 498
        misinformation effect, 498–500
        weapon focus, 495–496

F

Facebook, Internet self, 41–43
Facilitation, social, 311–314
Factorial experiments, 15–17
False consensus attribution bias, 95–96
Family
    disruption of, aggression and, 418–419
    reducing aggression in, 433–434
Fear appeal
    effectiveness of message and, 209–211
    extended parallel process model and, 211
    protection/motivation explanation of, 210–211
Fictional framing, 179
Field experiment, 20
Field research, 19–20
Field study, 19
Field survey, 19
First-level agenda setting, 180
Fixation time, attractiveness and, 363
Flexible correction model (FCM), 220
Foot-in-the-door technique, of compliance, 270–274
    definition of, 270
    hypotheses explaining, 271–273
Forgiveness, 380–381
Four horsemen of the apocalypse, relationship dissolution and, 382
Four walls technique, 272
Free choice, in dissonance theory, 230
Free riders, in group, 315
Friendships, 382–385
    diversity and, 360
    forgiveness and, 384
    gender differences in, 383–384
    over life cycle, 384–385
Frustration-aggression link, 406–411
    components of, 407–408
    factors mediating, 408–411
Fundamental attribution error, 92–94
    discriminatory stereotypes and, 141–142
    reasons for/correction of, 93–94

G

Gay and Lesbian Alliance Against Defamation (GLAAD), 157
Gender

    aggression and, 394–397
    authoritarianism and, 120–123
    communicator, persuasion and, 208–209
    conformity and, 264–265
    friendships and, 382–385
    leadership and, 328–330
    obedience and, 289
    prejudice and, 125–126
    rescue and, 478–479
Gender-domain effect, 208
Gender roles, in children's books, attitude formation and, 180
General adaptation syndrome (GAS), 517
General aggression model (GAM), 411
Genetic explanation
    of aggression, 399
    of altruism, 449–450
Genocide, 121, 135
Genovese, Kitty, death of, 451–452, 454–456
Glittering generalities, 244, 246
Global self-esteem, 53
Goebbels, Josef, 241–242, 244–246
Gratitude, helping behavior and, 462–464
Group(s), 307–338
    affiliative, 307
    characteristics of, 307–308
    cohesiveness of, 308
        group decision-making ability and, 333–334
    composition of, group decision-making ability and, 330–332
    control, definition of, 14
    decision making by, 323–325. *See also* Decision making, group
    definition of, 307
    deviates in, 310
    equivalence of, 14–15
    experimental, definition of, 14
    formation of, 309–310
    functional quality of, problem difficulty and, 325–327
    gender and leadership, 328–330
    individual versus group performance, 323–325
    influence on behavior, 311–317
    instrumental, 307
    in meeting basic needs, 309–310
    members of, obeying leaders, 329
    newcomers in, 310
    obedience and, 288
    participation in, performance and, 314–315
        enhanced, 314–315
        free rides and, 315
        social loafing and, 315
    polarization of, 334–335
    punishment by, 318–321
    racial composition, effects of, 331–332
    roles in, 310
    size of, group decision-making ability and, 333–334
    social, identification with, 317–318
    transactive memory systems of, 324
    use of information by, 326–327
    violence by, 321–323
Group justification theories, 139
Group norms, 308
Groupthink, 335–337

conditions favoring, 336
definition of, 335
symptoms of, 336–337

H

Hale, Matt, 121
Halo effect, 511
Happiness, optimism and, 524–525
Hate messages and hate groups, 133
Health, social psychology and, 515–527
    coping with stress, 519–521
        effects of positive mood, 522–523
        perceived control and self-efficacy beliefs, 520–521
        promoting healthier behavior, 525–527
        resilience, 519–520
        social support, 523–524
    perceived stress and health, 516–519
        appraisals of stress, 517–518
        life stressors and illness, 518–519
Heat effect, aggression and, 410–411
Hedonic contingency model (HCM), 219–220
Heider, Fritz, on attribution, 84–85
Heinrich, Ingo, 283
Help
    increasing the chance of receiving, 469
    receiving, reaction to, 485–488
    seeking, 483–485
        decision on, factors influencing, 484–485
Helping behavior
    altruistic, 443–488. *See also* Altruism
    biological explanation of, 449–450
    effect of seeing others help, 461–462
    egoism and, 444–448
    in emergencies, 451–468
    empathic, 477
    empathy-altruism hypothesis of, 444
    five-stage decision model of, 451–468
        applied to long-term helping, 482–483
    gratitude and, 462–464
    instrumental, 477
    long-term, 482–483
    mood and, 462
    in nonemergencies, 469–483
    race and, 466–468
    recipient of, 471
    rewards and costs of, 460–461
    sexual orientation and, 468
    victim characteristics, 464–466
Heritability factor, in attitude formation, 181–183
Heroism, 469–483
    civil heroes, 471
    defined, 470
    military heroes, 471
    personality and, 472–473
    righteous rescuers, 473–479
    situational and personal factors in, 479–483
    social heroes, 471
Heuristic and systematic information-processing model, 227
Heuristics
    availability, 99
    counterfactual thinking, 100
    definition of, 99

    judgmental, stereotypes as, 117–118
    representativeness, 99
Hidden profile paradigm, 326–327
Hierarchy, in U.S. Army, 160
Hindsight bias, 22
Hippler, Fritz, 244, 245
Historical differences, in conformity, 265–266
History, social psychology and, 8, 10
History of the Standard Oil Company, The (Tarbell), 168, 176
Hitler, Adolf, 244–246, 282, 473
Holdout, 332
Homeostatic theory, 228
Homophobia, 108, 125, 157
Hormonal influences, on aggression, 401–403
Hostile aggression, 393
Hostile sexism, 146, 147
Hyper-conformity, 261
Hypocrisy paradigm, 228
Hypothalamus, in aggression, 400
Hypothesis, definition of, 11

I

Ideal self, 55
Ideological-conflict hypothesis, 122
Ideology, 192–197
    behavior prediction and, 195–197
    as motivated social cognition, 195
    news reporting and, 182
    political polarization and, 193–195
    types of, 193
Ignorance, pluralistic, bystander effect and, 455
Illness, stress and, 518–519
Illusion(s)
    of efficacy, in small groups, 332
    of invulnerability groupthink and, 336
    of transparency, 66
    of unanimity, groupthink and, 337
Illusory correlations, stereotypes and, 140–142
Imagine other perspective, on empathy, 444
Imagine self perspective, on empathy, 444
Imagined intergroup contact, 156
Immersive Video Milgram Obedience Experiment, 291
Implicit Association Test (IAT), 109
Implicit attitudes, 172
Implicit personality theory, 97
Implicit prejudice, 107, 129
Implicit self-esteem, 54
Implicit stereotypes, 112–115
Imposter phenomenon, 34
Impression(s)
    accuracy of, 76
    body art and, 78–79
    constructing, 75–76
    first impressions in, 77–80
    formation of
        confidence and, 76–77
        social media and, 80
    heuristics in, 99–100
    on others, awareness of, 65–66
    of others on us, 75–76
    schemas in, 96–100
Impression formation, 74–83

Impression management, 62–63
    self-esteem and, 62
    self-monitoring and, 62–63
Inconsistency, cognitive dissonance and, 228–236
Incremental theories, of implicit stereotypes, 117
Independence, paths to, 257–258
Independent variable, 14
Indirect aggression, 394
Individual characteristics, in social behavior, 5–6
Individual self, 39
Induced compliance, 230
Industrial organizational psychology, 508–515
Inequity, perceived, aggression and, 409–410
Information, group use of, 326–327
Informational social influence, 254–255
Information-processing strategies for self-serving bias, 58–59
Informed consent, 25
In-group bias, 135–136
    biological perspective on, 137
    role of language in maintaining, 137–138
In-group comparisons, 152
Inhibition, social, 311
Injustice, perceived, aggression and, 409–410
Inoculation theory, 212–213
Instrumental aggression, 393
Instrumental groups, 307
Instrumental helping, 477
Instrumental values, 171
Integrated transactive memory system, 324
Intellective issue, social influence on, 262
Intent attributions, aggression and, 408–409
Intentionality, attributions and, 89
Interaction, defined, 16
Interactionist view, of altruism, 479–482
Interchain sequences, 373
Intergroup bias, 504–505
Internal attribution, 84
Internal validity, 15
Internalized false confessions, 506
Internet
    addiction, 358
    cyberbullying, 394
    hate groups and, 133
    relationships, 357–358
    self, 41–43
Interpersonal aggression, 391–436. *See also* Aggression
Interpersonal attraction
    determinants of, 356–369
    need for affiliation and, 345
    need for intimacy and, 345
    roots of, 344–346
Interpersonal cohesiveness, 332
Interpersonal dissonance, 233
Interpersonal forgiveness, 380
Intertwined model, 240
Intimacy
    love and, 349–350
    need for, 345
Intimate relationships. *See* Love; Relationships, close
Introspection, in self-knowledge, 34
Invulnerability, illusion of groupthink and, 335

J

Japanese, stereotypes of, 119
Jeopardy, TV show, 92
Jews
    discrimination against, in U.S., 118
    Nazi dehumanization and genocide of, 121, 156, 244–246
    prejudice against, 141–142, 156
    righteous rescuers and, 473–479
        five-stage decision model applied to, 482–483
        Irene Opdyke and, 441–443, 488
    stereotypes about, 141–142, 244–246
Jigsaw classroom, 156
Job analysis, 508
Judgment, distortion of, conformity and, 257
Judgmental heuristics, stereotypes as, 117–118
Judgmental issue, social influence on, 262
Juries
    conformity pressure and jury size, 502–503
    deliberation process, 503
    educating jurors about eyewitness testimony, 501–502
    effect of deliberation on individual opinion, 504
    group processes in, 502–504
    intergroup bias and, 504–505
    social influence in, 503–504
    use of eyewitness testimony by, 500–501
Just-world hypothesis, helping behavior and, 464

K

Kennedy, John F., assassination of, 284
Kin altruism, 450
King, Martin Luther, Jr., 284, 294
Knowledge, organizing, 45
Köhler effect, 316–317
Köhler motivation gain, 316
Koresh, David, 236–237
Ku Klux Klan, deindividuation and, 322

L

Laboratory research, 19
Language, in maintaining in-group bias, 137–138
Latitude of acceptance in social judgment theory, 214
Latitude of noncommitment in social judgment theory, 214
Latitude of rejection in social judgment theory, 214
Laughter, effect on health, 522–523
Law of primacy, 211
Leadership style, group decision making and, 327–330
Learning, observational aggression and, 412–413
    in attitude formation, 178
Left-wing authoritarianism (LWA), 122
Legitimacy, of leader, 329
Level playing field, 160
Lewin, Kurt, social behavior model of, 4–7
    expanding, 6–7
Liberalism, 193
Life cycle, friendships over, 384–385

Lilienfeld, Scott, 12–13
Limerence, 352
Lincoln, Abraham, 126
Linear conformity, 260
Lithuanian disobedience, 296
Loafing, social, group participation and, 315
Loneliness, 346–347
Lost-letter technique, in attitude assessment, 174
Love
    close relationships and, 349–355
    consummate, 352
    in lab, 381–382
    romantic, 351
    secret, 353
    triangular theory of, 349–351
    types of, 351–353
    unrequited, 352
    See also Relationships, close
Low-ball technique, of compliance, 276, 277
Lucifer Effect, 282

M

Maintenance phase, aggressive scripts, 414
Majority
    groups, 118
    minority influence on, 266–269
    size of, conformity and, 262–263
Majority and minority influence, in conformity, 266–268
Majority rule, 333
Man Who Mistook His Hat for His Wife, The (Sacks), 82
Marriages, kinds of, 381–382
Mask, importance of, 251–253, 299–300
Maslow's hierarchy of needs, 512–514
Mass media, in attitude formation, 178–181
Matching principle, in interpersonal attraction, 359
Mate
    how to attract, 367–369
    selection of, 366–367
McAuliffe, Christa, 305
Media, mass, in attitude formation, 178–181
Media violence, aggression and, 423–433
Mein Kampf (Hitler), 244
Memories in self-concept, 36–38
Memory
    conformity tasks, 259
    eyewitness, 498
    reconstructive, 498
Merchant of Venice, play, 142
Mere exposure effect, 175–176, 356
Mesomorphs, 364
Message(s)
    anti-smoking campaign, 219
    conflicting, about obedience, 288
    discrepancy of, from audience views, 213–215
    effectiveness of, 209–211
    elaboration of, attitude accessibility and, 223–224
    fitting of, to audience, 212
    inoculating audience against, 212–213
    one-sided versus two-sided, 212
    primacy versus recency effects, 211–212

    processing of
        mood and, 218–221
        personal relevance and, 221–223
    vivid versus nonvivid, persuasiveness of, 224–225
Michelangelo phenomenon, 377
Milgram, Stanley
    obedience studies of, 283–288
        authority figure presence and legitimacy in, 287
        cognitive narrowing in, 287
        conflicting messages in, 288
        critiques of, 292–294
        findings of, reevaluating, 292
        group effects in, 288
        participant's perspective on, 284–285
        power of situation in, 287
        predicted behavior in, 285
        proximity of victim in, 286–287
        reevaluating findings, 292
        results of, 285
        situational determinants in, 285–288
Mindfulness, 464
Mindguards, self-appointed, groupthink and, 337
Minnesota Multiphasic Personality Inventory, 124
Minority groups, 118
Minority influence, in conformity, 266–269
Minority slowness effect, 259
Mirth, effect of on helping, 462
Misattributions, 91–92
Misinformation effect, 498–500
Modern racism, 130–131
Mood
    helping and, 462
    processing of message and, 218–221
Moral idiots, 282
Moral monsters, 282
Mormons, prejudice and, 105–107, 160–161
Motivated social cognition, 195
Motivation, normocentric, 474
Motivation, at work, 512–514
Motivational strategy for self-serving bias, 58
Multiple audience problem, 215–216
My Lai massacre, 281
Myth of pure evil, 281

N

Naïve realism, attitudes and, 196–197
Nature of Prejudice, The (Allport), 145, 154
Nazis
    obedience and, 295–296
    propaganda and, 241–242, 244–246
    responsibility for evil deeds and, 283
    righteous rescuers and, 473–479
    role strain and, 295
    World War II and, 298
Need(s)
    for affect, 225–227
    for affiliation, 345
    for cognition, 225–227
    group formation and, 309–310
    for intimacy, 345
    physiological and psychological, 512
Negative correlation, 17

Negative mood regulation expectancies, 523
Neglect, child, aggression and, 417–418
Networks
    social, attitude formation and, 184–185
New Dawn reconciliation program, 157
Next Generation Science Standards, 11
Noncommitment, latitude of, in social judgment theory, 214
Nonrational actor, in attitude-behavior relationship, 190–192
    resolving rational actor with, 191
Norm(s)
    definition of, 254
    group, 308
    of reciprocity, 275
    social
        changing, 132–133
        as key to conformity, 255–256
        reducing expression of prejudice through, 157–158
    of social responsibility, 482
    subjective, behavioral intention and, 187
Normative accuracy, 75
Normative altruism, 474
Normative social influence, 254–255
Normocentric motivation, 474

O

Obedience, 278–294
    administrative, 290
    aggression or, 289
    conflicting messages about, 288
    constructive, 278
    culture and, 289–292
    definition of, 278
    destructive, 278–283
    Eichmann's fallacy, 282
    evil and, 279–283
    gender and, 289
    Milgram's experiments on, 283–288
    proximity and, 286–287
    situation and, 289–292
    time and, 289–292
    See also Disobedience
Obesity, stereotypes about, 364–366
Observational learning
    aggression and, 412–413
    in attitude formation, 178
Opdyke, Irene Gut, 441–443, 488
Openness to experience, prejudice and, 124
Operant conditioning, in attitude formation, 176–178
Optimal distinctiveness theory, 35
Optimism, 521–527
    cognitive, 521–522
    dispositional, 521
        happiness and, 524–525
    health and, 521–527
    improving level of, 522
Organizational citizenship behaviors, 514–515
Ortiz-Beck, Taj, 1, 2, 4
Ostracism, social, 318–321
Other-race effect, 504–505
Ought self, 55

Out-group homogeneity bias, 143
Out-groups, personalizing members of, in reducing prejudice, 156–157

P

Parenting
    aggressive, 414–417
    altruism and, 476–477
    in reducing aggression, 433–434
Parks, Rosa, 294
Participative leaders, 328
Passion, love and, 349–350
Pathological altruism, 448–449
Perceived behavioral control, behavioral intention and, 187
Perceived similarity, 361
Perception
    definition of, 5
    distortion of, conformity and, 257
    social, 71–101. *See also* Social perception
Perceptual contrast hypothesis, of foot-in-the-door effect, 272, 276
Performance
    audience effects on, 311–314
    enhanced performance and, 314–315
    free rides and, 315
    group participation and, 314–315
    social loafing and, 315
Performance appraisals, 510–511
    behavior-based scales, 511
    defined, 510
    halo effect, 511
    360-degree feedback model, 511
    trait-based scales, 511
Peripheral route processing, in message elaboration, 217–218
    mood and, 218–221
Persian Gulf War, 85
Personal attributes, self-concept and, 35–36
Personal dissonance, 233
Personal experience, direct, in attitude formation, 176
Personality
    altruism and, 479–483
    altruistic, 473
    authoritarian, 120–123
    courageous resistance and heroism and, 472–473
    prejudice and, 120–126
Personality psychology, aggressiveness and, 9
Personal relevance, goals and, 223
Person attribution, 86
Personnel selection, 508–510
    adverse impact, 510
    employee recruitment, 509
    employee screening, 510
    job analysis, 508
Persuasion, 201–247
    cognitive approach to, 216–227. *See also* Cognitive approach, to persuasion
    cognitive dissonance theory of, 227–240
    definition of, 203
    elaboration likelihood model of, 216–218
    group polarization from, 334–335

    heuristic model of, 227
    of masses, 241–246
        through propaganda, 241–246
    of multiple audiences, 215–216
    vividness of message and, 224–225
    Yale model of, 203–216. *See also* Yale communication model
Phrasing, attitude survey bias and, 173
Physical attack, prejudice as, 145
Physical attractiveness
    dimensions of, 362–364
    in interpersonal attraction, 361–366
Physical proximity effect, 356–358
Physiology, of aggression, 400–403
Physique, attractiveness bias and, 364–366
Planned behavior, theory of, 186–188
Pluralistic ignorance, bystander effect and, 455
Polarization
    group, 334–335
    political, 193–195
Political polarization, 193–195
Polygraph, 12
Population, attitude survey, 173
Pornography, 431
Positive bystander effect, 457
Positive emotions, 523
Positive correlation, 17
Positive illusions, 521
Positive mood, effect on health, 522–523
Postdecision dissonance, 231–234
Post-event rumination, 348
Prejudice, 105–161
    against African Americans, 126–133
    agreeableness and, 124
    authoritarianism and, 120–126
    cognitive roots of, 133–144
    color, historical view of, 120
    confirmation bias and, 142–143
    coping with, 151–154
        anticipating and confronting prejudice, 152–153
        compensating for prejudice, 153–154
        making in-group comparisons, 152
        raising the value of stigmatized groups, 151–152
    dark personality triad, 124
    definition of, 107
    dynamics of, 107–118
    explicit, 107, 129
    everyday, 145
    expecting to be a target of, 151
    false consensus and, 95–96
    forms of, 108–110
    against gays and lesbians, 157
    gender and, 125–126
    illusory correlations and, 140–142
    implicit, 107, 129
    against Jews, 141–142, 156
    jokes based on, 145–147
    against Mormons, 105–107, 160–161
    openness to experience and, 124
    perpetrators of, 109
    persistence and recurrence of, 118–120
    personality and, 120–126
    political orientation and, 122–123

Prejudice (*continued*)
  racism, 108–110
  reducing, 154–159
    contact between groups in, 154–156
    expression of, through social norms, 157–158
    personalizing out-group members in, 156–157
    through training, 158–159
  sexism, 108–110
  skin-tone bias, 110
  social dominance and, 123–124
  social roots of, 126–133
  stereotypes and, 110–118
  system justification and, 139–140
  targets of, 109, 151
  ways to express, 145
  See also Discrimination; Racism; Sexism; Stereotype(s)
Prevention strategies for promoting health, 525–527
  increasing self-efficacy, 526–527
  reframing behaviors, 526
  theory of planned behavior, 525–526
Primacy effect
  in impression-formation process, 77
  of message, 211–212
Primary compensation, 153
Priming, 296
Private key, 215
Problem-focused coping, 517
Process loss, group size and, 332
Propaganda, 241–246
  aims of, 243
  American Revolution and, 241, 243
  Catholic Church and, 242
  characteristics of, 242
  Communists and, 242, 244
  definition of, 241–242
  Hitler's rise to power and, 244–246
  in Nazi Germany, 241–242, 244–246
  techniques of, 243–244
  of U.S. government, WWII, 203
Prosocial behavior, in reducing aggression, 434
Prosocial model, children and, 461–462
Protection-motivation explanation of fear, 210–211
Pseudoscience, 12–13
Psychological characteristics, sexual aggression and, 432–433
Psychological field, in Lewin's model of social behavior, 4
Psychological reactance, 240
  independence and, 257–258
Psychology
  evolutionary, beauty and, 366
  of legitimacy, 329
  social. *See* Social psychology
  social psychology and, 8–10
Pueblo incident, 215
Punishment, by group, 318–321
Punitive ostracism, 319

Q

Question format, attitude survey bias and, 173
Quiz show phenomenon, 92, 141

R

Race
  concept of, 108
  helping behavior and, 466–468
  as socially constructed concept, 108
Racism
  aversive, 130
  changing social norms and, 132–133
  definition of, 108
  modern, 130–131
  skin tone bias, 110
  in U.S. Army, disarming, 160
  See also Discrimination; Prejudice; Stereotype(s)
Random assignment, 14
Rape, myths about, 431–432
Rational actor, 191
Rationalization, 238, 336–337
Reactance, psychological, 240
  independence and, 257–258
Reagan, Ronald, trustworthiness and, 204
Recency effect, of message, 211–212
Reciprocal altruism, 450
Reciprocity, norm of, 275
Reconstructive memory, 498
Reflected self-appraisal, 33
Reframing behaviors, 526
Reinforcement, vicarious, observational learning and, 413
Rejection, latitude of, in social judgment theory, 214
Relational aggression, 394
Relational devaluation, 348
Relational model, of legitimacy, 329
Relationships, close, 343–385
  attachment styles and, 354–355
  communal, 375
  dating scripts and relationship formation, 371–373
  development of, 370–371
  dissolution of, predicting, 382
  dynamics of, 369–382
  evaluating, 373–375
  formation of, 353–355
  friendships as, 382–385
  inequity in, 486
  Internet and, 357–358
  kinds of, 381–382
  love and, 349–355
  over time, 376
  responses of, to conflict, 378–381
  roots of, 344–346
  sculpting, 377–378
  working model of, 353
Relative deprivation theory, 153
Relevance, personal, message processing and, 221–223
Religion, influence on self, 40
Representativeness heuristic, 99
Representative sample, 15
  for attitude survey, 173
Rescuer
  becoming
    personality factors in, 476
    situational factors in, 475–476
  gender and, 478–479

righteous rescuers, 473–479
  five-stage decision model applied to, 482–483
Research, social psychological, 10–25
  applied, 21
  basic, 21
  correlational, 17–18
  ethics and, 24–25
  exceptions and, 23
  experimental, 13–17. *See also* Experimental research
  field, 19–20
  hindsight bias in, 22
  laboratory, 19
  settings for, 19–20
  theory in, 21–22
Resilience
  components of, 520
  defined, 520
  resources, 520
Resistance stage, 517
Responsibility, diffusion of, 288, 455
Retrieval and emission phase, aggressive scripts, 414
Revere, Paul, 243
Reverse incentive effect, in dissonance theory, 230
Righteous rescuers, 473–479
  five-stage decision model applied to, 482–483
Right-wing authoritarianism, 122
Role strain, disobedience and, 295
Romantic love, 351
Rosenberg Self-Esteem Scale, 53
Rugemer, Eduard, 441–443

S

Same norms–different adherence motivation, 256
Same-sex relationships, 158, 369–370
Sample, population, 15, 173
Sanctioned aggression, 394
Scapegoating, 121
Schema(s)
  aggressive, 414
  assimilating new information into, 97
  behavior and, 97–99
  definition of, 96
  heuristics and, 99–100
  origins of, 97
Schematic, defined, 45
Science
  defined, 11
  principles of, 11
Scientific method, definition of, 11
Second-level agenda setting, 180
Secondary compensation, 153
Secret love, 353–354
Self
  actual, 54
  collective, 40
  cultural influences on, 43–44
  enhancing, 49–50
  group influences on, 39–48
  ideal, 55
  individual, 39
  Internet, 41–43

ought, 55
religious influence on, 39
self-regulation, 55
self-schemas and, 45–48
social, 31–67. See also Social self
Self-affirmation theory, rationalization and, 238
Self-awareness, 60–61
self-knowledge and, 61
Self-categorization theory, discrimination and, 136–137
Self-censorship, groupthink and, 337
Self-concept, 33–48
definition of, 33
influence of groups and culture on, 39–48
memories and, 36–38
personal attributes and, 35–36
religion and, 39
self-knowledge and, 33–36
Self-consistency, maintaining, 59–60
Self-control, 54–58
cost and ironic effects of, 57–58
definition of, 55
self-regulation and, 54–57
Self-defense, as sanctioned aggression, 394
Self-disclosure, in relationship development, 371
Self-discrepancy theory, 55
Self-efficacy
defined, 520
in health promotion, 526–527
Self-esteem, 48–54
coping with disaster and, 50–51
cultural influences on, 53
definition of, 48
emotional intelligence and, 48–49
explicit, 54
high, benefits of, 53–54
implicit, 54
impression management and, 62
internal influences on, 48–51
maintaining, in interactions with others, 49–50
receiving help and, 485–488
self-evaluation maintenance theory, 49
stigma and, 51–53
Self-evaluation maintenance theory, 49
Self-focus, 60
Self-fulfilling prophecy, 97
Self-handicapping, 63–65
in academics, 65
definition of, 63
Self-identity
groups and, 317–323
identification with social group and, 317–318
Self-identity theory, 318
Self-knowledge
self-awareness and, 61
sources of, 33–36
Self-monitoring, impression management and, 62–63
Self-other oneness hypothesis, 447
Self-perception hypothesis, 271
Self-perception theory, 237–238
Self-presentation(s), door-in-the-face technique and, 276
managing, 61–65

manipulative strategies and, 63
self-esteem and impression management, 62
self-handicapping, 63–65
self-monitoring and impression management, 62–63
Self-regulation, self-control and, 54–57
Self-schema, 45–48
definition of, 45
sexuality and, 45–48
Self-serving bias, definition of, 58
Self-serving cognitions, 58–59
Self-threat model, 59
Self-verification, definition of, 59
September 11, 2001, terrorist attacks of, 22, 50–51, 281, 443
Sexism
benevolent, 146, 147
in children's books, attitude formation and, 180
definition of, 108–110
hostile, 146, 147
humor and, 146, 147
See also Discrimination; Prejudice; Stereotype(s)
Sexual aggression, 432–433
Sexuality, self-schemas and, 45–48
Sexual orientation
dating scripts and, 371–373
helping behavior and, 468
mate preferences and, 368
relationship characteristics and, 371–373
relationship formation and, 371–373
self-concept and, 47
sexual self-schemas and, 45–48
Sexual self-schema, 45–48
Sexual violence, viewing, impact on aggression, 430–433
SIDE model, 323
Similarity, interpersonal attraction and, 359–361
Simpson's Paradox, 118
Single-process model in majority and minority influence, 268–269
Situation-specific helping, 451
Situational attribution, 86
Situational factors, in becoming rescuer, 473–474, 479–483
Skin tone bias, 109–110
Sleeper effect, 206–207
Smith, Benjamin, 121
Smith College, 157
Smoking, and behavior change, 238
Social anxiety, 348–349
Social behavior
Lewin's model of, 4–7
expanding, 6–7
model for, 4–7
social psychology and, 2–7
understanding, 1–25
Social category relationship, 456
Social cognition
definition of, 5
motivated, 195
Social comparison
group polarization from, 334–335
need for, groups satisfying, 309

Social comparison process, 257
in self-knowledge, 34
Social compensation, in groups, 316–317
Social control behaviors, 458
Social dominance orientation, 123–124
Social exchange theory, 373–374
Social facilitation, 311, 312, 313–314
Social group, identification with, 317–318
Social identity, 35
Social identity theory, stereotypes and, 136
Social impact theory, 268–269
Social influence(s)
conformity and, 258–260
informational, 254–255
normative, 254–255
on self-knowledge, 39–43
Social information-processing view of aggression, 434
Social inhibition, 311
Social-interactional model, of aggression, 414–417
Social judgment theory, 214–216
Social learning explanation, of aggression, 411–423
Social learning theory, aggression and, 411–423
Social loafing, group participation and, 315
Social loneliness, 358
Social media
aggression and, 426–427
impression formation and, 80
Internet self, 41–43
Social networks, attitude formation and, 184–185
Social norms changing, 132–133
reducing expression of prejudice through, 157–158
Social ostracism, 318–321
Social penetration theory, 371
Social perception, 71–101
definition of, 5
Social psychology
applications of, 493–527
to health, 515–527
to the law, 494–508
to work, 508–515
definition of, 3
fields related to, 8–10
pseudoscience and, 12–13
research in, 10–25. See also Research, social psychological
understanding social behavior and, 2–7
Social readjustment rating scale (SRRS), 518
Social responsibility, norm of, 482
Social self, 31–67
Social situation, 4–5
Socialization, of aggression, 412–413
Sociobiology, aggression and, 398–399
Sociology, social psychology and, 8, 9
Spotlight effect, 66
Standard Oil Company, 167–168, 171, 176
Stein, Gertrude, 343–344, 356, 366, 369, 385
Stereotype(s)
accuracy of, 115–118
confirmation bias and, 142–143
content model, 111–112
definition of, 110

Subject Index I-21

Stereotype(s) (continued)
  of enemy, groupthink and, 337
  explicit, 112–115
  illusory correlations and, 140–142
  implicit, 112–115
  as judgmental heuristics, 117–118
  malleability of, 115–118
  prejudice and, 110–118
  of prejudiced and nonprejudiced individuals, 143–144
  in propaganda, 245
  relative deprivation theory and, 153
  social identity theory and, 153
  threat based on, 147–150
  See also Discrimination; Prejudice
Stereotype threat, 147–150
Stigma, self-esteem and, 51–53
Stigmatized groups, raising value of, 151–152
Stories, in conflict resolution, 378–379
Stranger anxiety, 9
Stratton, Spenser, 1, 2
Stress
  appraisals of, 517–518
  coping with, 519–521
    emotion-focused coping, 517
    perceived control and self-efficacy, 520–521
    positive mood and, 522–523
    problem-focused coping, 517
    promoting healthier behavior and, 525–527
    resilience and, 519–520
    social support and, 523–524
  general adaptation syndrome, 517
    alarm stage, 517
    exhaustion stage, 517
    resistance stage, 517
  illness and, 491
  life events and, 491
  mechanisms for coping with, 519–521
    perceived control, 520–521
    positive mood, 522–523
    resilience, 519–520
    self-efficacy beliefs, 520–521
    social support, 523–524
  perceived, health and, 516–519
    appraisals of stress, 517–518
    life stressors and illness, 518–519
  preventing, 525–527
  relationship between health and, 516–519
  sleep and, 519
  social readjustment rating scale (SRRS) and, 518
Subjective norms, behavioral intention and, 187
Superordinate goal, 155
Symbolic aggression, 394
System justification theory, 139–140
System variables, 495

T

Tarbell, Ida, 167–168, 169–171, 176, 177, 197
Task-based cohesiveness, 332–333
Television
  in attitude formation, 178–181
  in teaching aggression, 424–426
Terminal values, 171
Testosterone
  activation function, 401
  aggression and, 401–403
  organization function, 401
Theory
  application and, 22
  definition of, 21
  of planned behavior, 186–188
  research process and, 21
  in social psychological research, 21–22
Thin-slice methodology, 80
Thinking
  counterfactual, 100
  divergent, 268
Thompson, Jennifer, 493–494
Threat, stereotype-based, 147–150
Tiananmen Square incident, 296
Toklas, Alice, 343–344, 369, 385
Top-down perspective, 10
Training, reducing prejudice through, 158–159
Trait-based scales, 511
Transactional leaders, 328
Transactional model of stress and coping, 517
Transactive memory systems, of groups, 324
  differentiated, 324
  integrated, 324
Transformative leaders, 328
Transparency, illusion of, 66
Transphobia, 125
Trinidad Beach rescue, 1–2, 3, 4, 5, 9, 25
True partner effect, 263–264
Trustworthiness, of communicator, 204–205
Twelve Angry Men, film, 266, 268
Two-process model, in majority and minority influence, 268–269

U

Ultimate attribution error, 143
Unanimity, illusion of, groupthink and, 337
Unanimity rule, 333
Uniqueness, need for, 258
Unobtrusive measures, in attitude assessment, 174
Unrequited love, 352
U.S. Army, racism in, 160
U.S. Supreme Court, ideology of justices, 195–196

V

Validating couple, 381
Valley Transportation Authority (VTA), 391–393, 436
Value(s)
  attitudes as expression of, 171–172
  definition of, 171
  instrumental, 171
  terminal, 171
Variable(s)
  confounding, 15
  in experimental research
    dependent, 14
    independent, 14
    manipulating, 14
  extraneous
    controlling, 15
    definition of, 15
Vicarious dissonance hypothesis, 229
Vicarious reinforcement, observational learning and, 413
Victim characteristics, helping behavior and, 464–466
Video games, violence in, aggression and, 427–429
Vietnam War, 160, 298
Vincennes incident, 71–73, 99, 101
Violence
  culture and, 419–423
  group, 321–323
  sexual, viewing of, impact on aggression, 430–433
  on television
    aggression and, 424–426
    role in attitude formation, 178–181
  in video games, 427–429
  See also Aggression
Volatile couple, 381
Voluntary false confessions, 505

W

Wake Island, film, 241
War, as sanctioned aggression, 394
Watergate, 284, 298
Weak conformity, 260
Weapon focus, 495–496
Weibel, Narayan, 1, 2, 4
Williams, Serena, 31–33, 67
Williams v. Florida, 503
Wording, attitude survey bias and, 173
Working model, of close relationships, 353
Working self-concept, 36
World According to Garp, The, film, 499
World Church, 121
World Trade Center, attacks on, 50–51

X

Xenophobia, 137

Y

Yale communication model, 203–216
  audience in, 209–216
  communicator in, 203–207
  message in, 209–216
  social judgment theory and, 214–216
York, Adrian, 1, 2, 4